THE OXFORD HANDBOOK OF CRIMINOLOGY

The Oxford Handbook of Criminology

Edited by

MIKE MAGUIRE
ROD MORGAN
and
ROBERT REINER

CLARENDON PRESS · OXFORD

Oxford University Press, Walton Street, Oxford OX2 6DP
Oxford New York
Athens Auckland Bangkok Bombay
Calcutta Cape Town Dar es Salaam Delhi
Florence Hong Kong Istanbul Karachi
Kuala Lumpur Madras Madrid Melbourne
Mexico City Nairobi Paris Singapore
Taipei Tokyo Toronto
and associated companies in
Berlin Ibadan

Oxford is a trade mark of Oxford University Press

Published in the United States
by Oxford University Press Inc., New York

First published 1994
Paperback reprinted 1994 (twice)

British Library Cataloguing in Publication Data
Data available

Library of Congress Cataloging in Publication Data
Data available
ISBN 0-19-876242-9
ISBN 0-19-876241-0 (Pbk.)

Printed and bound in Great Britain by
Butler & Tanner Ltd, Frome and London

Contents

Notes on Contributors

ANDREW ASHWORTH is Edmund-Davies Professor of Criminal Law and Criminal Justice, King's College, University of London. He was formerly Fellow and Tutor in Law at Worcester College, Oxford, and an Associate of the Centre for Criminological Research, University of Oxford; before that he taught at Manchester University. He took his LLB at the London School of Economics (1968), followed by the BCL at Oxford University (1970) and a PhD at Manchester University (1973). In 1993 he was awarded a Doctorate of Civil Law by Oxford University, and was elected a Fellow of the British Academy.

He has published journal articles and made contributions to books on a wide range of topics in criminal law and criminal justice. He is author of *Sentencing and Penal Policy* (1983), and was one of five co-authors of *Sentencing in the Crown Court: An Exploratory Study* (1984). More recent books include *Principles of Criminal Law* (1991), *Sentencing and Criminal Justice* (1992), and, co-edited with Andrew von Hirsch, *Principled Sentencing* (1992). He has been editor of the *Criminal Law Review* since 1975, and was Chairman of the Council of Europe's Select Committee on Sentencing, 1989–92.

ANTHONY BOTTOMS is Wolfson Professor of Criminology and Director of the Institute of Criminology at the University of Cambridge (1983–); he is also a Fellow of Fitzwilliam College, Cambridge. After graduating in Law at Oxford University, he was successively a student on the first post-graduate course in Criminology at the Cambridge Institute (1961–2), a direct-entrant probation officer, and a member of the Institute's research contract staff. In 1968, he was appointed as the first Lecturer in Criminology in the Faculty of Law, University of Sheffield; subsequently he became professor of Criminology (1976–84) and Dean (1981–84) in the same Faculty. His interests within criminology are wide-ranging, and he has written on topics as diverse as: the pre-trial process as viewed by defendants; social inquiry reports; the nature and effectiveness of community penalties; prisons; the sociology of punishment; dangerousness; urban crime and environmental criminology; and crime prevention. He was a member of the Home Office's Research and Advisory Group on the Long-Term Prison System (1984–90), has been Editor of the *Howard Journal* (1975–81), and is currently an editor of the *Clarendon Studies in Criminology* (1993–), (OUP). He has also served as a member of editorial boards for criminological journals or book series in the United States, Sweden and The Netherlands.

David Downes is Professor of Social Administration at the London School of Economics. He has been a Senior Research Fellow at Nuffield College, Oxford, and an academic visitor at a number of universities in Europe and North America, including the University of Toronto, the University of California at Berkeley, the Free University of Amsterdam, and the University of Bologna. He has served on committees of the ESRC and NACRO and was editor of the *British Journal of Criminology*. He is the author, editor, and co-author of several works on delinquency, penal policy, and criminological theory. Among his more recent books is *Contrasts in Tolerance*, a study comparing British and Dutch penal policies.

Clive Emsley is Professor of History at the Open University. He was educated at the University of York and at Peterhouse, Cambridge. He has taught at the Open University since 1970, with temporary leaves at the University of Calgary, Alberta; Griffith University, Queensland; and the University of Paris VII (St Denis).

His publications include *Policing and its Context 1750–1870* (1983), *Crime and Society in England 1750–1900* (1987), and *The English Police: A Political and Social History* (1991).

David P. Farrington is Professor of Psychological Criminology at Cambridge University. He has been on the staff of the Institute of Criminology since completing his PhD in Psychology at Cambridge University in 1969. In addition to over 130 published papers on criminological and psychological topics, he has published eleven books, one of which, *Understanding and Controlling Crime* (1986), won the prize for distinguished scholarship of the American Sociological Association Criminology Section. He has been President of the British Society of Criminology, Vice-Chair of the US National Academy of Sciences Panel on Violence, and Chair of the Division of Criminological and Legal Psychology of the British Psychological Society. He is a Fellow of the British Psychological Society and of the American Society of Criminology, and received the Sellin–Glueck Award of the American Society of Criminology for international contributions to criminology.

David Garland is Professor of Penology in the Centre for Criminology and the Social and Philosophical Study of Law, Edinburgh University, and currently (1993/4) Visiting Professor at New York University School of Law. He has an LLB (1977) and a PhD (1984) from Edinburgh University, and an MA in criminology (1978) from Sheffield University. In 1984/5 he was a Davis Fellow at the Department of History, Princeton University, and in 1988 he held a Visiting Professorship in Boalt Law School at the University of California, Berkeley.

He is the author of *Punishment and Welfare: A History of Penal Strategies* (1985) and *Punishment and Modern Society: A Study in Social Theory* (1990), and the editor, with Peter Young, of *The Power to Punish* (1983). He is a member of the editorial board of the *British Journal of Criminology.*

LORAINE GELSTHORPE is a Lecturer in Criminology at the Institute of Criminology, University of Cambridge. She has a BA (Hons) from Sussex University (1977), and an MPhil in Criminology (1979) and a PhD in Criminology from Cambridge University (1983). Her books include *Women and Crime* (1981, co-edited with Allison Morris), *Gender Issues in Juvenile Justice* (1985), *Sexism and the Female Offender* (1989), and *Feminist Perspectives in Criminology* (1990, co-edited with Allison Morris). Other publications include papers and booklets on topics ranging from Attendance Centres to qualitative research methods.

She works with a range of national voluntary organizations on juvenile justice issues. She is editor of the British Society of Criminology *Newsletter* and Secretary of the Society's professional and Ethical Committee.

FRANCES HEIDENSOHN is Reader in Social Science and Administration in the Department of Social Policy and Politics at Goldsmiths' College, University of London. She graduated in sociology from the London School of Economics, where she was a lecturer first in the Sociology Department and later in the Department of Social Science and Administration. She was Director of Studies in Social Policy at the Civil Service before moving to Goldsmiths' College in 1979.

She is the author of *Women and Crime* (1985), *Crime and Society* (1989), *Women in Control?* (1992), and co-editor (with Martin Farrell) of *Crime in Europe* (1991). She was Associate Editor of the *British Journal of Criminology* 1985–93.

DICK HOBBS is a lecturer in the Department of Sociology and Social Policy at the University of Durham. He was formerly a Research Fellow at the Centre for Criminological Research, University of Oxford. He has an MSc in sociology (with distinction) from the LSE (1982), and a PhD from Surrey University (1986).

He is author of *Doing the Business* (1988), which won the Philip Abrams Prize in 1989, and editor (with Tim May) of *Interpreting the Field* (1993), *Policing Matters; Policing Changes* (1993), and *Professional Crime* (1994). He is a member of the council of the Howard League, and is on the editorial boards of the *Howard Journal* and *Youth and Policy.*

Michael Levi is Professor of Criminology at the University of Wales, College of Cardiff, where he has taught since 1975. A graduate of Oxford, Cambridge, and Southampton, he is the author of *The Phantom Capitalists* (1981), *Regulating Fraud: White-Collar Crime and the Criminal Process* (1987), *The Investigation, Prosecution, and Trial of Serious Fraud* (1993), and numerous articles on fraud, on policing, and on perceptions of crime seriousness. He has directed two local studies on violence: a study of assaults against the police in South Wales, and one on the prevention of alcohol-related disorder in Newport.

He is criminology editor of *Crime, Law, and Social Change*, assistant editor of the *Journal of Law and Society*, and a member of the editorial boards of the *Howard Journal* and the *European Journal of Criminal Policy and Research.*

Mike Maguire is a Senior Lecturer in Criminology and Criminal Justice at the University of Wales, Cardiff. He was formerly a Research Fellow at the Oxford University Centre for Criminological Research. In addition to over fifty articles and research reports on a range of criminological topics, he has written, co-authored or co-edited the following books: *Burglary in a Dwelling* (1982), *Accountability and Prisons* (1985) *The Effects of Crime and the Work of Victims Support Schmes* (1987), *Victims of Crime: A New Deal?* (1988), *A Study of the Police Complaints System* (1991) and *Prisons in Context* (1994). He has published in America, Canada, Holland and India, has given papers at many international conferences and has conducted major research projects on behalf of *inter alia* the Home Office, the Economic and Social Research Council and the Royal Commission on Criminal Justice. He was a member of the Parole Board of England and Wales for three years.

Tim May has been a lecturer in sociology and social policy at the University of Plymouth since September 1989. He originally trained and worked as an agricultural engineer and then moved into the retail sector during which time he undertook a return-to-study course. He has a BSc (Econ.) from the LSE (1985), an MSc in social research methods from Surrey University (1986), and a PhD in sociology and social policy from Plymouth Polytechnic (1990).

He is the author of *Probation: Politics, Policy and Practice* (1991) and *Social Research: Issues, Methods and Process* (1993), and the co-editor (with Dick Hobbs) of *Interpreting the Field: Accounts of Ethnography* (1993). He has also published articles on criminal justice and power, identity and organisational change. He is currently co-editing (with Tony Vass) *Working with Offenders: Themes and Perspectives*, as well as working on a social theory text and researching organizational change in social service departments.

Rod Morgan is Professor of Criminal Justice and Dean of the Faculty of Law at the University of Bristol. He is the author of several books and many articles on criminal justice issues. He was an Assessor to Lord Justice Woolf's inquiry into the 1990 prison riots, and he is an expert adviser to the Council of Europe Committee for the Prevention of Torture and to Amnesty International. He is co-editor of *Policing and Society* and a member of several advisory committees concerned with criminal justice issues, including the independent Committee of Inquiry into the Role of the Police jointly established in 1993 by the Police Foundation and the Policy Studies Institute.

Allison Morris is currently Director of the Institute of Criminology, Victoria University of Wellington, Wellington, New Zealand, on secondment leave from the Institute of Criminology, University of Cambridge. She has an LLB from the University of Edinburgh (1967), a diploma in Criminology (with distinction) from the University of Cambridge (1968), an LLM from Columbia University (1969), and a PhD in Criminology from the University of Cambridge (1985). She is author of *Juvenile Justice*? (1978, in collaboration with Mary McIsaac), co-author of *Justice for Children* (1980, with Henri Giller, Elizabeth Szwed, and Hugh Geach), *Care and Discretion* (1981, with Henri Giller) and *Providing Justice for Children* (1983, with Henri Giller). She co-edited *Women and Crime* (1981, with Loraine Gelsthorpe), *Women and the Penal System* (1988, with Christine Wilkinson) and *Feminist Perspectives in Criminology* (1990, with Loraine Gelsthorpe), and is author of *Women, Crime and Criminal Justice* (1987).

David Nelken is Professor of Sociology and Director of the Institute of Sociology at the University of Macerata in Italy. He is also Visiting Professor of Law (Criminology) at University College London where he was previously Reader in Law. He obtained his doctorate at the Institute of Criminology in Cambridge; his teaching at the Universities of Cambridge, Edinburgh, and London included courses in criminal law, criminal justice, criminology, sociology of law, and philosophy of law. He has written papers contributing to and trying to synthesize these fields. His book *The Limits of the Legal Process: A Study of Landlords, Law and Crime* (1983) gained an American Sociological Association Distinguished Scholar Award. He is currently working on an edited collection entitled *The Futures of Criminology*; a set of readings on *White-Collar Crime*; (in Italian) a book with N. Passas on *Controlling EEC Fraud*; and a book entitled *Law's Truth.* He is on the editorial boards of scientific journals in the UK, the USA, and Italy.

Geoffrey Pearson is Wates Professor of Social Work in Goldsmiths' College, University of London. An Associate Editor of the *British Journal of Criminology* and a former member of the National Council of the British Society of Criminology, he is a member of the Council of the Institute for the Study of Drug Dependence. His published work includes *The Deviant Imagination* (1975), *Hooligan: A History of Respectable Fears* (1983), *Young People and Heroin* (1986), and *The New Heroin Users* (1987).

Ken Pease is Professor of Criminology at Manchester University. A psychologist by first training, he has been consultant to the United Nations Crime Branch on crime trends, to the United Nations Drug Control Programme on drug seizure data, and to various criminal justice agencies in the UK and elsewhere. He has been Visiting Professor of Psychiatry at the University of Saskatchewan. He has served as a member of the parole Board and is currently the only academic member of the National Board for Crime Prevention. He has published on a variety of criminal justice topics, his books including *Crime and Punishment: Interpreting the Data* (with Keith Bottomley, Open University Press, 1986), *Police Work* (with Peter Ainsworth, British Psychological Society, 1987) *Sentencing Reform: Guidance or Guidelines?* (with Martin Wasik, Manchester University Press, 1987) and *Criminal Justice Systems in Europen and North America* (with Kristina Hukkila, HEVNI, 1990). He is currently particularly interested in the phenomenon of repeated victimisation of the same people.

Jill Peay is a barrister and Lecturer in Law at Brunel University. She was formerly a Research Fellow at the Centre for Criminological Research, Oxford, and Visiting Assistant Professor at the School of Criminology, Simon Fraser University, BC. She is a member of the Board of Directors of the International Academy of Law and Mental Health, and sits on the Advisory Council of the International Centre for Criminal Law Reform and Criminal Justice Policy.

Robert Reiner is Professor of Criminology in the Law Department, LSE. He was formerly Reader in Criminology at the University of Bristol, and at Brunel University. He has a BA in economics from Cambridge University (1967), an MSc in sociology (with distinction) from the LSE (1968), a PhD in sociology from Bristol University (1976), and a postgraduate diploma in law (with distinction) from City University, London (1985).

He is author of *The Blue-Coated Worker* (1978), *The Politics of the Police* (1985; 2nd edn. 1992), and *Chief Constables* (1991), and editor (with M. Cross) of *Beyond Law and Order* (1991). He has published nearly one hundred papers on policing and criminal justice topics. He is editor (with R. Morgan) of *Policing and Society: An International Journal of Research and Policy*, and review editor of *The British Journal of Criminology*. He is currently President of the British Society of Criminology.

PAUL ROCK is Professor of Sociology and Director of the Mannheim Centre for the Study of Criminology and Criminal Justice at the London School of Economics. He is editor of the *British Journal of Sociology*. He attained a BSc from the LSE (1964) and a DPhil (1970) as a student at Nuffield College, Oxford. He has been a Visiting Professor at Princeton University (1974–5), the University of California, San Diego (1972), Simon Fraser University (1976), and the University of British Columbia (1976); a Visiting Scholar at the Programs Branch of the Ministry of the Solicitor General of Canada (1981); and has frequently been a consultant to the Home Office.

He is author of *Making People Pay* (1973), *Deviant Behaviour* (1973), *The Making of Symbolic Interactionism* (1979), (with David Downes) *Understanding Deviance* (1982; 2nd edn. 1988), *A View from the Shadows: The Ministry of the Solicitor General of Canada and the Justice for Victims of Crime Initiative* (1987), *Helping Victims of Crime: The Home Office and the Rise of Victim Support in England and Wales* (1990), and *The Social wrold of an English Crown Court: Witnesses and Professionals in the Crown Court Centre at Wood Green* (1993). Jointly and singly, he has edited a comparable number of books. He is currently collaborating in the writing of a history of Holloway Prison.

ANDREW SANDERS is Lecturer in Criminal Justice at the Centre for Criminological Research, Oxford University, and a Fellow of Pembroke College. He was formerly a senior lecturer at Birmingham University and a lecturer at Manchester Metropolitan University (as it was not then called). He has an LLB from Warwick and a master's degree in Criminology from Sheffield, and was a member of the Parole Board from 1990 to 1993.

He has co-authored (with Lee Bridges, Adele Mulvaney, and Gary Crozier), *Advice and Assistance at Police Stations* (1989); (with Mike McConville and Roger Leng), *The Case for the Prosecution* (1991); (with Richard Young and Tim Moloney), *In the Interests of Justice?* (1992); and (with Richard Young) *Criminal Justice* (forthcoming). He has also written on many aspects of policing and prosecutions for a number of journals. He is a member of the editorial board of the *Clarendon Studies in Criminology* (OUP).

DAVID J. SMITH is Senior Fellow at the Policy Studies Institute (PSI), and Head of the Social Justice and Social Order Programme. After graduating in psychology and philosophy at the University of Oxford in 1963, he spent eight years as a market researcher, and joined the board of a market research agency in 1969. In 1972 he started a new career in social research with PEP, which later merged with another independent institute to form PSI. In 1988/9 he was Visiting Fellow of Lincoln College, Oxford.

He is the author of co-author of *Racial Disadvantage in Britain* (1977), *Police and People in London* (1983), *Evaluating Police Work* (1988), *The School Effect: A Study of Multi-Racial Comprehensives* (1989), *Inequality in Northern Ireland* (1991), and *Racial Justice at Work: The Enforcement of the Race Relations Act 1976 in Employment* (1991); co-editor of *Coming to Terms with Policing* (1989), and *Psychosocial Disorders of Youth: A Study of Cross-National Trends and Their Causes* (1993); and editor of *Understanding the Underclass* (1992). He has been an Additional Commissioner of the Commission for Racial Equality, and Specialist Adviser to both the Home Affairs Committee and the Employment Committee of the House of Commons.

NIGEL SOUTH is a lecturer in sociology at the University of Essex. He was formerly (1981–90) a research sociologist at the Institute for the Study of Drug Dependence, London. He received his BA (1976) and MA (1978) from University of Essex, and his PhD (1985) from Middlesex University.

Publications include many articles on drug-related issues and on the development of private and public policing. Books include *Policing for Profit* (1988), *Traffickers: Drug Markets and Law Enforcement* (with Dorn and Murji, 1992), *AIDS: Women, Drugs and Social Care* (ed. with Dorn and Henderson, 1992), and *A Land Fit for Heroin*? (ed. with Dorn, 1987). He is a member of the Editorial Advisory Group of the *Howard Journal* and of the International Editorial Board of the *International Journal on Drug Policy*.

IAN TAYLOR is Professor of Sociology at the University of Salford, Greater Manchester. He has previously taught at the Universities of Sheffield and Glasgow in the UK, and at Carleton University, Ottawa, Canada, where he was based between 1981 and 1989. He has also been a visiting professor at La Trobe University, Melbourne, Australia; McMaster University, Hamilton, Ontario, Canada; the University of Alberta, Canada; and the Institute of Criminology at Cambridge.

He is co-author of *The New Criminology* with Paul Walton and Jock Young (1973) and author of *Law and Order: Arguments for Socialism* (1981) and *Crime, Capitalism and Community* (1983). He has also co-edited *Politics and Deviance* (1973, with Laurie Taylor), *Critical Criminology* (1975, with Paul Walton and Jock Young), and *Relocating Cultural Studies* (1993, with Valda Blundell and John Shepherd). The volume most relevant to his concerns in his chapter in this volume is his edited collection *The Social Effects of Free Market Policies* (1991).

Jock Young is Professor of Criminology at Middlesex University, where he is the head of the Centre for Criminology. He graduated from the London School of Economics (BSc) in 1965 and received his MSc (1966) and PhD (1972) from the same institution. Among his publications are: *The Drugtakers* (1971), *The New Criminology*, with I. Taylor and P. (1973), *Critical Criminology*, edited with I. Taylor and P. Walton (1975), *Policing the Riots*, edited with D. Cowell (1982), *Confronting Crime*, edited with R. Matthews (1986), *Losing the Fight against Crime*, with R. Kinsey and J. Lea (1986), *The Islington Crime Survey*, with T. Jones and B. MacLean (1986), *Rethinking Criminology*, edited with R. Matthews (1992), *Issues in Realist Criminology*, edited with R. Matthews (1992), and *What is to be Done about Law and Order?*, with J. Lea (1993).

Lucia Zedner is Lecturer in Law, Law Department, and Assistant Director of the Mannheim Centre for Criminology and Criminal Justice at the LSE. She is also a research associate of the Centre for Criminological Research, University of Oxford, and in 1993 a Visiting Fellow of the Max-Planck Institute for foreign and International Criminal Law, Freiburg, Germany. She was formerly Prize Research Fellow at Nuffield College, Oxford. She has a BA in History (first class) from the University of York (1982), a DPhil in History from the University of Oxford (1988), and the Bar/Law Society CPE Part 1 (with Commendation) from City Poly (1991).

She is author of *Women, Crime and Custody in Victorian England* (1991); with Jane Morgan, *Child Victims: Crime, Impact and Criminal Justice* (1992); with L.H. Leigh, *The Royal Commission on Criminal Justice Research Study No. 1: The Administration of Justice in the Pre-Trial phase in France and Germany* (1992); and many articles on criminal justice. She is a member of the Editorial Advisory Group of the *Howard Journal.*

Introduction

ROD MORGAN, MIKE MAGUIRE, AND ROBERT REINER

In some senses, this text represents one of the most ambitious publishing enterprises ever attempted by British criminologists. The pages that follow contain twenty-five original, specially commissioned chapters, comprising approximately 400,000 words, by twenty-six British scholars. Between them they cover most of the major issues which preoccupy criminological researchers and which are taught to students of the subject. Anyone who has edited a text made up of diverse contributions from different authors will understand the dimensions of our task. It has taken more than three years to realize, from gleam in the eye to volume on the desk. It has been a major undertaking, the equivalent of a large research study and an onerous administrative responsibility rolled into one.

Yet despite the scale of the project and the effort involved, in other ways this is a rather more modest venture. There is no theoretical manifesto in these pages. We have not selected our authors according to some shared proseletyzing vision, nor have we sought to impose a common approach upon them. The text as a whole does not purport to be theoretically path-breaking, though some individual chapters within it undoubtedly are. In this respect it is less ambitious than some earlier texts which had also set out to chart the terrain of criminology. This is a collection of different voices, not a monolithic vision, though we intend it to be a comprehensive, state-of-the-art map of criminological analysis, research, and debate in Britain today. This combination of ambition and lack of ambition reflects more than our horizons as editors: it stems from the condition of contemporary criminology.

In this brief introduction we aim to explain: what the text was designed to achieve; how we set about the task of planning and commissioning it; and the degree to which we think we have succeeded in our objectives. Would we do it differently were we to start again? Or, rather, *will* we do it differently? For, as we shall explain, this is designed—both by us and our publishers—to be a continuing project.

THE PROBLEM

All three of us are long-serving members of British universities: we can muster between us well over half a century's experience of teaching and research in departments of sociology, social policy or administration, social work, and law. Most of our teaching has centred on criminology and/or the closely related subject which many now call 'criminal justice'—on the one hand, the study of crime, the manner in which we conceptualize and explain crime, its social definition, and its form and distribution; on the other, the manner in which (and reasons whereby) the various agencies that make up the criminal justice system respond to those behaviours labelled criminal.

However, within and around this core there has been much scope for change and variety. In response to changing theoretical emphases and audiences, over more than twenty years, we have taught courses variously called criminology, penology, criminal justice, crime control and public policy, the sociology of deviance, social censures, the sociology of legal order, and the sociology of law. We have also been involved in more specialized courses focusing in detail on issues which may only be touched on in general criminology courses: the sociology of medicine and psychiatry, patterns of crime, policing, criminal procedure, the philosophy of punishment, sentencing, community sanctions, prison administration, and even 'modern correctional methods'. The students we have taught have included not only undergraduate or postgraduate students pursuing general social science or law degrees, but also a variety of criminal justice professionals studying for more specialized qualifications, as well as laypersons with a non-vocational interest in one of the most controversial issues of our time. Our experience reflects a more general pattern, as Paul Rock's study of the social organization of contemporary British criminology in chapter 3 shows. Criminology in its various guises covers a multitude of theoretical and substantive issues and is taught in several social science and law contexts to students whose interest in the subject varies greatly.

There is now no shortage of respectable texts on most of the *specific* issues mentioned above, particularly on the more concrete topics like policing, victims, or the penal system. There are also several texts providing an accessible overview of the theoretical development of the subject.

However, we have regularly faced the problem of the absence of a single comprehensive textbook which covers sufficient ground in sufficient depth for a general criminological course to be built around it. The increasingly diverse topics which go to make up such courses are not encompassed within single texts: they are contained in many specialized books and an even greater number of articles. Hence, for each substantive topic it has been necessary to cite many separate references. Reading lists have grown longer and more daunting and it has become harder in good conscience to recommend books that students of limited means should buy as an essential source.

This was the gap we set out to fill. We wished to produce a criminology handbook which would provide students with authoritative overviews of the major issues that most criminology courses cover, whether taught in schools of law or social science, to undergraduates, postgraduates, or practitioners.

HISTORICAL AND THEORETICAL CONSIDERATIONS

It took us no time at all to decide that we could not write this text ourselves, but should instead invite quite lengthy contributions from a number of colleagues. The fact that we unanimously and speedily came to this conclusion says a good deal about how criminology has developed in recent years.

The criminological enterprise—both research and teaching—has expanded enormously. Forty years ago, Hermann Mannheim at the London School of Economics, Leon Radzinowicz at Cambridge, and Max Grunhut at Oxford were almost lone pioneering figures teaching criminology in British universities. Not until 1957 did the Home Office have a Research Unit (see Lodge 1974) and when the Cambridge Institute of Criminology was created with Home Office support and independent financial backing in 1959, it was the first postgraduate teaching and research centre of its kind. Prior to its formation (as the then Home Secretary, Lord Butler, who provided much of the impetus for the decision, was subsequently to recall), remarkably little had been spent by any government on criminological research and neither the University Grants Council nor the major trusts had shown much interest in the subject (Butler 1974: 3–6; see also Lodge 1974: 17–18). Moreover, at the time the creation of the Cambridge Institute was announced, there were only two journals—the *British Journal of Delinquency* (forerunner of the *British Journal of Criminology*) and the *Howard Journal*—devoted to publishing articles of a criminological nature. There were virtually no undergraduate courses, which is not surprising as there was a dearth of data and research studies on which teachers could draw. In the late 1950s lecturers preparing student reading lists had little difficulty incorporating most of the British official publications and independent research studies with which criminologists, whatever their substantive interests, might be familiar.

Today virtually no university social science faculty or law school is without a course which, either wholly or in part, covers the criminological terrain (though, as we have noted, it may not be titled as such). Taught postgraduate courses in the subject are proliferating apace, many of them directed at particular practitioner groups as well as geared to the teaching of research skills or advanced theory. Many universities now have research centres, some little more than letter-headings but an increasing number with real substance, which carry criminology, socio-legal, policing, criminal justice, or some cognate term in their titles. The biannual British Criminology Conference easily commands the attendance of over 400 delegates, most of them lecturers or research officers in social science or law departments. The recently formed Socio-Legal Studies Association, which so far mainly comprises lawyers, now attracts well in excess of 100 delegates to its annual meetings. International criminology events attract many more.

It is no longer possible, as once it was, for individuals to keep abreast of all this activity and output. Scores of research monographs and general texts of a criminological nature are published each year. At least a dozen British publishing houses carry a substantial list of criminology titles and many university centres have in-house monograph series. The Home Office Research and Planning Unit, together with its various offshoots, has itself several hundred research titles to its credit and the *British Journal of Criminology* and the *Howard Journal* now compete with at least a dozen other British-based academic journals carrying articles of a directly or tangentially criminological nature.

This explosion in academic activity is not surprising. The huge increase in recorded crime since the mid-1950s has led to considerable increases in the number of personnel employed in the various law and order services (see chapters 6, 15, and 19 in this volume). This has given rise to an increased demand for persons with some criminological training, which has in turn fuelled pressure for more research to be conducted on criminological issues. Academics are wont to complain about the level of financial support available for their work, and it is true that, in the same way that the increase in recorded crime has outstripped the additional personnel and resources of the criminal justice system, so too research funding has not kept pace either with crime or with the huge increase in public spending on 'law and order' services (see Home Office 1986; Home Office 1993). Nevertheless the growth of funding has been considerable, creating something of a boom in criminological research. In addition to the substantial programme of work conducted within or funded by the Home Office—now on an annual budget of approximately £8 million per year (of which £2 million is spent on external grants)—the Economic and Social Research Council has had a succession of programme initiatives directed wholly or partly at work of a criminological nature. A recent ESRC initiative on crime and modernity attracted no fewer than 180 applications from individuals or groups wishing to compete for the £2.3 million the Council had announced it intended to spend. Several of the major charitable foundations now regularly fund research on aspects of crime and criminal justice. In recent years, too, some local authorities and most criminal justice agencies have either set up their own research arms or contracted out work on aspects of crime or the performance of their own agencies.

There may be doubts, as there always have been, about the quality of some of this work. Much of the impetus behind the growth may have been self-serving. But teaching and research in criminology have become a significant industry in which many people now specialize. There has been an exponential growth in the amount of knowledge available about the nature and extent of criminal behaviour (see, especially, chapters 6–13 below) and the decision-making of the expanded agencies which respond to it (chapters 14–20).

Some idea of the extent of this growth—and hence of the size of the task we set ourselves and our contributors—can be obtained from the number of different references cited in this text: there are more than 3,000 of them. However, the complexity of the task does not derive merely from the volume of material which needs covering. The methodological and theoretical foundations of criminological discourse have also become more varied and technical. Many past students of criminology, and no doubt a good many contemporary teachers of the subject, will recognize the conceptually simplified, basically ahistorical periodization of the development of criminological discourse which has been the stock-in-trade of many introductory courses: classicism (1750–1870), positivism 1870–1960), interactionism (the 1960s), radical criminology (1970s onwards), all paraded as a kind of museum of quaint past perspectives. David Garland has incisively deconstructed this mythical history in the opening chapter of this text. The development of the subject was never so straightforward, nor were the affiliations of its practitioners ever so simple. In all its phases there have coexisted lively and cross-cutting debates and discourses about crime and justice. But if it was distorting to parcel up the work of criminological analyses into apparently neat theoretical boxes in the past, it is arguably even more problematic to attempt the same kind of division today. Most criminologists nowadays draw on a welter of theoretical perspectives in order to interpret their data. It becomes less and less possible to delineate clear-cut 'schools' of thought, let alone to isolate any one overarching dominant paradigm.

Criminology is the only highly developed social science which explicitly takes a social problem, and thus a political question (How should crime be defined and how much power should the state use in reaction?), as its defining subject matter. As a result, the tendency to claim political correctness and to label opponents or forebears as the occupiers of debased theoretical camps, at best politically naïve and at worst politically compromised, is probably more acute in criminology than in any other discipline. The best-publicized example of this phenomenon is the 'rift in

British criminology' occasioned by the setting up of the National Deviancy Conference in 1968. The birth of the NDC was eased by the forceps delivery of another group somewhat inchoately labelled 'traditional criminology' (see Wiles 1976), the existence and identity of which were apparently largely unrecognized by its membership.

'Traditional criminology', elsewhere referred to as 'establishment', 'mainstream', 'establishment' or 'official' criminology (see Cohen 1971: 13) was said by NDC adherents to have had the following characteristics. First, it was described as 'institutionally constrained', in that its research agenda was financially tied to its government paymaster, generally the Home Office. The implication was that ministers and civil servants, rather than academic researchers, were deciding what 'the problem' was. Criminologists, it was said, had not exhibited an appropriate scepticism regarding the connection between criminalizing and controlling behaviour: they did not regard the category 'criminal' as inherently problematic. Thus it was that at a conference organized by the Cambridge Institute of Criminology, whose programme of research was almost entirely funded by the Home Office, a decision to form the break-away NDC was taken.

Second, traditional criminology was labelled 'positivist'. It was said to be committed to the proposition that the methods of the natural sciences could appropriately be used to explain crime. This took the form largely of attempting to uncover differences between criminals and non-criminals in order to identify the sources of criminality. In this regard the criminological tradition was said to have had little connection with sociological theory, particularly with such theorists as Max Weber and Herbert Mead, who in different ways were concerned with the interpretation of the meaning of human action rather than with a deterministic quest for causes. Criminology was accused of neglecting problems of meaning, of failing to investigate and take seriously the question of how those labelled criminal view their actions. Criminologists were accused of treating criminals as objects whose behaviour could be categorized according to external absolutist definitions, generally those which were accepted and promoted by powerful social groups. In this way official criminology was said to have allowed ideological beliefs to permeate a spuriously objective and scientific discourse.

This critique led many adherents of the NDC to eschew the title criminology altogether: they preferred the 'sociology of deviance'. This description more appropriately highlighted the investigation of the symbolic worlds of meaning within which individuals shape their action, interact, develop a concept of self, and either attempt, or are subject to attempts by others, to apply the label 'deviant'. Criminal, it was pointed out, is merely one of the many labels that can be applied to deviants, albeit a particularly potent one, and one increasingly deployed in industrial societies. Thus, unlike 'traditional criminology', sociologists of deviance focused their research attentions not on designated 'delinquents' subject to treatment or 'criminals' locked away, but on relatively new and controversial arenas within which these powerful labels were being applied. They looked at the reactions to popular youth cults (Cohen 1972; Clarke *et al.* 1976), the recreational use of illegal drugs (Young 1971), sexually 'deviant' groups (Plummer 1975), football 'hooliganism' (Taylor 1971), and other sorts of marginal or exotic deviance. This agenda has been graphically if somewhat cuttingly characterized as the sociology of 'nuts, sluts and perverts' (Liazos 1972). They also began to focus on the agencies applying the labels—the police (Cain 1971, 1973), the social services (Bailey 1973), psychiatrists (Maddison 1973), coroners (Atkinson 1971), and so on.

Undoubtedly, the NDC assault on 'traditional criminology' was an important catalyst in the development of the discipline, attracting a number of talented young scholars into the field and stimulating a great deal of theoretical debate. However, labels such as 'traditional criminology' and 'positivism', though not without substance, were oversimplified typifications of a variety of theoretical and methodological approaches. Similarly, as leading members of the NDC soon acknowledged, the deviancy school 'probably never had any great degree of intellectual or political coherence': it was rather a 'generalised stance of institutional and intellectual opposition' (Wiles 1976: 13) that rapidly broke up into subgroups. Some of these groupings have remained self-referentially oppositional and radical. Others have been drawn into a realigned 'mainstream' criminology, now incorporating self-labelled 'critical' or even 'radical' elements to accommodate the returning prodigals in a field which is more inchoate and theoretically catholic in character than it was in the late 1960s.

There may still be some value in developing taxonomies of criminological work in order better to explore underlying assumptions and institutional affiliations, not least because many authors still seem unwilling, in spite of repeated pleas, to reflect publicly on the origins of their research agendas and the process of their realization and modification. In this volume, for example, Jock Young contrasts the principal features of 'left realism'—the school of thought which, during the past decade, he has done so much to champion—and 'right realism', a position which is not discernibly held by any group of criminologists, at least not in Britain, but is attributed mainly to the writings of J. Q. Wilson, a leading American theorist. Young has previously developed other ideal types in order to analyse criminological work. In a 1981 essay he distinguished 'classicism', 'positivism', 'conservatism', 'strain theory', 'new deviancy theory', and 'Marxism' along six dimensions: the position allegedly adopted by each with regard to human nature, social order, the definition of crime, its extent and distribution, its causes, and what should be done about it (Young 1981). Though he insisted that these were only ideal types, and that many theorists 'lack consistency'—presumably in the sense that their work combines or falls between paradigms—he equally insisted that the construction of such models allows us 'to create a usable vocabulary so that we can argue about crime in a serious and systematic fashion' (1981: 305). In later essays, notably one published as part of the important 1988 *British Journal of Criminology* special issue on the 'History of British Criminology', Young has drawn up firm lines of distinction between 'radical criminology' and 'establishment criminology', further charting how the former has progressed from 'left idealism' (for which read 'crude Marxism') to 'left realism', and the latter from 'positivism' to 'administrative criminology' (Young 1988: 175–7; see also Young 1986).

Whether it really makes sense—and is, ultimately, helpful—to subdivide criminological work in the way that Young does is an open question. Among the complexities which confuse the picture are his claims that 'radical criminology' is now the 'majority tendency' and that, though largely government-funded, the directors of the main university research centres are joined in a critique of the conservative 'administrative' agenda being pursued by the Home Office (Young 1988: 164, 177). Are these classifications too broad and in need of refinement, or does the enterprise itself inevitably result in the distorting pigeon-holing of work which actually draws on a range of theoretical perspectives?

Criminological discourse is extremely varied in character, some of it highly abstract and theoretical, some of it narrowly policy-orientated or technical. It ranges from work that is avowedly politically radical, committed to challenging seats of state power, to that which takes the authority of the law as the only necessary basis for evaluating what 'the problem' is and whether further control is necessary. The disciplinary orientations of those working in criminology include sociology, political science, law, psychology, psychiatry, geography, econometrics, and systems analysis. Yet whatever their intellectual backgrounds, they tend increasingly to draw on a variety of perspectives when forming and testing their hypotheses. We would suggest that the differences are often ones of emphasis rather than caused by fundamental disagreements about the agenda that criminology should be addressing.

It is because we doubt that most contemporary criminology can so easily be classified, and because our own orientation involves a catholicity of theoretical taste, that we decided against drawing up a manifesto in the present text. Nor did we seek to impose a blueprint on our authors, or seek out colleagues with particular perspectives. We did not think it appropriate to do so, and we doubt that those asked to contribute would have accepted on those terms. Rather, we invited leading criminologists, whose scholarship is widely recognized, to review the state of play in subject areas in which they have established expertise (though not necessarily those areas with which their names are most readily associated). It follows that all the chapters in this volume, whatever their specific subject-matter, are theoretically aware in the sense that they involve an appraisal of the theoretical perspectives and debates in the field, as well as an exposition of research findings.

Although we have avoided any narrow partisanship in the range of political or theoretical positions espoused by the contributors to this volume, this does not mean that we are indifferent about the outcomes of crime policy, nor that we embrace a fashionably postmodern relativism about truth or justice. All of the authors we have chosen share a commitment to rigorous scholarship and respect for evidence, as well as concern for clarity of analysis and exposition. Although there is certainly no shared political line, most authors appear to be sensitive both to the genuine damage which the behaviours commonly labelled criminal can wreak in people's lives (often on the most vulnerable in society), and to the grave dangers of injustice and oppression which the criminal justice system itself can pose. The reduction of the harm caused by crime is an important issue, but so is the accountability of the system formally established to control crime.

THE SUBSTANCE

How then did we decide what ground to cover? First, despite the temptation to take a global approach, we allowed discretion to overcome valour and resolved to concentrate first and foremost on coverage of *British* criminology. Although many refer extensively to theories and ideas developed abroad (particularly in the USA), all the contributors have spent most of their careers in British universities and have, at our request, focused their attention on crime and justice in this country. Having established this, we drew up a provisional list of topics to be covered and divided them into four broad areas: the theory and history of crime and criminology (chapters 1–6); forms of crime and criminality, and their explanation (7–13); crime control and criminal justice (14–20); and social dimensions (race, class, gender, mental health) of crime, justice and victimisation (21–25). We have retained these four topic categories as the basic sections of this text.

There then followed the most difficult decisions: the precise subjects for each and the identity of the authors to be approached. Our decisions are largely evident on the contents page of this text, but not entirely. The end product does not precisely match the original design, and some account is required of the disjunction.

First, we agreed with our publisher that the text should comprise one volume capable of being marketed at a price students can afford. This determined the overall word limit for the text. Second, we wanted to allow our contributors space sufficient for them both to review their subjects in depth *and* to react creatively in analysing what they found. That meant flexibility about the length of the essays, which in turn constrained the number that could be commissioned. Third, we decided against the detailed separate coverage of particular theoretical traditions. Since the available literature already included several cheap, accessible, and thorough exegetical and critical overviews of the theoretical paradigms that have informed criminology (e.g. Downes and Rock 1988), we saw no reason to repeat the exercise. Instead, we would assume some familiarity on the part of our readers with these.

Having established the ground rules, we made a final selection of those topics we considered essential for a general overview of criminology, and approached those colleagues we considered best equipped to undertake the task. Each of our letters of invitation sketched the ground we thought needed to be covered, but indicated that we wished to give all our contributors a good deal of discretion. Every essay should try to break new ground as well as provide readers with an accessible introduction to the subject-matter. Whether the right balance has everywhere been struck, we leave our readers to judge.

We were gratified by the response. It appears that our plan struck a common chord. Almost everyone we approached wished to contribute, though in the event not all did. Some colleagues had commitments which made their participation impossible in the end, and although substitute authors were found in one or two cases, this process meant that we lost three chapters from the original design. We had planned to include a separate chapter on the history of crime measurement in Section One. Our original outline for Section Three included two additional chapters, one on the nature of the criminal justice system as a whole and the relations among its various constituent agencies, and another on the effectiveness of sentences imposed by courts. We also planned a wide-ranging chapter on property crime to complement that on professional crime by Dick Hobbs. To some extent these topics have been covered in other chapters, though this is least the case with the planned chapter on the criminal justice system as system. Unfortunately, this was was a gap we were unable to plug within the time available.

An important issue arose about the handling of the dimensions of gender and race. Should we expect each of our contributors to discuss the significance of these factors? Should we *insist* that gender and race be thoroughly addressed in every chapter? Or should we assign them chapters for specialist coverage? Partly to avoid excessive repetition, and partly to maintain our general policy of leaving the balance of topics within individual essays to contributors' discretion, we chose the latter course. This ran the risk that these issues would not always, throughout the volume, receive the attention they deserve. In the event, many contributors have given them due prominence and, though some may dissent, we are reasonably happy with the outcome overall.

This raises another problem of balance within the volume, to which Jill Peay draws attention at the beginning of her chapter. Some of the imbalances in this collection reflect imbalances within criminology generally, which in turn reflect imbalances within academic life and society at large. Of the twenty-six authors, only five are women. While this proportion reflects the overall male–female ratio among criminologists (which Rock, in chapter 3 of this volume, estimates at around 20 per cent), it may still, we recognize, reflect some failure of imagination on our—three male editors'—part in the choice of authors. We can only respond that we chose potential contributors for each chapter separately, chiefly on the criterion of known expertise and interest in that particular area of criminology. The result, we believe, reflects the fact that, although there is now a healthier representation of women than ever before among the most distinguished British criminologists, a high proportion of these have established their reputations within an overlapping set of relatively new specialist interests, particularly in areas such as gender and crime, sexual and domestic violence, victimization, and fear of crime, which were previously neglected by most male criminologists. Finally, while the sex ratio among criminologists remains far from ideal, the discipline is even more impoverished (indeed, one could say, shamed) by the fact that very few black academics have yet established leading positions and reputations within the criminological field. None is represented here. If we were to repeat some or all of the exercise in a few years' time, we would hope that the situation would be very different in these respects.

THE FUTURE

It is in fact our hope, and that of our publishers, that this text represents the first edition in a continuing enterprise. It would be a foolish hostage to fortune to be too explicit about our aspirations. However, if those who teach, study, and practise criminology find this volume as much an asset as we planned it to be, then we envisage regularly revising the collection.

That means not just updating the reviews of particular topics, but amending the number and content of chapters to reflect developments in theory, research, and policy. For this reason we shall not pretend to be uninterested in the response this text evokes. On the contrary, we shall read the reviews avidly and we would urge our readers, whoever they may be, to let us know what they think of this volume and give us their suggestions for the next edition. In that way subsequent versions may move towards our aspiration of definitiveness, as well as to the development of understanding and action concerning issues which profoundly touch the lives of many people.

REFERENCES

ATKINSON, J. M. (1971), 'Societal Reactions to Suicide: The Role of Coroners' Definitions', in S. Cohen ed., *Images of Deviance.* Harmondsworth: Penguin.

BAILEY, R. (1973), 'Housing Alienation and Beyond', in I. Taylor and L. Taylor eds., *Politics and Deviance.* Harmondsworth: Penguin.

BUTLER, LORD (1974), 'The Foundation of the Institute of Criminology in Cambridge', in R. Hood ed., *Crime, Criminology and Public Policy.* London: Heinemann.

CAIN, M. (1971), 'On the Beat: Interactions and Relations in Rural and Urban Forces', in S. Cohen ed., *Images of Deviance.* Harmondsworth: Penguin.

—— (1973) *The Policeman in the Community.* London: Routledge.

CLARKE, J., HALL, S., JEFFERSON, T., and ROBERTS, B., eds. (1976), *Resistance through Rituals.* London: Hutchinson.

COHEN, S. (1971), 'Introduction', in S. Cohen, ed., *Images of Deviance.* Harmondsworth: Penguin.

—— (1972), *Folk Devils and Moral Panics: The Creation of the Mods and Rockers.* London: MacGibbon and Kee.

DOWNES, D., and ROCK, P. (1988), *Understanding Deviance*, 2nd edn. Oxford: Oxford University Press.

HOME OFFICE (1986), *Criminal Justice: A Working Paper* London: Home Office.

—— (1993) *Digest 2: Information on the Criminal Justice System in England & Wales.* London: Home Office Research and Statistics Department.

LIAZOS, A. (1972), 'The Poverty of the Sociology of Deviance: Nuts, Sluts and Perverts', *Social Problems*, 20: 102–20.

LODGE, T. S. (1974), 'The Founding of the Home Office Research Unit', in R. Hood, ed., *Crime, Criminology, and Public Policy* London: Heinemann.

MADDISON, S. (1973), 'Mindless Militants? Psychiatry and the University', in I. Taylor and L. Taylor eds., *Politics and Deviance.* Harmondsworth: Penguin.

PEARSON, G. (1983), *Hooligan.* London: Macmillan.

PLUMMER, K. (1975), *Sexual Stigma: An Interactionist Account.* London: Routledge.

TAYLOR, I. (1971), 'Soccer Consciousnessness and Soccer Hooliganism', in S. Cohen ed., *Images of Deviance.* Harmondsworth: Penguin.

Taylor, I., Walton, P., and Young, J. (1973), *The New Criminology*. London: Routledge.

Wiles, P. (1976), 'Introduction', in P. Wiles, ed., *The Sociology of Crime and Delinquency in Britain*. Oxford: Martin Robertson.

Wilson, J. Q., and Herrnstein, R. (1985), *Crime and Human Nature*. New York: Simon and Schuster.

Young, J. (1971), *The Drugtakers: The Social Meaning of Drug Use*. London: MacGibbon and Kee.

—— (1981), 'Thinking Seriously about Crime: Some Models of Criminology', in M. Fitzgerald, G. McLennan, and J. Pawson eds., *Crime and Society: Readings in History and Theory*. London: Routledge.

—— (1986), 'The Failure of Criminology: The Need for a Radical Realism', in R. Matthews and J. Young, eds., *Confronting Crime*. London: Sage.

—— (1988), 'Radical Criminology in Britain,' *British Journal of Criminology*, 28/2: 289–313.

PART 1

Theoretical and Historical Perspectives

1

Of Crimes and Criminals: The Development of Criminology in Britain

DAVID GARLAND

INTRODUCTION: THE CONTINGENCY OF THE CRIMINOLOGICAL PRESENT

This essay presents an interpretation of the historical development of criminology in Britain. Any such history is inevitably a contentious undertaking, entailing theoretical choices and rhetorical purposes as well as the selection and arrangement of historical materials. Whether they acknowledge it or not, histories of the discipline necessarily come up against fundamental issues—What is 'criminology'? What are its central features? How are its conceptual and historical boundaries identified? In what institutional, political, or cultural contexts should it be situated? It may therefore be useful to begin by outlining some of the theoretical assumptions which underpin the interpretation offered here.

I take criminology to be a specific genre of discourse and inquiry about crime—a genre which has developed in the modern period and which can be distinguished from other ways of talking and thinking about criminal conduct. Thus, for example, its claim to be an empirically grounded, scientific undertaking sets it apart from moral and legal discourses, while its focus upon crime differentiates it from other social scientific genres, such as the sociology of deviance and control, whose objects of study are broader and not defined by the criminal law. Since the middle years of this century, criminology has also been increasingly marked off from other discourses by the trappings of a distinctive disciplinary identity, with its own journals, professional associations, professorships and institutes. One of the central concerns of this essay will be to try to explain how such a discipline came to exist as an accredited specialism, supported by universities and governments alike.

I am grateful to the following friends and colleagues for their help with this essay: Stanley Cohen, Mitchell Duneier, James B. Jacobs, Dorothy Nelkin, Robert Reiner, Paul Rock, and Peter Young. Research for this project was assisted by the Lindsay Bequest Fund of the Edinburgh University Law Faculty and by the New York University School of Law.

My broad historical argument will be that modern criminology grew out of the convergence of two quite separate enterprises—'the governmental project' and 'the Lombrosian project'—which together provided a social and an intellectual rationale for the subject. By talking about a 'governmental project' I mean to refer to the long series of empirical inquiries, which, since the eighteenth century, have sought to enhance the efficient and equitable administration of justice by charting the patterns of crime and monitoring the practice of police and prisons. This tradition of inquiry was eventually to become a major part of the criminological enterprise and to provide criminology with its central claim to social utility. The 'Lombrosian project', in contrast, refers to a form of inquiry which aims to develop an etiological, explanatory science, based on the premise that criminals can somehow be scientifically differentiated from non-criminals.[1] Although each of these projects has undergone important revisions during the twentieth century, and the situation of criminology has been significantly altered by its entry into the universities, I will suggest that the discipline continues to be structured by the sometimes competing, sometimes converging, claims of these two programmes. One pole of the discipline pulls its members towards an ambitious (and, I have argued elsewhere—Garland 1985*b*—deeply flawed) theoretical project seeking to build a science of causes. The other exerts the force of a more pragmatic, policy-orientated, administrative project, seeking to use science in the service of management and control. Criminologists have sometimes sought to overcome this tension by rejecting one project in favour of the other—either giving up the search for causes in favour of a direct policy orientation, or else disengaging from governmental concerns in the name of a pure (or a critical) science. However, the combination of the two seems essential to criminology's claim to be sufficiently useful and sufficiently scientific to merit the status of an accredited, state-sponsored, academic discipline.

[1] I use the concept of a 'project' here to characterize an emergent tradition of inquiry which, despite a degree of variation, shares a cluster of aims and objectives. The 'governmental' project refers to those inquiries which direct their attention to the problems of governing crime and criminals. Studies which fall within this tradition are not necessarily official, state-sponsored studies, although, from the nineteenth century onwards, the state came to dominate work of this kind. Nor are these inquiries necessarily focused upon state practices (such as criminal laws, police, prisons, etc.), since the governance of crime and criminals also occurs through 'private' institutions such as the family, boys' clubs, settlement houses, and so on. As I discuss later, the study of crime and criminal justice practices was not at first separate from a much broader concern with the rational goverance of the population in all its aspects. (On the concept of governmentality, see Foucault 1979; Burchell *et al.* 1991.) The 'Lombrosian' project refers to that tradition of inquiry, begun by Lombroso, which aims to differentiate the criminal individual from the non-criminal. By naming the etiological project in this way I wish to emphasize the continuity in scientific objective which runs from Lombroso to the present, rather than to suggest a continuity of method or of substantive analysis: most etiological studies of the twentieth century have deemphasized the biological determinants which Lombroso took to be fundamental.

The coming together of these two projects was by no means inevitable. The historical record suggests that it took several decades for officials to accept that the Lombrosian search for the causes of crime had any relevance to their administrative tasks, and, in fact, Lombroso's criminology had to be extensively modified before it could be of service to policy-makers and state authorities. Beyond that, the very idea of a science devoted to 'the criminal' seems in retrospect to have been something of an historical accident, originally prompted by a claim that was quickly discredited: namely, that 'the criminal type' was an identifiable anthropological entity. Were it not for the contingency of that intellectual event there might never have been any distinctive criminological science or any independent discipline. As an historical counterfactual, it is perfectly plausible to imagine that crime and criminals could have remained integral concerns of mainstream sociology and psychiatry and that 'criminological' research undertaken for government purposes could have developed without the need of a university specialism of that name. If this is so, and criminology has a contingent rather than a necessary place in the halls of science, then its history becomes all the more relevant to an understanding of the discipline.

In the light of the assumptions and arguments I have outlined here, history becomes essential to an understanding of the modern criminological enterprise. If we are to understand the central topics which criminology has marked out as its own, if we are to understand the discipline's relation to institutional practices and concerns, if we are to understand some of the key terms and conceptions which structure the discourse, then we will have to ask genealogical questions about the constitution of this science and examine the historical processes which led to the emergence of an accredited disciplinary specialism. Moreover, the kind of historical inquiry required is one which is sensitive to context and contingency, and to the relation between intellectual developments and the social practices out of which they emerge. If my claim is correct, and criminology is a product of the convergence of certain ideas and interests, in a particular institutional context, then its history cannot be treated, as it so often is, as the gradual unfolding of a science which was always destined to appear. Such is the prevalence of this kind of history that it may be worth discussing the shortcomings of received accounts, before going on to sketch an alternative approach.

Textbook Histories

Criminology's history is most often constructed in the form of a preface. It appears, usually in a few compressed and standardized pages, as the opening section of a book or article, introducing the reader to the subject and placing the author's text within a longer tradition. Sometimes the prefatory history has a job to do, providing the reader with enough historical understanding to appreciate the significance and provenance of the text that follows. At other times it is merely decorative, a routine flourish with little real purpose beyond getting started in a way that has come to be expected of authors. Ironically, this routine repetition of conventional historical wisdom can have an influence quite out of keeping with its value as scholarship. The telling and retelling of the standard historical tale is a most effective way of persuading the discipline's recruits that whatever else may be contested, this much, at least, can be taken for granted.

Occasionally, textbooks, research monographs, or critical studies make a feature of their historical introductions, offering a more extensive (and usually more tendentious) account of the subject's history, which acts as a kind of framing device for subsequent arguments.[2] On such occasions, history becomes a way of conducting theoretical debate by other means. The recovery of a lost theoretical tradition, the reinterpretation of the subject's early history, claims and counter-claims about the true 'founders' of the discipline, or critical summaries of previous patterns of thought, are all ways in which the subject's history gets drafted into current controversies and made to do duty for one side or the other.

The history of the discipline has, on a few occasions, formed the central subject-matter for a book or an article. Most of these excursions into historical criminology are minor attempts to attribute importance to a particular author whose influence upon the subject is felt to have been slighted,[3] but some historical writings have more ambitious intentions. Books such as Mannheim's *Pioneers in Criminology* (1960) or Radzinowicz's *Ideology and Crime* (1966)—both published by leading figures in the process of discipline-building—played an important role in shaping the contours and self-consciousness of the discipline, and sought to enhance its status by invoking a distinguished Enlightenment past and a progressive scientific mission. The recent collection entitled *The History of British Criminology* (Rock 1988*a*)—edited by one of the sociologists who helped remake British criminology in the 1960s and 1970s—professes similar discipline-forming ambitions, aiming to introduce new generations of criminologists to a revised history more in keeping with contemporary interests and understandings. It is not just the textbooks which have to be adjusted when a discipline changes; history must also be rewritten.

The received history of the discipline, often simplified into a tale of icons and demons (Beccaria, Lombroso, Burt, Radzinowicz . . .), a few

[2] See e.g. the historical introductions to the following: Taylor, Walton, and Young 1973; Morris 1957; Matza 1964.

[3] See e.g. Savitz *et al.* 1977; also Lyell 1913, Levin and Lindesmith 1937.

key distinctions (classicism, positivism, radicalism . . .), and an overarching narrative in which ideological error is gradually displaced by the findings of science (e.g. the myth of the born criminal and its subsequent debunking), plays a small but significant role in shaping the horizons and reference points of contemporary criminology. A discipline's practitioners work with a sense of where their subject has come from and where it is going, which issues are settled and which are still live, who are the exemplars to imitate and who the anathemas to be avoided. Perhaps most importantly, the received history provides practioners with a standard-issue kit of collective terms and shared values. Thus, for example, anyone who learned about the discipline's history from the textbooks of the 1970s would find it hard to identify with the methods and aspirations of 'positivism', even though this term was broad enough to include virtually the whole discipline prior to the rise of 'labelling' theories and the associated anti-positivist critiques.[4]

The standard textbook account of criminology's history begins with the writings of criminal law reformers in the eighteenth century, particularly Beccaria, Bentham, Romilly and Howard. These writers are said to have characterized the offender as a rational, free-willed actor, who engages in crime in a calculated, utilitarian way and is therefore responsive to deterrent, proportionate penalties of the kind that the reformers preferred. This 'classical school of criminology', as it is usually called, was subsequently challenged, in the late nineteenth century, by writers of the 'positivist school' (Lombroso, Ferri, and Garofalo are usually cited) who adopted a more empirical, scientific approach to the subject, and investigated 'the criminal' using the techniques of psychiatry, physical anthropology, anthropometry, and other new human sciences. The positivist school claimed to have discovered evidence of the existence of 'criminal types' whose behaviour was determined rather than chosen and for whom treatment rather than punishment was appropriate. Subsequent research refuted or modified most of the specific claims of Lombroso, and restored the credibility of some of the 'classicist' ideas he opposed, but the project of a scientific criminology had been founded, and this enterprise continues, in a more diverse and sophisticated way, today.

This standard textbook history is, of course, broadly accurate—it would be very surprising if it were not. But the broad sweep of its narrative and the resounding simplicity of its generic terms can be profoundly misleading if they are taken as real history, rather than as a kind of

[4] See e.g. the discussions of 'positivism' in Taylor, Walton, and Young 1973 and in Matza 1964. The tradition of 'positivist criminology' has recently been re-evaluated and reaffirmed in the USA (see Gottfredson and Hirschi 1987), and in Britain, some of its sternest critics have modified their views and realigned themselves with some of its central concerns. For a discussion of the changing relationship between 'radical criminology' and 'positivism', see Young 1988.

foundational myth, developed for heuristic rather than historical purposes.

Misleading Categories

A major defect of these histories is their uncritical use of key terms which then subsequently enter into standard criminological discourse in an equally unselfconscious way. The term 'classicism', to take an important example, is used as a generic term to denote the criminology of Beccaria and Bentham, and eighteenthth-century thought more generally. It is also used, by extension, to describe modern theories which affirm the rationality and freedom of offenders' decision-making processes (see Roshier 1989). But, despite this conventional usage, it actually makes little sense to claim that these eighteenth-century thinkers possessed a 'criminology', given that they made no general distinction between the characteristics of criminals and non-criminals, and had no conception of research on crime and criminals as a distinctive form of inquiry. To use such a term to characterize eighteenth century thought seriously misrepresents the character of these writings and forcibly assimilates them to a project that was not invented until a century later.

The notion that these various writers all maintained the same rational, free-will view of the offender is also a distortion, derived from the polemics of late nineteenth-century positivists rather than from a reading of the eighteenth-century texts. There are, for example, quite major differences between authors such as Bentham and Howard on the questions of human nature and freedom of choice; and Beccaria, as a good Lockean empiricist, viewed human character and conduct as shaped by sense impressions and habit as well as by free will and reason.[5] Other eighteenth-century writers on crime approached the question from a quite different perspective, stressing the social conditions which shaped individual conduct and using a deterministic language to describe the process of becoming criminal.[6] The notion of 'classicism' thus tends to dissolve under close scrutiny, deriving any coherence it has not from the facts of intellectual history but from the requirements of contemporary criminological teaching.

'Positivism' holds up little better as a descriptive term, although, unlike classicism, it at least has the merit of having been the self-description of a school of criminologists. The use of this word to describe the specific claims of Lombroso and his *scuola positiva* in the late nineteenth century

[5] On the differences between Howard and Bentham, see Ignatieff 1978. On Beccaria as a Lockean empiricist, see Zeman 1981.

[6] See the discussion of writers such as Henry Dagge and Mannasseh Dawes in Green 1985.

(the born criminal, the constitutional and hereditary roots of criminal conduct, criminal types, etc.) and also to describe the huge and diverse range of criminological work which has been carried out within an empiricist framework (i.e. using 'theory-neutral' observation as a basis for inductive propositions, stressing measurement, objectivity, etc.) has been a source of great confusion in the discipline. Potted histories entrench this muddle whenever they talk indiscriminately about a 'positivist era' which stretched from the 1870s to the 1960s.

The Object of Inquiry

One of the most problematic issues to be addressed by any intellectual history is the question of criteria for inclusion and exclusion. If one is writing the history of criminology, what is to count as relevant? Where does the subject start and where does it stop? Textbook histories generally avoid the issue and simply begin with Beccaria, the arbitrariness of this decision being concealed by the fact that this is by now the traditional place to start. But one can see the problem much more clearly on those occasions when the intellectual history of criminology is the subject of a whole article or series of chapters. Thus, for instance, Israel Drapkin's essay in the *Encyclopedia of Crime and Justice* (Drapkin 1983)—like the more historically orientated textbooks by Bonger (1936) and Vold (1958)—seeks to provide a more serious, scholarly account of the subject's history. Drapkin traces criminology's intellectual history back through the early modern period, the Middle Ages, and the classical period to the ancient world and 'prehistoric times'. The problem here is that the selection criteria are unargued and hopelessly broad. Criminology's history becomes the history of everything that has ever been said or thought or done in relation to law-breakers, and the links between this amorphous past and the particular present remain vague and unspecified. Worse still, the writings of ancient and medieval authors are ransacked in search of 'criminological' statements and arguments, as if they were addressing the same questions in the same ways as modern criminologists, and we are introduced to anachronistic creatures such as 'early modern criminology' and St Thomas Aquinas' analysis of 'criminogenic factors' (Drapkin 1983: 550).

This criminology-through-the-ages style of history is objectionable on a number of grounds. First of all, it distorts the meaning of earlier writers and conceals the fact that their statements are structured by assumptions and objectives—not to mention institutional contexts and cultural commitments—which are quite different from those of modern criminology.[7]

[7] The classic discussion of this problem in the history of ideas is contained in Skinner 1969.

Secondly, it gives the false impression that criminology is our modern response to a timeless and unchanging set of questions which previous thinkers have also pondered, though with notably less success. Criminology is seen as a science which was waiting to happen, the end point of a long process of inquiry which has only recently broken through to the status of true, scientific knowledge. This progressivist, presentist view of things fails to recognize that criminology is, in fact, a socially constructed and historically specific organization of knowledge and investigative procedures—a particular style of reasoning, representing, and intervening—which is grounded in a particular set of institutions and forms of life. It is a 'discipline', a regime of truth with its own special rules for deciding between truth and falsity, rather than the epitome of right thought and correct knowledge. To adopt this fallacious way of thinking about the discipline's history is to cut off from view the other 'problematizations' (as Foucault would call them) that the historical record reveals, and to forget that our own ways of constituting and perceiving 'crime' and 'deviance' are established conventions rather than unchallengeable truths. An important purpose of writing history is to help develop a consciousness of how conventions are made and remade over time, and thus promote a critical self-consciousness about our own questions and assumptions. The myth of an emergent criminology, progressing from ancient error to modern truth, does little to improve our understanding of the past or of the present.

My remarks up to now have been directed against criminology's history as told by criminologists to criminologists. But in recent years our historical understanding of the subject has been considerably advanced by the work of 'outsiders' who owe no allegiance to the discipline and whose work is driven by quite different historical and critical concerns. The writings of Michel Foucault (1977), Robert Nye (1984), Daniel Pick (1989), Martin Wiener (1990) and others have, in their different ways, situated criminological discourse on a wider canvas, showing how this form of knowledge was grounded in quite specific institutional practices, political movements, and cultural settings. None of these authors provides an overall account of criminology's development, each one being concerned to understand the criminological ideas prevailing in a particular period or setting, rather than to produce a genealogy of the discipline. But the analyses of these and other writers are of great importance for the understanding of criminology's past and their work adds breadth and depth to the somewhat narrower, diachronic account which the present paper sets out. Similarly valuable is the recent work done in the newly developed field of the history of the human sciences by authors such as Nikolas Rose (1988), Roger Smith (1988), Kurt Danziger (1990), and Ian Hacking (1990). These writers have set out important methodological and theoretical guidelines for work in this area—guidelines which I have tried to follow in the present essay. They have also developed cogent historical analyses of disciplines such as psychology and statistics which are of great relevance for any account of criminology's development.[8]

ORIENTATIONS: A HISTORY OF THE PRESENT

I begin with the clear assumption that the phenomenon to be explained is a present-day phenomenon—the modern discipline of criminology—and that my task is to trace its historical conditions of emergence, identify the intellectual resources and traditions upon which it drew, and give some account of the process of its formation and development. This explicit concern to write a history of the present acknowledges that our contemporary problems and practices are quite distinct from those of the past; but equally, it recognizes that our present arrangements were constructed out of materials and situations which existed at earlier points in time. The present is continuous with the past in some respects, and discontinuous in others. It is the historian's job to identify the processes of transmutation which characterize change and, in particular, the generation of those differences which constitute our modernity.

Modern criminology, like any other academic specialism, consists of a body of accredited and systematically transmitted forms of knowledge, approved procedures and techniques of investigation, and a cluster of questions which make up the subject's recognized research agendas. These intellectual materials and activities are loosely organized by means of a 'discipline'—the standard form of academic organization. The discipline establishes and enforces appropriate norms of evidence and argument, evaluates and communicates research findings and other contributions to knowledge, fixes and revises the canon of theoretical and empirical knowledge, supervises the training of students, and distributes professional status and authority among accredited practitioners. These disciplinary functions are carried out, more or less effectively, by means of a variety of institutions—professional journals and associations, institutes and university departments, professional appointments, processes of peer review, letters of recommendation, training courses, textbooks, conferences, funding agencies, and so on—which make up the material infrastructure of the enterprise.[9] One has only to describe these taken-for-granted features explicitly to demonstrate that the modern discipline of criminology is indeed 'modern', and to pose the question of how such an institutional

[8] The history of anthropology also contains many suggestive parallels with that of criminology; see e.g. Darnell 1974.

[9] On scientific disciplines and their development, see Lemaine *et al.* 1976.

structure came to form itself around an intellectual specialism of this kind.

Modern criminology is a composite, eclectic, multidisciplinary enterprise. The subject is typically located in departments of law, sociology, or social policy—though there are now several independent centres of criminology in British universities—and training in criminology is normally at the postgraduate level, following on a first degree in a more basic field of study. In their research and teaching, criminologists draw upon a variety of other disciplines, most notably sociology, psychology, psychiatry, law, history, and anthropology—indeed, one of the major dynamics of modern criminology is the incessant raiding of other disciplines or ideologies for new ideas with which to pursue (and renew) the criminological project. They also address themselves to a wide range of research topics which somehow or other relate to crime and its control. Major areas of work include research on the incidence and distribution of criminal behaviour, inquiries about the causes or correlates of criminal conduct, clinical studies of individual delinquents and ethnographies of deviant groups, penological studies, victim studies, the monitoring and evaluation of criminal justice agencies, the prediction of future criminal conduct, the study of processes of social reaction, and historical work on changing patterns of crime and control. The list of 'central' topics is long and diverse, and each topic breaks down further into numerous sub-topics and specialisms. When one considers that these substantive areas have been approached using a variety of quantitative and qualitative methods, drawing upon the whole gamut of theoretical perspectives (psychoanalysis, functionalism, interactionism, ethnomethodology, Marxism, econometrics, systems theory, postmodernism, etc.) and ideological concerns (the implicit welfarism of most twentieth-century criminology, the radicalism of the 1970s, feminism, left realism, etc., etc.) it becomes apparent that modern criminology is highly differentiated in its theoretical, methodological, and empirical concerns.

The very diversity of the modern subject makes the question of its historical emergence and identity seem even more puzzling. How did this vast, eclectic bundle of disparate approaches, theories, and data come to acquire the status of a distinct academic specialism? At one level, the answer to this has already been set out above: the subject derives whatever coherence and unity it has from the exertions of its discipline-forming institutions. The danger of an exploding, unmanageable chaos of concerns is held in check by textbooks and teaching and a pattern of professional judgements which draw the subject together and establish its *de facto* boundaries. But this response begs a prior question, which is: Why has there emerged a discipline of this kind? What makes it possible and desirable to have a distinctive, specialist discipline of criminology in the first place? It seems to me that an answer to this question can be formulated if one has regard to the basic problem-structures or projects of inquiry which underlie these disparate investigations. My argument is, as suggested above, that criminology is structured around two basic projects—the governmental and the Lombrosian—and that the formation and convergence of these projects can be traced by studying the texts and statements which constitute criminology's historical archive. Criminology, in its modern form and in its historical development, is orientated towards a scientific goal but also towards an institutional field, towards a theoretical project but also towards an administrative task. Whatever fragile unity the discipline achieves emerges from the belief that these two projects are mutually supportive rather than incompatible, that etiological research can be made useful for administrative purposes, and that the findings of operational research further the ends of theoretical inquiry. Occasionally, criminologists lose this faith, and when they do, their arguments cast doubt on the very viability of the discipline.[10]

As with most 'human sciences', criminology has a long past but a short history.[11] Discourse about crime and punishment has existed, in one form or another, since ancient times, but it is only during the last 120 years that there has been a distinctive 'science of criminology', and only in the last fifty or sixty years has there been in Britain an established, independent discipline organized around that intellectual endeavour. My account of the emergence of the modern British discipline will be divided into four parts:

1. a brief discussion of what I will call 'traditional' representations of crime and criminals;
2. an outline of the empirical analyses that were brought to bear upon crime and criminal justice in the eighteenth and nineteenth-centuries, and which began the tradition of inquiry which I call the governmental project;
3. an account of the emergence of a positive, specialist 'science of the criminal'—the Lombrosian project—in the late nineteenth century, both in continental Europe and in Britain;
4. an account of how these two projects converged in a way and to an extent which facilitated the formation of a criminological discipline in Britain in the middle years of the twentieth century.

[10] See e.g. the debates surrounding the development of a radical criminology which aimed to disengage from the policy goals of the state—a development which, for some writers, came to imply the dissolution of criminology as a discipline. See Bankowski *et al.* 1976, Hirst 1975. See also the recent reflections on the relationship between criminology and criminal justice policy by Petersilia 1991 and Bottoms 1987.

[11] For a theoretical discussion addressing this issue in the history of psychology, see Smith 1988.

This order of exposition implies a certain developmental pattern, and to some extent that seems appropriate. Criminological thought and practice have developed, at least in some respects, in a 'scientific' direction, and the analysis presented here is concerned precisely to chart this evolution and to reconstruct the events and developments which played a role in that transmutation. The chronology of events is constructed in order to show how our particular ways of organizing thought and research have come into existence. But it needs to be emphasized that no overall process of progressive development is being asserted here, and there are no exclusive boundaries neatly separating the thought of one period from the thought of another. Some residues of the 'traditional' ideas to be found in the seventeenth century still circulate today in the form of common-sense and moral argument. Forms of thought and inquiry which flourished in the eighteenth and early nineteenth centuries have been rediscovered in the late twentieth and adapted to serve contemporary purposes. Conversely, certain ideas and arguments which appeared progressive and persuasive to criminologists at the start of the present century have come to seem pseudo-scientific and faintly absurd.

Criminology's history is not one of steady progress and refinement, although whenever a framework of inquiry has endured for a long enough time, such refinements have taken place. Instead, it is a story of constant reformulation in response to shifting political pressures, changes in institutional and administrative arrangements, intellectual developments occurring in adjacent disciplines, and the changing ideological commitments of its practitioners. The very fact that a basic orientation of the discipline links it to a field of social problems and to administrative efforts to govern that field imparts a certain instability to the subject and constantly transforms its objects of study. As a discipline criminology is shaped only to a small extent by its own theoretical object and logic of inquiry. Its epistemological threshold is a low one, making it susceptible to pressures and interests generated elsewhere.

TRADITIONAL REPRESENTATIONS OF CRIME

Social rules and the violation of them are an intrinsic aspect of social organization, a part of the human condition. Discourse about crime and criminals—or sin, villainy, roguery, deviance, whatever the local idiom—is thus as old as human civilization itself. Wherever generalized frameworks developed for the representation and explanation of human conduct, whether as myths, cosmologies, theologies, metaphysical systems, or vernacular common sense—they generally entailed propositions about aberrant conduct and how it should be understood. As we have seen, some writers have taken this recurring concern with law-breakers as sufficient licence to talk about a 'criminology' which stretches back to the dawn of time. But rather than see such writings as proto-criminologies struggling to achieve a form which we have since perfected, it seems more appropriate to accept that there are a variety of ways in which crime can be problematized and put into discourse, and that 'criminology' is only one version among others. The propositions about crime and criminals which appear in the writings of ancient and medieval philosophers, the theologies of the Church of Rome and the Protestant Reform tradition, the mythico-magical cosmologies of the Middle Ages, and the legal thought of the early modern period were not aspiring criminologies, even though their subject-matter sometimes bears a resemblance to that which criminology seeks to explain. These broad resemblances begin to appear less compelling when one looks in detail at what the discourses involved and their implicit assumptions about the world. Entities such as fate and demons, original sin and human depravity, temptation, lust, and avarice are the products of mental frameworks and forms of life rather different from our own.[12]

The differences between these mentalities and our own can be quite instructive, pointing up some of the peculiarities of our accustomed ways of thinking about crime. It is significant, for example, that the major tradition of Western thought—Christianity, in all its variants—did not separate out the law-breaker as different or abnormal, but instead understood him or her as merely a manifestation of universal human depravity and the fallen, sinful state of all mankind.[13] 'There but for the grace of God go I' is an understanding of things quite alien to much of the criminology that was written in the late nineteenth and early twentieth centuries. In the same way, the explicitly moral and spiritual terms in which the Christian tradition discusses individual wrongdoing, the lack of reference to systematically controlled empirical evidence, the invocation of the Devil, or demons, or divine intervention to account for human action, and the appeal to scriptural authority as proof for propositions are all starkly contrastive reminders of the rather different rules governing modern criminological discourse.

But traditional accounts of crime—Christian and otherwise—are not entirely remote from modern thinking about the subject. Scattered around in the diverse literature of the early modern period, in criminal biographies and broadsheets, accounts of the Renaissance underworld, Tudor rogue pamphlets, Elizabethan dramas and Jacobean city comedies,

[12] For a wide-ranging discussion, see Jean Delumeau's account (Delumeau 1990) of sin and fear in thirteenth- to eighteenth-century Europe.

[13] For developments of this point, see Zeman 1981; and also Faller 1987.

the utopia of Thomas More and the novels of Daniel Defoe,[14] one can discover rudimentary versions of the etiological accounts which are used today to narrate the process of becoming deviant. Stories of how the offender fell in with bad company, became lax in his habits and was sorely tried by temptation, was sickly, or tainted by bad blood, or neglected by unloving parents, became too fond of drink or too idle to work, lost her reputation and found it hard to get employment, was driven to despair by poverty or simply driven to crime by avarice and lust—these seem to provide the well-worn templates from which our modern theories of crime are struck, even if we insist upon a more neutral language with which to tell the tale, and think that a story's plausibility should be borne out by evidence as well as intuition.[15] Indeed, Faller's research (Faller 1987) suggests that what was lacking in these seventeenth- and eighteenth-century accounts was not secular or materialist explanations of the roots of crime, which were present in abundance alongside the spiritual explanations proffered by the church. What was lacking was a developed sense of differential etiology. Crime was seen as an omnipresent temptation to which all humankind was vulnerable, but when it became a question of why some succumbed and others resisted, the explanation trailed off into the unknowable, resorting to fate, or providence, or the will of God. When, in the late nineteenth century, the science of criminology emerged, one of its central concerns would be to address this issue of differentiation and subject it to empirical inqury.

'Traditional' ways of thinking about crime did not disappear with the coming of the modern, scientific age, though they may nowadays be accorded a different status in the hierarchy of credibility. These older conceptions—based upon experience and ideology rather than systematic empirical inquiry—have not been altogether displaced by scientific criminologies, and we continue to acknowledge the force of moral, religious and 'common-sensical' ways of discussing crime. Expert, research-based knowledge about crime and criminals still competes with views of the subject which are not 'criminological' in their style of reasoning or their use of evidence. Judges, moralists, religious fundamentalists, and populist leader-writers still offer views on criminological subjects which are quite innocent of criminological science. Unlike physics or even economics, which have established a degree of monopoly over the right to speak authoritatively about their subjects, criminology operates in a culture which combines traditional and scientific modes of thought and action.

[14] On criminal biographies and broadsheets, see Faller 1987; Sharpe 1985. On crime and criminals in Tudor rogue pamphlets and Jacobean city comedies, see Curtis and Hale 1981. For descriptions of the Elizabethan underworld, see Judges 1930; Salgado 1972.

[15] Matza (1969) analyses the recurring narratives of everyday discourse and shows how, in a slightly adapted form, these come to comprise the basic explanatory structures of contemporary criminological theory.

Intuitive, 'instinctive', common-sense views about crime and criminals are still more persuasive to many—including many in positions of power and authority—than are the results of carefully executed empirical research.

THE SCIENTIFIC ANALYSIS OF CRIME IN THE EIGHTEENTH AND EARLY NINETEENTH CENTURIES

In most criminological histories, the true beginnings of modern criminological thought are seen in writings of the eighteenth and early nineteenth centuries. Radzinowicz's monumental *History* (1948) begins in 1750, as does his historical essay on *Ideology and Crime* (1966). Mannheim's earliest 'pioneer' is Beccaria, whose *Of Crimes and Punishments* first appeared in 1764. Even *The New Criminology* (Taylor, Walton, and Young 1973), the radical and immensely influential textbook of the 1970s, begins its account with Beccaria and 'the classical school of criminology'. There are good grounds for choosing to emphasize the role of these eighteenth-century writings in the formation of criminology, but, as I suggested earlier, the connections are not as straightforward as is usually assumed. I have already argued that the writings of Beccaria, Bentham, and the others did not constitute a criminology. But despite this, they did establish and develop some of the key elements and conditions necessary for the subsequent development of the subject in its modern form. They are quite properly a part of criminology's genealogy, having been a direct source for some of the subject's basic aims and characteristics, as well as having produced a stock of propositions and arguments which would feature prominently in the criminological discourse which developed in the twentieth century.

There are several genealogical strands which link certain eighteenth- and early nineteenth-century writers with the criminology which followed. Most importantly, Enlightenment writers such as Beccaria, Bentham, and Howard wrote secular, materialist analyses, emphasizing the importance of reason and experience and denigrating theological forms of reasoning. They viewed themselves as proceeding in a scientific manner and dealing objectively with an issue which had previously been dominated by irrational, superstitious beliefs and prejudices. Members of the *scuola positiva* would later disparage the 'classical school' for its 'unscientific' reliance upon speculative reasoning rather than observed facts, but this is not how these writers viewed themselves. Indeed, it was the 'classicists' who first established the claim that crime and its control could be studied in a neutral, scientific manner.

Another important connection between the literature of the reformers and the criminology that followed was that the reformers of the late eighteenth and early nineteenth centuries were writing about a set of legal institutions which were becoming (partly through those reformers' efforts) recognizably modern. The institutional concerns which animated the writings of Beccaria, Bentham, Howard, and the rest are, in an important sense, modern concerns—about the systematic arrangement of criminal laws and procedures in order to promote social policy goals; about the sentencing choices of magistrates; about the organization and conduct of professional police; about the design and purposes of prison regimes. The interest of these writers in the psychology of offending, the nature of criminal motivation, the possibilities of deterrence and reform, and the most appropriate way for state institutions to regulate individual conduct, are also questions which were to be become quite central to later criminology. These issues gripped the imagination of eighteenth-century thinkers because they lived in a world caught up in the dynamics of modernization. This was the period which saw the emergence of the centralized administrative state, a national economy and a population inceasingly subject to governance, an autonomous, secular legal system, the political relations of liberalism, and institutional enclosures like the prison and the asylum with their reformative, disciplinary regimes. The writings of Beccaria, Bentham, and Howard—like those of Benjamin Rush in America—were the first soundings of a modernist discourse about crime. As intellectual responses to the challenge of crime in a newly urbanized market society, they were addressing problems of a novel type, quite unknown in traditional social thought. This new social and institutional environment, modified in certain ways, also formed the background against which the science of criminology would subsequently emerge, and in that respect there is a broad continuity of reference which makes eighteenth-century discourse 'modern' in a way that earlier writing is not. (Indeed, it is precisely because the reformist discourse of Beccaria *et al.* and the scientific discourse of Lombroso share a common institutional context that they are able to be viewed as 'opposites'. Each one entails a programme for directing the modern field of criminal justice.)

If one widens the lens to look beyond Beccaria and Bentham to some of the other discourses on crime and criminals dating from this period, one can detect other lines of affiliation. Patrick Colquhoun and Henry Fielding, as well as a large number of Parliamentary and private committees of the late eighteenth and early nineteenth centuries, used empirical evidence to situate and measure the extent of various crime problems ('the late increase in robbers', the relation between 'indigence' and crime, 'the alarming increase in juvenile delinquency', the 'police of the metropolis', and so on).[16] As Leon Radzinowicz (1956), and, more recently,

[16] See Colquhoun 1797, 1800, 1806, 1814; Fielding 1751; and the discussion of the parliamentary and private committees of inquiry of this period in Radzinowicz 1956.

Robert Reiner (1988) have pointed out, these inquiries formed part of a wider 'science of police' which flourished in this period, concerned not just with crime or criminals, but with the regulation and maintenance of the whole population in the interest of economy, welfare, and good governance (see also Foucault 1979; Pasquino 1978). John Howard's investigation of the state of the prisons was undertaken as a work of charity and reform, but his methods were doggedly empirical, and his study laid much stress on measurement and systematic observation as a basis for its findings.[17] Howard's work in the 1770s sparked the beginnings of a line of empirical penological inquiry which, from the 1830s onwards, became an increasingly important element in the British criminological tradition.

By the middle years of the nineteenth century this 'scientific' style of reasoning about crime had become a distinctive feature of the emergent culture of amateur social science. The papers delivered by Rawson W. Rawson, Joseph Fletcher, and John Glyde to the Statistical Society of London used judicial statistics and census data to chart the distribution and demography of crime, and to match up crime rates with other social indices—just as A. M. Guerry and Adolphe Quetelet had been doing in France and Belgium.[18] On the basis of carefully calculated correlations, they drew conclusions about the moral and social causes which influenced criminal conduct and presented their findings as instances of the new statistical science and its social uses. Henry Mayhew, writing in the middle years of the nineteenth century, was essentially a journalist concerned with 'the social question' and the problem of the poor. But unlike the moralists of a century earlier, his journalism was founded upon an empirical approach, using ethnographic and survey methods as well as life histories and statistical data; and his analyses of *London Labour and the London Poor* (1861–2) offered a series of empirically supported claims about the patterns and causes of professional crime in the city.[19]

Another line of inquiry which flourished in this period, and whose advocates would later be seen as progenitors of criminology, centred not upon the population and its governance by a well-ordered state, but instead upon individuals and their ability (or lack of ability) to govern themselves. As early as the 1760s and 1770s, Henry Dagge and Mannasseh Dawes argued that the law's notions of a free-willed offender were often enough fictions in the face of real social and psychological circumstances which limited choice and shaped human conduct, and they drew upon the new materialist psychologies of the time to explain how it

[17] See Howard 1973 [1777], 1973 [1789] and the discussion of his work in Ignatieff 1978.

[18] See the discussion of the work of Rawson, Fletcher, and Glyde in Morris 1957. Beirne (1993) provides detailed discussions of the work of Guerry and Quetelet and their place in the development of criminological thought.

[19] For a discussion of Mayhew's work and its relation to subsequent criminological analyses, see Morris 1957.

was that causal processes could be acknowledged without entirely destroying the belief in man's free will (see Green 1985). Indeed, both Thomas Zeman (1981) and Piers Beirne (1993) have recently shown that Cesare Beccaria's account of human conduct is shaped not by metaphysical assumptions about the freedom of the will, but instead by John Locke's empiricist psychology and the new 'science of man' developed by the thinkers of the Scottish Enlightenment.

During the nineteenth century this reconceptualization of human character and conduct was taken up and developed in the field of medicine, especially psychological medicine. The art of 'physiognomy'—which, it was claimed, enabled its practitioners to judge character and disposition from the features of the face and the external forms of the body—had been known since the seventeenth century, but the essays of J. C. Lavater purported to give a scientific foundation to this useful skill (Lavater 1792).[20] The craniometry and phrenology of F. J. Gall and J. C. Spurzheim made similar claims in the early nineteenth century, this time focusing upon the shape and contours of the human skull as an external index of character.[21] By the 1830s physiognomy and phrenology had lost much of their scientific credibility and had become the obsession of a few enthusiastic publicists, but the quest to uncover the links between physical constitution and psychological character was continued in a different and more important line of research: the new science of psychiatry.

The emergence of a network of private asylums in the eighteenth century led to the development of a new quasi-medical specialism which was at first called alienism and subsequently came to be known as psychological medicine or psychiatry. The writings of asylum managers about their patients—about their conduct, the antecedents of their madness, and the forms of treatment to which they responded—formed the basis for a major tradition of scientific investigation, and one which would subsequently be an important source of criminological data and ideas.

Attempts to link psychological characteristics to physical constitutions formed an abiding concern of this new discipline, but equally significant for our purposes, is its intense focus upon the insane individual—a focus permitted and encouraged by the long-term confinement of asylum patients under the daily gaze of the alienist (see Porter 1987). The new psychiatry produced a huge scientific literature concerned with the description of different mental types, case histories and causal analyses of how their madness developed, and detailed accounts of how they

[20] Richard Sennett (1977) provides an interesting account of various nineteenth-century efforts to judge character by outward appearance and describes the cultural predicament which prompted these concerns.

[21] On phrenology and its links to subsequent criminological studies, see Savitz *et al.* 1977. More generally, see Cooter 1981.

responded to various forms of 'moral' and medical treatment. What was developing here was a new kind of empirical psychology, concentrating upon pathological cases and their rational management. And because many of these cases involved criminal conduct (whether of a minor or a serious kind) one of the offshoots of this enterprise was a developing diagnostic and prognostic literature claiming to give a scientific account of certain kinds of individual criminals. Particularly after the Lunacy Acts of the mid-nineteenth century, when the asylum network was expanded to house the country's poor as well as the well-to-do, the new psychiatric profession had more and more to say about conditions such as 'moral imbecility', 'degeneracy', and 'feeblemindedness' which were deemed to be prevalent among the populations dealt with by the poor-houses and the prisons. Consequently, when a science of the criminal began to develop in the last decades of the century, there already existed a tradition of work whose concerns ran in parallel with its own and from which it could draw a measure of support and encouragement. Indeed, for about fifty years after the publication of Lombroso's *L'Uomo Delinquente* (1876) the journals of the psychiatric profession were virtually the only ones in Britain which took a serious interest in Lombroso's project.

If one were reviewing all of the ideas and undertakings of the eighteenth and early nineteenth centuries that bore a resemblance to elements which later appeared within the discipline of criminology, there would be other stories to tell. The various forms of charitable and social work with the poor, the societies for the care of discharged convicts, the management of workhouses, inquiries about the causes and extent of inebriety, investigations into the labour market, the employment and treatment of children, education, the housing of the poor, the settlement and boys' club movements, could all be identified as the roots of particular ingredients in the modern criminological mix. But one needs to recall that the ideas and forms of inquiry set out here did not add up to an early form of criminology for the simple reason that they did not 'add up' at all; nor could they until the later emergence of a form of inquiry centred upon the criminal, which drew together these various enterprises under the umbrella of a specialist criminological discipline. In their own time, they were discrete forms of knowledge, undertaken for a variety of different purposes, and forming elements within a variety of different discourses, none of which corresponds exactly with the criminological project that was subsequently formed. Beccaria, for example, developed his arguments about the reform of the criminal law within the broader context of a work on political economy. Colquhoun's writings about crime and police were, for him, one aspect of a treatise on government in which he addressed the changing problems of governance thrown up by the emergence of urbanized market society and the baleful effects of trade and luxury upon the manners of the people. Physiognomists, phrenologists, and psychiatrists were attempting to understand the physical and mental roots of human conduct rather than to develop a particular knowledge of offenders and offending. Like the utilitarian psychology developed by Bentham, these were attempts to capture the springs of human action in general, not to single out the criminal for special and exclusive attention. None of these discourses was struggling to create a distinctive criminological enterprise, though once such a subject was created, each formed a resource to be drawn upon, usually in a way which wrenched its insights about crime apart from the framework which originally produced them.

Certainly, if one looks back from the perspective of the present, one can glimpse the outlines of the governmental project and the Lombrosian project gradually taking shape in this period. Empirical studies of the police, of prisons, of crime rates and of the deterrent effects of criminal laws—the very stuff of criminology's governmental concerns—are already underway, conducted at first by amateurs but later by state officials utilizing the elementary tools of scientific method. However, these studies were not, at the time, viewed as distinct from other inquiries, into the market, morals, workhouses, or poverty. The broad concern animating all of these studies and more was a concern with governance and the use of empirical data and scientific methods to improve government's grip on the population. Only with the later professionalization and specialization of the various state agencies—and with the invention of 'criminology'—did the study of governance in criminal matters come to be viewed as distinct from the governance of the population in general. Similarly, one can see in the work of the nineteenth-century phrenologists and psychiatrists a concern to understand human conduct in scientific terms, to identify character types, and to trace the etiologies of pathological behaviours. But at this historical moment there was no focus upon the criminal as a special human type and no felt need for a specialism built around this entity. The splitting off of criminological studies, both in the administrative field and in the clinic, was a late nineteenth-century event which significantly changed the organization of subsequent thought and action.

Since the formation of criminology, its practitioners have repeatedly identified what they take to be their 'roots'—the various lines of descent which link their present practice to work done a century and more before. But this is perhaps the wrong way to look at things. A more accurate account might suggest that at the end of the nineteenth century the idea of a specialist criminological science emerged—centred, as it happens, on the figure of the 'criminal type'—and that, after a process of struggle, adaptation, and convergence, this subsequently led to the establishment, in a rather different form, of an independent criminological discipline. Since the discipline was characterized by an eclectic, multidisciplinary concern to pursue the crime problem in all its aspects, the subject is continually expanding to embrace all of the ways in which crime and criminals might be scientifically studied, and in so doing, it has constantly created new predecessors for itself. The connection between eighteenth- and twentieth-century discourse about crime is not a matter of tenacious traditions of thought which have survived continuously for 200 years. Rather, it is a matter of a certain broad similarity between forms of inquiry and institutional arrangements which prevailed in the eighteenth- and the twentieth centuries, together with the tendency of the modern discipline to embrace everything that might be scientifically said about crime and criminals. Each time a new element is added to the criminological armoury—be it radical criminology, ecological surveys, or sociological theory—someone sooner or later discovers that eighteenth- and nineteenth-century writers were doing something similar, and that this new approach should therefore be considered a central feature of the criminological tradition, albeit one that was temporarily (and inexplicably) forgotten. But this recurring 'recovery of tradition' is perhaps better understood as a bid for intellectual respectability and disciplinary centrality than as a serious claim about the development of the subject. After all, the crucial requirement of a genealogy is continuity of descent, and it is precisely this continuity which is missing wherever 'traditions' have to be 'rediscovered'.

If this account is accurate, and if criminology is a specific organization of knowledge which first emerged in the late nineteenth century, then the key problem is to try to describe its particularity and to explain the historical transmutation which produced this new form of enterprise. It has to be shown how the project of a specialized science emerged out of some other project or set of projects, and how it marked itself off from what went before. It is to that task that I now turn.

THE EMERGENCE OF A POSITIVE SCIENCE OF THE CRIMINAL

From Criminal Anthropology to the Science of Criminology

The idea of a specialist science of the criminal was born out of the interaction of a specific intellectual endeavour and a certain social context. As is often the case, a transmutation was produced in the history of ideas when a particular set of ideas and inquiries was found to have relevance to a field which had previously been regarded as quite separate. Ironically enough, the scientific work which led Cesare Lombroso to found a specialist 'science of the criminal'—a key ingredient in the formation of the modern discipline of criminology—was not, in fact, criminological in any sense that we would recognize. Lombroso's criminal science grew, somewhat accidentally, out of an anthropological concern to study humanity and its natural varieties, using the methods of anthropometry and craniometry to measure the physical features of human subjects. Influenced by the physical anthropology of Paul Broca and a Darwinian concern with species and their evolution, Lombroso's study of Italian army recruits and asylum and prison inmates was an attempt to identify different racial types and to subject them to scientific scrutiny and categorization (see Gould 1981). By the 1870s, however, the science of 'racial anthropology', like the science of degeneracy developed by Morel, had begun to overlap with potent social concerns, as is shown by its identification of 'types' such as the genius, the epileptoid, and the insane which were patently derived from social policy interests rather than evolutionary processes. Thus, when Lombroso 'discovered' the 'criminal type' he was extending a line of research which was already well established, and actually restating, in a more vivid form, an observation that had already been made by psychiatrists such as Maudsley and prison doctors such as J. Bruce Thomson.

But if Lombroso's 'discovery' was old news, the significance he gave to it was altogether novel. For him, the apparent distinctiveness of the criminal type prompted an idea that no one had imagined before: the idea of a distinctive science of the criminal. His conception of the criminal as a naturally occurring entity—a fact of nature rather than a social or legal product—led Lombroso to the thought of a natural science which would focus upon this entity, trace its characteristics, its stigmata, its abnormalities, and eventually identify the causes which make one person a criminal and another a normal citizen. And the startling thing about this Lombrosian project for the scientific differentiation of the criminal individual was that, despite its dubious scientific credentials, it immediately met with a huge international response. In the twenty years following the appearance of *L'Uomo Delinquente* in 1876 this strange new science came to form the basis of a major international movement, manifesting itself in an outpouring of texts, the formation of new associations, international congresses, specialist journals, national schools of thought, and interested officials in virtually every European and American state. At the same time, Lombroso himself became something of a household name, featuring in the fiction of Tolstoy, Musil, Bram Stoker, and Conan Doyle as well as in countless journalistic essays and scientific reports.[22]

[22] On the spread of the criminological movement at the end of the nineteenth century, see Garland 1985*a*; Nye 1984. On Lombroso in contemporary fiction, see Pick 1989; Gould 1981. On the development of criminal anthropology in the USA, see Rafter 1992. On the

In the years immediately following the publication of Lombroso's sensational claims a group of talented disciples gathered around him and a journal, *La Scuola Positiva*, was founded to publicize the new research and its practical implications. But disciples such as Enrico Ferri and Raffaele Garofalo were not content merely to repeat the master's formulations, and even the early work of this Italian school showed a considerable diversity and eclecticism, widening out the analysis to examine the social and legal aspects of criminality as well as its 'anthropological' character. This process of differentiation within the research enterprise was amplified by the formation of rival schools of inquiry, notably the 'French School' which emphasized the sociological and environmental determinants of crime and played down the role of fixed constitutional attributes, and the 'German school' which included the study of criminalistics and the development of new forensic techniques and procedures. A series of highly publicized international congresses, beginning in 1883, aired these disputes at length, with much acrimony on all sides, and resulted in the modification of most of Lombroso's original claims, particularly on the subject of the 'born criminal' and the fatalistic implications this notion was seen to have for the treatment and reform of offenders.

What eventually emerged from this process—especially in the writings of important second-generation figures like Prins, Saleilles, and Von Hamel—was a scientific movement which was much more eclectic and much more 'practical' than the original criminal anthropology had been (see Garland 1985*a*). One indication of the process of revision and modification whereby Lombroso's original formulations were reworked into a more acceptable form was the adoption of the term 'criminology', which came into general use in the 1890s. The term was originally used not as an exact synonym for criminal anthropology but as a neutral, generic term which avoided the partisanship implicit in the original term and others—such as 'criminal sociology', 'criminal biology', and 'criminal psychology'—which competed with it.

This new science of criminology, as it developed in the last decades of the nineteenth century, was characterized by a number of distinctive features.[23] It was an avowedly scientific approach to crime, concerned to develop a 'positive', factual knowledge of offenders, based upon observation, measurement, and inductive reasoning, and rejecting the speculative thinking about human character which had previously informed criminal

reception of Lombroso's work in Britain, see Radzinowicz and Hood 1986, which also provides the most detailed account of the indigeneous traditions of thinking about crime in the nineteenth century.

[23] For an analysis of the science of criminology and its early development, see Garland 1985*b*.

justice practices. In keeping with its Lombrosian origins, it focused its attentions upon the individual criminal, and in particular upon the characteristics which appeared to mark off criminals as in some way different from normal, law-abiding citizens. It assumed that scientific explanation amounted to causal explanation and therefore set itself the task of identifying the causes of crime, though it should be added that the notion of 'cause' was understood in a wide variety of ways, some of which were more 'determinist' than others, and the kinds of cause identified ranged from innate constitutional defects to more or less contingent social circumstances. Finally, it addressed itself to the investigation of a new, pathological phenomenon—'criminality'—which it deemed to be the source of criminal behaviour and which, in effect, became the subject's *raison d'être* and the target of its practical proposals.

This concern to produce a differential diagnosis of the individual criminal and the etiology of his or her offending behaviour was in turn linked to a definite programme of practical action, quite at odds with the legal principles which had previously underpinned criminal justice practice. The notion of the offender's free will was attacked as a metaphysical abstraction, as was the concept of legal responsibility. Uniformity of sentencing was viewed as a failure to differentiate between different types of offender, and the principle of proportionate, retrospective punishment was rejected in favour of a flexible system of penal sanctions adapted to the reformability or dangerousness of the specific individual. Criminal justice was to cease being a punitive, reactive system and was to become instead a scientifically informed apparatus for the prevention, treatment, and elimination of criminality. It was to be a system run by criminological experts, concerned to maximize social defence, individual reform and measures of security rather than to uphold some outdated legalistic conception of justice.

That such a radical programme of research and reform could be developed and become influential is testimony to the extent to which the new criminology resonated with the concerns and preoccupations of the political and cultural milieux in which it emerged.[24] The popularity of Lombroso's work is probably explicable in terms of the extent to which his conception of the criminal type chimed with deep-rooted cultural prejudices and offered scientific respectability to middle class perceptions of 'criminal classes' forming in the growing cities (see Sennett 1977). But the viability of the criminological movement, and the fact that it so quickly became an international phenomenon, are indications that it was a programme of thought and action which successfully meshed with the social politics and institutional practices which were becoming established at the

[24] For a detailed account of the British cultural milieu in which the new criminological science took hold, see Wiener 1990.

time. The increasing involvement of experts and scientists in the administration of social problems in the late nineteenth century, and the related development of statistical data as a resource for governing, is one background circumstance. So too is the developing concern on the part of governments, Poor Law administrators, police, and local authorities to classify and differentiate the populations they dealt with, seeking to identify and separate out dangerous elements while shoring up the social attachments of the 'deserving poor' and the 'respectable' working classes. In this specific context, the criminological programme offered certain regulatory and legitimatory possibilities which made it attractive to late nineteenth-century governments and administrators.

The regulatory advantages of the new criminology lay in its rejection of the formal egalitarianism that had previously shaped the practices of criminal law and its enforcement. Against the principle that everyone should be treated equally, criminology offered to differentiate between constitutional and accidental criminality, thus identifying the real sources of social danger and marking out the contours of the criminal class in a scientific rather than a moralistic way. Criminology also promised to provide a more extensive and a more effective form of intervention and regulation. Concerned to diagnose an individual's level of dangerousness rather than to judge whether or not he or she had yet broken the law, criminology offered the prospect of a system of control in which official measures need not wait for an offence to occur, or be limited by any principle of proportionality. At the same time, this more interventionist system could also claim to be more humane, in so far as its rationale was the promotion of individual and social welfare and not merely the infliction of retributive punishment (see Garland 1985*a*; Wiener 1990).

Finally, as is by now well documented, the new criminology met with extensive interest and social support because it was closely linked to the new prisons which had, by the late nineteenth century, become a prominent feature of all Western societies. As Michel Foucault (1977) has shown, the disciplinary, reformative practices of the penitentiary prison acted as a practical 'surface of emergence' for the individualizing, differentiating discourse of criminology. What Lombroso invented was a science of individual differences; but the data and social arrangements necessary for the production of this science, as well as the practical context in which such a knowledge would be practically useful, were already inscribed in the architecture and regimes of the disciplinary prison. In the prison setting inmates were arranged in individual cells, and subjected to constant, individual surveillance for long periods of time, their behaviour and characteristics being continually monitored in order that disciplinary measures could be adjusted to deal with individual reactions and peculiarities. The systematic and differentiating knowledge of offenders to which this gave rise formed the basis for the new science of criminology, which slowly fed back into the practices of imprisonment, refining the prison's classifications and techniques, and enhancing the authorities' understanding of the individuals that were held in custody (see Garland 1985*a*). The widespread use of disciplinary imprisonment in late nineteenth-century Europe and America thus provided a ready-made setting through which criminology could emerge and establish itself as a useful form of knowledge. As Sir Evelyn Ruggles-Brise (1924) put it, *la science penitentiaire* develops gradually into the science of the discovery of the causes of crime—the science of criminology'.[25] Lombroso's project was thus propelled not just by its own scientific logic but by a combination of institutional and cultural dynamics, a set of forces which were to sustain this form of inquiry long after Lombroso's own reputation was utterly destroyed.

The Development of Criminology in Britain

As was often pointed out at the time, British intellectuals and penal officials played very little part in the early development of this new criminological movement. Most of the relevant research and publication took place in Italy, France, and Germany, and the British were notable absentees at the international congresses held to debate the claims and counterclaims of the various schools. It was not until the Geneva Congress of Criminal Anthropology in 1896 that Britain first sent an official delegate—the prison inspector Major Arthur Griffiths—and Griffiths returned with a sceptical report (see Griffiths 1904) which confirmed the attitude of British officials to the claims of the new criminologists. Griffiths was later to write the first entry to appear on 'Criminology' in the *Encyclopaedia Britannica* (1910–11) in which he attacked the theory of criminal types, but went on to show a cautious interest in the penological ideas which were by then emerging from the movement.

The arm's-length attitude of the British penal establishment to the new criminology was something of a surprise to individual enthusiasts such as Havelock Ellis and William Douglas Morrison, both of whom did much to introduce continental ideas into this country. Ellis published a book entitled *The Criminal* in 1890 which was, in effect, a summary of the major ideas of criminal anthropology, and regularly reviewed foreign criminological publications for the *Journal of Mental Science* from 1890 to 1919; Morrison established and edited 'The Criminology Series' which published translations of works by Lombroso (1895), Ferri (1895) and Proal (1898), as well as publishing a number of his own works, including

[25] On the prison as a 'surface of emergence' for criminological knowledge, see Foucault 1977; also Garland 1992.

Juvenile Offenders (1896). One cause of this surprise was that many of the new criminologists, including Lombroso himself, pointed to earlier work published in Britain which appeared to contain the kinds of ideas which would later become central to the movement. Thus, in the 1860s the psychiatrist Henry Maudsley and the prison medical officer J. Bruce Thomson had written about 'the genuine criminal' and 'the criminal class', describing these individuals as 'morally insane', 'degenerate', 'defective in physical organisation . . . from hereditary causes' and 'incurable' in a way which appeared to be altogether 'Lombrosian' before Lombroso.[26]

But to describe Maudsley and Thomson as criminologists before the fact was misleading. Maudsley was engaged in a distinctively psychiatric endeavour (the development and application of typologies dealing with various mental disorders and pathologies) and Thomson's concern was to assess the impact of prison discipline upon the bodies and minds of prisoners (see Thomson 1867). Neither of them for a moment imagined that there was any justification for a distinctive scientific specialism centered upon the criminal. More importantly, during the 1870s and 1880s British medical and psychiatric opinion had shifted away from earlier attempts to characterize 'criminals' in such indiscriminating, pathological terms. From the 1870s onwards, prison doctors such as David Nicolson and John Baker set about redefining 'the morbid psychology of criminals', so as to differentiate a range of conditions rather than a single type. Nicolson (1878–9) emphasized that professional observation made it plain that only a minority of criminals were in any sense mentally abnormal, and he forcibly rejected any suggestion that offenders were generally 'incurable' or beyond the reach of prison reformation. During the same years, the nascent British psychiatric profession was learning that criminal courts would not tolerate psychiatric evidence which contradicted basic legal axioms about individual free will and responsibility, and it gradually developed a *modus vivendi* which aimed to minimize conflict between psychiatry and law. By the 1880s, leading figures of the new profession such as Needham, Hack Tuke, Nicolson, and Maudsley were taking pains to distance themselves from the embarrassing claims made by psychiatrists (Maudsley among them) in earlier years—claims which were now being

[26] Maudsley (1863: 73) refers to 'the criminal' as a 'fact in nature' and criminals as 'if not strictly a degenerate species, certainly . . . a degenerate variety of the species'. Thomson (1867: 341) states that 'all who have seen much of criminals agree that they have a singular family likeness or caste . . . Their physique is coarse and repulsive; their complexion dingy, almost atrabilious; their face, figure and mien, disagreeable. The women are painfully ugly; and the men look stolid, and many of them brutal, indicating physical and moral deterioration. In fact there is a stamp on them in form and expression which seems to me the heritage of the class.' For a discussion of these debates, see Garland 1988; also Radzinowicz and Hood 1986.

taken up again by criminologists with their talk of 'born criminals', 'the criminal type', atavism, and so on (see Nicolson 1878–9; Maudsley 1889; Tuke 1889; Needham 1889; Baker 1892; Nicolson 1895; Garland 1988).

The relationship between the new continental movement and the studies of criminals carried out in Britain by prison doctors and psychiatrists is a complex one, and the assumption (made by Ellis and others) that the two were continuous is a simplification which glosses over important differences. Unlike Lombroso's anthropology, British psychiatry was not concerned to isolate discrete human "types" and classify them by means of racial and constitutional differences. Instead, it was a therapeutically orientated practice based upon a system of classifying mental disorders which, like the disease model of nineteenth-century medicine, discussed the condition separately from the individual in whom it might be manifested. Within the classification schemes of morbid psychology there was a variety of conditions which criminals were said to exhibit, including insanity, moral insanity, degeneracy, and feeblemindedness (among others). But generally speaking, the criminal was not conceived of as a distinct psychological type.

More important than this theoretical difference was the way in which British psychiatry contrasted with Lombrosian anthropology in its practical commitments and its relationship to the institutions of criminal justice. In his early publications, Lombroso claimed that his ideas had great relevance for criminal law and penal policy, but, as his critics soon pointed out, he was not particularly well informed about the practical realities of crime and punishment.[27] In consequence, his penology was not just radical and at odds with current practices; it was also naïve and distorted, lacking a close familiarity with the normal range of offenders and the institutions that dealt with them. Lombroso's conception of the criminal type had emerged from the theoretical hypotheses of physical anthropology rather than extensive penological experience, and only gradually did he modify his views to bring them more into line with the way legal institutions worked. In contrast, the scientific thinking about the criminal which developed in British psychiatric and medico-legal circles was closely tied into professional tasks such as the giving of evidence before courts of law, or the decisions as to classification, diagnosis, and regimen which prison medical officers made daily. This practical experience was crucial in shaping the psychiatric approach to 'criminological' issues because it ensured that psychiatrists and prison doctors were well acquainted with the day-to-day realities of criminal justice and with the

[27] See, for instance, the review by Arthur St John (1912) of Lombroso's work, in which he contrasts Lombroso's naïvety to the experienced practical understanding of a prison doctor such as James Devon.

need to bring psychiatric propositions into line with the demands of courts and prison authorities.

The British tradition that was closest to the criminology developing on the continent was thus also somewhat hostile to it. The scientific studies conducted by British prison doctors and psychiatrists were, from an early stage, situated within an institutional framework which shaped their purposes and constrained their findings. In consequence, these studies were generally modest in their claims and respectful of the requirements of institutional regimes and legal principles. As far as most prison doctors and experienced psychiatrists were concerned, the majority of criminals were more or less normal individuals; only a minority required psychiatric treatment and this usually involved removing them from the penal system and putting them into institutions for the mentally ill or defective. And although the diagnostic and therapeutic claims of psychiatry changed over time, from an early stage there was a recognition that, for the majority of offenders, the normal processes of law and punishment should apply. Compared to the sweeping claims of criminal anthropology, the British medico-legal tradition was, by the 1890s, somewhat conservative, and generally dismissive of Lombrosian ideas. Senior psychiatric figures such as Maudsley and Conolly Norman referred publicly to the 'puerilities of criminal anthropology' and the 'lamentable extravagances' of the new theories (Norman 1895; Maudsley 1895). Sir Horatio Bryan Donkin, the first Medical Commissioner of Prisons, gave clear expression to the difference between the two traditions when he defined 'criminology', properly so-called, as the investigations undertaken by 'persons concerned in some way with the prison authorities who strive to discover just principles on which to base their work' and distinguished this from the newer 'doctrine and debate on the causation of crime' which he condemned as 'theories based on preconceived assumptions regardless of fact' (Donkin 1917).

So scientific research on individual criminals in Britain stemmed from a rather different root than did continental criminology, and inclined towards a more pragmatic, institutionalized approach to its subject. But, as I noted earlier, the international criminological movement tended to become more eclectic, more moderate, and more practical over time, gradually dissociating itself from extremist claims and adapting to the basic demands of the institutions it sought to influence. And as it became more respectable and more firmly established, the initial hostility of Britain's scientific and penological circles tended to fade. From the mid-1890s onwards, the English and Scottish Prison Commissions began to take an active interest in the movement, as did the leading psychiatric periodicals. Even the influential Gladstone Committee Report gave passing approval to the 'learned but conflicting theories' which have subjected 'crime, its causes, and treatment' to 'scientific inquiry' (Gladstone Committee 1895: 8). What seems gradually to have happened in Britain during the period leading up to the First World War is that 'criminology' ceased to be exclusively identified with its anthropological origins and instead became used as a general term to describe scientific research on the subject of crime and criminals. Grudgingly at first, but more and more frequently, prison officials, psychiatrists, and doctors began to refer to their researches as 'criminological', until this became the accepted name for a new scientific specialism. The irony is that, in Britain at least, criminology came to be recognized as an accredited scientific specialism only when it began to rid itself of the notion of the distinctive 'criminal type'—the very entity which had originally grounded the claim that a special science of the criminal was justified.

Most of the early British work which identified itself as criminological was actually a continuation of the older medico-legal tradition of prison research, now opened out to engage with an expanding criminological literature imported from Europe and North America. It is, for example, almost exclusively within the Reports of the Medical Commissioner of Prisons and of the various prison medical officers that one will find any official discussion of criminological science in the first few decades of this century, and most of the major scientific works on crime written in Britain before the 1930s were written by doctors with psychiatric training and positions within the prison service.[28] The first university lectures in 'criminology' delivered in Britain—given at Birmingham by Maurice Hamblin Smith in 1921—were directed at postgraduate medical students within a course entitled 'Medical Aspects of Crime and Punishment', and long before Hermann Mannheim began teaching at the London School of Economics in 1935 there were courses on 'Crime and Insanity' offered at London University by senior prison medical officers such as Sullivan and East.[29] In the absence of any specialist periodicals devoted to criminology, criminological articles and reviews appeared chiefly in the *Journal of Mental Science, The British Journal of Medical Psychology*, and the *Transactions of the Medico-Legal Association* (from 1933 *The Medico-Legal and Criminological Review*), although the *Howard Journal* also carried some reviews, as did the *Sociological Review*.

The institutionally based, medico-legal criminology which predominated in Britain for much of the nineteenth century and the first half of the twentieth was, by its nature, an evolving, adaptive tradition. The

[28] See *inter alia* Sutherland 1908; Quinton 1910; Devon 1912; Smith 1922; Sullivan 1924; East 1927.

[29] According to his own account, Cyril Burt had regularly given lectures on juvenile delinquency at Liverpool University between 1906 and 1914, but these had occurred in the context of a psychology class rather than one devoted to 'criminology'. See Mannheim 1957.

criminological texts which it generated grew out of practical contexts which were forever changing, since institutions continually redefined their operations and took on new concerns, and also because new methods, theories, and techniques became available to the professionals who administered them. Many of the criminological texts written in the nineteenth century focused upon the problems of classifying particular offenders—as psychiatric rather than criminal cases, as morally insane, feebleminded, and so on—and of course these problems had a direct bearing upon the practices of penal institutions. As the penal system diversified in the early part of the twentieth century, developing specialist institutions for the inebriate, habitual offenders, the feebleminded, and for juveniles, and becoming more refined and differentiated in the classification of adult prisoners, the criminological literature similarly began to address itself to these new diagnostic and classificatory problems.[30] Thus, although this line of research came close to the concerns of the Lombrosian project in its focus upon individuals and their differential classification, it lacked the scientific ambition and theory-building concerns of the latter, being almost exclusively focused upon knowledge which was useful for administrative purposes.

In 1919, the emphasis upon individual character and specialized treatment prompted by the Gladstone Committee report—together with concerns about large numbers of shell-shocked and mentally disturbed men returning from the war—led the Birmingham Justices to establish a permanent scheme for the clinical examination of untried adult offenders. Previously such work had been done on an occasional, *ad hoc* basis, and depended upon the skill and interest of the local prison doctor. By appointing Hamblin Smith and W. A. Potts, both psychiatrically trained prison doctors, and charging them with these new duties, the Justices effectively created a new specialism of applied criminology. Before long, Potts and Hamblin Smith were adapting the standard mental tests for use in this area, publishing the results of their clinical studies, and writing extensively about the need for this kind of investigation and its implications for the treatment and prevention of crime. In *The Psychology of the Criminal* (1922*b*) and in a series of articles in the *Journal of Mental Science*, the *Howard Journal*, and elsewhere, Smith emphasized the importance of criminological study, though for him this meant the clinical examination of individual offenders for the purpose of assessment and diagnosis. As Britain's first authorized teacher of 'criminology', and as the first individual to use the title of 'criminologist', it is significant that

[30] Works on alcoholism by W. C. Sullivan (1906), on recidivism by J. F. Sutherland (1908), and on the psychology of the criminal by M. Hamblin Smith (1922) and H. E. Field (1932) are significant examples of research derived from the developing penal-welfare complex.

Smith, like Donkin and Ruggles-Brise before him, rejected the search for 'general theories' in favour of the 'study of the individual'. It is also significant that the centres for criminological research and teaching which he proposed were envisaged as places where 'young medical graduates' would be trained to become expert in the medico-psychological examination and assessment of offenders (Smith 1922*a*).

Hamblin Smith was also one of the first criminological workers in Britain to profess an interest in psychoanalysis, which he used as a means to assess the personality of offenders, as well as a technique for treating the mental conflicts which, he claimed, lay behind the criminal act. In this respect Smith met with much official opposition, particularly from W. Norwood East; but there were others, outside the prisons establishment, who were more enthusiastic. In the winter of 1922–23 Dr Grace Pailthorpe assisted Smith in the psychoanalytic investigation of female offenders in Birmingham, and went on to complete a five-year study at Holloway, funded by a grant from the Medical Research Council. Her report (Pailthorpe 1932), which was completed by 1929, but held back by the MRC until 1932, claimed that crime was generally a symptom of mental conflict which might be psychoanalytically resolved. This radical approach met with some consternation in official circles (see East 1936: 319), but it excited the interest of a number of analysts and medical psychologists who formed a group to promote the Pailthorpe report and its approach. Out of their meetings emerged the Association for the Scientific Treatment of Criminals (1931), which, in 1932, became the Institute for the Scientific Treatment of Delinquency (ISTD) (see Glover 1960).

Most of the founder members of this group were involved in the new outpatient sector of psychiatric work, made possible by a developing network of private clinics, which included the Tavistock (1921) and the Maudsley (1923), the new child guidance centres, and, in 1933, the ISTD's own Psychopathic Clinic (which in 1937 was moved and renamed the Portman Clinic). This new field of practice gave rise to its own distinctive brand of criminological theory. The early publications of the ISTD emphasize the clinical exploration of individual personality, and in that sense are continuous with much previous work. But they also manifest a new preventative emphasis, which reflected the fact that the new clinics operated outside the formal penal system, and could deal with individuals before their disturbed conduct actually became criminal.[31]

[31] As the editors of the *British Journal of Delinquency* put it in the first issue: 'The names of James Devon, Hamblin Smith, Norwood East and others bear witness to the honourable part played by Prison Medical Officers in the development of scientific criminology in this country. But the activities of the "institutional" criminologist have been rather overshadowed in recent years by the expansion of what might be called the "ambulant" approach to delinquency, i.e. the application of diagnostic and, where necessary or possible, therapeutic

Eventually, the ISTD's emphasis upon psychoanalysis, and its open hostility to much official penal policy, ensured that it remained essentially an outsider body, operating at arm's length from the Home Office and the Prison Commission. This outsider status forms an important background to the later decision of the Home Office to establish a criminological institute at Cambridge, rather than under ISTD auspices in London, for although 'the formation of such a body was one of the original aims of the ISTD' (Glover 1960: 70), and the claims of the organization were canvassed to the Home Secretary in 1958, the Home Office appears not to have seriously considered such an option (see Radzinowicz 1988: 9).

Despite its subsequent neglect, the work of W. Norwood East, particularly *An Introduction to Forensic Psychiatry in the Criminal Courts* (1927) and *The Medical Aspects of Crime* (1936)—better represents the mainstream of British criminology in the 1920s and 1930s. East was a psychiatrically trained prison medical officer who became a leading figure in the 1930s as Medical Director on the Prison Commission and President of the Medico-Legal Society, and his views dominated official policy-making for a lengthy period. East was himself a proponent of a psychological approach to crime, but he considered its scope to be sharply delimited, and consistently warned against the dangers and absurdities of exaggerating its claims. Instead of theoretical speculation and scientific ambition he stressed the importance of 'day-to-day administration', and the practical impact of theoretical ideas. (Hence his criticism of deterministic ideas, which he thought promoted 'mental invalidism' instead of trying to build up a sense of social responsibility' (East 1931–2). In 1934 he established an extended experiment at Wormwood Scrubs prison, whereby those offenders deemed most likely to respond to psychological therapy—particularly sex offenders and arsonists—were subjected to a period of investigation and treatment. At the end of five years, East and Hubert's Report on *The Psychological Treatment of Crime* (1939) reaffirmed East's view that while 80 per cent of offenders were psychologically normal, and would respond to routine punishment, a minority might usefully be investigated and offered psychological treatment. The Report proposed a special institution to deal with such offenders—a proposal which was immediately accepted but not put into effect until the opening of Grendon Underwood prison in 1962. East and Hubert also recommended that this institution should function as a centre for criminological research, and it is significant that when a criminological centre is here

methods to early cases attending Delinquency Clinics, Child Guidance and Psychiatric Centres, etc., with or without probationary supervision. And to the extent that the Delinquency Clinic bridges the gap between the "non-delinquent" and the "recidivist", it is inevitable that the ambulant system should provide the most fruitful field for research into causes and methods of prevention' ('Editorial', *British Journal of Delinquency*, 1/1 (1950/1): 4).

proposed for the first time in an official report, it should be envisaged as part of a psychiatric institution, dealing only with a small minority of pathological offenders.

An important departure from this British tradition of clinically based psychiatric studies was *The English Convict: A Statistical Study*, published in 1913 by Dr Charles Goring under the auspices of the Home Office and the Prison Commission. This work was made possible by institutional routines, in so far as anthropometric methods were used in prisons for the identification of habitual offenders during the 1890s, and in fact one of its starting points was a desire to measure the impact of prison diet and labour upon the inmates' physiques. But the issues addressed by the final report went far beyond these institutional matters and engaged, for the first time in an official publication, with the theoretical claims of scientific criminology.

The analysis and tabulation of the vast quantity of data collected by the study was carried out in Karl Pearson's Biometrical Laboratory at the University of London—an unusual location for prison research but one which was well suited to the statistical and eugenic themes which dominated the final report. As its sponsors intended, the study gave a definitive refutation of the old Lombrosian claim that the criminal corresponded to a particular physical type, thus confirming the position which the British authorities had held all along. However, the significance of Goring's study went far beyond this negative and somewhat out-of-date finding. In fact, Goring's analysis began by *assuming* that there was no criminal type, and although it was not much noticed at the time, his study is chiefly notable for inventing a quite new way of differentiating criminals from non-criminals.

In the early part of the book, Goring set out extensive theoretical and methodological arguments which insisted that criminality should be viewed not as a qualitative difference of type, marked by anomaly and morbidity, but instead as a variant of normality, differentiated only by degree. Following the arguments of Manouvrier and Topinard, he pointed out that so-called criminal 'anomalies' are only 'more or less extreme degrees of character which in some degree are present in all men'. Moreover, he made it clear that his use of statistical method necessarily presupposed this idea of a criminal characteristic which is a common feature of all individuals, and he went on to name this hypothesized entity 'the criminal diathesis'. This conception of criminality as normal, rather than morbid or pathological, implied a new basis for criminological science, which Goring vigorously set forth. From now on, criminology could no longer depend on the clinical gaze of a Lombroso and its impressionistic identification of anomalies. (Goring had, in any case, provided a devastating critique of this 'anatomico-pathological method'.)

Instead it must be a matter of large populations, careful measurement, and statistical analysis, demonstrating patterns of differentiation in the mass which would not be visible in the individual or to the naked eye.

Goring's own application of these methods purported to reveal a significant, but by no means universal, association between criminality and two heritable characteristics, namely low intelligence and poor physique, and suggested that 'family and other environmental conditions' were not closely associated with crime. From these findings he drew a series of practical, eugenic conclusions, declaring that 'crime will continue to exist as long as we allow criminals to propagate' and that government should therefore 'modify opportunity for crime by segregating the unfit' and 'regulate the reproduction of those constitutional qualities—feeblemindedness, inebriety, epilepsy, deficient social instinct, insanity, which conduce to the committing of crime' (Goring 1913). Here, as so often in subsequent studies, we see Lombroso's specific claims rejected, only to find that his basic assumptions and project are being reasserted in some new, revised form.

Although *The English Convict* had a considerable impact abroad, and especially in the USA, in Britain it received a much more muted response. On the one hand, Goring's attack had been centred upon theoretical positions which had little support in this country, other than from maverick outsiders such as Havelock Ellis. On the other, it appeared to have policy implications—particularly the possibility that inherited traits would render reformative prison regimes impotent—which were not altogether welcome in official circles. The Prison Commissioners, while supporting the study's publication as a Blue Book, refused to endorse its conclusions (see Garland 1985*a*), and Sir Bryan Donkin (1919) distanced himself from the book altogether, arguing that 'even correct generalisations . . . concerning criminals in the mass are not likely to be of much positive value in the study or treatment of individuals'. In much the same way W. C. Sullivan, the medical superintendent at Broadmoor, argued in *Crime and Insanity* (1924) that clinical rather than statistical methods were the only reliable means of obtaining useful, policy-relevant knowledge.

These exchanges are revealing because they show the extent to which British criminology up to this point was shaped by the interests and assumptions of official policy-makers and the institutions that they served. In the years before the First World War, the medico-legal assessment of individual offenders played an explicit role in the trial process and in the disposition of offenders after conviction, so the promised benefits of clinical research were readily apparent in a way that was not true of statistical studies. Later on, when criminal justice officials came to realize how they could use the results of actuarial calculations—in predicting response to treatment, deploying police resources, calculating crime rates, and so on—the balance of interest shifted the other way. Though he did not live to see it (having died in 1919), Goring's argument for the importance of statistical method and mass data in criminological research was the one which was ultimately most persuasive to the British authorities. By the end of the 1930s, the Prison Commission and the Home Office had each embarked upon large-scale, statistically based projects, subsequently published as East (1942) and Carr-Saunders *et al.* (1942), and this became a characteristic form of government-sponsored research in the years after 1945.

If East's work exemplified the mainstream British tradition of medico-psychiatric criminological research (with the ISTD's more radical clinical studies forming an important tributary), and Goring inaugurated a new stream of statistical studies, there was also another significant line of inquiry which influenced criminological work in the post-war period. This third stream is best represented by the eclectic, multifactorial, social-psychological research of Cyril Burt. When later criminologists such as Mannheim and Radzinowicz looked back upon their predecessors, they spent little time discussing the merits of *The English Convict* or *The Medical Aspects of Crime*. Instead, they invariably picked out Cyril Burt's 1925 study, *The Young Delinquent*, as the first major work of modern British criminology and as an exemplar for the discipline that they were helping to create.[32] Like most criminological texts in this period, *The Young Delinquent* emerged from a specific field of practice—it was not until the 1960s that research took off from an academic base—but in marked contrast to the work of East, Hamblin Smith, Sullivan, and co., this field of practice was outside the penal system, rather than central to it. In his post as educational psychologist to the London County Council, Burt was responsible for the psychological assessment and advice of London's schoolchild population, which involved him in examining thousand of individual problem cases, many of them behavioural as well as educational, and making recommendations for their treatment. Consequently, his criminological study was built upon a wider than usual population, dealing mostly with 'pre-delinquents' rather than convicted offenders, and it was not constrained by the narrowly penal concerns that affected most contemporary studies. Rather than inquire about specific classifications or distinctions, Burt was interested to specify all the possible sources of individual psychological difference, and thereby to identify the causal patterns which precipitate delinquency and non-delinquency.

The Young Delinquent was based upon the detailed clinical examination

[32] See Mannheim (1949: 11); also Radzinowicz (1961: 173–6): 'it may be said that modern criminological research in England dates only from Sir Cyril Burt's study of *The Young Delinquent*, first published in 1925. Its excellence in method and interpretation was at once recognized and it has stood the test of rapidly advancing knowledge.'

of 400 schoolchildren (a delinquent or quasi-delinquent group and a control group), using a battery of techniques which included biometric measurement, mental testing, temperament testing, and psychoanalytic and social inquiries, together with the most up-to-date statistical methods of factor analysis and correlation. Its findings were expansively eclectic, identifying some 170 causative factors which were in some way associated with delinquency, and showing, by way of narrative case histories, how each factor might typically operate. From his analysis, Burt concluded that certain factors, such as defective discipline, defective family relationships, and particular types of temperament, were highly correlated with delinquency, while the influence of other factors, such as poverty or low intelligence, while not altogether negligible, had been seriously overstated in the past. His major proposition was that delinquency was not the outcome of special factors operating only on delinquents, but was rather the result of a combination of factors—typically as many as nine or ten—operating at once upon a single individual. In consequence, the study of criminality must be, above all, multicausal in scope, while its treatment must be tailored to fit the needs of the individual case. The influence of Burt's work, and especially its eclectic, multifactorial search for the correlates of individual delinquency, was to become something of a hallmark of British criminology in the mid-twentieth century, though ironically enough (in view of Burt's modern reputation) his most immediate impact was to shift attention away from the purported intellectual deficiencies of delinquents towards questions of temperament and emotional balance.

The scientific criminology which developed in Britain between the 1890s and the Second World War was thus heavily dominated by a medico-psychological approach, focused upon the individual offender and tied into a correctionalist penal-welfare policy. Within this approach there were a number of important variants, and the enterprise was differently understood by different practitioners; but compared to the subject which exists today, criminology operated within rather narrow parameters. Sociological work, such as that developed by Durkheim in France at the turn of the century, or in Chicago in the 1920s and 1930s (which treated crime rates as social facts to be explained by sociological methods), was virtually absent. Instead the 'social dimension' of crime was conceived of as one factor among many others operating upon the individual—a good example of how the criminological project transforms the elements which it 'borrows' from other disciplines. Nor was the radicalism of foreign criminologists such as Enrico Ferri and Willem Bonger much in evidence here; indeed, if British criminology can be said to have developed radical analyses during this period, they were inspired by Freud rather than by Marx.[33]

[33] See for instance the works by Glover (1941, 1960), Aichhorn (1951), and Friedlander (1947).

The major topics of scientific interest were those thrown up as problems for the courts, the prison and the Borstal system—such as the mentally abnormal offender, recidivists, and especially juvenile delinquents—and the central purpose of scientific research was not the construction of explanatory theory but instead the more immediate end of aiding the policy-making process. The governmental project dominated, almost to the point of monopolization, and Lombroso's science of the criminal was taken up only in so far as it could be shown to be directly relevant to the governance of crime and criminals. Such a pragmatic, correctionalist orientation was, of course, hardly surprising when one recalls that the authors of pre-war criminological research in Britain were, virtually without exception, practitioners working in the state penal system or else in the network of clinics and hospitals which had grown up around it. In Britain, before the mid-1930s, criminology as a university-based, academic discipline simply did not exist.

THE ESTABLISHMENT OF A CRIMINOLOGICAL DISCIPLINE IN BRITAIN

The transformation of British criminology from a minor scientific specialism—the part-time activity of a few practitioners and enthusiasts—into an established academic discipline took place comparatively late, occurring some time between the mid-1930s and the early 1960s. Even then, it was by no means an inevitable or necessary development. Indeed, had it not been for the rise of Nazism in Germany, and the appointment of three distinguished European emigrés, Hermann Mannheim, Max Grunhut, and Leon Radzinowicz, to academic posts at elite British universities, British criminology might never have developed sufficient academic impetus to become an independent discipline. But however contingently, the process of discipline formation did take hold in the post-war period and its symbolic culmination occurred in October 1961 with the inauguration of a postgraduate course for the training of criminological researchers and teachers at the new Institute of Criminology at Cambridge. In the intervening years, the other concomitants of disciplinary status had gradually come into being, initially as the result of private initiatives, and then, in the late 1950s, with the support and funding of government.

Criminology teaching in the universities began to expand from the late 1930s onwards, catering to the needs of the fast-growing social work and probation professions and attracting a first generation of research students (such as John Spencer, Norval Morris, Tadeuz Grygier, and John Croft) who would go on to become important figures in the new discipline.[34] Cambridge University established a Department of Criminal Science in 1941, which sponsored research projects as well as a book series, and eventually formed the base upon which the Institute of Criminology was built. In 1950 Britain's first specialist criminology journal, the *British Journal of Delinquency* (renamed the *British Journal of Criminology* in 1960), was established as 'the official organ of the ISTD' and set about the task of moulding a coherent discipline out of the scores of small-scale research efforts dotted around the country. Editorials by Mannheim and his co-editors Edward Glover and Emmanuel Miller identified key aspects of an emerging research programme and the journal carried extensive discussions of methodology and data sources as well as acting as a kind of bulletin board through which researchers could keep abreast of activities in the expanding field. In 1953, the ISTD also established the Scientific Group for the Discussion of Delinquency Problems, which acted as a forum for discussion for several years until younger members of the group—some of them with newly created university posts in criminology—grew dissatisfied with the clinical and psychoanalytical emphasis of leading figures such as Glover and split off to found the more academically orientated British Society of Criminology. In 1956, Howard Jones published the first British criminology textbook, *Crime and the Penal System*, a work much influenced by the teachings of Mannheim at the LSE. In its emphasis upon penological issues and its assumption of a reforming, welfarist stance it encapsulated an important and continuing strand of British criminological culture. (Such was the pace of change in this, the discipline's take-off phase, that the third edition of the book, appearing only nine years later in 1965, was described by an otherwise sympathetic reviewer as 'sadly out of date' (Taylor 1968).)

The Criminal Justice Act of 1948 provided for the regular allocation of Treasury funds for the purposes of criminological research, but in the years that followed only a tiny annual budget was actually made available. However, the 1950s saw the emergence of an explicit and continuing commitment by the British government to support criminological research, both as an in-house activity and as a university-based specialism. This, in effect, marked the point of convergence between criminology as an administrative aid and criminology as a scientific undertaking—the consolidation of the governmental and Lombrosian projects—and it

[34] According to the results of a survey carried out by Mannheim in the mid-1950s, twenty-one British universities claimed that criminology formed a part of their teaching curriculum, whether for undergraduate students or as a part of extension courses and diplomas taken by trainee social workers and probation officers (Mannheim 1957). From 1938 onwards, the ISTD was a centre for the University of London four-year Diploma Course in Social Studies, an evening course, of which the fourth year was devoted to criminology. Mannheim himself taught 'criminology as a separate subject in all its aspects' at the LSE from 1935 onwards.

represents a key moment in the creation of a viable, independent discipline of criminology in Britain. This new and closer relationship beween government and criminological science not only endorsed criminology's claim to be a useful form of knowledge; it also gave official and financial backing to criminology's claim to scientific status and university recognition. Thus the Home Office proceeded to set up not just an infrastructure for policy-led research—which it did in 1957 with the opening of the Home Office Research Unit (see Lodge 1974)—but also an academic institute, the Cambridge Institute of Criminology, sited in a prestigious university, with the explicit task of undertaking scientific research and training recruits for the newly founded discipline of criminology (see Radzinowicz 1988). As the 1959 White Paper '*Penal Policy in a Changing Society*' announced, 'the institute should be able, as no existing agency is in a position to do, to survey with academic impartiality . . . the general problem of the criminal in society, its causes, and its solution.' (Home Office 1959).

This new-found compatibility between traditions which had often pulled in different directions had a number of sources. In part it was testimony to the degree to which the scientific strand of criminological research had modified its ambitions and adapted its terms to fit the institutional realities and policy concerns which so heavily influenced the marketplace of criminological ideas. In part it was attributable to the fact that research concerned to differentiate criminals from non-criminals, and especially those who would recidivate from those who would not, was thought to be important for the development of effective sentencing decisions (especially Borstal allocations) and decisions regarding early release. Thus, for example, the prediction research which claimed so much attention in the late 1950s could appear to satisfy both the needs of administration and the ends of science, in so far as these studies sought to identify offender characteristics which were highly correlated with subsequent offending. (In the event, the most effective prediction tables made little use of clinical information about the offender, and actually discredited to some extent the whole project of etiological research.) One might also suggest, however, that this convergence between the search for useful knowledge and the search for scientific truth was actually more apparent than real, because, in the event, the research agenda pursued by the Cambridge Institute, at least in the early years, was heavily influenced by immediate policy needs. Indeed, for the most part, it was scarcely distinguishable from the in-house research of the Home Office—a fact that did not go uncriticized at the time.

If the emergence of a criminological discipline was the coming together of traditions of inquiry that had once been more distinct, it was also, and more immediately, the achievement of a few key individuals, backed by an alliance of interested organizations. These discipline-builders had to struggle with all sorts of resistance, but their decisive advantage was that they acted in a context in which government ministers and officials had become receptive to the idea that policy-making could be enhanced by the availability of systematic research and trained expertise. The shrewd political skills and institution-building energies of Leon Radzinowicz were particularly important (not least in persuading the Wolfson Foundation to fund the British discipline's first chair and provide the Cambridge Institute with the resources to become one of the world's leading centres of criminological work),[35] as was the influential teaching of Hermann Mannheim and the proselytizing work that he and the other ISTD members conducted in academic and practical circles. Similarly, the impressive body of research publications produced by these authors and others such as Burt, Bowlby, Grunhut, Sprott, Mays, and Ferguson created a strong case for the value of criminology as an academic subject.

The practical and educational benefits to be derived from establishing institutes and university departments of criminology were also canvassed by a number of influential political figures and associations. Senior government officials such as Alexander Paterson, Sir Lionel Fox, Sir Alexander Maxwell, and Viscount Templewood made public declarations about the need for criminology; Margery Fry and George Benson MP made representations to the Home Office to this effect; and at various times the Howard League, the Magistrates' Association, the British Psychological Society, the National Association for Mental Health, the Royal Medico-Psychological Association, and the United Nations European Seminar on Crime all added their weight to the campaign to obtain government sponsorship and university recognition for the subject (see Radzinowicz 1988). In the event, criminology's most influential supporter was R. A. Butler, who as Home Secretary in the late 1950s took a personal interest in the development of the subject and was instrumental in extending government funding for criminological research, and in setting up the Cambridge Institute (see Butler 1974).

The government's interest in sponsoring the creation of a viable criminological enterprise was a combination of immediate penological concerns and broader conceptions of how the policy-making process ought to be organized. In the years immediately preceding the Second World War, a concern about increasing rates of juvenile offending prompted the

[35] It is worth pointing out that the standard claim made by those who canvassed the British government to support the development of criminology—namely, that the UK was trailing far behind other countries in the pursuit of criminological research—was subsequently shown to be quite false. Radzinowicz's empirical survey of the state of criminology around the world suggested that, with the establishment of the Cambridge Institute and the Home Office Research Unit, British criminology probably enjoyed more official support than that of any other country, with the exception of the USA. See Radzinowicz 1961.

Home Office to arrange a series of conferences and research projects in order to estimate the extent of the problem and identify its social and psychological roots. When, in the post-war years, the high wartime rates of delinquent behaviour failed to decline, the problem attracted extensive political and press attention and provided a compelling rationale for the promotion of criminological research. (It is noteworthy that henceforth, juvenile delinquency was to become a central topic in British criminology.) Similarly, the gradual development of a penal philosophy of 'treatment and training', centred upon the Borstal system and relying for its effectiveness upon accurate assessment and classification procedures, led to a growing demand for criminological knowledge and advice. More generally, the wartime experience of operational research and the utilization of expertise in the formation of strategy, together with the growing professionalization of administration and social work in the new welfare state, gradually convinced post-war governments of the value of research and expertise as a basis for social policy.[36] The same governmental mentality which looked to Beveridge and Keynes to solve the social and economic problems of the nation came to recognize criminology as a form of knowledge which should be integrated into the institutions of government. Criminology thus became an integral part of the process of 'social reconstruction', a small element in the post-war settlement which sought to secure stability and capitalist growth by means of welfare provision and social democratic management (see Mannheim 1946; Taylor 1981).

One might add that this tendency to appeal to expert, 'scientific' knowledge as a source of solutions to social and personal problems was increasingly apparent not just in government but also in the wider culture. As the prestige of the traditional moral and religious codes continued to wane, the new figure of the 'popular expert' began to appear more regularly on the radio and in the press, teaching a mass audience how 'modern science' thought about age-old problems, including crime and delinquency.[37]

Once set in place, the component parts of the emergent discipline proceeded to establish the range of issues and research questions which was to characterize the subject. In hindsight, this research agenda is easily regarded as narrow and consensual, reflecting broad agreement about the importance of correctionalist aims and positivist methods and a traditional British bias against theoretical or sociological work (see Cohen

[36] For a contemporary discussion of these developments see National Association for Mental Health 1949. Ten years later, Barbara Wootton's review of the social sciences and their role in policy-making was severely critical of criminology's achievements in this respect (Wootton 1959). For a retrospective account, see Wiles 1976.

[37] See the transcripts of the BBC radio series on the causes of crime in *The Listener* of 1929 and 1934, especially the broadcasts by Cyril Burt on 'The Psychology of the Bad Child' (6 February 1929) and on 'The Causes of Crime' (2 May, 1934).

1981; Wiles 1976). However, there was actually a good deal of conflict and disagreement regarding the appropriate research agenda for the subject, and rather more diversity in intellectual style and policy orientation than the textbook histories have suggested. The major institutions in the newly created discipline—the Cambridge Institute and the Home Office Research Unit—were each, to differing degrees, tied into a framework of government-sponsored research which quickly assumed a distinctive pattern, although the Institute was home to other work as well, most notably Radzinowicz's monumental *History* (1948–86), and was careful to maintain its claim to academic independence. Neither organization concerned itself closely with the development of clinical studies of the causes of crime or with the task of theory-building, preferring instead to pursue knowledge which would be more readily obtained and more immediately accessible to the policy process. As Radzinowicz argued in 1961, 'the attempt to elucidate the causes of crime should be put aside' in favour of more modest, descriptive studies which indicate the kinds of factors and circumstances with which offending is associated. Using an interdisciplinary approach and a diversity of methods, research was to be focused upon 'descriptive, analytical accounts of the state of crime, of the various classes of offenders, of the enforcement of criminal law [and] of the effectiveness of various measures of penal treatment' (Radzinowicz 1961: 175).

This approach, well characterized by George Vold (1958) as 'administrative criminology', attracted harsh criticism at the time from those more attached to criminology's scientific and explanatory ambitions, particularly the psychoanalysts at the ISTD and the group of sociological criminologists that was forming around Mannheim at the LSE—just as it would later be criticized again in the 1970s, this time by a new generation of criminologists more attracted to critical and sociological theory. But to figures such as Radzinowicz, trying to establish a fledgling and still precarious discipline, the concern was to produce useful knowledge and produce it quickly, rather than risk the failure of a more ambitious programme of etiological research, a programme which, in any case, would depend on the production of a more accurate and wide-ranging description of criminal phenomena (Radzinowicz 1988).

This pragmatic vision of the criminological enterprise was echoed by the 1959 White Paper, which argued that etiological research 'is confronted with problems which are immense both in range and complexity', that 'there are no easy answers to these problems and progress is bound to be slow', and that consequently emphasis should be placed instead upon 'research into the use of various forms of treatment and the measurement of their results, since this is concerned with matters that can be analysed more precisely' (Home Office 1959: 5). The Home Office Research Unit began its work squarely within this newly constructed framework of science-for-government, using the methodologies of social science to measure and improve the effectiveness of penal treatments and trying to harness the concepts and classifications of academic criminology to the work of administering criminal justice institutions. Nor was it surprising that the paradigmatic study which shaped much of the unit's research in the first decade of its existence should be a prediction study—precisely the kind of work that formed a junction point between criminology's scientific and governmental concerns—and one, moreover, that focused on the Borstal, the British institution which more than any other embodied the correctionalist ideals of a scientific penology. The distinctive mixture of advanced statistical technique, correctively orientated classificatory concerns, and obvious policy relevance which characterized Mannheim and Wilkins' *Prediction Methods in Relation to Borstal Training* (1955) came to be the hallmark of the Research Unit's work throughout the 1950s and 1960s (see Clarke and Cornish 1983).

EPILOGUE

By the 1960s, then, one could say with confidence that a discipline of criminology had come into existence in Great Britain. Centred on the core institutions at Cambridge and London, but increasingly building a significant presence in universities and colleges throughout the country, the subject was well placed to benefit from the rapid expansion of higher education which occurred during this decade, and in the space of a few years criminology took on, rather suddenly, the character of a well-established discipline (see Rock 1988*b*). Indeed, such was the success of the new discipline in becoming a part of the academic scheme of things that many of its younger members seemed not to be aware of just how recently the battle for recognition had been won. Thus, in the critical writings which emerged in the late 1960s and 70s, in which a new generation of criminologists mounted a radical assault on all that had gone before, one gets the sense that what is being attacked is a very powerful criminological establishment, rather than a *parvenu* and somewhat precarious subject still in the process of constituting itself.[38]

Gaining a secure place in the institutions of higher education had a

[38] For examples of the radically self-critical criminology of this period, see Cohen 1971; Taylor and Taylor 1973; Taylor, Walton, and Young 1973; Taylor *et al.* (1975). In the context of these polemics—through which contemporary readers too often interpret the past—it is easy to forget that criminological writings had never been wholly uncritical of official practices. Most British criminological work has been framed by an ameliorist, social democratic politics, often sharply critical of state policies. Opposition to the death penalty was, for instance, a central concern for many criminologists in the period up to the 1960s. On the complex relationship of criminological knowledge to state power, see Garland 1992.

major and unanticipated impact upon the discipline, so that no sooner had it become 'established' than it began to transform itself in significant ways. Many of the developments of the 1960s and 1970s—particularly the reassertion of theoretical ambition, the emergence of a strongly critical discourse, and a widespread dissatisfaction with criminology's relationship to correctionalist policies—are explicable in terms of a discipline adjusting to its new situation, pulled between the demands of policy relevance and the aspiration for academic credibility. Thus the discipline became not only more diversified, more specialized, more professional, and more self-critical in these years, it also became bitterly divided between those who sought to pursue the 'traditional' criminological agenda (in either its etiological or its administrative variant) and those associated with the National Deviancy Conference, founded at York in 1968, who were deeply critical of the medico-psychological assumptions, social democratic politics, and atheoretical pragmatism of what they termed 'positivist criminology' (see Cohen 1981; Wiles 1976; Young, this volume, Chapter 2).

In those years, during which university funding seemed more secure than it would subsequently, and academic criminology momentarily enjoyed a degree of autonomy from government greater than at any time before or since, one of the repeated refrains of theoretical writing was that criminology had no epistemological warrant and that analytical considerations demanded that the discipline be dissolved into the broader concerns of sociology or social psychology. That such claims could be made, and made so forcefully, was a stark reminder of just how contingent was criminology's existence as a scientific subject. That they altogether failed to disturb the discipline and its continued expansion (see Rock, this volume, Chapter 3) is perhaps a measure of the social and institutional forces which have come to underwrite the existence of British criminology.

Selected Further Reading

P. Beirne, *Inventing Criminology: The Rise of 'Homo Criminalis'*. Albany, NY: State University of New York Press, 1993.

R. V. G. Clarke and D. B. Cornish, *Crime Control in Britain: A Review of Research*. Albany, NY: State University of New York Press, 1983.

S. Cohen, 'Footprints in the Sand: A Further Report on Criminology and the Sociology of Deviance in Britain', in M. Fitzgerald, G. McClennan, and J. Pawson, eds., *Crime and Society*. London: Routledge, 1981.

M. Foucault, *Discipline and Punish*. London: Allen Lane, 1977.

D. Garland, *Punishment and Welfare*. Aldershot: Gower, 1985.

D. Garland, 'Criminological Knowledge and its Relation to Power: Foucault's Genealogy and Criminology Today', *British Journal of Criminology*, 1992, 32/4: 403–22.

R. Hood, ed., *Crime, Criminology and Public Policy*. London: Heinemann, 1974.

H. Mannheim, ed., *Pioneers in Criminology*. London: Stevens, 1960.

P. Pasquino, 'The Invention of Criminology: Birth of a Special Savoir', in G. Burchell, C. Gordon, and P. Miller, eds., *The Foucault Effect: Studies in Governmentality*. London: Harvester Wheatsheaf, 1991.

D. Pick, *The Faces of Degeneration*. Cambridge: Cambridge University Press, 1989.

L. Radzinowicz, *Ideology and Crime*. London: Stevens, 1966.

Sir L. Radzinowicz, *The Cambridge Institute of Criminology: Its Background and Scope*. London: HMSO, 1988.

Sir L. Radzinowicz and R. Hood, *A History of the English Criminal Law and its Administration from 1750*, vol. 5: *The Emergence of Penal Policy*. Oxford: Oxford University Press, 1986.

P. Rock, ed., *A History of British Criminology*. Oxford: Oxford University Press, 1988.

M. Wiener, *Reconstructing the Criminal: Culture, Law and Policy in England, 1830–1914*. Cambridge: Cambridge University Press, 1990.

REFERENCES

AICHHORN, A. (1951), *Wayward Youth*. London: Imago.

BAKER, J. (1892), 'Some Points Connected With Criminals', *Journal of Mental Science*, 38: 364.

BANKOWSKI, Z., MUNGHAM, G., and YOUNG, P. (1976), 'Radical Criminology or Radical Criminologist?', *Contemporary Crises*, 1/1: 37–51.

BECCARIA, C. (1963 [1764]), *Of Crimes and Punishments*. Indiana: Bobbs-Merill. First published in Italian as *Dei Delitti e Delle Pene*.

BEIRNE, P. (1998), '*Inventing Criminology: The Rise of 'Homo Criminalis'*. Albany, NY: State University of New York Press.

BONGER, W. (1936), *An Introduction to Criminology*. London: Methuen.

BOTTOMS, A. E. (1987), 'Reflections on the Criminological Enterprise', *Cambridge Law Journal*, 46/2: 240–63.

BURCHELL, G., GORDON, C., and MILLER, P., eds. (1991), *The Foucault Effect: Studies in Governmentality*. London: Harvester Wheatsheaf.

BURT, C. (1925), *The Young Delinquent*. London: University of London Press.

—— (1929), 'The Psychology of the Bad Child', *The Listener*, 6 February.

—— (1934), 'Causes of Crime', *The Listener*, 2 May.

BUTLER, R. A. (1974), 'The Foundation of the Institute of Criminology at Cambridge', in R. Hood, ed., *Crime, Criminology and Public Policy*. London: Heinemann.

CARR-SAUNDERS, A., MANNHEIM, H., and RHODES, E. C. (1942), *Young Offenders*. Cambridge: Cambridge University Press.

CLARKE, R. V. G. and CORNISH, D. B. (1983), *Crime Control in Britain: A Review of Research*. Albany: State Univeristy of New York Press.

COHEN, S. (1981), 'Footprints in the Sand: A Further Report on Criminology and the Sociology of Deviance in Britain', in M. Fitzgerald, G. McClennan, and J. Pawson, eds., *Crime and Society*. London: Routledge.

COHEN, S., ed. (1971), *Images of Deviance*. Harmondsworth: Penguin.

COLQUHOUN, P. (1797), *Treatise on the Police of the Metropolis*, 4th edn. London: J. Mawman.

—— (1800), *Treatise on the Commerce and Police of the River Thames*. London: J. Mawman.

—— (1806), *Treatise on Indigence*. London: J. Mawman.

—— (1814), *Treatise on the Wealth, Power and Resources of the British Empire*. London: J. Mawman.

COOTER, R. (1981), 'Phrenology and British Alienists, 1825–1845', in A. Scull, ed., *Madhouses, Mad-Doctors and Madmen: The Social History of Psychiatry in the Victorian Era*. London: Athlone Press.

CURTIS, T. C., and HALE, F. M. (1981), 'English Thinking about Crime, 1530–1620', in L. A. Knafla, ed., *Crime and Criminal Justice in Europe and Canada*. Waterloo Ontario: Wilfred Laurier University Press.

DANZIGER, K. (1990), *Constructing the Subject: The Historical Origins of Psychological Research*. Cambridge: Cambridge University Press.

DARNELL, R. (1974), *Readings in the History of Anthropology*. New York: Harper & Row.

DELUMEAU, J. (1990), *Sin and Fear: The Emergence of a Western Guilt Culture 13th–18th Centuries*. New York: St Martin's Press.

DEVON, J. (1912), *The Criminal and the Community*. London: John Lane.

DONKIN, Sir H. B. (1917), 'Notes on Mental Defect in Criminals', *Journal of Mental Science*, 63.

—— (1919), 'The Factors of Criminal Action', *Journal of Mental Science*, 65: 87–96.

DRAPKIN, I. (1983), 'Criminology: Intellectual History', in S. Kadish, ed., *Encyclopedia of Crime and Justice*, ii. 546–56. New York: Free Press.

EAST, W. NORWOOD (1927), *An Introduction to Forensic Psychiatry in the Criminal Courts*. London: J. A. Churchill.

—— (1931–2), 'Report of the Medical Commissioner', in *Report of the Commissioners of Prisons and Directors of Convict Prisons, 1930*,' PP 1931–2, Cmd 4151, xii.

EAST, W. NORWOOD (1936), *The Medical Aspects of Crime*. London: J. A. Churchill.

—— (1942), *The Adolescent Criminal: A Medico-Sociological Study of 4,000 Male Adolescents*. London: J. A. Churchill.

EAST, W. NORWOOD, and HUBERT, W. H. DE B. (1939), *Report on the Psychological Treatment of Crime*. London: HMSO.

ELLIS, H. (1890), *The Criminal*. London: Walter Scott.

FALLER, L. (1987), *Turned to Account: The Forms and Functions of Criminal Biography in Late Seventeenth and Early Eighteenth Century England*. Cambridge: Cambridge University Press.

FERRI, E. (1895), *Criminal Sociology*. London: Fisher Unwin.

FIELD, H. E. (1932), 'The Psychology of Crime: The Place of Psychology in the Treatment of Delinquents', *British Journal of Medical Psychology*, 12: 241–56.

FIELDING, H. (1988 [1751]), *An Enquiry into the Causes of the Late Increase of Robbers . . . and Other Related Writings*, ed. M. R. Zircar. Oxford: Oxford University Press.

FOUCAULT, M. (1977), *Discipline and Punish*. London: Allen Lane.

—— (1979), 'On Governmentality', *Ideology and Consciousness*, 6: 5–23.

FRIEDLANDER, K. (1947), *The Psychoanalytical Approach to Juvenile Delinquency*. London: Kegan Paul.

GARLAND, D. (1985*a*), *Punishment and Welfare*. Aldershot: Gower.

—— (1985*b*), 'The Criminal and his Science', *British Journal of Criminology*, 25/2: 109–37.

—— (1988), 'British Criminology before 1935', in P. Rock, ed., *A History of British Criminology*. Oxford: Oxford University Press.

—— (1992), 'Criminological Knowledge and its Relation to Power: Foucault's Genealogy and Criminology Today', *British Journal of Criminology*, 32/4: 403–22.

GLADSTONE COMMITTEE (1895), *Report of the Departmental Committee on Prisons*. PP 1895, lvi.

GLOVER, E. (1941), *The Diagnosis and Treatment of Delinquency*. London: ISTD.

—— (1960), *The Roots of Crime*. London: Imago.

GORING, C. (1913), *The English Convict: A Statistical Study*. London: HMSO.

GOTTFREDSON, M. R., and HIRSCHI, T., eds. (1987), *Positive Criminology*. Newsbury Park, Ca.: Sage.

GOULD, S. J. (1981), *The Mismeasure of Man*. New York: Norton.

GREEN, T. A. (1985), *Verdict According to Conscience: Perspectives on the English Trial Jury, 1200–1800*. Chicago: University of Chicago Press.

GRIFFITHS, A. G. F. (1904), *Fifty Years of Public Service*. London: Cassell.

—— (1910–11), 'Criminology', in *Encyclopaedia Britannica*, 11th edn. London: Encyclopaedia Britannica.

HACKING, I. (1990), *The Taming of Chance*. Cambridge: Cambridge University Press.

HIRST, P. Q. (1975), 'Marx and Engels on Law, Crime and Morality', in Taylor *et al.*, eds., *Critical Criminology*. London: Routledge and Kegan Paul.

HOME OFFICE (1959), *Penal Practice in a Changing Society: Aspects of Future Development*, Cmnd 645. London: HMSO.

HOWARD, J. (1973 [1777]), *The State of the Prisons in England and Wales.* Montclair, NJ: Paterson Smith. First published Warrington: W. Eyres.

—— (1973 [1789]), *An Account of the Principal Lazarettos of Europe.* Montclair, NJ: Paterson Smith. First published Warrington: W. Eyres.

IGNATIEFF, M. (1978), *A Just Measure of Pain: The Penitentiary and the Industrial Revolution.* London: Macmillan.

JONES, H. (1956), *Crime and the Penal System.* London: University Tutorial Press.

JUDGES, A. V., ed. (1930), *The Elizabethan Underworld.* London: Routledge (repr. 1965).

LAVATER, J. C. (1792), *Essays on Physiognomy, Designed to Promote the Knowledge and Love of Mankind.* London: J. Murray.

LEMAINE, G., MACLEOD, R., MULKAY, M., and WEINGERT, eds., (1976), *Perspectives on the Emergence of Scientific Disciplines.* Paris: Maison des Sciences de l'Homme.

LEVIN, Y., and LINDESMITH, A. (1937), 'English Ecology and Criminology of the Past Century', *Journal of Criminal Law, Criminology and Police Science*, 27/6: 801–16.

LODGE, T. S. (1974) 'The Founding of the Home Office Research Unit', in R. Hood, ed., *Crime, Criminology and Public Policy.* London: Heinemann.

LOMBROSO, C. (1876), *L'Uomo Delinquente.* Turin: Fratelli Bocca. (No English translation was ever published, but see G. Lombroso-Ferrero, *Criminal Man: According to the Classification of Cesare Lombroso.* New York: Putnam, 1911; repr. Montclair, NJ: Paterson Smith, 1972.

—— (1895), *The Female Offender.* London: Fisher Unwin.

LYELL, J. H. (1913), 'A Pioneer in Criminology: Notes on the Work of James Bruce Thomson of Perth', *Journal of Mental Science*, 59.

MANNHEIM, H. (1946), *Criminal Justice and Social Reconstruction.* Oxford: Oxford University Press.

—— (1949), Contribution to the Proceedings of the Conference, in National Association for Mental Health, *Why Delinquency? The Case for Operational Research.* London: NAMH.

—— (1957), 'Report on the Teaching of Criminology in the United Kingdom', in UNESCO, *The University Teaching of Social Sciences: Criminology.* Lausanne: UNESCO.

—— ed. (1960), *Pioneers in Criminology.* London: Stevens.

MANNHEIM, H., and WILKINS, L. (1955), *Prediction Methods in Relation to Borstal Training.* London: HMSO.

MATZA, D. (1964), *Delinquency and Drift.* New York: Wiley.

—— (1969), *Becoming Deviant.* Englewood Cliffs, NJ: Prentice-Hall.

MAUDSLEY, H. (1863), 'Review of A Prison Matron's *Female Life in Prison*', *Journal of Mental Science*, 9: 69.

—— (1889), 'Remarks on Crime and Criminals', *Journal of Mental Science*, 34: 159, 311.

—— (1895), 'Criminal Responsibility in Relation to Insanity', *Journal of Mental Science*, 41: 657.

MAYHEW, H. (1861–2), *London Labour and the London Poor.* London: Griffin, Bohn & Co.

MORRIS, T. (1957), *The Criminal Area*. London: Routledge and Kegan Paul.

MORRISON, W. D. (1896), *Juvenile Offenders*. London: Fisher Unwin.

NATIONAL ASSOCIATION FOR MENTAL HEALTH (1949), *Why Delinquency? The Case for Operational Research*. London: NAMH.

NEEDHAM, D. (1889), 'Comments on Maudsley's "Remarks on Crime and Criminals"', *Journal of Mental Science*, 34: 311.

NICOLSON, D. (1878–9), 'The Measure of Individual and Social Responsibility in Criminal Cases', *Journal of Mental Science*, 24: 1, 249.

—— (1895), 'Crime, Criminals and Criminal Lunatics: The Presidential Address to the Medico-Psychological Association', *Journal of Mental Science*, 41; 567.

NORMAN, D. C. (1895), 'Comments on Dr. Nicolson's Presidential Address', *Journal of Mental Science*, 41: 487.

NYE, R. (1984), *Crime, Madness and Politics in Modern France*. Princeton: Princeton University Press.

PAILTHORPE, G. W. (1932), *Studies in the Psychology of Delinquency*. London: HMSO.

PASQUINO, P. (1978), 'Theatrum Politicum: The Genealogy of Capital, Police, and the State of Prosperity', *Ideology and Consciousness*, 5: 41–54.

PETERSILIA, J. (1991), 'Policy Relevance and the Future of Criminology: The American Society of Criminology 1990 Presidential Address', *Criminology*, 29/1: 1–15.

PICK, D. (1989), *The Faces of Degeneration*. Cambridge: Cambridge University Press.

PORTER, R. (1987), *Mind-Forg'd Manacles: A History of Madness in England from the Restoration to the Regency*. Cambridge, Mass.: Harvard University Press.

PROAL, L. (1898), *Political Crime*. London: Fisher Unwin.

QUINTON, R. F. (1910), *Crime and Criminals 1876–1910*. London: Longmans, Green.

RADZINOWICZ, L. (1948–86), *A History of the English Criminal Law and its Administration, from 1750*, 5 vols. (Vol. 5 with R. Hood). London: Stevens.

—— (1961), *In Search of Criminology*. London: Heinemann.

—— (1966), *Ideology and Crime*. London: Stevens.

—— (1988), *The Cambridge Institute of Criminology: Its Background and Scope*. London: HMSO.

RAFTER, N. H. (1992), 'Criminal Anthropology in the United States', *Criminology*, 30/4: 525–45.

REINER, R. (1988), 'British Criminology and the State', in P. Rock, ed., *A History of British Criminology*. Oxford: Oxford University Press.

ROCK, P., ed. (1988*a*), *A History of British Criminology*. Oxford: Oxford University Press.

—— (1988*b*), 'The Present State of Criminology in Britain;, in P. Rock, ed., *A History of British Criminology*. Oxford: Oxford University Press.

ROSE, N. (1988), 'Calculable Minds and Manageable Individuals', *The History of the Human Sciences*, 1/2: 179–200.

ROSHIER, B. (1989), *Controlling Crime: The Classical Perspective in Criminology*. Chicago: Lyceum Books.

RUGGLES-BRISE, Sir E. (1924), *Prison Reform at Home and Abroad: A Short History of the International Movement since the London Conference, 1872.* London: Macmillan.

SALGADO, G. (1972), *Cony-Catchers and Bawdy Baskets.* Harmondsworth: Penguin.

SAVITZ, L., TURNER, S. H., and DICKMAN, T. (1977), 'The Origin of Scientific Criminology: Franz Gall as the First Criminologist', in R. F. Meier, ed., *Theory in Criminology.* Beverley Hills: Sage.

SENNETT, R. (1977), *The Fall of Public Man.* London: Faber.

SHARPE, J. A. (1985), ' "Last Dying Speeches": Religion, Ideology and Public Execution in Seventeenth Century England', *Past and Present*, 107: 144–67.

SKINNER, Q. (1969), 'Meaning and Understanding in the History of Ideas', *History and Theory*,. 8/1: 3–53.

SMITH, M. H. (1922*a*), 'The Medical Examination of Delinquents', *Journal of Mental Science*, 68.

—— (1922*b*), *The Psychology of the Criminal.* London: Methuen.

SMITH, R. (1988), 'Does the History of Psychology have a Subject?', *The History of the Human Sciences*, 1/1: 147–78.

ST JOHN, A. (1912), 'Criminal Anthropology and Common Sense', *Sociological Review*, 5: 65–7.

SULLIVAN, W. C. (1906), *Alcoholism.* London: J. Nisbet.

—— (1924), *Crime and Insanity.* London: Edward Arnold.

SUTHERLAND, J. F. (1908), *Recidivism: Habitual Criminality and Habitual Petty Delinquency.* Edinburgh.

TAYLOR, I. (1981), *Law and Order: Arguments for Socialism.* London: Macmillan.

TAYLOR, I., and TAYLOR, L., eds. (1973), *Politics and Deviance: Papers from the National Deviancy Conference.* Harmondsworth: Penguin.

TAYLOR, I., WALTON, P., and YOUNG, J. (1973), *The New Criminology.* London: Routledge & Kegan Paul.

—— eds (1975), *Critical Criminology.* London: Routledge and Kegan Paul.

TAYLOR, R. S. (1968), 'Review of Jones' *Crime and the Penal System*, 3rd edn', *Howard Journal*, 12/3.

THOMSON, J. B. (1867), 'The Effects of the Present System of Prison Discipline on the Body and Mind', *Journal of Mental Science*, 12.

TUKE, H. (1889), 'Comments on Maudsley's "Remarks on Crime and Criminals" ', *Journal of Mental Science*, 34: 311.

VOLD, G. B. (1958), *Theoretical Criminology.* New York: Oxford University Press.

WIENER, M. (1990), *Reconstructing the Criminal: Culture, Law, and Policy in England, 1830–1914.* Cambridge: Cambridge University Press.

WILES, P. (1976), 'Introduction', in *The Sociology of Crime and Delinquency in Britain*, ii. Oxford: Martin Robertson.

WOOTTON, B. (1959), *Social Science and Social Pathology.* London: Allen and Unwin.

YOUNG, J. (1988), 'Radical Criminology in Britain: The Emergence of a Competing Paradigm', in P. Rock, ed., *A History of British Criminology.* Oxford: Oxford University Press.

ZEMAN, T. (1981), 'Order, Crime and Punishment: The American Criminological Tradition', Ph.D. thesis, University of California at Santa Cruz.

2

Incessant Chatter: Recent Paradigms in Criminology

JOCK YOUNG

THE PENDULUM OF IDEAS AND THE PROBLEM OF PARTIALITY

Two images of the criminal recur throughout the past hundred years: the moral actor, freely choosing crime; and the automaton, the person who has lost control and is beset by forces within or external to him or her. There is no necessary political evaluation to either picture: conservative and anarchist share the view of the moral criminal, but for one he is fallen humanity and for the other the hero; both Lombrosian and social reformer share the image of the determined criminal, but for one the causes are biological effects, for the other, defects in society. Images of free will, sometimes romanticized and always elevated as the universal essence of humanity, contrast with notions of pathology, of the 'sick' criminal, the person who, because of circumstances, *lacks* humanity.

The history of criminology is one of incessant competition between these two equally abstract images of humanity, each a caricature of reality. On one side there has been an idealism which granted the human actor free will, rationality, and unfettered moral choice; on the other, a vulgar materialism which portrayed the criminal as fully determined and non-rational, and regarded morality as a metaphysic. Thus the wilful, rational actor contrasts with the determined, propelled actor. One abstract metaphysic is set up against an equally absurd 'scientific' datum. These two gross abstractions have shadow-boxed with each other throughout the history of our subject, one mirror-image shaping itself up against the other. In the early days of criminology as a discipline, classicism and positivism arrayed themselves in such a fashion. The fight between structural functionalism and labelling theory had resonances of such a contest and, of course, today the re-emergence of new and idealistic forms of neo-classicism (e.g. the 'new administrative criminology') and virulent, if atavistic, forms of neo-positivism, (e.g. right realism) repeat the same combat with a ghastly inability to realize that history is repeating itself. And at each historical juncture the theorists claim paradigm change, from the positivist revolution of Enrico Ferri to the new scientific revolution of the 'born again' Lombrosians of the present period. This is exactly what Pitrim Sorokin described many years ago as a combination of 'amnesia' and 'the discoverers' complex', where the aspiring social scientist is unaware of (or forgets) the past and 'rediscovers' ideas already long known. And to this one might add that the *debates* of the past—for example, over the possibility (or not) of reducing the social to the biological—are also erased from the memory, so that the path of knowledge is not so much progressively linear, but rather forms a continuous circuit of *déja vu.*

It is important to stress at this juncture that this pendulum of fashion within the subject involves theories which are veritable mirror-images of each other as much as they are repeats of past ideas. As has been frequently pointed out, critique very often becomes mere conceptual inversion (see Young 1975, 1979; Bottomley 1979; Spitzer 1980).

Another manifestation of myopia among criminological theorists that characterizes much work of this kind is a chronic tendency towards partiality. This one-sidedness can involve taking the criminal at one single point of time and denying the past circumstances which brought about the crime or the future possibilities. It can involve a fixation on the distant past, so that present circumstances are annulled. It can involve a focus on the macro-structure of society and its legislation and ignore the rule-breaker altogether—and, of course, it can focus on the criminal as if he or she were independent of humanly created rules. It can produce criminal actors whose actions are prescribed by their bodies; it can produce those who exist in some airy limbo of symbolism without any bodies whatsoever. It can point to simple actors whose choices are an artefact of the spatial obstacles and opportunities confronting them; it can hold up criminals who exist outside of the physical world of space and opportunity. It can take one part of the square of crime—offender, victim, police, or informal control—and explain all crime in terms of one (or, at best, two) of these factors. It can be bone-headedly deterministic or can imbue human nature with pure reason. It can attempt to explain the criminological universe in terms of race, or class, or gender, or age, but scarcely ever a genuine, meaningful, cultural synthesis of them all.

In this essay I trace the development of recent dominant paradigms in criminology. There are, of course, and always have been, criminologists who believe they are merely adding to the stock of knowledge, free from ideological preconceptions. These are inevitably those most trapped within a paradigm—usually the positivist. The great Anglo-Saxon tradition of empiricism is a form of theoretical blindness: the parading of a hidden agenda of atomistic caricatures of human nature and simplistic notions of social order. It acts as if two centuries of social philosophy had never existed. Yet it is only by spelling out the logic of a theoretical position that we can clearly judge the ability of a perspective to grapple with the facts of crime and create workable policies. Social theory does not emerge out of the blue: it develops in distinct social and economic situations and is influenced by specific material problems, in the context of a particular array of ideas and socially defined problems.

Academic debate has both an interior and an exterior history. The interior history is the interchange between scholars buttressed by the material strength of departmental hierarchies and the underpinning of publishing outlets, together with access to external funding. But however autonomous this academic debate is considered to be by many of its participants, the interior dialogue is propelled by the exterior world. The dominant ideas of a period, whether establishment or radical; the social problems of a particular society; the government in power and the political possibilities existing in a society—all shape the interior discourse of the academic. Nowhere is this more evident than in criminology and the sociology of law. Exterior problems of crime, of law-making, of political options and current ideas, all profoundly shape the theories emanating from the interior world of academic criminology and legal scholarship. The establishment academic, propelled by the direction of local and national government funding, and the critical scholar, contesting the ever-changing orthodoxies of theory and practice, clash on a terrain determined by the specificity of their society. It is no accident, therefore—to take three radical currents—that abolitionist theory takes root in the liberal welfare democracies of Scandinavia and the Netherlands (Hulsman 1986; Scheerer 1986); that left realist theory emerges in a Britain concerned with a radical reappraisal of social democracy (Young and Matthews, eds. 1992); and that legal guaranteeism (Ferrajoli 1989) enthuses Latin American criminologists in countries where the rule of law is precarious and fragile.

None of this is to suggest a relativism of theory. Rather, it is to point to its reflexivity. That is, theory emerges out of a certain social and political conjuncture: this generates points of sensitivity and areas of blindness which inhibit the development of a general theory applicable even to all industrial societies, let alone the Third World. Yet theory, on the other hand, must be sharpened by its sense of locality if it is to gain purchase on the particular social and political terrain of which it is part. To take left realism as an example, Ray Michalowski (1991) quite correctly distinguishes between discussion of realism as a general theory and its practical applicability in the USA, as do David Brown and Russell Hogg (1992) in their discussion of the applicability of realism to the Australian context, whilst De Keseredy and Schwartz (1992) point accurately to the way in which the merging realist currents in Britain and the USA are shaped by the glaring social contrasts between the two countries.

Underlying this debate is the problem of specificity (Young 1992): namely, that generalizations about crime and justice (e.g. the relationship between unemployment and crime) can only be formulated in specific political and social contexts and cannot be made without specifying the particular social characteristics of offender and victim in terms of their respective positions on the major social axes of age, class, ethnicity, and gender. It is not possible simply to transpose findings from one country to another or to generalize from men to women, white to black, working class to middle class, etc. Such a localism does not preclude generalization, as many postmodernists would argue (e.g. Nicholson 1990); it merely stresses that sociological generalizations must be grounded in the lived realities of the human actors concerned.

THE ETIOLOGICAL CRISIS

Criminology and the sociology of deviance went through an intensive phase of development during the period from the late 1950s to the early 1970s. Labelling theory, new deviancy theory, conflict theory, subcultural theory, control theory, neo-classicism all blossomed in a most extraordinary creative ferment. It was a process which did not happen overnight: it happened in different ways and times in various advanced industrial countries, but in the long run it overturned the way in which not only criminologists but very many ordinary men and women in the street viewed crime.

In the immediate post-war period there was a consensus, stretching across a large section of informed opinion of various political persuasions, that one of the major causes of crime was impoverished social conditions. Anti-social conditions led to anti-social behaviour. This dominant paradigm was positivism or, more precisely, social democratic positivism: namely, the conviction that crime or other forms of anti-social behaviour can be greatly reduced by political interventions which seek to improve social conditions. The palpable failure of such theories, which I have termed the etiological crisis of criminology, is, to my mind, the key concept in understanding the development of criminology in industrial countries. What actually happened was the exact opposite to what the conventional wisdom decreed. Slums were demolished, education standards increased, full employment advanced and welfare spending increased—the highest level of affluence in the history of humanity was achieved: yet crime increased. In Britain, for example, in the years 1951–71, real disposable income per person in the UK increased by 64 per cent; in the same period, the number of crimes known to the police rose by more than double that—172 per cent.

Nowhere has the etiological crisis been expressed more pointedly than by James Q. Wilson, President Reagan's crime adviser and a writer with a new right perspective on the world:

> In 1960 if one had been asked what steps society might take to prevent a sharp increase in the crime rate, one might well have answered that crime could best be curtailed by reducing poverty, increasing educational attainment, eliminating dilapidated housing, encouraging community organization, and providing troubled or delinquent youth with counselling services.
>
> Early in the decade of the 1960s, this country began the longest sustained period of prosperity since World War II. A great array of programs aimed at the young, the poor and the deprived were mounted. Though these efforts were not made primarily out of a desire to reduce crime, they were wholly consistent with—indeed, in their aggregate money levels, wildly exceeded—the policy prescription that a thoughtful citizen worried about crime would have offered at the beginning of the decade.
>
> Crime soared. It did not just increase a little; it rose at a faster rate and to higher levels than at any time since the 1930s and, in some categories, to higher levels than any experienced in this century.
>
> It all began in about 1963. That was the year, to over-dramatize a bit, that a decade began to fall apart. (Wilson 1975: 3–4)

But it was not only on the conservative side of the political spectrum, nor only among Americans that the conventional wisdom on crime was in tatters.

The Nature of the Etiological Crisis

At this point the problem of the etiological crisis should be clarified. Basically, social democratic positivism maintains that crime is a result of poor social conditions: bad behaviour is a result of bad social background. Such a belief system was—and, of course, still is—a major component of contemporary social thought, and is a staple of the conventional wisdom with regard to crime. It underscores much of social work, of the thinking behind the role of the welfare state as ameliorating social problems, of the political attitudes of American 'liberals', Western democratic socialists, and Marxists in both East and West; and the consensus on this belief extends to the more 'wet' or progressive parts of conservative parties in Western democracies. In a weak form, social positivism merely argues that as affluence increases, and brings with it higher educational levels, better housing conditions, improved urban planning, etc., crime will automatically decrease. In the stronger social democratic form, it calls for the state to intervene to ensure that wealth is distributed equitably and for pockets of poverty to be eliminated, as well as for specific rehabilitative and integrative measures to be directed towards the offender. Social positivism thus believes that we must tackle what it sees as the *root* causes of crimes, and that these are social. The tradition of social positivism stretches right across the history of criminology, from the grounding of the discipline in the work of the moral statisticians such as Alphonse Quetelet (1842) in the first half of the nineteenth century, through the Chicago school, to modern subcultural theory.

Problems of etiology can, of course, occur from several directions, not merely the rise in crime coincident with affluence. A problem arises when:

(a) there is a decrease in crime over time with increased poverty or unemployment;
(b) crime or delinquency is found to be greater or equal among middle-class people than among the poor;
(c) crime is found to be greater in wealthy areas than in poor areas.

The particular way in which such anomalies present themselves to social positivism varies across time and place. For example, with Quetelet the difficulty was focused on the disparity between the wealthy urban and poor rural areas, while in modern American criminology the problem of middle-class juvenile delinquency has been important (see e.g. Schwendinger and Schwendinger 1985). But the major problem in most advanced industrial countries in the post-war period has been the existence of rising affluence and welfarism concomitant with increased crime and delinquency.

The Etiological Crisis and World Criminology

The etiological crisis, and attempts to explain or deny it, has been the major dynamic behind recent developments in criminology. This is not to say that it was uniformly felt across world criminology as a discipline To make such an assertion would be to ignore the way in which, criminologically, very different things were happening in different countries, and the way in which the discipline, as constituted, both emanates from and focuses upon a very select few countries. In some advanced industrial countries the etiological crisis was non-existent. In Japan, for example, up until recent years, the crime rate went according to plan—that is, it dropped with rising prosperity—and any 'normal scientist' of a social democratic mould would have found his or her world relatively unperturbed. In many parts of the Third World, particularly in Latin America, the crime rate has spiralled awesomely, as have gross poverty and immiseration. There are no surprises here.

In other countries the crisis arrived in very different guises: the persistence of crime in the Soviet Union after the 'achievement' of socialism was a different order of problem from the rise in crime in the USA, where the welfare state was comparatively minimal in its implementation. It also arrived at different times. It was an early puzzle to the socially reconstructed welfare states of Western Europe; and it was delayed in countries such as Spain and Portugal which until the mid-1970s remained in the thrall of fascism. Lastly, in some countries, particularly in Scandinavia, the rise in crime, although marked in percentage terms, started from such a low base that crime was never a really great problem as it was in other countries such as the USA.

The Rising Crime Rate in Europe in the Immediate Post-war Period

Let us start at the period just after the war in Europe. It is important to stress how rising crime rates in certain circumstances appear far from anomalous from the perspective of social democratic positivism. Initially, within the war-torn countries of Europe, the rise in the crime rate was seen as unsurprising (see Taylor 1981, ch. 2). As Hermann Mannheim put it, writing at the London School of Economics in 1947: 'It would be altogether wrong to regard the rise in crime as something extraordinary or particularly alarming. It is nothing but the natural result of six years of total war with all its inevitable moral, psychological and economic repercussions' (Mannheim 1955: 110). But the trend persisted; and the first explanation to gain currency involved a generational transposition of the war. It was argued that a 'delinquent generation' had been created which had passed through the early years of their lives during the war and whose delinquency was appearing ten or more years later (see, for Britain, Wilkins 1960; for Denmark, Christiansen 1964). Whatever rational kernel there maybe to the higher delinquency rates of certain birth years when compared to others, it is obvious that this particular theory had a very limited shelf-life. For the crime rate continued to increase, among both youngsters and adults, despite the receding aftermath of war.

The crime rate was most puzzling in Western European countries which had passed through a period of social reconstruction after the war. For a generation of committed European social democracies, post-war social reconstruction and the institution of the welfare state simply did not add up to an increase in the crime rate. Let us take John Barron Mays' important book, *Crime and Social Structure*, published in 1963:

> The drunkenness, despair and depravity of slum-dwellers in the midst of prosperous Victorian society led social reformers to the naive hope that if only the adverse physical and material conditions could be eliminated, criminality would also be checked and contained. Such hopes have been cruelly disappointed. For crime and higher living standards have advanced hand in hand, and the amount of known crime has actually about doubled over the past twenty years. (Mays 1963: 192–3)

T. R. Fyvel, writing at the same time, made much the same point in his best-selling book *The Insecure Offenders*: 'A generation ago it was still widely held that even if poverty was only one among the main causes, the delinquency figures would at least roughly follow the curve of economic dislocation and unemployment. Today this link has clearly been severed' (Fyvel 1963: 14). Fyvel noted that a paradoxical wave of criminality had occurred throughout Europe to such an extent as to give rise to the German word, *die Wohlstandskriminalität*. For, as Swedish criminologist Bo Svensson nicely put it, 'in the 20th century . . . the criminality of the destitute has been superseded by what may be called welfare criminality' (1986: 118).

The Immediate Reaction to the Crisis

But this has taken us too far ahead. Let us concentrate on the most immediate reaction to the etiological crisis. This involved a revival of the neo-classicist approach to crime and a reformulation of positivism from a social to an individual focus. Let us take the shift in positivism first. The failure of sociological positivism and the etiological crisis was evident, not just in the existence of crime and delinquency, which should simply not have been there, but in the changed prospects for policies based on social intervention. Steve Box captured this well when he wrote his famous essay on the discovery of the disease 'hyperactivity' in children:

> By the end of the seventies the promise of sociological positivism was either seen as counterfeit because programmes based on it failed to reduce delinquency and youthful misbehaviour or totally impractical because they required social reform on a scale that the dominant class was quite unprepared to contemplate. Thus, whilst lip service was still being paid to these types of programmes, there was already a preparedness to look elsewhere for alternative solutions to the delinquency problem. One of these was already under way and only required more funds and official certification to mushroom; this was a new version of biological determinism—the conception that delinquents and pre-delinquents were essentially ill, either mentally or, as in the case of hyperactivity, physically and organically, and required treatment, especially drug therapy. (Box 1980: 116–17)

Such a 'medicalization' of social problems, especially among juveniles, has continued and expanded to date and has provided the material basis for the continuing existence of biological positivism long after Lombrosianism had been—repeatedly—proclaimed dead. Indeed, some of the best known criminology books espouse a biological determinist position (e.g. Eysenck 1970; Jeffrey 1980). But there are limits to individual and biologically based determinism:

1. It can explain only a small proportion of the problem of crime and is particularly inadequate at dealing with its rise.
2. Individual therapy is expensive.
3. Biological reductionism is politically dynamite, even to politicians of the new right.

By far the most obvious and immediate reaction to the etiological crisis, in the face of the growing evidence of failure in terms of social democratic explanations and interventions in crime control, was a surge in neo-classicist methods of intervention: more police, more prisons, a 'more effective' justice system. None of this meant losing completely notions of conditions which predisposed people to delinquency; but these conditions came to be seen more as mitigating circumstances than as excuses for avoiding punishment.

In Britain, the most immediate move was the adoption of 'short, sharp, shock' treatment for a proportion of delinquents. Thus Fyvel writes:

> The unforeseen increase in delinquency in the male seventeen to twenty-one age-groups was reflected by an equivalent rise in the Borstal population which went up from 2,800 at the beginning of 1956, to over 5,000 at the end of 1960. Unprecedented measures had to be taken to absorb this new clientele, and Mr Butler's White Paper of January 1959 introduced the biggest prison-building programme for young adult offenders, including plans for the building of eight Borstals, together with eight of the new detention centres, designed to administer 'a short, sharp, shock' to the evidently more recalcitrant young offenders of the new age. (Fyvel 1963: 17)

The Crisis in Penality

If biological and individualistic explanations of crime had explanatory and political limits, neo-classicism had even greater problems which were to reverberate through criminology in the late 1970s. Indeed, it is possible to talk of a double-barrelled crisis in criminology: first the crisis of etiology in the 1960s, followed by a crisis in penality.

In the 1970s, faced with continuing rises in the crime rate and a fiscal crisis in the cost of police and prisons, politicians in the USA became greatly interested in the most effective use of resources. Research focused most strongly on police work, involving particularly the RAND organization and the Police Foundation. Their findings were to have a devastating effect on subsequent criminology. For they pointed out, among other things, that

(a) increased numbers of police do not necessarily reduce crime rates or increase clear-up;
(b) saturation policing does not reduce crime, but only increases displacement;
(c) improving response times to emergency calls does not affect the likelihood of arresting criminals;
(d) crimes are not solved primarily through criminal investigations but largely through public witnessing;
(e) the kinds of crime of which the public are most fearful are rarely encountered by the police on patrol;

(f) neither random motor patrols nor foot patrols had any effect on the crime rate.

This summary of findings I have culled from Jerome Skolnick and David Bayley's incisive book, *The New Blue Line*. They write:

> Those findings are devastating. They mean that the primary strategies followed by American police departments are neither reducing crime nor reassuring the public. The studies clearly imply that protection needs to be provided by citizens themselves, and that their assistance is essential in capturing and prosecuting the people who victimise them. The job for the police, therefore, is to work with the public so as to ensure that those things happen to develop specific and articulate approaches that can achieve results. (Skolnick and Bayley 1986: 5–6)

Here was a double-barrelled failure in both of the conventional wisdoms of crime control: social democratic positiFvism and neo-classicism. If better conditions did not work, neither did better (i.e. more apposite) punishment. If more housing did not reduce the crime rate, neither did more police. If the rehabilitative prison regime had failed, so had the 'short, sharp shock'. If there was on the left an etiologial crisis with regards to the causes of crime, there was a parallel intellectual crisis on the right over the failure of policing and prisons.

First Responses to the Crisis

The subsequent development of criminology is an attempt to come to terms with the crisis. It resulted in a wealth of debate and an intense level of dispute. But at the same time, there was a measure of agreement that the old ideas of social democratic positivism and neo-classicism had failed. It is difficult to imagine a criminology where Howard Becker, Richard Quinney, James Q. Wilson, and Ron Clarke were on the same side of the barricades, but this, to an extent, was what happened. Let us first look at the parameters of the debate.

The first response to the etiological crisis outside of the traditional paradigms of positivism and classicism was various varieties of what I call the 'great denial'. That is, criminologists simply deemed that there had not been a real increase in crime or criminality. For them at least, the etiological crisis had not occurred. Throughout the 1960s the US crime rate rose remorselessly and in Britain the increase had become seemingly inexorable. How could anyone in their right mind doubt that the curve was actually going up? They were able to do so because the interpretation of crime rates known to the police, on which official statistics are based, is a very complex business. The 'great denial' had many facets, all of which had in common the denial that crime or criminality had 'really' risen. It had gone up simply because there were more police or more laws, or more things to be stolen, or because people had more prosperous public lifestyles and thus were more exposed to crime, or we were less tolerant of crime. Typical replies to the question 'Why has the crime rate risen?' were:

More State Action	All that has happened is that because of rising numbers of police more people are being arrested; and, as there is a considerable dark figure of crime unknown to the police, the official statistics can rise without there being a rise in 'real' crime.
More Laws	Because there is more legislation on the statute book, there are more possible crimes.
More Sensitive	People have become more sensitive to crimes such as violence, therefore more are being reported to the police.
More Victims	Because of increased affluence there are more things to steal and people go out more, living more exposed lifestyles. As opportunities have risen, so have crimes.

And, of course, as well as theories based around denial, there were the conservative and social democratic theorists who believed that the rise was 'real' and involved an increase in numbers of offenders caused by, in the first instance, a welfare state that was soft on punishment and undermined authority and, in the second instance, a welfare state which had allowed relative inequalities to persist. In a way, the recent history of criminological theory is dominated by how the various social and political strands made sense of the early 1960s. They have spoken in many voices—some of them widespread and established, others restricted to tiny academic circles—but they all address, and are a response to, the etiological crisis and the associated problems of penality.

What is immediately apparent is that any of the changes noted above can affect the crime rate. For if we deconstruct the concept of 'crime rate' we will find we have the following variables:

(a) number of likely offenders;
(b) number of likely victims;
(c) variation in the tolerance levels of public or police about crime (that is, informal and formal definitions as to what is or is not serious crime);
(d) variation in the actual levels of control exerted by public and police on crime (that is, levels of informal and formal control).

Any one or a combination of these can alter the crime rate. The problem is that most theories have focused upon only one factor and largely ignored the others. None of them could be exclusively correct; all factors are undoubtedly involved, although the weighting one would give to each element is an empirical matter demanding investigation.

This was how the various theoretical traditions responded immediately to the etiological crisis and the crisis of penality in the period 1960–80. It is out of the ferment of this debate that the paradigms prominent in the last ten years arise.

CURRENT PARADIGMS IN CRIMINOLOGY

The four major approaches to criminology which have become predominant in the last ten years are: left idealism; the new administrative criminology; and realism of the right and of the left. They represent, once again, attempts to solve the crisis of etiology and penality. They take strands of the 1960s debate and weave them together in each of their discourses. They all represent responses to the etiological crisis and are all descendants of paradigms which emerged during the 1960s. Thus the ancestor of left idealism is labelling theory; of the new administrative criminology, control theory; of right realism, neo-positivism; and of left realism, subcultural theory. They have certain aspects in common: they all play down the role of the police in the control of crime and put a great stress on the public informal system of social control; they are all critical of the existing prison system; and they all reject traditional positivism and classicism.

In order to compare these theories systematically I will examine them under the following headings: concepts of human nature and social order; the causes of crime; the impact of crime; the role of the state agencies; the role of the public; and the crises in aetiology and penality. Because of the differing emphases of the various theories, not all these areas are covered in relation to each of them.

Left Idealism

> Whenever you scratch a twentieth century Marxist nine times out of ten he [*sic*] turns out to be a left idealist. (Timpinaro 1973: 101)

Left idealism is a spectrum that reaches from liberals to the hard left: it is part of a persuasive way of looking at the world which is evidenced not only in criminology but in every aspect of social life in Western society. In essence, it looks to the role of the state and of ideas emanating from it and other powerful institutions as a major way in which consciousness is structured and behaviour directed (see Young 1979; Lea and Young 1984).Its roots lie in American labelling theory, although its development has been greatest in Europe, where it is associated with an abolitionist position: that is, a policy which would take much 'crime' out of the orbit of criminal law and which would abolish the prison. Appropriately, its greatest development has been in countries with low crime rates, where the etiological crisis was experienced less dramatically than in the USA.

Left idealism is evident throughout the social sciences. In the sociology of education it is exemplified in the work of Bowles and Gintis (1976) in the USA and of Michael F. Young (1971) in the UK. In mass media studies it is associated with the work of the Glasgow Media Group (1976) and the radical phenomenologists (e.g. Tuchman 1978); and in social problems theory with the work of the social constructionists (Kitsuse and Spector 1973; Pfohl 1977). It is evident also in the work of radical feminists, both those working in the field of crime and those examining other areas of social life (e.g. Kelly and Radford 1987). Indeed, much radical feminist work parallels that of socialist criminologists, merely substituting women for the working class as a historical subject (see Nicholson 1990).

A central feature of left idealism is the priority of administration over structure. It views society as determined by the administration of the state rather than by the actual structural positions in which individuals find themselves. The youth is propelled by being labelled delinquent rather than by his impoverished circumstances; the pupil underachieves because of the school, not because of her class background and likely future; mental hospitals, not life outside, turn people mad; violence on television causes violence in the streets, rather than machismo violence being a product of the marginalization of working-class youth.

Human nature and social order

At heart left idealism is a form of radical social contract theory. People are equal, free, rational agents who, in a just society, would come together and form a consensus which would be the basis of state power and the organization of society. Yet the present world is palpably unjust: it is riven with the inequalities of class, gender, and race. Because of this, people in subordinate positions constantly create subcultures of resistance as they see through the inequalities of society. Yet the paradox remains: Why, in a world so palpably unfair, does capitalist society maintain itself? Why do not the vast majority of people subjugated by class, gender, and race come together and create a genuine social contract of equals? The left idealist answer to this stresses, first of all, the power of ruling-class ideas. A series of institutions, from the mass media to the school, from the criminal justice system to the panoply of 'consensus' politics, circulate a 'dominant ideology' (see Abercrombie *et al.* 1980) which upholds the values of capitalism, of the patriarchal nuclear family, of a Eurocentric notion of racial superiority. Institutionalized classism, sexism, and racism are encountered from cradle to grave. Our notions of 'normality', our images of appropriate gender roles, the contented consumer, the docile worker, or the honest citizen, are 'socially constructed' by these master institutions. To an extent such a consensus is a mystification, because the actual social world has a rainbow pluralism: a cultural diversity, differing definitions of sexuality, a plurality of 'family' structures and, above all, a constant fighting back by the resurgent subordinate orders. It is this fighting back which underlies the central need for coercion. The police, the courts, and the criminal justice system are ever necessary to control such an intransigent population. On one hand we have the inculcation of the 'normal', and on the other, the ever-present need to control and stigmatize the 'deviant'. The velvet glove of the soft, ideological machine of social control contains within it an iron fist of coercion. The various institutions of society, whether primarily ideological (the school and the mass media) or coercive (the criminal justice system) hang together in a *functioning* whole which perpetuates the present social order.

The causes of crime

For left idealists the causes of crime are obvious: deprivation in the poor and greed in the rich. It is not tied to one class and therefore the equation of more poverty with more crime is misleading, for in the case of the corporations and the rich, more crime is a product of affluence.

Working-class crime against property has, therefore, a quality of obviousness:

> The position of black labour, subordinated by the process of capital, is deteriorating and will deteriorate more rapidly according to its own specific logic. Crime is one potently predictable and quite comprehensible consequence of this process—as certain a consequence of how structures work, however 'unintended', as the fact that night follows day. (Hall *et al.* 1978: 390)

Note here a simple social positivism: crime is an obvious and inevitable consequence of the struggle to live; it is a product of absolute, rather than relative, deprivation. Such a belief is echoed in fine detail by revisionist historians who view both crime and the law as reflecting class interests (e.g. Hay 1975). Equally, if working-class crime is obvious, ruling-class crime, whether of corporations or the police, is both endemic and simple. The specificity of situation which creates crime among certain executives in particular corporations and at precise moments is ignored, while detailing the material predicaments which give rise to police malpractices is seen merely as a mistaken use of 'bad apple' theory.

The impact of crime

Crime is ubiquitous in an unequal society: criminal statistics showing a greater rate of crimes among the poor and ethnic minorities merely exhibit the bias of the police and judiciary against these groups. The rise in recorded crime is an epiphenomenon, a side-effect, of more police (see Carr-Hill and Stern 1979); there is no means of accurately telling if there has been any real rise in crime. Left idealism does not usually suggest that crime is *not* a problem (e.g. Scraton, 1985, 1987), but rather that the problem is grossly exaggerated and that this misleads people as to the real problems in society, e.g. poverty and exploitation. Indeed, by blaming the poor for crime, it ends up in blaming the poor for their poverty (see Ryan 1976). The poor are seen as double victims, both in their poverty and in that they are then stigmatized as offenders by the state.

The role of the state agencies

The police In left idealism the central role of the police is seen as not so much the control of crime as the control of order. Thus, English commentators on the 1984 miners' strike write: 'There can be little doubt that the British police force is primarily a public order force; its role in crime prevention and criminal apprehension is secondary' (Coulter *et al.* 1984: 135). The expansion of the police force is therefore seen as predominantly a response to problems of political order. Strikes, demonstrations, the control of those 'labelled' terrorists (in the UK, those active in the troubles in Northern Ireland), and the subjugation of the black and ethnic minority populations are seen as keys to understanding the development of policing (e.g. Brake and Hale 1992). Crime is used as an excuse to fuel the expansion of the police and the 'widening of the net' of social control. Even where seemingly positive initiatives are generated, hidden agendas are detected.

The prison The standard history of the prison, in the classicist tradition from Beccaria to Radzinowicz, was one of reform and its failure. Against this, a 'revisionist' reading of the history and development of the prison has grown, arguing that the real meaning of the prison, far from making humanitarian progress, was to create divisions with the working class (see Cohen and Scull 1985). This revisionist interpretation is shared by many socialist historians and left idealists today. In no other branch of radical criminology has functionalism taken such a root and developed such a taken-for-granted quality as in the debate on the possibility of prison reform. How can it be, it is asked, that such an inefficient instrument in terms of reform, with its high recidivism rate and its role as a 'university of crime' has continued for over a century of blatant failure? The answer to this, in the best tradition of functionalism, is that the prison is, in fact, far from a failure, but a functional necessity in the perpetuation of capitalism. All of the major radical writers on prisons explicitly take up a functionalist explanation of its persistence (e.g. Mathieson 1974; Fitzgerald 1977; Melossi and Pavarini 1981).

Such left functionalist theory of the failure of the prisons can be seen clearly in Jeffrey Reiman's brilliant polemic against the prison and the class society, *The Rich Get Richer and the Poor Get Prison*, where he describes what he calls the Pyrrhic Retreat Theory of the criminal justice system. Thus he writes: 'On the whole, Marxists see the criminal justice system as serving the powerful by successfully repressing the poor. My view is that the system serves the powerful by its failure to reduce crime, not by its success' (Reiman 1979: 6–7). He locates his position—as do many left idealists—as one influenced by Althusserian functionalism. And he indicates clearly that the function of the 'future' of the prison is to help divide and rule the working class:

> The Message is two-pronged: (1) By focusing on individual criminals, the criminal justice system diverts attention away from the irrationalities and injustices of our social and economic institutions. (2) By focusing on poor criminals, the criminal justice system diverts attention away from the rich and powerful who most profit from our social and economic institutions. (Reiman 1979: 167–8)

The capitalist system generates a surplus population who are unable to find labour. The criminalization and incarceration of this population has functions on a number of levels. First, it removes them from disturbing the productive process, then it blames such a need for 'sanitization' on their individual qualities. Second, it distracts the attention of the working class away from ruling-class crime and general social inequality on to this scapegoat population. Thus a failure of capitalism is turned ideologically into a success (see Fitzgerald 1977).

The role of the public

The public—at least, the working class and less powerful members of the community—are seen as being recipients of policing rather than instigators of demands on the police. The priorities of the police are those of the police bureaucracy or their government paymasters in the local and national state.

The effect of the stereotype of crime purveyed from the police, through the courts to the mass media, is to create moral panics in the population, creating an irrational fear of crime and justifying expenditure on the police.

The crisis of etiology

For left idealism there is no crisis in etiology—or in policing or prisons, for that matter. In fact, the intellectual task of left idealism is to challenge and expose this sham. Both aspects of the purported crisis are social constructs socially generated by the powerful. The crime statistics are a product of police preference: the reason why the prisons are full of working-class people, not middle-class people, is because working-class behaviour is defined as criminal, and working-class people are arrested rather than those higher up in society. The statistical rise in crime merely shows that more state resources are at the disposal of the police and the judiciary. Thus crime waves are moral panics engendered by the media and orchestrated by the police.

There is thus no etiological crisis: first because the rise in crime is exaggerated, second because the notion of crime being caused solely by the poor is false. There is a crisis in policing, on the other hand, but it is a crisis of the police getting out of hand. For example, the subtitle of Phil Scraton's 1985 book *The State of the Police* reads *Is Law and Order out of Control?* It is not a crisis of crime control, because this is not the primary role of the police in the first place (see Bunyan 1976). Finally, there is no crisis in penality, because the prisons are not there to succeed in terms of rehabilitation. They are there to segregate, to label, to stigmatize irrevocably. The high recidivism rate is a success story (see e.g. Foucault 1980; Mathieson 1976).

Preliminary criticisms of left idealism

The autonomy of the control institutions

It would be a bizarre type of theory that completely ignored that the expansion of the crime control system over the past two decades . . . is a direct response to increasing official crime rates. (Cohen 1985: 91)

Left idealists grant an extraordinary autonomy to the control institutions, whose expansion is seen to occur independently of crime itself. Yet even if the official rate of crime were a complete fiction, independent of the 'real' crime rate, the exponential rise in crimes known to the police in countries such as Britain and the USA must have a knock-on effect on the pressures on police caseloads, courts, and prison overcrowding. It turns causality on its head if we are to think otherwise. But all too many discussions of the police and the prison, whether by liberals or full-blown left idealists, seem to be fixated on the criminal justice system, as if the system began at the prison gate, or the courtroom, or the police encounter on the street, without extending to the incidence of crime itself. Thus the work of Steven Box and Chris Hale on the relationship between crime, unemployment, and the rate of imprisonment is often misleadingly interpreted as showing that the ideological fears of magistrates and judges concerning unemployment were the sole propellant of the expansion in incarceration. Yet they quite clearly state: 'This does not, of course, mean that unemployment is the major determinant of imprisonment levels: *clearly the crime and conviction rates have that honour*. Nonetheless, it is clear that the number of persons immediately imprisoned . . . would not be as high if the judiciary did not increasingly imprison persons in excess of that warranted by the conviction rate' (Box and Hale 1986: 86–7, emphasis added). Similarly, the phenomenon of 'widening the net', of the plethora of alternatives to prison expanding at the same time as the rise in numbers imprisoned (Vass 1990), is best seen as predominantly a bureaucratic response to an ever-increasing workload and the problem of the disposal of offenders. Indeed, as Tony Bottoms has clearly shown (1983), the proportional use of imprisonment in the UK has declined over the last fifty years, albeit with something of an upturn in the last decade. It is the numbers of those who have been convicted that has largely created the problem of prison overcrowding. Yet the attraction of elevating the machinations of the criminal justice system to a central causal role remains unabated. Indeed, as John Lowman wryly notes: 'Bizarre as it might be, Cohen does not, in fact, offer any analysis of changing rates of "crime" in discussing the expansion of control.' (1992: 158, n. 4).

The roots of crime: social disorganization and individualism Crime is, by and large, a result of the breakdown of social solidarity. This was as true in the nineteenth century as it is today. The claim, then, that the prison was introduced and continues to exist as a strategy of the powerful to individualize the collective fightback of the surplus population is one which remains at the level of appearances. It is correct on one level and completely inaccurate on another. First of all, it makes massive assumptions as to the collective nature of such cultures and their level of organization. Second, it assumes that more than a small amount of crime represents this collectivity. The truth is that the majority of crime is an individualistic response; it does not have to be individualized by the powers that be. One might not like the *sort* of individualistic analysis which nineteenth-century reformers (or contemporary members of the working class, for that matter) tacked on to offenders; but that is not the same thing as denying individualism and disorganization. Social and material situations can create individual, anti-social outcomes: to recognize this fact is not to hold any court for classicist or positivist theories. As we have seen, these theories pick upon one manifestation of a contradictory phenomenon and create from it either the abstraction of free-willed individualism or that of the pathological, determined criminal. Classicism and positivism, the two polarities of bourgeois thought, are each cast in the mode of analytical individualism—and each reflects a one-sided image of reality.

The reformers did not individualize the criminal, for crime was an individualistic mode of behaviour in the first place. They merely put it in an incorrect context. There is no reason, therefore, to invent a conspiracy on their part to turn collective resistance into individual effect. Furthermore, their interpretation struck ready chords within the working class and within offenders—and continues to do so today. This was the basis of its ideological effectiveness: its partial roots in reality. Thus Michael Ignatieff comments:

> If we return to what reformers said they were doing, it becomes clearer to me now than it was when I wrote *A Just Measure of Pain* (1978) that the adoption of the penitentiary in particular and the institutional solution in general cannot be explained in terms of their supposed utility in manufacturing social divisions within the working class. This is because at bottom reformers, like most of their own class, understood deviance in irreducible individual rather than collective terms; not ultimately as collective social disobedience, however much distress and collective alienation influenced individuals, but a highly personal descent into sin and error. Given this individualist's reading of deviance, the appeal of institutional solutions lay in the drama of guilt which they forced each offender to play out. (1985: 92)

A central problem with left idealist histories of the evolution of the prison and criminal law is their tendency to focus on the atypical instances where there was widespread collective opposition and ignore the vast majority of instances where no such resistance existed. Thus smugglers, costermongers, poachers, bootleggers became the focus of attention; not thieves, rapists, burglars, and murderers. John Langbein picks up this with venom when he writes of Douglas Hay's 1975 work on eighteenth-century English criminal procedure:

> We may come close to understanding how [he] went astray if we reflect upon [the way] in which Hay takes it for granted that the criminal law lacked the adherence of the lower orders. To be sure, there were corners of the criminal law that did not command universal regard. The source of Hay's undoing, I suspect, is that the only part of the substantive criminal law with which he was deeply acquainted when he wrote his essay was the uniquely class-based and arbitrary game law. There certainly was popular dissatisfaction with the game law (and not confined to the poor), but to extrapolate from that bizarre scheme (*much* of it misdemeanour) to the whole of the law of felony would be a grievous error, just as it would be folly in our own day to equate public attitudes towards marijuana offenses and, say, automobile theft.
>
> When Hay speaks indifferently of stealing wood from a Lord's park and sheep from a farmer's fold, he is making that sort of error. The property crimes that were of major consequence in the workload of 18th century criminal courts—in particular the theft of livestock, shop goods, and personal and household belongings—were those about whose blameworthiness there was a moral consensus that knew no class lines. That is why men of the non-elite could predominate (as prosecutors and jurors) in convicting persons who committed property crimes. (Langbein 1983: 15)

Division and agreement within the working class It is important to underline that the majority of crime is intra-class rather than inter-class. This is so today and it was so at the birth of the penitentiary in the nineteenth century. It is quite insufficient for idealist, revisionist authors to parade the fact that the majority of people in prison are working-class—for so are their *victims*. And, as victims, they frequently become involved in prosecuting other working-class people who offended against them. The history of criminal law—and of the police and prisons—involves a considerable degree of working-class complicity and co-operation. This is what makes the notion that the state manufactured crime within the working class so ludicrous. Ignatieff is very clear about this:

> As regards imprisonment, the divide-and-rule argument seems to me now to have fallen prey unwittingly to the problem inherent in what criminologists call 'labelling theory'. The notorious difficulty with this approach is that it makes the state's sanctions the exclusive source of the boundary between the deviant and the respectable. This would seem to ignore the degree to which, in the 19th as in the 20th century, the moral sanctions condemning murder, rape, sexual and personal assault were prior to and independent of the punitive sanction, commanding assent across class lines. In punishing these offences, the state simply ratified a line of demarcation already indigenous to the poor. Even in the case of petty property crime, it is not clear that the criminal sanction was labelling acts which the poor excused as an inevitable response to distress or which they justified in the vernacular of natural justice. The poor, no less than the rich, were victims of property crime, and any study of London police courts in the 19th century shows that they were prepared to go to law to punish members of their own class. If a constant process of demarcation was under way between criminals and the working classes, it was a process in which the working classes themselves played a prominent part. (1985: 90–1)

It might be argued that all that is being reflected is the division between the respectable working class and the poor—between the unemployed and the surplus population. The former support crime control: the latter are criminal. All of these distinctions are inaccurate. Most poor people are respectable; very few of the unemployed are committed criminals. Crime of a very professional nature is incontrovertibly a minority phenomenon; crime of a more minor nature is frequent among the lower working class, but is a product of disorganization and almost universally deplored. It is just another slur upon the unemployed to suggest that criminality is a generally approved mode of behaviour among them. As with so many of the conventional wisdoms of criminology, it is completely exploded when one adds the question of gender. A constant of the social disorganization of the slum is violence against women. This has always contributed approaching half of the homicide statistics, virtually all of the instances of rape, and a large proportion of serious assaults. All of these have always, rightly, been regarded as serious offences. Are we really to believe that the majority of poor people ever thought otherwise?

The indispensability of prison The problems with the left functionalist theory of the prisons parallel those of functionalist theory generally. As the prison is seen as essential to the functioning of capitalism, reform is not on the cards. This results in an inability to take alternatives seriously; or, indeed, to allow for the real difficulties in constructing alternatives to prison. Ignatieff, in a critique of the functionalism inherent in his earlier work, writes:

> When applied to prison history, this model implies that institutions 'work', whereas the prison is, perhaps, the classic example of an institution which works badly and which nonetheless survives in the face of recurrent scepticism as to its deterrent or reformative capacity. Instead of looking for some hidden function which prisons actually succeed in discharging, we ought to work free of such functionalist assumptions altogether and begin to think of society in much more dynamic and historical terms, as being ordered by institutions like the prisons which fail their constituencies and which limp along because no alternative can be found or because conflict over alternatives is too great to be mediated into compromise. (1985: 96)

Thus, if we wish to look at the causes of the prison, we can see them clearly in the interplay among the reformers' conception of crime—itself grounded partially in reality; conflicts and convergences between the demands for control from a wide section of the population; the fears of the propertied; and the economics of the situation. Similarly, the demands for alternatives today meet resistance from the working class, scepticism from government (both from the point of view of their own ideas on crime and from that of the possibility of losing votes), and extremely conflicting ideas of what should be done emanating from both the abolitionist and reformist camps. The mere suggestion of setting up a half-way house in a community sends shivers of apprehension down the public spine; and there are a thousand different approaches to running it successfully.

But none of this is to suggest that the prison is necessarily functional to the powers that be, let alone to the working class. This is a quite separate question from causality and has to be assessed accordingly. Thus it is important to assess dispassionately the likely deterrent effect of prison on various types of offenders (see e.g. Jill Box-Grainger's 1986 discussion of sentencing rapists). The deterrent effects on both offenders and would-be offenders are far from as obvious as both abolitionists and the law and order lobby would have us believe.

The limitations of idealism

> There has been around for a decade or more a general rhetoric which passes itself off as a 'Marxism'. Sometimes this is expressed in sophisticated intellectual form, sometimes an old-style Leninism, sometimes just as an un-examined vocabulary co-existing with other vocabularies . . . common elements in this rhetoric are some of the following: first, there is a platonic notion of . . . the ideal capitalist state . . . This state is inherently profoundly authoritarian, as a direct organ of capitalist exploitation and control, and any inhibitions upon its power are seen as

'masks' or disguises, or as tricks to provide it with ideological legitimation and to enforce its hegemony. It may . . . follow that any symptoms of authoritarianism are seen as disclosing a 'crisis of hegemony' and may even be welcomed as unmasking the 'true' (i.e. platonic) character of the state, and as signalling the 'conjuncture' in which a final class confrontation will take place . . . And this may . . . consort with a loose rhetoric in which civil rights and democratic practices are discounted as camouflage, or the relics of 'bourgeois liberalism'. And to cut short the list, this very often goes along with a wholesale dismissal of *all* law and *all* police and sometimes with the soppy notion that *all* crime is some kind of displaced revolutionary activity.

This is not the place to engage in philosophical wrangle. I will simply say that these are all half-truths which have a continual tendency to degenerate into rubbish. What is more to the point is that this rhetoric can be seen to unbend the springs of action, and to discount the importance of any struggle for civil rights. If *all* law and *all* police are utterly abhorrent, then it cannot matter much what *kind* of law, or what *place* the police are held within; and yet the most immediate and consequent struggles to maintain liberty are exactly about kinds and places, cases and precedents, and the bringing of power to particular account. (Thompson 1980: 166–7)

It is important to stress that the term 'idealist' refers to philosophical idealism: it is not a critique of utopian thinking (see MacLean 1991). Such thinking is idealist because its voluntaristic notion of action denies the material situations—with the exception of the intervention of the state—in which human beings construct their reality. It is, furthermore, idealist because it puts too strong an emphasis on social control through ideas, whether by mystification or hegemony. Hence its obsession with 'politically correct' language and the relabelling of deviant groups: the blind become redesignated 'visually challenged', etc.

It is idealist because it views the state as a platonic essence: not as the site of contradiction and struggle, nor as an entity which is responsive to changes in civil society. Hence the extraordinary autonomy which state agencies are seen to have from the problems which they are set up to tackle.

It is idealist because it romanticizes the norms and culture of subordinate groups (see Matza 1969). Rather than tracing how adverse material conditions create social disorganization among the poor and the underprivileged, it creates an unflawed historical subject, whether it is the working class, blacks, women, gays or ethnic minorities (Young 1983). It conjures up 'communities' where community is barely existent (e.g. Scraton 1985; cf. Pryce 1979), and it postulates alternative family structures where the family has been decimated (e.g. Lawrence 1982; cf. Wilson 1987).

Finally, it is idealist because it denies that human beings have a bodily reality which ages, differs by gender, and varies physiologically among individuals. It confuses the argument against biological reductionism with the rejection of biology.

The New Administrative Criminology

I have detailed elsewhere the emergence of the new administrative criminology as the major paradigm in establishment approaches to crime (Young 1986, 1988*a*). What is important to note is that its main thrust has been to sidestep the etiological crisis by suggesting that the causes of crime are either relatively unimportant or politically impossible to tackle. There is no need to explain the rise in crime: it is obvious that there is a rise. Rather, we must find ways of stemming its impact. The question becomes that of the most cost-effective way of making control interventions, with an emphasis 'on the purely technical cost-benefit ratio aspects of crime: the opportunities for crime available in the environment, and the high risks attached to criminal activity' (Downes and Rock 1982: 194).

It is important to note that the emergence of administrative criminology was a result of the double failure of orthodox criminology. This double crisis was quite clearly perceived in the research of Ron Clarke and his co-workers at the Home Office. The concept of situational crime prevention coupled with rational choice theory which they have pioneered to meet this challenge is—whatever its theoretical limitations—an innovative paradigm of great importance. Whatever else, it has hammered home the earthy facts of space and actual experienced choice at a particular time to a criminology all too content to live in abstractions.

The new administrative criminology was developed largely in Britain, centring on the work of a team of researchers at the Home Office. Since the early 1980s it has successfully supplanted social democratic positivism as the key theory of establishment criminology. Despite this, there are some striking similarities between left idealism and administrative criminology. Both would deny the etiological crisis, and both are, of course, opposed to the social democratic criminology of the immediate post-war period and to the penal and policing policies of neo-classicism.

Human nature and social order

This paradigm rejects both social positivism, with its search for the root causes of crime in problems of the wider society, and neo-classicism, with its emphasis on deterrence and the criminal justice system. Yet it is substantially rooted in neo-classicism—the 'administrative criminology' of the beginning of the century (Taylor *et al.* 1973; Vold 1958)—both in its notion of rational actors and in its conception of a resolved social contract: hence the appellation 'the new administrative criminology'. Its key revision on classicism is its notion of limited rationality. In this it was influenced by the economist Herbert Simon (1978) and his followers, who rejected the full rationality commonplace in economic theory and stressed that decision-making processes reflect 'the observed limitations on people's capacity to acquire and process information. In particular, it is thought that people tend to economize on this scarce capacity by adopting rules of thumb, or "standing decisions" which eliminate the need completely to analyse every new decision' (Cook 1980: 220; see also commentary in Trasler 1986). This idea is reinforced by work into the social psychology of a wide range of areas such as family planning, behaviour, voting, and consumer research (Tuck and Riley 1986; Fishbein and Coombs 1974; Tuck 1976).

Rationality is thus limited, whether one is talking of consumer choice in the supermarket or criminal choice in the housing estate. In neither instance does it involve the maximization of choice implicit in either micro-economics or classical legal theory. Consistent with classicism, however, is the insistence that 'normal' behaviour and criminal behaviour are not *per se* distinguishable and that the distinction made by traditional positivism between criminals and non-criminals is inadmissible. Much talk about crime is over-pathologized. Adherents of this theory do not maintain that pathology does not occur, only that it is greatly exaggerated; furthermore, it 'does not exclude the operation of pathological motives acting in concert with rational means to secure irrational ends' (Cornish and Clarke 1986*a*: 3). Here they are clearly correct: the activities of serial killers, for example, may combine extremely rational planning with incomprehensible ends. And here we have a distinct break with neo-classicist legal principles, involving a division between the rational and the non-rational actor, which, by invoking concepts of rationality such as *mens rea*, finds itself unable in the courtroom easily to classify the sanity of such criminals as Peter Sutcliffe or Brady and Hindley. Finally, these criminologists point to the fact that much expressive crime, whether it is 'wanton' vandalism, football hooliganism, domestic violence, or homicide, is distinctly rational in its patterning of timing, targets, and planned intentions (Cornish and Clarke 1986*b*).

With regard to the problem of social order, the new administrative criminologists rarely concern themselves with the wider question. Their affinity is clearly with Travis Hirschi's control theory (1969), which reverses the question of why people commit crimes and asks: Why do people not commit crime? Its characteristic answer is that of Hobbesian social theory, namely, that people will commit crime in the absence of restraints. Indeed, Hirschi (1986) details how both theoretical approaches share basic assumptions about human nature and social order. The problem of partiality is thus present: the focus is on social reaction (constraints), not on action (motivation). Yet an adequate theory must explain both: indeed, even the power of constraints is dependent on the motivation of actors and their appraisal of their legitimacy. And, of course, to view criminal action as merely an epiphenomenon of lack of restraints precludes discussion of the causes of crime in the wider context of the prevalent inequalities of wealth and power.

The causes of crime

Clarke, in his major statement of this position, writes:

> Conventional wisdom holds that crime prevention needs to be based on a thorough understanding of the cause of crime. Though it may be conceded that preventative measures (such as humps in the road to stop speeding) can sometimes be found without invoking sophisticated causal theory, 'physical' measures which reduce opportunities for crime are often thought to be of limited value. They are said merely to suppress the impulse to offend which will then manifest itself on some other occasion and perhaps in even more harmful form. Much more effective are seen to be 'social' measures (such as the revitalisation of communities, the creation of job opportunities for unemployed youth, and the provision of sports and leisure facilities) since these attempt to remove the root motivational causes of offending. These ideas about prevention are not necessarily shared by the man-in-the street or even by policemen and magistrates, but they have prevailed among academics, administrators and others who contribute to the formulation of criminal policy. They are also consistent with a preoccupation of criminological theory with criminal 'dispositions' and the purpose of this paper is to argue that an alternative theoretical emphasis on choices and decisions made by the offender leads to a broader and perhaps more realistic approach to crime prevention. (Clarke 1980: 136–7)

For administrative criminology the fatal flaw of social democratic positivism was the notion that crime is *caused* by social conditions. Rather, in the vast majority of instances, crime is not caused by antecedent conditions: it is opportunistic, being committed where situations arise which present possibilities for crime. All previous criminology is seen as being pervaded by 'a dispositional bias': a search for causes which dispose people to crime, whether these be social factors, as in positivism, or administrative labels, as in labelling theory. Most crime is not only opportunistic, it is much less strongly motivated than positivism—whether individualistic or social—has suggested. Because of this it can be deterred by structural barriers: for example, steering locks in cars, better locks and bolts on houses, greater surveillance from, for example, Neighbourhood Watch schemes or ticket inspectors.

The impact of crime

Administrative criminology does not deny that there has been an increase in crime, but holds this to be largely a product of more petty crimes being reported to the police than previously, while the number of opportunities for crime has risen in terms of possible targets and means of committing crimes (see Clarke 1984). Furthermore, it stresses the comparative rarity of crime in terms of the average risk of victimization (Hough and Mayhew 1983), and that serious crimes—especially violent crimes—form a very small part of all crimes (Hough and Mayhew 1985).

The major data base for the new administrative criminology has been the British Crime Survey, carried out in successive sweeps since 1982. The administrative criminologists saw their role as attempting to reduce exaggerated fears of crime. Thus Hough and Mayhew wrote of the thinking behind the British Crime Survey:

> It was thought within the Home Office that distorted and exaggerated ideas of crime levels, trends and risks were widespread among the public; information on crime risks would demonstrate the comparatively low risks of serious crime, and puncture inaccurate stereotypes of crime victims. In other words, the survey was envisaged in part at least as a way of achieving what might be called the 'normalisation' of crime—to help create a less alarmist and more balanced climate of opinion about law and order. (1988: 157)

Let us look at their empirical findings.

> The First British Crime Survey revealed:
>
> - that the typical victim is, in fact, very much like the typical criminal—not old, female and wealthy, but male, young, single, a heavy drinker, and involved in assaulting others.
> - that the fear of crime is greater than the reality. Crime is a minor risk in most people's lives (outside the inner city).
>
> On this basis, and assuming that the rates remain at 1981 levels, the survey showed that a 'statistically average' person aged sixteen or over can expect:
>
> - a robbery once every five centuries (not attempts)
> - an assault resulting in injury (even if slight) once every century
> - the family car to be stolen or taken by joy-riders once every sixty years
> - a burglary in the home once every forty years.
>
> The survey further argued that the popular picture fuelled by the politicians, the media, and even the police (as they campaign for more men and resources) is an exaggerated one. Most lawbreaking is petty and therefore the police would be better advised to adopt a preventive approach—to improve public and community relations—rather than the 'crimefighter' approach that predominates. (Slattery 1986: 70–1)

This is an extract from Martin Slattery's excellent introduction to 'official' social statistics, which sums up very well the position of the new administrative criminology on the effects of crime. Note the notion that fear of crime is a problem on a par with crime itself; and what we have termed the 'moral symmetry' conception of victimization (Lea and Young 1984), namely, that victims and offenders are very similar in social characteristics, in sharp contrast to the notion of the predatory offender and the innocent victim.

The role of the police

The new administrative criminologists recognize the limited role of the police in controlling levels of crime. In areas of serious crime the police are seen as effective, but in terms of the marginal effects of increasing the number of police officers on reducing the overall crime rate, these criminologists are sceptical. For example, in terms of beat policing, Clarke and Hough write in their summary of the literature: 'There is little evidence that increasing the frequency of foot patrols actually reduces crime—although this may achieve other important objectives in terms of public satisfaction and feelings of security' (1984: 6).

The police role is very much dominated by public demand. Over 90 per cent of crimes are brought to police attention by the public (Hough and Mayhew 1985: ch. 3). Furthermore, the range of public demands on the police is wide and includes crime only as a minority component. Service demands, such as lost property, advice, asking directions, etc. predominate over crime-related demands. Because of this it is deemed incorrect to measure police performance merely in terms of crime.

The role of the public

The public have a dominant role in policing. Clear-up of crimes, for which the public presses, is very greatly determined by public witnessing, and much less so by direct police detection. Because of this, simple increases in police manpower are not cost-effective in dealing with crime. What is vital is public–police co-operation, which is the reason for the emphasis on Neighbourhood Watch. Furthermore, the public themselves can prevent crime more directly and effectively than the police by 'target-hardening' their homes (making them more difficult targets for burglars) and by more cautious behaviour while outside their homes.

Thus situational crime prevention involves physical limitations (target hardening), physical changes which bring about greater informal surveillance (housing design which increases defensible space), and public surveillance (basic conditions, Neighbourhood Watch). What it does not involve is social crime prevention in the sense of changing social conditions which might lead to crime (e.g. unemployment, poor housing). Its advantages are that it stresses informal methods rather than policing as the major focus of control and, above all, that it emphasizes the actual spatial nature of crime, in terms of both opportunities and surveillance. Sociological criminology, like sociology in general, has been until recently extraordinarily remiss in the neglect of physical space as a major parameter of social—and criminal—interaction (see Gregory and Urry 1985).

The etiological crisis

For the administrative criminologists there is no etiological crisis. First of all, the notion of etiology—of crime being caused—is a dispositional bias. Second, the rise in crimes known to the police is, by and large, the effect of greater public reporting. It is the increase in public willingness to report less serious crimes which eats up the dark figure and largely causes the 'crime wave'.

Problems of causes and of displacement

The new administrative criminology restricts its interventions to only one side of the equation of crime: it is unwilling to countenance intervention on the level of causality. Such a restriction does not allow a full understanding of the motivation for crime; yet it is difficult to prevent crime if one does not know the underlying force behind the commitment of crime by the actors involved. Finally, it creates problems in fully understanding the phenomenon of displacement. While acknowledging that displacement exists, the commitment to the administrative solution to crime (the 'technical fix') does not allow proponents of this criminology to face up to criticisms that the underlying causes of crime will always lead it to emerging elsewhere.

In fact, any intervention has its costs. Different crime control measures have to be judged on several criteria:

1. How effective are they compared to each other?
2. How effective is the marginal increase in resources in one area rather than another?
3. What is the cost of the measure in terms of other desiderata, for example, the quality of life or the exercise of civil liberties?

A realistic policy must acknowledge that there are various methods which, if properly tested, monitored, and costed, can reduce crime. But any one method, however effective, will have declining marginal returns if taken too far and pursued too exclusively. Furthermore, any one method, be it public surveillance through Neighbourhood Watch, extra police on the streets, or target-hardening, will have costs which impact on the quality of life and the freedom of citizens. Present government policy, by putting too great an emphasis on target-hardening and ignoring the conditions which give rise to crime, has created an imbalance in intervention. It has focused on reducing the opportunities for crime, not on its causes; on one half of the equation rather than on both.

Every social intervention inevitably has unintended repercussions. The cost of crime control has to be measured against the degree of displacement of crime occurring and the effect on quality of life, from the aesthetics of target-hardening to the civil liberties aspect of intensive policing. An effective intervention will have a crime displacement which is quantifiably lower, qualitatively of a less serious nature, and directs crime away from the most vulnerable social groups. (In the area of drug control, see Dorn and South 1987). Its social cost will have to take account of any losses in the quality of life. Realistically, we have to decide politically what level of crime is tolerable when weighed against such social costs.

Right Realism: The Work of James Q. Wilson

James Q. Wilson is a central figure in recent American criminology. The author of the best-selling *Thinking about Crime* (1975) and of numerous articles and books on crime, he was also an adviser to the Reagan administration. His work is immensely influential both in the USA and in Britain. As we saw in the passage quoted at the beginning of this article, he engages himself precisely with the problem of the etiological crisis; and he sees himself as rejecting both 'liberal', social democratic positivist notions of crime prevalent in the USA of the 1960s, and the stance of those conservatives who merely believed in more police, more prisons, and more power to the judiciary.

What is interesting, from our point of view, is how different the response of establishment criminology in the USA to the etiological crisis is from that of Britain. For there is a wide gulf between British administrative criminology and American right realism. In part, this is because of the very different 'exterior' circumstances of the two countries, particularly the much higher crime rate in the USA and the existence of an American intellectual climate which is weak on the left but strong on the right.

The causes of crime

Wilson places his theory precisely in the main line of criminology. He does not deny 'causes' of crime, indeed, he admits himself almost 'overdetermining' in the number of causes he can muster. Despite this, Wilson is not eclectic, for the fundamental basis of his theory lies consistently in modern behaviouristic theories of conditioning. That is, his response to the crisis of etiology is not to retreat away from causality, as have the British administrative criminologists, but—together with Richard Herrnstein—to develop the theory of individual positivistic criminology pioneered by writers such as Hans Eysenck. Basically, this starts from the premise that the simplistic, hedonistic calculus proposed by classicist criminology, where the actor weighs up the rewards of crime compared to the punishments, would scarcely deter people from, say, stealing: for punishment is so uncertain that crime would be often undetected and usually in the individual's self-interest. However, this bleak possibility of a war of all against all is lessened by early conditioning in childhood, when rules are internalized. Here they agree with Eysenck's (1970) slogan that 'conscience is a conditioned reflex'. This being said, such a conscience depends on conditionability and the effectiveness of the family in conditioning the children: that is, on the individual's physical constitution and thus susceptibility to conditioning, and the quality of conditioning he or she receives, primarily in the family situation. Proceeding to the wider levels of analysis, the peer group, the work situation, the criminal justice system, and the culture itself will all play upon this basic conditioning process. As Wilson and Herrnstein succinctly put it: 'The larger the ratio of the rewards (material and non-material) of non-crime to the reward (material and non-material), the weaker the tendency to commit crimes. The bite of conscience, the approval of peers, and any sense of inequity will increase or decrease the total value of crime' (1985: 61). Important, then, are individuals' socialization and the possible rewards and punishments associated with crime. And these have changed over time.

> We suggest that long-term trends in crime rates can be accounted for primarily by three factors. First, shifts in the age structure of the population will increase or decrease the proportion of persons—young males—in the population who are likely to be temperamentally aggressive and to have short time horizons. Second, changes in the benefits of crime (the accessibility, density, and value of criminal opportunities) and in the costs of crime (the risk of punishment and the cost of being both out of school and out of work) will change the rate at which crimes occur, especially property crimes. Third, broad social and cultural changes in the level and intensity of society's investment (via families, schools, churches, and the mass media) in inculcating an internalised commitment to self-control will affect the extent to which individuals at risk are willing to postpone gratification, accept as equitable the outcomes of others, and conform to rules. (1986: 437)

It is important to stress Wilson's neo-positivism—greatly enhanced by his work with the psychologist Richard Herrnstein. Traditionally, the determinist base of positivism has been set against the voluntaristic nature of classicism. Thus a therapeutic approach to policy has contrasted with an emphasis on deterrence (Taylor *et al.* 1973; Vold 1958; Eysenck 1970). Such an opposition has no logical basis, for if positivism is based on a motivational structure generated by punishments and rewards in the process of primary socialization, there is no reason why such punishments and rewards (including deterrence) should not be effective in later life. Wilson's work acknowledges this, as does the recent shift in Eysenck's theory of criminality (Eysenck and Gudjonsson 1989), and the revitalization of positive criminology by Gottfredson and Hirschi (1987).

The impact of crime

Wilson has no problem accepting that the crime rate has gone up. His response is, therefore, very different from that of establishment criminology in Britain. His realism consists of recognizing the massive problem of crime in American society and the foolishness of those who would suggest otherwise. Thus he lampoons the liberal denial of the etiological crisis, the pretence that nothing had changed in terms of rates of crime, and even that the crime issue itself was merely a covert way of expressing racist sentiments. He notes wryly: 'However, by 1970, enough members of the liberal audience had had their typewriters stolen to make it difficult to write articles denying the existence of a crime wave' (1975: 83–4).

A conclusion one might draw from Wilson's analysis is that there is very little that can be done to tackle crime. Constitutional factors are difficult to deal with (the age of biological engineering is scarcely here yet); the proportion of young men in the population is a fixture which society has to live with; the effectiveness of child-rearing—particularly the incidence of single parents—is not something that can be changed overnight. Much of that which encourages crime in the USA, as Wilson freely admits, is part and parcel of the expressive and individualistic culture of modern America. That is not for changing. And as to the effects of policing and punishment, Wilson is in the forefront of those sceptical about their effectiveness. What do we need instead? Wilson's realism stresses the importance of marginal gains rather than utopian goals, and on carefully monitored intervention rather than 'throwing money' at the problem. Thus he writes:

> If we grant that it is possible to try to improve the criminal justice system without apologising for the fact that those efforts do not attack the 'root causes' of crime, the next thing to remember is that we are seeking, at best, marginal improvements that can only be discovered through patient trial-and-error accompanied by hard-headed and objective evaluations.
>
> Above all, we can try to learn more about what works and, in the process, abandon our ideological preconceptions about what ought to work. (1985: 253–4)

The role of the police

Wilson has developed an influential position on the relationship between policing and crime control. Baldly stated, the hypothesis is that policing is effective not through a direct effect on the control of crime, but rather in facilitating the maintenance of social order. Furthermore, where disorderly behaviour (for example, that of drunks or rowdy youths) is not controlled, the neighbourhood enters a spiral of decline in which the law-abiding emigrate from the area, informal social controls weaken, and crime itself begins to rise. So police involvement in 'order maintenance' facilitates, in the long run, the process of crime control. Police presence facilitates the growth of informal neighbourhood controls on crime by giving the area a general sense of security.

Wilson divides police work into three types: law enforcement, order maintenance, and public service. The last of these is concerned with traffic control, rescuing cats from trees, restoring lost property, and so on. Wilson sees it as mere historical contingency that the police should be concerned with such work and quickly eliminates this element from his analysis. It is the distinction between law enforcement and order main tenance that is central to his argument. For Wilson,

> The patrolman's role is defined more by his responsibility for maintaining order than by his responsibility for enforcing law. Any intervention by the police is at least under cover of the law and in fact might be viewed as an enforcement of the law. A judge, examining the matter after the fact, is likely to see the issue wholly in these terms. But the patrolman does not. Though he may use the law to make an arrest, just as often he will do something else, such as tell people to 'knock it off', 'break it up' or 'go home and sober up'. (1968: 16–17)

Order is a priority in police time; it involves, Wilson argues, three times as much time as law enforcement. It is a more difficult task, and yet it is the job at which the police are most effective. Putting extra police on the beat may not reduce the crime rate immediately, as George Kelling showed in his study of Newark, New Jersey, but it considerably reduces people's fear of crime. There are, according to this line of argument, several reasons for this apparent paradox. First, disorder itself frightens people. Second, in the long run disorder begets more disorder, and more disorder produces crime. That is, when order maintenance breaks down, the natural informal control mechanisms—the social antibodies of the community—are weakened, and real increases in crime ensue.

Historically, the police function, from city nightwatchmen onwards, has given priority to order. It is only, according to Wilson and Kelling, in response to the rapid rise in crime in the USA in the recent period that crime control has become of major importance. This has involved a shift from the police officer as maintainer of order, improvising the ground rules in accordance with the customs and habits of the community, to the police officer as functionary of the rule of law, directed by the justice department and hemmed in by legal rules and official procedures. This transition has been to the detriment of order. Strict justice and the rules of due process do not facilitate the maintenance of order. Wilson and Kelling write:

> Once we begin to think of all aspects of police work as involving the application of universal rules under special procedures, we inevitably ask: 'What constitutes an undesirable person?' . . . A strong and commendable desire to see that people are treated fairly makes us worry about allowing the police to rout persons who are undesirable by some vague parochial standard. And thus many of us who watch over the police are reluctant to allow them to perform, in the only way they can, a function that every neighbourhood wants them to perform. (Wilson and Kelling 1982: 35)

What is necessary, then, is to award priority to order, and not to judge the police solely on their ability as crime-fighters. We must concentrate our resources in those areas 'at the tipping point' and 'where the public order is deteriorating but not unreclaimable'—not necessarily those with the highest crime rates, which may have gone past the point of no return. Police officers must be trained in managing street life as much as in law and due process. And we must, Wilson and Kelling insist, oppose campaigns to decriminalize the so-called harmless behaviours: 'Public drunkenness, street prostitution, and pornographic displays can destroy a community more quickly than any team of professional burglars' (1982: 38).

It is important to note the political targets of such an analysis. Wilson and Kelling are opposed to traditional conservative policies of heavy policing. But, more revealing, they also set themselves against liberal notions of crime control. First, they oppose the decriminalization of minor crimes and so-called 'crimes without victims'. Second, their analysis widens the sphere for social control by seeing the control of deviant behaviour, both illegal and legal, as important in the maintenance of order. Third, it views the liberal emphasis on rights and due process as counter-productive and is critical of both the possibility and the desirability of right management controls on the police. Finally, the analysis emphasizes social control by both the community and the police as the key to crime control, rather than hoping to reduce crime through measures aimed at the elimination of poverty and deprivation.

The role of the public

Wilson thus sees informal control as the most powerful force of social control. The police role is, so to speak, to jump-start the informal control system back into action in those areas where it has broken down and which are, of course, *ipso facto*, high crime areas. Effective police work *per se*, in the traditional mode of detection, should be directed to the high-risk repeat offenders. Similarly, the courts and prisons should give high sentences to this small group of offenders in order to incapacitate them. Here Wilson agrees with his fellow conservative writer, Ernest van den Haag, that interests of order override those of justice. It is better to remove a recidivist from society proportionally to his criminal record than to judge him according to his last crime. The public, meanwhile, has an important role in Wilson's formulation of social control. Child-rearing itself is a vital part of the socialization process, as is peer group pressure, and much should be done in terms of citizen organized control, such as Neighbourhood Watch and self-help public patrols.

The etiological crisis: right realism and Realpolitik

As we have seen, Wilson directly confronts the etiological crisis. He highlights the dramatic rise in crime in the USA and pinpoints its causes. His realism addresses itself to (1) the limits of what can be done in terms of

possible intervention; (2) the paucity of our knowledge with regard to what works; and (3) the importance of marginal gains.

Wilson's right realism prioritizes order over justice. This can be illustrated in four areas:

1. Police intervention should occur in terms of order on the streets rather than crime itself. For it is here that intervention would be seen to be effective, despite the fact that the individuals concerned have committed the least serious crimes—if any crimes at all.
2. Public intervention should occur in those areas that have not yet 'tipped' into 'irrevocable' decay: that is, *not* towards the most deserving areas but towards those which are deemed rescuable.
3. Intervention to control drug use should be directed not at the addicts (who are past reclaiming), or at the dealers, but at the first-time users, who may be deterred: that is, against those who have the least culpability.
4. Repeat offenders, whom Wilson sees as making a particularly high contribution to the crime problem, should be 'incapacitated' by imprisonment on a dual-track basis: that is, they should be punished both in terms of the seriousness of their crime and in terms of the public interest.

The Left Realist Critique

Left realism, as a critique of existing criminological theory, emerged in the 1980s (see Lea and Young 1984; Currie 1985; Young and Matthews 1992). Its central aim is to be faithful to the reality of crime—to the fact that all crimes must, of necessity, involve rules and rule breakers (i.e. criminal behaviour and reaction against it) and offenders and victims. The problem with previous criminology, according to left realism, is that it is partial. It has tended to focus on only part of the process of crime and not to encompass all of it. We have already seen how the reactions of different critical traditions to the etiological crisis were partial. The focus was on the victim or on the offender, on the social reaction to crime or on the criminal behaviour itself. Left realism intends to bring together all aspects of the process: in this its approach emphasizes synthesis rather than simply dismissing opposing theories.

Although left realism is extremely critical of the right realism of James Q. Wilson, there are certain points of convergence between the two realisms which it is useful to highlight before we commence the critique.

1. Both see crime as really being a problem; both see the public's fear of crime as having a rational basis, in contrast to left idealism and administrative criminology.
2. Both believe that the reality of crime control has been misconceived, particularly the centrality of the public–police relationship.

3. Both are realistic about what can be done about crime and the limitations of our present-day knowledge. Neither disdains marginal gains, whilst both discount utopian solutions.
4. Both emphasize the need for closely monitored research and intervention and are critical of the widespread tendency to 'throw money' at the crime problem without attempting to measure cost-effectiveness (see Lea *et al.* 1988).

Crime, human nature and social order

The most fundamental tenet of realism is that criminology should be faithful to the nature of crime. That is, it should acknowledge the *form* of crime, the *social context* of crime, the *shape* of crime, its trajectory through *time*, and its enactment in *space*.

The form of crime The form of crime consists of two dyads, of a *victim* and an *offender*, and of *actions* and *reactions*: of crime and its control. This deconstruction gives us four definitional elements of crime: a victim, an offender, formal control, and informal control. Realism, then, points to a square of crime involving the interaction between police and other agencies of social control, the public, the offender, and the victim (see Fig. 2.1). Crime rates are generated not merely by the interplay of these four factors, but as *social relationships* between the various points on the square. It is the relationship between the police and the public which determines the efficacy of policing, the relationship between the victim and the offender which determines the impact of the crime, the relationship between the state and the offender which is a major factor in recidivism, etc. Furthermore, a hallmark of critical criminology is its pinpointing of the irony of the frequent symbiotic relationships between control agencies—whether formal or informal—and crime: for example, the way in which the burgled public create the informal economy which sustains burglary, or the police create, through illegalities, a moral climate which spurs delinquents into crime. Finally, the relationships among the four points of the square (offender, victim, state agencies, and the public) varies with differing types of crime (see Lea 1992).

It should be stressed that, in pointing to the fact that crime rates are produced by such an interaction, one is merely describing the process. To do so does not involve acceptance of the existing patterns of criminalization. Crime rates are a product, therefore, of changes in the number of putative offenders, the number of potential victims, and the changing levels of control exercised by the official agencies of control and the public. No explanation which does not embrace all these four factors can possibly explain crime rates. Let us focus, for the moment, on the relationship between social control in all its manifestations, and the criminal act

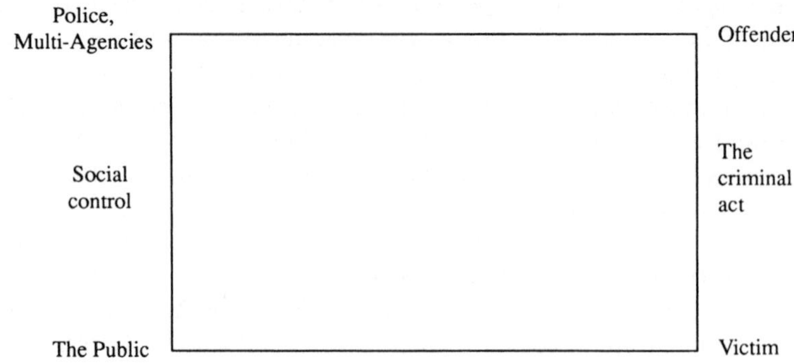

consisting of the dyad of victim and offender: that is, quite simply, on the criminal act and the reaction to it. If we examine changes over time, left realists would point to these *necessarily* being a product of changes in criminal behaviour *and* changes in reactions to crime. The increase in the rate of violent crime *by definition* must involve changes in violence. None of this makes it any the less 'real': for this is exactly what crime rates *really* are. This being said, the exponential increases in crimes occurring in most Western countries cannot merely be a product of increased sensitivity to crime. Any 'dark figure' of the crime unknown to the police would have been taken up long ago by the rise in crimes known to the police, and other indices, such as homicide rates and serious property crimes, indicate rises even if we use earlier thresholds as our measure. Thus, present rises in rates of violence in countries such as Britain may well be a product *both* of an increased sensitivity to violence *and* of a rise in violent behaviour.

Left realist criminology indicates that crime rates are a product of two forces: changes in behaviour and changes in the forces of social control and the definitions of what is seriously criminal. These two social dimensions are not necessarily covariant. It is quite possible, for example, for vandalism to increase but for people to become less concerned and more tolerant about litter, graffiti, etc. It is possible for acts of violence in a behavioural sense to decrease, yet for people to become more sensitive to violence. As Durkheim wrote:

> Imagine a society of saints, a perfect cloister of exemplary individuals. Crimes, properly so called, will there be unknown; but faults which appear venial to the layman will create there the same scandal that the ordinary offence does in ordinary consciousness. If, then, this society has the power to judge and punish, it will define these acts as criminal and will treat them as such. (1964: 68–9)

Durkheim's work has been interpreted by influential writers, such as K. Erikson (1966) and Leslie Wilkins (1964), to mean that there is always a *fixed* proportion of any behaviour which is defined as deviant within any normative community. Left realism rejects this. In our own time we have, in all probability, a tendency towards an *increase* in anti-social behaviour coupled with a *decrease* in the tolerance of deviance. A whole host of 'new crimes' have been discovered: violence against women, child abuse, racial violence. It is quite possible to argue for what Norbert Elias called the 'civilizing factor'—an increase in sensitivity to anti-social behaviour—while noting, at the same time, that there has been a decrease in civilized behaviour (cf. van Dijk 1989).

At heart, this points to the possible disjunction of definitions of what constitutes intolerable behaviour and the ability to control such behaviour. Thus the social reaction side of the equation consists of two distinct elements—often falsely conflated: the definitional element (i.e. the definitions of what is criminal and what tolerable behaviour) and the control element (i.e. the actual level of control that occurs with regards to any type of offending). It is quite possible, therefore, for definitions of crime to become less tolerant, while at the same time the ability to control criminal behaviour actually decreases.

Of course, social control and criminal behaviour are, in their substantive constituents, more elaborate than simply two formal dyads that make up the square of crime. Social control involves agencies, ranging from the state to the public, from the police, the educational system, social services, the mass media, the workplace, the family, and the peer group, to the informal control between strangers on the street. The recognition of the importance of informal, public systems of control and of the central place of non-policing agencies involved in the control of crime is a significant input of recent criminology. It goes without saying that the effectiveness of such a system of social control is dependent on the relationships between the various agencies (the police–public relationship being a vital area which has been widely analysed) and that conflicts exist—and will, in any democracy, *always* exist—between different agencies.

The social context of crime The social context consists of the immediate social interaction of these four elements and the setting of each of them within the wider social structure. Such an agenda was set out within *The New Criminology* (Taylor *et al.* 1973): namely, that the immediate social origins of a deviant act should be set within its wider social context and that such an analysis should encompass both actors and reactors. Left realism takes this a stage further, insisting not only that actions of offenders and of the agencies of the state must be understood in such a fashion, but that this approach must be extended to the informal system of social control (the public) and to victims.

Note the stark contrast here with right realism. For Wilson, potent causes of crime are seen as autonomous from the social structure. For example, the family and parents are blamed as if they did not exist within a social situation which undermines the family (see Currie 1985), and the 'permissive' ethos of modern society which he upbraids is seen as separate from the realities of a market society (see Currie 1990).

The shape of crime Crime is a series of relationships. Each type of crime presents a different network of relationships; if we compare illegal drug use, burglary, and assault, for example, we note markedly different structures. Drug dealing has a well-known pyramidal shape; burglary involves numerous victims and regular fences; assault may well be a one-off case of victimization. Furthermore, the natural history of crime involves differences in the content of these relationships. Crime involves both co-operation and coercion. In the case of drug use, every step of the pyramid is consensual; in the case of burglary, dealing in stolen goods is consensual and the actual act of stealing coercive; assault is a purely coercive act.

The trajectory of crime through time The temporal aspect of crime consists of the past of each of the four elements of the square of crime and their impact on each other in the future. A left realist approach sees the development of criminal behaviour over time. It breaks down this trajectory of offending into its component parts and notes how different agencies interact. Thus we can talk of (1) the *background causes* of crime; (2) the *moral context* of opting for criminal behaviour; (3) the *situation of committing crime*; (4) the *detection of crime*; (5) the *response to the offender*; (6) the *response to the victim*. Criminal careers are built up by an interaction of the structural position in which the offender finds him- or herself and the administrative responses to his or her various offences. These involve both material changes in the offender's structural position and the exchange of ideas (or 'rationalizations') for offending (see Cohen 1965; Matza 1964). But, of course, such moral careers are not confined to the offender. Other points of the square of crime change over time. Policing practices change in their interaction with offenders; the public's fear of crime in the city creates patterns of avoidance behaviour which consciously and unconsciously develop over time; victims—particularly repeated victims such as in domestic violence—change the patterns of their lives as a consequence of such an interaction.

Crime as an activity involves a moral choice at a certain moment in changing determinant circumstances. It has neither the totally determined quality beloved of positivism, nor the wilful display of rationality enshrined in classicist legal doctrine. It is a moral act, but one which must be constantly assessed within a determined social context. It is neither an act of determined pathology, nor an obvious response to desperate situations. It involves both social organization and disorganization. Left realism eschews both the romanticism of left idealism, which grants exaggerated levels of organization and rationality to deviant behaviour, and the desiccated scientism of positivist criminology, which does just the reverse (see Young 1987; Matza 1969).

The spatial dimension of crime The spatial dimension is the material space in which the process enacts itself. All crime has a spatial dimension, and the geography of crime varies widely. Drug-dealing has an international dimension, a national distribution, and a focus on specific areas of the city. Burglary occurs widely across a locality and subsists on a hidden economy which is locally based. Assault has no wider spatial dimension. It occurs, however, frequently in specific areas. For example, in the case of assault by a stranger, it has a pronounced geographical focus which is made evident both in the incidence of assault and in the fear of victimization, manifest in the avoidance of certain areas. Just as specific crimes involve differing structures of relationships, so they also involve particular structures in space.

Left realism, therefore, suggests that the control of crime must involve interventions at all points of the square of crime (e.g. through better policing, greater community involvement, protecting and empowering the victim, and dealing with the structural problems that cause offending). But it prioritizes intervention on the level of causes of crime over actions which take place *after* the crime has been committed (see Young and Matthews 1992).

Causes of crime

Left realism sees a potent cause of criminal behaviour in relative deprivation. Crime can, therefore, occur anywhere in the social structure and at any period, affluent or otherwise; it is simply not dependent on absolute levels of deprivation or on the level of the offender in the social structure (see Lea 1992). This being said, it is among particular segments of the poor, particularly the lower working class and certain ethnic minorities, who are marginalized from the 'glittering prizes' of the wider society, that the push towards crime is greater than elsewhere in the structure (see Lea and Young 1984).

To put an emphasis on relative deprivation as a cause of crime is not to retreat into monocausality. Of course, there are many causes of crime. Even within the tradition of anomie theory, subcultural theorists have tended to emphasize unduly relative deprivation, the disjunction between aspirations and opportunities, over anomie as a lack of limits, a product of an individualism where 'from top to bottom of the ladder, greed is aroused without knowing where to find its ultimate foothold. Nothing can colour it since its goal is far beyond all it can attain' (Durkheim 1952: 256). And certainly one can distinguish the anomie of the disadvantaged, which is largely concerned with relative deprivation, from the anomie of the advantaged, which is often a product of a limitless pursuit of money, status, and power (see Young 1974; Simon and Gagnon 1986; Taylor 1990). This being said, relative deprivation is an extremely potent cause of crime. For it is

(a) not limited to lower working-class crime, because relative deprivation can, and does, occur throughout the social structure;
(b) not merely concerned with economic crime, because subcultures of violence among the poor and the violence of better-off men occur precisely as a response to relative economic deprivation;
(c) not concerned with absolute poverty, and thus pinpoints the paradox of those crimes of the poor which focus on status goods. As Elizabeth Burney pointed out in her study of street robbery: 'Poverty is, nevertheless, not the immediate motive for street crime, since most offenders do not lack necessities: rather, they crave luxuries. The outstanding characteristic of young street offenders is their avid adherence to a group "style", which dictates a very expensive level of brand-name dressing, financed by crime' (1990: 63; see also Currie 1990).

As we have seen, the problem of the causes of crime is one which has perplexed criminologists and confused public opinion throughout the century. This is not the place to enter into the complexities of this subject, but it is pertinent to point to three notions which inform the debate: that is, absolute deprivation, total determinism, and mechanistic causation. All of these concepts are central to social democratic positivism and all are fundamentally mistaken.

There is no evidence that absolute deprivation (e.g. unemployment, lack of schooling, poor housing, etc.) leads *automatically* to crime. The crime rate was minute in the 1930s, despite very high levels of poverty. Left realist criminology points to *relative deprivation in certain conditions* as being the major cause of crime: that is, when people experience a level of unfairness in their allocation of resources and turn to individualistic means to attempt to right this condition. It is an unjust reaction to the experience of injustice. Needless to say, such an experienced injustice, coupled with an individualistic 'solution', can occur in different segments of society: like crime itself, it is certainly not a monopoly of the poor.

Such an individualistic response is particularly prevalent at certain times. It was at the heart of the dominant political ethic of mid-nineteenth-century *laissez-faire* capitalism, in a period which saw the crime rate at its highest in its history; it is the ascendent ethos of modern-day Britain, with its rising crime rate; and it is particularly prevalent in the USA, which has by far the highest crime rate of any advanced industrial society.

The notion that certain social conditions lead to crime is associated with the notion of total determinism. To say that poverty in the present period breeds crime is not to say that all poor people are criminals. Far from it: most poor people are perfectly honest, and many wealthy people commit crimes. Rather, it is to say that the rate of crime is higher in certain parts of society in certain conditions. Crime, like any other form of behaviour, involves moral choice in certain restricting circumstances. It is not inevitable in any particular circumstances. That is why an ethos of individualism has such an effect on public morality and the incidence of crime. Conversely, however, crime is not merely a matter of moral choice, a wickedness distributed randomly throughout the world. Material circumstances differ widely in present-day society—some would suggest far too widely—and this greatly affects crime rates.

To say that crime is causal is not, therefore, to suggest a mechanistic notion of causation, as for example, when we push a table and the table moves; rather, that, because of the subjective element, certain circumstances facilitate increases in crime among sections of the population. Because of this, simple attempts to relate social factors such as unemployment to crime will inevitably fail, however sophisticated their statistical techniques. Unemployment leads to discontent in those situations where people experience their circumstances as unjust, unnecessary, and, above all, *preventable*. Discontent leads to crime where individuals feel marginalized socially and politically. There are various, quite pronounced reasons why such marginalization and relative deprivation have increased in the present period. Furthermore, we have a generation which has grown up used to Keynesian interventions in the economy, and which consequently sees unemployment not as part of the natural order but as very much a political product. To them unemployment and relative impoverishment is no longer a fact of life, it is a failure of society and of government.

The common problem of mechanistic notions of crime causation is that they assume an *immediate* causation. But if we consider that it takes time for people to evaluate their predicaments and even longer for them to build up alternative solutions, then the notion of an immediate causation becomes ludicrous. Unemployment now does not relate to crime the day after tomorrow. Youth subcultures, for example, build up and develop appraisals of their situation, but they may not flourish until several years after the initial problem of unemployment. Perhaps even more significantly, the development of a hidden economy, including a level of illegal activity, will take a considerable time to build up. Thus, to correlate crime and unemployment at one moment completely obscures the fact that human evaluation and enterprise take time to develop.

The implications of this understanding of causality are of vital importance. Specifically, we have in our cities conditions of unemployment where no foreseeable future change for young people is in prospect and where the concept of 'youth' merely extends itself into those aged thirty and beyond. In such a situation relative deprivation is manifest in the contrast with the increasingly wealthy strata of those in work, and is underscored by the gentrification of our large cities which allows comparison to be easily available and, indeed, unavoidable.

The reality of the human predicament is the construction of choice in determinate circumstances. Because of this, causality presents itself as complex, sometimes distant, and, because of the human ability to reinterpret the world, always potentially reversible. It is not surprising that administrative criminology reacts to such complexity by simple disavowal or that left idealism *retrospectively* finds any choice obvious. Wilson's right realism is more of a problem; it does not deny causality, in fact, it embraces a multitude of causes. What he does deny, however, is the most palpable cause of crime: inequality of wealth and power.

Finally, with regard to Wilson's emphasis on human constitution and crime, left realism does not reject the fact of correlations between biology and crime, whether one is talking about body shape, hormone systems, size, or age. In rejecting biological reductionism, theories such as left idealism and labelling theory throw the baby out with the bathwater and reject biology itself. It is a fact that larger, more powerful people commit more violence than smaller people, that male hormones correlate strongly with violence, that the well muscled are more of a threat than the plump and unfit. You do not, after all, cross the street at night to avoid old ladies. Left realism does not deny the correlations between biology and crime: that men are more violent than women, and the young more violent than the old. Rather, it argues that the causes of patriarchal violence against women or the machismo of lower working-class youth are rooted in social situations, not biology, and that physical capacity to commit crime is merely an intervening variable.

The problem of specificity Both neo-positivism and the new administrative criminology seek generalizations which are independent of culture. A discussion of whether maternal deprivation leads to crime, or whether beat policing is effective, would be typical endeavours. Left idealism, with its sense of the obviousness of criminological generalization, enters the field of general laws with an abandon which would alarm the most staunch positivist. Of course unemployment leads to crime; it is self-evident that the recession has led to the rise in heroin use among young people; and so on. Such a mechanistic relationship between objective conditions and human behaviour is absurd. It is central to a left realist position that objective conditions are interpreted through the specific subcultures of groups involved. This is the nature of human experience and social action. Generalization is possible, but only given specific cultural conditions and social understandings. Thus, to be precise, the problem of specificity refers to extrapolating observations about crime, law, or victimization from one country or one social group and assuming that one's conclusions apply to all countries or social groups. It is being unable to see how general variables come together in a very specific form in any particular situation. This results in work which is not only inadequate as a generalization, but is lacking in its ability to cope with what is special about the precise constellation of factors which delineate any particular situation. Lack of specificity is a heuristic failure, on the level of both the general and the particular.

Left realism focuses on lived realities. It is concerned with the material problems which particular groups of people experience in terms of the major social axes of age, class, gender, and race, and spatially within their locality. It is these structural parameters which give rise to subcultures. Left realism has a close affinity with subcultural theory (e.g. Willis 1977; Cohen 1965). Subcultures are problem-solving devices which constantly arise as people in specific groups attempt to solve the structural problems which face them. The problems are evaluated in terms of the existing subculture and the subculture changes over time in order to *attempt* a solution to those perceived problems (see Lea and Young 1984: ch. 3; Young 1974). Crime is one form of subcultural adaption which occurs where material circumstances block cultural aspirations and where non-criminal alternatives are absent or less attractive.

Social constructionism, positivism, and everyday life In focusing upon lived realities, left realism stands in sharp contrast to both vulgar materialist explanations of crime (such as individual or social positivism) and idealist explanations. We may illustrate this by examining the explanation of opiate use offered by the left idealist tendency within social problem theory: social constructionism. Here opiate use is 'constructed' by the reactions of the powerful: by the material predicaments that they create for the user and the ideological categories with which they provide the user in order to explain his or her 'addiction'. The administration of opiate use, whether by the criminal justice system or the medical system, and the ideas which such institutions carry are given causal priority, whereas the structural causes of opiate use are virtually ignored.

The major problem of social constructionism is that it is not constructionist enough. The focus is almost entirely top-down. The mass media create moral panics; the identity of various deviant groups is forged for them by the powerful; the criminal justice system creates criminal statistics (e.g. Lidz and Walker 1980; Duster 1970; Hulsman 1986). In fact, all human behaviour is socially constructed. It is constructed by people in their everyday life, in the context of their subcultures, albeit in material circumstances only in part of their making, and in an idealistic context where pre-existing social scripts are widespread.

In the case of opiate use, the user takes opiates because it fits his or her subcultural problems or concerns. These, in turn, are a product of his or her structural position (see Young 1971). Subcultural theory posits the way in which individuals socially construct 'solutions' to the problems confronting them. Left realist subcultural theory accepts the fact that dominant ideas (such as the 'sickness' model) can gain currency in this construction; but only because such ideas fit the predicament of the user (see Auld *et al.* 1986). Different opiate users in different predicaments construct very different patterns of use. It is scarcely surprising, therefore, that social reactions to different types of use vary (e.g. to the nineteenth-century middle-class female opiate user; to the twentieth-century ghetto black junkie; to the physician addict), because they are engaging in totally different constructions of opiate use. None of this is to suggest that the various social reactions are appropriate. Indeed, left realism highlights the repeated, ineffective, and often counter-productive social reactions to opiate use, deviant behaviour, and crime in general. But social reactions, the constructions of the powerful, are inevitably geared to social constructions at ground level. You cannot write a history of social control without an adjacent history of changes in the crime to be controlled. Yet such top-down histories are the trademark of social constructionism.

Even more inaccurate is the notion that there is an essence of a phenomenon against which top-down social constructions simply vary. Troy Duster, for example, in his *Legislation of Morality* (1970) creates a scenario where he identifies the essence of opiate use (for him a relatively innocuous activity) and explains the different reactions against nineteenth-century, white, female opiate use and twentieth-century, black, heroin use as merely a function of the prejudice of the powerful. This displays what Woolgar and Pawluch (1985) have neatly termed 'ontological gerrymandering': that is, that there is a 'real' essential form of a particular type of deviant behaviour, usually located in the past (in this case, nineteenth-century opiate use), against which is contrasted that which is subsequently constructed by social intervention. In this fashion constructionism relapses into positivism—the very position which it seeks to criticize. Positivism, of course, posits the unchanging essence of phenomena (e.g. heroin use can be understood by looking up its characteristics in a pharmacopoeia). For positivists, crime is a 'fact out there', independent of values (see e.g. Eysenck and Gudjonsson 1989). Social definition is seen as merely reflecting the essence of the phenomenon, social intervention as having little intimate bearing on its nature.

Left realism, then, does not deal in abstractions: the principle of specificity demands that explanation be grounded. It is not just that the concept of 'crime' embraces a motley of types of behaviour and varieties of legal regulation; each 'type' of crime and each form of regulation must be specified if we are to make any progress in understanding their interaction. Opiate addiction, as we have seen, can mean many different things in particular subcultures. Burglary can involve the rational calculation of the professional or the opportunism of the young lad. Domestic violence can involve a variety of sub-species, each with its own life cycle. And, turning to social control, beat policing can involve many widely differing activities from the agressive to the consensual; Neighbourhood Watch can be a uniting or a divisive intervention. All of this suggests the necessity of typologies which cut across legal or formal definitions; but also, going further, that these typologies must be grounded in the particular lived realities of the phenomenon under investigation. It does not exclude generalization; it merely argues that generalization must be socially based and that explanations which are abstracted out of context have very little chance of etiological success because they ignore the very social context which determines them.

The impact of crime

Left realists are critical of the supposed disjunction between fear of crime and risk of crime which forms such a consistent background to the conventional thinking about crime. Many of the glaring 'irrationalities' centre around the high fear of crime among women and of old people despite the low risk rates. The contrast is always made with the low fear of crime of young men, despite their having the supposedly highest risk rates of any social grouping. Left realists point to the fundamental flaw of believing that there is an easy answer to the question of what is a 'rational' level of fear of crime.

The left realist method is not to look at the risk of crime in general (as administrative criminology does), for general rates obscure by adding very low-risk groups to groups with very high risks. Rather, the realist method delineates how crime is focused on certain geographical areas and certain groups within those areas, for example, blacks rather than whites, and poor people rather than rich. The most vulnerable in our society are not only at the greatest risk of crime, but also suffer a greater impact of crime because of their lack of money and resources. Finally, the people who suffer most from crime tend to suffer most from other social problems, for example, physical and mental illness, bad housing, etc. The effect of crime thus *compounds* with other problems.

If we are to unravel the relationship between anxiety about crime and risk of crime we should, therefore, substitute impact rates for risk rates.

We should note, also, that supposedly 'irrational' sectors of the at-risk population suffer from crimes which are 'invisible' to all but the most careful survey methods. Sexual crimes, domestic violence, and the harassment of women are cases in point, which generate much higher risk and impact rates than are usually presented. We should, then, make allowance for the fact that the supposed low-risk status of groups such as women and the elderly is in part a function of their high level of avoidance tactics. It would be interesting to know, for example, what the crime rate against women would be if they acted like men in their levels of avoiding crime. Finally, we must examine different tolerance levels to crimes such as violence. Why should women not have a greater intolerance of violence than men and hence a greater level of unease? Isn't the low level of fear of crime by young males simply a product of their own machismo values? (see Young 1988*b*).

None of this should suggest that attitudes to crime are simply a function of experience of crime. Obviously, for some subgroups fear of crime is, in part, a displacement of other forms of social unease (e.g. unemployment, racism, disquiet at the starkness of the built environment). Rather, anxiety about crime is one aspect of a particular subcultural position which includes different tolerance levels to social disorder, as well as a series of social anxieties, of which risk of crime is only one factor. 'Fear' of crime is, therefore, neither autonomous from, nor a simple reflex of, risk rates (Crawford *et al.* 1990).

The role of the police

Left realists argue that Wilson is wrong to suggest that crime control will be achieved by prioritizing order over justice. Society is held together to the extent that it is seen by its members to be just. When significant agencies of society, such as the police or the courts, act in a way which violates this sense of justice—by arbitrary arrest, harassment, or punishment incommensurate with the crime—then public alienation is likely to occur. And the part of the population most likely to be alienated is, paradoxically, the one most vital for social control. First of all, it includes those parts of the working class, particularly the young and often ethnic minorities, who have already suffered the economic marginalization of unemployment. The extra marginalization of harassment on the streets, etc., is often the last straw that breaks the camel's back—the point where economic marginalization is transferred into crime. Second, the effectiveness of the police is dependent on public co-operation, particularly a willingness to provide information and to witness in court. To the extent that the police and the courts develop a reputation as being arbitrary and unjust, they alienate a section of the community who, often extremely law-abiding themselves, are vital to the successful functioning of the judicial system.

Thus, while Wilson argues that control of order leads to control of crime, left realists argue that order achieved without justice can, in fact, foster crime. And when Wilson argues that the control and incapacitation of the 'dangerous' criminal are more important than the strict axiom of punishment fitting the crime, left realists argue that the precise reason why the judicial system does not at present work effectively is the systematic violation of standards of justice in the interests of order.

The role of the public

The reality of crime control is that the public play a central role, both in terms of the informal controls of daily life and in terms of their co-operation—or lack of it—with the police. Left realists point to the central problem of crime control as a breakdown of community in high crime areas. You cannot give the control of crime to the community, as left idealists would argue (e.g. Scraton 1985), for no such community exists. Furthermore, target-hardening is least likely to occur in the poorest areas because of the high costs involved. The privatization of crime protection which the administrative criminologists prefer is least likely to occur in the most crime-ridden areas: indeed, these areas are vulnerable to displacement from the target-hardened houses and areas of the wealthy. Left realists would agree with Wilson that the informal control system has to be built up, but point to the widespread evidence that his police-initiated schemes are likely to precipitate disorder rather than reinforce it (see Kinsey *et al.* 1986).

Left realism and the etiological crisis

Left realists are in no doubt that there has been a rise in crime, although they maintain that this reflects the reality of crime involving changes in both behaviour and tolerance of crime. It faces the crisis of etiology square on: crime is caused by inequalities in the social structure, but it is experienced injustice, relative deprivation—not absolute, 'objective' deprivation—which predisposes towards crime. And crime occurs in situations where there are no feasible alternatives to solving relative deprivation. This is why crime rates are higher in countries without social democratic alternatives (on the USA see Currie 1985).

For left realism, then, the control of crime involves interventions on all levels: on the social causes of crime, on social control exercised by the community and the formal agencies, and on the situation of the victim. Furthermore, that social causation is given the highest priority; while formal agencies, such as the police, do have a vital role, it is one which has been greatly exaggerated in the conventional literature. It is not the 'Thin Blue Line', but the social bricks and mortar of civil society which are the major bulwark against crime. Good jobs with a discernible future, housing estates of which tenants can be proud, community facilities which enhance a sense of cohesion and belonging, a reduction in unfair income inequalities, all create a society which is more cohesive and less criminogenic.

The distinguishing feature of left realism, when compared to the realism of the right, is the appraisal of the relationship between social order and social justice. For those on the right, order takes priority over justice: an orderly society will be one that is more just, however imperfect. And such a programme justifies unjust interventions such as selective incapacitation, a dual-track system of penality, the harassment, in order to maintain a neighbourhood, of those committing incivilities, etc. Left realists argue that it is wrong to suggest that crime control will be achieved by prioritizing order over justice. Society is held together to the extent that it is seen by its members to be just. When significant agencies of society, such as the police or the courts, act in a way which violates this sense of justice then public alienation is likely to occur. And, as we have seen, the parts of the population most likely to be alienated are those most vital to social control.

Left realists further distinguish themselves both from left idealists who oppose any net-widening of state intervention and from traditional conservatives who want to widen the net. There are areas of social control where the net should be drastically reduced (e.g. minor drug offences, juvenile 'status' crimes), and there are others where left realists would strongly call for net-widening: corporate crime, industrial pollution, racist attacks, child abuse, and domestic violence are a few of them. And, in general, the police and social service response to the poor is inadequate—in this case it is a *safety net* that needs widening. None of this need necessarily involve the traditional response of police and prisons, though in some cases it certainly would.

IN CONCLUSION: CRIME AND POLITICS

To solve the problem of crime involves political solutions. It is not that target-hardening and more locks and bolts do not help combat crime. Administrative criminology is effective, but only to an extent: for there are problems of crime being displaced elsewhere and distinct limits in terms of cost effectiveness. A recent DES Report on *Crime Prevention in Schools* indicates that the cost of target-hardening against vandalism soon becomes prohibitive, and, indeed, 'excessively target-hardened environments are thought to encourage more damage eventually than they prevent' (Department of Education and Science 1987: 37). For, after a certain stage, locks and bolts alienate and serve to feed sources of discontent rather than eliminate them. Furthermore, target-hardening has aesthetic and personal costs: we condemn many old people, for example, to virtual imprisonment in 'safe' houses, free from crime, but with a vista of iron bars and a barrier of answerphones. At some point women must reclaim the night: emphasis on safety, caution, and lifestyle restrictions are only temporary measures. In a civilized country women should be able to get out when they please. The solution to crime, as the left realists argue, is political. Strangely, other criminologists would agree: it is simply that they are unwilling or unhopeful as to the possibility of such political intervention occurring.

> We have learned that the factors in our lives and history that most powerfully influence the crime rate—our commitment to liberty, our general prosperity, our child-rearing methods, our popular values—are precisely the factors that are hardest or riskiest to change.
>
> In a sense, the radical critics of American society are correct: if you wish to make a big difference in crime, you must make fundamental changes in society. But they are right only in that sense, for what they propose to put in place of existing institutions, to the extent they propose anything at all except angry rhetoric, would probably make us yearn for the good old days when our crime rate was higher, but our freedoms were intact. (Wilson 1985: 250–1).

> Crime is intimately bound up with the social structure. If we seriously want to eliminate or greatly reduce its incidence, then we must alter the social system. But the price we will have to pay may be too high for many of us to contemplate.
>
> I would myself advocate the reconstitution of society. I would like to see our political institutions overhauled and renovated to bring them into line with agreed moral purposes. But I must confess that I see no prospect of this happening. It seems that the most we can reasonably hope for is that we should try to work out together some modus vivendi which will produce the minimum discomfort and crime with the least social dislocation for us all. (Mays 1963: 206–7)

Two writers: one an American right-winger writing in the 1980s; the other a British socialist writing in the 1950s; both in strange agreement across country, politics, and time. If you want to change the crime rate profoundly then you must profoundly change society. In the end, moral barometers are most easily affected by changes in political climate. One person steadfastly resists change; the other hoped for it but reluctantly surmised that such change was unlikely.

Crime involves politics: it does so because it is politics which determines the social conditions which cause crime, the degree to which the justice system is egalitarian, and the definition of what are crimes in the first place and what degree of gravity we allot to one crime against another. In a sense all criminologists recognize this. Wilson basically contends that if one wants the benefits of American capitalism, then one must put up with a certain (high) level of crime. Few British conservatives would have the gall to write this. But he is undoubtedly correct, although the benefits of a free enterprise culture are a matter for debate. Wilson then proceeds to evolve a series of measures which would step beyond the bounds of justice in order to defend the existing order. In a sense he is once again correct, as a conservative: if one does not wish fundamentally to restrict the economic and judicial system, then coercion and discipline are the only alternatives to maintain order. This frequently does not work: coercive policies tend to increase disrespect for law rather than the reverse, but it is at least the logical conservative alternative. The new administrative criminologists, on the other hand, hope that locks and bolts, better surveillance, tighter security will hold the world in check without changing anything. The policies of 'normalizing crime' seek to calm the public; the implementation of target-hardening seeks to make us safer. But whatever real gains can be made by situational crime prevention, there are limits. There is a point where the cost-effectiveness and impingement on freedom of security measures can become counter-productive.

For the left idealists nothing can be achieved outside of dramatic, political change. This prospect of waiting for a far and distant utopia is hardly consoling in the face of the real problems with which vulnerable sections of the population now have to deal. Left realism argues that gains are possible but that they must be part of a co-ordinated strategy involving a multi-agency approach. To tackle crime, interventions have to be made on the level of family support, employment, youth facilities, design change, changes in police patrol methods, target-hardening, victim support, and so on, involving many agencies including local authorities, the police, voluntary groups, educational authorities, and more (see Lea *et al.* 1988). Such a co-ordination must be democratic in its nature and attempt to effect the distribution of economic resources and judicial decisions. The etiological crisis is not solved simply by more money or better conditions, but by resources distributed equitably as part of a just politics. Such a policy of reform demands co-ordination, a democratic multi-agency approach, and careful monitoring. It is only where justice is seen to be done that the mainsprings of crime are severed.

Selected Further Reading

R. Clarke and P. Mayhew, eds., *Designing Out Crime*. London: HMSO, 1980.

D. Downes and P. Rock, *Understanding Deviance*. Oxford: Clarendon Press, 1988.

E. Currie, *Confronting Crime*. New York: Pantheon, 1975.

J. Lea and J. Young, *What is to be Done about Law and Order?*, rev. edn. London: Pluto, 1993.

M. Haralambos and M. Holborn, *Sociology*, 3rd edn., ch. 10. London: Collins, 1990.

P. Scraton, ed., *Law, Order and the Authoritarian State*. Milton Keynes: Open University Press, 1987.

K. Stenson and D. Cowell, eds., *The Politics of Crime Control*. London: Sage, 1991.

J. Q. Wilson, *Thinking about Crime*. New York: Vintage, 1985.

J. Young and R. Matthews, *Rethinking Criminology: The Realist Debate*. London: Sage, 1992.

REFERENCES

ABERCROMBIE, N., HILL, S., and TURNER, B. (1980), *The Dominant Ideology Thesis*. London: Allen and Unwin.

AULD, J., DORN, N., and SOUTH, N. (1986), 'Irregular Work, Irregular Pleasures', in R. Matthews and J. Young, eds., *Confronting Crime*. London: Sage.

BECKER, H. S. (1963), *Outsiders*. New York: Free Press.

BOTTOMLEY, A. K. (1979), *Criminology in Focus*. Oxford: Martin Robertson.

BOTTOMS, A. (1983), 'Neglected Features of Contemporary Penal Systems', in D. Garland and P. Young, eds., *The Power to Punish*. London: Heinemann.

BOWLES, S., and GINTIS, H. (1976), *Schooling in Capitalist America*. New York: Basic Books.

BOX, S. (1980), 'Where Have All the Naughty Children Gone?', in National Deviancy Conference, ed., *Permissiveness and Control*. London: Macmillan.

BOX, S., and HALE, C. (1986), 'Unemployment, Crime and Imprisonment', in R. Matthews and J. Young, eds., *Confronting Crime*. London: Sage.

BOX-GRAINGER, J. (1986), 'Sentencing Rapists', in R. Matthews and J. Young, eds., *Confronting Crime*. London: Sage.

BRAKE, M., and HALE, C. (1992), *Public Order and Private Lives*. London: Routledge.

BROWN, D., and HOGG, R. (1992), 'Law and Order Politics—Left Realism and Radical Criminology: A View from Down Under', in R. Matthews and J. Young, eds., *Issues in Realist Criminology*. London: Sage.

BUNYAN, T. (1976), *The Political Police in Britain*. London: Quartet.

BURNEY, E. (1990), *Putting Street Crime in its Place*. London: Centre for Inner City Studies, Goldsmiths' College, University of London.

CARR-HILL, R., and STERN, N. (1979), *Crime, The Police and Criminal Statistics*. London: Academic Press.

CHRISTIANSEN, K. (1964), 'Delinquent Generations in Denmark', *British Journal of Criminology*, 4.

CLARKE, R. (1980), 'Situational Crime Prevention: Theory and Practice', *British Journal of Criminology*, 20/2: 136–47.

—— (1984), 'Opportunity-based Crime Rates', *British Journal of Criminology*, 24/1: 74–83.

CLARKE, R., and HOUGH, M. (1984), *Crime and Police Effectiveness*. London: HMSO.

CLARKE, R., and MAYHEW, P., eds. (1980), *Designing Out Crime*. London: HMSO.

CLOWARD, R., and OHLIN, L. (1960), *Delinquency and Opportunity*. New York: Free Press.

COHEN, A. K. (1955), *Delinquent Boys*. New York: Free Press.

—— (1965), 'The Sociology of the Deviant Act: Anomie Theory and Beyond', *American Sociological Review*, 30: 5–14.

COHEN, S. (1985), *Visions of Social Control*. Cambridge: Polity Press.

COHEN, S., and SCULL, A., eds. (1985), *Social Control and the State*. Oxford: Basil Blackwell.

COOK, P. (1980), 'Criminal Deterrence', in M. Tonry and N. Morris, eds., *Crime and Justice*, vol. 2, Chicago: University of Chicago Press.

CORNISH, D. and CLARKE, R., eds. (1986*a*), *The Reasoning Criminal*. New York: Springer-Verlag.

—— (1986*b*), 'Situational Prevention, Displacement of Crime and Rational Choice Theory', in K. Heal and G. Laycock, eds., *Situational Crime Prevention*. London: HMSO.

COULTER, J., MILLER, S., AND WALKER, M. (1984), *State of Siege*. London: Canary Press.

CRAWFORD, A., JONES, T., WOODHOUSE, T., and YOUNG, J. (1990), *The Second Islington Crime Survey*. London: Middlesex University Centre for Criminology.

CURRIE, E. (1985), *Confronting Crime*. New York: Pantheon.

—— (1990), 'Crime and Market Society: Lessons from the United States', paper presented to the Conference on Crime and Policing, Islington, 26 November.

DE KESERDY, W., and SCHWARTZ, M. (1992), 'British and US Left Realism: A Critical Comparison', *International Journal of Offender Therapy and Comparative Criminology*.

DEPARTMENT OF EDUCATION AND SCIENCE (1987), *Crime Prevention in Schools*. London: HMSO.

DINITZ, S. (1979), 'Nothing Fals Like Success', in E. Sagarin, ed., *Criminology: New Concerns*. Beverley Hills: Sage.

DORN, N., and SOUTH, N. eds. (1987), *A Land Fit for Heroin?* London: Macmillan.

DOWNES, D., and ROCK, P. (1982), *Understanding Deviance*. Oxford: Clarendon Press.

DURKHEIM, E. (1952), *Suicide*. London: Routledge Kegan Paul.

—— (1964), *The Rules of Sociological Method*. New York: Free Press.

DUSTER, T. (1970), *The Legislation of Morality*. New York: Free Press.

ERIKSON, K. (1966), *Wayward Puritans*. New York: Wiley.

EYSENCK, H. (1964), *Crime and Personality*. London: Routledge Kegan Paul. 3rd edn. London: Paladin, 1970.

EYSENCK, H., and GUDJONSSON, G. (1989), *The Causes and Cures of Criminality*. New York: Plenum Press.

FELSON, M. (1987), 'Routine Activities and Crime in the Developing Metropolis', *Criminology*, 25: 911–31.

FELSON, M., and COHEN, L. (1981), 'Modelling Crime Rates: A Criminal Opportunity Perspective', *Research in Crime and Delinquency*, 18: 138–64.

FERRAJOLI, L. (1989), *Diritto e Ragione*. Bari: Laterza.

FINE, B., KINSEY, R., LEA, J., PICCIOTTO, S., and YOUNG, J. (1979), *Capitalism and the Rule of Law*. London: Hutchinson.

FISHBEIN, M., and COOMBS, F. (1974), 'Basis for Decision: An Attitudinal Analysis of Voting Behaviour', *Journal of Applied Social Psychology*, 4: 95–124.

FITZGERALD, M. (1977), *Prisoners in Revolt*. Harmondsworth: Penguin.

FITZGERALD, M., MCLENNAN, G., and PAWSON, J., eds. (1981), *Crime and Society*. London: Routledge Kegan Paul.

FOUCAULT, M. (1980), 'On Popular Justice', in C. Gordon, ed., *Power/Knowledge*. Brighton: Harvester.

FURLONG, V. (1985), *The Deviant Pupil*. Milton Keynes: Open University Press.

FYVEL, T. R. (1963), *The Insecure Offenders*. London: Penguin.

GLASGOW MEDIA GROUP (1976), *Bad News*. London: Routledge Kegan Paul.

GOTTFREDSON, M., and HIRSCHI, T., eds. (1987), *Positive Criminology*. London: Sage.

GOULD, L. (1969), 'The Changing Structure of Property Crime in an Affluent Society', *Social Forces*, 48: 50–9.

GREGORY, D., and URRY, J., eds. (1985), *Social Relations and Spatial Structures*. London: Macmillan.

HALL, S., CRITCHER, C., JEFFERSON, T., CLARKE, J., and ROBERTS, B. (1978), *Policing the Crisis*. London: Macmillan.

HAY, D. (1975), 'Property, Authority and Criminal Law', in D. Hay, P. Linebaugh, and E. P. Thompson, eds., *Albion's Fatal Tree*. London: Allen Lane.

HIRSCHI, T. (1969), *Causes of Delinquency*. Berkeley: University of California Press.

—— (1986), 'On The Compatability of Rational Choice and Social Control Theories of Crime', in D. Cornish and R. Clarke, eds., *The Reasoning Criminal*. New York: Springer-Verlag.

HOUGH, M., and MAYHEW, P. (1983), *The British Crime Survey*. London: HMSO.

—— (1985), *Taking Account of Crime*. London: HMSO.

—— (1988), 'Findings of the British Crime Survey', in M. Maguire and J. Pointing, eds., *Victims of Crime: A New Deal*. Milton Keynes: Open University Press.

HULSMAN, L. (1986), 'Critical Criminology and the Concept of Crime', *Contemporary Crises* 10/1: 63–80.

IGNATIEFF, M. (1978), *A Just Measure of Pain*. London: Macmillan.

—— (1985), 'State, Civil Society and Total Institutions', in S. Cohen and A. Scull, eds., *Social Control and the State*. Oxford: Basil Blackwell.

JEFFREY, C. (1980), 'Sociobiology and Criminology', in F. Sagarin, ed., *Taboos in Criminology*. Beverly Hills: Sage.

KELLY, L., and RADFORD, J. (1987), 'The Problem of Men: Feminist Perspectives on Sexual Violence', in P. Scraton, ed., *Law, Order and the Authoritarian State.* Milton Keynes: Open University Press.

KINSEY, R., LEA, J., and YOUNG, J. (1986), *Losing the Fight Against Crime.* Oxford: Blackwell.

KITSUSE, J., and SPECTOR, M. (1973), 'Towards a Sociology of Social Problems', *Social Problems*, 20: 407–19.

KLEIN, M. (1971), *Street Gangs and Street Workers.* Englewood Cliffs, NJ: Prentice-Hall.

LANGBEIN, J. (1983), 'Albion's Fatal Flaws', *Past and Present*, 98: 96–120.

LAWRENCE, E. (1982), 'Sociology and Black "Pathology"', in Centre for Contemporary Cultural Studies, ed., *The Empire Strikes Back.* London: Centre for Contemporary Cultural Studies.

LEA, J. (1992), 'Left Realism: A Framework for the Analysis of Crime', in J. Young and R. Matthews, eds., *Rethinking Criminology: The Realist Debate.* London: Sage.

LEA, J., JONES, T., WOODHOUSE, T., and YOUNG, J. (1988), *Preventing Crime: The Hilldrop Project.* London: Middlesex Polytechnic, Centre for Criminology.

LEA, J., and YOUNG, J. (1984), *What is to be Done about Law and Order?* London: Penguin. (Rev. edn. London, Pluto, 1993.)

LERMAN, P. (1975), *Community Treatment and Social Control.* Chicago: University of Chicago Press.

LIDZ, C., and WALKER, A. (1980), *Heroin, Deviance and Morality.* Beverly Hills: Sage.

LOWMAN, H. (1992), 'Rediscovering Crime', in J. Young and R. Matthews eds., *Rethinking Criminology: The Realist Debate.* London: Sage.

MACLEAN, B. (1991), 'On Critical Criminology', in B. MacLean and D. Milanovic, eds., *New Directions in Critical Criminology.* Vancouver: Collective Press.

MAGUIRE, M., and POINTING, J., eds. (1988), *Victims of Crime: A New Deal?* Milton Keynes: Open University Press.

MANNHEIM, H. (1955), *Group Problems in Crime and Punishment.* London: Routledge Kegan Paul.

MATHIESON, T. (1974), *The Politics of Abolition.* Oxford: Martin Robertson.

MATTHEWS, R., and YOUNG, J. eds. (1986), *Confronting Crime.* London: Sage.

—— (1992), *Issues in Realist Criminology.* London: Sage.

MATZA, D. (1964), *Delinquency and Drift.* New York: Wiley.

—— (1969), *Becoming Deviant.* Englewood Cliffs, NJ: Prentice-Hall.

MAYS, J. B. (1963), *Crime and Social Structure.* London: Faber.

MELOSSI, D., and PAVARINI, M. (1981), *The Prison and the Factory.* London: Macmillan.

MICHALOWSKI, R. (1991), '"Niggers, Welfare Scum and Homeless Assholes": The Problems of Idealism, Consciousness and Context in Left Realism' in B. MacLean and D. Milovanovic, eds., *Directions in Critical Criminology.* Vancouver: Collective Press.

MILLER, W. (1962), 'Preventive Work with Street Corner Groups', *Annals*, 7.

MORRIS, N., and HAWKINS, G. (1970), *An Honest Politician's Guide to Crime Control.* Chicago: Chicago University Press.

NICHOLSON, L., ed. (1990), *Feminism/Postmodernism*. New York: Routledge.
PFOHL, S. (1977), 'The Discovery of Child Abuse', *Social Problems*, 24: 310–24.
PRYCE, K. (1979), *Endless Pressure*. London: Penguin.
QUETELET, A. (1842), *A Treatise on Man and the Development of His Faculties*. Edinburgh: Chambers.
REIMAN, J. (1979), *The Rich Get Richer and the Poor Get Prison*. New York: Wiley.
RYAN, W. (1976), *Blaming the Victim*. New York: Vintage Books.
SCHEERER, S. (1986), 'Towards Abolitionism', *Contemporary Crises*, 10/1: 5–20.
SCHUR, E. (1973), *Radical Non-Intervention*. Englewood Cliffs, NJ: Prentice-Hall.
SCHWENDINGER, H., and Schwendinger, J. (1985), *Adolescent Subcultures and Delinquency*. New York: Praeger.
SCRATON, P. (1985) *The State of the Police: Is Law and Order out of Control?* London: Pluto.
—— ed. (1987), *Law, Order and the Authoritarian State*. Milton Keynes: Open University Press.
SIMON, H. (1978), 'Rationality as a Process and as a Product of Thought', *American Economic Review*, 8/2: 1–11.
SIMON, W., and GAGNON, J. (1986), 'The Anomie of Affluence: A Post-Mertonian Conceptual', *American Sociological Review*, 82: 356–78.
SKOLNICK, J., and BAYLEY, D. (1986), *The New Blue Line*. New York: Free Press.
SLATTERY, M. (1986), *Official Statistics*. London: Tavistock.
SPITZER, S. (1980), '"Left Wing" Criminology—An Infantile Disorder?', in J. Inciardi, ed., *Radical Criminology*. Beverly Hills: Sage.
SVENSSON, B. (1986), 'Welfare and Criminality in Sweden', in K. Heal and G. Laycock, eds., *Situational Crime Prevention*. London: HMSO.
TAYLOR, I. (1981), *Law and Order: Arguments for Socialism*. London: Macmillan.
—— (1990), *The Social Effects of Free Market Policies*. Hemel Hempstead: Harvester.
TAYLOR, I., WALTON, P., and YOUNG, J. (1973), *The New Criminology*. London: Routledge Kegan Paul.
—— (1975), *Critical Criminology*. London: Routledge Kegan Paul.
THOMPSON, E. P. (1980), *Writing by Candlelight*. London: Merlin.
TIMPANARO, S. (1975), *On Materialism*. London: New Left Books.
TRASLER, G. (1986), 'Situational Crime Control and Rational Choice', in K. Heal and G. Laycock, eds., *Situational Crime Prevention*. London: HMSO.
TUCHMAN, G. (1978), *Making News*. New York: Free Press.
TUCK, M. (1976), *How Do We Choose? A Study in Consumer Behaviour*. London: Methuen.
TUCK, M., and RILEY, D. (1986), 'A Theory of Reasoned Action: A Decision Theory of Crime' in Cornish and Clarke, Op Cit.
VAN DEN HAAG, E. (1975), *Punishing Criminals*. New York: Basic Books.
VAN DIJK, J. J. M. (1988), 'Penal Sanctions and the Process of Civilisation', paper presented to the Tenth International Congress of Criminology, Hamburg, 5 October.
VASS, A. (1990), *Alternatives to Prison*. London: Sage.
VOLD, G. B. (1958), *Theoretical Criminology*. Oxford: Oxford University Press.

WILKINS, L. (1960), *Delinquent Generations*. London: Home Office.
—— (1964), *Social Deviance*. London: Tavistock.
WILLIS, P. (1977), *Learning to Labour*. Farnborough: Saxon House.
WILSON, H., and HERBERT, G. (1978), *Parents and Children in the Inner City*. London.
WILSON, J. Q. (1968), *Varieties of Police Behavior*. Cambridge, Mass.: Harvard University Press.
—— (1975), *Thinking about Crime*. New York Vintage Books. 2nd edn. 1985.
WILSON, J. Q., and Herrnstein, R. (1985), *Crime and Human Nature*. New York: Simon and Schuster.
WILSON, J. Q., and KELLING, G. (1982) 'Broken Windows', *Atlantic Monthly*, March: 29–38.
WILSON, W. J. (1987), *The Truly Disadvantaged*. Chicago: Chicago University Press.
WOOLGAR, S., and PAWLUCH, D. (1985), 'Ontological Gerrymandering', *Social Problems*, 32/3: 214–27.
YOUNG, J. (1971), *The Drug-Takers*. London: Paladin.
—— (1974), 'New Directions in Subcultural Theory', in J. Rex, ed., *Approaches to Sociology*. London: Routledge Kegan Paul.
—— (1975), 'Working Class Criminology', in I. Taylor, P. Walton, and J. Young, eds., *Criminal Criminology*. London: Routledge Kegan Paul.
—— (1979), 'Left Idealism, Reformism and Beyond', in B. Fine *et al.*, eds., *Capitalism and the Rule of Law*. London: Hutchinson.
—— (1981), 'Thinking Seriously About Crime', in M. Fitzgerald, G. McLennan, and J. Pawson, eds., *Crime and Society*. London: Routledge Kegan Paul.
—— (1983), 'Striking Back against the Empire', *Critical Social Policy*, 8: 130–40.
—— (1986), 'The Failure of Criminology: The Need for Radical Realism', in R. Matthews and J. Young, eds., *Confronting Crime*. London: Sage.
—— (1987), 'The Tasks of a Realist Criminology', *Contemporary Crises*, 11: 337–56.
—— (1988*a*), 'Radical Criminology in Britain: The Emergence of a Competing Paradigm', *British Journal of Criminology*, 28: 159–83. Repr. in P. Rock, ed., *The History of British Criminology*. Oxford: Clarendon Press, 1988.
—— (1992), 'Ten Points of Realism', in J. Young and R. Matthews, eds., *Rethinking Criminology: The Realist Debate*. London: Sage.
YOUNG, J. and MATTHEWS, R., eds. (1992), *Rethinking Criminology: The Realist Debate*. London: Sage.
—— (1992), 'Asking Questions of Realism', in J. Young and R. Matthews, eds., *Rethinking Criminology: The Realist Debate*. London: Sage.
YOUNG, M. F. D., ed. (1971), *Knowledge and Control*. London: Collier Macmillan.

3

The Social Organization of British Criminology

PAUL ROCK

> What a bunch of old fogies we are. Richard Ingrams obviously had British criminologists in mind when he launched *The Oldie*.
>
> (A younger woman criminologist)

The evolution of scholarship is in part a *social* process, a process that mirrors and feeds the relations of those who constitute a discipline. In his description of what he labelled 'art worlds', Becker argued that art was shaped by elaborate dealings inside the communities and markets of artists, craftsmen, galleries, critics and publics (Becker 1984). So too with scholarship. An academic discipline is in substantial measure an institutionally bounded community, a tradition, a set of practices, a marketplace, a network of communication, and an organized way of seeing the world (see King and Brownell 1966).

Those who would wish to understand the history and significance of British criminology should think about its authors, teachers, and researchers as a population laid out in social and physical space, moving through time, and continually in interaction. They should see that population arrayed as if on a lattice-work that defines, unites, and severs relations not only between criminologists themselves but between criminologists and their significant others: the critics, readers, publishers, students, government officials, politicians, 'criminal justice practitioners' and their organizations, victims and victims' organizations, defendants and defendants' organizations, journalists, and the editors of journals and books (see Whitley 1969). They should examine criminology as a lattice composed not only of the obligations that bind patrons and clients, collaborators and colleagues, but also of the enmities and suspicions that keep people apart. They should examine how its organization sustains and is supported by the seminar and the conference, the consultancy and the commission. They should recognize criminology as a structure of power and politics, search-

I am grateful for funding provided by the Social Research Division of the London School of Economics, for the valuable work of data entry and preparation undertaken by Rebecca Daly and for the transcription of interviews performed by Seeta Persaud. I am particularly grateful to Robert Reiner with whom this chapter was originally planned to be written. He supplied many of the ideas and much of the work for the survey and it is unfortunate that pressure of work made it difficult for him to continue collaboration. Rebecca Daly, Janet Foster, Elaine Player, Robert Reiner, and Lucia Zedner read earlier drafts of this chapter, and I would like to thank them for their most helpful comments.

ing for the gatekeepers, the institutions, and the men and women who have the influence to determine who and what shall thrive in the discipline.[1] They should look for ensuing patterns of inclusion and exclusion that shape who is invited to attend colloquia, give broadcasts, or write papers—who, in effect, is allowed to be seen, heard, and known. They should see who discusses what with whom and where, searching for flows, confluences, and breaks in the transmission of knowledge, because only then will the character of criminology as an *artefact* become visible.

Criminology has a social organization, and it is an organization that has been shaped by all the structuring principles that affect any other substantial grouping: by generation, gender, and the rest. The study of such an organization may not explain everything of note about the discipline, but it is certainly likely to be illuminating enough to warrant exploration. It was for that reason that a beginning was made in the summer of 1992 by surveying all identifiable British criminologists, securing 106 replies out of 235, a response rate of 45 per cent.[2] This essay issues from that survey. It is a straightforward examination of a few of the more obvious bonds between the ideas and the social organization of criminology, and it focuses in particular on the demographic, the institutional, and the relational as a backdrop to some of the arguments in the rest of this handbook.

[1] Much will depend on the recruitment and workings of appointment committees, funding panels and editorial boards. See Crane 1969: 344.

[2] It could not be more than a beginning because a sample of 106 does not encompass all criminologists (and some of the inferences must in consequence be speculative) and because many of the more subtle and interesting questions about the connections between thought, practice, and relations cannot be answered by a simple questionnaire. Quite evidently a larger survey is needed, coupled with a programme of observation, reading, and interviewing that would lead to a thick description of criminology.

Robert Reiner and I sent questionnaires to all those whom we could identify as criminologists from available published sources such as the *Commonwealth Universities Yearbook*. We asked those we contacted to name any other colleagues who worked in the field and sent them questionnaires in turn. We could apply no strict definition of the term 'criminologist'. Rather, we employed our own and others' practical knowledge of the discipline and its members, allowing those we approached to accept or reject their inclusion in the survey. The inevitable result is that this chapter analyses the social organization of *academic* criminology, not the criminology of practitioners or those who have what Reiner called 'self-defined interests' in the subject. The survey was complemented by face-to-face interviews of a small group of six criminologists.

For obvious reasons, it is impossible to ascertain the representativeness of the sample. On the basis of limited information, it appears that the sample was representative in some matters but not others. Much the same proportions of men (79 per cent) and women (21 per cent) were evident among repliers as among non-repliers (81 per cent and 19 per cent), indicating no gender bias. Over half of those criminologists working in small and medium concentrations of up to eight replied, but there was an unusually low response rate of 31 per cent for those working in centres and institutions with the largest concentrations of nine or more criminologists. As I shall show, those concentrations are themselves atypical, accounting for only 20 per cent of all British criminologists, but their underrepresentation should be remembered when some of the analysis is considered.

THE FACE OF BRITISH CRIMINOLOGY IN THE EARLY 1990S

The education and recruitment of British criminologists were not paced evenly over time. They were clearly and fatefully bunched around the great expansion of higher education that took place in the 1960s and 1970s. Until 1950, the scale of higher education was modest indeed; but thereafter the existing twenty-nine British universities began to grow strongly, and they were to be joined by a welter of new institutions. Eight new universities were founded in the 1950s and fourteen in the 1960s (eight in 1966 and 1967 alone), polytechnics were established, and the student population grew. The number of home acceptance students more than doubled between 1963 and 1969, and increased by another 40 per cent by 1980. New staff were recruited, the body of university lecturers growing by 13 per cent in the 1970s. Thereafter, universities stagnated and declined as the state and its dependents were exposed to financial austerity. The numbers of teaching and research staff shrank by 11 per cent between 1979 and 1984. In retrospect, the 1970s stood apart as a golden age.[3]

The condition of British criminology waxed and waned in sympathy with that of the rest of higher education. Criminologists were educated principally in the late 1960s and early 1970s, and they moved into employment shortly thereafter, their careers tending to follow a larger pattern that has been described by Halsey and others.[4] They were conventionally trained in universities and polytechnics. Two of those we surveyed, men in their sixties, had no first degree, and fifteen had but one degree. Almost all the rest (75 per cent) were men or women in their late thirties or forties who had had a prolonged exposure to higher education. The majority had begun as sociologists (33 per cent had first degrees in sociology) or lawyers (18 per cent had first degrees in law). No other undergraduate training figured as prominently as those two disciplines: a mere 7 per cent of criminologists had been awarded psychology degrees and 6 per cent history degrees; the rest a spattering of other qualifications.[5] The study of crime was thus rooted in sociology and law as they were taught in the 1960s and 1970s (see Fig. 3.1).[6]

Like other academics, criminologists converged on a few institutions to take their first degrees. The largest single group (20 per cent) attended the University of London, the largest university: 8 per cent went to the LSE,

[3] That was certainly how I described it in an earlier paper: see Rock 1988.

[4] See Halsey 1992: 140–1; Geertz 1983. There are, however, some minor differences. For instance, as Lucia Zedner pointed out, in most disciplines training begins directly at undergraduate level, while that is not so of criminology.

[5] It must be recalled that the analysis reflects the sampling of academic criminologists known to us.

[6] None the less, the influence of academic law on criminology seems actually to have been rather slight until recently.

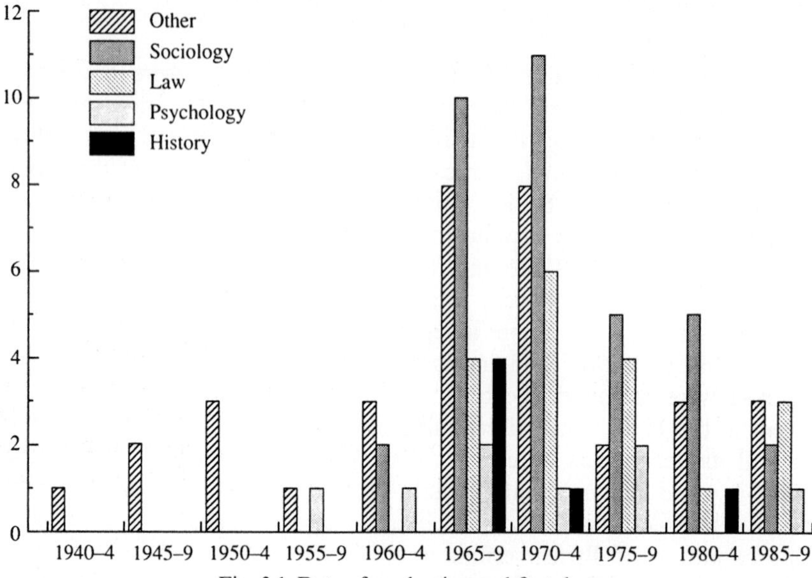

Fig. 3.1 Date of graduation and first degree

5 per cent to University College, and the rest to other colleges of that federal university. Of the others, 7.5 per cent attended the University of Oxford, 7 per cent the University of Cambridge, 6 per cent the University of Birmingham, and 4 per cent Lancaster University. Criminologists' further education as graduates was even more concentrated, in part because large, specialist departments and universities tend to retain their own (35 per cent of criminologists took their first and second degrees in the same institution), and in part because the decision to become a criminologist propelled students towards places where criminology was known to be had: 12 per cent of the ninety-seven criminologists with a higher degree went to the LSE, 11 per cent to the University of Cambridge, 10 per cent to the University of Oxford, and 6 per cent to the University of Sheffield. In short, some 40 per cent of criminologists had passed through a mere four institutions (58 per cent coming to those institutions from other universities, 42 per cent remaining in place) and their experience gave a pattern to the discipline. It was those institutions' conception of academic criminology, the groupings that formed within them, and their place in networks of patronage that fixed something of the character of the discipline. As Becher argued of the process at large, 'the disciplinary values with which [most academics] are first inculcated are . . . the values of the leading departments in their fields' (Becher 1989: 3). The LSE, Oxford, Cambridge, and Sheffield were—and are—British criminology for many practical intellectual purposes. A former LSE student remarked: 'I

wouldn't have said there was such a thing as a discipline [of criminology for me] . . . it was how my little world at LSE operated . . .'.

In their research, criminologists looked at criminal justice rather than at criminals, at prisons rather than courts, at men rather than women, at white men rather than black or Asian men, at criminality rather than at victimization. The graduate research undertaken by British criminologists covered a broad span, but it was also distinctively clumped. British criminologists undertook their apprenticeships as graduate students writing about the institutions and agencies of criminal justice and law enforcement rather than about criminals and crimes: 57 per cent studied such matters, while a mere 3 per cent claimed to have studied criminological theory, and only 8 per cent had written about crimes and criminals.

Graduate education engendered an array of lineages, lines of descent and tradition being mediated by scholars working in quasi-familial relation to one another. Criminology seems to be composed of many such networks that supply the materials for larger histories and maps of social organization. It was possible to discern one network of fourteen members organized loosely around the University of Oxford, LSE, and the University of Surrey; another with four generations and five members based in Edinburgh; and a third with six members based at Cambridge.[7] There were many others, but only the first group had any scale or complexity (although that may have been little more than a product of the way in which people were sampled). Those three fragmentary networks illustrate how supervision can join people formally and over time (see Fig. 3.2).

Students reading for a research degree characteristically combine a sense of the Promethean with passages of humility, anxiety, and loneliness. They are probably more susceptible to strong influence then than at any other stage in their academic career, and their supervisors, the men and women who instructed and judged them, can acquire prominence in proportion. Criminologists could confer exceptional significance on those who taught and advised them at such a formative time. One of the Oxford–LSE–Surrey network, a man I have named E, said: 'The major debt I owe is to C, who was the person who supervised me . . . he was the most conscientious and painstaking supervisor. . . . C was enormously supportive. He also gave me stuff that was coming over from the States quite a lot.' And one of E's students, H, talked about *him* and a colleague in like terms: D 'was very important in terms of shaping my perceptions . . . I see that the sort of association that I had with D and with E was actually very important for me because it opened the world up instead of making it very narrow.' There are thus clear and effective intellectual lines stretching from generation to generation, knitting the

[7] No doubt a more exhaustive survey would have revealed more elaborate organization, but it would not be right to move too far beyond the data.

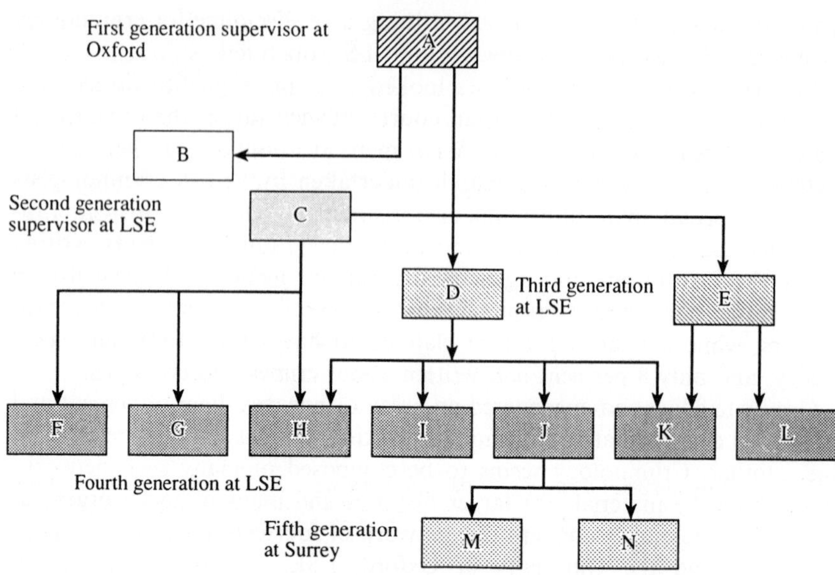

Fig. 3.2 Part of an Oxford–London–Surrey network

discipline and its members together.

Becoming a criminologist is probably not an obvious or commonplace ambition in Britain. Certainly, there was little enough criminology to be *seen* in the 1960s and 1970s, the period when most British criminologists drifted into the field. All the people interviewed talked of how it was rarely by design that they had moved into graduate research or paid employment. To paraphrase Goffman, it would seem that their decisions were shaped less by resolve than by contingencies. One distinguished scholar recalled that he had become a criminologist 'by accident really'. He had set out to become a social worker, but the admissions tutor who had read his application 'told me about some of the work that was going on in criminology at the time . . . I thought this was enormously exciting . . . for some reason criminology had never really occurred to me as an academic field in which research could go on . . .'. Another, a criminal lawyer, remembered how he had been asked to teach criminology on the retirement of a pioneering senior colleague. Although he had known little about the discipline, 'the head of the Law Department said "How would you like to do criminology along with criminal law?" . . . I was very reluctant. I thought about it for a weekend but I decided that it was better than doing more dull things like contract law and commercial law which he in fact threatened me with . . .'. Yet another, who was to become a senior member of the Home Office Research and Planning Unit, remembered how she had joined the Civil Service as an administrator, had found administration tedious, and had decided that 'I might as well be doing something which I enjoyed, which was research. I didn't really know anything about criminology. I just thought I would do research.' Her colleague declared that he 'fell into criminology because I wanted a research job and this happened to be a job in research and planning . . . I had no criminological expertise before I came here.'

Few (5 per cent) of the present population of British criminologists had been recruited before 1959. No doubt such a small number was made smaller still by death, migration, and retirement over the years, but it also reflects the very modest scale of higher education immediately after the war. A man, now retired, said simply that 'there weren't very many others' when he embarked on teaching criminology in 1955. Another who had come to criminology in the late 1950s recalled how he had found himself in an almost empty discipline:

> I was taken by surprise at how few people there were in the field. . . . I was staggered at how under-populated it was. Hermann Mannheim was the big name—he was . . . at LSE—there was John Mays in Liverpool, Terry [Morris]—and I was aware of the centre at Cambridge but it wasn't sociological at the time, so I didn't pay too much attention to it . . . And that was more or less it, I think, Liverpool and Cambridge and very little else going on.

Even fewer criminologists (3 per cent) were recruited in the first half of the 1960s. It was only in the latter half of the 1960s and in the 1970s, the great booming years after the Robbins Report, that most criminologists entered their posts (one lawyer recalled that it 'was a period of rapid growth and all the departments of law were interested in developing criminology and many other departments like sociology were interested too . . .'). Of our sample of criminologists, 14 per cent were recruited between 1965 and 1969; 22 per cent between 1970 and 1974; and 25 per cent between 1975 and 1979. Only 8 per cent of criminologists were hired in the five lean years between 1980 and 1984, a further 17 per cent in the years between 1985 and 1989, and 6 per cent between 1990 and the summer of 1992.

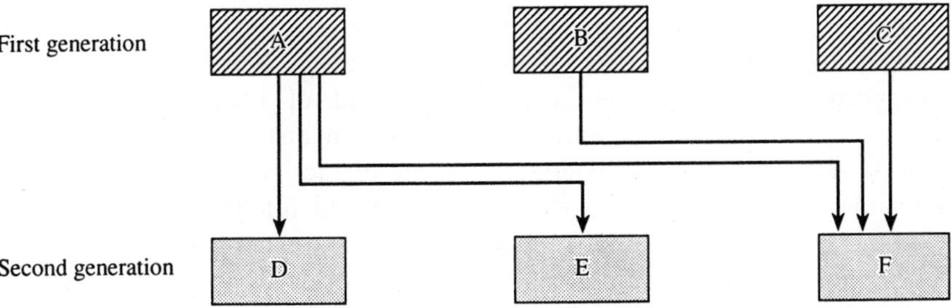

Fig. 3.3 Part of a Cambridge network

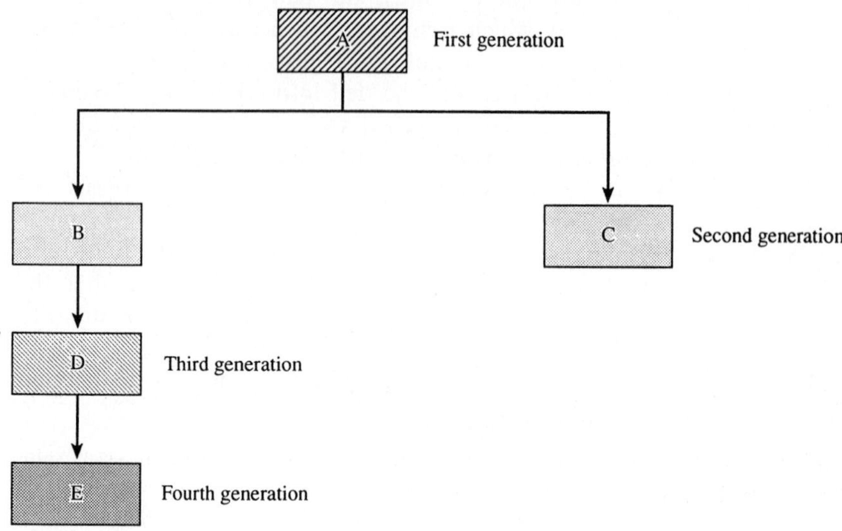

Fig. 3.4 Part of an Edinburgh network

Those recruited in the second half of the 1980s were 36 years old by mid-1992, and those entering between 1990 and mid-1992 were 30. Although criminology may be about to be replenished as law departments expand and become more diverse, to some the discipline seems to be at risk of becoming empty again. Sociological criminology in particular looks somewhat emaciated (a middle-aged man said 'there is a tremendous gap . . . there hasn't been recruitment . . . there has been an enormous gap which I think has done us a lot of harm').

In effect, two demographic waves have moved through post-war British criminology: the greater in the 1970s and the lesser in the latter half of the 1980s; and it was the greater that gave definition to the discipline. Criminologists educated and appointed in the late 1960s and 1970s form a distinct and self-conscious intellectual generation. Karl Mannheim once described a generation as 'a particular kind of identity of location, embracing related "age groups" embedded in a historical–social process' and he reflected that the generation 'is one of the indispensable guides to an understanding of the structure of social and intellectual movements' (Mannheim 1952: 292, 286–7). One generation's experience of the interlaced worlds of the criminologist's life, the worlds of scholarship, crime, politics, and mundane activity, can never be quite the same as that of another.

CRIMINOLOGY AND THE 'FORTUNATE GENERATION'

In an earlier survey of British criminologists, I wrote about the preponderance of the middle-aged members of the 'fortunate generation' who had been recruited in such large numbers in the 1960s and 1970s that they seemed to control the discipline (Rock 1988). This second survey shows that the fortunate generation remains in command six years later. Although it has been somewhat leavened by the younger recruits of the late 1980s, British criminology is still a middle-aged domain. The mean age of criminologists in 1992 was 43, the modal age being 46: 68 per cent of criminologists were older than 40, and only 6.5 per cent were younger than 30. The discipline is dominated by a group of men and women in their forties, who comprise just over half the total: erstwhile Young Turks, who are now perhaps not so young at all.

Criminologists themselves tend to acknowledge the centrality of the fortunate generation and the history and myths that gave it character. Chief among the group's formative events was the founding of the National Deviancy Conference (called by some the NDC) in November 1968, an event conventionally associated with what came to be known as

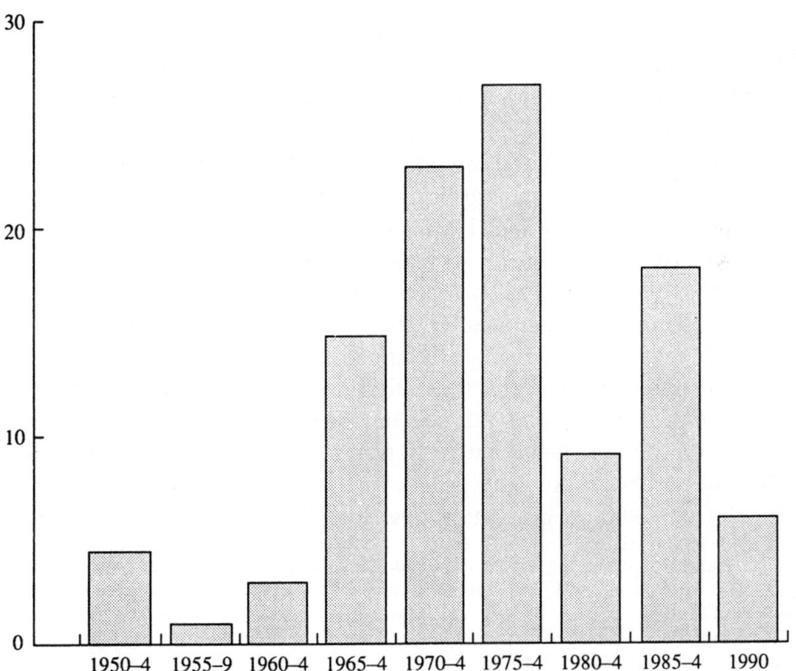

Fig. 3.5 Date of first appointment

the 'break from positivism' and the emergence of the sociology of deviance. One 'left realist' reflected: 'what really was interesting was the sociology of deviance—it wasn't criminology, and one wouldn't have called oneself a criminologist at the time.'[8] The founding of the National Deviancy Conference was regarded as unusually significant. It was the academic counterpart to the Big Bang, associated with frequent talk, accelerated theorizing, symbolic display, a burst of writing and publishing, and, afterwards, some nostalgia. Ideas, many of them imported from North America, were subjected to intense scrutiny, redrafted, stretched, realigned, synthesized and applied. Another middle-aged radical criminologist said: 'The parallel I always thought was with pop culture—we were taking American ideas and making them a lot more interesting—the fun way that we were actually transporting and translating in a way that was quite extraordinary . . .' It had been exciting, a time of expansiveness and youthful *braggadocio*. A middle-aged Home Office criminologist called it a 'glitzy' period. The moral density of the discipline undoubtedly increased during that time, bringing about an implosion and acceleration of social relations. Another middle-aged criminologist, himself a joint founder of the Conference, remarked that: 'Everybody says what was quite odd about the NDC days was how much people were in contact with each other . . . there were so many forums that you could meet up, you seemed always to be meeting on a level, and I remember actually how much the Americans were impressed by the level at which everyone was meeting.'

The fortunate generation came to see themselves as the special creatures of a theoretical revolution (see introduction to Cohen 1971); one said: 'We were doing something which was really, really interesting and I don't think it *is* as interesting any longer.' They were the members of a cohesive and vigourous social group[9] whose closeness was to be noted and dismissed long after by a younger Alison Young as 'internalized "cosiness" ' (Young 1991). They could not but interpret the world rather differently from the much smaller generation that came before, the older generation that had believed in 'planned collectivism' and talked about social reconstruction and the rehabilitation of the individual (see Morris 1989: esp. p. 21). They could not but view matters differently from a younger, smaller and comparatively fragmented generation that came to preoccupy itself with hunting grants for empirical research in the colder climate of the 1980s, a generation described by one of its members as 'not

[8] The return to criminology came soon enough with Taylor *et al.*'s *The New Criminology* (1973). The words 'new' and 'criminology' were used for ironic effect but criminology came back for all that.

[9] In Rock 1988 I reported that the wave of appointments was succeeded by a wave of publishing, most conspicuously in the years between 1976 and 1979 when 164 new books on deviance and criminology were mentioned by the journal *Sociology* in its lists of books received.

organized . . . there isn't enough of a critical mass . . . we're a fairly disparate bunch of people'.

The fortunate generation took themselves to be the pivot about which criminology turned. The collective representations of the 1970s and its happenings certainly made it seem so, and it was a somewhat self-regarding fortunate generation that framed those representations in its own teaching and writing. An Aristotelian demography of the discipline has been developed, a demography that talks of an all-important middle orbited by two small cohorts. A man in his mid-forties portrayed it thus:

> There is a small number of people older than me—well established political figures—but not very many—then there is a large wodge of people running from I suppose 35 to 50—and then there are people younger than that—I'm not aware of [those younger people] producing things that I think are really important bits of work, good stuff.

And a younger criminologist, a woman of 30, just about to embark on her own academic career, saw little of the small, older generation,[10] but she did mark the mass of middle-aged criminologists before her:

> The difficulty is that for somebody in my position there are so many heavyweights in the field who have been writing for so long that actually, it's very difficult for us to innovate in that way. You know the kind of exciting world that you were part of in the late sixties and early seventies allowed you to do something that's not possible for us to do. And I think we all feel rather cowed by the heavyweights.

The older generation itself, the generation that had existed before the Big Bang, had not had to contend at an impressionable age with the headiness of the 1970s, had not been part of a volatile and somewhat self-congratulatory mass, and had indeed sometimes formed the butt of that volatile mass. Above them was no visible and oppressively authoritative senior generation of supervisors and former supervisors armed with daunting ideas. Below them was a crowd of the young who could look a little undifferentiated, as all younger people do ('partly because I was always much older, you have this perception of people of fortyish and under, you don't discriminate very much . . .').

Theirs was a venerable criminology that had been practised long before the rise of interactionism,[11] feminism, and radicalism in Britain, the 'rather shallow theory which the criminologists had developed without sufficient awareness of philosophy, sociology, and psychology . . . There weren't any *really* intellectual criminologists, were there?' *They* did not describe the fortunate generation as 'heavyweights'. To the contrary: 'I've

[10] She was to ask: 'Are my generation too far removed from the pre- "Big Bangers" to recognize the importance of their work?'

[11] In the 1970s, one of the most senior of that senior generation told me firmly that symbolic interactionism was little more than a fad.

personally read X and Y [two of the "heavyweights" of the 1970s], but you see it's not just good enough is it? I mean, X's book, X doesn't deal with data properly and theoretically he is weak.' For them, the evolution of criminology did not appear to have been so dramatically shaken by the actions of a single group. Neither was that evolution discontinuous. A retired man remarked:

> It is all rather a seamless web of development and really what happened is a natural consequence of developments in universities and in the way we look at subjects . . . A few years ago, the period of the radical schools of criminology, there was more tension than there is today. I suppose the 1965 student trouble led to a radical reappraisal of all subjects and then crime, criminal law, criminology took its place in the analysis. But that is matured into a much more rounded view of crime and its consequences which you find today and I don't think there is this division.

Of our sample of criminologists, 71 per cent began work by teaching in universities; 16 per cent in polytechnics or colleges of higher education; 6 per cent in designated criminology research centres; and 6 per cent in the Home Office Research and Planning Unit. It is not surprising that the first degree conferred on criminologists tended to shape the choice of academic department in which they first worked: 46 per cent of the sociology graduates were to be found in sociology departments and 79 per cent of the lawyers in law departments. Many criminologists started in departments of law (twenty-six had done so, 25 per cent of the whole) or departments of sociology (again, twenty-six or 25 per cent). And there was a modest tendency for them to remain in the departments in which they had studied as graduates (22 per cent did so), confirming patronage and reproducing tradition. They were quite distinctively sociologists or lawyers at first.

That was to change a little over time: those working in departments of law have now come numerically to dominate the discipline, reflecting a more general drift among undergraduates towards the study of law.[12] Of the criminologists in the 1992 survey, 36 per cent (and 32 per cent of the non-respondents) may be found in departments of law, 19 per cent (and 18 per cent of the non-respondents) in departments of sociology, 2 per cent (and 15 per cent) in designated research centres,[13] 9 per cent (and 15 per cent) in social science departments and 7 per cent (and 8 per cent) in the Home Office Research and Planning Unit. Law departments are now recruiting criminologists with a wider range of qualifications, drawing them from sociology, psychology, social administration, and government—criminologists who could be said to be sailing under flags of con-

[12] There were 1398 home undergraduate students reading sociology in 1980, 1061 in 1991 (a decline of 24%). 3435 home students were accepted to read law in 1980, 4044 in 1991 (an increase of 18%). See successive reports by The University Central Council on Admissions, Cheltenham.

[13] This relatively large disparity reflected the tendency I have reported for those in large centres not to reply to the survey.

venience. That, and the broader intellectual pattern and style of recruitment of criminologists, can create multiple, crosscutting affiliations and identities. A young woman, trained in history and teaching criminology in a law department, asked: 'Do those in sociology departments think of themselves as criminologists or sociologists, likewise do those in law departments or with legal training call themselves lawyers? Or are criminologists simply more likely to wear different hats according to the occasion? I know *I* juggle "criminologist", "historian", and "lawyer".'

WOMEN IN CRIMINOLOGY

Above all, it was women who moved towards law departments. In part, their migration may be linked with a major diaspora from the Oxford Centre for Criminological Research at the end of the 1980s. This diaspora fed law departments at Brunel University, the LSE, King's College London, University College London, and the University of Sheffield. While five women criminologists had started their careers in law departments, eleven were to be found there by 1992, half of all the women in the survey.

Overall, women criminologists were outnumbered by men four to one (there were eighty-four males and twenty-two females in the survey), as they are in British higher education at large (see Universities' Statistical Record 1991: table 29). They had come to the field later than their male counterparts, 55 per cent having been recruited after 1980 compared with 25 per cent of the men, and they were correspondingly younger. Their average age was 42 (that of the men being 46); 41 per cent of them were under 40 (compared with 27 per cent of men).

Criminology has been affected by the manner in which those men and women have been distributed about the field. Feminists have maintained for some while that knowledge is sexually grounded, that men and women do not see the world alike, and that a criminology practised by males cannot be the same as that practised by females. They hold that being a woman or man now has implications for the theory and practice of criminology.

Gender certainly affected work and interests. One young woman reflected of a dissertation she had prepared as an undergraduate: 'I was looking at female delinquency as a young woman. What motivated me at that time was [anger] . . . it was an area that had been neglected and . . . women [were] treated in very stereotypical ways . . . that's what made me angry.' It marked the selection of themes for graduate research, male and female criminologists tending to study rather different problems as graduates. None of the males who had advanced to a second degree claimed specifically to have examined a problem affecting women, while 33 per cent of the women had done so, and it was the younger women, 40 per cent of those under 40, who had done so in disproportionately large numbers.

The study of women started as something of a woman's preserve in graduate work and it has remained so into current research. The survey found a continuing divide between those who studied women and those who did not. None of the men criminologists claimed in their current research to be working on the particular problems of women, while 14 per cent of the women criminologists did so.

Five of the twenty-two women in the survey described themselves as feminist, four being members of the nine-strong group aged 41–50. Neither of the two women older than 50 was a professed feminist; one remarked 'I was aware of the feminist school coming up and I read all those books . . . but I never actually found that very interesting, which may have something to do with my age. I'm 60 now . . . The questions that grabbed the feminists always seemed to be rather marginal questions.' And only one of the ten-strong group of younger women criminologists under 40 was avowedly feminist. There are undoubtedly some younger women who would assert that there is a contradiction between the projects of feminism and criminology, just as, in its heyday, some exponents of a totalizing Marxism denied criminology any pretensions to intellectual autonomy (see Hirst 1975).[14] There are other young women who find feminism to be confining; one observed that '[feminists] hardly ever refer to the rest of the literature . . . there is very little attempt to understand what's going on in the rest of the discipline, and we live in a society where there are men *and* women and it's too simplistic to chop off one section of the community and say I'm going to address *those* issues'.[15]

There were only two feminist men, but that is hardly remarkable. Feminism is predominantly a woman's pursuit, and male feminists are perhaps ontologically somewhat problematic. As one middle-aged man said: 'They have got you on both levels, haven't they? If you don't talk about problems with women, you're sexist, and if you do talk about it, you don't really have the right to do it *and* you're bound to do it wrong.' Feminism seems to be a position to which a great many men cannot wholly adhere. One man said:

> I think that we've restored the balance to some extent, the work that has been done on female crime which was no doubt neglected . . . I think the danger is that they overemphasized the feminist aspect and are in danger of distortion because there are male victims of sexual crime as we are now discovering . . . I

[14] One young woman said: 'Many . . . believe that feminism is more important than being appendages to a male criminology. They have a more explicit political agenda.'

[15] The small scale of express feminism disclosed here is perhaps another product of such a small survey. It certainly does not square with the very obvious productivity of feminist criminology and the stir that it is creating. My own impression is that feminism is more significant than the survey would have one think.

don't think it has yet reached the mature point of being a well-rounded critique and one waits and prays for the day when it will be restated for us in some kind of balanced way.

Faults in the line of succession have interfered with the smooth transmission and expansion of feminism. There was such a preponderance of men in the survey, and so middle-aged were they, that, in the main, criminology has passed from man to man; more rarely, from man to woman; and more rarely still, from woman to man. In only two instances did women criminologists report having had women supervisors, and that must have had consequences for the reproduction and elaboration of a world-view that is supposed ineluctably to be embedded in the very experience of gender. There was thus a Mendelian problem.

CHANGING RELATIONS AMONG CRIMINOLOGISTS

British criminologists are scattered throughout forty-three universities and twenty-one of the former polytechnics and colleges of higher education.[16] There are some important clusters: for example, twelve or 6 per cent of academic criminologists are to be found at the LSE; nine at the University of Sheffield; eight at the University of Wales; seven at Cambridge; and six at Manchester University. There is a gigantic concentration in the Home Office Research and Planning Unit. But most are to be found working in groups of a moderate size. Exactly 60 per cent of those with posts in higher education have no more than four criminologists as colleagues, and 26 per cent work either alone or with one other criminologist colleague only. The 'typical' criminologist is a member of a small work group.

The social relations of criminology are correspondingly diffuse. They seem to be constructed pragmatically out of contacts forged when criminologists were students and, later, with those who are usefully at hand as colleagues. In this sense, criminologists occupy institutionally defined neighbourhoods and it is neighbours who are their prime significant others, not a group of more remote sociometric stars. One helpful measure of the spread and organization of such relations is the frequency with which particular people claim to approach one another about intellectual problems and drafts of work. Routine discussion about those matters is the stuff of an academic discipline. Criminologists consult one another in dyads[17] and triads rather than advancing on just a few individuals with great piles of paper. Only seventeen of the eighty-seven

[16] This section is based on the addresses of the total population sampled rather than information contained in the replies received.

[17] Eighty per cent of names given were solitary choices.

named recipients of papers (19.5 per cent) were cited more than once, and only seven (5 per cent of the total) were cited more than twice. Criminologists consult colleagues in the same institution (in 27 per cent of the citations) and outside (in 73 per cent). But it is only when they are concentrated in groups of four or more that a critical mass seems to form and they begin to consult among themselves, preparing the structure of an internal net; in other cases, they go outside their institution for advice and support.

External nets of relations are forged out of the formal encounters that any academic will have experienced during a career: former research students consult their supervisors and, less often, their external examiners; former colleagues and fellow students maintain contact with one another, keeping old intra-mural networks alive (the dispersed members of the Oxford Centre for Criminological Research still confer, for instance); and criminologists communicate within networks defined by field and persuasion, radical speaking to radical and police specialist to police specialist across the boundaries of organizations.

Much the same pattern could be discerned in the claims criminologists made about the identity of those scholars, living and dead, domestic and foreign, who had influenced them intellectually. A total of 132 men and women of influence were so named: they included Thomas Luckmann and Karl Marx, Alvin Gouldner and Antonio Gramsci, Shoham Mednick and Thomas Mathiesen. Chief of them all was Robert Reiner, who was cited by ten criminologists; next was Michel Foucault with seven citations; Stan Cohen, Jock Young, and myself with six (together with the nomination of Reiner, a very gratifying artefact of the survey process); Tony Bottoms with five; Howard Becker, Stuart Hall, and Karl Marx with four; and Andrew Ashworth and Roger Hood with three. But what should be noted is that ninety-four names, 71 per cent of the total, were given just once, suggesting that influence was again dyadic, scattered, and local rather than massed in just a few dominant individuals. Just as in the other branches of what have been called the 'softer' disciplines, the social circles of criminology tend to be small (see Becher 1989: 67), loose, and open (see Crane 1969: 348).

British criminologists profess allegiance to a great abundance of theoretical schools that were founded in the 1960s and 1970s when they or their mentors were young. Echoes of the Big Bang continue to reverberate around the discipline: two criminologists in the survey called themselves discourse analysts; six were unabashed empiricists and two were male positivists; three (all under 50) followed the relatively recent Foucault; seven men and one woman said they were Marxists, and three claimed to be Weberians. There were two phenomenologists, two pragmatists, and two rationalists. However, it was symbolic interactionism and labelling theory, the old progenitors of the sociology of deviance, that still bulked large. Fifteen per cent of criminologists (fifteen men and two women) called themselves interactionist. No other grouping was as substantial. And seven of those fifteen were members of the youngest group, of men and women under 40. The voice of the Society for the Study of Social Problems and the National Deviancy Conference, of Lemert, Becker, and Matza, could still be heard in the 1990s.

Writings now considered important to the discipline also echo the Big Bang. They are eclectic, theoretical, critical, and declaratory, for the most part vehicles of the originating big ideas of the 1960s and 1970s, the hot matter that fed the intellectual explosion of British criminology. The interactionist manifesto, *Outsiders* (Becker 1963), was named most frequently as the publication that had had the greatest influence on them (receiving twenty nominations); it was followed by Taylor, Walton, and Young's radical manifesto, *The New Criminology*, published in 1973 (nineteen nominations); Foucault's structuralist *Discipline and Punish* of 1977 (twelve nominations); Garland's neo-Durkheimian, revisionist *Punishment and Modern Society* of 1990 (seven nominations); Carol Smart's feminist manifesto, *Women, Crime and Criminology*, of 1977 (seven nominations); Stan Cohen's *Visions of Social Control* of 1985 (six nominations), and David Matza's anti-positivist manifesto, *Delinquency and Drift*, published in 1964 (six nominations).

British criminologists are quite generous in acknowledging the significance of works whose arguments they may not necessarily support, and their approbation is both catholic and diffuse. There are no clear claques of radicals praising only radicalism or phenomenologists phenomenology. Thus feminists named *Outsiders* more frequently than they did *Women, Crime and Criminology*; and the interactionists were the largest single group to cite *The New Criminology*, the book that had dismissed them as naïve constructionists unable to recognize brute social reality (although they did so in part because of their sheer numbers, being the most sizeable group in the survey).

Approbation is affected by generation. The paradigm-breaking works of the 1960s and 1970s had not impressed the criminologists older than 50. The older generation had not been fired by the *grands événements* of those times. The 1960s had not been their times at all. *They* pointed to the works of their own and earlier generations, the books of Nigel Walker, Cesare Beccaria, Robert Merton, and Edwin Sutherland. However, the fortunate generation, now middle-aged, overwhelmingly cited the two books that had made them: *Outsiders* (31 per cent of the choices made by that group) and *The New Criminology* (22 per cent). They did so in much greater numbers than the younger criminologists, who gave only 8 per cent and 10 per cent of their choices to those works.

The young plumped rather for Foucault's *Discipline and Punish* (13 per cent of their choices were so made, compared with 5 per cent of those made by the middle-aged.)

It may be conjectured that the dispersal of criminologists, the attenuation of social relations, and the decentralization of theorizing are aspects of a single process. After the Big Bang of the late 1960s and the 1970s, criminological encounters have become more diffuse, infrequent, and cool. There no longer appears to be quite so much excited confrontation and disputation, nor so many meetings and debates, manifestos and counter-manifestos, criticisms and replies, and that is again a familiar phase in the evolution of a discipline (see Crane 1972: 37). Much of the theoretical argument that could have taken place within a small group, a group whose members know each other quite closely, *will* have taken place after the first few years. Controversy can begin to look threadbare and otiose ('you can't necessarily go on having intense theoretical debates all the time and I'm always suspicious of the big ideas,' said a man in his fifties). Intellectual innovation can begin to slow down ('it's difficult to see now anything very urgent going on theoretically . . . that's partly because a whole lot of theoretical options were explored, by no means exhaustively, in the sixties and seventies . . . to have a decade following, a decade of relative quiescence theoretically in which an awful lot of empirical work was going on on important policy and practical issues, I don't see that as a bad thing after two or three decades of intense theoretical debate'). And, at a time when a sense of collective excitement has begun to decline, when debates have petered out and criminological work has become more routine, members of the fortunate generation declare that they no longer find themselves convening and conversing so often: 'I don't seem to meet people as much as I used to . . . I always enjoy it and find it really quite odd that we don't meet as much.'

Paradoxically, too, the withering away of controversy has reduced intellectual, social, and symbolic distance. British criminologists are no longer incessantly at one another's throats. In the heady days of the Big Bang, intellectual fissures were magnified by a phenomenology of naming that separated, objectified, and essentialized the little schools that constituted (or were alleged to constitute) the discipline in Britain. It was as if scholars were possessed by a demonic urge to define, classify, reify, and master one another (see Caplow and McGee 1958: 87–8). Once they had tagged a rival, they went to extraordinary lengths to draw back and avoid being heard or seen ever to use his or her vocabulary. Words became magical. (Symbolic interactionists eschewed the term 'cause' and had little liking for 'social structure'. Functionalists did not talk about 'definitions of the situation'. Feminists had no love for 'victim precipitation'. Marxists did not care for 'consensus'.) There was an exaggeration of distance and distinction that brought about what Becher (1989: 22–3) described as 'tribalism'.

Levelling a charge of 'positivism',[18] 'scientism', or 'correctionalism' (see Matza 1969), for instance, used to be tantamount to an act of outcasting in some criminological circles. One middle-aged radical criminologist remembered how his intellectual development had been shaped by the need vigourously to confront the problem of 'positivism, there was entrenched positivism in the subject, Cambridge, the Home Office . . .'. And those charges of positivism, reaction, and empiricism stuck. A middle-aged Home Office researcher recollected how 'we carried this burden of guilt about the empirical requirements that we laboured under, rather than being more confident that empirical research was a valuable thing'. A colleague reflected that 'I was aware of a perception of the Unit—roughly what it felt like in those early years, in the seventies and early eighties, was that the Office was perceived as right-wing, Weberian, bureaucrats, [the] new administrative criminology,[19] and that . . . everybody outside was sort of libertarian . . . interested truly in freedom. And I thought this was just a very naïve conceptualization, sort of silly really.'

Perhaps what was principally at stake was the manufacture of a firm symbolic environment that could serve political and definitional purposes at a time of theoretical ferment. The criminological landscape was given artificially sharp contours and boundaries to confirm intellectual identities. A middle-aged academic criminologist argued:

> What struck me was that there was this attack on establishment criminology . . . and you got the impression that this was a really solid, strong, long-standing institution of great power and yet, if you think about it, it was really . . . vestigal. This establishment was virtually non-existent in so far as it was totally embryonic—the Cambridge Institute that only got started in the late fifties and the Home Office Research Unit which goes back to the mid-fifties or so. The establishment was hardly entrenched.

The age of the conflictual validation of self and position seems to have passed. The Big Bang has dissipated and British criminology is now much quieter and calmer, its structures having undergone a form of entropy:

> I think between those who were widely regarded as radical criminologists and those who were regarded as non-radical or whatever, there was a real divide. I

[18] Percy Cohen once observed that the use of intellectual classification can be as much denunciatory as expository. Being called a positivist, he declared, was not much different from being declared a fascist beast (see Cohen 1980). Jennifer Platt once searched for positivism in the pages of sociology and could find very little trace of it. Positivism, she thought, played little more than a demonological role in the myth-making of academic politics (see Platt 1981). It must, however, be said that positivism did have a more robust presence in criminology than in sociology. See, for instance, the importance which Hermann Mannheim assigned it in his introduction to *Pioneers in Criminology* (Mannheim 1960).

[19] 'Administrative criminology' is a term conventionally held to have been invented by Jock Young in the 1970s.

think the radical criminologists had a very strong network . . . but that is no longer so marked. With feminist criminologists, or just female criminologists—because some female criminologists reject the term or label 'feminist'—again, I wouldn't have thought there was such a tremendous separation.

One of the most formidable of the radical pugilists of the 1970s reflected that 'there is a sort of social democratic consensus, among the positivists as well. I don't think there is political dispute . . .' and a senior Home Office criminologist, a target of those earlier attacks, said 'it's finished. I think it's seen now as one community, don't you?'

British criminology certainly has no clear political markings now,[20] and it is not distinctively activist. The largest single group of all, thirty of the eighty-four men and thirteen of the twenty-two women, professed to practise their criminology outside any overriding political, religious, or moral frame. Theirs is not an overwhelmingly politicized or idealistic calling at all, although it is certainly prompted by humanistic and reforming aspirations. Elaine Player argued that 'many criminologists who have engaged in empirical work conceive of their findings in relation to a commitment to certain ideals, e.g. . . . to natural justice, racial equality, humane prisons etc., which are clearly political but not necessarily viewed as "political" or "moral" in a grand theory sense'.

Disinterestedness grows with age or changes with generation. A quarter of the twenty-eight younger men and 41 per cent of the forty-four middle-aged men between 41 and 50 were so detached. The more politically committed tended to call themselves by different labels of the left—there were twenty-two men and five women socialists (four 'left idealist' men, three between 41 and 50, and one elderly 'left idealist' woman; two 'left realist' men; three younger Marxist men and one younger Marxist woman; three middle-aged anarchist men; two feminist men and five feminist women). Nine criminologists were liberals and six Christians. No one claimed allegiance to Conservatism or to positions further to the right. A criminologist reflected that 'there is no conservative criminology' and a colleague concurred: 'The absence of a really, what you might call a redneck criminology, the absence of that in England is very important.'

If the fortunate generation has settled down and become less bellicose, it has been the lot of the generation that follows after, the young men and women appointed in the later 1980s and early 1990s, to find themselves not yet organized, massive, and confident enough to supply their own theories, politics, institutions, and meeting-places: 'You need to have a kind of critical mass of people around to discuss and exchange ideas with and so on, and it takes time, and we seem to live in this world now

[20] Of course, it may never have done so.

where everything is happening at such a rapid pace [that] it's not allowing us to do that . . .'

Criminologists now appear generally to be spread more widely apart, congregating in small working groups, existing in what looks like relative amity, tolerating dissent and diversity, no longer fulminating at every heresy, and joined together in a few major organizations. Forty per cent were members of the British Society of Criminology; 16 per cent were members of the British Sociological Association and 17 per cent of the Society of Public Teachers of Law, the associations of two big constitutive disciplines of criminology itself. No other associations bulked large, although 11 per cent were members of the Howard League and a few were members of the Institute for the Study and Treatment of Delinquency (8 per cent) and of NACRO (4 per cent). There was a common subscription to journals: 60 per cent read the *British Journal of Criminology*, 33 per cent the *Howard Journal*, and 21 per cent the *Criminal Law Review*.

THE EXHAUSTION OF THEORY?

In 'The Present State of British Criminology' (Rock 1988) I surmised that the criminological mind has sensed the exhaustion of theory and turned to the practical and the empirical. There has been much to push it towards engagement. A younger criminologist said: 'Theoretical criminology is dying a death amongst the younger generation and that's a terrible shame, and the reason it's dying a death is because of the way research is funded and the pressure that's being put . . . on the universities and polytechnics to do things in a particular way . . .' One of the discipline's patrons, the Economic and Social Research Council, has placed ever greater stress on the concrete and the policy-driven, only recently reversing the trend somewhat with the funding of a major initiative on the more theoretical theme of 'crime and modernity'. Another patron, the Home Office, quite inevitably and properly interested in 'policy-relevant research',[21] has loomed ever larger as it shapes questions, methods, and data. And criminological theorizing has itself been transformed by the brutal facts of riots and urban disorder, by the general victimization revealed in crime surveys and the particular victimization of women,

[21] One of the major figures in establishing the working tradition of the Home Office Research and Planning Unit wrote about 'formulating a programme of research in criminal justice, a programme designed for and applied to the requirements of those responsible for running the system . . .' (Croft 1978: 4). That emphasis remained fourteen-years later; in 1992 the Research and Statistics Department was described as 'an integral part of the Home Office, serving the Ministers and the department itself, its services, Parliament and the public through research, development and statistics'. See Home Office 1992: i.

publicized by feminism. Crime now looks more sober, abundant, and distressing than before, its sheer scale robbing those who would cry 'reformism' and 'correctionalism' of some of their power. And once such an intellectual dialectic begins, it tends to continue. The empirical has begun to *look* more interesting, exciting new questions and new lines of enquiry.

Current criminological research is monopolized, as graduate research was monopolized, by an interest in the institutions of law enforcement. Forty-eight per cent of criminologists claimed to be working on such institutions, dwarfing the rest. Another 10 per cent claimed an interest in 'theory' and another 10 per cent in crimes and criminals. A few of the more elderly men (4 per cent of the total) were working on the mentally disordered offender, and a few of the younger men and women (5 per cent of the total, all under 50) had become interested in victims. Those pursuits accounted for most of the work in progress.

Theoretical criminology may no longer seethe and flow but it is what British criminologists continue to teach. Variously called criminology and the sociology of deviance, it looms over all else. Over half the courses offered were so labelled and, in the main, they survey the accomplishments of the past. Thus the 'Theorizing about Crime' course, taught as part of one established MA in criminology, 'provides a basic overview of the development of criminological theory from its emergence in early 19th- century Europe, through its period of expansion in the first half of the 20th century . . . up to its present state of consolidation and diversification'. Other courses tend to be on aspects of criminology as they find expression in and around the teaching of law, and they are given a proliferation of names: jurisprudence; the English legal system; criminal justice; penology, crime, and penal policy; crime and sanctioning; and the like, totalling 31 per cent of the whole. It may be ventured that such a pattern again reveals traces of the Big Bang when contemporary criminology was born in and around theoretical argument, and theory is certainly the most general and obvious of all possible introductions to the discipline. I had originally speculated that the pattern would have been affected by the division of labour, criminologists being so scattered that, outside the few larger centres, there could be relatively little scope for the teaching of the more recondite and specialist subjects within the field. But theory is taught both by the solitary criminologist and by the criminologist with abundant colleagues. It is what criminologists *choose* principally to teach. Perhaps, even more importantly, and as Lucia Zedner has reminded me, it is what they inherited from the 1970s when their discipline was institutionalized in the universities.

CONCLUSION

Contemporary British criminology is laid out wide although there are a few large concentrations (particularly in the Universities of London, Sheffield, Oxford, and Cambridge) which attract, train, and channel recruits. Its cement is supplied in part by profuse webs of dyadic and triadic relations that mediate knowledge and social organization. What gave it special character was its birth in the intellectually volatile decade of the 1970s, a decade when most criminologists were recruited and educated. Almost all the books and theories which it celebrates now are those which were celebrated then, the symbolic interactionism, Marxism, and structuralism which the middle-aged first read twenty to thirty years ago. Criminology is a masculine discipline, and the other big idea of the 1970s, feminism, has not spread very far within it. But, in any event, and despite its nostalgia for the theoretical, it is no longer a discipline besotted with the idea of big ideas. There is instead what Reiner calls an 'underlying strain':

> What was once a social divide between groups seems to have become a personally internalized divide, a schizophrenia, between personal interest and commitment to 'Big Bang' and intellectual/theoretical approaches, expressed by teaching these things as the core, and the externally derived (funding-based) pressure to do policy-oriented, managerial criminal justice research and courses.

Selected Further Reading

S. Cohen, ed., *Images of Deviance*. London: Penguin, 1971.

F. Heidensohn, 'The Deviance of Women', *British Journal of Sociology*, June 1968.

P. Rock, ed., *A History of British Criminology*. Oxford: Oxford University Press, 1988.

P. Rock and M. McIntosh, eds., *Deviance and Social Control*. London: Tavistock, 1974.

C. Smart, *Women, Crime and Criminology*. London: Routledge and Kegan Paul, 1977.

I. Taylor, P. Walton, and J. Young, *The New Criminology*. London: Routledge and Kegan Paul, 1973.

REFERENCES

Becker, H. (1963), *Outsiders*. Glencoe, Ill.: Free Press.

—— (1984), *Art Worlds*. Berkeley: University of California Press, 1984.

Becher, T. (1989), *Academic Tribes and Territories*. Milton Keynes: Open University Press.

Caplow, T., and McGee, R. (1958), *The Academic Marketplace*. New York: Basic Books.

Cohen, P. (1980), 'Is Positivism Dead?', *Sociological Review*, 28/1: 141–76.

Cohen, S. (1971), *Images of Deviance*. Harmondsworth: Penguin.

Crane, D. (1969), 'Social Structure in a Group of Scientisits: A Test of the "Invisible College" Hypothesis', *American Sociological Review*, 34/3: 335–52.

—— (1972), *Invisible Colleges: Diffusion of Knowledge in Scientific Communities*. Chicago: University of Chicago Press.

Croft, J. (1978), *Research in Criminal Justice*. London: HMSO.

ESRC (1990), *Report for the Year Ending 31 March 1990*. Swindon: Economic and Social Research Council, 1990.

Foucault, M. (1977), *Discipline and Punish*. London: Allen Lane.

Garland, D. (1990), *Punishment and Modern Society*. Oxford: Clarendon Press.

Geertz, C. (1983), *Local Knowledge*. New York: Basic Books.

Halsey, A. (1992), *Decline of Donnish Dominion*. Oxford: Clarendon Press.

Hirst, P. (1975), 'Marx and Engels on Law, Crime and Morality', in I. Taylor, P. Walton, and J. Young, eds., *Critical Criminology*. London: Routledge and Kegan Paul.

Home Office (1992), *Research Bulletin*, Home Office Research and Statistics Department. London: Home Office.

King, A., and Brownell, J. (1966), *The Curriculum and the Disciplines of Knowledge*. New York: Wiley.

Mannheim, H. (1960), *Pioneers in Criminology*. London: Stevens.

Mannheim, K. (1952), 'The Problem of Generations', in *Essays on the Sociology of Knowledge*. London: Routledge and Kegan Paul.

Matza, D. (1969), *Becoming Deviant*. Englewood Cliffs, NJ: Prentice-Hall.

Morris, T. (1989), *Crime and Criminal Justice since 1945*. Oxford: Blackwell.

Platt, J. (1981), 'The Social Construction of "Positivism" and its Significance in British Sociology', in P. Abrams *et al.*, eds., *Practice and Progress*. London: Allen and Unwin.

Rock, P. (1988), 'The Present State of British Criminology', *British Journal of Criminology*, 28/2: 188–99.

Smart, C. (1977), *Women, Crime and Criminology*, London: Routledge and Kegan Paul.

Taylor, I., Walton, P., and Young, J. (1973), *The New Criminology*. London: Routledge and Kegan Paul.

Universities' Statistical Record (1991), *University Statistics 1989–90*. Cheltenham: Universities' Statistical Record.

Whitley, R. (1969), 'Communication Nets in Science: Patterns in Animal Physiology', *Sociological Review* 17/2: 219–33.

Young, A. (1991), 'Feminism and the Body of Criminology', unpublished paper delivered to the British Criminology Conference.

4

The History of Crime and Crime Control Institutions, c.*1770*–c.*1945*

CLIVE EMSLEY

Until the 1970s historians discussing developments in the area of crime control institutions in Britain tended to take a perspective formulated in terms of Whig notions of progress and drawing on a positivist approach to crime and criminals. Crime tended to be seen as an absolute: it was largely understood to mean theft and, to a lesser extent, violence; and as something perpetrated by 'criminals' on the law-abiding majority of the population. Improvements in the control mechanisms had been brought about by a progressive humanitarianism and the sensible, rational responses of reformers to abuses and inefficiencies. Since the 1970s these perspectives and interpretations have been subjected to critical examination by a new generation of social historians. Initially these historians began to work on court records in the hope of penetrating the lives of the poor and socially disadvantaged; they tended to concentrate on periods of social and economic upheaval such as the late sixteenth and early seventeenth centuries, or the years of industrialization and urbanization in the late eighteenth and early nineteenth centuries. They acknowledged that crime is something defined by the law, and that the law was changed and shaped by human institutions; they sought to relate crime and the control of crime to economic and social changes taking place in the country.

This chapter seeks to provide a synthesis of recent research into the history of crime and crime control in Britain from the late eighteenth century until the end of the Second World War. The period constitutes a long but nevertheless coherent unit, beginning with significant calls for reform in the system of punishment and for improvements in the policing of the metropolis, and ending with police and prisons poised for the major reorganizations of the 1960s and with crime beginning its dramatic post-Second World War increase. The chapter begins with an assessment of the scale of crime across the period, followed by a discussion of the changes in the way in which crime and the offender were perceived and understood by contemporaries and by subsequent historians. The focus then shifts to the solutions developed in response to these problems. A discussion of the origins of the police and their subsequent development is followed by a survey of the changes in the courts and the system of prosecution. The final main section explores the different means deployed to remove offenders from society and to punish and/or reform them.

Of necessity, given the research which has been done, the main focus of this chapter is on England and Wales; unfortunately, as yet, there has been little detailed research into developments within the independent Scottish legal system, while much of the work on Irish 'crime' has tended to concentrate on its manifestations within English cities.

THE EXTENT OF CRIME

Acknowledging that a crime is an action defined by the law, and one which, if detected, will lead to some kind of sanction being employed against the perpetrator, enables the historian to draw some conclusions about a society's priorities and its attitudes towards social groups, individuals, and property. But the problem which commonly affects contemporaries, and which has much vexed the new generation of historians of crime, is estimating the scale of crime. There are no official statistics for crime in England before 1805. Historians of the eighteenth century and earlier have sought to construct figures from court records, particularly the indictment membranes for assizes and quarter sessions. Recognizing that such figures cannot give any precise picture of the incidence of crime, it has nevertheless been forcefully argued that they can give an idea of the pattern. In 1810 the government decided to start collecting criminal statistics annually; the first collection went back to 1805, but in the early years the statistics registered only committals. The system was refined during the first half of the nineteenth century, notably in 1834 with the classification of offences into six main types:

1. offences against the person (ranging from homicide to assault);
2. offences against property involving violence (robbery, burglary);
3. offences against property without violence;
4. malicious offences against property (arson, machine-breaking, etc.);
5. offences against the currency;
6. miscellaneous offences (including riot, sedition, and treason).

Twenty-two years later an appendage to the County and Borough Police Act 1856 established the tripartite division of:

1. indictable offences reported to the police;
2. committals for trial, both on indictment and before summary jurisdiction;

3. the number of persons convicted and imprisoned.

There has been considerable debate over the value of all of these different forms of statistics for historians. J. J. Tobias and Rob Sindall have both maintained that because we cannot be sure why crimes were reported and prosecuted, and because of variations in recording practices across police jurisdictions, the figures are worthless for the purpose of serious historical analysis (Tobias 1972*a*: 18–25; Sindall 1990: 16–28). Others, notably John Beattie, V. A. C. Gatrell, and David Philips, have insisted that careful use of the figures can permit the construction of useful hypothetical graphs for the pattern of crime, and also enable conclusions to be drawn about the nature of crime and perceptions of criminality (Beattie 1981; Gatrell 1980; Philips 1977). The kind of graph which emerges from the statistical studies for the period under review shows a steady increase in crime, particularly property crime, in the late eighteenth century, becoming much sharper from the first decade of the nineteenth century until about 1850, when the pattern levels out—except, most noticeably, for the offence of burglary. After the First World War a steady, accelerating increase began again; it momentarily checked during the Second World War and the following decade, but then began to rise sharply once more.

This pattern tends to make sense when deployed alongside other social data. The eighteenth-century increase coincides with major shifts in the economy, with population increase, and with growing fears for the social order; the acceleration in the first part of the nineteenth century corresponds with the aggravation of these problems and new concerns generated by the example of the French Revolution and by the seemingly uncontrollable squalor of the new industrial cities. The question must remain as to whether these problems themselves caused more crime, or whether they simply made people more sensitive to offences and prompted them to report and/or prosecute more readily any crimes committed against them. The steady plateau of the second half of the nineteenth century coincides with what one historian dubbed the Victorian 'age of equipoise' (Burn 1964); it was a period of confidence and faith in both the future and the idea of progress. Moreover, the growth of international markets and reductions in the price of food meant that problems in the home market were generally less acute for both employers and employees than in the earlier years of the century; the coincidence of large-scale unemployment with high prices and food shortages became far less likely in the second half of the century and so, in consequence, did the necessity of stealing to survive. Burglary was one of the few offences which did not follow the general pattern in the second half of the nineteenth century; but the greater incidence of burglary itself may, in large measure, be a reflection of greater prosperity and the fact that ordinary people had more possessions in their homes. Both world wars witnessed a slight reduction of crime in the judicial statistics; this could be explained by the fact that the police had a myriad of other tasks with which to contend and therefore relegated ordinary crime to a lower place on their list of priorities; but it should also be noted that the needs of war shifted many of the young men often prone to committing criminal offences out of the country and subjected many of those who remained to new and stricter forms of control through the military. The steady increase of crime during the inter-war period might arguably reflect both the difficulties generated by the Depression and the temptations offered by the first inklings of a consumer society; it was during the inter-war years that motor vehicle ownership began to be widespread, and that concerns started to be expressed about the way in which motor vehicle offences were congesting the magistrates' courts.

But even if the statistical pattern makes some sense viewed against one set of social criteria, caution nevertheless remains necessary. The late eighteenth and early nineteenth centuries, which witnessed a marked increase in recorded crime, were also the key period of Britain's developments into an urbanized society with an economy rooted in industrial capitalism. Most contemporaries believed that the burgeoning towns were much more prone to crime than the countryside; however, the evidence for this is difficult to come by. Of course, there were different opportunities for theft in the towns and the goods stolen could be very different between town and country; but John Glyde's study of crime in mid-nineteenth-century Suffolk concluded that while one-third of the county's inhabitants were urban dwellers they were responsible for only about a fifth of the crime (Glyde 1856*a*: 146–7; 1856*b*: 102–6). The interrelationship between the growth of property crime and the growth of capitalism was a popular area of analysis for the first serious historians of crime and it has been restated with particular verve by Peter Linebaugh (1991). The work of these historians concentrated on thefts by poor men who were seen as resisting capitalism by their actions; but most of the studies of the 'perks' taken by workers from the raw materials with which they did their work reveal that the situation was far more complex than a simple class-struggle model might suggest. There were times when the purchaser, rather than the employer, was the victim of workplace fraud, and while the employer might, in such circumstances, have had some concern for the reputation of his business, this can scarcely be construed as an aspect of the struggle between capital and labour. It is possible that many workers preferred the steady wage which they earned under the capitalist system to a more traditional form of payment part in kind and part in wage; the continuing appropriation of goods, even in capitalizing textile industries, therefore, is less clearly a protest against new systems of payment and conditions of work. Employers did not always prosecute the appropriation of 'perks'. There continued to be a variety of other sanctions which they could employ; and occasionally they even took perks and fiddles into account when calculating pay rates (Davis 1989; Emsley 1987: ch. 5; Randall 1990). Furthermore, any simple conclusion that economic hardship prompted the working class to crime is undermined by the fact that there does not appear to have been anything other than a steady growth of offending during the inter-war period, in spite of the acute depression in many of the largest and traditional centres of industrialization. A more profitable line of inquiry delineating an interrelationship between capitalism and crime has been the exploration of the enormous scale of business and financial fraud during the nineteenth and early twentieth centuries (Robb 1992).

Overall the statistics suggest that property crime was the most common form of offence. Court records reveal that most thefts involved objects of relatively little monetary value. In the Hanoverian and Victorian periods, in the towns, these stolen articles were often taken to a pawn shop, or the less salubrious 'dolly shop', and exchanged for a small amount of ready cash. Statistically, violence declined over the period. But the suggestion, largely based on figures for homicide, that there has been a general decline in interpersonal violence since the Tudor period has excited a lively debate (Cockburn 1991; Sharpe 1985; Stone 1983, 1985). From the late eighteenth century at least, a large number of victims appear to have known their assailants or to have been related to them in some way; the major exception here were police officers who, from the origins of the new police, represented a disproportionate number of assault victims (Gatrell 1980).

THE OFFENDER

Whatever the statistics suggest about the predominance of petty theft, it was violent crime which frightened people and which newspaper editors knew sold their papers and vicariously enthralled their readers. The newspapers could contribute significantly to periodic scares by the way in which they chose to emphasize particularly horrific crimes, either for the sake of sales or for some crusading legislative purpose. The image of Jack the Ripper is a good example of the former. There is no precise evidence that the appalling murders committed in Whitechapel towards the end of 1888 were all committed by the same individual; and while only the most pathetic women in one very small district of East London appear to have been at risk, the panic about the Ripper spread far and wide, both geographically and socially. The garotting panic of 1862 provides an example of the latter, being an episode during which the press, and particularly the influential *Times*, built on concerns about offenders released on licence under the ticket-of-leave system and manufactured a scare from a few street robberies to encourage the passage of legislation authorizing harsh penalties against violent members of the 'criminal class' (Sindall 1990). There has been no systematic survey of crime reporting in the press from the mid-eighteenth to the mid-twentieth centuries, but it is clear that even before the advent of cheap newspapers towards the end of the Victorian period, the reading public was being fed on cases of 'orrible murder and outrage perpetrated by members of a criminal class outside of, and at war with, society.

The idea of a criminal sub-group was not new. Vagrants and beggars were perceived in this way and consequently legislated against at least as far back as the Tudor and Stuart periods (Beier 1985). The members of the criminal class portrayed in the writings of those interested in crime from the mid-eighteenth to the mid-nineteenth century had much in common with the Tudor 'sturdy beggar': they would not do an honest day's work because they sought a life of luxury and ease (Fielding 1751: 169; Hanway 1772: 38; Colquhoun 1796: 33). Yet during the first half of the nineteenth century in particular, events led to a significant shift in perceptions of crime and criminality. The wars against Revolutionary and Napoleonic France had severely limited access to foreign grain markets at a time when a series of bad harvests had led to food shortages, with resulting outbreaks of popular disorder and the need to increase poor rates. At the same time, the wars forced the propertied to dig deeper into their pockets for war taxes demanded by the national government, as well as for increased poor rates to assist the wives and children of poor men serving in the armed forces. For a variety of reasons, the restoration of peace in 1815 did not bring an end to this escalation of poor rates. The new national crime statistics, the first decade of which coincided with the last decade of the wars, while they only demonstrated an increase in committals and prosecutions, were taken as proof positive of a serious increase in crime. During the eighteenth century a crime was an individual action which the law sought to penalize; but against the background of the new statistics and resentment at increasing poor rates—which a harsh reading of Malthusian theory deemed unnecessary—crime increasingly acquired a symbolic meaning as a kind of disease within society, and a new stress was put on the pathological nature of the offender. By the 1840s the offender had become a member of the 'dangerous classes' lurking in the urban rookeries and slums; by the early 1860s the term 'criminal classes' was rather more in vogue (Stevenson 1983: 32 n. 4).

Social commentators like Henry Mayhew and Angus Bethune Reach made forays into the rookeries of these so-called criminal classes. The stigmatizing label, however, says more about these commentators and their readers than about the social group that they were studying, the individuals who committed crimes, or their motivation. Those labelled as the criminal class were generally the poorest sections of the working class, who eked out their existence in the uncertain casual labour market. Given their hard lives, their poor living conditions and inadequate diets, it is not surprising that members of this criminal class often died young. With their poor diet and shabby clothing they also looked different from those in steady work; in particular, they looked different from members of the growing middle class. The intrepid social investigators emphasized these differences by categorizing and describing the criminal classes for their readers as if they were members of strange tribes in far-away lands (Emsley 1987: 59–62).

The criminal class portrayed by these commentators was essentially male. Statistically, the number of offences committed by women was always very much smaller than that of offences committed by men, though independent women living in towns appear to have been more criminal than their sisters in the country—possibly because of greater family support and male protection in the rural districts, and possibly also because of the uncertain labour situation for single women in the town (Beattie 1975). The female equivalent of the male criminal was the prostitute, who was seen, even by sympathetic observers, to enter her trade for the same kind of reasons that men became criminals, notably idleness and the love of luxury; only very low on the list of supposed motivations came the probable spur to most prostitution, namely poverty. In her gaudy clothes and with her effrontery in propositioning potential clients, the archetypal prostitute was the antithesis of the ideal of Victorian womanhood. She also seemed much easier to apprehend than many male criminals. The notorious Contagious Diseases Acts, passed in the middle of the nineteenth century in an attempt to reduce the incidence of venereal disease in the armed forces, assumed that prostitutes were readily detectable, but inadvertently made thousands of ordinary working-class women the victims of officious and suspicious policemen (McHugh 1980; Walkowitz 1980).

The levelling out of the crime statistics, which implied a degree of success in the mechanisms of crime control, social Darwinism, and the advent of social science, led to a changing perception of the criminal classes as the century wore on. Criminals might still be characterized as those who shunned hard work and enjoyed the vagrant life, but they were also increasingly understood as individuals who turned to crime because of mental and physical, as well as moral, degeneracy: defects generally passed on through heredity. 'The ideal criminal has marked peculiarities of character,' proclaimed Francis Galton:

> His conscience is almost deficient, his instincts are vicious, his power of self control is very weak and he usually detests continuous labour. The absence of self control is due to ungovernable temper, to passion or to mere imbecility . . . he has neither sympathy for others nor the sense of duty both of which lie at the base of conscience . . . their vagrant habits, their illegitimate unions and extreme untruthfulness are among the difficulties of the investigator. It is however easy to show that the criminal nature tends to be inherited. (Galton 1907: 42–3)

Crime ceased to be seen as the work of a semi-organized criminal or dangerous class, and more that of, on the one hand, a small core of hardened professionals, and on the other, a much larger group of socially and mentally inadequate individuals who generally indulged in petty offences. This perception led to increasingly careful categorization as experts differentiated between the young and the habitual offender, the necessitous and the incorrigible, the opportunist and the professional (Wiener 1990).

The judicial statistics commonly revealed a large number of young offenders. These were rarely portrayed as part of the criminal class; from the early nineteenth century at least, they were increasingly perceived as a group which needed to be protected, both from immoral and uncaring parents and from hardened recidivists in prisons. Once the problem was identified a variety of expedients were tried either to reform the juvenile offender (industrial schools and reformatories) or to offer healthy alternatives (youth clubs and organizations) and thus to prevent this type of offending (Gillis 1975; Margery 1978; May 1973).

Mayhew had categorized his criminals by their various crafts, sometimes taking the argot verb for a particular offence and transforming it into a noun (Emsley 1987: 62). The garotting panic led some to assume that street robbers were professionals who specialized in a particular 'science of garotting' (Anon 1863). By the early twentieth century, criminal archetypes specializing in particular offences were commonly constructed in the press and by moral entrepreneurs: in the inter-war period there was the bag-snatcher, the motor bandit, and the razor gang; the Second World War saw the black-marketeer 'spiv'; in the aftermath of the war came the cosh-boy. Of course there were individuals who perpetrated each and every one of these offences; and in the inter-war period it is possible to identify something of an organized underworld involved in sexual vice, with groups like the Messina family in London's Soho, and the gangs working in gambling on the racetracks and at boxing matches, notably the Darby Sabini gang and the Brummagen Boys. This underworld could be vicious, but it generally fought among itself, as in the case of the Sheffield gang wars of the 1920s (Bean 1981; Jenkins and Potter 1988; Samuel 1981). But even including these gangs, it is unlikely that more than a very few offenders were 'professionals' for whom crime was the principal source of income. The creation of the archetype often clouded the understanding of the offence, and the situation became particularly serious when policy was made with reference to the archetype rather than the problem; as noted above, this problem arose with the enforcement of the Contagious Diseases Acts, and can be seen again subsequently in the preparation of much anti-gambling legislation (Dixon 1991: 37; Gatrell 1990: 306–10; Pearson 1983).

Since the eighteenth century at least, politicians and jurists have always claimed that all Englishmen and women are equal before the law. This, it has been argued, was a trick in Hanoverian England which enabled the ruling, propertied elite to run the country without a police force. The occasional example of an individual like Lord Ferrers, executed in 1760 for the murder of his steward, ensured the lower orders' faith in the law—a law which, for most of the time, was concerned with reinforcing and upholding an unequal division of property (Hay 1975). This argument has not gone unchallenged, and nineteenth-century governments became increasingly sensitive to accusations of class law. Yet the limited work which has been done on police practice and the sentencing policies of the courts suggests that both were influenced by the perception of stereotypes. Policemen, magistrates, and judges weighed up offenders according to their class, gender, and respectability, and how they conformed with the accepted social mores; they then acted accordingly (Conley 1991; Zedner 1991). By the same token, while financial fraud was widespread—one estimate has it that as many as one-sixth of the company promotions during the nineteenth century were fraudulent—the law was feeble in this area; the police were not geared up to pursuing such offenders, and such men as were convicted of major fraud were generally treated leniently in comparison with offenders from the 'criminal class' (Robb 1992: ch. 7).

THE POLICE

The traditional Whig historians who studied the origins of the English police accepted fairly uncritically the notion that crime was increasing significantly at the end of the eighteenth century and the beginning of the nineteenth. They also accepted, again uncritically, the claims of the early police reformers that the old system of parish constables and watchmen was totally inefficient and had quite outgrown its usefulness. The development of the new police, beginning with the creation of the Metropolitan Police in London in 1829, was therefore the logical solution of far-sighted men to a real and serious problem (Ascoli 1979; Critchley 1978; Reith 1938, 1943).

There were indeed problems with the old system of policing. Some parish constables were inefficient; they were chosen in a variety of different ways from among the respectable members of local communities, generally to serve for a year; few of them were professionals and most of them had still to conduct their full-time trade or profession while they served. It is little wonder, therefore, that some men sought to avoid the office, and that others were reluctant to put their duties as constable before the needs of their trade and livelihood. Some town watchmen, who were recruited by local authorities and paid to patrol the streets after dark, were also inefficient. But while the constables and watchmen of Hanoverian England still await detailed historical investigation, it is becoming increasingly clear that there were constables who took their role in the community seriously, that improvements were being made to the urban watches, and that, overall, the situation was by no means as bleak as it has been traditionally portrayed.

The chief focus of concerns over time and public order during the eighteenth century was London. It was the largest city in Europe, comprising the cities of both London and Westminster, and spreading out into the counties of Middlesex, Surrey, and Kent. It was a booming commercial centre as well as the seat of government. Contemporaries viewed it with pride for its obvious prosperity; but they also viewed it with trepidation for its slums and for the temptations which its wealth appeared to provide for those who lived in those slums. The parish watches in the metropolis began to be reorganized and improved from early on in the century (Tobias 1972*b*: 212–13). Private thief-takers established themselves to investigate offences for victims; they took rewards from victims for the return of stolen property, and they also cashed in on the rewards offered by government for the apprehension leading to conviction of offenders. Several unsavoury characters installed themselves in the entrepreneurial role of thief-taker, organizing both the theft and the apprehension of the offender (Howson 1970; Paley 1989*a*). Alongside these developments a new kind of magistrate began to emerge in the metropolis and on its fringes: the trading justice. Trading justices have received almost as bad a press as the entrepreneurial thief-takers, yet they were by no means all bad and, sitting regularly in their offices, they provided a much-needed service for the increasing numbers who wanted legal problems solved quickly and easily and who were prepared to pay the justice's fees (Landau 1984: 184–90). A marked step forward was made in the middle of the century when, under Henry Fielding and his blind half-brother Sir John Fielding, the magistrate's office in Bow Street became a model of how the trading justice might function. The Fieldings were supported by government money, which enabled them to keep their fees low; equally significant was their organization of half a dozen constables, the celebrated Bow Street thief-takers or 'Runners', and their experiment with night patrols organized to watch the main roads into the metropolis (Palmer 1988: 78–9).

The Gordon Riots of 1780, when the variety of civil powers in the metropolis showed themselves unable to cope with major disorder, prompted some to contemplate a centralized, professional system of policing. Indeed, in 1785 such a body was proposed in a bill presented to Parliament. But the bill was poorly drafted and poorly presented, and it provoked the fury of the powerful City of London which objected to having its authority over its own police replaced. The bill fell, though the system outlined in it was subsequently established in the city of Dublin. Seven years later a new bill was introduced to improve the policing of London; but rather than creating a centralized body of horse and foot answerable to government-appointed commissioners, this proposed only the creation of seven police offices along the lines of that in Bow Street. Each office was to be staffed by three stipendiary magistrates and six constables; the City of London was omitted from the proposal and continued with its own independent system. The Middlesex Justices Act successfully passed into law in 1792, and over the next thirty years government and private initiative built on the system. In June 1798, encouraged by Patrick Colquhoun, one of the new stipendiaries, a group of West India merchants established a private police force to protect the Thames dockyards; two years later the force was taken over by government as the Thames River Police. In 1805 a uniformed Horse Patrol began to be deployed from Bow Street. Refinements continued to be made in the foot patrol, and in 1822 it was augmented by a uniformed Day Patrol charged with supervising a small area of central London. A similar patrol was organized in the City, where, while a uniform of sorts had been available from 1791, it was not made compulsory until 1824.

By 1828 the policing of London was in the hands of some 300 patrolmen working out of the Bow Street office, about eighty men in the Thames River Police, the twenty-four stipendiaries and their constables, the two City of London Marshals and their constables and patrol, and the dozens of parish constables and nightwatchmen of the individual metropolitan parishes (Palmer 1988: 117–19, 143–7, 171–2; Rumbelow 1971: 104–5). The effectiveness and honesty of these various policemen varied from district to district depending on what pay was available, what recruitment policies were operated, and what systems of supervision were enforced: some nightwatchmen were young and fit and worked relatively short beats which they got to know well and policed conscientiously; but even the much-lauded Bow Street police succumbed to the kinds of corruption present among the old thief-takers as a succession of scandals in the aftermath of the Napoleonic wars revealed (Emsley 1987: 177, 196 n. 18).

The argument for sweeping aside such a motley system appeared a logical and forceful one to the traditional Whig historians of the police, especially since they believed that most parish constables and watchmen were useless. Yet there were, to contemporaries, strong arguments for maintaining the system: there was concern that a centralized police was something peculiarly foreign—worst of all, French—and that it would be a threat to liberty; there was even greater concern about central government encroaching on the rights of local government with a centrally directed police over which the localities would have no control. The police offices and the Bow Street patrols had been increasingly coordinated by the Home Office; but the Metropolitan Police, established in 1829, was a significant development in central government control.

The prime mover in the creation of the Metropolitan Police was the Home Secretary, Sir Robert Peel. He had first come to the Home Office in 1822 and during the mid-1820s had embarked on a major rationalization of the criminal law; in Peel's mind police reform had always been central to his law reforms. He brought with him to the Home Office his experience of Ireland, where he had served as Chief Secretary from 1812 to 1818 and where he had been instrumental in improving the police system. Manifestations of public disorder were different in the two countries. Ireland was overwhelmingly a peasant society; its Catholic minority was dominated by an Anglo-Irish gentry which was largely Protestant. In 1798 and again in 1803 there had been rebellions, and peasant guerrilla war continued to splutter on in the countryside. The magistracy was often reluctant to act in the face of disorder. Peel had created the Peace Preservation Force to help resolve these problems; one of his successors, Henry Goulburn, developed the force further in 1822 by legislation which established a French-style gendarmerie, the Irish Constabulary (Broeker 1970; Palmer 1988: 193–276). Peel remained in close touch with Goulburn throughout the latter's preparation of the Constabulary Bill, and while he recognized that the problems of the new industrial society in England were different from those of Ireland, that magistrates were often active, that local authorities were jealous of their independence, and that there would be ferocious hostility to a French-style military police, he nevertheless believed that some kind of national police system was desirable. Nor was he alone among the Tory Cabinet in this belief. Concerns about public order were probably central in most ministers' minds. While the duration and scale of the Gordon Riots had never been equalled since, there had been sporadic disorders in the metropolis and in the provinces both during and after the wars against Revolutionary and Napoleonic France. Yet it was not on the issue of maintaining public order that Peel chose to argue the need for a police force, but on the problem of increasing crime; and it is possible that Peel's reforms of the criminal law, which made it easier to prosecute offenders and reduced the amount of time lost by victim–prosecutors and their witnesses in the courts, had in themselves inflated the crime figures for the metropolis.

From the beginning in 1829 the constables of the new Metropolitan Police were informed that their first duty was the prevention of crime. It is arguable whether they were any more efficient at this than the more competent of the watches which preceded them, especially since in some areas they were less numerous on the ground (Paley 1989*b*: 114–17). But the new policemen did constitute a sizeable body which could be deployed across the metropolis to clear away street people and to suppress popular tumult. In their early years, also, Metropolitan Police officers and constables were commonly deployed in the provinces as a kind of national riot squad (Emsley 1991: 30, 39, 44, 52–3).

The Metropolitan Police provided a new model for consideration by those advocating police reform in the provinces. In the aftermath of the Napoleonic wars fear of disorder and of increasing crime was prompting a variety of developments in provincial policing. Some local Associations for the Prosecution of Felons organized private police; some towns improved their watches, either through private Acts of Parliament or, after 1833, by taking advantage of the Lighting and Watching Act of that year. The Municipal Corporations Act of 1835 sought to establish uniformity among the chartered boroughs by requiring each elected municipality to appoint a watch committee, and each watch committee to appoint a police force. In 1829 the County of Cheshire established, by Act of Parliament, a constabulary of paid professionals whose task it was to supervise the existing parish constables and to liaise with the developing police in the towns of the county and its neighbours. Yet these reforms were generally found wanting by the Royal Commission on a Rural Constabulary which deliberated between 1836 and 1839; and it was the conclusions of that Royal Commission which have informed the Whig police histories.

Three men served on the Royal Commission: Colonel Charles Rowan, one of the first two commissioners of the Metropolitan Police; Charles Shaw-Lefevre, a Whig MP and country gentleman; and Edwin Chadwick, the dynamic Benthamite reformer who had earlier played a key role in drafting the Poor Law Commissioners' Report of 1834. Chadwick's enthusiasm for a centralized system was controlled by the other two commissioners, but it is clear that Chadwick was primarily responsible for drafting the Constabulary Commissioners' Report, and in so doing he underplayed the extent to which developments were taking place in the provinces and ignored the wishes of the majority of the magistrates in the different quarter sessions who were opposed to the kind of sweeping changes which he favoured (Brundage 1986; Storch 1989). The Whig government, too, was opposed to the extent of the changes proposed by the Commissioners' Report, if for no other reason than that it recognized the impossibility of getting Parliament to agree to a national police force in which the control of local magistrates—then the unchallenged decision-makers for, and administrators of, the provinces through the medium of county quarter sessions—would be all but dispensed with. Instead, the government introduced legislation which enabled county magistrates to establish county police forces if they so wished, with the Home Office playing only a distant supervisory role.

It is difficult fully to assess the extent to which the county police legislation was adopted across England and Wales. Twenty-four counties appear to have adopted it during the first two years of its existence; another eleven did so over the next fifteen years, but nine of these seem to have appointed a constabulary for only parts of their jurisdiction (Foster 1982: 19). The causes of adoption varied, as did assessments of the success of the new constabularies. In the early 1840s there was considerable agitation in several counties for the abolition of the new forces, particularly because of their expense. In those counties which did not adopt the legislation various experiments were carried out with the aim of improving the existing system of parish constables, particularly by appointing professional superintending constables to oversee and organize their activities. Kent took the lead in these latter developments; yet when a parliamentary select committee investigated policing across the country in 1852 and 1853, no witnesses were called from that county.

The main fault with the superintending constables system seems to have been the way in which some magistrates sought to tie these policemen to petty sessions divisions and were jealous of requests that they be allowed to assist elsewhere in their county. By the early 1850s the dominant view in government circles was that the county was the natural unit of local government, and Lord Palmerston, first as Home Secretary and then as Prime Minister, was keen so see a national system of county-based police forces implemented, with only the larger towns maintaining their own independent police under watch committees. His initial ideas foundered on the hostility of the smaller boroughs, but in 1856 his Home Secretary, Sir George Grey, successfully negotiated the County and Borough Police Act through Parliament. This legislation made the creation of a police force obligatory on all counties of England and Wales and on all incorporated boroughs (even as late as this some small boroughs had not complied with the requirements of the Municipal Corporations Act). The Treasury was to pay one-quarter of the pay and clothing of efficient forces, and 'efficiency' was to be assessed by three new Inspectors of Constabulary whose duty it was to inspect each force annually and report to Parliament.

The Metropolitan Police remained separate from the new legislation. It continued to be answerable, not to any representatives of local government, but to the Home Secretary, and the Metropolitan Police Commissioner himself made an annual report to Parliament. In the provinces, however, the system established by the 1856 Act largely survived for the next hundred years. Borough police forces were answerable to their watch committees; in some instances these committees took a close interest in the day-to-day operations of their men, giving precise administrative and operational directives to their head constables. The chief constables of counties had more independence since the police committees of quarter sessions met far less frequently than watch committees, and this infrequency of meeting continued after the magistrates' police committees were replaced, under the local government reorganization of 1888, by standing joint committees made up equally of magistrates and elected members of the new county councils.

Parallel with developments in England and Wales, a similar system of policing emerged in Scotland. Towns were establishing their own forces by private legislation at the end of the eighteenth century and the beginning of the nineteenth; the first public enactment came in 1833 with further legislation fourteen years later. At least twelve out of the twenty-eight Scottish counties had set up some form of force by 1839 when an Act authorized them to levy an additional 'rogue money' assessment to create a constabulary. Lanarkshire was the only county of any significance which had not taken advantage of this legislation when an Act was passed in 1857 requiring the burghs and counties to establish police forces under terms similar to those of the earlier English and Welsh Act (Carson 1984, 1985; Carson and Idzikowska 1989).

While the form of local control over the police established under the 1856 and 1857 Police Acts and the 1888 Local Government Act remained in place for the next hundred years, the reality of this control was gradually undermined by the steady encroachment of the state. The Treasury grant to efficient provincial police forces was increased to half the cost of pay and clothing in 1874, specifically to give the Home Office a greater measure of control. But in general there was nothing conspiratorial in the steady encroachment of the state; rather, it was the logical development of the increasing perception of policemen, by Home Office functionaries and by the police themselves, as the professionals and experts in the job of 'policing'. This prompted a succession of circulars and Acts of Parliament by which central government required specific administrative duties to be undertaken by the police without reference to their local police committees. More dramatic, and more noticeable in their impact on the links between senior police officers and civil servants, were the central government's concerns about managing national emergencies, notably strikes, subversion, and world wars. During the 1830s and 1840s squads of Metropolitan Policemen had regularly been moved around the country to combat industrial disorder, agitation against the new Poor Law, Chartist demonstrations, and the Rebecca troubles in South Wales. But as time wore on the Home Office became increasingly reluctant to commit London policemen in this way, instead urging magistrates that they should establish their own police forces. As county forces developed there was some doubt about the extent to which any one such force might be moved out of its jurisdiction to assist another force, though by the last quarter of the nineteenth century concerns of this kind were long gone and by the last decade of the century the Home Office was urging police forces to enter into mutual aid agreements. Few such agreements appear to have been made, and the strike wave before the First World War witnessed an active Home Secretary, Winston Churchill, ordering both troops and police around the country to assist local forces against striking dockers, miners, and railwaymen. In Churchill's eyes these strikes, even where they were not national stoppages (as in the case of the South Wales coal strike), nevertheless threatened national security and supply, and consequently called for a national response. Churchill's more grandiose proposals for organizing police during strikes were defeated, and he himself moved from the Home Office in 1911. However, the outbreak of war in 1914 brought in its wake a much greater linkage between central government and local police (Emsley 1991: 52–3, 65, 106–12; Morgan 1987: chs. 3, 6; Weinberger 1991: chs. 3, 4).

The spy scares before the war had brought the provincial police forces into close contact with the embryonic secret service. The war itself strengthened these developments as the police were ordered to watch out first for German spies and saboteurs, then for subversives who had taken German gold to undermine the war effort. The Russian Revolution produced a new kind of subversive in the mind of the authorities—the Bolshevik agitator—and fear of this creature lasted long after the war. A few chief constables, notably in South Wales, had major confrontations with their standing joint committees when they equated Labour Party membership and industrial unrest with communism and Bolshevism; the Home Office backed the chief constables. Local police committees were bypassed by the Home Office as it communicated directly with chief constables in preparing to confront widespread industrial unrest. The Emergency Powers Act of 1920 was a key element in these changes, enabling the Home Secretary to deploy up to 10 per cent of the police force outside its own jurisdiction, not necessarily for mutual aid (Emsley 1991: ch. 6; Weinberger 1991: ch. 8).

Other developments, contemporaneous with the growing links between the police forces and the Home Office, also strengthened the idea of a single police service and undermined the local nature of the police. Towards the end of the nineteenth century the notion of policing as a skilled, professional trade, practised by men of similar origins with similar problems across the whole of the United Kingdom as well in the Empire, began to emerge. These ideas were fostered by trade newspapers such as the *Police Service Advertiser* and the *Police Review*, and by campaigns to establish a proper pension scheme applicable to all forces and a weekly rest day. While both of these campaigns were successful, there were many within the police forces who believed that a national police union would be the best means of ensuring a permanent voice for the rank and file in matters of pay, promotion, and discipline. The National Union of Police and Prison Officers was established in December 1913. The wartime pressures on the police, including longer hours and pay which was far outstripped by inflation, encouraged recruitment to the union which, while not acknowledged by the authorities, fought a successful strike in London in August 1918 over pay and conditions. However, a second strike, a year later, involving Birmingham and Liverpool as well as London, was a disaster for the union. All the strikers were dismissed, and the union itself was banned, to be replaced by a Police Federation to which all police officers up to and including the rank of inspector belonged. The Federation was refused the right to strike.

The Police Federation was among the recommendations of the commission appointed under Lord Desborough in the wake of the first police strike. Among the other proposals which it made, and which were accepted by the government, were that the pay and conditions of the police should be standardized and that half the total cost of the police, and not simply half the cost of pay and clothing, should be borne by the Treasury. Legal arguments, particularly Justice H. A. McCardie's controversial ruling in the case of *Fisher* v. *Oldham* in 1930, tended further to undermine local authority over the police. Yet local independence remained sufficiently strong throughout the inter-war years to check any hint of nationalization and, in particular, to prevent the forcible amalgamations of the smallest forces with their larger neighbours. It was the national emergency of the Second World War which provided the opportunity for central government to pass legislation enabling the Home Secretary to enforce amalgamations. The Labour government which came to power in 1945 was sufficiently impressed by the reports of the temporary wartime amalgamations to introduce legislation abolishing forty-five borough forces; this measure, together with four voluntary amalgamations, reduced the number of police forces in England and Wales to 131 by the end of 1947.

The argument for amalgamation and the abolition of the smaller forces was generally that such rationalization promoted efficiency. Yet police efficiency has always been notoriously difficult to estimate. The first Metropolitan Police constables were told that their principal task was the prevention of crime; and this instruction was taken up in the orders issued to the constables in provincial forces. The measurement of prevention is, of course, impossible; arrest statistics, however, are tangible. The new police were able to demonstrate their efficiency to watch committees, magistrates' police committees, and standing joint committees by arresting drunks, prostitutes, street sellers, and anyone else whose behaviour in a public place was offensive to Victorian perceptions of morality. Their presence may have had some impact on petty theft, particularly in public places, and may in consequence have contributed in some small measure to the levelling out of the crime statistics in the second half of the nineteenth century. Of course they did catch some offenders, but their methods were not particularly sophisticated. They appear to have accepted the notion of the criminal class and to have concentrated their efforts on containing stigmatized areas and the groups which lived in them; to paraphrase the explanation of one of the first commissioners of the Metropolitan Police to a parliamentary select committee, they guarded the elegant areas of St. James by watching the slums of St. Giles.

Practices changed little in the first half of the twentieth century. The use of scientific and technological developments depended on the awareness and determination of a chief constable and what he was able to persuade his police committee to purchase. But even when forces were equipped with radios, local pride and independence meant that they might not share frequencies with their neighbours. Detectives had been viewed with suspicion in the early nineteenth century, the man in plain clothes being feared as a spy; furthermore, the early Commissioners of the Metropolitan Police appear to have been wary of detective policemen since they were much more difficult to control and supervise than the uniformed constable patrolling a regular beat at a steady two-and-a-half miles an hour. A Home Office committee was appointed in 1933 to investigate detective policing; after deliberating for five years and investigating the situation elsewhere, particularly in North America, it concluded that England lagged far behind in training and in the deployment of scientific aids. The committee's report led to significant developments in training, the exchange of information between forces, and increased awareness of scientific aids; but the scale of the backwardness is demonstrated by the fact that even at the beginning of the Second World War some county forces, let alone the smallest borough forces, had no CID.

A lack of sophistication, however, was one of the main positive attributes of the image of the British 'bobby' as it developed during the nineteenth and early twentieth centuries. By the middle of the Victorian period he was perceived as solid and dependable; his ability to pull himself up by hard work and diligence from constable third class to superintendent or, in one of the smaller borough forces, to head constable, made him, in the perception of the Victorian middle class, a working-class role model in Samuel Smiles's self-help mould. At the same time the bobby was seen as a mainstay of the British constitution, which Victorians liked to think of as a model for the rest of the world; politicians, journalists, and senior policemen commonly reported the British police to be the best in the world. There were occasions when this image crumbled, and it was probably never particularly strong among the poorer sections of the working class. Furthermore, as the ownership of private motor vehicles increased during the inter-war period, so, for the first time, the police were brought more and more into direct confrontation with 'respectable' members of society.

PROSECUTION AND THE COURTS

Just as policing increasingly became the preserve of experts and professionals from the mid-eighteenth century, so too did the system of prosecution and the activity within the courtroom. Throughout the eighteenth century the decision to prosecute an offender in England and Wales was generally taken by the victim, or by the victim's relations or friends. In Scotland, by the beginning of the century, the Procurators-fiscal, subordinated to the Lord Advocate, had largely taken over the prosecution of all serious crimes; but in England, representatives of the central government rarely intervened (the occasional exceptions were coining cases, commonly prosecuted by the Treasury Solicitor, and those few cases of treason or sedition which threatened the state and which were conducted by the Attorney-General).

One of the problems with the English system was the expense: the prosecutor had to find fees and pay for a variety of legal documents. This appears often to have encouraged the victim to settle with the offender outside the courtroom, though compounding a felony with a monetary payment was itself an offence. The expense of prosecution also prompted men of property to organize themselves into subscription insurance clubs, known as Associations for the Prosecution of Felons, which met any prosecution costs that a member might incur (King 1989; Philips 1989). Legislation of 1752 authorized the payment of expenses to poor prosecutors in felony cases when the accused was convicted, and sixteen years later this payment was extended to all prosecutors. Peel's Criminal Justice Act of 1826 extended the provision to witnesses, and permitted such payment in some misdemeanour cases, notably assaults. These developments probably contributed to the increase in the number of prosecutors who came forward with charges, but well into the nineteenth century some victims still refused to prosecute: sometimes through fear, sometimes because of anxiety about the loss of time from work, sometimes because the whole procedure seemed inconvenient. In the case of sexual offences, embarrassment, and the oppressive climate of Victorian morality which had little time for women who could not demonstrate their adherence to the expected norms of female behaviour, probably dissuaded many women from reporting, let alone prosecuting, an offender.

The Scottish system had its advocates in nineteenth-century England, but the idea of a public prosecutor was perceived as European, and more particularly French; it was lumped together with political police and regarded similarly as alien to English common-law and constitutional traditions. However, it is apparent that, as the nineteenth century wore on, the new police increasingly took on the role of prosecutor, though under the continuing official insistence that the English system was one of private prosecution. In the beginning the police assumed this role, at least in some instances, partly to uphold their own authority; but they also appear to have acted when no one else came forward or when the victim was poor or a woman. The pattern of police involvement as prosecutor varied among the different force jurisdictions: nevertheless, by the last quarter of the nineteenth century prosecutors seem invariably to have been policemen, and the senior officers of municipal forces were often formally presenting cases to the courts, much to the fury of another growing body of professionals—the lawyers (Emsley 1987: 149–50; 1991: 217–18; Hay and Snyder 1989: 36–47).

Criminal prosecutions were heard in three different kinds of court, each developing its distinctive style of practice between the mid-eighteenth and the mid-twentieth century. The most serious cases went before the county assize courts, which until the early twentieth century generally met only twice a year, at Lent and in the summer. In London these cases were heard at the Old Bailey, more properly known as the Central Criminal Court after 1834; but the pressure of business in the metropolitan area meant that the courts here met far more frequently. County quarter sessions met four times a year and heard felony cases; but, unlike the judges at the assizes, the magistrates of the county bench did not have the authority to hear capital offences. Less serious offences went before the summary jurisdiction of magistrates meeting in petty sessions. During the eighteenth century new legislation had permitted more and more cases to be heard summarily; the trend increased in the following century, particularly with the Juvenile Offenders Acts of 1847 and 1850 (which empowered magistrates to try summarily any juvenile charged with simple larceny), the Criminal Justice Act of 1855, and the Prevention of Crime Act of 1879. These courts of petty sessions became more and more formal as the century progressed, and, in consequence of their growing workload and greater formality, the role of the quarter sessions declined. The formal petty sessions were increasingly known as police courts, something which concerned members of the legal profession, and others who were worried that this implied some linkage between the police and the courts.

In both the assize courts and the courts of quarter sessions, cases were heard before juries. However, one of the most significant developments over the period was the shift in the role of the jury from that of an active participant in a trial, with its members interrupting and asking questions, to that of an audience whose task was simply to reach its verdict after watching the adversarial contest between professional lawyers. The process was gradual. It was not the result of any legislation or key legal rulings; rather, it was the corollary of the growing authority of the legal profession. At the beginning of the eighteenth century it was rare for a man with legal training to prosecute, still less defend, in a run-of-the-mill criminal case. However, by the 1730s prosecution counsel were appearing in increasing numbers, and defence counsel to a slightly lesser extent. It is not clear why the development occurred, especially since counsel increased the costs of a case markedly, but by the 1840s the lack of prosecuting counsel at an assize could provoke caustic comments from the presiding judge. Poor defendants had problems with this system; not only could they not give evidence on oath until after 1898, but there was no provision for legal aid until the Poor Prisoners' Defence Act of 1903. During the nineteenth century any defendant seeking a professional defence could get cheap counsel through the 'dock brief' system by which, for the fee of a guinea, he or she could obtain the services of a barrister without the mediation of a solicitor; but the services obtained in this way were rarely of much quality (Beattie 1986: 352–62; Emsley 1987: 152–3).

The shift to summary jurisdiction may have speeded up the process from arrest, through trial to verdict, but it also brought anxieties. The legal profession complained about the impact on the fees, and consequently on the livelihood, of its members. More seriously, there was disquiet about the fact that an increase in summary trials meant a decrease in the number of defendants who had their cases heard before that keystone of the British constitution—the jury. The latter concern was compounded, first, by the fear that magistrates, as men of property (women were not eligible to serve until 1918), might adjudicate in their own interest, and second, by the fact that so many magistrates were laymen with no formal training in the law. In a few instances some magistrates did hear cases in which they themselves were involved; but this practice was frowned upon and always provoked critical comment. It was much more common for a magistrate to step down from the bench if he was involved in a case; but this, of course, did not always ensure an unbiased verdict, since all magistrates were appointed from the same social class. No government contemplated instituting the requirement of legal training for the men appointed as magistrates; it was simply accepted that they could take the advice of their clerks, who did have legal training. Furthermore, increasingly in the nineteenth century magistrates were bolstered by recorders, who were barristers, and by stipendiaries, who were also trained in the law. Indeed, the pressure of business meant that the police courts in the cities came to be dominated by stipendiaries.

Tangentially it should be noted that the increasing shift to summary jurisdiction and the development of professional, bureaucratic police forces contributed to a significant change in the role of the magistrate. During the eighteenth century he had an administrative as well as a judicial role. The former was reduced by the development of elected local government, in the boroughs by the Municipal Corporations Act 1835 and in the counties by the Local Government Act 1888. It was further reduced as the new police assumed more and more responsibility for making decisions in cases where disorder and riot had to be suppressed.

PUNISHMENT

It used to be popular to think in terms of a steady mitigation in the punishment of offences from the notorious 'Bloody Code' of the eighteenth century, with over 200 capital statutes, to the final abolition of the death penalty in 1965, going hand in hand with a steady recognition of the need to reform the offender, manifested by the development of the prison. Unfortunately, historical processes have rarely moved in such a convenient linear fashion, and the changes in the punishment and reformation of offenders are no exception.

The number of capital statutes did increase in the eighteenth century, but consolidation and codification were alien to the English legal tradition and consequently there were not 200 completely distinct offences for which persons could be executed; often separate statutes covered virtually the same offence but referred to a separate part of the country or tidied up an outstanding problem left over from an earlier law. Furthermore, even though the number of capital statutes increased, the number of executions declined over the century. Since the second half of the seventeenth century judges had been exercising their discretion to ensure that convicted offenders were not all executed. The Transportation Act of 1718, which authorized the sending of offenders to the American colonies, provided the best alternative means of getting rid of offenders.

As the eighteenth century wore on, only those offences deemed to be the most aggravated were likely to be punished by death. This punishment was to be a terrible example to others. As a consequence, while sensibilities decreed that fewer should hang, the need for terrible examples, following concerns about violent crime in London in the middle of the century, led to the passage of the 1752 Murder Act which, in order to deter potential offenders, instructed that the bodies of convicted murderers be delivered to surgeons for dissection or, at the judge's discretion, be hanged in chains; furthermore, while there were usually two or three weeks between sentence and execution, under the Murder Act sentence was to be carried out the next day but one after the verdict.

The shifting sensibilities which questioned the reliance on the death penalty seem to have been linked with developing arguments about the nature of God. The traditional view assumed a link between God assessing sinners on the Day of Judgement and judges assessing offenders in the courts; as one cleric explained in 1739, there would be great 'confusion' in the state 'where men only stand in awe of them that can kill the body, and trouble not at the displeasure of that Almighty Being, who after he hath killed, hath power to cast into hell!'. However, increasingly during the eighteenth century, God, rather than being the god of wrath and vengeance, was understood as the benevolent Creator; He had never intended barbarous punishments, and consequently, far more appropriate than the gallows was the prison conducted on humane principles to encourage the offender's reformation (McGowen 1988).

Prisons were not a new departure. From Tudor times petty offenders, vagrants, and prostitutes could have found themselves sentenced to a period in a bridewell or house of correction; and those awaiting trial on an indictment for felony were kept in prison, often for several months, awaiting trial. The use of imprisonment to punish simple felonies had however been largely abandoned after the Transportation Act of 1718. Interest was revived during the 1760s and early 1770s, at least in part because the combination of the occasional example on the gallows and transportation did not appear to be effectively deterring crime. The outbreak of the American War of Independence in 1775 forced the issue; the courts might still sentence felons to transportation, but now there was nowhere that the sentence might be carried out. By the end of the 1780s the government had settled on the colony of New South Wales as its receptacle for felons; however, by then moves for creating prison where the offender might be reformed were already under way, partly through local initiative, but also with significant moves on the part of central government.

The attempt to pinpoint the reasons behind the growth of the prison has given rise to considerable debate. On one level there are the arguments which tie its development in with an interrelationship between forms of knowledge and the shifting strategies and institutions through which power is exercised; thus the prison becomes interlinked with the new expertise of medicine and psychiatry and with a new, enclosing and restricting orientation towards the body (Foucault 1977). For others the emergence of the prison ties in with the needs of a new industrial order and its desire for a controllable, disciplined workforce (Ignatieff 1978). On a more prosaic level there were obvious, practical difficulties which fostered change and reform. Typhus broke out in the crowded gaols made still more crowded by the temporary halt to transportation. The periodic bacchanalia at Tyburn not only threatened order but also suggested that the traditional argument behind this kind of punishment, that it served to deter, was unconvincing; such suspicions fused with the changing view of God and the Enlightenment's perception of man as a rational being who could, through reason, be taught good behaviour. In 1767 Cesare Beccaria's *Dei Delitti e delle Pene*, already widely praised on the continent, appeared in English translation; it was warmly received for its criticisms of the barbaric punishments of the past and its exhortation to create a rational system within which punishment was certain, and fitted the crime. Ten years later John Howard published his detailed and depressing account of *The State of the Prisons in England and Wales*. Rather than changing men's minds, both of these books probably crystallized thoughts and ideas already in motion. In 1779 Parliament passed the Penitentiary Act, providing for the construction of two prisons in the metropolis, one for 600 men and the other for 300 women who, instead of being transported, were to be reformed and taught the habits of industry. However, financial retrenchment following the war against the American colonists and the enormous expense of the Revolutionary and Napoleonic wars slowed and constrained national developments along these lines. Millbank, the first national penitentiary, was not begun until 1812 and not opened until 1816.

The Revolutionary and Napoleonic wars compelled the government to take on the management of large numbers of prisoners. On the one hand there were the felons, held in increasing numbers on aged, dismasted warships (known as the 'hulks') because of the difficulties which war imposed on their shipment to Australia; on the other there were the large numbers of prisoners of war who had to be accommodated—the prison at Princeton on Dartmoor was opened in 1809 for 6,000 such. At the same time the chorus of demands for reform of the system of punishment became ever more shrill, driven by determined individuals such as Sir Samuel Romilly and by evangelical reformist bodies such as, most notably, the Society for the Improvement of Prison Discipline and the Reformation of Juvenile Offenders, established in 1815. Parliament, by no means the diehard reactionary institution it is sometimes portrayed as for this period, responded by reducing the number of capital statutes and by limiting the opportunities for graft and corruption among prison governors and their turnkeys. During the 1820s Peel successfully reformed and rationalized the criminal law. In 1833 a body of Criminal Law Commissioners was appointed to establish a rational system of punishment whereby punishment was to fit the crime; but their attempts foundered on the sheer complexity of the task.

Prison reform reached a climax in the 1830s with debates between the advocates of the separate system (wherein convicts were separated from each other in the belief that, in the quiet of their solitary cells, with their Bible, the exhortation of the chaplain, and their work at a hand crank, they would reach a realization of their wrongdoing and consequent repentance) and those of the silent system (wherein a strict discipline of silence would bring the prisoner to a similar recognition). The former, urged by William Crawford, a member of the Society for the Improvement of Prison Discipline, and by the Revd. Whitworth Russell, the chaplain of Millbank, who were both appointed to a new inspectorate of prisons in 1835, resulted in the opening of Pentonville in 1842. Pentonville was a bleak, dehumanizing establishment from which, in its early years, an annual toll of between five and fifteen of the 450 inmates were taken away to the asylum; and others sought escape through suicide. But while the separate and silent systems were experimented with in varying degrees across the county, the majority of prisons remained under the control of local authorities, and developments here were constrained by local government finance and the pressures from ratepayers.

It was also during the 1830s that the number of offenders who were transported reached a peak of about 5,000 a year. There had always been debate about the effectiveness of transportation. During the eighteenth century there were a few who protested that, rather than punishing the offender, transportation gave him, or her, an undeserved opportunity to start a new life. By the early nineteenth century it was being alleged that some individuals were committing crimes deliberately so as to get themselves transported to a pleasant environment where the shortage of labour promised opportunity for profit and advancement. In reality, the convict settlements in Australia could be harsh and cruel; yet the very fact that such allegations could be made in itself served to undermine the deterrent effect of the punishment. Furthermore, as free settlers and the children of the convicts began to form the majority of citizens in the Australian colonies, so their opposition grew to the mother country foisting its dregs upon them. Dissatisfaction with transportation, both in Britain and in the colonies, brought about a steady reduction in the numbers dispatched during the 1840s, and even more so in the following decade until, in 1857, it was abolished as a judicial sentence (though small numbers of offenders continued to be sent to Western Australia until 1867).

The annual criminal statistics reveal that, by the 1860s, over 90 per cent of those convicted of indictable offences were being sentenced to terms of imprisonment, and the gradual ending of transportation confirmed the prison as the principal form of punishment. But the same period witnessed increasing concerns about what to do with offenders once they were released from gaol. In many respects the popular assumptions about a separate 'criminal class' tended to undermine the notions of moral reformation which were central to prison policy during the second quarter of the century. Men stamped with the stigma of a prison term often found it difficult to find work, and this could be aggravated by the police marking them out as 'known offenders'. The Penal Servitude Act of 1853 attempted to address some of the problems. It extended sentences and toughened the discipline in prisons in lieu of transportation; it also formally introduced the ticket-of-leave system whereby convicts could be released on licence following good behaviour. A succession of Acts followed seeking to fine-tune the system; but penal servitude, while it remained on the Statute Book until 1948, was never precisely defined, and the problems for the police in supervising those on tickets of leave, not to mention the threat which this supervision suspended over an ex-convict's head, were enormous.

It was popularly assumed that the garotting attacks of the 1850s and early 1860s were the work of members of the criminal class on tickets of leave. The panic prompted a further hardening of penal discipline with the Security from Violence Act of 1863, popularly known as the 'Garotter's Act'; this legislation also introduced flogging as a punishment for street robbery in addition to a prison term; like penal servitude, this provision remained on the Statute Book until 1948. The recommendations of a House of Lords Select Committee chaired by Lord Carnarvon, also in 1863, led to a further tightening of discipline within the national convict prisons: long-term prisoners sentenced to penal servitude now spent an initial nine months in solitary confinement in Millbank or Pentonville before being moved to one of the public works prisons of Chatham, Dartmoor, Portland, and Portsmouth. The Scottish equivalent of these institutions was the General Prison in Perth, begun in 1840, opened in 1843, and completed in 1859. But in Scotland, as well as in England and Wales, the majority of gaols continued to be not these national institutions but smaller, local ones. Only in 1877 did legislation sweep away local management and, in consequence, begin to reduce the number of prisons. The Prisons Act of that year appointed prison commissioners, responsible to the Home Secretary, who were to superintend all prisons and submit annual reports to Parliament.

Centralization under the prison commissioners brought into being a uniform system of punishment across the country, which had been the aim of many reformers at least since the early nineteenth century; and punishment was now to be in private: not for the Victorians the public spectacle to deter potential offenders. Floggings and, after 1868, executions were to be carried out behind prison walls. But no sooner was the uniformity of punishment achieved than it began to be queried, as the authorities sought to come to terms with the individuals who did not fit the criminal stereotype for whom the prison system had been designed, notably juveniles, women, and offenders from the higher social classes such as some of the Irish Nationalists and the gentlemen convicted of various forms of commercial fraud or embezzlement. At the same time the number of recidivists committed to prison was increasing, and while the decline of first offenders and the levelling out of the crime statistics suggested that the Victorian war against crime was a success, the recidivists were regarded as evidence of the prison's overall failure to deter or to reform criminals. The problem became linked to the changing perception of professional criminals less as a 'class' and more as a small hard core bolstered by a much larger number of social inadequates who constituted that part of the population least able to cope with the pressures of modern life, especially modern urban life. This changing perception increasingly worked its way into sentencing policy and policy-making in general, notably with the report of the Gladstone Committee in 1895 and the direction pursued by the second chairman of the prison commissioners, Evelyn Ruggles-Brise. Alternatives to incarceration were sought, and, rather than seeking to eradicate the evil habits of a class, the treatment of offenders began to be geared more and more to what were perceived as the needs of particular individuals. Probation was introduced for first offenders in 1887 and was put on a more general footing twenty years later with social workers, in the form of probation officers, seeking to help the inadequate, petty criminal member of society to adjust to the community without being taken away from that community. Borstals were developed for young offenders: these particularly, but also to some degree the conventional prisons, were encouraged to employ what were, in contemporary parlance, scientific systems of therapeutics (Wiener 1990: chs. 8, 9).

The amelioration of the prison system during the inter-war period was gradual. The Victorian prison uniform with its broad arrows, the silence rule, and the punitive labour were all moderated in the 1920s. But the food and living conditions of prisoners remained poor and provoked a serious 'mutiny' among the inmates of Dartmoor in 1932. The policy of reducing incarceration and the search for alternatives was maintained, and the overall success of this approach appeared to be underlined by the prison commissioners' ability to continue closing prisons but, at the same time, to maintain a surplus capacity. In 1951 the chairman could boast that it had been necessary to build only two institutions since the beginning of the century: Camp Hill on the Isle of Wight and Lowdham Grange Borstal (Fox 1952: 98). In many respects the Criminal Justice Act of 1948, which swept away most of the severe vestiges of the Victorian system, was the climax of the shift towards rehabilitating individual offenders. It showed something of a liberal consensus among Labour and Conservative politicians, the penal reform lobby, and the professionals working in the system. The Act abolished corporal punishment; it provided preventive detention for the worst recidivists, but 'corrective training' for others; detention centres were created for young offenders who were felt to require something stiffer than probation, but not as severe as Borstal; and attendance centres were established for a variety of petty offenders of all ages who could be required to attend in their free time and participate in a variety of activities not necessarily of their own choosing (Bailey 1987: 302–5).

SHIFTS AND CONTEXTS

The two hundred years surveyed here witnessed a shift from crime control mechanisms which were essentially local, personal, and (since constables, thief-takers, justices, and gaolers took fees from their clients and charges) entrepreneurial to crime control institutions which were bureaucratic, largely impersonal, and increasingly centralized. This shift took place against the background of a move from a predominantly agrarian economy with a largely rural population to an industrial, capitalist economy, with, from about 1850, a majority of people living in towns. The growing economy resulted in more moveable possessions owned by a greater variety of individuals, and this provided new and probably greater opportunities and temptations for theft; and it is not necessary to accept arguments about anomie leading to crime to note that the more complex, impersonal nature of towns probably also offered greater opportunities and temptations for crime. The question remains, however: What, if anything, was the relationship between economic and social change and the developing institutions of crime control?

Exploring the institutional developments in the light of the economic and social changes has been illuminating: clearly economic and social ideas influenced the understanding of offences and offenders; the growth of London and other big cities, together with fears about the new urban population, contributed to the creation of police forces; parallels can be detected between the nature of, and the supporters and advocates of, the prison, the new workhouse, and the factory. Yet the development of crime control institutions has not been unique to liberal capitalist societies like Britain. Where Britain has been unique is in the perception of the state. During the nineteenth century, unlike the most influential and powerful of its continental neighbours, the British state acquired an aura of stability, success, and, above all, benevolence. The extent to which this state acted in the interests of a new capitalist class remains a moot point; certainly businessmen as tax- and ratepayers were often reluctant to provide the money for new police and prisons, and government, both central and local, often disappointed reformers by not raising the money necessary for their cherished projects. Yet the Victorian state and its successors did grow; and, in the name of greater efficiency and rationalization which, it was claimed, would benefit the population as a whole, it centralized. The men driving this growth—reformers, politicians, and civil servants—believed in progress and their own humanitarianism; the gradual amelioration of the penal system from the late nineteenth century, in itself, is an indication of the power of these beliefs. The same world-view also influenced the first historians of these institutions, who celebrated the police and prison systems as the achievements of a beneficent, progressive state and society. A more cynical, more pessimistic age is also more critical of its institutions, and the contemporary historians of crime and crime control cannot so readily share an explanation for the changes they explore.

Selected Further Reading

The five volumes of Leon Radzinowicz, *A History of English Criminal Law and its Administration From 1750* (London: Stevens, 1948–86) is an invaluable reference work for the whole period, though students may find it a little daunting. Those looking for a gentler introduction to the subjects discussed above could usefully turn to the following:

J. M. Beattie, *Crime and the Courts in England 1660–1800*. Oxford: Clarendon Press, 1986.

Clive Emsley, *Crime and Society in England 1750–1900*. London: Longman, 1987.

Clive Emsley, *The English Police: A Political and Social History*. Hemel Hempstead: Wheatsheaf, 1991.

Douglas Hay and Francis Snyder, eds., *Policing and Prosecution in Britain 1750–1850*. Oxford: Clarendon Press, 1989.

Martin J. Wiener, *Reconstructing the Criminal: Culture, Law and Policy in England 1830–1914*. Cambridge: Cambridge University Press, 1990.

Lucia Zedner, *Women, Crime, and Custody in Victorian England.* Oxford: Clarendon Press, 1991.

REFERENCES

ANON. [H. W. Holland] (1863), 'The Science of Garrotting and Housebreaking', *Cornhill Magazine*, 7: 79–92.

ASCOLI, D. (1979), *The Queen's Peace: The Origins and Development of the Metropolitan Police 1829–1979*. London: Hamish Hamilton.

BAILEY, V. (1987), *Delinquency and Citizenship: Reclaiming the Young Offender 1914–1918*. Oxford: Clarendon Press.

——, ed. (1981), *Policing and Punishment in Nineteenth-Century Britain*. London: Croom Helm.

BEAN, J. P. (1981), *The Sheffield Gang Wars*. Sheffield: D and D Publications.

BEATTIE, J. M. (1975), 'The Criminality of Women', *Journal of Social History*, 8: 80–116.

—— (1981), 'Judicial Records and the Measurement of Crime in Eighteenth-century England', in L. A. Knafla, ed., *Crime and Criminal Justice in Europe and Canada*, 127–45. Waterloo, Ontario: Wilfred Laurier University.

—— (1986), *Crime and the Courts in England 1660–1800*. Oxford: Clarendon Press.

BEIER, A. L. (1985), *Masterless Men: The Vagrancy Problem in Britain 1560–1640*. London: Methuen.

BROEKER, G. (1970), *Rural Disorder and Police Reform in Ireland, 1812–1836*. London: Routledge and Kegan Paul.

BRUNDAGE, A. (1986), 'Ministers, Magistrates and Reformers: The Genesis of the Rural Constabulary Act of 1839', *Parliamentary History: A Yearbook*, 5: 55–64.

BURN, W. L. (1964), *The Age of Equipoise: A Study of the Mid-Victorian Generation*. London: Allen and Unwin.

CARSON, W. G. (1984), 'Policing the Periphery: The Development of Scottish Policing 1795–1900, Part I', *Australian and New Zealand Journal of Criminology*, 17: 207–32.

—— (1985), 'Policing the Periphery: The Development of Scottish Policing 1795–1900, Part II', *Australian and New Zealand Journal of Criminology*, 18: 3–16.

CARSON, W. G., and IDZIKOWSKA, H. (1989), 'The Social Production of Scottish Policing, 1795–1900', in D. Hay and F. Snyder, eds., *Policing and Prosecution in Britain 1750–1850*, 267–97. Oxford: Clarendon Press.

COCKBURN, J. S. (1991), 'Patterns of Violence in English Society: Homicide in Kent 1560–1985', *Past and Present*, 131: 70–106.

COLQUHOUN, P. (1796), *A Treatise on the Police of the Metropolis*, 3rd edn. London: C. Dilly.

CONLEY, C. A. (1991), *The Unwritten Law: Criminal Justice in Victorian Kent*. New York: Oxford University Press.

CRITCHLEY, T. A. (1978), *A History of Police in England and Wales*, 2nd edn. London: Constable.

DAVIS, J. S. (1984), ' "A Poor Man's System of Justice": The London Police Courts in the Second Half of the Nineteenth Century', *Historical Journal*, 27: 309–35.

—— (1989), 'Prosecutions and their Context: The Use of the Criminal Law in Later Nineteenth-Century London', in D. Hay and F. Snyder, eds., *Policing and Prosecution in Britain 1750–1850*, 397–426. Oxford: Clarendon Press.

DELACY, M. (1986), *Prison Reform in Lancashire, 1700–1850: A Study in Local Administration*. Manchester: Manchester University Press.

DIXON, D. (1991), *From Prohibition to Regulation: Bookmaking, Anti-Gambling and the Law*. Oxford: Clarendon Press.

EMSLEY, C. (1987), *Crime and Society in England 1750–1900*. London: Longman.

—— (1991), *The English Police: A Political and Social History*. Hemel Hempstead: Wheatsheaf.

FIELDING, H. (1751), *An Enquiry into the Late Increase of Robbers*. London: A. Millar.

FORSYTHE, W. J. (1987), *The Reform of Prisons, 1830–1900*. London: Croom Helm.

—— (1991), *Penal Discipline, Reformatory Projects and the English Prison Commission, 1895–1939*. Exeter: University of Exeter Press.

FOSTER, D. (1982), *The Rural Constabulary Act 1839: National Legislation and the Problems of Enforcement*. London: Bedford Square Press/NCVO.

FOUCAULT, M. (1977), *Discipline and Punish: The Origins of the Prison*. London: Allen Lane.

FOX, Sir L. (1952), *The English Prison and Borstal Systems*. London: Routledge and Kegan Paul.

GALTON, F. (1907), *Inquiries into Human Faculty*, 2nd edn. London: Dent.

GATRELL, V. A. C. (1980), 'The Decline of Theft and Violence in Victorian and Edwardian England, in V. A. C. Gatrell, B. Lenman, and G. Parker, eds., *Crime and the Law: The Social History of Crime in Western Europe since 1500*, 238–370. London: Europa.

—— (1990), 'Crime, Authority and the Policeman State', in F. M. L. Thompson, ed., *The Cambridge Social History of Britain 1750–1950*, iii: 243–310. Cambridge: Cambridge University Press.

GILLIS, J. R. (1975), 'The Evolution of Juvenile Delinquency in England, 1890–1914', *Past and Present*, 67: 96–126.

GLYDE, J. (1856*a*), *Suffolk in the Nineteenth Century: Physical, social, moral, religious and industrial*. London.

—— (1856*b*), 'Localities of Crime in Suffolk', *Journal of the Statistical Society*, 19: 102–6.

HANWAY, J. (1772), *Observations on the Causes of the Dissoluteness which Reigns among the Lower Classes of People: the Propensity of some to Petty Larceny: and the Danger of Gaming, Concubinage, and an Excessive Fondness for Amusement in High Life*. London: J. and F. Rivington.

HAY, D. (1975), 'Property, Authority and the Criminal Law', in D. Hay, P. Linebaugh, E. P. Thompson, *et al.*, *Albion's Fatal Tree: Crime and Society in Eighteenth-Century England*, 17–63. London: Allen Lane.

HAY, D., and SNYDER, F., eds. (1989), *Policing and Prosecution in Britain 1750–1850*. Oxford: Clarendon Press.

HOWSON, G. (1970), *Thief-taker General: The Rise and Fall of Jonathan Wild*. London: Hutchinson.

IGNATIEFF, M. (1978), *A Just Measure of Pain: The Penitentiary in the Industrial Revolution 1750–1850*. London: Macmillan.

INNES, J., and STYLES, J. (1986), 'The Crime Wave: Recent Writing on Crime and Criminal Justice in Eighteenth-century England', *Journal of British Studies*, 25: 380–435.

JENKINS, P., and POTTER, G. W. (1988), 'Before the Krays: Organised Crime in London, 1920–1960', *Criminal Justice History: An International Annual*, 9: 209–30.

JONES, D. J. V. (1982), *Crime, Protest, Community and Police in Nineteenth-century Britain*. London: Routledge and Kegan Paul.

—— (1992), *Crime in Nineteenth-century Wales*. Cardiff: University of Wales Press.

KING, P. J. R. (1989), 'Prosecution Associations and their Impact in Eighteenth-century Essex', in D. Hay and F. Snyder, eds., *Policing and Prosecution in Britain 1750–1850,* 171–207. Oxford: Clarendon Press.

LANDAU, N. (1984), *The Justices of the Peace 1679–1760*. Berkeley, University of California Press.

LINEBAUGH, P. (1991), *The London Hanged: Crime and Civil Society in the Eighteenth Century*. London: Allen Lane.

MCCONVILLE, S. (1981), *A History of English Prison Administration*, i: 1750–1877. London: Routledge and Kegan Paul.

MCGOWEN, R. (1988), 'The Changing Face of God's Justice: The Debates over Divine and Human Punishment in Eighteenth-century England', *Criminal Justice History: An International Annual*, 9: 63–98.

MCHUGH, P. (1980), *Prostitution and Victorian Social Reform*. London: Croom Helm.

MARGERY, S. (1978), 'The Invention of Juvenile Delinquency in Early Nineteenth-century England', *Labour History*, 34: 11–27.

MAY, M. (1973), 'Innocence and Experience: The Evolution of Juvenile Delinquency in the Mid-nineteenth century', *Victorian Studies*, 17: 7–29.

MORGAN, J. (1987), *Conflict and Order: Labour Disputes in England and Wales 1900–1939*. Oxford: Clarendon Press.

PALEY, R. (1989*a*), 'Thief-takers in London in the Age of the McDaniel Gang, *c.*1745–1754', in D. Hay and F. Snyder, eds., *Policing and Prosecution in Britain, 1750–1850*, 301–41. Oxford: Clarendon Press.

—— (1989*b*), ' "An Imperfect, Inadequate and Wretched System"? Policing London before Peel', *Criminal Justice History: An International Annual*, 10: 95–130.

PALMER, S. H. (1988), *Police and Protest in England and Ireland 1780–1850*. Cambridge: Cambridge University Press.

PEARSON, G. (1983), *Hooligan: A History of Respectable Fears*. London: Macmillan.

Philips, D. (1977), *Crime and Authority in Victorian England: The Black Country 1835–1860*. London: Croom Helm.

—— (1989), 'Good Men to Associate and Bad Men to Conspire: Associations for the Prosecution of Felons in England, 1760–1860', in D. Hay and F. Snyder, eds., *Policing and Prosecution in Britain, 1750–1850*, 113–70. Oxford: Clarendon Press.

Radzinowicz, L. (1948–86), *A History of the English Criminal Law and its Administration from 1750*, 5 vols.: i (1948) *The Movement for Reform*; ii (1956) *The Clash between Private Initiative and Public Interest in the Enforcement of the Law*; iii (1956) *Cross-currents in the Movement for the Reform of the Police*; iv (1968) *Grappling for Control*; v (1986, with R. Hood) *The Emergence of Penal Policy in Victorian and Edwardian England*. London: Stevens and Sons.

Randall, A. J. (1990), ' "Peculiar Perquisites and Pernicious Practices": Embezzlement in the West of England Woollen Industry *c*.1750–1840', *International Review of Social History*, 35: 193–219.

Reith, C. (1938), *The Police Idea*. Oxford: Oxford University Press.

—— (1943), *British Police and the Democratic Ideal*. Oxford: Oxford University Press.

Robb, G. (1992), *White-collar Crime in Modern England: Financial Fraud and Business Morality 1845–1929*. Cambridge: Cambridge University Press.

Rumbelow, D. (1971), *I Spy Blue: The Police and Crime in the City of London from Elizabeth I to Victoria*. London: Macmillan.

Samuel, R. (1981), *East End Underworld: Chapters in the Life of Arthur Harding*. London: Routledge and Kegan Paul.

Sharpe, J. A. (1985), 'The History of Violence in England: Some Observations', *Past and Present*, 108: 206–15.

Sindall, R. (1990), *Street Violence in the Nineteenth Century: Media Panic or Real Danger?* Leicester: Leicester University Press.

Stevenson, S. J. (1983), 'The "Criminal Class" in the Mid-Victorian City: A Study of Policy Conducted with Special Reference to Those made Subject to the Provisions of 34 & 35 Vict. c. 112 (1871) in Birmingham and East London in the Early Years of Registration and Supervision', D.Phil. thesis, University of Oxford.

Stone, L. (1983), 'Interpersonal Violence in English Society, 1300–1980', *Past and Present*, 101: 22–33.

—— (1985), 'A Rejoinder', *Past and Present*, 108: 216–24.

Storch, R. D. (1989), 'Policing Rural Southern England before the Police: Opinion and Practice, 1830–1856', in D. Hay and F. Snyder, eds., *Policing and Prosecution in Britain, 1750–1850*, 211–66. Oxford: Clarendon Press.

Tobias, J. J. (1972*a*), *Crime and Society in the Nineteenth Century*. Harmondsworth: Penguin.

—— (1972*b*), 'Police and Public in the United Kingdom', *Journal of Contemporary History*, 7: 201–19.

Walkowitz, J. R. (1980), *Prostitution and Victorian Society: Women, Class and the State*. Cambridge: Cambridge University Press.

Weinberger, B. (1991), *Keeping the Peace? Policing Strikes in Britain 1906–1926*. Oxford: Berg.

WIENER, M. J. (1990), *Reconstructing the Criminal: Culture, Law and Policy in England, 1830–1914*. Cambridge: Cambridge University Press.

ZEDNER, L. (1991), *Women, Crime and Custody in Victorian England*. Oxford: Clarendon Press.

5

'Hostages to Fortune'? The Politics of Law and Order in Post-War Britain

DAVID DOWNES AND ROD MORGAN

INTRODUCTION

The politics of law and order is a vast subject, and we should state at the outset certain limits we have set to its scope and definition for the purposes of this chapter. First, we cannot deal at all adequately with the micro-politics of law and order as they are articulated in family, neighbourhood, agency, and institutional contexts. Every household, school, street corner, marketplace, shop, office, workplace, and leisure setting generates law and order talk and discourse which are the very tissue of deviance and control. To subsume this terrain within our topic would be virtually and, in our view, falsely to equate the politics of law and order with the sociology of deviance and control. Second, we must differentiate the politics of law and order from the processes of criminal justice policy-making. In so far as the two are linked, we attempt to address key aspects of the connections between them. However, while the making of a particular policy—that concerning victim support, for example (see Rock 1990)—may illuminate the nature of the political context, and vice versa, it is important to retain a sense of their analytical distinctiveness. Third, though we make reference to Scotland and Northern Ireland, our focus is overwhelmingly on England and Wales since 1945.

What, then, *do* we regard as our subject? We take the term 'the politics of law and order' to mean the public contestation of the dynamics of crime, disorder, and their control. The key players in this matrix are: the major political parties, in particular successive Home Secretaries and their ministerial and Opposition teams; senior civil servants who, despite their non-political role, bear crucial advisory responsibilities; pressure and interest groups in the criminal justice field; and the mass media. The private, off-stage, often confidential and even secretive processes of discussion, negotiation, and exchange, which provide the ingredients of public utterance and action, remain implicit rather than spelt out in what

The authors would like to thank Paul Rock, Vincenzo Ruggiero, and Mick Ryan for helpful comments and constructive criticism.

follows. We assume, however, that readers will realize that terms such as 'the Conservative Party' or 'the Labour Party' are not meant to propagate the fallacy of misplaced concreteness but are necessary abbreviations for the welter of possible responsibilities for actions and policies that may be the work of many thousands of individuals. Nor, in quoting the words of ministers or other politicians, do we assume that perfect comprehension can be achieved—if it ever can be—without much more provision of detail about timing, context, multiple purposes, encoding and decoding artfulness, and much else. We assume that our readers will grasp that a limited purpose is pursued in making quotations and examples, namely, to demonstrate a point rather than to convey some total reality.

OVERVIEW

Compared with the contested party politics of the economy, foreign affairs, defence, health, housing, and education, those of 'law and order' are of remarkably recent origin: they emerged in the mid-1960s, but came decisively to the fore only with the 1979 election campaign. This long-standing absence from party political discourse and contention is in itself somewhat remarkable. Law and order are highly emotive and fundamentally political issues. Few topics can routinely arouse such passionate debate—a phenomenon taken by Durkheim a century ago as the basis for his functionalist theses on crime and punishment. That law and order were relatively insulated from the realm of party politics for so long testifies perhaps to the strength of belief that crime, like the weather, is beyond political influence; and that the operation of the law and criminal justice should be above it. This is not to deny that criminal law reform has long been regarded as the prerogative of Parliament. But once laws are enacted, the liberal doctrine of the separation of powers holds that their enforcement is the preserve of the police and the judiciary. Hence, bipartisanship has been the rule rather than the exception in the twentieth century on such matters as the response to crime, the nature of policing, sentencing in the courts, and the character of imprisonment. Even at the fringes of political life, few challenges were made to so profound a consensus.

The nature of and the reasons for the change from a broadly bipartisan to a sharply contested politics of law and order are therefore central to our concerns in this chapter. But the prelude to that change was not without deep significance, because the nature of the consensus itself was both complex and far from apolitical. This was, however, a politics more of nuance and inflection than of explicit difference. Also, the politics of law-breaking are not necessarily those of order-defiance (cf. Elder 1984), and the latter has a far more developed history, particularly in the realm of industrial conflict (Dixon and Fishwick 1984). Friction over public order legislation and its enforcement has throughout the period been far more evident than that concerning straightforward criminality. It was the achievement of 'Thatcherism' to blur the difference between the two, and even to fuse them symbolically to political effect. And the consequences of the change have been more than a simple matter of the major parties taking up starkly opposing stances across the range of relevant issues. Despite new, overt differences, a species of second-order consensus has emerged to replace former orthodoxies. Moreover, the politics of law and order are not confined to the party sphere. Extra-parliamentary processes have often been more vigorous than those within the confines of Westminster, and developments at local government level, or formulations by pressure groups and lobbies, have frequently been the stimulus for national attention. Finally, the eruption of particular scandals and concerns, via a rapidly changing media framework, have consistently proved catalysts for changing policies.

In what follows, we shall address these topics in turn.

BRITISH GENERAL ELECTIONS AND 'LAW AND ORDER', 1945–1992

In 1945, Britain was 'a society both exhausted and exhilarated' (Morris 1989: 13). The awesome task of post-war reconstruction led the three main parties to contend overwhelmingly about the priorities of rebuilding the economy and constructing the 'welfare state'. Despite fundamental ideological differences, out of this period was evolved a form of consensus, usually known as 'Butskellism',[1] which set limits to the scope of political conflict. Full employment, core welfare rights in health, housing, income maintenance, and education, and economic growth on Keynesian assumptions, were broadly accepted as shared goals, as was a mixed economy—though strong differences persisted over the nature of the mix. Crime and criminal justice were minor, taken-for-granted aspects of this consensus.

Our analysis of trends in the salience of 'law and order' as an issue in British politics is heavily reliant on party manifestos for, and campaigning during the relatively short (generally three-week) run-up to, general elections. The method has obvious advantages. Such material provides a time series of supremely public character which has enabled political

[1] 'Butskellism' was the word coined in the early 1950s to convey the similarity and continuity of economic policy between the outgoing Labour Chancellor of the Exchequer, Hugh Gaitskell, and the new Conservative Chancellor, R. A. Butler. See Marwick (1990: ch. 6.)

analysts to chart the changing complexion of party policies and their intended and actual appeal. The work of David Butler and his colleagues has furnished a thorough guide to the complexities and problems of interpretation. Against this view, it can be said that manifestos are purely formal exercises in party rhetoric which are little read and, as such, provide highly problematic guides to party thinking and influence. Such a view seems to us too dismissive of their value. Manifestos are not only highly accessible documents; they are also a major part of the process of democratic accountability. After elections they are constantly referred to by opponents of the government, and the notion of a mandate to pursue policies is heavily dependent on their prior legitimation by majority (or winning minority) vote by an electorate which has, in principle, had prior warning of party thinking and intentions. That electoral promises are far from sacrosanct does not alter the basis on which they rest: that voters have had the chance to assess the worth and credibility of party strategy.

In the first part of this section we describe and compare the way in which successive post-war manifestos and campaigns developed 'law and order' issues; we then attempt to discern the underlying reasons for the distinctive pattern that emerges.

The Post-War Manifestos and Campaigns

Not until 1959 did any party mention in a manifesto anything to do with topics of law and order, though in both 1955 and 1959 issues of legal aid and betting and gaming legislation were raised. In 1959, the new note struck by the Conservatives was simply 'to review the system of criminal justice and to undertake penal reforms which will lead offenders to abandon a life of crime. A scheme for compensating the victims of violent crime for personal injuries will be considered' (Conservative Party 1959). In 1964, the Conservative manifesto extended its coverage to include; strengthening the police; the (abortive) Royal Commission on the Penal System; tougher measures against hooliganism; and supporting family ties to counteract delinquency. The Liberal Party implicitly attacked the inadequacy of the government's record by switching the emphasis, on combating crime to prevention and rehabilitation (Liberal Party 1964). Yet even in 1964, after thirteen years of continuous Conservative government, the Labour Party said nothing about law and order, or the government's record in the face of crime rates which had risen steeply since the mid-1950s. This self-denial was all the more noteworthy because in 1963, in the run-up to the coming election, Harold Wilson had convened a study group on crime and criminal justice under the chairmanship of Lord Longford. Though the group's reports, *Crime—A Challenge To Us All*, became available only as Labour was taking up office in 1964, it was presumably known in advance that its members were 'breaking new ground' (Morris 1989: 114), mainly on penal reform, the treatment of juveniles (see chapter 20 in this volume) and capital punishment.

In 1966, however, after two years in government, the Labour Party for the first time devoted as much space to 'law and order'; policy as the Conservatives. The preamble to their pledge to strengthen the police, reform juvenile justice, and modernize the prison system was implicitly critical of the Conservatives: 'For years Britain has been confronted by a rising crime rate, overcrowded prisons and many seriously undermanned police forces' (Labour Party 1966). The Conservatives were also keen to 'beat the crime wave' in 1966, announcing policies which differed from Labour only in that they favoured the formation of national police forces and greater use of compensation orders by the courts. On one issue, however, they signalled a disagreement with Labour that was to persist for many years. Whereas the Labour reforms, drawing on the report of the Longford Committee, envisaged the end of juvenile courts and their powers, by contrast the Conservatives would 'preserve the juvenile courts and expand the methods available for dealing with the problems of young people' (Conservative party 1966: see Chapter 20 in this volume). It should be stressed that, as previously, no party manifesto suggested that the level or form of crime was itself attributable to the politics of the party in government.

All that changed in 1970. In ways that mark this election rather than that of 1979 as the real watershed in the policies of 'law and order', all three major parties devoted more space than ever before in their manifestos to these issues. Moreover, the Conservatives, albeit in restrained fashion, argued that 'the Labour Government cannot entirely shrug off responsibility for the present situation'. The 'situation' was 'the serious rise in crime and violence' and increased fear of both (Conservative Party 1970; for contemporary examinations of the nature of these problems see Downes 1966; Cohen 1972; Hall *et al.* 1978). While the Conservatives laid this situation at the door of the Labour government, pointing to their having restricted 'police recruitment at a critical time' (a contentious argument, since full employment in the whole post-war period had bedevilled police pay levels and their effects on recruitment—see Bottoms and Stevenson 1992), 1970 also saw them draw a clear connection between crime, protest, and disorders associated with industrial disputes. The law, the Conservative manifesto proclaimed, 'needs modernising and clarifying, and needs to be made less slow and cumbersome, particularly for dealing with offences—forcible entry, obstruction and violent offences connected with public order—peculiar to the *age of demonstration and disruption*' (Conservative Party 1970, n. 25, emphasis added). Against this thinly veiled linkage of issues of law-breaking and order-defiance that had hitherto been quite distinct in political discourse, Labour asserted its recognition that it was 'the first duty of government to protect the citizen against violence, intimidation and crime', and undertook to prosecute 'vigorously . . . the fight against vandals and law breakers'. However, Labour decried the breakdown of bipartisanship about crime: 'Nothing could be more cynical than the current attempts of our opponents to exploit for Party political ends the issue of crime and law enforcement' (Labour Party 1970). Indeed, the Labour manifesto sought to reassure the electorate that 'the streets of our cities are as safe today as those in any throughout the world. They must remain so' (ibid.: 26).

The chords struck in the 1970 election campaign persisted and grew more insistent in those of 1974 and 1979. In that of February 1974, the Conservative Party further increased the amount of space devoted to law and order issues in its manifesto, claiming some success during their period of office in reducing crime (the rate had barely risen between 1970 and 1973, though it was to soar in 1974). These 'encouraging signs' were attributed to the growth in police manpower, tougher penalties for offences involving firearms and vandalism, and the ability of the courts to impose compensation orders. More of the same types of measure were promised if the Party were re-elected (Conservative Party 1974*a*). By contrast, the Labour Party, back in opposition, said nothing on law and order: it promised nothing and said nothing about the government's record (Labour Party 1974*a*). The Liberal Party also said nothing on this area of policy though, continuing its well-established tradition, it advocated a Bill of Rights (Liberal Party 1974).

The outcome of the February 1974 election—a narrow Labour victory with a hung Parliament in which the Labour government depended on Liberal support—led to a second election in October 1974. The Labour Party, once again, said little about law and order, and what it did say was couched in generalities and promised no specific measures (Labour Party 1974*b*). The Conservative Party, by contrast, once again devoted a substantial part of its manifesto to law and order issues. It vigorously pursued the approach of attacking the government's record, but with a significant difference. On this occasion, it was the government's integrity rather than its policies and priorities that was condemned. Following the traditional defence of the need for law and the protection it affords the weak against the strong, they continued: 'But recently the law has been under attack and these attacks have all too often been condoned and even endorsed by members and supporters of the present Government' (Conservative party 1974*b*). This veiled reference to the support given to the National Union of Mineworkers, in their successful deployment of mass picketing in 1973, by Labour MPs and key members of the then Shadow Cabinet, such as Tony Benn, gave the Conservative Party a crucial opening. The Clay Cross affair, in which the Labour government refused to prosecute Labour local councillors who had refused to increase rents in line with Conservative legislation during their period of office, was another lever to be deployed in prising apart the image of Labour and the wholehearted, not selective, support for the law without which there could be no freedom. A detailed array of specific policies were put forward in relation to policing, young offenders, and crime prevention, including the commitment to amend the Labour government's Children and Young Persons Act 1969, 'to deal more effectively with persistent juvenile offenders—for example, soccer hooligans—and the range of available institutions must be improved' (ibid.).

It is apparent, therefore, that by the mid-1970s it had been established that law and order issues could assume as much prominence in major party election manifestos as, for example, housing, transport, and urban renewal policy. However, while 'law and order' was not a question on which only the Conservatives pronounced, the manner in which the major parties dealt with the issues was increasingly different. The Conservatives were refashioning their traditional claim to be the natural party of government representing the order of established authority (Honderich 1990), a claim which had lost much credibility as a result of the Conservative defeats in the 1974 elections, following the huge loss of face involved in the miners'; strike of 1973. By emphasizing respect for the law, the Conservatives—now under the leadership of Mrs Thatcher—were laying claim to a clear moral and practical ascendancy in this field. By contrast, Labour was experiencing difficulties in mounting a convincing counter-attack and, in the two 1974 elections, in effect ducked the issue. Since Labour nevertheless won those elections, that strategy seemingly paid off. The clear difficulty for Labour was the success with which the Conservatives were fusing the issues of law-breaking and order-defiance in the industrial relations field. Labour felt inhibited from unequivocally condemning disruptive and at times aggressive strike-related actions by its principal constituency, trade unionists. During the late 1970s, following the forced loan from the International Monetary Fund and especially during the strike-ridden 'Winter of Discontent' of 1978–9,[2] it seems probable that a number of anxieties symbolizing national decline came to be associated with Labour government: lack of economic competitiveness; fear of crime; fear of inner-city decay; fear of an explosion of black criminality; fears of youthful extremism (embodied in both the brief rise of the punks and far-right street demonstrations that culminated in the murder

[2] In autumn 1978, it was widely predicted that the Labour government, then with a much reduced majority, would call an election. It was not called. But a plethora of strikes ensued, notably in the health and other public services. The number of days lost from work rose above those recorded during the General Strike of 1926. See Marwick (1990: 261).

of Blair Peach at Southhall[3]); and fears that the authorities could not cope with the array of problems thus presented. It was at this time that many an editorial was written on the 'ungovernability' of Britain. It was out of these ingredients that the major differences between the parties on 'law and order' assumed their most polarized form in the 1979 election.

In 1979 the Labour government knew, because the Conservative Party had long signalled the fact, that its record in office was to be attacked on this front. In its manifesto, Labour devoted space to law and order issues but dealt with them *within* the context of its objective of creating 'one nation' by eliminating the evils of inequality, poverty, and racial bigotry (Labour Party 1979). It invoked the need to 'fight against crime and violence', protect citizens' rights and liberties, and continue to back the police more strongly than the Tories had done. Its focus was on attacking 'the social deprivation which allows crime to flourish'. Labour's 'law and order' policy was therefore implicitly to be found elsewhere in the manifesto, in its social and economic policies, though it gave such specific, if low-key, undertakings as to provide more law centres and extend legal aid and help for victims.

By contrast, the Conservatives made restoring the 'rule of law', which they claimed that the Labour Party 'in government as in opposition . . . have undermined', one of their five major tasks; and they undertook to do so by implementing specific 'law and order' policies (Conservative Party 1979). First, they would 'spend more on fighting crime even while we economise elsewhere. Second, they would improve the pay and conditions of the police and, in particular, 'implement in full the recommendations of the Edmund–Davies Committee', which the Labour government had said it would implement in two stages rather than at once.[4] Third, the police would be relieved of many non-crime-fighting duties. Fourth, provision would be made for more effective sentencing, 'tough sentences . . . for violent criminals and thugs'; but also 'a wider variety of sentences' should be available for those offenders for whom 'long prison terms are not always the best deterrent'. Such measures would range from experiments with 'short, sharp shock' regimes in detention centres to making more compulsory attendance centres available 'for hooligans'. Finally, MPs would be given an early free vote on the restoration of capi-

[3] On 23 April 1979 the National Front held a meeting at the Town Hall, Southall. It was a deliberate provocation to the predominantly Asian local community. An estimated 3,000 anti-National Front demonstrators gathered to protest, and approximately 4,000 police were drafted in to confront them. During the mêlée that ensued a white teacher, Blair Peach, was killed, possibly after having been struck by a member of the Metropolitan Police Special Patrol Group. See Marwick (1990: 221).

[4] The Edmund–Davies Committee of Inquiry (1978) had been set up by the Labour government primarily to advise on problems of low police recruitment and high wastage. The Committee recommended, *inter alia*, that police pay be increased and thereafter index-linked.

tal punishment. Two other aspects of note were, first, in a substantial section on trade union reform, a proposal to revise the law on picketing to prevent 'violence, intimidation and obstruction'; and second, eight specific undertakings were given to achieve 'firm immigration control' which was said to be 'essential for racial harmony'. The 1979 Conservative manifesto brought 'law and order' to the fore as a major election issue and dispelled any lingering trace of bipartisan consensus.

By 1983, the party political battle over 'law and order' had been firmly joined. The Conservatives listed their achievements in office (all inputs as opposed to outputs) as giving the police 'every possible backing'; being in the process of revising their powers (in the Police and Criminal Evidence [PACE] Bill); giving the courts 'tougher and more flexible sentencing powers'; and embarking on a major prison building programme (Conservative Party 1983). Finally, broadening the scope of any law and order discussion, and widening responsibility for it, they pronounced:

> Dealing with crimes, civil disobedience, violent demonstrations and pornography are not matters for the police alone. It is teachers and parents—and television producers too—who influence the moral standards of the next generation. There must be close co-operation and understanding between the police and the community they serve.

The law and order issue was thus extended to embrace not only law-violation and order-defiance, but also present and future morality.

Labour's 1983 manifesto (Labour Party 1983) was the longest it had ever produced and twice as long as the Conservatives'. It devoted more space than ever before to law and order issues, spelling out a detailed programme of reform for reducing the prison population by non-custodial measures; for improving prison conditions, regimes, and prisoners' rights; and for enabling citizens to activate their rights under the law. Though stressing the need for support for the police, Labour pledged to repeal the PACE Act and replace it with a framework for police accountability which would 'protect the rights of individual suspects' and create elected police authorities.[5] Labour's programme made no reference to punishment, deterrence, or particular categories of heinous offenders. The

[5] The first PACE Bill was widely held by the left (civil liberties groups and the Labour Party) significantly to increase police powers without providing adequate safeguards for suspects. Further, the alleged safeguards that were provided were predicted to be of little worth in practice. Following the inner-city public disorders in St Pauls, Bristol, in 1980 and Brixton and elsewhere in 1981 (see Scarman Report 1981), increased police use of paramilitary equipment and tactics, without that use having been sanctioned by public debate in either Westminster or police authority fora, led to major disputes between some police authorities and their chief constables. This in turn led to calls from the left for the full democratization of local police authorities and the empowerment of police authorities to determine general police policy (see Christian 1983; Spencer 1985; Downes and Ward 1986; Lustgarten 1986; Reiner 1992: ch. 6; chapter 15 in this volume).

policies they advocated were directly at variance with the existing and projected programme of the Conservative administration. Otherwise, the Labour manifesto maintained the 'one nation' perspective and focused on 'healing the wounds' brought about by unemployment and cuts in public expenditure.

Both major parties displayed a greater realism and restraint in the 1987 election. The Labour Party manifesto (Labour Party 1987) said nothing about the much amended Police and Criminal Evidence Act 1984, nor about the penal and criminal justice systems. Though elected police authorities figured once more as a pledge, police responsibility for 'all operational matters' was guaranteed. Social crime prevention schemes in the community were massively endorsed. However, for the first time in any but the most glancing way, the Labour Party shaped up to attack the Conservative 'law and order' record; 'eight years of rising crime, of greater insecurity on the streets and housing estates and in the home'. Labour attributed the continued steep rise in recorded crime directly to Conservative policies (though not necessarily those on 'law and order').

The Conservative manifesto (Conservative Party 1987) was no more confrontational than Labour's for the first time since law and order emerged as an electoral issue. Though making no concessions to the structural inequalities typically cited by Labour as producing crime, the Conservatives no longer implicitly claimed that their own policies would readily lead to lower crime rates or safer streets. Instead, responsibility for fighting crime was—in line with the 1983 manifesto—extended to 'all of us'; and the worsening crime rate was a problem 'not just in Britain but in most other societies too'. Its origins lie 'deep in society' (a rare reference to this hitherto taboo collectivity), though *not* in any form of social differentiation such as wealth or income inequalities: rather, in poor parental support; in poor school discipline; and in the glamorization of violence and the attack on traditional values. The mobilization of communities to support the police by such schemes as Neighbourhood Watch, and tough measures against, *inter alia*, drug traffickers in the envisaged Criminal Justice Bill, betokened a persistently resolute stance against crime. Control of drug abuse and immigration—topics perhaps unfortunately discussed in adjacent sections of the manifesto—were priorities.

The Liberal/SDP Alliance produced the most radical law and order manifesto of 1987 (Liberal/SDP Alliance 1987), after two elections in which the Liberals had adopted a position either compromising between Conservative and Labour (1979) or little different from the latter (1983). They advocated a Bill of Rights incorporating the European Convention of Human Rights;[6] the establishment of local 'Crime Crisis Areas': a

[6] The European Convention of Human Rights and Fundamental Freedoms is conventionally assumed in Britain to be an extremely liberal framework, but in some respects is

Ministry of Justice; a strengthened Judicial Studies Board to lay down sentencing guidelines; a Royal Commission on Violence in the Media; and a requirement on local authorities to set up Crime Prevention Units.

The period immediately before the election of 1992 suggested the likely and lively engagement by the opposition parties with the government's record on law and order. The Labour Party produced a criminal justice policy document, *Seven Steps to Justice*, which represented its most ambitious thinking since the 1964 document *Crime—A Challenge to Us All* and seemed likely to provide much of the material for the law and order part of the Labour manifesto. The Conservative government produced a flurry of measures to tackle 'bail bandits' (Morgan and Jones 1992), car theft, and 'hotting',[7] and teenage crime in general was addressed by 'work camps'. The Home Secretary, Kenneth Baker, termed Labour 'soft and flabby on crime'. His Shadow, Roy Hattersley, persistently called for more police strength (in part to neutralize that attack), and invoked social measures to stem the unprecedented rise in the crime rate. A sign that the Conservative Party may, for the first time, have been vulnerable on the law and order front was to be discerned in opinion poll findings that showed little difference between the two major parties on these issues. This presumably reflected two consecutive years, 1990 and 1991, during which recorded crime rose by an unprecedented and much-publicized 36 per cent. Whether or not these rises were 'real' (a vast critical literature exists on this question; see chapter 6 in this volume), they are generally regarded as indicating gross trends. As such, they may be seen as 'real' in their political consequences.

In the event, somewhat anti-climactically, Labour chose to fight the 1992 election on a smaller front and fewer issues than any since 1945. Its manifesto (Labour Party 1992) devoted only one half-column in a document of over twenty pages to law and order issues, focusing on crime prevention involving local authorities (who had been marginalized on this front by Conservative Governments) and on implementing the Woolf Inquiry recommendations on prisons (see below). It was a recipe for reform that could have been culled from the eighteenth-century works of Henry Fielding and John Howard. By contrast, the Conservative

open to different interpretations. For example, its provisions allow for the use of lethal force in the recapture of non-dangerous escaping prisoners; and for the use of the death penalty, despite the fact that no member state retains capital punishment. The support enjoyed by the Convention among critical commentators in Britain may owe as much to the lack of domestic remedies as to the liberality of the Convention and the European Commission and European Court of Human Rights which determine the outcome of petitions under the Convention.

[7] 'Hotting' refers to a fashion for racing stolen cars around local estates. A related craze for 'ram-raiding', using stolen cars as battering rams for forcing entry into shops and even houses, also caused much concern during this period. See Webb and Laycock 1992; Light *et al.* 1993.

document (Conservative Party 1992) devoted five of its fifty pages to 'Freedom Under Law', siting crime prevention in 'communities', Neighbourhood Watch schemes, and community policing, without mention of local authorities; listing a number of modest reforms in each criminal justice field; and making the claim to have 'reversed the Labour Party's neglect of the prison service in the 1970s'. The Liberal Democratic Party's manifesto (1992) brought rising crime rates and soaring expenditure on police and prisons together in dramatic montage, listing reforms such as the creation of a Ministry of Justice as necessary for a more coherent policy-making process. The most striking feature of the campaign period, however, was Labour's disengagement from this whole terrain: even more strikingly than in 1983 and 1987, it was a clear case of 'the dog that did not bark'.

Election campaign analysis substantially bears out these trends. According to the Nuffield studies, 'law and order' topics (that is, if broad industrial relations issues are excluded) did not figure at all in the elections of 1945, 1950, 1951, 1955, and 1959. In their apparently exhaustive scrutiny of election broadcasts, leaders' speeches, and press coverage, as well as constituency election addresses, there is not a single reference to a law and order topic—crime, policing, *or* immigration—by any of the three major parties (McCallum and Readman 1946; Nicholas 1951; Butler 1952, 1956; Butler and Rose 1960). Neither the 'race riots' in Nottingham and Notting Hill in 1958 nor the Street Offences Act of 1959 impinged on the 1959 election campaign. Even in that of 1964, with the notable exception of the campaign at Smethwick, where exploitation of the fear of immigration led to the defeat of Patrick Gordon Walker, Labour's Shadow foreign affairs spokesman, by Peter Griffith, who 'almost invariably linked immigration with violence, crime and disease', such issues were surprisingly marginal and all three party leaders were keen that it should remain so (Butler and King 1965). Despite rising crime rates, and heavy media coverage of the youth cults of the day and the disturbances in which they regularly engaged, there was no attempt by the party leaderships to exploit either law and order or immigration as an issue with which to belabour the opposition.

Nevertheless, 1966 saw the emergence of 'law and order' as a clear Conservative issue, more so in the campaigns than in the manifestos: 40 per cent of Conservative addresses mentioned crime, compared with none for Labour and only 2 per cent of Liberal addresses (Butler and King 1967). Yet immigration appears to have been less of an issue in 1966 than in 1964, perhaps due to Labour's acceptance, in a White Paper in August 1965, of the need for immigration control: only 11 per cent of Conservative addresses mentioned it compared to none among both Labour and Liberal addresses. It is not clear why such a high proportion of Conservative election addresses mentioned crime in 1966 when, according to the Nuffield studies, none had in any previous post-war election. However, the most plausible explanation is that substantial media coverage of youth cults (see, for example, Cohen 1972) and organized crime—the 1964–6 period was the climax of the notoriety of the Kray and Richardson gangland 'empires' (see chapter 10 in this volume)—led to a groundswell of concern that was translatable into Conservative, though not Labour and Liberal, discourse.

Whatever the explanation for the party differences in 1966, they were amplified in 1970. As we have seen, the Conservatives decided in 1970, for the first time, to attack the Labour government's 'law and order' record. There was incident enough on which the Conservatives could draw: 1968–9 saw, *inter alia*, the great 'permissive society' debate on homosexual and abortion law reform; the end of censorship by the Lord Chamberlain; the Paris and UK student demonstrations and occupations; the Rolling Stones drug furores; Enoch Powell's 'rivers of blood' speech against immigration (and for repatriation); anti-apartheid demonstrations (during the election campaign itself) against the South African rugby tour; and a spate of strikes which led to the abortive Labour government response of *In Place of Strife*.[8] It is not too surprising, therefore, that 'law and order' appears to have figured for the first time in the media coverage of an election. But the Nuffield analysis of constituency election addresses shows a clearly marked difference between the parties: 60 per cent of Conservative addresses compared to only 15 per cent of Labour mentioned law and order questions. 'Law and order' was now sixth in the Conservative 'top ten' of topics: it did not figure in the Labour top ten (Butler and Pinto-Duschinsky 1971). The Conservatives won a handsome majority, an outcome hardly expected until, late in the campaign, opinion polls registered the decisive shifts.

The trend set in 1966 and 1970 continued in the two elections of February and October 1974. In that of February, the industrial relations crisis led the Conservatives to fight on a 'Who Governs?' front (Butler and Kavanagh 1975*a*). When the narrow win by Labour left them without an overall majority, they went to the country again in October. Once more, 60 per cent of Conservative addresses mentioned 'law and order' compared to only 2 per cent of Labour and 7 per cent of Liberal. Though the Conservatives lost more heavily, Labour policies on immigration and defence were rated by polling respondents more negatively than

[8] *In Place of Strife* (Cmnd 3888, 1969) was the White Paper discussion document aimed at curbing the trade unions' right to strike by proposing a Commission to look at disputes; a secret ballot before a strike could be called; and a cooling-off period of up to two months between a strike threat and its implementation. Resistance from the trade unions led to the withdrawal of the proposals and, arguably, to Labour's unexpected defeat in the 1970 election.

those of the Conservatives (unfortunately, the parties' popularity on 'law and order' was not examined: see Butler and Kavanagh 1975*b*).

It is apparent, therefore, that the seminal and much-analysed 1979 election represented the heightening of a trend in relation to 'law and order' issues which was already well established. In 1979, the Conservatives successfully promoted their positive public image on law and order and all the evidence suggests that they did so to the great detriment of Labour. Nor was this lead simply a matter of the wounds inflicted on Labour by the 'Winter of Discontent' of 1978–9. 'Maintaining law and order' moved from sixth to fourth in the list of 'biggest failures of the present government' in the regular Gallup polls during 1975–8 (Butler and Kavanagh 1980: 37–8). Across a range of policy issues tested by MORI polls between August 1978 and April 1979, *no* policy placed the Conservatives so far ahead of Labour as 'law and order': a thirty-point lead compared with eleven points for 'unemployment' and little difference for 'prices/inflation' and even 'industrial relations/strikes' (ibid.: 131). One-third of Labour voters and almost one-half of Liberal voters expressing a clear preference on the issue thought that the Tories had a better 'law and order' policy than their own parties (ibid.: 163).

The salience of the 'law and order' issue for the Conservatives was heightened during the election period itself by a number of events and developments, such as the killing of a leading Conservative MP, Airey Neave, by an IRA bomb in the Palace of Westminster; the Southall Riot in the wake of a march by the National Front; and a number of statements by leading 'law and order' figures, such as Robert Mark, the then recently retired Commissioner of the Metropolitan Police, and Lord Denning, Master of the Rolls, asserting respectively that the unions enjoyed a Nazi Party-like immunity from the law and were 'almost above the law' (quoted in ibid.: 187). Press coverage, mostly in support of the Conservative Party, boosted the issue more than ever before. 'Law and order' emerged, not surprisingly, as a favourite topic in Conservative candidates' election addresses: an astonishing 87 per cent issued tough calls for action. By contrast, 66 per cent of Labour addresses were silent on the subject and those that did take it up argued that only social reform could tackle crime (ibid.: 297). Moreover, 35 per cent of Tory addresses mentioned the death penalty, compared to none among Labour (ibid.: 297). *During* the campaign, the Nuffield analysts conclude, the growth in Tory support on this issue was greater than for any other issue. 'Law and order' had become what political scientists term a 'valence issue'; that is, party and voters alike agree on the objectives, but doubt whether the party has the capacity to affect the issue. The voters of 1979 judged that the Tories put 'law and order' first, of which they overwhelmingly approved: they doubted whether Labour did so. Labour lost a substantial degree of its traditional working-class vote and got only half the trade unionists' vote. The Conservatives won a sizeable majority.

By 1983, law and order had begun to assume a less prominent role, but it remained a central card in a way in which, until the 1970s, it never had been. No party could afford to cede this ground to the opposition, and all parties felt obliged to address it in some way during the campaign. By 1987, a kind of second-order consensus had been evolved whereby all parties asserted their support for the police and the need to increase their effectiveness; all parties agreed that crime prevention and victim support were priorities; and all parties accepted the logic of 'bifurcation' (Bottoms 1977), according to which extended custodial sentences are appropriate for the most serious offenders, but an enhanced range of non-custodial measures for the less serious should be used. By 1987, 65 per cent of Labour, 74 per cent of Conservative, 74 per cent of Social Democrat, and 65 per cent of Liberal addresses mentioned the topic. Yet significant differences remained in the manner in which they dealt with an issue which *all* now felt obliged to discuss. Substantial minorities of Conservative addresses called for tougher sentences (30 per cent) or capital punishment (19 per cent), or claimed that Labour was anti-police (14 per cent). By contrast, Labour Party addresses talked of the crime which pervaded a divided society, a Britain divided by the Tories' social and economic policies. In 1987, the local election addresses comprehensively mirrored the presentational stances which, throughout the 1980s, had been developed in the national manifestos. It was a configuration that seemed likely to play a prominent role in the election of 1992. In the event, as we have seen, Labour chose to remain content with the neutralization of the issue, rather than its contestation, a strategy which arguably left the Conservative Party in a position of inert supremacy as the guardians of law and order.

Explaining the Trends: Images, Philosophies, and Constraints

Frank Parkin argued over two decades ago that the principal strength of the Conservative Party was its capacity to claim oneness with the bastions of traditional British sovereignty: the monarchy, the aristocracy, property, the armed forces, the ancient universities, the land, and the law (Parkin 1967). The only countervailing force to this ruling-class ideology was that offered by the Labour Party as representative of the working-class labour movement and its trade union organization. Yet this constituency was always deviant with respect to the core values and most cherished allegiances of British traditionalism. The Labour Party could flourish only in direct relation to movement away from their sites, most typically in a single-occupation, one-class urban area like a mining town. Against the Tory

Party's keystone value of what Macpherson termed 'possessive individualism' (Macpherson 1962), the Labour Party rests on an appeal to the alternative morality of redistributive social justice and community.

These ideological differences translated readily into quite distinct policy choices in the post-war period. The Conservative preference for owner-occupation in housing has contrasted sharply and successfully with Labour's emphasis on municipal rented accommodation. On the other hand, Labour's development of the National Health Service can still command such widespread support that the Conservatives had striven to resist the claim that their policies amount to 'privatization'. In taxation, Labour supports progressive direct taxation of income and wealth; the Conservatives favour regressive indirect taxes on spending. The choices are fairly distinct. Yet issues of 'law and order' do not lend themselves to such clear-cut articulation along party lines. This asymmetry is not due to the absence of sharp differences between the parties in their *explanations* of the underlying causes of crime. For Conservatives, these inhere in the realms of individual pathology and/or lax authority whether imposed at parental or institutional level. For Labour, they derive far more from social and economic realities: inequality, deprivation, marginalization, and outright poverty. For Labour, the task of political persuasion is therefore to make connections between crime and public issues, such as trends in employment and welfare. For the Conservatives, the task is to *disconnect* them, to contest, indeed, the very act of making such connections as inimical to law and order maintenance (Downes 1989*a*). In Conservative rhetoric, 'explanation' amounts to 'excuse', an equation Labour has failed to challenge at all effectively. Throughout the 1980s, Mrs Thatcher successfully deployed this philosophically unacceptable elision by using the rhetoric of moral outrage. Thus, her statement that 'rioting can never be justified by unemployment' (or poverty, or racism, or police malpractices) always overrode the logical objection—rarely voiced—that nevertheless such realities may help to explain it. Edged by such tactics into appearing to be 'soft' on crime, Labour reacted consistently not by challenging the image but by claiming equal hardness to—if not greater hardness than—the Conservatives.

An attempt to resolve this impasse appeared in a speech given in February 1993 by Tony Blair, Labour Shadow Home Secretary. Addressing public anger and unease following the adbuction and murder in Liverpool of a two-year-old boy, Blair set out Labour's policy on law and order as being 'tough on crime, tough on the causes of crime'. As yet, only the first part of the policy has been outlined, entailing support for the government on the need to provide more secure places for serious juvenile offenders, but disagreeing on their character and location. It remains to be seen how the second part of the policy will be developed.

It follows that party policies on law and order can be related only tenuously to their ideological foundations. Image—associations of ideas and mythology—lent the Conservatives weight as *the* party of 'law and order'. No warrant for this assumption can be found in any indicator of actual performance. If anything, the reverse holds true, since periods of Labour government have seen lower rises in the recorded crime rate, both relatively and absolutely, than have Conservative administrations (Downes and Young 1987; Downes 1989*b*; Young 1992). Despite the similarity or even superiority of Labour by comparison with the Conservative record on law and order, Labour have nevertheless proved vulnerable on this front due to various hostages to fortune derived from their association with, and implicit need to defend, several key constituencies.

These hostages to fortune on the left are bound up integrally with the origins and continuing role of the Labour Party as the parliamentary voice of the trade unions, on the one hand, and as the major vehicle for progressive intellectuals of a non-Marxist, socialist persuasion, on the other. The uneasy alliance between the labour movement and Fabian-style intellectuals is the chief strand in the story of the Labour Party, each involving the party in a set of distinctive concerns on the 'law and order' front which have exposed it to accusations from the right of undermining the 'rule of law'. Paradoxically, though the right also bears hostages to fortune in distinct (though fewer) respects, these can be handled in ways that strengthen rather than weaken their association with the forces of law and order.

Trade Unions and Labour

The labour movement both launched and proved the main ballast of Labour Party history, but in the period 1978–85 arguably almost sank it. This is no place to essay analysis of the long and tangled history of the relationship between the Party and the movement. The major point is that the struggle to win basic labour rights, from assembly to picketing to the very process of unionization itself, of a kind now accepted as legitimate in all democratic states, entailed a great deal of order-defiance and law-violation. In the immediate post-war period, however, the dominance of the right wing within the labour movement lent it a new respectability. Two pivotal factors eventually led to the situation whereby, in the late 1970s and 1980s, trade unionism could be equated with hooliganism and violence.

First, the electoral, though not numerical, defeat of the Labour government under Attlee in 1951 ushered in a period during which Britain, unlike any other western European country, enjoyed the fruits of post-war prosperity under a right-wing government. The association of ideas between Toryism and prosperity has proved lasting. Despite intervening periods in office, Labour appeared to be the party of the austerity years, with union links that could 'threaten' economic growth. By contrast, trade unions in Scandinavia and West Germany were seen as playing an essential part in the process of economic recovery and expansion.

Second, the peculiar nature of capitalist law in Britain (and the USA) places unique emphasis on the overriding priority to be accorded the rights of shareholders in company development. Again by contrast, such rights in West Germany, Japan, Scandinavian, and other industrial societies are tempered by the requirement to give far more consideration to two other entities: the community and the employees (see e.g. Dore 1992, on Japan; Schneider-Lenné 1992, on Germany). Rights, conditions, amenities, and wage levels which were granted relatively smoothly by a process of negotiated settlements in these countries were in Britain too often wrung from reluctant employers by protracted conflict involving strike action. The litany of protracted industrial conflict in Britain embraces manufacturing industries in historic decline as well as light industries in the ascendant after the Second World War. In the 1970s, the left in Britain came to associate success in industrial conflict with militancy, a strategic choice which heightened the linkages made by the right between the labour movement, violence, and lawlessness. The eventual climax to this sequence of events was the so-called 'Winter of Discontent' of 1978–9 (see note 2 above), which ushered in the downfall of the Labour government and the Thatcherite era.

The unions at times colluded in the process. For example, the print unions presided over the notorious Fleet Street ghost worker scandal, whereby workers who were already relatively well paid also drew wages for non-existent employees (see Martin 1981). Perhaps the most tragic instance was the misconduct of the National Union of Mineworkers in 1983 in embarking on a national strike without the legally prescribed ballot of members. This tactic split the miners' otherwise united front, legitimized the government's pursuit of the union's funds by sequestration, and neutralized the likelihood of open Labour Party support for the strike. These factors arguably led to the miners' defeat after eighteen months of bitter strike action, in which the union was hauled through the courts, hundreds of miners were unwarrantedly harassed or victimized by the police, and the strikers' cause was marred by occasional acts of outright criminality and, in one case, manslaughter. The fact that the dire predictions by the NUM leadership, under Arthur Scargill, of pit closures and mass redundancies have been cruelly vindicated by events, with a labour force of 220,000 in 1983 reduced to 41,000 in 1992 and a further thirty-one pits threatened with closure in 1993–4, does not nullify the association of ideas between trade union militancy and law-violation that resulted.

The New Underclass?

The concept and formation of a new underclass is vigorously contested (see e.g. Abercrombie and Ward, 1988; Dahrendorf 1987; Macnicol 1987; and, on the USA, Jencks and Peterson 1991). What is not disputed is that deindustrialization has fractured the links between steady manual work and the stable communities which it once sustained. Further, the official statistics attest to the fact that the least wealthy half of the population now holds a lower proportion of overall wealth than it did a decade ago and that income differentials between households have grown. The rich have become richer, the poor poorer. To the extent that there can be said to be an underclass, it comprises groups as diverse as impoverished single parents; discriminated-against minority groups; the long-term unemployed; the never-have-been-employed youth of the poorer housing estates; and, as ever, those who, as Henry Mayhew put it, 'will not work' (Mayhew 1862). The old working class has decayed. High, endemic unemployment and non-employment rates have provided the tinder from which—from 1980 onwards—riots have been kindled by policing which may have been insensitive but was rarely outlandish: the real cause lies in the economic marginalization and political exclusion of disadvantaged youths in particular, whether black, white or both (Lea and Young 1984). Relations between underclass and authority are inherently conflict-ridden at any time, since the lot of underclass people is to be underprotected and overcontrolled (Downes and Ward 1986).

The key problem for the Labour Party is unfortunately much the same as that for sociologists; how to connect private troubles with public issues (Mills 1959). When riots as vicious as that at the Broadwater Farm Estate in North London flare up, and a police officer is hacked to death, the best way to make the connection is hardly to announce that 'the police got a good hiding'. This remark by Bernie Grant, the local black Labour MP for a constituency with a large black population, was perhaps the biggest single hostage to fortune handed to the Conservatives by a left-wing source. The 1987 Labour strategy on policing was watered down from a policy of local accountability (strongly opposed by the police) to one of local consultation (little different from Conservative policy), due to fears that this and similar 'anti-police' remarks by left-wing sources would otherwise be quoted endlessly by the Conservatives in their campaigning: much the same backing-off process arguably occurred in 1992. However, Mr Grant did have a problem: how to supply a sound-bite at the scene and under pressure which, by putting the events in context—that of racism, unemployment, and the oppressive policing resulting in the death of Mrs Groce, a West Indian mother of a black male suspect in a minor case of car theft, that had triggered the riot—did more than simply condemn the rioters. That he got it so resoundingly wrong in the event is in part a testimony to the massive difficulties in transcending sheer condemnation and moving on to explanation and constructive action. Given the constituencies involved, this was far more of a problem for Mr Grant and the Labour Party than for the Conservative government.

Working-class trade unionists demonstrate and take industrial action in pursuit of recognizable, collective ends, in ways—such as mass picketing—which may verge on or constitute law-violation under certain circumstances. The new underclass is incapable of such organizational feats. Riot and criminality may conceivably be interpreted as impoverished routes to these ends, but they are hardly recognizable or shared, and explanation in these terms all too easily sounds like special pleading. In short, the more the organized labour movement and the trade unions are pushed off the stage by endemic mass un- and non-employment, and by rapid technological change, the more the emergent underclass presents the Labour Party with a massive problem of translation. For example, despite widespread and articulate opposition across the social spectrum, even the poll tax presented the Labour opposition with a particularly nasty version of the 'law and order' paradox, whereby the iniquitous character of the law would only be changed by strong public reaction, including non-compliance (since compliance would be taken by the government as confirming public acquiescence).[9] However, for the opposition to support non-compliance would have been denounced as inciting people to violate the law, an accusation that was indeed levelled against several Labour MPs who advocated it despite official Labour policy on the issue. Non-compliance would also have deprived Labour-controlled local authorities of essential income.

Civil Disobedience

Civil disobedience has been a substantial and usually honourable strand in the history of the Labour Party. The inter-war period was notable for such events as George Lansbury's imprisonment in 1921 for leading the non-payment of local precepts by Poplar Council in protest against the burden placed on local government to provide poor relief, the 1926 General Strike, and the 'hunger marches' of the 1930s Depression years, all of which were actively supported by Labour MPs (see Mowat 1955). It might have been expected that, as Labour formed the government for

[9] The so-called 'poll tax', or community charge, introduced by the Conservative government in 1988 to replace local authority rates, levied the same tax per capita regardless of income, wealth, or size of property. The only major exemptions concerned people on income support and students, who were charged 20 per cent of the tax.

seventeen of the post-war years, old habits would have died and indeed, for the first decade after the war, that seemed to be so. However, the Suez Crisis of 1956 revived the tradition, and the Campaign for Nuclear Disarmament, formed in the same year, founded the annual march to London from the first American forces nuclear base at Aldermaston (see Taylor 1988). Left-wing Labour MPs were prominent figures on these demonstrations which, although eminently peaceful, were increasingly drawn into association with extra-legal activities, such as the exposure by an Anarchist group on the 1961 march of the hitherto secret Regional Seats of Government bases (see *Anarchy* 1963). The formation of the Committee of 100 in 1961 brought a new repertoire to civil disobedience: the systematic violation of the law by leading and usually left-wing intellectuals to focus attention on the nuclear disarmament cause.

The Vietnam War from 1964 onwards provided the target for a rising crescendo of demonstrations which, with the rise of the student movement in the USA and its spread to Europe in the mid-1960s, added site occupations to the armoury of protest. Labour, which formed the government from 1964 to 1970, pursued a policy of damage-limitation with respect to the policing of such forms of protest. Media coverage of the October 1968 Grosvenor Square demonstration, however, lent a new imputation to reportage: the expectation that the potential for violence implicit in any mass movement would be realized. As Halloran *et al.* (1970) pointed out, the press greatly exaggerated such violence as did occur on that march.

After Grosvenor Square, and the student demonstrations in Paris in May 1968 which almost led to the collapse of the French Government, the die was cast. No left-wing cause had street credibility without a march, demonstration, or occupation. The Clydebank occupation of 1972 firmly associated industrial militancy with key figures in the Labour Party following the much publicised conversion of Tony Benn to the merits of such direct action.[10] The case of the 'Shrewsbury Three' in 1974 embodied the ease with which direct action by pickets could turn ugly and involve criminal prosecutions.[11] It was also in 1974 that the newly elected

[10] Three shipyards on the Clyde owned by Upper Clyde Shipbuilders got into financial difficulties and sought assistance from the government. Assistance was refused and the firm went into liquidation, whereupon the workforce, led by shop steward Jimmy Reid, staged a prolonged 'work-in' of the yards.

[11] This *cause célèbre* arose out of a strike in the building industry and the use of 'flying pickets'. The Director of Public Prosecutions approved the prosecution of six pickets for the common-law offences of unlawful assembly, affray, and conspiracy to intimidate workers, in addition to the substantive offences of assault and criminal damage. All six were convicted of some offences including three, by a majority of the jury, of conspiracy to intimidate. These three received sentences of three years' imprisonment, much longer sentences than they would have been likely to receive on the substantive charges. The Court of Appeal dismissed appeals against both charges and sentence and the case was subsequently the subject

Labour government's Director of Public Prosecutions failed to prosecute Labour councillors in Bolsover who had refused to raise rents in accordance with the previous Conservative government's Rent Act. Another *cause célèbre* was the Grunwick strike and several months' long mass picket of 1976–7, which even right-of-centre Labour ministers such as Shirley Williams felt the need to attend, in solidarity with a workforce largely composed of Asian women who had been denied the right to unionize by their employer. The 1970s were characterized by a plethora of such events, the policing of which was frequently contentious and costly, and at times tragically counter-productive.

In the 1980s, street protest turned sour. The symbolism had become devalued to the point where the absence of a demonstration or march against a measure was taken for popular compliance with it. The threshold for media coverage was raised to the point at which, unless a demonstration involved violence, little reportage could be expected. The poll tax riots of 1989–90 were the climax of these developments. By this juncture, however, the 'freedom of the streets' had been greatly constrained. The strategy brought diminishing returns of publicity and, in the face of disruption and traffic congestion, of public support and interest. Bans on marches by the extreme right had been extended to all unless stringent criteria of stewardship and route-taking were met. If the increasing frequency and size of demonstrations heralded the eclipse of a Conservative government in 1974, their decreasing salience and vigour has marked the ascendancy of the neo-Conservative regimes since 1979. In so far as Labour is associated with both the decline and the unwanted side-effects of taking to the streets, its image as upholder of law and order is at risk. Only when the politics of the street are actively welcomed as a symbol of peaceable and healthy democracy is such a risk neutralized. Without them, the arena for the legitimate expression of views is greatly reduced.

Libertarian Criminal Law Reform

Though Labour Party history has been marked by a libertarian strand which has surfaced from time to time, the late 1960s witnessed a sustained programme of criminal law reform under a Labour government: the decriminalization of male homosexuality and abortion; the substantial relaxation of the censorship laws; the abolition of capital punishment; and the resolution of key problems threatening the legalization of casino gaming. The last of these stemmed from the sweeping legalization of gaming carried out by the Conservative government of Harold Macmillan in 1960 and 1963; a government which also decriminalized attempted sui-

of protest resolutions at both the TUC and Labour Party Annual Conferences (see Wallington 1975).

cide in 1963. It was left to a Labour Lord Chancellor, Gerald Gardiner, systematically to push the reform through, however. Two decades later, the entire period of liberalizing achievement by both Conservative and Labour was to be derided by the new right of Thatcher and Tebbit as the 'permissive society', having achieved nothing more than a slackening of authority and an unwonted release of baser passions. What was, by most standards, a major period of reform promoting greater tolerance and freedom of expression came to figure in the popular press and in right-wing ideology as the source of unprecedented rises in criminality in the 1980s.

What had been a relatively clear-cut battle between the 'progressive liberals'—who in the 1960s had migrated to the Labour Party to a much greater extent than before or since—and the forces of reaction, had in the 1980s become more complex, however. First, certain forms of backlash arose from unexpected quarters. For example, radical feminists, including such leading Labour MPs as Clare Short, and leading traditionalists, such as Mary Whitehouse, ranged themselves, albeit for different reasons, against pornography and the exploitation of women as exemplified on page three of the *Sun*. The porn merchants had made far narrower and more profitable use of the new-found liberties of expression of the 1960s than the exponents of liberalization had ever predicted. The average suburban newsagent carried a far greater spread of female nudity in the 1980s than the average Soho pornshop in the 1950s. Second, gay militancy had found forms of political expression which included material for primary schools. The resulting backlash included legal constraints such as s. 28 of the Education Act 1988, which expressly forbade the inclusion of family imagery in school material other than that connoting the heterosexual nuclear family.

In sum, once basic freedoms had been won, the complications to which their extension gave rise tended to saddle Labour with the worst of both worlds, able neither to defend such developments as 'gay' schoolbooks nor to define where the line should be drawn afresh. Such defensiveness left such minorities as gays feeling betrayed, on the one hand, and the 'silent majority' feeling that Labour had allowed too much scope for deviant viewpoints, on the other. Conversely, Labour spokespersons who opposed such phenomena as the 'page three nude' could be castigated as killjoys. One notorious election-day ploy in the *Sun* (9 April 1992) was the substitution for the usual page three model of a stereotypically reverse image, a flabby parody of coquettishness. The caption read: 'Here's How Page 3 Will Look Under Kinnock.' Labour could be blamed for both the unwanted developments of libertarianism and the negative aspects of the selective backlash against them.

In the face of such wide-ranging attacks on the potential for order-defiance and law-violation of several of its key constituencies, Labour reacted defensively, content to neutralize the appeal of the Conservatives wherever possible as *the* party of law and order, but backing away from outright contention on the issues involved. The scope for Labour to turn the tables on the Conservatives on these terms was limited by the simple 'rule of law' principle to which the latter adhered quite uncritically. Thus, the law-violations of the extreme right, or those endemic in the operations of the commercial–financial world of the City of London, or those emanating from flawed police procedures, could always be explained in terms of individual pathology, a 'few bad apples'. The kind of challenge to the very terms of the debate which Labour had mounted in some respects in the 1960s was increasingly foregone as anxieties about the electoral liabilities of the hostages to fortune rose.

By any objective standard, the period of Conservative government since 1979 has been a conspicuous failure in crime control terms. In spite of a host of crime prevention initiatives[12] and real increases in spending on the so-called 'law and order' services, increases greater than in any other branch of government expenditure—more police, better paid and with more powers; more courts with an increased range of penalties at their disposal; more prisons and more prisoners in them—the fear of crime has increased, there have been larger than normal rises in recorded crime, and a sequence of urban disturbances has occurred unprecedented in their ferocity this century (see chapters 6 and 15 in this volume). And yet, the polls suggest, the Conservative Party retains its supremacy as the party of 'law and order'. It has managed to persuade a large section of the electorate that the rising tide of crime is not to be explained by the widened divide between rich and poor, the undermining of public goods and services, the emasculation of local government, and the lauding of competitive individualism to the detriment of collective responsibility. Rather, crime is to be ascribed to evil individuals or persons; generally young persons, subject to insufficient control by parents who have a duty to police their behaviour. Either way, criminals are to get their just deserts, punishment proportionate to their culpability and the harm they have caused. Explanatory references to structural forces—poverty, unemployment, discrimination, oppression, social and economic hopelessness, and alienation—are castigated as damaging to the ethos of personal responsibility on which the maintenance of law and order is said ultimately to depend. The question at stake is whether the hegemony of the philosophy of individual pathology, a philosophy closely allied to the paramountcy of the market in Conservative economic policy, can be sus-

[12] These have included the development of Neighbourhood Watch and numerous other Watch schemes, the Safer Cities initiative, and the encouragement of multi-agency schemes of various types: see chapter 14 in this volume.

tained in the face of further increases in crime and disorder, and whether the Labour Party will continue to adopt a defensive law and order policy on the terrain that the Conservative Party has mapped out; or whether the tide will turn and the opposition successfully call into question the moral basis of the political economy which current law and order policies are designed to support.

PRESSURE-GROUP AND INTEREST-GROUP POLITICS

As Bottoms and Stevenson (1992) argue, the fundamental variable in any assessment of 'What went wrong?' in post-war criminal justice policy and practice is the rise and rise of the crime rate. From the mid-1950s onwards, this almost unbroken increase in crime of 5–6 per cent annually beggared explanation in terms of simple poverty and deprivation, as both were manifestly on the decline. With the rise in crime despite the rise in welfare and increasing prosperity came rises in criminological and pressure-group activity, attempts respectively to account for crime and to improve the nature of responses to it. The system which proved barely adequate for a million offences a year and 20,000 prisoners broke down at crucial points when handling several million crimes and 50,000 prisoners—despite increasing resources and a plethora of innovations and reforms.

The proliferation of pressure groups was not unique to the law and order field but was a trend in British politics as a whole in this period.

> Beneath the apparent restoration of the structure of two-party politics in Britain, there were signs that the fabric of British political life had been permanently changed by the events of the Thatcher decade. The emergence of the Greens in the European elections of 1989 underlined the degree of this change. For not merely did the growth in electoral support for the Greens (jumping to 15 per cent of the total vote from 0.5 per cent registered in the European elections of 1984) signal the continuing volatility of the public and the willingness to switch to a new party; more importantly it signalled the capacity of single issues to alter electoral behaviour and the extent to which the electorate might be mobilised by short-term factors which had gained publicity rather than long-term factors such as class identity. (Peele 1990: 69–70)

Gamble concludes that this trend is of even wider significance:

> The emergence of new social movements . . . and new issues can only with difficulty be forced within the straitjacket of the old, class-based, two-party system. A new political agenda centred on Europe, disarmament, the environment, the quality of public and private services, and citizenship rights has already become well established in many countries of the European Community. (Gamble 1990: 353)

Perhaps because law and order issues had never fitted that straitjacket to any marked extent, pressure groups in this field often bore pedigrees going back to before the Thatcher decade, though some—notably Inquest (founded 1981) and the Prison Reform Trust (founded 1982)—are of very recent origin. The oldest, the Howard League for Penal Reform, emerged in 1921 from the amalgamation of the original Howard Association, founded in 1866, and the more militant Penal Reform League, formed in the wake of the suffragette movement in 1907 (see Ryan 1978). It has counterparts in many Commonwealth countries. Until the foundation of the National Association for the Care and Resettlement of Offenders (NACRO) in 1966, it had no real contenders in the field of penal reform. From the late 1960s, however, new pressure groups flourished: Radical Alternatives to Prison (RAP) in 1969 (Ryan 1978); the Legal Action Group (LAG) in 1971; and—within the Labour Party—the Labour Campaign for Criminal Justice in 1978. Justice had, however, preceded even NACRO: founded by Tom Sargent, it was a remarkably successful pressure group in its highly focused pursuit of legal reform. On occasion, alliances between two or more of these groups enhanced their effectiveness, as with the battle of the Howard League, Justice and NACRO to expunge certain classes of ex-offender records in the Rehabilitation of Offenders Act 1974 (see Ryan 1978: 60–3).

The concept of the campaigning consortium was most successfully adopted between 1978 and 1983 when New Approaches to Juvenile Crime—a grouping of NACRO and the principal social work and probation practitioner organizations—chaired by Baroness Faithful, herself an ex-director of social services and prominent Conservative in the House of Lords, did much to generate the climate of opinion which led to the dramatic decline in the use of custody for juvenile offenders in the 1980s. The group was formed in the run-up to the 1979 election in response to the suggestion that the Labour government had been soft on juvenile crime when the evidence indicated the opposite. The group used all the informational techniques which have made NACRO a force to be reckoned with: briefing papers and associated press releases were regularly produced; deputations to ministers were arranged; meetings with magistrates were held; and regular parliamentary briefings were organized. It was Lady Faithful who, against government wishes, introduced amendments to the Bill which became the custody criteria for young offenders in the Criminal Justice Act 1982, s. 1: this measure has led to a greatly reduced use of custody. Moreover, though cause and effect can never precisely be established, there seems little doubt that New Approaches to Juvenile Crime did much to counter the rhetoric of the early 1980s in support of the experimentally punitive 'short, sharp shock' regimes in detention centres—the courts used these centres less rather than more—

and helped to lay the foundation whereby the DHSS funded more than 100 Intermediate Treatment programmes from 1983 onwards.

The most recent pressure grouping is the Penal Affairs Consortium, a lobbying collective which comprised thirteen organizations when it was formed in 1989 and which currently comprises twenty-four, ranging from the Prison Governors' and the Prison Officers' Associations to NACRO, the Prison Reform Trust, the Howard League, and Liberty—a previously unthinkable combination.

Some single-issue pressure groups, such as the National Campaign for the Abolition of the Death Penalty (1955), rise and fall as the issue around which they are built waxes and wanes. The extent of pressure-group activity in 1990 can be gauged from the (by no means exhaustive) catalogue of such groups listed as having given evidence to the Woolf Inquiry into the prison disturbances of April that year. They ranged from the Aids and Prison Consortium Project to the Mental Health Foundation to Women in Prison and included some sixty-five groups in all, as well as professional associations, public service unions and ministries, and agencies of central and local government.

The sheer proliferation of such groups is striking, but less salient than the impressive professionalization of the major organizations in the field, particularly NACRO, the Prison Reform Trust, and the Howard League. Before 1970, the date assigned by Bailey (1987) to the final break-up of the post-war consensus on delinquency, pressure-group activity metaphorically sought to influence policy by a well-informed word in the ministerial ear. From that date, reformers increasingly began to beat on the ministerial door in a far more public, confrontational way, albeit one which was, if anything, even more highly informed. Douglas Hurd, Home Secretary from 1984 to 1988, remarked that such clamour was counter-productive. However, this metaphor should not be allowed to obscure the growth, especially in the 1980s, of myriad links between the Home Office and the pressure groups. In conferences, media debates, seminars, and the regular call for expert evidence on penal matters in particular, opportunities abound for the groups to inform penal policy-making processes. None of these processes, either singly or in total, however, equalled the kind of unforced access that the Howard League enjoyed in its heyday of close informal as well as formal contact with the Home Office (see Ryan 1978) or the strong role for criminological expertise provided by the Advisory Council on the Penal System (1966–80) and its predecessor the Advisory Council on the Treatment of Offenders (1944–64). The abolition of the ACPS in 1980 signalled the end of the inside track enjoyed by the more Establishment academic liberal reformers, adding to the scope for pressure-group activity. That inside track had, of course, carried the danger that research might uphold punitive measures, and inhibit strong contestation of government policy, as in the example of Max Grunhut's long gestation of a project which eventually reported in favour of detention centres, to the detriment of the Howard League's stance on the issue (Ryan 1978: 83–4). Further, in its final years, the ACPS produced more and more lengthy reports—on *Young Adult Offenders* in 1974 and *Sentences of Imprisonment* in 1978—which attracted critical academic judgement as well as ministerial impatience (see Morgan 1979). In the 1980s the government replaced advice from Royal Commissions and standing advisory bodies with official inquiries set up whenever a need was perceived.

Most of the main pressure groups in the law and order field—NACRO, the Prison Reform Trust, the Howard League, Justice, Liberty, and a number of small groups such as Inquest, RAP, and PROP—are thus of recent formation and, even when they are beneficiaries of substantial government funding (as NACRO is), they are more or less critical of successive governments' policies. They are differently constituted. For example, Liberty and the Howard League are membership organizations, wholly independent of the state; the Prison Reform Trust is essentially a voluntarily funded single-issue pressure group; NACRO is an organization funded by central government to provide community services but which, with trust funding for specific purposes, has also developed into a powerful campaigning group and authoritative information service. Despite these differences, all are to some degree liberal or radical reformist groups (see Ryan 1978, 1983) favouring:

(a) explanations of crime which stress social and economic inequality and individual vulnerability;
(b) use of social policy in general rather than criminal justice policy in particular to prevent or control crime;
(c) scepticism as to the value of police powers and punitive methods (particularly imprisonment) as crime control measures—indeed, generally stressing the discriminatory and unjust consequences of such methods for repressing already oppressed minorities.

Thus, though there are substantial differences between these groups regarding their ideological commitments, constitutional form, access to policy-makers, and credibility with government, they have a good deal in common. They are generally perceived as left of centre, generally have allegiances with Liberal or Labour rather than Conservative politicians (though NACRO and the Prison Reform Trust are always scrupulously careful to involve politicians of all major parties on their councils), and tend, in spite of the consortia arrangements referred to above, also to have fragile relationships with the practitioner sectional groups, such as the Prison Officers' Association, the Police Federation, the Association of Chief Police Officers (ACPO), and the Magistrates' Association. The latter tend to adopt policies emphasizing the 'thin blue line' and the importance of their members' powers to safeguard the community from crime.

Given these dissonances, it is notable how much interchange has occurred between the groups and the government since 1979. In other fields of social policy, such as education, where pressure groups of comparable expertise are largely lacking, ideologically driven changes since 1979 have arguably met with less resistance, despite strong interest-group and practitioner unease or hostility. Given the immense imbalance of power between the groups and the Home Office, the latter could be said to have little to lose and much to gain from such contacts. The pressure groups provide positive feedback services for governments in furnishing early warnings of probable trouble, in canvassing feasible reforms, and in heightening the legitimacy of the governmental process itself. In a complex society, pressure-group and interest-group activities are the major avenues for active citizen participation in democratic decision-making. In the 1980s, pressure groups also fitted the ideological predispositions of the Thatcher administrations to accord client-based and consumerist agencies a better hearing, albeit at the expense of local government (which still harboured socialist residues), the trade unions, and the demise of Quangos and Royal Commissions, which were seen as stifling government and citizen initiative. The Woolf Inquiry of 1990 was a model of democratic participation by an informed citizenry (by comparison with, say, the average Royal Commission), holding seminars at which the views and evidence of different groups were debated rather than simply presented *seriatim*—though the views of prisoners were separately canvassed and, to that extent, somewhat devalued (Morgan 1991; Sim forthcoming). At those hearings, the expertise of NACRO and the Prison Reform Trust was especially impressive, not least by comparison with that of the Prison Service. This consultative model was subsequently adopted by the Committee of Inquiry into Complaints about Ashworth Hospital in 1991–2, with similarly radical impact (Blom-Cooper Report 1992; see also Richardson 1993).

Nevertheless, the huge imbalance of power remains a political reality. When 'pressured', the Home Office can brush aside any protest, as exemplified by the recent acceleration of prison privatization, a policy opposed vehemently by all the groups cited as well as the Prison Officers' and Prison Governors' Associations. To compensate for the deficit, the pressure groups have striven to deploy their expertise in two novel respects: media influence and the appeal to comparative criminology.

Media influence is important to the pressure groups, not only for the impact it may enable them to bring to bear on policy-making, but also for its sheer publicity value. 'As Frances Crook of the Howard League said to us: "a lot of members will say 'Oh yes, you seem to be doing a lot. I've seen your name in the paper again'. The higher profile we get, the more members we get"' (quoted in Schlesinger and Tumber 1992: 190). Similarly, Paul Cavadino of NACRO, who also plays a crucial linking role as Secretary of the All-party Parliamentary Penal Affairs Group, saw the potential of media influence for persuading public opinion to take more note of the problems facing ex-offenders: 'in an unpopular area like ours, that is the constructive treatment of offenders, what is important is that if people are in favour of what we are doing and of the sorts of things we are saying, to try and make sure that they do not feel they are completely out of step with everyone else' (ibid.: 191). The Home Office and the police are not immune from pursuing much the same strategy. Greater openness by police and prison staff in the 1980s was in part inspired by the demand thus generated for more resources.

Comparative criminology has been increasingly used by the pressure groups to highlight the extent to which prisoners in Britain are both relatively more numerous and worse served by prison conditions than prisoners in virtually all other Western European countries. The NACRO league table of numbers of prisoners per head of population (drawing on Council of Europe data) has been a feature of their briefings for the past decade. Analyses comparing Britain's current penal conditions unfavourably with those of the Netherlands (Tulkens 1979; Downes 1982, 1988), West Germany (Feest 1988), the Netherlands and Japan (Rutherford 1984), and those of Britain in the recent past (King and McDermott 1989, 1991, 1992) were drawn on by the pressure groups, as well as by criminologists in general, including those working within the Home Office Research and Planning Unit (Graham 1988). The Woolf Inquiry (1991) broke new ground by interviewing British prisoners abroad, in Spain, the Netherlands, and West Germany, as well as drawing on comparative evidence for the second part of the Report. In 1989 Prison Reform International (PRI) was formed with, significantly, Vivien Stern, Director of NACRO, as its Secretary General. PRI currently has an expanding membership drawn from almost fifty countries: the information pooled by that membership is providing an increasingly international backcloth to the shape of penal pressure-group politics in Britain.

The micro-politics of law and order are intimately bound up with the processes whereby the goals and agendas set by ministers are translated into policies and specific directives by civil servants. They are also creatively authored in key respects by senior civil servants, whose briefings and policy formulations have a distinct part to play in formal policy-making. As Rock (1990) has shown, policy formation within the Home Office is typically a matter of written argument developing creatively. For example, the 1991 Criminal Justice Act was the outcome of a lengthy, decade-long process of casting about for the most appropriate means of reducing the level of the prison population without either eroding the independence of the judiciary or offending the more reactionary wing of the Conservative Party. David Faulkner was a Deputy Under-Secretary at the Home Office from 1982, and for much of the decade he pursued that brief with the *imprimatur* of the Permanent Secretary, Sir Brian Cubbon. In the context of the demise of the rehabilitative policies that dominated the progressive field up to 1970, to be replaced by the 'just deserts' model pioneered in the USA (see e.g. American Friends Service Committee 1971; von Hirsch 1976; Martinson 1974). Faulkner sought a compromise which would respect judicial independence and yet persuade sentencers to reduce their resort to imprisonment. The provision of *more* non-custodial measures had failed to achieve this effect in the 1970s. They had simply tended to be used as alternatives to *other* alternatives to custody. The major reason always given by sentencers for this result was that the existing alternatives were 'too soft'. Logically, tougher versions of existing community measures, especially probation, might succeed where the provision simply of extra alternatives had failed. That informed guesswork has now, after much sounding and debate, been incorporated in the 1991 Criminal Justice Act. Whether or not the Act succeeds, it testifies to the active working through of such measures by civil servants still stereotyped as passive bureaucrats. By their creation of a 'symbolic environment' (Edelman 1971), by their active refinement of current issues, and by their deployment of arguments culled from gatherings as diverse as international conferences and informal discussion groups, it is possible, even in Britain, for senior civil servants such as Faulkner and, in an earlier period, Morrell (in connection with the Children and Young Persons Act 1970) to energize the field (see Rock 1986, 1990; Bottoms 1974).

It would, however, be mistaken to assume that the benign hand of some concerned civil servant is always to be found behind major legislative and policy-making processes, or that policy initiatives are the outcome of an increasingly open and well-informed discussion between ministers and their advisers on the one hand and experts and practitioners working with a growing array of penal pressure groups on the other. Just as important, if not more commonplace, is the process of masterly inactivity or just plain drift. For example, analysis of the history of one penalty, the senior attendance centre order, has found little by way of cumulative rationality or systematic planning in its development (Mair 1991). Other relevant processes at work can be found in the Select Committee stages of drafting legislation. The often painstaking scrutiny involved in this stage of a Bill's enactment can be the means for its profound amendment or effective termination by delay. For example, the Police and Criminal Evidence Act 1984 was a vastly different affair from the 1983 Bill which lapsed on the calling of the 1983 general election, after a clause-by-clause challenge to its composition by the opposition parties (see Ryan 1983 for a searching analysis of parliamentary processes in this field). Such major transformations as a result of detailed parliamentary scrutiny are, however, increasingly the exception rather than the rule. Within a matter of months of the implementation of the Criminal Justice Act 1991, the then Home Secretary, Kenneth Clarke, conceded, in the face of criticism from the judiciary and magistracy, that some of the detail within the legislation required amendment: critics argued that the Bill had received altogether too little parliamentary scrutiny.

By contrast, some policy innovations emerge out of the blue because of a minister's personal enthusiasm, or are the product of almost haphazardly won concessions granted during the committee stage of a bill, or are adopted following vigorous lobbying by small groups of backbenchers, sometimes with the support of one or another of the Select Committees of the House of Commons. For example, s. 58 of the Criminal Justice Act 1991, which provides for parents to be bound over if the court is satisfied that to do so would be desirable in the interests of preventing the commission of further offences by a young offender, would almost certainly not have been included in the Bill had it not been for the enthusiasm, against the tide of practitioner and pressure-group opinion, of John Patten, then a junior minister in the Home Office. Mr Patten originally proposed a much more drastic measure in order to ensure parental control of their children, a prophylactic he considered lacking. In March 1989 he proposed that it should be made a criminal offence for parents to fail to make reasonable efforts to prevent their children from committing offences. This proposition encountered considerable opposition and was dropped. The bind-over provision of s. 58 was the barely acceptable substitute. It is also doubtful whether either the experiment which preceded the Act, or the provision in the Act (s. 12), for electronic tagging would have happened had it not been for the personal enthusiasm of Mr Patten. The idea was not supported by practitioners, the experimental tagging in 1989 of suspects granted conditional bail was a conspicuous failure (Mair and Nee 1990), the penal pressure groups were universally hostile to the proposal, and though tagging had been in use in some US states (Ball *et al.* 1988), no other country in Europe appears seriously to have considered following their example. Mr Patten has since moved from the Home Office and, significantly, it has been announced that there are no plans to set up schemes which would enable the courts to make use of s. 12.

The enthusiasms of backbench MPs and peers may also carry the day, if they are backed by influential groups. We have already noted the example of Baroness Faithful backed by the juvenile justice lobby. A contrasting example is to be found in s. 84 of the Criminal Justice Act 1991. This provides for the contracting out of the management of prisons and could in principle mean that every prison currently run by the Prison Service might be turned over to the private sector through the affirmative resolution procedure of s. 84(5). This is an astonishing provision given that, as recently as 1987, the then Home Secretary, Douglas Hurd, informed the House of Commons that he did not 'think that there is a case, and I do not believe the House would accept that there is a case, for auctioning or privatising the prisons, or handing over the business of keeping prisoners safe to anyone other than government servants' (Hansard HC, 16 July 1987, vol. 119, col. 1299). The about-turn is explained by the fact that in 1986–7 the Select Committee on Home Affairs produced a brief report in which the majority of the Committee recommended that there should be experimentation on contracting out the management of prisons (Home Affairs Committee 1987). By skilful lobbying (see Ryan and Ward 1989 for background detail) various members persuaded a reluctant government to insert a clause providing for the contracting-out of remand prisons, a restrictive provision arrived at after consultation following a Green paper on the question (Cm 434, 1988). However, a backbench Conservative MP introduced an amendment to the Bill during the report stage, permitting the contracting-out of *any* existing or future prison, and the amendment was carried. Though the government maintained that it would not consider contracting out any prison other than the new remand prison at the Wolds, until that experiment had been carefully evaluated, it has already been announced that the management of the rebuilt prison at Strangeways, Manchester, is to be contracted out and that other institutions are likely to follow. The additions to s. 84 seem likely to be used radically to change the shape of the penal system.

This discussion suggests, gratifyingly perhaps, that Parliament is frequently the site of innovatory discussion and intervention on aspects of criminal justice and penal policy. Unfortunately, many aspects of policy development receive remarkably little parliamentary scrutiny or debate. It needs to be emphasized that because so much contemporary legislation (the Prison Act 1952, for example) is permissively diffuse, granting ministers and thus departments substantial discretionary powers, many important policy developments are preceded by virtually no public debate, parliamentary or otherwise (see Richardson 1993). Much policy is made by stealth or is announced as a *fait accompli*, challengeable only *ex post facto*, if it is challenged at all. For example, in 1983 the then Home Secretary, Leon Brittan, was able fundamentally to change parole policy without consulting either Parliament or the Parole Board and, in the event, his power to do so was upheld by the House of Lords following judicial review. In response to what he saw as growing public concern about the rise in violent crime, Mr Brittan announced in a speech to the Conservative Party Conference that he intended to use his discretion to ensure that certain classes of prisoners—serving sentences of five years or more for drug-trafficking or violence—would not get parole. Moreover, certain categories of murderer would in future serve at least twenty years. Needless to say, Mr Brittan's speech was well received by his immediate audience, though it caused much controversy elsewhere, not least because some prisoners, already transferred to open prison conditions with the expectation that they would soon be released, fell foul of the new guidelines and were sent back to closed prisons. Two such prisoners challenged the new policy by way of judicial review but the House of Lords ruled, contrary to a first instance opinion, that since the Home Secretary had taken account of the relevant considerations of deterrence, retribution, and public confidence, he was under no obligation to consult even the Parole Board before making the changes (*Re Findlay* (1985) AC 318).

Policing provides a much broader example of the absence of parliamentary debate. Policing policy arguably underwent a sea-change in the early 1980s, with increased reliance on mutual aid between forces, sometimes under the direction of the National Reporting Centre (Spencer 1985; Lustgarten 1986); the deployment of new paramilitary equipment and techniques (Jefferson 1990; Waddington 1991); and the adoption of neighbourhood crime-prevention strategies (Bennett 1990; Rosenbaum 1988), without the benefit of research or public debate. Again, when police authorities sought to challenge some of these policies by judicial review, the High Court upheld the power of chief constables and the Home Secretary to make such far-reaching decisions. Or, to take a recent example, the discretionary significance of which has yet to be tested, the Criminal Justice Act 1991 incorporates no definition of a pivotal term, a 'serious offence': that term has yet to be interpreted by the Court of Appeal (though the same term is the subject of limited case law following its introduction in relation to young offenders in s. 1 of the Criminal Justice Act 1982). Yet on the court's interpretation substantially hangs the future size and complexion of the prison population!

It is precisely because so much policy is made and implemented without adequate public debate of its implications that many analysts of criminal justice and penal policy insist that statutes should in future state much more precisely what objectives agencies should pursue and what specific powers decision-makers should have, and provide for procedural rights for those citizens—suspects, prisoners, and mental hospital patients—caught up in the system (Richardson 1993). Ideally, accountability should begin with Parliament and end with the day-to-day answerability of practitioners.

MATTERS OF SCANDAL AND CONCERN

The remaining variable is the unpredictable realm of scandal and concern. For all their pretensions, both parliamentary and extra-parliamentary groupings can be utterly outpaced by events which explode in such a way that unusual responses are called for by 'public opinion'—a phenomenon for which media attention is often taken to be the proxy. In the penal realm, for example, two major sets of events seemingly dwarf all others in their impact on the 'public': the escapes of Ronald Biggs and George Blake in 1965–6;[13] and the rioting at Strangeways and other prisons in 1990. The former led to a greatly increased emphasis on prison security and the latter prompted the Woolf inquiry, the policy impact of which remains to be seen (see chapter 19 in this volume). In the realm of public order, the riots in Brixton (1981; see Scarman Report 1981) and on the Broadwater Farm Estate (1985; see Gifford Report 1986) far transcended other disturbances in their evocation of profound unease. Lord Scarman's Report on the events at Brixton led to the development of formal police-community consultation (see Morgan 1992). At the time of writing (February 1993) the Home Secretary has announced, in the wake of the horrific murder of two-year-old James Bulger, allegedly by two juveniles, and a sustained police campaign regarding offences committed (particularly by juveniles) while on bail (see P. Morgan 1992; Morgan and Jones 1992), that he intends introducing custodial measures for chronic serious juvenile offenders which directly contravene principles only just implemented in the Criminal Justice Act 1991. However, not all scandals translate into calls for reform or change: for example, the so-called Moors Murders of the early 1960s, in which several children were fatal victims of sadistic sexual practices, were the source of heightened moral fears, but also of sheer bafflement.

As Bottoms and Stevenson argue:

> It is a fact well known to students of social policy that reforms of the system often take place not so much because of careful routine analysis by ministers and civil servants in the relevant Department of State, nor even because of a critique or exposé by an outside journalist or pressure group, but because one or more individual incident(s) occurs, drawing public attention to some underlying imperfections of policy in a dramatic way which seems to demand change. Very often an inquiry is set up after such incidents, and it is the report of the inquiry that sets the agenda for subsequent reforms; but the reforms would not have taken place without the public attention created by the original incident. (1992: 23–4)

[13] Ronald Biggs, sentenced to thirty years' imprisonment was one of those responsible for the notorious 'Great Train Robbery' of 1963: he escaped from Wandsworth Prison. He was the second of the train robbers to escape; George Wilson, also sentenced to thirty years, got out of Birmingham Prison in 1964. George Blake, who had spied for the Russians and had recently received the longest determinate sentence ever imposed, forty-two years, escaped dramatically from Wormwood Scrubs Prison in October 1966. Two days after Blake's escape, the Home Secretary appointed Lord Mountbatten to conduct a review of prison security (Mountbatten Report 1966).

It is worth embellishing this point a little. Such incidents tend to generate change only when they discredit institutions so drastically and dramatically that their credibility and effectiveness—and, by extension, those of the government and the state—risk serious erosion unless changes are made. The damage is not simply symbolic, a matter of reputation and belief, though declining public confidence carries grave implications for the agencies of control and the caring professions. The authority of the modern state rests heavily on its claims to expertise (Giddens 1984). Practical effects include the predictable increase in, for example, escape attempts in the wake of successful breakouts, and increasing dismissal rates in courts where juries no longer unquestioningly accept police evidence. As the latter point suggests, scandals can and should result in improved policy and practice. The abolition of capital punishment is arguably an example of 'things going right' in criminal justice and penal policy after a series of executions that caused public disquiet. Much hinges on the character of the response; and, we argue below, the trend has recently been towards specific and limited rather than wide-ranging and searching modes of inquiry. Nor are scandals randomly scattered throughout the system: the police and the prisons have produced far more than, for example, probation and after-care.

Prisons: Mountbatten to Woolf

The prison escapes of 1965–6 (see note 11 above) transformed the prison system. Until the mid-1960s, little was thought to be awry with the prison system, apart from its legacy of Victorian architecture and authoritarian regimes. Nothing was amiss that a fresh building programme and the development of more therapeutic regimes would not redress. The famous White Paper of a reforming Conservative Home Secretary, R. A. 'Rab' Butler, *Penal Practice in a Changing Society*' (1959) seemed—despite Tory backbench disquiet—to have set the agenda for the next few decades. But the escapes made a 'public laughing-stock' of the Prison Department (Bottoms and Stevenson 1992: 25) and the Labour Home Secretary, Roy Jenkins, felt that anxieties could be assuaged only by a rapid inquiry. This was conducted by Lord Mountbatten (Mountbatten Report 1966) and resulted in a tough but perceptive report which discerned the major problem as a combination of insufficiently secure provision for the tiny minority of high-escape-risk prisoners and over-security for the great majority. Concentrating the high risks within one or two purpose-built top-security prisons, with the stress on perimeter control, would enable both to experience more relaxed regimes. In the event, liberal anxiety about the so-called 'Alcatraz' effect of these proposals led the Home Office to refer the matter to the Advisory Council on the Penal System for a further inquiry, chaired by Professor Leon Radzinowicz. Its Report (Advisory Council on the Penal System 1968) led to the 'dispersal' of top-security risks among several maximum-security prisons. The unwanted side-effects of these directives were to heighten security across the system, prioritize control and surveillance at the expense of other objectives (such as work, training, education, recreation, and better rights and conditions), and, in combination with the impact of adverse research findings, halt the spread of therapeutic regimes while leaving intact the differentiation between local and training prisons based upon that ideology (see King and Morgan 1980 for a detailed inventory; also chapter 19 in this volume).

The growth of what Rutherford (1984) has termed 'high-cost squalor' in the penal system advanced most dramatically in the 1970s and 1980s, mainly because the new strategy was both labour-intensive and overly security-based. Running conflicts between prisoners and staff, on the one hand, and staff and Prison Department officials, on the other, became endemic. The May Committee was appointed to resolve a pay dispute but widened its brief to look at the overall context. Its report (May Report 1979) led to only one innovatory gain, an inspectorate independent of the Prison Department. The prisons continued to fester, conditions manifestly deteriorating on virtually all fronts (King and McDermott 1989), locked into a logically endless drift born of rising numbers and costs in a policy vacuum. When it came, however, the frequently predicted climax of two decades of often serious outbreaks of prison unrest took even informed observers by surprise in its scope and ferocity. A large local prison, Strangeways in Manchester, was completely taken over and destroyed by its inmates, an occupation lasting over two weeks that became a veritable media event as prisoners humiliated the authorities by their rooftop defiance. One death, a host of injuries, and the terrorization of sex offenders occurred. Several other prisons erupted in a sequence of less sustained rioting.

The Woolf Inquiry into these disturbances broke new ground in several respects. Lord Justice Woolf reported in two stages: the first covered the disturbances themselves, and addressed questions of responsibility and culpability; the second, with HM Chief Inspector of Prisons, Judge Steven Tumim, examined the causes of so signal a system failure. This process enabled them to look in depth at the massive mismatch between needs and resources in the system; at the myriad ways in which containment fell far short of the humane; and at remedies in the short and longer terms (Woolf Report 1991). Unusually, as mentioned above, comparative evidence was gathered at first hand from prisoners (including British prisoners) abroad, in the Netherlands, the USA, and Spain. Uniquely, five open public seminars were held at which specialists from government, the Prison Service, academe, pressure groups, and other bodies debated key issues. The Report was widely acknowledged to have advanced the most comprehensive agenda for radical change in the penal system since the Gladstone Report of 1895. It pioneered a process for democratic accountability and debate on urgent problems that should serve as a model for inquirites in all fields, not simply penal affairs.

Nevertheless, the Inquiry was debarred by its terms of reference from exploring one subject of utmost relevance to the topic, namely the judicial framework of sentencing policy. In one sense, the Prison Service is correct in stating that it cannot be held responsible for all aspects of its performance, since one key variable—that is, the actual number of prisoners it is called upon to contain—is utterly beyond its control. That responsibility lies with the judiciary, and the prisons are under a statutory obligation to accept all those who are sent there by the courts. Unlike the case of schools, hospitals, or any other institution, and the prison systems of such other countries as the Netherlands, no legal limit is placed on the numbers any prison can be called upon to hold. Certified Normal Accommodation (CNA) is a formal baseline that is normally exceeded by several thousands. The power of the judiciary to stand aloof from the entire debate about penal policy is perhaps the most salient feature of the politics of law and order, since all agendas for reform must bow to their refusal to take part in any such process. This refusal is justified by the judicial elite in terms of the essential independence of the law from politics. However, their interpretation of that independence to embrace not simply their judgment of cases—where indeed it is vital—but the entire conspectus of sentencing trends and practices—where it is not—forces all other components of the criminal justice system to adjust to their often ill-coordinated actions. This feature of the system has led many to see better coordination as an end in itself, the attainment of which will automatically bring improvement. But unless some agreed objective, such as a reduction in the numbers in prison, is laid down, then coordination is simply a means without an end. It is around these issues that the arguments for and against some version of a Sentencing Council have been made (Ashworth 1983; Cavadino and Dignan 1992: ch. 4), but the judiciary have so far managed to keep themselves insulated from, while influential in, the policy process.

Policing: Dixon to Robocop

The conventional wisdom about policing tends to the apocalyptic. Things have fallen apart since the Golden Age of Policing in the 1950s, embodied in the film *The Blue Lamp* and the folk heroism of its central character, PC George Dixon, later even more celebrated as the linchpin of the community in the long-running TV serial *Dixon of Dock Green*. Nowadays, in Reiner's vivid contrast, the image of the police constable is more like Darth Vader or Robocop, a barely human presence within a visored technological armour, holding a seething mob at bay with advanced weaponry (see chapter 15 in this volume). The real story is more complex and less sensational. The Golden Age of policing was a myth based upon blind faith in authority and ignorance of actual police work at a time of relatively harmonious community relations. Declining public confidence in the police is due to rates of crime that have soared for social, economic, and cultural reasons that affect but hardly originate in policing; the exposure of forms of corruption that were customary rather than novel; and the growth of problems such as terrorism and drug trafficking which are unparalleled this century in their scale and viciousness. We are only now coming to grips with age-old problems that defy short-term solutions. The police are now in a healthier state than before, but look worse because far more is known about their shortcomings, thanks to a mixture of scandals, research, and the gradual move towards more stringent forms of both legal and political accountability.

The three cases which have come to dramatize public concerns about policing most vividly are those of the Guildford Four, the Maguire Seven, and the Birmingham Six. In all three cases, Irish suspects were convicted of causing explosions that killed multiple victims. Outrage as expressed through the media, placed immense pressure on the police to get 'results'. The sentences of life imprisonment were accompanied by recommendations that at least twenty years be served in several cases. Only fifteen to seventeen years later were the verdicts declared 'unsafe', and the prisoners freed, as a result of the tireless campaigning of family support groups aided by a few maverick MPs, lawyers, and journalists. Despite the discrediting of the forensic evidence and the increasing grounds for serious doubts about the methods of interrogation used by senior detectives, the verdicts were declared unsafe only after a protracted series of re-examinations of the evidence and grounds for appeal had been turned down by the Home Secretary. These and other cases of similar magnitude so eroded public confidence in the police and the courts, as shown by opinion polls, that a Royal Commission on Criminal Justice was appointed in 1991, the first Royal Commission for fourteen years, to inquire into the procedural issues involved and suggest remedies.

These cases exemplify the tendency for matters of notoriety to originate in taken-for-granted practices that are exposed as a result of unusual degrees of pressure or modes of scrutiny, rather than being in themselves exceptional instances of individual pathology—a 'few bad apples'. 'Constructing the suspect' by embellishing the evidence against him or her and ignoring countervailing evidence is standard police practice (see e.g. Leng *et al.* 1992; cf. McBarnet 1981). Once socialized into an occupational culture which affirms such practices as not only a necessary evil but also a professional skill, designed ultimately to secure conviction in the ornate adversarial exchanges in open court, it is a small step for the police officer to fabricate evidence and 'lose' counter-evidence. The appeal of such procedures is the greater when the suspect has 'previous' and is construed as 'overdue' for conviction. The logic of methodical suspicion casts certain groups more readily into the suspect role than others. The moral economy of police work reinforces these images of deviance, certain groups being seen as 'slag', 'rubbish', and 'police property' (Reiner 1992). If such variables as age, sex, ethnicity, demeanour, degrees of cooperativeness with the police, and the reputation of areas are consequential in routine offending, how much larger they loom when intense pressures for a 'result' are generated. Another example of unusual modes of inquiry bringing new focus to established practices was Roger Graef's 1982 TV documentary series on the Thames Valley police. The public outcry at the merciless grilling by detectives of a female rape victim led to rapid changes in the procedures for the processing of similar cases. The impetus had also led to the heightened awareness and changing practices in cases of domestic violence (see Stanko 1990; Dobash and Dobash 1992; chapter 6 in this volume).

Northern Ireland and its Impact

The context for the most notorious recent miscarriages of justice is of course the political quagmire of Northern Ireland and its ramifications for the control of terrorism in Britain. Since 1969, 'nearly 3,000 people have died because of political violence in northern Ireland . . . The conflict has often spilled outside the borders of the region, leading to the deaths of approximately 200 people in Great Britain, the Republic of Ireland, and sites elsewhere in Europe, ranging from Gibraltar to Western Germany' (O'Leary and McGarry 1993). As these authors point out, 3,000 dead may seem a relatively small toll over two decades. 'However, scale matters. The population of Northern Ireland in the 1981 census . . . was estimated as 1,488,077. If the equivalent ratio of victims to population had been produced in Great Britain in the same period some 100,000 people would have died, and . . . in the USA . . . over 500,000, or about ten times the number of Americans killed in the Vietnam War' (ibid.: 2). Comparatively speaking, 'the death-toll in Northern Ireland alone made the UK absolutely the most violent liberal democracy during the same time-span' (ibid.: 4). Close to one in fifty of the population have suffered serious injuries over the period. The costs in law enforcement, paramilitary measures, compensation, and legal processes have been huge. One audit in 1985 estimated the annual direct costs of violence in Northern Ireland at £1,194 million per annum (ibid.: p. 22). The costs in terms of negative effects on public trust in British political institutions have been incalculable.

The granting of strong emergency powers to the legal authorities under the regularly renewed Emergency Provisions Act in Northern Ireland and the Prevention of Terrorism Act throughout the UK has meant that departures from traditional English legal procedures have become normal in Northern Ireland and spill over into aspects of crime control in Britain (as, for example, in the short-lived 'control units' for recalcitrant prisoners in two English prisons in the 1970s, whose regimes paralleled forms of sensory deprivation used in Northern Ireland). 'Since 1973 no-jury single-judge courts have presided over cases arising from "scheduled offences", i.e. "terrorist offences", on the grounds that jury-trials are not safe from perverse verdicts or the intimidation of jurors and witnesses. Confessions are admissible as the sole basis for conviction on charges "of this kind"' (O'Leary and McGarry 1993: 24). The rise and discrediting of 'supergrass' evidence in the 1980s; the abandonment of the 'right of silence' in 1988; the regular delay of several years in holding inquests on persons killed by the security forces (Amnesty International 1978); and the violation of the European Convention on Human Rights on a number of fronts concerning interrogation and time held in custody; have all severely eroded the belief, both nationally and internationally, in the impartiality of British justice. They also provided the context within which routine police practices for constructing the suspect escalated into 'the greatest twentieth-century crisis of confidence in the administration of justice in Great Britain' (ibid.). Even the most rigorous and wide-ranging Royal Commission will be sorely pressed to tackle such deep-rooted problems, though it is gratifying that a start has been made by its establishment.

Forms of Official Inquiry

The appointment of that Commission, and the unusually open and searching nature of the Woolf Inquiry, go against the grain of the trend, especially notable during the Thatcher years, increasingly to use the *ad hoc*, highly specific, departmental inquiry as a policy-making mechanism. Such inquiries were internal, as when HM Chief Inspector of Prisons was asked to consider the prison disturbances of 1986 (Her Majesty's Chief Inspector of Prisons 1986); or external, conducted either by a committee, as in the case of the Prior Committee on prison discipline (Prior Report 1985), or by an individual, usually a judge, as in the case of the Woolf Inquiry. The latter embrace both statutory inquiries, as in the cases of Lord Scarman's investigation of the Brixton disturbance in 1981 under s. 32 of the Police Act 1964 (Scarman Report 1981) or Sir Louis Blom-Cooper's investigation of Ashworth Special Hospital 1991 under s. 125 of the Mental Health Act 1983 (Blom-Cooper Report 1992), and non-statutory inquiries, as in the case of the Woolf Report.

Such inquiries may be resorted to for a variety of political reasons (see Morgan 1991) but, unlike statutory or even non-statutory standing consultative bodies and Royal Commissions, they have the merit for ministers of being focused, relatively short-term, and manageable. Their terms of reference are precise and often, though not invariably, narrowly technical. By contrast, standing bodies, like the Advisory Council on the Penal System, are liable to take a robust view of their terms of reference; and Royal Commissions tend to be wide-ranging and long-lasting. Which mechanism is resorted to depends on the seriousness of the incident(s), the degree of loss of public confidence, and whether ministers have a clear objective, wish to distance themselves from a potentially unpopular solution, or play for time. What is clear is that straightforward assumptions about the political methodology likely to be adopted in relation to one mechanism or another can no longer be made. The Woolf and Blom-Cooper Inquiries were unusually open and consultative in their methods. It was widely anticipated that the 1992 Royal Commission on Criminal Justice would be the same, particularly since Sir John May's inquiry into the 'Guildford Four' miscarriage of justice (an inquiry eventually incorporated by the Royal Commission) had indicated his readiness to hold public seminars. In the event, the Royal Commission, though it has taken oral evidence in the usual manner and commissioned a good deal of research, has been relatively orthodox: it has held no seminars. The 1992 Sheehy Committee on police ranks, structure and conditions of employment (which at the time of writing has still to report) held at least one, but under conditions of excessive secrecy. Such pointers, coupled with the recent rumours of Home Office plans to substitute representatives from the business world for those of the elected local authorities on police committees, signal a highly managerial and undemocratic strategy for 'law and order' into the 1990s. If that is indeed the case, the second-order consensus alluded to above will be short-lived indeed.

CONCLUSIONS

The politics of law and order in the post-war period have been massively shaped by the nature of responses to the continuous rise in rates of recorded crime and to the unforeseen explosion of politically inspired terrorism and illicit drug trafficking. Two phases can be discerned in the party political sphere. First, up to 1970, a consensus prevailed whose terms, heavily influenced by 'liberal progressive' ideology (Bailey 1987) implicitly rested on the non-partisan character of crime and on the merit of gradual shifts towards rehabilitative policies for its control. This consensus was not shared, other than for a range of juvenile offenders, by the judiciary, who continued to adhere to broadly retributive and deterrent principles of sentencing, except for a small minority of clinically diagnosed mentally ill offenders. Governments of both left and right shared a strong reluctance to intrude into the judicial realm. The 1970 election was a watershed which, by 1979, had swept away the main supports of non-partisanship. The second phase, of sharp and growing contention between the parties for the 'law and order' terrain, saw the Conservative Party emerge relatively unscathed from Labour's attempts to link rising crime with the social and economic effects of growing inequality and unemployment: the 'hostages to fortune' which Labour Party attachments to the trade unions and to libertarian causes entail, have led its leaders to seek to neutralize, rather than sharply contest, the Conservative hegemony on this issue.

Though the elements of a 'second-order consensus' have been discernible in some respects—bifurcation, the need to reduce prison overcrowding, victim support, and crime prevention are examples—the routes to those ends have often differed. One instance is the much greater emphasis placed by the Labour Party on the role of local authorities as the linchpin of crime prevention initiatives of a social (rather than a purely situational) kind. The Conservatives have stressed a host of alternative frameworks—Neighbourhood Watch, Safer Cities, and crime prevention through environmental design (see Clarke and Mayhew 1980; chapter 14 in this volume)—which bypass local authorities rather than engage them in community crime prevention schemes: indeed, they have founded an independent organization, Crime Concern, to evangelize their approach. The stress on 'active citizenship' and the 'community' was evolved in the mid-1980s as a form of recognition by the government that reliance on the 'rule of law' alone was no longer serving as a credible strategy (Reiner and Cross 1991). Crime rates and public disorder alike were reaching new heights. These new watchwords and strategies were intended to signify fresh thinking and active concern, on the one hand, and a refusal to countenance the role of social and economic variables, on the other. The irony is that the Home Office under the Conservatives has, since 1979, assembled a criminal justice and penal policy which, however, unevenly, shares broad cross-party support. Yet the government is struggling to put that policy into effect in a context rendered peculiarly unfavourable in crime control terms by the impact and character of their social and economic policies. For the Labour Party the real Conservative enemy in crime control terms is not the Home Office but the Treasury, the Department of Trade and Industry, and the ethos embodied in successive leaders (notably Mrs Thatcher) who deny the existence of 'society' and state that—as far as offenders are concerned—'we should understand less and condemn more' (Mr Major in 1993). In other words, it is not so much that the Conservatives have tightened the screws on civil liberties and citizenship rights; in some ways they have even formally extended them. It is rather that they have effectively excluded far larger numbers of people from any conceivable activation of those rights—by doubling unemployment, quadrupling homelessness, increasing inequalities of wealth and income, and draining local authorities of both power and resources (see Stewart 1992; Brake and Hale 1992). The problem for the opposition parties is that they have yet to find ways of convincing the electorate that these connections exist and can be influenced by political decision-making in the medium to long term. This formidable task has so far eluded them, not least because the effects of criminal victimization appear supremely short-term.

In what has been, for the most part, a policy vacuum following the eclipse of rehabilitation as a salient goal, the penal pressure groups have played an increasingly significant role in policy-making and public debate processes. They have in general backed policies favouring the reduction in the prison population, greater police accountability and greater responsiveness to the needs of both offenders and victims in the criminal justice process. Practitioner interest groups have, again in general, favoured the *status quo* or sought to strengthen it, as in the support of ACPO for the National Reporting Centre during the 1984–5 coal dispute. In many ways, the real adversarial politics of the second phase have been those between the pressure and interest groups. Finally, matters of scandal and concern have surfaced throughout the entire period as triggers for change. In the past two decades, the responses have become increasingly circumscribed, a symptom paradoxically of a state of affairs in which matters of law and order are, in general, far less 'under control' than was then the case. In short, despite the recent ascendancy in the penal sphere of a mildly reductionist philosophy and practice, the situation remains highly volatile. The road to the second millenium may well be marked by a sharp reversal of this trend, a switch to the American model of lengthy incapacitation and punitive responses to what are defined as essentially matters of individual rather than collective responsibility. As things stand, this option has not been ruled out sufficiently firmly for it to be safely discounted.

Selected Further Reading

M. Brake and C. Hale, *Public Order and Private Lives: The Politics of Law and Order*. London: Routledge, 1992.

D. Downes, ed., *Unravelling Criminal Justice*. London: Macmillan, 1992.

R. Hood, ed., *Crime, Criminology and Public Policy: Essays in Honour of Leon Radzinowicz*. London: Heinemann, 1974.

T. P. Morris, *Crime and Criminal Justice in Britain since 1945*. Oxford: Blackwell, 1989.

P. Norton, ed., *Law and Order and British Politics*. Aldershot: Gower, 1984.

B. O'Leary and J. McGarry, *The Politics of Antagonism: Understanding Northern Ireland*. London: Athlone, 1993.

R. Reiner and M. Cross, eds., *Beyond Law and Order: Criminal Justice Policy into the 1990s*. London: Macmillan, 1991.

M. Ryan, *The Politics of Penal Reform*. London: Longman.

REFERENCES

ABERCOMBIE, N., and WARDE, S., eds. (1988), *Contemporary British Society*. Cambridge: Polity.

ADVISORY COUNCIL ON THE PENAL SYSTEM (1969), *The Regime for Long-term Prisoners in Conditions of Maximum Security*. London: HMSO.

AMERICAN FRIENDS SERVICE COMMITTEE (1971), *Struggle for Justice*. New York: Hill and Wang.

AMNESTY INTERNATIONAL (1978), *Report of an Amnesty International Mission to Northern Ireland*. London: International Secretariat, Amnesty International.

Anarchy (1963), *The Spies for Peace Story*, no. 29 (July). London: Freedom Press.

ASHWORTH, A. (1983), *Sentencing and Penal Policy*. London: Weidenfeld and Nicholson.

BAILEY, V. (1987), *Delinquency and Citizenship: Reclaiming the Young Offender, 1914–1948*. Oxford: Clarendon Press.

BALL, A. B., HUFF, C. R., and LILLY, J. R. (1988), *House Arrest and Correctional Policy: Doing Time at Home*. Newbury Park, Ca.: Sage.

BENNETT, T. (1990), *Evaluating Neighbourhood Watch*. Farnborough: Gower.

BLOM-COOPER REPORT (1992), *Report of the Committee of Inquiry into Complaints about Ashworth Hospital*, Cm 2028. London: HMSO.

BOTTOMS, A. E. (1974), 'On the Decriminalization of English Juvenile Courts', in R. Hood, ed., *Crime, Criminology, and Public Policy*. London: Heineman.

—— (1977), 'Reflections on the Renaissance of Dangerousness', *Howard Journal*, 16: 70–96.

BOTTOMS, A. E., and STEVENSON, S. (1992), 'What Went Wrong?: Criminal Justice Policy in England and Wales, 1945–70', in D. Downes, ed., *Unravelling Criminal Justice*. London: Macmillan.

BRAKE, M., and HALE, C. (1992), *Public Order and Private Lives: The Politics of Law and Order*. London: Routledge.

Butler, D. (1952), *The British General Election of 1951*. London: Macmillan.
——(1956), *The British General Election of 1955*. London: Macmillan.
Butler, D., and Kavanagh, D. (1975*a*), *The British General Election of February 1974*. London: Macmillan.
—— (1975*b*), *The British General Election of October 1974*. London: Macmillan.
—— (1980), *The British General Election of 1979*. London: Macmillan.
—— (1988), *The British General Election of 1987*. London: Macmillan.
Butler, D., and King, A. (1965), *The British General Election of 1964*. London: Macmillan.
—— (1967), *The British General Election of 1966*. London: Macmillan.
Butler, D., and Pinto-Duschinsky, M. (1971), *The British General Election of 1970*. London: Macmillan.
Butler, D., and Rose, R. (1960), *The British General Election of 1959*. London: Macmillan.
Cavadino, M., and Dignan, J. (1992), *The Penal System: An Introduction*. London: Sage.
Christian, L. (1983), *Policing by Coercion*. London: GLC Police Support Unit.
Clarke, R. V. G., and Mayhew, P. (1980), *Designing Out Crime*. London: HMSO.
Cohen, S. (1972), *Folk Devils and Moral Panics*. London: MacGibbon and Kee.
Conservative Party (1959), *The Next Five Years*. London: Conservative Party.
—— (1966), *Actions not Words*. London: Conservative Party.
—— (1970), *A Better Tomorrow*. London: Conservative Party.
—— (1974*a*), *Firm Action for a Fairer Britain*. London: Conservative Party.
—— (1974*b*), *Putting Britain First*. London: Conservative Party.
—— (1979), *The Conservative Manifesto*. London: Conservative Party.
—— (1983), *The Challenge of Our Times*. London: Conservative Party.
—— (1987), *Our First Eight Years: The Next Moves Forward*. London: Conservative Party.
—— (1992), *The Best Future for Britain*. London: Conservative Party.
Craig, F. W. S. (1975), *The British General Election Manifestos 1900–1974*. London: Macmillan.
Dahrendorf, R. (1987), 'The Underclass and the Future of Great Britain', lecture delivered at Windsor Castle, 27 April.
Dixon, D., and Fishwick, E. (1984), 'The Law and Order Debate in Historical Perspective', in P. Norton, ed., *Law and Order and British Politics*. Aldershot: Gower.
Dobash, R. E., and Dobash, R. D. (1992), *Women, Violence and Social Change*. London: Routledge.
Dore, R. P. (1992), *Japanese Capitalism, Anglo Saxon Capitalism: How Will the Darwinian Contest Turn Out*? London: LSE Centre for Economic Performance, Occasional Paper no. 4.
Downes, D. M. (1966), *The Delinquent Solution*. London: Routledge and Kegan Paul.
—— (1982), 'The Origins and Consequences of Dutch Penal Policy since 1945: A Preliminary Analysis', *British Journal of Criminology*, 22: 325–62.
—— (1988), *Contrasts in Tolerance: Post-War Penal Policy in the Netherlands and England and Wales*. Oxford: Clarendon Press.

—— (1989*a*), 'Only Disconnect: Law and Order, Social Policy and the Community', in M. Bulmer, J. Lewis, and D. Piachaud, eds., *The Goals of Social Policy*. London: Unwin Hyman.

—— (1989*b*), 'Thatcherite Values and Crime', *Samizdat*, May/June.

Downes, D. M., and Ward, T. (1986), *Democratic Policing*. London: Labour Campaign for Criminal Justice.

Downes, D. M., and Young, J. (1987), 'A Criminal Failure', *New Society*, 13 May.

Edelman, M. (1971), *Politics as Symbolic Action*. Chicago: Markham.

Edmund-Davies Report (1978), *Report of the Committee of Inquiry on the Police*, Cmnd 7283. London: HMSO.

Elder, N. C. M. (1984), 'Conclusion', in P. Norton, ed., *Law and Order and British Politics*. Aldershot: Gower.

Feest, J. (1988), *Reducing the Prison Population: Lessons from the West German Experience*? London: National Association for the Care and Resettlement of Offenders.

Gamble, A. (1990), 'The Thatcher Decade in Perspective', in P. Dunleavy, A. Gamble, and G. Peele, eds., *Developments in British Politics*, 3. London: Macmillan.

Giddens, A. (1984), *The Constitution of Society*. Cambridge: Polity.

Gifford Report (1986), *The Broadwater Farm Inquiry: Report of the Independent Inquiry into Disturbances of October 1985 at the Broadwater Farm Estate, Tottenham*. London: Karia Press.

Graham, J. (1988), 'The Declining Prison Population in the Federal Republic of Germany', *Home Office Research and Planning Unit Research Bulletin*, 24: 47–52.

Hall, S., Critcher, S., Jefferson, T., Clarke, J., and Roberts, B. (1978), *Policing the Crisis: Mugging, the State, and Law and Order*. London: Macmillan.

Halloran, J. D., Elliott, P., and Murdock, G. (1970), *Demonstrations and Communications*, Harmondsworth: Penguin.

Her Majesty's Chief Inspector of Prisons (1987), *Report of an Inquiry into the Disturbances in Prison Service Establishments in England between 29 April and 2 May*, HC 42. London: HMSO.

Home Affairs Committee (1987), *Fourth Report of, Contract Provision of Prisons*. London: HMSO.

Home Office (1988), *Private Sector Involvement in the Remand System*. London: HMSO.

Honderich, T. (1990), *Conservatism*. London: Hamish Hamilton.

Jefferson, T. (1990), *The Case against Paramilitary Policing*. Milton Keynes: Open University Press.

Jencks, C., and Peterson, P. E., eds. (1991), *The Urban Underclass*. Washington DC: Brookings Institution.

King, R. D., and McDermott, K. (1989), 'British Prisons 1970–97: The Ever-Deepening Crisis', *British Journal of Criminology*, 29/2: 107–28.

—— (1991), 'A Fresh Start: Managing the Prison Service', in R. Reiner and M. Cross, eds., *Beyond Law and Order*. London: Macmillan.

King, R. D., and McDermott, K. (1992), 'Security, Control and Human Containment in the Prison System in England and Wales', in D. Downes, ed., *Unravelling Criminal Justice*. London: Macmillan.

King, R. D., and Morgan, R. (1980), *The Future of the Prison System*. Farnborough: Gower.

Labour Party (1959), *Time for Decision*. London: Labour Party.

—— (1966), *Time for Decision*. London: Labour Party.

—— (1970), *Now Britain's Strong—Let's Make it Great to Live in*. London: Labour Party.

—— (1974*a*), *Let Us Work Together—Labour's Way out of the Crisis*. London: Labour Party.

—— (1974*b*), *Britain Will Win with Labour*. London: Labour Party.

—— (1979), *The Labour Way is the Better Way*. London: Labour Party.

—— (1983), *New Hope for Britain*. London: Labour Party.

—— (1987), *Britain Will Win*. London: Labour Party.

—— (1992), *It's Time to Get Britain Working Again*. London: Labour Party.

Lea, J., and Young, J. (1984), *What Is to Be Done About Law and Order?* Harmondsworth: Penguin.

Leng, R., McConville, M., and Sanders, A. (1992), 'Researching the Discretions to Charge and to Prosecute', in D. Downes, ed., *Unravelling Criminal Justice*. London: Macmillan.

Liberal Party (1964), *Think for Yourself: Vote Liberal*. London: Liberal Party.

—— (1974), *Change the Face of Britain*. London: Liberal Party.

Liberal Democratic Party (1992), *Changing Britain for Good*. London: Liberal Democratic Party.

Liberal/SDP Alliance (1987), *Britain United: The Time Has Come*. London: Liberal/SDP Alliance.

Light, R., Nee, C., and Ingham, H. (1993), *Car Theft: The Offender's Perspective*, Home Office Research Study no. 130. London: HMSO.

Lustgarten, L. (1986), *The Government of the Police*. London: Sweet and Maxwell.

McBarnet, D. (1981), *Conviction*. London: Macmillan.

McCallum, R. B., and Readman, A. (1946), *The British General Election of 1945*. Oxford: Oxford University Press.

Macnicol, J. (1987), 'In Pursuit of the Underclass', *Journal of Social Policy*, 16: 293–318.

Macpherson, C. B. (1962), *The Political Theory of Possessive Individualism*. Oxford: Oxford University Press.

Mair, G. (1991), *Part-Time Punishment: The Origins and Development of Senior Attendance Centres*. London: HMSO.

Mair, G., and Nee, C. (1990), *Electronic Monitoring: The Trials and their Results*, Home Office Research Study no. 120. London: HMSO.

Martin, R. (1981), *New Technology and Industrial Relations in Fleet Street*. Oxford: Oxford University Press.

Martinson, R. (1974), 'What Works?—Questions and Answers about Prison Reform', *The Public Interest*, 35 (Spring): 22–54.

Marwick, A. (1990), *British Society since 1945*. London: Penguin.

MAY REPORT (1979), *Report of the Committee of Inquiry into the United Kingdom Prison Services* (Chairman, Mr Justice May), Cmnd 7673. London: HMSO.

MAYHEW, H. (1862), *Those That Will Not Work*, vol. 4 of *London Labour and the London Poor* (1851–62). London: Griffin. Repr. ed. P. Quennell, *London's Underworld*; London: Spring Books, 1955.

MILLS, C. W. (1959), *The Sociological Imagination*. New York: Oxford University Press.

MORGAN, P. (1992), *Offending While on Bail: A Survey of Recent Studies*, Home Office Research and Planning Unit Paper no. 65. London: HMSO.

MORGAN, R. (1979), *Formulating Penal Policy: The Future of the Advisory Council on the Penal System*. London: National Association for the Care and Resettlement of Offenders.

—— (1991), 'Woolf: in Retrospect and Prospect', *Modern Law Review*, 54: 713–25.

—— (1992), 'Talking about Policing', in D. Downes, ed., *Unravelling Criminal Justice*. London: Macmillan.

MORGAN, R., and JONES, S. (1992), 'Bail or Jail', in E. Stockdale and S. Casale, eds., *Criminal Justice under Stress*. London: Blackstone.

MORRIS, T. P. (1989), *Crime and Criminal Justice in Britain since 1945*. Oxford: Blackwell.

MOUNTBATTEN REPORT (1966), *Report of the Inquiry into Prison Escapes and Security by Admiral of the Fleet, the Earl Mountbatten of Burma*, Cmnd 3175. London: HMSO.

MOWAT, L. W. (1955), *Britain between the Wars, 1918–1940*. London: Methuen.

NICHOLAS, H. G. (1951), *The British General Election of 1950*. London: Macmillan.

O'LEARY, B., and MCGARRY, J. (1993), *The Politics of Antagonism: Understanding Northern Ireland*. London: Athlone.

PARKIN, F. (1967), 'Working-Class Conservatives: A Theory of Political Deviance', *British Journal of Sociology*, 18/3: 278–90.

PEELE, G. (1990), 'Parties, Pressure Groups and Parliaments', in P. Dunleavy, A. Gamble, and G. Peele, eds., *Developments in British Politics, 3*. London: Macmillan.

PRIOR REPORT (1985), *Report of the Departmental Committee on the Prison Disciplinary System* (Chairman, Mr Peter Prior), Cmnd 9641. London: HMSO.

REINER, R. (1992), *The Politics of the Police*, rev. edn. Brighton: Wheatsheaf.

REINER, R., and CROSS, M. (1991), 'Introduction', in R. Reiner and M. Cross, eds., *Beyond Law and Order: Criminal Justice Policy into the 1990s*. London: Macmillan.

RICHARDSON, G. (1993), *Law, Custody and Process: Prisoners and Patients*. London: Hamish Hamilton.

ROCK, P. (1986), *A View from the Shadows: The Ministry of the Solicitor General of Canada and the Justice for Victims of Crime Initiative*. Oxford: Clarendon Press.

—— (1990), *Helping Victims of Crime: The Home Office and the Rise of Victim Support in England and Wales*. Oxford: Clarendon Press.

Rosenbaum, D. (1988), 'A Critical Eye on Neighbourhood Watch: Does it Reduce Crime and Fear?', in T. Hope and M. Shaw, eds., *Communities and Crime Reduction*. London: HMSO.

Ruggiero, V. (1991), 'Public Opinion and Penal Reform in Britain', *Crime, Law and Social Change*, 15: 37–50.

Rutherford, A. (1984), *Prisons and the Process of Justice*. London: Heinemann.

Ryan, M. (1978), *The Acceptable Pressure Group—Inequality in the Penal Lobby: A Case Study of the Howard League and RAP*. Farnborough: Saxon House.

—— (1983), *The Politics of Penal Reform*. London: Longman.

Ryan, M., and Ward, T. (1989), *Privatization and the Penal System*. Milton Keynes: Open University Press.

Scarman Report (1981), *The Brixton Disorders 10–12 April 1981*. London: HMSO.

Schlesinger, P., and Tumber, H. (1992), 'Crime and Criminal Justice in the Media', in D. Downes, ed., *Unravelling Criminal Justice*. London: Macmillan.

Schneider-Lenné, E. R. (1992), 'Corporate Control in Germany', *Oxford Review of Economic Policy*, 8: 11–23.

Sim (1993), 'Reforming the Penal Wasteland?: A Critical Review of the Woolf Report', in E. Player and M. Jenkins eds., *Prisons After Woolf*, London: Routledge.

Spencer, S. (1985), *Called to Account*. London: National Council for Civil Liberties.

Stanko, E. A. (1990), *Everyday Violence*. London: Unwin Hyman.

Stewart, J. D. (1992), *Accountability to the Public*. London: European Policy Forum.

Taylor, R. K. S. (1988), *Against the Bomb: the British Peace Movement 1958–1965*. Oxford: Clarendon Press.

Tulkens, H. (1979), *Some Developments in Penal Policy and Practice in Holland*. London: National Association for the Care and Resettlement of Offenders.

von Hirsch, A. (1976), *Doing Justice: The Choice of Punishments*. New York: Hill and Wang.

Waddington, P. A. J. (1991), *The Strong Arm of the Law*. Oxford: Oxford University Press.

Wallington, P. (1975), 'Criminal Conspiracy and Industrial Conflict', *The Industrial Law Journal*, 4: 69–88.

Webb, B., and Laycock, G. (1992), *Tackling Car Crime: The Nature and Extent of the Problem*, Crime Prevention Unit Paper no. 32. London: Home Office.

Woolf Report (1991), *Prison Disturbances April 1990: Report of an Inquiry by the Rt Hon. Lord Justice Woolf (Parts I and II) and His Honour Judge Stephen Tumim (Part II)*, Cm 1456. London: HMSO.

Young, J. (1992), 'The Rise in Crime in England and Wales 1979–1990', Middlesex Polytechnic: Centre for Criminology.

6

Crime Statistics, Patterns, and Trends: Changing Perceptions and their Implications

MIKE MAGUIRE

At heart the extent of crime is a political as well as a behavioural matter . . . The figures for crime . . . are not 'hard facts' in the sense that this is true of the height and weight of physical bodies. They are moral not physical statistics.

(Young 1988*b*: 175)

INTRODUCTION

This chapter explores a number of interrelated questions regarding the state of our knowledge about 'crime levels', 'crime patterns', and 'crime trends'. These range from what may sound like (but are not) straightforward empirical and methodological questions, such as 'How much crime is there?', 'How is it changing?' and 'How do we find out?', to broader questions about the relationship between, on the one hand, the kinds of data which are collected and published about crime and, on the other, the perceptions, ideas, and theories which are formed about it.

A Changed Picture

There is no doubt that the picture of crime painted by such data in Britain in the early 1990s is very different from the image which was presented to our predecessors in, say, the early 1950s by the information available at that time. Most obviously, it differs in terms of the quantity of criminal offences known to have taken place. The annual totals of offences officially recorded by the police and published in *Criminal Statistics* are now more than eleven times greater (over five and a half million, compared with around half a million).[1] Moreover, repeated 'sweeps' of the British Crime Survey, (conducted in 1982, 1984, 1988, and 1992) have established beyond doubt that the official totals reflect only

[1] The total number of notifiable offences recorded in 1992 was 5,594,000. Even when increased population is taken into account, the increase has been more than tenfold, from just over one offence per 100 population in 1950 to 10.6 per 100 in 1992.

the tip of an iceberg of crimes known to victims, the majority of which go unreported and unrecorded.

Equally important, the present picture is composed of considerably different types and patterns of crimes. This is quite striking even among officially recorded offences: for example, crimes involving motor vehicles, relatively rare in the 1950s when there were few cars on the roads, now make up a quarter of the total; crimes of violence against the person have overtaken sexual and fraudulent offences, both of which clearly exceeded them in the early 1950s; and offences of criminal damage, then an almost negligible category, now total over 800,000 per year, around 15 per cent of all recorded crime. However, the difference is much more dramatic if one looks beyond police statistics and beyond the British Crime Survey (which focuses on a limited set of standard offences), to the studies of criminologists. As noted in the introduction to this volume, the growth of criminology has been remarkable over the last forty years: from a few lone scholars and a small Institute in London to over 300 academics engaged in teaching and research countrywide (many in specialist 'Centres'), regular funding of empirical research, and a flourishing market for publications.[2] As greater resources have been devoted to research, so more and more kinds of criminal activity which formerly remained largely hidden from police and public view have been described and analysed in depth. Important among these are intra-household offences (such as domestic violence and sexual abuse of children), 'white-collar' and corporate offences, and crimes between consenting parties (notably drug offences), none of which attracted any sustained attention in the 1950s.

A third major difference lies in our perceptions of 'criminals'. In the early 1950s, offenders tended to be represented by experts, as well as by politicians and the media, almost as a breed set apart from the rest of society. Conviction for a criminal offence was a relatively rare occurrence in most communities and was likely to bring opprobrium and ostracism from family and neighbours (Morris 1989). Those convicted—in the main, young males from lower-class backgrounds—were seen by most

[2] The Institute referred to was the Institute for the Study and Treatment of Delinquency, whose members were chiefly engaged in medical or psychological studies of convicted offenders (see Saville and Rumney 1992). This was not only the sole criminological centre in Britain, but published the main academic journal, the British Journal of Delinquency, later to become the British Journal of Criminology.

As stated, the picture is quite different now. In 1993, for example, about 180 papers were given at the now biannual British Criminology Conference; at least ten major publishers commissioned several books each in the criminological field; and, in addition to the substantial Home Office funding of external research, criminologists received grants totalling over £2 million from the Economic and Social Research Council's initiative on crime and social disorder. For useful accounts of the growth of post-war criminology, see Rock's (1988) edited special issue of the British Journal of Criminology.

people who described themselves as criminologists, as well as by many working within the criminal justice system, as suffering from something akin to a medical condition—caused, ultimately, by some form of social and/or emotional deprivation—and in need of 'treatment' to reduce their chances of reconviction (see e.g. Bowlby 1953). Forty years later, though media stereotypes of 'criminals' still abound, possession of a criminal conviction is by no means unusual and is much less likely to be stigmatizing: indeed, it is now known from cohort studies[3] that over one-third of all males (though only 8 per cent of females) born in 1953 had acquired at least one criminal conviction for an indictable offence by the age of 31 (Home Office 1989). Furthermore, in-depth and ethnographic research—as well as high publicity for particular cases—has helped to bring about wider recognition that criminal behaviour is not a near-monopoly of poor and deprived young males. For example, the sexual abuse of children (Baker and Duncan 1985), domestic violence (Dobash and Dobash 1992), football hooliganism (Murphy *et al.* 1990), workplace theft (Ditton 1977; Mars 1982), and drug offences (Pearson 1987) have all been shown to be committed by people from a wide range of age groups and social classes—though, as will be discussed later, much less so by females than males—while a series of major frauds, some with direct financial consequences for large numbers of ordinary people (BCCI, Maxwell, Barlow Clowes, etc.) have demonstrated for all to see that criminals are to be found in suites as well as on the streets (Levi and Pithouse 1992).

None of this is to deny that there exist identifiable groups and individuals, many of them young males from deprived and disturbed backgrounds, who commit substantial numbers of the highly visible 'predatory' kinds of offence like burglary and car theft which make up the bulk of recorded crimes. Indeed, the authors of the Home Office cohort studies have estimated that as many as 65 per cent of all court convictions acquired by the cohort for indictable crimes are accounted for by just 7 per cent of its members, each convicted on six or more occasions (Home Office 1989). Nor is to deny that such persistent offenders, whose activities often seriously damage their own and their victims' lives, are worthy of special attention by researchers. However, it should make us wary of accounts and explanations which proceed as though virtually *all* crime were akin to predatory street crime and *all* offenders were afflicted by social or psychological 'problems'.

In at least three important respects, then—dramatically higher totals of

[3] Such studies trace the progress of a given group of people over a long period of time, often from birth to maturity, collecting new data on them at regular intervals. The best known in criminology include cohorts followed by the Gluecks (1950) and by West and Farrington (e.g. 1969), as well as the more recent Home Office studies referred to in the text.

known offences, revelations of major 'new' kinds of criminal activity in previously unprobed areas of the social world, and recognition that many offenders are neither psychologically abnormal nor young males from the lower social classes—the phenomenon of crime appears very different to the informed observer in 1993 than it did to his or her counterpart forty or so years ago. (On a different tack, it is also worth flagging here a fourth difference—much greater awareness of the experience of crime from the *victim*'s point of view—the importance of which will be discussed later.)

Of course, the $64,000 question which remains is how much the differences reflect 'real' changes in behaviour over this period and how much they are simply a function of new, improved, or differently tuned channels of communication about what is happening 'out there'. No satisfactory answer to this could be expected without a wide-ranging search for relevant (and mainly obscure) historical evidence; nor, equally importantly, without a thorough consideration of complex epistemological questions which underlie the differences between what Bottomley and Coleman (1981) call the 'realist' and the 'institutionalist' approaches to crime data—tasks which (though the latter questions will be touched upon) are clearly beyond the scope of this one chapter. The more modest aim here is simply to examine the kinds of data on which our perceptions of the phenomenon of crime are built, outlining some of the main developments in criminology, as well as in other sources of information about crime, which have helped to transform and broaden these perceptions. A few general comments will also be made about how convincing or otherwise some of the theories of crime causation which were put forward in earlier years, without the benefit of current sources of data, appear to remain in the light of that new knowledge.

Painting by Numbers

The empirical data most often used by modern criminologists, as well as by policy-makers in the Home Office and elsewhere, derive from three main sources: statistical records routinely compiled by the police and criminal justice agencies; large-scale surveys (usually directly commissioned by government); and small-scale surveys and studies conducted by academic and other researchers.

With notable exceptions, the central feature of this raw material, and of the use made of it, is the predominance of *numbers* as a descriptive medium. Indeed, a salient feature of almost all modern forms of discourse about crime is the emphasis placed upon terms associated with its quantification and measurement: 'volume', 'extent', 'growth', 'prevalence', 'incidence', 'trends', and so on. In political and media debates, trends in aggregate crime figures are often put forward as evidence of failures or successes in criminal justice policy, or are treated as a sort of social barometer, supposedly indicative of, for example, declining standards of parenting or schooling. Among policy-makers, arguments for an initiative in response to a particular form of crime are unlikely to cut any ice without a convincing numerical representation of 'the scale of the problem'. Criminologists, too, are well aware of the power of the 'language of figures', and even those orientated primarily towards qualitative research methods routinely produce quantitative data to reinforce and 'legitimate' their findings.

If their limitations are fully recognized, crime-related statistics offer an invaluable aid to understanding and explanation. On the other hand, not only can they can be highly misleading if used incorrectly, but, if presented in mechanical fashion, without any deeper comprehension of their relationship to the reality they purport to represent, they can grossly distort the social meaning of events as understood by those experiencing or witnessing them. Ultimately, indeed, one may ask whether 'crime' (or any particular category of crime) is a phenomenon which can sensibly be described merely by adding up totals of diverse actions and incidents.

It is also important to note that, while changes in regularly compiled statistics have a considerable impact on our perceptions of the crime problem, these are by no means the only—nor necessarily the most influential—sources of information or insights about it. In fact, systematic data collection often *follows*, rather than generates, new insights and perspectives. Spectacular instances of forms of criminal behaviour hitherto considered of only marginal importance may suddenly attract attention from the media and spark off a trawl for similar events, thus 'uncovering' (or, from another perspective, 'creating') a new 'crime problem'. Examples from Britain in the 1980s and early 1990s include the surge in public, academic, and official attention to 'child sex abuse' produced by the Cleveland case (see e.g. Morgan 1988), to 'corporate crime' by the Robert Maxwell pensions fraud, and to 'police malpractice' by the Guildford Four, Birmingham Six, and other major cases revealed as miscarriages of justice (Woffinden 1987; Rozenberg 1992).

Some writers—among the best known being Hall *et al.* (1978)—have argued further that 'crime waves' may be deliberately manufactured (with assistance from the police and the media) by governments suffering unpopularity during economic recessions, when the legitimacy of the class-based economic system is weakened. Hall *et al.*'s main example was the 'mugging' scare in the early 1970s, which was created, they claim, to focus public hostility upon, and justify greater social control over, the unemployed young black populations of inner cities. They pointed out that 'mugging' is a term which does not correspond to a legal offence category, and that the racially differentiated statistics from the Metropolitan Police Department figures which fuelled the scare were highly unreliable (for further discussion, see chapter 7 in this volume).

Finally, more gradual changes in perception may be brought about either by the dissemination of the work of criminologists with original ideas or by the persistence of groups campaigning to get a particular form of behaviour taken more seriously by the police and criminal justice system, as has happened in the case of racial attacks and domestic violence. But whatever the source of the initial attention, once sufficient public or media interest in a type of crime is generated, researchers are not usually slow to seek grants to investigate the scale of the problem in a more systematic way, while policy-makers may ask agencies to keep new kinds of records. The results, in turn, are likely to feed back into the political domain, thus promoting and continuing a dynamic process of 'amplification'.

Fundamental Problems

The above examples serve as a useful introduction to some of the fundamental problems associated with the study of crime, which demand careful attention from anyone wishing to make general statements about its nature and extent. They help, especially, to illustrate the point that the core object of study—'crime'—is, ultimately, a *social construct*. Looked at as an abstract formal category, it consists of a diverse set of behaviours which have in common (perhaps only) the fact that they are proscribed by the criminal law. The law, of course, changes over time, new offences being created and others being redefined or decriminalized, so that, even if we had god-like vision to spot every possible transgression, it would be difficult to make definitive comparisons between the 'true level of crime' at different points over a period of years (let alone to compare levels in countries with significantly different laws). More importantly, though, such an exercise would lack social meaning, which derives from the application in the real world of the label 'crime' or 'criminal' to specific incidents and people, *out of a much wider set of possible candidates for such a label.* This necessitates recognition by those involved in (or witnessing or hearing about) an incident, both that a crime has been committed and that this fact is of some significance to them or others; in most cases, too, for the event to have any publicly visible consequences requires its notification to the police and subsequent incorporation into official records. As will be illustrated later, despite the apparently precise wording of legislation, such categorization is anything but mechanical and value-free: it is highly selective and value-laden, the product of complex social, political, and organizational processes.

One of the recurrent criticisms made of criminology (particularly by sociologists) has been that, despite the daunting implications of the above points for the status of empirical knowledge in the subject, 'crime' has too often been treated as an unproblematic concept. Partly because of the importance of direct government grants in the funding of research, it has been pointed out, the overall 'agenda' of criminology—including the determination of the range of behaviours to be studied or analysed—has always been heavily influenced, explicitly or implicitly, by relatively short-term, policy-related concerns. Yet criminologists have often forgotten or ignored this, claiming a spurious 'scientific' status for their subject-matter (for an extensive historical critique, see Taylor *et al.* 1973; see also Cohen 1974; Bottomley 1979; Garland's chapter in this volume). While such criticism is less fair nowadays than in the past, it is still easy, for example, for those engaged in government-funded research to be pulled into unquestioning acceptance of policy-driven definitions of particular 'crime problems'. There is also a tendency to present the accumulation of data about unreported crime as the gradual unveiling of more and more of the 'complete picture', the 'true total' of criminal offences committed, when a more appropriate metaphor might be the constant repainting of a canvas of indeterminate size, with new areas highlighted and depicted in greater detail.

Awareness of the shaky foundations of criminological knowledge does not mean that one should abandon the pursuit of statistical data about it: on the contrary, these are vital to the development and testing of ideas, as well as to the very necessary task of description. The important point to stress, however, is that no conclusions should be drawn from any such data without careful qualification and very clear definition of terms.

CHANGING PERSPECTIVES: KEY INFLUENCES

To gain a broader understanding of how and why perceptions of crime—and approaches to its measurement—have changed, it is necessary to begin by reiterating one or two general points about the nature of criminology in the earlier part of this century and to refer to the crucial upheaval in the subject which occurred in the late 1960s and early 1970s. (These issues are discussed in varying degrees of detail by several other contributors to this volume; see particularly the chapters by Garland and Young.) Two other significant influences will then be briefly discussed: the growing focus, during the 1980s, upon victims of crime; and the increased attention given in Home Office policy to crime prevention and opportunity reduction through alteration of the environment. Both of these, it will be pointed out, played a part in shifting the focus of many criminologists' interests from the mental state of *offenders* to the physical circumstances and distribution of *offences*.

The Paradigm Shift in the 1970s

For much of the twentieth century, British criminology remained a small and somewhat insular discipline, dominated (though by no means monopolized; see chapter 1 in this volume) by what has since been widely, and often disparagingly, referred to as the 'positivist' tradition.[4] Most early criminologists were people with backgrounds in medicine or psychiatry, for whom the central goal was to understand and explain—and hence point the way to 'treatment' for—the 'criminality' of individual offenders. This was regarded by some as a real and discoverable condition, a propensity towards criminal or other anti-social behaviour, somewhat akin to a disease. Research was typified by the use of supposedly 'scientific' methods, such as systematically comparing the physical or psychological characteristics of groups of 'known offenders' (usually prisoners) with those of 'non-criminal' control groups, in order to identify factors which appeared to distinguish them and might therefore provide clues to the elusive 'causes of crime'. Biological explanations (variants on Lombroso's notion of the 'born criminal') had been largely discounted by the 1920s, being replaced by a variety of psychological and psychiatric theories. Later, as more academics with social science backgrounds entered criminology, interest shifted to 'social' factors such as family structure or unemployment, but the primary focus still tended to be on their possible influence upon individuals' propensity to commit offences—an equally deterministic approach, in which people continued to be seen as passive objects of extraneous forces, rather than as exercising choice, and in which no heed was paid to their own understanding of events. The dominant positivist method of enquiry thus remained essentially unchanged, continuing to thrive well into the 1970s.[5]

Despite their professed commitment to 'science', most British criminologists sought findings with direct relevance to the immediate goals of policy-makers and practitioners. Consequently, positivist criminology was further characterized by the acceptance of narrow, conventional definitions of 'the crime problem'. Many were content to restrict their inquiries entirely to officially defined offenders, focusing upon the predominantly male, lower-class 'recidivists' (repeat offenders) who provided

[4] Positivism as a distinct, self-proclaimed 'school' is principally associated with the work of Italian scholars such as Ferri (1913) and Garofalo (1914), who had a major influence in the institutionalisation of criminology in the USA in the early years of the twentieth century.

[5] Indeed, the tradition still has some distinguished and unapologetic exponents (see Farrington's chapter in this volume).

the bread-and-butter work of the police and courts, and the majority of whom were convicted of a limited range of predatory property crimes such as burglary and petty theft. Others preferred to define their focus of inquiry, as advocated by Sellin (1938), according to social, rather than legal, categories of disapproved behaviour, using terms such as 'delinquent' or 'anti-social' or 'socially harmful' behaviour, rather than 'crime' (see e.g. Burt 1944; Bowlby 1953; West and Farrington 1969). However, this clearly involved value-laden choices about what to include: again—particularly during the late 1950s and early 1960s as middle-class fears of the 'youth culture' increased—attention was directed at readily visible kinds of norm-violation, especially in cultural forms commonly displayed by working-class adolescents.[6] In either case, with the emphasis upon finding out what was 'wrong with' those who engaged in such activities, there was relatively little curiosity about other, more 'hidden' forms of crime, particularly those practised by more powerful social groups; and 'crime' itself continued to be treated essentially as an unproblematic concept.

However, since the late 1960s, when, galvanized by a new generation of scholars with a strong interest in sociological theory, the discipline began to expand and burst out of its positivist straitjacket, the task of understanding and explaining crime has been interpreted in a variety of new ways. The immediate impetus came from the work of American sociologists, including the influential 'labelling' theorists (e.g. Becker 1963; Kitsuse 1964), who popularized the argument that 'crime' (or 'deviance') was not an independently existing phenomenon, but simply a label attached for a variety of reasons to diverse forms of behaviour. In the words of Erikson (1964): 'Deviance is not a property inherent in certain forms of behaviour, it is a property conferred upon those forms by the audience which directly or indirectly witness them.'

The influence of these writers, mediated at first in Britain through the work of 'deviancy' theorists such as Rock (1973) and Cohen (1974), helped to initiate a broad shift in the focus of inquiry and level of explanation, away from 'the pathology of the criminal' towards 'the social construction of crime'—the social and political processes by which particular forms of activity and the actions of particular groups within society are (or are not) 'criminalized'. The way was thus opened to the growth of new academic schools such as interactionism, radical criminology, and socio-legal studies, which, though deeply split on many other grounds,

[6] Many 'delinquency' studies included behaviour such as under-age smoking or drinking, 'horseplay' in groups on the street, truanting, and even rudeness to schoolteachers (see e.g. West and Farrington 1969; Belson 1968). Apart from general concern about 'rebelliousness', another reason for the concentration on youth was that this was regarded as one of the areas in which policy intervention was most likely to have an impact.

shared this basic interest. Some writers engaged in macro-level analyses of the relationships between the interests of the ruling classes, the state, and the shaping of 'crime' through the criminal law (see Taylor *et al.* 1973). Others, influenced by the work of other American sociologists such as Skolnick (1966), Cicourel (1968) and Manning (1977), conducted micro-level studies of the daily interactions through which legal and social rules are interpreted and deviant or criminal identities are created. This included exploration of systematic biases by the police and criminal justice system in the invocation and enforcement of legal rules (see Holdaway 1979; Bottomley and Coleman 1981).

Among their many other influences, such approaches made virtually all criminologists distinctly more wary of accepting, as representations of an 'objective reality', broad pictures of crime and criminals derived from official police and court records. These data, it became widely understood, created not just an *incomplete* picture of crime—the problem, already familiar to all criminologists, of the missing 'dark figure' of crimes which are not reported to the police—but a *systematically biased* picture of crime. Criminal statistics had to be analysed as the product, not of a neutral fact-collecting process, but of a record-keeping process which is geared first and foremost to organizational (primarily police) aims and needs. As such, they may tell us more about the organization producing them than about the 'reality' they are later taken to describe. In the words of Wiles (1971: 188):

> Criminal statistics are based on data collected not by agencies designed to collect information about crime, but agencies designed to enforce the law. The statistics which result are part of the attempt to achieve that goal. The nineteenth century political economists were right in seeing the collection of statistics by such agencies as part of the process of government, but the implication of this for the sociological study of crime is that statistics themselves must be explained, rather than that they provide data for the explanation.

This line of argument led some writers to conclude that there was no point in analysing crime figures for the purpose of finding out anything about the extent of any kind of illegal behaviour—if, indeed, it made any sense to speak of 'real' crime rates at all. For them, crime rates were simply 'indices of organisational processes' (Kitsuse and Cicourel 1963) or 'an aspect of social organisation' (Black 1970), worthy of study only to help one understand the agency producing them.[7] This 'institutionalist', as opposed to 'realist', approach was also broadly the starting position adopted by Bottomley and Coleman (1981) in a major empirical study of crime-recording processes in police stations. However, although the study

[7] An alternative view was put forward by Taylor *et al.* (1973), who argued that the statistics could be usefully analysed to reveal truths about the importance attached to various forms of property under a capitalist economy.

revealed a great deal about the influence of specific police interests, attitudes and decisions in the creation of official statistics, the authors also reached the important conclusion that the decisions of many other people and agencies (notably personal and commercial victims, who between them initiate the vast majority of recorded crimes) had as much, if not more, to do with the overall 'shaping' of the figures.

The growing belief that official statistics should be studied as an object of sociological enquiry, rather than as a means of describing criminal activity, had the further important effect of raising criminologists' awareness of the rich potential of alternative sources of information about crime, such as ethnographic or participant observation studies and data from agencies other than the police. It also encouraged studies of previously neglected and largely hidden areas of 'deviant' and/or 'criminal' activity, such as drug-taking, workplace 'fiddles', and, later, corporate crime, domestic violence, and sexual violence against women (examples being, respectively, Young 1970; Ditton 1977; Levi 1981; Dobash and Dobash 1979; Hanmer and Saunders 1984).

The New Focus on Victims

The search for new forms of knowledge generated a fertile period for criminology in terms of theory and ideas, but it should be stressed that, with the emphasis upon understanding social processes rather than upon description or measurement, it did not immediately produce much new information in *statistical* form. On the contrary, there was a period when the climate in many parts of the discipline was distinctly *anti*-statistical, those who employed quantitative methodologies frequently being derided as 'mere empiricists'. In many cases, then, the new information acquired was qualitative (based, for example, on small numbers of detailed case studies) rather than quantitative.

A marked change came about in the early to mid 1980s, fuelled to a large extent by a growth in attention to crime *victims*. This perspective, initially given impetus by feminist campaigns in the USA in the 1970s, has since been embraced in a variety of ways by criminologists from all parts of the political spectrum, informing debates about, *inter alia*, the welfare and rights of victims, policing policy, crime prevention, court processes, mediation, racial harassment, and sexual oppression (for overviews, see the chapter by Zedner in this volume; Walklate 1989; Heidensohn 1989; Lurigio *et al.* 1990; Maguire 1991). More important for our purposes here, it has had the general effect of focusing attention much more upon the *offence* (and its impact) than upon the *offender*, and hence encouraging systematic analyses of where, when, and against whom different types of crime are likely to be committed.

An early British example of this kind of study was Maguire and Bennett's work on residential burglary (Maguire 1982).[8] The researchers described it as a 'crime-specific' study: a detailed look at one particular form of crime, the circumstances under which it is committed, the motives and behaviour of those committing it, and the experiences of its victims. They mapped every burglary recorded by the police over various periods in three separate areas and conducted 'in-depth' interviews with as many of the victims as possible about the precise circumstances of the incident. They also collected information from the police about the known or suspected offenders and interviewed some of those who had been convicted. A number of recurrent patterns were found, such as that burglaries tended to be clustered in poorer housing areas or close to arterial roads on the edges of towns; and that individual houses were more likely to be burgled if situated near road junctions or if they offered good cover (e.g. high hedges or fences) or access (e.g. rear or side alleys) to potential offenders. These patterns were tentatively explained in terms of interactions between, on the one hand, variations in the attractiveness of targets and in the risks and opportunities they offered and, on the other, the aims, thought processes, and behaviour patterns of different types of offender (juvenile and adult, local and travelling, and so on). The findings were generally consistent with offending behaviour as purposive and instrumental in pursuit of gain, rather than as irrational or expressive of psychological disturbance.

Many of these findings were echoed and amplified in further studies (e.g. Winchester and Jackson 1982; Bennett and Wright 1984), which also contributed to interest in the general concept of 'crime as opportunity' (Mayhew *et al.* 1976) or as a by-product of 'routine activity' (Cohen and Felson 1979), as well as in the responses of potential offenders to various kinds of opportunities to steal, the latter finding theoretical expression in, among other approaches, 'rational choice theory' (Cornish and Clarke 1986). They also fuelled new thinking about crime prevention (see next section). All of these approaches, it should be noted, are significantly removed from traditional concerns of criminology, in that they tend to direct attention to questions about the distribution of criminal events and about the physical circumstances in which they take place, rather than to questions about the mental state of those committing them. Interesting and important as the new questions are, the main academic criticism they attract is that they leave on the back burner the theoretical task which many crimi-

[8] Several North American studies, illustrating the value of attempting to understand patterns of crime through detailed information from or about victims, had been carried out considerably earlier. These include von Hentig's (1948) classic *The Criminal and his Victim*, Wolfgang's (1959) work on criminal homicide, and Amir's (1971) controversial study of forcible rape. Specifically on burglary, there were similar studies by Reppetto (1974) and Waller and Okihiro (1978).

nologists would still consider to be the ultimate goal of criminology, that of explaining why people commit crime at all (for further comment on these points, see the chapters by Garland and Young in this volume).

Moreover, whatever their usefulness in opening up new lines of thought, the obvious methodological weakness of the above mentioned burglary studies, as of similar research in North America (e.g. Reppetto 1974; Waller and Okihiro 1978; Brantingham and Brantingham 1975) and of other crime-specific studies in the UK (e.g. Banton 1985 on robbery), remains their reliance upon offences recorded by the police. Later in the chapter we shall look at what was probably the most significant development in criminological research in Britain during the 1980s, whereby systematic information has been built up about patterns of *unrecorded* crime: the advent and acceptance of the 'victim survey' (latterly more often called 'crime survey') as a standard method of data collection. Initially conceived primarily as a means of counting crimes not reported to the police, crime surveys have developed into a flexible and rewarding research tool, gathering all kinds of details about the circumstances of offences, the relationships between offenders and victims, and the reactions of victims to what happened. Indeed, so successful have they been, it is already clear that the danger with such surveys, as in the past with official crime figures, lies in the temptation to regard their results as objective reflections of the overall state of crime in the country. This is plainly wrong, not least because surveys measure a limited range of criminal activity and, even within this range, are better suited to eliciting information about some types of offence—and some types of victim—than others. These and other issues will be discussed in a substantial section of this chapter devoted to the British Crime Survey and to the various local surveys which have made their own distinct contribution in recent years, while further comment will be found in chapter 25.

New Thinking about Crime Prevention

Another strand of the shift of focus towards the offence, rather than the offender, was the growing disillusionment among influential policy-makers with the idea that crime can be controlled solely—or even principally—through the actions of the police and criminal justice system (cf. Brody 1976; Clarke and Hough 1984). Faced with the apparent failure of the police, courts, and prisons to stem rising crime rates, the Home Office Research Unit, under the headship of Ronald Clarke, began a clear policy shift in the late 1970s towards research and initiatives in the area of crime prevention, in the sense of attempting to alter the physical environment, rather than the offender. This led eventually to the formation of a separate research unit, the Home Office Crime Prevention Unit.

The distinctive contribution of Home Office research during the early and mid-1980s was the development of 'situational crime prevention'. Eschewing any interest in what Clarke (1980) called 'dispositional' theories of crime (which assert that certain people have a predisposition to offend and hence that the key to crime prevention lies in changing them), it set out to use detailed crime pattern analysis to pinpoint areas of the environment which could be altered in such a way as to make it less easy or less attractive for potential offenders to commit particular types of crime. The alteration might take the form of extra physical security, increased surveillance, the marking of property, and so on (for overviews and examples, see Clarke and Mayhew 1980; Bennett and Wright 1984: Heal and Laycock 1986: and Pease chapter 14 in this volume).

This 'targeting' approach necessitated detailed knowledge about the prevalence and the geographical and temporal patterning, as well as the physical 'mechanics', of particular offences, thus stimulating more empirical research in these areas. At the same time, the already fast declining proportion of Home Office funding which was granted for research into subjects connected with the psychology or social problems of individual offenders, dwindled virtually to zero.

For these and other reasons, then—including a general expansion of interest in issues such as public sector accountability and managerial efficiency, which led to more research examining the data collection practices of crime-related agencies—criminology began to benefit from a rapidly growing storehouse of empirical data about the frequency, location, and physical circumstances of specific kinds of criminal incidents. Since the beginning of the 1980s there have been, *inter alia*, four national crime surveys, several substantial local crime surveys, various 'victimization' surveys of businesses, 'in-depth' interview studies of victims of specific types of offence, analyses of police message pads (as opposed to the traditional dependence on crime files), and trawls of data held by ethnic minority welfare groups, hospitals, and other agencies to which people reveal 'hidden crimes'. The most influential of these sources will be discussed in some detail below. However, before commenting further on the explosion of new knowledge, it is time to take a closer look at the traditional sources of information and the basic picture of crime they produce.

THE OFFICIAL PICTURE

The key official publication in respect of crime figures is *Criminal Statistics*, the annual compilation of data derived from police and court records throughout England and Wales, which is collated and tabulated by the Home Office Research and Statistics Department.[9] Despite the caution with which they are now treated by criminologists and Home Office statisticians alike, and despite the increasingly high profile given in *Criminal Statistics* to comparative data from the British Crime Survey (see below), these statistics remain the primary 'barometer of crime' used by politicians and highlighted in the media. They are also—a use to which they are much better suited—influential in the resource and strategic planning of the Home Office and police forces. We shall now consider, briefly, how the police-generated statistics are constructed and what they indicate about the total volume of crime, the relative frequencies of different offences, their geographical distribution, and broad trends over recent years. Later in the chapter, we shall also examine what the statistics based on court records appear to tell us about the characteristics of offenders.

Total Volume of Crime

The latest official figures available at the time of writing (Home Office 1993*a*) indicate that the total number of 'notifiable offences' recorded by the police in England and Wales in 1992 was just under 5.6 million. Although this is the global figure referred to in most public debates about the extent of crime, it has to be emphasized that, *even as a record of criminal offences officially known to the authorities*, it is anything but complete (unreported offences are another matter, as discussed below). Notifiable offences are largely, though not fully, coterminous with offences which may be tried in the Crown Court.[10] This means that a large number of *summary* offences (i.e. those triable only in magistrates' courts) do not appear in the figures. No records are kept of the totals of such offences, although some statistics are available on the numbers of people officially sanctioned for them. For example, in 1990, about 1.3 million people were convicted or formally cautioned for summary offences: a total, it is worth noting, almost three times that of people convicted or cautioned for notifiable offences.[11]

In addition, the 'official crime figures' do not include offences recorded by police forces for which the Home Office is not responsible, notably the British Transport Police, Ministry of Defence Police, and UK Atomic

[9] Mention should also be made of the relatively new Digest of Information on the Criminal Justice System (Home Office 1991, 1993*a*), which provides an excellent 'user friendly' summary of key statistics, using coloured graphs, bar charts, and pie charts.

[10] Known as 'indictable' and 'triable either way' offences (see *Criminal Statistics* 1990: 21).

[11] See *Criminal Statistics* 1990: 14. More than half of the summary offences were motoring offences, but even excluding these, more people were convicted or cautioned for summary than for indictable offences.

Energy Authority Police, who between them recorded about 80,000 notifiable offences in 1992.[12] Nor, more significantly in terms of numbers, do they include numerous cases of tax and benefit fraud known to agencies such as the Inland Revenue, Customs and Excise, and Department of Social Security, which have investigative and prosecutional functions but which deal with the vast majority of cases by using their administrative powers to impose financial penalties (Levi 1993). Again, while such agencies keep internal records of the numbers of people dealt with in these ways, or of the total amounts of revenue saved, they do not record the total numbers of 'offences' coming to their notice—a task which, given that a single offender may repeat the same kinds of fraud numerous times over a period, would require complex counting rules.

It might be argued that, for all practical purposes, it is perfectly adequate to judge the size of 'the crime problem' by the total of notifiable offences recorded by the police, on the grounds that these embrace the most serious crimes, for which the vast majority of prison sentences are passed. However, they also include large numbers of incidents which it is difficult to claim are any more serious than many of the summary offences and the offences dealt with administratively, referred to above. For example, among the largest categories of notifiable offences, together making up well over a third of the total recorded, are theft from a vehicle, criminal damage, and theft from shops: most cases in these categories involve relatively small amounts of loss or damage. Again, attempts to commit notifiable offences are included along with completed crimes. Meanwhile, not only do unprosecuted tax and benefit frauds often involve considerable sums of money, but among the uncounted summary offences are common assault, assault on a police officer, cruelty to children, 'drink-driving', and indecent exposure, all of which include acts arguably more serious than many of the abovementioned notifiable offences.

Changing views about the seriousness or otherwise of particular kinds of offence have led on occasion to changes in Home Office decisions about what to include in or exclude from the official crime totals. Most notably, offences of criminal damage of £20 or less—which were not indictable—were not counted prior to 1977, but since that date have been defined as notifiable and included. This decision immediately raised the 'total volume of crime' by about 7 per cent.[13]

In addition to the issue of which categories of offence are included,

[12] A number of these, in fact, overlap with offences recorded by the police, owing to joint operations or joint processing of cases. These agencies have published separate totals of notifiable offences since 1989.

[13] This is recognized in *Criminal Statistics*; when comparisons are required between pre- and post-1977 figures, adjustments being made to the relevant tables. However, such comparisons are further complicated by the problem of inflation.

there are important questions to ask about how individual crimes are counted. Some kinds of offence tend to be repeated many times within a short period, to the extent that, though there may be several separate actions or people involved, they may be considered to form part of one concerted criminal incident. For example, a thief may go through twenty trouser pockets in a changing-room, or try the doors of a whole row of cars, or steal a cheque card and use it many times to obtain goods or cash. Equally, a large affray—for example, at a demonstration or a football match—may involve numerous assaults by many people on many others; or a man may assault his partner virtually every night for a period of months or years.

Prior to 1968, there was little consistency between police forces on how many offences were to be recorded when events of these kinds came to their notice. Following the recommendations of the Perks Committee in 1967, clearer 'counting rules' were established (Home Office 1971),[14] which tidied up some of the discrepancies between forces, but at the same time they appear fairly arbitrary and, undoubtedly, understate the relative frequency of some offences. The general rule is now that, if several offences are committed 'in one incident', only the most serious is counted—unless violence is involved, in which case the rule is 'one offence for each victim'. There is also a broad (and by no means clear) guideline stating that only one offence will be counted in a 'continuous series of offences, where there is some special relationship, knowledge or position that exists between the offender and the person or property offended against which enables the offender to repeat the offence'. Thus, in the above examples, the changing room thief, the cheque fraudster, and the spouse abuser are likely to be credited with only one crime apiece, while the affray may produce quite a large number of offences. If the rule were changed, for example, to allow all cheque frauds to be counted separately, the overall 'official' picture of crime might look significantly different.

The illustrations given here all demonstrate that statements about the 'total volume of crime' have to be hedged about with qualifications, even when they purport only to describe crimes officially known to state agencies: if different notification or counting rules were adopted (let alone new offences being created by legislation), the total could be raised or lowered significantly at a stroke.

However, the problems of police statistics are by no means restricted to formal questions of definition or rules of inclusion and exclusion. Not only do the figures (obviously) not include offences known to the public which fail to come to police notice, but a great deal of discretion remains

[14] These were revised again in 1980.

in police hands about whether and how to record possible offences which do come to their notice. Reports from the public—which are the source of over 80 per cent of all recorded crimes (McCabe and Sutcliffe 1978; Bottomley and Coleman 1981)—may be disbelieved, or considered too trivial, or deemed not to refer to a criminal offence, with the result that they either are not recorded at all, or are officially 'no crimed' later. They may also be excluded ('cuffed') for less defensible reasons, such as to avoid work or to improve the overall clear-up rate (Bottomley and Coleman 1981).[15] Calculations from crime survey data indicate that about 40 per cent of 'crimes' reported to the police do not end up in the official statistics, for good or bad reasons (Mayhew and Maung 1992).

Equally, the numbers of offences 'discovered' by the police themselves—either in the course of patrols or observation, or through admissions by arrested offenders—are subject to all kinds of fluctuation. For example, planned operations against a particular type of offence will usually result in a considerable increase in arrests and the uncovering and recording of many new offences. This is particularly true of operations against 'victimless' crimes: for example, a pop festival is almost guaranteed to generate a sudden dramatic boost in an area's recorded drug offences. Conversely, numbers may fall owing to a withdrawal of police interest in a particular type of crime, as in the late 1950s and early 1960s when, pending anticipated legislation to legalize homosexuality, most forces turned a blind eye to instances of 'indecency between males' and the recorded total of such offences declined to half the level previously regarded as 'normal' (Walker 1971).

Types of Crime

Criminal Statistics currently lists the notifiable crimes recorded by the police under a total of seventy-one headings, each of them assigned a Home Office classification number (murder is no. 1, attempted murder no. 2, threat or conspiracy to murder no. 3, and so on). These are grouped under eight broader headings, namely 'offences of violence', 'sexual offences', 'robbery', 'burglary', 'theft and handling stolen goods', 'fraud and forgery', 'criminal damage', and 'other notifiable offences'. Most of these groups contain a considerable variety of offences, in terms of both context and seriousness, but most are dominated numerically by just one or two. Thus the category 'violence' includes offences as diverse

[15] The more 'hopeless' cases, in terms of their potential for detection, that are omitted from the figures, the higher the proportion detected (the clear-up rate) is likely to be. If a division's or force's clear-up rate is exceptionally low, officers (especially those in the CID) can expect criticism from management as well as, in some cases, the media. There is thus some incentive to 'massage' local crime statistics to avoid such criticism (Young 1991).

as murder, causing death by reckless driving, and concealment of birth, but over 90 per cent of its total is accounted for by what is referred to in the tables as 'other wounding etc.'—ie mainly offences of s. 47 assault (which tend to involve fists or feet rather than knives or other weapons). Similarly, 'sexual offences' range from rape to bigamy to indecency between males, but over half consist of indecent assault on a female. In other words, a relatively small number of offence categories play a major part in determining both the overall crime total and the size of each offence group in relation to the others. Moreover, trends in these dominant offence types tend to disguise countertrends in less prolific offences.

Table 6.1 Notifiable offences recorded by the police, 1992

Offence group	No. (to the nearest 10,000)	%
Theft of/from vehicles	1,540,000	29
Other theft	1,300,000	24
Burglary	1,360,000	25
Criminal damage	690,000	13
Violence (inc. robbery)	250,000	5
Fraud and forgery	170,000	3
Sexual offences	30,000	<1
Other	40,000	<1
Total	5,380,000	100

Source: Adapted from Home Office 1993*a*.

Table 6.1 shows in simplified form the contributions of the main offence groups to the total number of offences recorded by the police in 1992. It also separates out 'auto crime' (the theft or unauthorized taking of, or theft from, motor vehicles) from other forms of theft.

If one looks at the figures as a whole, the picture of the 'crime problem' which emerges is one dominated by property offences, and above all by theft associated with vehicles. The 'theft and handling' group as a whole, with 2,844,548 recorded offences, constituted well over half of the sum total, with 'auto crime' alone accounting for 29 per cent. Burglary—primarily a property offence, though with the added (and often disturbing) element of trespass—makes up another quarter of the total. The numbers of fraudulent, violent, and sexual offences appear very small in comparison.

The fact that offences against the person make up such a small proportion of all recorded crime has quite often been quoted in a reassuring tone, especially to support the argument that the popular media focus too strongly upon violence and distort its importance within the overall crime picture. However, two points need to be made in this context. First, as pointed out above, the published figures do not include sizeable numbers of offences of common assault or assault on a police officer, which are not indictable crimes. Secondly—a more fundamental problem—the statistics can be misleading without an acknowledgement of the relative importance of violent offences judged by criteria other than sheer numbers: for example, in terms of public concern, the effects upon victims, or the number and length of prison sentences they attract. Sexual assaults, robberies, and woundings have been found to have a profound emotional impact on much higher proportions of victims than is the case with offences of theft (Maguire and Corbett 1987). Fear of violence also severely restricts the social lives of many people (Maxfield 1984; Zedner, chapter 25 in this volume). Strikingly, too, on any one day one cares to select, well over 40 per cent of the total population of convicted prisoners will be found to be serving sentences for violent or sexual offences. By contrast, people sentenced for the much more common offences of theft, handling, fraud, and forgery together make up under 12 per cent of the convicted prison population.[16]

Related comments can be made about fraud. First, as explained earlier, the counting rules cause a great number of repetitive fraudulent acts, especially those involving cheque cards and false entries in accounts, to be recorded as only one or two 'sample' offences. Second, many fraudulent tax or benefit offences are dealt with administratively by the Inland Revenue, Customs and Excise, or Social Security Department. Third, if one measures the importance of property offences in terms of the value of goods stolen, rather than the quantity of incidents, fraud comes out as of enormously greater significance than other categories. For example, Levi (1993) points out that the *minimum* value threshold for a case to be accepted for investigation by the Serious Fraud Office is a fraud of £5 million and that in April 1992, the Frauds Divisions of the Crown Prosecution Service were supervising cases involving nearly £4 billion. By contrast, the combined costs of the common offences of 'auto crime' and burglary for 1990 were estimated by the Association of British Insurers at under £1.3 billion. (Levi also points out that the alleged fraud in any one of several major cases—Barlow Clowes, Guinness, Maxwell, BCCI, Polly Peck—*alone* exceeded the total amount stolen in thefts and burglaries recorded by the police.)

This problem of minor offences 'counting' the same as major offences was recognized many years ago by Sellin and Wolfgang (1964),

[16] In June 1990, for example, 14,800 out of 34,800 convicted prisoners were serving sentences for violence against the person, sexual offences or robbery, while 4,100 were serving sentences for theft, handling, fraud, or forgery (Home Office 1992). It should be noted that the proportion of violent offenders among receptions into prison is considerably lower: their prominence among the population reflects the disproportionate length of their sentences.

who devised a weighted index, based on the notional gravity of each recorded offence, which could be used to present an alternative picture of crime in any jurisdiction. This, they argued, would allow more realistic comparisons of the seriousness of the crime problem, either over time or in different cities, states, or countries. In brief, the authors attached a different score to each category of crime, based upon ratings of seriousness derived from interviews with random samples of the population. They found a fair degree of agreement among raters, both about the order in which they placed offences and about the degree of difference in 'seriousness' between them.

Various comparisons were carried out in the USA between changes in officially recorded crime rates and changes in 'crime rates' as measured by the Sellin–Wolfgang index. Some interesting results emerged—for example, Normandeau (1969) found some contrary trends in robbery in Philadelphia, as measured by the index and by the official Uniform Crime Rates—but eventually most criminologists abandoned the index as of both dubious validity and dubious utility. Lesieur and Lehman (1975), for example, doubted whether seriousness is 'one kind of thing' that can be ordered along a scale as on a ruler, let alone whether adding up the scores would produce a total which had any meaning at all (see also Nettler 1978). Such questions, of course, are also pertinent to the current debate about 'just deserts' sentencing systems based on scales of punishment supposedly related to the seriousness of each type of offence (for contrasting views, see Von Hirsch 1986; Hudson 1987).

Finally, a long-standing criticism of the presentation of official statistics (see e.g. McLintock and Avison 1968) has been that they do not give a clear picture of the social or situational context of crimes. For example, 'robbery' includes actions as diverse as an organized bank raid, the theft at knifepoint of the contents of a shopkeeper's till, and a drunken attempt to snatch a handbag or necklace in the street. Knowing that 52,894 robberies were recorded in 1992, or that this represented an increase of 16.7 per cent over 1991, tells us very little about the events, nor whether different styles of robbery are declining or becoming more prevalent. Until recently, the only offences for which any attempt was made in *Criminal Statistics* to illustrate the context were homicide and offences involving firearms. Information is regularly provided in homicide cases about the age and sex of the victim, the relationship between the principal suspect and the victim, and the method of killing used. For example, in 1991 the highest victimization rate, expressed in terms of deaths per million population in each age group, was found among males under the age of one year (53 per million);[17] or, again, 41 per cent of

[17] The lowest was found among males between 5 and 16 (three per million). Overall, females (11) were calculated to be at slightly less risk than males (15).

female victims were killed by a current or former spouse, cohabitant, or lover, most commonly by means of strangulation.

A further step in the direction of providing 'context' has been taken in recent years, with the analysis of data (from a small number of police forces) on offences of violence. For example, recorded assaults are subdivided into 'street brawls' (the largest group for male victims), 'pub brawls', 'attacks on a public servant', and 'domestic violence' (the largest group for female victims). There are all kinds of doubts about even the factual accuracy of these data. Nevertheless, particularly when compared to crime survey findings—which show a rather higher proportion of domestic violence—they still raise some interesting questions, both about relationships between gender and violence and about how domestic violence is responded to by the police (for further discussion of this topic, see Levi, chapter 7 in this volume).

Geographical Distribution

Criminal Statistics does not include detailed breakdowns of the distribution of recorded crime across the country, but basic figures are supplied separately for each of the forty-three police forces in England and Wales. Some forces, of course, are much larger than others and in order to afford a ready means of comparison, crime rates are expressed for each in terms of numbers of recorded offences per 100,000 population. This is by no means a fully satisfactory way of compensating for the differences between police force areas, as it takes no account of possible difference in the *compositions*, as opposed to the sizes, of the relevant populations. As Bottomley and Pease (1986: 11–12) point out in relation to changes in the same area over time:

> We should beware of easily reaching the conclusion that 'people commit crime, therefore more people can be expected to commit more crime' so that if the ratio between crime and population is unchanged then there can be nothing which requires an explanation. It can be seen at once that underlying such an assumption is an emergent theory about rates of offending, and possibly about rates of victimization, which leaves itself wide open to a series of supplementary questions such as whether all members of a population are equally 'at risk' of offending . . . what significance should be attached to the gender composition of the population . . . [and] given the change in the pattern of criminal opportunities, should one adjust for social changes like the number of cars registered.

It should also be noted that the crime rates produced may not reflect important differences between areas *within* forces. Nevertheless, they do offer some fairly consistent patterns. The most obvious difference between forces lies between those covering metropolitan areas and those covering predominantly rural counties. Table 6.2, which gives the figures for forces which fall clearly into one or other of these groups, shows that the rate in 'metropolitan' forces is consistently higher than, and sometimes double, that of 'rural' forces.

Table 6.2 Selected police force areas: notifiable offences recorded per 100,000 population, 1991

	Offences per 100,000 population
'Metropolitan' forces	
Cleveland	14,137
Durham	10,881
Greater Manchester	14,700
Humberside	13,831
Merseyside	10,309
MPD (London)	12,855
Northumbria	15,798
W. Midlands	11,584
W. Yorkshire	14,273
'Rural' forces	
Cheshire	6,913
Devon and Cornwall	7,224
Dyfed–Powys	5,508
Norfolk	8,541
North Wales	6,804
North Yorkshire	7,086
Suffolk	6,201
Wiltshire	6,998

Source: Adapted from Home Office 1992*c*: table 2.6.

Apart from those shown in Table 6.2, there was only one force in the country where the recorded crime rate exceeded 10,000 per 100,000 population: Nottinghamshire showed a rate of 14,810, the second highest in the country. This was not a new phenomenon. Indeed, Nottinghamshire has long been an object of curiosity for its unexpectedly high crime rates and, more recently, has been held up as a prime example of the potentially misleading nature of official statistics. Farrington and Dowds (1985) published a detailed study of police recording practices in the county, from which they concluded that its apparently huge crime rate relative to its neighbouring counties of Leicestershire and Staffordshire (which are socially not dissimilar to Nottinghamshire) was a function of (a) a much greater number and proportion of recorded crimes originating from admissions to the police (25 per cent, compared to 4 per cent and 8 per cent in the neighbouring forces); (b) a greater number and proportion of recorded crimes involving property of little value (48 per cent valued at £10 or under, compared with 29 per cent and 36 per cent); and (c) a somewhat higher 'true' crime rate, indicated by a public survey. The researchers stated:

> 'It is reasonable to conclude that between two-thirds and three-quarters of the difference in crime rates . . . reflected differences in police reactions to crime, while the remaining one-third reflected differences in criminal behaviour . . .
>
> The research shows once again the difficulties of interpreting official statistics. Almost certainly, Nottinghamshire has never been the most criminal area in the country. (Farrington and Dowds 1985: 70–1)

Interestingly, Nottinghamshire fell from its top place in the national table in 1981 to fifth place in 1982, a change which, Farrington and Dowds claim, 'is almost certainly attributable to changes in police policies for recording offences, which may have been caused partly by this research project'.

The foregoing discussion provides us with two messages about the capacity of the official statistics to reflect patterns of crime across the country. On the one hand, they show broad consistency in indicating differences in crime rates between the extremes of rural and metropolitan areas—differences one would expect according to most theories of crime causation, as well as in the light of ordinary experience. On the other hand, as the Nottinghamshire example shows, variations in recording practices can have such a great effect on the totals produced as to render 'face value' comparisons between individual areas meaningless. It is only when one probes deeply into the practices generating police statistics that they begin to yield valuable insights.

Trends

Although graphic references to the volume of offences (e.g. 'A Burglary Every Twenty Seconds') are not uncommon, the kinds of statistic most likely to feature in newspaper headlines are those referring to apparent *trends* in recorded crime (e.g. 'Burglary Up 20 Per Cent'). In many cases, such figures refer only to a rise or fall relative to the previous year, or even the previous quarter, paying no attention to the relationship between the latter and the situation in earlier years. Thus—even leaving aside the doubts about whether changes in recorded crime levels reflect real changes in criminal behaviour—they can be highly misleading in terms of longer term trends. Sometimes, too—a practice which, if used deliberately, is simply dishonest—commentators refer to a percentage fall or increase since a particular year (to take a real example, 'burglary has risen over 60 per cent since 1989'), selecting as their baseline year one in which the official total had deviated significantly from the underlying trend.

Serious attempts to identify trends in recorded crime use figures produced at regular intervals over longer periods, and may represent the trend either in the form of a graph or through devices such as 'moving averages'. They also try to take account of changes in recording practice, such as allowing for the exclusion of minor offences of criminal damage prior to 1977, referred to above, as well as adjusting for legislative changes—the most important in the post-war years being the Theft Act 1968, which radically redefined a number of key offences including burglary (Maguire 1982: 8–9).

As can be seen from Fig. 6.1, the main features of trends in official crime statistics since their inception in 1876 have been a relatively unchanged picture until the 1930s, a clear rise up to and through the Second World War (though tailing off a little in the early 1950s), and an extremely sharp and sustained increase from the mid-1950s onwards. This saw a doubling of the figures within ten years (from roughly half a million crimes in 1955 to a million in 1964), another doubling over the next ten years, and yet another by 1990.

It should be kept in mind that parallel spectacular rises were recorded in most other western democracies over the same period.[18] Indeed, it was from this time on that criminologists worldwide, hitherto used to fairly stable, if gradually increasing, crime rates, began to be faced for the first time with a phenomenon which laid down a serious challenge to most of the 'positivist' explanations of crime which had been put forward and gained broad acceptance during the 'quieter' years. Most of these, as mentioned earlier, postulated some form of pathology in individual offenders, caused by some form of deprivation. How, it began to be asked, in a time of rising prosperity—which would, if anything, predict a *decrease* in crime according to such theories—could there be such an apparently massive increase in individuals with 'problems'?

Other features of the growth in recorded crime since the legal changes in definitions introduced by the 1968 Theft Act include the following:

1. The average annual rate of increase has been in the region of 5 per cent, but there have been many fluctuations, ranging from a rise of 18 per cent in 1974 to a 3 per cent fall in 1979. The late 1980s saw a period of relatively little change, but this was followed by exceptionally sharp rises (of 17 and 16 per cent) in 1990 and 1991.
2. The greatest *percentage* increase has been in offences of criminal

[18] An interesting exception was Switzerland, which produced such low crime rates that a distinguished American criminologist (Clinard 1978) wrote a book attempting to explain why.

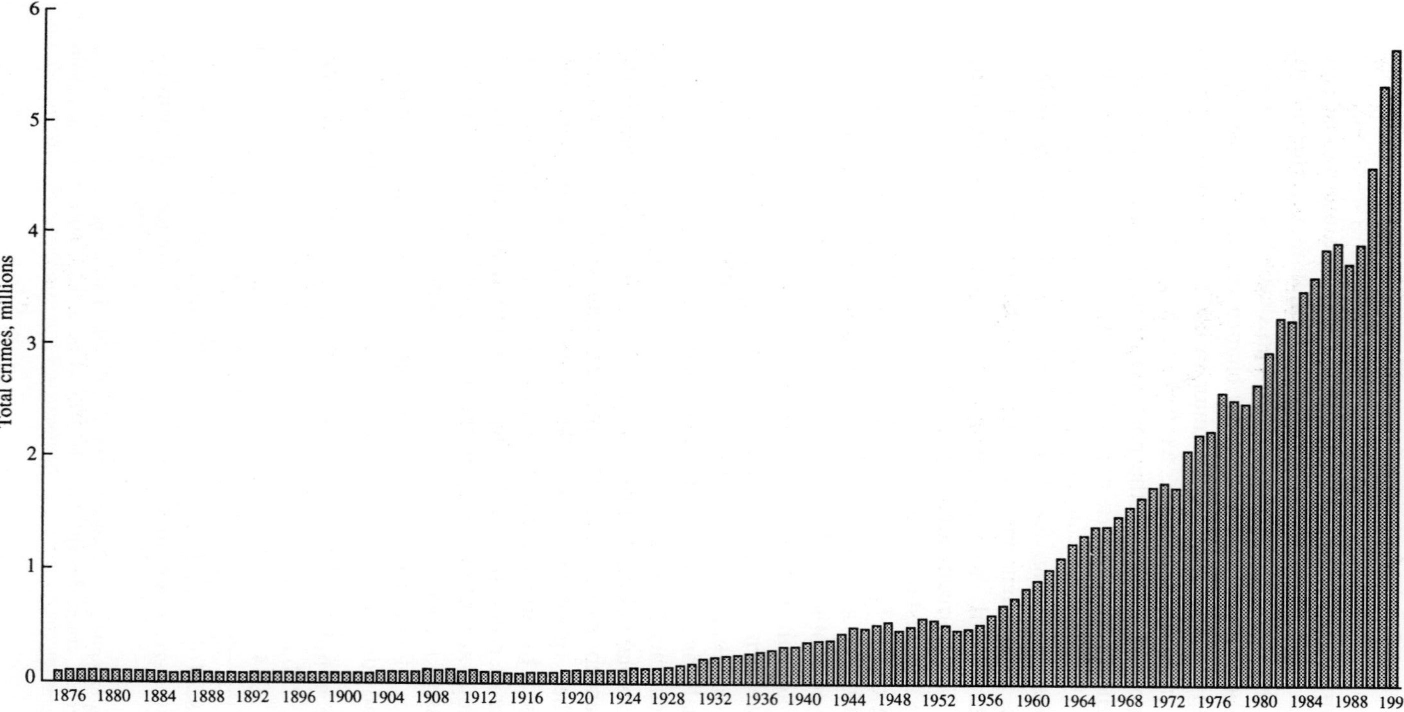

Fig 6.1 Crimes recorded by the police, 1876–1992
Source: Home office 1993*b*.

damage: from about 13,000 in 1969 to over 900,000 in 1992 (or 690,000 if offences of value £20 and below are excluded, as in 1969), a massive rise of more than 6,000 per cent. In *numerical* terms, as one would expect, the largest increases have been in various categories of theft, especially those involving vehicles. There were around two million more theft offences recorded in 1992 than in 1969.

3. During the 1980s, the offences which appeared to rise most sharply were rape and trafficking in controlled drugs, both exhibiting average annual increases of over 10 per cent. There appear to be special reasons, associated with police practice, in both cases: publicized improvements in the treatment of—and a greater willingness to believe—rape victims (Blair 1985) may have affected both reporting and recording behaviour, while more police and Customs resources have been put into operations against drug trafficking (which, of course, tends to be recorded only when arrests are made).

All other major categories of crime showed more gradual increases over the 1980s, until the figures for theft, burglary, and fraud 'took off' quite dramatically in 1990 and 1991, with 'auto crime' leading the way. In 1992, however, the increases returned to a relatively modest rate.

THE ADVENT OF CRIME SURVEYS

Prior to the advent of national crime surveys in the early 1980s, criminologists used to spend a great deal of time debating whether or not the trends apparent in recorded crime reflected 'real' changes in levels of offending, or were primarily a function of changes in the propensity of the public to report crimes and/or of the police to record them. At the extreme, some argued that the 'rises in crime' regularly deplored in newspaper headlines were largely, if not totally, illusory: the result of, *inter alia*, increases in the number of police officers (more people to uncover and record offences), the installation of telephones in more and more houses (thus making reporting easier), the spread of insurance (reporting being necessary to support a claim), reduced levels of public tolerance to violence, and the break-up of traditional communities (the last two factors making people more inclined to call in the police rather than 'sort the problem out themselves'). Hal Pepinsky, in a brief unpublished study in a British city in the late 1970s, produced the interesting finding that local crime rates appeared to have varied in relation to fluctuations in police morale and disputes about resources, offering the interpretation that the figures were manipulated, consciously or unconsciously, for 'political' reasons, such as to support arguments for increased manpower.[19] He claimed, for example, that almost half the year's increase in recorded thefts in one subdivision had been produced by a single prolific offender who stole bottles of milk from doorsteps, efforts having been made (arguably in contravention of the counting rules) to identify and record separately large numbers of his minor criminal acts. At the same time, he found, officers working 'on the ground' had not noticed any difference in levels of criminal activity in the area. Selke and Pepinsky (1984) produced a similar kind of analysis in relation to crime figures in Indiana which, they claimed, had risen and fallen almost entirely in relation to the political needs of the party in power.

While few went as far as Pepinsky in doubting that any 'real' increase at all in conventional forms of criminal activity had been taking place, criminologists in the 1970s generally remained highly sceptical, at least, of the *rates* of increase indicated by police returns. Certainly, little academic writing or debate was devoted to analysis of 'the rise in crime' as a genuine and pressing social problem. By the early 1990s, such sceptical attitudes have become much less common, it having been broadly accepted throughout the discipline that the incidence of certain forms of crime, at least, has substantially increased. This change has been influenced by several factors, not least the high profile of and acceptance achieved by crime surveys, to which we now turn. Other factors, such as the currency achieved in the 1980s by 'left realist' ideas (e.g. Matthews and Young 1986), will be referred to later.

National Surveys

In the mid-1960s, the first serious attempts were made to assess the extent of the 'dark figure' of crimes which were either not reported to the police or, having been reported, were not officially recorded by the police. Two substantial experimental surveys were conducted in the USA (Ennis 1967; Bidermann and Reiss 1967), wherein members of a random sample of households were asked whether anyone in the house had been the victim of a crime within the previous year and, if so, whether the matter had been reported to the police. A similar experiment was carried out in three areas of London in the early 1970s (Sparks *et al.* 1977).

In both countries, despite the many methodological problems identified by the researchers, governments were sufficiently persuaded of the value of such surveys to invest considerable sums of money in running them officially on a large scale. In the USA, the Department of Justice funded regular surveys at both a national and local level from 1972, and while the Home Office was slower off the mark, its crime sur-

[19] Pepinsky, an American professor of criminology, was at the time a visiting fellow at the Oxford University Centre for Criminological Research.

veys have moved rapidly into a position where they now rank alongside *Criminal Statistics* as a source of data on crime and crime trends in Britain. Other European countries are quickly following suit. Indeed, the notion of regular *international* crime surveys, building upon those co-ordinated by van Dijk *et al.* (1990) and Van Dijk and Mayhew (1992), is by no means an idle dream.

The British Crime Survey (BCS), undertaken by members of the Home Office Research and Planning Unit, was first conducted in 1982, with further 'sweeps' (the radar metaphor consistently used by its authors) in 1984, 1988, and 1992. The main rationale for the survey—and, in particular, for its expensive repetition at regular intervals—is that, by asking samples of the public to describe crimes committed against them within a given recent period, the vagaries of crime-reporting behaviour and police recording behaviour are neatly avoided, and the responses can be grossed up into an alternative, 'fuller'—and hence, by implication, more 'valid'—picture of crime and its trends in Britain.

Before discussing its shortcomings in this respect, let us look briefly at the way the data from the BCS are compiled and presented (further comment on this may be found in chapter 25 in this volume). The basic format of the part of the questionnaire which elicits information about crimes known to respondents, and the framework for presenting the figures, were established in the 1982 survey and have changed relatively little since.[20] Respondents, who are residents of households over the age of 16 (though see note 20), are first asked whether 'you or anyone else now in your household' have been the victim of any of a series of crimes, each described to them in ordinary language, since 1st January of the previous year.[21] They are then asked whether 'you personally' have suffered any of a number of other offences. If any positive answers are received, interviewers complete a detailed 'Victim Form' for each incident, though with an upper limit of five. The results of this exercise are analysed to produce estimated national totals of both 'household offences' and 'personal offences', based on calculations using, respectively, the total number of households and the total adult population of England and Wales.[22]

[20] However, the follow-up questionnaire, which asks questions of a more general nature, has been altered significantly on each 'sweep', while extra self-completion forms asking about people's own involvement in crime, and a special form for offences against children, were introduced in 1992.

[21] The survey is usually conducted in January or February, to allow comparisons to be made with the whole of the previous year's official crime figures.

[22] As the total interview sample deliberately includes an over-representation of households from denser urban areas (to maximize the chances of finding 'victims' to interview), the calculated victimization rates are weighted to take account of this.

Table 6.3 Estimated totals of offences in England and Wales, 1991, as derived from the 1992 British Crime Survey and 1991 *Criminal Statistics* where possible comparing crime groups

	BCS No.[a]	(%)	*Police*[b] No.	(%)
Comparable offence groups				
Theft of/from vehicles	3,807,000	(25)	1,263,000	(24)
Vandalism	2,730,000	(18)	410,000	(8)
Burglary	1,365,000	(9)	625,000	(12)
Wounding	626,000	(4)	157,000	(3)
Robbery/theft from person	622,000	(4)	82,000	(2)
Bicycle theft	564,000	(4)	225,000	(4)
Subtotals	9,713,000	(65)	2,762,000	(52)
BCS offences not comparable with police data				
Other household theft	1,838,000	(12)	–	
Common assault	1,757,000	(12)	–	
Other personal theft	1,744,000	(12)	–	
Police-recorded offences not covered by/comparable with BCS				
Burglary not dwelling	–	–	595,000	(11)
Vandalism of public property	–	–	410,000	(8)
Theft from a shop	–	–	281,000	(5)
Fraud and forgery	–	–	175,000	(3)
Theft of/from commercial vehicles	–	–	132,000	(3)
Other	–	–	921,000	(17)
Totals	15,052,000	(100)	5,276,000	(100)

[a] All figures are rounded to the nearest 1,000; percentages may not total precisely owing to rounding.

[b] The 'comparable' police figures follow adjustments made by Mayhew and Maung (1992), which include adding some offences recorded by the British Transport Police. These are not included in the overall police total given, so the 'Other' figure in the 'non-comparable' section (921,000), which was arrived at by subtraction from this total, is a slight underestimate.

Sources: Mayhew and Maung 1992; Home Office 1992*c*.

The offence categories produced by the BCS are shown in Table 6.3. The first important point to note is that by no means all are coterminous with police categories. In fact, when making direct comparisons of 'official' and 'BCS' crime rates, only about two-thirds of the BCS-generated 'offences' can justifiably be used (Mayhew and Maung 1992).[23]

[23] Those not directly comparable are 'common assaults', 'other household thefts' (for example, thefts of milk from doorsteps, the type of minor and very common incident identified by Pepinsky as a potentially misleading element in police statistics) and 'other personal thefts'. Some thefts involving commercial vehicles and vandalism against public and corporate property are also reported to the BCS, but excluded from the analysis.

And, vice versa, there are many categories of offence covered in the police-derived statistics which are not measured by the BCS. These include crimes against commercial or corporate victims (notably shoplifting, burglary, and vandalism), fraud, motoring offences, and so-called 'victimless' crimes such as possession of or dealing in drugs. The main BCS schedule also excludes offences against victims under age 16 (though the 1992 'sweep' was designed to generate more information about these: see note 20 above). And sexual offences, though asked about, are reported to BCS interviewers so infrequently that no reliable estimations can be produced.

In other words, as their authors freely admit (see e.g. Hough and Mayhew 1985: ch. 1), national surveys are much less successful in obtaining information about some types of incident than others. They do not produce an overall figure purporting to represent the 'total volume of crime', but concentrate instead upon selected categories of offence, which are usually analysed and discussed individually or in sub-groups. It cannot be too heavily stressed, therefore, that the BCS provides an *alternative*, rather than a directly *comparable*, overall picture of crime to that offered by police statistics: it is 'fuller' than the latter in some respects, but 'narrower' in others.

Let us look first at the areas where the two data sets do overlap, and then at the BCS 'picture of crime' in the round. The main value of being able to compare estimated totals derived from the BCS with police-recorded totals in the equivalent offence categories is that some tentative statements can be made about the famous 'dark figure' of unreported and unrecorded crime—or, more accurately, about the 'dark figure' in each of these categories.

The authors of the initial BCS summarized the results of this exercise as follows:

> Only for one category—thefts of motor vehicles—were the figures similar. For instance, the survey indicated twice as many burglaries as were recorded by the police; nearly five times as much wounding; twelve times as much theft from the person; and thirteen times as much vandalism (or criminal damage) . . . The overall ratio *for incidents which had been compared* was one in four. (Hough and Mayhew 1983: 10; emphasis added)

It will be noted from the first section of Table 6.3 that—though vandalism is an important exception (see below)—most of the above ratios were found to be relatively unchanged in the 1991 survey.

As the authors rightly went on to point out, there is a strong temptation to interpret such figures as showing that there is 'four times as much crime' as the official records suggest: a trap into which many people have duly fallen. The problem lies in the wide variations between offences in terms of their reporting and (to a lesser extent) recording rates. These variations mean that the choice of offence groups to include in any comparison can significantly affect the overall ratio between the survey figures and the police figures. For example, if the comparison included survey data covering some of the offences in the final section of Table 6.3—let us say, estimates of instances of shoplifting or pilfering from work or cheque frauds, derived from surveys of employers or shopkeepers or bank employees—where the proportions which end up in police records are known to be tiny (see e.g. Martin 1962; Levi 1993), the overall 'dark figure' would emerge as a very much larger one. (In fact, the overall 'dark figure' estimated by Sparks *et al.* (1977) in their pioneering survey was one of eleven times the police figure, in contrast to the 'four times' estimate of the BCS. The main reason for this seems to be the different spread of offences covered.) These remarks are highly pertinent to the difference between the 'image' of crime presented by the BCS and that presented by some local surveys, which will be discussed in the next section.

How, then, can we summarize the main picture of crime that has emerged from the British Crime Survey? First, the central message sent out by its authors during the initial passage of its results into the public domain was, in essence: the bad news is that there is a lot more crime than we thought, the good news is that most of it is petty. The emphasis upon 'the petty nature of most law-breaking' (Hough and Mayhew 1983: 33) was designed to deflect a possible moral panic in reaction to the huge amount of 'new' crime revealed by the survey,[24] but it also reflected the finding that unreported crimes generally involve much lower levels of financial loss, damage, and injury than those reported to the police.

Secondly, the four 'sweeps' of the BCS, like most surveys in the USA, together suggest that, overall, increases in crime have been less steep than police figures suggest. Between 1981 and 1991, among the sub-set of offences which are comparable, the number of recorded crimes increased by 96 per cent, while those uncovered by the BCS rose by only 49 per cent. This is partly explained by an increase in 'reporting rates'—i.e. the proportion of offences known to victims which get reported to the police—from 36 per cent to 50 per cent (among the comparable sub-set). However, Mayhew and Maung (1992) point out that the increase in reporting was especially marked in the case of vandalism, a factor which significantly distorts the overall picture. In fact, what they call 'acquisitive crime' (burglary, vehicle-related theft, and other personal thefts) appears

[24] This message has been sent less loudly latterly as (a) the media and the public have become more used to the idea that there is a great deal of unrecorded crime, and (b) the notion of 'trivial' crimes has become less easy to defend as the general level of tolerance for petty theft appears to have fallen. This has been reflected in 1993 in vocal opposition to clauses in the Criminal Justice Act 1991 which appear to allow petty persistent offenders to escape prison, as well as in several cases of 'vigilantism' against suspected local thieves.

from BCS results to have increased at a rate close to that indicated by police figures.

Thirdly, the BCS produces a picture of crime not wildly dissimilar in its broad 'shape' to that projected by police records: both sets of figures are dominated by 'auto crime' and both indicate low levels of violent offences in relation to property offences. The main difference in respect of directly comparable offences is that vandalism is more prominent among BCS offences than in the official statistics: it appears that only about one in seven cases known to victims ends up in the police figures.

Finally, and more fundamentally, the BCS, perhaps even more so than the police figures, promotes a picture dominated by the types of crime that are generally *committed by strangers,* as it were 'out of the blue'. Most incidents reported to the survey consist of discrete events in which individuals suddenly and unexpectedly suffer the theft of or damage to a piece of their property, or an illegal entry into their house. Crime in this mode takes on an appearance in many ways akin to an accident, or an 'act of God'—an almost random event which can strike anyone at any time, but which is relatively rare in the life of any individual. This image was strengthened in the first BCS report by the calculation of the 'average risks' of falling victim to various types of offence:

> a 'statistically average' person aged 16 or over can expect:
>
> * a robbery once every five centuries (not attempts)
> * an assault resulting in injury (even if slight) once every century
> * a family car to be stolen or taken by joyriders once every 60 years
> * a burglary in the home once every 40 years.
>
> . . . These risks can be compared with the likelihood of encountering other sorts of mishaps: the chances of burglary are slightly less than the chances . . . of a fire in the home; the chances a household runs of car theft are smaller than the chances . . . of having one of its members injured in a car accident. (Hough and Mayhew 1983: 15)

This manner of describing crime may correspond to many people's experience of it, especially among the middle classes. However, as will be discussed in the next section, it tends to leave out of the picture a number of very different kinds of experience. First of all, there are areas (poor inner city areas, particularly) where even predatory, stranger-to-stranger offences like burglary are suffered by individuals far more often than the above figures suggest. Secondly, there are important kinds of criminal behaviour, inadequately measured by the BCS, which are closely tied up with *continuing relationships between 'offender' and 'victim'*. These include assaults resulting from disputes between neighbours, the battery of women by their partners, and the sexual and physical abuse of children, all of which tend to be suffered many times by the same victims. They also include the repeated threats and harassment from local gangs suffered in some areas by members of racial minorities and by other individuals who become targeted as 'different'.

Local Surveys and the Radical Critique

Concerns about the tendency of the BCS to distort 'real' experiences of crime—especially those of women, ethnic minorities, and the very poor—have been raised by several writers (see e.g. Matthews and Young 1986; Stanko 1988; Genn 1988; Dobash and Dobash 1992). They have also strongly influenced the design of a number of local crime surveys (eg Kinsey 1984; Hanmer and Saunders 1984; Jones *et al.* 1986, 1987; Crawford *et al.* 1990), funded mainly by Labour councils, which have aimed to uncover areas of criminal behaviour not seriously touched by the BCS and, equally important, to examine and emphasize the extent to which victimization is *unequally distributed* among the population.

Some aspects of the distribution of risk were considered in the BCS from the start, but the main angle from which this topic was approached in the first report attracted a good deal of criticism. The main findings highlighted by the authors were that, for crimes of violence, males had higher victimization rates than females, and younger people higher than older; and that the risks were further related to lifestyle—for example, people who frequently went out drinking were more likely to be assaulted. From these findings they concluded, first, that offenders (or, at least, known offenders) and victims of violence shared several of the same social characteristics—the survey, wrote Hough and Mayhew (1983: 25) 'paints a . . . coherent picture of assault victims, in which the people they most resemble are their assailants'; and, second, that, this being the case, the fears of street violence expressed by both women and the elderly (which were much greater than those of young men) were to some extent out of proportion to the actual risks they faced. As will be discussed shortly, this latter point became a key target for some radical critiques of the BCS and the message it appeared to be sending out.

Other points from the first survey which received less attention included the finding that, where burglary was concerned, council properties were more vulnerable than owner-occupied dwellings (Hough and Mayhew 1983, 1985). Preliminary results from the 1992 survey confirm this in more detail, indicating that residents of 'the poorest council estates' face a burglary risk 2.8 times the average and twelve times that of people living in agricultural areas (Mayhew and Maung 1992).[25] Similar

[25] These are identified in the survey by means of the ACORN classification, which assigns every dwelling to one of 11 categories based on the demographic, housing, and employment characteristics of its immediate surrounding area.

patterns obtain for 'auto crime around the home' and robbery/theft from the person, though the greatest risk for the latter appears to be in 'mixed inner metropolitan areas'. The 1988 survey paid particular attention to differences in risk between racial groups. It was found that both Afro-Caribbeans and Asians were more at risk than whites for many types of crime, the latter being particularly vulnerable to vandalism and robbery or street theft committed by strangers (Mayhew *et al.* 1989).

Although these are all important findings, their impact has to some extent been diluted among the welter of other figures emerging from the surveys. By focusing chiefly upon inner city districts, local crime surveys have brought out much more vividly than the BCS the extent to which crime is concentrated in some small areas—predominantly those blighted by poverty—and, moreover, how particular forms of crime are suffered disproportionately by particular social groups within those areas. For example, the first Islington Crime Survey (Jones *et al.* 1986) indicated that a third of all households had been touched by burglary, robbery, or sexual assault within the previous twelve months (a situation light years away from that of the notional 'statistically average' person referred to in the BCS). It also indicated that young, white females in the area were twenty-nine times more likely to be assaulted than white females over 45. As Young (1988: 171) observes, such massive differences between subgroups illustrate 'the fallacy of talking of the problem of women as a whole, or of men, blacks, whites, youths, etc.' Rather, he insists, criminological analysis should 'start from the actual subgroups in which people live their lives'.

Writing in the same volume, two of the founders of the BCS acknowledged that the increased attention given in later 'sweeps' of the BCS to the distribution of risk was to some extent prompted by criticism of the superficial approach taken earlier on, and in particular of the handling of questions about the relationship between risk of victimization and fear of crime (Mayhew and Hough 1988).[26] Much of this criticism was led by Jock Young and others broadly adhering to the 'left realist' school of criminology (cf Matthews and Young 1986; Young 1988).[27] They attacked in particular the inference, mentioned above, that fear of crime was in some senses 'irrational' because both women and the elderly, who were less likely to be attacked, expressed greater fear than the young men who were 'objectively' at the greatest risk. Young (1988: 173–5) points out that such an approach, like the argument that fears are exaggerated

[26] A special analysis of BCS data on this topic (Maxfield 1988) was also commissioned by the Home Office.

[27] In fairness to the authors of the BCS, it should be pointed out that they had anticipated several of the criticisms in qualifications to their original conclusions (which were anyway tentative), though these qualifications tended to be forgotten in the later controversy.

because much crime is 'trivial' in terms of loss or injury, obscures the fact that what are 'objectively' similar events can have enormously different meanings and consequences for different people:

> People differ greatly in their ability to withstand crime . . . The 'same' punch can mean totally different things in different circumstances . . . Violence, like all kinds of crime, is a social relationship. It is rarely random: it inevitably involves particular social meanings and occurs in particular hierarchies of power. Its impact, likewise, is predicated on the relationship within which it occurs . . .
>
> The relatively powerless situation of women—economically, socially and physically—makes them more unequal victims than men.

The other main strand of criticism concerned the extent to which some forms of crime still remained largely 'hidden' to the BCS, even though questions were asked which appeared to cover them. Efforts to put this right were central to the design of the local crime surveys mentioned above. Perhaps the most significant aspect was the attention given to ways of obtaining more information about sexual and other assaults on women. These included less restrictive wording of questions and greater emphasis on sensitive approaches to these areas in the training and selection of interviewers. The results stand in considerable contrast to the BCS findings: in the first Islington survey, for instance (Jones *et al.* 1986), significantly higher levels of sexual assault were found, while over one-fifth of reported assaults were classified as 'domestic'—more than twice the proportion identified by the BCS. Moreover, questions were asked about incidents which would not necessarily be classified by the police as 'crime', but may be experienced as serious by victims, namely sexual and racial 'harassment'. It was found, for example, that over two-thirds of women under the age of 24 had been 'upset by harassment' in the previous twelve months.

A number of special surveys of women, most conducted by feminist writers, have also found high levels of actual or threatened sexual violence. For example, Hanmer and Saunders (1984) found that 59 per cent of 129 women surveyed in Leeds had suffered some form of threat, violence, or sexual harassment within the previous year; and Hall (1985) and Radford (1987) have produced even more startling figures. Among the most challenging of all has been a survey by Painter (1991), based on a representative sample of over 1,000 married women, which suggests that 14 per cent had been raped by their husbands at some time during their marriage, over 40 per cent of them perceiving the incident as 'rape' at the time.[28]

[28] The question used was 'Have you ever had sex with your present husband (or previous husband) against your will, when you had clearly insisted that you did not want to and refused your consent?' This is a legal definition of rape, though despite court decisions which mean that a man can be convicted of raping his wife, it is unlikely that many police

Of course, there are major questions of definition to be tackled in relation to all the above findings, as well as to those of the BCS discussed earlier. Clearly, different surveys are 'measuring' different things. The large government-run surveys in Britain and elsewhere, while prepared to experiment, have broadly held on to the definitions of crime and the counting rules used by the police in compiling official statistics: this is to allow direct comparison and hence a convincing statement of the 'dark figure' and its fluctuations over time. The surveys carried out by academics have moved further away from official definitions of crime, towards alternative definitions favoured by their designers—which, the latter would claim, are also much closer to 'social reality' and the perceptions and priorities of ordinary people. Thus the 1992 BCS 'filter' question on sexual offences was simply: 'Since 1st January 1991, have you been sexually interfered with, assaulted or attacked, either by someone you knew or by a stranger?', while most local surveys have used much broader definitions in their questions, including threats and 'pestering' behaviour.

Finally, a graphic illustration of the kinds of definitional and counting problems we have been discussing is provided by Genn (1988). Prompted by worries that the survey method leads to serious undercounting of certain types of crime, Genn revisited some of the female respondents to the pilot crime survey in which she was involved, all of whom had said they had been victimized many times. She gives an eye-opening account of the way in which the lives of these women, in severely deprived areas of London, were blighted by frequent sexual and physical assaults, thefts, burglaries, and other forms of mistreatment, many of them from people with whom they had some sort of continuing relationship. Yet this kind of 'multiple victimization', she notes, is lost from view in most surveys, partly because—in order to create comparability with police recording practices—they tend to impose artificial limits (five, in the case of the BCS) upon the number of crimes that can be counted for any one victim, and partly because such victims may be less likely than others to respond to the survey or to admit their victimization to interviewers. (Similar comments could be made about other marginalized groups—the homeless, the mentally ill, those who drift from bed-sitter to bed-sitter, and so on—whose voice is not often heard in the large surveys which draw their samples from the Electoral Register. Such people may also be subject to exceptionally high levels of victimization.) At the same time, Genn raises fundamental questions, touched on earlier in this chapter, about how meaningful it is to 'count' certain crimes at all. She writes:

> In asking respondents about their experiences of crime, victim surveys have tended to use an approach which Skogan has termed 'the events orientation': that

officers would arrest on allegations of refused consent by a wife living with her husband, without evidence of violence.

which conceptualises crime as *discrete incidents*. This . . . can be traced back to one of the original primary objectives of victim surveys: the estimation of the 'dark figure' of unrecorded crime for direct comparison with police statistics. In order to accomplish this . . . information obtained from victims had to be accommodated within a rigid 'counting' frame of reference. *Although isolated incidents of burglary, car theft or stranger attacks may present few measurement problems, for certain categories of violent crime and for certain types of crime victim, the 'counting' procedure leads to difficulties. It is clear that violent victimization may often be better conceptualized as a process rather than as a series of discrete events.* This is most evident in cases of prolonged and habitual domestic violence, but there are also other situations in which violence, abuse and petty theft are an integral part of victims' day-to-day existence. (Genn 1988: 91, emphasis added)

THE 'OFFENDER POPULATION': YOUNG, MALE, AND POOR?

Throughout this chapter we have looked at crime mainly from the point of view of those who experience it and of those who chart its incidence, the focus being upon where, against whom, and in what circumstances it is known and perceived to occur. Of course, what is glaringly absent from most of the discussion so far is information about the *perpetrators* of all these crimes. While it is important to conclude our account with some comments on this topic, these will be kept to a minimum, to avoid trespassing too much on David Farrington's territory (see chapter 12 in this volume) and partly because studies of offenders have become much rarer over the past two decades as criminologists' interests have leaned more towards victims, offence patterns, and the operations of the criminal justice agencies.

Just as the annual statistics compiled by the police produce an 'official' account of the extent of crime, to which victim surveys offer various alternative pictures, so the statistics compiled from court records (together with police cautioning records) produce a picture of all those officially held responsible for recorded offences, while various other studies and surveys—notably 'self-report studies'—have similarly provided alternative pictures of the offender population.

In looking at all those convicted of or cautioned for indictable offences in any given year, the first point to note is that their total is very much lower than the total of offences recorded. Moreover, it has become proportionally lower in recent years: despite the virtual doubling of the recorded crime rate, the numbers of people convicted or cautioned have changed little since the late 1970s.[29] In 1991, for example, about 337,000

[29] In 1980, for example, 556,000 people were convicted or cautioned for indictable offences. In 1990, the total was around 540,000. The fact that these figures have hardly changed while the totals of crimes 'cleared up' by the police have risen (in absolute num-

were sentenced in court and a further 180,000 were cautioned—small figures compared with the recorded crime total of over five and a half million offences. Taking into account the fact that some offenders are charged with more than one offence, this means that not many more than one in ten offences recorded by the police result in a caution or conviction: in other words, in the vast majority of cases, nothing is officially known about those responsible. Indeed, it has been further calculated (Home Office 1993*a*: 29) that only about one in fifty of the comparable crimes identified by the BCS result in a conviction—a figure which drops as low as one in 200 where 'vandalism' (criminal damage) is concerned.

This being the case, it can obviously not simply be assumed that the characteristics of 'offenders' as a whole can be inferred from those of adjudicated offenders—a central point which we shall return to in a moment. First, though, let us look at the official figures.

The basic profile of the half million or so offenders convicted or cautioned for indictable offences in 1991 was as follows: 82 per cent were male and 46 per cent were under the age of 21. The 'peak age' for males was 18 and for females it was 15 (Home Office 1992*c*).[30] It is also known from cohort studies using the Home Office Offenders' Index that a high proportion of those convicted will have had a number of previous convictions: as noted earlier, it has been calculated that two-thirds of all convictions are accounted for by male offenders who have already been before the courts six or more times (Home Office 1989).

Another, more detailed, picture of adjudicated offenders—in this case, the sub-group thought to have offended seriously enough to warrant detention in a custodial institution—is provided by analysis of information held in prison records. The National Prison Survey (Walmsley *et al.* 1992) gives a breakdown of the social characteristics of 10 per cent of all male, and 20 per cent of all female, prisoners over the age of 17 held in custodial institutions in England and Wales in early 1991.[31] Like the sentenced and cautioned population, the prison population was shown to be predominantly young: excluding juveniles in both cases, 62 per cent of inmates were aged below 30, compared with 25 per cent of the general

bers, not percentages) seems to be explained by the growth of practices such as 'prison write offs' and 'informal cautions', whereby minor crimes are 'cleared' in a bureaucratic fashion, with a minimum of fuss and expense.

30 That is, 18-year-old males constitute the age group with the highest proportion of its population cautioned or convicted for indictable offences. In fact, the peak age for males has changed recently, from 15 to 18. Farrington and Burrows (1993) note that this is due mainly to a significant fall in the number of boys under 16 cautioned or convicted for shoplifting—itself explained by a growing tendency of the police to use alternative, informal ways of dealing with them.

31 The survey included remand prisoners as well as those convicted, so was not strictly speaking a sub-group of all adjudicated offenders (a relatively small proportion will subsequently have been found not guilty).

population. Males were even more strikingly overrepresented, making up 96 per cent of all prisoners.

Disproportionate numbers of prisoners also came from ethnic minorities: 15 per cent of male prisoners and as many as 23 per cent of female prisoners described themselves as black or Asian.[32] Where social class was concerned, 41 per cent of males had had unskilled or partly skilled jobs, compared with 18 per cent of the general population.

Other noteworthy findings included the revelation that over a quarter of prisoners had at some time been in local authority care (compared with an estimated 2 per cent of the general population); 40 per cent of male prisoners had left school before the age of 16 (compared with 11 per cent of all British males); and 13 per cent had been 'of no fixed abode' before coming into prison (for further details, see the chapter by Morgan in this volume).

Taken overall, these data clearly illustrate that the social characteristics of people who are arrested and processed by the criminal justice system—and particularly of offenders who are eventually sent to prison—present a very different pattern from that found in the general population. There are many more males, young people, black people, poor people, poorly educated people and people with disturbed childhoods than one would find in a random sample.

Of course, as pointed out above, if only 2 per cent of known crimes end in a conviction, it is important to ask whether the other 98 per cent are likely to have been committed by a similarly skewed section of the population (or, indeed, by the very same people). This is the province of self-report studies—the technique by which samples of the population are asked in confidence whether they have committed crimes for which they have not been caught. On the one hand, these suggest that crime is committed by a much larger proportion of the population than is officially held responsible for it. On the other hand, convicted offenders tend to admit to both *more serious* and *more frequent* offending behaviour than people who have not been convicted.

Depending upon the age, location, and other social characteristics of the sample questioned, as well as upon the wording of the questions, self-report studies have generally found that between 50 and almost 100 per cent will admit to having committed at least one criminal offence during their lifetime. Most such studies have used samples of young males, often schoolchildren or students. For example, in one of the best early studies, Elmhorn (1965) found that 92 per cent of a random sample of teenage

32 For a full discussion of the massive overrepresentation of black people in prisons in the USA and England and Wales, see Tonry (forthcoming). Hood (1992) and Smith's chapter in this volume provide more general discussions of the disproportionate black–white ratios, and the probable extent of racial bias, at each stage of the criminal justice process.

schoolboys in Stockholm admitted to at least one offence, while 53 per cent admitted to at least one 'serious' offence (roughly the equivalent of an indictable crime in Britain), principally theft. Methodologically sound studies of adults are rare, although Farrington (1989) found that 96 per cent of the birth cohort used in the long-term Cambridge delinquency studies—which contains a higher than average proportion of working-class urban males—admitted to having committed at least one criminal offence by the age of 32. Like the authors of most other self-report studies, however (e.g. Short and Nye 1958; Christie *et al.* 1965; Elmhorn 1965; Huizinga and Elliott 1986), Farrington found that a much smaller proportion—predominantly, those who had criminal convictions—admitted to large numbers of offences (see also Farrington 1973). Hence, the general conclusion reached over 20 years ago by Hood and Sparks (1970: 51), after a summary of results of self-report studies from several countries, seems to remain valid today: 'While it may be correct to say that to commit one or two delinquent acts is "normal behaviour" for boys, to be involved in frequent criminal acts is apparently relatively rare.'

An important qualification, however, is that self-report studies have generally covered a limited range of offences, chiefly the less serious forms of street crime. Many, too, have included vaguely defined 'delinquent' or 'anti-social' acts, such as 'defying parents' authority' or 'a fist fight with one other person' (Short and Nye 1958), which would be unlikely to qualify as crimes if reported to the police. These features of their methodology have played a part in what has been the most controversial issue surrounding the results of self-report studies, that of the social class of offenders.

The argument was started in earnest by the abovementioned study by Short and Nye (1958), which indicated that middle-class boys were as likely as lower-class boys to be involved in delinquent acts, despite the fact that adjudicated offenders are predominantly working-class. This finding, supported by some (but contradicted by other) subsequent studies, suggested that there must be some major form of class bias in the processes of arrest and prosecution by which offenders come to official notice. A lively debate ensued over many years, focusing particularly on the reliability of the methodologies employed. Questions were raised about the representativeness of the samples used, the suitability of the method of administering the questions (for example, self-completion questionnaires may elicit a fuller response from middle-class than working-class people), the doubtful status as 'crime' of many of the acts asked about, the possibility of respondents telling lies and, indeed, the definition of 'lower class'—including the possible significance of differences between the urban and the rural working classes (for more detailed accounts of these problems and the related arguments, see Hood and Sparks 1970;

Braithwaite 1979; Bottomley 1979; Hindelang *et al.* 1979; Bottomley and Pease 1986; and the chapter by Farrington in this volume).

Perhaps the most thorough review of the evidence has been that provided by Braithwaite (1979), who analysed forty-one self-report studies as well as over 250 other studies concerning the relationship between social class and crime. He concluded that, although the evidence was often contradictory and confusing, although police bias probably exaggerates the relative extent of working-class delinquency, and although self-report studies tend to exaggerate the relative extent of middle-class delinquency, the following statements may be made with some confidence:

1. Lower-class adults commit *those types of crime which are handled by the police* at a higher rate than middle-class adults.
2. Adults living in lower-class areas commit *those types of crime which are handled by the police* at a higher rate than adults who live in middle-class areas.
3. Lower-class juveniles commit crime at a higher rate than middle-class juveniles.
4. Juveniles living in lower-class areas commit crime at a higher rate than juveniles living in middle-class areas.

(Braithwaite 1979: 62, emphasis added)

Aside from membership of the lower class, statistical correlations have been claimed between many other social (as well as psychological and physical) factors and self-reported or officially defined offending. No more will be said here about the wide range of factors which are identified and discussed in depth by Farrington in this volume as distinguishing serious and persistent offenders from non-offenders or occasional minor offenders, except to reiterate the point (also emphasized by Braithwaite 1979 in relation to the social class of offenders) that the offences covered in the studies to which he refers are chiefly the common and visible predatory street offences like burglary and 'auto crime'—almost by definition the 'crimes of the poor'—rather than the more hidden kinds of crime which happen within the private space of the commercial world or within the household. Nor will any more be said here about the complex issue of race and crime, which is tackled by Smith in chapter 22 in this volume. However, although a fuller discussion can be found in Heidensohn's contribution (chapter 21), it is important to make a few general points about what is perhaps the most interesting phenomenon of all to emerge from all statistics on offenders: *the overwhelming preponderance of males over females.*

This imbalance seems to be a universal feature of the criminal justice records of all modern countries, enduring over time, and confirmed by self-report studies and other research methods (Heidensohn 1985): it happens, for example, that the male–female ratio of convictions was almost precisely the same in 1892 as in 1992 (Home Office 1993*c*). Gender differences are also apparent when one looks at the types of offence for which males and females are convicted. For example, 69 per cent of all females cautioned or convicted in England and Wales in 1990 had committed theft, compared with 41 per cent of males; and much smaller proportions of females than males were held responsible for burglaries or violent offences (Home Office 1992*b*: 7).[33]

There has, it is true, been a very gradual upward trend since the 1960s in the proportion of females among those convicted or cautioned, as well as some small shifts in the pattern of female convictions which suggest greater involvement by women and girls in offences such as robbery and burglary—trends which gave rise to some controversy in the 1970s and early 1980s, around Adler's (1975) argument that the 'emancipation of women' was responsible for a greater number of women engaging in criminal activity, just as it had allowed women to engage in a wider range of legitimate economic and social activities. However, the rise in female cautions and convictions has not been strongly sustained: since the end of the 1970s, the female 'share' of officially defined offenders has fluctuated mainly between 16 and 17 per cent, reaching a high point of 17.6 in 1991, while the total numbers—like those of males—have slightly declined. (Moreover, several writers have commented, with regard to Adler's hypothesis, that the assumed 'female emancipation' is neither a proven phenomenon nor easily measurable—see e.g. Box 1983.)

The argument that the official statistics grossly distort the 'true picture' and that a disproportionate amount of female crime remains 'hidden', likewise finds little evidence to support it. As Heidensohn rightly points out:

> There is little or no evidence of a vast shadowy underworld of female deviance hidden in our midst like the sewers below the city streets. As we have become increasingly aware in modern times, *quite the opposite is true*. There is a great deal of crime which is carefully hidden from the police, from families, friends and neighbours. Much of this takes the form of domestic violence, the abuse of children both physically and sexually, incest and marital rape. *The overwhelming majority of such cases involve men*, usually fathers and husbands injuring or abusing their wives and children. (1989: 87, emphasis added)

Similar points can be made about another major area of crime which remains largely unrevealed by both police statistics and conventional crime surveys: that of corporate crime. As few women are in the high-level positions from which markets can be manipulated or business frauds

[33] The equivalent proportions for burglary were three per cent compared with 13 per cent, and for offences of violence they were 10 per cent compared with 18 per cent.

perpetrated, it is safe to assume that this genre of crime, too, is overwhelmingly a male province.

To sum up, there now appears to be relatively little dispute about the broad validity of the general picture, as reflected in the official statistics, of the relative 'contribution' as offenders of males and females, but there is much more argument about the relative contributions of other major social groups, particularly black people and white people, and people from different social classes. Where the *persistent commission of common predatory street offences* is concerned, it is true, both 'official' and 'self-reported' offenders emerge with a broadly similar profile (partly, one may presume, because few persistent burglars or car thieves succeed in escaping conviction entirely). However, this does not alter the vital point that, just as victim surveys are vastly more effective in revealing 'hidden' instances of some kinds of crime than of others, so the perpetrators of different kinds of offence are not equally well 'revealed' through the medium of self-report studies. Thus, while the (usually young and all-male) respondents tend to be asked in great detail about the relatively visible kinds of anti-social activity which are associated with the court appearances of adolescents, they are not asked whether they have assaulted their partners or sexually abused their children, nor whether they have perpetrated a significant financial fraud. It may be, as many writers on the subject claim, that intra-family violence and abuse are much more evenly distributed throughout the population (see e.g. Morgan 1988; Morgan and Zedner 1992; Dobash and Dobash 1992). And without doubt, the social class distribution of people involved in business fraud is skewed in a different direction from that of burglary and street robbery.

STUDIES OTHER THAN SURVEYS

Although the bulk of information relating to the 'crime picture' nationwide comes, by virtue of the vastly greater resources spent on gathering them, from data gathered by the police and criminal justice agencies or by major government-run surveys rather than by individual criminologists, it is important to end this account with some (necessarily brief) mention of empirically based criminological studies which have not used survey methods and have been conducted in only one or two areas, yet have had a considerable influence on how we perceive crime.

At the extreme opposite end from national surveys are ethnographic or 'participant observation' studies of particular small groups or individuals. Most of these have been based upon groups of offenders, although a few have focused upon the lives of victims (especially women subjected to assault by men—see e.g. Genn 1988; Counts *et al.* 1992). Such studies do not use numbers at all, but try to convey the essence of their subjects' lifestyles, behaviour and experiences by means of qualitative analysis, based on field notes acquired through close observation over a substantial period of time. Criminology has a long tradition in this kind of work, rooted in the 'Chicago' studies of the 1930s, which brought to life the dominant lifestyles, motivations, and *modi operandi* of, for example, the 'jack-roller' (Shaw 1930) and the street corner gang (Thrasher 1927; Whyte 1955). However, apart from a period of prominence in the 1960s and early 1970s, this tradition has never really flourished in Britain, remaining largely a 'lone furrow' ploughed by a small number of talented ethnographers.

Even so, studies of this kind have produced important insights which have informed a great deal of other work, both theoretical and empirical. For example, Young's illuminating ethnography of small groups of drug-takers (Young 1970) helped greatly to develop the important concept of 'deviancy amplification'—the process by which deviant behaviour 'escalates' as deviants and control agencies react to each other. Other such studies have done much to reflect the reality of teenage petty theft and 'joy-riding' in an inner-city area (Parker 1974), gang life in Glasgow (Patrick 1973), and violence among female gangs (Campbell 1984). More recently, Hobbs's (1988) ethnographic study conducted in the East End of London produced original ideas about the influence upon both crime and policing of the unusual working-class entrepreneurial tradition in the area.

More common than purely ethnographic studies have been field research studies based on a catholic mixture of quantitative and qualitative methods, usually including face-to-face interviews with samples of offenders and/or victims using a semi-structured questionnaire. The samples may be drawn up primarily from official criminal justice records (like Maguire and Bennett's 1982 and Bennett and Wright's 1984 samples of 'burglars'), recruited from a variety of community schemes for offenders (as in Light's 1993 study of car thieves), or created via a 'snowballing' process of asking interviewees for introductions to potential new informants (as in Cromwell *et al.*'s (1991) study of burglars). While open to question about the 'representativeness' of their samples, such studies have usually carried more weight with policy-makers than have ethnographic studies, owing to the scope they give for producing statements of magnitude (e.g. '50 per cent of burglars interviewed said . . .'). At the same time, they have the advantage over large-scale surveys that they allow the researchers more scope to build up a rapport with those they interview, exploring matters in more depth and teasing out the subject's own understanding of events. Direct quotations from interviews can then be used to counterbalance any tendency of the figures and percentages to lose or distort the reality.

Studies of this kind have played a part in altering both criminologists' and policy-makers' perceptions of various kinds of crime. For example, Dobash and Dobash's (1979) study altered many people's notions of the scale and seriousness of domestic violence; Maguire and Bennett's (1982) study drew attention simultaneously to the relatively minor loss or damage suffered in most burglaries and the severe emotional impact that burglary has on many victims; and Pearson's (1987) study has widely changed the view of heroin use as a swift and automatic path to addiction and dissolution, to one of a culture in which some people can handle regular use of the drug over a long period while still leading an otherwise 'normal' life. In each case, the studies have performed to some extent a 'myth-breaking' function, showing that the picture is not so simple as was previously thought. Other studies have shed new light upon scarcely known fields of crime and victimization, such as Ditton's (1977) and Mars' (1982) examinations of almost routine thefts by employees in all kinds of industries, Levi's (1981) work on long-firm fraud and Morgan and Zedner's (1992) study of child victims. Finally, while one or two scholars (e.g. van Duyne 1993) have made a laudable start, there remains a major gap in our knowledge about the important area of highly organized cross-border crime—activities associated particularly with drug-smuggling and money-laundering, but also many other kinds of illegal financial manipulation at an international level (e.g. frauds involving European Community funds). British criminologists, who have generally focused their attention upon crime within the UK, have only recently begun to identify such cross-border offences as an area of any serious relevance to their field of study (cf. Croall 1992; Levi and Maguire 1992).

CONCLUDING COMMENTS

One of the central themes of this chapter has been the extent to which knowledge about 'crime' in all its manifestations has not only greatly expanded, but has shifted in focus over the last twenty or thirty years. A Rumplestiltskin-like criminologist, waking up after, say, a 35-year sleep ready to resume his (he would almost certainly be male) task of 'explaining crime', would find himself confronted with a situation so foreign that he would have difficulty in finding a theoretical perspective in his toolbag with which to make sense of what he saw. Let us end the chapter with a few brief, speculative thoughts about how he might react. These are put forward as no more than quick and crude illustrations of how theoretical work, far from developing in a vacuum, has to take account of developments in criminal statistics and empirical research.

We have identified several major features of the changes with which our criminologist would have to come to terms. First of all, instead of well under a million 'conventional' property and violent crimes, he would have to explain over 15 million (the BCS estimated total). Second, he would be confronted with evidence of widespread intra-familial crime, mainly sexual and physical abuse by men of women and children living with them. Third, he would have to explain numerous massive corporate frauds and many other lesser forms of 'white-collar crime'. Fourth, he would have to explain an apparently major increase in international organized crime, much of it based on the smuggling and distribution of illegal drugs and the laundering of money from that trade. Fifth, he would be confronted with a general switch of interest from 'what makes offenders tick' to how criminal events are distributed in time and space. Sixth, he would find as much written about the institutions which define or respond to crime—the police, courts, and prisons (and, latterly, the media)—as about crime and offenders themselves, all of which draws attention to the extent to which the shape of 'the crime problem' is socially and politically constructed. Seventh, he would find widespread interest in the relevance of gender issues to crime—in why, for example, the sex distribution of victims and offenders is significantly skewed in many different types of crime. Finally, he would be confronted with ample evidence of the stark unpleasantness of crime from the point of view of the victim—and, moreover, the fact that a great deal of it is suffered by the poorest and most vulnerable members of society.

Faced with a picture so much more complex than it had been in the 1950s, he would probably soon abandon any lingering hopes he might still have had then of finding the 'criminologist's stone'—the single 'cause' of crime. The wisdom of embarking upon such a search has been thrown into serious doubt since the 1960s by a combination of the insights of the deviancy and labelling theorists, the revelation of many 'new' kinds of crime in all sections of society, and the continuing upward trend in 'conventional' offences like burglary. To begin with, if, as many of his contemporaries did, our man from the 1950s saw individuals' criminal behaviour as caused primarily by economic and social deprivation, he would have expected crime figures (especially those of minor theft, which make up the bulk of officially recorded crime) to have declined significantly from the mid-1950s onwards, as people generally became wealthier, education and housing improved, and so on. He would therefore immediately encounter serious problems in trying to explain why the trend had gone dramatically in the opposite direction. This unexpected phenomenon was the crux of what Young (1986) has called the 'etiological crisis'—a crisis which seriously undermined positivist criminology. (It should, however, be pointed out that deprivation-based explanations become more convincing when applied to crime trends in more recent years when, although living standards may have increased for the majority, there has been an increase in poverty—both relative and absolute—among those at the lower end of the economic scale: for discussion of these issues, see Taylor, chapter 11 in this volume.)

Similarly, our criminologist would also certainly begin to question whether any physiological or psychological theory of why certain people offend and others do not could ever aspire to accounting for both the range and the extent of criminal behaviours now known about. This is particularly true of physiological theories, especially those arguing that crime is genetically determined, which, though they may be defensible where specific forms of behaviour are concerned, would have to assume almost a mutation of the species to explain the overall picture (for reviews of such theories, see Wilson and Herrnstein 1985; Moffitt 1990; Farrington's chapter in this volume). Similar comments apply to single-factor psychological explanations. For example, Bowlby's (1953) work linking juvenile delinquency with the separation of children from their mothers in the early years of childhood—originally attractive by virtue of the coincidence of a rise in delinquency with the arrival at adolescence of the generation of children who had been evacuated during the Second World War—not only became increasingly unconvincing as later generations apparently exhibited more delinquency than the evacuees, but is far too simplistic to take proper account of the complexities of modern forms of family life (for further discussion, see the chapter by Pearson in this volume).

Moreover, our criminologist's new knowledge would probably cause him to have reservations about the normative 'strain' theories which were being discussed and developed in the USA in his era—Merton's 'anomie' theory, Albert Cohen's subcultural theory, and subsequently Cloward and Ohlin's subcultural/differential opportunity theory, and so on—which were built on the assumption that crime is committed by people whose legitimate channels to status and success are blocked (for good brief summaries of these theories see, *inter alia*, Chambliss 1988; Heidensohn 1989; see also Garland's chapter in this volume). Neither 'crimes of the powerful' nor intra-familial crimes fit these models; nor, indeed, is there any convincing evidence of an unprecedented growth in specific subcultures expressing a search for goals other than those espoused by the dominant middle-class culture. At the same time, the greater awareness now of gender issues—and the more widespread readiness to challenge assumptions in this area—would force the by now confused time-traveller to face such difficult questions as why, if young men turn to crime when their opportunities are blocked, women do not do so to the same degree.

How might he be helped, then, by catching up on later writers? First of all, he would certainly gain a great deal of insight by reading the early 'labelling' and 'deviancy' theorists, who would direct his attention to the role of 'powerful others' in defining certain acts and people as 'crimes' and 'criminals'—a perspective useful in making sense of the shifting patterns of media and public concern about particular forms of behaviour. But while they might help him understand the weaknesses of positivism, the analyses of these writers were much more convincing in relation to the 'marginal' kinds of crime (recreational drug-taking, sexual deviance, and so on) which occupied most of their attention, than they would be in relation to types of behaviour (of more interest to modern criminologists, owing to the apparently enormous increase in their incidence) which would be almost universally described and recognized as criminal, not least by those engaging in them: crimes, that is, such as burglary, robbery and car theft.

He would also find valuable insights in some of the Marxist analyses of crime which were prominent in the late 1970s, although he might be less impressed by their ability to explain some important pieces of empirical data. For example, little evidence has emerged to support the image they often projected of offenders as proto-revolutionaries or latter-day 'Robin Hoods': on the contrary, the evidence of crime surveys, as we have seen, suggests that most criminal victimization is *intra*-class rather than *inter*-class (see also the chapter by Emsley in this volume). However, he might find more persuasive the general perspective of the 'left realists', who start from criticism of 'the great denial' in which, they claim, criminology (particularly the criminology of the 'idealist' left) became involved in the 1970s—denial, that is, of the seriousness and high incidence of crime. While maintaining a radical approach—in the sense of (a) recognizing that criminal statistics are social constructs, not hard facts, and (b) locating the roots of crime in the fundamental social relationships of class and patriarchy—they have adapted their thinking more than most other theorists to the new evidence about crime that we have been discussing. They have constructed new ideas around questions raised by victim surveys. They have acknowledged unequivocally that crime is a very real social problem which, moreover, most afflicts the poorest and most vulnerable groups. They have taken gender issues seriously. They have also stressed the importance of studying the subjective understandings and choices of those who become involved in crime, rather than seeing offending in purely deterministic terms as the mechanistic product of some biological, psychological, or social force (for overviews of the left realist position, see Young 1986, 1988*a*; Kinsey *et al.* 1986). While their theories of why people commit crime remain undeveloped in several respects—indeed, many would argue that left realism is a 'perspective' rather than a theory—adherents of this school have certainly taken criminology forward by trying to come to terms with the 'facts' of crime as understood in recent years.

Similar points can be made about feminist theories of crime, one of the main growth areas of criminology in the 1980s and early 1990s (for an overview, see the chapter by Heidensohn in this volume). Feminists, more than the proponents of any other approach, have followed through at a theoretical level the implications of the many research findings which locate a great deal of crime within the home, and of those which show huge imbalances between the sexes in both the commission of crime and the experience of victimization.[34]

Finally, if he wished to eschew radicalism and embrace some very broad theory of individual offending behaviour, our criminologist might be drawn in the general direction of control theory, which starts from the other end, as it were, by asking why some people do *not* commit crime. The assumption that the 'natural' state is one in which, without some form of control being applied, everyone would do so, at least fits with the findings of self-report studies that criminal offences are committed by virtually everyone at some time. However, whether he would agree with the chief progenitor of this theory, Travis Hirschi (Hirschi 1969), that the main mechanism of control is that of 'bonding' with parents, school, or some other body which disapproves of crime, is more doubtful, there being little strong empirical evidence for this (see Garland's chapter in this volume).

More likely, though, coming from an era in which statistical analysis was a central feature of almost all criminologists' work, he would eventually follow the sizeable number of his modern colleagues who, finding a waning of interest in the search for the 'ultimate causes of crime', have switched their attention from data about convicted offenders to the vast amounts of numerical data which have accumulated about the incidence of criminal events, employing their skills to seek explanations for patterns and trends in crime and victimization. The kinds of explanation investigated have included, for example, shifts in economic conditions (Field 1990), patterns of crime in relation to unemployment (Box 1987) and housing (Smith 1986), crime opportunity structures created by routine social activities (Cohen and Felson 1979), and the 'geography' of offence patterns (Evans and Herbert 1989).

Interesting as these avenues have proved to explore, however, he might ultimately find that, despite the vast amount of data generated, there was

[34] Feminist theory, it should be noted, has also contributed a great deal in the socio-legal field, in particular to the understanding of how social biases and inequalities are built into definitions of crime, the creation of legal rules, and the operation of the criminal justice system.

still something lacking: perhaps a sense of genuine understanding of how those most directly involved—offenders, victims, and criminal justice officials—perceive and experience crime. What seems to be missing, now as in his own time, is good qualitative material about offending, gleaned through the most difficult kind of research of all where crime is concerned—that based upon direct observation and ethnographic methods.

If one broad conclusion can be drawn from the discussion in this chapter, it is that while we may know a lot more about crime, we are less sure about the implications of our knowledge. In 'postmodern' fashion, old certainties have disappeared, and both the phenomenon of crime and explanations of it have become fractured, patterns appearing transient and illusory. Criminological research has become a far more complex and demanding enterprise and there is no clear consensus on the questions that should be tackled or how to tackle them. In sum, the 1980s saw increasing sophistication in data collection techniques and, in particular, important advances in knowledge about previously 'hidden' forms of crime; the challenge of the 1990s seems to be to find new theoretical frameworks to make sense of it.

Selected Further Reading

A. K., Bottomley and C. A. Coleman, *Understanding Crime Rates*, Farnborough: Saxon House, 1981.

A. K. Bottomley and K. Pease, *Crime and Punishment: Interpreting the Data*, 1986.

L. E. Cohen and M. Felson, 'Social change and crime rate trends: a routine activity approach' *American Sociological Review*, 1979, Vol 44, 588–608.

D. J. Evans and D. T. Herbert, *The Geography of Crime*. London: Routledge, 1989.

D. P. Farrington, 'Self-reported and official offending from adolescence to adulthood' in M.W. Klein (ed.) *Cross-national Research in Self-reported Crime and Delinquency*, Dordrecht, Netherlands: Kluwer, 1989.

D. P. Farrington and E. A. Dowds, 'Disentangling Criminal Behaviour and Police Reaction' in D. P. Farrington and J. Gunn eds., *Reaction to Crime: the Public, the Police, Courts and Prisons*. Chichester: John Wiley, 1985.

S. Field, *Trends in Crime and Their Interpretation: A Study of Recorded Crime in Post War England and Wales*. Home Office Research Study No. 119, 1990.

H. Genn, 'Multiple Victimization' in M. Maguire and J. Pointing eds., *Victims of Crime: A New Deal?*. Milton Keynes: Open University Press, 1988.

F. M. Heidensohn, *Crime and Society*. London: Macmillan, 1989.

Home Office, *Criminal and Custodial Careers of those born in 1953, 1958 and 1963*. Home Office Statistical Bulletin 32/89. London: Home Office, 1989.

Home Office, *Criminal Statistics, England and Wales 1991*. London: HMSO, (annual).

Home Office, *Digest 2: Information on the Criminal Justice System in England and Wales*. London: Home Office Research and Statistics Department, 1993.

T. Jones, B. Maclean and J. Young, *The Islington Crime Survey: Crime, Victimization and Policing in Inner City London*. Aldershot: Gower, 1986.

P. Mayhew, N. A. Maung and C. Mirrless-Black, *The 1992 British Crime Survey*. Home Office Research and Planning Unit, London: HMSO, 1993.

E. Stanko, 'Hidden violence against women' in M. Maguire and J. Pointing eds., *Victims of Crime: A New Deal?*. Milton Keynes: Open University Press, 1988.

J. J. M. van Dijk, P. Mayhrew and M. Killias, *Experiences of Crime Across the World: Key Findings of the 1989 International Crime Survey*, 1990.

R. Walmsley, L. Howard and S. White, *The National Prison Survey 1991: Main Findings*. Home Office Research Study No. 128, London: HMSO, 1992.

J. Young, 'Risk of crime and fear of crime: a realist critique of survey-based assumptions', in M. Maguire and J. Pointing eds., *Victims of Crime: A New Deal?*. Milton Keynes: Open University Press, (1988).

REFERENCES

ADLER, F. (1975) *Sisters in Crime*. New York: McGraw-Hill.

AMIR, M. (1971), *Patterns in Forcible Rape*. Chicago: University of Chicago Press.

BAKER, A., and DUNCAN, S. (1985), 'Child Sexual Abuse: A Study of Prevalence in Great Britain', *Child Abuse and Neglect*, 9: 457–67.

BANTON, M. (1985), *Investigating Robbery*. Aldershot: Gower.

BECKER, G. (1974), 'Crime and Punishment: An Economic Approach', in *Essays in the Economics of Crime and Punishment*. New York: National Bureau of Economic Research.

BECKER, H. S. (1963), *Outsiders: Studies in the Sociology of Deviance*. London: Macmillan.

BELSON, W. A. (1968), 'The Extent of Stealing by London Boys and Some of its Origins', *The Advancement of Science*, 25: 171–84.

BENNETT, T, and WRIGHT, R. (1984), *Burglars on Burglary*. Aldershot: Gower.

BIDERMANN, A. D., and REISS, A. J. (1967), 'On Explaining the "Dark Figure" of Crime', *Annals of the American Academy of Politics and Social Science*, November.

BLACK, D. J. (1970), 'The Production of Crime Rates', *American Sociological Review*, 35: 4, 733–48.

BLAIR, I. (1985), *Investigating Rape: A New Approach for Police*. London: Croom Helm.

BOTTOMLEY, A. K. (1979), *Criminology in Focus*. London: Martin Robertson.

BOTTOMLEY, A. K., and COLEMAN, C. A. (1981), *Understanding Crime Rates*. Farnborough: Saxon House.

BOTTOMLEY, A. K., and PEASE, K. (1986), *Crime and Punishment: Interpreting the Data*. Milton Keynes: Open University Press.

BOWLBY, J. (1953), *Child Care and the Growth of Love*. Harmondsworth: Penguin.

BOX, S. (1983), *Power, Crime and Mystification*. London: Tavistock.

——(1987), *Recession, Crime and Punishment*. London: Macmillan Education.

BRAITHWAITE, J. (1979), *Inequality, Crime and Public Policy*. London: Routledge and Kegan Paul.

BRANTINGHAM, P. J., and BRANTINGHAM, P. L. (1975), 'The Spatial Patterning of Burglary', *Howard Journal*, 14: 11–23.

BRODY, S. (1976), *The Effectiveness of Sentencing*, Home Office Research Study no. 35. London: HMSO.

BURT, C. (1944), *The Young Delinquent*. London: University of London Press.

CAMPBELL, A. (1984), *The Girls in the Gang*. Oxford: Blackwell.

CARSON, W. G. (1982), *The Other Price of Britain's Oil*. Oxford: Martin Robertson.

CHAMBLISS, W. J. (1988), *Exploring Criminology*. New York: Macmillan.

CHRISTIE, N. (1977), 'Conflicts as Property', *British Journal of Criminology*, 17: 1, 1–15.

CHRISTIE, N., ANDENAES, J., and SKIRBEKK, S. (1965), 'A Study of Self-Reported Crime' in K. O. Christiansen, ed., *Scandinavian Studies in Criminology*. London: Tavistock.

CICOUREL, A. V. (1968), *The Social Organization of Juvenile Justice*. New York: Wiley.

CLARKE, R. V. G. (1980), 'Situational Crime Prevention: Theory and Practice', *British Journal of Criminology*, 20: 136–47.

CLARKE, R. V. G., and HOUGH, M. (1984), *Crime and Police Effectiveness*, Home Office Research Study no. 79. London: HMSO.

CLARKE, R. V. G., and MAYHEW, P., eds. (1980), *Designing Out Crime*. London: HMSO.

Clinard, M. (1978), *Cities with Little Crime*. Cambridge: Cambridge University Press.

Cohen, L. E., and Felson, M. (1979), 'Social Change and Crime Rate Trends: A Routine Activity Approach' *American Sociological Review*, 44: 588–608.

Cohen, S. (1974), 'Criminology and the Sociology of Deviance in Britain', in P. Rock and M. McIntosh, eds., *Deviance and Social Control*. London: Tavistock.

Counts, D. A., Brown, J. K., and Campbell, J. C. (1992), *Sanctions and Sanctuary: Cultural Perspectives in the Beating of Wives*. Oxford: Westview Press.

Corbett, C., and Maguire, M. (1988), 'The Value and Limitations of Victim Support Schemes', in M. Maguire and J Pointing, eds., *Victims of Crime: A New Deal?* Milton Keynes: Open University Press.

Cornish, D. B., and Clarke, R. V. G. (1986), 'Situational Prevention, Displacement of Crime and Rational Choice Theory', in K. Heal and G. Laycock, eds., *Situational Crime Prevention: From Theory into Practice*. London: HMSO.

Croall, H. (1992), *White Collar Crime*. Milton Keynes: Open University Press.

Crawford, A, Jones, T, Woodhouse, T., and Young, J. (1990), *Second Islington Crime Survey*. London: Middlesex Polytechnic.

Cromwell, P. F., Olson, A., and Avary, D. W. (1991), *Breaking and Entering: An Ethnographic Analysis of Burglary*. Newbury Park: Sage.

Ditton, J. (1977), *Part-time Crime*. London: Macmillan.

Dobash, R. E., and Dobash, R. P. (1979), *Violence against Wives*. London: Tavistock.

—— (1992), *Women, Violence and Social Change*. London: Routledge.

Elmhorn, K. (1965), 'Study in Self-Reported Delinquency among School Children in Stockholm', in K. O. Christiansen, ed., *Scandinavian Studies in Criminology*. London, Tavistock.

Ennis, P. (1967), *Criminal Victimization in the United States, President's Commission on Law Enforcement and Administration of Justice, Field Surveys III*. Washington, DC: US Government Printing Office.

Erikson, K. T. (1964), 'Notes on the Sociology of Deviance', in H. S. Becker, ed., *The Other Side: Perspectives on Deviance*. New York: Free Press.

Evans, D. J., and Herbert, D. T. (1989), *The Geography of Crime*. London: Routledge.

Farrington, D. P. (1973), 'Self-Reports of Deviant Behaviour: Predictive and Stable?', *Journal of Criminal Law and Criminology*, 64: 99–110.

—— (1989), 'Self-Reported and Official Offending from Adolescence to Adulthood', in M. W. Klein, ed., *Cross-National Research in Self-Reported Crime and Delinquency*. Dordrecht: Kluwer.

Farrington, D. P., and Burrows, J. N. (1993), 'Did Shoplifting Really Increase?' *British Journal of Criminology*, 33: 57–69.

Farrington, D. P., and Dowds, E. A. (1985), 'Disentangling Criminal Behaviour and Police Reaction' in D. P. Farrington and J. Gunn, eds., *Reaction to Crime: The Public, the Police, Courts and Prisons*, Chichester: Wiley.

Ferri, E. (1913), *The Positive School of Criminology*. Chicago: C.H. Kerr.

FIELD, S. (1990), *Trends in Crime and their Interpretation: A Study of Recorded Crime in Post War England and Wales*, Home Office Research Study no. 119. London: HMSO.

GAROFALO, R. (1914), *Criminology*. Boston: Little, Brown.

GENN, H. (1988), 'Multiple Victimization', in M. Maguire and J. Pointing, eds., *Victims of Crime: A New Deal?* Milton Keynes: Open University Press.

GLUECK, S. and GLUECK, E. (1950), *Unravelling Juvenile Delinquency*. New York: Commonwealth Fund.

GOVERNMENT STATISTICAL SERVICE. (1992), *Criminal Justice: Key Statistics in England and Wales 1991*. London: HMSO.

HALL, R. (1985), *Ask Any Woman: A London Enquiry into Rape and Sexual Assault*. Bristol: Falling Wall Press.

HALL, S., CRITCHER, JEFFERSON, T., CLARKE, J., and ROBERTS, B. (1978), *Policing the Crisis*. London: Macmillan.

HANMER, J., and SAUNDERS, S. (1984), *Well-Founded Fear*. London: Hutchinson.

HEAL, K., and LAYCOCK, G., eds. (1986), *Situational Crime Prevention: From Theory into Practice*. London: HMSO.

HEIDENSOHN, F. M. (1985), *Women and Crime*. London: Macmillan.

—— (1989), *Crime and Society*. London: Macmillan.

HIRSCHI, T. (1969), *Causes of Delinquency*. Berkeley: University of California Press.

HOBBS, R. (1988), *Doing the Business: Entrepreneurship, the Working Class and Detectives in the East End of London*. Oxford: Oxford University Press.

HOLDAWAY, S., ed. (1979), *The British Police*. London: Edward Arnold.

HOME OFFICE. (1971), *Instructions for the Preparation of Statistics Relating to Crime*. London: HMSO.

—— (1989), *Criminal and Custodial Careers of those Born in 1953, 1958 and 1963*, Home Office Statistical Bulletin, 32/89. London: Home Office.

—— (1991), *A Digest of Information on the Criminal Justice System.*_London: Home Office Research and Statistics Department.

—— (1992*a*), *Criminal Justice: Key Statistics in England and Wales 1990*. London: Government Statistical Service.

—— (1992*b*), *Gender in the Criminal Justice System*. London: Home Office.

—— (1992*c*), *Criminal Statistics, England and Wales 1991*, Cmnd 2134 London: HMSO.

—— (1993*a*), *Notifiable Offences, England and Wales, 1992, Home Office Statistical Bulletin*, 9/93. London: Government Statistical Service.

—— (1993*b*), *Digest 2: Information on the Criminal Justice System in England and Wales*. London: Home Office Research and Statistics Department.

—— (1993*c*), *Criminal Justice Statistics 1882–1892*, Home Office Statistical Findings, 1/93. London: Home Office Research and Statistics Department.

HOOD, R. (1992), *Race and Sentencing: A Study in the Crown Court*. Oxford: Clarendon Press.

HOOD, R., and SPARKS, R. (1970), *Key Issues in Criminology*. London: Weidenfeld and Nicolson.

HOUGH, J. M., and MAYHEW, P. (1983), *The British Crime Survey*, Home Office Research Study no. 76. London: HMSO.

HOUGH, J. M., and MAYHEW, P. (1985), *Taking Account of Crime: Key Findings from the Second British Crime Survey*, Home Office Research Study no. 85. London: HMSO.

HUDSON, B. (1987), *Justice through Punishment*. London: Macmillan Education.

HUIZINGA, D., and ELLIOTT, D. S. (1986), 'Reassessing the Reliability and Validity of Self-Report Measures', *Journal of Quantitative Criminology*, 2: 293–327.

JONES, T., LEA, J., and YOUNG, J. (1987), *Saving the Inner City: the First Report of the Broadwater Farm Survey*. London: Middlesex Polytechnic.

JONES, T., MACLEAN, B., and YOUNG, J. (1986), *The Islington Crime Survey: Crime, Victimization and Policing in Inner City London*. Aldershot: Gower.

KINSEY, R. (1984), *Merseyside Crime Survey: First Report*. Liverpool: Merseyside Metropolitan Council.

KINSEY, R, LEA, J., and YOUNG, J. (1986), *Losing the Fight Against Crime*. Oxford, Blackwell.

KITSUSE, J. I. (1964), 'Societal Reactions to Deviant Behaviour: Problems of Theory and Method', in H. S. Becker, ed., *The Other Side: Perspectives on Deviance*. New York: Free Press.

KITSUSE, J. I., and CICOUREL, A. V. (1963), 'A Note on the Uses of Official Statistics', *Social Problems*, 11: 131–9.

LESIEUR, H. R., and LEHMAN, P. M. (1975), 'Remeasuring Delinquency: A Replication and Critique', *British Journal of Criminology*, 15: 69–80.

LEVI, M. (1981), *The Phantom Capitalists: The Organization and Control of Long-Firm Fraud*. London: Heinemann.

—— (1993), *The Investigation, Prosecution and Trial of Serious Fraud*, Research Study no. 14. London: Royal Commission on Criminal Justice.

LEVI, M., and MAGUIRE, M. (1992), 'Crime and Cross-Border Policing in Europe', in J. Bailey, ed., *Social Euorpe*. London: Longman.

LEVI, M., and PITHOUSE, A. (1992), 'The Victims of Fraud', in D. Downes, ed., *Unravelling Criminal Justice*. Basingstoke: Macmillan.

LIGHT, R. (1993), *Car Theft: The Offender's Perspective*, Home Office Research Study no. 130. London: HMSO.

LURIGIO, A., SKOGAN, W. G., and DAVIS, R. C. (1990), *Victims of Crime: Problems, Policies and Programs*. New York: Sage.

MCCABE, S., and SUTCLIFFE, F. (1978), *Defining Crime: A Study of Police Decisions*. Oxford: Blackwell.

MCLINTOCK, F., and AVISON, N. H. (1968), *Crime in England and Wales*. London: Heinemann.

MAGUIRE, M. (1991), 'The Needs and Rights of Victims of Crime', in M. Tonry, ed., *Crime and Justice: A Review of Research*, vol. 14. Chicago: University of Chicago Press.

MAGUIRE, M., in collaboration with BENNETT, T. (1982), *Burglary in a Dwelling: The Offence, the Offender and the Victim*. London: Heinemann Educational.

MAGUIRE, M., and CORBETT, C. (1987), *The Effects of Crime and the Work of Victim Support Schemes*. Aldershot: Gower.

MANNING, P. (1977), *Police Work*. Cambridge, Mass.: MIT Press.

MARS, G. (1982), *Cheats at Work*. London: Allen and Unwin.

MARTIN, J. P. (1962), *Offenders as Employees*. London: Macmillan.

MATTHEWS, R., and YOUNG, J., eds. (1986), *Confronting Crime*. London: Sage.

MAXFIELD, M. G. (1984), *Fear of Crime in England and Wales*, Home Office Research Study no. 78. London: HMSO.

—— (1988), *Explaining Fear of Crime: Evidence from the 1984 British Crime Survey*, Home Office Research and Planning Unit Paper no. 43. London: HMSO.

MAYHEW, P., CLARKE, R. V. G., STURMAN, A., and HOUGH, J. M. (1976), *Crime as Opportunity*, Home Office Research Study no. 34, London: HMSO.

MAYHEW, P., ELLIOTT, D., and DOWDS, L. (1989), *The 1988 British Crime Survey*. Home Office Research Study no. 111. London: HMSO.

MAYHEW, P., and HOUGH, J. M. (1988), 'The British Crime Survey: Origins and Impact', in M Maguire and J. Pointing, eds., *Victims of Crime: A New Deal?* Milton Keynes: Open University Press.

MAYHEW, P., and MAUNG, N. A. (1992), *Surveying Crime: Findings from the 1992 British Crime Survey*, Home Office Research and Statistics Department, Research Findings no 2. London: HMSO.

MOFFITT, T. E. (1990), 'The Neurophysiology of Juvenile Delinquency: A Review', in M Tonry and N Morris, eds., *Crime and Justice*, vol 12. Chicago: University of Chicago Press.

MORGAN, J. (1988), 'Children as Victims', in M. Maguire and J. Pointing, eds., *Victims of Crime: A New Deal?* Milton Keynes: Open University Press.

MORGAN J., and ZEDNER, L. (1992), *Child Victims: Crime, Impact and Criminal Justice*. Oxford: Oxford University Press.

MORRIS, T. (1989), *Crime and Criminal Justice since 1945*. Oxford: Blackwell.

MURPHY, P., WILLIAMS, J., and DUNNING, E. (1990), *Football on Trial: Spectator Violence and Developments in the Football World*. London: Routledge.

NETTLER, G. (1978), *Explaining Crime*. New York: McGraw-Hill.

NORMANDEAU, A. (1969), 'Trends in Robbery as Reflected by Different Indexes', in T. Sellin and M. E. Wolfgang, eds., *Delinquency: Selected Studies*. New York: Wiley.

PAINTER, K. (1991), *Wife Rape, Marriage and the Law: Survey Report*. Manchester: University of Manchester Faculty of Economic and Social Science.

PARKER, H. (1974), *View from the Boys: A Sociology of Downtown Adolescents*. Newton Abbot: David and Charles.

PATRICK, J. (1973), *A Glasgow Gang Observed*. London: Eyre Methuen.

PEARSON, G. (1987), *The New Heroin Users*. Oxford: Blackwell.

RADFORD, J. (1987), 'Policing Male Violence', in J. Hanmer and M. Maynard, eds., *Women, Violence and Social Control*. London: Macmillan.

REPPETTO, T. (1974), *Residential Crime*. Cambridge Mass.: Ballinger.

ROCK, P. (1973), *A Sociology of Deviance*. London: Hutchinson.

—— (1988), 'The History of British Criminology', special issue of the *British Journal of Criminology*, 28/2.

ROZENBERG, J. (1992), 'Miscarriages of Justice', in E. Stockdale and S. Casale, eds., *Criminal Justice under Stress*. London: Blackstone Press.

SAVILLE, E., and RUMNEY, D. (1992), *A History of the ISTD*. London: Institute for the Study and Treatment of Delinquency.

SELKE, W., and PEPINSKY, H. (1984), 'The Politics of Police Reporting in Indianapolis 1948–78', in W. J. Chambliss, ed., *Criminal Law in Action*. New York: Wiley.

SELLIN, T. (1938), *Culture, Conflict and Crime*. New York: Social Science Research Council.

SELLIN, T., and WOLFGANG, M. E. (1964), *The Measurement of Delinquency*. New York: Wiley.

SHAW, C. (1930), *The Jack Roller: A Delinquent Boy's Own Story* Chicago: University of Chicago Press.

SHORT, J. F., and NYE, F. I. (1958), 'Extent of Unrecorded Juvenile Delinquency', *Journal of Criminal Law, Criminology and Police Science*, 49: 296–302.

SKOLNICK, J. H. (1966), *Justice Without Trial: Law Enforcement in Democratic Society*. New York: John Wiley.

SMITH, S. (1986), *Crime, Space and Society*. Cambridge: Cambridge University Press.

SPARKS, R., GENN, H., and DODD, D. (1977), *Surveying Victims*. Chichester: Wiley.

STANKO, E. (1988), 'Hidden Violence against Women', in M. Maguire and J. Pointing, eds., *Victims of Crime: A New Deal?* Milton Keynes: Open University Press.

TAYLOR, I., WALTON, P., and YOUNG, J. (1973), *The New Criminology*. London: Routledge and Kegan Paul.

THRASHER, F. M. (1927), *The Gang*. Chicago: Phoenix Press.

TONRY, M. (forthcoming), 'Racial Disproportion in US Prisons', in R. King and M. Maguire, eds., *Prisons in Context*. Oxford: Oxford University Press.

VAN DIJK, J. J. M., and MAYHEW, P. (1992), *Criminal Victimization in the Internationalized World: Key Findings of the 1989 and 1992 International Crime Surveys*. The Hague, Netherlands: Directorate for Crime Prevention, Ministry of Justice.

VAN DIJK, J. J. M., Mayhew, P., and Killias, M. (1990), *Experiences of Crime Across the World: Key Findings of the 1989 International Crime Survey*. Boston: Kluwer.

VAN DUYNE, P. C. (1993), 'Organized Crime and Business Crime-Enterprises in the Netherlands' *Crime, Law and Social Change*, 19: 103–42.

VON HENTIG, H. (1948), *The Criminal and his Victim*. New Haven: Yale University Press.

VON HIRSCH, A. (1986), *Past or Future Crimes*. Manchester: Manchester University Press.

WALKER, N. D. (1971), *Crimes, Courts and Figures: An Introduction to Criminal Statistics*. Harmondsworth: Penguin.

WALKLATE, S. (1989), *Victimology: The Victim and the Criminal Justice System*. London: Unwin Hyman.

WALLER, I., and OKIHIRO, N. (1978), *Burglary: The Victim and the Public*. Toronto: University of Toronto Press.

WALMSLEY, R., HOWARD, L., and WHITE, S. (1992), *The National Prison Survey 1991: Main Findings*, Home Office Research Study no. 128. London: HMSO.

WEST, D. J., and FARRINGTON, D. P. (1969), *Present Conduct and Future Delinquency*. London: Heinemann.

WHEELER, S. (1967), 'Criminal Statistics: A Reformulation of the Problem', *Journal of Criminal Law, Criminology and Police Science*, 58: 317–24.

WHYTE, W. F. (1955), *Street Corner Society*, 2nd edn. Chicago: University of Chicago Press.

WILES, P. N. P. (1971), 'Criminal Statistics and Sociological Explanations of Crime', in W. G. Carson and P. N. P. Wiles, ed., *The Sociology of Crime and Delinquency in Britain*. London: Martin Robertson.

WILSON, J. Q., and HERRNSTEIN, R. J. (1985), *Crime and Human Nature*. New York: Simon and Schuster.

WINCHESTER, S., and JACKSON, H. (1982), *Residential Burglary*, Home Office Research Study no. 74. London: HMSO.

WOFFINDEN, R. (1987), *Miscarriages of Justice*. London: Hodder and Stoughton.

WOLFGANG, M. (1959), *Patterns in Criminal Homicide*. Philadelphia: University of Pennsylvania Press.

YOUNG, J. (1970), *The Drugtakers*. London: McGibbon and Kee.

—— (1986), 'The Failure of Radical Criminology: The Need for Realism', in R. Matthews and J. Young, eds., *Confronting Crime*. London: Sage.

—— (1988*a*), 'Risk of Crime and Fear of Crime: A Realist Critique of Survey-Based Assumptions', in M. Maguire and J. Pointing, eds., *Victims of Crime: A New Deal?* Milton Keynes: Open University Press.

—— (1988*b*), 'Radical Criminology in Britain: The Emergence of a Competing Paradigm', *British Journal of Criminology*, 28/2: 289–313.

YOUNG, M. (1991), *An Inside Job*, Oxford: Clarendon Press.

PART 2

Crime and Causation

7

Violent Crime

MICHAEL LEVI

INTRODUCTION

This chapter is concerned principally with how much violent crime of various kinds, including sexual violence, there is (focusing mainly on England and Wales), the extent to which such crimes have been rising, and how violent crimes can best be explained. The implications of these data for the control of violence will then be reviewed. The first decision is what sorts of behaviours should be included within the category 'violent crime'. Do we mean only acts prosecutable as homicide, grievous bodily harm, wounding, or actual bodily harm? Are we going to extend our category to cover crimes such as common assault or assault against the police which are triable only at magistrates' courts and are not normally included in Home Office classifications of serious crime? What about deaths and injuries on the roads? And deaths and injuries following breaches of health and safety regulations in factories and mines, or on offshore oil rigs and car ferries? Are we going to include sexual violence, which is classified as 'sexual' rather than 'violent' crime in the criminal statistics? And what about acts such as racial or sexual harassment that induce the *fear* of violence without necessarily hitting someone? What about genocide or wars? Or those sado-masochistic sexual acts between adults which result in serious injuries that the 'victims' agreed beforehand to experience? Or the activities of the 'Nashville Footstomper', a man convicted of assault in 1977 for stamping on the toes of twenty-four women? Did he somewhow misinterpret the drive to stamp out violent crime?

How we construe 'violent crime' makes a big difference to the task of explanation. When the popular media write, as they regularly do, about the 'rising tide of violence', they generally refer to violence in public places and to violence against the police, and sometimes to superficially non-violent crimes such as domestic burglary which awaken apprehensions of *potential* violence. However, they relatively seldom refer to violence in the home, to vehicular assaults by those 'motormuggers' who are driving their *own* vehicles (as contrasted with the frequently publicized 'tragic murders' by so-called 'joyriders'), to 'accidents' at work, or—

except in the context of a court case or demonstration—to violence *by* the police.[1] In so far as they ever make connections between these forms of injury at all, lawyers and police officers often attempt to distinguish between 'violent crime', on the one hand, and 'bad driving' and health and safety at work, on the other, on the grounds of intentionality differences and supposed public sentiment: the former are described as *mala in se* (bad in themselves); the latter, particularly the business crimes, as *mala prohibita* (or 'regulatory offences' which are criminalized only for pragmatic reasons). However, as Lacey *et al.* (1990) argue, this distinction assumes a level of *un*intentionality (or what I might term 'accidentality') that is inappropriate, especially in many health and safety cases. Moreover, one might further argue, it assumes a level of intentionality in 'ordinary' violent crime that may not be there: for example, some quarrels escalate into fights in a way that was not planned by any of the parties. Culture shapes the conditions under which we attribute responsibility and blame to individuals whose acts result in harmful consequences, even though there may be high agreement across different cultures and over time. For example, the criminal law defines provocation in homicide as requiring a *sudden and temporary* loss of self-control by the killer, but many argue that the experience by some women who kill of *long-term* abuse ought to be construed as excusable provocation.[2]

For reasons of space, and despite the high rate of robbery in some inner city areas,[3] I intend to exclude instrumental violence where financial gain is the motive, even though many robbers also obtain a high from the violence or threats they employ (Katz 1988).[4] I intend also to devote little attention to collective violence, though the presence of significant others

[1] This is not just a reflection of the pro-police and pro-business bias of the media. There are sometimes sound pragmatic reasons in defamation law for this reluctance to label such acts as 'crimes', where individuals are indentifiable as plausible targets of allegations of misconduct that are not being made as part of a report of criminal proceedings. This emphasizes the significance of court and public disciplinary proceedings as means by which 'elite violence' can be reported. Huge sums are awarded to the respectable as compensation for libel.

[2] *Thornton* [1982] Crim LR 54 and *Ahluwalia* [1983] Crim LR 63, where the courts have ruled that delayed reaction to abuse makes the defence of provocation less plausible but not unarguable. The 'overcontrolled' males in Megargee's (1983) typology likewise are slow-burning 'explosives', so this phenomenon is not gender-specific though it may account for a larger proportion of killings by women. Historically the law, judges, and jurors have been more sympathetic to men who claim that sexual jealousy made them lose control than to women who kill in 'lukewarm blood': but what level of irritation is acceptable to lead us to deem killings or woundings to be excusably provoked? Should the test of provocation be 'objectively' behavioural or in the mind of the killer? If the latter, particularly, how do we test the claim?

[3] Including robberies of shopkeepers, reported by Hibberd (1993) as affecting one in six Midlands and one in four London small shops in one year.

[4] Conversely, however, I will be including 'violence in the workplace', even though the savings in failing to ensure safe working conditions could be said to constitute a financial motive.

can act as a key trigger to the individual propensity to behave aggressively.[5] It is hard to separate the limits of what we mean by 'violent *crime*' from notions of *justifiability* and *excusability*. (Justifiable means we were right to do what we did; excusable means what we did was wrong but was not really blameworthy.) Good examples include violence against women and assaults involving the police. In discussions with some colleagues about our research on assaults *against* the police (Christopher *et al.* 1989), I was informed confidently that surely these were really assaults *by* the police (or if not, that we *ought* to be studying violence by the police). Sparks (1980) found that the reason why most prison inmates rated assaults on the police as non-serious was that they took it for granted that such assaults were provoked; and feminist authors likewise point out the interconnectedness of perceptions of victim culpability with both the causes of and social reactions to violence against women.

In short, our conception of both the content and the causes of 'the violent crime problem' is socially constructed. Hall *et al.* (1978) and subsequent *marxisant* writers argue that intensified stories about mugging during the 1970s formed part of a combined police and media attempt to associate 'the crime problem' with young blacks, with the objective of justifying police repression in the interests of capitalist control; others might eschew the broad ideological rationale as over-theorized, but might accept that there were conscious and/or unconscious alliances between police (to justify inner city police operations) and crime reporters (to increase newspaper sales and produce popular, cheap 'voyeuristic' programmes such as *Crimewatch UK* and *True Crimes* which appeal to, and exacerbate, the underlying fears of the public). Moreover, the struggle for control of the working-class (and 'ethnic') city, if necessary by violent means (Holdaway 1983), is as important to police morale and culture as it is to organized criminals who seek immunity from police intervention.

Cohen (1981) deployed the phrase 'moral panic' to point up the way in which campaigning groups amplified some social problems, using the media to whip up anxieties.[6] In rough historical order of their original appearance, there have been 'moral panics' about child physical abuse, mugging, battered women, rape, racial violence, child (including satanic) sex abuse, rural violence, assaults against the police, and 'joyriding', all of which have resurfaced as 'new and/or growing problems' in various media

[5] The mere fact that some people behave violently while others do not is not itself evidence of differential 'inner propensities' to violence: it can simply reflect different situational pressures, some of which—policing, housing, and family relationships, for example—may be consistent over time. See Waddington (1992) for an overview of collective violence.

[6] A neglected feature of Cohen's work is that the initial fear of crime had a genuine basis in experience: indeed, there is a serious conceptual problem in whether we can ever discredit fears as 'irrational' and—if we can so discredit some fears—in how we can do so consistently. See also Young (1988).

more frequently than the 25-year cycle of concern about the supposedly 'unprecedented' problem of 'rebellious youth' noted by Pearson (1983). It should be apparent from the above list that many of these mobilizations of 'public concern' have been generated by liberal and feminist groups as well as by those on the political right. They produce partial shifts in the conceptualization of 'the violent crime problem' among policy-makers responding to what they see as public sentiments, and they sometimes impact on police resource allocation and strategies.[7]

However, not all issues are given equal prominence in the popular media, and it is possible that neither they nor government surveys of the 'dark figure' of patterns of victimization capture accurately the meaning of violent crime to the individuals or 'community' experiencing it. Thus wife battery and racial harassment may be particularly frightening because of their unrelenting or unpredictable nature, creating what Stanko (1990) terms 'climates of unsafety'.[8] Perceived threats and verbal abuse may be no less intimidating than actual physical harm; Pearson *et al.* (1989) assert that ethnic groups are and feel themselves to be particularly vulnerable, and although there is scope for argument about whether the term 'racial' or 'racist' is properly applied to minority attacks on majority group members, older white people sometimes *do* see themselves as 'victims of racial attacks' and as a 'community under threat'. Those same perceptions may trigger racial violence by members of the supposedly 'threatened community'. I stress here the difficulty of being consistent in discrediting some perceptions while granting others credibility. It is tempting, but ethically perilous, to privilege some definitions of the situation over others, whatever the theoretical justifications for so doing.

MEASURING VIOLENCE: SOME PRELIMINARY COMMENTS

It is sometimes helpful to start with the data and spread outwards into explanations. Let us start with the criminal statistics, and see what light they can throw on these phenomena, and then move to consider the

[7] Indeed, some of them appear to be directed at obtaining greater police resources overall: police, like other pressure groups, have to mobilize the concerns of politicians to achieve organizational objectives. For example, the national publicity given to the very serious wounding of a woman police constable in Merseyside in December 1992 was used to justify the introduction in relatively rural Dorset of longer batons, which the Home Secretary had earlier resisted despite police desire for the greater protection they supposedly afford to them.

[8] The decline in the amount of affordable council housing means that there are fewer places for victims—or, in current terminology, 'survivors', though not all do survive—to relocate. The effects depend partly on the context of expectations and past experiences: as a child, I vividly recall the traumatic effect on my father, a concentration camp survivor, of a swastika painted outside our front door, even though no overt threats, still less actual violence, occurred.

result of 'victimization surveys' in which people are asked about their experiences of crime irrespective of whether or not these have been reported to the police. It should not be forgotten that crime statistics are a major battleground on which media, official, and local concern can be mobilized. For example, the US National Study of the Incidence and Severity of Child Abuse and Neglect initially used an operational definition of 'child maltreatment' that did not specify how much harm was required before a case counted as maltreatment, and 30 per cent of all children were classed as victims. When a minimum degree of demonstrable harm was specified, the proportion dropped to 1 per cent (Burgdorf and Eldred 1978)! If the latter percentage had been reported initially, would child abuse have become such a major social issue?

'Notifiable' offences of wounding, robbery, and sexual offences comprised 6 per cent of all crime (recorded and unrecorded) measured by the 1988 British Crime Survey (Mayhew *et al.* 1989); another 11 per cent were less serious 'common assaults'. In 15 per cent of all the above assaults, the victims needed some medical attention; in 1 per cent of cases, victims needed to go to hospital. Homicide statistics are generally considered to be among the most reliable of crime figures. Yet, as my discussion earlier suggests, there are problems over what acts constitute homicide, for 'being a victim of violence' carries with it some claim to retribution or deterrence, or at least compensation and social sympathy, which campaigning groups covet. Omitted from the Home Office classification of homicides are not only the 313 offenders convicted in 1990 of causing death by reckless driving, but also those whose reckless driving may have caused deaths on the roads but who were *not* so charged—over 5,000 people a year die on the roads—and innumerable cases of reckless driving which *by coincidence* did not result in death or even injury.[9]

Despite the fact that some 346 deaths at work occurred in 1990,[10] the only such deaths included in the criminal statistics for homicide are those where police or prison officers are victims: one per annum in the most recent years for which figures are available, 1989 and 1990. Indeed, as Bergman (1991) observes, in the previous nine years only one workplace fatality out of the 4,217 which occurred resulted in a director or manager facing charges of manslaughter; only one out of 1,016 workplace deaths in 1988–90 resulted in a criminal investigation by the police (as contrasted with the Health and Safety Executive; the police investigate only if there is a coroner's verdict of 'unlawful killing' at an inquest); and despite the fact that the *de facto* criterion of prosecution is at least serious

[9] Should these be categorized as 'reckless attempts'?

[10] The figure for 1991/2 is expected to reach some 320 when final figures are available (Health and Safety Commission 1992).

negligence, only 35 per cent of deaths in the workplace led to a company being prosecuted, the average fine being £1,940. Just as there are very few drunken drivers who want to hurt other road users, almost no business-people positively want their workers to be injured; but since many deaths at work involve regulatory breaches which could have been prosecuted, one may legitimately treat them at least as avoidable harmful acts, and plausibly as 'violent crimes' whose consequences follow from the insufficient value placed on safety in relation to cost (though this can become tautological). Safety guards may be taken off machinery because the latter shuts down 'too readily' in response to 'minor triggers' of extraneous substances, one of which may be a trapped hand; training about the hazards of underground electric cables may not be given because managers are 'too busy' or it is 'too costly'; safety measures are resisted by workers *partly* because employers choose to pay them at piece-work rates, and taking precautions slows down their work rate, reducing their income. The rise in the use of child labour due to their poverty and the drive for profit maximization (or business survival) may lead to less skilful, untrained children carrying out dangerous mechanical tasks like cutting vegetables with sharp knives. In short, though it smacks of moral entrepreneurialism, there is a good arguable case for treating many deaths in the workplace as a special kind of 'violent crime'.[11]

Even setting aside the above areas that are not normally considered as part of 'the violent crime problem', are all homicides recorded? There are conflicts over whether some 'deaths in police custody' should not in fact be recorded as homicides committed by the police. Moreover, just speculate on how many of Dennis Nilsen's homosexual drifter victims would have been classified as homicide victims if he had not—somewhat fortuitously—been caught because their decomposing bodies blocked up the drains at his home (Masters 1986)? There are thousands of runaways, some of whom may well have been murdered but are just 'missing persons' in police records. Elderly people with known heart conditions may be given death certificates specifying 'death by natural causes' when in fact they have been unlawfully killed (or 'euthanased') by members of their families, whether for their money or out of humanitarianism.

The position is even more complex if we look at homicide rates historically or compare First and Third World countries. For the official homicide rates have been affected by the advance of medical science and routine autopsies (for ascertaining causes of death), and by improved medical skills and speed of transport (for turning potential deaths into operable injuries). Despite former President Reagan's famous comment that 'guns don't kill people; people kill people', the sort of weapon avail-

[11] For a legal critique of current corporate criminal liability, see Wells (1993).

able in the room where the conflict occurs (or a malfunctioning ambulance or police computer dispatch system) can turn a minor wounding into a homicide; and the accidental striking of a head against a sharp or hard object can turn the slapping of a baby into a 'dead battered child'. Thus many features other than the intent of the 'offender' can affect the rate of serious injury. This also raises questions about how meaningful is the distinction between 'serious violence' and the rest, for the physical consequences of risky behaviour—whether in the operation of manufacturing or commercial transport, in personal motoring, or in fighting—vary from nothing to death.

THE RISK OF VIOLENCE

According to the 1988 British Crime Survey, the overall risk per 10,000 population of becoming a victim of violence in 1987 was 372 for common assault, 141 for wounding, 44 for robbery, and 79 for 'theft from the person' such as bag-snatching (Mayhew *et al.* 1989; for a discussion of the strengths and weaknesses of the survey method through which such results are produced, see Maguire in this volume Chapter 6). Some of the above are multiple victims, whether of the same or different forms of violent crime, but it is unlikely that fewer than one in thirty people were assaulted *in that year alone*; the rates in some areas are very much higher (see also Young 1988). At an individual or group level, the chance of violence occurring can be related to the lifestyle adopted by the victim, whether voluntarily (e.g. going out to a party) or partly voluntarily but constrained by cultural or economic pressures (e.g. returning from a party on foot or by public transport because one cannot afford a car or cab).[12] 'Accidents' in the workplace also relate to the kind of work being done: the Health and Safety Commission (1992) attributes much of the reduction in fatal and non-fatal injury rates at work in recent years to the decline of coal-mining and other heavy industries.

Though there may be dispute about the causes of death, and about the role of socio-economic factors in both mortality and morbidity rates which lie concealed behind medical pronouncements of 'cause of death', mortality statistics are among the most reliable statistics we have. Table 7.1 reviews the annual risk of death from various causes per million of the population at risk.[13] The presented data in this table may surprise

[12] Analogous to the latter are those who 'choose' to work in dangerous jobs rather than draw income support or do very much worse-paid jobs. For discussion of the 'lifestyle' approach, see Garofalo (1987) and Chapter 14 in this volume by Ken Pease.

[13] However, there are problems about determining the number of people at risk from road accidents and terrorism, in particular, and time at risk is not allowed for as a variable here. The risks are very unevenly distributed.

Table 7.1. The annual risk of death per million population in England and Wales, 1989

Cause of death/occupation	No. of deaths per million
Offshore oil and gas industries	1,250
Deep-sea fishing	840
Coal mining	145
Construction industries	100
Road accidents	98
Agriculture (employees)	74
Manufacture of bricks, pottery, cement, etc.	60
Manufacture of vehicles	12
Homicide	12
Homicide from terrorism (1982–90)	0.2

some readers. One theme that emerges from modern analysis is that perceptions of riskiness involve much more than merely the estimated fatalities in some unit of time such as those given in the table: other factors include an activity's voluntariness, its personal controllability, and its familiarity, in ways not captured by the models traditionally used in mathematical risk assessment (Royal Society 1992: 91). Risk research suggests that we should take people's perceptions of risk seriously, rather than treat them as an 'error' which experts should correct or ignore. This has important implications for the use of victimization risk data, which are often used by the Home Office to suggest that people's estimates are exaggerated. Even in the first British Crime Survey (1981), an attempt was made to reassure the public by showing that someone would be burgled 'only' once every forty years: yet one might respond that twice in an average woman's lifetime is hardly reassuring! In making collective risk assessments on behalf of 'society' (for example over police resource allocation, including policies on racial harassment, domestic violence, and investigations of 'accidents' at work), policy-makers implicitly or explicitly weight the opinions of particular individuals or groups as to which crimes are serious and which should be dealt with through the criminal process.

Despite the efforts of Scandinavian criminologists such as Christie (1981) to get us to set 'limits to pain' and to think collectively about how we want to deal with offenders, tolerating a risk of violent (or any other) crime is not the same sort of decision as judging whether a toxic waste plant which could have harmful (violent?) effects should be built: the latter is a decision on concrete issues affecting the future, whereas crime is already with us and we tolerate it because 'on balance', for whatever reasons, we do not want to/cannot move home. However, in other respects violent crime, like a nuclear accident, is a high-consequence, low- (in most places) probability event, and some insights may be obtained from the approach taken following the public inquiry into the Sizewell B nuclear plant, where the Health and Safety Executive concluded (1988: 1) that 'tolerability' does not mean 'acceptability'. It refers to the 'willingness to live with a risk in order to secure certain benefits and in the confidence that it is being controlled. To tolerate a risk means . . . something we need to keep under review and reduce still further if and as we can.' Understanding the behavioural causes of accidents and disasters involves analysing not just individual slips and lapses but patterns of management and organizational failings: this may be useful also in understanding violence by the police and others in collective violence settings. Fischhoff (1989: 270) observes that 'what is commonly called the conflict between actual and perceived risk is better thought of as the conflict between two sets of risk perceptions: those of ranking scientists performing within their field of expertise and those of anybody else'. Given that—as we shall see—many violent crimes arise out of quarrels, mistakes over actual risk can lead to people becoming offenders as well as becoming victims.

One study discovered that Americans only slightly underestimated the risk of homicide and, taken in the context of other judgements, it was noted that the grossest overestimates of fatality tended to be made by those who also envisaged vivid or imaginable causes of death (Lichtenstein *et al.* 1978). More generally, Tversky and Kahneman (1973) suggest that the easier it is to recall or imagine an event, the more likely we are to judge that it is risky or happens frequently (see also Kahneman and Tversky 1982). This perceptual process applies not only to crime victims but also to police and parole decision-takers, whether dealing with violence or any other type of crime. Mass media reportage serves as a substitute for direct experience—though research shows that people typically are active interpreters rather than passive consumers of what they see—and it is in this context that the viewing of violent incidents must be considered.

In a general (Dutch) population study that was larger and more representative than the mostly student-based studies by psychologists, Vlek and Stallen (1981) observed that the acceptability of risks depends more on their estimated benefits than on the perceived dangers. It seems plausible that general perceptions of technological risks are often associated with social benefits in a way that violent crime is not, the limited exception being that if we are asked whether we are willing to tolerate going out at night despite there being violence in the area, those who value highly what they intend to do while out—drinking, dancing, a chance of finding someone with whom to have sex, evening classes, or whatever—may be more willing to run the risk than those who do not much care (and who may not want to go out anyway). As Sparks *et al.* (1977) observed, fear of crime may act as a surrogate for all sorts of disparate psychological and social phenomena: fear of getting old, poor health, social change, declining community, job insecurity, etc.[14] Thus positive motivation factors, rather than simply underestimation of risks, may account for why so many young people—particularly young males—go out at night in spite of their high incidence of victimization.[15] Another group of people who are prepared to take a serious risk of violence are prostitutes: consider, for example, their behaviour in staying in business when there are 'known but unidentified' serial killers or rapists about.[16]

In general, people are more fearful about risks over which they feel they have no control: an example is the greater concern about being killed or injured in public transport accidents than when driving (even taking into account the effect of seeing larger numbers injured or killed in individual public transport than in private motoring accidents). This would make more understandable the preoccupation of the public (as well as the media) with out-of-the-blue sexual or non-sexual attacks by strangers, even though the number of assaults by acquaintances is higher.[17] Neither the young men nor the prostitutes in the cases noted above feel helpless: older people and women less used than prostitutes to manipulating potential threats from 'punters' are less confident (or less reckless), a phenomenon that may be reinforced by the socialization of women into passivity in patriarchal societies. The results of these risks may be seen in the patterns of recorded and of unreported violence. Davidoff and Greenhorn (1991) reveal that the most common known act leading to a *recorded* violent crime in England and Wales is a street brawl, followed by domestic violence, a pub brawl, and an attack on a

[14] These also fuel racist attitudes, which have longer histories.

[15] I use the term 'incidence' rather than 'risk' here, because properly examined, the risk of street victimization should be a proportion of the occasions on which people go out: it is entirely possible that over-sixties have a higher rate than young people of being mugged as a proportion of the times they go out, even though the proportion of over-sixties who are mugged is much lower than the proportion of young people mugged.

[16] Although their motivation here is money for themselves and/or their pimps, who may be coercing them to stay at work.

[17] This does not mean automatically that the *risk* of being attacked by an acquaintance is higher. As a proportion of the number of times that one is *plausibly* at risk of being attacked, the ratio of attacks to opportunities may be higher for strangers than for acquaintances. In practice, applying the concept of 'opportunities' here is far from easy, given the bizarre sorts of circumstances that can trigger sexual attacks. For example, if going shopping counts as an 'assault opportunity' for every stranger one passes, the chance of being attacked per 'person opportunity' falls to an extremely low level, even if a high proportion of women who lead an active night life are assaulted.

public servant (41 per cent of violent crimes recorded were not classified by the police).

I turn now to consider the risks of violence facing particular categories of person. This selection of 'appropriate' categories for analysis is inevitably subjective, though my choice reflects topics of academic and social debate. 'Blaming the victim' is a common preoccupation, particularly in violent and sexual crime, even to the extent that the Criminal Injuries Compensation Board can deny compensation to those whose characters or way of life are judged to make them 'undeserving' (Miers 1990). The concept of 'victim-precipitated violence' has received considerable criticism from feminists, party because of the policy uses to which it has been put by some and partly because the phrase appears to suggest that what happened was really the victim's fault. However, it is worth noting here that as a matter of formal theory, any explanation of any type of crime which neglects the way potential victims behave is incomplete: as McIntosh (1975) puts it, the study of the organization of crime is the study of the organization of society from the standpoint of its bearing upon crime. What makes the issue of incorporating victim behaviour into explaining crime so emotive is the difficulty in practice of separating out the perceptions of victims' behaviour held by actual and theoretically potential offenders from social judgements of the *culpability* of victims' behaviour. As a matter of sociological fact, blaming victims occurs in a relatively narrow range of behaviour, principally violent crime (against young men as well as, more unreasonably, against women) and crimes against corporations (Levi and Pithouse 1992; for an overview, see also Walklate 1990).[18]

Ethnicity and Risk

The development of racial/racist assaults as a social problem in Britain has been analysed thoughtfully by Bowling (1993). There are very substantial variations within ethnic groups (Young 1988), but the 1988 British Crime Survey found that even after taking into account social and demographic factors, non-white people were more at risk from violence than were whites. The fact that overall, risks of assault for Afro-Caribbeans and of threats for Asians were substantially greater than their equivalents for whites was accounted for largely by age, sex, marital status, and area of residence. Furthermore, the victims believed (rightly or wrongly) that 44 per cent of assaults directed at Asians and a third of

[18] One might go further and use as examples of victim-blaming the condemnation of the poor, and particularly the black, for acts of aggression which themselves partly reflect the inferior economic and social situation in which they are confined. In this sense, we may speak of there being 'chains of victims'.

those directed at Afro-Caribbeans (plus about half the threats) had been racially motivated. They judged this because of racist language (particularly the Afro-Caribbeans) and/or because they (particularly the Asians) thought the violence was specifically directed at their group or had happened to them before. As regards the risk of violent crime for gain, people of Afro-Caribbean or Asian origin were about three times as likely as whites to be victims of robbery or theft from the person. In the case of Asians, though not Afro-Caribbeans, ethnicity was a significant factor in victimization (Mayhew *et al.* 1989).

Social Class and Risk

There is surprisingly little material on social class and risk, largely because official statistics on recorded crime or offenders are not collected on that basis. Victimization survey data do yield important information, though they are not free from problems of differential interpretation among social classes of physical acts as 'violent' ones. It is common for studies of violence against women and against children to observe that violence is no respecter of social class and is spread throughout society. This is true but misleading, for it tells us nothing about variations in the *proportions* of different social groups who become victims. There is also fierce debate among feminists about the salience of class and ethnicity, as contrasted with gender alone, for violence. As regards rape, a study of a representative sample of over 1,000 English married women by Painter (1991a) observes that wife rape is something that can happen regardless of social class and economic position, but that women in social class DE were twice as likely to be raped and three times more likely to be raped with violence than were women in social class AB. The same women, when asked if they had been raped outside marriage, displayed similar social class patterns: working-class women were more than three times as likely as middle-class ones to be raped by a stranger or by someone they knew (other than a boyfriend). However, possibly because less physical violence was used against them, the middle-class women were less likely to see what happened to them as 'rape' than were the working-class ones. Painter's survey found also that working-class women (classes DE) were twice as likely (43 per cent) as women in social classes AB (16 per cent) and C1 (23 per cent) to report that they had been hit by their husbands, and three times more likely to state that they had been threatened by them. Social class is inferred only indirectly from housing type, but the evidence from the British Crime Surveys indicates significant social class differences in vulnerability to other forms of violence, including mugging. In the USA, survey data suggest that rates of child abuse are 40 per cent higher in blue-collar than in white-collar families, and are 62 per cent higher among the very poor (Straus *et al.* 1980). At least in the USA, there is a stronger relationship between social class (and ethnicity) and non-family violence than between social class and family violence (Weis 1989); but even outside the family, most violence everywhere is intra-class.

Homicide offers the most valid *recorded* crime data set for ascertaining the social class of victims, but there are no systematic English studies. However, a review of the home circumstances in major inquiries into death as a result of child abuse supports the hypothesis that significant social class variations in risk exist there too: it is implausible that these differences are the result of definitional bias by doctors and coroners. Both Australian (National Committee 1990) and American (Greene and Wakefield, 1979) studies indicate that homicide victims come disproportionately from the lower social classes; and, since most homicides—*a fortiori* the 'family killings'—are 'cleared up' and are intra-class, it seems evident that the poor are most likely to be injured and killed, whether by violence (including terrorism) as conventionally defined, or by injury at work.[19]

Age and Risk

The 'lifestyle' approach to victimization relates risk to the patterns of living in which people engage (see Pease Chapter 14 in this volume). An important factor influencing such lifestyles is age (which can also act as a masking variable for marital and parental status, which affects the extent to which women, in particular, go out in the evening). The rise of 'the child victim' has been lucidly examined by Morgan and Zedner (1992) and by Parton (1985, 1990), but it should be noted that for socio-cultural reasons, children make the purest victims among any of the categories reviewed here, being (in popular and media perceptions) 'too young to be blamed' for becoming victims.

Here, as in other realms, there are politically contested definitions of what constitutes 'abuse'. Gil (1975: 347) states that child abuse is 'inflicted gaps or deficits between circumstances of living which would facilitate the optimum development of children, to which they should be entitled, and to their actual circumstances, irrespective of the sources or agents of the deficit.' By that criterion, the amount of child abuse would be vast, even if we could agree on what constituted 'the optimum development of children', which seems unlikely. At a substantially more prosaic level, a 1990 survey of local authorities in England showed that they

[19] The latter is close to being a tautology: only those in consumer complaints departments would be likely to become victims of assault, for white-collar staff would seldom work on scaffolding, chop materials in workshops, etc.

registered 3.6 children per 1,000 as being 'at risk' of abuse: 39,200 in England as a whole, of whom about one in seven were registered as sexual abuse risks. Those under one year old have the highest homicide risk of any age group in England: 44 deaths per million children in 1990.[20] However, popular discussion of 'violence against children' often reviews the age range 0–17 as if it were a homogeneous category, all being technically juveniles. This is dramatically powerful but analytically unhelpful, since the lifestyle patterns of relatively independent teenagers are enormously different from those of parentally dependent under-fives.

In 1989, according to the official statistics, the age group 16–24 had the highest rate of victimization;[21] the lowest rates were for those aged 0–9 and 60 or over. The rise in the proportion of victims of violence who were aged 25–39, from 27 per cent to 33 per cent over the period 1984–9, may be attributable to the increased willingness of women to report and of the police to record violence against women.

Official statistics and victim surveys agree that all but 10 per cent of rape victims are aged under 40 and all but 5 per cent of indecent assault victims are 40 or over. According to recorded crime figures, in relation to their numbers in the population, the age group 10–15 is most at risk, with forty-two per 100,000 population being raped and 310 per 100,000 being indecently assaulted in 1989. Next comes the 16–24 group, with a rate of thirty-nine per 100,000 for rape and 118 for indecent assault. Then patterns diverge, the under-10s having a rate of five per 100,000 for rape and 105 for indecent assaults, while the 25–39 age group has a higher rape rate (fifteen) but a lower indecent assault rate (thirty-three per 100,000); and the 40–59 group has a four in 100,000 chance of being raped and a ten in 100,000 chance of being indecently assaulted.

Relatively little work has been done on the victim experiences of under-16s in England, though more will be known when the results of the 1991 British Crime Survey are fully analysed (see Maguire Chapter 6 in this volume). In the USA, 12–19-year-olds were estimated to have suffered 1.8 million crimes annually: roughly twice the rate of the adult population, though those aged 16–19 were far more likely to be victims of rape, robbery, and assault than were those aged 12–15 (National Crime Survey

[20] The rate drops to nine per million for 1–4-year-olds and to three per million for 5–15-year-olds, and rises to fifteen per million—the second highest risk—for those aged 16–29; fourteen for those aged 30–49; eleven for those aged 50–69; and eight for those aged 70 or more. Some socio-biologists would account for the vulnerability of the very young in terms of its being more sensible to reject offspring before rather than after much economic and emotional investment has been made in them; others might have a more situational explanation, as we shall examine later. In most respects these are parallel accounts at different levels.

[21] The British Crime Surveys also found that in 1981 and 1987, the 16–24 age group had the highest risk of becoming victims of violence. Young males in this age group accounted for 57 per cent of all assaults measured by victim surveys.

1986). The older the victims were, the more likely they were to be attacked by strangers and to suffer serious injuries. A survey of 11–15-year-olds in Edinburgh found that half the young people surveyed had been victims of an assault, threatening behaviour, or theft from the person over the previous nine months; the proportion who had been 'touched up' or had been 'flashed at' was higher for girls than for boys, varying from 14 per cent for 11–12-year-old boys (declining thereafter) to 17 per cent for 11–12-year-old girls and 30 per cent for 14–15-year-old girls. Only 14 per cent of assaults, 8 per cent of threatening behaviour, 16 per cent of thefts from the person were reported to the police, and only slightly higher percentages of sexual crimes were reported to other adults, let alone to the police (Anderson *et al.* 1990).

In general, young people are more at risk of becoming victims of any form of violence except spouse abuse, and this is related to the general patterns of life they lead, including the kinds of group drinking and quarrels in public places they get into (Tuck 1989).

Occupation and Risk

Increasing attention is being paid to the risks of violence among different occupational groups while at work, though these almost invariably omit the sort of 'corporate violence' risks discussed earlier. The 1988 British Crime Survey informs us (Mayhew *et al.* 1989: 32) that 16.8 per cent of male workers aged 16–30 and 17 per cent of male workers aged 31–45 had experienced verbal abuse by the public over the previous fourteen months, and that occupations with three or more times the average risk of violence included not only the police but also welfare workers, nurses, female office managers, and 'entertainment managers' such as publicans and 'bouncers'.[22] An earlier study by Rowett (1986) had shown that one in ten social workers were assaulted each year: in inner city areas, the proportion was one in four, though residential social workers were more at risk than their community colleagues (see also Norris 1990). However, Painter (1991b: 161) criticizes these 'objective' measures of violence because they trivialize threats and exaggerate the impact of hitting:

> a physical assault by an elderly, female geriatric patient in an acute surgical ward upon a young, physically robust, male staff nurse is not the same as a random, unprovoked, physical attack by a young, male, outpatient in accident and emergency, upon a middle-aged female nurse. The statistics may show that two assaults have taken place but give no indication of their relative seriousness as defined by the victim.

[22] Except for office managers, the same categories had a three times greater than average risk of being threatened at work. Teachers, whose risk of assault was no greater than average, were three times as likely as the average to have been threatened at work.

Occupational crime: a case study of the UK police The police are in a special category of socially construed 'deserving victims', sustaining a constant media barrage of sympathetic coverage of their proneness to the risk of violence while acting 'on behalf of society'. Like prison officers and psychiatric nurses, constraining 'the violent' is part of their job, and this differentiates them from those who are exposed to the risk of violence without any professional (and highly paid) motive. Technically, an assault against the police is committed every time that a member of the public touches a police uniform in a way that could be interpreted as aggressive. On the other hand, just as many young people (particularly blacks) complain of low-level verbal harassment by the police (Bowling 1993), so too one may observe in many 'hard' areas after pub or club closing time a stream of verbal insults against the police which reinforces their sense of righteousness against 'scumbags'. Prior to 1988, force orders for the South Wales Constabulary defined 'assault' as follows for the purpose of collation:

Any assault on an officer whilst he is on duty whereby:
1) any injury, however slight, is inflicted, and/or
2) it was the assailant's intention to injure the officer although no actual injury was caused.
(An unintentional assault e.g. pushing or struggling whilst arresting a drunk is excluded.)

Before 1990, the term 'assault on police' was inconsistently defined by different forces. On average, if the figures published in *Police Review* are to be believed, one in seven officers on the mainland were assaulted during 1988. Data from the 1988 British Crime Survey (Mayhew *et al.* 1989: 69) show that during 1987, just over one in twenty adults were victims of common assault or wounding: the equivalent categories to assaulting police.[23] So—without allowing for the vagaries of police recording procedures for assaults on police—it appears that police officers run a three times greater risk of being assaulted than does the average member of the public. The 1988 British Crime Survey shows that almost one in three males aged 16–24 and over one in twenty males aged 25–39 were assaulted. Consequently, the analytically appropriate police/public differential is much smaller, and, taken as a group, police officers may actually stand a *lower* chance than young men generally of being assaulted, though not necessarily of being assaulted with the same level of severity.

Looked at another way, research in South Wales—one of the highest-risk force areas in England and Wales—shows that one in every 740 inci-

[23] Woundings rose by 7.6 per cent annually but common assaults by only 1.1 per cent annually since 1983, indicating the importance of looking at levels of seriousness when reviewing trends.

dents a police officer attends results in an incident defined as an assault on the officer. In any year, the likelihood of an officer being *seriously* injured—as defined by him or her—on duty is 1:7,000. An average South Wales police officer will be assaulted once every four years and will be seriously assaulted once every forty-four years (i.e. substantially less often than once in the maximum working life of an officer). These figures, it should be emphasised, do not take into account the far smaller number of officers *actually* 'at risk' through being on the sort of street policing and police station duties that our research shows are most likely to occasion assaults: *their* risk of assault will be substantially higher (and the risk of others correspondingly lower).

'Corporate' death and injury Finally, some comments are appropriate about the 'corporate death and injury rates' in different occupations. Eight police and prison officers were killed on duty in England and Wales in the period 1986–90, an average of one per 100,000 annually. Partly because of the 1988 *Piper Alpha* explosion, by far the highest risk per 100,000 employees was in oil and gas extraction, with 87.3 deaths annually per 100,000 over the period 1986–92. The construction industry ranked fifth per 100,000, but had the largest *number* of fatalities. Coal mining, followed by the railways, had the highest injury rates (Table 7.1).

There are some genuine as well as perceived differences in intentionality which are important components of 'the crime problem'. The fact that the police and prison officers are paid more than they would otherwise get to take on the risk of violence may only be an intriguing consequence of this perception as well as of their social role: but given these occupational death rates, why do most of us see their work as more dangerous and 'violent' than that of miners and building workers?

Gender and Risk

We are often informed (e.g. Dobash and Dobash, 1979, 1992; Dobash *et al.* 1992) that discussions of 'domestic violence' neglect the essential issue that this is primarily violence against women. This point is correct. However, a more general look at English homicide data reveals that although men are the primary offenders, they are also the primary victims: for no age group are there more females than males killed per million population, and only in the 1–5 age group are the rates equal. Altogether, in 1990, 381 males and 228 females were victims of homicide in England and Wales.[24] The gender difference is less when we look at

[24] In the USA the numbers of male and female victims are roughly equal (Wilson and Daly 1992). Compare this with the gender distribution and level of violence in Colombia, where there were approximately 29,000 homicide victims in 1992, and Kenya where, during 1992, there were some 800 homicides arising out of political conflict alone. Most of these victims were male.

violence by those acquainted—234 males as against 181 females (for strangers, ninety males and twenty-six females)—but it still remains. In cases where there was no suspect, fifty-seven males and nineteen females were killed: we may plausibly assume that these were not family killings. The proportion of killings by people who know each other has risen from 64 per cent in 1980 to 80 per cent in 1990: the proportion of killings by partners rose from 20 per cent to 38 per cent.

If we break the data down further, patterns begin to appear. Nineteen men and eighty-six women were victims of killings by spouses or cohabitants, past or present. To this may be added the non-cohabiting lovers by whom fourteen men and eleven women were killed. So plainly, women are more at risk of being killed by their partners than are men.[25] On the other hand, men are more at risk than women from their parents, from other family members, and particularly from friends or acquaintances and from 'other associates'. Moreover, men are more at risk from strangers: eighty males and twenty-six females were so killed, in acts other than terrorism. These risk data *may* have a gender dimension: because females are more tightly controlled in their leisure activities—by parents, by jealous partners, or by childcare arrangements—they are less 'at risk' outside the home because they are less often out (or allowed to go out) in dangerous situations. On the other hand, for socio-cultural reasons connected with challenges to masculinity, it seems implausible that if women went out as often as men, they would be victims of homicide outside as often as men.[26] The notion of risk depends properly on the lifestyle people lead, but, except to some advocates of natural selection, that lifestyle is only modestly the product of nature, and is very substantially the consequence of socio-economic, ethnic, and gendered influences.

Once we move beyond homicide, the violence data become much more problematic. As regards recorded violent crime, the proportion of victims who were female rose to 33 per cent in 1989 compared with 27 per cent in 1984–7. This may reflect a rising trend in the *reporting* of such assaults: British Crime Survey data suggest that the proportion of domestic assaults against women that are reported increased from one in five in 1981 to one in two in 1987. (However, a survey of 1,000 men and women in North London by Mooney (1993) found that only 22 per cent of the women experiencing domestic violence in their lifetime had reported it to the police.) The greater the physical injury, the more likely the victim was to be male: 71 per cent of victims of serious violence were male, com-

[25] This is confirmed by cross-national data on inter-spousal homicide, though the ratios vary considerably, being 6:1 in Denmark, 3.3:1 in Canada, and only 1.3:1 in the USA. For the latter, see Wilson and Daly (1992).

[26] Given current cultural values, it is far more probable that if women went out more, the number of cases of sexual violence would increase.

pared with 67 per cent for less serious offences. Excluding the effects of their different lifestyles, young men were twice as much at risk as young women of becoming victims of non-sexual violence.[27]

The British Crime Survey (BCS) estimated that in 1987, just over a third of those assaulted were women: an only slightly higher proportion than that found in recorded cases of violence. In about half the cases reported to the BCS interviewers, the victim and offender were known to each other: this too is similar to the data on recorded violence compiled by the Metropolitan Police (1990) where, in 1989, 13,119 offenders were known to victims and 15,048 were not. Eighteen per cent of BCS-reported assaults involved family, lovers, or ex-lovers, though this is likely to be an underestimate.

BCS data do understate levels of unreported family violence, but it would take a very substantial rise in the underreporting of adult family violence compared with non-family violence to make family violence into even half the 'true' total of violent crime (though a rise in reporting can make a substantial impact on its proportion of recorded crime).[28] Though the BCS data are not broken down in this way, given that offences outside the family are typically male on male, the implication is that the role in total violent behaviour played by male on female intra-family violence has been overstated by feminist critics. Although 46 per cent of female victims were assaulted in the home of victim or suspect compared with 14 per cent of male victims (Davidoff and Greenhorn 1991), the greater number of male than female victims overall means that over a third of recorded victims of domestic assault are male. Likewise, the BCS data reveal that more than half the assaults against women but only one in twelve of those against men were 'domestic', though the fact that there were so many more male than female victims of violence almost evened out the actual number of 'domestic' male and female victims. These data do *not* mean that male on female violence is any less important socially, nor that women do not need extra protection from men: confirmation of the latter may be found from a study (Mooney 1993) which revealed that 10 per cent of North London women (of whom four fifths were injured) had experienced violence from their partners during 1992, and that 5 per cent of women had had a bone broken during their lifetime as a result of this. (The 'lifetime prevalence rate' of marital violence was over a quarter in this study, which did not examine female on male violence.) Nor do

[27] In the highest-risk age group, 16–24 years old, the rates of recorded violence were 1,288 for males and 601 for females per 100,000 population. No data are kept on gender risks of sexual violence but we may reasonably assume that nearly all victims are female, even though male assaults on gay men and/or on men in institutions are unlikely to be reported or, until recently, if reported taken seriously by the police.

[28] It would be more analytically defensible to describe 'family violence' as violence between intimates, but I have adopted the phrase in common usage.

the data imply anything about the deserts of female victims compared with male assault victims. Despite the subjective nature of such constructions, it may be, for example, that most male victims 'provoke' their assaults, whereas female victims do not: see Dobash *et al.* (1992). But the information about assaults and homicides does at least raise some questions that deserve exploration.

The pattern of circumstances of recorded violence was different for male and female victims. Thirty-two per cent of female but only 6 per cent of male victimizations arose within the home (Davidoff and Greenhorn, 1991).[29] The fact that attacks on public servants accounted for 8 per cent of male and 3 per cent of female victims in 1989 may reflect low female representation in violence-prone occupations other than social security counter work and the social work professions.[30]

There is no breakdown by gender of the reasons why some violence is not reported. But one important question is whether women are more likely than men to be *multiple* victims of violence, but not to report it because of practical problems in finding alternative accomodation, etc., and/or because they have been socialized into 'learned helplessness' and are unable to cope without 'their' man: social stigma is part of the latter aspect. There is substantial evidence that women are prone to multiple victimization, but there is little evidence on male multiple victimization in the home, data on which have not been collected in the UK. (On female multiple victimization, see further Dobash and Dobash 1992; Genn 1988; and Maguire and Pease Chapters 6 and 14 in this volume.)

Unsurprisingly, the direction of 'domestic violence' has been the subject of enormous controversy. The findings of research by Straus and Gelles (1990) in the USA based on two large national surveys exclusively on violence in the home appear to reveal first, as many male as female victims (about 12 per cent of each gender), and second, that men are more likely than women to be victims of severe violence by their partner (a 'fact' unsupported by English homicide data cited earlier). This research has been criticized (Dobash and Dobash 1992: ch. 9; Dobash *et al.* 1992) on grounds both of methodological adequacy and of negative effects on the provision of help for women.[31] It should be noted that more general victimization surveys in the USA, Canada, and Britain—which themselves have been criticized for undercounting sexual violence against women—

[29] Street brawls account for 32 per cent of male and 22 per cent of female victims; pub brawls for 11 per cent of male and 5 per cent of female victims.

[30] Modes of dangerous employment are one factor, for instance, that affects the relative risks of serious violence for women and men. One unintended effect of low female employment in mining, oil, and deep-sea fishing is their low 'corporate violence' victimization rate.

[31] Although there is no reason in principle why provisions for women should depend on the rate of male victimization, and if there were not also good methodological criticism, such policy consequences would be technically irrelevant.

(Young 1988) find that over 80 per cent of violence between partners involves men assaulting women. While, despite some Canadian findings, it seems plausible that the rate of male non-reporting would be greater than female non-reporting on any one occasion (because of the stigma attached to reporting for men), it seems implausible that men would be repeat victims to the same extent as women.

SEXUAL VIOLENCE

The term 'sexual violence' has expanded from a rape or unwanted physical 'fondling' of someone to whom the suspect was not married, to include rape in marriage,[32] child sexual abuse, and—in the view of some—sexual harassment, i.e. behaviour and language by men which makes women feel uncomfortable. It is difficult to know how to approach an explanation of sexual violence without clarifying what the boundaries are of the behaviour we wish to explain. One of the key questions here is how far we wish to push the test of *women's perceptions* as against the more conventional criminal law test of *men's awareness* of sexual intimidation. If we base our analysis on women's perceptions (or transcend even women's perceptions, since they may be suffering from indoctrination into acceptance of exploitation), then we may have a very broad category of what Box (1983) terms 'exploitation rape' (i.e. any sexual intercourse between people of unequal power). However, while this may be superficially attractive, in so far as it should be acknowledged that many women are made very uncomfortable by sexual approaches from bosses, police officers, teachers, or others in positions of power, and that some women feel obliged to have sex with such men (or, indeed, with gay women) for fear that they be disadvantaged, let us reflect upon it a little harder. It would mean, for example, that a police officer could not have heterosexual intercourse with anyone (except a superior female officer or—depending on one's construct of power relativities—an elite woman). This surely points to some bizarre consequences of the concept of 'exploitation rape'. Some women and (men) presumably do find particular powerful men or women attractive: how are we to allow their free choice if all such intercourse is automatically deemed rape? And if not all sex between unequals is rape, how are men to know whether consent is genuine or simply the result of fear (whether fear of violence, of prosecu-

[32] After more than two centuries in which men could not be convicted of raping their wives—though in law they could have been convicted of indecent assault and non-sexual violent crimes—the English courts finally held that husbands were liable to conviction, the old common law being declared to be 'a fiction which had become anachronistic and offensive': see *R.* v. *C. (Rape: Marital Exemption)* [1991] 1 All ER 755; and *R.* v. *R.* [1991] 2 WLR 1065, affirmed by the House of Lords [1991] 3 WLR 767.

tion, of job disadvantage, or of lower exam grades)? Moving to the concept of 'indecent assault', one could agree that actions (such as a kiss or a 'grope' without express or 'reasonably implied' permission) should be criminalized on preventive grounds, even though some such behaviour is sometimes welcomed, but unless it can be made clear *at the moment of the assault or harassment* which acts are allowable/welcome and which are not, it would be retributively unjust to punish people for performing them.

This outline contains an element of caricature, because there are so many acts of gross aggression which are not in practice punished currently, but some analytic clarity is required. A study of married women by Painter (1991*a*) found that wives raped with threatened or actual violence were more likely than women who had insisted that they did not want sex to consider that they had been raped; they also differentiated having sex when 'disinclined' (because uninterested or unwell) from having sex following coercion. However, given the sexual and non-sexual tensions between many partners that exist in current or reasonably foreseeable societies, it cannot always be self-evident whether women's reports of sexual assault are true or untrue, particularly among cohabitees where forensic evidence is unlikely to be determinative.[33]

In short, counting rape and other sexual assaults is not as easy as we might imagine, and unless we do adopt a test based on women's perceptions *irrespective* of men's subjective awareness of those perceptions, women's sincere statements that they have been raped are *not* definitive as a measure of offending, even if we wish (entirely properly) to take them as a measure of victimization. The difference may depend on what we want to do with the data. If, by attitude-changing campaigns or by some work-based complaints mechanisms, we want to reduce harassment of women, then it seems reasonable to take victims' perceptions as the baseline. If men are to be sent to prison for at least six years (as was the median sentence for rape in England and Wales in 1990), then what do we want to require as the minimum degree of subjective awareness on the part of the accused? A further area of contention is the aggregation of different levels of victimization into the generic term 'sexual violence'. It is clearly right to complain that serious acts like forced anal sex or vaginal sex using objects other than a penis are not legally 'rape':[34] but are unwanted sexual propositions or even being 'touched up' always 'the same sort of thing' as rape,

[33] It seems plausible that the number of wrongly disbelieved reports will vastly outnumber the wrongly believed ones: our view of which set of potential miscarriages of justice—unjust deserts for victims or for offenders—is the less undesirable may depend on our general attitudes towards the offence and towards civil liberties, as well as on our gender. See Lacey *et al.* (1990) on sexuality and the criminal law.

[34] They have always been prosecutable as wounding and grievous bodily harm, though there are no data on actual prosecutions for this.

even though the attitude-set of males may be similar to those involved in rape? (If the 'touching up' were part of a persistent pattern, for example at work, the seriousness would increase markedly.)

How much Sexual Violence is there?

Using recorded crime data for England and Wales, there were thirteen rapes and fifty-nine indecent assaults per 100,000 population in 1989: if these data reflected the amount of sexual violence—which they do not—it would mean that females have a one in 8,000 chance of being raped and a one in 1,660 chance of being indecently assaulted in any one year. Going beyond recorded crime, victimization survey data on sexual violence for the UK are poor in quality. Extraordinarily, the 1983 British Crime Survey found that only one attempted rape (and seventeen indecent assaults) in a sample of about 5,000 women was reported to researchers, a result that is generally acknowledged to be a serious underestimate, possibly reflecting embarrassment, the absence of under-16s in the sample, and the fact that interviewees were not always alone in the house. Most surveys have found that one in four of those reporting to rape crisis centres have reported to the police: the same proportion as in a *Woman's Own* survey in 1986 and in American studies (Scully 1990). Since there were 4,046 recorded rapes (including attempts) and 15,800 recorded indecent assaults on females in 1991, this would imply a 'grossed up' figure of at least 80,000 sexual assaults outside marriage in England and Wales during 1991. It should not be assumed that all indecent assaults are of the same perceived seriousness as rapes, nor that most of the offenders would have gone on to rape if they had had the opportunity: as we shall examine later, they may have seen the sexual aggression as a 'try on' to generate what they saw as 'consent', however passive, while baulking at an act that 'clearly' (to them) did not involve consent.[35]

The survey of 1,007 married women in the UK by Painter (1991*a*) suggested that 14 per cent of women had been raped by their husbands at some time during their marriage: in 44 per cent of these cases, violence was used, and half the wives so raped had been raped six times or more. Among married women, rape by husbands is twice as likely as rape by acquaintances or boyfriends, and seven times more likely than rape by strangers[36]. Mooney's study in North London (1993) found that 6 per

[35] One should add whatever multiplier is deemed appropriate for the 389 incest, the 1,142 gross indecency with a child, and—assuming a lack of consent—the 314 unlawful sexual intercourse with a girl under 13 cases that were recorded in 1991. Studies indicate that all offences against young people, mostly female, are seriously underreported because of manipulated fear and guilt.

[36] Women are, of course, 'at risk' for much longer periods with their husbands than they are with other potential rapists.

cent of women had been forced to have sex—2.4 per cent by violence—with their partners during the previous twelve months.

Levels of rape in the USA appear to be much higher: in 1980, the per capita recorded rape rate in the USA was eighteen times that in England and Wales (West 1983). This does *not*, however, mean that the UK would be found to have similar rates if only our research were better. Americans have generally much higher rates for most violent crimes. Estimates of the proportion of rapes reported to the police in the USA vary from half (National Crime Survey 1986) to 10 per cent (Russell 1984). Without suggesting that attempted rape is not serious, the rape and attempted rape data in police records should be disaggregated, for Chappell *et al.* (1977) noted that (at least at that time) the Los Angeles police tended to overcharge relatively modest indecent assaults as 'attempted rape' to try to induce a plea bargain by defendants.

As one might expect statistically, a number of American researchers who have asked about lifetime experiences have found much higher rates of sexual assault than are found by victim surveys which ask only about one year's experiences, and women's fear of sexual violence may not depend on their own actual experience, or that of anyone they know, of rape or attempted rape (Stanko 1990). Johnson (1980) suggested that almost a third of girls then aged 12 would suffer a violent sexual attack (including from their partners) in their lifetime, while Russell's survey in San Francisco (Russell 1984) estimated this proportion at almost half, noting also that 14 per cent of women who had ever been married reported that their husband or ex-husband had raped them.

Societies vary enormously in their rape rates, matrifocal ones tending to have low rates (Sanday 1981; Scully 1990). Recorded rape statistics for 1990 show that the rape rate in England was 130 per million; in France, 81.8 per million; in India, 7.65 per million; in Italy, 22.8 per million; in Russia, 89 per million; in South Africa, 630 per million; and the United States, 600 per million. These figures may tell us more about cultural variations in the reporting and recording of rape than about rape itself. However, to the extent that expected and actual social reaction to crime affect the rate of criminal behaviour, the task of explaining the causes of crime is linked to unpacking the nature of the stigmatization and crime-recording processes.

IS VIOLENT CRIME GETTING WORSE?

Victims seldom feel better or worse because they would have stood a greater or lesser chance of being beaten up or raped a year earlier. Nevertheless, the theme of social deterioration is an important one in general explanations, particularly since it is often asserted that 'in the good old days', when 'we had the death penalty and corporal punishment', there was less violent crime. In fact, the homicide rate today has been put at roughly half what it was in the mid-seventeenth century, though the pattern of homicide is very different, being much more intra-familial now than then (Nuttall, personal communication). Gatrell (1980) has shown that the Victorian era did witness a significant fall in the level of violent crime (at least outside the home), and Gurr's review (1990) points to large fluctuations in both American and English rates of violence within a general decline attributable to the 'civilizing process'. Recorded crime data for both counties suggest an increase in violence from the relatively peaceful early 1950s.

Whether measured by official statistics or victimization surveys (which commenced only in 1981 in England and Wales), there seems little doubt that there was a substantial increase in violent crime during the 1980s in England. For example, the recorded victimization rate for violence against the person increased during the period 1984–9 from 348 to 482 per 100,000 population for males, and from 119 to 223 per 100,000 for females. Davidoff and Greenhorn (1991: 4) note that the male rate rose by 40 per cent while the female rate rose 90 per cent. However, one might add that the *numerical* increase in male recorded victimization was 134 per 100,000, while that for females was 104 per 100,000; so the rise in recorded violence against men was actually higher than that against women, though using percentages rather than raw numbers made it appear to be lower. The recorded victimization rate for rape more than doubled between 1984 and 1989, from six to thirteen per 100,000 population. The indecent assault rate rose by 40 per cent, from forty-two to fifty-nine per 100,000 population, over the same period.[37] Davidoff and Dowds (1989) point out that the BCS data show a slight increase (3 per cent) in common assaults over 1981–7, and that the greater willingness of the public to report them has artificially boosted the recorded violence data.

The 1991 British Crime Survey suggests that robbery and wounding have increased by a fifth since 1981, while recorded offences have almost doubled. There has been an increase in recorded sexual violence, but there is nothing either to support or to falsify the claim that the 1981–91 rise in recorded rape from 1,170 to 4,046 and indecent assault from 10,634 to 15,800 is mainly the result of enhanced confidence in the police rather than being, at least in part, a real increase. (The police *have* improved their attitude to rape and to domestic violence since the late 1980s, and observation indicates that the proportion of offences reported

[37] It is always easier to get a higher percentage rise from a low 'base rate' figure than from a higher one.

that are recorded as crime and prosecuted has increased substantially. However, what effect this has had on the recorded rape rate is uncertain.)

What causes these changes in rates of violent crime? Farrington and Langan's review of victim survey data (1992) shows that the rate per 1,000 persons rose from 4.2 to 4.4 for robbery and 13.1 to 14.1 for assault over the period 1981–7 in England and Wales; the corresponding figures for 1981–6 in the USA were a drop in robbery (from 7.4 to 5.1), in assault—different from the UK, where serious assaults include cuts other than from a weapon—(from 3.2 to 2.9), and in rape (from 1.8 to 1.3). These differential national changes are cautiously attributed to the increased conviction and imprisonment rates in America and to the only very slight rise in the corresponding rates in England.

As for what one might term 'corporate violence' (whether or not it is corporate 'crime'), the number of deaths at work has not been increasing, though there was a 'freak' high total of 590 in 1988/9 due to the death of 192 people on the *Herald of Free Enterprise* ferry. During the 1980s there were fewer than three fatal injuries per 100,000 employees in manufacturing, though the number of major reported injuries in manufacturing and construction—which could easily have become deaths—rose markedly during the 1980s. Indeed, the fatality rate dropped to 1.5—the lowest ever—in 1991/2. Theoretically, since the population in the workforce fluctuates more than the general population, any number of deaths should be expressed as a proportion of the number of workers in 'dangerous occupations', a number which has been falling substantially due to the recession and to the general switch to less hazardous service and finance industries: people in energy and water extraction have a twenty times greater chance of being killed or seriously injured at work than do banking and finance workers. The way in which both the business cycle and the strength of unionization *vis-à-vis* capital affect the rate of industrial injuries is the subject of heated debate. It is agreed that the rate of accidents is related positively to increased industrial activity, but despite the criticisms by Nicholls (1991), it seems plausible that the attack on unions by the Thatcher government did lead to reduced safety at work (Tombs 1992), though one might expect that, irrespective of unionization, fear of unemployment inhibits concern about *expensively* avoidable harms, while payment principally by piece-work rates inhibits safe working behaviour irrespective of the financial cost of safety measures.

Turning our attention to assaults on the police over a longer time-span, we note the findings of Gatrell (1980: 276) that

> popular hostility to the police could erupt in riot in the 1850s and 1860s, and police-baiting remained a popular and approved sport among London juveniles even in the Edwardian years. None the less growing acquiescence in the police presence . . . is eloquently witnessed in . . . the rate of assaults against the police.

Trials for this offence declined steadily from an average annual rate of some 67 per 100,000 . . . in 1856–60 to a rate which by 1910–14 was nearly a third of that, namely 24. . . . The policeman's uniform had palpably acquired its now traditional potency when in 1853 a Durham police superintendent was said single-handedly to have calmed a thousand angry men 'merely from his being dressed as a policeman'.

So the rate of assaults against the police (as measured by trials) fell by 64 per cent between the late 1850s and the years before the First World War.

Figures published by *Police Review* for 1988 reveal that in England and Wales, 16,090 officers were assaulted: 12.5 per cent of the numbers in the force. In 1903, 20 per cent of the Metropolitan police were assaulted (Gatrell 1990); and the Royal Commission on the Police (1929: para. 296) found that between 1920 and 1927, the annual average of assaults against the police in London was 12 per cent. By 1988, the proportion of police assaulted there had dropped to 15 per cent on the *Police Review* figures and 6 per cent in officially recorded figures (Metropolitan Police, 1989), whose respective definitions are uncertain. In other words the assaults per officer ratio today is lower than that in 1910–14 and much lower than that in 1891. The number of homicides of police and prison officers in England and Wales has remained virtually unchanged since 1964: altogether, forty-six officers have been killed in twenty-six years.[38]

ATTITUDES TO VIOLENCE

As a society, we are obsessed with violent crime, particularly murder, as a look at the bookshelves in the 'True Crime' section of any bookshop will confirm. Contrary to initial preconceptions on the part of conflict theorists, the results of seriousness surveys in the West tend to show a high degree of consensus in ratings of property and violent offences among people of different social classes. There are variations by age, older people generally viewing all offences more seriously. Contrary to 'subculture of violence' theory (Wolfgang and Ferracuti 1967), except where the parties are acquainted, people of colour are no more tolerant of violence than are whites (Sparks *et al.* 1977; Hough and Mayhew 1985). Analysing the 1984 British Crime Survey, Pease (1988) found almost perfect concord among people of different ages, sexes, and socio-economic groupings. Nor did it make any difference whether or not they had been victims of crime. On the gender dimension, for example, the following are the proportions of the public rating as 'very serious' the loose crime descriptions

[38] To give some comparative context, this is about the same as the number of South African police officers killed in Soweto (South Africa) alone in 1992.

below: a woman being raped: 97 per cent males, 96 per cent females; a woman being sexually molested or pestered: 84 per cent males, 83 per cent females; someone being attacked by strangers: 72 per cent males, 76 per cent females; someone repeatedly driving a car while over the legal alcohol limit: 65 per cent males, 73 per cent females; someone being insulted or bothered by strangers but not in a sexual way: 14 per cent males, 17 per cent females. However, despite the well-tested methodology of such surveys, there may be socio-economic and gendered differences in what people *mean* by such ratings, particularly where justifiability and excusability are involved.

Levi and Jones (1985) surveyed a random area household sample of 960 members of the public (aged 14 and above) and 368 police officers in two English police force areas. One of the questions researched was the rating of a variety of offences. Violent crime was rated more seriously than property crime, though both the police and public regarded the offence of theft by a police officer from the scene of a burglary as being more serious than 'mugging'. The police rated more highly than did the public all the violent offences.

However, the social construction of 'violent crime' requires more careful thought than has been given hitherto. A number of seriousness surveys have shown that the public construe 'white-collar offences' that result in serious injury as being just as serious as 'normal' violent crimes. Thus, if a pharmaceutical company *knowingly* manufactures a drug known to be harmful, this is as bad as or worse than a street killing (Schrager and Short 1980; Cullen *et al.* 1982; Miethe 1984). Yet what is problematic about corporate homicide is precisely its intentionality, and we may be deceived by public seriousness ratings which are made on the basis of the offence being described as being deliberately and knowingly harmful. Quite apart from any vagaries in corporate homicide legislation, many individual suspects in alleged corporate crime cases escape prosecution or conviction precisely because their *personal* blameworthiness is in doubt: our perceptions of risk-taking are much more ambivalent than our perceptions of evil!

EXPLAINING VIOLENCE

The conceptual issue of what acts count as violence does not cause too many difficulties for criminologists in practice *because they usually ignore it*. Almost all the literature on explaining violent crime focuses exclusively on violence as conventionally delimited, at the most drawing analogies between violent crime and rape (which has been included in this chapter as a form of violent crime, even though it would be wrong to argue that there is nothing sexual about it). Interestingly, where criminologists seek to go beyond this, they seldom attempt any genuine theoretical integration: for example what we are offered by Kempe and Kempe (1978) in their text *Child Abuse* is a series of *types* of child abuse without a very clear idea of the ways in which the same explanation will or will not do for all.[39] Feminist literature attempts the highest level of theorizing violence across the board, but it seldom includes violence in the workplace and for obvious reasons concentrates substantially on crimes against women. (Though machismo or a compulsion to assert a threatened self-concept of masculinity may lead also to violent crimes against other men.) Furthermore, feminist scholarship neglects areas of violence for gain such as robbery, although in a different sense of 'crime for gain' it is arguable that male violence against women is economically as well as emotionally instrumental in obtaining sexual and domestic services at less than market rates. Given the enormous heterogeneity of forms of violence discussed earlier in this chapter, is it plausible that any one theory or theoretical paradigm can account for all these manifestations, or even serve as a common thread in all of them? (I exclude as explanations tautologies or unfalsifiable hypotheses of the form 'all violence derives from the need to control people by physical means'.)

As in the other areas of crime discussed in this volume, there is disagreement over what sort of explanation we are seeking. An explanation of why this person did that crime and when and where it happened? (The criminologist's 'whydunnit'?) Are we searching for an explanation of different *rates* of violence in different geographical areas or different countries? Or for different rates of victimization, by occupation, age, ethnicity, and gender (as discussed earlier); locations; weather; motivation? Different sorts of answers are required for different levels of explanation, which partly explains the enormously varied attention paid to items as diverse as autonomic nervous systems, circulating hormones (such as testosterone and corticosterone), electro-encephalogram readings, social and economic status (absolute or by level of social inequality), gender, ethnicity, media coverage, and level of victim precipitation (i.e. the role of the victim in 'provoking' the violent incident, which some think should be discussed only when women kill men).[40] One of the persistent difficulties

[39] We are also treated to an attempt to apply the evocative term 'violence' to emotional hurt, without any clarification of the outer limits of unjustificable distress: children may cause as well as receive emotional hurt, a complication which is readily ignored or trivialized.

[40] Attribution theorists have shown female victim deserts to be such an integral part of the patriarchal culture that such defensiveness by feminists is appropriate. Nevertheless, it is questionable whether female violence against partners is always justifiable: the phrase 'protective reaction violence' is uncomfortably close to the justification given by the former US government for the bombing of Kampuchea! Victim precipitation can apply to workplace injuries, for example, the link between the machismo of refusing to wear safety clothing and

with many approaches to explaining violence (and, for that matter, victimization risks) is that though they may lay down social indicators or 'marker variables'—some of which illuminate the dynamics of the phenomenon—they seldom generate anything close to a causal account which makes sense of *non*-violence as well as of violence. The accounts that come closest to helping us understand why this person committed that crime on that particular occasion are retrospective reviews: the configuration of circumstances thus described is usually vastly more common than the number of actual violent incidents.

Socio-cultural Explanations of Violence

Gartner (1990) has conducted some cross-national research in developed countries to see what factors best account for variations in homicide rates. She concludes that more micro-level research is required, but observes that

> Nations with greater material deprivation, more cultural heterogeneity, more family dissolution, higher female labor force participation, and greater exposure to official violence generally have higher homicide rates . . . A disproportionate number of teens and young adults was not associated with higher homicide rates for any age group, among these 18 nations . . . Female labor force participation may influence homicide by raising the motivations for female and child homicide, rather than by weakening controls. (Gartner 1990: 102)

Braithwaite (1989) likewise focuses on economic inequality as a primary predictor of homicide rates. Links between unemployment and criminality are stronger for property crime than for violent crime, but more sophisticated sociological accounts might separate out the unemployed into those who are psychologically integrated into 'straight society' and those who see themselves as part of an 'underclass' (and are policed as if they were). Burgess and Draper (1989) examine family violence in evolutionary terms, arguing that under certain conditions child maltreatment has a benefit in helping the fittest survive: moreover, hostility towards stepchildren, for example, may be explicable in terms of our being prepared to act in a more hostile way towards people who share none of our genes,[41] while greater rates of violence against poor and 'physically challenged' children are understandable in relation to competition for scarce resources and optimizing future individual reproductive potential.[42] (They explicitly state, however, that violence may currently be maladaptive.)

an enhanced risk of injury among manual workers, though piece-work payment systems also increase risk.

[41] One might add that most so-called 'family violence' is committed by intimates who do not share the genes of their victims but rather are relatives by marriage.

[42] Natural selection arguments take into account epidemiological data but, like most

One of the earliest attempts at a comprehensive explanation of violence was the 'subculture of violence' theory (Wolfgang and Ferracuti 1967). While not providing a plausible account of why the supposed subculture developed in the first place, the authors showed that many acts of violence arise from incidents that are trivial in origin—an insult, a curse, or a jostle—whose significance is blown out of all proportion in poor neighbourhoods where self-esteem is low. A more micro-sociological successor to their approach is the 'lifestyle' theoretical paradigm, based on victimization survey research, which shows that offenders and victims of street violence not only are the same 'sort of people'—for example, two-thirds of those who attacked 16–24-year-olds were in the same age group (Davidoff and Greenhorn 1991)—but actually are *the same people.*

Curtis (1975) later developed the 'subculture of violence' approach to account for the higher incidence of black than of white violence, arguing *inter alia* that black people were expected to have a lower 'boiling point' and that their identities were much more fragile precisely because of racism and economic discrimination in the wider society: a point developed also by Blau and Blau (1982) and by Currie (1985). Messner and Golden (1992) observe that a high degree of racial inequality is strongly associated with higher homicide rates among whites as well as among blacks. Daly and Wilson (1988: 128) observe, partly caricaturing Wolfgang:

> A seemingly minor affront is not merely a 'stimulus' to action, isolated in time and space. It must be understood within a larger social context of reputation, face, relative social status, and enduring relationships. Men are known by their fellows as 'the sort who can be pushed around' or 'the sort who won't take any shit', as guys whose girlfriends you can chat up with impunity or guys you don't want to mess with. In most social milieus, a man's reputation depends in part upon the maintenance of a credible threat of violence.

Feminist critics express concern that the focus on social stratification evades the central issue about violent crime, which is that it is committed primarily by men. Feminist theories of male violence against women stress the social construction of masculinity, violence, and sexuality in patriarchal society, whose object is to reproduce and maintain the relative status and authority of men over women (Hanmer *et al.* 1989; Scully 1990; Dobash *et al.* 1992). Thus, while most victims of homicide are male (though women are by far the predominant victims of sexual violence),

functionalist explanations, tend towards the tautological. Selection operates at the level of the individual person or even the individual gene, rather than in terms of 'reproducing the population': the latter is simply an aggregated consequence of individual selections. One problem posed for natural selection theory is the high prevalence of unrecorded incest. Another problem is how to account for variations in violence such as the alleged increase in attacks upon disabled people in Germany during the 1990s.

there seems little doubt that men are overwhelmingly the offenders.[43] Wife battery, for example, is seen as an interactive process in which—even discounting the effects of rosy retrospection on early stages of relationships -the women started out feeling loved and interpreted male possessive behaviour as a gesture of commitment: only later did this sense of possession escalate into paranoid violence at the least threat to his control or 'patriarchal rights' (Dobash and Dobash 1979). Unfortunately, with some notable exceptions (Morgan 1987), these explanations are weak when we consider variations in violence against women (and men) over time or in different societies. Feminists are far from agreed upon the role of race and class, as contrasted with gender, in violent crime (Hanmer *et al.* 1989). However, though race and class factors are more pronounced in non-family than in spousal or parent–child violence, the data cited earlier indicate that theories based solely on gender seriously overpredict levels of violent crime both within and between societies. Whether or not men are biologically more aggressive than women, the level and manifestation of machismo is culturally variable.

The Home Office (or rather, the police) classify homicides by apparent motive. Though such situational classifications omit the history of relationships (e.g. did the woman kill the man after she had been bullied for years?), this is important for estimation of issues such as rationality and deterrability. Quarrels and revenge which lead to loss of temper or calculated killing are the predominant motives between acquaintances, comprising in 1989 66 per cent of homicides by acquaintances and 30 per cent of those by strangers. Theft or gain—an important issue, since this is often the kind of scenario used in the debate on capital punishment—were motives in 4 per cent of acquaintance and 11 per cent of stranger homicides (seventeen and twenty-one killings respectively). Also relevant was the fact that 'only' one person was killed while the killer was resisting or evading arrest.[44]

What do these findings on previous convictions—and data discussed in the later section on incapacitation strategies—signify in *explanatory* terms? Very little. They do not, for example, enable us to test the relative roles of heredity, family socialization, peer group influences, or even generalized learning of masculinity.

Accounting for Rape

Explanations of rape are predominantly socio-cultural, generally arguing that rape reflects more general attitudes by men towards women in any

[43] About 90 per cent of English killers are male, roughly half of whom were aged 18–29 at the time of their conviction.

[44] There were thirteen such killings in the period 1980/90.

particular society (Sanday 1981). What sort of men rape and what circumstances give rise to this form of violence? A study by Smith (1989) in two London boroughs showed that (as in the USA) almost two-thirds of rapists were under 30 and that Afro-Caribbeans are strongly over-represented compared with their numbers in the population. Most rape is intra-racial, so the 'true proportion' of rapists from ethnic groups depends on reporting rates, which may differ among ethnic groups but are hardly likely to be much higher among black females than among white ones: Asian and Oriental women stereotypically may be more reluctant to report than other ethnic groups, for reasons of stigma and because they do not wish to involve the police.

In at least 60 per cent of recorded rape and 50 per cent of recorded indecent assault offences in England and Wales in 1989, the suspect knew the victim. Under a third of the rapists were known to be strangers. The Islington Crime Surveys show that about two-thirds of victims knew the offenders, which accounts for the fact that the most common place for rape to occur is in the home. Eight out of ten rapes occurring in the home were at the victim's home, the remainder being at that of the suspect; the corresponding proportion for indecent assaults was seven out of ten. Although rape in some societies is directed towards women who display most independence (Sanday 1981), thereby attracting the explanation that it occurs to keep all women subjugated (Brownmiller 1975), rape in the West occurs disproportionately against young, relatively poor women. Unless they are the target group for subjugation by those males who have few economic goods to exchange for (relative) monogamy, or by wealthy men who do not fear the criminal law or for their social reputation, such a distribution of victims is hard to explain in terms of *collective* male interests.[45] There is insufficient detail to enable most of these instances to be described as 'date rapes', but the data support the argument that the explanation for sexual violence must be sought in male misperceptions of females' attitudes towards them and/or in their beliefs that if they 'go too far' in such situations, the consequences will not be very serious (see Chappell 1989).

On the basis of interviews with American rapists, Scully (1990: 91) observes that rapists have nothing in their background to predict rape specifically but rather are typical of non-white-collar felons, with similar

[45] Natural selection theorists would regard it as nonsensical to suggest that there could be a gene which generated behaviour which benefited a group as a whole. The high proportion of young females as victims, 'explained' by some socio-biologists as an attempt to maximize offenders' reproduction—though today, given female contraception, this would be a maladaptive response—also owes much to their more active night life. Older women go out less, having responsibility for child-care under current gender roles. The situational opportunity factors are omitted from most socio-biological accounts (see e.g. Thornhill and Thornhill 1992).

attitudes towards women, though rapists (and some non-rapists) were particularly prone to have 'double standards' about what they would expect from women. From the perspective of the rapists, almost no act—however brutal—is a 'real' rape and almost no man is a rapist. The key to justifying violence to others (and to themselves) is to make what was in fact rape appear ambivalent in terms of consent. Those who (after conviction) denied rape were less likely to have attacked strangers, to have had a weapon, to be multiple rapists, and to be convicted of group rape: the presence of any of the above factors makes the claim of consent less plausible even to chauvinists.[46] Forty-three per cent of admitters, though 'only' 34 per cent of deniers, were convicted of or admitted to more than one rape.[47] Deniers were likely to understate the amount of violence and to make what they did appear as 'normal' sexual aggression. They were also prone to believe, or at least to assert, that women found them particularly desirable. Among the deniers, almost half stated that they had no feelings at all after the rape; and a quarter each stated that they felt scared and felt satisfied. Admitters, on the other hand, while denying that they themselves were 'essentially' rapists, were much more aware of the emotional impact and took satisfaction in the belief that their victims felt powerless, humiliated, or degraded. Neither group felt guilt or shame during or after the rape, nor did they feel empathy for their victims at the time. Indeed, the desire to dominate a woman is also a major component of rapists' sexual fantasies, though rape in the context of longstanding relationships raises questions about whether men totally depersonalize their victims when they rape them. ('Depersonalization' can be a tautological term in this context.)

Research studies generally link rape to the culture of gender stereotyping and emphasize the variability of motives for rape while stressing—somewhat tautologically—the 'objectification' of women. Some men use rape as a means of revenge and punishment, suggesting the *collective* liability of women. For some, rape is an afterthought or a bonus that they add to a burglary or robbery, as 'another thing to take'. For some, it is a means to gain access to unavailable or unwilling women (such as when a date says 'no'): this is the explanation offered by LaFree (1982) for the substantial rate of black-on-white rape in the USA. Some men rape in groups as a male bonding activity, while others do so to make a fantasy come true to control and dominate impersonally. Women are jokes, objects, targets, sexual commodities: 'pieces of property to be used and conquered . . . Since actions directed at meaningless objects do not evoke

[46] Although in Scully's sample, 69 per cent of those who denied rape had had a weapon or had injured the victim.

[47] The amount of undetected recidivism among British rapists has not been researched, but reconvictions for rape are few: see the discussion of incapacitation later in this chapter.

feelings, emotions fail to constrain their sexually violent behaviour' (Scully, 1990: 166). This is an important contribution to our understanding of the mindsets of rapists and their relationship with the general culture. However, socio-cultural explanations grossly overpredict the amount of rape, and even individuals' attitudes towards women fail to account for the fact that few rapists rape as frequently as our analysis of their individual and gendered value systems would lead us to expect. The question of why most men who could rape do not do so remains unresolved. One could hypothesize that non-rapists fear more than rapists for their social reputations, for the expected future feelings of the prospective victim, or for the direct and indirect socio-economic consequences of arrest and conviction; but these concepts lack analytical specificity. The natural selection hypothesis that rape is an historical adaptation which substitutes for lawful access to reproductive mates is difficult to falsify, but many rapists do in fact enjoy access to consenting (or at least uncomplaining) females, and their generalized aggressiveness to people and to property suggests that 'the selfish gene' is not restricted to the desire to reproduce genetically.

The Culture of Masculinity and Violence Involving the Police

Comments from senior police officers and politicians, and media reports of violent incidents, sometimes depict violent outcomes as the result of interactive social processes, but they normally have little difficulty in blaming the public (or rather, some 'hooligan' section of the public which is hostile to the police). By contrast, in the specific area of violence in which police are hurt, early American research by Toch (1969) observed that many police victims of assault become so because they are personally insecure and wish to prove to themselves and others that they are 'real men' by daring others to defy them. (In societies such as the USA with ready recourse to fatal weapons this desperate search for challenges can be very dangerous.) This explanatory approach is also generalized to other contexts, such as inmate–inmate and inmate–officer violence in prison:

> The term 'brawling' is used advisedly, because, as this man sees it, his conflicts with officers are 'fights'. In other words, they are disputes which are settled physically, as disputes must be settled among men. This view is partially shared and reinforced by the officers, who repeatedly describe in vivid detail the wrestling holds they deploy to neutralize the man . . . The man is said to have 'communication problems' and these are reciprocal . . . The central issue often appears to be that the man feels himself treated like a child, and that his version of *machismo* holds that no man must be ordered about by another man, and that it is demeaning and insulting to be told to do things, particularly when you have explained why you do not wish to do them or would have explained if you could have.

The issue of the man's reactions to uniforms does not necessarily enter the equation because the man sees encounters between himself and officers as personal, and perceives custodial instructions as originating in whims and expressions of disdain or disrespect. When the man feels disdained or disrespected in this way he reacts at the first available opportunity, which makes his behaviour unpredictable, because his reaction does not necessarily coincide with the move that originates the offence to which he reacts. (Toch 1979: 272–3)

Some might seek to dismiss the Toch approach to explaining police-precipitated assaults as the product of 'American culture': British Bobbies are immune from such identity problems! But we should not be surprised that *some* British police should have these masculinity anxieties and express them through challenges to 'hard men' in the community. Police officers still come predominantly from the working classes, who are shown by most reliable evidence to be more likely to behave violently and to be tolerant of physical aggression. Police recruits are prone to have authoritarian views about the social value of conformity under authority, and they are socialized into a 'street cop' subculture in which the vital importance of 'controlling the beat', by force if 'necessary', is emphasized (Reiner 1992). Police recruiting officers claim that they root out the 'rogue' officers at the initial entry and probation stages, but there is an inherent tension in the police culture between the need to avoid 'unnecessarily aggressive' policing by sustaining the 'peace officer' role and the belief that at times one needs to act positively and show command, 'law officer' qualities.[48] Poor pay in the 1970s led to some 'tough' officers who might not now be selected attaining managerial positions from which they exert 'negative peer influence' on their colleagues. Consequently, the 'higher quality' entrants from the 1980s and 1990s find themselves faced with a choice between joining the 'rough' subculture that is scattered around or seeking to remain aloof and risking isolation from their colleagues and supervisors.

A focus on the *police* contribution to their own victimization—which I label here the 'public-excusing theory'—would therefore follow the lines of a general or force or area or shift police subculture in which aggressive policing was encouraged or, at least, was not actively *dis*couraged. Adherents to this 'Dirty Harry' subculture believe—along with detectives who 'strengthen' evidence against those they 'know' to be guilty—that unless they act firmly 'things will get out of hand', and that they must especially clamp down on 'known troublemakers' in their area who set a bad example to others by demonstrating 'contempt of cop'. How do they know who the troublemakers are? Every police officer who joins an area has these individuals or families pointed out to him by supervisors either

[48] The times at which the latter are deemed appropriate vary considerably between officers of the same and different ranks.

in the police station or out on the beat. Other prime candidates are young 'ethnics', bikers, and other potential 'rowdies'. So, the 'public-excusing' theory would have us believe that the police pick on those who either are labelled for them by prior personal or subculture-derived prejudicial stereotypes, or in some other way fail to show the right attitude to police control over the area or to the seriousness of their offence.

By contrast, the 'public-blaming' theory would maintain that in the great majority of cases of assault on police, members of the public who may be more generally anti-social and anti-authority become the worse for wear on drink and, fortified by the low penalties attached to attacks (principally a small fine) as well as by the expected low (and lower than in 'the old days') probability of bystander intervention on behalf of the police, indulge in untrammelled violence which is generally unprovoked by any misconduct on the part of the police. Assailants are hostile members of the public who without any good reason attack the police who are just doing their job in a normal, restrained way. In the minds of the beleaguered officers, the large amount of low-level verbal abuse and hostility to their presence in some licensed premises and city centres late at night makes it necessary to intervene to stop these districts turning into 'no-go' areas. Whether or not police and public are right in believing that there is less respect for the police nowadays and that society is getting more violent, these beliefs impinge upon police anxieties about loss of control and can result in 'heavy-handed policing', particularly if (a) their supervisory and senior officers encourage 'active' policing and (b) the members of the public they are dealing with are seen as 'criminal' and/or 'anti-police' types who belong to a 'subculture of violence'. It is tempting to explain the rise in assaults against the police since the tranquil early 1950s in terms of the greater ease with which modern communications enable a police officer to get to the scene of the 'disturbance' while it is still in its upswing: a view with which some older police officers concur. However, this is to ignore the high assault rates in the period 1850–1927, when communications were slow. To the extent that assaults against the police *have* been increasing in recent years, this may also be because police legitimacy in the eyes of the public has diminished—something which the police acknowledge has happened but do not usually attribute to a general deterioration in police behaviour—and/or because the police have become less skilful in the handling of relations with the public (see *Which* 1990; Skogan 1990; Reiner 1992). The process of desubordination to authority is a generalized feature which is implicated in assaults against a variety of personnel—police, prison officers, social workers, teachers—all of whom pose a threat to the desire for autonomy. This may be extended to others who threaten or are expected, reasonably or unreasonably, to threaten in the future the self-gratification of the offender. Looked at in this way, what may look like individual paranoia may be understood to have some socio-cultural roots.

Some, though comparatively few, assaults appear to be wholly unrelated to anything the individual officer—or possibly any other officer—did at that time or in the past: they are 'out of the blue' attacks on strangers and it cannot be stated with confidence whether the wearing of the police uniform or the officer's interpersonal skills made any difference to the individual's propensity to assault. (The police may have displaced violence from some other target of—to me, inexplicable—anger.) Others are clearly motivated by the desire to escape arrest and its consequences, though the large number of recorded assaults in police vans and stations would appear to be irrational methods of achieving that objective. More generally, however, interviews with assailants and observation of police work support Toch's (1969) view that the way the police approach the public—such as appearing to pick on them, making them face humiliation in front of their friends or their girlfriends to whom they wish to present a tough image;[49] or standing physically very close, thereby (a) winding them up psychologically, and (b) bringing themselves within ready head-butting range—is an important dimension in understanding assaults against the police.

Katz (1988) plausibly argues that the kind of 'high' or 'righteous rage' experienced by those who are violent is a significant phenomenon, and it may be that the relatively high rate of violent reoffending in our sample (Christopher *et al.* 1989) is evidence of the reinforcing effect of such pleasure as well as of the tendency of police to single out those diagnosed by them as 'dangerous offenders' (or 'scumbags') when they threaten to misbehave in public. Bernard (1990) likewise concludes that a subculture of angry aggression arises under conditions when serious social disadvantage is combined with individual social isolation.[50]

At the level of individual incidents and area/class rates of violence, police attitudes towards the public and public attitudes towards the police, the *general* violence-using styles of citizens, and lifestyles which expose people to differential risks of negative encounters with the police are all salient. Beyond this, however, it remains easier to disentangle and demystify the background behind the social control of violence against the police than to explain why some people commit it when they do. This applies to most forms of violent crime, as I have noted above. It seems undeniable that some people obtain powerful reinforcement from the

[49] Research suggests that most of those who are convicted of assault against the police have friends present with them who believe that such behaviour is justified (Christopher *et al.* 1989).

[50] See also Shepherd (1990) for similar conclusions reached from an interesting survey of hospital casualty admissions in Bristol.

pleasure of causing pain, and it may be simply chance or, more likely, subculturally approved or at least ambiguous values, which determines whether rape or armed robbery or overseas war or all three represent the venue within which that 'high' is obtained and reinforced. Peer activity routines, once established, are likely to account for the immense social class and status group and gender variations in the prevalence of all these different forms of violence. Let us now turn to what research indicates about individual involvement in violence.

Individual-level Predictors of Violence

Self-reports of offending suggest that assault is quite prevalent: only 12 per cent of males (and 33 per cent of those males who had a conviction) in an inner city were convicted of violent offences between the ages of 10 and 32, but even when violence was decreasing—between ages 27 and 32—over a third admitted physical assault (Farrington 1989). In London, 70 per cent of offenders with a conviction for violence were convicted for only one offence of violence. (Similar findings exist for Scandinavia, but the proportion of recidivists is greater in the USA.) These data suggest that individual-level accounts of violent crime must cope with enormous variation in the frequency of violence among those who do behave violently.

Even given a conventional view of what constitutes 'violent crime' (Wilson and Herrnstein 1985), controversy rages about the role of genetic factors. Some people behave violently for a long time in a variety of settings: although the manifestations of aggression vary, a child who is top of the distribution for aggression at age 8 is likely to be near the top twenty years later. Psychological research has tended to focus upon the role of 'temperament', which is obscure in origin but seems to be a relatively stable phenomenon. Children who are extremely inhibited or uninhibited at twenty-one months are likely to be similarly classified at age 7.5. Farrington (1989) has argued that when they are children, violent offenders tend to be high on hyperactivity–impulsivity–attention deficit, tend to be restless and lacking in concentration, lack empathy (the ability to identify with others' feelings), and find it difficult to defer gratification. This may look like a caricature of the 'feckless poor' but is an *intra*-class discriminator of aggression levels.

There is much popular belief in the intergenerational aspect of child abuse, but even if the great majority of 'child abusers' were abused children, it would be possible that only a tiny proportion of abused children grow up to abuse their children. Many child-abusing parents misperceive their children's culpability and treat the baby as if it were an adult who 'made a mess' *deliberately* (Frude 1989); however, some children are objectively more difficult to handle, cry more, and give less affection, thereby making a cycle of escalating violence more probable. Situational opportunity variables are also salient to baby-battering: modern nuclear families are far more isolated than extended families found in many Third World countries, where parents are seldom alone in the house. (Different considerations apply to physical punishment of older children, who are considered in many cultures, in extended or in nuclear families, to be properly blameworthy and 'reformable' by being beaten. Systematic incest patterns also are found in extended families.)

Are violent offenders specialists? Because of the distortions generated by non-reporting and non-prosecution of family violence (and injuries in the workplace), criminal career data based on official statistics are prone to specific distortions. American research suggests that violent offenders have longer criminal careers and are less likely to stop in the early stages of their offending than are property criminals (Blumstein *et al.* 1986). Nearly all London offenders studied by Farrington (1989) were convicted of non-violent as well as violent crimes, and only a quarter of their crimes were violent. Essentially, then, violent offenders are frequent 'generalist' offenders. They commit their violent offences at a later age than their property offences. In London, the majority of juvenile violent offenders did go on to commit adult violent offences (and most of those who did not committed non-violent offences as adults). Home Office (1989) data on the prospective and retrospective criminal careers of rapists suggest similar generalized offending. Of those convicted of rape in 1985, 55 per cent had previous convictions for theft and 43 per cent for burglary.[51] Though many of these offences will have been against men, just under half had previous convictions for one or more offences involving violence: a third of these were for sexual offences, but only 3 per cent had rape convictions.

However, since the majority of offenders are not convicted of more than one violent offence, ideas such as 'careers of violence' are not very useful, at least outside the family context and, it is suggested, among some *extra*-familial paedophiles. Even within the family violence context, there are dangers in generalizing from the repetitive violence suffered by women who go to refuges and those interviewed by researchers such as Dobash and Dobash (1979) to recidivism in attacks on wives generally. Fagan's (1989) review of the cessation of family violence notes that three-quarters of spouse abusers stop following legal sanctions, but for how long they stop is uncertain, since the follow-up periods are not long. The shorter the time before cessation and the less severe the battering, the more likely people are to stop beating. (Sherman and Smith 1992, observe

[51] No statistics are kept, but in the UK, unlike the USA, burglary–rape is rare.

that this effect is found only for 'respectable' batterers.) These findings of low recidivism for violence (see also Farrington, Chapter 12 in this volume) have, or ought to have, important implications for those who believe in 'incapacitating the violent offender'.

Psychological approaches to explaining individual-level violence have moved from the relatively crude frustration–aggression approach (later refined to suggest that frustration raises arousal which may be interpreted as anger), through social learning theory (Bandura 1973), according to which aggression is learned vicariously through watching unless accompanied by punishment (though this too has been criticized for overinterpretation of play as aggression), to more cognitive and behavioural theories. Huessman and Eron (1989) argue that aggressive behaviour is largely controlled by programmes or 'scripts' about what events are likely to occur, how the person should react to the events, and what will result. These 'scripts' have been learned during the child's early development and are retrieved from memory on the appropriate environmental cues. Children are likely to be influenced by parents' own cognitive processes, so people who are 'paranoid' and view the world as hostile reinforce the child's scripts. (People may learn 'rape scripts' in a like manner.) Such individual-level accounts emphasize the interactive nature of much violent behaviour, although the behavioural cues which 'trigger' the violent conduct may vary not only with the general cognitive state of that person but also with the drugs, including alcohol and tranquillizers, that s/he has consumed. In research on non-sexual child abuse, for example, Frude (1989) notes that the child's behaviour may influence the aggression levels of the parent(s) and may also provide a less responsive feedback to parental discipline methods, though the negative attitudes of parents towards their children, as well as factors such as social isolation, poverty, etc., were salient to the risk of abuse.

Toch (1969) has usefully distinguished several types of violent offender: the 'self-image demonstrator', who uses violence to demonstrate toughness which he believes will be admired by his peers; the 'self-image defender', who tends to feel easily slighted or disparaged and will react to defend his ego; and the 'reputation defender', who acts as a member of a group to defend the values of the group when s/he believes them to be threatened. All these involve various methods of coping with fragile self-concepts: this fragility may be linked to class or status-group, in so far as those who are used to commanding social resources and respect may be less prone than poor whites or people of colour to having their self-image undermined. On the other hand, some high-status people expect respect and may react aggressively—for example, by firing staff or 'freezing' partners—when contradicted or thwarted: whether this ever comes to be defined as 'violence' or 'violent crime' depends upon what they do and how they do it.

'SUBSTANCE ABUSE' AND VIOLENT CRIME

Most people know others who behave much more aggressively when they have been drinking heavily or, much more rarely, while under the influence of illegal drugs. Though some violent offenders report (to this author) that they choose to get 'tanked up' with alcohol to put themselves in an appropriate mood for the fight they desire anyway (that is, drink is an enjoyment enhancer as a well as disinhibitor), heavy drinking permeates almost every venue in which violence occurs. However, it is very rare for such people to be violent every time that they consume those substances, so it cannot be said, for example, that the drink is a sufficient or even a necessary explanation of their violence, even if one disregards powerful cross-cultural evidence that the relationship between substance use and aggression depends upon social norms and expectations (Collins 1989; Fagan 1990). Adolescents who drink or use drugs are more likely than those who do not to commit violent acts. Likewise, there is a positive correlation between (a) the severity and frequency of violent delinquency and (b) the seriousness and frequency of drug-taking (Fagan 1990). American research indicates a positive relationship between alcohol use and violence, both against wives (Frieze and Browne 1989) and generally. British research indicates a strong relationship between crimes of violence and beer consumption (Field 1990), though this may be an artefact of street violence occurring where young people cluster and become embroiled in disputes when they leave drinking places (Tuck 1989). Drinking and drug-taking can be indulged in as trauma-free fun, but although some offenders are part of a peer culture in which 'handling it' without aggression is expected, frequent 'poly-substance abusers' tend to be people with low self-esteem who find it difficult to confront problems in relationships. Common accompaniments are violence to self and to others, as well as generalized aggression. Collins (1989) observes that individuals with alcohol disorders frequently have other personality disorders, including crippling anxiety or sudden changes in relationships and mood.

As regards illicit substances, though there may be 'commercial' violence resulting from a desire to dominate drugs distribution or extort money from sellers, there is no evidence that the *pharmacological* effect of cannabis, hallucinogens, or opiates makes people violent: if anything, the reverse is true. There is a more plausible link between violence and amphetamines and solvents but, as with alcohol, demonstrating the causal link is confounded by the intervening personality variables. A thoughtful overview by Fagan concludes that

> intoxication affects cognitive processes that shape and interpret perceptions of both one's own physiology (i.e. expectancy) and the associated behavioral

response. The cognitive processes themselves are influenced by cultural and situational factors that determine the norms, beliefs, and sanctions regarding behaviors following intoxication . . . Propensity toward aggression reflects explanations regarding the use of personal power to resolve perceived conflicts. (Fagan 1990: 299)

DEALING WITH VIOLENT CRIME

It is not my objective here to set out a normative account for how 'we' should deal with the large range of offences grouped artificially as 'violent crime', but some brief comments on the implications of theory and data for strategies of control are appropriate.[52] Clearly, there are major differences in modes of control, depending on whether one believes in punishing wrongdoing because it is retributively just to do so or whether one is seeking primarily to reduce future violence. Many people believe that severe penalties will achieve both objectives, but the evidence for this is scant. As regards retribution, it may be pointed out that in the area of corporate 'violence' at work and 'risky motoring', retributivism has never been practised as a dominant response: a socially equitable approach to retributivism would require a massive expansion of resources in prosecuting corporate crime, but Braithwaite and Pettit (1990) argue that this would lead to less rather than more safety. As regards reducing the rate of violent crime, it seems evident that some major socio-economic and cultural changes need to occur: the question is how we get from here to there.

Field (1990) suggests that the strong relationship between violent crime and per capita consumption reflects the fact that affluence leads people to go out more, increasing their risk of victimization, while a reduction in unemployment slightly counteracts what otherwise would be a stronger rise in violence. But going beyond the mechanical lifestyle risk approach—opportunities to go out drinking are not a *sufficient* condition for crime—the general social and economic insecurity in the 1980s and 1990s is plausibly connected with an increased prevalence of tensions in interpersonal relationships, which sometimes give rise to violent behaviour—some of it unrecorded, in the home—as well as to verbal aggression and unhappiness. Battles between drug-dealers in criminally disorganized neighbourhoods apart, the cultural focus on highly competitive individual enterprise characteristic of the Thatcher and Reagan eras may not have directly caused any increase in violence: no minister has stated that eliminating one's competitors *physically* was a socially approved method of

[52] I shall deal with only some aspects of the prevention of violence: see further Farrell (1992) and Pease, Chapter 14 in this volume.

wealth creation. However, the devaluation of the social and the caring in favour of the 'stressed society' (albeit with 'individual responsibility') as a method of freeing up the spirit of enterprise may have made it easier for people so inclined to excuse their own violence. Whether such verbalizations really increase (or are necessary conditions for) violent crime or any other type of crime, or whether their role is mainly to make offenders feel better about themselves, is a fundamental analytical problem for social explanation.

We do not know whether the fall in female workforce participation due to the recession has exacerbated family violence (by making households poorer and therefore more tense, as well as giving women fewer options for leaving) or has eased it (by reassuring the machismo spouses that their control of women is not under threat). But despite official acceptance of the ideology of equal opportunities for women, the power of the imagery of the 'traditional family' remains great, and in the opinion of some men justifies male control over women. Moreover, the cultural expectation continues among working-class males that fighting is a central method of attaining and maintaining social prestige. The virtual abolition of opportunities for traditional unskilled labouring work has reduced the incentives for conformity, but those unacquainted with the role of socialization and prevalent social controls might be surprised that violence (and crime for gain) among the underclass is so low, rather than that it is so high.

There is evidence to suggest that a focus upon multiple victims is a sensible as well as a humane approach to crime reduction. As regards domestic violence, initial research in the USA suggested that irrespective of subsequent action, a routine arrest policy might have a preventive effect on repeat offenders. However, replications of that research have found that arrest had no overall effect on reducing repeat violence, whether measured by victim interviews or by official statistics. Indeed, possibly because it made them more angry at their partners, arrests *increased* recidivism among unemployed and unmarried people with a low stake in conformity, though it reduced it among the married and employed (see *inter alia* Sherman and Smith 1992.) The research suggests that legal controls depend upon a bedrock of commitment to informal control rather than being an effective substitute for it.

At the level of penal policy, violent crime has long been at the forefront of debate, being used as a superficially coherent category to justify severe sanctions on all principles of punishment, the dominant principle being that which yields the greatest severity. For example, where, as for most 'domestic murderers', the expected reoffending rate is extremely low and there is little to suggest either an individual or a general deterrent point in severe punishment, denunciatory and retributivist principles—

sometimes allied with assertions about general deterrent 'needs'—are used to justify not letting offenders out at the earliest possible date. (Though such offenders typically are released earlier than others.) Where the expected reoffending rate is higher, incapacitative principles are added to this list, particularly where retributive grounds alone would not be sufficient to keep someone in custody. The Criminal Justice Act 1991 makes mandatory the just deserts approach to sentencing, but how one works out the 'proper' rank ordering and absolute levels of just sentencing in an unjust society is a subject on which there is little consensus, despite much debate.[53] Despite relaxations in the desert principles and in the salience of previous convictions, under the Act special rules apply to sexual and violent crime, which enable sentencers lawfully to take into account expected future harm as well as past harm.[54]

Despite the rhetoric of seriousness with which violent crime is surrounded, the fine is actually the most common sentence for violence, even for offences such as assaulting the police which might have been expected to attract magisterial wrath. Governments have hitherto (1993) resisted the abolition of the mandatory life sentence for murder, but the growth in convictions for violent crime and the long sentences such offenders serve means that roughly four-fifths of the long-term prison population are inside for violence. This includes rapists, who almost never receive non-custodial sentences and whose sentence lengths have been increasing during the 1980s and 1990s.[55] Whether many offences of rape and violence other than for financial gain are really deterrable by long sentences is questionable: if 'power' is really the motivation, then why should a

[53] For non-conservative advocates of retributivism, see further von Hirsch (1986) and Ashworth (1992).

[54] This is the latest stage in the 'bifurcation tendency' in punishment which has occurred over this past two decades. S. 2 (2) of the Criminal Justice Act 1991 states: '(2) The custodial sentence shall be (a) for such term (not exceeding the permitted maximum) as in the opinion of the court is commensurate with the seriousness of the offence, or the combination of the offence and other offences associated with it; or (b) where the offence is a violent or a sexual offence, for such longer term (not exceeding that maximum) as in the opinion of the court is necessary to protect the public from serious harm from the offender.' It is unlikely that judges would construe health and safety offences as 'violent crime' within this sub-section.

[55] In 1990, the median sentence for rape was six years; sixteen out of 538 offenders sentenced were not jailed or given hospital orders, though such cases understandably receive heavy publicity. Whereas in 1984, 30 per cent of convicted rapists received sentences of five years or longer, by 1987, following the guideline judgement *R.* v. *Billam* [1986] 1 WLR 349, the proportion receiving such sentences rose to 80 per cent in 1987. In *Attorney-General's Reference (No. 7 of 1989)* [1990] 12 Cr App R (S) 1, a man convicted of the rape of his former cohabitee had a two-year sentence increased to four and a half years. Armed bank robbers would expect to get longer sentences, and retributivists might find this to be wrong, though on pure deterrence grounds the difference might be defensible. Box (1983) and others are technically correct in asserting that most rapists do not go to prison, but only in the grossly misleading tautological sense that unconvicted offenders do not receive custodial sentences.

five-year spell deter more than, say, a short prison sentence? If the motivation is more sex than power, then a large means-related fine ought to have the same (or no less) effect, provided that it was much greater than the cost of equivalent 'commercial sex'. There are strong retributivist grounds for punishing rapists severely, but there is nothing in research on the impact of violence on actual victims or on the general public (via fear of crime) to suggest that those who commit sexual or non-sexual violence against women are *uniquely* appropriate targets for severe retribution. Treatment programmes for sex offenders have been very poorly provided for in the past, though they are now widespread (Barker and Morgan 1993), and claims for effectiveness by entrepreneurs are largely unsubstantiated (West 1983). (For a review of programmes on violence against women, see Dobash and Dobash 1992.)

Incapacitating the Violent Offender

Most of the sentencing debate has been over what do about serious violence (excluding serious corporate and motoring 'violence'), where—at least among academics, who seem more troubled than politicians about justifications for punishment—arguments rage about whether 'dangerous offending' can be predicted and what accuracy of prediction would justify keeping people in custody to prevent future crimes (Floud and Young 1981; Haapanen 1990). Morris and Miller (1985: 15–16) note that 'with the best possible predictions of violent behavior we can expect to make one true positive prediction of violence to the person for every two false positive predictions', but go on to observe that a group of three people, one of whom will soon commit an act of serious violence, is a very dangerous group indeed. To cause problems for the most liberal of consciences, we have only to consider what we would do about someone who had 'only' committed an assault but warned us that he would kill us personally if he had the chance. Dangerousness is a probabilistic condition, not an event, and even if the person does not turn out to injure someone, s/he may remain 'dangerous' to some degree. (It is helpful to think of dangerousness/non-dangerousness as a spectrum of risk rather than as a binary concept.)

Morris and Miller (1985: 21) observe that the 'societal decision, the moral decision, is not whether to place the burden of avoiding the risk on the false positives, but how to balance the risk of harm to society and the certain intrusion on the liberty of each member of the preventively detained group. At some level of predicted harms from the group, the intrusions on each individual's liberty may be justified.' The decision may, however, be affected by confidence in the accuracy of the predictions, though we seldom have the opportunity of discovering what those incapacitated would have done had they been released, thereby making it difficult to test the validity of our expectancy rates. Morris and Miller argue that it is proper to take the dangerousness of the group into account in sentencing, provided that no individual is sentenced to longer than s/he otherwise would have deserved and that individuals are properly allocated to the groups estimated as dangerous. However, s. 2(2)(b) of the Criminal Justice Act 1991 specifically permits individuals to be sentenced for longer than they retributively deserve on the basis of their perceived individual dangerousness. How the criteria involved in that prediction are to be regulated is in the hands of the Court of Appeal (Sentencing Division) and the Judicial Studies Board.

Setting aside the question of whether in theory we ought to (or in practice would be likely to) incapacitate rapists but not other offenders, the general incapacitative grounds for imposing long rape sentences in the UK are not very strong. An early study of sexual offending showed that reoffending rates for sexual violence were low (Radzinowicz, 1957). A neglected study by Soothill *et al.* (1976) shows that the reoffending rate for rapists convicted in 1951 was 6 per cent over a 22-year follow-up period, although those rapists who did reoffend were just as dangerous a decade after their conviction as they had been earlier. The Home Office (1989) study of 264 people convicted of rape in 1972 showed that nine of them had been reconvicted of rape within five years of discharge, and twelve, i.e. 4.5 per cent, by 1985.[56] These are very low figures by comparison with other offenders.

It is possible that both the proportion of the population who offend and the number of violent offences they commit may be greater today than they used to be: the rate of violent offending by the cohort born in 1958 in Philadelphia exceeded that of the 1945 Philadelphia cohort by a factor of 3:1 for homicide, 1.7:1 for rape; and 2:1 for aggravated assault and burglary, and they were more likely than the 1945 cohort to be violent recidivists (Tracy *et al.* 1990: 276, 281). The 7.5 per cent of the 1958 cohort described as 'chronic offenders' accounted for 61 per cent of the homicides, 75 per cent of the rapes, 73 per cent of the robberies, and 65 per cent of the aggravated assaults: the 1945 'chronics' had committed an even higher proportion of cleared-up violent crimes, presumably because violence was more widespread among the later group. In contemporary British sexual culture, and despite longer sentences,[57] the rate of

[56] Over a quarter were reconvicted for violence within five years of discharge, one in five for theft and one in six for burglary: this supports the view that rape is part of a general profile of aggression, not all of it towards women. Altogether, one in three convicted of rape were reconvicted for some offence within two years and 54 per cent within five years of discharge. Even these percentages are lower than for offenders generally.

[57] If Sherman and Smith's (1992) finding that arresting those without major social ties for domestic violence *increased* their hostility applies also to rape, the rise in reoffending might be partly *because* of longer sentences.

reoffending may be higher among those convicted today than it was among the 1951 and 1972 rape cohorts: but there is no evidence yet that it actually is higher, and certainly none that it is as high as it is among American sex offenders, up to a third of whom commit further rapes after release.

Some of the rapists in the reconviction studies—like any other set of offenders—are likely to have committed other, unreported crimes against women or, because the prosecution was not allowed to tell the jury of their prior sexual convictions, may have escaped conviction or even prosecution for rapes they had in fact committed. But given the police predilection for 'rounding up the usual suspects' for serious offences like rape which have a high police priority once recorded, their unconvicted recidivism would have to be enormous to bring the rape reoffending rate up to one quarter. Home Office (1989) data indicate that 'only' 3 per cent of those convicted of rape in 1985 had previous convictions for rape, so even if they were incapacitated, this alone would have little impact upon the total volume of rape unless there were also a general deterrent effect.

As regards the effect on the homicide rate of incapacitating killers, it is significant that fewer than 2 per cent of those convicted for homicide in 1989 had previous convictions for killing: this does not, of course, reflect the *inherent* unlikelihood of homicides to reoffend—for more might have killed again if they had been released earlier—but the number of 'repeat killers' constituted 0.03 per cent of the number of released killers at liberty altogether. Those who killed strangers were much more likely than those who killed acquaintances to have been convicted of some form of crime before, and they were twice as likely as those who killed a family member to have been convicted before. Whether family killers would be more likely to have previous convictions if their previous involvements in 'domestic' violence had been prosecuted is unknown, but their 43 per cent previous conviction rate is not far above the norm for males. Offenders convicted of s. 2 (diminished responsibility) manslaughter within the family had the lowest percentage of prior convictions (28 per cent), which actually is lower than the average for the male population at large. (We should note that 7 per cent of the male population have convictions for violence by age 31.) Of those convicted of homicide, only one in six had previous convictions for offences of violence against the person, sexual offences, or robbery, so unless there is a general deterrent effect as well as an incapacitative one, the homicide rate would be reduced by 'only' one-sixth even if one kept out of circulation every convicted violent offender. (Though among those with six or more previous convictions, 75 per cent had at least one prior conviction for violence.)

What does the reoffending rate have to be to justify general incapacitation for violent crime? This is a political (and financial) question, but in anything approaching a rational world, information about risks ought to be relevant to it. There remains the possibility of refining categories of violent offender so that we can discover which 'sorts of people' are most likely to become serial rapists or killers, but the claims made for offender profiling far outstrip their actual predictive value, particularly in the UK where sufficiently detailed information on offenders has not been kept. With the possible exception of men who have sex with young boys outside their families, who appear (from self-reports in the USA) to be the most recidivistic among any set of violent and/or sex offenders (Abel *et al.* 1987), this is true *a fortiori* of the selective incapacitation of particular individuals within these categories of violence. It is generally agreed that the diagnosis of individuals as 'dangerous' by clinicians has very little basis (Brody and Tarling, 1981): a serious problem also for the theory of parole decisions as individualized rehabilitation judgements.

More generally, the dilemmas in what we decide to do about violence or any other type of crime depend on how painful our interventions are to those who have offended or whom we predict will become offenders. There are far fewer objections to crime reduction strategies if our predictions lead us to improve the quality of life and job prospects in inner cities, and/or to provide better lighting and transport for residents and potential victims, than if they lead us to play 'electronic tag' with those who might go out at night and commit offences, or to keep relatively minor offenders in prison for lengthy periods in case they commit further offences. Those involved in parole and sentencing decisions, particularly politicians, are usually much more afraid of being blamed for letting out someone who reoffends than they are of keeping someone inside whom no one will ever know would *not* have reoffended. That is the personal and political reality which underlies the continuing popularity of incapacitation for violent crime.

CONCLUSIONS

Few of the accounts of violent crime examined in this review are mutually exclusive, though they may have been competing for theoretical and ideological primacy as models of how we should go about the task of explanation and how we determine what the most serious forms of violence are. I have stressed, perhaps *ad nauseam*, the enormous variation within that all too often simplified term, 'violent crime'. Much of the criminological progress during the 1980s and 1990s has been in refining our understanding of the risks of crime for different groups and the way in which this relates to their lifestyles. Fuelled by feminist research and campaigns for action, fear of crime and the impact of crime on victims (see Zedner Chapter 25 in this volume) have been major growth areas of study.

By contrast with this focus on 'the victim', the causes of violence have received comparatively little criminological attention. This is not simply because victims are easier to get to (both physically and mentally) than are offenders and because the discovery of the victim has been a major area of criminal policy interest. In part it also reflects the greater theoretical simplicity of generating interesting facts about patterns of victimization than of explaining fundamentally why violence happens where and when it does (and not in other places at other times). The 'ethos of masculinity' is one analytical thread that runs through much of the etiological discussion, but though the concept of machismo may be theoretically coherent, it is far from being theoretically complete: it is not readily applied in practice and its completeness, in my judgement, would require us to account for (a) the non-violence of all males most of the time, and (b) the non-violence of the majority of adult working-class and middle-class males all of the time. The personal and cultural dynamics of what constitutes a challenge 'requiring' a violent response have been explored, and have been accounted for largely in terms of sophisticated social learning theory, including expectancy theory. Although it seems inappropriate to dignify with the sobriquet 'rational' the decision to head-butt a complete stranger because 'I didn't like the way he looked' (and, in some cases, to do this fairly regularly to other strangers), much apparently 'mindless' violent behaviour is understandable in the context of the emotional needs of offenders for respect, which may have its psychodynamic roots in miserable (and/or misogynistic) family relationships but may also often have functional consequences for that person's status and control within the family and/or peer group. (Although men in prison, for example, are expected to be able to handle much 'hassle' without immediate explosion.) Though it may also attract the hostile attention of police or prison officers, a reputation for extreme violence may be very useful in deterring other predators in 'dangerous' neighbourhoods or prisons, and in obtaining, by extortion, money or sex. Violence is more functional to those who practise it in poor neighbourhoods than in middle-class ones, where self-control is valued and aggression is more likely to be channelled into business competition (which may have unintended consequences for workers, consumers, or environmental safety). The poor go in for punch-ups in pubs; upper-class 'hearties' do so on the field at Twickenham or on rugby or rowing club 'binges'; while in review articles such as this, the punier among the academicians parody delinquent gang members by 'trashing' the analytic abilities of their rivals, or fight for their friends' academic reputations. Each group has its own culturally approved outlets for aggression.[58]

Outside of a wartime context of ethnic or national oppression,[59] serial killers or rapists cannot properly be described as 'normal' personalities, though before being arrested they may not be identified by workmates or families as 'weirdos' (or as any more weird than many non-serial rapists or killers). Few of even the most hardened chauvinists or 'rape myth subscribers' would seek to justify such serial violence in peacetime, and offenders receive almost no cultural support, since their behaviour lacks any remotely plausible pretence of ambiguity. Without a climate in which sexual anxieties and 'double standard' expectations of women were prevalent, there would be far fewer cases in which women became the 'appropriate' victims of delusions of power and humiliation. But the fact that most known violence occurs between young working-class males suggests that violence has both expressive and instrumental functions in status competition between males, as well as having the intended or unintended value of 'keeping women in their place'.

We have learned a great deal in recent decades about patterns of violent behaviour and the factors that influence them, such as social class, ethnicity, and gender. The learning from role models on screen and in (ever more fractured) families and neighbourhoods about how to respond to tensions, plus differences in individual temperament and life circumstances, play a major part in accounting for variations in rates of violence. Retrospective accounts by killers and rapists help us to make sense of 'why it happened'. However, why—outside of learned and/or biological gender variations—people, even sometimes those from the same family and brought up apparently similarly, turn out to have different temperaments and cognitive sets remains mysterious. Becker (1973), in an attempt to mitigate attacks on the idea that the labelling of people as 'criminals' intensified their involvement in crime, observed that he had not really meant to put forward a 'theory', merely a 'perspective' in which he would 'illuminate things formerly obscure'. This introductory overview has posed more questions than it has answered, but I am less apologetic than was Becker for these theoretical inadequacies: violent crime is a subject which is usually accompanied by more heat than light, and the

[58] Personally, I would rather receive a bad academic review, however unmerited, than have my face smashed in.

[59] Examples of the former include the alleged rapes of thousands of Muslim women by Serbs during the fight over Bosnia in 1992–3 (see Brownmiller 1975 on earlier wars). The complex of motives include the desire to humiliate and demoralize the enemy; the desire to increase one's own and group reproduction rate by inseminating 'the enemy's womenfolk'—pregnant women appear deliberately to have been spared from being raped (*The Independent*, 8 February 1993); and the heightened erotic sense that, among males, sometimes accompanies total power.

specification of areas of uncertainty is worthwhile in itself. If this discussion of the causes of violent crime is ultimately unsatisfying, much of the reason lies in the inherent difficulty of teasing out the interaction between the myriad influences on human aggression and its specific outlet in violent crimes of different kinds. Whether ultimately it will be possible to resolve these difficulties is a subject for a much larger analytical project.

Selected Further Reading

T. Bernard, 'Angry Aggression among the 'Truly Disadvantaged', *Criminology*, 1990, 28/1: 73–93.

M. Daly and M. Wilson, *Homicide*. New York: de Gruyter, 1988.

L. Davidoff and L. Dowds, 'Recent Trends in Crimes of Violence against the Person in England and Wales', *Home Office Research Bulletin*, 1989, 27: 11–17.

R. E. Dobash and R. P. Dobash, *Women, Violence, and Social Change*. London: Routledge, 1992.

D. Farrington, 'Childhood Aggression and Adult Violence: Early Precursors and Later Life Outcomes', in D. Pepler and K. Rubin, eds., *The Development and Treatment of Childhood Aggression*. Hillsdale, NJ: Erlbaum, 1991.

K. Howells and C. Hollin, eds., *Clinical Approahces to Violence*. Chichester: John Wiley.

J. Katz, *The Seductions of Crime: The Moral and Sensual Attractions of Doing Evil*. New York: Basic Books, 1988.

N. Morris and M. Miller, 'Predictions of Dangerousness', in M. Tonry and N. Morris, eds., *Crime and Justice*, vol. 6. Chicago: Chicago University Press, 1985.

L. Ohlin and M. Tonry, eds., *Family Violence*, Chicago: University of Chicago Press.

D. Scully, *Understanding Sexual Violence*. London: HarperCollins, 1990.

L. Sherman and D. Smith, 'Crime, Punishment, and Stake in Conformity: Legal and Informal Control of Domestic Violence', *American Sociological Review*, 1992, 57: 680–90.

H. Toch, *Violent Men*. London: Penguin, 1969.

C. Wells, *Corporations and Criminal Responsibility*. Oxford: Oxford University Press, 1993.

D. West, *Sexual Crimes and Confrontations*. Aldershot: Gower, 1983.

N. Wiener and M. Wolfgang, eds., *Pathways to Criminal Violence*. Newbury Park, Ca: Sage.

REFERENCES

ABEL, G., BECKER, J., MITTELMAN, M., CUNNINGHAM-RATHNER, J., ROULEAU, J-L., and MURPHY, W. (1987), 'Self-reported Sex Crime of Non-incarcerated Paraphiliacs', *Journal of Interpersonal Violence*, 2/6: 3–25.

ANDERSON, S., KINSEY, R., LOADER, I., and SMITH, C. (1990), *Cautionary Tales: A Study of Young People and Crime in Edinburgh*. Edinburgh: Centre for Criminology.

ASHWORTH, A. (1992), *Sentencing and Criminal Justice*. London: Weidenfeld and Nicholson.

BANDURA, A. (1973), *Aggression: A Social Learning Analysis*. Englewood Cliffs, NJ: Prentice-Hall.

BARKER, M., and MORGAN, R. (1993), *Sex Offenders: A Framework for the Evaluation of Community-Based Treatment*. London: Home Office.

BECKER, H. (1973), *Labelling Theory Reconsidered*. New York: Free Press.

BERGMAN, D. (1991), *Deaths at Work: Accidents or Corporate Crime*? London: Workers' Educational Association.

BERNARD, T. (1990), 'Angry Aggression among the "Truly Disadvantaged" ', *Criminology*, 28/1: 73–93.

BLAU, J., and BLAU, P. (1982), 'The Cost of Inequality: Metropolitan Structure and Violent Crime', *American Sociological Review*, 47: 114–29.

BLUMSTEIN, A., COHEN, J., ROTH, J., and VISHER, C. (1986), *Criminal Careers and 'Career Criminals'*. Washington, DC: National Academy Press.

BOWLING, B. (1993), 'Racial Harassment and the Process of Victimization: Conceptual and Methodological Implications for the Local Crime Survey', *British Journal of Criminology*, 33/1.

BOX, S. (1983), *Power, Crime, and Mystification*. London: Tavistock.

BRAITHWAITE, J. (1989), *Crime, Shame, and Reintegration*. Cambridge: Cambridge University Press.

BRAITHWAITE, J., and BRAITHWAITE, V. (1980), 'The Effects of Income Inequality and Social Democracy on Homicide', *British Journal of Criminology*, 20: 45–53.

BRAITHWAITE, J., and PETTIT, P. (1990), *Not Just Deserts: A Republican Theory of Criminal Justice*. Oxford: Oxford University Press.

BRODY, S., and TARLING, R. (1981), *Taking Offenders out of Circulation*. London: HMSO.

BROWNMILLER, S. (1975), *Against Our Will*. Harmondsworth: Penguin.

BURGDORF, K., and ELDRED, C. (1978), *System of Operational Definitions*. Rockville, Md.: Westat.

BURGESS, R., and DRAPER, P. (1989), 'The Explanation of Family Violence: The Role of Biological, Behavioral, and Cultural Selection', in L. Ohlin and M. Tonry, eds., *Family Violence*. Chicago: University of Chicago Press.

CHAPPELL, D. (1989), 'Sexual Criminal Violence,' in N. Wiener and M. Wolfgang, eds., *Pathways to Criminal Violence*. Newbury Park, Cal.: Sage.

CHAPPELL, D., GEIS, G., SCHAFER, S., and SIEGEL, L. (1977), 'A Comparative Study of Forcible Rape Offenses Known to the Police in Boston and Los Angeles', in D. Chappell, R. Geis, and G. Geis, eds., *Forcible Rape*. New York; Columbia University Press.

CHRISTIE, N. (1981), *Limits to Pain*. Oxford: Martin Robertson.

CHRISTOPHER, S., NOAKS, L., and LEVI, M. (1989), 'Assaults upon the Police: the Assailant's Perspective', unpublished paper. London: Home Office.

COHEN, S. (1981), *Folk Devils and Moral Panics*, 2nd edn., London: Paladin.

COLLINS, J. (1989), 'Alcohol and Interpersonal Violence: Less than Meets the Eye', in N. Weiner and M. Wolfgang, eds., *Pathways to Criminal Violence*. Newbury Park, Cal.: Sage.

CULLEN, F., LINK, B., and POLANZI, C. (1982), 'The Seriousness of Crime Revisited', *Criminology*, 20: 83–102.

CURRIE, E. (1985), *Confronting Crime: An American Challenge*. New York: Pantheon Books.

CURTIS, L. (1975), *Violence, Race and Culture*. Lexington: Lexington Books.

DALY, M., and WILSON, M. (1988), *Homicide*. New York: de Gruyter.

DAVIDOFF, L., and DOWDS, L. (1989), 'Recent Trends in Crimes of Violence against the Person in England and Wales', *Home Office Research Bulletin*, 27: 11–17.

DAVIDOFF, L., and GREENHORN, M. (1991), 'Violent Crime in England and Wales', paper presented at the British Criminology Conference, York.

DOBASH, R. E., and DOBASH, R. D. (1979), *Violence against Wives*. New York: Free Press.

—— (1992), *Women, Violence, and Social Change*. London: Routledge.

DOBASH, R. E., DOBASH, R. D., DALY, M., and WILSON, M. (1992), 'The Myth of Sexual Symmetry in Marital Violence', *Social Problems*, 39/1: 71–91.

FAGAN, J. (1989), 'Cessation of Family Violence: Deterrence and Dissuasion', in L. Ohlin and M. Tonry, eds., *Family Violence*. Chicago: University of Chicago Press.

—— (1990), 'Intoxication and Aggression', in M. Tonry and J. Wilson, eds., *Drugs and Crime*. Chicago: University of Chicago Press.

FARRELL, G. (1992), 'Multiple Victimisation: Its Extent and Significance', *International Review of Victimology*, 2: 85–102.

FARRINGTON, D. (1989) 'Early Predictors of Adolescent Aggression and Adult Violence', *Violence and Victims*, 4: 307–31.

—— (1991), 'Childhood Aggression and Adult Violence: Early Precursors and Later Life Outcomes', in D. Pepler and K. Rubin, eds., *The Development and Treatment of Childhood Aggression*. Hillsdale, NJ: Erlbaum.

FARRINGTON, D., and DOWDS, E. (1985), 'Disentangling Criminal Behaviour and

Police Reaction', in D. Farrington and J. Gunn, eds., *Reactions to Crime: The Public, the Police, Courts and Prisons*, 41–72. Chichester: John Wiley.

FARRINGTON, D., and LANGAN, P. (1992), 'Changes in Crime and Punishment in England and America in the 1980s', *Justice Quarterly*, 9/1: 5–31.

FIELD, S. (1990), *Trends in Crime and their Interpretation*. London: HMSO.

FISCHHOFF, B. (1989), 'Risk: A Guide to Controversy', appendix C in *Improving Risk Communication*. Washington D.C.: National Academy Press.

FLOUD, J., and YOUNG, W. (1981), *Dangerousness and Criminal Justice*. London: Heinemann.

FRIEZE, I., and BROWNE, A. (1989), 'Violence in Marriage', in L. Ohlin and M. Tonry, eds., *Family Violence*. Chicago: University of Chicago Press.

FRUDE, N. (1989), 'The Physical Abuse of Children', in K. Howells and C. Hollin, eds., *Clinical Approaches to Violence*, 155–82. Chichester: Wiley.

GAROFALO, J. (1987), 'Reassessing the Lifestyle Model of Personal Victimisation', in M. Gottfredson and T. Hirschi, eds., *Positive Criminology*. London: Sage.

GARTNER, R. (1990), 'The Victims of Homicide', *American Sociological Review*, 55/1: 92–107.

GATRELL, V. (1980), 'The Decline of Theft and Violence in Victorian and Edwardian England', in V. Gatrell, B. Lenmna, and G. Parker, eds., *Crime and the Law: The Social History of Crime in Western Europe since 1500*. London: Europa.

—— (1990), 'Crime, Authority, and the Policeman-State, 1750–1950', in F. Thompson, ed., *The Cambridge Social History of Britain, 1750–1950*. Cambridge: Cambridge University Press.

GENN, H. (1988), 'Multiple Victimisation', in M. Maguire and J. Pointing, eds., *Victims of Crime: A New Deal?*, 90–100. Milton Keynes: Open University Press.

GIL, D. (1975), 'Unravelling Child Abuse', *American Journal of Orthopsychiatry*, 45/3: 345–56.

GREENE, E., and WAKEFIELD, R. (1979), 'Patterns of Middle and Upper Class Homicide', *Journal of Criminal Law and Criminology*, 70/2: 172–81.

GURR, T. (1990), 'Historical Trends in Violent Crime: A Critical Review of the Evidence', in N. Wiener, M. Zahn, and R. Sagi, eds., *Violence: Patterns, Causes, Public Policy*, 15–37. San Diego: Harcourt Brace Jovanovich.

HAAPANEN, R. (1990), *Selective Incapacitation and the Serious Offender*. New York: Springer-Verlag.

HALL, S., CRITCHER, C., JEFFERSON, T., CLARKE, J., and ROBERTS, B. (1978), *Policing the Crisis*. London: Macmillan.

HANMER, J., RADFORD, J., and STANKO, E. (1989), *Women, Policing, and Male Violence: An International Perspective*, London: Routledge.

HEALTH AND SAFETY COMMISSION (1992), *Annual Report, 1991/92*. London: HMSO.

HEALTH AND SAFETY EXECUTIVE (1988), *The Tolerability of Risk from Nuclear Power Stations*. London: HMSO.

HIBBERD, M. (1993), *Violent Crime in Small Shops*. London: Police Foundation.

HOLDAWAY, S. (1983), *Inside the British Police*. Oxford: Basil Blackwell.

HOME OFFICE (1989), *Statistics on Offences of Rape 1977–1987, Statistical Bulletin* 4/89. London: Home Office.

HOUGH, M. and MAYHEW, P. (1985), *Taking Account of Crime: Key Findings from the 1984 British Crime Survey*. London: HMSO.

HUESSMAN, L., and ERON, L. (1989), 'Individual Differences and the Trait of Aggression', *European Journal of Personality*, 3: 95–106.

JOHNSON, A. (1980), 'On the Prevalence of Rape in the United States', *Signs*, 6: 136–46.

JONES, S., and LEVI, M. (1987), 'Law and Order and the Causes of Crime: Some Police and Public Perspectives', *Howard Journal*, 26/1: 1–14.

KAHNEMANN, D., SLOVIC, P., and TVERSKY, A. (1982), *Judgment under Uncertainty: Beuristics and Biases*. Cambridge: Cambridge University Press.

KATZ, J. (1988), *The Seductions of Crime: The Moral and Sensual Attractions of Doing Evil*. New York: Basic Books.

KEMPE, R., and KEMPE, C. (1978), *Child Abuse*. London: Fontana.

LACEY, N., WELLS, C., and MEURE, D. (1990), *Reconstructing Criminal Law*. London: Weidenfield and Nicolson.

LAFREE, G. (1982), 'Male Power and Female Victimization: Toward a Theory of Interracial Rape', *American Sociological Review*, 88: 311–28.

LEVI, M., and JONES, S. (1985), 'Public and Police Perceptions of Crime Seriousness in England and Wales', *British Journal of Criminology*, 25/3: 234–50.

LEVI, M., and PITHOUSE, A. (1992), 'Victims of Fraud', in D. Downes, ed., *Unravelling Criminal Justice*, 229–46. London: Macmillan.

LICHTENSTEIN, S., SLOVIC, P., FISCHHOFF, B., LAYMAN, M., and COMBS, B. (1978), 'Judged Frequency of Lethal Events', *Journal of Experimental Psychology (Human Learning and Memory)*, 4: 551–78.

MCINTOSH, M. (1975), *The Organisation of Crime*. London: Macmillan.

MASTERS, B. (1986), *Killing for Company*. London: Jonathan Cape.

MAYHEW, P., ELLIOTT, D., and DOWDS, L. (1989), *The 1988 British Crime Survey*. London: HMSO.

MEGARGEE, E. (1983), 'Undercontrolled and Overcontrolled Personality Types in Extreme Antisocial Aggression', *Psychological Monographs*, 80/3, whole no. 611.

MESSNER, S., and GOLDEN, R. (1992), 'Racial Inequality and Racially Disaggregated Homicide Rates: An Assessment of Alternative Theoretical Explanations', *Criminology*, 30/3: 421–37.

METROPOLITAN POLICE (1989), *Annual Report of the Commissioner of the Metropolis, 1989*. London: HMSO.

MIERS, D. (1990), *Compensation for Criminal Injuries*. London: Butterworths.

MIETHE, T. (1984), 'Types of Consensus in Public Evaluations of Crime: An Illustration of Strategies for Measuring "consensus"', *Journal of Criminal Law and Criminology*, 75/2: 459–73.

MOONEY, J. (1993), *The North London Domestic Violence Survey*. London: Middlesex University.

MORGAN, D. (1987), 'Masculinity and Violence', in J. Hanmer and M. Maynard, eds., *Women, Violence, and Social Control*. London: Macmillan.

MORGAN, J. and ZEDNER, L. (1992), *Child Victims*. Oxford: Clarendon Press.

MORRIS, N., and MILLER, M. (1985), 'Predictions of Dangerousness', in M. Tonry and N. Morris, eds., *Crime and Justice*, vi. Chicago: Chicago University Press.

NATIONAL COMMITTEE (1990), *Violence: Directions for Australia*. Canberra: Australian Institute of Criminology.

NATIONAL CRIME SURVEY (1986), *Teenage Victims: A National Crime Survey Report*. Washington DC: US Government Printing Office.

NICHOLLS, T. (1991), 'Industrial Injuries in British Manufacturing Industry and Cyclical Effects: Continuities and Discontinuities in Industrial Injury Research', *Sociological Review*, 39/1: 131–9.

NORRIS, D. (1990), *Violence against Social Workers: The Implications for Practice*. London: Jessica Kingsley.

PAINTER, K. (1991*a*) *Wife Rape, Marriage and the Law*. Manchester: Manchester University.

—— (1991b) 'Violence and Vulnerability in the Workplace: Psychosocial and Legal Implications', in M. Davidson and J. Earnshaw, eds., *Vulnerable Workers: Psychosocial and Legal Issues*, 159–78. Chichester: Wiley.

PARTON, N. (1985), *The Politics of Child Abuse*. London: Macmillan.

—— (1990) 'Taking Child Abuse Seriously', in The Violence against Children Study Group, eds., *Taking Child Abuse Seriously*. London: Unwin Hyman.

PEARSON, G. (1983), Hooligan. London: Macmillan.

PEARSON, G., SAMPSON, A., BLAGG, H., STUBBS, P., and SMITH, D. (1989), 'Policing racism', in R. Morgan and D. Smith, eds., *Coming to Terms with Policing*. London: Routledge.

PEASE, K. (1988), *Crime Seriousness: Findings from the British Crime Survey*. London: Home Office Research and Planning Unit.

RADZINOWICZ, L., ed. (1957), *Sexual Offences*. London: Macmillan.

REINER, R. (1992), *The Politics of the Police*, 2nd edn., Hemel Hempstead: Wheatsheaf.

ROWETT, C. (1986), *Violence in the Context of Local Authority Social Work*. Cambridge: Institute of Criminology.

ROYAL COMMISSION ON THE POLICE (1929), *Report*. London: HMSO.

ROYAL SOCIETY (1992), *Risk: Analysis, Perception, Management*. London: Royal Society.

RUSSELL, D. (1984), *Sexual Exploitation*. Beverly Hills: Sage.

SANDAY, P. (1981), 'The Socio-cultural Context of Rape: A Cross-cultural Study', *Journal of Social Issues*, 37/4: 5–27.

SCHRAGER, L., and SHORT, J., (1980), 'How Serious a Crime? Perceptions of Organizational and Common Crimes', in G. Geis and E. Stotland, eds., *White-collar Crime: Theory and Research*. Beverly Hills: Sage.

SCULLY, D. (1990), *Understanding Sexual Violence*. London: HarperCollins.

SHEPHERD, J. (1990), 'Violent Crime in Bristol: An Accident and Emergency Department Perspective', *British Journal of Criminology*, 30/3: 289–305.

SHERMAN, L., and SMITH, D. (1992), 'Crime, Punishment, and Stake in Conformity: Legal and Informal Control of Domestic Violence', *American Sociological Review*, 57: 680–90.

SKOGAN, W. (1990), *The Police and Public in England and Wales: A British Crime Survey Report*. London: HMSO.

SMITH, L. (1989), *Concerns about Rape*. London: HMSO.

SOOTHILL, K., JACK, A. and GIBBENS, T. (1976), 'Rape: A 22-year Cohort Study', *Medicine, Science, and the Law*, 16/1: 62–9.

SPARKS, R. (1980), 'Crime and Punishment', unpublished paper presented at American Society of Criminology Conference, San Francisco.

SPARKS, R., GENN, H., and DODD, D. (1977), *Surveying Victims*. Chichester: Wiley.

STANKO, B. (1990), *Everyday Violence*. London: Unwin Hyman.

STRAUS, M. and GELLES, R., (1990) 'How Violent are American Families? Estimates from the National Family Violence Survey and other Studies', in M. Straus and R. Gelles, eds., *Physical Violence in American Families*. New Brunswick, NJ: Transaction.

STRAUS, M., GELLES, R., and STEINMETZ, S. (1980), *Behind Closed Doors*. New York: Anchor Press.

THORNHILL, R., and THORNHILL, N. (1992), 'The Evolutionary Psychology of Men's Coerceive Sexuality', *Behavioural and Brain Sciences*, 15: 363–421.

TOCH, H. (1969), *Violent Men*. Harmondsworth: Penguin.

—— (1979), 'Perspectives on the Offender', in H. Toch, ed., *Psychology of Crime and Criminal Justice*. London: Holt, Rinehart and Winston.

TOMBS, S. (1992), 'Safety, Statistics, and Business Cycles: A Response to Nichols', *Sociological Review*, 40/1: 132–45.

TRACY, P., WOLFGANG, M., and FIGLIO, R. (1990), *Delinquency Careers in Two Birth Cohorts*. New York: Plenum Press.

TUCK, M. (1989), *Drinking and Disorder: A Study of Non-Metropolitan Violence*. London: HMSO.

TVERSKY, A., and KAHNEMANN, D. (1973), 'Availability: A Heuristic for Judging Frequency and Probability', *Cognitive Psychology*, 4: 207–32.

VLEK, C., and STALLEN, P. (1981), 'Judging Risks and Benefits in the Small and in the Large', *Organizational Behaviour and Human Performance*, 28: 235–71.

VON HIRSCH, A. (1986), *Past or Future Crimes?* Manchester: Manchester University Press.

WADDINGTON, D. (1992), *Contemporary Issues in Public Disorder*. London: Routledge.

WALKLATE, S. (1990), *Victimology*. London: Unwin Hyman.

WALMSLEY, R. (1986), *Personal Violence*. London: HMSO.

WEIS, J. (1989), 'Family Violence Research Methodology and Design', in L. Ohlin and M. Tonry, eds., *Family Violence*. Chicago: University of Chicago Press.

WELLS, C. (1993), *Corporations and Criminal Responsibility*. Oxford: Oxford University Press.

WEST, D. (1983), *Sexual Crimes and Confrontations*. Aldershot: Gower.

Which (1990), 'The Police', *Which?*, May: 258–61.

WILSON, J., and HERRNSTEIN, R. (1985), *Crime and Human Nature*. New York: Simon and Schuster.

WILSON, M., and DALY, M. (1992), 'Who Kills Whom in Spouse Killings: On the Exceptional Sex Ratio of Spousal Homicides in the United States', *Criminology*, 30/2: 189–214.

WOLFGANG, M., and FERRACUTI, F. (1967), *The Subculture of Violence*. London: Tavistock.

YOUNG, J. (1988), 'Risk of Crime and Fear of Crime: A Realist Critique of Survey-based Assumptions', in M. Maguire and J. Pointing, eds., *Victims of Crime: A New Deal?*, 164–76. Milton Keynes: Open University Press.

8

White-Collar Crime

DAVID NELKEN

INTRODUCTION

In April 1992 Carlo De Benedetti, chairman of Olivetti and architect of its recent growth as one of Italy's major corporations, rang his head office from Switzerland to ask how Olivetti's shares were doing. He was not pleased to be told that they had gone down in value. 'Is this because of a general fall in prices on the Milan exchange?' he asked. 'No', came the reply, 'it is because you have just been sentenced to six years in prison for your role in the Banco Ambrosiano crash of 1982.' This story exemplifies what is typically conjured up by a certain idea of white-collar crime. Successful business or professional people are apparently caught out in serious offences, quite often for behaviour which they did not expect to be treated as criminal, and for which it is difficult to secure a conviction. (It should be added for the record that De Benedetti, who remains in charge at Olivetti, is widely considered to have been, if anything, one of those least guilty of misconduct in the crash of the bank, and is more than likely to have his conviction overturned in the next stage of the judicial process.) The Jekyll-and-Hyde nature of crime committed by the respectable raises questions unlike those posed by other types of criminal behaviour. Why do they do it when they have so much to lose? How representative are they or their practices of other business-people or business life in general? How likely are they to be caught? Is there one law for the rich and another for the poor? Criminological research has something to offer in answer to these questions, but, as so often, it also suggests some rethinking of the way the questions are formulated.

One of the biggest difficulties in approaching this subject is to find a way of putting dramatic and newsworthy cases of business misbehaviour in some sort of context and proportion. Study of the distribution and frequency of white-collar crimes is made problematic by the fact (not in itself unimportant) that, especially in the common-law countries where the concept was first formulated, most white-collar crimes are not included in the official statistics which serve as the basis for debates about 'the crime problem'. The usual difficulties of interpreting the statistics of crime are greatly magnified here (Levi 1985). The information recorded by specialized enforcement agencies (often not even made public) serves mainly as a source for describing methods of control rather than the misbehaviour being controlled. Nor can it be assumed that there is any uniformity in the meaning of data obtained in this way. A few agencies are reactive, depending on complaints others are proactive; but the level of enforcement is restricted by limited resources. (In Britain factories are inspected for safety offences on average once every four years.) Much regulation is geared to using prosecution as a last resort, and thus the number of prosecuted offenders says little about the likely level of crime; conversely, the number of visits or warnings cannot be used as an index of the incidence of deliberate law-breaking. There is a danger of double-counting where the same behaviour is dealt with by different agencies or where one firm has more sub-units than another. This also creates problems about defining recidivism—which were ignored by Sutherland in his pioneering study (Sutherland 1949). There are problems of classifying the date and location of some of these offences (a factor which often helps secure the offender's immunity.) Changes in legislative mandates, and in the number, expertise, politics, and motivation of enforcers make a treacherous basis for studies of changes in offending patterns over time. Finally, supplementing official statistics with victim reports is difficult because the victims are often unaware of their victimization; and even where this is not the case, as in organizations subject to fraud, there is often unwillingness to admit to vulnerability.

These difficulties mean that discussions of the subject in textbooks are forced to rely unduly on newspaper reports or on the activities of crusading journalists (see e.g. Coleman 1985). Obtaining information in this way complicates the task of assessing the accuracy, frequency, or representativeness of the cases reported. Newspapers, or those who feed them their stories, initiate crime control campaigns for reasons which may have little to do with the long-term trend in the misbehaviour at issue. It is therefore hard to tell, for example, whether business or financial crimes are increasing or are just more newsworthy, or to decide if any change is the result of an increase in this kind of misbehaviour or of a trend towards the use of formal and legal, rather than informal, means to deal with it.

Despite these problems, some useful quantitative studies have been made, for example using agency records to survey the rate of corporate offending (Clinard and Yeager 1980), or court records to establish the type of offenders normally apprehended for what the authors call 'middle-class crimes' (Weisburd *et al.* 1991). What we know about white-collar crime also comes from interviews with enforcers as well as observation of their work (e.g. Carson 1970; Hawkins 1984; Hutter 1988; cf. also Nelken 1991); interviews with businessmen (e.g. Lane 1953; Braithwaite

1984); biographies of and retrospective accounts by offenders (e.g. Geis 1968); participant observation in offending organizations (e.g. Nelken 1983: ch. 2), and experimental techniques such as those used by consumer organizations (Green 1990: ch. 2), as well as other sources (and for useful methodological hints on researching these type of offences see Levi 1985).

Although most of the literature on white-collar crime is American (as is true of criminology in general), major contributions have been made by other English-language scholars such as Braithwaite, Carson, and Levi. The equivalent term for white-collar crime is also widely found in other languages, and even used in foreign court proceedings. There are also interesting contributions, some in foreign languages, which could serve as a useful starting-point for comparative research (e.g. Tiedemann 1974; Cosson 1978; Magnusson 1985; Clarke 1990; Delmas-Marty 1990; Zigler 1990; Punch 1991; Van Duyne 1993; Passas and Nelken 1993). But, despite the similarities among modern industrialized economies, there may also be important differences in general and legal culture which affect the response to white-collar crime. American outrage over business misbehaviour may be connected to what Mills (1963 [1943]) saw as the small-town values of American social reformers, as well as to a peculiar American love–hate relationship with big businesses (are they the ultimate proof of capitalist success or a threat to the market and to the individual?). In civil-law countries such as Italy there are few of the special enforcement agencies used to deal with occupational offences found, for example, in America, Britain, and Australia. Instead, normal police forces, often spearheaded by specialized financial police, conduct investigations of safety and pollution cases, and businessmen or politicians with white collars regularly see the inside of prisons (though few seem to stay there for long).

Much of the literature on white-collar crime continues to be concerned to demonstrate the seriousness and diffuseness of such offending, and to show that its costs and damages dwarf those of conventional, or 'ordinary', crime. Colossal fines and settlements are imposed in cases of some financial crimes: for example, Michael Milken, the 'junk bond king', paid over $650 million even before sentence. The collapse of the savings and loan institutions (similar to British building societies) in the United States in the late 1980s may end up costing a trillion dollars. Contrary to what is supposed by some definitions (e.g. Edelhertz 1970), there is also no reason to exclude violence and death from the province of white-collar crime (Hills 1988). There are a number of case studies which document this, even without going into more controversial calculations of the overall number of fatal accidents or diseases occurring at work which could have been prevented and prosecuted (Box 1983: 28 ff; Slapper 1991). Carson's study of the loss of life in the exploration for oil in the North Sea (confirmed by later events, such as the loss of the *Piper Alpha* oil rig in 1988 at a cost of 168 lives), for instance, showed that many lives could have been saved by rudimentary attention to safety considerations (Carson 1981). The devastating consequences of the nuclear disaster at Chernobyl or the chemical explosion at Bhopal, the suffering caused by the sale of the drug thalidomide, or the contraceptive known as the Dalkon shield, are other well known examples.

Despite all this evidence, white-collar crimes are still subjected to very different interpretations. It might seem odd that sociologists familiar with Durkheim's argument that society considers dangerous those behaviours it responds to as criminal, rather than the other way round, should keep trying to prove that white-collar crime is really criminal simply because it causes great harm. The answer must be that they hope in this way to influence the social definition of such conduct. But debates over the nature of white-collar crime cannot simply be reduced to different political evaluations of the misdeeds of business or capitalism. They also reflect more specific disagreements over the nature of the behaviour at issue. This can be well demonstrated if we compare the different lessons drawn from roughly similar materials even by authors who do not otherwise seem to disagree much politically. In the course of this chapter I shall be referring in particular to two recent overviews by writers who offer sharply contrasting assessments of the subject, though neither seems interested in using it to cast doubt on the normal operations of capitalist forms of production and organization. Green's *Occupational Crime* (1990) is a comprehensive American textbook devoted to systematizing the now voluminous data on white-collar crime and its control. It uses the same categories of criminological analysis and explanation which serve for other types of crime. White-collar crime is seen both as more criminal than ordinary crime and at the same time as more likely to escape control; as Geis argues in his foreword, 'occupational crime is without a doubt more dangerous, both in physical and in fiscal terms, than street crime' (Geis 1990: xv). Considerable attention is therefore devoted to discovering more effective ways of bringing criminal penalties to bear on this type of conduct. On the other hand, Clarke's *Business Crime* (1990*b*), though considering much the same data, is largely devoted to showing the differences between these sorts of offences and those more usually handled as crimes. For Clarke:

> Business crime, however, in the sense in which it is used here, covers a much wider range of misconduct, which may be none the less damaging and otherwise undesirable, resulting from duress, incompetence, negligence, lack of training, lack of clarity in the rules, opportunism, technical infraction, or sheer muddle-headedness, rather than calculated deceit motivated by greed. (Clarke 1990*b*: 16)

It follows that such crime should not be handled in the same way as ordinary crime:

> Pursuing business crime as fraud, through criminal prosecution, though appropriate for a minority of cases, is irrelevant and impossible for the majority. Furthermore if criminal prosecution is pursued as the sole or even the principal means of control, it will fail to achieve anything more than public hysteria and expense, and the jailing of a few of the less lucky and competent villains. (Clarke 1990*b*: 16)

SEVEN TYPES OF AMBIGUITY

Why is there still so much disagreement over white-collar crime? As with the equivocal designs produced by Gestalt psychologists, do we find it difficult to see 'the criminal' and 'the respectable person' in one and the same figure? Following Aubert (1952), I shall argue that ambiguity about the nature of white-collar crime and the best way of responding to it, forms an essential key to the topic and can be used to provide insights into this type of crime as well as into the 'ordinary' crime to which it is contrasted. As the subject has become more established, scholars have tended either to abandon Aubert's insight or to concentrate on only one or two of the sources of ambiguity which will be considered here. They also tend to divide somewhat dogmatically into those, on the one hand, who point to the ambiguous features of white-collar crime so as to explain and justify special treatment for this misbehaviour, and those, on the other, who claim that ambiguity is a socially constructed smokescreen which ought to be dispelled. In this chapter I do not purport to settle the question of how far the features which supposedly make white-collar crime more ambiguous than ordinary crime are (merely) socially constructed. I shall, however, try to do something to clarify the uncertainties produced by the literature itself by offering a critical review both of those arguments that assert that ambiguity is intrinsic to the misbehaviour itself and of those which attempt to prove that white-collar crime is 'essentially' the same as ordinary crime but is transformed by the social reaction to it.

To provide a common thread to the following overview of what has been written about the *definition* of, *causes* of, and *responses* to white-collar crime I shall seek to illustrate seven different sources of ambiguity which surround this topic. (I use the term ambiguity loosely to embrace the various forms of equivocalness, uncertainty, and ambivalence referred to in and produced by discussions of the characteristics of white-collar crime.) The first ambiguities I shall consider arise in trying to define what is meant by white-collar crime. The ambiguous way the concept is used in the criminological literature means that it is not clear what range of crimes is being referred to. From the outset Sutherland's concept has also been criticized for seeking to apply the crime label to behaviours whose definition as crime is legally or sociologically controversial. The second set of ambiguities belongs more to discussions of the causes of white-collar crime. While many scholars try to apply the usual criminological frameworks of explanation to this kind of offending, others have used the topic precisely so as to place these schemes in doubt. Ambiguity also surrounds discussions of the commission of these offences. Thus some writers stress the point that this type of offending behaviour takes place in a more respectable context than most other crimes, and that it is the product of more ambiguous intentions than is the case for ordinary crime. The third set of ambiguities derives from the regulation and handling of white-collar crime. White-collar crimes are often controlled in a different and more ambivalent way from ordinary crime, and it is controversial how far this reflects, reinforces, or even creates its ambiguity. The uncertain status of these crimes may also be seen to reflect a process of transition and social change in which the public is not yet ready for more outright criminalization of these behaviours. It is also argued that control of these offences is hampered by problems of competing values and social costs which do not arise in repressing ordinary crime.

I shall be taking these various ambiguities one by one (in numbered sequence throughout the remainder of the essay), partly for purposes of exposition and partly because there are important differences among the sources and types of ambiguity. Taken as a whole, however, many of these ambiguities are mutually reinforcing and thus help shape the perceived character of white-collar crime as a social phenomenon. If, for example, different and predominantly administrative methods of enforcement are used in dealing with white-collar as opposed to ordinary crime, this will shape public opinion concerning their relative seriousness. But, at the same time, such (alleged) differences in public attitudes also serve as justifications offered by legislators and enforcers for their different treatment of white-collar crimes. On the other hand, any given source of ambiguity may have implications under a number of different headings. That white-collar crimes generally take place in private settings represents a special feature of their causation which may facilitate their commission; but it also serves as an impediment to normal policing methods which helps explain the use of other means and forms of enforcement. The importance of respecting 'privacy' as a value also figures as an argument in policy debates over the appropriateness of strengthening controls.

WHITE-COLLAR CRIME AS A CONTESTED CONCEPT

1. If Sutherland merited a Nobel Prize, as Mannheim thought, for pioneering this field of study, he certainly did not deserve it for the clarity or serviceableness of his definition. What, if anything, is there in common between the marketing of unsafe pharmaceuticals, the practice of insider trading, long-firm fraud, computer crime, bank embezzlement and fiddling at work? Though Sutherland claimed to be interested in reforming criminological theory rather than changing society, the appeal of this topic, particularly through the 1970s and 1980s, was unquestionably linked to its progressive connotations and its implicit accusations of bias in the making and enforcing of criminal law (Yeager 1991: ch. 1). The apparent success of the label in finding public acceptance, while lacking a clear or agreed referent, may testify less to its coherence than to its capacity to name a supposed threat (as with the term 'mugging'). Not all instances of white-collar crime are ambiguous (embezzlement, for example, is not), just as not all ambiguous deviance is white-collar crime. But considerable disagreement over the range of misbehaviour referred, to, as well as doubts about the coherence of those behaviours it does include, make the category as a whole rather ambiguous. And, peculiarly enough, those white-collar offences whose criminal character seems most unambiguous—such as bank embezzlement or (on some definitions) credit-card fraud—are the ones least likely to illustrate the theoretical or policy-relevant features of white-collar crime in which Sutherland and his successors have been most interested.

The basic ambiguity in Sutherland's definition of white-collar crime as a crime committed by a person of high status in the course of his or her occupation (1949: 9) is that it does not distinguish crimes committed *for* an organization or business from those carried out *at its expense* (his empirical studies focused mainly on the former). Later writers sympathetic to the topic have almost universally divided it up to highlight this distinction (as, for example, by distinguishing corporate and occupational crime). A number of other problems derive from his definition of the white-collar offender. We need not take the expression 'white-collar' too seriously (attempts to develop other sartorial typologies of crime, such as blue-collar, red-collar, blue-coated, or khaki-coated crime, have all met with deserved neglect). The objection is rather that this term combines definition and explanation, and that 'building theory on the back of definition' makes it impossible actually to investigate the empirical correlation between high status and criminality (Braithwaite 1985). Sutherland's reason for adopting the term was probably that he was trying to focus on 'crimes of the powerful' rather than all cases of technically criminal behaviour taking place in and around occupations—such as the numerous cases of employee theft. But even he stretches his idea of high-status offenders by including discussions of such misbehaviour as the selling tricks used by shoe salesmen. Status and respectability are in any case not the best sociological criteria to use: some argue that a focus on class would be more fruitful; others stress the opportunity to use organizational resources (to manipulate money) as the key variable (Weisburd *et al.* 1991). In a recent theoretical reappraisal it has been persuasively suggested that it would be better to concentrate on offence criteria rather than the characteristics of offenders (Shapiro 1989). Sutherland is in any case inconsistent in his focus on offenders: he describes companies as recidivist on the basis of their recorded violations, while using a criminological explanation—differential association—which refers to the behaviour of individuals.

There are other more substantive objections to the classic definition: it is too readily assumed that crimes committed by high-status offenders are aimed at the poor (just as it wrongly used to be presumed that crimes of the poor were mainly at the expense of the rich). Greatest access to organizational resources for doing harm does not always exist in parallel with highest status. The connection between crime and enterprise is not limited to those of high status (Mars 1982; Hobbs 1986). In any case, social changes since the time Sutherland wrote mean that the proportion of the population engaged in white-collar as compared to blue-collar jobs has steadily increased, and with it the opportunity for various forms of fraud and peculation.

Sutherland's definition also lacks internal coherence. As Fig. 8.1 illustrates, this is because it is built on the *overlap* of (at least) three different types of misbehaviour (crimes). The first refers to any crime committed by a person of high status (whether or not in the course of their occupation); the second to crimes committed on behalf of organizations (by people of any status); and the third to crimes committed against organizations (whether or not these are carried out by people working in the same organization, another organization, or no organization at all). Sutherland focuses on that area of overlap in which people of high status use organizations to commit crimes for their organization—against workers, consumers, or other organizations including competitors and the government. But whatever there may be in common among the offences highlighted by this focus it is probable that, for each of the three types of misbehaviour on which his definition draws, there will be even more in common between the behaviour which fits into his central category and the *other* examples of behaviour of the same type which fall outside his definition. This creates a continual tension in trying to develop typologies of white-collar crime.

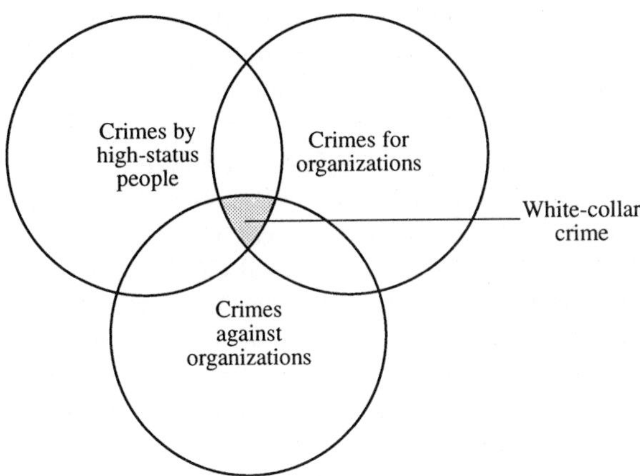

Fig. 8.1 Sutherland's concept of white-collar crime

The problem of definition cannot just be put aside in order to get on with more interesting matters because it determines the findings of any investigation. This is seen clearly in the most recent attempt, by Weisburd *et al.* (1991), actually to test the relationship between white-collar crime and the class background of those convicted for such crimes. Their findings (1991: 184 ff.) are that 'contrary to the portrait generally presented we find a world of offending and offenders that is very close to the everyday lives of typical Americans'. The majority of offenders 'do not necessitate nor do their defences rely upon elite social status'. The authors argue that small frauds are as normal a part of the business context as street crimes are in poor communities and conclude that 'the people we studied are the core American criminals whose ranks will grow as society becomes more middle class, as credit cards and credentialling grows, and television continues to hammer home the message of consumption'. The study is of great value in showing us that common crime and white-collar crime lie on a continuum and in proposing (inductively) a new category of offending intermediate between common and corporate crime. But the definition of white-collar crime used in this work, based as it was on criminal convictions rather than administrative proceedings, and biased towards smaller-scale frauds (the crimes they selected included securities fraud and antitrust; bribery; embezzlement; mail fraud; tax fraud; false claims and accounting; and credit fraud) was almost bound to produce the picture of middle-class crime which the authors describe.

There are a number of ways of trying to break up or reformulate the topic of white-collar crime which do not simply rely on selecting the most appropriate-seeming crimes from the official criminal statistics. One common inductive strategy is to start from the data produced by the non-police administrative agencies generally entrusted with dealing with business offences (especially in common-law countries). This was the source of data used in the comprehensive study by Clinard and Yeager (1980) which focused on various US federal regulatory bodies. Non-police agencies in Britain include the Post Office, British Transport Police, Customs and Excise, water authorities, local government, and the Ministry of Agriculture, among others (see Royal Commission on Criminal Procedure 1980). But though these agencies may have some enforcement practices in common it would be quite wrong to describe all the types of offenders they prosecute as white-collar criminals. Another strategy is to seek to develop typologies of different kinds of crime which fit under the general heading of white-collar crime. The difficulty here is that the categories thus created are still likely to end up as containers for somewhat disparate behaviours. Green (1990), for example, distinguishes among organizational occupational crime, state authority occupational crime, professional occupational crime, and so on. But these headings cannot pretend to be either theoretically defined or even coherent classifications of types of crime. The offences considered as state crime range from bribe-taking to genocide, while the chapter on individual occupational crime—which is admitted to be a catch-all category—includes behaviour as different as employee theft and securities crimes. On the other hand, the organization of the chapters can lead to artificial distinctions, as when it separates bribe-givers from bribe-takers.

There has also been a variety of attempts to rethink Sutherland's concept in a more deductive fashion. Some of these are deliberately modest, such as Clarke's extended definition of business crime in terms of its distinguishing features (Clarke 1990*b*: ch. 3). In the rest of the book Clarke seeks to illustrate the applicability of his definition to a series of different arenas of misbehaviour (and justifies a refusal to develop typologies partly on the somewhat odd grounds that opting for any one typological scheme would exclude another which might be more appropriate for other purposes). Despite the richness of his descriptions, his approach can be criticized for already building in as part of his definition of business crime those controversial features of the social response which are less geared to prosecution than in the case of ordinary crime. It is also unclear why the book is entitled *Business Crime* when the thrust of the argument is intended to undermine this label.

There are also more ambitious efforts aimed at finding a key theoretical variable which could produce a coherent focus for further research. Recent examples (which go beyond the somewhat unimaginative 'crimes of the powerful', 'crimes of the upperworld' or 'elite crimes') include Shapiro's focus on the increasing need to trust agents and the consequent exposure to various forms of abuse of such trust in which agents subordinate the interests of their principals to their own gain (Shapiro 1989). Coleman and others stress the importance of the growth of organizational actors in what has been called the 'asymetric society' (Gross 1980; Coleman 1992). These approaches may include more or less than the offences that Sutherland covered; Shapiro's proposal, for example, seems particularly tied to her previous empirical research interests in securities frauds and would not be applicable, say, to pollution crimes; its focus on agents also lets principals off the hook. But they promise to be theoretically more productive than Sutherland's concept.

2. If there are basic uncertainties about what is being referred to when talking of white-collar crime, there are also long-standing doubts whether or not all the misbehaviours discussed under this rubric can be considered to count as crime. Most of the continuing controversy, as well as the original interest, generated by this topic is due to the fact that it appears to straddle the crucial boundary between criminal and non-criminal behaviour. Since this is a well-aired problem, and the debates can be found in all the readers on this subject (e.g. Geis 1968), I will confine myself to drawing out their relevance to the issue of ambiguity. Many scholars have argued that the (mis)behaviours discussed by Sutherland or his followers do not always satisfy the legal criteria for crime; some even go so far as to insist on the necessity for a penal conviction at court (e.g. Tappan 1947). It is admittedly ironic that Sutherland himself was unable to publish the names of the companies whose administrative violations he described in his book, because of his publisher's fears that he would then be exposed to claims of libel for describing them as criminal (this was only remedied in the uncut version published much later; see Sutherland 1983). Restricting attention to those crimes found in the ordinary criminal statistics, however, too easily robs the term of all its sense. The results of following such a definition make it possible to argue that white-collar crime is an otiose category and that white-collar criminals, like all ordinary criminals, are young, feckless, and unsuccessful (See Hirschi and Gottfredson 1987, 1989; and the criticism by Steffensmeier 1989). Others have made virtually the opposite point, complaining that many white-collar crimes are merely technically criminal and are not socially considered on a par with ordinary crimes; hence they do not satisfy the requirements of a sociological definition of crime (see e.g. Burgess 1950, criticizing Hartung 1950). While this is a more acute criticism it tends to assume the unchanging circularity of social definitions and underestimates the potential for change (a process in which criminology can play a part).

The fact that such opposite criticisms can be raised is confirmation of the ambiguity of this concept—which is also reflected in the use of descriptions such as 'regulatory crimes' or *mala prohibita*. Sutherland, and many later scholars, chose to include in their definition of white-collar crime not only misbehaviours with criminal penalties, but also those which carried only civil or administrative sanctions. This was done precisely so as not to beg the question whether the choice of these generally lighter sanctions was justified (or only a sign of the power of the offenders involved). But it is only a small (if significant) step from this to argue for the inclusion in the category of white-collar crime of other types of harmful business behaviour which have succeeded (through much the same political and economic pressures) in avoiding being subject to any sanctions at all. Must we use law to draw the line? One of the contributions made by the topic of white-collar crime to criminology lies in this very difficulty of assimilating all that Sutherland was getting at without breaking the boundaries of the discipline. Should the definition of crime adopted for sociological purposes be the same as that of the law? What are the dangers of tying criminology to a starting point defined by another discipline? If we allow the political process to define what counts as crime, is this a politically conservative choice? Is it just good tactics—a way to avoid alienating the 'liberals' (as Box 1983 argues)? It is now assumed that we must refer to the law because otherwise it would be impossible to decide who is to define (business) deviance (Coleman 1987). But this was exactly the decision that the labelling perspective tried to force criminologists to face. The topic of white-collar crime thus illustrates the possibility of divergence between legal, social and political definitions of criminality—but in so doing it reminds us of the artificiality of all definitions of crime.

EXPLAINING THE CAUSES OF WHITE-COLLAR CRIME

3. Can white-collar crime be explained using the normal frameworks of criminological explanation? Certainly, more needs to be done in studying the 'how'—the *modus operandi*—rather than the 'why' of such misbehaviour (Levi 1985). The closeness of the class backgrounds of many criminologists to those of these offenders may make it difficult to gain the correct distance from which their behaviour could be seen as sufficiently puzzling. A leading theoretical textbook assures us that 'the question of why white-collar offenders behave the way they do can be answered in a relatively straightforward way; they want to make a profit' (Vold and Bernard 1986: 338). But this is perilously close to accounting for bank robbery in terms of the money to be gained from this activity. The question remains why most businessmen apparently channel their profit-making activities in other ways. Because of the political distaste felt for

'crimes of the powerful' there are also hardly any attempts to 'appreciate' the point of view of such criminals. More generally, the continuing problem of *what* exactly needs to be explained continues to confuse the search for causes. Is white-collar crime conventional or unconventional behaviour for those who commit it? Why is so much effort put into keeping criminal activities secret even from other members of the same organization (Hirschi and Gottfredson 1987)? Where the explanatory approach adopted is to look for the individual motivations of what is taken to be clearly criminal behaviour, white-collar crime becomes just another test of standard theories of crime causation. Its novelty, if it has any, is tied to the emergence of new opportunities, for new groups, to commit old offences—for example, through the use of computers to carry out frauds (Tapper 1987). Where, instead, the issue becomes the criminogenic properties of business, of capitalism or organizational behaviour in general, then the normative fabric of everyday business life seems placed in doubt and the actual evidence of white-collar crime seems to fall far short of what would be predicted.

These difficulties have not discouraged a series of attempts to explain the causes of white-collar crime, and there are even a number of good reviews of such work (see e.g. Braithwaite 1985, who concludes, however, that 'only banal generalisations are possible', or Coleman 1987, who furnishes a (banal?) synthesis of existing work in terms of opportunity and motivation theory). I shall comment on explanations concerned with the whole area of white-collar crime. But, as already noted, the search for causes may be limited to typologies of crime, such as crimes by professional people or even to specific offences. And, obviously, where the topic is theoretically reformulated this will affect what needs to be explained. For Shapiro, for example, attention must turn to the rising need to rely on agents and the consequent increased exposure to the risks of their malpractices. The study of white-collar crime therefore belongs to the wider study of the maintenance and abuse of trust. Trust is required in so far as it is difficult to tell when agents are putting their self-interest above that of their principals, especially as they tend to be the 'repeat players', and to act at a distance; but efforts to limit their discretion are self-defeating. An understanding of causation therefore calls for 'the marriage of a systematic understanding of the distribution of structural opportunities for trust abuse with an understanding of the conditions under which individual or organisational fiduciaries seize or ignore these illicit opportunities' (Shapiro: 353).

The concept of white-collar crime was certainly not invented in order to provide support for standard approaches to causation in criminology. Sutherland hoped to use these misbehaviours as ammunition against the reigning tendency to explain crime in terms of individual or social pathology. By ridiculing the idea that businesses or businessmen could be said to misbehave because of their difficult childhoods he intended to 'reform criminological theory' and show that only his theory of 'differential association' could account for all forms of criminal behaviour. There is ample evidence of the diffusion of definitions favourable to white-collar forms of lawbreaking in business circles, whether these are based on loyalty to the firm, the alleged requirements of business life, or dislike of government regulation. But Sutherland's theory is nevertheless now regarded as flawed and superficial and the search for a universal theory of crime has lost its attractions. Ironically, those who are most committed to the subject of white-collar crime are now under attack by criminologists who argue that there is no need for this special category of criminal behaviour precisely because it gets in the way of general explanations of the crime phenomenon (Hirschi and Gottfredson 1987; Gottfredson and Hirschi 1990: ch. 9).

Proponents both of 'strain' and of 'control' theories have tried to make sense of white-collar crime. Whatever his original focus may have been, most strain theories find their inspiration in Merton's concept of anomie, which is applied to corporate crime in particular. White-collar crimes can be seen, for example, as an 'innovative' response on the part of businesses (or particular roles such as middle management) to the strain of conforming to cultural prescriptions to maintain profits even in difficult circumstances (Passas 1990). The strain may be located in the business environment itself, in particular industries, or in particular firms. For example, the conditions under which the major car manufacturers in the USA constrain their car dealers to operate is such as to pressurize them to cut corners if they want to survive economically (Leonard and Weber 1970); other situations may facilitate rather than directly coerce criminal solutions (Needleman and Needleman 1979). Control theories are premised on the initial question why don't we all commit crimes when the temptations are so strong? It replies that most of us, the non-deviants, have too much invested in relationships and in legal society. This approach might therefore seem a weaker candidate for explaining white-collar crime. It finds it difficult to account for how middle-class criminals (and even most of those who find themselves in a position to embezzle) ever achieved their social positions in the first place. It also needs to show why they were willing to risk their investment. One line of argument could be based on the idea of 'over-investment'. Weisburd and his colleagues, in their sample of middle-class criminals, found that 'many of our offenders have the material goods associated with successful people but may barely be holding their financial selves together' (Weisburd *et al.* 1991: 65) This could be interpreted as meaning that such offenders are so strongly tied to social expectations and obligations that they are willing to offend to maintain their position (and so anomie and control theories meet up). In any case, a number of more particular ingredients of control theory are regularly deployed, such as the importance placed on the neutralization of social controls through the use of justifications learned within or outside the company. Typical theoretical syntheses in textbooks dealing with white-collar crime draw, on the one hand, on the 'strain' elements of capitalist competition and striving for business or individual success, and, on the other, on a variety of such 'techniques of neutralisation, (see e.g. Box 1983; Coleman 1987; Green 1990).

The labelling approach has, strangely, been comparatively neglected in the study of white-collar crime, even though it would seem peculiarly relevant given the relative recency of many laws regulating business, the sharp swings between political projects of regulation and deregulation, and the divergent views of different groups as to the appropriateness of criminalization. The reason could be that criminologists here line up with those doing the labelling (see Katz 1980, Yeager 1991: ch. 1). But few would now deny the importance of legislative or other battles over the labelling of business misbehaviour. Moreover, attention has recently turned to the success of techniques of 'non-labelling' or 'de-labelling' in diluting or avoiding the imposition of the criminal label, for example, in shaping the (mis)behaviour involved in some tax-avoidance schemes (McBarnet 1991). However, my earlier study (1983) of the social construction of landlord crime remains one of the few works to have examined the process of labelling and de-labelling in the same area of business misbehaviour (though see also Cook 1989). I showed there that those actually apprehended for landlord crime were small immigrant landlords involved in disputes with their tenants (for similar findings for other white-collar crimes see Hutter 1988; Croal 1989). With some effort it was possible to portray their self-help methods as criminal, but the malpractices characteristic of large business landlords stayed immune to criminalization because of their similarity to ordinary business behaviour—a 'limit' of the legal process which was, paradoxically, concealed by actually exaggerating the capacity of law to control such behaviour (Nelken 1983).

The attempt to explain white-collar crime within the 'normal science' approaches used in criminology shows itself not only in theories of causation but also in the positivist search for the peculiar characteristics associated with offenders and offences and the methodology appropriate to this task. Sutherland (1949, 1983) himself was keen to show the widespread nature of white-collar offences. He discovered pursuit of fair labour practices by General Motors; violations of laws against the restraint of trade, especially common in the major companies in the film industry; and infringements of patents, and misrepresentation in advertising by household names such as Bayer aspirin, Quaker Oats, Carnation milk, Phillips milk of magnesia, Hoover vacuum cleaners, and the *Encyclopaedia Britannica*. He particularly stressed the duration of some offences and the 'recidivism' of some of the companies concerned. Clinard and Yeager (1980), in the most wide-ranging documentary study of corporate crime to date, examined all the federal administrative, civil, and criminal actions initiated in 1975 and 1976 by twenty-five federal agencies against 582 of America's largest corporations. The violations they examined were divided into non-compliance with agency regulations; environmental pollution; financial crimes, such as illegal payments or tax offences; labour discrimination, including unsafe working practices; manufacturing offences, such as the distribution of unsafe products; and unfair trading practices, including price-fixing arrangements. Unlike Sutherland, they tried to control comparisons for the time available to commit offences and the differential size of the companies they investigated. They found that three-fifths of their sample had had charges brought against them in the period studied. While 13 per cent of the companies accounted for just over half the violations, large, medium, and small companies were all well represented among the violators. Where Sutherland had found the film, mercantile, and railroad industries particularly engaged in violations, Clinard and Yeager found their black sheep in the oil, pharmaceutical, and motor vehicle industries, all of which had more than their proportional share of violations. The oil industry, for example, was involved in three-fifths of all serious violations, with twenty-two of twenty-eight oil-refining firms guilty of at least one violation in the period under consideration; car manufacturers were responsible for one-sixth of all the violations discovered and a third of the manufacturing violations overall; pharmaceutical manufacturers accounted for one-tenth of all violations and all seventeen companies in this sector were found to have committed at least one violation.

Some of Clinard and Yeager's findings were artefacts which resulted from using data which depended on the vagaries of regulatory regimes: the higher offending rates of diversified firms, for example, may simply mean that they were exposed to more regulatory agencies (though the firms concerned may also have faced problems in maintaining oversight of their different operations). Their investigation produced some statistical support for the proposition that violations increased as financial performance became poorer; this was particularly marked for environmental and labour offences. On the other hand, firms with higher than average growth rates were more likely to have engaged in manufacturing violations. The authors admitted that the causal variables on which they concentrated—size, growth rate, diversification, and market power and resources—had only limited predictive power. Even the more confident of their claims concerning crime rates and economic performance have now been questioned in the later literature (Braithwaite 1985). Their study was unable to allow for the complicating factor of why and when agencies choose to uncover violations, and has been criticized for taking agency records as the measure of corporate crime and for failing to see such behaviour as endemic to capitalism (Young 1981).

A central debate among scholars of white-collar crime in fact concerns the extent to which corporate and business crime should be seen as an inevitable corollary of capitalism. Box (1983), in a Marxist-influenced application of Merton, argues that corporations are criminogenic because if legal means are blocked they will resort to illegal means so as to maintain or increase profitability. As and when necessary they will use techniques aimed at competitors (e.g. industrial espionage or price-fixing), at consumers (e.g. fraud or misleading advertising), or at the public in general (e.g. environmental pollution). Those recruited to work in corporations learn to justify such behaviour on the grounds that 'business is business' (cf. Pearce 1976). This is particularly true for those who rise to the top and who then have a disproportionate influence over the ethos of their firms (although they generally take care not to be directly involved in or informed of the illegal activities made necessary by their drive for profit). For those who subscribe to this theory, businesspeople comply with the law in so far as they see it enforced strictly (thereby denying competitive advantage to those who would break it). Where there are few effective controls, as in the Third World, capitalism shows its true face, selling unsafe products, paying low wages, and exploiting the complaisance of poor and corrupt governments and regulators.

On the other hand, a number of attempts have been made to question the idea that capitalism itself is criminogenic. If Merton's anomie theory is to be pressed this far it is at least necessary to go on to discuss the alternative, non-criminal modes of responding to 'strain', and (which Merton did not do) offer an explanation of why or when each mode is chosen. The argument appears to predict too much crime and makes it difficult to explain the relative stability of economic trade within and between nations, given the large number of economic transactions, the many opportunities for committing business crimes, the large gains to be made, and the relative unlikelihood of punishment. This theory also has difficulty in accounting for improvements in safety and increases in the quality of goods under capitalism. If it is somewhat oversimplified to argue that only a small proportion of businessmen and women are 'bad apples' it is not much more convincing to assume that all businesses act as 'amoral calculators' and would choose to offend but for the availability of serious sanctions (Pearce and Tombs 1990, 1991). The desire to continue in business, to maintain self-respect and the goodwill of fellow businesspeople, goes a long way towards explaining reluctance to seize opportunities for a once-only windfall. Trading competitors (as well as organized consumer groups) can serve as a control on illicit behaviour for their own reasons. It can often be definitely in the competitive interests of companies to abide by the law. Braithwaite (1985) illustrates how American pharmaceutical companies able to obtain Federal Drug Administration authorization for their products are in this way guaranteed lucrative markets in countries which cannot afford their own expensive drug-testing facilities. It could be said that the clear evidence of exploitation and the sale of dangerous goods in Third World countries reflects an anomalous situation and is at least partly the result of the freedom of manœuvre of powerful multinational companies which are not exposed to sufficient competition.

Marxist theory in any case has no need to assume that all business crime will be tolerated. Many forms of business misbehaviour made into crimes may reflect changing forms of capitalism or inter-class conflict. At any given period some corporate crimes, such as anti-trust offences, will not be in the interest of capitalism as a whole; it is therefore important to distinguish what is in the interests of capitalism from what suits particular capitalists. Even if the latter may succeed in blocking legislation or effective enforcement, at least in the short term, this does not prove that it is capitalism *per se* which requires the continuation of specific forms of misbehaviour. Moreover, capitalism is a set of practices and not just an important set of social actors. Practices may remain free from effective control even if the group concerned is not particularly economically powerful. The relative immunity from control of abuses of the Rent Acts by private business landlords has been attributed less to their importance within the social structure and more to objective difficulties in controlling their behaviour without affecting normal commercial transactions (Nelken 1983). When professional criminals succeed in getting away with serious forms of business-related crime such as long-firm fraud, it is implausible to say that this is in the interest of any capitalist group (Levi 1985).

Without underestimating the fruitfulness of hypotheses based on the capacity of capitalism to generate business crime, it seems wise to add that all organizations can be criminogenic in so far as they tend to reward achievement even at the expense of the outer environment. This would help explain why public organizations such as the army, the police or government bureaucracies also generate crime and corruption (these behaviours are increasingly being included in textbooks on white-collar crime). Likewise the far from positive record of the former communist regimes in matters of worker safety, environmental pollution, or corruption cannot be blamed on the pressures of competition. Even in capitalist societies it is often the *absence* of market pressures which explains some types of business misbehaviours, such as the ease with which government subsidy programmes are diverted to improper uses.

4. We have seen so far that there are, on the one hand, doubts about how far the same explanations will work for white-collar crime as for ordinary crime, and, on the other hand, risks of over-explanation in accounts which relate it too closely to ordinary business behaviour. For some commentators, however, the central issue to be addressed concerns the extent to which white-collar crimes come about in ways similar to other criminal behaviour. Clarke's book about 'business crime', for example, argues strongly that these misbehaviours are typically 'less criminal' in their inception and motivation than much ordinary crime (Clarke 1990*b*). Whereas many textbook presentations of white-collar crime simply list a variety of dangerous behaviours in a way which emphasizes their harmful consequences and implies that these are incurred deliberately or at least recklessly, Clarke attempts to recover their sense by putting them back into their everyday business context.

For Clarke there is a series of factors which distinguish the commission of business crimes (see also Punch 1991). Their location in the midst of ordinary business and occupational activity both facilitates their achievement and helps prevent their detection by colleagues and superiors as well as by outside authorities. In contrast to ordinary crimes such as burglary, the perpetrator has every justification for being present at the scene of the crime. Indeed, Clarke claims that unlike ordinary crimes, where presence at the scene is a crucial clue, with white-collar crimes the problem is not so much to identify the culprit as to discover whether there has been an offence. Police or regulatory agencies are reluctant to enter private settings without invitation and are often not called upon even where an offence has been committed. White-collar crimes are frequently what we could call 'complainantless crimes' and those who suffer the consequences of them cannot be relied upon to act as a reliable source of criminal intelligence. Clients of professionals are often unable to assess their performance—this is why they need to turn to them in the first place. Workers may simply be unaware of the risks to which they have been exposed; consumers will often not appreciate what they have lost; competitors will be unaware of collusive practices. The behaviour which constitutes white-collar crime is often indistinguishable on its surface from normal legal behaviour. For example, for fraud to succeed, it must obviously succeed in mimicking the appearance of legitimate transactions, and it is not unusual for those guilty of this crime to remain undetected for years, even a lifetime. Unlike all except 'victimless crimes' the involvement of the victim is apparently voluntary (though sometimes the result of the lure of easy money).

A further claim concerning the supposed distinctiveness of white-collar crime is virtually true by definition. The criminal aspects of the business or occupational activities under consideration are often *secondary* or *collateral* features, both in priority and in the succession of events, of an undertaking pursued for other, legitimate, purposes. Criminal consequences, such as damage to the health of workers or to the environment, often come about either as a result of omissions or because of financial pressures or unanticipated opportunities for gain; they are not inherent in the economic activity itself. Such criminality is difficult to recognize (in time) because of the narrow and constantly changing line between acceptable and unacceptable business behaviour. Even such essential features of outrightly crooked schemes as the deliberate withholding of payment to creditors may exist as practices in the legitimate world of business—for example as a desperate manœuvre by small businesses trying to survive on tight margins, or as a more cynical use of market strength by large enterprises exploiting the dependence of small contractors on their patronage. This makes it difficult for all concerned—creditors, regulators, and others—to tell whether, or at what point, the intention permanently to avoid payment was formed.

Ambiguity surrounds not only the goals of the activity in the midst of which white-collar crime is encountered but also, it is argued, the degree of intention involved. There are certainly notorious cases of cold-blooded calculation: for example, the way in which Ford went ahead with its dangerous design for the Ford rear engine because it estimated that the potential payment of damages would be less than the cost of recalling the cars (Dowie 1988); or the manner in which P&O disregarded repeated requests for the installation of bow warning lights to improve safety on their on–off ferries. But, it is argued, these are the exceptions (and even these cases did not end in criminal convictions). More commonly it is difficult to distinguish malevolence from incompetence; and, as Clarke insists, in business and professional life we are often more concerned about the harmful effects of the latter. A professional is specifically valued for her competence rather than for her honesty as such (which is perhaps taken for granted); in large organizations and bureaucracies there is considerable scope for laziness or lack of interest which may have tragic consequences. These points, it is said, are less true of ordinary crime.

On the other hand, many scholars would insist that these aspects of the setting and commission of white-collar crimes mainly point to problems of detection, without negating the essential similarities between these and ordinary crimes. Businesses involved in offending behaviour often do their best to organize in such a way as to minimize the costs of their infractions (concealing compromising knowledge from directors, appointing 'vice presidents responsible for going to jail', etc.). Conversely, there are also occasions where enforcement against ordinary crime has to overcome similar difficulties of categorization. The difficulty of identifying the 'really' criminal cases is not unique to white-collar crime. The definition of 'dishonesty' in the English law of theft, for example, leaves it to the jury to decide whether the behaviour at issue demonstrates the requisite level of criminal intent in terms of what ordinary people would consider stealing: the business world would probably be capable of answering a similar question. Many ordinary crimes, such as assault, also fall on a continuum that runs from accidental to deliberate, but we do not let this place the appropriateness of criminal sanctions in doubt. Indeed, we take trouble to hold individuals responsible for the consequences of their assaults even when this exceeds their intention or even their foresight (for a recent example see *R* v. *Le Brun* 1991 3 WLR 653 CA (Criminal Division). Much also depends on the time-frame adopted for identifying the commission of an offence. For example, the conduct that causes a serious breach of health or safety standards may have been unintended at the time of the accident but deliberate when the choice was made not to install up-to-date and costly measures of prevention (Kelman 1981). Philosophical studies of when we choose to describe an action as voluntary or not assert that (because of the difficulty of defining what is meant by 'will') this is itself a way of indicating our evaluation of the actions in question rather than simply a description of them.

Like so much concerning the social definition of white-collar crime, the question of intention therefore easily lends itself to social construction. Much ambiguity—or, conversely, the provision of a cover of ostensible legality—is a contingent product of social processing. Thus accountants and barristers may use their professional skills to help businesses construct tax-avoidance schemes which must then appear as anything but deliberate attempts to evade tax (McBarnet 1991). If a case reaches trial, defence lawyers work hard to redefine the misconduct as not having been deliberate (Mann 1985). White-collar criminals may even find they have allies in the redefinition of their behaviour in those trying their misbehaviour. In the course of research into deviance by professionals I made a study of the (confidential) proceedings of English family practitioner tribunals, which deal with cases where dentists (and other professionals) are alleged not to have complied with their National Health contracts. Here everything is done to avoid the impression that potentially criminal behaviour is at issue, even though in cases where misconduct is proved fixed withholdings from payment serve the function of fines. In one case, for example, a dentist admitted to 'fraud' in deliberately claiming for more work than he had done, only to find the tribunal members pleading with him to retract his admission (and claim inadvertence) so that they could retain jurisdiction.

While it is debatable how far the ambiguous aspects alleged to characterize the commission of white-collar crime are intrinsic features restricted to this type of misbehaviour, there are certainly some important cases where criminals deliberately exploit the appearance of legitimate business. In fact the overlap between white-collar crime and more clear-cut kinds of crime, such as organized crime, has so far been relatively neglected in comparison with the attention given to the boundary between white-collar crime and ordinary business behaviour (but see e.g. Smith 1980). Professional or organized criminals may *create* ambiguity by fostering the impression of genuine business enterprises, if necessary by trading normally for an initial period. At other times they may penetrate legitimate companies, especially when these have fallen on hard times, and use them to launch purely criminal activities such as long-firm frauds (Levi 1981). Organized criminal businesses may seek to monopolize the market for legitimate goods and services, such as public construction projects or waste-processing, beating their competitors with their lower marginal costs and using violence or corruption against competitors or those with the power to award lucrative contracts, as with Camorra enterprises in the Campania area of Italy and the activities of many of the *cosche* of the New Mafia (Arlachi 1985). The division of labour between legitimate and illegitimate business, on the other hand, can also represent an attempt to disguise the criminal presuppositions of legal enterprises. Legitimate business may call upon the service of criminals for particular operations such as loan repayment, money laundering, or tax evasion (Block 1991: chs. 5, 6). They may take advantage of the operation of international criminals—for example, major electrical companies apparently find it financially profitable to buy and resell (at the expense of other wholesalers) examples of their own products illegally smuggled on to the market (Van Duyne 1993). Legal enterprise may rely on organized criminals to supply a disciplined workforce, as in the New York construction industry (New York State Organised Crime Task Force 1988), or to get rid of industrial waste-products in illegal ways so as to reduce their external costs of production (Szasz 1986). With the growth of concern about the environment and the explosion of new regulatory crimes in this and other areas, (cf. Sgubbi 1990), we may predict a considerable increase in this sort of collaboration. Conversly, organized criminals may call upon legitimate businesses such as printers or supermarkets in developing major frauds, such as those against the EEC agricultural subsidy programmes (Passas and Nelken 1993); such symbiosis is also essential for the purpose of recycling money earned in illegal activities. The steady growth in international and transnational trading—and the changing face of national and economic borders in Europe—is also leading to an increase in different types of criminals seeking to profit from the opportunities these changes offer them (Passas and Nelken 1993; Van Duyne 1993). Future research on white-collar crime will therefore need to look more closely at the relationships between legal, semi-legal, and illegal economic activities. Such work will need to involve a comparative dimension, both because these relationships differ among countries and because many of these crimes have an international dimension (Nelken 1994). Appreciation of the political and economic structures conducive to such operations requires the criminologist to be open to concepts pioneered in disciplines other than sociology, including ideas about clientilism in political science, legal and illegal monopolies in economics, and risk analysis in accounting and management science.

THE AMBIVALENT RESPONSE TO WHITE-COLLAR CRIME

5. As the above discussion will already have shown, there are various ways in which the control of white-collar crime can also play a part in its causation. Government and business may share similar imperatives which coincide to favour offending. Carson's description of the importance of speed in the calculations of both the Treasury and the oil companies in the exploitation of North Sea oil, and the consequent sacrifice of ordinary safety standards, is an extreme example of such objective coincidence of interests (Carson 1981). The Bank of England may be caught between its duties as regulator of the banking system and its desire not to compromise the credibility of one of the major clearing banks (*The Economist* 1992). But even where government and offenders are clearly opposed, weak regulatory regimes or moves towards deregulation may provide an incentive to offend. One common situation which leads to increased crime is the combination of removing legal or informal constraints on a business sector with the simultaneous resort to (new) criminal penalties to be available as a last resort. Complex and changing regulatory regimes, especially those involving government payment schemes, may in themselves provide the opportunity for crime (Vaughan 1983, Passas and Nelken 1993).

The methods adopted in responding to white-collar crime play a particularly important part in shaping this type of behaviour, inasmuch as the difficulty of relying on complainants means that the accent must be put on prevention and proactive enforcement. In this way our information about these types of misbehaviour often tells us more about the theories and priorities of the controllers than anything else (for example, the belief that small firms are more likely than large ones to bend the rules will inevitably find confirmation in the statistics of violations discovered). However, the main issue which needs to be discussed under this heading is the charge that the different enforcement methods used to respond to white-collar as compared to ordinary crimes reinforce their ambiguous status and indirectly contribute to their causation. Is the difference in handling the cause or consequence of the distinctiveness of white-collar crime? Many scholars stress the fact that white-collar crimes are difficult to detect and control. It is difficult to prove intention when dealing with decisions taken within an organization (and legal thinking has not yet caught up with the importance of organizations); trials are long and expensive, juries have problems in understanding the evidence in complex fraud cases; professional advisers acting for businesspeople can delay or defeat prosecution. Extra powers for obtaining evidence given to the Department of Trade inspectors or the recently established Serious Fraud Office go only some of the way to dealing with these difficulties, as demonstrated by the spectacular collapse of the recent Blue Arrow prosecutions, amongst others. A premium is therefore placed on achieving compliance without the need for prosecution (although this is used as a threat, the need to resort to it is seen as failure.) It is considered still better to rely on self-regulation by an industry or by the business itself. But reliance on self-policing can easily lead to conflicts of interest: for example, banks find themselves both potential participators in money laundering and also required to detect and deter it (Levi 1991*a*, *b*).

Some scholars (such as Clarke 1990*b*, but here his views are more widely shared) argue that the way white-collar crimes are handled reflects the special circumstances of these offences. It makes sense to use compliance in the regulation of occupations because offenders can easily be found at their place of occupation and it is feasible to put repeated pressure on them. Violations of safety or pollution standards are difficult and costly to conceal. Even the apparently paradoxical practice of giving advance warning of inspection visits does not therefore lead to concealment of offending. The difficulty in respect of other business offences, Clarke argues, is to identify the commission of an offence rather than to find the offender. But even here offenders in organizations do tend to leave a 'paper trail' of their actions.

Different interpretations of the nature of white-collar crimes lead to corresponding views concerning the best way to handle them. Clarke argues that an approach based on criminal prosecution is inappropriate for all but a few cases of business crime. Complainants are mainly interested in recompense and go to the police only if all else fails; the criminal process polarizes the parties, involves delay, carries risks of failure, and, above all, does nothing to secure future improvement in the relevant working practices. Existing enforcement practices make more sense; suggestions for improvement, should be based mainly on trying to internalize better methods of control within businesses themselves rather than increasing prosecution (Stone 1975 is a classic discussion of this theme). But the opposite point of view is also well supported. Green summarizes an extensive American literature which offers various proposals for improving the effectiveness of prosecution against white-collar crimes (Green 1990: ch. 8; see also Groves and Newman 1986). The assumption behind much of this work is that business behaviour is in fact particularly well suited to the application of deterrent criminal sanctions. Offences (it is alleged) are strictly instrumental and offenders have much to lose from prosecution; prison, if only it were to be used regularly, would be more potent than for ordinary criminals. The main problem in current practice is that of producing a level of fines sufficient actually to deter business from crime. Solutions such as stock dilution, equity fining, ceding shares to the state may all work, but in cases where there has been physical injury may give the wrong message that everything can ultimately be paid for. Informally and formally initiated negative publicity is unlikely to put a firm out of business but can and does have collateral effects and may help produce beneficial procedural changes within firms (Fisse and Braithwaite 1985). Green's discussion is thin on the questions which are central for Clarke concerning the possible counter-productive effects of using the normal criminal process for white-collar crime. On the other hand, many of Clarke's arguments against the use of prosecution could also be made regarding ordinary crime—certainly the victim usually gains little from the criminal process and seems rather to be used by the system to serve its own ends.

For many observers the difficulties of controlling white-collar crime, and the need to rely on compliance techniques, should rather be attributed to a lack of political will to provide the resources necessary for a full-blown prosecution approach. In Britain proportionally few police officers are assigned to the fraud squad, the prestige of such assignments is low, and the term of service short (Levi 1987). For the United States Calavita and Pontell argue that the savings and loans crash in the United States was due in part to the lack of trained thrift examiners and the excess workload of FBI agents directed to clear up the scandal (Calavita and Pontell 1992). Even the famous and feared American Securities and Exchange Commission, according to Shapiro, is forced to choose between detection or enforcement and only uses the criminal sanction in around 11 per cent of cases (Shapiro 1984).

The actual combination of objective difficulties and political priorities in decisions over prosecution is often concealed by ideologically loaded communication. Much white-collar crime is subject to regulation under the heading of strict liability by which, in theory, even unintentional offending can be held criminally culpable. Criminal law textbooks and philosophical writers discuss whether or not this is justified by the difficulty of proving intention in complex modern industrial processes. However, investigations of the 'logic in use' of the inspectorates responsible (at least in common-law countries) for some of the most important areas of social regulation, such as those concerning worker safety or environmental pollution, tell a different story. In practice, apart from cases in which accidents have taken place, breaches of rules will normally be sanctioned only if *mens rea* and even recidivism has been shown by a refusal to correct matters pointed out by the inspector in warning visits and letters (Carson 1970; Hawkins 1984; Hawkins and Thomas 1984; Hutter 1988). The inspectors involved in such enforcement activity refuse to see themselves as 'industrial policemen' and see their role rather as one geared to advising and cajoling the majority of fundamentally law-abiding businessmen. One consequence (perhaps even an intended one; see Carson 1974, 1980) of this difference between theory and practice is that the imposition of strict liability reduces the stigma associated with these offences so as to reinforce the impression that they represent behaviour which is merely *mala prohibita* rather than *mala in se*. Enforcement techniques which concentrate on consequences rather than intentions by collapsing the distinction between incompetence and deliberateness thus often end up diluting rather than extending criminal stigma.

Difficulties of enforcement may be exaggerated to conceal other decisions (or 'non-decisions') about responding to criminal behaviour by economically influential groups. In an important later study Carson argued convincingly that the causes of accidents on North Sea oil rigs were little different from those which lead to accidents in factories or on construction sites (Carson 1981). The claim that the high level of injuries was due to the difficulty of regulating activities operating 'at the frontiers of technology' at hitherto untried depths of oil exploration at sea was not supported by his careful examination of the relevant case-records. The crucial issue was the fact that the responsibility for ensuring compliance with the normal standards of safety had been assigned not to the factory inspectors of the Health and Safety Inspectorate (here seen in more heroic light than in Carson's earlier work) but to the Department of Energy. Since this was also the body responsible for encouraging oil exploration to proceed as fast as possible in the interests of the British balance of payments, there was an inevitable conflict of interests in which the interests of the weakest groups were sacrificed.

Since Sutherland the subject of white-collar crime has also been the focus of attempts to prove that the rich and powerful are treated more favourably by the criminal justice system. Some caveats should be entered here. The main basis for the relative immunity of businesspeople in the criminal process (at least in Anglo-American jurisdictions) derives from political choices regarding which behaviour to make criminal in the first place, and only to a lesser extent from the way their offences are categorized. Those effectively criminalized for business-related offences tend to be small businesspeople, quite often from immigrant backgrounds (Nelken 1983; Croal 1989). It is a mistake to confuse the macro (legislative) and micro (enforcement) logics which keep criminality and respectability apart. Many of those working in the criminal justice system would actually be interested (and have an interest) in successful prosecutions of 'the powerful'. Thus apparently ineffective legislative outcomes are often best studied as a product of 'coherence without conspiracy' (Nelken 1983). This does not mean, of course, that there cannot also be more explicit cases of prejudice, and there have rightly been many attacks on alleged bias and injustice in the handling of white-collar crimes, from enforcement to trial and beyond. As with most accusations of bias, however, the difficulty is ensuring that like is being compared with like.

A recent debate over the alleged leniency involved in using 'compliance' methods for dealing with white-collar regulatory offences is that between Pearce and Tombs, on the one hand, and Hawkins, on the other (Pearce and Tombs 1990, 1991; Hawkins 1990, 1991). But although the argument represented opposing positions, each of which is quite widely shared, it did not take matters much further. Pearce and Tombs began by criticizing Hawkins's and other recent descriptions of the compliance approach for giving the appearance of being persuaded by the 'logic in use' of those whose enforcement strategy they described. In this way, it was alleged, they (indirectly) confirmed an unfair status quo instead of supporting the adoption of stricter methods which could reduce the level of harm caused by such offences. Hawkins fiercely challenged this as a misreading of the role of interpretative sociology (which was not directed towards policy evaluation), but then went on to endorse the compliance strategy in general terms without necessarily agreeing with all its tactics or the severity of the sanctions applied. For their part, Pearce and Tombs recommended that prosecution should begin at an earlier stage, favoured the imposition of (low) fines rather than simply warning notices, and wanted there to be more use of other sanctions such as the withdrawal of licences. In his reply, Hawkins pointed out that very few of the violations noted in routine proactive enforcement do eventually turn out to be the cause of serious harm and that it is not possible to predict which will do so. Unless Pearce and Tombs really want to cut back sharply on enforcement discretion, their proposals are unlikely to produce much change in current practice. To insist on legal action each time a violation is revealed, as was tried for a time by the American OSHA mines authority, tends to be counter-productive in terms of destroying the goodwill of those being regulated. It also risks producing a political backlash leading to deregulation, as happened in the case of this agency.

As this summary suggests, this and similar debates fail to make progress mainly because the policy arguments of Hawkins and others like him assume as givens exactly those political realities which their critics would like to see changed. A valuable study which points out this moral is Cook's comparison of the harsh response to those suspected of social security fraud with that meted out to those engaged in tax frauds of very similar kinds (Cook 1989). The very different treatment received by the two groups does not so much relate to the practical possibilities of enforcement (more or less the same for both), or to fears of counter-productive effects from tougher penalties, but rather follows from a set of associated beliefs about the relative worth and importance of maintaining the goodwill of each set of offenders.

Some of the most fruitful proposals for strengthening the control of white-collar crime, which acknowledge the force of both sides of this debate, are currently being developed by Braithwaite on the basis of his research into the successes and failures of regulation in very different industries and businesses, such as drug manufacturing, coal mining, and nursing homes. He suggests that businesses (beyond a certain size) should be obliged by government to write a set of rules tailored to the unique contingencies of their firm. These rules should be submitted for comment and amendment to interest groups, including citizen groups. Firms should have their own internal compliance units with statutory responsibility on the director to report cases of violation and the function of government inspectors would be to audit and if necessary sanction the performance of this unit (see e.g. Braithwaite 1989).

It might be thought that the study of bias in the prosecution and trial of white-collar crimes should be more straightforward than an evalution of the justifiability of its special style of enforcement; but even here there is no consensus. Analysis of the penalties meted out for serious frauds in Britain as compared to other types of crime certainly suggests that these are the crimes which are the most rewarding (Levi 1991*c*). Shapiro, in her study of securities offenders in the USA, detected a tendency for higher-status offenders to be less likely to receive criminal penalties instead of being dealt with by administrative or civil measures (Shapiro 1984, 1989). But in their more comprehensive American study Weisburd *et al.* (even after double-checking) found that higher-status offenders were more likely to receive prison sentences (Weisburd *et al.* 1991: 7). In their earlier study Wheeler *et al.* (using a sample of pre-1980 American social inquiry reports and case files) showed that penalties for white-collar crimes depended on the criteria normal for other crimes: prior record, seriousness of crime, degree of involvement of offender, the nature of and harm to the victim, etc., though there was also some limited evidence of judges identifying with the offender more than in cases of ordinary crimes, especially if the latter involve personal violence (Wheeler *et al.* 1988). They left it open whether the judges were merely reproducing (unconsciously or deliberately) the biases of the wider population.

Instead of demanding that white-collar criminals be treated like ordinary criminals we could argue the reverse (though this is rarely done). Why not apply the methods used for dealing with businesspeople and professionals to ordinary criminals? Much of what purports to be regulation or self-regulation of white-collar crime is bogus or ineffectual and deserves to be attacked as such. But there is also much to be learned from the variety of forms of regulation and self-regulation designed to reduce violations without criminalizing the offender. Even if it would probably be impossible to model the handling of ordinary crime too closely on that of business crime, the differences are not as great as is often claimed. All non-police agencies—even when not dealing with powerful offenders—put the emphasis on recovering money rather than securing convictions (Royal Commission on Criminal Procedure 1980). The problem of apprehending and maintaining pressure on ordinary criminals is not as great as it seems: the police do know just where to lay their hands on juvenile delinquents and quite a few other criminal suspects. And in a sense compliance does already get used with ordinary criminals: (Pearce and Tombs mention police control of prostitution and gambling as an example of compliance (though they use these examples to show the danger of collusion and corruption in the use of such methods). The role of social work and diversion (before trial) and probation or other techniques of rehabilitation (after conviction) is similar. And the choice between co-operation and compulsion is repeatedly offered to ordinary criminals from the stage of pleading guilty to that of obtaining parole. A crucial difference, however, is that it is usually necessary for an offender accused of ordinary crime to suffer the stigma of a conviction before consideration is given to compliance, whereas the opposite is true for business offenders handled in this way. The temptation is to believe that, beyond a certain point, enforcement against ordinary crime is geared precisely to maximizing stigma even at the expense of effectiveness. Pearce and Tombs do seem correct in tracing the difference in approach to the (untested) assumption that businesspeople are basically disposed to respond to a compliance approach (whereas ordinary criminals are presumed to require punishment)—though they prefer the equally untested assumption that businesspeople should be dealt with as 'amoral calculators'. It is reasonable to conclude that practical considerations regarding effective enforcement provide insufficient justification for the extent of the present contrast between methods used for ordinary and business crimes. A considerable merit of Braithwaite's long-standing search for an effective as well as just approach to the control of all types of crime—what he calls 'reintegrative shaming' (Braithwaite 1989)—is that it builds in a series of attempts at compliance as a prelude to prosecution.

6. Whatever the reasons or justifications for the methods used to control white-collar crime, the ambivalence of the social response to this sort of behaviour is also related to wider social factors which have both objective and subjective dimensions. For Aubert (as well as for writers such as E. A. Ross who anticipated Sutherland's ideas on this topic) the ambiguity of white-collar crimes reflected the objective fact that they were the index of important transitions in social structure. A good example of this phenomenon is the practice of 'insider trading' on the stock exchange and in other financial institutions, which has recently come to be penalized in Britain, but is still not criminal in all European countries. As Clarke argues,

> It would have perplexed leading members of these institutions up to the end of the 1950s to be told that they were doing anything reprehensible in acting on such information. It was precisely because of the access to such information that one was part of the City, and one was part of the City in the clear expectation of making a considerable amount of money. (Clarke 1990*b*: 162)

The crime of insider trading therefore nicely symbolizes the change from a time when there were only 'insiders' (see also Stanley 1992).

Ambiguity thus results from a situation in which previously legal behaviour has only recently been redefined; and it is exacerbated when the boundaries are changed in ways which are to some extent outside the control of the community being regulated. But we could extend Aubert's analysis by saying that social and legal definitions of crime may be out of joint either because public attitudes have not caught up with the legal recognition of important economic and social changes or because the law has not yet recognized the seriousness of behaviour which causes public concern (in both cases these processes will be mediated by interest and pressure groups). As a further complication we should note that economic and legal definitions will not always coincide (insider trading is still seen as economically useful by some economists). Conversely, at any given time there will be some practices which are quite legal but of dubious economic value, a current example being corporate raiding so as to bid up the price of a business and sell on at a profit. It is therefore not always easy to tell when the time has arrived at which particular business practices have lost all economic justification. In a stimulating recent paper Calavita and Pontell discuss the economic justifications for the type of practices which were the subject of financial scandals and prosecutions during and after the Reaganite period of relaxation of economic controls in the 1980s (Calavita and Pontell 1992). This period saw the breaking down of barriers between banks and other financial institutions and a great increase in the scale and internationalization of financial transactions. Drawing on the idea of the French economist Allais, they argue that much of what is produced in what he calls the 'casino economy' is of illusory economic benefit. If, for example, it only takes $12 billion of commercial trade to generate $400 billion of foreign exchange transactions, the amounts of money that can be manipulated are far in excess of the goods to which they correspond. The system is kept going only by trust in the backing of these transactions; equally, an excess of confidence can bring about disaster if it allows the production of 'junk bonds' or helps sustain unsound financial institutions. Calavita and Pontell point to various characteristic abuses of this period, such as corporate takeovers, currency trading and futures trading, 'land flips', 'daisy chains' and other forms of property speculation, and the switching of loans to confuse auditors regarding actual assets. Emblematic for them was the accumulation of enormous uncollectable loans relying on federal deposit insurance in the massive 'savings and loans' scandal.

Provocative as their argument is, Calavita and Pontell may none the less be wrong in thinking that the practices from which these scandals arose (which they associate with finance capital as opposed to industrial capital) can be controlled severely without risk to jobs or to economically sound activities. Much of what they describe, shorn of obvious abuses (and it should be noted that the savings and loans fiasco was as much the result of over-generous government guarantees to bank investors as it was of speculation and financial mismanagement), may point to changes in what makes economic sense in a world where the costs of production increasingly favour countries outside the USA and Western Europe. They themselves may be relying on an outdated model of industrial capitalism as the only proper conception of a functioning economy.

A more subjective source of ambivalence in the social response to white-collar crime is the assumption that there is less public concern about these behaviours and therefore less support for severe sanctions than is the case with more familiar 'street crimes'—especially those involving violence (though this may be the result of existing methods of control). A series of studies have therefore sought to demonstrate that the public in fact ranks examples of these crimes quite severely as compared to ordinary crimes (see e.g. Cullen *et al.* 1983; Green 1990: 47–57). Harsh attitudes towards such conduct, going well beyond the penalties actually meted out, can be documented in cases of culpable disasters caused by white-collar offenders (Calavita *et al.* 1991). On the other hand, some recent attempts to measure public attitudes to white-collar crime do reveal greater leniency in public attitudes (see e.g. Goff and Nason-Clarke 1989). Much depends on the way questions about different crimes are phrased and the extent to which effort is made to refer to the possible side-effects of the use of certain sanctions. But, even if it were to be shown that there was greater public ambivalence towards white-collar crimes than towards ordinary crimes, writers such as Box would only regard this a further challenge 'to sensitize people to not seeing processes in which they are victimised as disasters or accidents' (Box 1983: 233).

7. Many of the sources of ambiguity discussed so far can also be related to the value conflicts and policy dilemmas so often cited as explaining, and even justifying, a cautious response to white-collar crime. The regulation of white-collar crime has been seen as the locus of a number of different awkward policy choices. Risk-taking is said to be the motor of the capitalist economy; but someone has to pay the price of the inevitable failures. The pursuit of greater health and safety has costs in terms of national and international competitiveness and jobs, and this explains (justifies?) the acceptance of no more than a 'reasonable' level of safety or pollution. In many areas of business crime, enforcers are obliged to choose between going for punishment (and stigmatization) and achieving compliance or maximizing the amount of revenue recovered. Other dilemmas are more particular. If we are worried about money laundering does this mean that we want to see banks become a crucial part of the justice system? What about the rights to privacy and confidentiality (Levi 1991*a*, *b*)? On the other hand, we should not assume that such *post hoc* philosophical dilemmas or justifications are the actual movers of political action. To explain the actual social weight given to these conflicting values we also need to provide a sociology of public policy choices. Starting from a Marxist perspective, Snider, for example, examines the dialectic between the state, business interests, pressure groups, public opinion, etc. in an attempt to explain the contrasting fate of different types of regulation (Snider 1991). She argues that the resistance to effective implementation of legislation concerning health and safety at work is explicable in terms of the fact that these laws are not in the interests of business itself (except where they can be used by large businesses to beat off the competition of smaller firms). Industry tends—with the collusion of the State—to balance the safety of workers against the increased costs of production. The victims of these crimes are diffuse, though not as diffuse as the victims of crimes against the environment. Anti-trust legislation has more success because the state is interested in bringing down its costs as a major purchaser from the private sector, and at least parts of the business world are in favour of such laws. On the other hand, the monopolies and cartels which already control many major markets provide firm resistance; and, of less importance, unions may be ambivalent because of the threat to jobs which could follow the break-up of large conglomerations. Insider trading and stock-market fraud, she claims,

should encounter least resistance (as the success of the American Securities and Exchange Commission supposedly illustrates) because here the interests of the state and business coincide. Business needs to be able to raise money on the stock market and government does not want to have to bail out defrauded investors. We will be reminded of the social determination of these policy dilemmas if we accept that the control of ordinary crime may also have a number of negative side-effects, on the offender, his or her family, and the community, which tend to be ignored when the crucial criterion of policy choice is reduced to the need to continue business as usual.

The potential of criminology to contribute to shaping public policy concerning the best way to regulate white-collar crime is likely to increase in importance but it is unlikely to be univocal in its recommendations. There will also always be a need for denouncing the crimes of the 'powerful' and their many illegal (as well as semi-legal and legal) ways of causing harm. But experience as well as theoretical considerations would suggest that there are severe difficulties in using the criminal law to control the groups most powerful within a given society (quite apart from the danger that tougher measures may have counter-productive effects for their victims). It is extremely difficult to get laws passed which represent a real threat to current economic interests; and, even when such laws exist, when it comes to enforcement the choice may lie between stigmatization without effective regulation or regulation without stigmatization. On the other hand, as we have seen, it is too easily taken for granted that treating white-collar crime as crime, or fitting it into the usual paradigm of criminological explanation, goes hand in hand with a belief in the appropriateness of actually using criminal sanctions to reduce the behaviour; this is one reason why the argument over ambiguities has tended to get pulled one way or the other depending on the practical conclusions the analyst wanted to draw. Yet there are many precedents for criminological explanations which do not indicate the individual offender as the key causal factor or the appropriate point of intervention (e.g. blocked opportunity theories of juvenile delinquency). Most of those who offer explanations which refer to capitalism or other structural factors of ordinary business life do as it happens also want to criminalize the offender (see e.g. Box 1983). But, as Cohen has argued, a focus on crime in organizations needs to avoid seeking to assign blame in identifying the important links relevant to organizational outcomes (Cohen 1977). Whether it is right for law to attach criminal penalties to certain behaviours, and to seek to enforce such penalties when this misses the underlying causes of such behaviour, is a question which goes beyond the scope of criminology. But it is certainly not a question confined to white-collar crimes, nor irrelevant to many more ordinary ones.

Selected Further Reading

S. Box, *Power, Crime and Mystification*. London: Tavistock, 1983.

W. G. Carson, *The Other Price of Britain's Oil*. Oxford: Martin Robertson, 1982.

H. Croal, *White Collar Crime*. Milton Keynes: Open University Press, 1992.

M. Clarke, *Business Crime: Its Nature and Control*. Cambridge: Polity, 1990.

M. Levi, *Regulating Fraud*. London: Tavistock, 1987.

D. Nelken, ed., *White-Collar Crime*. Aldershot: Dartmouth, 1994.

S. Shapiro, 'Collaring the Crime, not the Criminal: Reconsidering "White-Collar Crime"', *American Sociological Review*, 1989, 55: 346–65.

E. H. Sutherland, *White Collar Crime: The Uncut Version*. New Haven: Yale University Press, 1983.

REFERENCES

ARLACHI, P. (1985), *Mafia Business*. Oxford: Oxford University Press.

AUBERT, V. (1952), 'White Collar Crime and Social Structure', *American Journal of Sociology*, 58: 263–71.

BLOCK, A. (1991), *Perspectives on Organising Crime*. Boston/London: Kluwer.

BOX, S. (1983), *Power, Crime and Mystification*. London: Tavistock.

BRAITHWAITE, J. (1984), *Corporate Crime in the Pharmaceutical Industry*. London: Routledge and Kegan Paul.

—— (1985), 'White-Collar Crime', *Annual Review of Sociology*, 11: 1–25.

—— (1989), *Crime, Shame and Integration*. Cambridge: Cambridge University Press.

BURGESS, E. (1950), 'Comment to Hartung', *American Journal of Sociology*, 56: 25–34.

CALAVITA, K. *et al.* (1991), 'Dam Disasters and Durkheim', *International Journal of the Sociology of Law*, 19: 407–27.

CALAVITA, K., and PONTELL, H. (1992), 'The Savings and Loans Crisis' in *Corporate and Governmental Deviance* (M. Erdmann and R. Lundman eds.) Oxford: Oxford University Press.

CARSON, W. G. (1970), 'White Collar Crime and the Enforcement of Factory Legislation', *British Journal of Criminology*, 10: 383–98.

—— (1974), 'Symbolic and Instrumental Dimensions of Early Factory Legislation', in R. Hood, ed., *Crime, Criminology and Public Policy*, 107–38. London: Heinemann.

—— (1980), 'The Institutionalisation of Ambiguity: The Early British Factory Acts', in G. Geis and E. Stotland, eds., *White Collar Crime: Theory and Research*, 142–73. London/New York: Sage.

—— (1981), *The Other Price of Britain's Oil.* Oxford: Martin Robertson.

Clarke, M. (1990*a*), 'The Control of Insurance Fraud: A Comparative View', *British Journal of Criminology*, 30.

—— (1990*b*), *Business Crime: Its Nature and Control.* Cambridge: Polity Press.

Clinard, M., and Yeager, P. (1980), *Corporate Crime.* New York: Free Press.

Cohen, A. K. (1977), 'The Concept of Criminal Organization', *British Journal of Criminology*, 18: 97–111.

Coleman, J. W. (1985), *The Criminal Elite: The Sociology of White Collar Crime.* New York: St Martin's Press.

—— (1987), 'Toward an Integrated Theory of White Collar Crime', *American Journal of Sociology*, 93: 406–39.

—— (1992), 'The Assymetric Society', in M. Erdmann and R. Lundman, eds., *Corporate and Governmental Deviance.* Oxford: Oxford University Press.

Cook, D. (1989), *Rich Law, Poor Law.* Milton Keynes: Open University Press.

Cosson, J. (1978), *Les Industriels de la Fraude Fiscale.* Paris: Éditions du Seuil.

Croal, H. (1989), 'Who is the White-Collar Criminal?' *British Journal of Criminology*, 29: 157–74.

Cullen, F. *et al* (1983), 'Public Support for Punishing White-Collar Criminals', *Journal of Criminal Justice*, 11: 481–93.

Delmas-Marty, M. (1990), *Droit Pénal des Affaires*, 2 vols. Paris: Presses Universitaires de France.

Dowie, M. (1988), 'Pinto Madness', in Stuart L. Hills, ed., *Corporate Violence: Injury and Death for Profit.* Totowa, NJ: Rowman and Littlefield.

The Economist (1992), 'The Blue Arrow Affair', 7 March 23.

Edelhertz, H. (1970), *The Nature, Impact and Prosecution of White-Collar Crime.* Washington, DC: US Government Printing Office.

Fisse, B., and Braithwaite, J. (1985), *The Impact of Publicity on Corporate Offenders.* Albany, NY: State University of New York Press.

Geis, G. (1968), 'The Heavy Electrical Equipment Anti-Trust Cases of 1961', in G. Geis, ed., *White-Collar Crime.* Atherton Press.

—— (1990), 'Foreword', in G. S. Green, *Occupational Crime.* Chicago: Nelson-Hall.

Goff, C., and Nason-Clarke, N. (1989), 'The Seriousness of Crime in Fredericton, New Brunswick: Perceptions toward White Collar Crime', *Canadian Journal of Criminology*, 31: 19–34.

Gottfredson, M., and Hirschi, T. (1990), *A General Theory of Crime.* Stanford: Stanford University Press.

Green, G. S. (1990), *Occupational Crime.* Chicago: Nelson-Hall.

Gross, E. (1980), 'Organisational structure and Organisational Crime',in G. Geis and E. Stotland, eds., *White-Collar Crime: Theory and Research.* London/New York: Sage.

Groves, W. B., and Newman, G. eds. (1986), *Punishment and Privilege.* Albany, NY: Harrow and Heston.

Hartung, F, (1950), 'White Collar Offences in the Wholesale Meat Industry in Detroit', *American Journal of Sociology*, 56: 25–34.

Hawkins, K. (1984), *Environment and Enforcement: Regulation and the Social Definition of Pollution.* Oxford: Clarendon Press.

—— (1990), 'Compliance Strategy, Prosecution Policy, and Aunt Sally: A Comment on Pearce and Tombs', *British Journal of Criminology*, 30: 444–66.

—— (1991), 'Enforcing Regulation: More of the Same from Pearce and Tombs', *British Journal of Criminology*, 31: 427–30.

Hawkins, K., and Thomas, J. M., eds. (1984), *Enforcing Regulation.* Nijhoff: Kluwer.

Hills, S. L., ed. (1988), *Corporate Violence: Injury and Death for Profit.* Totowa, NJ: Rowman and Littlefield.

Hirschi, T., and Gottfredson, M. (1987), 'Causes of White-Collar Crime', *Criminology*, 25: 949–74.

—— (1989), 'The Significance of White-Collar Crime for a General Theory of Crime', *Criminology*, 27: 359–72.

Hobbs, D. (1986), *Doing the Business.* Oxford: Clarendon Press.

Hutter, B. (1988), *The Reasonable Arm of the Law?* Oxford: Clarendon Press.

Katz, J. (1980), 'The Social Movement against White Collar Crime', *Criminology Review Yearbook 1980*: 161–84.

Kelman, S. (1981), 'Substantive Interpretation in the Criminal Law', *Stanford Law Review*, 33: 591–67.

Lane, R. (1953), 'Why Businessmen Violate the Law', *Journal of Criminal Law, Criminology and Police Science*, 44: 151–65.

Leonard, W. N., and Weber, M. G. (1970), 'Automakers and Dealers: A Study of Criminogenic Market Forces', *Law and Society Review*, 4: 407–24.

Levi, M. (1981), *The Phantom Capitalists.* London: Gower.

—— (1985), A Criminological and Sociological Approach to Theories of and Research into Economic Crime', in D. Magnuson, ed., *Economic Crime: Programs for Future Research*, 32–72. Stockholm: National Council for Crime Prevention, Report no. 18.

—— (1987), *Regulating Fraud.* London: Tavistock.

—— (1991*a*), 'Pecunia Non Olet: Cleansing the Money Launderers from the Temple', *Crime, Law and Social Change*, 16: 217–302.

—— (1991*b*), Regulating Money Laundering', *British Journal of Criminology*, 31: 109–25.

—— (1991*c*), 'Fraudulent Justice? Sentencing the Business Criminal', in P. Carlen and D. Cook, eds., *Paying for Crime*, 86–108. Milton Keynes: Open University Press.

McBarnet, D. (1991), 'Whiter than White Collar Crime: Tax, Fraud Insurance and the Management of Stigma', *British Journal of Sociology*, 42: 323–44.

Magnusson, D., ed. (1985), *Economic Crime: Programs for Future Research.* Stockholm: National Council for Crime Prevention, no. 18.

Mann, M. (1985), *Defending White Collar Crime.* New Haven: Yale University Press.

Mars, G. (1982), *Cheats at Work.* London: Allen and Unwin.

Mills, C. W. (1963 [1943]), 'The Professional Ideology of Social Pathologists', in *Power, Politics, and People*, 525–22. New York: Oxford University Press.

Needleman, M. L., and Needleman, C. (1979), 'Organizational Crime: Two Models of Criminogenesis', *Sociological Quarterly*, 20: 517–28.

NELKEN, D. (1983), *The Limits of the Legal Process: A Study of Landlords, Law and Crime*. London: Academic Press.

—— (1990), 'Why Punish?', *Modern Law Review*, 53: 829–34.

—— (1994), 'The Future of Comparative Criminology', in D. Nelken, ed., *The Futures of Criminology*. London: Sage.

NEW YORK STATE ORGANISED CRIME TASK FORCE (1988), *Corruption and Racketeering in the New York City Construction Industry*. New York: Cornell University Press.

PASSAS, N. (1990), 'Anomie and Corporate Deviance', *Contemporary Crises*, 14: 157–78.

PASSAS, N., and NELKEN, D. (1993), 'The Thin Line between Legitimate and Criminal Enterprise: Subsidy Frauds in the European Community', *Crime, Law and Social Change*, 19: 223–43.

PEARCE, F. (1976), *Crimes of the Powerful: Marxism, Crime and Deviance*. London Pluto.

PEARCE, F., and TOMBS, S. (1990), 'Ideology, Hegemony, and Empiricism: Compliance Theories of Regulation', *British Journal of Criminology*, 30: 423–43.

—— (1991), 'Policing Corporate "Skid Rows" ', *British Journal of Criminology*, 31: 415–26.

PUNCH, M. (1991); 'Tackling Business Crime in Europe and the USA', paper presented at the University of Liverpool conference on Fraud, Corruption and Business Crime, 17–19 April.

ROYAL COMMISSION ON CRIMINAL PROCEDURE (1980), *Prosecutions by Private Individuals and Non-Police Agencies*, Research Study No. 10. London: HMSO.

SGUBBI, F. (1990), *Il Reato Come Rischio Sociale*. Bologna: Il Mulino.

SHAPIRO, S. (1984), *Wayward Capitalists*. New Haven: Yale University Press.

—— (1989), 'Collaring the Crime, not the Criminal: Reconsidering "White-Collar Crime" ', *American Sociological Review*, 55: 346–65.

SLAPPER, G. (1991), 'Corporate Manslaughter: An Examination of Prosecutorial Policy', LL.M. dissertation, University College, London.

SMITH, D. J., jun. (1980), 'Paragons, Pariahs and Pirates: A Spectrum-Based Theory of Enterprise', *Crime and Delinquency*, 26: 358–86.

SNIDER, L. (1991), 'The Regulatory Dance: Understanding Reform Processes in Corporate Crime', *International Journal of the Sociology of Law*, 19: 209–36.

STANLEY, C. (1992), 'Serious Money: Legitimation of Deviancy in the Financial Markets', *International Journal of the Sociology of Law*, 20: 43–60.

STEFFENSMEIER, D. (1989), 'On the Causes of White Collar Crime: An Assessment of Hirschi and Gottfredson's Claims, *Criminology*, 27: 345–58.

STONE, C. (1975), *Where the Law Ends: The Social Control of Corporate Behaviour*. New York: Harper & Row.

SUTHERLAND, E. H. (1949), *White Collar Crime*. New York: Holt Rinehart and Winston.

—— (1983), *White Collar Crime: The Uncut Version*. New Haven: Yale University Press.

SZASZ, D. (1986), 'Corporations, Organised Crime and the Disposal of Hazardous Waste: An Examination of the Making of a Criminogenic Regulatory Structure', *Criminology*, 24: 1–27.

TAPPAN, P. (1947), 'Who is the Criminal?', *American Sociological Review*, 12: 96–102.

TIEDEMANN, K. (1974), 'Kriminologische und Kriminalistische Aspekte der Subventionserschteichung', in H. Schäfer, ed., *Grundlagen der Kriminalistik*, 13/1: *Wirtschaftskriminalität, Weissen-Kragen Kriminalität*. Hamburg: Steintor.

VAN DUYNE, P. (1993) 'Organised Crime and Business Crime Enterprises in the Netherlands', in *Crime, Law and Social Change*, 19: 103–43.

VAUGHAN, D. E. (1983), *Controlling Unlawful Organizational Behaviour*. Chicago: University of Chicago Press.

VOLD, G. and BERNARD, T. (1986), *Theoretical Criminology*, (3rd edn. Oxford: Oxford University Press.

WHEELER, S., MANN, K., and SAPET, A. (1988), *Sitting in Judgement:The Sentencing of White-Collar Crimes*. New Haven: Yale University Press.

WEISBURD, D., WHEELER, S., WARING, E., and BODE, N. (1991), *Crimes of the Middle Classes: White Collar Offenders in the Federal Courts*. New Haven/London: Yale University Press.

YEAGER, P. C. (1991), *The Limits of Law: The Public Regulation of Private Pollution*. Cambridge: Cambridge University Press.

YOUNG, T. R. (1981), 'Corporate Crime: A Critique of the Clinard Report', *Contemporary Crises*, 5: 323–36.

ZIGLER, J. (1990), *La Suisse Lave Plus Blanc*. Amsterdam: Uitgeverij Balanss.

9

Drugs: Control, Crime, and Criminological Studies

NIGEL SOUTH

The dynamics of crime and criminology [in Britain] have often been at odds. For example, until very recently, . . . the anticipated stream of research into drug dependence has not materialised. With a few exceptions, . . . sociologists were not engaged by the drugs issue. Alcohol remains almost totally neglected as a topic. Despite high levels of productivity much remains to be mapped.

David Downes, in P. Rock, ed., *A History of British Criminology* (1988)

This chapter will review studies of the use, distribution, and control of illegal drugs, with some reference to alcohol. The focus of the chapter is the UK experience but I shall also refer to some international developments.[1] The structure of the chapter is as follows. A brief discussion of the legal status and properties of drugs is followed by a social history of contemporary drug use in Britain. The chapter then reviews the control of drugs in Britain (and internationally) and the evidence concerning the relationship between drugs, alcohol, and crime. A conclusion considers some emerging trends.

STATUS AND PROPERTIES OF DRUGS

This chapter is principally concerned with *illegal* drugs, that is, those designated illegal for purposes of possession or use or trade according to various domestic laws and international agreements and treaties (Brunn *et al.* 1975). In Britain the classification of illegal drugs is a tiered system reflecting official perceptions of their relative harmfulness. Thus Class A includes heroin and other strong opiates, cocaine, LSD, and MDMA (Ecstasy); Class B includes cannabis, amphetamines, and barbiturates; and Class C, tranquillizers and some mild stimulants. Maximum penalties are highest for Class A, lowest for Class C.

I am particularly grateful to the staff of the libraries of the Institute for the Study of Drug Dependence (ISDD) and Alcohol Concern and to Geoff Pearson and Nicholas Dorn for providing various works and suggestions.

[1] It should be noted that here, and generally throughout the literature, reference to the UK or Britain tends to mean England and Scotland. There seems to be a lack of substantial work on Wales and Northern Ireland; the latter may, of course, present particular problems for researchers interested in clandestine activities (but see Murray 1993).

Various texts describe the properties and effects of illegal and legal drugs, the most accessible, authoritative review being ISDD's *Drug Abuse Briefing* (1991*a*). In terms of general effects, drugs such as alcohol, barbiturates, tranquillizers, and heroin have a depressant effect on the nervous system, while caffeine, amphetamines, cocaine, and tobacco are stimulants. Cannabis, LSD, and MDMA distort perception, cannabis having a relaxing effect and LSD producing hallucinogenic effects, while MDMA and similar drugs may produce restlessness and mild visual distortions. However, actual behaviour and subjective experience will be strongly shaped by other influences, such as culture, context, and expectations.

A SOCIAL HISTORY OF CONTEMPORARY DRUG USE

In this section I shall review information on the prevalence and incidence of contemporary drug use, then discuss variations relating to gender, class, ethnicity, and age, and finally, evidence relating to correlations with social factors such as unemployment, deprivation, and housing circumstances. (A thorough review of many of these issues is Giggs 1991.) I shall concentrate here on illegal drugs, but we should note that prescribed and 'over-the-counter' (OTC) drugs also create dependency: recent estimates suggest there are between 0.25 million and 1.25 million people experiencing problems with tranquillizer-type drugs (Lacey and Woodward 1985; Cooper 1987; Gabe and Bury 1988), and the mass marketing of these substances ensures a level of availability which inevitably leads to seepage of such drugs into the illegal market.

Undoubtedly, the Royal College of Psychiatrists (1986, 1987) is correct to call alcohol 'our favourite drug' (Bunton 1990). According to Alcohol Concern,

> UK alcohol consumption reached a postwar peak of 7.7 litres per head of total population in 1979, falling by more than 10% to 6.9 litres per head in 1982 but with a strong recovery to 7.4 litres in 1988. . . . Overall alcohol consumption is . . . twice as high as in the mid 1950s, but still much lower than in the 18th and 19th centuries. (1991: 8)

By contrast with deaths caused by illicit drugs—a few hundreds per year—mortality associated with alcohol is considerably higher, with annual estimates ranging from 5,163 to 40,000 (Alcohol Concern 1991: 4–6).

Tobacco has only relatively recently faced widespread social disapproval; in Britain about 32 per cent of people over 16 smoke tobacco (ISDD 1991*a*: 44). A common estimate is that up to 100,000 premature deaths per year are linked to tobacco-related illnesses. By contrast, Fazey

(1991: 19) notes that for 1987 (during the peak period of concern about rising heroin use) only 230 deaths were associated with drug dependence or abuse (*Parliamentary Debates*, 1987–8).

However, such comparisons do not constitute straightforward support for the view that illegal drugs should be decriminalized because 'they cause less harm than legal drugs'. The point is that legal drugs are widely available, illegal drugs are not; the health-related consequences of widespread availability of currently illegal drugs are not known. Furthermore, the legality of some drugs does not mean that they do not contribute to 'legal harms', i.e. crime. Alcohol, for example, contributes to crimes of violence and social disturbance, and drink-driving offences (including manslaughter deaths); while both alcohol and tobacco, despite their legal status, are commodities which attract smuggling activity to profit from avoidance of taxation, as well as hijacking and theft.

A Short History of Drug Use Trends since the Second World War

I shall discuss the popular usage of opium and opiate preparations during the nineteenth century, and the subsequent development of moral, medical, and legal reactions to this popularity, in the section below on the control of drugs. Here I shall describe aspects of the British (and US) experience in the post-war period.

During the Second World War, illegal drug use attracted little attention. Trafficking routes were obviously disrupted worldwide and in the USA, where heroin and opium had been causes of concern before the war, supply was diminished. Interestingly amphetamine, a focus of recent concern, achieved unusual, if limited, approval in the war—and again later in the Vietnam conflict—being used by servicemen and flyers to relieve fatigue and anxiety.

The 1950s

During the early 1950s in Britain, relative inactivity seems to have characterized both drug availability and official response to drugs. However, by the mid-point of the decade an 'emerging drug subculture' seemed to be detectable in the West End of London, associated with one particular supplier (Spear 1969: 254) and bohemian and jazz cultures were associated with some drug use (MacInnes 1985; Spear 1969). The availability of cannabis and of heroin, albeit in limited circles, was sufficient to move the Ministry of Health to bring together in 1958 an interdepartmental committee on drug addiction under Sir Russell Brain. The Committee reported in 1961. Meanwhile, in the USA resurgence of popular concern (and legislative response) was rather more evident—as reflected in 'popular accounts' of the new youth fashions of the 1950s and a purported 'link' between rock and roll, the mixing of black and white youth, communism, and drugs (Inciardi 1986: 103–4).

The 1960s

The period of the 1960s saw expressions of artistic and political protest, mistrust of establishment values, and rejection of enforced conformity in both popular and youth cultures. Use of drugs (particularly cannabis, amphetamines, and heroin) increased among youthful groups drawn from the middle- and working-class mainstream.

In 1961 the Brain Committee reported that drug supply was 'almost negligible' and it seemed that Britain had no drug problem to speak of (Ministry of Health 1961: 9). Its policy was a continuing success. However, as Spear (1975) has observed, the 1960 addict statistics were not completed in time for the committee to consider them and, in fact, the number of addicts known to the Home Office was rising (Mott 1991: 78); moreover, it continued to rise, from a 1960 figure of 454 to 753 by 1964 (ibid.: 79). While these were extremely modest rises compared to later developments in the 1980s, they suggested that a new group of addicts had appeared who were not in touch with the medical services: new and younger British users, as well as a group of Canadian heroin addicts who had arrived in London in the late 1950s. The Brain Committee was reconvened in 1964 to report on these changes and its recommendations, produced in 1965, were to have a major impact upon the British response to serious drug use (Mott 1991: 78–9; Pearson 1991: 176–8).

In September 1967, quantities of 'Chinese' heroin were seized by the Metropolitan Police (Mott 1991: 82), while around this time several doctors had started prescribing methedrine ampoules (methylamphetamine) on a large scale, a practice which had fed a growing illicit market (ibid.; Leach 1991). For others, cannabis and psychedelic drugs (LSD) 'fitted' (Young 1971; Willis 1978) with the style, values, and music of the hippy counter-culture (Auld 1981).

From the 1970s to the 1980s

Between 1973 and 1977, only 4,607 new narcotic drug users came to official notice (Giggs 1991: 153). With regard to use of opiates, then, much of the 1970s presented a picture of relative stability, low rate of growth, and localized concentration, predominantly in the London area. By the tail end of the decade, however, there were signs of change, and the 1980s presented a profoundly different picture.

During the late 1970s, new sources of heroin were noted. Contrary to official perceptions that increasing availability was once again a sign of seepage from generous prescribing on to an illegal market (DHSS 1984), in fact a whole new era was beginning. Political shifts in the Golden Crescent region of south-west Asia (Iran, Pakistan, and Afghanistan) had opened up new supply routes, while Iranian exiles had converted capital into heroin after the downfall of the Shah and imported it to Britain. Cheap, high-purity heroin was becoming readily available, and with a tighter prescribing policy adopted by the new Drug Dependency Units or DDUs (see below) and police success in dealing with the Chinese heroin market, the new sources of availability stimulated the market (Mott 1991: 85). Of crucial importance for the spreading popularity of heroin use in the next few years was that the new heroin imports could be *smoked*, the prepared drug being heated and the smoke being inhaled ('chasing the dragon'), snorted, or sniffed (Auld *et al.* 1986). These methods overcame the deep psychological barrier posed for many by use of the needle for injecting: suddenly, use of the most fascinating drug of all was more accessible and the mode of administration familiar and 'ordinary': 'compared to injecting it doesn't feel addictive, it's clean, it's easy' (O'Bryan 1985; Mott 1991: 85–6). For some, familiarity with sniffing amphetamine or cocaine made the move from 'one white powder to another', heroin, seem easy (Hartnoll *et al.* 1984). 'Scoring smack' (Lewis *et al.* 1985) was not difficult in the new drug markets; further, it was of higher purity and cheaper in real terms than it had been four to five years before (Mott 1991: 87–8). For the period 1981 to 1985, Home Office notifications of 'new addicts' came to 21,030 (Giggs 1991: 153) and their spatial distribution around the country represented such an unanticipated spread that many commentators adopted an 'epidemic' analogy (but for a critical view of this analogy see Young 1987: 426–8).

Studies of heroin use expansion in provincial sites afford interesting longitudinal and 'snapshot' pictures of trends in the 1980s and also display methodological innovation in moving away from sole reliance on Home Office and other formal statistical indicators of drug use. Instead, studies have increasingly adopted a 'multi-agency' approach, drawing upon the information resources of various local agencies and groups, as well as street-level interview data collection (e.g. Drug Indicators project, 1985). Ditton and Speirits (1981, 1982) were among the first to note and discuss the 'new wave' of heroin addiction in areas beyond London, in this case the Glasgow metropolitan area. Subsequent work by Haw (1985) provided further examination of prevalence in Glasgow and Taylor (1993) updated the local picture with a particularly useful emphasis upon the drug-using patterns of women. Work in Edinburgh has been carried out against the background of extremely high rates of HIV transmission between drug injectors and partners in this area (Robertson 1987; Morrison, 1988, 1989). This work and that of Parker *et al.* (1987, 1988) examining trends in the Wirral, Merseyside, confirm a picture of rapidly spreading heroin use. However, caution about accepting the 'epidemic' model without reservation is suggested by the data of Peveler *et al.* (1988), which indicated little change in the prevalence of heroin use in Oxford between 1969 and 1984–5—the point at which such use was peaking at an all-time high in some other areas. Giggs (1991) usefully reviews other locality, urban, and area studies.

Studies *across* areas or regions are rare and should have been encouraged. Pearson *et al.* (1986), for example, are able to consider differences across northern England, the responses of different services, and the socio-economic profiles of localities (see also Dorn, James, and South 1987; Donoghoe *et al.* 1987). Such studies demonstrate the limitations of official data on numbers of 'notified' 'new addicts'. Based on the breadth of available data, ISDD (1990: 9) suggests that 'using a multiplier of five, it can be estimated that between 74,000 and 112,000 people in the UK were dependent on opiates at some time in 1989'.

The late 1980s also saw considerable official and popular concern over 'crack'. This was prompted by alarmist warnings from a visiting representative of the US Drug Enforcement Administration. In fact, available data for the end of the 1980s suggested that use of 'crack' in Britain appeared to be quite limited (Shapiro 1989). More recent reviews suggest an increase in crack availability and use; but it seems to remain the case that, putting the matter in perspective—in Britain at least—'crack is only a minor part of the cocaine market, itself a minor part of the overall drugs market' (ISDD 1991*b*: 33). Despite a rise in numbers of seizures of crack, from 30 in 1988 to 350 in 1990, 'these were still less than a fifth of all cocaine seizures and netted less than a kilo of the drug' (Shapiro 1991: 40).

Overall, at the end of the 1980s, there seems to have been relative stability in the British drug market, with heroin still important, cocaine increasing in availability but still of *relatively* minor concern, and the market dominated by cannabis and amphetamines (ISDD 1990: 9).

Into the 1990s and towards 2000

In contrast to the dominant focus on heroin of the mid-1980s, research in that decade and into the 1990s shows that Britain has a 'poly-drug' culture in which many users, while perhaps having a preferred 'drug of choice', none the less use a variety of illegal and legal drugs (Davis and Ditton 1990). Heroin availability is still high but there are signs that its use is in decline. The reasons are unclear, but may include effectiveness of policing responses (arrests and convictions; new policies of cautioning and diverting away from the criminal justice system: Dorn *et al.* 1990), increased penalties (Dorn, Murji, and South 1992), the impact of media and educational campaigns (Andrew Irving Associates 1986; Power

1989*a*), or decreased fashionability (Fraser and George 1988). But despite the rise of multi-drug use, including the use of newly fashionable drugs such as Ecstasy and increasing availability of previously scarce drugs such as cocaine and crack (Mirza *et al.* 1991), it would be premature to assume that heroin has had its day. Certainly, the culture of injection has not evaporated, as some might have expected, with the risk posed to injectors by HIV/AIDS (Power 1989*b*; Hart 1990; Stimson *et al.* 1988*a*, *b*, 1989; *British Journal of Addiction* 1992). Amphetamine and other drugs long administered intravenously remain popular, while certain prescription drugs and preparations for pain relief or travel sickness can be prepared from pill form for injection, with attendant serious health problems (Gilman *et al.* 1990). Drug injection is all too clearly still a major means of administration—and heroin injection may yet rise again.

The picture now is one of continuing widespread availability of a great variety of drugs, use being shaped by familiar factors such as local supply (Fraser and George 1988; George and Fraser 1989; Giggs 1991: 171), fashion (Newcombe 1992), contexts of use (Auld 1981; Becker 1963; Zinberg 1984; Peele 1985), preferred styles of consumption (Auld *et al.* 1986; Pearson 1987*a*), and purpose or intent, e.g. sociability, 'retreatism', 'energy' supply, and so on (Pearson 1992*a*).

Some recent research has reported on drug use trends at the beginning of the 1990s. Most crack or cocaine users in Britain would seem to be poly-drug users (Shapiro 1991: 42; Mirza *et al.* 1991; Ditton *et al.* 1991), not using excessively and not developing heavy dependence (*Druglink* 1992*a*: 6). Evidence is mixed about the degree to which crack and cocaine are becoming favoured drugs among Afro-Caribbean users (see discussion in Shapiro 1991: 42). Current trends suggest that London, the south-east, and several major cities around the UK (including Manchester and Birmingham) have the highest concentrations of cocaine use; that enforcement and treatment statistics probably underestimate the amount of cocaine and crack available on the market (with some specialist drug squad officers suggesting that there are certain localities where crack/cocaine is highly visible and very available[2]); but that consumption is unlikely to increase dramatically in the foreseeable future (Shapiro 1991: 44).

Further features of the poly-drug scene include a resurgence of LSD and amphetamine use, alongside the popularity of 'new' drugs such as Ecstasy and Ketamine, which have all become a part of post-acid house 'rave' music and style trends (Pearson *et al.* 1991; Fraser *et al.* 1991; Dorn *et al.* 1991*a*; Gilman 1991; Newcombe 1992; *Druglink* 1992*b*: 6; Shapiro 1992: 7)—predictably accompanied by a familiar degree of

[2] Personal communication, Metropolitan Police.

'moral panic' (*Druglink* 1992*c*: 5) as well as providing genuine grounds for concern (*Druglink* 1992*d*: 5).

Social Divisions and Drug Use: Class, Gender, Ethnicity, and Age

Data here are thin. In the USA and Canada regular national surveys of drug use are carried out; for Britain we must rely on the evidence of small-scale, localised and cross-sectional studies (Giggs, 1991: 165; but see ISDD, 1987, 1990, 1991*b*).

Class

Historically, illegal drug use has always crossed class boundaries. During the 1920s, users of opiates were frequently 'professional' addicts, who had abused their access to such drugs. 'Therapeutic' addicts, of various class backgrounds, were those who had become dependent during the course of painkilling treatment with opiate-type drugs. Recreational users of illegal drugs were relatively few in number. Some within the *demi-monde* and on the bohemian fringes of society experimentally dabbled. Within the working class, Chinese and other opium smokers were to be found in Limehouse while across London in the West End some young, white, male criminals and female prostitutes were using cocaine recreationally (Parssinen 1983: 216–17; Kohn 1992). However, the concern over drugs in this period hardly seems justified by the evidence of use.

The 1960s represent the next significant period of class and drug use change. Alarm over the (modest) rise in availability of opiate drugs in the West End of London was in part related to the emergence of a new type of user—young and working class. Middle-class youth also used heroin but were particularly associated with images of a counter-culture: the 'hippy' lifestyle and drugs such as cannabis and the hallucinogen LSD.

By the late 1970s, drug use was clearly a 'classless' phenomenon. Indeed, it may be argued that one of the generators of alarm in the mid-1980s was that it was not just the youth of the council estates that were using heroin or at risk, but also the youth of the middle and upper classes.

Gender

Studies of women and drug use (illegal or legal) are relatively rare (for an important feminist review, see Ettorre 1992; see also Bowker 1978; Cuskey 1982; Cuskey *et al.* 1972; Erickson and Watson 1990; Ettorre 1986; Goldstein 1979; Gomberg 1982; Griffin 1991; Henderson 1990; Inciardi 1980; Laycock 1991; McConville 1991; Perry 1979; Rosenbaum 1981*a*, *b*; Silverman 1982; Taylor 1993). There is, however, general agreement that research shows a lower prevalence of problem drug use for women than for men, except in relation to tranquillizers. Recent British data indicate that the gender imbalance is not fixed, and from 1973 to 1985 the 'proportions of females in the total known narcotic drug addict population rose from 24.6% . . . to 29.8%' (Giggs 1991: 166). However, it seems to remain a fair constant that drug *use* and, particularly, drug *dealing* are predominantly male pursuits. There is some evidence to suggest that heroin use is not significantly related to partnership status (i.e. whether a user lives alone or with a partner; Parker *et al.* 1987; Bean *et al.* 1987; Giggs 1991: 167). But some studies show that the familiar social pattern of an unequal burden of care falls upon female partners or relatives (principally mothers) of male heroin users (Auld *et al.* 1986; Dorn and South 1988; Dorn, Henderson, and South 1992).

Ethnicity

Drug use within ethnic minorities has received even less research attention than drug use by women. Pryce (1979) discusses cannabis in the context of Afro-Caribbean youth and street culture and Oswald (1982) provides a very useful account of the significance of 'ganja' for Rastafarian youth and some of the cultural reasons for its use among other young blacks. Pearson (1991: 187) notes that possession of cannabis by black youth, and police 'stop and search' tactics, have been a background factor in several instances of inner-city unrest in the 1980s—St Paul's (Bristol) in 1980, Brixton (London) in 1981, and Handsworth (Birmingham) in 1985 (Scarman 1981; Ashton and Shapiro 1982: 11–12; Benyon and Solomos 1987). More recently, manufacture and sale of 'crack' have been associated by the police and media with illegal Jamaican immigrants involved in 'yardie' gangs (Home Affairs Committee 1989: 47; Silverman, 1991: 24–5). Whatever the (questionable) extent of such an association, it is cannabis that is most widely used in the Afro-Caribbean community and it is for possession of this drug rather than any other that black people are most likely to face arrest. Recent research in Lewisham by Mirza *et al.* (1991) suggests some cocaine use in the black community, very little amphetamine use, and that heroin and other opiates account for only about 20 per cent of main drug use. Indeed, amid the 'epidemic' of heroin use in Britain in the 1980s, one striking feature was the relative absence of black users.

Prison and probation service statistics suggest that a high proportion of ethnic minority individuals (compared to the white population) have come to the attention of the criminal justice system for drug-related reasons. However, while such statistics tell us something about, for example, policing and the high number of court cases involving cannabis, they tell us little or nothing about actual patterns of drug use. One reason why we know so little about drug use is that the counselling and advice services which provide information about street-level use among white clients (Dorn and South 1985) simply do not seem to attract ethnic minority clients. Only recently has research attempted to understand why this should be so (Awiah *et al.* 1990, 1992; but see also *Druglink*, 1992*e*: 5).

Age

Use of illegal drugs seems to be largely confined to the young. This was not the case when currently illegal drugs were legal in the nineteenth century, and we do not yet know whether a significant proportion of the 'new' drug users of the 1980s and 1990s will continue their use into middle age (or beyond). However, with fluctuations over time and in different areas, the majority of drug users can be described as young, relatively few being over 35, regardless of class or gender. Limited data relating to ethnicity means that no firm conclusions can be drawn on this point, but cannabis use by some Afro-Caribbean smokers may not relate so clearly to age (cf. Oswald 1982).

The endeavour to chart drug-using 'careers' has led to a preoccupation for many studies with the question: 'When did drug (legal and illegal) use start?' Evidence suggests that teen (and early teen) years are significant (see Swadi 1988; Plant *et al.* 1985; Giggs 1991). Most studies suggest that for most young people, experimentation (and little more) with illegal drugs involves cannabis, amphetamine, and other Class 'B' drugs, although use of Ecstasy and LSD (Class A) is sufficiently widespread in the early 1990s to be added to this list. 'Escalation' to 'harder' drugs and continued use is confined to a minority.

Debates about the Correlation between Drug Use and Social Factors: Unemployment, Deprivation, Housing

Various studies in the 1980s undertook an examination of hypothesized links between rising drug use in certain areas and local and national socio-economic conditions. In one significant study, Peck and Plant (1986) offer analysis of data on average annual unemployment statistics, cautions and convictions for drug offences, and notifications of users in treatment between 1970 and 1984, and conclude that there are significant and positive correlations between these variables. Other studies are reminiscent of the 'ecological' approach of the Chicago School (e.g. Dai 1970 [1937]). Pearson *et al.*'s 1986 study in the north of England found that areas with a high concentration of use frequently exhibited very high figures for unemployment, single-parent families, limited mobility, and other indices of social disadvantage. Further, multiple deprivation and drug use may be mutually reinforcing in an area that is already socially deprived: drug use may flourish, resulting in deterioration of the general social and economic 'reputation' of the areas (see also Giggs 1991; Unell 1987; Plant 1989; Pearson 1987*b*, 1989). However, while Pearson *et al.* (1986) found high rates of drug use associated with high rates of deprivation, they also found some localities with high indices of deprivation but low rates of use *and* comfortable middle-class areas with high rates of use. The explanatory variable proposed here, and one which probably has fairly universal validity, is that of availability. Where supply and distribution conduits are well developed then class and other social factors may have diminished significance in predicting onset and spread of use. A related consideration is remarked upon by Forsyth *et al.*

> drugs are often linked with deprivation and crime, . . . this association may in fact derive from where drugs are sold, rather than who takes them. Just as American drinkers in the Prohibition era tended to consort with gangsters and frequent disreputable speakeasies, so the drug users of today are most visible in the deprived areas where they go to score. Counting drug users present in deprived areas is likely to exaggerate their prevalence, because many live elsewhere. (1992: 306)

THE CONTROL OF DRUGS IN BRITAIN (AND INTERNATIONALLY)

The Nineteenth and Early Twentieth Centuries

During the nineteenth century, opiate preparations were commonly marketed and widely used in Britain (Berridge and Edwards 1981); the same was true in other parts of Europe and in the USA (Musto 1973). On both sides of the Atlantic, opiate-based medicines and tonics were used as analgesics, as sedatives, as febrifuges, as remedies for cholera, and as children's 'quieteners'. Apart from such therapeutic use, reports between the 1830s and 1860s describe the *recreational* use of opiates in factory districts, seaports, and the Fenlands (Parssinen 1983: 212; Berridge 1977), and the literature of the period indicates experimentation and familiarity with the drug in literary and bohemian circles (Berridge and Edwards 1981; Hayter 1988). The question of *control* was, however, emerging.

The industrial revolution and other social developments promoted interest in the subject of 'public health', particularly in relation to the fitness of the urban working class. In this context, the use of opiates gave rise to some concern (although use of opiates for pleasure and pain relief among the middle class apparently received less disapproval and attention: Berridge and Edwards 1981; Pearson 1991). A different provocation of public discussion about opiates was their common use as a means of sedating children, a practice which led to many cases of children dying of opium poisoning (Parssinen 1983: 207; Pearson 1991: 170). Additionally, from around the 1870s onwards, sensational accounts of Chinese 'opium dens' in the Limehouse area of London's East End provided a sinister stereotype of corruption and alien culture to associate with opium use, along with ideas of oriental conspiracy and 'clandestine organisation' (Kohn 1992: 18–20; Pearson 1991). There is, however, considerable irony in the idea of the Chinese as a corrupting influence, given that it was Britain that was the principal sponsor of the international trade in opium. Although not the first power to engage in the trade, Britain developed the export of opium from India to China into a large and highly profitable enterprise (Inglis 1975; Berridge and Edwards 1981) and in terms of the history of drug control it is worth noting that Britain's first efforts in this regard were aimed precisely at *preventing* such control, engaging in wars (1839–42 and 1856–8) with China to stop its attempt to reduce opium importation from British-controlled India, and its rising problem of addiction (ibid.; Brunn *et al.* 1975: 8–12).

In the light of this connection, it is perhaps less surprising to find that domestic control over opiate use in Britain was of a limited nature. None the less, in the latter half of the century, moral opposition to opium use and Britain's opium trade was growing. Further, there was a shift in perception of opium use from seeing it as an indulgence or habit, as in the first part of the nineteenth century, to viewing it as a 'problem', classifiable in various ways by the new medical discourses (Berridge 1979). The new 'clinical gaze' (Foucault 1973) could diagnose *social* as well as biological pathology and asserted the status of doctors as the professional body appropriate to exert control (Hart 1990). Thus, for example, medical practitioners attempted to bring the treatment and control of those dependent upon opium within the provisions of the 1888 Inebriates Act which applied to the voluntary detention of 'habitual drunkards'. In this particular endeavour to extend professional power they failed, but pharmacists fared better: the 1868 Pharmacy Act removed morphine and opium derivatives from the shelves of general stores and provided regulations under which pharmacists could sell them, a system eventually extended to patent medicines by the 1908 Poisons and Pharmacy Act (Pearson 1991: 171). Modest restrictions on supply developed but control of *use* remained unaddressed by legislation. 'Insanity' certified to be the result of addiction could lead to institutionalization and the 1890 Lunacy Act was sometimes applied, but only with the passing of the 1913 Mental Deficiency Act did legislation embrace 'any sedative, narcotic or stimulant drug' within the definition of an 'intoxicant' and thereby allow for the detention of 'moral imbeciles' in asylums or under the guardianship of another (Pearson 1991: 171; Berridge and Edwards 1981: 119–22, 165–9, 212–15).

As well as medical entrepreneurs, moral crusaders were also fairly consistent in seeking the introduction of new control measures. In 1874 the Society for the Suppression of the Opium Trade was formed, the twin themes of its campaign over the next few decades being 'sin' and 'exploitation', as illustrated by the title of a pamphlet of 1898 called *The Unchangeableness of Sin: The Slave Trade a Century Ago and the Opium Revenue Today*. In 1906, the new Liberal government committed Britain to phasing out opium exports to China—a development that can be seen as a triumph for morality or as a reflection of political and economic compromise in view of apparently falling revenue from the trade.

By the early years of the twentieth century a polarity had emerged between the medical view of drug use as addictive or a 'disease', and the moral view of it as a vice to be controlled by law and punishment (Berridge 1979; Smart 1984; Pearson 1991). However, the concerns about vice that finally introduced the first real penal response to drug use in Britain arose not as a result of peacetime lobbying but in the context of wartime emergency. During the early years of the First World War, press and public were aroused by threats to the troops posed by prostitution and cocaine (Kohn 1992: 23–66). Similarly, concern about the productivity of war workers in the factories prompted calls for restriction of alcohol availability. Therefore, in 1916 an amendment to the Defence of the Realm Act (DORA), Regulation 40B, made possession of cocaine or opium a criminal offence except for professionals such as doctors, or where supplied on prescription (Kohn 1992: 44). DORA Regulations also introduced the licensing laws, restricting opening times of public houses and regulating alcohol sales (relaxed only in the 1980s). Of course, it is the latter measure which had the greater impact, but with regard to the cocaine 'Threat', legal control was now exercised and unauthorized possession was criminalized. A significant step had been taken and the role of the Home Office was brought to centre stage in the control of drugs (Pearson 1991: 172; Berridge 1978: 293; on DORA and alcohol policy see Dorn 1983: 64–5).

Subsequently, various influences—such as the US push for prohibitionist policies, its increasing ability to set the agenda for drug control (but not alcohol control, in which the largely European League of Nations had no interest, and the peculiar *de facto* ratification of the 1912 Hague Convention on Opium through ratification of the post-war Versailles Treaty, Article 295 (Delevingne 1931: 54–5; Bruun *et al.* 1975: 12)—encouraged further government legislation in the form of the Dangerous Drugs Acts of 1920 and 1923. These made possession of opiates and cocaine illegal except where prescribed by a doctor. The Home Secretary gained powers to regulate the manufacture, distribution, and legitimate sale of these drugs, and policing practice and public perception reflected the new status of illegal drugs as a criminal matter (Stimson and

Oppenheimer 1982: 25; Parssinen 1983: 217; Pearson 1991: 172; Kohn 1992).

Control in relation to alcohol went in the opposite direction, however. DORA regulations were at first ignored and then lifted; and as Steele (1986: 7) puts it, 'The Licensing Act of 1921 set the seal upon a movement which continues to this day. . . . The 1961 Act matched with the 1964 elimination of retail price maintenance provided a drink entrepreneurs charter. Outlets of all kinds could, and did, multiply.'[3]

'The British System'

The official response to illegal drug misuse in the UK is often referred to as 'The British system' (Strang and Gossop 1993) and is frequently held up as a model that the USA should have followed. The generally cited origin of this 'system' is the 1926 report of the departmental committee on morphine and heroin addiction, chaired by Sir Humphrey Rolleston, popularly known as the Rolleston Committee Report. The brief for the committee was to define the circumstances in which prescription was appropriate and the precautions to be taken to avoid the possibility of abuse (Ministry of Health 1926: 2; Pearson, 1991: 173). The committee offered recommendations allowing for prescription of heroin and morphine to enable gradual withdrawal, or to 'maintain' a regulated supply to those judged unable to break their dependence or those whose lives would otherwise suffer serious disruption (Pearson 1991: 173).

Given the influential view that this development represents a profoundly different path from that taken by the US authorities, it is important to make two points. First, in Britain, the number of people considered to be addicted or potentially addicted was *extremely small*, perhaps a few hundreds. Second, as Parssinen argues,

> Although the Harrison Act (of 1914) probably strengthened the connections between narcotics addiction and the urban underworld, these connections were firmly in place long before 1914. The increasingly hard-line American enforcement and treatment policy during the 1920s was less cause than effect of the emerging criminal-addict. (1983: 219; see also Inciardi, 1986: 16–17)

In other words, in terms of drug users, the British and US experiences seem to have been diverging already, ahead of the passing and subsequent interpretation of legislation.[4]

[3] On the history and discussion of alcohol control policy see Bunton 1990; Dorn 1983; Williams and Brake 1980; and the report by the Central Policy Review Staff 1989, denied publication in Britain.

[4] How the Harrison Act was interpreted is interesting. In intention, it was a taxation and regulatory code, not a penal measure aimed at users. It was the practice of the US Treasury and decisions of the Supreme Court in interpreting the Act that set the conditions for expansion of the illegal drug market (Inciardi 1986: 14–15).

In any case, in Britain at least, the issue being contested was actually one that was going away even as the Rolleston Committee deliberated. The committee itself found that medical and recreational addiction seemed to be in decline and by the late 1920s the cause for concern was over. Press and public fascination persisted and sensational stories still made news (Kohn 1992), but generally, such subcultures of use as had existed were fragile and easily broken up by police efforts. Scarcity and expense seem to have deterred both users and suppliers of cocaine and opiates. Thus, Parssinen argues, 'in Britain as in America, drug policy was less a cause than it was the effect of the addict population. Put simply, narcotic drug maintenance was accepted in Britain in the 1920s because the addict population was small, elderly and dying off' (1983: 220). Despite generally uncritical interpretations of this period of drug policy debate, some recent writers (Smart 1984; Pearson 1991; Dorn and South 1992*a*; Kohn 1992) agree that the apparently dominant medical discourses of the time were in fact shadowed and influenced by strong moral and penal positions. None the less, one reason for a general acceptance of the success of the Rolleston recommendations is that through the 1930s to the late 1950s, Britain did indeed experience no serious problems with illegal drugs.

The 1960s were to prove a very different decade, however, and new controls were at the heart of international and domestic developments of considerable significance. In March 1961 in New York, the UN Single Convention on Narcotic Drugs was signed, drawing together provisions of nine previous treaties signed between 1912 (the Hague Convention) and 1953 and extending control to cover the plants poppy, coca, and cannabis.[5] The UN International Narcotics Control Board was established the same year to monitor the working of the Convention.

Back in London, with evidence of new patterns of drug availability, the Brain Committee was reconvened (see above). Amphetamine availability was a new problem ('pep pills' and 'purple hearts' were associated with new youth cultures) and new legislation—the 1964 Drugs (Prevention of Misuse) Act and accompanying regulations—was introduced to control possession, production, and supply. This Act also introduced aspects of the Single Convention into British law and a 1966 modification added LSD to its provisions for control. In 1965 the Dangerous Drugs Act ratified the Single Convention and the Brain Committee published its new report. This was to lead to major legislation in the form of the Dangerous Drugs Act 1967. Prescribing was to continue but medical practitioners were to be more tightly controlled by regulations and were to 'notify' to the Home Office new addicts not previously in treatment.

[5] See Bruun *et al.* 1975: 20–1 for a tabulation of multilateral treaties between 1912 and 1972.

Specialist Drug Dependency Units or 'Clinics' (introduced in 1968 and initially centred in London) would become the centres of expertise in treatment of addiction, and henceforth only their doctors could prescribe heroin and cocaine. It should, however, be noted that general practitioners were not in fact barred from prescribing drugs such as methadone and diconal (dipipanone) for treatment and GPs have actually played an expanding role in working with users (Ashton 1987; Glanz and Taylor 1986; Pearson 1991: 182; Greenwood 1992: 8–9).

In practice, the new clinics sought to break client dependence on such drugs by prescribing injectable (soon changed to oral) methadone as a drug without the same attractions and thought suitable for planned detoxification and cessation of prescribing, or 'maintenance' (Stimson and Oppenheimer 1982). Thus medical *management* of addiction was endorsed, within a framework which also placed doctors in a role with responsibility for regulating supply and controlling the spread of dependence (Pearson 1991: 178–81; Stimson and Oppenheimer 1982)—a role which effectively included policing or 'disciplinary' and epidemiological or 'surveillance' functions (cf. Foucault 1977). Thus, despite the perceived liberalism of many legislative developments in these 'permissive' years, drugs received rather conservative treatment: even a call by the respectable Advisory Council on Drug Dependence (the Wootton Committee, 1968) for liberalization of the law relating to cannabis was dismissively rejected (Young 1971: 198–201).

Debates around the dichotomies of 'soft' and 'hard' drugs, and 'users' and 'dealers', during the 1960s were reflected in the 1971 Misuse of Drugs Act, which made an important distinction between possession offences and supply offences. Drug users could be characterized as sad and weak types corrupted by drug dealers who were very bad types; the former needed counselling or treatment, the latter deserved the harshest punishment. Ironically, in the early 1970s drug-related corruption in police services also caused some alarm and prompted inquiries in London and New York (Cox *et al.* 1977; Knapp Commission 1972). In Europe, the Pompidou Group was established in 1971 to exchange information on drug problems (Hartnoll 1989) and at the UN a Convention on Psychotropic Substances included drugs not covered by the Single Convention (such as amphetamine and LSD).

The recent status of drug control as a 'war' on drugs can perhaps be traced to the mobilization in the USA of public and official sentiment against drugs by President Nixon (Inciardi 1986: 117–18). In the early 1970s crime was ranked as pre-eminent among the urban problems of the USA, with drugs close behind. The political benefits of the 'war' metaphor and the increased power accruing to White House-directed resources, are clear (ibid.). Perhaps this lesson was one not lost on a subsequent conservative President, Ronald Reagan, who launched a new (or renewed) 'war on drugs' in the 1980s. The coincidence of the conservative politics of the British prime minister, Margaret Thatcher, and President Reagan, set the tone for the rhetoric—but not all of the practice—of drug control in the 1980s.

In Britain in the 1980s drugs became a political and politicized issue (Stimson 1987), yet one which attracted a political consensus that persists (Berridge 1991: 179; *Druglink* 1992*f*: 4). Several cross-party parliamentary committees (e.g. Social Services Committee 1985; Home Affairs Committee 1985) were in agreement in warning of the dangers facing Britain from heroin and cocaine trafficking. Such consensus enabled the government to take the earlier proposals of the Hodgson Committee (convened in 1980, reporting in 1984) to make provision for the recovery of the profits of crime, jettison its liberal recommendations relating to sentencing, and introduce the far-reaching Drug Trafficking Offences Act (DTOA) of 1986 (in force from 1987); see Dorn, Murji, and South 1992: ch. 10; Dorn and South 1991.[6]

Overall, the DTOA and the high profile given to enforcement responses generally reflected the balance of emphasis in the government's 'strategy document' *Tackling Drug Misuse* (first published 1985), which proposed five fronts for action:

1. reducing supplies from abroad;
2. making enforcement even more effective;
3. maintaining effective deterrents and tight domestic controls;
4. developing prevention;[7]
5. improving treatment and rehabilitation.

Law Enforcement and Drugs: Success or Failure?

Police and customs were now expected to show what they could do with enhanced resources. Organizational changes followed (Dorn, Murji, and South 1992: 152–8; 1991*b*). The National Drugs Intelligence Unit (NDIU)

[6] The Hodgson Committee was set up in the wake of the 'Operation Julie' trial of manufacturers of LSD when it was found, on appeal, that the Misuse of Drugs Act 1971 could not provide for the forfeiture of criminally generated assets. The committee was sponsored by the Howard League and presented the case that where money or property was forfeited this amounted to punishment that should be taken into account in calculating sentences. The 1985 Home Affairs Committee, on the other hand, sought an emulation of 'American practice', 'to give the courts draconian powers in both civil and criminal law to strip drug dealers of all the assets acquired from their dealings in drugs' (1986: iv–vi; Stimson 1987: 44; Rutherford and Green 1989: 21). For fuller discussion of the Act and its significance see Dorn and South 1991; Zander 1989).

[7] This initiative included the designation of specialist teachers as Local Education Authority Drugs Education (later Health Education) Co-ordinators. In the early 1990s funding for such posts seems likely to melt away (*Druglink*, 1992*g*: 4).

was established in 1985 at New Scotland Yard as a joint police and customs services' 'clearing house' for the collation and networking of information relevant to enforcement operations.

There had previously been a Central Drugs and Illegal Immigration Unit at Scotland Yard since 1973 (an interesting linking of two issues). This had become the Central Drugs Intelligence Unit in 1974, serving the UK as a whole but remaining part of the Metropolitan Police, reflecting the feeling of the time that drugs were largely a London problem. The NDIU replaced this body, while throughout the country the regional crime squads established seventeen specialist drugs wings to help them undertake investigations that crossed local police force boundaries. These developments reflected the recommendations of the Association of Chief Police Officers' Broome Committee report (appendix in Dorn, Murji, and South 1992: 214–15).

Internationally, co-operation was highlighted, customs liaison officers were posted abroad (Berridge 1991: 181), and Britain's encouragement of drug crop substitution or eradication programmes and rural development projects was given a higher profile.

In 1992 the new National Criminal Intelligence Service came into operation (Dorn, Murji, and South 1992: 154–5; Hebenton and Thomas 1992), drawing together various police intelligence databases, including the NDIU. The command of regional crime squads now falls under an Executive coordinator overseen by a committee drawn mostly from ACPO, representing a significant 'further step in the development of the autonomy of the police' (Dorn 1991: 4).

Such organizational changes in drugs enforcement often herald other changes in the criminal justice system, yet outside the USA there seems to have been little English-language research on drugs law enforcement (Waymont and Wright 1989; Grieve 1987; Anderson 1989). For Britain, Dorn, Murji, and South (1992, 1991*b*) examine the development of enforcement practice 'on the street', and in terms of intelligence refinement and organizational change. However, an attempt to provide an economic appraisal of the cost-effectiveness of expenditure on police and customs enforcement argued that such a task is seriously hampered by the inadequacy of the empirical data available (Wagstaff and Maynard 1988).

Enforcement statistics

One way of measuring the 'impact' of enforcement could be to look at the detection of drugs—reflected, it is presumed, in annual seizure statistics. This is, of course, a partial measure, but it is one on which government, enforcement agencies, and media place great emphasis. Years of high seizure are greeted as either (a) a sign of the increased success of enforcement efforts and/or (b) a reflection of an increasing incoming tide of drugs that requires investment of yet further enforcement resources to stem it. Whatever view is taken, seizure statistics should be treated with caution: just one or two seizures of very large amounts can inflate the figures unrepresentatively; correspondingly, low seizure figures do not mean low importation or distribution, for several large consignments may have avoided enforcement agencies' attention. Generally, customs and the police (in most countries) are unlikely to feel able to claim much more than a 10 per cent interception rate (Stimson 1987: 49–50).

Law enforcement statistics, then, are subject to severe limitations. They can reflect only detection, seizures, and convictions; drugs offences are rarely reported in the same way as robberies or assault (ISDD 1990: 15).

Sentencing

There are few studies analysing sentencing in relation to drugs offences and drug-related crime in Britain. Goodsir (1986: 10–11) reported on a survey of solicitors that indicated serious variations in sentencing practices across geographical areas and unfocused police operations resulting in small-scale offenders bearing the brunt of the law. The findings concerning low levels of cautioning may now be dated following changes in many force policies, but a similar sentencing trend was also found in Scotland by Haw (1988, 1989), who showed that length of custodial sentences for even fairly minor drug offences went up in the mid-1980s. These reviews of sentencing are exceptions, however, and data on national sentencing trends have not been the subject of much scrutiny. Dorn, Murji, and South (1992: ch. 10) discuss the rising trend in penalties, noting their expressive and symbolic function as well as how their escalation runs counter to more general trends to try to reduce use of custody.

Briefly, this escalation has developed as follows. In 1972, i.e. before the 1971 Misuse of Drugs Act (MDA) had come into effect, sentences were frequently of between six months and two years. By 1976, when the MDA had been in operation for three years, the numbers of persons receiving a prison sentence had approximately doubled by comparison with 1972 and of these, the majority received sentences of between six months and three years. From 1983 onwards, the courts could refer to the Lord Chief Justice's guidelines (from *R.* v. *Aramah*; Kay 1988) which suggested a raised tariff, subsequently amended upward as a result of *R.* v. *Bilinski* (Dorn, Murji, and South 1992: 185–6). In practice, sentences of ten years or more have become common, the 1985 Controlled Drugs (Penalties) Act raised the maximum penalty for trafficking in Class A drugs from fourteen years to life imprisonment, and with the implementation of the 1986 DTOA such sentences may also include asset confiscation (see Rutherford and Green 1989; Dorn and South 1991; Zander

1989; Fortson 1988; Bucknall and Ghodse 1989; discussion of use of financial investigation powers and sentence provisions can be found in Levi 1991).

According to the parole release scheme, up to 12,000 problem drug users are received into custody each year (Trace 1988: 8; a 1989 Home Office figure estimated 6,500 but this was limited to notifiable addicts (ACMD 1991; see *Druglink* 1992*h*: 7, n. 3). Generally, Home Office data on 'offenders dealt with' (Home Office 1991) show a consistent rise in the number of persons 'found guilty, cautioned or dealt with by compounding for drugs offences' between 1986 and 1990 (the last date for which figures are available). The pattern is not the same for all drugs offences; e.g. heroin declines, while cocaine, LSD, and cannabis all rise. But, overall, for 'all drugs', the trend is upwards, with over half the UK drug offender population in 1990 being aged between 17 and 24, and the great majority being young men (*ibid.*; ISDD 1991*b*: 26, tables 10, 11).

Conclusions about the impact of sentencing are difficult to draw; referring to heroin users, Mott (1989: 32) observes that 'there has been very little research specifically aimed at investigating the effect of court sentences, or of different types of sentence, on the subsequent drug using and criminal behaviour of heroin users. What there is suggests that sentences of imprisonment may have little effect.'

DRUGS, ALCOHOL, AND CRIME

Drugs and Crime

The illegality of certain drugs obviously makes their possession, supply, preparation, or manufacture an offence (McBride and McCoy 1982: 145). But evidently, the debate about the drugs-crime relationship is wider than this.

Drug-related crime is typically non-violent and acquisitive, involving theft, shoplifting, forgery, or burglary (Chaiken and Chaiken 1991) or prostitution (Plant 1990; Goldstein 1979; Datesman and Inciardi 1979; Inciardi and Pottieger 1986; Marshall and Hendtlass 1986). More serious drug-related crimes of violence, murder, large-scale trafficking, and money laundering occur and may be increasing in Britain—although by comparison with the USA they remain relatively infrequent. (On the US experience see Stephens and Ellis 1975; Johnson *et al.* 1985; Drug Enforcement Report 1990; US Senate Foreign Relations Committee 1990; Goldstein 1985; Hamid 1990; various essays in Weisheit 1990, and in Tonry and Wilson 1990.) The majority of criminological studies since the 1960s have focused on heroin and have largely excluded the casual and recreational use of drugs, especially 'soft' drugs such as cannabis (McBride and McCoy 1982: 143; but see Mott 1985 and, on amphetamine and crime, the major review by Greenberg 1976).

The 1980s rise in heroin use prompted new (or renewed; see Mott and Taylor 1974) debate over the nature of the relationship between drug use and dealing/trafficking, and crime. In the USA this debate has had a lengthier history, producing a substantial body of work (Gandossy *et al.* 1980; Research Triangle Institute 1976; Chaiken and Chaiken 1991; Tonry and Wilson 1990; Greenberg and Adler 1974; Richards 1982; Watters *et al.* 1985; Nurco *et al.* 1985). It is not disputed that in many circumstances drug use and criminal behaviour are in some way linked. It is the causal nature of this link that researchers contest—whether drug use leads to criminality or criminal associations lead to drug use. An important caveat to enter here is that the majority of studies on drugs and crime are actually studies of *men*, drugs, and crime. Generally, as in criminology more broadly, drugs research has been partial in pursuing its concerns. Research on *women*, drugs, and crime is discussed by Rosenbaum (1981*a*, *b*), Silverman (1982), and Erickson and Watson (1990).

'Involvement in criminal activity leads to drugs use'

Some studies (e.g. Mott and Taylor 1974) provide evidence that a high proportion of heroin users were already involved in delinquent or criminal activities before they started using heroin or other drugs. McBride and McCoy (1982: 145) note that Eldridge (1952) argued that because heroin use was illegal, and the source and distribution of heroin was part of a criminal underworld . . . few non-criminal innocents were seduced into the initiation of heroin use (also see Stephens and Ellis, 1975: 487).' Thus the argument would be that (a) involvement in deviant/criminal-oriented subcultures or groups would be likely to lead a person to encounter the availability of drugs sold within that culture; (b) they would have a deviant lifestyle which would accommodate deviant drug use with relative ease; and (c) while money from criminal activity might then pay for the drugs, it was not drug addiction or use which led to the perpetration of crime.

Auld *et al.* (1986) have reported on a small study, based on accounts of common but irregular heroin use among a group of North London young working-class men. Findings here supported the argument that 'criminal/deviant lifestyles' can lead to heroin and other drug use. In this context of an irregular 'street' economy of petty crime, hustling, wheeling and dealing, business 'off the books', etc. (Henry 1978; Hobbs 1988) heroin had become just one commodity among many circulating in this illegal economy. Those involved in this culture therefore came across the drug, had the contacts to get it, and had the lifestyle in which risk-taking was valued and in which heroin would therefore fit as a deviant indulgence (see also Burr, 1987; Pearson 1987*b*).

Work in this vein confirms the findings of—and, it must be acknowledged, has often been influenced by—the classic research in New York published by Preble and Casey as 'Taking Care of Business' (1969), a study which emphasized that it is the activity and lifestyle surrounding drug use as much as the drug-taking itself which is attractive to users. As described in this tradition of ethnographic and ecological perspectives, the hustling, enterprising, dynamic life of the street user is quite the opposite of the stereotyped portrayal of the dazed and dozing junkie (see also Feldman 1968; Agar 1973; Johnson *et al.* 1985; Gilman 1988).

In Britain, a series of studies by the Strathclyde University Addiction Research Group provide evidence to challenge the view that heroin use is a direct causal determinant of criminal activity (Hammersley *et al.* 1989). Rather, they find that although the two are related, use of other drugs is also related to crime (an obvious but often neglected point); and, furthermore, a prior history of criminality is the more important determinant of crime frequency. Thus, considering teenage drug users' involvement in crime, they observe that 'explanations of delinquency are likely to be more relevant . . . than explanations invoking "drug addiction"' (Hammersley *et al.* 1990: 1592).

The prominent place occupied by heroin in popular and official perceptions of the drug–crime link may be traced to historical influences such as the development of drugs legislation and also the belief of users themselves that they *need* certain amounts of heroin to avoid withdrawal: the cost of such supplies being expensive, more frequent criminal activity is encouraged. Importantly, Hammersley *et al.* found that moderate heroin users were not significantly more criminal than cannabis/alcohol users.

'Involvement in drug use causes crime'

Of course, other research argues that there is strong evidence to support the thesis that the direction of causality is 'drug use (particularly heroin use) causes crime' (Gandossy *et al.* 1980; Chaiken and Chaiken 1991: 204). Some crimes seem to have a clear relationship with drug use. In the early 1980s (and in the 1960s to a lesser extent) there was concern about break-ins to pharmacies with stocks of controlled drugs (Laycock 1984; Mott 1986). Jarvis and Parker (1989) argue that their finding that the criminal convictions of one group of heroin users doubled after they started using heroin regularly is firm evidence of the proposition that addiction leads to acquisitive crime. Related work carried out on the Wirral reported a direct correlation between a dramatic rise in local burglaries (compared to national figures) between 1979 and 1985 and the rise of heroin use (Parker and Newcombe 1987; Parker *et al.* 1988).

Home Office analysis of statistics (1985; 1987) suggests that a higher level of involvement in *acquisitive* crime will be recorded for both notified addicts *and* drugs offenders, compared to other groups. On the other hand, the groups represented by these two sets of statistics are *minorities* within the larger population of drug users in that they have entered into a treatment arrangement which has led to their notification as an addict and/or been processed through the criminal justice system. Caution is therefore advisable in using such a finding to draw firm conclusions (Mott 1986; Pearson 1991: 190). Certainly, it cannot be held that causality is demonstrated.

Indeed, in the Jarvis and Parker (1989) study, it was also the case that some young people appearing in court had been engaged in criminal activity *before* they started to use heroin. So, despite the emphasis that Parker *et al.* place upon the 'drugs cause crime' argument, their data also seem to support the view that criminal involvement leads to drug use. As Pearson (1991: 191) observes, these mixed findings would 'appear to have squared the circle, reconciling the two sides of the long standing argument as to whether "heroin use causes crime" or "crime causes heroin use"'. But, as Pearson (ibid.) also points out, these findings relate to *acquisitive* crime—when typical non-acquisitive crimes such as joy-riding or vandalism are considered, there does not seem to be any similar evidence of a relationship with heroin use (Parker and Newcombe 1987). Perhaps Nurco *et al.* (1985: 101) have a point worth emphasizing when they argue that 'the long and continuing controversy over whether narcotic addicts commit crimes primarily to support their habits or whether addiction is merely one more manifestation of a deviant and criminal lifestyle seems pointless in view of the fact that addicts cannot be regarded as a homogeneous group'.

Drugs, crime, and drug markets

Overall, the drugs–crime debate in the British context remains inconclusive. However, the *association* between drugs and crime seems to be moving *some* way closer to the pattern familiar in the USA (Pearson 1991: 192). For example, diversity and sophistication of organization are evident (Dorn and South 1990; Dorn, Murji, and South 1992; Pearson *et al.* 1986); use of violence and of firearms by traffickers has reportedly been rising. For some participants involved in trafficking/dealing, high rates of profit are achievable, although for users engaging in non-drug crimes (e.g. burglary, theft, forgery, fraud) the returns per crime may be quite small and the total gain per annum quite modest (see Johnson *et al.* 1985). Finally, money laundering has developed in various ways (Levi 1991; South 1992).

On the other hand, the familiar US image of drug markets controlled by supranational syndicates has been challenged by research there (Reuter 1983) and in Britain (Dorn, Murji, and South 1992; Dorn and South 1990). One of the central arguments of this research is that the reality of the development of drug markets does not conform at all to the image of monopolistic or oligopolistic structures dominated by Mr Bigs or controlling cartels. If all-powerful cartels *did* exist, it would seem logical to expect that imperatives to maximize profit would ensure continued supply, price fixing, and relatively well assured purity levels (punitively disciplining those suppliers adulterating street-level 'deals' for purpose of extra profit) This, clearly, is not what happens. While *some* situations and trafficking groups or networks may exhibit tendencies towards attempts to establish monopolistic or oligopolistic control over local and/or regional drug markets, countervailing tendencies (e.g. the need for security, mobility) and law enforcement efforts push the market into a competitive, fluctuating, and fractured state, generally ensuring many small entrepreneurial participants (Reuter 1983; Ruggiero and Vass 1992; Dorn and South 1990; Dorn, Murji, and South 1992; Anderson and Tollison 1991). The policy implication is that enforcement efforts must develop strategic responses targeted at the specific vulnerabilities of the different participants in drug markets. Furthermore, consideration of the characteristics of these different groups may suggest new ways of looking at the costs and benefits of enforcement efforts—a subject still in need of more in-depth research and open debate (see Wagstaff and Maynard 1988; *British Journal of Addiction* 1989).

Treatment, rehabilitation, drugs, and crime

A different kind of cost–benefit analysis might be applied to the issue of treatment of drug users by the medical system: namely, what kinds of treatment are most efficacious in (a) reducing reliance on the illegal market for drug supply and (b) reducing related criminal activity engaged in to generate funds for purchasing drugs? Unfortunately, as Jarvis and Parker (1990: 29) have remarked, 'evidence of the efficacy of medical treatment, whatever form it might take, is neither plentiful nor conclusive'.

One key underlying assumption of the practice of 'maintaining' drug users on methadone or other substitutes (or even heroin and cocaine) has been that this will remove the need to resort to criminal activity and erode the profitability of an illegal market in drugs (Mott 1989: 32). Weipert *et al.* (1979) report on 575 users receiving treatment between 1968 and 1975, while Bennett and Wright (1986) report on a sample studied in 1983. Weipert *et al.* found that DDU attendance and treatment for up to 8.5 years had no impact upon crime rates overall, and the later study concluded that neither long-term heroin maintenance nor a regime of methadone reduction resulted in the cessation of criminal activity. One careful and important study (Hartnoll *et al.* 1980) compared the effect of prescribing injectable heroin versus oral methadone on users' criminal activity and, with various qualifications, concluded that there was no indication of 'a clear overall superiority of either [{treatment}] approach' in terms of achieving abstinence or of reducing illicit drug use and associated criminal activity (Mott 1989: 32). Of course, drug users in treatment are the minority: during the 1970s, moves towards a more disciplinary style of managing drug-user patients meant less chance of a prescription for heroin and more of methadone maintenance, or detoxification with reducing doses (Stimson and Oppenheimer 1982). These options were and are unattractive to many users, discouraging take up of treatment by some and encouraging drop-out by others. Fazey's 1992 study of a 'flexible' drug treatment regime suggests that certain approaches to treatment *can* retain patients *and* reduce criminal activity. She concludes that

> As long as patients stay in treatment their criminal behaviour reduces, but whether they stay in treatment or not seems strongly related to the type of treatment they receive. If they do not see it as meeting their needs—even if the medical practitioner thinks that it does—then they vote with their feet, and go back to committing more crime to finance their street habit. (ibid.: 161; cf. Mott 1989: 32–3)

Jarvis and Parker (1990: 32) similarly suggest that 'the more flexible and "user-friendly" the treatments offered are, the more likely it seems to be that young heroin users will come forward'. However, these authors acknowledge that their study provides only 'limited grounds' for regarding medical treatment as successful in reducing drug-related crime. If studies clearly and unequivocally showed that treatment results in decline in criminal activity, then the case for *compulsory* treatment would, no doubt, be put forward more frequently and with more force (for a statement of this view see Johnson 1989). However, the evidence does not provide such certainty. For example, in the Jarvis and Parker study, many users felt they were growing out of drugs' or were weary of 'hassle' from the police. Hence the reasons users were receiving treatment and the success of treatment outcomes (measured as less likelihood of using illicit sources of drugs or committing offences) may have less to do with treatment *per se* and more to do with personal biography and situation.

In summary, studies are by no means unanimous in their conclusions about the impact of treatment upon crime behaviour, suggesting that abstinence (generally the medically desired outcome[8]) is achievable by some users while others find acceptance of such medical regimens to be

[8] Although the challenge of AIDS/HIV has given strong support to maintenance and harm-minimization approaches (Strang and Stimson, 1991; Buning *et al.* 1992).

too difficult, resulting in rejection of the 'therapeutic goals', possibly increased involvement in crime, and a 'chaotic' lifestyle (Hartnoll *et al.* 1980; Stimson and Oppenheimer 1982; Pearson 1991). Neither treatment *per se* nor participation (voluntary or otherwise) in it is guaranteed to reduce criminal activity (Bennett and Wright 1986; Bean and Wilkinson 1988), although other studies offer more optimistic conclusions, albeit tentatively so (Jarvis and Parker 1990), and some reviews offer strong support for methadone maintenance as effective in helping to reduce drug-related crime and injecting (Ball and Ross 1991; Ward *et al.* 1992).

A key concept for practice in the 1980s and 1990s has been that of 'harm minimization'. Arguably not a new idea (ISDD 1981; Berridge 1991; Velleman and Rigby 1990), and familiar in relation to alcohol ('Don't Drink and Drive!'), the concept has been developed further in relation to illegal drugs and concerns about HIV transmission: the aim is to reduce legal, social, and financial, as well as health, harms. Harm minimization first received 'official' endorsement in the pre-AIDS report by the Advisory Council on the Misuse of Drugs entitled *Prevention* (ACMD 1984). This report concluded that policy and practice should be developed (a) to reduce the risk of initial drug misuse and (b) to reduce the harm associated with misuse.

However, it is most evidently in the wake of the HIV/AIDS threat and the considerable impact this has had on British drug policy that the concept has influenced practice. Again, ACMD reports (1988, 1989), this time on AIDS, supply legitimation; but agencies on the ground had been developing the practice for some years. Syringe exchange schemes were approved by the Department of Health, initially on an experimental basis, to try to draw injecting users into contact with services, supply clean injecting equipment, and provide harm minimization advice about injecting and safer-sex practices (Stimson *et al.* 1988*a*, *b*, 1989; for a broad review of the sex, HIV, and drugs issues, see Donoghoe 1992). A major contribution to the success of such initiatives has been changes in policies adopted by the police service in many areas (Berridge 1991: 194; Dorn *et al.* 1990).

State and corporate involvement in drug crime

Finally, it should be noted that examination of the experiences of North (and South) America raises other dimensions to the drugs and crime question. First there is the issue of what Dorn and South (1990) call 'state sponsored' traders in drugs (cf. Chambliss 1989). The most notable example might be CIA involvement in the transportation of opium during the Vietnam era of US cold war politics—historically something of an emulation of past British and French colonial practices. US support for south-east Asian interests which were profiting from the opium trade might seem odd when this Golden Triangle area was the principal source of supply to US and European markets, but conflicts of interest, public ignorance, and the prioritization of US foreign policy over domestic concerns may explain this situation—and the more recent history of relations with Panama and various South American countries (Pearce 1976: 151–2; McCoy *et al.* 1972; Chambliss 1989: 188–9; Dorn and South 1992*b*).

At a similar level of state-sponsored criminality, Levi (1991: 301) notes 'internal contradictions in money laundering controls' which mean that while some US government departments are busy negotiating with (and pressurizing) other countries to tighten controls against money laundering, state agencies such as the CIA have been using banks like BCCI (Bank of Credit and Commerce International) for the disbursement of funds, legally and illegally. At the same time, clandestine operations like the Iran–Contra affair require such a manipulable (and to some extent acquiescent) international banking system (South 1992). In such blurred and murky activities, the mixing, laundering, and movement of money from government, from traffickers, and from arms dealers takes us into a world of political crime and international corruption that is beyond the scope of this chapter. However, studies so far produced about 'narco-terrorism' (e.g. Henze 1986; Frost 1986) would seem to be rather one-sided if they concentrate solely on the drug-crime violence of South American traffickers, international terrorists, and communist conspiracies, to the exclusion of the double-edged activities of US law enforcers.

Alcohol and Crime

Since the 1960s, road accidents and deaths related to drinking and driving have attracted increasing attention from the police and various community groups. Stronger public emphasis on the problem and tougher enforcement and penalties seem to have had an impact, and fatalities and serious injuries attributable to drinking and driving fell significantly between 1979 and 1989 (Alcohol Concern 1991: 24–6). However, groups such as Alcohol Concern argue that much public education still needs to be done and that the criminal justice system needs to develop new initiatives (based for example upon models tried in Germany) which include assessment of convicted drink-drivers and their involvement in educational, counselling, and treatment courses.

During the 1980s, further concern and discussion arose about the health problems and social harm caused by alcohol, and particularly its use by young people (British Medical Association 1986; Royal College of Psychiatrists 1986; Mott 1990). A recurrent theme was the extent to which alcohol consumption could be held responsible for certain forms of criminal behaviour. This has been a concern of long-term, follow-up studies examining criminal careers and drinking careers. These suggest that 'criminality and alcohol abuse tend to run in parallel, as both have their peak incidence in young adults and tend to diminish with age. Those who continue with heavy drinking and petty crime into mid-life tend to become habitual drunkenness offenders' (d'Orban 1991: 298). The latter present both the criminal justice and health systems with considerable problems. In 1987, 83,000 persons were found guilty or cautioned for drunkenness offences in England and Wales, according to Home Office statistics.

Of course, concerns about the relationship between alcohol and crime are not new. According to Lombroso:

> Alcohol . . . is a cause of crime, first because many commit crime in order to obtain drinks, further, because men sometimes seek in drink the courage necessary to commit crime, or an excuse for their misdeeds; again, because it is by the aid of drink that young men are drawn into crime; and because the drink shop is the place for meeting of accomplices, where they not only plan their crimes but squander their gains . . . it appears that alcoholism occurred oftenest in the case of those charged with assaults, sexual offences, and insurrections. Next came assassinations and homicide; and in the last rank those imprisoned for arson and theft, that is to say, crime against property. (Lombroso, 1968 [1911]: 95–6)

As Collins (1982: xvi) observes, dominant opinions about the role of alcohol in criminal behaviour have probably changed little, more research may have been done but its sophistication has not necessarily improved greatly, and the prisoners Lombroso interviewed for his research have been followed by later generations of prisoners, asked similar questions, despite greater awareness of the problems inherent in generalizing from such respondent groups. An indication of the amount of literature generated on the alcohol–crime 'connection' can be found by consulting the collection of US reviews edited by Collins (1982). Conclusive findings seem elusive, however: Collins (ibid: 289) writes: 'The consistency and strength of the alcohol–crime empirical association is sufficient to justify the inference that alcohol is *sometimes* causally implicated in the occurrence of serious crime. Questions of *how* alcohol exerts its criminogenic influence have not been satisfactorily answered' (emphasis added).

In the British context, Evans (1986) considers the role of alcohol as a causal factor in impairing judgement about acceptable and risk-taking behaviour, as well as the interaction between alcohol and other drugs and the relationship between alcoholism and violence (see also Evans 1980). D'Orban (1991: 296) observes that 'studies of offences of violence show that the majority of the offenders, the victims or both, had consumed alcohol prior to their offence'. Other commentators note that whatever the alcohol *consumption* levels of the offenders (be they higher or lower than average), consideration of their drinking 'must be related to *specific* criminal incidents' (emphasis added) (Mott 1990: 25; Murphy 1983). For example, Myers (1982) examined the drinking of Scottish, adult male prisoners convicted of acquisitive or violent crime and found that unplanned offences were more likely to have been committed by those drinking immediately before the offence, thus ' "spontaneous" offenders reported drinking more alcohol than the rest [of the sample] on the day their offence was committed' (Mott 1990: 25). Less conclusively, McMurran and Hollin (1989) looked at the drinking habits of 100 English young offenders and found that where drinking and delinquency are 'functionally related, the drinking can be an antecedent to the commission of the delinquent act, or it can be a consequence of the crime' and that 'the same degree of involvement between drinking and delinquency was evident for younger and older offenders' (ibid.: 386).

As with illegal drug consumption, *belief* about how alcohol is 'supposed' to affect behaviour, coupled with the influences of immediate social context and wider culture, are as important for the behavioural outcome as the amount of alcohol consumed (Mott 1990: 25; Hauge 1984; Royal College of Psychiatrists 1986; Pearson 1992*a*). The Cambridge Study on Delinquent Development (West and Farrington 1977; Mott 1990: 25) described offenders who reported heavy drinking and engaging in fights as 'less socially restrained, more hedonistic, more impulsive, more reckless, and more aggressive than their non-delinquent peers. They smoked more, they drank more, they gambled more. They had a faster lifestyle, they went out more, they visited bars, discotheques and went to parties more often' (Mott 1990). Data from the British Crime Survey have shown that young men who have been drinking heavily are more likely than moderate drinkers to become involved in minor violent offences and, further, are more likely to be victims of some crime of violence (Gottfredson 1984; Mott 1990: 25–6). Evidence from a number of studies associates disorderly conduct offences with recent alcohol consumption (Mott 1990: 26), and the location of violent or disorderly conduct offences to be in or near licensed premises in 20–30 per cent of cases (Hough and Sheehy 1986), with the timing of such offences to be likely to follow the end of licensing hours, occur on a Friday or Saturday night, and involve young men (Mott 1990: 26). Similar findings resulted from investigation of the wave of 'lager lout' outbreaks of disorderly conduct which ACPO (1988) and the media portrayed as a serious problem in the normally quiet towns and villages of rural England (Tuck 1989).

However, the question of causality is again problematic. Brain (1986) examines (among other matters) 'the recurrent media claim that alcohol causes a percentage of the aggression we see in our everyday lives' and observes that 'the question "Does alcohol cause aggression" is . . . grossly over-simplistic' (ibid.: ii). This view might fruitfully inform further research on the role of alcohol in crimes of sexual assault and rape (Coid 1986*a*). To some, 'alcohol abuse' is an appealing social explanation for violence against women, but it should not be allowed to overshadow the importance of masculinity as a source of values and behaviours injurious to women (Stanko 1985; Kelly 1988).

Socialization and cultural expectations, stereotypes and labelling, circumstances and significant others all play their part in shaping people's identities as 'aggressive' and as 'drinkers'. Such definitions are not 'fixed' but change over time and across cultures (Levine 1983; Coid 1986*b*). Modern media also play an influential part in shaping positive and negative images of alcohol use (Coid 1986*b*; Dorn and South 1983).

CONCLUSIONS: TRENDS AND FUTURES

Theory

Theoretical issues have lain outside the scope of this chapter. However, any cursory review of the sociological and criminological literature would note a continuing reliance on anomie, subculture, and labelling theories, albeit modified in varying ways (see e.g. Gabe and Bury 1991). These perspectives were developed in the USA between the 1920s and the 1960s, and one question must surely be whether these approaches are adequate and applicable in the European context at the end of the twentieth century? Marxist and other critical perspectives must also be open to revision and critique.

International Developments

It is possible that the new Democratic administration in the USA will offer a slightly different stance from past Republican positions on drug policy, but (perhaps unsurprisingly) pre-election statements did not suggest that major changes are in store. European fora and other international bodies continue to place enforcement high on their agendas (Hartnol 1989: 39), while a recent European Community study of legislation and judicial practice in member states has noted discrepancies between countries and urged more effective co-ordination (Leroy 1992). 'Harmonisation' in the EC after 1992 will bring further international agreements between law enforcement agencies: the creation of a 'Europol' agency is a current proposal on the agenda (for a review of related issues, see Hebenton and Thomas 1992). This is part of a trend towards globalization of law enforcement concerned with illegal drugs. Anti-terrorist and anti-money-laundering strategies and agreements are already developing fast (Levi 1991). One view might be that this is an old trend, dating back to the anti-opium conventions of the early part of the century (Bruun *et al.* 1975), but new currents in social theory (such as postmodernism) might suggest that the globalization of social issues is an accelerating trend in the late twentieth century.

Domestic Enforcement

Trends in enforcement will include further development of intelligence-gathering and processing capabilities, perhaps involving the security service MI5. Among the techniques being employed is that of monitoring the sale of 'precursor chemicals', i.e. those used in the refining, preparation, and manufacture of illegal drugs. Previously a technique about which the British police have wanted to remain silent, the strategy has now been discussed in the international literature and was in any case a known aspect of US efforts against cocaine production in South America since 1984.

Current behind-the-scenes and parliamentary committee reports suggest that we may be on the way to something from which Britain has always shied away—a national police force. In relation to drugs, a national system of co-ordinating law enforcement efforts (operational and intelligence-gathering) could evolve into a division of a national 'serious crimes' police agency or force, like the US FBI or a national CID, dovetailing with an enhanced role for the security service.

At street level, there is increasing support for a model of 'low-level policing' which might disrupt street markets and divert users from criminalization to counselling and treatment (Pearson and Gilman 1991; Dorn and Murji 1992). This is a development encouraged by recent policy recommendations (ACMD 1991).

Overall, enforcement and other drug control policies must confront the likelihood that the war on drugs is not one that can be won. If drug markets cannot be eradicated, then perhaps we should be asking 'what kind of drug markets are *least* undesirable?' and trying to shape them in that direction (Dorn and South 1990).

Domestic Policy

Domestically, sentencing seems to have followed the harsh pattern the law enables, particularly with regard to drug couriers (Green 1991); and the new Criminal Justice Act (1992) widens the power of the courts with regard to trafficking, asset confiscation, and money laundering. However, it is encouraging that the development of a pragmatic harm minimization response has been taken up by various police (for example, in Merseyside and London) and probation services (Bild 1992), including for example the spread of police referral and other forms of diversion scheme (Dorn *et al.* 1990). This kind of development will be encouraged further, following proposals for non-custodial sentences in the 1990 White Paper *Crime, Justice and Protecting the Community*, which suggested that many 'problem drug users' should be dealt with in the community rather than prison by requiring them to attend a drugs advice agency for counselling. Similar and further recommendations in the recent report of the ACMD (1991) include the possibility of court orders for treatment; adoption of harm minimization goals by probation, sentencers, and agencies; training; the need to ensure availability of treatment options; and steps to lessen disincentives to offenders admitting drug use, with special attention paid here to women with children and ethnic minority offenders (*Druglink* 1992*i*: 5). Within this and broader initiatives, the criminal justice system must respond to and develop new approaches to accommodate the problems posed by AIDS/HIV and drugs. Offenders coming to the attention of various agencies and being processed through the system must be afforded appropriate treatment: the challenge has been noted (ACMD 1988, 1989; Trace 1990; Inciardi 1990; Hammett *et al.* 1991) but the way forward is not yet clear.

The preoccupation of both policy and practice with heroin, cocaine, and now Ecstasy and amphetamine-type drugs should not exclude consideration of other drug use. The predominance of cannabis in the enforcement statistics, arguments about the extent to which it is a relatively harmless rather than dangerous drug (ACMD 1982; Ashton and Shapiro 1982: 9–10), its evident popularity, and the question of whether it justifies the enforcement resources expended upon it, all suggest that while the 'legalize cannabis' lobby is not at present attracting a great deal of attention in Britain, it still has a case to put, and that it would be unsurprising to find it re-emerging, as it sporadically does (Ashton and Shapiro 1982; *Druglink* 1991: 5; Release, 1992).

More broadly, the debate about overall decriminalization or legalization of drugs may gather further momentum in the 1990s and beyond (Mason 1992; Farr 1990; Kraska 1990). Proponents (e.g. Nadelman 1989; Stevenson 1990, 1991; Graham 1991; Trebach 1991; Release 1992) argue that the costly, counter-productive, and unsuccessful efforts of law enforcement as a response to drug use suggest legalization is a wiser alternative. It is suggested that availability would not mean unacceptable rises in use and that taxation of legal supply would provide funds for educational, health, and counselling responses. Regulation would ensure purity levels and hence reduce health hazards caused by adulterants, and legal availability would remove the profit motive that drives the criminal market. Opponents (e.g. Inciardi and McBride 1989; Wilson 1990) argue that legalization *would* increase use, thereby increasing serious costs to society. Commentators between these two positions suggest that the impact of legalization and commercialization on Third World producer countries could be highly negative (Dorn 1992) and that the frequently cited example of *de facto* decriminalization of cannabis—the Netherlands—is actually a case of a policy aimed at preserving 'market separation', keeping cannabis supply distinct from supply of drugs with an 'unacceptable risk' (ibid.: 111; Mol and Trautmann 1991: 17). At present, however, proposals for decriminalization and legalization are unpopular, impractical, and extremely unlikely to find favour with any individual government, let alone be accorded agreement at an international level (Dorn 1992; Pearson, 1992*b*).

Overall, though it is tiresome to read conclusions which suggest that 'more research is needed', this is precisely the case. A better picture of local drug use may be made available by a new national database system (Donmall 1990) and crime, enforcement, health, and HIV-related research will undoubtedly continue. However, at present, British criminology and broader policy and practice are ill served by the limited (albeit generally excellent) research upon which we can draw.

Selected Further Reading

General: H. Becker, *Outsiders* (Glencoe: Free Press, 1963); N. Dorn and N. South, *A Land Fit for Heroin?: Drug Policies, Prevention and Practice* (1987); S. MacGregor, ed., *Drugs and British Society* (London: Routledge, 1989); D. Whynes and P. Bean, eds., *Policing and Prescribing: The British System of Drug Control* (London: Macmillan, 1991); E. Ettorre, *Women and Substance Use* (London: Macmillan, 1992); J. Strang and M. Gossop, eds., *Responding to Drug Misuse: The British System* (1993).

On history: V. Berridge and G. Edwards, *Opium and the People* (New Haven: Yale University Press, 1981); D. Courtwright, *Dark Paradise: Opiate Addiction in America before 1940* (Cambridge, Mass.: Harvard University Press, 1982); M. Kohn, *Dope Girls: The Birth of the British Drug Underground* (London: Lawrence and Wishart, 1992).

On drugs and crime: M. Tonry and J. Q. Wilson, eds., *Drugs and Crime* (Chicago: University of Chicago Press, 1991); N. Dorn, K. Murji, and N. South, *Traffickers: Drug Markets and Law Enforcement* (London: Routledge, 1992); B. Johnson *et al.*, *Taking Care of Business: The Economics of Crime by Heroin Abusers* (Lexington Mass.: Lexington Books, 1985).

On alcohol and crime-related problems: J. Collins, ed., *Drinking and*

Crime (London: Tavistock, 1982); P. Brain, ed., *Alcohol and Aggression* (London: Croom Helm, 1986).

On drugs and AIDS: *British Journal of Addiction*, special issue on *AIDS, Drug Misuse and the Research Agenda*, 1992, 87/3; J. Strang and G. Stimson, eds., *AIDS and Drug Misuse* (London: Routledge, 1991).

Researchers will also find the libraries of the Institute for the Study of Drug Dependence and of Alcohol Concern, both in London, of great assistance.

REFERENCES

ACMD (1982), *Report of the Expert Group on the Effects of Cannabis Use*. London: Home Office (Advisory Council on the Misuse of Drugs).

—— (1984), *Prevention*. London: HMSO.

—— (1988), *AIDS and Drug Misuse, Part 1*. London: HMSO.

—— (1989), *AIDS and Drug Misuse, Part 2*. London: HMSO.

—— (1991), *Drug Misusers and the Criminal Justice System, Part 1*. London: HMSO.

ACPO (1988), 'Public Disorder outside Metropolitan Areas', unpublished paper. London: Association of Chief Police Officers.

Agar, M. (1973), *Ripping and Running: A Formal Ethnography of Heroin Addicts*. New York: Seminar Press.

Alcohol Concern (1991), *Warning: Alcohol Can Damage Your Health*. London: Alcohol Concern.

Anderson, G., and Tollison, R. (1991), 'The War on Drugs as AntiTrust Regulation', *Cato Journal*, 10/3: 691–701.

Anderson, M. (1989), *Policing the World: Interpol and the Politics of International Police Cooperation*. Oxford: Clarendon Press.

Andrew Irving Associates (1986), *Anti-Heroin Misuse Campaign: Qualitative Evaluation Research Report*. London: AIA.

Ashton, M. (1987), 'Treatment Trends', *Druglink*, 2/5: 12–13.

Ashton, M. and Shapiro, H. (1982), 'Cannabis stalemate, Part 1: Cannabis and Health', *Druglink*, 17 (Winter): 8–10.

Auld, J. (1981), *Marijuana Use and Social Control*. London: Academic Press.

Auld, J., Dorn, N., and South, N. (1986), 'Irregular Work, Irregular Pleasures: Heroin in the 1980s', in R. Matthews and J. Young, eds., *Confronting Crime*, 166–87. London: Sage.

Awiah, J., Butt, S., and Dorn, N. (1990), '"The Last Place I Would Go": Black People and Drug Services in Britain', *Druglink*, 5/5: 14–15.

Awiah, J., Butt, S., Dorn, N., Pearson, G., and Patel, K. (1992), *Race, Gender and Drug Services*. London: Institute for the Study of Drug Dependence.

Ball, J., and Ross, A. (1991), *The Effectiveness of Methadone Maintenance Treatment*. Washington, DC: Springer-Verlag.

Bean, P., and Wilkinson, C. (1988), 'Drug Taking, Crime and the Illicit Supply System', *British Journal of Addiction*, 83: 533–9.

BEAN, P., WILKINSON, C., GIGGS, J., and WHYNES, D. (1987), *Drug Taking in Nottingham and the Links with Crime*, Report to the Home Office Research and Planning Unit. Nottingham: Nottingham University.

BECKER, H. (1963), *Outsiders: Studies in the Sociology of Deviance*. Glencoe: Free Press.

BENNETT, T., and WRIGHT, R. (1986), 'The Impact of Prescribing on the Crimes of Opioid Users', *British Journal of Addiction*, 81: 265–73.

BENYON, J., and SOLOMOS, J., eds. (1987), *The Roots of Urban Unrest*. London: Pergamon.

BERRIDGE, V. (1977), 'Fenland Opium Eating in the Nineteenth Century', *British Journal of Addiction*, 72: 275–84.

—— (1978), 'War Conditions and Narcotics Control: The Passing of the Defence of the Realm Act Regulation 40B', *Journal of Social Policy*, 7/3: 285–304.

—— (1979), 'Morality and Medical Science: Concepts of Narcotic Addiction in Britain, 1820–1926', *Annals of Science*, 36: 67–85.

—— (1991), 'AIDS and British Drug Policy: History Repeats Itself . . .?', in D. Whynes and P. Bean, eds., *Policing and Prescribing: The British System of Drug Control*, 176–99. London: Macmillan.

BERRIDGE, V., and EDWARDS, G. (1981), *Opium and the People: Opiate Use in 19th-Century England* (2nd edn. 1987). New Haven: Yale University Press.

BILD, M. (1992), 'Probation, Harm Reduction and Drug Services', *Druglink*, 7/2: 10–12.

BOWKER, L. (1978), 'Woman and Drugs: Beyond the Hippie Subculture', in L. Bowker, ed., *Women, Crime and the Criminal Justice System*. Lexington, Mass.: Lexington Books.

BRAIN, P., ed. (1986), *Alcohol and Aggression*. London: Croom Helm.

British Journal of Addiction (1989), 'Economic Aspects of Illicit Drug Problems' (A. Wagstaff and A. Maynard on 'Economic Aspects of the Illicit Drug Market and Drug Enforcement Policies in the United Kingdom: Summary of Report', followed by commentaries), *British Journal of Addiction*, 84: 461–75.

—— (1992), 'Special Issue: AIDS, Drug Misuse and the Research Agenda', *British Journal of Addiction*, 87/3.

BRITISH MEDICAL ASSOCIATION (1986), *Young People and Alcohol*. London: BMA.

BRUUN, K., PAN, L., and REXED, I. (1975), *The Gentlemen's Club: International Control of Drugs and Alcohol*. Chicago: University of Chicago Press.

BUCKNALL, P., and GHODSE, A. (1989), *Misuse of Drugs and Drug Trafficking Offences Act*, Supplement 3. London: Waterlow.

BUNING, E., DRUCKER, E., O'HARE, P., and NEWCOMBE, R., eds. (1992), *Reduction of Drug-Related Harm*. London: Routledge.

BUNTON, R. (1990), 'Regulating our Favourite Drug', in P. Abbot and G. Payne, eds., *New Directions in the Sociology of Health*, 104–17. London: Falmer.

BURR, A. (1987), 'Chasing the Dragon: Heroin Misuse, Delinquency and Crime in the Context of South London Culture', *British Journal of Criminology*, 27: 333–57.

CENTRAL POLICY REVIEW STAFF (1979), 'Alcohol Policies', unpublished paper. London: Cabinet Office. Repr. and published as *Alcohol Policies in the United Kingdom* (1982), Stockholm: Sociologiska Institutionen, Stockholm University.

Chaiken, J., and Chaiken, M. (1991), 'Drugs and Predatory Crime', in M. Tonry and J. Wilson, eds., *Drugs and Crime*, 203–40. Chicago: University of Chicago Press.

Chambliss, W. (1989), 'State Organised Crime', *Criminology*, 27/2: 183–208.

Coid, J. (1986*a*), 'Alcohol, Rape and Sexual Assault', in P. Brain, ed., *Alcohol and Aggression*, 161–83. London: Croom Helm.

—— (1986*b*), 'Socio-Cultural Factors in Alcohol-related Aggression', in P. Brain, ed. *Alcohol and Aggression*, 184–211. London: Croom Helm.

Collins, J. ed. (1982), *Drinking and Crime: Perspectives on the Relationships between Alcohol Consumption and Criminal Behaviour*. London: Tavistock.

Collins, J., and Bailey, S. (1987), 'Early Drug Use and Criminal Careers', mimeo. Research Triangle Park, NC: Research Triangle Institute.

Cooper, J. (1987), 'Benzodiazepine Prescribing: The Aftermath', *Druglink*, 2/5: 8–10.

Courtwright, D. (1982), *Dark Paradise: Opiate Addiction in America before 1940*. Cambridge, Mass.: Harvard University Press.

Cox, B., Shirley, J., and Short, M. (1977), *The Fall of Scotland Yard.* Harmondsworth: Penguin.

Cuskey, W. (1982), 'Female Addiction: A Review of the Literature', *Focus on Women*, 3/1: 3–33.

Cuskey, W., Premkumar, T., and Sigel, L. (1972), 'Survey of Opiate Addiction among Females in the United States between 1850 and 1970', *Public Health Reviews*, 1: 6–39.

Dai, B., (1970 [1937]), *Opium Addiction in Chicago*. Montclair, NJ: Patterson Smith.

Datesman, S., and Inciardi, J. (1979), 'Female Heroin Use, Criminality and Prostitution', *Contemporary Drug Problems*, 8: 455–73.

Davis, J., and Ditton, J. (1990), 'The 1990s: Decade of the Stimulants?', *British Journal of Addiction*, 85: 811–13.

Delevingne, M. (1931), 'Drug Addiction as an International Problem', *British Journal of Inebriety*, 29/2: 54–9.

DHSS (1984), *Medical Working Group on Drug Dependence: Guidelines on Good Clinical Practice in the Treatment of Drug Misuse*. London: Department of Health and Social Security.

Ditton, J., Farrow, K., Forsyth, A., Hammersley, R., Hunter, G., Lavelle, T., Mulen, K., Smith, I., Davies, J., Henderson, M., Morrison, V., Bain, D., Elliot, L., Fox, A., Geddes, B., Green, R., Taylor, J., Dalgarno, P., Ferguson, I., Phillips, S., and Watt, S. (1991), 'Scottish Cocaine Users: Wealthy Snorters or Delinquent Smokers?', *Drug and Alcohol Dependence*, 28: 269–76.

Ditton, J., and Speirits, K. (1981), *The Rapid Increase in Heroin Addiction in Glasgow during 1981*, background paper 2. Glasgow: University of Glasgow, Department of Sociology.

—— (1982), 'The New Wave of Heroin Addiction in Britain', *Sociology*, 16/4: 595–8.

Donmall, M. (1990), 'Towards a National Drug Database', *Druglink*, 5/2: 10–12.

Donoghoe, M. (1992), 'Sex, HIV and the Injecting Drug User', *British Journal of Addiction*, 87: 405–16.

DONOGHOE, M., DORN, N., JAMES, C., JONES, S., RIBBENS, J., and SOUTH, N. (1987), 'How Families and Communities Respond to Heroin', in N. Dorn and N. South, eds., *A Land Fit for Heroin? Drug Policies, Prevention and Practice*, 95–124. London: Macmillan.

D'ORBAN, P. (1991), 'The Crimes Connection: Alcohol', in I. Glass, ed., *The International Handbook of Addiction Behaviour*, 295–300. London: Routledge.

DORN, N. (1983), *Alcohol, Youth and the State: Drinking Practices, Controls and Health Education*. London: Croom Helm.

—— (1991), 'Central Drug Squad Quits Met.', *Druglink*, 6/2: 4.

—— (1992), 'Clarifying Policy Options on Drug Trafficking: Harm Minimization is Distinct from Legalization', in E. Buning, E. Drucker, P. O'Hare, and R. Newcombe, eds., *Reduction of Drug Related Harm*, London: Routledge.

DORN, N., HENDERSON, S., and SOUTH, N., eds. (1992), *AIDS: Women, Drugs and Social Care*. London: Falmer.

DORN, N., JAMES, C., and SOUTH, N. (1987), *The Limits of Informal Survillance: Four Case-Studies on Identifying Neighbourhood Heroin Problems*. London: Institute for the Study of Drug Dependence.

DORN, N., and MURJI, K. (1992), 'Low Level Drug Enforcement', *International Journal of Sociology of Law*, 20: 159–171.

DORN, N., MURJI, K., and SOUTH, N. (1990) 'Drug Referral Schemes', *Policing*, 6: 482–92.

—— (1991*a*), 'Abby, the Ecstasy Dealer', *Druglink*, 6/6: 14–15.

—— (1991*b*), 'Mirroring the Market? Police Reorganisation and Effectiveness Against Drug Trafficking', in R. Reiner and M. Cross, eds., *Beyond Law and Order*, (1–106. London: Macmillan.

—— (1992), *Traffickers: Drug Markets and Law Enforcement*. London: Routledge.

DORN, N., RIBBENS, J., and SOUTH, N. (1987), *Coping with a Nightmare: Family Feelings about Long-Term Drug Use*. London: Institute for the Study of Drug Dependence.

DORN, N., and SOUTH, N. (1983), *Message in a Bottle: Theoretical Overview and Annotated Bibliography of the Literature on Mass Media and Alcohol*. Aldershot: Gower.

—— (1985), *Helping Drug Users: Social Work, Advice Giving, Referral and Training Services of Three London 'Street Agencies'*. Aldershot: Gower.

—— (1988), 'Drugs and Leisure, Prohibition and Pleasure: From Subcultures to the "Drugalogue"', in C. Rojeck, ed., *Leisure for Leisure: Critical Essays*, 171–90. London: Macmillan.

—— (1990), 'Drug Markets and Law Enforcement', *British Journal of Criminology*, 30/2: 171–88.

—— (1991), 'Profits and Penalties: New Trends in Legislation and Law Enforcement Concerning Illegal Drugs', in D. Whynes and P. Bean, eds., *Policing and Prescribing: The British System of Drug Control*, 125–41. London: Macmillan.

—— (1993*a*), 'The Power Behind Practice: Drug Control and Harm Minimisation in the Inter-Agency and Criminal Law Contexts', in *Responding to Drug Misuse: The British System*, J. Strang and M. Gossop, eds., Oxford: Oxford University Press.

DORN, N., and SOUTH, N. (1993*b*), 'After Mr Bennett and Mr Bush: US Foreign Policy and the Prospects for Drug Control', in F. Pearce and M. Woodiwiss, eds., *Global Crime Connections*, 72–90. London: Macmillan.

——, eds. (1987), *A Land Fit for Heroin? Drug Policies, Prevention and Practice*. London: Macmillan.

Drug Enforcement Report (1990), 'Drug Related Murders Are On the Increase, Say Reports', *Drug Enforcement Report*, 8 August: 7.

DRUG INDICATORS PROJECT (1985), *Drug Problems: Assessing Local Needs*. London: Drug Indicators Project, Birkbeck College, University of London.

Druglink (1991), 'Law Reform Group Rejects Decriminalisation', *Druglink*, 6/1: 5.

—— (1992*a*), 'Low Dependence and Use Typical of British Cocaine/Crack Users', *Druglink*, 7/3: 6.

—— (1992*b*), 'Ketamine Supplements Ecstasy at the Rave', *Druglink*, 7/3: 6.

—— (1992*c*), 'Grant Frozen after Ministers See Ecstasy Leaflet: Tabloid Press Urge Parents To "Dump" Author in Mersey', *Druglink*, 7/2: 5.

—— (1992*d*), '"Heatstroke" Cause of Ecstasy Deaths: Surprise Evidence of Liver Damage after Repeated Use', *Druglink*, 7/5: 5.

—— (1992*e*), 'Ethnic Minorities "Not Under-represented" Says Report', *Druglink*, 7/5: 5.

—— (1992*f*), 'Parties Neck and Neck on Drugs', *Druglink*, 7/2: 4.

—— (1992*g*), 'Drug Education Funding Axed', *Druglink*, 7/5: 4.

—— (1992*h*), 'Ground Rules Published for New Criminal Justice "Partnership"', *Druglink*, 7/5: 7.

—— (1992*i*), 'ACMD Urges Cooperation with the Courts', *Druglink*, 7/1: 5.

ELDRIDGE, W. (1952), *Narcotics and the Law*. New York: American Bar Foundation.

ERICKSON, P., and WATSON, V. (1990), 'Women, Illicit Drugs and Crime' in L. Kozlowski *et al.*, eds., *Research Advances in Alcohol and Drug Problems*, vol. 10, 251–72. New York/London: Plenum Press.

ETTORRE, B. (1986), 'Women and Drunken Sociology', *Women's Studies International Forum*, 9/5: 515–20.

—— (1989), 'Women, Substance Abuse and Self Help', in S. MacGregor, ed., *Drugs and British Society: Responses to a Social Problem in the 1980s*, 101–15. London: Routledge.

ETTORRE, B. (1992), *Women and Substance Use*, London: Macmillan.

EVANS, C. (1980), 'Alcohol, Violence and Aggression', *British Journal on Alcohol and Alcoholism*, 15: 104–17.

—— (1986), 'Alcohol and Violence: Problems Relating to Methodology, Statistics and Causation', in P. Brain, ed., *Alcohol and Aggression*, 139–60. London: Croom Helm.

FARR, K. (1990), 'Revitalizing the Drug Decriminalization Debate', *Crime and Delinquency*, 36/2: 223–37.

FAZEY, C. (1991), 'The Consequences of Illegal Drug Use', in D. Whynes and P. Bean, eds., *Policing and Prescribing: The British System of Drug Control*, 17–34. London: Macmillan.

—— (1992), 'An Empirical Study of the Relationship between Heroin Addiction, Crime and Medical Treatment', in P. O'Hare, R. Newcombe, A. Matthews,

E. Buning, and E. Drucker, eds., *The Reduction of Drug Related Harm*, 154–61. London: Routledge.

FELDMAN, H. (1968), 'Ideological Supports to Becoming and Remaining a Heroin Addict', *Journal of Health and Social Behaviour*, 9: 131–9.

FORSYTH, A., HAMMERSLEY, R., LAVELLE, T., and MURRAY, K. (1992), 'Geographical Aspects of Scoring Illegal Drugs', *British Journal of Criminology*, 32/3: 292–309.

FORTSON, R. (1988), *The Law on the Misuse of Drugs*. London: Sweet and Maxwell.

FOUCAULT, M. (1973), *The Birth of the Clinic: An Archaeology of Medical Perception*. London: Tavistock.

—— (1977), *Discipline and Punish: The Birth of the Prison*. London: Allen Lane.

FRASER, A., GAMBLE, L., and KENNETT, P. (1991), 'Into the Pleasuredome', *Druglink*, 6/6: 12–13.

FRASER, A., and GEORGE, M. (1988), 'Changing Trends in Drug Use: An Initial Follow-up of a Local Heroin-using Community', *British Journal of Addiction*, 83/6: 655–63.

FROST, C. (1986), 'Drug Trafficking, Organised Crime and Terrorism: The International Cash Connection', in V. Raanan, R. Pfaltzgraff, R. Shultz *et al.*, eds., *Hydra of Carnage*, 189–98. Lexington, Mass.: Lexington Books.

GABE, J., and BURY, M. (1988), 'Tranquillisers as a Social Problem', *Sociological Review*, 26: 321–51.

—— (1991), 'Drug Use and Dependence as a Social Problem: Sociological Approaches', in I. Glass, ed., *The International Handbook of Addiction Behaviour*, 25–33. London: Routledge.

GANDOSSY, R., WILLIAMS, J., COHEN, J., and HARWOOD, H. (1980), *Drugs and Crime: A Survey and Analysis of the Literature*. Washington, DC: US Department of Justice, National Institute of Justice.

GEORGE, M., and FRASER, A. (1989), 'Changing Trends in Drug Use: A Second Follow-up of a Local Heroin-using Community', *British Journal of Addiction*, 84/12: 1,461–6.

GIGGS, J. (1991), 'The Epidemiology of Contemporary Drug Abuse', in D. Whynes and P. Bean, eds., *Policing and Prescribing: The British System of Drug Control*, 145–75. London: Macmillan.

GILMAN, M. (1988), 'Joining the Professionals', *Druglink*, 3/2: 10–11.

—— (1991), 'Beyond opiates . . . and into the '90s', *Druglink*, 6/6: 16–18.

GILMAN, M., and PEARSON, G. (1991), 'Lifestyles and Law Enforcement', in D. Whynes and P. Bean, eds., *Policing and Prescribing: The British System of Drug Control*, 95–124. London: Macmillan.

GILMAN, M., TRAYNOR, P., and PEARSON, G. (1990), 'The Limits of Intervention: Cyclizine Misuse', *Druglink*, 5/3: 12–13.

GLANZ, A., and TAYLOR, C. (1986), 'Findings of a National Survey of the Role of General Practitioners in the Treatment of Opiate Misuse: Extent of Contact with Opiate Misusers', *British Medical Journal*, 293: 427–30.

GOLDSTEIN, P. (1979), *Prostitution and Drugs*. Lexington, Mass.: Lexington Books.

—— (1985), 'The Drugs/Violence Nexus: A Tripartite Conceptual Framework', *Journal of Drug Issues*, 15/4: 493–506.

GOMBERG, E. (1982), 'Historical and Political Perspectives: Women and Drug Use', *Social Issues*, 38/2: 9–23.

GOODSIR, J. (1986), 'Trends in Drug Enforcement', *Druglink*, 1/3: 10–11.

GOTTFREDSON, M. (1984), *Victims of Crime: The Dimensions of Risk*, Home Office Research Study no. 81. London: HMSO.

GRAHAM, G. (1991), 'Criminalisation and Control', in D. Whynes and P. Bean, eds., *Policing and Prescribing: The British System of Drug Control*, 245–60. London: Macmillan.

GREEN, P. (1991), *Drug Couriers*. London: Howard League for Penal Reform.

GREENBERG, S. (1976), 'The Relationship between Crime and Amphetamine Abuse: An Empirical Review of the Literature', *Contemporary Drug Problems*, 5/2: 101–30.

GREENBERG, S., and ADLER, F. (1974), 'Crime and Addiction: An Empirical Analysis of the Literature, 1920–1973', *Contemporary Drug Problems*, 3: 221–70.

GREENWOOD, J. (1992), 'Unpopular Patients: GPs' Attitudes to Drug Users', *Druglink*, 7/4: 8–9.

GRIEVE, J. (1987), 'Comparative Police Strategies: Drug Related Crime', unpublished M.Phil. thesis, Cranfield Institute of Technology.

GRIFFIN, L. (1991), 'More Than a Mother', *Alcohol Concern Magazine*, 7/2: 12–13.

HAMID, A. (1990), 'The Political Economy of Crack-Related Violence', *Contemporary Drug Problems*, Spring: 31–78.

HAMMERSLEY, R., FORSYTH, A., and LAVELLE, T. (1990), 'The Criminality of New Drug Users in Glasgow', *British Journal of Addiction*, 85: 1583–94.

HAMMERSLEY, R., FORSYTH, A., MORRISON, V., and DAVIES, J. (1989), 'The Relationship between Crime and Opioid Use', *British Journal of Addiction*, 84: 1029–44.

HAMMETT, T., HUNT, D., GROSS, M., RHODES, W., and MOINI, S. (1991), 'Stemming the Spread of HIV Among HIV Drug Users, their Sexual Partners, and Children: Issues and Opportunities for Criminal Justice Agencies', *Crime and Delinquency*, 37/1: 101–24.

HART, G. (1990), 'Say No to Drugs, but Yes to Clean Syringes?', in P. Abbott and G. Payne, eds., *New Directions in the Sociology of Health*. London: Falmer.

HARTNOLL, R. (1989), 'The International Context', in S. MacGregor, ed., *Drugs and British Society: Responses to a Social Problem in the 1980s*, 36–51. London: Routledge.

HARTNOLL, R., MITCHESON, M., BATTERSBY, A., BROWN, G., ELLIS, M., FLEMING, P., and HEDLEY, N. (1980), 'Evaluation of Heroin Maintenance in Controlled Trial', *Archives of General Psychiatry*, 37: 877–84.

HARTNOLL, R., LEWIS, R., and BRYER, S. (1984), 'Recent Trends in Drug Use in Britain', *Druglink*, 19: 22–4.

HAUGE, G. (1984), *Alcohol and Crime*. Strasbourg: Council of Europe.

HAW, S. (1985), *Drug Problems in Greater Glasgow*. Glasgow: Standing Conference on Drug Abuse.

—— (1988), 'The Sentencing of Drug Offenders in Scottish Courts', paper presented to Drug Questions Research Conference, ISDD, London, April.

—— (1989), *Patterns of Sentencing of Drug Offenders Convicted in Scottish Courts*, Report to the Scottish Home and Health Department, Criminological Research Division, Edinburgh.

HAYTER, A. (1988), *Opium and the Romantic Imagination: Addiction and Creativity in De Quincey, Coleridge, Baudelaire and Others*. Wellingborough: Crucible.

HEBENTON, B., and THOMAS, T. (1992), 'Rocky Path to Europol', *Druglink*, 7/6: 8–10.

HENDERSON, S., ed. (1990), *Women, Drugs, HIV: Practical Issues*. London: Institute for the Study of Drug Dependence.

HENRY, S. (1978), *The Hidden Economy*. Oxford: Martin Robertson.

HENZE, P. (1986), 'Organised Crime and Drug Linkages', in V. Raanan, R. Pfaltzgraff, R. Shultz, *et al.*, eds., *Hydra of Carnage*, 171–87. Lexington, Mass.: Lexington Books.

HOBBS, D. (1988), *Doing the Business: Entrepreneurship, the Working Class and Detectives in the East End of London*. Oxford: Clarendon Press.

HOME AFFAIRS COMMITTEE (1985), *Misuse of Hard Drugs: Interim Report*. London: HMSO.

—— (1989), *Crack: The Threat of Hard Drugs in the Next Decade (Interim Report)*. London: HMSO.

HOME OFFICE (1985), *Criminal Convictions of Persons First Notified as Narcotic Addicts in 1979–81, Home Office Statistical Bulletin*, 19/85. London: Home Office.

—— (1987), *Criminal Convictions of Persons Convicted of Drug Offences in 1980–81, Home Office Statistical Bulletin*, 31/87. London: Home Office.

—— (1991), *Statistics of the Misuse of Drugs: Seizures and Offenders Dealt with, United Kingdom, 1990, Home Office Statistical Bulletin*, 19/91. London: Home Office.

HOUGH, M., and SHEEHY, K. (1986), 'Incidents of Violence: Findings from the British Crime Survey', *Home Office Research and Planning Unit Bulletin*, 20: 20–6.

INCIARDI, J. (1980), 'Women, Heroin and Property Crime', in S. Dotesman and F. Scarpitti, eds., *Women, Crime and Justice*. New York: Oxford Press.

—— (1986), *The War on Drugs: Heroin, Cocaine and Public Policy*. Palo Alto, Ca.: Mayfield.

—— (1990), 'AIDS and Drug Use: Implications for Criminal Justice Policy', in R. Weisheit, ed., *Drugs, Crime and the Criminal Justice System*, 303–23. Cincinatti: Anderson.

INCIARDI, J., and MCBRIDE, D. (1989), 'Legislation: A High Risk Alternative in the War on Drugs', *American Behavioural Scientist*, 32/3: 259–89.

INCIARDI, J., and POTTIEGER, A. (1986), 'Drug Use and Crime among Two Cohorts of Women Narcotics Users: An Empirical Assessment', *Journal of Drug Issues*, 12: 91–106.

INGLIS, B. (1975), *The Forbidden Game: A Social History of Drugs*. London: Hodder and Stoughton.

ISDD (1981), *Teaching About a Volatile Situation*. London: Institute for the Study of Drug Dependence.

—— (1987), *Surveys and Statistics on Drugtaking in Britain*. London: Institute for the Study of Drug Dependence.

ISDD (1990), *Drug Misuse in Britain: National Audit of Drug Misuse Statistics*. London: Institute for the Study of Drug Dependence.

—— (1991*a*), *Drug Abuse Briefing*. London: Institute for the Study of Drug Dependence.

—— (1991*b*), *Drug Misuse in Britain: National Audit of Drug Misuse Statistics*. London: Institute for the Study of Drug Dependence.

Jarvis, G., and Parker, H. (1989), 'Young Heroin Users and Crime', *British Journal of Criminology*, 29: 175–85.

—— (1990), 'Can Medical Treatment Reduce Crime amongst Young Heroin Users?', *Home Office Research Bulletin*, 28: 29–32.

Jeffs, B., and Sanders, W. (1983), 'Minimizing Alcohol-Related Offences by Enforcement of the Existing Licensing Legislations', *British Journal of Criminology*, 29: 386–94.

Johnson, B. (1989), 'Crime and Compulsory Treatment', *Druglink*, 4/3: 12–13.

Johnson, B., Goldstein, P., Preble, E., Schmeidler, J., Lipton, D., Spunt, B., and Miller, T. (1985), *Taking Care of Business: The Economics of Crime by Heroin Abusers*. Lexington, Mass.: Lexington Books.

Kay, L. (1988), 'Aramah and the Street Value of Drugs', *Criminal Law Review*, December: 814–20.

Kelly, L. (1988), *Surviving Sexual Violence*. Cambridge: Polity Press.

Knapp Commission (1972), *The Knapp Report on Police Corruption*. New York: George Braziller.

Kohn, M. (1992), *Dope Girls: The Birth of the British Drug Underground*. London: Lawrence and Wishart.

Kraska, P. (1990), 'The Unmentionable Alternative: The Need for, and the Argument against, the Decriminalization of Drug Laws', in R. Weisheit, ed., *Drugs, Crime and the Criminal Justice System*, 111–37. Cincinnati: Anderson.

Lacey, R., and Woodward, S. (1985), *That's Life! Survey on Tranquillisers*. London: BBC/MIND.

Last, J. (1982), *A Dictionary of Epidemiology*. Oxford: Oxford University Press.

Laycock, G. (1984), *Reducing Burglary: A Study of Chemist's Shops*, Crime Prevention Unit paper 1. London: Home Office.

Laycock, C. (1991), 'Breaking down the Drinking Myth', *Alcohol Concern Magazine*, 7/2: 10–11.

Leach, K. (1991), 'The Junkies' Doctors and the London Drug Scene in the 1960s: Some Remembered Fragments', in D. Whynes and P. Bean, eds., *Policing and Prescribing: The British System of Drug Control*, 35–59. London: Macmillan.

Leroy, B. (1992), 'The EC of 12 and the Drug Demand', *Drug and Alcohol Dependence*, 29: 269–81.

Levi, M., (1991), '*Pecunia non olet*: Cleansing the money-launderers from the Temple', *Crime, Law and Social Change*, 16: 217–302.

Levine, H. (1983), 'The Good Creature of God and the Demon Rum: Colonial American and 19th Century Ideas About Alcohol, Crime and Accidents', in R. Room and G. Collins, eds., *Alcohol and Disinhibition: Nature and Meaning of the Link*, 347–73. Rockville, Md.: National Institute on Alcohol Abuse and Alcoholism.

LEWIS, R., HARTNOL, R., BRYER, S., DAVIAUD, E., and MITCHESON, M. (1985), 'Scoring Smack: The Illicit Heroin Market in London, 1980–83', *British Journal of Addiction*, 80: 281–90.

LINDESMITH, A. (1967), *The Addict and the Law*. New York: Vintage Books.

LOMBROSO, C. (1968 [1911]), *Crime: Its Causes and Remedies*. Montclair, NJ: Patterson Smith.

MCBRIDE, D., and MCCOY, C., (1982), 'Crime and Drugs: The Issues and Literature', *Journal of Drug Issues,* Spring: 137–51.

MCCONVILLE, B. (1991), *Women under the Influence: Alcohol and its Impact*. London: Grafton.

MCCOY, A., READ, C., and ADAMS, L. (1972), *The Politics of Heroin in South-East Asia*. New York: Harper and Row.

MACGREGOR, S., ed. (1989), *Drugs and British Society: Responses to a Social Problem in the 1980s*. London: Routledge.

MACINNES, C. (1985), *City of Spades*. London: Alison and Busby.

MCMURRAN, M., and HOLLIN, C. (1989), 'Drinking and Delinquency', *British Journal of Criminology*, 29/4: 386–93.

MARSHALL, N., and HENDTLASS, J. (1986), 'Drugs and Prostitution', *Journal of Drug Issues*, 16: 237–48.

MASON, P. (1992), 'The Drug War: Signs of a Tactical Retreat?', *Druglink*, 7/4: 11.

MINISTRY OF HEALTH (1926), *Report of the Departmental Committee on Morphine and Heroin Addiction*. London: HMSO.

—— (1961), *Drug Addiction: Report of the Interdepartmental Committee*. London: HMSO.

MIRZA, H., PEARSON, G., and PHILLIPS, S. (1991), *Drugs, People and Services in Lewisham*, Final Report of the Drug Information Project. London: Goldsmiths College, University of London.

MOL, R., and TRAUTMANN, F. (1991), 'The Liberal Image of Dutch Drug Policy', *International Journal on Drug Policy*, 2/3: 16–21.

MORRISON, V. (1988), 'Drug Misuse and Concern about HIV Infection in Edinburgh: An Interim Report', in N. Dorn, L. Lucas, and N. South, eds., *Drug Questions: Annual Research Register*, no. 4. London: Institute for the Study of Drug Dependence.

—— (1989), 'Psychoactive Substance User and Related Behaviour of 135 Regular and Illicit Drug Users in Scotland', *Drug and Alcohol Dependence*, 23: 95–101.

MOTT, J. (1985), 'Self-Reported Cannabis Use in Great Britain in 1981', *British Journal of Addiction,* 80: 37–43.

—— (1986), 'Opioid Use and Burglary', *British Journal of Addiction*, 81: 671–77.

—— (1989), 'Reducing Heroin Related Crime', *Home Office Research Unit Bulletin*, 26: 30–3.

—— (1990), 'Young People, Alcohol and Crime', *Home Office Research Bulletin* (Research and Statistics Department), 28: 24–8.

—— (1991), 'Crime and Heroin Use', in D. Whynes and P. Bean, eds., *Policing and Prescribing: The British System of Drug Control*, 77–94. London: Macmillan.

MOTT, J., and TAYLOR, M. (1974), *Delinquency amongst Opiate Users*, Home Office Research Study, no. 23. London: HMSO.

Murphy, D. (1983), 'Alcohol and Crime', *Home Office Research Bulletin*, 15: 8–11.

Murray, M. (1993), 'Use of Illegal Drugs in Northern Ireland', in J. Strang and M. Gossop, eds., *Responding to Drug Misuse: The British System*. Oxford: Oxford University Press.

Musto, D. (1973), *The American Disease: Origins of Narcotics Control*. New Haven: Yale University Press.

Myers, T. (1982), 'Alcohol and Violent Crime Re-examined', *British Journal of Addiction*, 77: 399–414.

Nadelman, E. (1989), 'Drug Prohibition in the United States: Costs, Consequences and Alternatives', *Science*, 245: 939–47.

Newcombe, R. (1992), 'A Researcher Reports from the Rave', *Druglink*, 7/1: 14–16.

Nurco, D., Ball, J., Shaffer, J., and Hanlon, T. (1985), 'The Criminality of Narcotic Addicts', *The Journal of Nervous and Mental Disease*, 173/2: 94–102.

O'Bryan, L. (1985), 'The Cost of Lacoste: Drugs, Style and Money', in A. Henman, R. Lewis, and T. Malyon, eds., *Big Deal*. London: Pluto.

Oswald, P. (1982), 'The Healing Herb?' *Youth in Society*, 68: 21–2.

Parker, H., and Newcombe, R. (1987), 'Heroin Use and Acquisitive Crime in an English Community', *British Journal of Sociology*, 38: 331–50.

Parker, H., Newcombe, R., and Bakx, K. (1987), 'The New Heroin Users: Prevalence and Characteristics in Wirral, Merseyside', *British Journal of Addiction*, 82: 147–57.

—— (1988), *Living with Heroin: The Impact of a Drugs 'Epidemic' on an English Community*. Milton Keynes: Open University Press.

Parssinen, T. (1983), *Secret Passions, Secret Remedies: Narcotic Drugs in British Society, 1820–1930*. Manchester: Manchester University Press.

Pearce, F. (1976), *Crimes of the Powerful*. London: Pluto.

Pearson, G. (1987*a*), *The New Heroin Users*. Oxford: Blackwell.

—— (1987*b*), 'Social Deprivation, Unemployment and Patterns of Heroin Use', in N. Dorn and N. South, eds., *A Land Fit for Heroin? Drug Policies, Prevention and Practice*, 62–94. London: Macmillan.

Pearson, G. (1989), 'Heroin Use in its Social Context', in D. Herbert and D. Smith, eds., *Social Problems and the City: New Perspectives*. Oxford: Oxford University Press.

—— (1991), 'Drug Control Policies in Britain', in M. Tonry and N. Morris, eds., *Crime and Justice: A Review of Research*, vol. 14, 167–227. Chicago: University of Chicago Press.

—— (1992*a*), 'The Role of Culture in the Drug Question', in G. Edwards, M. Lader, and C. Drummond, eds., *The Nature of Alcohol and Drug Related Problems*. Oxford: Oxford University Press.

—— (1992*b*), 'Drugs and Criminal Justice: A Harm Reduction Perspective', in E. Buning, E. Drucker, P. O'Hare, and R. Newcombe, eds., *Reduction of Drug Related Harm*, 15–29. London: Routledge.

Pearson, G., Ditton, J., Newcombe, R., and Gilman, M. (1991), 'Everything Starts with an "E": An Introduction to Ecstasy Use by Young People in Britain', *Druglink*, 6/6: 10–11.

PEARSON, G., GILMAN, M., and MCIVER, S. (1986), *Young People and Heroin: An Examination of Heroin Use in the North of England.* London: Health Education Council; Aldershot: Avebury (1987).

PECK, D., and PLANT, M. (1986), 'Unemployment and Illegal Drug Use: Concordant Evidence from a Prospective Study and National Trends', *British Medical Journal*, 293: 929–32.

PEELE, S. (1985), *The Meaning of Addiction.* Lexington, Mass.: Lexington Books.

PERRY, L. (1979), *Women and Drug Use: An Unfeminine Dependency*, ISDD briefing paper. London: Institute for the Study of Drug Dependence.

PEVELER, R., GREEN, R., and MANDELBROTE, B. (1988), 'Prevalence of Heroin Misuse in Oxford City', *British Journal of Addiction*, 83: 513–18.

PLANT, M. (1989), 'The Epidemiology of Illicit Drug Use and Misuse in Britain' in S. MacGregor, ed., *Drugs and British Society: Responses to a Social Problem in the 1980s*, 52–63. London: Routledge.

—— (ed.) (1990), *AIDS, Drugs and Prostitution*, London: Routledge.

PLANT, M., PECK, D., and SAMUEL, E. (1985), *Alcohol, Drugs and School Leavers.* London: Tavistock.

POWER, R. (1989*a*), 'Drugs and the Media: Prevention Campaigns and Television', in S. MacGregor, ed., *Drugs and British Society: Responses to a Social Problem in the 1980s*, 129–42. London: Routledge.

—— (1989*b*), 'Methods of Drug Use: Injecting and Sharing', in P. Aggleton, G. Hart, and P. Davies, eds., *AIDS: Social Representations, Social Practices.* Lewes: Falmer.

PREBLE, E., and CASEY, J. (1969), 'Taking Care of Business: The Heroin User's Life on the Street', *International Journal of The Addictions*, 4/1: 1–24.

PRYCE, K. (1979), *Endless Pressure: A Study of West Indian Lifestyles in Bristol.* Harmondsworth: Penguin.

Release (1992), *A Release White Paper on Reform of the Drug Law.* London: Release.

RESEARCH TRIANGLE INSTITUTE (1976), *Drug Use and Crime: Report of the Panel on Drug Use and Criminal Behaviour.* Springfield, Va.: National Technical Information Service, Research Triangle Institute.

REUTER, P. (1983), *Disorganised Crime: Illegal Markets and the Mafia.* Cambridge, Mass.: MIT Press.

RICHARDS, L. (1982), 'Drugs and Crime: Theory Engagement after a Forced Marriage', *Contemporary Drug Problems*, Winter: 461–73.

ROBERTSON, J. (1987), *Heroin, AIDS and Society.* London: Hodder and Stoughton.

ROSENBAUM, M. (1981*a*), *Women on Heroin.* New Brunswick, NJ: Rutgers University Press.

—— (1981*b*), 'Sex Roles among Deviants: The Woman Addict', *International Journal of the Addictions*, 16: 859–77.

ROYAL COLLEGE OF PSYCHIATRISTS (1986), *Alcohol: Our Favourite Drug.* London: Tavistock.

—— (1987), *Drug Scenes: A Report on Drugs and Drug Dependence by the Royal College of Psychiatrists.* London: Gaskell.

RUGGIERO, V., and VASS, T. (1992), 'Heroin Use and the Formal Economy: Illicit

Drugs and Licit Economies in Italy', *British Journal of Criminology*, 32/3: 273–91.

Rutherford, A., and Green, P. (1989), 'Illegal Drugs and British Criminal Justice Policy', in H. Allbrecht and A. Kalmthout, eds., *Drug Polices in Western Europe*. Freiburg: Max Planck Institute.

Scarman, Lord (1981), *Brixton Disorders, 10–12 April, 1981: Report of an Inquiry Presented to Parliament by the Secretary of State for the Home Department*. London: HMSO.

Shapiro, H. (1989), *Crack: A Briefing*. London: Institute for the Study of Drug Dependence.

—— (1991), 'Contemporary Cocaine Use in Britain', in ISDD, ed., *Drug Misuse in Britain*, 40–5. London: Institute for the Study of Drug Dependence.

—— (1992), 'Ketamine Factsheet', *Druglink*, 7/3: 7.

Silverman, I. (1982), 'Women, Crime and Drugs', *Journal of Drug Issues*, Spring: 167–83.

—— (1991), 'Crack Magic Puts Us Under its Spell', *New Statesman and Society*, 25 October: 24–5.

Smart, C. (1984), 'Social Policy and Drug Addiction: A Critical Study of Policy Development', *British Journal of Addiction*, 79: 31–9.

Social Services Committee (1985), *Misuse of Hard Drugs: Fourth Report of the Committee*. London: HMSO.

South, N. (1992), 'Moving Murky Money: Drug Trafficking, Law Enforcement and the Pursuit of Criminal Profits', in D. Farrington and S. Walklate, eds., *Offenders and Victims: Theory and Policy*, 167–93. London: British Society of Criminology.

Spear, B. (1969), 'The Growth of Heroin Addiction in the UK', *British Journal of Addiction*, 64: 245–55.

—— (1975), 'The British Experience', *The John Marshall Journal of Practice and Procedure*, 9: 67–98.

Stanko, E. (1985), *Intimate Intrusions: Women's Experiences of Male Violence*. London: Unwin Hyman.

Steele, D. (1986), 'Alcohol and Drugs: Unsuitable Attachment?', *Druglink*, 1/3: 7.

Stephens, R., and Ellis, R. (1975) 'Narcotic Addicts and Crime: An Analysis of Recent Trends', *Criminology*, 12: 474–88.

Stevenson, R. (1990), 'Can Markets Cope with Drugs?', *Journal of Drug Issues*, 20/4: 659–66.

—— (1991), 'The Economics of Drug Policy', in D. Whynes and P. Bean, eds., *Policing and Prescribing*: The British System of Drug Control, 200–16. London: Macmillan.

Stimson, G. (1987), 'The War on Heroin: British Policy and the International Trade in Illicit Drugs', in N. Dorn and N. South, eds., *A Land Fit for Heroin? Drug Policies, Prevention and Practice*, 35–61. London: Macmillan.

Stimson, G., Dolan, K., Donoghoe, M., and Aldritt, L. (1988*a*), 'Syringe Exchange, 1', *Druglink*, 3/3: 10–11.

Stimson, G., Donoghoe, M., Aldritt, L., and Dolan, K. (1988*b*), 'Syringe Exchange 2: The Clients', *Druglink*, 3/4: 8–9.

STIMSON, G., DOLAN, K., DONOGHOE, M., ALDRITT, L., and LART, R. (1989), 'Syringe Exchange 3: Can Injectors Change?', *Druglink*, 4/1: 10–11.

STIMSON, G., and OPPENHEIMER, E. (1982), *Heroin Addiction: Treatment and Control in Britain*. London: Tavistock.

STRANG, J., and GOSSOP, M., eds. (1993), *Responding to Drug Misuse: The British System*. Oxford: Oxford University Press.

STRANG, J., and STIMSON, G., eds. (1991), *AIDS and Drug Misuse*. London: Routledge.

SWADI, H. (1988), 'Drug and Substance Abuse among 3,333 London Adolescents', *British Journal of Addiction*, 83: 935–42.

TAYLOR, A. (1993), *Women Drug Users: An Ethnography of a Female Injecting Community*. Oxford: Clarendon Press.

TONRY, M., and WILSON, J. Q., eds. (1990), 'Drugs and Crime' in M. Tonry and N. Morris, eds., *Crime and Justice: A Review of Research,* vol. 13. Chicago: University of Chicago Press.

TRACE, M. (1988), 'Why Not Work in Prison?', *Druglink*, 3/5: 6–8.

—— (1990), 'HIV and Drugs in British Prisons', *Druglink*, 5/1: 12–15.

TREBACH, A. (1991), 'Rethinking American Drugs Policy: A Bundle of Peaceful Compromises', in D. Whynes and P. Bean, eds., *Policing and Prescribing: The British System of Drug Control*, London: Macmillan.

TUCK, M. (1989), *Drinking and Disorder: A Study of Non-Metropolitan Violence*, Home Office Research Study no. 108. London: HMSO.

UNELL, I. (1987), 'Drugs and Deprivation', *Druglink*, 2/6: 14–15.

US SENATE FOREIGN RELATIONS COMMITTEE (1990), *Drug Money Laundering, Banks and Foreign Policy*, Report to the Foreign Relations Committee. Washington DC: US Government Printing Office.

VELLEMAN, R., and RIGBY, J. (1990), 'Harm Minimisation: Old Wine in New Bottles?', *International Journal on Drug Policy*, 1/5: 22–3.

WAGSTAFF, A., and MAYNARD, A. (1988), *Economic Aspects of the Illicit Drug Market and Drug Enforcement Policies in the United Kingdom*, Home Office Research Study no. 95. London: HMSO.

WARD, J., MATTICK, R., and HALL, W. (1992), *Key Issues in Methadone Maintenance Treatment*. New South Wales University Press.

WATTERS, J., REINARMAN, C., and FAGAN, J. (1985), 'Causality, Context and Contingency: Relationships between Drug Abuse and Delinquency', *Contemporary Drug Problems*, Fall: 351–73.

WAYMONT, A., and WRIGHT, A. (1989), *Drug Enforcement Strategies and Intelligence Needs*, draft report. London: Police Foundation.

WEIPERT, G., D'ORBAN, P., and BEWLEY, T. (1979), 'Delinquency by Opiate Addicts Treated at Two London Clinics', *British Journal of Psychiatry*, 134: 14–23.

WEISHEIT, R., ed. (1990), *Drugs, Crime and the Criminal Justice System*. Cincinatti: Anderson.

WEST, D., and FARRINGTON, D. (1977), *The Delinquent Way of Life*. London: Heinemann.

WHYNES, D., and BEAN, P. eds. (1991), *Policing and Prescribing: The British System of Drug Control*. London: Macmillan.

WILLIAMS, P., and BRAKE, T. (1980), *Drink in Great Britain, 1900–1979*. London: Edsel.

WILLIS, P. (1978), *Profane Culture*. London: Routledge.

WOOTTON COMMITTEE (1968), *Cannabis: Report by the Advisory Committee on Drug Dependence*. London: HMSO.

YOUNG, J. (1971), *The Drugtakers: The Social Meaning of Drug Use*. London: Paladin.

—— (1987), 'Deviance', in P. Worsley, ed., *The New Introducing Sociology*, 407–50. London: Penguin.

ZANDER, M. (1989), *Confiscation and Forfeiture Law: English and American Comparisons*. London: Police Foundation.

ZINBERG, N. (1984), *Drug, Set and Setting: The Basis for Controlled Intoxicant Use*. New Haven: Yale University Press.

10

Professional and Organized Crime in Britain

DICK HOBBS

How I admired the life of taking pains, of living in defiance of a government that did not like you and did not want you and wanted to destroy you so that you had to build out protections for yourself with money and men deploying armaments, buying alliances, patrolling borders as in a state of secession, by your will and wit and warrior spirit living smack in the eye of the monster, his very eye. (Doctrow 1989: 67)

The phenomenon of professional and organized crime in Britain has received relatively little attention from academics. One of the principal restraints upon researchers is the vagueness of the terms 'professional' and 'organized' when applied to criminality, and one of the tasks of this chapter will to be unpack the terminology by way of highlighting changes and continuities in the political economy of crime. However, it is worth making some preliminary comments on definitional problems that might set the scene for the ensuing, at times necessarily contentious, arguments that follow.

THE NATURE OF ORGANIZED AND PROFESSIONAL CRIME

Edwin Sutherland's (1937) seminal study of a professional thief laid the foundations for a number of studies that focused upon the craft involved in the committal of specific crimes against property. Subsequent work, notably Maurer's (1964) study of professional pickpockets, followed on in a similar vein, utilizing similar key notions of craft and professionalism. The essential thread that runs through this mode of theory is best summed up by Sutherland, who claims that professional criminals possess 'a complex of abilities and skills, just as do physicians, lawyers or bricklayers' (1937: 197; see also Clinard and Quinney 1967). Critics have pointed out the ambiguity of the terms (Cressey 1972: 45–6), the apparent lack of skill of many practitioners (Lemert 1958), and the lack of consensus among such individuals (Gould *et al.* 1966). However, the notion of a full-time commitment to crime does emerge from Sutherland's work as a useful starting-point (Mack 1964; McIntosh 1971, Roebuck and Windham 1983).

Defining organized crime is perhaps more problematic. For Sutherland

(1949), white collar crime was organized crime because white-collar criminality took place within organizations apparently grounded in the first place in legal enterprise. The inadequacy of this definition is underlined by Block, who points out that contemporary serious criminality involves 'organised criminals often doing white collar type crime, and white collar criminals frequently acting like racketeers' (Block 1991*b*: 3). Block is here referring sceptically to the normative use of the term 'organized crime' which concentrates on 'Mafia-type' structures, often of a syndicated nature, of which Cressey has been the most influential exponent (1969, 1972). For Cressey, organized crime *is* the Mafia or Cosa Nostra, and he outlines a number of key characteristics (1969: 314–15). The debate concerning the existence of the Mafia is referred to later in this chapter; partly as a way of dealing with this issue, and partly as a means of explaining this chapter's approach, organized crime will be referred to in terms of its relationship to the marketplace. Block's 'serious crime community' (1991*b:* 1–26) is a more flexible tool with which to probe the cultural forms that are ill served by the imposition of legalistically defined categories.

Professional and organized crime are particularly problematic phenomena for social scientists. Not the least of these problems is that of methodology, for professional criminals have little to gain from exposing themselves to academic viewing. Further, researchers will inevitably become at the very least party to guilty knowledge (Polsky 1971: 138) and as a consequence ethical obstacles, both personal and professional, need to be surmounted (Fountain 1993; Hobbs 1988: ch. 1). Whether these ethical problems are greater than in more conventional administrative-based criminological concerns is, however, contentious, for ethical traps lurk in studies of similar environments that also make extraordinary demands upon researchers (cf. Norris 1993; Humphreys 1975, Van Maanen 1978; Fielding 1981).

The covert, non-institutionalized base from which professional and organized crime operates favours the use of a range of largely interpretative techniques. Until gangsters, armed robbers, fraudsters and their ilk indicate their enthusiasm for questionnaires or large-scale social surveys, ethnographic research, life histories, oral histories, biographies, autobiographies and journalistic accounts will be at a premium. While ethnography has a long-standing tradition of exploiting a range of research opportunities within the study of crime, and both oral histories (Plummer 1983: 25–6; Samuel 1981; Thompson 1978) and life histories (Plummer 1983; Thomas and Znaniecki 1958; Klockars 1975; Spradley 1970; Sutherland 1937) have been widely used, this chapter also features some rather more unconventional sources.

Biographies, autobiographies and journalism offer narrative accounts that are often ignored, particularly by British criminologists; their American counterparts exploit such data far more readily (see e.g. Marx 1988; Katz 1988). However, the intransigence of a positivism that colludes so closely with administrative analysis ignores narrative accounts at the cost of a considerable loss of detail, tone and depth. Yet their use in this chapter is due to more than a dearth of more conventional material. If an armed robber writes a memoir surely it is essential for relevant scholars to include it in any cumulative database, in the same way that scholars of the police would value the biography of a prominent policeman, or political scientists the memoirs of an eminent politician. For biographies offer unique glances into worlds otherwise uncharted. As Blumer noted, 'human documents [are] accounts of individual experience which reveal the individual's experience as a human agent and as a participant in social life' (Blumer 1979: 27).

The lack of corroborating evidence from more orthodox data sources, however, does put a considerable stress on the need to provide readings of these narratives that are essentially against the grain, thus objectivifying subjectively orientated data by cross-referencing with other accounts. For instance, one might compare the differing accounts of professional criminal ideologies given in a study of a top-security prison in the late 1960s (Cohen and Taylor 1972) and in the pungent autobiographies of Probyn (1977) McVicar (1979), and Richardson (1992). All four studies are to varying degrees concerned with F wing of Durham prison, yet offer divergent viewpoints. Another example of reading against the grain would be to compare the biography of the Kray twins, (Pearson 1973) with an autobiography of a former member of the Kray gang (Dickson 1986), the autobiography of the Kray twins' elder brother (Kray and Sykes 1976), and the autobiography of one of the twins (Kray 1991).

Most biographies and accounts of professional criminals have been written at the end of successful careers that have usually been cut short by a lengthy prison sentence (Kray 1991; Richardson 1992) or some other criminal justice intervention (Pileggi 1987; Hohimer 1981). In McVicar's case a portion of the text was written as a crucial part of his legal defence (McVicar 1979). Some of the accounts are driven by a hard-boiled narrative that led to their being adapted for the cinema. Pileggi (1987) was the basis for the highly successful *Goodfellas*, Hohimer (1981) became *Violent Streets*, and McVicar (1979) was made into a film of the same name. The subjective nature of these and similar accounts needs to be acknowledged, but should in no way diminish their value, any more than the career patterns and funding strategies of normative criminologists detract from the quality of their work.

Another feature of this chapter is that, in the face of a dearth of indigenous data, material from the USA is used extensively. Cross cultural applications are problematic in that much of the literature, from a range of sources, refers to phenomena that are culturally specific; this is particularly true of American studies of organized crime, which in their classic form tend to refer to large-scale organizd criminality of the syndicated variety (Cressey 1969, 1972). Making use of this literature is, however, no more problematic than making use of the narrative accounts, if it is read critically. Indeed, the lack of empirical evidence that typifies many of the classic American studies of organized crime (cf. Block 1977) underlines the need both to read all data critically and, more importantly, to create a substantive and generating base for studies concerned with the subjective worlds of professional and organized crime.

THE DEVELOPMENT OF ORGANIZED AND PROFESSIONAL CRIME

The practice of crime as a full time occupation can be traced to the decline of the feudal system in England, and to a need for those leaving the land to develop alternative forms of economic subsistence within the context of urbanization and the emergence of capitalism (Roebuck and Windham 1983). Studies of early urban professional criminals, some of them displaying elements of organization, indicate an emerging universe of deviant commitment featuring a range of activities (Aydelote 1913; Salgado 1977). However, professional and organized crime—particularly its changes and contingencies—can be understood only by comprehending the context in which these particular forms of action are enacted. As Chambliss has noted, 'Crime is not a by-product of an otherwise effectively working political economy: it is a main product of that political economy' (1978: 2). The master context for professional and organized crime is the marketplace, and the marketplace that emerged from the early years of British urbanization created, for instance, a demand for game which in turn led to a flourishing poaching trade (Munsche 1981; Hay 1975). Fulfilling this need required considerable organization (Sharp 1984) and a link between rural and urban cultures that was based upon intra-market dependency. The onset of industrialism introduced an acceptance of commercialism as a central ethic upon which a whole range of individuals could organize and justify their actions (Hobbs 1988: chs. 4, 5; Perkin 1992). The vast criminal organization of Jonathan Wild is an exemplary case of an individual exploiting the dominant rhetoric of the era (Defoe 1901; Pringle 1958; Howson 1971). As Klockars indicates, 'On the eve of the industrial revolution, Wild adopted the methods of modern business' (Klockars 1975:14).

By the eighteenth century professional and organized criminals had established their presence in Britain, particularly in London, where the marketplace was most affluent (Low 1982) and regimentation of the emerging working class was most ineffective (Hobbs 1988; Stedman Jones 1971). After the demise of Wild and his organization, the principal focus of both professional and organized crime was that of the fence. Often the fence would introduce some instruction to his (often juvenile) cohorts, yet his primary function as a buyer and seller of stolen goods was carried out within strict commercial guidelines (Tobias 1974).

While the marketplace can be seen to define and shape professional and organized criminal activity, criminal practice was often affected by changes in the law (Klockars 1975: ch. l; Hay 1975; Munsche 1981) and by subtle changes in technology or cultural preference. Indeed, these latter changes often resulted in de-skilling—as in the 1860s, when changes in fashion led to men ceasing to expose silk handkerchiefs to the subtle skills of marauding pickpockets. This fashion innovation coincided with the introduction of reformatories for wayward youth that enforced upon its charges manual tasks which 'ruined for ever the delicacy of touch necessary for a pick-pocket' (Lloyd Baker 1889: 23). Consequently there was an increase in violent street crime, most notably garrotting (Sindall 1990).

However, with the notable exception of Jonathan Wild's highly structured criminal 'firm', there is little evidence of substantial criminal organizations during the eighteenth and nineteenth centuries. As Low has noted: 'There were some big criminal entrepreneurs, but on the whole the criminal underworld was not organised, or even much influenced by its leading citizens: fortunately for the rest of society it remained essentially a community of small operators' (Low 1982: 195). Industrialization and urbanization created a regulation of markets, both legal and illegal (McIntosh 1971). Even 'social crimes', of which poaching (particularly after the repeal of the Corn Laws in 1846) was the most easily absorbed into the new demand-led marketplace, were greatly transformed by the construction and subsequent physical location of the demand for goods and services (Jones 1982). It is from this milieu that our perception of both 'professionalism' and 'organization' in relation to crime has emerged.

As a consequence both of this environmental specificity and of the informal nature of criminal actions and social structures, the term 'professional' bears little relation to its formal definitional usage in sociology (Carr-Saunders and Wilson 1933). However, the attribution of professional status to criminals is far more significant than, as Letkemann (1973) suggests, mere layman's terminology. While lacking in the formal entry requirements of doctors, lawyers, or academics, professional criminals are marked out by their singular commitment to criminal activity. Crime becomes an ideal partly detached from pecuniary advantage, whose essential rationality is located in the pursuit of status (Hughes

1971). As McVicar has noted of his own criminal career: 'Money has always been a secondary goal; crime has always been directed to more powerful objectives' (1979: 197).

Craft crime (McIntosh 1971) responds to restraints imposed by the market or by technology (McIntosh 1975; Letkemann 1973; Hobbs forthcoming), rather than those imposed by organizational codes. Indeed, even armed robbery, an activity regarded by McIntosh as essentially project crime (involving planning, high risk, and specialist skills), is typified during its heyday (Campbell 1991*a*) by a similar emphasis on individualism, autonomy, and a belief in the sanctity of one's own practice. This existential tendency is exemplified in the following quote from convicted bank robber Bertie Smalls:

> The nervous tension I used to feel before a job didn't stay with me all the time, only till I got started. Once I start I feel completely calm, one hundred per cent, everything comes brilliant to me . . . I might be fogged up a minute or two before but the minute its on its like the sun coming out from behind a cloud. (Ball *et al.* 1978: 183)

Minimal planning (Ball *et al.* 1978) and a reliance upon key personnel, as opposed to organizational traits, were the prime characteristics of robberies during what is often projected as something of a 'Golden Age' (McVicar 1979; Campbell 1991*a*: 13–26). This commitment to an ideal, coupled with a 'moral exercise of competence' (Gouldner 1971: 156) is typified by the professional armed robber. This does not, however, constitute an identifiable, self-contained subculture of specialists (Einstadter 1969). Indeed, such an essentially romantic view can be seriously misleading, especially in view of periodic changes in policing, as in the proliferation of supergrasses during the 1970s (Ball *et al.* 1978; Taylor 1984; Campbell 1991*a*), a direct result of a collaborative policy manufactured by the police and the Director of Public Prosecutions (Jennings *et al.* 1990: 48–57), or the implementation of new security technology that makes one group of criminals redundant and puts the emphasis upon another group. For instance, improved safe technology and difficulty in obtaining explosives after an upsurge of politically motivated bombings combined to make safebreakers redundant, and give a new impetus to armed robbery (McIntosh 1971; Hobbs forthcoming; Byrne 1991). To suggest that deviant adaptions are somehow subcultural ignores the fertility of the ideological base from which working-class crime emerges. For instance, the 'Great Train Robbers' who in 1963 robbed the Glasgow to London train of over £2.5 million were a motley collection of committed robbers, generalists or 'rounders' (Shover 1983), jump-up merchants, and petty thieves, who could hardly have displayed the kind of ideological coherence or consistency of practice suggested by Einstadter (1969; cf.

Read 1979; Biggs 1981; McIntosh 1971: 124; Williams 1973; Hobbs 1988: 47–50). Einstadter was concerned with the social organization of professional robbery, and stresses a self-contained hierarchy and rigid co-ordination of tasks. This subcultural approach effectively ignores the parent culture that fosters the cultural base from which professional criminals emerge. This cultural base is in turn a communal response to the collective experience of the market of which the workplace is a crucial segment.

As Katz has noted, professional criminals often use skills which are basic to the experience of many working-class occupations: 'the safe-cracker's expertise copies that of a locksmith, the robber's strong arm is usually the night-time variation of the strength of the day labourer, and the pickpocket's and the booster's manual dexterity does not rise above levels that are customary in traditional crafts and on many assembly lines' (Katz 1988: 211). Professionals will inevitably belong to networks of like-minded individuals who are informed by a similar commitment to criminal activity, thus monopolizing a segment of social activity and its concomitant knowledge. These networks will in turn inform the marketplace but not organize it; the networks imbue action with a significance that is common to individuals engaging in many types of illicit activity (Pileggi 1987; Katz 1988: 209–15) and constitutes what is often labelled as 'the underworld'. While elements of organization may exist in such a milieu (Tobias 1974; Defoe 1901), this will only be the case where the marketplace demands it. Therefore, armed robbery is typically a disorganized activity (Walsh 1986), formulated around the immediate environment of its enactment, with the focus resting upon violence or its potential (cf. Katz 1988: ch. 5). Other groups of professionals may find that the peculiar demands of their chosen form of criminal action require elements of enacted, as opposed to market, organization—for instance pickpockets (Maurer 1964) or professional shoplifters (Taylor 1984: ch. 5). Enacted organization relates to selected categories of action that will enable competent performance of the crime, while market organization refers to competent engagement with a crucial market subsequent to the criminal act.

The idea of an underworld populated by criminals and those with 'too little moral restraint to starve' (Archer 1865) is inextricably linked to the notion of an urban underclass. In Britain, certain locations became associated with areas of sanctuary and of alms distribution and, as a consequence, the emerging working class became segmented and its rump became 'that dangerous class which is found occupying a position between pauper and convict' (Archer 1865). The work of Dickens (1986) and particularly Mayhew (1861) further emphasized the essential criminality of the 'undeserving poor', while Booth (1902) mapped their geographical location. Yet even the most cursory examination of the data reveals a cornucopia of crime and unemployment inextricably linked to begging, casual work, and self-employment (Stedman Jones 1971). Mayhew's work in particular exposes the range of strategies available to a population who throughout the nineteenth century were increasingly defined by their location in distinct urban areas (Rock 1973: 30). Crime was part of a repertoire of responses to coercive market forces, and emerged indistinct from other culturally refined strategies (see Hobbs 1988: ch. 5). Within such an environment, 'everyone [is] "at it" and some are "at it" more than most. They were the professional criminals' (Hobbs 1988: 8). The enacted networks of professional criminals are then indistinguishable from the entrepreneurial networks of a distinctive milieu (cf. Messinger 1966), and that milieu will act as an enabling environment for a range of (in working-class terms) high-status concerns such as crime and self-employment.

Within this environment, a commitment to the discourse of entrepreneurship will dominate, and while pecuniary spoils serve as a definite status indication, some professional criminals, notably those engaging in activity requiring qualities of 'gameness' (McVicar 1979) 'gemmie' (Patrick 1973: 84–7), or courage (Taylor 1984: 101), will evolve into an elite. Yet the entrepreneurial pursuit of profit is the sovereign aim and a combination of the businessman and the hard man represents the zenith of working-class entrepreneurship. This potent combination is demonstrated in the following quotation from Pileggi's biography of a professional criminal all-rounder, which stresses the role of the hard man as hardnosed businessman who always collects his debts, no matter what: 'You got no business? Fuck you, pay me. You had a fire? Fuck you, pay me. The place got hit by lightning and World War Three started in the lounge? Fuck you, pay me' (Pileggi 1987: 53–4). The ideal type hard man/hard-nosed businessman is to be found in Pileggi's Jimmy Burke, who dominated a range of networks by exploiting a violent reputation to pursue not only profit but also prestige and respect within a plethora of settings (Pileggi 1987: 96–105). These settings—in British terms, pubs, clubs, restaurants, dog tracks, boxing arenas (Pruis and Irini 1980)—constitute a very public stage for the performance of elite working-class entrepreneurship, where the aura of successful violent action in the pursuit of profit gets top billing (see Hebdige 1977). The professional criminal is a member of a working-class elite who is expected to exploit his status in a culture of conspicuous narcissism that is a subterranean version of normative leisure (cf. Matza and Sykes 1961). The narcissistic essence of this lifestyle is captured here by professional burglar Frank Hohimer: 'Travelling first class jet, driving Caddy convertibles, Chrysler Imperials and Lincoln Continentals. Staying in fifty-dollar-a-night hotels and motels. I changed cars and women like most people change socks' (Hohimer 1981: 19).

Other writers confirm the importance of such conspicuous consumption (Taylor 1984; McVicar 1979; Pileggi 1987), for it is within this quasi-leisured culture that entrepreneurial networks touch and alliances are formed. Further, overt narcissism establishes the successful entrepreneur and marks him out from mere 'punters' (Hobbs 1988: 7). 'Life was lived without a safety net' (Pileggi 1987: 39), but in terms of maintaining entrepreneurial success, it is necessary to stress the viability of one's enterprise, to hint at the cultural collateral available. In this way, market information and investment opportunities manifest themselves as part of the social milieu. The trappings of excellence are crucial instrumental tools within entrepreneurial networks, yet they also serve to distinguish the entrepreneur from straight society, who are 'a greedy ignorant mob of mug punters, simply asking to be taken' (Taylor 1984: 169). As drug-dealer and convicted murderer and armed robber Robby Wideman explained:

> Straight people don't understand. I mean, they think dudes is after the things straight people got. It ain't that at all. People in the life ain't looking for no home and grass in the yard and shit like that. We the show people. The glamour people. Come on the set with the finest car the finest woman, the finest wines. Hear people talking about you. Hear the bar get quiet when you walk in the door. Throw down a yard and tell everybody drink up . . . You make something out of nothing. (Wideman 1985: 131, quoted in Katz 1988: 315)

Competence and the ability to wear it well are crucial as the professional criminal organizes his life around entrepreneurship both as a career and as a source of self-esteem.

The skilled craftsman, whose highly specialized practice has parallels with the legitimate world of craft production (Sutherland 1937; Maurer 1955; Clinard and Quinney 1967) is a rarity in contemporary Britain. Certainly the current marketplace has little room for such romantic outsiders. It is a market geared to rationalization and dominated by a single commodity: drugs. Within such a marketplace networks of specialized professionals, for instance car thieves (Hobbs forthcoming), armed robbers (Campbell 1991*a*), specialist burglars (Hobbs forthcoming; Hohimer 1981; Shover 1973; Maguire 1982), or small-scale drug-dealers can, if they confine the scope and scale of their operations to generic entrepreneurial networks, continue to function. However, to engage in mainstream contemporary felony, drug-dealing or its enabling activities such as commercial fraud, VAT fraud, or non-narcotic smuggling, require levels of market organization that transcend the enclaves of petit-bourgeois entrepreneurial networks.

ORGANIZED CRIME IN BRITAIN: A CHRONOLOGY

The outstanding characteristic of organized crime in Britain is the local orientation of both its practice and its street-level practitioners, despite the increasing influence of other nationalities. The neighbourhood provides new recruits by way of the local delinquent subculture (Vigil and Chang 1990: 157–58; Chin 1990: 120–45) and is organized around markets that manifest themselves indigenously; commuting to work is a rarity (Samuel 1981; Bean 1981). During the Second World War, shortages of food, clothing, and raw materials, and subsequent rationing, led to the creation of a 'black market' which supplied goods and services for which there was a demand (Smithies 1982). The organization of this illegal market can be seen to be 'filling in gaps left by other forms of commerce' (Quinney 1975: 244).

The basic frameworks of British organized crime were built during the Second World War on the foundations of parochial networks of violence that had been established by the pre-war racecourse gangs (Greene 1943; Lucas 1969: 19–27; Samuel 1981: 175–86; Bean 1981; see also Jenkins and Porter 1988). These gangs operated several forms of protection racket. The gangs controlled the pitches, renting them at extortionate prices to the on-course bookmakers. Sheets of horses running, chalk, stools, and other accoutrements were sold or rented to bookmakers exclusively by the gangs. Fights were deliberately started if payment was slow and non-repayable loans were demanded. Profits were enormous, for instance, Samuel states that the gang led by Darby Sabini would glean £15,000–£20,000 on Derby Day (Samuel 1981: 184). The Sabini gang prospered from 1910 until the Second World War, by which time they had expanded into greyhound racing and various drinking and gambling clubs in the West End of London (Hill 1955; Chinn 1991). The Sabinis were interred as enemy aliens on the outbreak of war, and their organization never recovered.

Thus at the outbreak of war those best equipped to exploit the opportunities profferred by a besieged wartime economy were incarcerated. The outstanding criminal feature of the wartime years was the 'black market', the illegitimate market in state-controlled goods or commodities that were in short supply. Unavailability of or restricted access to both essential goods, such as food and clothing, and luxuries, such as alcohol and cigarettes, led to their illegal provision by groups of criminals, many of whom had established their reputations in the pre-war racetrack gangs (Smithies 1982; Mannheim 1955). Competent criminals of the Second World War found that the post-war market hardly differed from its wartime equivalent, and they were able to extend their operations well into the 1950s.

Two of these criminals of the post-war era were Jack 'Spot' Comer and Billy Hill: both made their names as neighbourhood men of violence in the 1930s, made their money in the 1940s, and made the Kray twins in the 1950s. Their contribution to the demonology of organized crime in Britain, and in particular Hill's career, deserves more attention than it has been afforded by criminologists. Comer and Hill 'acted very much like businessmen, drawing their profits from a discreet monopoly, carefully preserving good relations with the police' (Pearson 1973: 85). Their 'discreet monopoly' covered protection, gambling, prostitution, and what remained of the black market. Violent conflict was a rarity and to be avoided at all costs, as confidence in the status quo was paramount to good business practice. Essential to the maintenance of this status quo was the avoidance of police attention by preventing 'trouble'.

> If any two mobs started trouble the guv'nor of the CID usually got busy and wanted to know what it was all about. Then when their reports went into the Yard the high-ups down there got on to the uniformed branch whose job it was to supervise all clubs and spielers. So gang warfare didn't do anyone any good.' (Hill 1955: 149)

The process of succession which saw the Kray twins' rise to power, Hill return to Spain, and Comer get a job filling sausages (Kray and Sykes 1977: 100) has been played out numerous times all over Britain. The Krays were initially employed as bodyguards by Comer. After he had received ninety stitches following a razor attack administered by two allies of Hill, Frank Frazer and Bob Warren, Comer retired, initially to run a furniture business. The Kray twins were then taken under the wing of Hill, who taught them the intricacies of club management and introduced them to the possibilities of the gambling industry.

The subsequent rise and fall of the Kray twins has been well documented (Pearson 1973; Kray and Kray 1989; Kray and Sykes 1977; Kray 1991; Cater and Tullett 1990; Kelland 1987; Hobbs 1988; Campbell 1991*a*; Cale, 1989; Dickson 1986; Hebdige 1974). The peculiarity of their rise is however marked only by its glamorous, high-profile location. The same use of muscle in the exploitation of markets defined by a combination of legislation, economics, and leisure culture is to be found elsewhere. Their fall, despite featuring characteristics that were peculiar to the Kray twins, does highlight the centrality of traditional working-class cultural traits in maintaining organized crime structures that endure beyond one generation.

The Kray twins' various enterprises had served to reinforce a local order built upon a solid foundation of independence, autonomy, and tough masculinity. As crucial agents of this indigenous local order, their potential for violence remained discreet and firmly situated within geographical and economic parameters which in turn stressed the primacy of the culture's key focal concerns: trouble, toughness, smartness, excitement, and autonomy (Miller 1958: 7). However, 'when issues emerged from beyond the parameters of these concerns, then offences were committed that the police could no longer ignore. Mental illness and homosexuality were two such alien issues' (Hobbs 1988: 58). It is apparent that while organized crime personnel remain within the parameters of the enterprise's parent culture, it is business as usual. Yet issues such as mental illness and homosexuality, which contributed to two non-instrumental murders, or engaging in taboo activities, such as, in some instances, narcotics enterprises (Pileggi 1987), can lead to punitive responses by members of the same culture. Similarly the Richardson brothers, who operated from working-class neighbourhoods in South London during the 1950s and 1960s, were moving towards corporate criminal success of some magnitude (Parker 1981; Richardson 1992) before a murder of little instrumental value to anyone made it impossible for the police to ignore their activities (Hobbs 1988). However, the Kray twins (aided by their most underrated allies, the Nashes) did compete for a lucrative market. The Krays had been in an ideal position to identify and exploit changes in the gambling laws in 1961, and had subsequently established themselves as market leaders in London's gambling and night-club industries. The Richardsons' attempted involvement in this market was imminent at the time of their arrest (Pearson 1973), although their activities had by the late 1960s spread way beyond London (Parker 1981).

Competition for lucrative markets was a redundant concept throughout the 1970s. Across Britain, organized criminal groups co-existed with each other with few examples of intensive conflict. Markets were divided up largely according to proximity to the neighbourhood, which remains to this day the fulcrum of organized criminal activity. One of the few commentators on contemporary organized crime has suggested that the old neighbourhood firms 'have been replaced by multinationals of uncertain ownership, branches throughout the world, profits disposed of through myriad outlets' (Campbell 1991*a*: 8). However, this assertion is based on the mistaken premise that the convictions of the Kray and Richardson gangs marked the end of something more than an era. While the Krays undoubtedly had territorial control over east, west, and parts of north London, the breadth and strength of the Richardsons in the south achieved nothing like the Krays' monopoly. As a consequence, organized crime in north and east London became fragmented and a vacuum was created in the west. East End organizations learned to keep their heads down and avoid the temptation to expand, for the marketplace during most of the 1970s was based on the indigenous neighbourhood, with the exception of a small elite of armed robbers whose activities could barely be classed as organized (see Taylor 1984; Ball *et al.* 1978; Campbell 1991*a*: 13–26). Expansion of the kind that made the Kray twins rich was too overt and dramatic, and any group that appeared remotely to resemble the Krays (in family structure, neighbourhood orientation, overt use of violence) was nipped in the bud (see Wickstead 1985). However, in south London the Richardsons' demise had left neighbourhood crime cells untouched, and powerful criminal dynasties were able to carry on in their traditional relatively restrained manner.

This is not to suggest that organized crime was dormant during this period, despite lacking a formal hierarchical structure. British organized criminals used traditional neighbourhood bases to exploit a multitude of market opportunities. There was no unifying structure and no unifying market. Normative entrepreneurial activity became increasingly prevalent during this period as parallel, alternative, and hybrid strains of entrepreneurship were practised (see Catanzaro 1985). Markets for pornography, a well established and highly lucrative source of income, grew, as a result of both increased demand and a massive expansion in the home video market (Tomkinson 1982; Cox *et al.* 1977; Kelland 1987), while counterfeiting (Humphrey 1992; UK Anti-Piracy Group 1986; Rice 1991) and VAT fraud (Levi 1987: 185–6) became popular, relatively low-risk options, particularly for armed robbers seeking secure investments and a less strenuous alternative to 'leaping over counters, grabbing and running' (Campbell 1991*a*: 17). VAT fraud involving the buying and selling of gold coins was facilitated by the government in 1979, when it removed VAT on gold coins. Criminals were able to buy gold in the name of bogus commercial concerns, trade, and disappear with both the profit and the VAT. Huge sums of money were acquired in this way, and it was a favoured method of acquiring the capital necessary for major drug importation (Jennings *et al.* 1991: 136–7). British society was no longer an environment hostile to piratical mavericks of an entrepreneurial persuasion (Hobbs 1991) and the discourse of enterprise culture had become one of the major articulating principles of the age (Burrows 1991: 17). The drugs market that emerged during the 1980s was as stone-cold rational as the slave trade had been in the sixteenth century. It was the most perfect example of capitalism at work: a commodification of commercial and personal oblivion.

As Dorn and South (1990) have suggested, drug distributors in contemporary Britain can be categorized into seven distinct types. Of these, the 'business sideliners', 'retail specialists', and 'criminal diversifiers' display elements of organizational form. However, it is the last group that warrants the most considered attention on the grounds of their lineage and the sense of continuity suggested by their activities. During the 1970s the traditional neighbourhood family firms quietly prospered via their discreet coalitions with specialized professionals (robbers, fraudsters), generalists (Shover's 'rounders': Shover 1983); and an assortment of entrepreneurial types. During this period, the adoption of fraud as a generic criminal form began and merged seamlessly with the consolidation of funds into normative business enterprises (Hobbs forthcoming). This process is distinct from the often-cited phenomenon of 'going legit'. Illegal funds were not being 'laundered' (Levi 1987: 123–4); rather, the activities of organized criminals were made indistinct from normative enterprise. This was achieved by a process of entrenchment in the parent culture, proprietorship of local businesses, and the periodic confirmation of violent potential. The process was enhanced during the mid- to late 1970s by armed robbers and gangsters who had retired, been released from prison, or deemed it prudent to diversify (Jennings *et al.* 1991). Subsequently the 'Great Train Robbers' Frank Fraser, Charlie and Eddie Richardson, and others returned to their working-class entrepreneurial homeland in South London. This consolidation of 'faces' from the 1960s with 'powerful criminal families' (Campbell 1991*b*) proved a powerful entrepreneurial dynamic for an expanding drug market at the turn of the decade.[1]

These consolidations of past and present entrepreneurial networks were complemented in the 1970s by a potent black 'hustling' culture. This culture, although it has many precedents in the USA, has taken on a distinctive character which is specific to the experience of black Britons: 'The hustle, for the hustler, makes up for all the intrinsic and extrinsic deprivation of work . . . It restores the hustler's sense of pride and his feeling of mastery and autonomy . . . The hustle is the ideal alternative to legal work because it is the complete antithesis' (Pryce 1986: 58; cf. Headley 1989). Black involvement in both organized and 'irregular' (Dorn *et al.* 1992) drug-dealing is a comparatively recent phenomenon and its course does appear to be changing rapidly (Robins 1992). Manchester, in particular, attracted much attention during the late 1980s and early 1990s after a series of shootings stemming from disputes in the heroin trade. The subsequent concern of both mass media and the police with Jamaican 'yardies' was provoked by a spate of cocaine-related killings in London from 1986 to 1988 (Darbyshire 1988). Undoubtedly, British yardie activity has been a reality since at least 1985, but the 'shanty town gangs' (Johnson and Murtagh 1988) have since proved of rather less significance than gangs of 'irregulars' (Dorn *et al.* 1992) or 'jump-up merchants' (Hobbs 1988) coagulating around the peculiar demands of a specific

[1] The career of Roy Garner, and in particular his progression from armed robbery to VAT fraud and drug importation via property development and club ownership, represents the post-Kray criminal career *par excellence* (Jennings *et al.* 1991).

marketplace. Although there is some evidence of yardie activity in Britain (Sweeney 1989), the disbanding of the Metropolitan Police's yardie squad and its immediate reconstitution as an anti-crack unit suggests a tendency during the late 1980s to label any Afro-Caribbean criminal activity as a case of organized yardie crime (Cashmore and McLaughlin 1992: 11). The overall picture is not one of ethnically differentiated groups of dealers competing for markets, for as Dorn *et al.* (1992) have noted, rivalry tends to take place within different ethnic communities rather than between them: 'They [the white and black gangs] tend to keep away from each other. Its that sort of respect, you know, "you don't bother us and we don't bother you". And that's the way it seems to work unless that's infringed upon and if somebody does cross that line then something happens' ('Eileen', quoted in Dorn *et al.* 1992: 246).

The outstanding feature of British organized crime is its conservatism and consistency with the past. Although there are now, largely due to the drugs trade, well-established links among criminal practitioners in London, Manchester, Birmingham, Bristol, and Glasgow (among others), the elder statesmen of British crime have shown a marked resilience in maintaining their place among the market leaders. Eddie Richardson was jailed for twenty-five years in 1991 for his role in importing a shipment of cocaine. Likewise, in August 1989 two of the Great Train Robbers, Tommy Wisby and Jimmy Hussey, were sent down for seven and ten years for cocaine dealing, while in 1990 their ex-colleague, Charles Wilson, was murdered at his villa in Spain following a dispute regarding drug trafficking (Sweeney 1990; cf. Shover 1985). The most remarkable resilience of all has been shown by Frank Fraser. Coming to prominence first in 1956 as the primary attacker of Jack 'Spot' Comer, he worked closely with the Richardson brothers during the 1960s and was present at the Mr Smith shooting which proved the downfall of the south London organization.[2] Both in and out of prison, Fraser earned the respect not only of his ex-colleagues (Richardson 1992: 70–2) but also of old foes (Kray 1991: 137–8). In 1991, aged 63, he was taken to hospital in London suffering from a gunshot wound to the head following a shooting at a pub in east London.

This apparent consistency with the neighbourhood-based organized crime structures of the 1950s was assured while old markets and their consequent territories were adhered to, since competition was kept to a minimum, especially during the 1970s and most of the 1980s. However, the drug market has introduced levels of extreme competition which has resulted in unprecedented violence (Campbell 1991*b*). The demands of

[2] Mr Smith's drinking and gambling club was the site of a fatal shooting in 1966 as the result of a territorial dispute between the Richardsons and another group (Pearson 1973; Parker 1981: 276–82).

this unfamiliar marketplace also place an emphasis upon the formation of alliances across cities, countries, and even continents, which has in turn also put pressure on the sanctity of the neighbourhood firm. New alliances with shippers or manufacturers can be risky (Leigh 1988), but more importantly the rhetoric of normative commerce in the shape of 'business sideliners' (especially in the case of heroin), 'diversifies', and 'retail specialists' (Dorn and South 1990; Dorn *et al.* 1992) has encouraged traditional criminal organizations to spread their entrepreneurial wings. As a consequence, the drugs trade is now a generic profit-making exercise, forming the commercial bedrock for future criminal enterprises that will be organized around markets rather than increasingly symbolic neighbourhoods (Hobbs forthcoming).

The other generic criminal activity that forms the basis of organized criminal enterprise in Britain is fraud. Fraud is no longer a 'crime of the powerful' (Pearce 1976), so much as a crime of those in the know. Particularly through the seminal work of Levi (1981, 1987), it is possible to observe a merging of 'upper and underworld' (Levi 1987: 194). Long firm fraud in particular offers an introduction to fraudulent possibilities while exploiting the opportunity structures of urban entrepreneurial elites (Levi 1981; Pearson 1973: 154–5). Yet Levi's description of long firm fraud as 'down market' (Levi 1987: 205) is in itself misleading as it is this activity, along with VAT fraud, which has in the 'post-robber age' provided the essential capital for even more lucrative action. The merging of upper and underworlds, and the importance of fraud as an enabling commercial device as well as an end in itself, was greatly assisted during the 1980s by key structural changes in the marketplace, notably the deregulation of the Stock Exchange (the 'Big Bang') in 1986. Additionally, technological innovations such as 'computers . . . international direct dialling, telephones, telexes, computer aided despatch systems and facsimile senders' (Levi 1987: 3) have enabled fraudsters to engage with targets from a distance (cf. Cornwall 1987; Bose and Gunn 1989). Such innovations empower criminals to attack information and/or money where it is most vulnerable in a way similar to that of the thermic lance or the shotgun during previous eras (McIntosh 1971).[3]

THE MAFIA

In 1969 Donald Cressey published *Theft of the Nation* (Cressey 1969), a book based upon a report that Cressey had produced for the President's

[3] There will always be occasions when crime of a more traditional working-class nature will pay off, however, and the Security Express and Brinks-Mat robberies of 1983 and 1984 respectively were spectacularly untypical examples of classic project crimes that were carried out (comparatively) successfully (cf. Hogg *et al.* 1988).

Commission on Law Enforcement and Administration of Justice. In this book Cressey claimed that the Sicilian Mafia had been exported to the 'United States [where] criminals have managed to put together an organisation which is at once a nationwide illicit cartel and a nationwide confederation' (Cressey 1969: 1). According to Cressey, this organization consists of twenty-four 'families', all of Italian or Sicilian descent, and the system is known to members as the Cosa Nostra. The families are hierarchically structured and controlled by a 'Commission' made up of the leaders of the most powerful families (Cressey 1969: x–xi). This and subsequent work by Cressey (1972) stresses an essentially alien criminal conspiracy that permeates every aspect of American economic and political life, from labour unions and commercial monopolies to the judicary, all levels of the legislature, and monopolies of illegal gambling, loan sharking, extortion, prostitution, theft, and aspects of the narcotics trade.

Subsequent criticism of this view has taken a number of forms. According to Hess (1970) there is no organized, secret, hierarchical criminal society called the Mafia. In response to the Kefauver Commission of 1951, which stressed the national and international nature of Mafia influence, Bell dismissed the evidence as 'hearsay' (1976), while Block (1977, 1991a) and Chambliss (1978) argue forcefully that the database for the Mafia conspiracy thesis is both small and unreliable. Block in particular has noted that informer Joe Valachis's 1963 evidence to the McClellan Committee was based on a series of fabrications, most notably the apparent invention of the term Cosa Nostra (Block 1991*a*, 1983; see also Hawkins 1969).

Throughout the 1980s and 1990s some spectacular court cases in the USA, including the prosecution of what was claimed to be the Mafia's entire National Commission in 1986 (Balsamo and Carpozi, 1988), the Sicilian Mafia's alleged use of pizza restaurants across the USA to sell narcotics (Blumenthal 1988; Alexander 1988), and—most illuminating of all—the high-profile prosecution of alleged New York Gambino family boss John Gotti (Cummings and Volkman 1991; *New York Times*, 3 February—8 April 1992) would appear to confirm the existence of 'big conspiracies and plenty of interaction among primarily Italian-American criminal syndicates and their associates' (Block 1991*a*: 13). Confirmation of a rigidly disciplined hierarchical structure of co-operating gangs is something that we await. Meanwhile, however, the work of Pileggi (1987), Arlaachi (1986), Sterling (1991), Blumenthal (1988), Mustain and Capeci (1988), and Block (1991*b*) portray the apparent manifestation of organizations within which 'the business of crime is planned, contacts are made, some crimes are carried out, the fruits of crime are often enjoyed, and the methodologies for the integration of organised criminals into civil society are established' (Block 1991*b*: 15; cf. Block 1977). Consequently the term 'Mafia' is used in this paper as a form of shorthand for the structures described above which have apparent Sicilian-American roots.

Knowledgeable commentators have for some time questioned the existence of the Mafia in Britain (Mack and Kerner 1975; Dorn *et al.* 1992). However, the Sabini family mentioned above were rumoured to have Mafia links (Morton 1992: 10), and one prominent member of the racecourse gangs, Alberto Dimeno (Albert Dimes), was an associate of Philadelphia Mafia boss Angelo Bruno (Morton 1992: 55–8; Read 1991; 124–5). Further, one of the founders of the Mafia's American branch, Meyer Lansky, was the owner of London's Colony Club, and there is considerable evidence of affiliations and attempted affiliations between American and British organized criminals during the 1960s (Pearson 1973: 175–6; Kray 1991; Richardson 1992: 155; Block 1991*b*: 46–9). Additionally, there was solid evidence during the mid-1980s of the Mafia using legitimate businesses as a front for drug importation (*Times*, 19 August 1987). Yet a case perhaps more indicative of the sophistication and flexibility of the Mafia is that of the plot uncovered at London's Heathrow Airport in 1988. This involved a project to import over 100 kilos of Bolivian cocaine per week into Britain welded into heavy plant machinery. The project was orchestrated by the Sicilian Mafia operating out of Detroit (*Times*, 12 October 1988; Sterling 1991: 48). It would be a mistake to discount Mafia involvement in Britain merely because the organization's operatives are not prominent at street level. The Sicilian Mafia's dominance in partnership with other organizations over the world heroin market (Sterling 1991: chs. 4, 5, 6; Lewis 1985; Arlaachi 1986: ch. 8) and their underrated role as syphons for both cocaine and cocaine profits (Sterling 1991: ch. 7; Eddy *et al.* 1989), apart from their involvement in the importation of other drugs and their success in fraud (Levi 1987: 143), therefore generating capital for further drug investment (cf. Block 1991*b*), should not be ignored. The existence of powerful, albeit neighbourhood-based, criminal entrepreneurial groups in Britain, and a recognition of their cultural and capital constraints and capabilities, means that the Mafia must be considered significant players in a game that is parochial only at street level. For instance, in September 1992 200 people were arrested worldwide, including three in the UK, as part of a cocaine-smuggling operation purportedly involving organized criminals in the USA, Colombia, Canada, Costa Rica, Italy, and Spain (*Guardian*, 29 September 1992). At the multinational level the Sicilian Mafia and their partners in Asia (Sterling 1991: 409–10; Booth 1990: 141–2; President's Commission 1984), South America (Sterling 1991: ch. 7), and the USA (Gosch and Hammer 1974; Blumenthal 1988; Alexander 1988) are powerful influences over British crime markets. They have no monopolies within Britain, but their dominance of crucial articulated world economies means that some level of manipulation by the Mafia and/or their affiliates in Turkey, Pakistan, and elsewhere is inevitable. This is a case of an organized multinational enterprise enabling the manifestation of indigenous crime to be essentially disorganized in character (cf. Reuter 1984). However, the early 1990s have been marked by crucial alterations in the organization of markets, and criminal as well as legitimate commercial enterprises will have to adapt to survive.[4]

PROSPECTS, CHANGES AND CONTINUITIES

You will not find any baseball bats, you won't find any broken bodies. This is simply a business case, no matter the names and nasty things they call Tommy Gambino. (Defence lawyer Michael Rosen addressing the court during the trial of Thomas Gambino: *New York Times*, 5 February 1992)

In the near future it will become impossible to distinguish for any other than academic purposes between the categories of organized crime and white-collar crime. The increased bureaucratization of the drugs trade and its accelerating trend towards corporatism, marked by the rationalization of white powder networks and their consolidation and centralization in South America (Ross 1992), will be controlled by individuals whose collars are white, pristine, and hand-stitched in silk. Corporatism and its subsequent effect on world economies as money is laundered and invested will generate a milieu of enterprise that will flourish regardless of legality. Legality will be increasingly irrelevant in an international market immune to any moral perspective other than profit. As Lord Young, former Minister of Trade and Industry has noted, 'One of the characteristics of the enterprising spirit is that it can never be satisfied' (Young 1992: 34); and organized crime, having used the 1980s to establish markets and trading networks that will endure well into the twenty-first century, is full of enterprise.

The elimination of national boundaries within the EC since 1992 will expose the entire marketplace; 'Men of Honor and their associates will then be able to move undisturbed from the Mediterranean to the Baltic, and from the Danube to the Atlantic coast of Ireland' (Sterling 1991: 392). An increasingly hegemonized international drug market will, it would appear, be co-existing with crucial socio-economic changes that

[4] A comparatively recent phenomenon has been the use of conventional organized criminality by paramilitary groups in Northern Ireland, structured around the exploitation of both community resources, in the form of extortion, and community needs, by controlling lucrative leisure outlets. As Dillon has noted, this amounts to a symbiotic relationship via criminality between paramilitaries and legitimate representatives of the state (Dillon 1991: 418–25). For further discussion of this largely ignored area see Adams (1986); Dillon (1991: chs. 16, 17); Bishop and Mallie (1988); Cranshaw (1984).

could have been deliberately manufactured to accommodate both its product and its market practices. As Reuter *et al.* have noted, in 1969 in the USA the unemployment rate for inner-city black males aged 16–24 was 13 per cent; by 1985, the year that marked the beginning of New York's crack epidemic, the rate was 37.1 per cent (Reuter *et al.* 1990: 2–3). The subsequent attractions of the crack trade as an alternative career can only become more apparent as the drug establishes itself alongside amphetamines as a drug of choice in the inner cities (Williams 1989). Although crack cocaine has never measured up to the panic of 1989, orchestrated by the Home Office (Home Affairs Committee 1989), it is firmly established on British housing estates and the British trade in crack shows some similarities with the USA, specifically in terms of the violence that is associated with the commerce related to the drug, if not with its pharmacological effect (cf. Mirza *et al.* 1991; Williams 1989; *Guardian* 1992).

It is difficult to reconcile the contemporary British professional criminal with Sutherland's Chic Conwell. Sutherland (1937)—and, to a great extent, Maurer (1964)—stress technical skill, status, a shared ideology, differential association, and organization as being the prime characteristics of professional crime. However, these characteristics were afforded primacy by the demands of the marketplace. The contemporary British marketplace requires little technical skill, and notions of shared ideology and differential association need to be considered in terms of the contemporary entrepreneurial culture that has pervaded all aspects of British life (Burrows 1991; Healas and Morris 1992; MacDonald and Coffield 1991; Curran and Blackburn 1991; Keat and Abercrombie 1991). Organization, however, is crucial, and it is from one's adeptness within the organizational frame (albeit in most British cases a frame restrained by indigenous contextual precedent) that status is acquired. To a great extent violence has replaced technical skill as an indicator of professionalism. Sutherland's eschewing of violence as a resource for the professional has already been questioned by Abadinsky (1983), who has indicated that a professional contemporary of Chic Conwell, a safecracker, habitually carried and used a gun as a tool of his trade. To establish and maintain a niche in the contemporary marketplace, violence is a key resource. Its utility is particularly important in drug markets that are recreational and youth-orientated, when both trade and consumption are carried out in the same symbolic locations, such as clubs and discotheques—locations which are normally removed from the well-established neighbourhood bases. Total control of these environments is required, and as organized groups of professionals move out of their old bases in order to establish monopolies in locations that had previously been regarded as neutral, the willingness to use extreme violence becomes not a skill or a craft, but an expression of personal and market sovereignty (Hobbs forthcoming). Although this consistent utility of violence may seem to contradict the move to white-collar crime, it does provide a base line from which to operate; a market sanction for potential bankrupts.

In Britain the master status of professional criminal can be acquired and retained only by operating within a shadow economic order that, like its counterpart in the 'straight' world, is vulnerable to the whims of multinational corporations with head offices in Europe, Asia, and America. The economic structure of professional crime demands an adherence to enacted markets and to the moral economy of these markets. To survive and prosper, therefore, it will be increasingly important to be 'businesslike', for, as Chambliss has noted, 'One of the reasons we fail to understand crime is because we put crime into a category that is separate from normal business. Much crime does not fit into a separate category. It is primarily a business activity' (Chambliss 1978: 53).

The future of professional crime in Britain lies with entrepreneurial alliances operating within an amalgam of markets that maintain both operational and ideological allegiances to working-class culture. The attraction of life as a professional criminal remains that, for most working-class people, the alternative is 'No more action. I have to wait around like everyone else. I'm an average nobody. I get to live the rest of my life like a shnook' (Pileggi 1987: 270).

Selected Further Reading

J. Albini, *The American Mafia*. New York: Appleton-Century-Crofts, 1971.

A. Block, *Masters of Paradise*. New Brunswick: Transaction, 1991.

D. R. Cressey, *Criminal Organisation*. London: Heinemann, 1972.

N. Dorn and N. South, 'Drug Markets and Law Enforcement', *British Journal of Sociology*, 1990, 30/2: 171–88.

C. Klockars, *The Professional Fence*. London: Tavistock, 1975.

P. Letkemann, *Crime as Work*. New Jersey: Prentice-Hall, 1973.

M. McIntosh, 'Changes in the Organisation of Thieving', in S. Cohen, ed., *Images of Deviance*. London: Penguin, 1971.

N. Pileggi, *Wise Guy*. London: Corgi, 1987.

P. Reuter, *Disorganised Crime*. Cambridge, Mass.: MIT Press, 1984.

N. Shover, 'The Social Organisation of Burglary', *Social Problems*, 1973, 20: 499–514.

E. Sutherland, *The Professional Thief*. Chicago: Chicago University Press, 1937.

T. Williams, *The Cocaine Kids*. Reading, Mass.: Addison-Wesley, 1989.

REFERENCES

ABADINSKY, H. (1983), *The Criminal Elite*. Westport, Conn.: Greenwood.

ADAMS, J. (1986), *The Financing of Terror*. London: New English Library.

ALBINI, J. (1971), *The American Mafia*. New York: Appleton-Century-Crofts.

ALEXANDER, S. (1988), *The Pizza Connection*. New York: Weidenfield and Nicolson.

ARCHER, T. (1865), *The Pauper, the Thief and the Convict*.

ARLACHI, P. (1986), *Mafia Business*. London: Verso.

AYDELOTE, F. (1913), *Elizabethan Rogues and Vagabonds*. Oxford: Clarendon Press.

BALL, J., CHESTER, L., and PERROTT, R. (1978), *Cops and Robbers*. London: Andre Deutsch.

BALSAMO, W., and CARPOZI, G. (1988), *Crime Incorporated*. London: W. H. Allen.

BEAN, J. P. (1981), *The Sheffield Gang Wars*. Sheffield: D. & D. Publications.

BELL, D. (1965), 'Crime as an American Way of Life', in D. Bell, *The End of Ideology*. New York: Free Press.

BIGGS, R. (1981), *His Own Story*. London: Sphere.

BISHOP, P., and MALLIE, E. (1988), *The Provisional IRA*. London: Corgi.

BLOCK, A. (1977), 'Some Thoughts on the State of Comparative Research in the Study of Organised Crime', paper presented at the annual meeting of the Society for the Study of Social Problems, Chicago.

—— (1983), *East Side–West Side: Organizing Crime in New York, 1930–1950*. Newark, NJ: Transaction.

—— (1991*a*), *The Business of Crime*. Boulder: Westview.

—— (1991*b*), *Masters of Paradise*. New Brunswick: Transaction.

BLUMENTHAL, R. (1988), *Last Days of the Sicilians*. London: Bloomsbury.

BLUMER, H. (1979), Introduction to the Transaction edition, in *Critiques of Research in the Social Sciences: An Appraisal of Thomas and Znaniecki's* The Polish Peasant in Europe and America. New Brunswick: Transaction.

BOOTH, C. (1902), *Life and Labour of the People*. London: Macmillan.

BOOTH, M. (1991), *The Triads*. London: Grafton.

BOSE, M., and GUNN, C. (1989), *Fraud*. London: Unwin Hyman.

BRAKE, M., and HALE, C. (1992), *Public Order and Private Lives*. London: Routledge.

BURROWS, R. (1991), *Deciphering the Enterprise Culture*. London: Routledge.

BYRNE, R. (1991), *Safecracking*. London: Grafton.

CALE, C. (1989), 'Twin Myths of the Krays', *Living Marxism*, 13/10 (November).

CAMPBELL, D. (1991*a*), *That was Business, this is Personal*. London: Mandarin.

—— (1991*b*), 'Gangland Britain', *Guardian*, 14 December.

CARR-SAUNDERS, A. M., and WILSON, P. A. (1933), *The Professionals*. Oxford: Clarendon Press.

CASHMORE, E., and MCLAUGHLIN, E., eds. (1992), *Out of Order? Policing Black People*. London: Routledge.

CATANZARO, R. (1985), 'Enforcers, Entrepreneurs and Survivors: How the Mafia has Adapted to Change', *British Journal of Sociology*, 35/1: 34–57.

CATER, F., and TULLETT (1990), *The Sharp End*. London: Grafton.

CHAMBLISS, W. J. (1978), *On the Take*. Bloomington: Indiana University Press.

CHIN, K. L. (1990), 'Chinese Gangs and Extortion', in R. Huff, ed., *Gangs in America*, 129–45. Beverly Hills: Sage.

CHINN, C. (1991), *Better Betting with a Decent Feller*. Hemel Hempstead: Harvester Wheatsheaf.

CLINARD, M., and QUINNEY, R. (1967), *Criminal Behaviour Systems: A Typology*. New York: Rinehart & Winston.

COHEN, S., ed. (1971), *Images of Deviance*. Harmondsworth: Penguin.

COHEN, S., and TAYLOR, L. (1972), *Psychological Survival*. Harmondsworth: Penguin.

CORNWALL, H. (1987), *Data Theft*. London: Heinemann.

COX, R., SHIRLEY, J., and SHORT, M. (1977), *The Fall of Scotland Yard*. Harmondsworth: Penguin.

CRANSHAW, M. (1984), 'The Persistence of IRA Terrorism', in Y. Alexander and A. O'Day, eds., *Terrorism in Ireland*. London: Croom Helm.

CRESSEY, D. R. (1969), *Theft of the Nation*. New York: Harper & Row.

—— (1972), *Criminal Organisation*. London: Heinemann.

CUMMINGS, J., and VOLKMAN, E. (1991), *Mobster*. London: Futura.

CURRAN, J., and BLACKBURN, R., eds. (1991), *Paths of Enterprise*. London: Routledge.

DARBYSHIRE, N. (1988), 'London Cocaine War: Two Killed', *London Standard*, 8 July.

DEFOE, D. (1901), *The King of the Pirates, Including the Life and Actions of Jonathan Wild*. New York: The Jason Society.

DICKENS, C. (1986), 'On Duty with Inspector Field', in N. Philip and V. Newbury, *Charles Dickens: A December Vision*, 26–41. London: Collins.

DICKSON, J. (1986), *Murder without Conviction*. London: Sidgwick & Jackson.

DILLON, M. (1991), *The Dirty War*. London: Arrow.

DOCTROW, E. L. (1989), *Billy Bathgate*. London: Picador.

DORN, N., MURJI, K., and SOUTH, N. (1992), *Traffickers*. London: Routledge.

DORN, N., and SOUTH, N. (1990), 'Drug Markets and Law Enforcement', *British Journal of Criminology*, 30/2: 171–88.

EDDY, P., WALDEN, S., and SABOGAL, H. (1989), *The Cocaine Wars*. London: Arrow.

EINSTADTER, W. J. (1969), 'The Social Organisation of Armed Robbery', *Social Problems*, 17: 64–83.

FIELDING, N. (1981), *The National Front*. London: Routledge.

Fijnaut, C. (1990), 'Organized Crime: A Comparison between the United States of America and Western Europe', *British Journal of Criminology*, 30/3: 321–40.

Fountain, J. (1993), 'Dealing in Data', in D. Hobbs and T. May, eds., *Interpreting Fieldwork*, Oxford: Oxford University Press.

Franklin, P. (1991), *Profits of Deceit*. London: Mandarin.

Gerth, H., and Mills, C. W. (1948), *From Max Weber: Essays in Sociology*. London: Routledge.

Gosch, M., and Hammer, R. (1974), *The Last Testament of Lucky Luciano*. Toronto: Little, Brown.

Gould, L., Walker, A., and Crane, L. (1967), *Crime as a Profession*. Washington, DC: Office of Law Enforcement, US Dept of Justice.

Gouldner, A. (1971), *The Coming Crisis of Western Sociology*. London: Heinemann.

Greene, G. (1943), *Brighton Rock*. Harmondsworth: Penguin.

Guardian (1992), 'Cocaine Blitz Traps Top Dealers', *Guardian* 29 September.

Hawkins, G. (1969), 'God and the Mafia', *The Public Interest*, 14 (Winter): 24–51.

Hay, D. (1975), 'Property, Authority and the Criminal Law', in D. Hay, *et al. Albion's Fatal Tree*. London: Allen Lane.

Hay, D., Linebaugh, P., and Thompson, E. P. (1975), *Albion's Fatal Tree*. London: Allen Lane.

Headley, B. (1989), 'War In a Babylon: Dynamics of the Jamaican Informal Drug Economy', *Social Justice*, 15/3–4: 61–86.

Hebdige, D. (1974), 'The Kray Twins: A System of Closure', stencilled occasional paper no. 21, Centre for Contemporary Cultural Studies, Birmingham University.

—— (1977), 'Sub-Cultural Conflict and Criminal Performance in Fulham', stencilled occasional paper no. 25, Centre for Contemporary Cultural Studies, Birmingham University.

Heelas, P., and Morris, P., eds (1992), *The Values of the Enterprise Culture*. London: Routledge.

Hess, H. (1970), *Mafia*. Tübingen: Mohr.

Hill, B. (1955), *Boss of Britain's Underworld*. London: Naldrett.

Hobbs, D. (1988), *Doing the Business: Entrepreneurship, the Working Class and Detectives in East London*. Oxford: Clarendon Press.

—— ((1991), 'Business as a Master Metaphor', in R. Burrows, ed., *Deciphering the Enterprise Culture*. London: Routledge.

—— (1993), 'Peers, Careers, and Academic Fears', in D. Hobbs and T. May, eds., *Interpreting Fieldwork*. Oxford: Oxford University Press.

—— (forthcoming), *Mutant Enterprise*. Oxford: Oxford University Press.

Hogg, A., McDougall, J., and Morgan, R. (1988), *Bullion Brinks-Mat*. Harmondsworth: Penguin.

Hohimer, F. (1981), *Violent Streets*. London: Star.

Home Affairs Committee (1989), *Crack: The Threat of Hard Drugs in the Next Decade*. London: HMSO.

Howson, G. (1971), *Thief Taker General*. New York: St Martins Press.

Huff, R., ed. (1990), *Gangs in America*. Beverly Hills: Sage.

Hughes, E. C. (1971), *The Sociological Eye*. Chicago: Aldine-Atherton.

HUMPHREY, L. (1992), 'Counterfeiting and Anti-Counterfeiting: The Case of Taiwan', unpublished dissertation, University of Durham.

HUMPHREYS, L. (1975), *Tea-Room Trade*. Chicago: Aldine.

IANNI, F., and IANNI, E. (1972), *A Family Business*. London: Routledge.

JENKINS, P., and PORTER, G. W. (1988), 'Before the Krays: Organised Crime in London 1920–1960', *Criminal Justice History*, 9: 209–30.

JENNINGS, A., LASHMAR, P., and SIMSON, V. (1990), *Scotland Yard's Cocaine Connection*. London: Arrow.

JOHNSON, A., and MURTAGH, P. (1988), 'Shanty Town Gangs that Met want to Nip in the Bud', *Guardian*, 25 February.

JONES, P. J. V. (1982), *Crime, Protest Community and the Police in Nineteenth Century England*. London: Routledge and Kegan Paul.

KATZ, J. (1988), *Seductions of Crime*. New York: Basic Books.

KEAT, R., and ABERCROMBIE, N., eds. (1991), *Enterprise Culture*. London: Routledge.

KELLAND, G. (1987), *Crime in London*. London: Grafton.

KLOCKARS, C. (1975), *The Professional Fence*. London: Tavistock.

KRAY, C., and SYKES, J. (1977), *Me and My Brothers*. London: Everest.

KRAY, R. (1991), *Born Fighter*. London: Arrow.

KRAY, R., and KRAY, R. (1989), *Our Story*. London: Pan.

LEIGH, D. (1988), Howard Marks, *His Life and High Times*, rev. edn. London: Unwin.

LEMERT, E. (1958), 'The Behaviour of the Systematic Check Forger', *Social Problems*, 6: 141–9.

LETKEMANN, P. (1973), *Crime as Work*. Englewood Cliffs, NJ: Prentice-Hall.

LEVI, M. (1981), *The Phantom Capitalists*. Aldershot: Gower.

—— (1987), *Regulating Fraud*. London: Tavistock.

LEWIS, R. (1985), 'Serious Business: The Global Heroin Economy', in A. Henman, R. Lewis, and T. Malyon, *Big Deal*. 5–49. London: Pluto.

LLOYD BAKER, T. B. (1889), *War with Crime*. London.

LOW, D. A. (1982), *Thieves' Kitchen: The Regency Underworld*. London: Dent.

LUCAS, N. (1969), *Britain's Gangland*. London: Pan.

MCARTHUR, A., and LONG, K. (1964), *No Mean City*. London: Corgi.

MACDONALD, R., and COFFIELD, F. (1991), *Risky Business*. London: Falmer.

MCINTOSH, M. (1971), 'Changes in the Organisation of Thieving', in S. Cohen, ed., *Images of Deviance*, 98–133. Harmondsworth: Penguin.

—— (1975), *The Organisation of Crime*. London: Macmillan.

MACK, J. (1964), 'Full time miscreants, Delinquent Neighbourhoods and Criminal Networks', *British Journal of Sociology*, 15: 38–53.

MACK, J., and KERNER, H. (1975), *The Crime Industry*. Lexington, Mass: Lexington Books.

MCVICAR, J. (1979), *McVicar By Himself*. London: Arrow.

MAGUIRE, M. (1982), *Burglary in a Dwelling*. London: Heinemann.

MANNHEIM, H. (1955), *Group Problems in Crime and Punishment*. London: Routledge.

MARX, G. T. (1988), *Undercover: Police Surveillance in America*. Berkeley: University of California Press.

MATZA, D., and SYKES, G. (1961), 'Delinquency & Subterranean Values', *American Sociological Review*, 26/5: 712–19.

MAURER, D. (1964), *Whiz Mob*. New Haven, Conn.: College & University Press.

MAYHEW, H. (1861), *London Labour and the London Poor*, 4 vols. London: Dover; facsimile edition 1968.

MESSINGER, S. L. (1966), 'Some Reflections on Professional Crime in West City', mimeographed personal communication, cited in J. Roebuck and G. Windham, 1983.

MILLER, W. (1958), 'Lower Class Culture as a Generating Milieu of Gang Delinquency', *Journal of Social Issues*, 14: 5–19.

MIRZA, H., PEARSON, G., and PHILLIPS, S. (1991), *Drugs, People and Services in Lewisham: Final Report of the Drug Information Project*. London: Goldsmiths College.

MORTON, J. (1992), *Gangland*. London: Little, Brown.

MUNSCHE, P. B. (1981), *Gentleman and Poachers*. Cambridge: Cambridge University Press.

MUSTAIN, G., and CAPECI, J. (1988), *Mob Star*. New York: Franklin Watts.

NORRIS, C. (1993), 'Some Ethical Considerations on Fieldwork with the Police', in D. Hobbs and T. May, eds., *Interpreting Fieldwork*. Oxford: Oxford University Press.

PARKER, R. (1981), *Rough Justice*. London: Fontana.

PATRICK, J. (1973), *The Glasgow Gang Observed*. London: Eyre Methuen.

PEARCE, F. (1976), *Crimes of the Powerful*. London: Pluto.

PEARSON, J. (1973), *The Profession of Violence*. London: Panther.

PERKIN, H. (1992), 'The Enterprise Culture in Historic Perspective: Birth, Life, Death and Resurrection', in P. Heelas and P. Morris, eds., *The Values of the Enterprise Culture*, 36–60. London: Routledge.

PILEGGI, N. (1987), *Wise Guy*. London: Corgi.

PLUMMER, K. (1983), *Documents of Life*. London: Unwin Hyman.

POLSKY, N. (1971), *Hustlers, Beats and Others*. Harmondsworth: Pelican (1st edn. 1967).

PRESIDENT'S COMMISSION ON ORGANISED CRIME (1984), *Organised Crime of Asian Origin*. New York: US GPO.

PRINGLE, P. (1958), *The Thief Takers*. London: Museum Press.

PROBYN, W. (1977), *Angel Face*. London: Allen & Unwin.

PRUIS, R., and IRINI, S. (1980), *Hookers, Rounders and Desk Clerks: The Social Organisation of a Hotel Community*. Toronto: Gage.

PRYCE, K. (1986), *Endless Pressure*. Bristol: Bristol Classical Press.

QUINNEY, R. (1975), 'Crime Control in Capitalist Society', in I. Taylor, P. Walton, and J. Young, eds, *Critical Criminology*, 181–202. London: Routledge.

READ, L. (1991), *Nipper*. London: MacDonald.

READ, P. P. (1979), *The Train Robbers*. London: Coronet.

REUTER, P. (1984), *Disorganised Crime*. Cambridge, Mass.: MIT Press.

REUTER, P., MACCOUN, R., and MURPHY, P. (1990), *Money from Crime*. Santa Monica, Ca.: Rand Corporation.

RICE, F. (1991), 'How Copycats Steal Billions', *Fortune*, 22 April: 77–80.

RICHARDSON, C. (1992), *My Manor*. London: Pan.

ROBINS, D. (1992), *Tarnished Vision: Crime and Community Action in the Inner City*. Oxford: Oxford University Press.

ROCK, P. (1973), *Deviant Behaviour*. London: Hutchinson.

ROEBUCK, J., and WINDHAM, G. (1983), 'Professional Theft', in G. P. Waldo, *Criminal Careers*. Beverly Hills: Sage.

ROSS, T. (1992), 'Colombia Tackles New Threat from Poppy Fields', *The Independent*, 8 February: 11.

SALGADO, G. (1977), *The Elizabethan Underworld*. London: Dent.

SAMUEL, R. (1981), *East End Underworld: The Life and Times of Arthur Harding*. London: Routledge and Kegan Paul.

SHARP, J. A. (1984), *Crime in Early Modern England 1550–1750*. London: Longman.

SHOVER, N. (1973), 'The Social Organisation of Burglary', *Social Problems*. 20: 499–514.

—— (1983), 'Professional Offender: Major Offender', in S. H. Kadish, ed., *Encyclopaedia of Crime and Justice*, 1263–71. New York: Free Press.

—— (1985), *Aging Criminals*. Beverly Hills: Sage.

SINDALL, R. (1990), *Street Violence in the Nineteenth Century*. Leicester: Leicester University Press.

SMITHIES, E. (1982), *Crime in Wartime*. London: Allen and Unwin.

SPRADLEY, J. (1970), *You Owe Yourself a Drunk*. Boston: Little, Brown.

STEDMAN JONES, G. (1971), *Outcast London*. Oxford: Oxford University Press.

STERLING, C. (1991), *The Mafia*. London: Grafton.

SUTHERLAND, E. (1937), *The Professional Thief*. Chicago: Chicago University Press.

—— (1949), *White Collar Crime*. New York: Holt, Rinehart and Winston.

SWEENEY, J. (1989), 'Heirs to the Krays', *Observer Magazine*, 25 June: 27–30.

—— (1990), 'Silencing the Silent Man', *Observer*, 29 April: 19.

TAYLOR, L. (1984), *In the Underworld*. Oxford: Blackwell.

THOMAS, W. I., and ZNANIECKI, F., (1958), *The Polish Peasant in Europe and America*. New York: Dover. (1st edn 1918–20).

THOMPSON, P. (1978), *The Voice of the Past: Oral History*. Oxford: Oxford University Press.

THRASHER, F. (1927), *The Gang*. Chicago: Chicago University Press.

TOBIAS, J. J. (1974), *Prince of Fences: The Life and Crimes of Ikey Solomons*. London: Valentine Mitchell.

TOMKINSON, M. (1982), *The Pornbrokers*. London: Virgin Books.

UK ANTI-PIRACY GROUP (1986), *International Piracy*. London: UK Anti-Piracy Group.

VAN MAANEN, J. (1978), 'Watching the Watchers', in P. Manning and J. Van Maanen, *A View from the Streets*. Santa Monica, Ca.: Goodyear.

VIGIL, J. D., and YUN, S. C. (1990), 'Vietnamese Youth Gangs in Southern California', in R. Huff, ed., *Gangs in America*, 146–62. Beverly Hills: Sage.

WALSH, D. (1986), *Heavy Business*. London: Routledge and Kegan Paul.

WICKSTEAD, B. (1985), *Gangbuster*. London: Futura.

WIDEMAN, J. E. (1985), *Brothers and Keepers*. New York: Penguin.

WILLIAMS, F. (1973), *No Fixed Address: The Great Train Robbers on the Run*. London: W. H. Allen.

Williams, T. (1989), *The Cocaine Kids*. Reading, Mass.: Addison-Wesley.
Young, Lord (1992), 'Enterprise Regained', in P. Heelas and P. Morris, eds., *The Values of Enterprise Culture*, 29–35. London: Routledge.

11

The Political Economy of Crime

IAN TAYLOR

INTRODUCTION

In the mid- to late eighteenth century, in England, Scotland, and continental Europe, in the writings of John Stuart Mill, Charles Montesquieu, David Hume, Adam Ferguson, Adam Smith, and many others, the term 'political economy' actually referred to a powerful literature focusing on what we would now identify as the field of moral or political philosophy—a literature which was concerned, in particular, with the relationship between forms of economic organization and the question of the 'good society', the rights and duties of citizenship, and the question of individual and state obligation. By the late nineteenth century, sadly, much of this literature had effectively been forgotten, as the rapid changes wrought by the rise of industrial society and, in particular, the street violence and thieving of the 'dangerous classes' presented established authority with an immediate set of problems with respect to social control in society as it was then organized. The triumph of liberal and 'scientific' modes of social thought in the late nineteenth century, challenged by a few lone voices of conservative (e.g. Arnold 1965 [1869]) or utopian (e.g. Ruskin 1985 [1862]) persuasion, was also a triumph of a largely pragmatic, philosophically uninquisitive, and actually rather narrow conception of the proper scope of 'political economy'.

In this chapter, my concern is to survey the literature of nineteenth- and twentieth-century criminology, and associated social scientific fields, in respect of the issue of 'political economy' and 'crime'. What will very rapidly be apparent is that a large amount of this literature works from within the perspective just described—that of a pragmatic, theoretically uncritical notion of the proper scope of 'political economy'. In particular, the criminological literature is replete with studies that purport simply to confirm, illustrate, or sometimes elaborate what George Vold in 1958 called 'the economic determinist approach', namely, 'the proposition that economic life is fundamental and therefore the determining influence upon which all social and cultural arrangements are made' (Vold 1958: 159–60). In particular, the concern of this literature seems very often to have been to point up the existence of causal relations between 'economic crisis', 'the business cycle', or other departures from 'normal' economic relationships or processes and the outgrowth of crime. There is often very little curiosity, in this tradition, as to the ways in which the routine or successful functioning of economies organized around the capital–labour relation or around individual self-interest may in itself be a factor in crime. These issues have surfaced occasionally in the broader literatures of social theory, most notably in the work of Merton (see below), and they were once the subject of commentary by Marx himself—often thought of as the original 'economic determinist'—in a famous, ironic disquisition on the productivity of crime under capitalism (Marx 1969). One of the themes in this survey on the issue of political economy and crime is the need to retrieve the broad set of issues that are raised by social theory and moral philosophy in any serious examination of these themes, especially at an historical moment like the present, with the transition from a world dominated by nation-states pursuing essentially Keynesian economic policies to a deregulated international 'free market economy', divided into competing economic blocs, all but complete.

Partly with this argument in view, but partly, also, for ease of reading and consultation, this chapter is organized into four discrete, but connected, sections, on (1) crime rates and economic conditions: the issue of the business cycle; (2) the political economy of inequality and crime; (3) the costs of crime: the partial vision of utilitarian economic theory; and (4) crime and free market societies. The main concern is to provide an overview of a significant selection of the literature, but there is also an argument, running throughout this chapter, about the need to broaden out debate and to return to an earlier notion of what constitutes a powerful, responsible consideration of the field of political economy.

CRIME RATES AND ECONOMIC CONDITIONS: THE ISSUE OF THE BUSINESS CYCLE

The earliest investigation of the relationship between economic conditions and crime (which is nearly always acknowledged in the recognized literature of applied criminology) is that published, by André-Michel Guerry in his *Statistique morale d'Angleterre comparée avec la statistique morale de la France* (1833)—an examination of the first ever set of criminal statistics, released by the government of France in 1827. Guerry's analysis (and that of Adolphe Quetelet, published in 1835) presented an extremely detailed, statistically organized set of ecological maps of France, representing the rates of crime in relationship to geographical location and climate, levels of education, and occupation and employment. Quetelet's and Guerry's analyses were particularly important for the demonstration they provided that relationships among economic activity, geographical location, and crime were reproduced over several years: there was, in other words, a law-like relation between economic and ecological factors and crime—a 'constancy of crime' under specific economic or other conditions.

The nineteenth-century proliferation of interest in the production of social and economic statistics also gave rise to a series of studies as to the relationship between 'the economic cycle' (which was being understood, rather tentatively, as an inevitable aspect of industrial capitalist society) and rates of crime. An early study of court statistics in England and Wales during the 1840s by Whitworth Russell found a strong, positive relation between the general 'commercial and manufacturing distress' obtaining in 1842, in particular, and the number of prisoners appearing before the higher courts (Russell 1847). A few years later, however, a study of committals to the House of Correction in Preston, Lancashire, over the period 1835–54 challenged this early attempt at a straightforward correlation between 'the business cycle' and crime rate. According to John Clay, the author of this particular study, 'economic hard times' may have added a few cases to the courts' workload, but 'good times' had produced a much more significant increase (Clay 1855: 79). In Clay's view, the increase in summary convictions which occurred in the 1850s—subsequent to the travails of the 'hungry 1840s'—was a function of 'the intemperance which high wages encourage among the ignorant and the sensual'.

The project of trying to demonstrate a strong statistical relationship between economic cycles and crime has been reasserted in scholarly work in criminology, as well as in popular political discussion, throughout the late nineteenth century and into the twentieth. One of the most influential studies, by Georg von Mayr (1867)—attempting to correlate the price of rye in Bavaria over the period 1835–61 and the numbers of offences against the person over the same period—concluded, with considerable authority, that 'for every halfpenny increase in the price of rye there would be one theft per 100,000 persons, and for every drop in the price of rye there would be a corresponding decrease in the crime of theft' (von Mayr 1867, quoted in Vold 1958: 167). Von Mayr's insistence on such a close, determinate relation between the price of a staple food commodity and crime helped to establish a piece of criminological received wisdom of the first half of the twentieth century—specifically, that the level of crime known to the police is an expression, more or less directly and straightforwardly, of the level of 'economic distress' in society (particularly in respect of the poorest sections of society).

In twentieth-century criminology, probably the best-known attempt at exploring the impact of the economic cycle on crime has been Georg

Rusche and Otto Kirchheimer's examination of the relation between unemployment and *imprisonment* (1939).[1] Rusche and Kirchheimer's analysis of penal policies and *crime rate* in England, France, Germany, and Italy in the period between 1911 and 1928, and in Italy and Germany in the first years of fascism (1928–36), is actually quite complex in its various conclusions, but the most usual interpretation of their overall argument is 'that prisons help to control the labour supply by jettisoning inmates when labour is scarce and filling up when labour is abundant' (Box and Hale 1982: 21). Similar findings have been reported in two separate studies of the relationship between unemployment and imprison-

[1] Rusche and Kirchheimer's analysis has been subject to close critical examination in Box and Hale (1982, 1985) and in a more extended fashion in Box (1987). Box and Hale concluded that while 'the total population' under immediate sentence of imprisonment was 'sensitive to the level of unemployment', the really important significance of the increase in unemployment in the 1930s in Italy and Germany—as well as in the UK in the 1980s—was that it was 'an *ideologically motivated* response to the perceived threat of crime posed by the swelling population of economically marginalised persons' (Box and Hale 1982: 22). According to this analysis, then, it is not that there is a direct relation between cycles of unemployment and levels of imprisonment, explicable in terms of the dynamics of political economy (the prison population never comprises more than a small minority of the unemployed: it cannot directly 'take up' the reserve army of labour); it is rather that the cycles of the economy are associated with shifts in the ideological mood consequent on what another analyst of these issues, Dario Melossi, calls the 'political business cycle' (Melossi 1985). The relationship between economic cycles, crime, and punishment must be investigated as a topic *in social and political ideology*.

It is worth noting here, also, a closely associated debate conducted by criminologists in the 1970s with respect to the move taking place towards deinstitutionalization or decarceration of various socially marginal populations, from the mentally ill to the pre-delinquent. A particularly important text here is Andrew Scull (1977). Scull challenged the conventional, liberal account of this pronounced move towards decarceration, with its emphasis on the newly developed capacities of psychotropic drugs to control individuals in non-institutional settings and the associated 'humanist' critique of total institutions, by insisting that the most powerful explanation of decarceration must be sought in the developing fiscal crisis of the capitalist state. A similar argument was later developed by Spitzer (1983) in an attempt to argue that capitalist political economy involves the 'marginalization' of a significant fraction of the reserve army of labour, and that the control of a certain proportion of the marginal population *within the community* is necessary whenever the costs of incarceration become prohibitive. Later research findings suggesting that control within the community can actually be as costly as institutional control have, however, posed a challenge to explanations of control strategies that depend entirely on 'a political economy'. In a more recently published piece, Spitzer argues that 'as it moves along its twisted course, capitalism requires an *ever-changing* ensemble of strategies to meet new crises' (Spitzer 1983: 328, emphasis added).

The move away from explanations of 'the logic of social control' based on *political economy* to explanations based on a theoretical understanding of *ideologies of marginalization* is perhaps most strongly developed in Jeffrey Reiman's *The Rich Get Richer and the Poor Get Prison* (1979). In this powerful account of American penal policy and practice, Reiman's concern is to argue that there is an ideological requirement that the enormous capital investment involved in prisons, police, and other measures of crime control *must fail*—that they must sustain what he dubs 'a pyrrhic defeat'—because, in this failure, the criminal justice system confirms the real seriousness of the danger which is posed by 'criminals', the fearful 'other' against which working people and the propertied middle class alike can unite in common struggle.

ment in Canada (Greenberg 1977; Kellough *et al.* 1980) and by Jankovic (1977) in an analysis of Californian imprisonment in the early 1970s.

In this view, it is not simply that capitalist economies experience continual cycles of boom and slump and that slumps tend to produce significant increases in crime: it is also, quite specifically, that capitalist economies systematically give rise to—*or even require*—instability in the employment chances of a section of the working population (a 'reserve army' of labour). When the business cycle throws this reserve army out of work, prisons fill up with unemployed workers attempting to maintain themselves through theft and other crime. In this respect, the political economy of unreformed capitalist societies is a factor in the cyclical production of crime and also the 'workload' of the criminal justice system itself.

A criminological wisdom of this kind, focused on the close and essentially determinate relationship between crime, imprisonment, and economic distress, lies at the core of nearly all the socially reformist, Keynesian, and even Marxist theoretical and analytic writing on crime that emerged in North America and in Europe from the mid-twentieth century through to the later 1970s. It is a tradition that has been reasserted, in recent years, in the work of Harvey Brenner.

Harvey Brenner is widely known among sociologists of health and illness, epidemiologists, social work lobby groups, and others in the United States and in England for a variety of studies which purport to demonstrate the existence of a close causal relationship between unemployment and mortality and morbidity rates. His work is distinctive for its adoption of 'time series regression analysis', wherein the analyst 'lags' the effects of unemployment over a period of years and thereby avoids the necessity of demonstrating the immediate, temporal coincidence of unemployment and its hypothesized effects. One of the most widely quoted of Brenner's findings in the USA was a study published in 1977, concluding that 'the 1.4 per cent rise in unemployment during 1970 [was] directly responsible for some 51,570 total deaths, including 1,740 additional homicides, 1,540 additional suicides, and for 5,520 additional state mental hospitalizations' (Brenner 1977: 4).

Earlier, in evidence presented to the Joint Economic Committee of the US Congress, Brenner had argued that every 1 per cent increase in unemployment in that country had meant that 4.3 per cent more men and 2.3 per cent more women were introduced into state mental hospitals for the first time; 4.1 per cent more people committed suicide; 5.7 per cent more were murdered; and 4 per cent more entered state prisons. In the next six years, in addition, 1.9 per cent would die from heart disease, cirrhosis of the liver, and other stress-related chronic ailments (Brenner 1971). Research undertaken by Brenner in Liverpool in the late 1970s purported to demonstrate a similar type of causal relationship between income level and mortality, with every decline in income resulting in increased numbers of deaths, except in respect of homicide. The relationships identified by Brenner between level of parental income and infant mortality, on a one-year 'lag', and suicide, over two years, were significant, as was the relationship between unemployment in men over 40 and cirrhosis of the liver and cardiovascular mortality (Brenner 1977). Brenner experienced greater difficulty in the attempts he made in his work (most of it done on American data) to relate unemployment specifically to crime and delinquency, since the official rates of both have tended to increase exponentially *throughout* the post-war period, irrespective of the stage of the economic cycle (Brenner 1978). Brenner's overall analysis has, in any case, been subjected to significant critique, notably by Jon Stern, on the issue of causal order (does unemployment produce illness or can the relationship work the other way round?) and also in respect of the warrantability of his choice of different lag periods (Stern 1982). Eyer, and other critics, have also pointed specifically to the problems involved in using a three-year lag in attributing pathologies of health or social disorder to economic downturns (or unemployment) as distinct from the impending upturn of the business cycle, and the opportunities (and stresses and strains) associated with such an upturn (Eyer 1977, 1981).[2]

Exactly these same issues—of advancing a causal argument as distinct from offering merely correlational analysis—had been highlighted thirty years earlier in a well-known study, by Paul Wiers, of the fluctuating relationship between juvenile court cases and a variety of indices of economic conditions in Wayne County, Detroit, in the period between 1921 and 1943 (Wiers 1945). In this particular study, Wiers found a particularly strong positive correlation between 'non-agricultural employment', department store sales, gross national product, and industrial production, on the one hand, and the number of delinquent court cases, on the other. As George Vold was subsequently to observe, these results were in direct contradiction of von Mayr's famous study of 1867—suggesting, as they did, a strong positive relation between crime and economic *prosperity* rather than distress.

Attempts to relate economic conditions to crime rate gained popularity again in the early 1990s in both Britain and North America, consequent on the continuing and severe recessions in the economies of those two

[2] An earlier study which used econometric techniques to try to estimate the determinate relationships between unemployment and crime, focusing in particular on levels of police activity (Carr-Hill and Stern 1979), has been widely quoted as suggesting that unemployment and crime are not related; but a later reanalysis of the data by Hakim (1982) 'confirms the association between crime and unemployment', suggesting that what Carr-Hill and Stern really analysed was 'the contribution of unemployment to explaining the number of police in each area' (Hakim 1982: 452).

societies. In Britain, where there were 5.3 million offences known to the police in 1991 (compared to 2.4 million in 1979) and a record annual increase of 19 per cent in the twelve months to September 1991, a study by Simon Field suggested that the increases of the previous twelve years were most marked in respect of property crime (theft, burglary, and car crime) in the years where spending power decreased, and that in contrast the increases in crimes of violence (assault, armed robbery, and sex offences) were more marked in the years of economic boom. Field particularly noted a close correlation between economic boom, consumption of beer, and violent offences (Field 1991).

THE POLITICAL ECONOMY OF INEQUALITY AND CRIME

The last section was concerned with reviewing the criminological literature focusing on the determinate effects of the economic cycle on crime (and on incarceration) and dealing therefore with the relation between absolute levels of economic distress or deprivation and levels of crime and delinquency. There is also a distinct body of (usually quite specifically sociological) literature, however, which has been more interested in thinking about *inequalities in the distribution of economic return or economic well-being*, and the broad social effects of such inequalities, e.g. in respect of crime. In this approach it is not so much the 'volatility' of political economy which is at issue as the systematic or ongoing production of unequal opportunity or of actual poverty.

Interest in the relationship between poverty, or 'absolute inequality', and crime predates the emergence of the discipline of criminology in the nineteenth century; it can be seen, for example, in the teaching of Christian leaders from St Paul to Thomas More (1478–1535). In the late nineteenth century, the exact same set of concerns with respect to the general consequences of poverty, in particular, on the prevalence of unruly begging, 'mendacity', and street crime infused the urban commentaries of Henry Mayhew, the 'fiction' of Charles Dickens and Charles Kingsley, and the utopian pamphleteering of late nineteenth-century critics of industrial capitalism like Edward Carpenter and John Ruskin.[3] Enrico Ferri (1856–1929), one of the founding fathers of the Italian *scuola positiva*, is remembered for his insistent emphasis in his *Criminal Sociology* on social and economic deprivation as one of the primary causes of crime, and for his advocacy of political action by the state to reduce deprivation and inequality as a policy measure made legitimate in terms of its effect on levels of crime.

[3] For further discussion of the one criminological intervention made by the nineteenth-century utopian socialist Edward Carpenter, see Taylor (1991*a*).

Willem Bonger

In the first half of the twentieth century, probably the best-known criminological dissertation on the relation of deprivation and inequality to crime was that advanced by the Dutch Marxist criminologist, Willem Bonger (1876–1940). Along with many other socialist writers on crime and prison in the first half and middle of the twentieth century,[4] Bonger's search for the causes of crime in industrial capitalist society began with a serious attempt to understand not just the impact of the economic cycle but also workers' *routine* experience of insecurity within the capital–labour relationship. In the last years of the nineteenth century and early years of the twentieth century, wage labour was never secure. According to Bonger: 'The proletarian is never sure of his existence: like the sword of Damocles, unemployment is constantly hanging over his head' (1969 [1916]: 49). In the periods of forced idleness which are imposed on workers, and also in economic downturns in the demoralizing work which is often required of workers during periods of employment, there is no real incentive for workers to develop any overall moral code or sense of collective social life and responsibility. The result is a growth of what Bonger calls 'egoistic' sentiments among workers, evidenced, on the one hand, in the carelessness of securely employed working people with respect to saving money, and also, on the other, the relative willingness of workers to engage in crime for material survival, particularly in response to periods of unemployment or penury.

Bonger's extended analysis of working-class 'egoism' in relation to a vast range of offence categories has been variously described in later literature as a kind of crude materialistic psychology or economic determinism. In fact, his analysis of offence types and offender behaviour was significantly more elaborate than either description would allow: his work is particularly noteworthy for the attention it gave to the routine subjection and inequality of women in early twentieth-century capitalist societies (and the powerful sense that patriarchal structures were very closely linked to the structures of capital), and also for the attention it gave to the relationship between the militarized character of capitalist states in the early twentieth century and the prevalence of violence in civil society even in periods of peace.

It is fair, however, for subsequent critics to see a certain kind of rigidity in Bonger's attempt to read off a single psychological predisposition from the experience of uncertainty, or absolute levels of poverty, experi-

[4] A list of other socialist writers who wrote on crime as a function of poverty must also include, in England, Robert Blatchford, the editor of *Clarion* newspaper, in his *Not Guilty: a Defence of the Bottom Dog* (1906); and, in the USA the IWW (International Workers of the World) leader Eugene Debs in his *Walls and Bars* (1927) and, of course, the Black Panther Party leader, George Jackson, in his famous polemic *Soledad Brother* (1970).

enced by working people caught up in the logic of capitalist political economy. And inasmuch as Bonger's work 'like many other straightforwardly socialist accounts in its time' could be read as suggesting that the 'roots of crime' lay in some *absolute* level of deprivation or poverty, it was an account which lost power and influence when improved economic circumstances in the mid- to late 1930s did not seem to produce any radical reduction in the scale of the problem of crime. The instructive contrast, perhaps, is with the attempt made by Robert K. Merton, the American sociologist, writing in the 1930s, to try to explain the overall relation between the dynamic of an individual economy, the *culture* within which it is experienced, and the wide *variety of individual adaptations* which may arise.

Robert K. Merton

First published in 1938, but subsequently revised for inclusion in *Social Theory and Social Structure* (1957), Merton's classic essay on 'Social Structure and Anomie' advances an explanation of crime, delinquency, and other deviant individual adaptations based on the strains that were produced in mid-twentieth-century American society by the unequal distribution of legitimate means available to the population in general for the attainment of the dominant cultural goal of material success (Merton 1963 [1938]).

For Merton, modifying the nineteenth-century work of Émile Durkheim, the key issue in explaining crime might be the existence of a condition of normlessness or *anomie*, particularly at times of economic downturn, when the opportunities for individual Americans to strive for, and attain, material success were blocked, as a result of the restriction of opportunities in the labour market and/or the opportunities for upward mobility through education. In this vision of anomie, the emphasis was not only on a *structure* of unequal opportunity—evident in the blockages placed before individuals in different class, ethnic, or other social positions; it was also on the strains produced in *individuals* at particular levels of the social formation who had been unable to achieve any sense of the material wealth which had been so heavily prioritized as the dominant success goal of the society. Among those social groups who experience such a blockage of opportunity it was therefore not surprising, Merton argued, to find widespread evidence of 'innovation' in respect of the means for achieving material success (theft, burglary, or other forms of property crime) or alternatively a 'retreatism' (for example, into drug abuse or vagrancy) on the part of those who had given up on the possibility of material success for themselves. The other adaptations to the mix of cultural goals and institutional opportunity structure confronting individuals identified by Merton (of 'conformity', 'ritualism', or 'rebellion') were understood by him to be heavily influenced by individuals' relationship to the political–economic *structure* of opportunity, though also to involve those individuals' interpretation of cultural pressures and demands.

The emphasis on blockage of institutionalized means—or on a 'political economy of unequal opportunity'—is probably less important, however, in Merton's essay than his critical discussion of the lack of regulation of the moral basis of economic activity itself. In the early half of the twentieth century, there had emerged in America 'a heavy emphasis on wealth as a basic symbol of success without a corresponding emphasis upon the [legitimacy of the] avenues on which to march towards this goal' (Merton 1963 [1938]: 139). It was a culture in which 'money [had] been consecrated as value in itself, over and above its expenditure for articles of consumption or its use for the enhancement of power' (ibid.: 136).

The enormous value placed on money as a value itself—without regard to the intrinsic value of the activity through which pecuniary success had been realized—was accompanied by no obvious moral or legal qualification on such success: Al Capone was by no means an unwelcome guest in all social circles (especially at the baseball park) in 1930s Chicago. Americans of all backgrounds were, in effect, invited to pursue material success even by 'illegitimate means' without fear of social exclusion. For Merton, this essentially unregulated political economy was a significant source of crime and instability in the body of American society; and it was especially destabilizing because the lack of moral regulation meant that there could never be a settled sense of achievement or accomplishment:

> In the American Dream there is no final stopping point. The measure of 'monetary success' is conveniently indefinite and relative. At every income level . . . Americans want just about twenty-five per cent more (but of course this 'just a bit more' continues to operate once it is obtained). In this flux of shifting standards, there is no stable resting point, or rather, it is the point which manages to be 'just ahead'. (Merton 1963 [1938]: 63)

In a society dominated by this American Dream, then, there is a constant condition of unease and anxiety: a ceaseless striving for *more* income and/or material possessions as the only possible personal goal. This is a cultural condition which would tend to produce a radically egoistic individual, indifferent to the consequences of this individualistic pursuit of material success on others' material or personal and psychological security or their associated 'quality of life'.

The importance of Merton's essay—and the advance it marked on Bonger's economic determinism and materialist psychology—lies in the dynamic and contradictory capacity of the theory of anomie there developed to lay bare the links between the condition of a political economy and what Merton himself calls 'the cultural structure' of the broad society within which that economic activity was pursued, and then to produce a sociological account of some of the individual adaptations or effects (including crime) across the whole social formation. It was a classic essay—not only in the sense that it offered a framework, derived from an understanding of the political economy of American capitalism at the time, within which to theorize systematically the overall effects of inequality within civil society, but also in making the links, specifically, between political economy, the dominant cultural goals of the society, unequal structures of opportunity, and patterns of crime.

Richard Cloward and Lloyd Ohlin

The most celebrated exposition of these links within the post-war American criminological literature is to be found in Richard Cloward and Lloyd Ohlin's *Delinquency and Opportunity: A Theory of Delinquent Gangs*, published in 1960. Cloward and Ohlin retained much of Merton's functionalist stress on the importance of universalistic cultural goals in ensuring the survival of a dynamic 'industrial society' in America, but, also like Merton, they were aware of the potentially disorderly consequences of structural blockages to individual achievement:

> If a cultural emphasis on unlimited success-goals tends to solve some problems in the industrial society, it also creates new ones. A pervasive feeling of position-discontent leads men to compete for higher status and so contributes to the survival of the industrial order, but it also produces acute pressure for deviant behaviour. (Cloward and Ohlin 1960: 81–2)

Cloward and Ohlin went on to argue that the absence from particular neighbourhoods of legitimate opportunities for self-advancement (in the form of stable employment, albeit of a low-paid kind, for high-school leavers or, alternatively, the chance to go to college for the purpose of training or accreditation) creates the conditions for the emergence of delinquent youth subcultures. The precise shape and character of the subcultures emerging in particular neighbourhoods will be a function of the presence, or absence, in those neighbourhoods of stable 'illegitimate' criminal enterprises. Where such enterprises do exist, and involve significant numbers of the adult population, youthful delinquent activity will tend to be drawn towards, or be parasitic upon, such adult criminal enterprise (in the form, for example, of more or less organized theft or burglary). In such circumstances, recruitment into these youthful criminal subcultures might be the first stage of the recruitment of the young into a career of adult crime. In areas where such stable adult criminal enterprises do not exist, and opportunities for this kind of advancement are therefore blocked, young men will gravitate instead into the local 'fighting gang'—or what Cloward and Ohlin call the 'conflict subculture'. Young men who fail to win acceptance in either a criminal or a conflict subculture will be drawn, as a result of this 'double failure', into drug use, alcohol abuse, or other forms of eventually self-destructive hedonism, in the context of what Cloward and Ohlin called the 'retreatist subculture'.

Cloward and Ohlin's analysis of delinquency has been subjected to extensive critical discussion in the subsequent criminological literature, both in North America and elsewhere. There is debate over whether the three models of delinquent subculture now have, or ever did have, any demonstrable empirical reference, and also over the model that is proposed by Cloward and Ohlin of the *sequence* through which young men are said to be recruited into the criminal, conflict, and retreatist subcultures. There has also been debate, especially among conservatively minded criminologists in the 1980s, over whether this model could still be said to apply to a free market society like the USA, in which the problems of the broad society are, it is argued, no longer those of blocked opportunity.[5] Outside America, there has always been concern as to whether the Mertonian model adopted by Cloward and Ohlin could ever be transferred to societies (like Britain) where there is nothing like the dominant ideology of egalitarianism that characterizes the United States.[6] There have also been a host of other queries about the Cloward and Ohlin thesis, for example, in respect of the lack of interest shown in the dynamics of lower-class culture itself, the organization of the lower-class family, and problems at the level of schools in lower-class neighbourhoods. One of the best-known criticisms of Cloward and Ohlin (and also of other writers on subcultures in the 1960s) is of the complete lack of interest in that literature in issues of gender: women are present in the subcultural texts only in their role as mothers. The impact of the facts of political economy and the associated 'structures of opportunity' on adolescent girls in lower-class neighbourhoods is never a topic for discussion in this literature, and the result is that the idea of the masculine role *per*

[5] For one attempt to revise Merton's typology of deviant adaptation with a view to understanding a social condition of 'unanticipated affluence' in the USA in the mid-twentieth century, and its differential social effects, especially 'at higher economic levels', see Simon and Gagnon (1976).

[6] Probably the most famous discussion of the inapplicability of American subcultural theory to the analysis of delinquency and youth subcultures in Britain is to be found in Clarke *et al.* (1978). The argument advanced is that the different youth subcultures emerging in post-war Britain were actually an attempt to resolve essentially unresolvable, brute facts of class and generational inequality experienced by every youthful cohort *in their imaginary lives* i.e. at the level, simply, of style. This is largely because, instead of there being a widespread experience of what Cloward and Ohlin call 'position-discontent' in Britain, there was a widespread sense of the *inevitability* of the rigid division of the society by class.

se, and the priorities that have traditionally been given in lower-class neighbourhoods in the USA as well as in Britain to young men getting jobs, are never problematized. For present purposes, the most important feature of Cloward and Ohlin's application of Merton to the analysis of youthful delinquency is the unambiguous emphasis they place on the influence of blocked opportunity—of inequality of 'life chances'—in the recruitment of young men into careers of delinquency and crime.

This connection was to be highly influential in the USA in the 1960s, especially in informing the inner-city job-creation programme, Mobilization for Youth; it also had some influence in Britain, notably in the Labour Party pamphlet of 1964, *Crime: A Challenge to Us All*, written by Lord Longford prior to the election of the 1964–70 Wilson government, although the argument in this pamphlet also exhibited concern, in a characteristically English Fabian fashion, over the pathological failure of working-class families to grasp what opportunities were presented to them for advancement (Longford 1964). Mobilization for Youth was to prove relatively short-lived in the USA, encountering fairly quickly the resistance of private and public employers to the employment within their organizations of young people of low skill and inappropriate social or personal attributes (Jones 1971). The English Fabian project of mobilizing ameliorist social work intervention into 'dysfunctional' or 'problem' working-class families ran up against the twin traditions within the English working class of insubordination towards authority on the one hand and a kind of inward-looking conservatism on the other—traditions that quite accurately reflected the working-class scepticism towards the possibility of fundamental change in their life possibilities.

The Political Economy of Post-War Youthful Unemployment

One other reason for the relatively short-lived interest in the United States in the Mobilization for Youth programme, with its Mertonian emphasis on tackling inequalities of opportunity for youth, may have been a recognition that these problems were not merely a matter of cultural prejudice or the uneven capacity of government agencies to help. What was beginning to become apparent to many observers in the USA in the late 1960s and early 1970s was that youth unemployment was taking on the character of an organic structural problem that was going to bedevil the American economy for the foreseeable future. In a classic analysis of the youth employment problem in the USA first published in 1970, John and Margaret Rowntree demonstrated that US unemployment had been concentrated among young people throughout the 1950s and 1960s and also that the unemployment figures for young people would have been even higher had it not been for the rapid expansion of the education system and the military. Between 1950 and 1965, there was an increase in enrolment of 3.68 million in schools and universities in the USA and an increase of 960,000 enrolments in the armed forces. (Rowntree and Rowntree 1970: 11). The overall impact on the pattern of employment of young people was considerable:

> In 1950, only about 22.8 per cent of all men between the ages of 20 and 24 years were either in the armed forces or in schools; in 1965, the figure was 40 per cent. . . . for men 18 to 24 years old, the data are even more impressive; of these 52.1 per cent, or more than half, were in school or college, the military or unemployed. . . . The figures for young women follow the same pattern: in 1950, 24.3 per cent of young women aged 18 and 19, and 4.5 per cent of women aged 20 to 24, were in school or college: by 1965 the figures had increased to 37.7 per cent and 11.8 per cent respectively. (Ibid.: 16)

The point which Rowntree and Rowntree wanted to emphasize, through this analysis of the American labour market between 1950 and 1965, was that 'if [young people] did venture outside army or school, they encountered unemployment rates two to five times the [national US] average'.

Analysis of the American labour market in the later 1960s and early 1970s by Harry Braverman suggests that the problem of structural unemployment intensified during this period, partly as a result of labour-saving technological innovation in the workplace and partly through the export of jobs beyond the American borders by multinational corporations (Braverman 1974). One consequence of these changes was a significant 'de-skilling' of the American workforce, consequent on the replacement of workers in manufacturing industry by machines and the rise of low-skill consumer industries. An increasingly obvious feature of the urban landscape, and the broad labour market, was the existence of a surplus population of unskilled and largely unemployable people, many of them young, and very many of them black. According to Braverman, this 'surplus population' of the 'de-skilled' was the contemporary form assumed by the famous 'reserve army of labour' discussed by writers like Rusche and Kirchheimer in the 1930s—an army of people whose insecure labour market position, and insecure life chances, are a function of the organization of industrial production according to the logic of capital.

Phil Cohen: The Upward and Downward Options

Something of the same kind of argument is apparent in the account presented by Phil Cohen of the 'social effects' of the reconstruction of the British economy during the post-war years (Cohen 1972). Like Braverman, Cohen places particular emphasis on the effects of automation in the 1950s in replacing skilled workers with machines:

> Craft industries . . . were the first to suffer; automated techniques replaced the traditional hand skills and their simple division of labour. Similarly the economics of scale provided for by the concentration of craft resources meant that the small scale family business was no longer a viable unit. Despite a long rearguard action many of the traditional industries . . . and many of the service and distributive trades . . . rapidly declined or were bought out. (Cohen 1972: 18)

The consequence, overall, was

> a gradual polarisation in the structure of the labour force—on the one side, the highly specialised, skilled and well-paid jobs associated with the new technology and the high growth sectors that employed them; on the other, the routine, dead end, low paid and unskilled jobs associated with the labour-intensive sectors, especially the service sectors. (ibid.)

One effect of this development in the political economy of production was to accentuate and intensify the division that had always existed between the stable or 'respectable' sections of the working class (organized labour, the artisan class) and those who have variously been described as the disorganized and residual, rough, sections of the working class. Specifically, the technological reorganization of work clearly identified what Cohen called an 'upward option' for some sections of the class, who were able to move up from the shop floor into office positions or minor research and development roles. But it also helped to redefine a large set of 'downward options'—into residual, insecure, poorly paid jobs that offered little or no training or other opportunities for self-development or for a career. One key aspect of the 'downward option', from the mid-1960s onwards, was the clear expectation of regular periods of unemployment.

Cohen clearly demonstrates how this reorganization of the post-war labour market was related to other aspects of working-class experience in Britain—in particular, in its effects on working-class neighbourhood and community. From the late 1950s onwards, large numbers of established working-class communities (of terraced housing built around the local corner store and public house)—now identified in popular discussion as 'slums'—were gradually broken up, and large proportions of the 'slum-dwellers' rehoused in large council estates or high-rise developments. The areas left behind drifted downwards, slipping into multiple occupation and a new role as 'transitional zones' for incoming immigrant populations. The newly created public housing developments had a chequered history, with the high-rise developments almost a complete failure in respect of creating or sustaining any sense of community, and some inner-city estates likewise. The belief that a sense of community and personal well-being could be constructed on estates or in high-rise buildings whose populations had rather unwillingly been uprooted from the neighbourhoods of their birth may have been a mistake. But perhaps equally crucially, it should be remembered this wholesale rehousing of the working class of Britain occurred against the background of the polarization of the labour market described by Cohen. Just as thousands of new jobs opened up for young people who had worked their way up to the 'upward options' described by Cohen, so also the 'downward' alternatives were increasingly apparent, in the decline in openings in manufacturing industry, in apprenticeships, and in other lower-level labour market opportunities. The official unemployment rate rose from 2.2 per cent in 1960 to 4.1 per cent in 1972 (Sinfield 1981: 14). It may be no coincidence—and some kind of support for the Mertonian emphasis on the relationship between crime and inequality—that it was at just such a juncture that the annual criminal statistics started to show really very marked increases in the number of offences committed by young people. In 1968, for example, the increase in the number of offences known to the police in England and Wales was greater than any year since 1957, with the largest percentage increases in convictions occurring among 17–21-year-old males.

The Demise of Mass Manufacturing

The polarization of the labour market in the USA, Britain, and other western industrial societies that was produced by technological advances in the 1950s and 1960s was relatively insignificant, however, by comparison with the convulsions that occurred in the 1980s. Taking the official unemployment rate as the most immediate expression of these changes, there is no escaping the calamitous increase in unemployment that has occurred in Britain: on official figures—which quite notoriously have been subjected to a series of definitional changes, all of which have had the effect of deflating the overall official figure—unemployment increased from 4.1 per cent of the labour force in 1972 to 10.3 per cent in 1981. Official figures suggst that the highest level of unemployment in the 1980s in Britain was 12.4 per cent in 1983, declining to 6.8 per cent in 1990 (but with a new increase in 1991 to 8.7 per cent)—though all official estimates of the 'real' level of unemployment, including those 'discouraged' from job search, indicate much higher figures. Long-term worklessness (unemployment for more than a year) of individuals increased exponentially in both Britain and the USA, particularly in the older industrial regions. In Britain, the numbers of people out of work for over a year averaged about 34,000 throughout the 1950s; by 1987 this number had risen to 1.3 million—about 40 per cent of all those claiming unemployment benefit (Sinfield 1992: 102). In the USA, a society which, as we have seen, had been used to seeing itself as providing more or less unlimited economic opportunity, unemployment rose steadily throughout the 1980s and early 1990s, and in November 1992, the month when President Bush was defeated by the Democratic candidate, Bill Clinton, was at 7.4 per cent. On various other measures of economic prosperity and well-being—average family income, average industrial productivity, personal investment, and optimism—there was widespread evidence of fundamental decline. Many of the fundamental assumptions about the continuing capacity of the American economy, and by extension other western economies, to produce economic growth, and to guarantee a basic and civilized standard of living for all citizens, were suddenly in doubt, as anxious discussion of the length of 'the recession' turned into even more agitated fear of 'slump'.

In rehearsing some of the evidence about the increases in the size of the 'reserve army of labour' or unemployment during the 1960s and, again, in the late 1970s through to the present, we are associating ourselves with one of the key assumptions intrinsic to the approach of political economists of the late eighteenth and early nineteenth century: namely, that there is *some kind* of determinate relationship between the onset of mass unemployment and the loss of the sense of economic and personal security and well-being involved in worklessness, and the involvement of people in crime. This association is of course challenged by philosophers of the right and by Conservative politicians—most famously by Prime Minister Margaret Thatcher, during the riots in England's inner cities in the summer of 1981, in her resounding declaration that 'unemployment was no excuse'. There may be some basis on which one could attribute moral blame to rioters; but we should not be blind to the truth that the riots of 1981, like those that followed on intermittently throughout the 1980s and early 1990s, occurred in areas of extraordinarily high unemployment (such as the north-east of England), much of it spread over long periods of time. It is clear that unemployment in and of itself would not be a sufficient explanation of the occurrence of these riots (or, indeed, of the very high rates of theft, car crime, and assaults—the 'long slow riot of crime', as Jock Young has called it—which characterises many of these areas): unemployment was just as high, on official measures, in many of these self-same areas in the 1920s without there being anything like the same rate of interpersonal and property crime reported to the police that was being reported in the 1980s (Lea and Young 1984: 90–3).

It is also true that the continuing outbreaks of crime and riot in America's ghetto areas, as well as in the inner cities of Britain, have been subject to an alternative cultural and sociological explanation, namely the theory of the underclass, particularly in the works of the American conservative commentator, Charles Murray (1990). Murray's approach is behavioural, in the sense that he wants to identify the emergence of a pathological type of behaviour and then explain that pathological behaviour in terms of its most immediate conditions of existence. For him, the source of much of the crime and dislocation in the inner city and the ghetto lies in the welfare policies that have been adopted by successive governments in Britain and the USA, which have made it possible for deprived or disadvantaged people to survive outside the labour force. Not only have such welfare policies not provided the support for further initiative and personal development on the part of their clients which may have been thought to be their original rationale; the argument is that they have encouraged a form of 'welfare state dependency' in which the recipients of welfare remain content with their minimal conditions of life and do not take responsibility for improving those conditions. But the second, associated development, which gives cause for further concern, is the way in which young women, in such circumstances, knowingly become pregnant—as a means of ensuring, in Britain, their access to public housing, staying out of the labour market and, in both the USA and Britain, obtaining state benefits over and above basic unemployment support. Murray points, for example, to the increase in illegitimate births in Britain from 10.6 per cent of all live births in 1979 to 25.6 per cent in 1988. The consequence of this, in Britain as in America, is a rather rapid increase in the number of single-parent female-headed households, with what Murray argues are disastrous effects in terms of the routine socialization of the children brought up in such circumstances. The third element in Murray's definition of the underclass is its disproportionate involvement in crime, and especially violent crime. For Charles Murray, the bulk of the 60 per cent increase in crimes of violence reported in the English criminal statistics between 1980 and 1988 is attributable to the activities of young men from the underclass, who, deprived of the dignity and the life-project of work in support of a family, tend to engage in other ways of expressing themselves:

> when large numbers of young men don't work, the communities around them break down, just as they break down when large numbers of young women have babies. The two phenomena are intimately related. Just as work is more important than merely making a living, getting married and raising a family are more than a way to pass the time. Supporting a family is a central means for a man to prove to himself that he is a 'mensch'. Men who do not support families find other ways to prove that they are men, which tend to take various destructive forms. As many have commented through the centuries, young males are essentially barbarians for whom marriage—meaning not just the wedding-vows, but the act of taking responsibility for a wife and children—is an indispensable civilising force. (Murray 1990: 22–3)

Murray's theses about the underclass in America and Britain have found many critics in both countries, not least because the policy sub-text of his writing is always the withdrawal of benefits from populations who are already officially in poverty in the context of recession and deindustrialization. Writers in Britain like Frank Field and Alan Walker accuse Murray of inventing an essentially ideological category (i.e. of lower-class people who are to be differentiated in terms of their conditioned behaviour from the rest of the working class—a resurrection of the Victorian distinction between the 'deserving' and 'undeserving' poor), for which there is no real evidence, and then ignoring the broad patterns of government policies that generate poverty among pensioners and the elderly, single parents in general, and the disabled. Curiously enough, however, Murray's earlier concern to recognize the differential responses of sections of the lower class in America (now translated to his work on the underclass in Britain) to the collapse of the industrial labour market and other developments in the 1980s do find some support in the work of the pioneering black scholar in America working on such issues, William Julius Wilson (1987). In contrast to many liberal scholars, Wilson squarely confronts the data on the disproportionate involvement of the black population of America in violent crime, and also recognizes the extraordinary increase in illegitimate births and in female-headed households in the black community in America. But where Murray would want to claim that these developments must be an expression of generous and self-defeating welfare programmes, especially for the single mother, Wilson shows that the real value of such benefits has declined throughout the 1980s. Where liberal scholars then turn to racism as an explanation of blacks' involvement in violent crime and other dysfunctional, anti-social behaviour, Wilson insists that such racism was far worse in earlier periods than it was in the 1980s. For Wilson, explanation of these contemporary phenomena of violent crime and labour force drop-out among large sections of the black lower class in America must lie in an understanding of what he calls *historic discrimination*—a long-term systemic process of subordination and subjugation, as distinct from the immediate presenting symptoms involved in individual acts of discrimination or prejudice. To think that these long-term processes can have evolved without real structural effects—in cutting whole sections of the black population off, over generations, from adequate training and education, and also imprisoning such people into tightly bounded ethnic ghettoes in which maladaptive individual behaviours were common—is merely naïve. Wilson wants to point up not the 'culture of poverty' so beloved of earlier critics of the poor but rather a culture of exclusion and subordination which has had long-term, crippling cultural effects, which are not accessible to a quick policy fix, especially in competitive free market conditions. In Britain, throughout the 1980s and in the early 1990s, these processes of deindustrialization have had quite extraordinarily sudden and fundamental effects. Unemployment—measured in the same terms as it was before 1979—reached about 4 million in November 1992 (in contrast to the 'official' measure of 2.8 million) and adult male unemployment was firmly stuck at a level not seen since the 1930s (Hutton 1992). All the different measures of income distribution and inequality were continuing to show ever-widening gaps between the richest and poorest sections of the society, and, in the meantime, levels of crime known to the police continued to escalate, nearly doubling in the decade from 1981 to 1991. There were particularly steep increases in the numbers of attempted thefts reported to the police over this period (336 per cent) and in vehicle thefts. Burglaries increased by about 75 per cent—an increase apparent in British Crime Survey findings as well as in police statistics (Mayhew and Maung 1992; see Maguire this volume, Chapter 6, for a broad discussion of recent trends).

It matters enormously, in conditions of increasing economic polarization and crime, how analysts attempt to explain the relationship between these developments. Murray lays himself open, in many ways, to accusations of 'blaming the victim', particularly in his strictures on the problems posed by unmarried mothers in respect of the socialization they provide for their offspring and the overall character of 'family life' in such households. But he is also clear-headed, in ways not recognized by his critics, about the real problems that are presented by the 'unreconstructed masculinity' of the unemployed working class (especially the youthful unemployed) in deindustrialized societies. These problems are plain to see on the streets of England in the 1990s, especially on Saturday nights. With Petras and Davenport (1991), however, and in contrast to Charles Murray, I want to insist that the development of these problems in lower-class urban environments must be approached, first, through an understanding of the absolutely destructive effects that the structural unemployment resulting from deindustrialization have had on the lives of individuals and on communities, and that these destructive processes have been magnified, rather than modified, throughout the 1980s by the dogged and unyielding pursuit by governments, especially in Britain and the United States, of free market economic policies as a matter of faith, and without any real care for the human consequences of this particular experiment in social engineering. The human effects of the free market experiment are clear and inescapable on the streets of Los Angeles and other parts of southern California (Currie 1990*a*, *b*) in the 'Rust Belt' of the northern industrial cities of the USA (Henry and Brown 1990), and in the older industrial cities of the north of England and the lowlands of Scotland. All such areas, in the 1990s, are plagued by previously unknown levels of theft and burglary, car stealing, interpersonal violence, and a crippling sense of fear and insecurity, which cuts thousands of their residents off from the pleasures of the broader consumer society and also from the compensations of friendship and neighbourhood; and it is also worth pointing out that they are plagued by quite extraordinary levels of personal and family poverty, by poor physical health resulting from bad diet, and also by the increasing levels of suicide and early death associated with loss of a personal sense of morale and self-regard. Following the same line of thought as William Julius Wilson, an understanding of the political economy of unemployment in the 1980s and 1990s must be supplemented, especially in respect of an understanding of crime among the lower class, by an analysis of how the *long-term* effects of inequality and subordination—in England, in respect of the unskilled working class—now find a more urgent and nihilistic expression among young white working-class males left behind in the deindustrialization of the 1980s (the new 'poor whites'); for only through such an understanding can one understand the defensive and paranoid character of the adaptations of such a section of the population.

There are a number of accounts on offer as to the source and character of the developments in western economies in the 1980s, with some key differences among these accounts as to whether a *fundamental* change is taking place in respect of the familiar structures of industrial-capitalist society. Some accounts point to continuities between the present and earlier moments in the history of industrial society. Anthony Giddens, for example, believes that we are experiencing a highly developed stage of capitalism, which he describes as High Modernity, in which there are many risks and dangers, but in which long-established patterns of conflict and accommodation still pertain (Giddens 1991). John Urry and Scott Lash point to what they call a 'disorganized capitalism', characterized by the growth of world markets, the emergence of a service class, a declining working class, and national wage bargaining, large monopolies overriding nation-state controls, diminution of class politics, increased cultural fragmentation and pluralism, decline of employment in extractive and manufacturing industries and regionally specialized industry, and a decline in plant size and industrial cities (Lash and Urry 1987). For Lash and Urry, there are all kinds of changes in the character of capitalism, but these changes coexist, often rather uneasily, with established forms. In other accounts, the emphasis is on the radical character of the transformations of the 1980s. Stuart Hall and many other commentators speak of the move towards what are called post-Fordist methods of production and accumulation, and the terminal decline of traditional plant-level industrial organization and of whole economies organized around single industries (Hall and Jacques 1990). Jürgen Habermas accepts this kind of analysis, and points up one of its key consequences as being the subversion of the utopian or reformist hopes of the traditional labour movement, with the 'exhaustion of the Welfare State' and its associated institutions of social care and protection (Habermas 1989). Piore and Sabel, two prominent American economists, argue in a highly influential analysis that the 1980s actually witnessed 'the demise of mass production' as the engine of growth and capital accumulation (Piore and Sabel 1984). In the developed world in general, they argue, domestic consumption of the goods produced by manufacturing industry had begun to encounter limits in the 1960s. By the mid-1970s, something over 90 per cent of all American households had TV sets, refrigerators, toasters, washing machines, and vacuum cleaners. Manufacturing industries began to move, with increasing urgency, into world markets in search of customers; but, in the meantime, there was a driving down of wage bills in western economies through redundancies and other labour-saving measures. This process of deindustrialization was accelerated by a set of precipitating circumstances, of which the two most important were the abandonment of the Bretton Woods agreement in 1971, and the oil crises of 1974 and 1979.

The Bretton Woods agreement had been struck at the end of the Second World War, when the US government, confident in the future of the American economy, agreed to underwrite a system of fixed exchange rates among its European wartime allies, to provide a framework for economic recovery from the war through trade. This system came to pose great strain on the American economy in the 1960s and was abandoned. In its place has emerged a much more uncertain situation, in which investors move money around the world at enormous speed, in response to daily signals about the health of particular companies or national economies. The power of unaccountable and amorphous international financial forces is becoming far more evident than the power of any national Government, and the idea that individual governments can act effectively in terms of a purely national economic policy (e.g. to reduce unemployment) increasingly problematic. It is an extremely volatile situation, and also one in which the limited capacity of individual governments to engage in effective projects of social reform or economic regeneration must be having effects at the level of popular morale.

The second set of precipitating circumstances producing the major transformation in international political economy were the so-called oil shocks of 1974 and 1979. The OPEC embargo of 1974, in particular, is seen as having shifted the epicentre of economic expansion from the developed world to the oil-rich countries of the developing world; the huge incomes which were then earned by the OPEC countries are seen, by Piore and Sabel and many other commentators, as the primary reason for the vast expansion in the 'Eurodollar market'. Eurodollars are a new kind of money, according to Piore and Sabel, completely outside the control of any individual government and enmeshed in the vast network of international banks and financial institutions which have grown up as a result of the collapse of the fixed exchange-rate system.

The international economic situation which has developed through the 1980s is highly volatile and competitive, as major investors and financial institutions move enormous sums of money—sometimes in excess of any one nation's gross national product—around the international stock exchanges, which are now open twenty-four hours a day, at the slightest hint of a change in interest rates in a single jurisdiction or in the fortunes of particular corporations. In a world in which there is no secure store of value *all* players in the market, including national governments, are placed under pressure to take risks and to make increasingly rapid decisions in the search for competitive advantage. Individual multinational corporations have adapted to the uncertainties by diversifying their sphere of operations both horizontally and vertically into different markets (the phenomenon of 'flexible accumulation'), but this is not an option that is always available to national governments. The deregulation of stock exchanges in individual countries in the early 1980s (in London, on 'Big Bang' day, 27 October 1986) was one means available to governments, given the globalized character of economic competition and accumulation activities, to attract the investment of overseas investors and financial institutions into their countries. So also is the resort to what must be identified as free market policy by national governments within their own countries, rolling back the state's direct involvement in the kind of economic or social planning which was demanded during the earlier post-war period, and rationalizing significantly the state's involvement in the provision of public goods in areas like health and welfare, transport, housing, and urban planning. It is important to note that, while the development of flexible accumulation strategies and the move towards 24-hour stock exchange trading are international phenomena, the adoption of *rigorously* free market policies at the national level has been specific to Britain, in what is usually discussed as 'Thatcherism', and the USA, in respect of the decade of 'Reagonomics', culminating in the defeat of George Bush in November 1992 (see the discussion below of Elliott Currie's work on the connection between 'free market society' and crime).

Any coherent political economy of crime in the 1980s must be able to make a connection between the 'liberalization' and internationalization of major speculative financial activity across most western capitalist societies in the early 1980s, and the sudden emergence of major frauds and other serious economic crimes that were thrust into public view, in short order, in the immediately ensuing period.

Crimes of the International Finance Market in the 1990s

Probably the most widely publicized set of these economic and financial offences were those involving the offence of 'insider trading', particularly those cases in the USA involving sums of money beyond all previous experience. In May 1986, the Securities and Exchange Commission (SEC) accused Dennis Levine, a prominent US stockbroker, of making $12.6 million profit by making trades on information gained (through espionage and bribes) from insiders in particular companies. In November of the same year, Ivan Boesky, another prominent broker, agreed to pay the SEC a penalty of $100 million to settle the charges of insider trading it was going to bring against him (in 1987 Boesky was sentenced to three years in prison). In September 1988 the SEC accused one of the top Wall Street firms of stockbrokers, Drexel Burnham Lambert, and one of its top executives, Michael Milken, of even more substantial insider trades as well as a variety of other stock market manipulations, outright frauds, and other violations of federal securities laws, particularly in respect of the marketing of so-called 'junk bonds'; in December 1988 Drexel agreed to plead guilty to six felonies and settle the SEC charges by paying back $650 million. In November 1990 Michael Milken, having been indicted on ninety-eight charges of racketeering and securities fraud, was sentenced to ten years in prison (Stewart 1991).

The scale of these insider trading frauds, in which individual investors were trading in monies equivalent to those of some national government departments, ensured that these American cases attracted international attention. But insider-trading cases were also common in many other western societies. In France, in February 1989, Max Theret and Roger Patrice Pelat, business associates of President Mitterrand, were accused of using advance information on an American takeover bid of $1.26 billion to trade in shares of Pechiney-Triangle Industries. In Britain, on a rather smaller scale, Michael Collier, the chairman of Morgan Collier, was prosecuted in 1986 for making an instant profit of £15,000 on an insider trade, and the following year a Conservative MP, Keith Best, was similarly accused.

Another major activity in the international financial market receiving some public attention in this period was the activity of money laundering. Simply put, the concern of those involved in this activity is to shield money from tax within individual national jurisdictions, and also to disguise the origins or sources of the money as well as its ownership. The 1980s saw the proliferation throughout the world of a number of identifiable 'tax havens' or offshore banking systems for this purpose: the Cayman Islands, for example, which in 1964 had two banks, had by 1987 become the home of 360 foreign banks and 8,000 registered companies, and had more fax machines than any other country in the world (Blum 1984: 22). Much of the money circulating through these havens is known to have originated from the international drug trade, but, even before the well-publicized collapse of the Bank of Credit and Commerce International in 1991, it was clear that these havens had been used for speculative accumulation by major banks and other legitimate financial institutions, including the major national Italian bank, the Banco Ambrosiano, which actually failed in 1984 as a result of such speculative activity (Santino 1988). The scale of this laundering of 'hot money' through the international economy at the end of the 1980s was causing considerable concern among national governments: a Financial Action Task Force, set up by fifteen western governments in 1989, reported in April 1990 that some £43 billion was being laundered through the banking system, and feared for the stability of the system, particularly in respect of the smaller banking institutions (*The Independent*, 12 April 1990).

The publicity given to insider trading and money laundering in the late 1980s (sometimes as a result of investigative journalism and sometimes as a result of 'whistle-blowing' by competitors of those involved in such activities) should not detract attention from the wide range of other fraudulent activities that began to be identified, in the same period, across a large number of financial fields. The problem of 'insurance fraud'—by insurance salespeople as well as by claimants—was an important developing field of economic crime in this period, as also were the problems of credit card, VAT, customs, and pension scheme fraud. There was also evidence of widespread fraudulent dealing in time-share holiday and retirement homes and a variety of other related activities in the financial services market, including the banks and other major financial institutions. (cf. *inter alia* Levi 1988) By the early 1990s, in Britain, a large number of voices were proclaiming that the system of 'self-regulation' that had been established in the Financial Services Act 1986 had palpably failed, and that a system of reregulation, like that which had been instituted even in the USA, was now required.

It should be obvious that a criminology of the international financial markets that grew up in the 1980s would look very different from the political economy of crime that was drawn up, by criminologists like Willem Bonger or sociologists like Robert Merton, at a very different historical juncture in the first half of the twentieth century. In the first instance, such a contemporary criminology would need to be focused on the powerful corporate institutions and individuals at the core of the major crimes in the new international markets, rather than being focused, narrowly, on the street-corner delinquents who were the focus of earlier political-economic studies. But, secondly, it seems clear that the explanatory burden of such a political economy should focus on the broad structures of international economic development and corporate activity and the way in which the crimes of the period (money laundering, insider trading, etc.) are a systemic product, in a key sense, of these newly competitive, international economic conditions—as well as understanding the cultural environment (stressing 'enterprise' and individualism above all other values) that has accompanied such economic developments in societies like the USA and Britain. In this sense, a political economy of contemporary market crime would want to advance beyond the essentially social-psychological approach adopted by the American student of 'white-collar crime', Edwin H. Sutherland, in his famous 1948 study of that name. And, thirdly, it should be apparent that any such political economy of crime in the contemporary market would have to be international in scope, like the activity it seeks to comprehend and/or control, and not be thought through, in the manner of most criminology of this century, in terms only of *national* policy and practice. It is quite clear, for example, that the control of money laundering in the 1990s can be achieved only through internationally co-ordinated activity that is capable of intruding into the activities of national banking systems and financial institutions. (For an extended review of many of the issues discussed in this section, see Nelken, this volume, Chapter 8).

The Political Economy of the International Drug Trade

To insist that any contemporary political economy of crime must focus on the large-scale processes of economic change, and on the powerfully placed institutions that have been engaged in innovative forms of capital accumulation—sometimes in contravention of conventions, and legal and other regulations, that have been prized by national governments and some of their competitors—is not, however, to suggest that these large-scale economic processes do not have major impact on the lives and practices of the lower class, the population that is the accustomed focus of more traditional criminology. It surely is no accident that the largest reported increases in crime, particularly those associated with the mushrooming problem of hard drugs, are reported in precisely those urban centres in North America and Europe that have suffered the greatest job losses as a result of what Piore and Sabel describe as 'the demise of manufacturing industry'. Michael Davis's account of the emergence of the gang wars and cocaine trade in Los Angeles, published some three years before the major Los Angeles riots of June 1992, shows how the context for the dislocation of the black community in that city in the 1980s was the 'sectoral deindustrialization' of southern California as a whole, with the subsequent haemorrhaging away of high-wage industrial jobs, especially for young black men. The slow growth in the service sector, in the meantime, threw up employment disproportionately for young women; but blacks of both sexes continued to be excluded from those jobs thrown up in service outlets in the suburbs (Davis 1988). With their opportunity for gainful employment in the legitimate business sector destroyed by deindustrialization and their search for alternatives obstructed by institutional racism, many young blacks began to innovate—after the fashion of many more fortunately placed entrepreneurs in the 1980s—and move into the lucrative business of the drug trade. The *opportunity* to enter this alternative form of productive employment arose as a result of the rerouting of the so-called 'cocaine trail' from Florida into California around 1984: and, with the development and dissemination of the techniques for distilling and cutting crack cocaine in so-called 'crack houses', the conditions of existence of the massive illegitimate business that is the southern Californian drug trade were laid. By 1988, the Los Angeles Attorney-General's Department was estimating that there was a 'hard-core gang' membership in Los Angeles of between ten and fifteen thousand, and gang-related killings in the city were running at one a day.

The importance of a political-economy approach to understanding the drug trade that emerged in American cities in the 1980s is underlined by the insight which such an approach also yields into the circumstances of the continuing production of the cocoa plant in countries like Colombia and Peru on the South American continent and Sri Lanka and Burma in south-east Asia. It is precisely these countries which have been disadvantaged in the new international global political economy, in part because they have not developed an indigenous industrial or financial commercial class, and now rely on whatever agricultural product they can produce, with minimal technology, and also sell. The really powerful demand, and the highest market prices, are for drugs; and hence, for all the attempts of the US government to stem the production of the coca crop in Colombia and Peru (through defoliation raids and other measures), the international trade in such drugs continues to expand (McConohay and Kirk 1988).

Explaining the conditions of existence of coca *production* in south America, and the conditions of existence of the illegitimate business that organizes the *distribution* of cocaine and other drugs, especially in deindustrialized American cities, does not constitute an exhaustive explanation of drug-related crime. It is necessary also to explain the conditions of existence of the *demand* for such drugs, especially as this demand is not confined to desperate inner-city or ghetto areas—and this may involve a critical understanding of cultural conditions in the deindustrialized, competitive, and individualistic labour market that has existed throughout much of America during the 1980s and is now embracing Britain (cf. Taylor 1992). Davis's account of the development of the drug trade in Los Angeles, later to be replicated by Elliott Currie in his interviews with 'delinquent youth' elsewhere in California (Currie 1991), cannot be transferred wholesale to the British situation, but none the less, there is no mistaking the parallels with certain inner-city areas in Britain (like Moss Side in Manchester), with reports of firearm use and other violence linked to struggles over territory between different gangs involved in the drug trade. The relationship between such drug-related violence and other activities involved in the 'long, slow riot of crime' in Britain's inner cities (car theft and 'joyriding' and 'ram-raiding', burglary, and assaults) may take on a rather different form from that in the United States—not least because the deprivation of the inner city, and also on problem council estates, now extends deeply into a population of poor whites, unaccustomed to their now undeniable position as an underclass.

It is clear, however, that any adequate account of the international trade in drugs, and its impact within individual societies, must not only take account of the interpenetration between street-level criminal enterprise and organized crime, but also pay attention to the ways in which the international economic conditions of the 1980s have encouraged many legitimate businesses into innovative or risky enterprise, some of it conducted 'offshore' through the new international banking systems. One of the really difficult tasks for any internationally organized fraud squad in the early 1990s would be the identification of the real source or ownership of particular flows of 'hot money' it encounters moving through the banking systems. The definitive analytical problem confronting a political economy of the international drug trade in the 1990s might be that of demonstrating the precise interconnectedness, in this sphere of social problems, of the risk-taking enterprise of ostensibly legitimate brokers and traders, on the one hand, and more recognizably illegitimate criminals, on the other. (For further discussion of international drug markets, see South, this volume, Chapter 9.)

THE COSTS OF CRIME: THE PARTIAL VISION OF UTILITARIAN ECONOMIC THEORY

Standing in complete contrast to the kind of political-economic analyses of crime undertaken by critically minded social scientists discussed in the previous section are the approaches to the analysis of crime adopted by economists working within the classical or utilitarian perspective. This approach first came to be applied to crime in an influential fashion in the USA as a consequence of the publication in that country of a famous essay by the economist Gary Becker in 1968. Isaac Ehrlich subsequently extended the economic approach to the study of punishment and deterrence (Ehrlich 1973), and Kenneth Avio and Scott Clark reworked these studies using Canadian economic and crime data (Avio and Clark 1976).

Much of this early North American literature on the political economy of crime is informed by generalized political concern at the extraordinary costs to the state (and, therefore, to taxpayers) of the continuing post-war expansion in the criminal justice system (provoked, according to a common-sense view, by the rapid and accelerating increases in crime). Some of the literature is also informed, however, by the use of the analytic techniques of applied economics (and, specifically, econometrics) in the attempt to investigate the equally problematic issue of measuring the *effectiveness* of particular social control interventions in reducing the incidence of humanly and economically costly crime. The concern of this literature is often not only to try to measure the *differential* costs and benefits of different social control interventions on crime, but also to try to measure the cost of achieving a radical reduction—even to an outcome 'no crime'—in certain crimes. In the work of Lehtinen (1977), for instance, cost–benefit analysis is applied, more or less without qualification, to the disposition of convicted murderers in the USA; her analysis of the differential costs of long-term imprisonment versus execution results in firm support for the economic benefits of execution. In some of this literature, there is also an attempt to apply techniques of cost–benefit analysis to the measurement of the specifically *deterrent* effects of executions or other forms of punishment, as distinct from the costs of disposition *per se*.

In the early 1980s, the work undertaken by economists on crime and punishment finally began to find an echo among certain applied criminologists and social scientists, some of whom attempted to develop the economic approach in the direction of a theory of criminal action. In Britain the development of what came to be known as 'rational choice theory' was undertaken by Derek Cornish and Ron Clarke, most notably in a monograph entitled *The Reasoning Criminal: Rational Choice Perspectives on Offending* (1986). The central argument advanced, quite straightforwardly, was that many people engage in crime because the opportunity presents itself so to do. The situational decision to engage in an act of theft, for example, is taken in circumstances when people think the risk is worth taking—that is, when the opportunity is clear and the chances of being observed and caught are small. This notion of the exercise of reasoned choice is a diluted version of the famous Benthamite calculus of human action being simultaneously deterred by pain and driven by pleasure. What Cornish and Clarke tried to do in *The Reasoning Criminal*, as well as in an earlier paper of 1985, was to try to model the kinds of choices that people will make in different situations of opportunity, in relation to particular forms of crime.

The rational choice theorists have in common with the classical, utilitarian economists, from whom their work derives, a real indifference with respect to the larger questions of political economy discussed by Ferguson, Hume, and others in the eighteenth century—namely, the relationship between the kinds of choices which are presented to people in respect of conformity and crime and the moral or social organization of the broad society (for example, in respect of equality of life chances); and this indifference does mean that the rational choice theorists (like classical economists as well) effectively abstain from examining the ability of particular forms of economic organization to generate *productive work* or *paid employment* for the mass of citizens. Where classical economists do speak of the issue of unemployment, it is usually in an idealist rather than analytical fashion—that is to say, they bemoan the underdevelopment of the free market or of the enterprise culture (which has in some way been prevented from working its magic) as the self-evident source of the unemployment problem of the 1980s. Mass unemployment cannot be admitted as an empirical demonstration of the failure of free market arrangements (cf. Taylor 1991*b*).

Rational choice theorists in criminology also seem largely indifferent—unlike the control theorists with whom they are sometimes confused (cf. Hirschi and Gottfredson 1986)—to the processes that might be thought to produce the personal quality of 'criminality' (or 'criminal propensity') in individuals or in particular neighbourhoods. The overwhelming interest of rational choice criminologists is in the *situations of opportunity* that can be analysed to arrive at the way in which they produce crime as an outcome. Thus, one of the first published studies of the rational choice school centred on Cornish and Clarke, working at the Home Office Research Unit in London in the early 1980s, was a study of the deterrent effects of steering-column locks in cars (Mayhew *et al.* 1976). Subsequent work has ranged widely across the newly established field of 'situational crime prevention', attempting to measure the consequences of different crime-prevention measures (for example, in the redesign of car parks, entrances to buildings in residential areas, lighting and security systems) on the level of crime. There has been a rediscovery of interest (inspired to some extent by the earlier work of Isaac Ehrlich) in the deterrent effects of punishment, and specifically the proposition that an increase in the level of sanction could have effects on the calculations engaged in by the offender at the key situational moment of opportunity (Silberman 1976; Tittle 1977, 1980).

In one subsequent study working within this overall framework, Piliavin *et al.* conducted a sophisticated empirical test in order to question this proposition: their conclusion is that increases in sanctions do *not* feed through to potential offenders' perceptions, but they do nonetheless argue that there is support for what they called 'the reward component of the rational choice model'—namely, the idea that when the rewards for engaging in a criminal act are significant, this will substantially outweigh most of the reasons for abstaining (Piliavin *et al.* 1986). It surely is no surprise, given our earlier discussion of Merton, to find that young people in low-paid employment in the service industries or on welfare in the USA of the 1980s (the golden era of 'feel-good' Reaganomics, and the unleashing of free market policies in that country) were often persuaded in the later 1980s that the rewards accruing from some forms of property crime were more compelling than the benefits of legitimate employment or the weekly welfare cheque, or alternatively that they were a very useful supplement to these legitimate opportunities. In another study conducted from within the rational choice framework, Philip J. Cook (1986) suggested that the emphasis in that literature on 'target-hardening' was making many private homes and public buildings far less vulnerable to criminal attacks, and he wondered whether this might be having the effect on 'displacing' crime on to other targets. He speculated that the displacement effect might, in fact, be different for different types of offence, and that this needed detailed research. There is certainly evidence of this kind of displacement effect at work in studies of the policing of prostitution in both Britain and Canada. It is not so much that the reduction of opportunities in one place reduces the overall prevalence of the offence behaviour; it is rather that the offending behaviour comes to be reorganized elsewhere in response to intrusive neighbourhood responses and intrusive policing (Lowman 1989; Matthews 1986).

Application of this kind of cost–benefit analysis to crime and to crime control is replete with methodological and theoretical problems.[7] Not the least of these problems is the continuing lack of interest among utilitarian economists in models of human action other than those of the 'rational' Economic Man. Sociologists in general, and most sociologically informed criminologists, would see any such model as far too one-dimensional and as far too inattentive to the symbolic and cultural dimensions of social life. But it is interesting, on the other hand, to note the interest in rational choice theory shown by such an influential social thinker as Anthony Giddens. For Giddens,

> situational interpretations of crime can quite easily be connected to the labelling approach, because they clarify one feature of criminality about which labelling theory is silent: why many people who are in no way 'abnormal' choose to engage in acts which they know could be followed by criminal sanctions. (1989: 133)

[7] For discussion of some of the issues involved in cost–benefit analysis of the deterrent effects of punishment, especially in the work of Ehrlich (1973), see Beyleveld (1980).

Closely associated with this difficulty is the problem of the continuing insistence of economic analysts on extraordinarily restrictive and essentially quite ideological notions of 'social costs', usually referring to the 'costs' of crime (or other socially problematic human activities) on propertied individuals or institutions within societies as currently and unequally constituted.[8] In the later 1980s, however, there was a perceptible shift in the debate around the social costs of crime and crime control. Both in the USA and in Britain, there was an increasingly widespread recognition that the extraordinary level of state investment in crime control was demonstrably an ineffective kind of investment, inappropriate in a political culture in which all other forms of public expenditure were subject to increasingly stringent scrutiny.

In Britain these concerns were first voiced, ironically enough, by the so-called left realist school in respect of the declining efficiency of a police force which had been in receipt, from the early 1980s, of increasingly generous state support—particularly as measured by the paltry clear-up rates in offences reported by the public (the consumer) to the police (the service-provider) (Kinsey *et al.* 1986). In the USA, particular attention was rapid to the continuing contradiction between the massive increase in the prison population that occurred in that country in the 1980s, with 673,565 sentenced prisoners in state and federal institutions in June 1989, compared to 128,466 in 1974 (Greenberg 1990: 40) and the continuing escalation in crimes of violence, robberies, and other disruptive and disorderly behaviours on American streets. Edwin Zedlewski, an economist based at the National Institute of Justice, published two studies (1985, 1987) arguing that these increases in numbers imprisoned were indeed 'cost-effective'. But these studies have subsequently been subjected to a close critical examination by Greenberg, who shows that Zedlewski's computatations of both costs and benefits are highly ideological (Greenberg 1990). In particular, Zedlewski's computation of the costs of imprisonment does not include or measure the costs of imprisonment to the imprisoned, and no normative argument is advanced to justify this exclusion. Nor is his computation of the benefits accruing to 'society' from imprisonment placed within any *comparative evaluation* of the benefits—in terms of reduction in crime and in public anxieties, and an increased sense of well-being—that might result from state expenditures in respect of health, education, transportation, or other areas of the 'public good'.

The cost of crime to the British state, though not at the level identified by Zedlewski for the USA in 1989 ($61.4 billion), is certainly of increasing significance. According to a Home Office Working Group reporting

[8] For discussion of the concept of social cost in the propagandist literature of free market economists from the mid-1970s to the present day, see Taylor (1991*b*).

in 1988 (Home Office 1988: 30–2), computation of the overall 'costs of crime' in the United Kingdom in the late 1980s would have to include:

1. *Compensation to victims of crime* £52,042,521 (excluding Northern Ireland), plus £7 million administrative costs of the Criminal Injuries Compensation Board.
2. *Policing* Overall cost of policing England and Wales in 1987: £3,500 million.
3. *Crown Prosecution Service* £170 million for 1987/8.
4. *Legal aid in criminal cases* £200 million in 1986/7.
5. *Criminal courts* Expenditure on Crown Court in 1986/7: £144 million; on magistrates' courts in 1986/7: £179 million.
6. *Probation service* Total costs of probation service in 1986/7 (in England and Wales only) £215 million.
7. *Prison service* Expenditure in 1986/7: £698 million (England and Wales).

The Home Office's figures, all from the late 1980s, do not claim to cover the overall cost to the state of crime (it does not include the cost of social workers), but, even on such an incomplete account (and recognizing that expenditure on policing may be seen as incurred for purposes other than the control of crime alone), it is apparent that the costs of these criminal justice institutions in England and Wales must comprise at least £5,000 million per year. It is unsurprising that analysts have begun to apply some version of cost–benefit analysis to these expenditures and, in particular, that social scientists with a critical interest in the larger issue of the public (rather than merely private) good have begun to ask whether these expenditures justify themselves—particularly in comparison to other imaginable patterns of expenditure of public monies in the interest of crime reduction in neighbourhoods and public territories and the creation of a sense of safety and civility in everyday public life.

Before leaving the discussion of the application of utilitarian analysis to crime, attention should be drawn to some of the other issues that are usually ignored in the application of such an approach to crime and crime control. Probably most important of all is the complete absence of attention to the substantive social inequalities that are entailed in the routine operation of the political economies of Western free market capitalist societies—inequalities that are more obvious in Britain in terms of class, and in the USA in terms of race, but inequalities (of opportunity and position) that are also quite fundamental in terms of gender. This inattention to substantive inequalities extends to a complete lack of curiosity on the part of cost–benefit analysts with respect to the inequalities that routinely structure the application of penal discipline and other measures of social control. In the United States, for example, recent figures have shown that one in four black men in the 20–29 age group is in prison, on probation, or on parole, compared to one in sixteen whites (Walker 1991). In the UK, recent research has shown that entirely different assumptions inform the policing of tax evasion and other forms of fraud by the well off, on the one hand, and fraudulent supplementary benefit (welfare) claims by the poor, on the other (Cook 1989*a*, *b*). In 1987/8, for example, there were only 322 Inland Revenue presentations for tax fraud and evasion, compared with 9,847 prosecutions by the DHSS for supplementary benefit fraud (Cook 1989*b*: 120). In 1982, according to a study by the National Association for the Care and Resettlement of Offenders, 268 'social security offenders' had actually been imprisoned, compared to only thirty-two tax evaders (Cook 1989*a*: 160), and subsequent analysis does not suggest any marked shift away from this differential application of punishment. The relationship between the everyday operation of these systems and the broad society's definition of itself as a democratic and just social formation is starkly posed. Although this is an issue which conventional proponents of cost–benefit analysis have almost entirely ignored, it is one which is attracting more attention as the routine costs of a repressive and expansive criminal justice system continue to escalate.

CRIME AND FREE MARKET SOCIETIES

A key feature of the utilitarian economic analysis of the costs and benefits of crime discussed in the last section is its continuing reification of 'the economy', separated off, in this kind of analysis, from the kinds of social and political relations which help to arrange and structure economic life, and the outcomes for individuals of particular patterns or economic activity that obtain in particular societies at particular times. It is not only that this kind of analysis is insensitive, in a descriptive and empirical sense, to broad historical change—from the period of imperial pioneer capitalism in the late nineteenth century, via the period of Keynesian or welfare state mixed economies in the mid-twentieth century (variously referred to as the period of compromise between capital and labour or the period of social reconstruction) to the contemporary period of deregulation and privatization (the 'free market experiment'). It is also that it shows no interest in *evaluating*, in a theoretical, interrogatory, or morally curious fashion, the kinds of relationship that could be thought to exist between particular types of political economy and the character of social relations (including crime and the broader, connected question—now very much on the agenda in most free market societies—of the 'quality of life').

In an unpublished lecture originally given in London in November 1990, the social democratic American criminologist, Elliott Currie, observed that post-war America was, in effect, a kind of 'natural laboratory' for examining the social effects of the freeing of market forces now under way in Europe, and he noted how the extraordinary triumphalist celebration of these free market policies within the USA during the 1980s had also been accompanied by quite frightening newspaper and television reports of crime on the 'ominous underside' of these policies (Currie 1990*a*).[9] These stories could not fail to acknowledge the growth of poverty and homelessness (signified, in the USA, by the phenomenon of the 'bag lady'), the sudden increases in preventable illnesses, and galloping inner-city drug abuse, in addition to the continuing sharp rises in the 'already staggering levels of violent crime, which [had] long set [America] apart from every other advanced industrial nation' (Currie 1990*a*: 3). Currie proceeded to argue that there was, indeed, a kind of causal relationship between the advent of 'market society' and the acceleration of violent crime, drug abuse, and other forms of social dislocation in America. This revolved around at least five 'links' or connections (Currie 1990*a*: 10–20).

1. The promotion in market society of increased inequality and concentration economic depression.
2. The erosion by market society of the capacity of local communities for informal support, mutual provision, and effective supervision of the young.
3. Market society's promotion of crime via the stress and fragmentation it produces in the family.[10]
4. Market society's promotion of crime via its withdrawal of public provision of basic services from those it has already stripped of livelihoods, economic security, and community support.
5. Market society's promotion of crime via its magnification of a culture of Darwinian competition for status and resources and its encouragement of a level of consumption it cannot provide for everyone through legitimate channels.

Many of these links or connections are illustrated and, some would argue, confirmed in Mike Davis's extraordinary account of the growth of

[9] For two different elaborations of the social democratic critique of free market economies in the USA, see Currie (1990*b*) and Henry and Brown (1990).

[10] Currie's use of the term 'family' here (rather than household) should not identify him as an apologist for patriarchy, as his work as a whole is notably attentive to the particularly destructive effects on women of the pursuit of free market goals in the USA. In Britain, Pat Carlen has been at the forefront of the attempt to link the 'feminization of poverty' resulting from the Thatcher experiment with the increasing problems of women with respect to crime and the imposition of social control. The proportionate use of imprisonment for women has doubled in Britain in the last ten years and there is now a significant tendency for women to be sent to prison for less serious offences than men (Carlen 1988: 4).

gang violence and the drug trade in Los Angeles consequent on the de-industrialization of southern California in the early to mid-1980s (Davis 1990). Many of them are also evident in the continuing acceleration of property crime and violence in many inner-city areas and council estates in Britain in the early 1990s. They may also find expression, of course, in the explosion in the number and variety of forms of fraud and market crime coming to public attention, as the Darwinian struggle for material self-aggrandizement that characterized the deregulation of the early to mid-1980s translates into a recessionary struggle for economic survival.

We cannot conclude, however, that the current explosion of property crime and violence in Britain, coincident as it undoubtedly has been with the free market experiment of the Thatcher government, is proof positive of a straightforward, law-like relation between the free market economy and something called crime. In the mid-1970s, conservatively minded criminologists like James Q. Wilson in the USA and Patricia Morgan in Britain wanted to argue, by complete contrast, that there was a relationship between the post-war development of a welfare state and of Keynesian intervention into the economy, on the one hand, and a generalized cultural condition of 'state dependency', on the other. They also argued that this form of dependency—which Morgan, in particular, associated with 'social democracy'—produced a kind of amoral self-interest in society, particularly in the so-called underclass (Wilson 1975; Morgan 1978). In this perspective there was also a causal relationship between the social democratic belief in state intervention *per se* as an answer to both economic and social problems, and the failure of parents and the state education system to provide appropriate moral socialization and education of the young. What neither Wilson or Morgan may have anticipated were the extraordinary debacles involved in the deregulation of financial markets in the 1980s, from the Boesky affair in 1986 to the collapse of the Bank of Credit and Commerce International in 1991, and the subsequent difficulties posed for proponents of the free market economy themselves in addressing the issue of moral socialization 'by example'.

These are large issues, but *contra* the assumptions of many practitioners of the tired discipline of applied economics, they are absolutely the stuff of a proper political economy, applied broadly to discussions of moral and social order. So also, it must be said, are the issues posed in respect of 'the economy' and 'crime' by the kind of sociological project initiated in the work of Robert Merton, aimed at making sense of the cultural strains involved in particular forms of economic organization at particular historical moments. Ironically enough, the advent of the free market economy in North America and Britain in the 1980s, with its extraordinarily negative impact on levels of economic equality, may actually have undermined the credibility of material success as a viable success goal in many segments of the social formation. It may also, simultaneously, have created the conditions for the explosion of a large variety of new forms of 'white-collar' enterprise crime, from insider trading to the international laundering of drug money. The investigation of these developments is properly a responsibility of contemporary sociology. There are, in fact, pressing issues of causal explanation, as well as profound challenges in respect of moral argument, involved in understanding the working of free market political economies. They are issues of profound importance, too, for criminology in the 1990s and beyond.

Selected Further Reading

Elliott Currie, *Confronting Crime: An American Challenge*. New York: Pantheon, 1985.

Elliott Currie, 'Heavy with Human Tears: Free Market Policy, Inequality and Social Provision in the United States', in Ian Taylor, ed., *The Social Effects of Free Market Policies*. Hemel Hempstead: Harvester Wheatsheaf, 1991.

Mike Davis, *City of Quartz*. London: Verso, 1992.

Ian Taylor, 'Left Realist Criminology and the Free Market Experiment in Britain', in Jock Young and Roger Matthews, eds., *Rethinking Criminology: The Realist Debate*. London: Sage, 1992.

REFERENCES

ARNOLD, M. (1965 [1869]), *Culture and Anarchy*, ed. R. H. Super. Ann Arbor: University of Michigan Press.

AVIO, K., and CLARK, S. (1976), *Property Crime in Canada: An Econometric Study*. Toronto: University of Toronto Press.

BECKER, G. S. (1968), 'Crime and Punishment: An Economic Approach', *Journal of Political Economy*, 76: 169–217.

BEYLEVELD, D. (1980), *A Bibliography on General Deterrence Research*. Farnborough: Saxon House.

BLATCHFORD, R. (1906), *Not Guilty: A Defence of the Bottom Dog*. London: Clarendon Press.

BLUM, R. H. (1984), *Offshore Haven Banks, Trusts and Companies: the Business of Crime in the Euromarket*. New York: Praeger.

BONGER, W. (1969 [1916]), *Criminality and Economic Conditions*. Bloomington: Indiana University Press.

BOX, S. (1987), *Recession, Crime and Punishment*. London: Macmillan.

Box, S., and Hale, C. (1982), 'Economic Crisis and the Rising Prisoner Population in England and Wales', *Crime and Social Justice*, 17: 20–35.

—— (1985), 'Unemployment, Imprisonment and Prison Over-crowding', *Contemporary Crises*, 9: 209–28.

Braverman, H. (1974), *Labour and Monopoly Capital: The Degradation of Work in the Twentieth Century*. New York: Monthly Review Press.

Brenner, H. (1971), *Time Series Analysis of Relationships Between Selected Economic and Social Indicators, vol. 1: Texts and Appendices*. Washington, DC: US Government Printing Office.

—— (1977), 'Health Costs and Benefits of Economic Policy', *International Journal of Health Services*, 7: 581–623.

—— (1978), 'Impact of Economic Indicators on Crime Indices', in *Unemployment and Crime*, hearing before the Subcommittee on the Judiciary, House of Representatives, 59th Congress, first and second sessions. Serial no. 47: 20–54.

Carlen, P. (1988), *Women, Crime and Poverty*. Milton Keynes: Open University Press.

—— (1989), 'Introduction' in P. Carlen and D. Cook, eds., *Paying for Crime*. Milton Keynes: Open University Press.

Carlen, P. and Cook, D., eds. (1989), *Paying for Crime*. Milton Keynes: Open University Press.

Carr-Hill, R., and Stern, J. (1979), *Crime, the Police and Criminal Statistics*. New York: Academic Press.

Clarke, J., Crichter, C., Hall, S., and Jefferson, T. (1978), 'Subcultures, Cultures and Class', in S. Hall and T. Jefferson, eds., *Resistance through Rituals*', 99–102. London: Hutchinson.

Clarke, R. V. G., and Cornish, D. B. (1985), 'Modelling Offenders' Decisions: Framework for Research and Policy', in M. Tonry and N. Morris, eds., *Crime and Justice: An Annual Review of Research*, 147–86. Chicago: University of Chicago Press.

Clay, J. (1855), 'On the Effect of Good or Bad Times on Committals to Prison', *Journal of the Statistical Society of London*, 18: 74–9.

Cloward, R. E., and Ohlin, L. E. (1960), *Delinquency and Opportunity: A Theory of Delinquent Gangs*. New York: Free Press.

Cohen, P. (1972), 'Subcultural Conflict and Working Class Community'. *Working Papers in Cultural Studies*, 2: 5–52.

Cook, D. (1989*a*), *Rich Law, Poor Law: Different Responses to Tax and Supplementary Benefit Fraud*. Milton Keynes: Open University Press.

—— (1989*b*), 'Fiddling Tax and Benefits: Inculpating the Poor, Exculpating the Rich', in P. Carlen and D. Cook, eds., *Paying for Crime*, 109–27. Milton Keynes: Open University Press.

Cook, P. J. (1986), 'The Demand and Supply of Criminal Opportunities', in M. Tonry and N. Morris, eds., *Crime and Justice: An Annual Review of Research*, vol. 7, 1–27. Chicago: University of Chicago Press.

Cornish, D. B., and Clarke, R. V. G. (1986), *The Reasoning Criminal: Rational Choice Perspectives on Offending*. New York: Springer-Verlag.

Currie, Elliott (1990*a*), 'Crime and Free Market Society: Lessons from the United States', unpublished lecture given to international conference on

'Crime and Policing 1992: A Global Perspective', Islington, London, November.

—— (1990*b*), 'Heavy with Human Tears: Free Market Policy, Inequality and Social Provision in the United States', in Ian Taylor, ed., *The Social Effects of Free Market Policies*, 299–318. Hemel Hempstead: Harvester Wheatsheaf.

—— (1991), *Dope and Trouble: Portraits of Delinquent Youth*. New York: Pantheon.

DAVIS, M. (1988), 'Nightmares in Los Angeles', *New Left Review* 170 (July/August): 37–60.

—— (1990), *City of Quartz: Excavating the Future in Los Angeles*. London: Verso.

DEBS, E. (1927), *Walls and Bars*. Chicago: Socialist Party.

EHRLICH, I. (1973), 'Participation in Illegitimate Activities: A Theoretical and Empirical Investigation', *Journal of Political Economy*, 81: 531–67.

EYER, J. (1977), 'Review of Mental Illness and the Economy', *International Journal of Health Services*, 6: 139–48.

—— (1981), 'Prosperity as a Cause of Death', *International Journal of Health Services*, 7: 125–50.

FIELD, S. (1991), *Trends in Crime and their Interpretation: A Study of Recorded Crime in Post-war England and Wales*, Home Office Research Study no. 119. London: HMSO.

GIDDENS, A. (1989), *Sociology*. Cambridge: Polity Press.

—— (1991), *Modernity and Self-Identity*. Cambridge: Polity.

GREENBERG, D. (1977), 'The Dynamics of Oscillatory Punishment Processes', *Journal of Criminal Law and Criminology*, 68: 643–51.

—— (1990), 'The Cost–Benefit Analysis of Imprisonment', *Social Justice*, 17: 49–75.

GUERRY, A.-M. (1833), *Statistique morale d'Angleterre comparée avec la statistique morale de la France*. Paris.

HABERMAS, J. (1989), 'The New Obscurity: The Crisis of the Welfare State and the Exhaustion of Utopian Energies', in Shierry Weber Nicholsen, ed., *The New Conservatism: Cultural Criticism and the Historians' Debate*, 48–70. Cambridge: Polity Press.

HAKIM, C. (1982), 'The Social Consequences of High Unemployment', *Journal of Social Policy*, 11: 433–67.

HALL, S. and JACQUES, M., eds. (1990), *New Times: The Changing Face of Politics in the 1990s*. London: Lawrence and Wishart.

HENRY, S. and BROWN, J. (1990), 'Something for Nothing: The Informal Outcomes of Free Market Policies', in Ian Taylor, ed., *The Social Effects of Free Market Policies*, 319–48. Hemel Hempstead: Harvester Wheatsheaf.

HIRSCHI, T., and GOTTFREDSON, M. (1986), 'The Distinction between Crime and Criminality', in T. F. Hartnagel and R. A. Silverman, eds., *Critique and Explanation: Essays in Honour of Gwynn Nettler*. New Brunswick, NJ: Transaction.

HOME OFFICE (1988), *Report of the Working Group on the Costs of Crime* (Standing Conference on Crime Prevention, 6 December). London: Home Office.

Hutton, W. (1992), 'How Whitehall Cut the Dole Queues', *The Guardian*, 11 November.

Jackson, G. (1970), *Soledad Brother*. Penguin: Harmondsworth.

Jankovic, I. (1977), 'Labour Market and Imprisonment', *Crime and Social Justice*, 9: 17–31.

Jones, J. A. (1971), 'Federal Efforts to Solve Social Problems', in Ervin O. Smigel, ed., *Handbook on the Study of Social Problems*, 547–90. Chicago: Rand McNally.

Kellough, D. G., Brickney, S. L., and Greenaway, W. K. (1980), 'The Politics of Incarceration: Manitoba 1918–1939', *Canadian Journal of Sociology*, 5: 253–71.

Kinsey, R., Lea, J., and Young, J. (1986), *Losing the Fight against Crime*. Oxford: Blackwell.

Lash, S., and Urry, J. (1987), *The End of Organized Capitalism*. Cambridge: Polity.

Lea, J., and Young, J. (1984), *What is to be Done about Law and Order*? London: Penguin.

Lehtinen, M. (1977), 'The Value of Life: An Argument for the Death Penalty', *Crime and Delinquency*, 23: 237–52.

Levi, M. (1988), *Regulating Fraud: White Collar Crime and the Criminal Process*. London: Tavistock.

Longford, F., ed. (1964), *Crime: A Challenge to Us All*. London: The Labour Party.

Lowman, J. (1989), *Street Prostitution: Assessing the Impact of the Law in Vancouver*. Ottawa: Department of Justice.

McConohay, M. J., and Kirk, R. (1988), 'Over There: America's Drug War Abroad', *Mother Jones*, 14/2: 36–9.

Marx, K. (1969 [1862–3], 'The Apologist Conception for the Productivity of All Professions', in *Theories of Surplus Value*, vol. 1, 387–8. Moscow: Foreign Languages Publishing House.

Matthews, R. (1986), *Policing Prostitution: A Multi-Agency Approach*. Middlesex Polytechnic Centre for Criminology Paper no. 1. London: Middlesex Polytechnic.

Mayhew, P. M., Clarke, R. V. G., Sturman, A., and Hough, J. M. (1976), *Crime as Opportunity*, Home Office Research Paper no. 34. London: HMSO.

Mayhew, P., and Maung, N. A. (1992), *Surveying Crime: Findings from the 1992 Crime Survey*. London: Home Office Research and Statistics Department.

Melossi, D. (1985), 'Punishment and Social Action: Changing Vocabularies of Motive Within a Political Business Cycle', *Current Perspectives in Social Theory*, 6: 169–97.

Merton, R. K. (1963 [1938]), 'Social Structure and Anomie', *American Sociological Review*, 3: 672–82; repr. in *Social Theory and Social Structure*, Glencoe: Free Press, 1957; rev. edn. 1963.

Morgan, P. (1978), *Delinquent Fantasies*. London: Temple Smith.

Murray, C. (1990), *The Emerging British Underclass* (with responses by Frank Field, Joan C. Brown, Nicholas Deakin, and Alan Walker). London: IEA Health and Welfare Unit.

PETRAS, J., and DAVENPORT, C. (1991), 'Crime and the Development of Capitalism', *Crime, Law and Social Change*, 16: 155–75.

PILIAVIN, I., GARTNER, R., THORNTON, C., and MATSUEDA, R. L. (1986), 'Crime, Deterrence and Rational Choice' *American Sociological Review*, 51: 101–19.

PIORE, M., and SABEL, C. (1984), *The Second Industrial Divide*. New York: Basic Books.

QUETELET, A. (1835), *Sur l'homme et le developpement de ses facultés; essai de physique sociale*. Paris: Bachelier.

REIMAN, J. (1979), *The Rich get Richer and the Poor get Prison: Ideology, Class and Criminal Justice*. New York: Wiley (2nd edn. 1984).

ROWNTREE, J. and ROWNTREE, M. (1970), 'The Political Economy of Youth', *Our Generation*, 6/1–2; repr. in pamphlet form by the Radical Education Project, Ann Arbor, Michigan.

RUSCHE, G., and KIRCHHEIMER, O. (1939), *Punishment and Social Structure*. New York: Russell and Russell.

RUSKIN, J. (1985 [1862]), *Unto this Last*, ed. Clive Wilmer. Harmondsworth: Penguin.

RUSSELL, W. (1847), Abstract of the 'Statistics of Crime in England and Wales from 1839 to 1843', *Journal of the Statistical Society of London*, 10: 38–61.

SANTINO, U. (1988), 'The Financial Mafia: The Illegal Accumulation of Wealth and the Financial-Industrial Complex', *Contemporary Crises*, 12/3: 203–44.

SCULL, A. (1977), *Decarceration*. Englewood Cliffs, NJ: Prentice-Hall.

SELLIN, T. (1937), *Research Memorandum on Crime in the Depression*. New York: Social Science Research Council, *Bulletin* no. 27.

SILBERMAN, M. (1976), 'Towards a Theory of Criminal Deterrence', *American Sociological Review*, 41: 442–61.

SIMON, W., and GAGNON, J. H. (1976), 'The Anomie of Affluence: A Post-Mertonian Conception', *American Journal of Sociology*, 82/2: 356–77.

SINFIELD, A. (1981), *What Unemployment Means*. Oxford: Martin Robertson.

—— (1992), 'The Impact of Unemployment upon Welfare', in Z. Ferge and J. E. Kolberg, eds., *Social Policy in a Changing Europe*. Frankfurt: Campus; Boulder: Westview Press.

SPITZER, S. (1975), 'Toward a Marxian Theory of Deviance', *Social Problems*, 22: 638–51.

—— (1983), 'The Rationalization of Crime Control in Capitalist Society', in S. Cohen and A. Scull, eds., *Social Control and the State*, 312–34. Oxford: Martin Robertson.

STERN, J. (1982), 'Does Unemployment Really Kill?', *New Society*, 10 June: 421–2.

STEWART, J. B. (1991), *Den of Thieves*. New York: Simon and Schuster.

SUTHERLAND, E. H. (1948), *White Collar Crime*. New Haven: Yale University Press.

TAYLOR, I. (199*a*), 'A Social Role for the Prison: Edward Carpenter's "Prisons, Police and Punishment" (1905)', *International Journal of the Sociology of Law*, 19: 1–26.

—— (1991*b*), 'The Concept of Social Cost in Free Market Theory and the Social Costs of Free Market Policies', in Ian Taylor, ed., *The Social Effects of Free Market Policies*', 1–26. Hemel Hempstead: Harvester Wheatsheaf.

Taylor, I. (1992), 'The International Drug, Trade and Money-Laundering: Border Controls and Other Issues, *European Sociological Review*, 8/2: 181–93.

Tittle, C. (1977), 'Sanctions, Fear and the Maintenance of Social Order', *Social Forces*, 55: 579–96.

—— (1980), *Sanctions and Social Deviance: The Question of Deterrence*. New York: Praeger.

Vold, G. V. (1958), *Theoretical Criminology*. New York: Oxford University Press.

von Mayr, G. (1867), *Statistik der Gerichtlichen Polizei im Königreiche Bayern und in einigen anderen Länderen*. Munich.

Walker, M. (1991), 'Sentencing System Blights Land of the Free', *The Guardian*, 19 June.

Wiers, P. (1945), 'Wartime Increase in Michigan Delinquency', *American Sociological Review*, 10: 515–23.

Wilson, J. Q. (1975), *Thinking about Crime*. New York: Basic Books.

Wilson, W. J. (1987), *The Truly Disadvantaged: The Inner City, the Underclass and Public Policy*. Chicago: University of Chicago Press.

Zedlewski, E. W. (1985), 'When Have We Punished Enough?', *Public Administration Review*, 45: 771–9.

—— (1987), *Making Confinement Decisions*. Washington, DC: US Department of Justice.

12

Human Development and Criminal Careers

DAVID P. FARRINGTON

The aim of this chapter is to review what is known about human development and criminal careers. A 'criminal career' is defined as the longitudinal sequence of offences committed by an individual offender. 'Offences' in this chapter are defined as the most common types of crimes that predominate in the official criminal statistics, including theft, burglary, robbery, violence, vandalism, and drug use. 'White-collar' crime is not included here, because there has been little attempt as yet to study it from the perspective of human development and criminal careers.

A criminal career has a beginning (onset), and end (desistance), and a career length in between (duration). Only a certain proportion of the population (prevalence) has a criminal career and commits offences. During their careers, offenders commit offences at a certain rate (frequency) while they are at risk of offending in the community (e.g. not incarcerated or hospitalized). For offenders who commit several offences, it is possible to investigate how far they specialize in certain types of offences and how far the seriousness of their offending escalates over time.

The criminal career approach is essentially concerned with human development over time. However, criminal behaviour does not generally appear without warning; it is commonly preceded by childhood anti-social behaviour (such as bullying, lying, truanting, and cruelty to animals) and followed by adult anti-social behaviour (such as spouse assault, child abuse and neglect, excessive drinking, and sexual promiscuity). The word 'anti-social', of course, involves a value judgement; but it seems likely that there would be general agreement among most members of western democracies that these kinds of acts were antipathetic to the smooth running of western society.

It is argued that offending is part of a larger syndrome of anti-social behaviour that arises in childhood and tends to persist into adulthood. There seems to be continuity over time, since the anti-social child tends to become the anti-social teenager and then the anti-social adult, just as the anti-social adult then tends to produce another anti-social child.

In order to understand and explain the development of offending and anti-social behaviour from childhood to adulthood, it is important to bring together knowledge from the disparate fields of developmental psychopathology and criminal career research, and this is one of the aims of this chapter. (For other efforts to unite these two fields, see Loeber and LeBlanc 1990; Tonry *et al.* 1991.) Just as it is possible to investigate the onset, desistance, frequency, and duration of the types of behaviour defined as offences, it is also possible to study the onset, desistance, frequency, and duration of other types of anti-social acts. This chapter reviews knowledge about onset and other career features of offending and anti-social behaviour.

In studying development, it is important to investigate developmental sequences over time, for example where one behaviour facilitates or acts as a kind of stepping-stone to another. It is desirable to identify non-criminal behaviours that lead to criminal behaviours, and long-term developmental sequences including types of offending. For example, hyperactivity at age 2 may lead to cruelty to animals at 6, shoplifting at 10, burglary at 15, robbery at 20, and eventually spouse assault, child abuse and neglect, alcohol abuse, and employment and accommodation problems later on in life. Typically, a career of childhood anti-social behaviour leads to a criminal career, which often coincides with a career of teenage anti-social behaviour and leads to a career of adult anti-social behaviour. The criminal career is a legally defined subset of a longer-term and more wide-ranging anti-social career. A deeper understanding of the development of the criminal career requires a deeper understanding of the wider anti-social career.

This chapter also reviews risk factors that influence the development of anti-social and criminal careers. Fortunately or unfortunately, there is no shortage of factors that are significantly correlated with offending and anti-social behaviour; indeed, literally thousands of variables differentiate significantly between official offenders and non-offenders and correlate significantly with reports of anti-social behaviour by teenagers, peers, parents, and teachers. In this chapter, it is possible only to review briefly some of the most important risk factors for offending and anti-social behaviour: individual difference factors such as high impulsivity and low intelligence, family influences such as poor child-rearing and anti-social parents, socio-economic deprivation, peer influences such as having delinquent friends, school factors, community characteristics such as social disorganization, and situational factors. Because of the chapter's focus on human development, unchanging variables such as sex and race are not reviewed.

The chapter ends with a brief review of the theoretical and policy implications of research on human development and criminal careers. An attempt is made to propose a simple theory that accounts for as much of the complex reality as possible, and implications for crime prevention and crime control are discussed. The emphasis is on anti-social behaviour by males; most research on offending and anti-social behaviour has concentrated on males, because they commit most of the serious predatory and violent offences. The review is limited to research carried out in the UK, the USA, and other western democracies. In light of the scope of this handbook, most research quoted here is on offending rather than on other types of anti-social behaviour.

Within a single chapter, it is obviously impossible to review everything that is known about the development of offending and anti-social behaviour. (For more detailed reviews of risk factors, see Rutter and Giller 1983; Wilson and Herrnstein 1985.) I will be very selective in focusing on some of the more important and replicable findings obtained in some of the more methodologically adequate studies, especially longitudinal studies of large community samples.

In studying human development, it is essential to carry out prospective longitudinal surveys. I will refer especially to knowledge gained in the Cambridge Study in Delinquent Development, which is a prospective longitudinal survey of over 400 London males from age 8 to age 32 (Farrington and West 1990). However, similar results have been obtained in similar projects elsewhere in England (e.g. Kolvin *et al.* 1988, 1990), in the USA (e.g. McCord 1979; Robins 1979), in the Scandinavian countries (e.g. Wikström 1987; Pulkkinen 1988), and in New Zealand (e.g. Moffitt and Silva 1988*a*). While most longitudinal surveys of offending and anti-social behaviour focus primarily on lower-class and urban samples, some are based on large representative samples from the whole population (e.g. Wikström 1987; Moffitt and Silva 1988*a*).

CONCEPTUAL AND METHODOLOGICAL ISSUES

The Anti-social Syndrome

While the acts defined as offences are heterogeneous, it nevertheless makes sense to investigate the characteristics of offenders. This is because offenders are predominantly versatile rather than specialized (e.g. Klein 1984; Farrington, Snyder, and Finnegan 1988). In other words, people who commit one type of offence have a significant tendency also to commit other types. For example, 86 per cent of convicted violent offenders in the Cambridge Study also had convictions for non-violent offences (Farrington 1991*b*).

Just as offenders tend to be versatile in their types of offending, so they also tend to be versatile in their anti-social behaviour generally. In the Cambridge Study, delinquents tended to be troublesome and dishonest in their primary schools, tended to be aggressive and frequent liars at age

12–14, and tended to be bullies at age 14. By age 18, delinquents tended to be anti-social in a wide variety of respects, including heavy drinking, heavy smoking, using prohibited drugs, and heavy gambling. In addition, they tended to be sexually promiscuous, often beginning sexual intercourse under age 15, having several sexual partners by age 18, and usually having unprotected intercourse (Farrington 1992*d*).

West and Farrington (1977) argued that delinquency (which is dominated by crimes of dishonesty) was only one element of a larger syndrome of anti-social behaviour which arose in childhood and usually persisted into adulthood. They developed a scale of 'anti-social tendency' at age 18, based on factors such as an unstable job record, heavy gambling, heavy smoking, drug abuse, drunk driving, sexual promiscuity, spending time hanging about on the street, anti-social group activity, violence, and anti-establishment attitudes. Their aim was to devise a scale that was not based on the types of acts (thefts and burglaries) that predominantly led to convictions, and they showed that convicted males were usually anti-social in several other respects. For example, two-thirds (67 per cent) of those convicted up to age 18 had four or more of these anti-social features at that age, compared with only 15 per cent of the unconvicted males.

Farrington (1991*a*) developed more comprehensive scales of 'anti-social personality' at ages 10, 14, 18, and 32, based on offending and on other types of anti-social behaviour. For example, the scale at age 14 included convictions, high self-reported delinquency, stealing outside the home, regular smoking, having sexual intercourse, bullying, frequent lying, frequent disobedience, hostility to police, frequent truancy, daring, and poor concentration/restlessness. All these measures tended to be interrelated. However, the last two measures, of impulsivity, are arguably causes of anti-social behaviour rather than indicators of it. They were included for consistency with psychiatric criteria of anti-social personality disorder; but impulsivity will be reviewed later in this chapter as a risk factor for anti-social behaviour. It is often difficult to distinguish between causes, consequences, and indicators of anti-social personality.

The links between offending and other types of anti-social behaviour have also been found in numerous other studies. For example, in a St Louis survey of black males, Robins and Ratcliff (1980) reported that juvenile delinquency tended to be associated with truancy, precocious sex, drinking, and drug abuse. In two American studies separated by thirteen years, Donovan *et al.* (1988) concluded that a single common factor accounted for the positive correlations among a number of adolescent anti-social behaviours, including problem drinking, marijuana use, precocious sexual intercourse, and delinquent behaviour. Hence, as Jessor and Jessor (1977) argued, there is a syndrome of problem behaviour in adolescence.

In the literature on childhood psychopathology, it is also common to find a single syndrome including stealing, lying, cheating, vandalism, substance abuse, running away from home, and truancy (Achenbach *et al.* 1987). A key issue is how far aggressive acts are part of this syndrome. Conduct disorder is sometimes divided into an aggressive or overt type and a non-aggressive or covert type (Loeber and Schmaling 1985). Since aggressive individuals tend to be serious and versatile in their anti-social behaviour, it seems likely that the difference between overt and covert individuals may be a difference in degree rather than in kind. The difference may also reflect stages of development. Children who are non-aggressive at an early age may escalate to aggression later.

The Criminal Career Approach

The criminal career approach is not a criminological theory but a framework within which theories can be proposed and tested (see Blumstein *et al.* 1986; Blumstein and Cohen 1987). Dictionary definitions of the term 'career' specify two different concepts: a course or progress through life, and a way of making a living. The term is used in the first sense here. A 'criminal career' describes a sequence of offences committed during some part of an individual's lifetime, with no necessary suggestion that offenders use their criminal activity as an important means of earning a living.

The criminal career approach emphasizes the need to investigate such questions as why people start offending (onset), why they continue offending (persistence), why offending becomes more frequent or more serious (escalation), and why people stop offending (desistance). The factors influencing onset may differ from those influencing other criminal career features such as persistence, escalation, and desistance, if only because the different processes occur at different ages. Indeed, Farrington and Hawkins (1991) in the Cambridge Study found that there was no relationship between factors influencing prevalence (official offenders versus non-offenders), those influencing early versus later onset, and those influencing desistance after age 21; and Loeber *et al.* (1991) in the Pittsburgh Youth Study reported no relationship between factors influencing onset and those influencing escalation.

In order to understand the causes of offending, it is important to study developmental processes such as onset, persistence, escalation, and desistance. However, it is also important not to restrict this study narrowly to offending, but to study as well the onset, persistence, escalation and desistance of other types of antisocial behaviour. Loeber and LeBlanc (1990) used many other concepts to describe developmental processes in anti-social careers, including acceleration and deceleration, diversification, switching, stabilization, and de-escalation. For example, 'retention' (escalating to serious acts while still committing trivial acts) was more common than 'innovation' (escalating and giving up trivial acts).

The criminal career approach is essentially concerned with human development over time. Most criminological theories focus on instantaneous or cross-sectional differences between official offenders and non-offenders, or on cross-sectional correlates of the frequency or variety of self-reported offending. Furthermore, most criminological theories aim to explain offending when it is in full flow, in the teenage years. However, the criminal career approach focuses on within individual changes over time and on the predictors of longitudinal processes such as onset and desistance, recognizing that the same person can be an active offender at one age and a non-offender at another. It also aims to explain the development of offending over all ages.

Criminal career research seeks to investigate whether aggregate career features are the same as or different from individual features (Blumstein *et al* 1988). For example, the age–crime curve over all individuals shows that the aggregate rate of offending increases to a peak in the teenage years and then decreases. The shape of this curve may reflect changes in the prevalence of offenders at each age (the proportion of individuals who offend, out of the total population), or changes in the frequency of offending (by those who are offenders at each age), or some combination of these. Most of the existing British and American evidence suggests that the aggregate peak age of offending primarily reflects variations in prevalence, and that individual offenders commit offences at a tolerably constant frequency during their criminal careers (Farrington 1986*a*). On this model, a 30-year-old offender commits offences at roughly the same rate as an 18-year-old offender, although offenders are more prevalent in the population of 18-year-olds than in the population of 30-year-olds. Therefore, the flat age–crime distribution for individual offending frequency is quite different from the peaked distribution for prevalence and from the peaked aggregate age–crime curve.

Putting this point in a slightly different way, a key issue in criminal career research is to determine how far aggregate changes with age or during the course of a criminal career reflect changes within individual offenders as opposed to changes in the composition of the offending population. For example, juvenile offenders primarily commit their crimes with others, whereas adult offenders primarily commit their crimes alone (Reiss and Farrington 1991). Does this finding mean that offenders change their methods of offending as they get older, switching from co-offending to lone offending? Or does it mean that one population of co-offenders desists (drop out) and is replaced by a new population of lone offenders? The answer to this kind of question, which arises very frequently, has important theoretical and policy implications. Generally, the evidence suggests that changes occur within one population of offenders at different ages, rather than some offenders desisting and being replaced at later ages by a new population of offenders.

Similarly, criminal career researchers emphasize that different career features may be differently related to age. It has already been pointed out that prevalence peaks in the teenage years but that the individual offending frequency may not. Blumstein *et al.* (1982) found that the residual length of a criminal career (the time remaining up to the point of desistance) peaked between ages 30 and 40. While teenage offenders are quite prevalent in the teenage population, the average teenage offender does not commit offences at a particularly high frequency and tends to have only a relatively short criminal career remaining. Hence, the peak prevalence in the teenage years does not imply that criminal justice measures such as incapacitation should be especially targeted on teenagers. In contrast, 30-year-old offenders are much less prevalent in the population of 30-year-olds, but the average 30-year-old offender tends to have a relatively long criminal career remaining. Looked at developmentally, 30-year-old offenders tend to be a subset of teenage offenders. Most teenage offenders desist from offending before age 30.

A key feature of the criminal career approach is its emphasis on the development of explicit mathematical models and the testing of quantitative predictions (for more details, see Farrington 1992*a*). These predictions are usually probabilistic rather than deterministic. The aim is to propose models that are simplifications of reality but that explain complex data. For example, it is unlikely that the individual offending frequency is exactly constant over time, but it is possible to fit criminal career data on this simple assumption. Most models are stochastic, assuming that the occurrence of measured offences (e.g. convictions) depends to some extent on chance processes.

Definitions and Measurement

Anti-social behaviour covers a multitude of sins. It includes acts prohibited by the criminal law, such as theft, burglary, robbery, violence, vandalism, and drug abuse; as already mentioned, the definition of 'offending' in this chapter focuses on these types of acts. It also includes other clearly deviant acts such as bullying, reckless driving, heavy drinking, and sexual promiscuity, and more marginally or arguably deviant acts such as heavy smoking, heavy gambling, employment instability, and conflict with parents. All of these acts tend to be interrelated, in the sense that people who commit any one of them have a considerably increased risk of committing any of the others (West and Farrington 1977).

Certain types of anti-social behaviour are used as diagnostic criteria for the psychiatric category of 'conduct disorder' in the International Classification of Diseases of the World Health Organization, ICD-10, and in the *Diagnostic and Statistical Manual* of the American Psychiatric Association, DSM-IIIR (see e.g. Robins 1991). The major types are stealing, running away from home, lying, arson, truancy, burglary, vandalism, forced sex, fighting, robbery, and cruelty to people and animals. Conduct disorder is currently diagnosed when the disturbed behaviour persists for at least six months and includes at least two (ICD-10) or three (DSM-IIIR) of the specified behaviours. Although this is usually termed childhood conduct disorder, the diagnosis can be made up to age 17, and hence often reflects teenage anti-social behaviour.

The psychiatric category of 'anti-social personality disorder' in DSM-IIIR (American Psychiatric Association 1987) was influenced by Robins's work (e.g. 1979) and applies to adults who fail to maintain close personal relationships with anyone else, perform poorly in their jobs, are involved in crime, fail to support themselves and their dependants without outside aid, drive recklessly, tend to change their plans impulsively, and lose their tempers in response to minor frustrations. According to DSM-IIIR, adult anti-social personality disorder is diagnosed if the anti-social adult displays four out of ten specified symptoms and had shown conduct disorder before age 15. This latter requirement was included because Robins's research showed that, while no more than half of conduct-disordered children became anti-social adults, virtually all anti-social adults had previously shown at least one symptom of conduct disorder. For anti-social adults, the average age of the first childhood symptom was 8 (Robins *et al.* 1991).

The category of adult anti-social personality disorder is closely related to the construct of psychopathy. The best known psychometric measure of this latter construct is the 'Psychopathy Checklist' of Hare (1980, 1986). This focuses slightly more on personality factors than DSM-IIIR, which focuses more on indicators of anti-social behaviour. The Psychopathy Checklist includes criteria such as: superficial charm or conning; an inflated ego; boredom, risk-taking, and excitement-seeking; pathological lying; lack of remorse; cold, lacking emotions and lacking empathy; a parasitic lifestyle; easily becoming angry and aggressive; promiscuous sexual behaviour; child behaviour problems and delinquency; impulsivity and failure to honour financial and family commitments; failure to accept responsibility for actions; and a variety of different offences committed. Despite its slightly different emphasis, Psychopathy Checklist scores in adults are highly correlated with the diagnosis of anti-social personality disorder (e.g. a point-biserial correlation of 0.67 was reported by Hare, 1985).

In England, definitions of psychopathy are more subjective than in North America, and explicit diagnostic checklist criteria have not been developed. In the 1959 and 1983 Mental Health Acts, psychopathic disorder is defined as a persistent disorder 'which results in abnormally aggressive or seriously irresponsible conduct'. According to Walker (1985), British psychiatrists reserve the label of 'psychopath' for persons who show unusual (e.g. sadistic, compulsive) impulses, or who have unusually weak self-control, or who commit crimes without remorse or anxiety about the consequences.

Whether conduct disorder, anti-social personality disorder, and psychopathy should be regarded as illnesses or diseases is arguable. Robins *et al.* (1991) thought that they should, because the symptoms are highly intercorrelated, because they are recognized in different times and places, and because they have genetic components. However, Blackburn (1988) argued that personality characteristics and anti-social behaviour were different and should be carefully distinguished. It is certainly true that intercorrelations between symptoms and interrater reliabilities are high (e.g. Hare 1985; Klinteberg *et al.* 1992). Also, the factor structure of the symptoms typically holds up well in cross-national comparisons (e.g. Raine 1985; Achenbach *et al.* 1987; Harpur *et al.* 1988). However, it is difficult to claim that genetic, physical, or biological causes of the syndromes have been established conclusively.

Anti-social behaviour is usually measured by conducting interviews with or obtaining ratings from parents, peers, teachers, or the subjects themselves. Psychiatric diagnoses such as conduct disorder or anti-social personality disorder are usually made on the basis of clinical interviews. However, conduct disorder can also be measured by having parents, teachers, or adolescents complete checklists of specific symptoms (e.g. Achenbach and Edelbrock 1984). Structured psychiatric interviews which can be administered by non-clinicians, such as the Diagnostic Interview Schedule (DIS) and the Diagnostic Interview Schedule for Children (DISC), and ratings based on systematic observation are also used. There is usually quite high concordance between different measurement methods in identifying disordered individuals (e.g. Boyle *et al.* 1987; Edelbrock and Costello 1988).

Offending is commonly measured using either official records of arrests or convictions, or self-reports of offending. The advantages and disadvantages of official records and self-reports are to some extent complementary. In general, official records include the worst offenders and the worst offences, while self-reports include more of the normal range of delinquent activity. Self-reports have the advantage of including undetected offences, but the disadvantages of concealment and forgetting. The key issue is whether the same results are obtained with both methods. For example, if official records and self-reports both show a link between parental supervision and delinquency, it is likely that supervision is related to delinquent behaviour (rather than to any biases in measurement). This chapter focuses on such replicable results.

Generally, the worst offenders (taking account of frequency and seriousness) according to self-reports tend also to be the worst offenders according to official records (e.g. Farrington 1973; Huizinga and Elliott 1986). For example, in the Cambridge Study, 11 per cent of the males between ages 15 and 18 admitted burglary, and 62 per cent of these males were convicted of burglary (West and Farrington 1977). The predictors and correlates of official and self-reported burglary were very similar (Farrington 1992*c*).

The results obtained in criminal career research depend on the methods of defining and measuring crime that are adopted. Most criminal career researchers focus on official records of arrests or convictions for relatively serious offences rather than on self-reports of relatively trivial infractions. Most criminal career results quoted in this chapter are based on arrests or convictions. With official records of relatively serious offences, the measured prevalence and frequency of offending are lower and the age of onset of offending is later. In principle, there is no reason why the criminal career approach could not be applied to self-reports of relatively trivial offences. It could also be extended (as an 'anti-social career' approach) to cover measures of anti-social but non-criminal behaviour such as cheating, lying, truancy, reckless driving, and getting drunk. In comparing official records and self-reports of the same behaviour, the underlying criminal career parameters (such as the individual offending frequency) might remain the same in each analysis, but the relationship between these parameters and the observed behaviour (e.g. convictions or self-reports) would vary.

Criminal career research requires exact information about the timing of offences. This is available in official records (e.g. of convictions), but not usually in self-reports. It would be convenient for criminal career researchers if offenders would keep regular diaries listing all their offences, but it is difficult to obtain large-scale, demonstrably valid data using this method. It is clear that retrospective self-reports covering long periods of ten years or more are not accurate (see e.g. Yarrow *et al.* 1970). For example, in a systematic comparison of prospective repeated self-reports and long-term retrospective self-reports of offending by the same males, Farrington (1989*c*) found that an average of 46 per cent of all offences admitted prospectively between ages 10 and 25 were denied retrospectively (in response to 'ever' questions) at age 32. The most frequent offenders are likely to have the greatest difficulty in providing valid retrospective self-reports of their offending careers, especially if they have low intelligence and are alcohol or drug abusers. Hence, prospective longitudinal data are needed.

DEVELOPMENT OF OFFENDING AND ANTI-SOCIAL BEHAVIOUR

Prevalence at Different Ages

One of the distinctive contributions of criminal career research has been to demonstrate the high cumulative prevalence of arrests and convictions of males (for a review, see Visher and Roth 1986). For example, in Philadelphia, Wolfgang *et al.* (1987) found that 47 per cent of males were arrested for a non-traffic offence up to age 30, including 38 per cent of whites and 69 per cent of non-whites. In London, Farrington and West (1990) reported that 37 per cent of males were convicted for criminal offences up to age 32, when these were restricted to offences normally recorded in the Criminal Record Office. In Sweden, Stattin *et al.* (1989) discovered that one-third of males (and 7 per cent of females) were officially registered for non-traffic offences by age 30. The curves showing the cumulative prevalence up to age 25 of offending by working-class males in London and Stockholm were remarkably similar (Farrington and Wikström 1993).

The cumulative prevalence of self-reported offences is even higher. In the Cambridge Study, Farrington (1989*c*) showed that 96 per cent of the males had committed at least one of ten specified offences (including burglary, theft, assault, vandalism, and drug abuse) by age 32. Many males commit minor acts, especially in their teenage years, that might, strictly speaking, be classified as offences. In order to compare offenders and non-offenders, it is necessary to set a sufficiently high criterion for 'offending' (e.g. in terms of frequency, seriousness, or duration, or in terms of arrests or convictions) so that the vast majority of the male population are not classified as offenders. Alternatively, more and less serious offenders could be compared.

An important focus of criminal career research is the relationship between age and crime. Generally, the 'point prevalence' of offending at each age increases to a peak in the teenage years and then declines. The age–crime curve obtained by following up a cohort of people over time (the same people at different ages) is often different from the cross-sectional curve seen in official statistics (which reflects different people at different ages; see Farrington 1990*a*). Farrington (1986*a*) proposed a mathematical model for the age–crime curve, with three parameters. The first determined the speed of increase of the curve up to the peak, the second determined the speed of decrease of the curve after the peak, and the third determined the height of the peak.

In the Cambridge Study, the peak age for the prevalence of convictions was 17 (Farrington 1992*b*). The median age of conviction for most types of offences (burglary, robbery, theft of and from vehicles, shoplifting) was 17, while for violence it was 20 and for fraud 21. Similarly, in the Philadelphia cohort study of Wolfgang *et al.* (1987), the arrest rate increased to a peak at age 16 and then declined. In the Cambridge Study, the peak age of increase in the prevalence of offending was at 14, while the peak age of decrease was at 23. These times of maximum acceleration and deceleration in prevalence draw our attention to times in people's lives when important life events may be occurring that influence offending. They also indicate that the modal age of onset of offending is probably 14 and the modal age of desistance is probably 23.

Self-report studies also show that the most common types of offending decline from the teens to the twenties. In the Cambridge Study, the prevalence of burglary, shoplifting, theft of and from vehicles, theft from slot machines, and vandalism all decreased from the teens to the twenties, but the same decreases were not seen for theft from work, assault, drug abuse, and fraud (Farrington 1989*c*). For example, burglary (since the last interview) was admitted by 13 per cent at age 14, 11 per cent at age 18, 5 per cent at age 21, and 2 per cent at both age 25 and age 32. In their American National Youth Survey, Elliott *et al.* (1989) found that self-reports of the prevalence of offending increased from 11–13 to a peak at 15–17 and then decreased by 19–21.

The prevalence of other types of anti-social behaviour also varies with definitions and methods of measurement. According to the DSM-IIIR manual, about 9 per cent of American males and 2 per cent of American females under age 18 meet the diagnostic criteria for conduct disorder. The most extensive information about the prevalence of psychiatric disorders in children and adolescents was collected in the large-scale Ontario Child Health Study in Canada (Offord *et al.* 1989). This was a survey of about 3,300 children. About 7 per cent of males and 3 per cent of females aged 12–16 were conduct-disordered in the previous six months, according to reports by teachers and by the adolescents themselves.

Detailed figures for the prevalence of individual symptoms were provided by Offord *et al.* (1986). For example, for 12–16-year-olds, 10 per cent of males and 9 per cent of females admitted cruelty to animals, while 14 per cent of males and 8 per cent of females admitted destroying other people's things. In the same survey, Boyle and Offord (1986) provided detailed figures for the prevalence of smoking, drinking, and drug abuse. Extensive information about the prevalence of different anti-social symptoms at different ages between 4–5 and 15–16 can be found in Shepherd *et al.* (1971) for English children and in Achenbach and Edelbrock (1983) and Loeber *et al.* (1989) for American children.

According to the DSM-IIIR manual, about 3 per cent of American males and less than 1 per cent of American females meet the diagnostic criteria for adult anti-social personality disorder. However, the prevalence was greater than this in the large-scale Epidemiological Catchment Area project carried out in five sites in the United States. The lifetime prevalence was 7.3 per cent for males and 1.0 per cent for females (Robins *et al.* 1991).

Individual Offending Frequency

Since the pioneering research of Blumstein and Cohen (1979), much criminal career research has been concerned to estimate the individual offending frequency of active offenders during their criminal careers (for a review, see Cohen 1986). For example, on the basis of American research, Blumstein and Cohen concluded that the average active Index (more serious) offender committed about ten Index offences per year free, and that the individual offending frequency essentially did not vary with age. Furthermore, the average active Index offender accumulated about one arrest per year free.

The British and American studies reviewed by Farrington (1986*a*) indicated that the individual offending frequency did not vary greatly with age or during criminal careers. More recently, however, Loeber and Snyder (1990) concluded that it increased during the juvenile years up to age 16, and Haapanen (1990) found that it decreased during the adult years. Furthermore, in the Stockholm Project Metropolitan, Wikström (1990) showed that frequency peaked at age 15–17, and in retrospective self-report research with Nebraska prisoners Horney and Marshall (1991) concluded that it varied over time within individuals. Since there are several studies indicating on the contrary that frequency is stable with age (e.g. Home Office 1987; LeBlanc and Frechette 1989), more research is clearly needed to establish the conditions under which it is relatively stable or varies with age.

If periods of acceleration or deceleration in the individual offending frequency could be identified, and if the predictors of acceleration or deceleration could be established, as Farrington (1987*b*) suggested, these could have important implications for theory and policy. Barnett and Lofaso (1985) found that the best predictor of the future offending frequency in the Philadelphia cohort study was the past offending frequency.

There are many life events or conditions that might lead to an increase in the individual offending frequency. For example, using retrospective self-reports, Ball *et al.* (1981) found that Baltimore heroin addicts committed non-drug offences at a higher rate during periods of addiction than during periods when they were off opiates, suggesting that addiction caused an increase in offending. Using official records, Farrington *et al.* (1986*b*) showed that London males committed offences at a higher rate during periods of unemployment than during periods of employment. This difference was restricted to offences involving material gain, suggesting that unemployment caused a lack of money, which in turn caused an increase in offending to obtain money. However, neither of these studies adequately disentangled differences in prevalence from differences in frequency.

The individual offending frequency cannot be estimated from aggregate data simply by dividing the number of offences at each age by the number of arrested or convicted persons at each age, because some persons who have embarked on a criminal career may not sustain an official record at a particular age. Barnett *et al.* (1987) tested several mathematical models of the criminal careers of the Cambridge Study males, restricting the analyses to persons with two or more convictions. They found that models assuming that all offenders had the same frequency of offending were inadequate. Hence, they assumed that there were two categories of offenders, 'frequents' and 'occasionals'. The data showed that both categories incurred convictions at a constant (but different) rate during their active criminal careers. Barnett *et al.* did not suggest that there were in reality only two categories of offenders, but rather that it was possible to fit the actual data with a simple model assuming only two categories.

The average 'street time' interval between offences is the reciprocal of the individual offending frequency. Generally, this time interval decreases with each successive offence in a criminal career (e.g. Hamparian *et al.* 1978; Tracy *et al.* 1985). This decrease could mean either that the individual offending frequency was speeding up with each successive offence or that relatively low-frequency offenders were gradually dropping out of the offending population, so that this population was increasingly composed of high-frequency offenders at each successive offence transition. With the Philadelphia cohort data, Barnett and Lofaso (1985) concluded that offenders were not speeding up; offending frequencies stayed relatively constant over time, and the decreasing time intervals reflected a changing population of offenders.

Most prior studies of recidivism have used reconviction or no reconviction (or rearrest or no rearrest) within a short follow-up period of two or three years as the key dependent variable to be predicted. However, this is a rather insensitive measure. The individual offending frequency and the associated (reciprocal) time intervals between offences would be a more sensitive measure, and might give researchers a better chance of detecting the effect of sentencing or penal treatment on recidivism.

Onset

Criminal career research on onset using official records generally shows a peak age of onset between 13 and 15. For example, in the USA, Blumstein and Graddy (1982) found that the age of onset curve for arrests of both white and non-white males peaked at age 15. In the Swedish Project Metropolitan, Fry (1985) reported that the peak age of first arrest for both males and females was 13. In the Cambridge Study, the peak age of onset was 14; 4.6 per cent of the males were first convicted at that age (Farrington 1992*b*). The onset curves up to age 25 of working-class males in London and Stockholm were quite similar (Farrington and Wikström 1993).

Rather than presenting the onset rate with all persons in a cohort still alive as the denominator, it might be better to present a 'hazard' rate. This relates the number of first offenders to the number of persons still at risk of a first offence, excluding those with a previous onset. Farrington, Loeber, Elliott, *et al.* (1990) presented both hazard rates and onset rates for convictions in the Cambridge Study. The hazard rate showed a later peak at age 17; 5.5 per cent of the males still at risk were first convicted at that age. Basically, the peak hazard rate was later and greater than the peak onset rate because of the decreasing number of males still at risk of a first conviction with increasing age (the denominator). McCord (1990) showed how hazard rates varied according to social background variables. In the Cambridge Study, Farrington and Hawkins (1991) found that the best childhood predictors of an early versus a later onset of offending were: rarely spending leisure time with the father; high troublesomeness; authoritarian parents; and high psychomotor impulsivity.

In reality, and in a mathematical model, the true age of onset of offending will precede the age of the first conviction. By knowing the true individual offending frequency (which can be estimated from time intervals between offences), it is possible to estimate the true age of onset from the measured age of onset. For example, if the true individual offending frequency was two per year, and the measured age of onset (the first recorded offence) was 13.0 years, the true age of onset would be 12.5 years (since the average time to the first offence would be 0.5 years).

It would also be desirable to study sequences of onsets, to investigate how far the onset of one type of offence is followed by the onset of another type. The age of onset varies with different types of offences. In a study of Montreal delinquents, LeBlanc and Frechette (1989) discovered that shoplifting and vandalism tended to occur before adolescence (average age of onset 11), burglary and motor vehicle theft in adolescence (average onset 14–15), and sex offences and drug trafficking in the later teenage years (average onset 17–19). It is also well established that early substance abuse predicts later serious drug use. For example, Yamaguchi and Kandel (1984) showed that alcohol use preceded smoking cigarettes, which in turn preceded marijuana use, which in turn preceded other illicit drug use.

Judging from average ages of onset, the onset of shoplifting or vandalism might provide an early opportunity to detect future serious criminal offenders. However, the onset of childhood anti-social behaviour such as cruelty to animals might provide an even earlier indication. On the basis of retrospective reports by parents of clinic-referred boys, Loeber *et al.* (1992) found that rule-breaking at home tended to occur at a median age of onset of 4.5 years, then cruelty to animals (5.0), bullying (5.5), lying, stealing, fighting (6.0), vandalism (6.5), and eventually burglary (10.0). It is desirable to investigate whether these sequences of onsets occur within individuals. Onset sequences might suggest stages when interventions can be introduced to prevent escalation to more serious behaviour.

In the Cambridge Study, the average age of the first conviction was 17.5. The males first convicted at the earliest ages (10–13) tended to become the most persistent offenders, committing an average of 8.1 offences leading to convictions in an average criminal career lasting 9.9 years (Farrington 1992*b*). Similarly, Farrington and Wikström (1993), using official records in Stockholm, and LeBlanc and Frechette (1989) using both self-reports and official records in Montreal, showed that the duration of criminal careers decreased with increasing age of onset. It is generally true that an early onset of anti-social behaviour predicts a long and serious anti-social career (Loeber and LeBlanc 1990). Reitsma-Street *et al.* (1985) found that anti-social teenagers in Ontario had initiated smoking, drinking, drug use, and sexual behaviour on average over two years before their non-anti-social siblings.

Clearly, an early age of onset foreshadows a long criminal career (see also Home Office 1987). Whether it also foreshadows a high frequency of offending is less clear. Hamparian *et al.* (1978), in a study of violent juveniles in Ohio, reported that there was a (negative) linear relationship between the age of onset and the number of offences. Neglecting the possibility of desistance, this suggests that the offending frequency may be tolerably constant between onset and the eighteenth birthday. However, Tolan (1987) found that the frequency of current self-reported offending was greatest for those with the earliest age of onset.

It is important to establish why an early age of onset predicts a long criminal career and a large number of offences. Following Gottfredson and Hirschi (1986), one possibility is that an early age of onset is merely one symptom of a high criminal potential, which later shows itself in persistent and serious offending. On this theory, an early age of onset has no effect on underlying theoretical constructs. Another possibility is that an early age of onset in some way facilitates later offending, perhaps because of the reinforcing effects of successful early offending or the stigmatizing effects of convictions. In other words, an early onset leads to a change in an underlying theoretical construct such as the probability of persistence. Nagin and Farrington (1992*a*) concluded that the inverse relationship between age of onset and persistence of offending in the Cambridge Study was entirely attributable to the persistence of a previously existing criminal potential, and that an early age of onset had no additional impact on persistence.

An onset offence of a particular type might predict a later frequent or serious criminal career. For example, the Home Office study (1987) showed that an onset offence of burglary or theft was particularly predictive of persistence in offending. This type of information might be useful in identifying at first arrest or conviction those at high risk of progressing into a persistent and serious criminal career.

Desistance

The true age of desistance from offending can only be determined with certainty after offenders die. In the Cambridge Study up to age 32, the average age of the last offence, according to official records, was 23.3. Since the average age of the first offence was 17.5, the average length of the recorded criminal career was 5.8 years, with an average of 4.5 recorded convictions per offender during this period (Farrington 1992*b*).

In the Philadelphia cohort study, Wolfgang *et al.* (1972) showed how the probability of reoffending (persistence as opposed to desistance) increased after each successive offence. This probability was 0.54 after the first offence, 0.65 after the second, 0.72 after the third, and reached an asymptote of 0.80 after six or more arrests. Assuming a probabilistic process with a probability p of persisting after each offence, and conversely a probability $(1 - p)$ of desisting, the expected number of future offences after any given offence is $p/(1 - p)$, which at the asymptote (p = 0.80) is 4. Several other researchers have replicated these results by showing the growth in the probability of recidivism after each successive offence (see Blumstein *et al.* 1985; Farrington and Wikström 1993).

Barnett *et al.* (1987) proposed a more complex mathematical model for the Cambridge Study data, aiming to explain time intervals between convictions as well as recidivism probabilities. They distinguished 'frequents' and 'occasionals' who differed both in their rates of offending and in their probabilities of desisting after each conviction. The longitudinal sequences of convictions were fitted best by assuming persistence probabilities after each conviction of 0.90 for frequents and 0.67 for occasionals.

These models assume that desistance does or does not occur immediately after each conviction. Hence there is an implicit assumption that something connected with the conviction (e.g. the penalty) has an effect, with a certain probability. An alternative model is that, after onset, desistance occurs continuously as an annual process. With this assumption in the London data, the annual rate of desistance for the frequents (0.11) was not significantly different from that of the occasionals (0.14). It is difficult to distinguish between these alternative models on the basis of conviction sequences alone. However, they have very different theoretical and policy implications.

Barnett *et al.* (1989) also carried out a predictive test of their model with the Cambridge Study data. The model was developed on conviction data between the tenth and twenty-fifth birthdays and tested on reconviction data between the twenty-fifth and thirtieth birthdays. Generally, the model performed well, but it seemed necessary to assume that there was some intermittency (desisting and later restarting) in criminal careers. Some of the frequents ceased offending at an average age of 19 and then restarted after a period of 7–10 years with no convictions. It is important to establish why this restarting occurs.

Several projects have explicitly investigated why offenders desist. For example, in the Cambridge Study, getting married and moving out of London both fostered desistance (Osborn 1980; West 1982). Shover (1985) explicitly asked retrospective questions about desistance to older men who had given up offending. The main reasons advanced for desistance focused on the increasing costs of crime (long prison sentences), the importance of intimate relationships with women, increasing satisfaction with jobs, and becoming more mature, responsible, and settled with age. Some policy implications of desistance research are that ex-offenders should be helped to settle down in stable marital relationships and in stable jobs, and helped to break away from their criminal associates.

Chronic Offenders

In the Philadelphia cohort study, Wolfgang *et al.* (1972) showed that 6 per cent of the males (18 per cent of the offenders) accounted for 52 per cent of all the juvenile arrests, and labelled these 6 per cent the 'chronic offenders'. These 'chronics' accounted for even higher proportions of serious offences: 69 per cent of all aggravated assaults, 71 per cent of homicides, 73 per cent of forcible rapes, and 82 per cent of robberies. Frequency and seriousness of offending are generally related. Other researchers have essentially replicated these results. For example, in the Cambridge Study, Farrington (1983*a*) found that about 6 per cent of the males accounted for about half of all the convictions. Furthermore, when convictions of all family members (fathers, mothers, sons, and daughters) were added together, it was discovered that less than 5 per cent of the families accounted for half of all the convictions (West and Farrington 1977). In Stockholm, Wikström (1987) showed that only 1 per cent of Project Metropolitan cohort members (6 per cent of all offenders) accounted for half of all the crimes, while Pulkkinen (1988) in Finland found that 4 per cent of males and 1 per cent of females accounted for half of all the convictions.

The chronic offenders who account for a disproportionate number of all offences are clearly prime targets for crime prevention and control. However, a lot depends on how far they can be identified in advance. Blumstein *et al.* (1985) pointed out that Wolfgang *et al.* (1972) identified the chronics retrospectively. Even if all the arrested boys were truly homogeneous in their underlying criminal potential, chance factors alone would result in some of them having more arrests and others having fewer. Because of these probabilistic processes, those with the most arrests—defined after the fact as the chronics—would account for a disproportionate fraction of the total number of arrests. For example, if an unbiased dice were thrown thirty times and the five highest scores added up, these would account for a disproportionate fraction of the total score obtained in all thirty throws (thirty out of 105, on average; 16.7 per cent of the throws accounting for 28.6 per cent of the total score).

A key question is whether the chronic offenders differ prospectively from the non-chronic offenders in their individual offending frequency. Blumstein *et al.* (1985) investigated this in the Cambridge Study. They used a seven-point scale of variables measured at age 8–10, reflecting child anti-social behaviour, family economic deprivation, convicted parents, low intelligence, and poor parental child-rearing behaviour. Of fifty-five boys scoring four or more, fifteen were chronic offenders (out of twenty-three chronics altogether), twenty-two others were convicted, and only eighteen were not convicted. Hence, it was concluded that most of the chronics could have been predicted in advance on the basis of information available at age 10. It is true that only a minority of the high-scoring boys became chronics; however, as will be explained below, the remainder should not all be regarded as 'false positives' or mistakes in prediction.

Blumstein *et al.* (1985) developed a mathematical model in which all the London males were classified as 'innocents', 'desisters', or 'persisters'. The best fit to the recidivism probabilities in the survey was obtained by assuming that the probability of persisting after each conviction was 0.87 for persisters and 0.57 for desisters. The proportion of first offenders who were persisters was 28 per cent. Persisters and desisters differed in their *a priori* probabilities of persisting, not in their *a posteriori* number of convictions (as chronics did).

Interestingly, the number of predicted chronics among the offenders (thirty-seven scoring four or more on the seven-point scale) was similar to the hypothesized number of persisters (36.7) according to the mathematical model. Furthermore, the individual process of dropping out of crime of the predicted chronics closely matched the aggregate drop-out process for persisters predicted by the mathematical model with parameters estimated from aggregate recidivism data. Hence, the predicted chronics might be viewed as equivalent to the persisters. According to the mathematical model, because of probabilistic processes, 18.3 of the 36.7 persisters should survive to have six or more convictions by age 25 (and hence be classified as 'chronics'). Actually, fifteen of the thirty-seven offenders who were predicted to be chronics became actual chronics. The mathematical model shows that it is inappropriate to view the other twenty-two offenders as 'false positives', because this concept reflects deterministic prediction. Most of the discrepancy between predicted and actual chronics (18.4 in the model, out of the actual discrepancy of twenty-two) reflects probabilistic desistance processes rather than errors in identification.

Duration

There has been less research on the duration of criminal careers. Farrington and Wikström (1993) found that, up to age 25, working-class boys had similar average career lengths in London (3.9 years) and in Stockholm (3.5 years). As already mentioned, the boys first convicted at the earliest ages (10–13) in the Cambridge Study tended to be the most persistent offenders, with an average career length close to ten years up to age 32. Those first convicted at age 10–11 had an average career length of 11.5 years (Farrington 1992*b*). Over a quarter of all convicted males had criminal careers lasting longer than ten years. The average duration of criminal careers declined precipitously from age 16 (7.9 years) to age 17 (2.9 years), suggesting that those males first convicted as juveniles were much more persistent offenders than those first convicted as adults.

Barnett *et al.* (1987) estimated career lengths in the Cambridge Study using their mathematical model. On average, the frequents had a duration of 8.8 years and the occasionals had a duration of 7.4 years. (Both groups included only males with two or more convictions, in order to estimate time intervals between offences.) Hence, the frequents and occasionals did not differ much in their career lengths, although they differed considerably in their individual offending frequencies. Little is known about the predictors and correlates of criminal career duration.

Another important concept is the residual length of a criminal career at any given moment. Blumstein *et al.* (1982) used a life-table method to estimate residual career length and, as already mentioned, found that it increased to a peak between ages 30 and 40. One area where knowledge about residual career length is important is in estimating the incapacitative effects of imprisonment. If the average time served exceeds the residual career length, people would be imprisoned beyond the point at which they would have stopped offending anyway. Hence, valuable prison space might be wasted by incarcerating those who would in any case have desisted from offending.

Continuity

Generally, there is significant continuity between offending in one age range and offending in another. In the Cambridge Study, nearly three-quarters (73 per cent) of those convicted as juveniles at age 10–16 were reconvicted at age 17–24, in comparison with only 16 per cent of those not convicted as juveniles (Farrington 1992*b*). Nearly half (45 per cent) of those convicted as juveniles were reconvicted at age 25–32, in comparison with only 8 per cent of those not convicted as juveniles. Furthermore, this continuity over time did not merely reflect continuity in police reaction to crime. Farrington (1989*c*) showed that, for ten specified offences, the significant continuity between offending in one age range and offending in a later age range held for self-reports as well as official convictions.

Other studies (e.g. McCord 1991) show similar continuity. For example, in Sweden, Stattin and Magnusson (1991) reported that nearly 70 per cent of males registered for crime before age 15 were registered again between ages 15 and 20, and nearly 60 per cent were registered between ages 21 and 29. Also, the number of juvenile offences is an effective predictor of the number of adult offences (Wolfgang *et al.* 1987). Farrington and Wikström (1993) showed that there was considerable continuity in offending between ages 10 and 25 in both London and Stockholm.

It is not always realized that relative continuity is quite compatible with absolute change. In other words, the relative ordering of people on some underlying construct such as criminal potential can remain significantly stable over time, even though the absolute level of criminal potential declines on average for everyone. For example, Farrington (1990*a*) in the Cambridge Study showed that the prevalence of self-reported offending declined significantly between ages 18 and 32, but that there was a significant tendency for the worst offenders at 18 also to be the worst offenders at 32.

There are two major alternative reasons for the continuity between past and future offending (Nagin and Farrington 1992*b*). One is that it reflects a stable underlying construct such as criminal potential; this was termed the 'persistent heterogeneity' explanation. The second is that the commission of one crime leads to an increase in the probability of commission of future crimes, perhaps because of reinforcement or stigmatization; this was termed the 'state dependence' explanation. In predicting convictions during each age range in the Cambridge Study, the best model included age, intelligence, daring, convicted parents, and poor child-rearing, but did not include prior convictions. Hence, prior convictions did not predict future convictions independently of background factors and age, so that the persistent heterogeneity explanation was supported. In other words, the continuity between past and future convictions reflected continuity in an underlying criminal potential.

These results are in agreement with the idea that there tends to be persistence of an underlying 'anti-social personality' from childhood to the teenage years and into adulthood. Robins (e.g. 1986) has consistently shown how a constellation of indicators of childhood anti-social behaviour predicts a constellation of indicators of adult anti-social behaviour. In several longitudinal studies, the number of different childhood symptoms predicted the number of different adult symptoms, rather than there being a linkage between any specific childhood and adult symptoms (Robins and Wish 1977; Robins and Ratcliff 1978, 1980). Numerous other studies also show that childhood conduct problems predict later offending and anti-social behaviour (e.g. Loeber and LeBlanc 1990). For example, Spivack *et al.* (1986) in Philadelphia discovered that troublesome behaviour in kindergarten (age 3–4) predicted later police contacts; and Ensminger *et al.* (1983) in Chicago and Tremblay *et al.* (1988) in Montreal showed that ratings of aggressiveness by teachers and peers in the first grade (age 6–7) predicted self-reported offending at age 14–15.

Similarly, in the Cambridge Study there was evidence of continuity in anti-social behaviour from childhood to the teenage years. The anti-social personality scale at age 10 correlated 0.50 with the corresponding scale at age 14 and 0.38 with the scale at age 18 (Farrington 1991*a*). The second-best predictor of the anti-social tendency scale at age 18 was childhood troublesomeness (getting into trouble at school, e.g. for bad behaviour or laziness) at age 8–10, rated by peers and teachers (Farrington 1993*b*); the best predictor was having a convicted parent by age 10. With regard to specific types of anti-social behaviour, troublesomeness was the only factor measured at age 8–10 that significantly predicted bullying at both ages 14 and 18 (Farrington 1993*d*). Again, troublesomeness at age 8–10 was the best predictor of both truancy and aggression at age 12–14 in the secondary schools (Farrington 1980, 1989*a*).

There is also continuity in anti-social behaviour at younger ages. For example, Rose *et al.* (1989) in New York City found that externalizing scores on the Achenbach Child Behaviour Checklist (reflecting a broad-band anti-social syndrome; see Achenbach and Edelbrock 1983) were significantly correlated (r = 0.57) between ages 2 and 5. Furthermore, a mother's ratings of her boy's difficult temperament at age six months significantly predicted (r = 0.31) his externalizing scores at age 8 years in the Bloomington longitudinal survey (Bates *et al.* 1991). It might possibly be argued that these kinds of relationships reflected the stability of the parent's personality rather than of the child's behaviour, but similar results are obtained even with different data sources (parents at an earlier age and teachers later). In outer London, Richman *et al.* (1985) reported that behaviour problems tended to persist between ages 3 and 8, and in New Zealand White *et al.* (1990) showed that externalizing scores and being difficult to manage at age 3 predicted anti-social behaviour at age 11.

There is also continuity in anti-social behaviour from the teenage to the adult years. In the Cambridge Study, a measure of adult social dysfunction at age 32 was developed, based on (in the previous five years) convictions, self-reported offending, poor home conditions, poor cohabitation history, child problems, poor employment history, substance abuse, violence, and poor mental health (a high score on the General Health Questionnaire; see Farrington *et al.* 1988*a*, *b*, and Farrington 1989*b*). This measure of adult social dysfunction at age 32 was significantly predicted by the anti-social tendency measure at age 18 (Farrington 1993*b*). Similarly, a measure of anti-social personality at age 32 was developed which was comparable with the anti-social personality measures for earlier ages. Anti-social personality at age 18 correlated 0.55 with anti-social personality at age 32 (Farrington 1991*a*).

Expressing this another way, 60 per cent of the most anti-social quarter of males at age 18 were still in the most anti-social quarter fourteen years later at age 32. Bearing in mind the very great environmental changes between ages 18 and 32, as the males left their parental homes, went through a period of unstable living arrangements, and eventually settled down in marital homes, this consistency over time seems likely to reflect consistency in the individual's personality rather than consistency in the environment. It is often found that about half of any sample of anti-social children persist to become anti-social teenagers, and that about half of any sample of anti-social teenagers persist to become anti-social adults. Comparing the 0.55 correlation between ages 18 and 32 with the 0.38 correlation between ages 10 and 18, it is interesting that there was increasing stabilization of anti-social personality with age.

Zoccolillo *et al.* (1992), in a follow-up study of children who had been in care, also demonstrated the continuity between childhood conduct disorder (at age 9–12) and adult social dysfunction (at age 26) in the areas of work and social and sexual relationships. For example, 81 per cent of those with three or more symptoms of conduct disorder showed adult dysfunction in two or more areas, compared with only 21 per cent of those with 0–2 symptoms of conduct disorder. Approaching half (40 per cent) of the males with three or more symptoms of conduct disorder showed persistent anti-social behaviour after age 18 and fulfilled the psychiatric criteria for adult anti-social personality disorder.

The continuity in anti-social personality does not mean that it is not desirable to study influences on criminal career features such as onset and desistance. Unlike Gottfredson and Hirschi (1990), I would not argue that all criminal career features reflect only one underlying construct of criminal potential. Also, the persistence of anti-social personality does not mean that there is no scope for change. The correlations between measures of anti-social personality at different ages (e.g. the 0.55 correlation between 18 and 32), and the fact that only about half of anti-social children become anti-social adults, show that a great deal of relative change is occurring. This makes it possible to investigate factors that might encourage anti-social children to become less anti-social as they grow older, or that might foster early desistance.

There is specific as well as general continuity in anti-social behaviour from the teenage to the adult years. In the Cambridge Study, Farrington (1990*a*) developed measures of absolute change and relative consistency between ages 18 and 32. For example, the prevalence of marijuana use declined significantly, from 29 per cent at age 18 to 19 per cent at age 32. However, there was a significant tendency for the users at age 18 also to be users at age 32 (44 per cent of users at age 18 were users at age 32, whereas only 8 per cent of non-users at age 18 were users at age 32). Other researchers (e.g. Ghodsian and Power 1987) have also reported significant consistency in substance abuse between adolescence and adulthood.

In contrast, the prevalence of binge drinking and drunk driving increased significantly between ages 18 and 32, but there was again significant consistency over time; the prevalence of heavy smoking did not change significantly between ages 18 and 32, but there was again significant consistency over time. Therefore, relative consistency could coexist with absolute increases, decreases, or constancy in anti-social behaviour in the Cambridge Study. In the Netherlands, Verhulst *et al.* (1990) also reported relative stability and absolute changes in childhood anti-social behaviour.

There is usually specific as well as general continuity in aggression and violence from the teenage to the adult years. In the Cambridge Study, aggression at age 16–18 was the best predictor of fighting at age 32 (Farrington 1989*a*). Spouse assault at age 32 was significantly predicted by teacher-rated aggression at age 12–14, and by the anti-social personality measures at ages 14 and 18, but not (surprisingly) by aggression at age

18 (Farrington 1993*a*). Bullying at 32 was specifically predicted by bullying at 14 and 18 independently of the continuity between aggression at 14 and 18 and aggression at 32 (Farrington 1993*d*). Furthermore, a male's bullying at 14 and 18 predicted bullying by his child when he was 32, showing that there was intergenerational continuity in bullying. In their New York study, Eron and Huesmann (1990) also found that a boy's aggression at age 8 predicted not only his aggression and spouse assault at age 30 but also the aggressiveness of his child.

Specialization and Escalation

In the Cambridge Study, Farrington (1991*b*) investigated how far violent offenders specialized. About one-third of the convicted males (fifty out of 153) were convicted of violence (assault, robbery, or threatening behaviour). They committed a total of eighty-five violent offences (an average of 1.7 each), but they also committed 263 non-violent offences (an average of 5.3 each). Only seven of the fifty violent offenders had no convictions for non-violent offences. Other researchers (e.g. Hamparian *et al.* 1978; Snyder 1988) have also found that the majority of recorded offences of violent offenders are non-violent. Farrington (1991*b*) tested a model that assumed that violent offences occurred at random in criminal careers. Since the data fitted this model, it was concluded that offenders did not specialize in violence. Furthermore, violent offenders and non-violent but persistent offenders were virtually identical in childhood, adolescent, and adult features. Hence, violent offenders are essentially frequent offenders.

Using criminal career data collected in the South East Prison Survey, Stander *et al.* (1989) investigated specialization with offence-to-offence transition matrices. Generally, these matrices did not change (were 'stationary') during the criminal career. Stander *et al.* studied whether the offending sequences could be viewed as a first-order Markov chain (i.e. whether the probability of one offence following another was not influenced by the prior offending history), but concluded that they could not. While there was a great deal of generality in offending, there was some specialization superimposed on it. Stander *et al.* used the Forward Specialization Coefficient of Farrington, Snyder, and Finnegan (1988) to quantify the degree of specialization. They found that sex offenders were the most specialized, and that specialization in fraud was especially marked for persistent offenders. Other criminal career research also suggests that there is a small degree of specificity superimposed on a great deal of generality or versatility in offending (see Farrington, Snyder, and Finnegan, 1988). There is also some indication of increasing specialization (decreasing diversification) with age.

There has been less research on escalation, partly because of the prevailing belief in versatility and in the fact that different types of offences seem to be committed almost at random during criminal careers. In the Philadelphia cohort study, Tracy *et al.* (1990) found that the average seriousness of offences increased as offenders became older and with each successive offence. More information about escalation, and especially about the predictors of escalation, is needed.

Co-offending and Motives

Past criminal career research has mainly focused on prevalence, frequency, onset, desistance, duration, and specialization. However, there are many other features of offences that might be studied in criminal career research. These include whether a person commits an offence alone or with others; the location of the offence, and the distance travelled by offenders to commit it; motives for committing offences, including how far they are planned in advance; characteristics of victims; methods of committing crimes, including use of psychological or physical force; the offender's subjective probability of being caught by the police, convicted, and sentenced to imprisonment; and the offender's subjective utilities of the costs and benefits of offending. Except for the work of LeBlanc and Frechette (1989), there has been little research on these topics within the criminal career perspective, despite their potential relevance. Many distinctive features of offences might help in detecting offenders, for example through 'offender profiling' (e.g. Canter 1989), but I will focus here on co-offending and motives.

In the Cambridge Study, Reiss and Farrington (1991) found that about half of all offences were committed with (usually one or two) others, and that the incidence of co-offending was greatest for burglary and robbery. Co-offending declined steadily with age from 10 to 32. As already mentioned, this was not because co-offenders dropped out but because the males changed from co-offending in their teenage years to lone offending in their twenties. Males who committed their first offence with others tended to have a longer criminal career than those who committed their first offence alone, but this was largely because first offences with others tended to be committed at younger ages than first offences alone, and of course those with an early age of onset tended to have a longer criminal career. Transition matrices showed that there tended to be some consistency in co-offending or lone offending between one offence and the next.

Burglary, robbery, and theft from vehicles were especially likely to involve co-offenders. Generally, co-offenders were similar in age, sex, and race to the males themselves, and lived close to the males' homes and to the locations of the offences. However, the similarity between the males and their co-offenders, and their residential propinquity, decreased with age. Co-offending relationships tended not to persist for very long: rarely more than one year. About one-third of the most persistent offenders continually offended with less criminally experienced co-offenders, and hence appeared to be repeatedly recruiting others into a life of crime. Recruiting was especially common for burglary offences. (For a review of research on co-offending, see Reiss 1988.)

West and Farrington (1977) found that the most common motives given for property offences (46 per cent of self-reported offences, 43 per cent of offences leading to convictions) were utilitarian, rational, or economic ones: offences were committed for material gain. The next most common motives (31 per cent of self-reported offences, 22 per cent of conviction offences) might be termed hedonistic: offences were committed for excitement, for enjoyment, or to relieve boredom. In general, utilitarian motives predominated for most types of property offences such as burglary and theft, except that vandalism and motor vehicle theft were committed predominantly for hedonistic reasons, and shoplifting was partly utilitarian and partly hedonistic. Offences at younger ages (under 17) were relatively more likely to be committed for hedonistic reasons, while offences at older ages (17 or older) were relatively more likely to be committed for utilitarian reasons.

These results are similar to those reported by Petersilia *et al.* (1978) in a retrospective survey of about fifty armed robbers imprisoned in California. The main motives given for their crimes committed in the juvenile years were thrills and peer influence, but the main motive given for their crimes committed in the adult years was to obtain money—for drugs or alcohol or to support themselves or their families. Similar findings were obtained by LeBlanc and Frechette (1989) in Montreal. (For a review of research on motivation, see Farrington 1993*c*.)

In the Cambridge Study, Farrington *et al.* (1982) also studied motives for aggressive acts (physical fights). They found that the key dimension was whether the male fought alone or in a group. In individual fights, the male was usually provoked, became angry, and hit out in order to hurt his opponent and to discharge his own internal feelings of tension. In group fights, the male often said that he became involved in order to help a friend or because he was attacked, and rarely said that he was angry. The group fights were more serious, occurring in bars or streets, and they were more likely to involve weapons, produce injuries, and lead to police intervention. Fights often occurred when minor incidents escalated, because both sides wanted to demonstrate their toughness and masculinity and were unwilling to react in a conciliatory way. Similarly, Berkowitz (1978) interviewed convicted violent offenders and found that most incidents arose out of arguments and were angry outbursts intended primarily to hurt the victim; the second most frequent cause was a friend's need for assistance.

In the future, criminal career research should be expanded to study a wider range of career features. For example, if utilitarian motives increase and hedonistic motives decrease with age, is this because hedonistically motivated people stop offending (and if so why?) or because hedonistically motivated people change to become utilitarian (and if so why?)? Prospective longitudinal research would be needed to resolve these kinds of criminal career issues.

INFLUENCES ON CRIMINAL CAREERS

Risk Factors

Risk factors are prior factors that increase the risk of occurrence of events such as the onset, frequency, persistence, or duration of anti-social behaviour. In order to establish the ordering of risk factors and criminal career features, longitudinal data are required. The focus in this chapter is on risk factors for the onset or prevalence of offending and anti-social behaviour. Few studies have examined risk factors for persistence or duration. However, in the Cambridge Study, Farrington and Hawkins (1991) investigated factors that predicted whether convicted offenders before age 21 persisted or desisted between ages 21 and 32. The best independent predictors of persistence included the boy rarely spending leisure time with his father at age 11–12, low intelligence at age 8–10, employment instability at age 16, and heavy drinking at age 18. Indeed, nearly 90 per cent of the convicted males who were frequently unemployed and heavy drinkers as teenagers went on to be reconvicted after age 21.

It is also difficult to decide whether any given risk factor is an indicator (symptom) or a possible cause of anti-social behaviour. The problems raised by impulsivity have already been mentioned. As other examples, do heavy drinking, truancy, unemployment, and divorce measure anti-social tendency, or do they cause (an increase in) it? It is important not to include a measure of the dependent variable as an independent variable in causal analyses, because this will lead to false (tautological) conclusions and an overestimation of explanatory or predictive power (see e.g. Amdur 1989).

It is not unreasonable to argue that some factors may be both indicative and causal. For example, long-term variations *between* individuals in anti-social tendency may be reflected in variations in alcohol consumption, just as short-term variations *within* individuals in alcohol consumption may cause more anti-social behaviour during the heavier drinking periods. The interpretation of other factors may be more clear-cut. For example, being exposed as a child to poor parental child-rearing techniques might cause anti-social tendency but would not be an indicator of it; and burgling a house might be an indicator of anti-social tendency but would be unlikely to cause it (although it might be argued that, when an anti-social act is successful in leading to positive reinforcement, this reinforcement causes an increase in the underlying anti-social tendency).

Cross-sectional studies make it impossible to distinguish between indicators and causes, since they can merely demonstrate correlations between high levels of one factor (e.g. unemployment) and high levels of another (e.g. offending). However, longitudinal studies can show that offending is greater (within individuals) during some periods (e.g. of unemployment) than during other periods (e.g. of employment). Because within-individual studies have greater control over extraneous influences than between-individual studies, longitudinal studies can demonstrate that changes in unemployment within individuals cause offending with high internal validity in quasi-experimental analyses (Farrington 1988*b*; Farrington, Gallagher, Morley, *et al.* 1986). Longitudinal studies can also establish whether factors such as unemployment have the same or different effects on offending when they vary within or between individuals. Implications for prevention and treatment, which require changes within individuals, cannot necessarily be drawn from effects demonstrated only in between-individual (cross-sectional) research.

It is unfortunate that the static model of relationships between independent and dependent variables has dominated research and theories of offending and anti-social behaviour. This model may have a veneer of plausibility in a cross-sectional study, at least if problems of causal order are neglected. However, it is not easily applied to longitudinal or criminal career data, where all presumed explanatory constructs and all measures of anti-social behaviour and criminal career features change continuously within individuals over different ages. Relationships between an explanatory factor in one age range and a measure of anti-social behaviour in another age range may vary a great deal according to the particular age ranges, and this needs to be systematically investigated by researchers.

The major risk factors for offending and anti-social behaviour that are reviewed in this chapter are the individual difference factors of impulsivity and intelligence, and family, socio-economic, peer, school, community, and situational factors. These factors often have additive, interactive, or sequential effects, but I will consider them one by one.

Impulsivity

In the Cambridge Study, the boys nominated by teachers as lacking in concentration or restless, those nominated by parents, peers, or teachers as the most daring, and those who were the most impulsive on psychomotor tests all tended to be juvenile but not adult offenders (Farrington 1992*c*). Later self-report questionnaire measures of impulsivity (including such items as 'I generally do and say things quickly without stopping to think') were related to both juvenile and adult offending. Daring, poor concentration, and restlessness were all related to both official and self-reported delinquency (Farrington 1992*d*). Daring at age 8–10 was an important independent predictor of anti-social tendency at age 18 (Farrington 1993*b*) and of violence and spouse assault at age 32 (Farrington 1989*a*, 1993*a*). Poor concentration or restlessness at age 8–10 was an important independent predictor of adult social dysfunction at age 32 (Farrington 1993*b*).

Many other investigators have reported a link between the constellation of personality factors termed 'hyperactivity–impulsivity–attention deficit' or HIA (Loeber 1987) and offending. For example, Satterfield (1987) tracked HIA and matched control boys in Los Angeles between ages 9 and 17, and showed that six times as many of the HIA boys were arrested for serious offences. Similar results were reported by Gittelman *et al.* (1985) in New York. Other studies have shown that childhood hyperactivity predicts adolescent and adult anti-social behaviour and substance use (e.g. Barkley *et al.* 1990; Mannuzza, Klein, and Addalli, 1991; Mannuzza, Klein, Bonagura *et al.* 1991).

A key issue is how far HIA is a cause or an indicator of anti-social behaviour, and more specifically whether HIA and conduct disorder reflect the same or different underlying constructs (Taylor 1986). Farrington, Loeber, and Van Kammen (1990) in the Cambridge Study developed a combined measure of HIA at age 8–10 and showed that it significantly predicted juvenile convictions independently of conduct problems at age 8–10. Hence, it might be concluded that HIA is not merely another measure of anti-social personality, but is a possible cause, or an earlier stage in a developmental sequence. Richman *et al.* (1985) found that restlessness at age 3 predicted conduct disorder at age 8, while McGee *et al.* (1991) showed that hyperactivity at age 3 predicted a variety of child disorders at age 15. Other studies have also concluded that hyperactivity and conduct disorder are different constructs (e.g. McGee *et al.* 1985; Blouin *et al.* 1989). Similar constructs to HIA, such as sensation seeking, are also risk factors for delinquency (e.g. White *et al.* 1985); and Gottfredson and Hirschi (1990) argued that individual propensities to commit crimes and other types of anti-social acts arose from the similar construct of low self-control.

It has been suggested that HIA might be a behavioural consequence of a low level of physiological arousal. Offenders have a low level of arousal according to their low alpha (brain) waves on the EEG, or according to autonomic nervous system indicators such as heart rate, blood pressure, or skin conductance, or they show low autonomic reactivity (e.g. Venables and Raine 1987). In his Swedish longitudinal survey, Magnusson (1988) demonstrated that low adrenalin levels at age 13, reflecting low autonomic reactivity, were related to aggressiveness and restlessness at that age and to later adult offending. Olweus (1987) also found that aggressive juveniles in Sweden tended to have low adrenalin levels. The causal links between low autonomic arousal, consequent sensation seeking, and offending are brought out explicitly in Mawson's (1987) theory of transient criminality.

Heart rate was measured in the Cambridge Study at age 18. While a low heart rate correlated significantly with convictions for violence (Farrington 1987*a*), it was not significantly related to delinquency in general. In addition, being tattooed was highly related to self-reported and official offending in the Cambridge Study (Farrington 1992*d*). While the meaning of this result is not entirely clear, tattooing may reflect risk taking, daring, and excitement seeking.

Intelligence

Loeber and Dishion (1983) and Loeber and Stouthamer-Loeber (1987) extensively reviewed the predictors of male delinquency. They concluded that poor parental child-management techniques, offending by parents and siblings, low intelligence and educational attainment, and separations from parents were all important predictors. Longitudinal (and indeed cross-sectional) surveys have consistently demonstrated that children with low intelligence are disproportionately likely to become offenders. Low intelligence and attainment are also related to childhood anti-social behaviour (e.g. Rutter *et al.* 1970).

In the Cambridge Study, one-third of the boys scoring ninety or less on a non-verbal intelligence test (Raven's Progressive Matrices) at age 8–10 were convicted as juveniles, twice as many as among the remainder (Farrington 1992*d*). Low non-verbal intelligence was highly correlated with low verbal intelligence (vocabulary, word comprehension, verbal reasoning) and with low school attainment at age 11, and all of these measures predicted juvenile convictions to much the same extent. In addition to their poor school performance, delinquents tended to be frequent truants, to leave school at the earliest possible age (which was then 15) and to take no school examinations.

Low non-verbal intelligence was especially characteristic of the juvenile recidivists (who had an average IQ of 89) and those first convicted at the earliest ages (10–13). Furthermore, low intelligence and attainment predicted self-reported delinquency almost as well as convictions (Farrington

1992*d*), suggesting that the link between low intelligence and delinquency was not caused by the less intelligent boys having a greater probability of being caught. Similar results have been obtained in other projects (e.g. Moffitt and Silva 1988*a*; Wilson and Herrnstein 1985). Low intelligence and attainment predicted both juvenile and adult convictions (Farrington, 1992*c*). Low intelligence at age 8–10 was an important independent predictor of anti-social tendency at age 18 (Farrington 1993*b*) and of spouse assault at age 32 (Farrington 1993*a*), while early school leaving was an important independent predictor of anti-social personality at age 32 (Farrington 1992*e*). Low intelligence and attainment predicted aggression and bullying at age 14, and poor reading ability at age 18 was the best predictor of having a child bully at age 32 (Farrington 1989*a*, 1993*d*).

The key explanatory factor underlying the link between intelligence and delinquency is probably the ability to manipulate abstract concepts. People who are poor at this tend to do badly in intelligence tests such as the Matrices and in school attainment, and they also tend to commit offences, probably because of their poor ability to foresee the consequences of their offending and to appreciate the feelings of victims (i.e. their low empathy). Certain family backgrounds are less conducive than others to the development of abstract reasoning. For example, lower-class, poorer parents tend to talk in terms of the concrete rather than the abstract and tend to live for the present, with little thought for the future, as Cohen (1955: 96) pointed out many years ago. A lack of concern for future consequences, which is a central feature of Wilson and Herrnstein's (1985) theory, is also linked to the concept of impulsivity.

Modern research is studying not just intelligence but also detailed patterns of cognitive and neuropsychological deficit. For example, in a New Zealand longitudinal study of over 1,000 children from birth to age 15, Moffitt and Silva (1988*b*) found that self-reported delinquency was related to verbal, memory, and visual–motor integration deficits, independently of low social class and family adversity. Neuropsychological research might lead to important advances in knowledge about the link between brain functioning and offending. For example, the 'executive functions' of the brain, located in the frontal lobes, include sustaining attention and concentration, abstract reasoning and concept formation, anticipation and planning, self-monitoring of behaviour, and inhibition of inappropriate or impulsive behaviour (Moffitt 1990). Deficits in these executive functions are conducive to low measured intelligence and to offending. Moffitt and Henry (1989) found deficits in these executive functions especially for delinquents who were both anti-social and hyperactive.

Family Factors

Loeber and Stouthamer-Loeber (1986) completed an exhaustive review of family factors as correlates and predictors of juvenile conduct problems and delinquency. They found that poor parental supervision or monitoring, erratic or harsh parental discipline, parental disharmony, parental rejection of the child, and low parental involvement with the child (as well as anti-social parents and large family size) were all important predictors.

In the Cambridge–Somerville study in Boston, McCord (1979) reported that poor parental supervision was the best predictor of both violent and property offenders. Parental aggressiveness (which included harsh discipline, shading into child abuse at the extreme) and parental conflict were significant precursors of violent offenders, while the mother's attitude (passive or rejecting) was a significant precursor of property offenders. Robins (1979), in her long-term follow-up studies in St Louis, also found that poor supervision and discipline were consistently related to later offending, and Shedler and Block (1990) in San Francisco reported that hostile and rejecting mothers when children were aged 5 predicted frequent drug abuse at age 18.

Other studies also show the link between family factors and offending. In a Birmingham survey, Wilson (1980) concluded that poor parental supervision was the most important correlate of convictions, cautions, and self-reported delinquency. In their English national survey of juveniles aged 14–15 and their mothers, Riley and Shaw (1985) found that poor parental supervision was the most important correlate of self-reported delinquency for girls, and the second most important for boys (after delinquent friends). Similarly, family dysfunction is related to conduct disorder (e.g. Offord *et al.* 1989).

In the Cambridge Study, West and Farrington (1973) found that harsh or erratic parental discipline, cruel, passive, or neglecting parental attitude, poor supervision, and parental conflict, all measured at age 8, all predicted later juvenile convictions. Farrington (1992*d*) reported that poor parental child-rearing behaviour (a combination of discipline, attitude, and conflict), poor parental supervision, and low parental interest in education all predicted both convictions and self-reported delinquency. Poor parental child-rearing behaviour was related to early rather than later offending (Farrington 1986*b*), and was not characteristic of those first convicted as adults (West and Farrington 1977). Hence, poor parental child-rearing behaviour may be related to onset but not persistence. Poor parental supervision was related to both juvenile and adult convictions (Farrington 1992*c*), and was the strongest correlate of anti-social personality at age 10 (Farrington 1992*e*).

Offenders tend to have difficulties in their personal relationships. The Cambridge Study males who were in conflict with their parents at age 18 tended to be juvenile offenders. Both juvenile and adult offenders tended to have poor relationships with their wives or cohabitees at age 32, or to have assaulted them, and they also tended to be divorced and/or separated from their children (Farrington 1992*c*).

In agreement with the hypothesis that being physically abused as a child foreshadows later violent offending (Widom 1989), harsh parental discipline and attitude at age 8 significantly predicted later violent as opposed to non-violent offenders in the Cambridge Study (Farrington 1978). However, more recent research showed that it was equally predictive of violent and frequent offending (Farrington 1991*b*).

Broken homes and early separations are also risk factors for offending. In the Newcastle Thousand Family Study, Kolvin *et al.* (1990) reported that parental divorce or separation up to age 5 predicted later convictions up to age 33. McCord (1982) carried out an interesting study of the relationship between homes broken by loss of the natural father and later serious offending. She found that the prevalence of offending was high for boys reared in broken homes without affectionate mothers (62 per cent) and for those reared in united homes characterized by parental conflict (52 per cent) irrespective of whether they had affectionate mothers. The prevalence of offending was low for those reared in united homes without conflict (26 per cent) or in broken homes with affectionate mothers (22 per cent).

These results suggest that it is not so much the broken home (or a single-parent female-headed household) which is criminogenic as the parental conflict which causes it. Similarly, Fergusson *et al.* (1992), in the Christchurch (New Zealand) Child Development Study, found that parental separation before a child was 10 did not predict self-reported offending independently of parental conflict, which was the more important factor. However, teenage child-bearing combined with a single-parent female-headed household seems conducive to the development of offending in children (Morash and Rucker 1989). Single-parent families tended to have conduct-disordered and substance-abusing children in the Ontario Child Health Study, although such families tended to overlap with and were difficult to disentangle from low-income families (Blum *et al.* 1988; Boyle and Offord 1986).

The importance of the cause of the broken home is also shown in the British national longitudinal survey of over 5,000 children born in one week of 1946 (Wadsworth 1979). Boys from homes broken by divorce or separation had an increased likelihood of being convicted or officially cautioned up to age 21 in comparison with those from homes broken by death or from unbroken homes. Remarriage (which happened more often after divorce or separation than after death) was also associated with an increased risk of offending.

In the Cambridge Study, both permanent and temporary (more than one month) separations before age 10 predicted convictions and self-reported delinquency, providing that they were not caused by death or hospitalization (Farrington 1992*d*). However, homes broken at an early age (under age 5) were not unusually criminogenic (West and Farrington 1973). Separation from a parent before age 10 predicted both juvenile and adult convictions (Farrington 1992*c*), and was an important independent predictor of adult social dysfunction and spouse assault at age 32 (Farrington 1993*a*, *b*). After anti-social personality at 10, it was the best predictor of anti-social personality at 14 (Farrington 1992*e*).

Criminal, anti-social, and alcoholic parents also tend to have delinquent sons, as Robins (1979) found. For example, in her follow-up study of over 200 black males in St Louis (Robins *et al.* 1975), arrested parents tended to have arrested children, and the juvenile records of the parents and children showed similar rates and types of offences. McCord (1977), in her thirty-year follow-up study of about 250 boys in the treatment group of the Cambridge–Somerville study, reported that convicted fathers tended to have convicted sons. Whether there is a specific relationship in her study between types of convictions of parents and children is not clear. McCord found that 29 per cent of fathers convicted for violence had sons convicted for violence, in comparison with 12 per cent of other fathers, but this may reflect the general tendency for convicted fathers to have convicted sons rather than any specific tendency for violent fathers to have violent sons. Craig and Glick (1968) in New York City also showed that the majority of boys who became serious or persistent delinquents (84 per cent) had criminal parents or siblings, in comparison with 24 per cent of the remainder. Criminal parents tended to have conduct-disordered children in the Ontario Child Health Study (Offord *et al.* 1989), and substance use by parents predicted substance use by children in the Rutgers Health and Human Development project (e.g. Johnson and Pandina 1991) and in the west of Scotland longitudinal study (Green *et al.* 1991).

In the Cambridge Study, the concentration of offending in a small number of families was remarkable. As already mentioned, West and Farrington (1977) discovered that less than 5 per cent of the families were responsible for about half of the criminal convictions of all family members (fathers, mothers, sons, and daughters). West and Farrington (1973) showed that having a convicted mother, father, or brother by a boy's tenth birthday significantly predicted his own later convictions. Furthermore, convicted parents and delinquent siblings predicted self-reported as well as official offending (Farrington 1992*d*). Therefore, there is intergenerational continuity in offending.

Unlike most early precursors, a convicted parent was related less to offending of early onset (age 10–13) than to later offending (Farrington 1986*b*). Also, having a convicted parent predicted those juvenile offenders who went on to become adult criminals and those recidivists at age 19 who continued offending (West and Farrington 1977). Hence, a convicted parent seemed to be a risk factor for persistence rather than onset. Having a convicted parent was the best predictor of anti-social tendency at age 18 and of spouse assault at age 32, and was also an important independent predictor of bullying at age 14 and adult social dysfunction at age 32 (Farrington 1993*a*, *b*, *d*). After earlier measures of anti-social personality, a convicted parent was the best predictor of anti-social personality at 18 and 32 (Farrington 1992*e*). These results are concordant with the psychological theory (e.g. Trasler 1962) that anti-social behaviour develops when the normal social learning process, based on rewards and punishments from parents, is disrupted by erratic discipline, poor supervision, parental disharmony, and unsuitable (anti-social or criminal) parental models. However, some part of the link between anti-social parents and anti-social children may reflect genetic transmission (see e.g. Wilson and Herrnstein 1985; Eysenck and Gudjonsson 1989).

Just as early family factors predict the early onset or prevalence of offending, later family factors predict later desistance. For example, it is often believed that male offending decreases after marriage, and there is some evidence in favour of this (e.g. Bachman *et al.* 1978). In the Cambridge Study, there was a clear tendency for convicted males who got married at age 22 or earlier to be reconvicted less in the next two years than comparable convicted males who did not get married (West 1982). However, in the case of both the males and their fathers, convicted males tended to marry convicted females, and convicted males who married convicted females continued to offend at the same rate after marriage as matched unmarried males. Offenders who married convicted females incurred more convictions after marriage than those who married unconvicted females, independently of their conviction records before marriage. Hence, it was concluded that the reformative effect of marriage was lessened by the tendency of male offenders to marry females who were also offenders. Rutter (1989) has drawn attention to the importance of studying turning-points, such as marriage, in people's lives.

Socio-economic Deprivation

Most delinquency theories assume that offenders come disproportionately from lower-class social backgrounds, and aim to explain why this is so. For example, Cohen (1955) proposed that lower-class boys found it hard to succeed according to the middle-class standards of schools, partly because lower-class parents tended not to teach their children to delay immediate gratification in favour of long-term goals. Consequently, lower-class boys joined delinquent subcultures by whose standards they could succeed. Cloward and Ohlin (1960) argued that lower-class children could not achieve universal goals of status and material wealth by legitimate means and consequently had to resort to illegitimate means.

Generally, the social class or socio-economic status (SES) of a family has been measured primarily according to rankings of the occupational prestige of the family breadwinner. Persons with professional or managerial jobs are ranked in the highest class, while those with unskilled manual jobs are ranked in the lowest. However, these occupational prestige scales may not correlate very highly with real differences between families in socio-economic circumstances. The scales often date from many years ago, when it was more common for the father to be the family breadwinner and for the mother to be a housewife. Because of this, it may be difficult to derive a realistic measure of SES for a family with a single parent or with two working parents (Mueller and Parcel 1981).

Over the years, many other measures of social class have become popular, including family income, educational levels of parents, type of housing, overcrowding in the house, possessions, dependence on welfare benefits, and family size. These may all reflect more meaningful differences between families in socio-economic deprivation than occupational prestige does. For example, in his California self-report survey of over 4,000 children, Hirschi (1969) concluded that offending was related to the family being on welfare and the father being unemployed, but not to the occupational or educational status of the father. Family size is highly correlated with other indices of socio-economic deprivation, although its relationship with delinquency may reflect child-rearing factors (e.g. less attention given to each child) rather than socio-economic influences.

In many criminological research projects, delinquents and non-delinquents are matched on SES, or SES is controlled first in regression analyses. This reflects a widespread belief in the importance of SES, but of course it often prevents the correctness of this belief from being tested. Unfortunately, as Thornberry and Farnworth (1982) pointed out, the voluminous literature on the relationship between SES and offending is characterized by inconsistencies and contradictions, and some reviewers (e.g. Hindelang *et al.* 1981) have concluded that there is no relationship between SES and either self-reported or official offending.

Beginning with the pioneering self-report research of Short and Nye (1957), it was common in the USA to argue that low social class was related to official offending but not to self-reported offending, and hence that the official processing of offenders was biased against lower-class youth. However, British studies have reported more consistent links between low social class and offending. In a British national survey, Douglas *et al.* (1966) showed that the prevalence of official juvenile delinquency in males varied considerably according to the occupational prestige and educational background of their parents, from 3 per cent in the highest category to 19 per cent in the lowest. Also, Wadsworth (1979) reported that offending increased significantly with increasing family size in this survey. A similar link between family size and anti-social behaviour was reported by Kolvin *et al.* (1988) in their follow-up study of Newcastle children from birth to age 33, by Rutter *et al.* (1970) in an Isle of Wight survey, and by Ouston (1984) in an inner London survey.

Numerous indicators of SES were measured in the Cambridge Study, both for the male's family of origin and for the male himself as an adult, including occupational prestige, family income, housing, employment instability, and family size. Most of the measures of occupational prestige (based on the Registrar-General's scale) were not significantly related to offending. However, in a reversal of the American results, low SES of the family when the male was aged 8–10 significantly predicted his later self-reported but not his official delinquency. Should we therefore conclude that official processing is biased in favour of lower-class youth?

More consistently, low family income, poor housing, and large family size predicted official and self-reported, juvenile and adult offending (Farrington 1992*c*, *d*). Large family size at age 10 was an important independent predictor of anti-social tendency at age 18 and teenage violence, while low family income at age 8 was the best independent predictor of adult social dysfunction (Farrington 1989*a*, 1993*b*). Low-income families also tended to have conduct-disordered children in the Ontario Child Health Study (Offord *et al.* 1989).

Socio-economic deprivation of parents is usually compared with offending by sons. However, when the sons grow up, their own socio-economic deprivation can be related to their own offending. In the Cambridge Study, official and self-reported delinquents tended to have unskilled manual jobs and an unstable job record at age 18. Just as an erratic work record of his father predicted the later offending of the Study male, an unstable job record of the male at age 18 was one of the best independent predictors of his convictions between ages 21 and 25 (Farrington 1986*b*). Also, having an unskilled manual job at age 18 was an important independent predictor of adult social dysfunction and anti-social personality at age 32 (Farrington 1992*e*, 1993*b*). Also, as already mentioned, the Study males were convicted at a higher rate when they were unemployed than when they were employed (Farrington *et al.* 1986*b*), suggesting that unemployment in some way causes crime, and conversely that employment may lead to desistance from offending.

It seems clear that socio-economic deprivation is an important risk factor for offending and anti-social behaviour. However, low family income, poor housing, and large family size are better measures and produce more reliable results than low occupational prestige.

Peer Influence

The reviews by Zimring (1981) and Reiss (1988) show that delinquent acts tend to be committed in small groups (usually of two or three people) rather than alone. In the Cambridge Study, as already mentioned, most officially recorded juvenile offences were committed with others, but the incidence of co-offending declined steadily with age from 10 years onwards (Reiss and Farrington 1991). When the Study males had brothers of similar age, they tended to offend with their brothers. In Ontario, Jones *et al.* (1980) discovered that male delinquents tended to have a preponderance of brothers, and proposed that there was male potentiation of anti-social behaviour.

A major problem of interpretation is whether young people are more likely to commit offences while they are in groups than while they are alone, or whether the high prevalence of co-offending merely reflects the fact that, whenever young people go out, they tend to go out in groups. Do peers tend to encourage and facilitate offending, or is it just that most kinds of activities out of the home (both delinquent and non-delinquent) tend to be committed in groups? Another possibility is that the commission of offences encourages association with other delinquents, perhaps because 'birds of a feather flock together' or because of the stigmatizing and isolating effects of court appearances and institutionalization. It is surprisingly difficult to decide among these various possibilities, although most researchers argue that peer influence is an important factor. For example, the key construct in Sutherland and Cressey's (1974) theory is the number of persons in a child's social environment with norms and attitudes favouring delinquency.

There is clearly a close relationship between the delinquent activities of a young person and those of his friends. Both in the USA (Hirschi 1969) and in England (West and Farrington 1973), it has been found that a boy's reports of his own offending are significantly correlated with his reports of his friends' delinquency. In the American National Youth Survey of Elliott *et al.* (1985), having delinquent peers was the best independent predictor of self-reported offending in a multivariate analysis. In the same study, Agnew (1991) showed that this relationship was greatest for teenagers who were most strongly attached to their peers and felt most peer pressure.

Unfortunately, if delinquency is a group activity, delinquents will almost inevitably have delinquent friends, and this result does not necessarily show that delinquent friends cause delinquency. In other words, delinquent friends could be an indicator rather than a cause. Longitudinal research is needed to establish the causal ordering between delinquent friends and delinquency. In the American National Youth Survey, Elliott and Menard (1988) concluded that having delinquent peers increased a person's own offending and that a person's own offending also increased his likelihood of having delinquent peers. Hence, both effects seemed to be operating.

In the Cambridge Study, association with delinquent friends was not measured until age 14, and so this was not investigated as a precursor of offending (which began at age 10). However, it was a significant independent predictor of convictions at the young adult ages (Farrington 1986*b*) and of teenage violence at age 16–18 (Farrington 1989*a*). As already mentioned, the recidivists at age 19 who ceased offending differed from those who persisted, in that the desisters were more likely to have stopped going round in a group of male friends. Furthermore, spontaneous comments by the youths indicated that withdrawal from the delinquent peer group was seen as an important influence on ceasing to offend (West and Farrington 1977). Therefore, continuing to associate with delinquent friends may be an important factor in determining whether juvenile delinquents persist in offending as young adults or desist.

Delinquent peers are likely to be most influential where they have high status within the peer group and are popular. However, studies both in the USA (Roff and Wirt 1984) and in England (West and Farrington 1973) show that delinquents are usually unpopular with their peers. It seems paradoxical for offending to be a group phenomenon facilitated by peer influence, and yet for offenders and especially aggressive youths to be largely rejected by other adolescents (Parker and Asher 1987). However, it may be that offenders are popular in anti-social groups and unpopular in pro-social groups, or that rejected children band together to form adolescent delinquent groups (Hartup 1983).

School Factors

It is clear that the prevalence of offending varies dramatically among different secondary schools, as Power *et al.* (1967) showed more than twenty years ago in London. However, what is far less clear is how much of the variation should be attributed to differences in school climates and practices, and how much to differences in the composition of the student body.

In the Cambridge Study, Farrington (1972) investigated the effects of secondary schools on offending by following boys from their primary schools to their secondary schools. The best primary-school predictor of offending was the rating of troublesomeness at age 8–10 by peers and teachers. The secondary schools differed dramatically in their official offending rates, from one school with 20.9 court appearances per 100 boys per year to another where the corresponding figure was only 0.3. However, it was very noticeable that the most troublesome boys tended to go to the high-delinquency schools, while the least troublesome boys tended to go to the low-delinquency schools.

All the schools had overlapping catchment areas. The low-delinquency-rate secondary schools were oversubscribed, because parents who were most interested in their children's education, who tended to have high-achieving, well-behaved children, were very concerned that their children should go to these schools. Taking account of reports from primary schools, the head teachers of these secondary schools could pick and choose the best children out of all the applicants, leaving the high-delinquency schools with lower-achieving, worse-behaved children. Hence, it was clear that most of the variation in delinquency rates among schools could be explained by differences in their intakes of troublesome boys. The secondary schools themselves had only a very small effect on the boys' offending.

The most famous study of school effects on offending was carried out, also in London, by Rutter *et al.* (1979). They studied twelve comprehensive schools, and again found big differences in official delinquency rates among them. Schools with high delinquency rates tended to have high truancy rates, low-ability pupils, and parents of low social class. However, the differences in delinquency rates among the schools could not be entirely explained by differences in the social class and verbal reasoning scores of the pupils at intake (age 11). Therefore, Rutter *et al.* argued, they must have been caused by some aspect of the schools themselves or by other, unmeasured factors.

In trying to discover which aspects of schools might be encouraging or inhibiting offending, Rutter *et al.* (1979) developed a measure of 'school process' based on school structure, organization, and functioning. This was related to school misbehaviour, academic achievement, and truancy independently of intake factors. However, it was not significantly related to delinquency independently of intake factors. Many aspects of the schools were not related to their delinquency rates: the age of the buildings, the number of students, the amount of space per student, the staff/student ratio, the academic emphasis (e.g. amount of homework or library use), the rate of turnover of teachers, the number of school outings, the care of the school buildings, and so on. The main school factors that were related to delinquency were a high amount of punishment and a low amount of praise given by teachers in class. However, it is difficult to know whether much punishment and little praise are causes or consequences of anti-social school behaviour, which in turn is probably linked to offending outside school.

The research of Rutter *et al.* (1979) does not show unambiguously that school factors influence offending. This is partly because of the small number of schools involved in the study (only nine containing boys), and partly because far more is known about individual-level risk factors for offending than about school-level risk factors. Because this was a pioneering study, important school-level risk factors may not have been measured. In order to advance knowledge about possible school effects on offending, longitudinal research is needed in which many factors are measured for primary school children, who are then followed up to a large number of secondary schools. This might make it possible convincingly to identify school factors that explained differences in offending rates independently of individual-level factors present at intake.

Community Influences

Offending rates vary systematically with area of residence. For example, Clark and Wenninger (1962) compared four areas in Illinois and concluded that self-reported offending rates were highest in the inner city, lower in a lower-class urban area, lower still in an upper-middle-class urban area, and lowest of all in a rural farm area. In their national survey of American juveniles, Gold and Reimer (1975) also found that self-reported offending was highest for males living in the city centres and lowest for those living in rural areas. More recently, Shannon (1988) documented how police contact rates over a long period were highest in the inner city (of Racine, Wisconsin) and lowest in the more peripheral areas.

The classic studies by Shaw and McKay (1942, 1969) in Chicago and other American cities also showed that juvenile delinquency rates (based on where offenders lived) were highest in inner-city areas characterized by physical deterioration, neighbourhood disorganization, and high residential mobility. A large proportion of all offenders came from a small proportion of areas, which tended to be the most deprived. Furthermore, these relatively high delinquency rates persisted over time, despite the effect of successive waves of immigration and emigration of different national and ethnic groups in different areas. Shaw and McKay concluded that the delinquency-producing factors were inherent in the community: areas had persistently high offending rates partly because of the cultural transmission of anti-social values and norms from one generation to the next and partly because of the ineffective socialization processes to which children were exposed in deprived areas. Both of these factors were consequences of the social disorganization of an area, or the poor ability of local institutions to control the behaviour of local residents (Bursik 1988).

Jonassen (1949) criticized Shaw and McKay's conclusions about the unimportance of national and ethnic origins. He pointed out that it was desirable not only to compare delinquency rates of the same ethnic group in different areas (as Shaw and McKay did) but also to compare those of different ethnic groups in the same area. Jonassen argued that Shaw and McKay's published data showed that northern and western Europeans had lower delinquency rates than southern and eastern Europeans living in the same areas of Chicago. Jonassen also noticed that Shaw and McKay had found that orientals had low delinquency rates even when they lived in the most deteriorated areas of the city, whereas blacks had high delinquency rates in all areas where they lived (see also Gold 1987).

Later work has tended to cast doubt on the consistency of offending rates over time. Bursik and Webb (1982) tested Shaw and McKay's cultural transmission hypothesis using more recent data in Chicago and more sophisticated quantitative methods. They concluded that the ordering of area delinquency rates was not stable after 1950, but reflected demographic changes. Variations in delinquency rates in different areas were significantly correlated with variations in the percentages of non-whites, of foreign-born whites, and of overcrowded households. The greatest increase in offending in an area occurred when blacks moved from the minority to the majority, as indeed Jonassen (1949) and Short (1969) had noticed earlier. These results suggested that Shaw and McKay's ideas, about community values which persisted irrespective of successive waves of immigration and emigration, were incorrect. It was necessary to take account both of the type of area and of the type of individuals living in the area (e.g. Simcha-Fagan and Schwartz 1986).

Similar ecological studies have been carried out in the UK (for a review, see Baldwin 1979). For example, Wallis and Maliphant (1967) showed that in London official offender rates correlated with rates of local authority renting, percentage of land used industrially or commercially, population density, overcrowded households, the proportion of non-white immigrants, and the proportion of the population aged under 21. However, offender rates were negatively related to suicide and unemployment rates and not related to illegitimacy or mental illness rates. Power *et al* (1972) carried out a similar study in one lower-class London borough and found that official delinquency rates varied with rates of overcrowding and fertility and with the social class and type of housing of an area.

In Wallis and Maliphant's (1967) project, it was generally true that crime rates were higher in the inner city, and it is important to investigate why this is so. One of the most significant studies of inner-city and rural areas is the comparison by Rutter and colleagues (Rutter, Cox, *et al.* 1975; Rutter, Yule, *et al.* 1975) of 10-year-old children in inner London and in the Isle of Wight. They found a much higher incidence of conduct disorder in their inner London sample. However, they also showed that the differences between their inner-city and rural areas disappeared after they controlled for family adversity (based on parental conflict, family breakdown, criminal parents, and large family size). Rutter (1981) concluded that rates of conduct disorder were higher in inner London purely because family adversities were more common there. Any effects of inner-city residence on children's anti-social behaviour were indirect and sequential: communities affected families, which in turn affected children.

It is not invariably true that offender rates are highest in inner-city areas. Baldwin and Bottoms (1976) found that in Sheffield the key factor influencing where offenders lived was the type of housing. Offender rates were lowest in owner-occupied areas and highest in areas of council housing and private renting, and the high-crime areas were not all near the centre of the city. They concluded that council housing allocation policies played a role in creating areas with high offender rates. This again raises the issue of how far offender rates reflect the influence of the area or the kinds of individuals who happen to be living there.

Reiss (1986) pointed out that a key question was why crime rates of communities changed over time, and to what extent this was a function of changes in the communities or in the individuals living in them. Answering this question requires longitudinal research in which both communities and individuals are followed up. The best way of establishing the impact of the environment is to follow people who move from one area to another, thus using each person as his own control. For example, Osborn (1980) in the Cambridge Study found that moving out of London led to a significant decrease in convictions and self-reported offending. This decrease may have occurred because moving out led to a breaking up of co-offending groups, or because there were fewer opportunities for crime outside London. Also, Rutter (1981) showed that the differences between inner London and the Isle of Wight held even when the analyses were restricted to children reared in the same area by parents reared in the same area. This result suggests that the movement of problem families into problem areas cannot be the whole explanation of area differences in offending.

Clearly, there is an interaction between individuals and the communities in which they live. Some aspects of an inner-city neighbourhood may be conducive to offending, perhaps because the inner city leads to a breakdown of community ties or neighbourhood patterns of mutual support, or perhaps because the high population density produces tension, frustration, or anonymity. There may be many interrelated factors. As

Reiss (1986) argued, high-crime areas often have a high concentration of single-parent female-headed households with low incomes, living in low-cost, poor housing. The weakened parental control in these families—partly caused by the fact that the mother had to work and left her children unsupervised—meant that the children tended to congregate on the streets. In consequence, they were influenced by a peer subculture that often encouraged and reinforced offending. This interaction of individual, family, peer, and neighbourhood factors may be the rule rather than the exception.

Situational Factors

It is plausible to suggest that criminal and anti-social behaviour results from the interaction between an individual (with a certain degree of underlying anti-social tendency) and the environment (which provides criminal opportunities). Given the same environment, some individuals will be more likely to commit offences than others, and conversely the same individual will be more likely to commit offences in some environments than in others. Criminological research typically concentrates on either the development of criminal individuals or the occurrence of criminal events, but rarely on both.

As already mentioned, delinquents are predominantly versatile rather than specialized. Hence, in studying delinquents it seems unnecessary to develop a different theory for each different type of offender. In contrast, in trying to explain why offences occur, the situations are so diverse and specific to particular crimes that it probably is necessary to construct different explanations for different types of offences.

The most popular theory of offending events suggests that they occur in response to specific opportunities, when their expected benefits (e.g. stolen property, peer approval) outweigh their expected costs (e.g. legal punishment, parental disapproval). For example, Clarke and Cornish (1985) outlined a theory of residential burglary which included such influencing factors as whether a house was occupied, whether it looked affluent, whether there were bushes to hide behind, whether there were nosy neighbours, whether the house had a burglar alarm, and whether it contained a dog. Several other researchers have also proposed that offending involves a rational decision in which expected benefits are weighed against expected costs (e.g. Farrington and Kidd 1977; Cook 1980; Trasler 1986).

While it is obvious that offences require opportunities, it is also probable that some individuals are more likely than others to seek out and create opportunities for offending and to select suitable victims. The 'routine activities' theory of Cohen and Felson (1979) attempts to explain how opportunities for crime arise and change over time. They argue that criminal opportunities vary with routine activities that provide for basic needs such as food and shelter. For example, the increase in the number of working women, coupled with the increase in the number of single-parent female-headed households, has created increasing numbers of houses left unoccupied during the day, thus providing more numerous opportunities for burglary.

In the Cambridge Study, as already mentioned, the most common motives given for offending were rational or utilitarian ones, suggesting that most property crimes were committed because the offenders wanted the stolen items (West and Farrington 1977). In addition, a number of cross-sectional surveys have shown that low estimates of the risk of being caught were correlated with high rates of self-reported offending (e.g. Erickson *et al.* 1977). Unfortunately, the direction of causal influence is not clear in cross-sectional research, since committing delinquent acts may lead to lower estimates of the probability of detection as well as the reverse. A number of studies carried out by Farrington and Knight (1980), using experimental, survey, and observational methods, suggested that stealing involved risky decision-making. Hence, it is plausible to suggest that opportunities for delinquency, the immediate costs and benefits of delinquency, and the probabilities of these outcomes, all influence whether people offend in any situation.

THEORETICAL AND POLICY ISSUES

Explaining the Development of Offending

In explaining the development of offending, a major problem is that most risk factors tend to coincide and tend to be interrelated. For example, adolescents living in physically deteriorated and socially disorganized neighbourhoods tend disproportionately also to come from families with poor parental supervision and erratic parental discipline and tend also to have high impulsivity and low intelligence. The concentration and co-occurrence of these kinds of adversities make it difficult to establish their independent, interactive, and sequential influences on offending and anti-social behaviour. Hence, any theory of the development of offending in the present state of knowledge is inevitably speculative.

A first step is to establish which factors predict offending independently of other factors. In the Cambridge Study, it was generally true that measures in each of six categories of variables (impulsivity, intelligence, parenting, anti-social family, socio-economic deprivation, child anti-social behaviour) predicted offending independently of measures in each other category (Farrington 1990*b*). For example, Farrington and Hawkins (1991) reported that the independent predictors of convictions between ages 10 and 20 included high daring, low school attainment, poor parental child-rearing, convicted parents, poor housing, and troublesomeness. Hence, it might be concluded that impulsivity, low intelligence, poor parenting, anti-social family, and socio-economic deprivation, despite their interrelations, all contribute independently to the development of delinquency. Any theory needs to give priority to explaining these results.

Some of the most important theories of delinquency have already been mentioned in this chapter. These include Cohen's (1955) status frustration–delinquent subculture theory, Cloward and Ohlin's (1960) opportunity–strain theory, Trasler's (1962) social learning theory, Hirschi's (1969) control–social bonding theory, Sutherland and Cressey's (1974) differential association theory, Wilson and Herrnstein's (1985) discounting future consequences theory, Clarke and Cornish's (1985) situational decision-making theory, and Gottfredson and Hirschi's (1990) self-control theory. The modern trend is to try to achieve increased explanatory power by integrating propositions derived from several earlier theories (e.g. Elliott *et al.* 1985; Hawkins and Weis 1985; Pearson and Weiner 1985). My own theory of offending and anti-social behaviour (Farrington, 1986*b*, 1992*c*, 1993*c*) is also integrative, and it distinguishes explicitly between the development of anti-social tendency and the occurrence of anti-social acts. The theory suggests that offending is the end result of a four-stage process: energizing, directing, inhibiting, and decision-making.

The main long-term energizing factors that ultimately lead to variations in anti-social tendency are desires for material goods, status among intimates, and excitement. The main short-term energizing factors that lead to variations in anti-social tendency are boredom, frustration, anger, and alcohol consumption. The desire for excitement may be greater among children from poorer families—perhaps because excitement is more highly valued by lower-class people than by middle-class ones, in turn because poorer children think they lead more boring lives, or because poorer children are less able to postpone immediate gratification in favour of long-term goals (which could be linked to the emphasis in lower-class culture on the concrete and present as opposed to the abstract and future).

In the directing stage, these motivations produce anti-social tendency if socially disapproved methods of satisfying them are habitually chosen. The methods chosen depend on maturation and behavioural skills; for example, a 5-year-old would have difficulty stealing a car. Some people (e.g. children from poorer families) are less able to satisfy their desires for material goods, excitement, and social status by legal or socially approved methods, and so tend to choose illegal or socially disapproved methods. The relative inability of poorer children to achieve goals by legitimate methods could be attributable to their tendency to fail in school and to have erratic, low-status employment histories. School failure in turn may often be a consequence of the unstimulating intellectual environment that lower-class parents tend to provide for their children, and their lack of emphasis on abstract concepts.

In the inhibiting stage, anti-social tendencies can be inhibited by internalized beliefs and attitudes that have been built up in a social learning process as a result of a history of rewards and punishments. The belief that offending is wrong, or a strong conscience, tends to be built up if parents are in favour of legal norms, if they exercise close supervision over their children, and if they punish socially disapproved behaviour using love-orientated discipline. Anti-social tendencies can also be inhibited by empathy, which may develop as a result of parental warmth and loving relationships. The belief that offending is legitimate, and anti-authority attitudes generally, tend to be built up if children have been exposed to attitudes and behaviour favouring offending (e.g. in a modelling process), especially by members of their family, by their friends, and in their communities.

In the decision-making stage, which specifies the interaction between the individual and the environment, whether a person with a certain degree of anti-social tendency commits an anti-social act in a given situation depends on opportunities, costs, and benefits, and on the subjective probabilities of the different outcomes. The costs and benefits include immediate situational factors such as the material goods that can be stolen and the likelihood and consequences of being caught by the police, as perceived by the individual. They also include social factors such as likely disapproval by parents or spouse, and encouragement or reinforcement from peers. In general, people tend to make rational decisions. However, more impulsive people are less likely to consider the possible consequences of their actions, especially consequences that are likely to be long delayed.

Applying the theory to explain some of the results reviewed here, children from poorer families are likely to offend because they are less able to achieve their goals legally and because they value some goals (e.g. excitement) especially highly. Children with low intelligence are more likely to offend because they tend to fail in school and hence cannot achieve their goals legally. Impulsive children, and those with a poor ability to manipulate abstract concepts, are more likely to offend because they do not give sufficient consideration and weight to the possible consequences of offending. Children who are exposed to poor child-rearing behaviour, disharmony, or separation on the part of their parents are likely to offend because they do not build up internal controls over socially disapproved behaviour, while children from criminal families and those with delinquent friends tend to build up anti-authority attitudes and the belief that offending is justifiable. The whole process is self-perpetuating, in that poverty, low intelligence, and early school failure lead to truancy and a lack of educational qualifications, which in turn lead to low-status jobs and periods of unemployment, both of which make it harder to achieve goals legitimately.

The onset of offending might be caused by increasing long-term motivation (an increasing need for material goods, status, and excitement), an increasing likelihood of choosing socially disapproved methods (possibly linked to a change in dominant social influences from parents to peers), increasing facilitating influences from peers, increasing opportunities (because of increasing freedom from parental control and increasing time spent with peers), or an increasing expected utility of offending (because of the greater importance of peer approval and lesser importance of parental disapproval). Desistance from offending could be linked to an increasing ability to satisfy desires by legal means (e.g. obtaining material goods through employment, obtaining sexual gratification through marriage), increasing inhibiting influences from spouses and cohabitees, decreasing opportunities (because of decreasing time spent with peers), and a decreasing expected utility of offending (because of the lesser importance of peer approval and the greater importance of disapproval from spouses and cohabitees).

The prevalence of offending may increase to a peak between ages 14 and 20 because boys (especially lower-class school failures) have high impulsivity, high desires for excitement, material goods, and social status between these ages, little chance of achieving their desires legally, and little to lose (since legal penalties are lenient and their intimates—male peers—often approve of offending). In contrast, after age 20, desires become attenuated or more realistic, there is more possibility of achieving these more limited goals legally, and the costs of offending are greater (since legal penalties are harsher and their intimates—wives or girlfriends—disapprove of offending).

Risk Factors and Prevention

Methods of preventing or treating anti-social behaviour should be based on empirically validated theories about causes. In this section, implications about prevention and treatment are drawn from some of the risk factors and likely causes of anti-social behaviour listed above. The major focus is on the early social prevention of offending. (For more extensive reviews of this topic, see Kazdin 1985; Gordon and Arbuthnot 1987; McCord and Tremblay 1992.) The implications reviewed here are those for which there is some empirical justification, especially in randomized experiments. The effect of any intervention on delinquency can be demonstrated most convincingly in such experiments (Farrington 1983*b*; Farrington, Ohlin, and Wilson 1986).

It is difficult to know how and when it is best to intervene, because of the lack of knowledge about developmental sequences, ages at which causal factors are most salient, and influences on onset, persistence, and desistance. For example, if truancy leads to delinquency in a developmental sequence, intervening successfully to decrease truancy should lead to a decrease in delinquency. On the other hand, if truancy and delinquency are merely different behavioural manifestations of the same underlying construct, tackling one symptom would not necessarily change the underlying construct. Experiments are useful in distinguishing between developmental sequences and different manifestations, and indeed Berg *et al.* (1979) found experimentally that decreases in truancy were followed by decreases in delinquency.

The ideas of early intervention and preventative treatment raise numerous theoretical, practical, ethical, and legal issues. For example, should prevention techniques be targeted narrowly on children identified as potential delinquents or more widely on all children living in a certain high-risk area (e.g. a deprived housing estate)? It would be most efficient to target the children who are most in need of the treatment. Also, some treatments may be ineffective if they are targeted widely, if they depend on raising the level of those at the bottom of the heap relative to everyone else. However, the most extreme group may also be the most resistant to treatment or difficult to engage, so there may be a greater pay-off from targeting those who are not quite the most in need. Also, it might be argued that early identification could have undesirable labelling or stigmatizing effects, although the most extreme cases are likely to be stigmatized anyway and there is no evidence that identification for preventative treatment is in itself damaging; the degree of stigmatization, if any, is likely to depend on the nature of the treatment. In order to gain political acceptance, it may be best to target areas rather than individuals.

The ethical issues raised by early intervention depend on the level of predictive accuracy and might perhaps be resolved by weighing the social costs against the social benefits. For example, Farrington *et al.* (1988*a*, *b*) found that three-quarters of vulnerable boys identified at age 10 were convicted. It might be argued that, if preventative treatment had been applied to these boys, the one-quarter who were 'false positives' would have been treated unnecessarily. However, if the treatment consisted of extra welfare benefits to families, and if it was effective in reducing the offending of the other three-quarters, the benefits might outweigh the costs and early identification might be justifiable. Actually, the vulnerable boys who were not convicted had other types of social problems, including few or no friends at age 8 and living alone in poor home conditions at age 32. Therefore, even the unconvicted males in the survey might have needed and benefited from some kind of preventative treatment designed to alleviate their problems.

Impulsivity and other personality characteristics of offenders might be altered using the set of techniques termed cognitive–behavioural interpersonal skills training, which has proved to be quite successful (e.g. Michelson 1987). For example, the methods used by Ross to treat juvenile delinquents (see Ross *et al.* 1988; Ross and Ross 1988) are solidly based on some of the known individual characteristics of delinquents: impulsivity, concrete rather than abstract thinking, low empathy, and egocentricity.

Ross believes that delinquents can be taught the cognitive skills in which they are deficient, and that this can lead to a decrease in their offending. His reviews of delinquency rehabilitation programmes (Gendreau and Ross 1979, 1987) show that those which have been successful in reducing offending have generally tried to change the offender's thinking. Ross carried out his own 'Reasoning and Rehabilitation' programme in Canada, which aimed to modify the impulsive, egocentric thinking of delinquents, to teach them to stop and think before acting, to consider the consequences of their behaviour, to conceptualize alternative ways of solving interpersonal problems, and to consider the impact of their behaviour on other people, especially their victims. He found (in a randomized experiment) that it led to a significant decrease in reoffending for a small sample in a nine-month follow-up period.

If low intelligence and school failure are causes of offending, then any programme that leads to an increase in school success should lead to a decrease in offending. One of the most successful delinquency prevention programmes was the Perry pre-school project carried out in Michigan by Schweinhart and Weikart (1980). This was essentially a 'Head Start' programme targeted on disadvantaged black children, who were allocated (approximately at random) to experimental and control groups. The experimental children attended a daily pre-school programme, backed up by weekly home visits, usually lasting two years (covering ages 3–4). The aim of the programme was to provide intellectual stimulation, to increase cognitive abilities, and to increase later school achievement.

The pre-school children were significantly better in elementary school motivation, school achievement at 14, teacher ratings of classroom behaviour at 6–9, self-reports of classroom behaviour at 15, and self-reports of offending at 15. Furthermore, a later follow-up study of this sample by Berrueta-Clement *et al.* (1984) showed that, at age 19, the experimental group was more likely to be employed, more likely to have graduated from high school, more likely to have received college or vocational training, and less likely to have been arrested. Hence, this pre-school intellectual enrichment programme led to decreases in school failure and to decreases in delinquency.

If poor parental supervision and erratic child-rearing behaviour are causes of delinquency, it seems likely that parent training might succeed in reducing offending. Many different types of family therapy have been used (see e.g. Kazdin 1987), but the behavioural parent-management training developed by Patterson (1982) in Oregon is one of the most hopeful approaches. His careful observations of parent–child interaction showed that parents of anti-social children were deficient in their methods of child-rearing. These parents failed to tell their children how they were expected to behave, failed to monitor the behaviour to ensure that it was desirable, and failed to enforce rules promptly and unambiguously with appropriate rewards and penalties. The parents of anti-social children used more punishment (such as scolding, shouting, or threatening), but failed to make it contingent on the child's behaviour. Patterson attempted to train these parents in effective child-rearing methods, namely noticing what a child is doing, monitoring behaviour over long periods, clearly stating house rules, making rewards and punishments contingent on behaviour, and negotiating disagreements so that conflicts and crises did not escalate. His treatment has been shown to be effective in reducing stealing and anti-social behaviour by children over short periods in small-scale studies (Dishion *et al.* 1992; Patterson *et al.* 1982, 1992).

If having delinquent friends causes offending, then any programme which reduces their influence or increases the influence of pro-social friends could have a reductive effect on offending. Several studies show that school children can be taught to resist peer influences encouraging smoking, drinking, and marijuana use. (For detailed reviews of these programmes, see Botvin 1990; Hawkins *et al.* 1992.) For example, Telch *et al.* (1982) in California employed older high-school students to teach younger ones to develop counter-arguing skills to resist peer pressure to smoke, using modelling and guided practice. This approach was successful in decreasing smoking by the younger students, and similar results were reported by Botvin and Eng (1982) in New York City. Murray *et al.* (1984) in Minnesota used same-aged peer leaders to teach students how to resist peer pressures to begin smoking, and Evans *et al.* (1981) in Houston used films with the same aim.

Using high-status peer leaders, alcohol and marijuana use can be reduced as well as smoking (e.g. Klepp *et al.* 1986; McAlister *et al.* 1980). Botvin *et al.* (1984) in New York compared the application of a substance use prevention programme by teachers and peer leaders. The programme aimed to foster social skills and teach students ways of resisting peer pressure to use these substances. They found that peer leaders were effective in decreasing smoking, drunkenness, and marijuana use, but teachers were not. A large-scale meta-analysis by Tobler (1986) of 143 substance-use prevention programmes concluded that programmes using peer leaders were the most effective in reducing smoking, drinking, and drug abuse. These techniques, designed to counter anti-social peer pressures, could also help to decrease offending.

Criminal Careers and Crime Control

The implications of criminal career research relate mainly to crime control. With regard to prevalence, if offending is spread widely throughout the whole community, primary prevention measures targeting the 'root causes' of crime, such as those described above, are likely to be most appropriate. On the other hand, if offending is narrowly concentrated among a few problem families, then criminal justice measures such as rehabilitation, individual deterrence, and incapacitation might be more effective. There is some justification for both these approaches in criminal career research, since a high overall prevalence of offending coexists with a small minority of 'chronic' offenders who account for a substantial proportion of the crime problem.

Estimates of the magnitude of criminal career features such as the individual offending frequency and career duration are needed to assess criminal justice policies such as selective incapacitation (Blumstein *et al.* 1988). All studies of the individual offending frequency have concluded that it differs markedly between individuals. These differences were shown most graphically in the Rand research on self-reports of prisoners in California, Michigan, and Texas (Greenwood and Abrahamse 1982). While the majority of offenders reported relatively low offending rates, a small number reported exceptionally high rates. For example, over all active offenders the median offending frequency for burglary was five offences per year, but the top 10 per cent of burglars averaged at least 232 per year; and while the median offending frequency for robbery was again five per year, the top 10 per cent of robbers averaged at least 87 per year. Greenwood and Abrahamse (1982) developed a seven-point scale to investigate how far it was possible to predict the high-rate offenders, on the basis of previous convictions and incarceration, the juvenile record, drug use, and unemployment history. This scale proved to be very efficient in discriminating among the offenders. For example, for California burglars, the median annual burglary rate was 1.4 for those scoring 0–1 on the scale, 6.0 for those scoring 2–3, and 92.9 for those scoring 4–7. Their results were replicated in New Orleans by Miranne and Geerken (1991).

Greenwood and Abrahamse (1982) went on to assess the value of a sentencing policy of selective incapacitation that involved lengthening the time served by predicted high-rate offenders and shortening the time served by predicted low-rate offenders. For California robbers, they estimated that such a policy might achieve a 15 per cent reduction in the robbery rate together with a 5 per cent reduction in the population incarcerated for robbery. For California burglars, the best selective incapacitation policy required a 7 per cent increase in the prison population to achieve a 15 per cent decrease in crime. The conclusions about the benefits of selective incapacitation for California robbers were largely replicated in the reanalysis by Visher (1986), but she concluded that a 13 per cent decrease in crime might be achieved with no increase in the prison population. The results in Texas were less impressive, because of the lower offending frequencies.

Recommendations about selective incapacitation based on criminal career research have proved highly controversial. Several objections were raised (see Visher 1986), some focusing on the ethics of sentencing according to predicted behaviour. Also, it was pointed out that all the information was derived from self-reports, and that offenders would be unlikely to provide valid self-reports if their sentence length or time served were dependent on them. Furthermore, predictive efficiency had probably been overestimated in this research, because the prediction instrument had not been constructed in one sample and applied to a different (validation) sample.

Chaiken and Chaiken (1984) analysed the same data but came to different conclusions. They argued that the low-rate offenders could be identified more accurately than the high-rate ones. Hence, they advocated that the predicted low-rate offenders should be diverted from prison to community programmes, and that this could be done with minimal risk to the public. Also, Rolph and Chaiken (1987) showed that optimistic conclusions about selective incapacitation were not warranted when official records were used to identify high-rate serious offenders, because of inadequacies in the records, and Greenwood and Turner (1987) concluded that the seven-point scale did not correlate with past or future arrests as highly as with self-reports. One problem is that offending frequencies based on arrests can never be as skewed as those based on self-reports. For example, Greenwood and Turner showed that, in self-reports, the offending frequency of the top 10 per cent of offenders was more than fifteen times the median frequency, but in arrest data the offending frequency of the top 10 per cent was less than four times the median frequency. The self-report frequencies seem likely to be closer to the truth.

Two important policy implications might be drawn from the growth in persistence probabilities after each successive offence. The first is that, since a high proportion of offenders desist after the first or second offence, significant criminal justice system interventions might be delayed until the third offence (Wolfgang *et al.* 1972). Diversionary measures might be appropriate after the first or second offence. The second is that desistance is uncommon after six or more arrests, at least for juveniles. Indeed, Barnett and Lofaso (1985) argued that virtually all apparent desistance of the chronic offenders in Philadelphia was illusory, caused by the truncation of the data at the eighteenth birthday. The high probability of reoffending by persistent offenders shows that they are important targets for crime control measures.

An important implication of the generally low degree of specialization by offenders is that it will be difficult to prevent a particular type of offending by targeting a particular type of offender. For example, special incapacitative, individually deterrent, or rehabilitative sentences applied to persons convicted of violence will not necessarily have a disproportionate effect in reducing violent crimes, because frequent offenders currently convicted of non-violent crimes will be as likely to commit violent crimes in the future as persons currently convicted of violent crimes. It would be more effective to target frequent or chronic offenders rather than any particular type of offender.

Co-offending has important implications for crime control. If an offence is committed by a group, criminal justice measures targeted on one member of the group will not necessarily prevent the offending. It is important to investigate under what circumstances individually focused control efforts do or do not prevent offending. For example, measures targeted on group leaders might prevent group offending. The recruiters are primary targets for control measures, and more research is needed to establish how far recruiters can be identified at an early age and what are their characteristics. In so far as recruiters lead formerly innocent people into criminal careers, successful crime control measures targeted on recruiters could have a disproportionate impact on the prevalence of offending.

LeBlanc and Frechette (1989) argued that there were two types of offenders, situational and chronic, who required two types of intervention strategies. Situational offending was infrequent, opportunistic, and minor, whereas chronic offending was part of an anti-social lifestyle. They proposed that situational offenders should be treated with social tolerance, diversion, conciliation, protection, and support, whereas chronics needed judicial control, intensive supervision, and social re-education. Following their criminal career model of two types, it might be proposed that early social prevention measures should be used with situational (or occasional) offenders, and criminal justice measures should be used with chronic (or frequent) offenders. Further research is needed on when and how it is possible to distinguish between these two categories.

CONCLUSIONS

Research on criminal careers has greatly advanced knowledge about the prevalence, frequency, onset, persistence, and desistance of individual offending. For example, the peak age of offending in the teenage years primarily reflects a peak in prevalence; the individual offending frequency is relatively constant at different ages, and residual career length reaches a peak at age 30–40. The peak onset rate is at age 13–15, while the peak desistance rate is at age 21–25.

An early onset of offending predicts a long and serious criminal career, because of the persistence of an underlying criminal potential. In the Cambridge Study, more than a quarter of all convicted males had a recorded criminal career lasting more than ten years. A small group of chronic offenders account for a large proportion of the crime problem, and these chronics might have been identified with reasonable accuracy at age 10. Most offenders are versatile, but there is a small degree of specialization superimposed on a great deal of versatility. Co-offending and hedonistic motives decrease from the teens to the twenties, while lone offending and utilitarian motives increase.

The criminal career approach also has important implications for criminological theories, which should address developmental processes. The theory proposed here suggested that offending depended on energizing, directing, inhibiting, and decision-making processes. In addition to explaining differences between individuals in the prevalence or frequency of offending, theories should explain changes within individuals: why people start offending, why they continue or escalate their offending, and why they stop offending. For example, onset may depend primarily on poor parental child-rearing behaviour, persistence may depend on criminal parents and delinquent peers, and desistance may depend on settling down with spouses and cohabitees.

There are a number of ways in which criminal career research might be extended and improved. Existing research is largely based on official records of offending. Future projects are needed that obtain information about offending, including exact dates, by the self-report method in prospective longitudinal surveys. Existing research tends to group together all kinds of crimes, largely because of the versatility of offending; future research should devote more attention to studying different kinds of crimes separately. This is more feasible with self-reports than with official records (because of the low prevalence and frequency of any given offence type in official records). Existing research focuses mainly on males. More studies are needed that systematically compare different criminal career patterns of different categories of people (e.g. males versus females, whites versus blacks, lower class versus upper and middle class). Existing research focuses on individuals, but there could also be studies of the criminal careers of larger units, such as families, gangs, communities, and places.

Offending is one element of a larger syndrome of anti-social behaviour that arises in childhood and tends to persist into adulthood, with numerous different behavioural manifestations. However, while there is continuity over time in anti-social behaviour, changes are also occurring. It is commonly found that about half of a sample of anti-social children go on to become anti-social teenagers, and about half of anti-social teenagers go on to become anti-social adults. More research is needed on factors that vary within individuals and that predict these changes over time. Research is especially needed on changing behavioural manifestations and developmental sequences at different ages. In particular, more efforts should be made to identify factors that protect vulnerable children from developing into anti-social teenagers.

A great deal has been learned in the last twenty years, particularly from longitudinal surveys, about risk factors for offending and other types of anti-social behaviour. Offenders differ significantly from non-offenders in many respects, including impulsivity, intelligence, family background, peer influence, and socio-economic deprivation. These differences may be present before, during, and after criminal careers. Since most is known about risk factors for prevalence and onset, more research is needed on risk factors for frequency, duration, escalation, and desistance. While the precise causal chains that link these factors with anti-social behaviour, and the ways in which these factors have independent, interactive, or sequential effects, are not known, it is clear that individuals at risk can be identified with reasonable accuracy.

Research is needed on methods of preventing and treating this anti-social personality syndrome. Some promising techniques were reviewed in this chapter: cognitive–behavioural interpersonal skills training, pre-school intellectual enrichment programmes, behavioural parent-management training, and peer influence programmes. However, the preventative effects on offending are often small in magnitude, demonstrated with small samples, and not proved to be long-lasting. Larger-scale tests of these techniques, using randomized experiments and long-term follow-up periods, are clearly warranted and needed. More systematic research is needed to establish with what samples and in what circumstances different techniques are optimally effective.

The major policy implications of criminal career research focus on criminal justice measures such as incapacitation, individual deterrence, and rehabilitation. It is essential for criminal justice decision-makers to know the likely future course of criminal careers for different categories of offenders, and to know how far these careers can be predicted. Special attention could be paid to categories of offenders who are likely to re-offend quickly, who are likely to commit serious offences in the future, and who are likely to have a long future criminal career. On the other hand, categories of offenders who are likely to desist, or who are likely to have a long interval before their next offence, might be treated differently.

Similarly, it is essential for sentencers to know the relative effects of different sentences on aspects of the future criminal career, after controlling for aspects of the past criminal career. This information would assist judges in selecting optimal sentences for different categories of offenders. Very few studies have even attempted to relate sentences to recidivism probabilities with minimal controls for other criminal career variables (one example is Walker *et al.* 1981). Also, few studies have investigated the impact of official processing as opposed to no official action, but Farrington (1977) found an increase in offending frequency after first convictions. This again suggests that first offenders might be better diverted than convicted.

To advance knowledge about human development and criminal careers, Farrington (1988*a*) argued that a new generation of multiple-cohort longitudinal studies was needed. For example, Tonry *et al.* (1991) recommended that seven cohorts should each be followed up for eight years, beginning during the pre-natal period (with a sample of pregnant women) and at ages 3, 6, 9, 12, 15, and 18. This kind of project would advance knowledge about the development of offending and other types of anti-social behaviour from before birth up to the mid-twenties, covering the major periods of onset, persistence, and desistance of criminal careers. One attraction of this design is that, by amalgamating data from adjacent cohorts, conclusions about twenty-five years of development could be drawn in a project taking only ten years from start to finish (including preparatory work, analysis, and writing up). Indeed, preliminary conclusions about development from before birth up to age 21 could be drawn in the first five years of the project. It is also important to include experimental interventions within longitudinal studies, to distinguish between causes and indicators and to investigate the effects of prevention or treatment measures on criminal career features (Farrington 1992*f*).

The Home Office currently focuses on short-term narrowly policy-orientated research and seems disinclined to sponsor long-term fundamental research on the development and causes of offending. Assuming that offending and anti-social behaviour are indicators of mental health problems, it would be highly desirable for a health funding body to take over as the lead agency for sponsoring this type of research. This is most obviously justifiable in studying violence, which is clearly a public health problem (Shepherd and Farrington 1993). As with offending and anti-social behaviour, investigations of the causes and prevention of cancer and heart disease often require prospective longitudinal studies, the identification of risk factors and developmental sequences, and randomized clinical trials to evaluate the success of methods of prevention and treatment.

This chapter shows that much has been learned in the past two decades about human development and criminal careers. With a major investment in new longitudinal studies, there can be considerable further advances in knowledge and theory, and consequent improvements in crime prevention and control. Because of the link between offending and numerous other social problems, any measure that succeeds in reducing offending will have benefits that go far beyond this. Any measure that reduces offending will probably also reduce alcohol abuse, drunk driving, drug abuse, sexual promiscuity, family violence, truancy, school failure, unemployment, marital disharmony, and divorce. It is clear that problem children tend to grow up into problem adults, and that problem adults tend to produce more problem children. Major efforts to advance knowledge about and reduce offending and anti-social behaviour are urgently needed.

Selected Further Reading

R. Blackburn, *The Psychology of Criminal Conduct*. Chichester: Wiley, 1993.

A. Blumstein, J. Cohen, J. A. Roth and C. A. Visher, eds., *Criminal Careers and 'Career Criminals'*. Washington, DC: National Academy Press, 1986.

D. P. Farrington and D. J. West, 'The Cambridge Study in Delinquent Development: A Long-term Follow-up of 411 London Males', in H. J. Kerner and G. Kaiser, eds., *Criminality: Personality, Behaviour, Life History*, 115–38. Berlin: Springer-Verlag, 1990.

R. Loeber and M. LeBlanc, 'Toward a Developmental Criminology', in M. Tonry and N. Morris, eds., *Crime and Justice*, vol. 12, 375–473. Chicago: University of Chicago Press, 1990.

J. McCord and R. E. Tremblay, eds., *Preventing Antisocial Behaviour*. New York: Guilford Press, 1992.

D. J. Pepler and K. H. Rubin, eds., *The Development and Treatment of Childhood Aggression*. Hillsdale, NJ: Erlbaum, 1991.

L. N. Robins and M. Rutter, eds., *Straight and Devious Pathways from Childhood to Adulthood*. Cambridge: Cambridge University Press, 1990.

M. Tonry, L. E. Ohlin and D. P. Farrington, *Human Development and Criminal Behaviour*. New York: Springer-Verlag, 1991.

J. Q. Wilson and R. J. Herrnstein, *Crime and Human Nature*. New York: Simon and Schuster, 1985.

REFERENCES

ACHENBACH, T. M., and EDELBROCK, C. S. (1983), *Manual of the Child Behaviour Checklist and Revised Child Behaviour Profile*. Burlington, Vt.: University of Vermont Department of Psychiatry.

—— (1984), 'Psychopathology of Childhood', *Annual Review of Psychology*, 35: 227–56.

ACHENBACH, T. M., VERHULST, F. C., BARON, G. D., and ALTHAUS, M. (1987), 'A Comparison of Syndromes Derived from the Child Behaviour Checklist for American and Dutch boys aged 6–11 and 12–16', *Journal of Child Psychology and Psychiatry*, 28: 437–53.

AGNEW, R. (1991), 'The Interactive Effects of Peer Variables on Delinquency', *Criminology*, 29: 47–72.

AMDUR, R. L. (1989), 'Testing Causal Models of Delinquency: A Methodological Critique', *Criminal Justice and Behaviour*, 16: 35–62.

AMERICAN PSYCHIATRIC ASSOCIATION (1987), *Diagnostic and Statistical Manual of Mental Disorders*, 3rd rev. edn. Washington, DC: American Psychiatric Association.

BACHMAN, J. G., O'MALLEY, P. M., and JOHNSTON, J. (1978), *Youth in Transition*, vol. 6. Ann Arbor: University of Michigan Institute for Social Research.

BALDWIN, J. (1979), 'Ecological and Areal Studies in Great Britain and the United States', in N. Morris and M. Tonry, eds., *Crime and justice*, vol. 1, 29–66 Chicago: University of Chicago Press.

BALDWIN, J., and BOTTOMS, A. E. (1976), *The Urban Criminal*. London: Tavistock.

BALL, J. C., ROSEN, L., FLUECK, J. A., and NURCO, D. N. (1981), 'The Criminality of Heroin Addicts: When Addicted and When Off Opiates', in J. A. Inciardi, ed., *The Drugs–Crime Connection*, 39–65. Beverly Hills: Sage.

BARKLEY, R. A., FISCHER, M., EDELBROCK, C. S., and SMALLISH, L. (1990), 'The Adolescent Outcome of Hyperactive Children Diagnosed by Research Criteria, I: An 8-year Prospective Follow-up Study', *Journal of the American Academy of Child and Adolescent Psychiatry*, 29: 546–57.

BARNETT, A., BLUMSTEIN, A., and FARRINGTON, D. P. (1987), 'Probabilistic Models of Youthful Criminal Careers', *Criminology*, 25: 83–107.

—— (1989), 'A Prospective Test of a Criminal Career Model', *Criminology*, 27: 373–88.

BARNETT, A., and LOFASO, A. J., (1985), 'Selective Incapacitation and the Philadelphia Cohort Data', *Journal of Quantitative Criminology*, 1: 3–36.

BATES, J. E., BAYLES, K., BENNETT, D. S., RIDGE, B., and BROWN, M. M. (1991), 'Origins of Externalizing Behaviour Problems at 8 Years of Age', in D. J. Pepler and K. H. Rubin, eds., *The Development and Treatment of Childhood Aggression*, 93–120. Hillsdale, NJ: Erlbaum.

BERG, I., HULLIN, R., and MCGUIRE, R. (1979), 'A Randomly Controlled Trial of Two Court Procedures in Truancy', in D. P. Farrington, K. Hawkins, and S. Lloyd-Bostock, eds., *Psychology, Law and Legal Processes*, 143–51. London: Macmillan.

BERKOWITZ, L. (1978), 'Is Criminal Violence Normative Behaviour? Hostile and Instrumental Aggression in Violent Incidents', *Journal of Research in Crime and Delinquency*, 15: 148–61.

BERRUETA-CLEMENT, J. R., SCHWEINHART, L. J., BARNETT, W. S., EPSTEIN, A. S., and Weikart, D. P. (1984), *Changed Lives*. Ypsilanti, Michigan: High/Scope.

BLACKBURN, R. (1988), 'On Moral Judgements and Personality Disorders: The Myth of Psychopathic Personality Revisited', *British Journal of Psychiatry*, 153: 505–12.

BLOUIN, A. G., CONNERS, C. K., SEIDEL, W. T., and BLOUIN, J. (1989), 'The Independence of Hyperactivity from Conduct Disorder: Methodological Considerations', *Canadian Journal of Psychiatry*, 34: 279–82.

BLUM, H. M., BOYLE, M. H., and OFFORD, D. R. (1988), 'Single-Parent Families: Child Psychiatric Disorder and School Performance', *Journal of the American Academy of Child and Adolescent Psychiatry*, 27: 214–19.

BLUMSTEIN, A., and COHEN, J. (1979), 'Estimation of Individual Crime Rates from Arrest Records', *Journal of Criminal Law and Criminology*, 70: 561–85.

—— (1987), 'Characterizing Criminal Careers', *Science*, 237: 985–91.

BLUMSTEIN, A., COHEN, J., and FARRINGTON, D. P. (1988), 'Criminal Career Research: Its Value for Criminology', *Criminology*, 26: 1–35.

BLUMSTEIN, A., COHEN, J., and HSIEH, P. (1982), *The Duration of Adult Criminal Careers*. Washington, DC: National Institute of Justice.

BLUMSTEIN, A., COHEN, J., ROTH, J. A., and VISHER, C. A., eds. (1986), *Criminal Careers and 'Career Criminals'*, vol. 1. Washington, DC: National Academy Press.

BLUMSTEIN, A., FARRINGTON, D. P., and MOITRA, S. (1985), 'Delinquency Careers: Innocents, Desisters and Persisters', in M. Tonry and N. Morris, eds., *Crime and Justice*, vol. 6, 187–219. Chicago: University of Chicago Press.

BLUMSTEIN, A., and GRADDY, E. (1982), 'Prevalence and Recidivism in Index Arrests: A Feedback Model', *Law and Society Review*, 16: 265–90.

BOTVIN, G. J. (1990), 'Substance Abuse Prevention: Theory, Practice and Effectiveness', in M. Tonry and J. Q. Wilson, eds., *Crime and Justice*, vol. 13: *Drugs and Crime*, 461–519. Chicago: University of Chicago Press.

BOTVIN, G. J., BAKER, E., RENICK, N. L., FILAZZOLA, A. D., and BOTVIN, E. M. (1984), 'A Cognitive-Behavioural Approach to Substance Abuse Prevention', *Addictive Behaviours*, 9: 137–47.

BOTVIN, G. J., and ENG, A. (1982), 'The Efficacy of a Multicomponent Approach to the Prevention of Cigarette Smoking', *Preventive Medicine*, 11: 199–211.

BOYLE, M. H., and OFFORD, D. R., (1986), 'Smoking, Drinking and Use of Illicit Drugs among Adolescents in Ontario: Prevalence, Patterns of Use and Socio-Demographic Correlates', *Canadian Medical Association Journal*, 135: 1113–21.

BOYLE, M. H., OFFORD, D. R., HOFMANN, H. G., CATLIN, G. P., BYLES, J. A., CADMAN, D. T., CRAWFORD, J. W., LINKS, P. S., RAE-GRANT, N. I., and SZATMARI, P. (1987), 'Ontario Child Health Study, I: Methodology', *Archives of General Psychiatry*, 44: 826–31.

BURSIK, R. J. (1988), 'Social Disorganization and Theories of Crime and Delinquency: Problems and Prospects', *Criminology*, 26: 519–51.

BURSIK, R. J., and WEBB, J. (1982), 'Community Change and Patterns of Delinquency', *American Journal of Sociology*, 88: 24–42.

CANTER, D. (1989), 'Offender Profiles', *The Psychologist*, 2: 12–16.

CHAIKEN, M. R., and CHAIKEN, J. M. (1984), 'Offender Types and Public Policy', *Crime and Delinquency*, 30: 195–226.

CLARK, J. P., and WENNINGER, E. P. (1962), 'Socio-Economic Class and Area as Correlates of Illegal Behaviour among Juveniles', *American Sociological Review*, 27: 826–34.

CLARKE, R. V., and CORNISH, D. B. (1985), 'Modelling Offenders' Decisions: A Framework for Research and Policy', in M. Tonry and N. Morris, Eds., *Crime and Justice*, vol. 6, 147–85. Chicago: University of Chicago Press.

CLOWARD, R. A., and OHLIN, L. E. (1960), *Delinquency and Opportunity*. New York: Free Press.

COHEN, A. K. (1955), *Delinquent Boys*. Glencoe, Ill.: Free Press.

COHEN, J. (1986), 'Research on Criminal Careers: Individual Frequency Rates and Offence Seriousness', in A. Blumstein, J. Cohen, J. A. Roth, and C. A. Visher, eds., *Criminal Careers and 'Career Criminals'*, vol. 1, 292–481. Washington, DC: National Academy Press.

COHEN, L. E., and FELSON, M. (1979), 'Social Change and Crime Trends: A Routine Activity Approach', *American Sociological Review*, 44: 588–608.

COOK, P. J. (1980), 'Research in Criminal Deterrence: Laying the Groundwork for the Second Decade', in M. Tonry and N. Morris, eds., *Crime and Justice*, vol. 2, 211–68. Chicago: University of Chicago Press.

CRAIG, M. M., and GLICK, S. J. (1968), 'School Behaviour Related to Later Delinquency and Non-Delinquency', *Criminologica*, 5: 17–27.

DISHION, T. J., PATTERSON, G. R., and KAVANAGH, K. A. (1992), 'An Experimental Test of the Coercion Model: Linking Theory, Measurement and Intervention', in J. McCord and R. Tremblay, eds., *Preventing Antisocial Behaviour*, 253–82. New York: Guilford.

DONOVAN, J. E., JESSOR, R., and COSTA, F. M. (1988), 'Syndrome of Problem Behaviour in Adolescence: A Replication', *Journal of Consulting and Clinical Psychology*, 56: 762–5.

DOUGLAS, J. W. B., ROSS, J. M., HAMMOND, W. A., and MULLIGAN, D. G. (1966), 'Delinquency and Social Class', *British Journal of Criminology*, 6: 294–302.

EDELBROCK, C., and COSTELLO, A. J. (1988), 'Convergence between Statistically Derived Behaviour Problem Syndromes and Child Psychiatric Diagnoses, *Journal of Abnormal Child Psychology*, 16: 219–31.

ELLIOTT, D. S., HUIZINGA, D., and AGETON, S. S. (1985), *Explaining Delinquency and Drug Use*. Beverly Hills: Sage.

ELLIOTT, D. S., HUIZINGA, D., and MENARD, S. (1989), *Multiple Problem Youth*. New York: Springer-Verlag.

ELLIOTT, D. S., and MENARD, S. (1988), 'Delinquent Behaviour and Delinquent Peers: Temporal and Developmental Patterns', unpublished manuscript.

ENSMINGER, M. E., KELLAM, S. G., and RUBIN, B. R. (1983), 'School and Family Origins of Delinquency', in K. T. van Dusen and S. A. Medrick, eds., *Prospective Studies of Crime and Delinquency*, 73–97. Boston: Kluwer-Nijhoff.

ERICKSON, M., GIBBS, J. P., and JENSEN, G. F. (1977), 'The Deterrence Doctrine and the Perceived Certainty of Legal Punishment', *American Sociological Review*, 42: 305–17.

ERON, L. D., and HUESMANN, L. R. (1990), 'The Stability of Aggressive Behaviour—Even Unto the Third Generation', in M. Lewis and S. M. Miller, eds., *Handbook of Developmental Psychopathology*, 147–56. New York: Plenum.

EVANS, R. I., ROZELLE, R. M., MAXWELL, S. E., RAINES, B. E., DILL, C. A., GUTHRIE, T. J., HENDERSON, A. H., and HILL, P. C. (1981), 'Social Modelling Films to Deter Smoking in Adolescents: Results of a Three-year Field Investigation', *Journal of Applied Psychology*, 66: 399–414.

EYSENCK, H. J., and GUDJONSSON, G. H. (1989), *The Causes and Cures of Criminality*. New York: Plenum.

FARRINGTON, D. P. (1972), 'Delinquency Begins at Home', *New Society*, 21: 495–7.

—— (1973), 'Self-Reports of Deviant Behaviour: Predictive and Stable?', *Journal of Criminal Law and Criminology*, 64: 99–110.

—— (1977), 'The Effects of Public Labelling', *British Journal of Criminology*, 17: 112–25.

—— (1978), 'The Family Backgrounds of Aggressive Youths', in L. Hersov, M. Berger, and D. Shaffer, eds., *Aggression and Antisocial Behaviour in Childhood and Adolescence*, 73–93. Oxford: Pergamon.

—— (1980), 'Truancy, Delinquency, the Home and the School', in L. Hersov and I. Berg, eds., *Out of School: Modern Perspectives in Truancy and School Refusal*, 49–63. Chichester: Wiley.

—— (1983*a*), 'Offending from 10 to 25 Years of Age', in K. T. Van Dusen and S. A. Mednick, eds., *Prospective Studies of Crime and Delinquency*, 17–37. Boston: Kluwer-Nijhoff.

—— (1983*b*), 'Randomized Experiments on Crime and Justice', in M. Tonry and N. Morris, eds., *Crime and Justice*, vol. 4, 257–308. Chicago: University of Chicago Press.

—— (1986*a*), 'Age and Crime. in M. Tonry and N. Morris, eds., *Crime and Justice*, vol. 7, 189–250. Chicago: University of Chicago Press.

—— (1986*b*), 'Stepping Stones to Adult Criminal Careers', in D. Olweus, J. Block, and M. R. Yarrow, eds., *Development of Antisocial and Prosocial Behaviour*, 359–84. New York: Academic Press.

—— (1987*a*), 'Implications of Biological Findings for Criminological Research', in S. A. Mednick, T. E. Moffitt, and S. A. Stack, eds., *The Causes of Crime: New Biological Approaches*, 42–64. Cambridge: Cambridge University Press.

—— (1987*b*), 'Predicting Individual Crime Rates', in D. M. Gottfredson and M. Tonry, eds., *Crime and Justice*, vol. 9: *Prediction and Classification: Criminal Justice Decision Making*, 53–101. Chicago: University of Chicago Press.

Farrington, D. P. (1988*a*), 'Advancing Knowledge about Delinquency and Crime: The Need for a Coordinated Programme of Longitudinal Research, *Behavioural Sciences and the Law*, 6: 307–31.

—— (1988*b*), 'Studying Changes within Individuals: The Causes of Offending', in M. Rutter, ed., *Studies of Psychosocial Risk*, 158–83. Cambridge: Cambridge University Press.

—— (1989*a*), 'Early Predictors of Adolescent Aggression and Adult Violence', *Violence and Victims*, 4: 79–100.

—— (1989*b*), 'Later Adult Life Outcomes of Offenders and Non-Offenders', in M. Brambring, F. Losel, and H. Skowronek, eds., *Children at Risk: Assessment, Longitudinal Research, and Intervention*, 220–44. Berlin: De Gruyter.

—— (1989*c*), 'Self-Reported and Official Offending from Adolescence to Adulthood', in M. W. Klein, ed., *Cross-National Research in Self-Reported Crime and Delinquency*, 399–423. Dordrecht: Kluwer.

—— (1990*a*), 'Age, Period, Cohort, and Offending', in D. M. Gottfredson and R. V. Clarke, eds., *Policy and Theory in Criminal Justice: Contributions in Honour of Leslie T. Wilkins*, 51–75. Aldershot: Avebury.

—— (1990*b*), 'Implications of Criminal Career Research for the Prevention of Offending', *Journal of Adolescence*, 13: 93–113.

—— (1991*a*), 'Antisocial Personality from Childhood to Adulthood', *The Psychologist*, 4: 389–94.

—— (1991*b*), 'Childhood Aggression and Adult Violence: Early Precursors and Later Life Outcomes', in D. J. Pepler and K. H. Rubin, eds., *The Development and Treatment of Childhood Aggression*, 5–29. Hillsdale, NJ: Erlbaum.

—— (1992*a*), 'Criminal Career Research: Lessons for Crime Prevention', *Studies on Crime and Crime Prevention*, 1: 7–29.

—— (1992*b*), 'Criminal Career Research in the United Kingdom', *British Journal of Criminology*, 32: 521–36.

—— (1992*c*), 'Explaining the Beginning, Progress and Ending of Antisocial Behaviour from Birth to Adulthood', in J. McCord, ed., *Advances in Criminological Theory*, vol. 3: *Facts, Frameworks and Forecasts*, 253–86. New Brunswick, NJ: Transaction.

—— (1992*d*), 'Juvenile Delinquency', in J. C. Coleman ed., *The School Years*, 2nd edn., 123–63. London: Routledge.

—— (1992*e*), 'Psychosocial Influences on the Development of Antisocial Personality', paper given at the Third European Conference on Law and Psychology, Oxford, September.

—— (1992*f*), 'The Need for Longitudinal-Experimental Research on Offending and Antisocial Behaviour', in J. McCord and R. E. Tremblay, eds., *Preventing Antisocial Behaviour*, 353–76. New York: Guilford.

—— (1993*a*), 'Childhood, Adolescent and Adult Features of Violent Males', in L. R. Huesmann, ed., *Aggressive Behaviour: Current Perspectives*. New York: Plenum, in press.

—— (1993*b*), 'Childhood Origins of Teenage Antisocial Behaviour and Adult Social Dysfunction', *Journal of the Royal Society of Medicine*, 86: 13–17.

—— (1993*c*), 'Motivations for Conduct Disorder and Delinquency', *Development and Psychopathology*, 5: 225–41.

—— (1993*d*), 'Understanding and Preventing Bullying', in M. Tonry and N. Morris, eds., *Crime and Justice*, vol. 17. Chicago: University of Chicago Press, in press.

FARRINGTON, D. P., BERKOWITZ, L., and WEST, D. J. (1982), 'Differences between Individual and Group Fights', *British Journal of Social Psychology*, 21: 323–33.

FARRINGTON, D. P., GALLAGHER, B., MORLEY, L., ST LEDGER, R. J., and WEST, D. J. (1986), 'Unemployment, School Leaving, and Crime', *British Journal of Criminology*, 26: 335–56.

—— (1988*a*), 'A 24-Year Follow-Up of Men from Vulnerable Backgrounds', in R. L. Jenkins and W. K. Brown, eds., *The Abandonment of Delinquent Behaviour*, 155–73. New York: Praeger.

—— (1988*b*), 'Are There any Successful Men from Criminogenic Backgrounds?', *Psychiatry*, 51: 116–30.

FARRINGTON, D. P., and HAWKINS, J. D., (1991), 'Predicting Participation, Early Onset, and Later Persistence in Officially Recorded Offending', *Criminal Behaviour and Mental Health*, 1: 1–33.

FARRINGTON, D. P., and KIDD, R. F. (1977), 'Is Financial Dishonesty a Rational Decision?', *British Journal of Social and Clinical Psychology*, 16: 139–46.

FARRINGTON, D. P., and KNIGHT, B. J. (1980), 'Four Studies of Stealing as a Risky Decision', in P. D. Lipsitt and B. D. Sales, eds., *New Directions in Psycholegal Research*, 26–50. New York: Van Nostrand Reinhold.

FARRINGTON, D. P., LOEBER, R., ELLIOTT, D. S., HAWKINS, J. D., KANDEL, D. B., KLEIN, M. W., MCCORD, J., ROWE, D. C., and TREMBLAY, R. E. (1990), 'Advancing Knowledge about the Onset of Delinquency and Crime', in B. B. Lahey and A. E. Kazdin, eds., *Advances in Clinical Child Psychology*, vol. 13, 283–342. New York: Plenum.

FARRINGTON, D. P., LOEBER, R., and VAN KAMMEN, W. B. (1990), 'Long-term Criminal Outcomes of Hyperactivity–Impulsivity–Attention Deficit and Conduct Problems in Childhood', in L. N. Robins and M. Rutter, eds., *Straight and Devious Pathways from Childhood to Adulthood*, 62–81. Cambridge: Cambridge University Press.

FARRINGTON, D. P., OHLIN, L. E., and WILSON, J. Q. (1986), *Understanding and Controlling Crime*. New York: Springer-Verlag.

FARRINGTON, D. P., SNYDER, H. N., and FINNEGAN, T. A. (1988), 'Specialization in Juvenile Court Careers', *Criminology*, 26, 461–87.

FARRINGTON, D. P., and WEST, D. J. (1990), 'The Cambridge Study in Delinquent Development:' A Long-Term Follow-Up of 411 London Males', in H. J. Kerner and G. Kaiser, eds., *Criminality: Personality, Behaviour and Life History*, 115–38. Berlin: Springer-Verlag.

FARRINGTON, D. P., and WIKSTRÖM, P-O. (1993), 'Criminal Careers in London and Stockholm: A Cross-National Comparative Study', in E. Weitekamp and H. J. Kerner, eds., *Cross-National and Longitudinal Research on Human Development and Criminal Behaviour*. Dordrecht: Kluwer, in press.

FERGUSSON, D. M., HORWOOD, L. J., and LYNSKEY, M. T. (1992), 'Family Change, Parental Discord and Early Offending', *Journal of Child Psychology and Psychiatry*, 33: 1059–75.

Fry, L. J. (1985), 'Drug Abuse and Crime in a Swedish Birth Cohort', *British Journal of Criminology*, 25: 46–59.

Gendreau, P., and Ross, R. R. (1979), 'Effective Correctional Treatment: Bibliotherapy for Cynics', *Crime and Delinquency*, 25: 463–89.

—— (1987), 'Revivification of Rehabilitation: Evidence from the 1980s', *Justice Quarterly*, 4: 349–407.

Ghodsian, M., and Power, C. (1987), 'Alcohol Consumption between the Ages of 16 and 23 in Britain: A Longitudinal Study', *British Journal of Addiction*, 82: 175–80.

Gittelman, R., Mannuzza, S., Shenker, R., and Bonagura, N. (1985), 'Hyperactive Boys almost Grown Up', *Archives of General Psychiatry*, 42: 937–47.

Gold, M. (1987), 'Social Ecology', in H. C. Quay, ed., *Handbook of Juvenile Delinquency*', 62–105. New York: Wiley.

Gold, M., and Reimer, D. J. (1975), 'Changing Patterns of Delinquent Behaviour among Americans 13 through 16 Years Old: 1967–72', *Crime and Delinquency Literature*, 7: 483–517.

Gordon, D. A., and Arbuthnot, J. (1987), 'Individual, Group and Family Interventions', in H. C. Quay, ed., *Handbook of Juvenile Delinquency*, 290–324. New York: Wiley.

Gottfredson, M., and Hirschi, T. (1986), 'The True Value of Lambda would Appear to be Zero: An Essay on Career Criminals, Criminal Careers, Selective Incapacitation, Cohort Studies, and Related Topics', *Criminology*, 24: 213–33.

—— (1990), *A General Theory of Crime*. Stanford: Stanford University Press.

Green, G., MacIntyre, S., West, P., and Ecob, R. (1991), 'Like Parent like Child? Associations between Drinking and Smoking Behaviour of Parents and their Children', *British Journal of Addiction*, 86: 745–58.

Greenwood, P., and Abrahamse, A. (1982), *Selective Incapacitation*. Santa Monica: Rand.

Greenwood, P., and Turner, S. (1987), *Selective Incapacitation Revisited*. Santa Monica: Rand.

Haapanen, R. A. (1990), *Selective Incapacitation and the Serious Offender*. New York: Springer-Verlag.

Hamparian, D. M., Schuster, R., Dinitz, S., and Conrad, J. P. (1978), *The Violent Few*. Lexington, Mass.: Heath.

Hare, R. D. (1980), 'A Research Scale for the Assessment of Psychopathy in Criminal Populations', *Personality and Individual Differences*, 1: 111–19.

—— (1985), 'Comparison of Procedures for the Assessment of Psychopathy', *Journal of Consulting and Clinical Psychology*, 53: 7–16.

—— (1986), 'Twenty Years of Experience with the Cleckley Psychopath', in W. H. Reid, D. Dorr, J. I. Walker, and J. W. Bonner, eds., *Unmasking the Psychopath: Antisocial Personality and Related Syndromes*, 3–27. New York: Norton.

Harpur, T. J., Hakstian, A. R., and Hare, R. D. (1988), 'Factor Structure of the Psychopathy Checklist', *Journal of Consulting and Clinical Psychology*, 56: 741–7.

Hartup, W. W. (1983), 'Peer Relations', in P. H. Mussen ed., *Handbook of Child Psychology*, vol. 4, 103–96. Toronto: Wiley.

HAWKINS, J. D., CATALANO, R. F., and MILLER, J. Y. (1992), 'Risk and Protective Factors for Alcohol and other Drug Problems in Adolescence and Early Adulthood: Implications for Substance Use Prevention', *Psychological Bulletin*, 112: 64–105.

HAWKINS, J. D., and WEIS, J. G. (1985), 'The Social Development Model: An Integrated Approach to Delinquency Prevention', *Journal of Primary Prevention*, 6: 73–97.

HINDELANG, M. J., HIRSCHI, T., and WEIS, J. G. (1981), *Measuring Delinquency*. Beverly Hills: Sage.

HIRSCHI, T. (1969), *Causes of Delinquency*. Berkeley: University of California Press.

HOME OFFICE (1987), *Criminal Careers of Those Born in 1953: Persistent Offenders and Desistance, Home Office Statistical Bulletin* no. 35/87. London: Home Office.

HORNEY, J., and MARSHALL, I. H. (1991), 'Measuring Lambda through Self-Reports', *Criminology*, 29: 471–95.

HUIZINGA, D., and ELLIOTT, D. S. (1986), 'Reassessing the Reliability and Validity of Self-Report Measures', *Journal of Quantitative Criminology*, 2: 293–327.

JESSOR, R., and JESSOR, S. L. (1977), *Problem Behaviour and Psychosocial Development*. New York: Academic Press.

JOHNSON, V., and PANDINA, R. J. (1991), 'Effects of the Family Environment on Adolescent Substance Use, Delinquency and Coping Styles', *American Journal of Drug and Alcohol Abuse*, 17: 71–88.

JONASSEN, C. T. (1949), 'A Re-evaluation and Critique of the Logic and Some Methods of Shaw and McKay', *American Sociological Review*, 14: 608–14.

JONES, M. B., OFFORD, D. R., and ABRAMS, N. (1980), 'Brothers, Sisters and Antisocial Behaviour', *British Journal of Psychiatry*, 136: 139–45.

KAZDIN, A. E. (1985), *Treatment of Antisocial Behaviour in Children and Adolescents*. Homewood, Ill.: Dorsey.

—— (1987), 'Treatment of Antisocial Behaviour in Children: Current Status and Future Directions', *Psychological Bulletin*, 102: 187–203.

KLEIN, M. W. (1984), 'Offence Specialization and Versatility Among Juveniles', *British Journal of Criminology*, 24: 185–94.

KLEPP, K-I., HALPER, A., and PERRY, C. L. (1986), 'The Efficacy of Peer Leaders in Drug Abuse Prevention', *Journal of School Health*, 56: 407–11.

KLINTEBERG, B. A., HUMBLE, K., and SCHALLING, D. (1992), 'Personality and Psychopathy of Males with a History of Early Criminal Behaviour', *European Journal of Personality*, 6: 245–66.

KOLVIN, I., MILLER, F. J. W., FLEETING, M., and KOLVIN, P. A. (1988), 'Social and Parenting Factors Affecting Criminal-Offence Rates: Findings from the Newcastle Thousand Family Study (1947–1980)', *British Journal of Psychiatry*, 152: 80–90.

KOLVIN, I., MILLER, F. J. W., SCOTT, D. M., GATZANIS, S. R. M., and FLEETING, M. (1990), *Continuities of Deprivation*? Aldershot: Avebury.

LEBLANC, M., and FRECHETTE, M. (1989), *Male Criminal Activity from Childhood through Youth*. New York: Springer-Verlag.

LOEBER, R. (1987), 'Behavioural Precursors and Accelerators of Delinquency', in W. Buikhuisen and S. A. Mednick, eds., *Explaining Criminal Behaviour*, 51–67. Leiden: Brill.

LOEBER, R., and DISHION, T. (1983), 'Early Predictors of Male Delinquency: A Review', *Psychological Bulletin*, 94: 68–99.

LOEBER, R., GREEN, S. M., LAHEY, B. B., CHRIST, M. A. G., and FRICK, P. J. (1992), 'Developmental Sequences in the Age of Onset of Disruptive Child Behaviours', *Journal of Child and Family Studies*, 1: 21–41.

LOEBER, R., and LEBLANC, M. (1990), 'Toward a Developmental Criminology', in M. Tonry and N. Morris, eds., *Crime and Justice*, vol. 12, 375–473. Chicago: University of Chicago Press.

LOEBER, R., and SCHMALING, K. B. (1985), 'Empirical Evidence for Overt and Covert Patterns of Antisocial Conduct Problems', *Journal of Abnormal Child Psychology*, 13: 337–352.

LOEBER, R., and SNYDER H. N. (1990), 'Rate of Offending in Juvenile Careers: Findings of Constancy and Change in Lambda', *Criminology*, 28: 97–109.

LOEBER, R., and STOUTHAMER-LOEBER, M. (1986), 'Family Factors as Correlates and Predictors of Juvenile Conduct Problems and Delinquency', in M. Tonry and N. Morris, eds., *Crime and Justice*, vol. 7, 29–149. Chicago: University of Chicago Press.

—— (1987), 'Prediction', in H. C. Quay, ed., *Handbook of Juvenile Delinquency*, 325–82. New York: Wiley.

LOEBER, R., STOUTHAMER-LOEBER, M., VAN KAMMEN, W. B., and FARRINGTON, D. P. (1989), 'Development of a New Measure of Self-Reported Antisocial Behaviour for Young Children: Prevalence and Reliability', in M. W. Klein, ed., *Cross-National Research in Self-Reported Crime and Delinquency*, 203–25. Dordrecht: Kluwer.

—— (1991), 'Initiation, Escalation and Desistance in Juvenile Offending and their Correlates', *Journal of Criminal Law and Criminology*, 82: 36–82.

MCALISTER, A., PERRY, C., KILLEN, J., SLINKARD, L. A., and MACCOBY, N. (1980), Pilot Study of Smoking, Alcohol and Drug Abuse Prevention', *American Journal of Public Health*, 70: 719–21.

MCCORD, J. (1977), 'A Comparative Study of Two Generations of Native Americans', in R. F. Meier, ed., *Theory in Criminology*, 83–92. Beverly Hills: Sage.

—— (1979), 'Some Child-Rearing Antecedents of Criminal Behaviour in Adult Men', *Journal of Personality and Social Psychology*, 37: 1477–86.

—— (1982), 'A Longitudinal View of the Relationship between Paternal Absence and Crime', in J. Gunn and D. P. Farrington, eds., *Abnormal Offenders, Delinquency, and the Criminal Justice System*, 113–28. Chichester: Wiley.

—— (1990), 'Crime in Moral and Social Contexts', *Criminology*, 28: 1–26.

—— (1991), 'Family Relationships, Juvenile Delinquency, and Adult Criminality', *Criminology*, 29: 397–417.

MCCORD, J., and TREMBLAY, R. E. (1992), eds., *Preventing Antisocial Behaviour*. New York: Guilford.

MCGEE, R., PARTRIDGE, F., WILLIAMS, S., and SILVA, P. A. (1991), 'A Twelve-Year Follow-Up of Preschool Hyperactive Children', *Journal of the American Academy of Child and Adolescent Psychiatry*, 30: 224–32.

MCGEE, R., WILLIAMS, S., and SILVA, P. A. (1985), 'Factor Structure and Correlates of Ratings of Inattention, Hyperactivity and Antisocial

Behaviour in a Large Sample of 9-Year-Old Children from the General Population', *Journal of Consulting and Clinical Psychology*, 53: 480–90.

MAGNUSSON, D. (1988), *Individual Development from an Interactional Perspective*. Hillsdale, NJ: Erlbaum.

MANNUZZA, S., KLEIN, R. G., and ADDALLI, K. A. (1991), 'Young Adult Mental Status of Hyperactive Boys and their Brothers: A Prospective Follow-Up Study', *Journal of the American Academy of Child and Adolescent Psychiatry*, 30: 743–51.

MANNUZZA, S., KLEIN, R. G., BONAGURA, N., MALLOY, P., GIAMPINO, T. L., and ADDALLI, K. A. (1991), 'Hyperactive Boys Almost Grown Up, V: Replication of Psychiatric Status', *Archives of General Psychiatry*, 48: 77–83.

MAWSON, A. R. (1987), *Transient Criminality*. New York: Praeger.

MICHELSON, L. (1987), 'Cognitive-Behavioural Strategies in the Prevention and Treatment of Antisocial Disorders in Children and Adolescents', in J. D. Burchard and S. N. Burchard, eds., *Prevention of Delinquent Behaviour*, 275–310. Beverly Hills: Sage.

MIRANNE, A. C., and GEERKEN, M. R. (1991), 'The New Orleans Inmate Survey: A Test of Greenwood's Predictive Scale', *Criminology*, 29: 497–518.

MOFFITT, T. E. (1990), 'The Neuropsychology of Juvenile Delinquency: A Critical Review', in M. Tonry and N. Morris, eds., *Crime and Justice*, vol. 12, 99–169. Chicago: University of Chicago Press.

MOFFITT, T. E., and HENRY, B. (1989), 'Neuropsychological Assessment of Executive Functions in Self-Reported Delinquents', *Development and Psychopathology*, 1: 105–18.

MOFFITT, T. E., and SILVA, P. A. (1988*a*), 'IQ and Delinquency: A Direct Test of the Differential Detection Hypothesis', *Journal of Abnormal Psychology*, 97: 330–3.

—— (1988*b*), 'Neuropsychological Deficit and Self-Reported Delinquency in an Unselected Birth Cohort', *Journal of the American Academy of Child and Adolescent Psychiatry*, 27: 233–40.

MORASH, M., and RUCKER, L. (1989), 'An Exploratory Study of the Connection of Mother's Age at Childbearing to her Children's Delinquency in Four Data Sets. *Crime and Delinquency*, 35: 45–93.

MUELLER, C. W., and PARCEL, T. L. (1981), 'Measures of Socio-Economic Status: Alternatives and Recommendations', *Child Development*, 52: 13–30.

MURRAY, D. M., LUEPKER, R. V., JOHNSON, C. A., and MITTELMARK, M. B. (1984), 'The Prevention of Cigarette Smoking in Children: A Comparison of Four Strategies', *Journal of Applied Social Psychology*, 14: 274–88.

NAGIN, D. S., and FARRINGTON, D. P. (1992*a*), 'The Onset and Persistence of Offending', *Criminology*, 30: 501–23.

—— (1992*b*), 'The Stability of Criminal Potential from Childhood to Adulthood', *Criminology*, 30: 235–60.

OFFORD, D. R., ALDER, R. J., and BOYLE, M. H. (1986), 'Prevalence and Sociodemographic Correlates of Conduct Disorder', *American Journal of Social Psychiatry*, 6: 272–8.

OFFORD, D. R., BOYLE, M. H., and RACINE, Y. (1989), 'Ontario Child Health Study: Correlates of Disorder', *Journal of the American Academy of Child and Adolescent Psychiatry*, 28: 856–60.

OLWEUS, D. (1987), 'Testosterone and Adrenaline: Aggressive Antisocial Behaviour in Normal Adolescent Males', in S. A. Mednick, T. E. Moffitt, and S. A. Stack, eds., *The Causes of Crime: New Biological Approaches*, 263–82. Cambridge: Cambridge University Press.

OSBORN, S. G. (1980), 'Moving Home, Leaving London, and Delinquent Trends', *British Journal of Criminology*, 20: 54–61.

OUSTON, J. (1984), 'Delinquency, Family Background, and Educational Attainment', *British Journal of Criminology*, 24: 2–26.

PARKER, J. G., and ASHER, S. R. (1987), 'Peer Relations and Later Personal Adjustment: Are Low Accepted Children at risk?', *Psychological Bulletin*, 102: 357–89.

PATTERSON, G. R. (1982), *Coercive Family Process*. Eugene, Oregon: Castalia.

PATTERSON, G. R., CHAMBERLAIN, P., and REID, J. B. (1982), 'A Comparative Evaluation of a Parent Training Programme, *Behaviour Therapy*, 13: 638–50.

PATTERSON, G. R., REID, J. B., and DISHION, T. J. (1992), *Antisocial Boys*. Eugene, Oregon: Castalia.

PEARSON, F. S., and WEINER, N. A. (1985), 'Toward an Integration of Criminological Theories', *Journal of Criminal Law and Criminology*, 76: 116–50.

PETERSILIA, J., GREENWOOD, P. W., and LAVIN, M. (1978), *Criminal Careers of Habitual Felons*. Washington, DC: National Institute of Justice.

POWER, M. J., ALDERSON, M. R., PHILLIPSON, C. M., SHOENBERG, E., and MORRIS, J. N. (1967), 'Delinquent Schools?', *New Society*, 10: 542–43.

POWER, M. J., BENN, R. T., and MORRIS, J. N. (1972), 'Neighbourhood, Schools, and Juveniles before the Courts', *British Journal of Criminology*, 12: 111–32.

PULKKINEN, L. (1988), 'Delinquent Development: Theoretical and Empirical Considerations', in M. Rutter, ed., *Studies of Psychosocial Risk*, 184–99. Cambridge: Cambridge University Press.

RAINE, A. (1985), 'A Psychometric Assessment of Hare's Checklist for Psychopathy on an English Prison Population', *British Journal of Clinical Psychology*, 24: 247–58.

REISS, A. J. (1986), 'Why are Communities Important in Understanding Crime?', in A. J. Reiss and M. Tonry, eds., *Crime and Justice*, vol. 8: *Communities and Crime*, 1–33. Chicago: University of Chicago Press.

—— (1988), 'Co-offending and Criminal Careers', in M. Tonry and N. Morris, eds., *Crime and Justice*, vol. 10, 117–70. Chicago: University of Chicago Press.

REISS, A. J., and FARRINGTON, D. P. (1991), 'Advancing Knowledge about Co-offending: Results from a Prospective Longitudinal Survey of London Males', *Journal of Criminal Law and Criminology*, 82: 360–95.

REITSMA-STREET, M., OFFORD, D. R., and FINCH, T. (1985), 'Pairs of Same-Sexed Siblings Discordant for Antisocial Behaviour', *British Journal of Psychiatry*, 146: 415–23.

RICHMAN, N., STEVENSON, J., and GRAHAM, P. (1985), 'Sex Differences in the Outcome of Pre-school Behaviour Problems', in A. R. Nicol, ed., *Longitudinal Studies in Child Psychology and Psychiatry*, 75–89. Chichester: Wiley.

RILEY, D., and SHAW, M. (1985), *Parental Supervision and Juvenile Delinquency*. Home Office Research Study no. 83. London: HMSO.

ROBINS, L. N. (1979), 'Sturdy Childhood Predictors of Adult Outcomes:

Replications from Longitudinal Studies', in J. E. Barrett, R. M. Rose, and G. L. Klerman, eds., *Stress and Mental Disorder*, 219–35. New York: Raven.

—— (1986), 'Changes in Conduct Disorder over Time', in D. C. Farran and J. D. McKinney eds., *Risk in Intellectual and Social Development*, 227–59. New York: Academic Press.

—— (1991), 'Conduct Disorder', *Journal of Child Psychology and Psychiatry*, 32: 193–212.

ROBINS, L. N., and RATCLIFF, K. S. (1978), 'Risk Factors in the Continuation of Childhood Antisocial Behaviour into Adulthood', *International Journal of Mental Health*, 7: 96–116.

—— (1980), 'Childhood Conduct Disorders and Later Arrest', in L. N. Robins, P. J. Clayton, and J. K. Wing eds., *The Social Consequences of Psychiatric Illness*, 248–63. New York: Brunner/Mazel.

ROBINS, L. N., TIPP, J., and PRZYBECK, T. (1991), 'Antisocial Personality', in L. N. Robins and D. Regier, eds., *Psychiatric Disorders in America*, 258–90. New York: MacMillan/Free Press.

ROBINS, L. N., WEST, P. J., and HERJANIC, B. L. (1975), 'Arrests and Delinquency in Two Generations: A Study of Black Urban Families and their Children', *Journal of Child Psychology and Psychiatry*, 16: 125–140.

ROBINS, L. N., and WISH, E. (1977), 'Childhood Deviance as a Developmental Process: A Study of 223 Urban Black Men from Birth to 18', *Social Forces*, 56: 448–73.

ROFF, J. D., and WIRT, R. D. (1984), 'Childhood Aggression and Social Adjustment as Antecedents of Delinquency', *Journal of Abnormal Child Psychology*, 12: 111–26.

ROLPH, J. E., and CHAIKEN, J. M. (1987), *Identifying High-Rate Serious Criminals from Offical Records*. Santa Monica: Rand.

ROSE, S. L., ROSE, S. A., and FELDMAN, J. F. (1989), 'Stability of Behaviour Problems in Very Young Children', *Development and Psychopathology*, 1: 5–19.

ROSS, R. R., FABIANO, E. A., and EWLES, C. D. (1988), 'Reasoning and Rehabilitation', *International Journal of Offender Therapy and Comparative Criminology*, 32: 29–35.

ROSS, R. R., and ROSS, B. D. (1988), 'Delinquency Prevention through Cognitive Training', *New Education*, 10: 70–5.

RUTTER, M. (1981), 'The City and the Child', *American Journal of Orthopsychiatry*, 51: 610–25.

—— (1989), 'Psychosocial Risk Trajectories and Beneficial Turning Points', in S. Doxiadis, ed., *Early Influences Shaping the Individual*, 229–39. New York: Plenum.

RUTTER, M., COX, A., TUPLING, C., BERGER, M., and YULE, W. (1975), 'Attainment and Adjustment in Two Geographical Areas, I: The Prevalence of Psychiatric Disorder', *British Journal of Psychiatry*, 126: 493–509.

RUTTER, M., and GILLER, H. (1983), *Juvenile Delinquency*. Harmondsworth: Penguin.

RUTTER, M., MAUGHAN, B., MORTIMORE, P., and OUSTON, J. (1979), *Fifteen Thousand Hours*. London: Open Books.

RUTTER, M., TIZARD, J., and WHITMORE, K. (1970), *Education, Health and Behaviour*. London: University of London Press.

RUTTER, M., YULE, B., QUINTON, D., ROWLANDS, O., YULE, W., and BERGER, M. (1975) 'Attainment and Adjustment in Two Geographical Areas', III: Some Factors Accounting for Area Differences', *British Journal of Psychiatry*, 126: 520–33.

SATTERFIELD, J. H. (1987), 'Childhood Diagnostic and Neurophysiological Predictors of Teenage Arrest Rates: An 8-year Prospective Study', in S. A. Mednick, T. E. Moffitt, and S. A. Stack, eds., *The Causes of Crime: New Biological Approaches*, 146–67. Cambridge: Cambridge University Press.

SCHWEINHART, L. J., and WEIKART, D. P. (1980), *Young Children Grow Up*. Ypsilanti, Michigan: High/Scope.

SHANNON, L. W. (1988), *Criminal Career Continuity*. New York: Human Sciences Press.

SHAW, C. R., and MCKAY, H. D. (1942), *Juvenile Delinquency and Urban Areas*. Chicago: University of Chicago Press.

—— (1969), *Juvenile Delinquency and Urban Areas*, rev. edn. Chicago: University of Chicago Press.

SHEDLER, J., and BLOCK, J. (1990), 'Adolescent Drug Use and Psychological Health', *American Psychologist*, 45: 612–30.

SHEPHERD, J. P., and FARRINGTON, D. P. (1993), 'Assault as a Public Health Problem', *Journal of the Royal Society of Medicine*, 86: 89–92.

SHEPHERD, M., OPPENHEIM, B., and MITCHELL, S. (1971), *Childhood Behaviour and Mental Health*. London: University of London Press.

SHORT, J. F. (1969), 'Introduction to the Revised Edition', in C. R. Shaw and H. D. McKay (1969), *Juvenile Delinquency and Urban Areas*, rev. edn. Chicago: University of Chicago Press.

SHORT, J. F., and NYE, F. I. (1957), 'Reported Behaviour as a Criterion of Deviant Behaviour', *Social Problems*, 5: 207–13.

SHOVER, N. (1985), *Aging Criminals*. Beverly Hills: Sage.

SIMCHA-FAGAN, O., and SCHWARTZ, J. E. (1986), 'Neighbourhood and Delinquency: An Assessment of Contextual Effects', *Criminology*, 24: 667–703.

SNYDER, H. N. (1988), *Court Careers of Juvenile Offenders*. Washington, DC: Office of Juvenile Justice and Delinquency Prevention.

SPIVACK, G., MARCUS, J., and SWIFT, M. (1986), 'Early Classroom Behaviours and Later Misconduct', *Developmental Psychology*, 22: 124–31.

STANDER, J., FARRINGTON, D. P., HILL, G., and ALTHAM, P. M. E. (1989), 'Markov Chain Analysis and Specialization in Criminal Careers', *British Journal of Criminology*, 29: 317–35.

STATTIN, H., and MAGNUSSON, D. (1991), 'Stability and Change in Criminal Behaviour up to Age 30', *British Journal of Criminology*, 31: 327–46.

STATTIN, H., MAGNUSSON, D., and REICHEL, H. (1989), 'Criminal Activity at Different Ages: A Study Based on a Swedish Longitudinal Research Population', *British Journal of Criminology*, 29: 368–85.

SUTHERLAND, E. H., and CRESSEY D. R. (1974), *Criminology*, 9th edn. Philadelphia: Lippincott.

TAYLOR, E. A. (1986), 'Childhood Hyperactivity', *British Journal of Psychiatry*, 149: 562–73.

TELCH, M. J., KILLEN, J. D., MCALISTER, A. L., PERRY, C. L., and MACCOBY, N. (1982), 'Long-Term Follow-Up of a Pilot Project on Smoking Prevention with Adolescents', *Journal of Behavioural Medicine*, 5: 1–8.

THORNBERRY, T. P., and FARNWORTH, M. (1982), 'Social Correlates of Criminal Involvement: Further Evidence on the Relationship between Social Status and Criminal Behaviour', *American Sociological Review*, 47: 505–18.

TOBLER, N. S. (1986), 'Meta-analysis of 143 Drug Treatment Programmes: Quantitative Outcome Results of Programme Participants Compared to a Control or Comparison Group', *Journal of Drug Issues*, 16: 537–67.

TOLAN, P. H. (1987), 'Implications of Age of Onset for Delinquency Risk', *Journal of Abnormal Child Psychology*, 15: 47–65.

TONRY, M., OHLIN, L. E., and FARRINGTON, D. P. (1991), *Human Development and Criminal Behaviour*. New York: Springer-Verlag.

TRACY, P. E., WOLFGANG, M. E., and FIGLIO, R. M. (1985), *Delinquency in Two Birth Cohorts*. Washington, DC: Office of Juvenile Justice and Delinquency Prevention.

—— (1990), *Delinquency Careers in Two Birth Cohorts*. New York: Plenum.

TRASLER, G. B. (1962), *The Explanation of Criminality*. London: Routledge and Kegan Paul.

—— (1986), 'Situational Crime Control and Rational Choice: A Critique', in K. Heal and G. Laycock, eds., *Situational Crime Prevention: From Theory into Practice*, 17–24. London: HMSO.

TREMBLAY, R. E., LEBLANC, M., and SCHWARTZMAN, A. E. (1988), 'The Predictive Power of First-Grade Peer and Teacher Ratings of Behaviour: Sex Differences in Antisocial Behaviour and Personality at Adolescence', *Journal of Abnormal Child Psychology*, 16: 571–583.

VENABLES, P. H., and RAINE, A. (1987), 'Biological Theory', in B. J. McGurk, D. M. Thornton, and M. Williams, eds., *Applying Psychology to Imprisonment*, London: HMSO.

VERHULST, F. C., KOOT, H. M., and BERDEN, G. F. M. G. (1990), 'Four-Year Follow-Up of an Epidemiological Sample', *Journal of the American Academy of Child and Adolescent Psychiatry*, 29: 440–8.

VISHER, C. A. (1986), 'The Rand Inmate Survey: A Reanalysis', in A. Blumstein, J. Cohen, J. A. Roth, and C. A. Visher, eds., *Criminal Careers and 'Career Criminals'*, vol. 2, 161–211. Washington, DC: National Academy Press.

VISHER, C. A., and ROTH, J. A. (1986), 'Participation in Criminal Careers', in A. Blumstein, J. Cohen, J. A. Roth, and C. A. Visher eds., *Criminal Careers and 'Career Criminals'*, vol. 1, 211–91. Washington, DC: National Academy Press.

WADSWORTH, M. (1979), *Roots of Delinquency*. Oxford: Martin Robertson.

WALKER, N. (1985), *Sentencing: Theory, Law and Practice*. London: Butterworths.

WALKER, N. D., FARRINGTON, D. P., and TUCKER, G. (1981), 'Reconviction Rates of Adult Males after Different Sentences', *British Journal of Criminology*, 21: 357–60.

WALLIS, C. P., and MALIPHANT, R. (1967), 'Delinquent Areas in the County of London: Ecological Factors', *British Journal of Criminology*, 7: 250–84.

WEST, D. J. (1982), *Delinquency: Its Roots, Careers and Prospects*. London: Heinemann.

WEST, D. J., and FARRINGTON, D. P. (1973), *Who Becomes Delinquent*? London: Heinemann.

—— (1977), *The Delinquent Way of Life*. London: Heinemann.

WHITE, H. R., LABOUVIE, E. W., and BATES, M. E. (1985), 'The Relationship Between Sensation Seeking and Delinquency: A Longitudinal Analysis', *Journal of Research in Crime and Delinquency*, 22: 197–211.

WHITE, J. L., MOFFITT, T. E., EARLS, F., ROBINS, L. N., and SILVA, P. A. (1990), 'How Early Can We Tell? Predictors of Child Conduct Disorder and Adolescent Delinquency', *Criminology*, 28: 507–33.

WIDOM, C. S. (1989), 'The Cycle of Violence', *Science*, 244: 160–6.

WIKSTRÖM, P-O. (1987), *Patterns of Crime in a Birth Cohort*. Stockholm: University of Stockholm Department of Sociology.

—— (1990), 'Age and Crime in a Stockholm Cohort', *Journal of Quantitative Criminology*, 6: 61–84.

WILSON, H. (1980), 'Parental Supervision: A Neglected Aspect of Delinquency', *British Journal of Criminology*, 20: 203–35.

WILSON, J. Q., and HERRNSTEIN, R. J. (1985). *Crime and Human Nature*. New York: Simon and Schuster.

WOLFGANG, M. E., FIGLIO, R. M., and SELLIN, T. (1972), *Delinquency in a Birth Cohort*. Chicago: University of Chicago Press.

WOLFGANG, M. E., THORNBERRY, T. P., and FIGLIO, R. M. (1987), *From Boy to Man, from Delinquency to Crime*. Chicago: University of Chicago Press.

YAMAGUCHI, K., and KANDEL, D. B. (1984), 'Patterns of Drug Use from Adolescence to Young Adulthood, II: Sequences of Progression', *American Journal of Public Health*, 74: 668–72.

YARROW, M. R., CAMPBELL, J. D., and BURTON, R. V. (1970), *Recollections of Childhood: A Study of the Retrospective Method*, Monographs of the Society for Research in Child Development, serial no. 138, vol. 35, no. 5.

ZIMRING, F. E. (1981), 'Kids, Groups and Crime: Some Implications of a Well-Known Secret', *Journal of Criminal Law and Criminology*, 72: 867–85.

ZOCCOLILLO, M., PICKLES, A., QUINTON, D., and RUTTER, M. (1992), 'The Outcome of Childhood Conduct Disorder: Implications for Defining Adult Personality Disorder and Conduct Disorder', *Psychological Medicine*, 22: 971–86.

13

Environmental Criminology

ANTHONY E. BOTTOMS

In a 'trend report' on urban sociology, published in 1989, Rosemary Mellor noted an enduring scepticism, in much post-war British sociology, about the 'urban' as a rewarding field of study; hence, most ordinary people's 'everyday recognition of places or neighbourhoods as having different potential for living in, or for investment, found no place in a discipline that sought status in generalisation and assumed the "urban" as a uniform context' (Mellor 1989: 242). Paradoxically, however, towards the end of the twentieth century, when developments in telecommunications technology and the ready availability of rapid transport have rendered many people's home locations a less all-embracing milieu for daily living than our grandparents would have thought possible, there has been, within sociology, a rediscovery of the importance of places and of local context. This change apparently has at least two sources. The first is the geographical 'unevenness of development in a modernising economy' (Mellor 1989: 244).[1] The second, which derives more from within social theory itself, is essentially a product of some sociologists' novel (but welcome) emphasis upon the centrality of mundane daily social practices to the reproduction of social systems (see especially Giddens 1984), an emphasis which is of relevance in the present context since—as the ordinary lives of all of us readily attest—place, spatial differentiation, and time are of considerable importance to the business of doing the things we have to do each day. In short, therefore, and to the surprise of some, there is now

> a re-entry of the 'local' . . . into the sociological mainstream of debates over class, status, racism, the social division of labour, welfare and power. Urban sociology cannot disappear under the sociological umbrella, rather, the reverse. Sociology has to be alert to the issues of urbanisation and, in particular, to the routine appreciation of localities as conferring social power . . . [Increasingly], localism *and* mobility define everyday life. (Mellor 1989: 253)

[1] This refers to the general shift away from manufacturing/extractive industries, the importance of regional economies, etc.; and towards a more information and service-based economy, multinational corporations selectively locating their business to reduce costs and/or avoid local labour resistances, and so on. See generally Lash and Urry (1987).

It can be plausibly argued that most sociology of crime in modern Britain has not adequately come to terms with these developments. Of course, 'left realists' have in an important way developed the local victim survey as a methodological tool (see e.g. Jones *et al.* 1986; Painter 1992), but even in these studies the importance of specific local milieux is not always recognized or adequately theorized (though there are exceptions; see e.g. the Edinburgh Crime Survey's highlighting of the city centre as a site for victimization and harassment: Anderson *et al.* 1990: ch. 5). Indeed, it might not be going too far to say that many British criminologists would be quite content to leave aside issues of crime and place as a worthwhile (but ultimately peripheral) 'sub-specialism', which can be safely left to the few criminologists who have shown a particular interest in it—and, of course, to the geographers.[2]

It is a central contention of this chapter that such attitudes to environmental criminology,[3] where they exist, are profoundly mistaken. Crime and criminality are, as we shall see, highly geographically skewed, and an understanding of this uneven spatial distribution is of crucial importance both to the explanation of *crimes* and to the social production of *offenders*. A serious grappling with issues of place and of space[4] in criminological explanation very quickly uncovers a number of important explanatory issues, relevant to criminological theorization in general, which are all too easily forgotten when the spatial dimension is not addressed.[5] That being the case, mainstream criminologists need to take environmental criminology seriously.

The two central concerns of environmental criminology are *explaining the spatial distribution of offences* and *explaining the spatial distribution of*

[2] Social geographers in Britain have in fact been quite prolific in their writings on crime in recent years: see e.g. Davidson (1981), Herbert (1982); Smith (1986); Evans and Herbert (1989); Evans *et al.* (1992).

[3] Though it is not without its problems, especially in an era of 'green' issues, I have used the term 'environmental criminology' throughout this chapter as the most convenient generic description of analyses of the relationship between place, crime, and offending. Other such descriptions include 'the geography of crime', 'the ecology of crime', etc.; most of these descriptions carry with them more difficulties than the term used here.

[4] 'Place' is not the same as 'space'. The former concept refers to a geographical location, with fairly definite boundaries, within which people may meet, engage in various activities, etc. 'Space' is a much broader concept, but environmental criminologists are interested in it because some social activities have become quite markedly *spatially differentiated* (e.g. the 'zoning' policies of some urban planners); on the other hand, modern transport and telecommunications allow for individuals (and social systems) to bridge spatial separation to a much greater extent than in previous generations.

[5] It can be powerfully argued that the concept of *time* should also be of central importance in environmental criminology; and indeed the careful reader will note the significance of temporal variables at several points in examples given in this chapter. However, as there is only a relatively weak existing literature on this topic, I have followed the convention of most enviromental criminology in restricting the substantive focus of the chapter to issues of place and space in relation to crime. For an interesting pioneering study on temporal variables, see Cohn (1991).

offenders; hence, sections on these topics will form the core of this chapter. These central sections will, however, be preceded by a historical introduction and some methodological comments; and they will be followed by sections on community change and crime, and on environmental criminology and the future. The important but specialized topic of design and crime has had to be omitted for reasons of space.[6] Similarly, although some of the findings of environmental criminology are relevant for crime prevention, it has not been practicable within this chapter to consider the policy implications of the subject.

ENVIRONMENTAL CRIMINOLOGY: A BRIEF HISTORY

As a number of authors have pointed out, environmental criminology is nearly as old as the study of crime itself. In the first half of the nineteenth century, Guerry and Quetelet studied the newly published criminal statistics of France, discovering *inter alia* some marked areal variations in crime rates. Subsequently, Henry Mayhew's (1862) comprehensive social survey of Victorian London, *London Labour and the London Poor*, provided much ethnographic detail on various 'rookeries' (slum criminal quarters); and in the work of others, concern about the 'dangerous classes' thrown up by the industrializing and urbanizing developments of the nineteenth century also led to a focus on various specific localities. (On this nineteenth-century background see generally Morris 1957: ch. 3; Radzinowicz 1966: ch. 2; Tobias 1972.)

In a chapter of this kind, these early precursors of environmental criminology can necessarily receive only brief mention. But more sustained attention must be paid to the next major development in the subject, because of the extent of its subsequent influence.

In the period between the two world wars, the Chicago School of Sociology constituted an immensely creative group of scholars, of a varied kind, which made 'by far the most important American contribution to dissolving the stratification of sociology into theoretical sociologists and empirical sociologists' (Bulmer 1984: 221). The most enduring criminological contribution from within the Chicago School came from Clifford Shaw and Henry McKay, whose *magnum opus* on juvenile delinquency in urban areas is still read, half a century on (Shaw and McKay 1942). As well as making a theoretical contribution themselves—notably through the theory of 'social disorganization' (see below)—Shaw and McKay's research heavily influenced much other criminological theory in the 1930s, notably Thorsten Sellin's (1938) 'culture conflict' theory and

[6] Among the most important literature on design and crime, see Newman (1973); Poyner (1983); Coleman (1985, 1989); Poyner and Webb (1992); Taylor and Gottfredson (1986).

Edwin Sutherland's theory of differential association (see Cressey 1964). But Shaw and McKay's main contribution to criminology was empirical, and here their research embraced two very different styles, always seen by the authors themselves as complementary. In the first place, they meticulously mapped the residences of juvenile delinquents, first of all in Chicago itself at different points in time, and then also in other American cities. Secondly, they also tried, in the tradition of the Chicago School more generally, to stay close to the life of the people and the communities about which they were writing, particularly through the use of the life history method (see e.g. Shaw 1930).

For present purposes, we can concentrate mainly on Shaw and McKay's mapping of delinquent residences. In developing this research, they drew upon the more general work in urban sociology of the Chicago School, notably that of Robert E. Park and Ernest W. Burgess, the dominant concept of which was 'human ecology'. Human ecology was seen as the study of the spatial and temporal relations of human beings as affected by the selective, distributive and accommodative forces of the environment; the concept was derived, by analogy, from the botanical sub-discipline of plant ecology. Shaw and McKay drew only to a limited extent upon the most explicitly quasi-biological elements of Park's urban sociology (see Alihan 1938: 83), but they made quite central use of Burgess's zonal theory of city development. According to this theory, the typical city could be conceptualized as consisting of five main concentric zones (see Fig. 13.1), the innermost of which was described as the non-residential central business district (or 'loop'), which was then circled by a 'zone in transition', where factories and poorer residences were intermingled, and finally by three residential zones of increasing affluence and social status. New immigrants, it was postulated, would move into the cheapest residential areas of the city (in the 'zone in transition') and then, as they became economically established, migrate outwards. This would be a continuous process, so that the 'zone in transition' would (as its name implies) have a high residential mobility rate. In the case of a rapidly expanding city, particular districts which had once been peripheral and affluent might become, in time, part of the zone in transition within the larger metropolis (see e.g. Rex and Moore 1967 on Sparkbrook, Birmingham).

Applying this zonal model to their empirical data, Shaw and McKay made the following three central discoveries (see Finestone 1976, p. 25):

1. The rates of juvenile delinquency residence conformed to a regular spatial pattern. They were highest in the inner-city zones and tended to decline with distance from the centre of the city; and this was so not only in Chicago but in other cities as well (see Table 13.1).

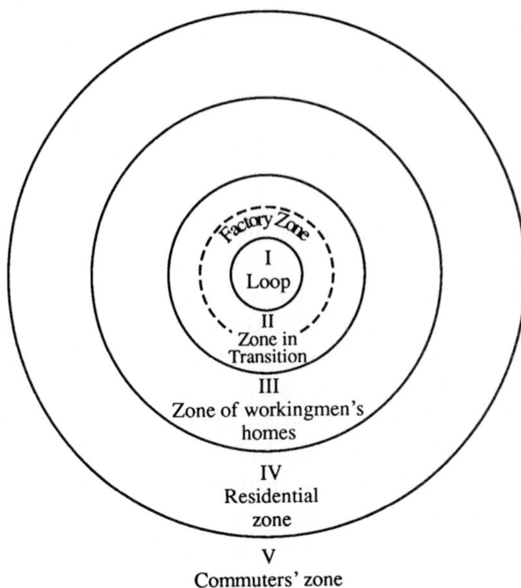

Fig. 13.1 E. W. Burgess's zone model of urban development
Source: Burgess (1925).

Table 13.1. Delinquency Residence Rates for the Concentric Zones of Seven American Cities, c.1930

	Zone 1	Zone 2	Zone 3	Zone 4	Zone 5
Chicago	10.3	7.3	4.4	3.3	–
Philadelphia	11.6	6.8	4.4	3.5	3.4
Richmond	19.7	12.2	6.4	–	–
Cleveland	18.3	10.2	7.8	7.0	5.1
Birmingham	14.1	6.9	6.4	–	–
Denver	9.4	7.1	4.2	3.7	3.2
Seattle	19.1	9.7	7.6	6.1	–

Source: Brantingham and Brantingham (1981: 14), collating data from various tables in Shaw and McKay (1931).

2. The same spatial pattern was shown by many other indices of social problems in the city.
3. The spatial pattern of rates of delinquency showed considerable long-term stability, even though the nationality make-up of the population in the inner-city areas changed greatly from decade to decade (with successive waves of migration to American cities in the early twentieth century).

In seeking to explain these striking findings, Shaw and McKay focused especially upon the observed *cultural heterogeneity* and the *constant population movements* in the 'zone in transition'. As Robert Bursik (1986: 38) has pointed out, economic mobility lay at the heart of the process they described, but they did not posit a direct relationship between economic factors and rates of delinquency; rather, areas characterized by economic deprivation and physical deterioration were seen as also having population instability and cultural fragmentation, and it was these factors which especially influenced delinquency through a process which they called 'social disorganization'. This process, as seen by Shaw and McKay, was later well summarized by Finestone (1976: 28–9) in a passage that is worth quoting in full:

> The same selective processes which made it relatively easy for the first generation of newcomers to the city to become aggregated in inner-city areas also permitted the location there of many illegitimate enterprises and deviant moral worlds. Such moral diversity within the inner-city areas meant that it was difficult if not impossible for immigrant communities to insulate themselves from illegitimate and criminal enterprises and influences. In the face of many centrifugal pulls, the traditional institutions, the family, the church, and the local community, became incapable of maintaining their solidarity. Their inability to organise effectively in defence of conventional values meant that they were unable to resist or limit the influence exercised upon their youth by the diverse value systems which became rooted in such areas. Continued high rates of delinquents in inner-city areas were a product of the joint operation of locational and cultural processes which maximized the moral diversity of population types at the same time as they weakened the collective efforts of conventional groups and institutions to protect their own integrity.

Hence, in Shaw and McKay's thinking, 'social disorganisation exists in the first instance when the structure and culture of a community are incapable of implementing and expressing the values of its own residents' (Kornhauser 1978: 63); and this process of disorganization was seen as strongly related to the genesis of juvenile delinquency. However, at various points in their writings, Shaw and McKay also speak of another and rather different theoretical approach to the explanation of criminality, namely that of *criminal subcultures*, linked to the *cultural transmission of delinquent values*. The precise relationship between these two varied theoretical strands of Shaw and McKay's work was not always made fully clear in their writings (see Kornhauser 1978: ch. 3).

The subsequent history of the social disorganization concept is a tangled one, and can be pursued only to a limited extent in this chapter. A number of writers have argued that criminality might in certain circumstances stem from *organization* rather than disorganization, especially in areas with organized crime syndicates or well-entrenched criminal subcultures; those who take this view point out that just because actions are morally disapproved of, that does not mean that they are necessarily any less related to social organization, and not all groups share conventional value systems. Other critics have suggested that social disorganization theory pays insufficient attention to the distribution of power in society (see Snodgrass 1976; cf. Bursik 1986: 61); while yet others have suggested that the theory can be tautologous—that is, social disorganization theorists have sometimes used a single indicator (such as a delinquency rate) both as an example of disorganization and as an effect allegedly caused by disorganization. Finally, like a number of other early sociological theories of crime, it has been argued that social disorganization theory is over-deterministic and therefore over-predictive of crime (see e.g. Matza 1964). Despite these various criticisms, the concept of social disorganization remains a live one in contemporary criminology: for example, not long ago its status was fully reviewed by Bursik (1988), while Sampson and Groves (1989) have recently attempted to test the social disorganization element in Shaw and McKay's work using data from the first British Crime Survey.

It is a measure of the standing and achievement of Shaw and McKay that, in the quarter-century immediately after the end of the Second World War, there were relatively few major new developments in environmental criminology, despite the publication of some significant individual research monographs (e.g. Lander 1954; Morris 1957). Moreover, throughout this period the relationship between crime and place was routinely referred to as 'the ecology of crime', in effect accepting the Chicagoans' biological analogy for the working of urban society, and hence implicitly acknowledging their intellectual pre-eminence in the field (interestingly, this nomenclature is not dead even today).[7] But this post-war lack of challenge to the supremacy of the Chicago School was accompanied also by some loss of interest, among mainstream criminologists, in the spatial dimension of the study of crime. Accordingly, in 1965 a leading criminologist in Britain, Hermann Mannheim, commented in

[7] Cf. Baldwin (1979: 34): 'the term [ecology] is still used to characterise subsequent research even when the researchers in question would vehemently eschew the Burgess framework . . . the term is certainly confusing, and it would be more appropriate to refer to "areal" studies of crime than to "ecological" studies.'

his major textbook that 'ecological theory . . . reached the peak of its popularity in the period between the two world wars, but has gradually retreated into the background in the decades after 1945' (Mannheim 1965: 532).[8]

But the 1970s were to see environmental criminology given fresh impetus; and in this respect two main developments were perhaps of particular importance.

The first of these might be described as the *rediscovery of the offence*. Shaw and McKay's work had been all about *areas of delinquent residence*, i.e. the areas where the juvenile delinquents lived. But these *high offender rate areas* (to adopt the usual technical term) are in fact not necessarily the same as *high offence rate areas* (i.e. areas with a high rate of offence commission), since offenders do not necessarily commit offences close to their homes (see further below). This important point had been made very crisply in the 1950s by Morris (1957: 20–1), referring to an unpublished doctoral dissertation of 1946 on juvenile delinquency in Egypt, where the author had distinguished between the 'breeding grounds' of crime (the slum areas where offenders lived) and the wealthier shopping centres ('attracting areas') where they tended to commit their crimes. Nor was this the first such comment: as Brantingham and Jeffery (1981) have interestingly shown, a very early article by Burgess (1916) had, thirty years beforehand, made much the same observation in a study of a small Kansas town. But despite these examples, until the 1970s most work on crime and place (including that of Shaw and McKay) had shown very little systematic interest in offence locations: 'This fact should not be surprising because, . . . sociological criminology was, for long decades, primarily concerned with the origins and epidemiology of criminality [as opposed to specific offences]. The findings of [Burgess's] article have nothing to say about criminality' (Brantingham and Jeffery 1981: 230).

Various different criminological developments of the 1970s combined to re-focus attention on *crimes* rather than *offenders* (see generally Brantingham and Brantingham 1981*a*, introduction). These included the early work of the Home Office Research Unit on 'crime as opportunity' (Mayhew *et al.* 1976), leading in due course to the more sophisticated development of 'situational crime prevention' theory (see Clarke 1983, 1992); the work of the architect Oscar Newman (1973) and others on design and crime ('defensible space'); and C. Ray Jeffery's (1971) influential book *Crime Prevention through Environmental Design*. In the wake of these new strands of work, by 1981 Paul and Patricia Brantingham were able to open their influential edited book on environmental criminology with the following offence-centred paragraph—though apparently without

[8] See Baldwin (1979) for an overview of early post-war research in the field.

realizing that their definition of 'environmental criminology' actually excluded most of Shaw and McKay's massive endeavours:[9]

A crime is a complex event. A crime occurs when four things are in concurrence: a law, an offender, a target, and a place. Without a law there is no crime. Without an offender, someone who breaks the law, there is no crime. Without some object, target, or victim, there is no crime. Without a place in time and space where the other three come together, there is no crime. These four elements—law, the offender, the target, and the place—can be characterized as the four dimensions of crime. Environmental criminology is the study of the fourth dimension of crime. (Brantingham and Brantingham 1981: 7)

It will become apparent later in this chapter that this 'rediscovery of the offence' in environmental criminology has been of major importance in the field. Moreover, the careful synthesis of work on the explanation of *who commits offences* (offender-based theory) with work on the explanation of *where and why offences are committed* (offence-based theory) can be regarded as an issue of central significance in contemporary criminology (see for example Gottfredson and Hirschi 1990; Bottoms 1993).

The second major development of the 1970s came in the field of explaining offender rates. Once again, it had its precursors. In his pioneering 1957 book, Terence Morris (1957) carried out an empirical study of Croydon and showed that the areal rates of offender residence in that borough did not conform particularly well to the Chicago zonal hypothesis, not least because of the existence of high offender rate council estates located at a considerable distance from the urban centre.[10] Commenting on this point—a product, of course, of post-1920 British housing policy—Morris (1957: 130) shrewdly observed that:

where the provision of housing is not solely within the province of the market, and the local authority has stepped in to provide housing as a social amenity for a not inconsiderable proportion of the population, then [what the Chicago School described as] the natural ecological processes of selection manifesting themselves in the cycle of 'invasion-dominance-succession' are likely to be severely modified by social policy, with strikingly different results.

[9] To be fair, in this source the Brantinghams (1981; 8) do refer to the 'movements that bring the offender and the target together at the same site', and to the question of 'how the fourth dimension of crime interacts with the other three dimensions'. It is nevertheless striking that their *definition* of environmental criminology does not embrace the study of the location of offender residence.

[10] For those unfamiliar with the British housing context, 'council estates' are areas in which tenants rent from the local authority (a 'council'): i.e. they are a form of public housing. They reached their peak of importance around 1980, at which stage about a third of households in Great Britain were council tenants; hence this tenure form is much more extensive in Britain than in the United States (for a history and full account, see Merrett 1979). Since 1980, various aspects of national government policy have led to some decline in the proportion of council tenants nationally.

All these points were to be confirmed and strengthened in work in the city of Sheffield, published in the 1970s (Baldwin and Bottoms 1976). Fig. 13.2 illustrates the adult offender rates found in that city: while there is indeed still something of a clustering of high offender rate areas around the central business district, the data overall show 'no tidy zonal model . . . [rather], areas with high and low offender residence rates were distributed throughout the city in apparently haphazard fashion' (Brantingham and Brantingham 1984: 322). In seeking to explain the offender rate patterns found, the Sheffield researchers were drawn increasingly towards the exploration of the *direct and indirect conse-*

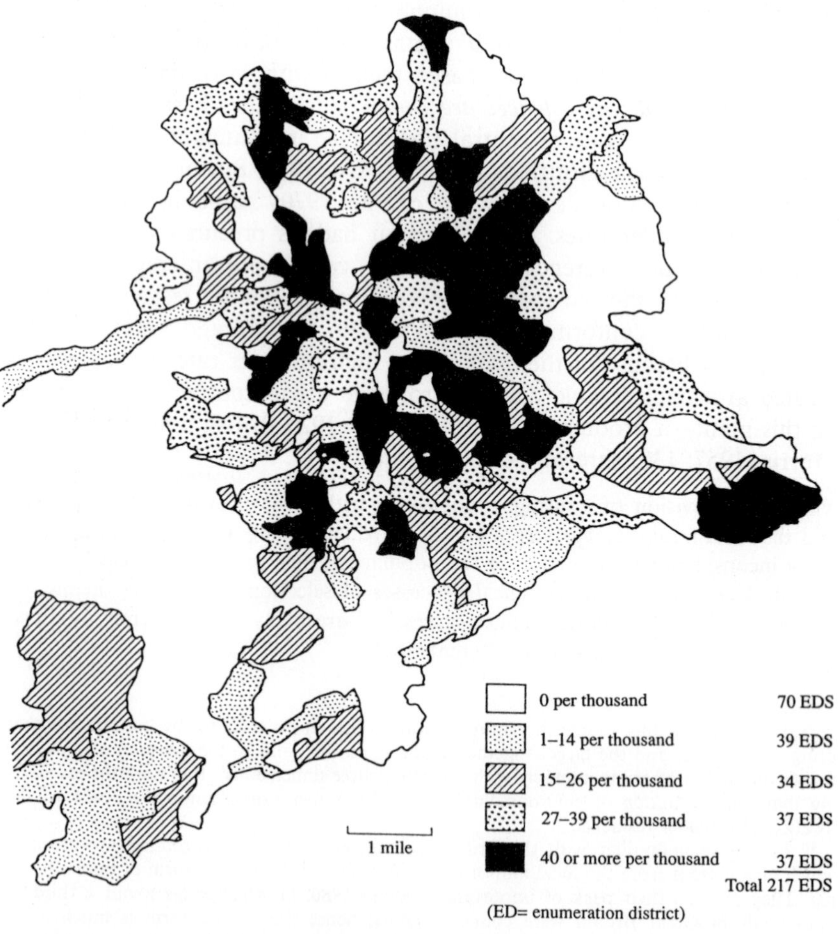

Fig. 13.2 Areal distribution of adult male offender residences in Sheffield, 1966
Source: Baldwin and Bottoms (1976: 75).

quences of the operation of the housing market (see e.g. Bottoms and Wiles 1986). As we shall see in a later section of this chapter, this emphasis on housing markets has also been taken up by other researchers (some influenced by the Sheffield research, and others working independently), and has been found to be of particular significance when assessing change in offender and offence rates in residential areas. These considerations have taken some researchers working on crime-related topics deep into analyses of the complex housing market contexts of particular local areas (see e.g. Taub *et al.* 1984; Bottoms *et al.* 1992).

The *rediscovery of the offence* and the *discovery of the significance of housing markets* have, between them, done much to revivify environmental criminology in the last quarter-century. It is essentially these developments, in interaction with some theoretical issues to be described in more detail in later sections of this chapter, that underpin the claim that mainstream criminologists need to take environmental criminology seriously if they are truly interested in the explanation of crimes and criminality.

PRELIMINARY METHODOLOGICAL ISSUES

But before we turn to substantive research findings, three key methodological issues in environmental criminology must be briefly addressed: they are the offence/offender distinction, the validity of official statistics, and the so-called 'ecological fallacy'.

The offence rate/offender rate distinction has been highlighted above. It is an absolutely central issue in environmental criminology, as will quickly become apparent if one compares a map of offence locations in Sheffield (see Fig. 13.3) with a map of adult offender residences in the same year (refer back to Fig. 13.2). It is very clear from these maps that one certainly cannot assume that high offender and high offence rate areas are identical—although, interestingly, further work in Sheffield has shown that if one excludes areas such as the city centre and industrial districts, then there is a high (but not perfect) correlation between offender and offence rates in *residential* areas (Mawby 1979).[11]

One should further note (see Bottoms and Wiles 1986: appendix) that, in any given geographical area, both the offence rate and the offender rate are in principle measurable both by official (police-recorded) data and by research-generated data seeking to improve upon official statistics (namely, victim surveys in respect of offence rates, and self-report studies in respect of offender rates). In practice, however, self-report studies

[11] Unfortunately, some research studies of the 1950s did not adequately appreciate the importance of the offence/offender rate distinction, with sometimes confusing results: see Brantingham and Brantingham (1981: 17).

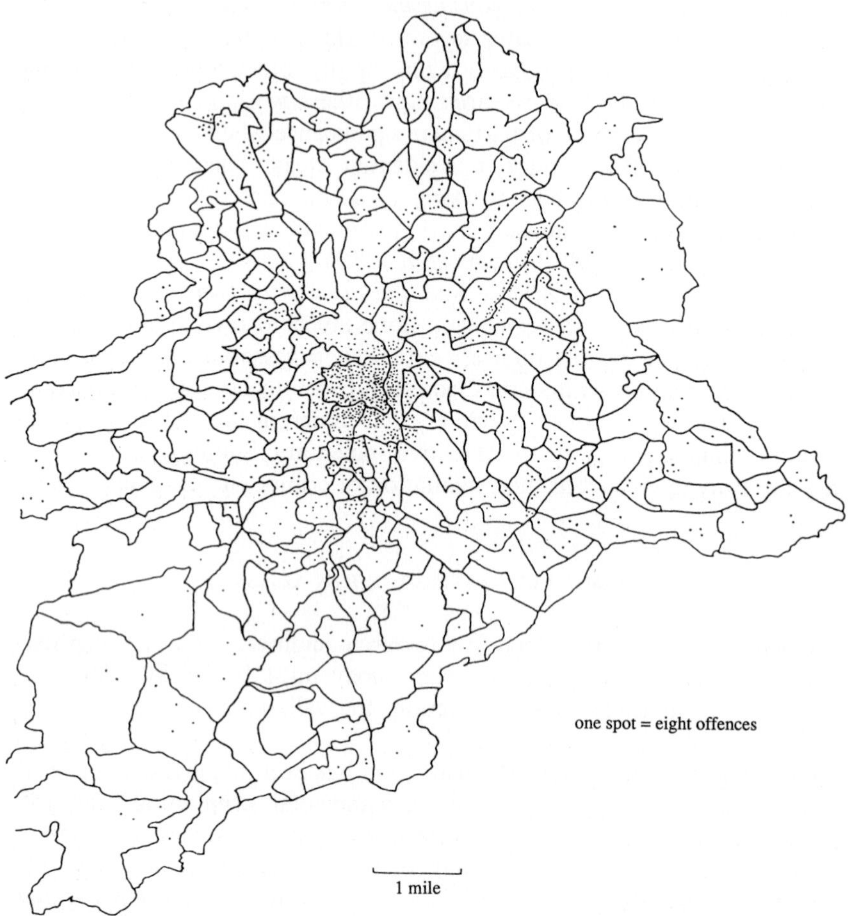

Fig. 13.3 Areal distribution of indictable offences in Sheffield, 1966
Source: Baldwin and Bottoms (1976: 58).

carried out on a small-area basis in defined neighbourhoods are extremely rare. One should also be aware that there is an important distinction in principle between an *area offence rate* and an *area victimization rate*. The former measures all offences committed in an area, whether against businesses, individual residents, or individuals who are visiting the area; the latter measures all offences committed against a defined population (e.g. respondents to a household victim survey living in a particular residential district), *wherever those offences were committed.* Because of this conceptual difference, particular care must be taken in comparing total police-recorded offence rates for an area (which will be geographically bounded, but will include offences against businesses and individual visitors to the area) with overall rates generated from a household victim survey carried out in the same area (which will exclude crimes against businesses and individual victims visiting the area, but will *include* crimes committed against residents of the area when they have ventured outside the district, e.g. to the city centre or their place of work).

These considerations take us straight to the second methodological issue, that of the validity of official criminal statistics in relation to area-based data. There has been and continues to be a lively debate on this issue, with particular scepticism about the validity of official statistics being expressed during the heyday of labelling theory in the 1970s (for a useful historical overview of the debate, see Mawby 1989). Commenting on this debate in a small space is difficult; but to begin with the uncontroversial, there is now little doubt that, on a large-area basis—for example, as between different large counties—the message conveyed by official criminal statistics can be seriously misleading (see e.g. the study by Farrington and Dowds 1985 in Nottinghamshire and comparable counties), owing especially to different police investigative and recording practices in different administrative areas, and perhaps to differential levels of public reporting of crime to the police. On a smaller-area, within-city basis, however, as Mawby (1989) points out, there are two main grounds for believing that differential police-recorded offence and offender rates as between different areas might often express a basically true difference in crime or criminality levels.

First, the results of victim surveys have consistently shown a higher crime victimization rate for inner-city areas and poor council estates than for more affluent suburbs, exactly as shown in official police data (see for example the Merseyside crime survey, Kinsey 1985, and the aggregated area-based results from different parts of England and Wales in the British Crime Survey: Hope and Hough 1988). (Note, however, in respect of these results the previously-mentioned distinction between victimisation and offence rates.)

Secondly, as part of the Sheffield project, a careful area-based analysis of the validity of official criminal statistics on offences and offenders in nine small areas was carried out by Mawby (1979) (see also Bottoms *et al.* 1987 for a related victim survey). Mawby, who had begun his work expecting to find major police-generated differences in official statistics by area (based on the propositions of labelling theory), in fact found that a careful analysis of various aspects of police processing (for example, the discovery, reporting, and recording of crime, and the process of detection) forced him 'to question widespread assumptions that police forces create area differences in crime rates . . . the recorded information [showed] no indication of area [offence and offender rate] differences being radically altered due to the different actions of the police (or indeed the public) in different areas' (Mawby 1979: 182).

One must, however, be quite careful in interpreting the above results. On the one hand, the research cited certainly shows that differential official offence and offender rates in different small areas of cities can sometimes be valid indicators of real differences in crime/criminality levels. On the other hand, it is important not to over-state the results, nor to over-generalize from them. The Sheffield results, for example, largely concerned offences that were policed reactively rather than proactively, and different issues arise in respect of proactively policed offences such as prostitution (cf. Lowman 1986). Moreover, Brantingham and Brantingham's somewhat grandiose claim (1991: 4) that the Sheffield results appear 'to have established that official statistics are valid Euclidean indicators of area crime rate differences in that city, creating a working presumption that such might be the case in other places as well' unfortunately goes beyond the evidence of the Sheffield study.[12] The more modest truth is that official crime and offender data often seem to reflect real differences between sub-areas of cities, but that in any given case this cannot be taken for granted and must be investigated.

The third preliminary methodological issue to consider is the so-called 'ecological fallacy', discussed mathematically in a famous article by Robinson (1950). This fallacy, which was sometimes unfortunately evident in early studies in environmental criminology (see Baldwin 1979 for some examples), occurs where 'the assumption [is] made that the descriptive characteristics of *areas* having high proportions of offenders resident also [identify] . . . the *individuals* who are likely to commit crimes' (Brantingham and Brantingham 1981: 17). To take a simple example of the fallacy, in the 1960s various British research studies demonstrated that recorded crime rates were highest in areas with a relatively high rate of recent ethnic minority immigration (mostly from the Caribbean and the Indian sub-continent), but research also showed, at that time, that on an individual basis such immigrants had on the whole rather low offending rates (for references relating to this example see Baldwin and Bottoms 1976: 37–8). While Janson (1993) has recently argued that examples where ecological and corresponding individual correlations move in opposite directions are the exception rather than the rule, it is nevertheless clear that the wise researcher would do very well to avoid the fallacy, in

[12] This is most obvious in the 1980s follow-up study of one pair of areas (see Bottoms, Claytor and Wiles 1992); but even in the original 1970s small-area study, the ratio of survey-reported crime to officially recorded differences was substantially higher in a pair of high-rise council estates than in other comparable areas studied (see Bottoms *et al.* 1987, table 5, row 4, and commentary at pp.138–9).

any instance where he/she has access primarily to area-based data (e.g. Census data) rather than individual data.

Having considered these three methodological issues, we can now turn to the substantive results of modern environmental criminology.

EXPLAINING THE LOCATION OF OFFENCES

We begin with the explanation of the location of offences. A preliminary problem here concerns how to measure areal offence rates, as opposed to offender rates. When measuring areal offender rates, the denominator for the rate calculation is straightforward: it is the total population of the studied area, or, preferably, the total *relevant* population of the area (i.e. standardizing for possible differential sex ratios, differential representation of various age-groups in the populations of different areas, etc.). However, when measuring offence rates, the use of the resident population as a denominator is often not very helpful at all, and the development of alternative denominators is frequently necessary (see e.g. Harries 1981). To appreciate the force of this point, the reader is invited to consider the obvious inappropriateness of using the resident population as a denominator for a study of, say, thefts of and from cars in commuter car parks at semi-rural outer-city railway stations which draw their passengers from a wide hinterland.

Wikström (1991), in a comprehensive areal study of recorded offences in Stockholm, carefully considered the denominator problem for different kinds of offence. He distinguished between the 'suggested best denominator' for each offence (i.e. what he considered the most appropriate denominator if full information were available) and the best practicable denominator within the data available for his own study (called 'the chosen denominator'). His choices in these two categories are shown in Table 13.2. I shall not discuss these denominators in detail, and readers should be aware that other choices could have been made; but careful study of Table 13.2 will clearly illustrate the nature of the denominator problem when constructing areal offence rates.

Wikström's study, using these denominators, provides one of the clearest illustrations in the research literature of the way in which offences are locationally distributed in a major city. We have already seen from the overall distribution of offences in Sheffield (Fig. 13.3) that offences in general tend, in traditional cities, to be very much clustered around the city centre;[13] and the offence rates in Wikström's study (see Fig.

[13] In fact in Sheffield in 1966 24 per cent of recorded offences were committed within a half-mile radius of the centre of the city, though this area constituted less than 3 per cent of the total land area in the city (Baldwin and Bottoms 1976: 57).

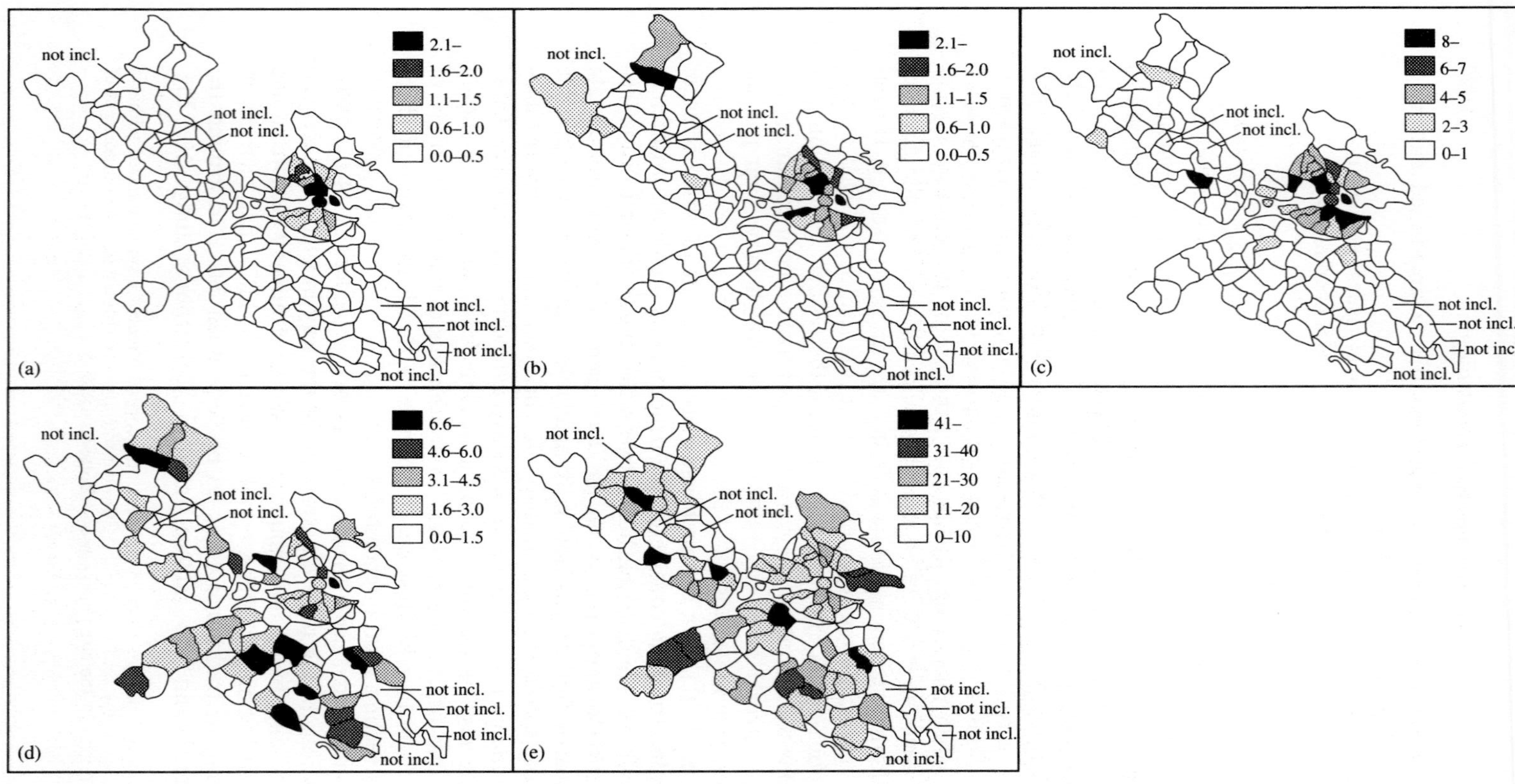

Fig. 13.4 Areal offence rates for selected type of crime, Stockholm, 1982: (a) violence in public per hectare; (b) vandalism in public per hectare; (c) thefts of and from cars per hectare; (d) family violence per 1,000 households; (e) residential burglaries per 1,000 residences

Source: Wilkström (1991: 203–6).

Table 13.2. Per-Olof Wikström's suggestions for appropriate denominators in area studies of offence rates

Crime	Suggested best denominator	Chosen denominator
Family violence	No. of households	No. of households
Non-family violence and vandalism in residences	No. of residences	No. of residences
Violence in public	No. of meetings between people	Hectare
Vandalism in public	?	Hectare
Residential burglaries	No. of residences	No. of residences
Cellar/attic burglaries	No. of residences in multi-storey houses	No. of residences in multi-storey houses
Non-residential burglaries	No. of companies and public institutions	No. of people working in area
Thefts of and from cars	No. of cars	Hectare

Source: Wikström (1991: 196).

13.4(a)–(c)) show this to be especially the case for violence in public, vandalism in public, and theft of and from cars. (Wikström does not present data concerning shoplifting or thefts from the person, but other research studies show that these offences also are often concentrated in city centres.) However, it should be noted that there is nothing necessarily immutable about such patterns: for example, in cities that develop large shopping or entertainment complexes on peripheral sites (as many cities have increasingly tended to do in recent years), one would expect some corresponding modification of the traditional geographical pattern.

Turning to offences in residential areas, the distributions of family violence and residential burglaries in Wikström's study are shown in Fig. 13.4(d) and (e). The highest rates of family violence were found in certain outer-city wards, and further analysis showed that there was a strong positive correlation (at an area level) between (i) an area's rates of recorded family violence and (ii) its score on a factor (derived from a factor analysis of social areas in Stockholm) which was labelled by Wikström as 'problem residential areas' (Wikström 1991: 226).[14] Hence,

[14] This was derived from a factor analysis not including offence or offender data. The main loadings on the factor were: (i) positive loadings: percentage on public welfare assistance; immigrants (foreign citizens); non-profit housing; children with single working parents; and percentage blue-collar workers; (ii) negative loadings: old residences; mean income; flats in smaller houses; large residences; and percentage people over 60 (Wikström 1991: 123–4).

and perhaps not surprisingly, police-recorded family violence was heavily concentrated in poorer public housing areas. A further inspection of the maps at in Fig. 13.4(d) and (e) indicates, however, that the distribution of offences of residential burglary was substantially different from that of family violence, and additional analysis by Wikström (1991: 226–7) showed that residential burglaries in fact tended to occur in areas of high socio-economic status, and especially in districts where there were nearby high offender rate areas. This finding, while not unique in the literature,[15] conflicts with the results of some other research studies which suggest that rates of residential burglary are greatest in, or in areas close to, socially disadvantaged housing areas (for a summary, see Maguire and Bennett 1982: 20–1; see also Hope and Hough 1988: 33, 42). Possible reasons for these conflicting results will become apparent as the discussion proceeds.

Wikström's study fairly conclusively demonstrates, at any rate as regards crimes as measured by official data, first that there are marked geographical skews in the patterning of offence locations, and secondly that these can vary significantly by type of offence. This general message has been heavily reinforced, at a micro level of analysis, by some research on so-called 'hotspots' of crime by Lawrence Sherman *et al.* (1989). Using 'police call data' for the city of Minneapolis for 1985/6, the authors found, *inter alia*, (i) that just 3.3 per cent of specific addresses or intersections in the city generated 50 per cent of crime-related calls to the police to which cars were despatched, and (ii) that there was considerable variation in the victimization rate (as measured by call data) of specific micro-locations even *within* high crime rate areas—that is, even high-crime areas have their relatively safe specific locations, as well as their 'hotspots' where the public are likely to be especially vulnerable.

The above discussion of offence locations has been primarily descriptive. We need now to attempt to explain the variations discussed; and we will begin with the related concepts of opportunity and routine activities.

Opportunity theory and routine activities theory

In his analysis of residential burglary in Stockholm (see above), Wikström (1991: 227) went beyond descriptive maps, and demonstrated that there was a significant positive correlation, on an areal basis, between the burglary rate and the percentage of households with an

[15] See e.g. Baldwin and Bottoms (1976: 63); Winchester and Jackson (1982: 18–19). It should be pointed out that these studies, like Wikström's, are based on data recorded by the police, and it is likely that they proportionately overstate the number of high-value burglaries, since value is known to be related to the decision to report.

annual income of Kr 200,000 (approximately £20,000) or more. On the basis of this finding, he concluded that 'area target attractiveness' had an important influence on the residential burglary rate.

The concept of 'target attractiveness', however, needs a little elaboration. In the instance cited above (and see note 15), it refers to the *potential availability of lucrative goods to steal*; but in other instances it might refer instead to the *relative absence of adequate surveillance*. This latter point is well illustrated from an analysis by a crime prevention team in Croydon of the risk rates for car crime from different multi-storey car parks in the town centre (reported in Liddle and Bottoms 1993): it was shown (see Table 13.3) that the three short-stay car parks which were used primarily by shoppers (and therefore had a constant stream of passers-by acting as a form of natural surveillance) had substantially lower crime rates than the long-stay car parks, primarily used by London commuters who would leave their cars all day in parks near the railway station where, in the nature of the case, there was much less coming and going by members of the public.[16]

Table 13.3. Croydon town centre multi-storey car parks: car crime risk rates per car, and crimes per space, by type of car park

	Capacity	Daily turnover[a]	Est. no. of cars using park in 8 months (000s)	Recorded Crimes in 8 months	Risk rate per 1,000 vehicles (8 months)	Est. crimes per car park space p.a.
(a) *Longer-stay*						
A	1,300	0.86	233.9	170	0.73	0.196
B	'918	0.91	175.6	79	0.45	0.130
(All)			(409.5)	(249)	(0.61)	(0.168)
(b) *Shorter-stay*						
C	867	2.88	825.0	40	0.05	0.069
D	618	5.66	735.0	20	0.03	0.048
E	1,140	2.89	693.0	25	0.04	0.033
(All)			(2253.0)	(85)	(0.04)	(0.049)

[a] Number of cars using car park daily, divided by capacity.
Source: Liddle and Bottoms (1993).

[16] A complicating variable here is that each car on average stayed longer in the commuter car-parks (= greater opportunity through target availability); note however (last column of table) that even when one calculates the rate as 'per car park space' (in effect controlling for this difference), the commuter car parks had substantially higher car crime rates.

Other (and similar) examples of the importance of natural surveillance can be found in the literature on the location of offences: for example, public telephones in places such as pubs or launderettes suffer much less vandalism than street-located callboxes (Clarke 1983: 239), while in driver-only double-decker buses vandalism has been shown to be twenty-five times higher on the (unsupervised) top deck than on the lower deck (Mayhew *et al.* 1976).

The two aspects of 'target attractiveness' considered above (i.e. potentially lucrative targets and the apparent absence of surveillance) can of course both be described as falling also within the broader concept of *opportunity*. But that concept embraces one additional dimension which is not related to target attractiveness, namely *the availability or otherwise of the means to commit crimes*. That this point might be criminologically important can be seen from the commonsense observation that, in a heated quarrel, the availability of a gun might mean that a homicide will result, while if there is no loaded weapon to hand, then perhaps no crime at all (or at most a minor assault) might be committed (and see Cook 1983). This 'means to commit crime' factor might be of at least indirect importance for environmental criminology, in that it clearly might affect offence rates in specific micro-locations where the availability of 'means to crime' is of special importance (as with e.g. the reduction in hijackings since the introduction of more stringent airport security; consider also the possible effects of provision of plastic drinking receptacles rather than traditional glasses in British pubs: Clarke 1983: 244).

The multi-faceted 'opportunity' approach to the explanation of crime patterns, as outlined above, is very closely related to so-called 'routine activities theory', originally developed in an article by Cohen and Felson (1979) and subsequently elaborated mostly by Marcus Felson (see e.g. Felson 1992). The central hypothesis of routine activities theory is that 'the probability that a violation will occur at any specific time and place might be taken as a function of the convergence of likely offenders and suitable targets in the absence of capable guardians (Cohen and Felson 1979: 590). However, of the three elements identified in the above quotation, routine activities theory (as developed by its advocates) has in practice concentrated very heavily on the second and third (suitable targets and capable guardians).[17] That being so, the link with opportunity theory is self-evident; but there are nevertheless two features of the routine activities approach which develop and in a sense extend the straightforward concept of 'opportunity'.

[17] See Cohen and Felson (1979: 589): 'Unlike many criminological enquiries, we do not examine why individuals or groups are inclined criminally, but rather we take criminal inclination as given and examine the manner in which the spatio-temporal organisation of social activities helps people to translate their criminal inclinations into action.'

First, there is a strong interest within routine activities theory in *the day-to-day activities of potential victims of crime, and of those potentially able to offer 'natural surveillance'*. There is therefore seen to be an interdependence between the varied social organization of daily life patterns (for example, in different decades, and/or in different places, and/or among different social groups in the same area) and the spatial–temporal structuring of illegal activities. For example, in their original article, Cohen and Felson presented data supportive of the fact that, in the post-war years (1947–74), crime rate variations in the United States were related to a major shift of routine activities away from the home and towards both labour force participation and participation in other activities away from home (1979: 593). To put it simply, if there are general changes in social life such that people spend less time in their homes, then there might be more crimes against unattended residential property, especially if those residential properties contain increasing quantities of valuable and easily moved goods.

Secondly, routine activities theory has an explicitly spatial dimension which, while implicitly present in simple opportunity theory, has not always been much developed by writers of that school (though cf. for example Poyner 1983). Routine activities theory, precisely because of its interest in the everyday lives of potential victims of crime and of potential 'natural guardians', specifically emphasizes 'the fundamental human ecological character of illegal acts as *events* which occur at specific locations in *space* and *time*, involving specific persons and/or objects' (Cohen and Felson 1979: 589, emphasis in original).

In sum, routine activities theory in effect embeds the concept of opportunity within the routine parameters of the day-to-day lives of ordinary people, and in doing so also emphasizes the spatial–temporal features of opportunity. For those interested in social theory, these features of Cohen and Felson's work present an intriguing parallel with Anthony Giddens's (1984) 'theory of structuration'—a major contemporary approach to some fundamental questions about the nature of human action in its relationship to social structures—since Giddens's theory also includes among its innovative features (i) a greater emphasis on routine daily social practices than is to be found in most social theory, and (ii) an unusual insistence (for a modern writer) that space–time issues lie at the heart of the concerns of social theory, and are not merely 'a particular type or "area" of social science which can be pursued or discarded at will' (Giddens 1984: 110).

Once one begins—as in Cohen and Felson's approach—to link the opportunity concept to that of the routine activities of victims and of potential 'natural guardians', then other relevant issues in considering the spatial distribution of offences also begin to become apparent. One of the most important is the issue of *self-policing*, as it affects potential offences against the person. There is perhaps a tendency, among some opportunity theorists, to concentrate especially upon property offences, and upon issues such as 'target-hardening', leaving property unguarded, etc. But the concept of opportunity is also of relevance in offences against the person: for example, a group of youths in a city centre intent on personal attacks linked to thefts (of wallets, handbags, etc.) will, other things being equal, probably be more likely to select as a victim a person walking alone than an accompanied person. Potential victims can of course respond to possible opportunities of this sort by 'self-policing' or 'avoidance' behaviour, so that the opportunity to attack an unaccompanied person is not presented. Since there is clear empirical evidence of substantially greater harassment of women (especially younger women) in the public spaces of cities (see e.g. Anderson *et al.* 1990: 23–4; Painter 1992), and since this harassment is not unnaturally regarded by many women as threatening potential future personal victimization, it is hardly surprising that women especially are likely to engage in 'self-policing' activities of this kind as regards their use of public space—for example, by completely avoiding certain areas of the city, especially at night, or by avoiding certain specific locations within an area, or by going out only with a companion (e.g. Ramsay 1989: 6–8). Unfortunately, such routine self-policing activities might themselves have further social consequences of an unintended kind—hence Kate Painter (1992: 181), for example, suggests that what she calls 'women's space evasion at night' might have the unintended consequence of compounding the fears of other women (who may see very few women using certain kinds of public space), and also perhaps helping to undermine, by degrees, the overall quality of life in parts of the urban environment (see below on dynamic processes of social decline in specific neighbourhood contexts).

Taking all the evidence of this sub-section together, there is not much doubt that the broad concept of 'opportunity' (understood here as incorporating the routine activities approach) powerfully influences crime locations. But is it the *only* relevant variable to be considered in explaining the spatial distribution of offences? A booklet published by the Home Office Crime Prevention Unit seemed to imply that it was:

> Most crimes do not occur at random but tend to be concentrated in particular places or to occur at particular times of the day. This is a reflection of the fact that crime is most likely to occur where the opportunities for it are greatest. A housing estate renowned for the insecurity of its doors and windows, or a car park dimly lit and protected from public view will almost certainly attract the criminal. It is the link between opportunity and crime which explains the crime patterns revealed through . . . a crime profile [drawn from police crime data]. (Home Office 1988: 15)

Unfortunately, the research literature suggests that matters are more complex than this. To begin to see why that is so, let us first consider a recently published ethnographic study of active burglars in a Texas city (Cromwell *et al.* 1991). These authors found, congruently with opportunity theory, that offenders weighed potential gains, levels of guardianship (e.g. signs of occupancy), and risks of detection at possible sites of residential burglary (see also Bennett and Wright 1984). Hence, *active weighing of the opportunity factor at the potential crime site* was a significant factor in the ultimate decision whether or not to commit a particular crime. On the other hand, the Texas study also found that:

1. there were variations between different burglaries, some being more opportunistic and some more carefully planned (again see Bennett and Wright 1984);[18]
2. there were also some complex group effects (for example, burglars working in groups were more likely to engage in multiple—offence burglary 'sprees' on a single outing, because of increased levels of arousal; on the other hand, group discussions at a specific crime site could tend to result in more cautious decisions than an individual's solo decision would have done, probably because more eyes could perceive more potential risks of detection);
3. drugs issues could additionally influence decision-making (not only in terms of incentives to burgle, but also in terms of differential risk-taking as between non-drug users, cocaine users, and heroin and marijuana users);
4. sometimes effects on burglary decisions could arise from interactions between burglars and fences, the latter often 'amateur or avocational' rather than professional.

This range of factors suggests some quite complex decision-making processes, and hence clearly tends to indicate that a monocausal 'opportunity' model of crime locations will be too simple. This point is well appreciated by Cromwell and his colleagues, who conclude from their study that, overall, perhaps 'the most fertile paradigm' of explanation for the observed patterns of burglary offending might be 'a cognitive analysis of subroutines, [taking] into account drug and group effects within the larger template model' (Cromwell *et al.* 1991: 94).

In speaking here of 'subroutines', Cromwell *et al.* are of course referring to the routine activities of *offenders*. As previously noted, that is a subject in which the proponents of 'routine activities theory' have shown rather little interest (see note 17); but, as we shall now see, others have considered the topic, not least in a spatial context—and with interesting

[18] Note, however, that Cromwell and his colleagues used a different (and wider) definition of 'opportunistic' than did Bennett and Wright; see Cromwell *et al.* (1991: 48).

results that can be used to complement the insights of the opportunity and routine activities theorists.

Offenders' Use of Space

It is a commonplace of criminological textbooks that much crime is committed close to offenders' homes, though, not surprisingly, that is more likely to be true for juvenile delinquents than for adult offenders (see e.g. Baldwin and Bottoms 1976: ch. 3). However, while a number of so-called 'crime and distance' studies may be found in the literature, empirically exploring the data on detected offenders' distance from home when committing offences, it can be plausibly argued that this issue is in fact rather less interesting than is the related question of *the relationship of the place of the offence to the offender's habitual use of space*. To put the matter in non-technical terms, perhaps it is really of little significance that offenders A and B are one mile from home, while offenders C and D are three miles from home, when they commit offences in the city centre, which they all regularly frequent. On the other hand, the difference between a burglar who commits offences in an area he knows well, and one who is prepared to search carefully for a suitable target in a completely unknown residential area, might be a subject of much greater criminological importance and interest.

In preliminary exploration of this issue, let us first note that there are some purely *opportunist* crimes,[19] where a person responds 'there and then' to a set of attractive environmental cues (e.g. a teenage boy calls at a friend's house and finds the back door open and £20 unguarded on the table); and also some *affectively spontaneous* crimes, where a person commits, say, an assault in the course of a sudden heated argument with an acquaintance. These offences, by definition, must occur in the place where the offender happens to be, as a result of his/her daily life choices. More than a decade ago, however, Patricia and Paul Brantingham (1981) proposed, in a very interesting hypothetical paper, that the offender's daily life patterns might influence the location of offending behaviour even where the offender was engaging, to some degree, in a search pattern for a suitable target, having already decided in principle that he/she was willing to commit an offence (as, perhaps, in burglary). All of us, it was argued by these authors, carry in our heads 'cognitive maps' of cities where we live. Some parts of the city we will know extremely well (e.g. the areas immediately around our home, near our workplace, and in the city centre where we go for shopping and entertainment purposes); and we will also tend to know well the roads linking these various areas. On

[19] This uses Bennett and Wright's (1984) definition of 'opportunist': see note 18 above.

the other hand, there will be some areas of the city which we hardly know at all, such as residential areas (away from main roads) in which we have no social acquaintances. Patricia and Paul Brantingham innovatively postulated that most offenders will not commit offences in poorly known areas; hence offences, even 'search pattern' offences, were, they argued, most likely to occur where *criminal opportunities* intersected with *cognitively known areas*. This hypothesis is schematically illustrated in Fig. 13.5.

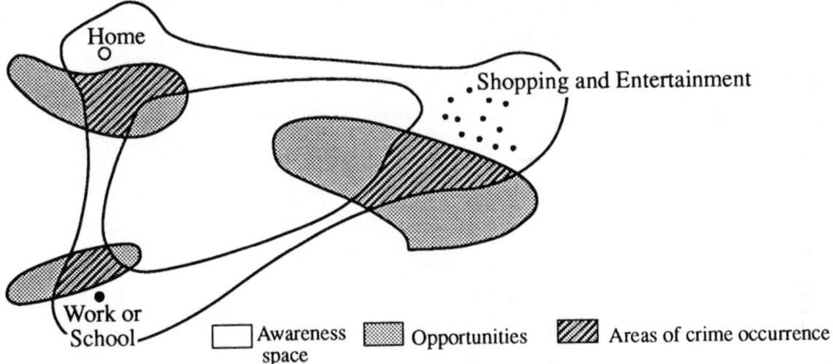

Fig 13.5 The Brantingham's hypothetical model of intersection of criminal opportunities with offender's cognitive awareness space
Source: Brantingham and Brantingham (1984: 362).

While the degree of empirical testing of this hypothetical model has not been extensive, what evidence we have tends clearly to support it, at least for many crimes (see for example Rhodes and Conly 1981; Brantingham and Brantingham 1991: 1–5, 239–51; Figlio *et al.* 1986: pt. 2). To illustrate this, we may look briefly at two small-scale studies of burglars, both carried out in the United States.

Rengert and Wasilchick (1985: ch. 3) carried out an interview study of imprisoned adult burglars from Delaware County, Philadelphia. Figure 13.6(a) provides a map of that county, and shows that the burglars' home residences tended to be located in the south of the county, while the high residential property values tended to lie in the north. Burglars were asked to rate each area of the county on a rating scale for familiarity: the results are shown in Fig. 13.6(b), and indicate, not surprisingly, that the areas near to offenders' homes were better known than other areas.[20] When further asked, in interview, for a scaled evaluation of each area of the county as a potential burglary site (using for this exercise only those areas with which the respondent claimed some familiarity), the results

20 Two areas were an exception to this: one was the seat of the county's criminal court, and the other the location of its prison!

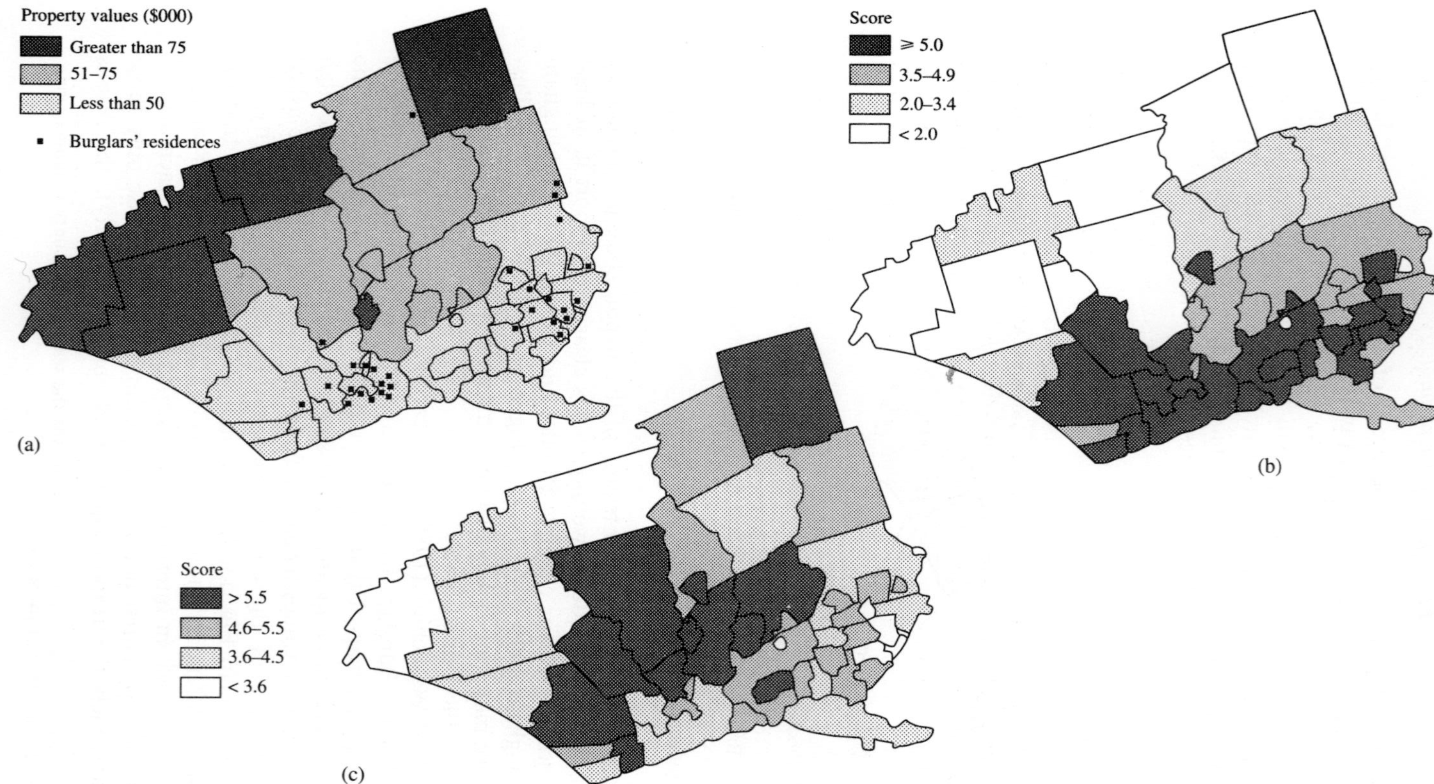

Fig 13.6 Aspects of burglary in Delaware County, Philadelphia (I): (a) location of burglars' homes in relation to residential property values; (b) burglars' knowledge of areas; (c) burglars' interview-based choice of areas for criminal activity

Source: Rengert and Wasilchick (1985: 58, 60, 61).

were as given in Fig. 13.6(c): that is, the stated preferred areas for crime sites were generally not the burglars' home areas, but neither (with one exception) were they the most affluent areas of the county. Interestingly, when these interview-based 'preferred' areas were compared with burglars' known offence locations (in their prior criminal records), there was a strong correlation, except that burglaries in the affluent north-eastern area were very rare.

The adult recidivist burglars in this study, then, tended to avoid the low-status areas of the south (because of poor target attractiveness), but they also avoided the unfamiliar affluent territory to the north of the county.[21] Developing the analysis further, Rengert and Wasilchick obtained from their respondents details of their day-to-day journeys when not in prison (to their work, their usual recreational sites, etc.). Figure 13.7(a) and (b) show (i) the *distance* from the offender's home to his place of employment (Fig. 13.7(a)), leisure resorts (Fig. 13.7(b)), and known crime locations (both diagrams)—distance from home being measured from the central point to the edge of the diagram, in every direction; and (ii) the *direction* from home towards the burglary site, assessed in relation to the offender's workplace or his stated leisure sites (on this directional issue, note that all the work and recreational sites are positioned on the 0° axis in the diagrams: a crime committed in the opposite direction from the offender's normal route to work would therefore be shown as 180° in Fig. 13.7(a), while a crime committed on a site at right angles to the home–workplace axis would be shown as 90°. It will be seen from these diagrams that there is a strong directional bias of burglary sites, which were clustered very disproportionately in the segment of the respective diagrams closest to offenders' normal routes to work and to recreational sites (thirty-one out of forty offences in this segment in Fig. 13.7(a); twenty out of thirty-five in Fig. 13.7(b)). By contrast, a very different directional pattern was observed for the few burglaries in the sample committed not as a result of the offender's own search pattern, but because a secondary source (e.g. a fence) told the offender about an appropriate opportunity for crime (see Fig. 13.7(c)). Overall, therefore, Rengert and Wasilchick's evidence can be seen clearly to support the hypotheses of the Brantinghams, while also showing that for some offences (Fig. 13.7(c)), their propositions may be of little relevance.

An earlier study in Oklahoma City had found some similar results. Carter and Hill (1979) interviewed eighty-three imprisoned property

[21] The following point, concerning the symbolic meaning of space, is also worth noting from this study: 'a cultural barrier to spatial movement [to the north of the county] seems to be West Chester Pike [a main road] . . . although the highway can be crossed easily, it seems to act as a perceptual dividing line between northern and southern parts of the county' (Rengert and Wasilchick 1985: 62).

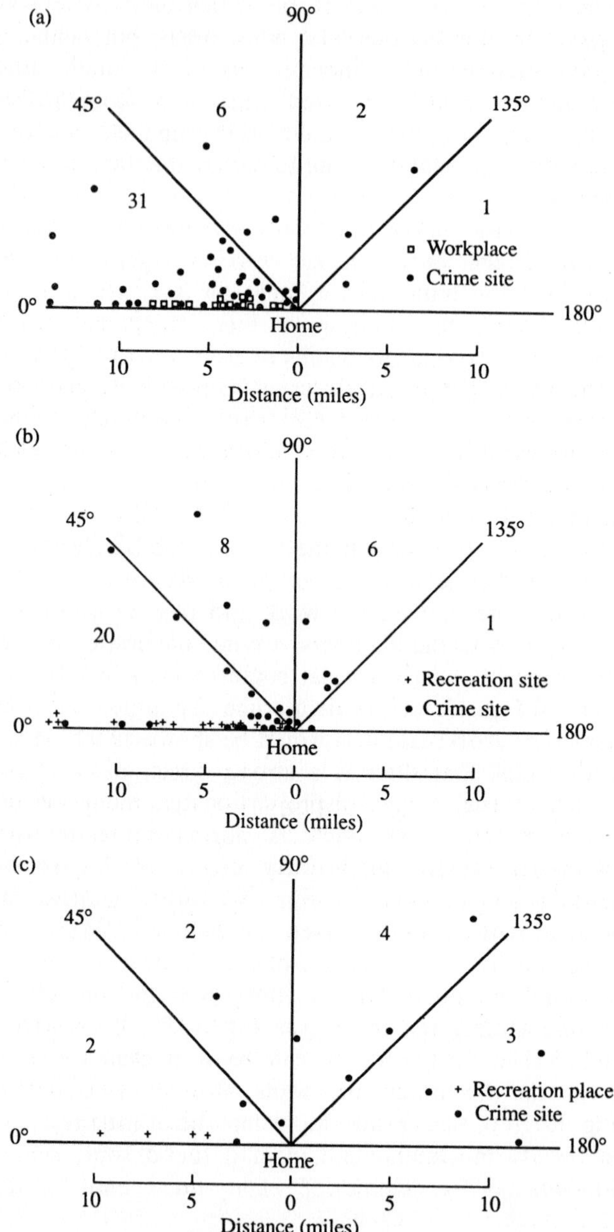

Fig. 13.7 Aspects of burglary in Delaware County, Philadelphia (II): (a) directional bias of burglaries toward offender's workplace; (b) directional bias of burglaries towards offender's recreational sites; (c) direction of burglaries suggested by a third party

Source: Rengert and Wasilchick (1985: 70, 71, 73).

offenders, and found that, for both black and white offenders, 'the social status dimension [of areas], which indicates wealth variations in the city, was negatively associated with their number of crimes. In other words, *there was a systematic tendency to avoid neighborhoods where the take was likely to be especially high*' (Carter and Hill 1979: 63, emphasis added).

Oklahoma City is a racially divided city, and neither black nor white offenders ventured much into residential areas inhabited predominantly by the other ethnic group. Moreover, both groups of offenders committed offences predominantly in areas with which they were familiar, and where they felt comfortable ('ontologically secure', in sociological language). These facts, plus the fact that most blacks (offenders and non-offenders) in Oklahoma City had only a restricted familiarity with the city at large, explained 'the dense pattern of black [offenders'] crimes around their home neighborhoods' (Carter and Hill 1979: 62). White offenders were (in general) familiar with more areas of the city, so their offences were more widely geographically spread.

On the basis of these findings, Carter and Hill (1979: 49) proposed an interesting distinction between 'strategic' and 'tactical' choices in search-pattern property crimes. 'Tactics' refer to 'short-term operational considerations for a specific crime', and may well be very strongly influenced by opportunity factors such as the expectation of the 'take' (from the visual external appearance of the property), ease of access, signs of occupancy, degree of surveillance, etc. However, these 'tactical' decisions will be taken, suggest Carter and Hill, only within a geographical search-pattern framework already set by 'strategic' considerations. These 'strategic' considerations—related especially to the issues of familiarity and ontological security referred to above—are based on intuitive feelings or images [concerning certain areas] which are difficult to articulate . . . Guided by his environmental image, the criminal will concentrate his activities in those areas towards which he has a favorable feeling' (Carter and Hill 1979: 49).

The offenders' lack of ability to articulate their 'strategic' choices is well illustrated in conversational extracts printed by Carter and Hill (1979: 47–8).[22] These extracts suggest that, to use the language of Giddens's structuration theory, offenders' broad choice of locations often seems to take place essentially in the realm of that *practical consciousness* which is so essential to the daily lives of all of us. 'Practical consciousness', in Giddens's terms, refers to the fact that human subjects largely act within a domain which cannot be expressed in terms such as 'motives' or 'reasons', but which 'consist of all the things which actors know tacitly

[22] For example: 'they agreed that it is a lot of things, but no one thing in particular. One said, "you've got to look at the pros and cons of the situation". [But] what are they?—"I don't know . . . I just gotta feeling"' (Carter and Hill 1979: 48).

about how to "go on" in the context of social life without being able to give them direct discursive expression' (Giddens 1984: xxiii); it must be distinguished from 'discursive consciousness', which is 'what actors are able to say, or give expression to, about social conditions, including especially the conditions of their own action' (Giddens 1984: 374).

As with Rengert and Wasilchick's work, therefore, we find in Carter and Hill's study some confirmatory evidence for the Brantinghams' hypotheses (note, for example, the fit between Carter and Hill's 'strategic'/'tactical' distinction and the conceptual apparatus of Fig. 13.5). We have also, however, begun to open up some fresh theoretical avenues, by linking Carter and Hill's work with the concepts of 'ontological security' and 'practical consciousness', as used in structuration theory. We shall return briefly to the significance of these links at a later point in the chapter. For the moment, it is appropriate to re-emphasize the main message of this sub-section: that is, that just as Cohen and Felson (1979) very helpfully developed the relevance to criminological explanation of the routine activities of potential crime victims, so the work of the Brantinghams and others (including Cromwell *et al.* 1991, considered at the end of the preceding sub-section) focuses attention on the routine (non-criminal) activities of *offenders* in seeking to provide an explanation for the location of offences. The introduction of this dimension clearly complicates the explanatory task well beyond the boundaries of what we can now see as the over-simplistic opportunity theory espoused in 1988 by the Home Office Crime Prevention Unit (see above).

Multiple Victimization

At this point, we must further complicate the emerging picture by drawing attention to a topic that has, until very recently, been systematically neglected in criminological explanation, namely the issue of *multiple victimization.*

In the first household victimization study to be carried out in Britain, the late Richard Sparks and his colleagues (1977) drew attention to the fact that victimization patterns in the studied areas were quite skewed—that is, while many residents had (reportedly) no crimes committed against them in the relevant year, some had a significant number. The true importance of this point was not, however, recognized until the late 1980s and early 1990s, when multiple victimization became a key focus for a number of important British crime prevention programmes (for an overview, see Farrell 1992; Pease 1993).

Farrell (1992: 91 ff.) has usefully re-analysed the results of the 1982 British Crime Survey (BCS) to show the statistical importance of multiple victimizations. As shown in Table 13.4, taking all offences together one-third of the sample (31.9 per cent) reported a criminal victimization during the year 1981; but nearly half of these victimized respondents (44 per cent) reported more than one victimization. Translated into a count of *incidents* rather than *respondents* (see right-hand column of table), this meant that 71 per cent of all offences reported in the BCS occurred to respondents multiply victimized during the year—a point that needs to be set alongside the fact that two-thirds of all respondents reported no victimizations. Interestingly, however, in the BCS (see Table 13.4) multiple victimization was more evident among property crimes than among crimes against the person, though this finding might be at least partly artefactual[23]. Overall, the highly skewed distribution of BCS victimizations is very evident from these data, and the evidence it provides is highly congruent with the work of Sherman *et al.* (1989) on the 'hotspots' of crime in Minneapolis (see above).

Table 13.4. % Distribution of victimization for all offences: 1982 British Crime Survey

	Respondents			Incidents (all offences)
No. of times victimized	Personal offences	Household offences	All offences	
0	91.7	72.3	68.1	0.0
1	6.0	16.9	17.8	29.1
2	1.0	5.0	6.2	20.3
3	0.4	2.6	3.1	15.2
4	0.3	1.3	1.8	11.8
5+	0.6	1.9	2.9	23.7
	100	100	100	100
% of all respondents multiply victimized (i.e. '2+' in table)	2.3	10.8	14.0	n/a
% multiple victimization among all victimized respondents (or, in col. 5, all victimizations)	27.2	38.9	43.9	70.9

Source: Gottfredson (1984: appendix B) and Farrell (1992: 92), plus supplementary calculations.

[23] This is because domestic violence is known to be under-reported in formal crime surveys.

The BCS data cited refer, of course, to the whole of England and Wales, and until very recently the geographical distribution of multiple victimization had received little attention. However, in 1992 Trickett *et al.* published a secondary analysis of the 1982 British Crime Survey which demonstrated that the areas with the highest rates of criminal victimization also had the highest rates of multiple victimization: 'the number of victimisations per victim rises markedly as area crime rate increases' (Trickett *et al.* 1992: As shown in Table 13.5, re-examination of the data for within-area household offences in a published local-area victimization study in Sheffield—using smaller areas than in the Trickett *et al.* analy-

Table 13.5. Incidence and prevalence rates for within-area household offences in six contrasting small areas of Sheffield, 1975

	Low-rise Council housing areas		High-rise Council housing areas		Predominantly Privately rented areas	
	High Crime	Lower Crime	High Crime	Lower Crime	High Crime	Lower Crime
Prevalence (% households victimized)	33	19	32	24	42	26
Incidence (total survey-based rate for these offences)[a]	58	29	67	51	94	45
Incidence/ prevalence ratio	1.8	1.5	2.1	2.1	2.2	1.7

[a] Rate is expressed as mean no. of offences per 100 households.

1. Given the definitions of incidence and prevalence, it follows that the 'incidence/prevalence ratio' is a measure of the extent of multiple victimization in each area, for the offences described (i.e. within-area household offences).
2. The six areas in this study were selected as three pairs of high and low crime rate areas (on official data), but of contrasting housing type. In the first two (council) pairs, the high and low areas were geographically adjacent; in the third (rented) pair they were not Size of total population of each area was 2,000–3,000. For a fuller discussion of the areas, see the original source; in this regard, note also that for the privately rented pair, the comparison made here is between the area known as RHH (but excluding the student population of the area), and the sub-area known as RHL(D) (which was closer to RHH in terms of housing tenure than was the other sub-area, RHL(0)).

Source: Derived from data in Bottoms *et al.* (1987: tables 6, 7).

sis—gives a similar result, except in the case of one low-crime area which comprised a high-rise residential complex. However, in this area the multiple victimization was largely confined to vandalism offences, suggesting perhaps the need for a closer look at the extent to which vandalism might dominate general multiple victimization data in areas of this type.

The Quantitative Criminology Group at Manchester University, which developed the Trickett *et al.* (1992) paper, has subsequently taken forward its work by applying similar analyses to the 1988 British Crime Survey, and also by examining changes over time (from 1982 to 1988) on an areal basis. A preliminary paper by Pease (1993) reports the results as follows:

> The variation among areas in level of crime victimisation has increased [between 1982 and 1988]. The high crime areas are characterised by increasingly more property crime victimisation than the low crime rate areas as time passes. *Inequality amongst areas has increased . . .* However, the difference in [each respondent's] probability of victimisation by area has not increased. [On this prevalence measure] the areas have remained roughly as unequal in 1988 as they had been in 1982. *What has changed is the difference between areas in the number of victimizations per victim.* (emphasis added)

In other words, according to the Manchester group's analysis, between 1982 and 1988 virtually the whole of the increased inequality in crime incidence as between different geographical areas in England and Wales was attributable to multiple victimization. This is an extraordinarily interesting result, which (together with the earlier finding about the greater concentration of multiple victimization in high-crime areas) clearly demonstrates the potential importance of multiple victimization analyses for environmental criminology in the future. As yet, however—as the Manchester group would be the first to admit—the full meaning of these results has not been fully explicated. One important issue, for example, is to try to disentangle how far area differences in multiple victimization are influenced by the *individual characteristics* of victims and their lifestyles (to give an exceptional example to make the point, bouncers in nightclubs might be expected to be the subject of repeated assaults, regardless of where they live), and how far they are the product of the *social context and characteristics* of residential areas. While preliminary work by the Manchester group suggests that both individual and area characteristics are important, these analyses have not yet (as I understand it) been extended to the specific task of seeking to explain more fully the role of multiple victimization in the increased inter-area inequality between 1982 and 1988.

All of the data reported above assess multiple victimization without specific regard to crime type—hence, a family would count as multiply victimized in the BCS if they had suffered, in the course of a year, a burglary at their home, their car being taken, and a brick through the window of their garage (criminal damage). It can however be argued that multiple victimization is likely to be of greatest criminological interest when it is offence-specific; and, while common sense might lead one to expect multiple victimization patterns to occur for certain particular kinds of offence (e.g. domestic violence,[24] fraud against a company by an employee), other crimes might intuitively seem less likely to produce such patterns. Yet, even on an offence-specific basis, multiple victimization does appear to be a very important feature of many crimes: for example, in an unpublished survey of non-domestic burglaries in Lisburn, Northern Ireland, it was shown that 16 per cent of the burgled premises (1 per cent of all premises) accounted for 40 per cent of the burglaries (reported in Pease 1993; see also Polvi *et al.* 1990 on domestic burglaries, Sampson and Phillips 1992 on racial attacks, and Burquest *et al.* 1992 on serious property crime against schools).

Data of this sort raise starkly the question: why does offence-specific multiple victimization occur? Leaving aside offences (such as domestic violence) where the answer is unfortunately obvious, there seem to be three main possibilities,[25] and burglary is (in principle) a good offence upon which to test them. The possibilities are:

1. That multiple victimization is explicable through opportunity factors. From opportunity theory one would expect some premises to be more vulnerable than others (e.g. because of a better potential 'take', relatively long periods of non-occupancy, or poor natural surveillance); that being the case, one might expect, on a random chance basis, that different offenders (each operating within an opportunity framework) would separately choose the same premises to burgle, thus creating, over time, a multiple victimization pattern.
2. It is of course possible that the same offender(s) is/are responsible for the repeat victimization.
3. It is possible that the original offender(s) might discuss the vulnerability of the specific premises with others, who then commit the repeats (or they in turn might speak to their friends, who then commit the repeats).

To the best of my knowledge, there is no reported empirical study which specifically examines the distribution of multiple victimization as

[24] See the comment by Lorna Smith (1989: 16): 'despite disagreement over many aspects of domestic violence by various researchers, one of the few things about which there is almost universal agreement is that it escalates in frequency and intensity over time. Numerous studies have exploded the myth that serious injuries seldom occur or that weapons are seldom used. *If violence happens once it is likely to happen often*' (emphasis added).

[25] These are mentioned in Pease (1993), and follow a discussion between Professor Pease and the present author.

between these three possibilities. However, a small study by Polvi *et al.* (1990) on the time-course of repeated domestic burglary victimizations in Saskatoon, Canada, showed a time-pattern for the repeated victimization that was very heavily skewed towards an early repeat (see Fig. 13.8).[26] While this study is based on small numbers, and therefore needs to be treated with caution as a basis for generalized statements, nevertheless it is of great interest that the time-course pattern it displays is clearly not at all consistent with the first of the three possibilities outlined above, i.e. the straightforward 'opportunity' thesis. In the same context, it is also worth noting a Dutch study (cited in Winkel 1991: 257) which suggests that around one-third of domestic burglars return again to the same house to commit a further offence.

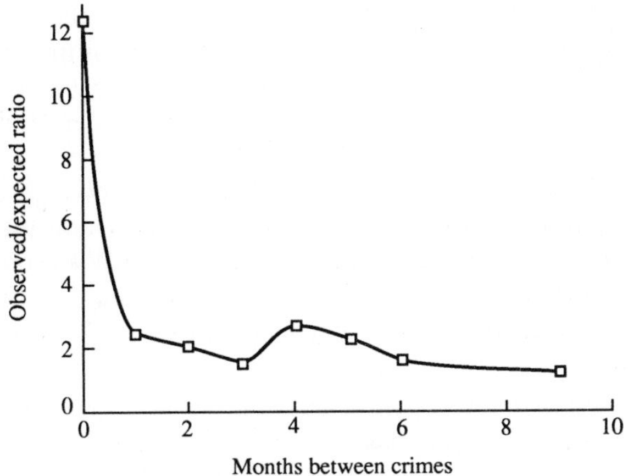

Fig. 13.8 Ratio of observed to expected repeat break and enter offences, Saskatoon, 1987, by months between crimes
Source: Polvi *et al.* (1990: 10).

It will be clear from much of the above that our knowledge of the multiple victimization phenomenon remains, at this stage, patchy. However, it should also be clear that the subject is potentially extremely important to criminological explanation, including the explanatory tasks of environmental criminology. Among other things, the time-course data seem to provide further evidence against a simple opportunity thesis in relation to

[26] It should be noted that Fig. 13.8 includes data calculated only on the basis of the calendar month: hence 'zero' means two burglaries within the same calendar month, 'one' means burglaries in adjacent months (January/February), and so on. A more sensitive comparison would obviously be to calculate exact numbers of days between victimizations.

the location of property offences; and, at the same time, they direct us again to an exploration of offenders' routines and their patterns of everyday thinking (and, possibly, also to their 'grapevine' discussions of potential crime-sites with friends and acquaintances). Meanwhile, the Manchester group's findings concerning the major contribution of multiple victimization to the increased cross-area crime inequalities of the 1980s inevitably directs attention to a macro-level of analysis concerning possible relationships between crime trends and general social trends,[27] linked to studies in environmental criminology: a point to which we must return.

Wikström's Tentative Model for Explaining Offence Locations

So far, in this major section on explaining the location of offences, we have discussed opportunities, the routine activities of the general population, the routine activities of offenders, and the role of multiple victimization. It is now time to try to draw some threads together, and seek to develop, if possible, some overall framework for understanding the way in which offences are geographically distributed.

Such a task has recently been attempted by the Swedish criminologist Per-Olof Wikström (1990), as a prelude to a major and (at the time of writing) continuing study of crime in Stockholm. Wikström's 'tentative model', as he calls it, for the explanation of variations in crime rates and types of crime in the urban environment, is set out in Figure 13.9.

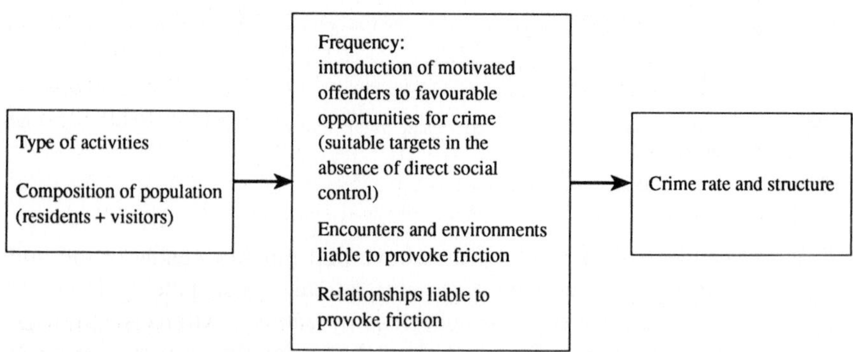

Fig. 13.9 Wilkstrom's tentative model for explaining variations in crime rate and types of crime in the urban environment
Source: Wilkström (1990:2 4)

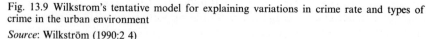

[27] See Walker and Walker (1987) on growing social inequality in Britain.

This model begins (see left-hand box) by emphasizing basic *variations in land use* within the urban environment. This feature has two aspects: first, the types of activities which take place in the area (e.g. whether the area is predominantly residential or non-residential; if the latter, whether it is a shopping/industrial/leisure area, etc.); and secondly, the composition of the population at any given time (including here both residents and victims). In drawing attention to these matters, Wikström also rightly emphasizes that particular areas may be host to different kinds of activities (and/or populations) on different days of the week, or at different times of the day (in this respect consider the difference in most city centres between weekday commercial hours, weekday evenings, and Friday and Saturday evenings).

Wikström's model then postulates that the *variations in land use* of the left-hand box will directly influence a number of criminologically very relevant social interactions (see central box). The first of these is (following the familiar Cohen and Felson formulation) the 'introduction of motivated offenders to favourable opportunities for crime', i.e. 'suitable targets in the absence of direct social control'. Within this formulation, Wikström intends to embrace not only Cohen and Felson's emphasis on the routine activities of the general population, but also the Brantinghams' (1981) work, discussed above, on the cognitive spatial awareness of offenders (see Wikström 1990: 21).

Wikström goes on to point out, however, that Cohen and Felson's concept of 'suitable targets', as developed by them, focuses principally upon theft and theft-related offences, since in discussing this concept they mention especially value (material or symbolic), ease of access, physical visibility, and 'the inertia of a target against illegal treatment', including portability (Cohen and Felson 1979: 591). Cohen and Felson do, it must be said, make some allowance for personal crimes within these categories (for example, in the last of the four factors, they include 'the physical capacity of personal victims to resist attackers with or without weapons'). However, what they envisage here seems clearly to be focused upon what might be called *instrumental personal crimes* (e.g. robbery, stranger rape), and, as Wikström suggests:

> research on the social context of criminal episodes . . . enables us to conclude that whereas the concept of a 'suitable criminal target' can generally be applied without much difficulty to instrumental categories of crime . . . it is less obviously applicable in the case of expressive crimes (the majority of assaults and malicious damage). In this category of crime, the question of a considered 'choice' of target hardly arises; rather, it is a matter more of how situations (or relations) arise which may lead to violence or damage than of motivated offenders taking advantage of a suitable opportunity for crime with which they may have been confronted or themselves sought out. (Wikström 1990: 22–3)

Developing this insight, Wikström then adds to the central box in his 'tentative model' both 'encounters and environments liable to provoke friction' and 'relationships liable to provoke friction'. It hardly needs to be spelled out that the addition of these dimensions reinforces the overall emphasis on routine activities within the explanation of offence location.

Wikström's 'tentative model' for explaining the location of offences is of very great interest and value. However, a number of points perhaps need to be made in elaboration and modification of the model.

In the first place, we should note that Wikström's model effectively begins with *variations in land use* in the city, taking this as essentially given. Elsewhere, Wikström (1991: ch. 6) has carried out a sophisticated statistical analysis of the 'factorial social ecology of Stockholm', so he is very well aware of the complexity of the task of describing and analysing the considerable diversity of sub-areas within a given urban environment. Conceptually, however, it is perhaps worth taking this process a stage further by trying to set urban sub-areas within a wider sociological and geographical framework, in an attempt to explain more fully the types of activities and population composition found within specific areas (in other words, such a framework will ask questions logically prior to the matters raised in the left-hand box in Fig. 13.9). A useful framework for this kind of exercise has been suggested by the geographer David Herbert (1982: 26): see Fig. 13.10. While some of Herbert's specific concepts are, in my view, contestable, the framework as a whole has some very valuable features, which include the following:

First, the framework emphasizes that the particular kinds of activities occurring in specific geographical sub-areas may be powerfully affected by social forces originating well outside the sub-area, including *macro-level material and political factors* (for example, the nature of regional, national, and international economic developments, and the political power structures of a given country) and *pervasive macro-level ideological features* such as societal values and traditions, i.e. what Anthony Giddens (1984: 283) calls the 'structural principles' of a given society, namely the principles underpinning its overall institutional alignments. (To appreciate the importance of this latter dimension, consider, for example, some of the very different 'structural principles' of Japanese and Western societies, which are by no means irrelevant to criminological explanation (Moriyama 1993); or, in a related vein, compare the differing structural principles of urban and of traditionally rural societies).

Secondly, Herbert's framework emphasizes the role of *allocative processes* within a given society, in relation to the geography of crime. Later sections of this chapter will provide several examples of the importance of such processes; for the present, let us simply note, in general terms, that land use decisions by city planners (for example, as regards

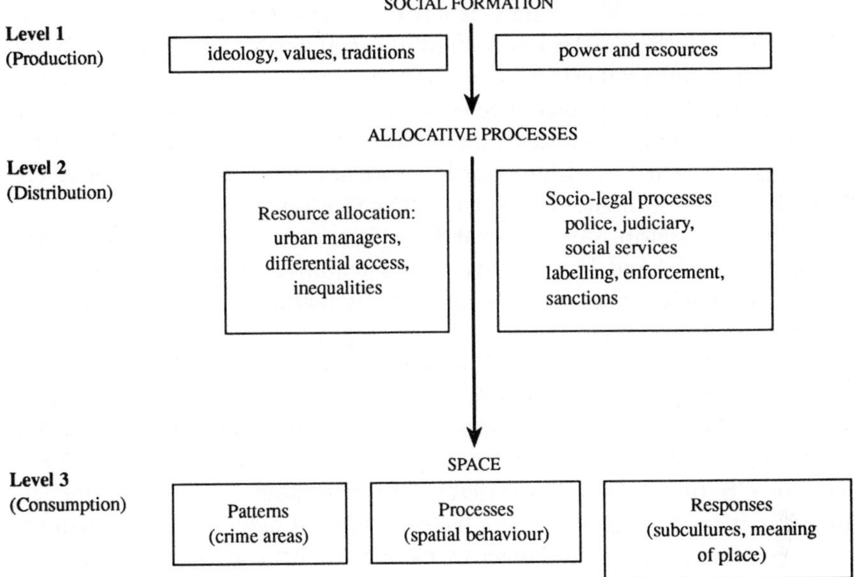

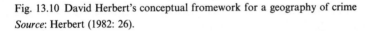

Fig. 13.10 David Herbert's conceptual fromework for a geography of crime
Source: Herbert (1982: 26).

the creation of dedicated industrial estates in segregated zones, as opposed to allowing a mixture of small-scale industrial plant and residential development in certain areas) could clearly be of considerable importance as regards the location of offences, and indeed as regards the overall level of offending in a given city.

Thirdly, Herbert's framework includes *inter alia* (at the lowest level of the diagram) both *spatial behaviour/processes* and the *meaning of place*. The first of these concepts very obviously links up with the central importance of routine activities as regards offence locations, as discussed in previous sub-sections. The second concept, the meaning of place, is an important issue, which has not always been given adequate attention by environmental criminologists. Its importance derives from the fact that, to real-life actors, places are very often not just neutral locations for social interactions. They may be, in symbolic terms, pregnant with meaning (e.g. perhaps the decor indicates that this is a place only for the young, or only for the rich), and/or they may be intimately linked to aspects of actors' personal biographies (and cf. note 21). Such matters are often very subtle and nuanced, but they can crucially affect (in an interactive way) the kinds of variables outlined in both the left-hand and the central boxes in Wikström's 'tentative model' (Fig. 13.9).

Fourthly, Herbert's framework usefully emphasizes the intimate *interconnections* between the three levels that he specifies. As a point of criticism, however, the interconnections are, in this framework, seen as unidirectional (in a downwards direction), whereas in fact they should be drawn as interactive (in other words, processes developing at lower levels can have effects at higher levels, as well as vice versa).

In short, therefore, to understand the land use and population variations in the left-hand box of Wikström's tentative model (Fig. 13.9), we need a complex understanding of the interacting macro-, meso- and micro-social processes in society at large (Fig. 13.10).

Three further points about Wikström's model may finally be made, each of which seeks to supplement his essentially quantitative and factorial approach (based on his statistical study of Stockholm: Wikström 1991) with more qualitative and processual insights relevant to the subject (see also Bottoms and Wiles 1992). The first point is that the model, based as it is on a set of specific factors ('type of activities', 'composition of population', etc.), is in danger of paying too little attention to the perceptions and daily life choices of individual actors within the city, and the way in which these come together to build up the aggregate statistical patterns that the model seeks to portray. In this sense, the model by implication raises the general (and very difficult) issue of how best to conceptualize the relationship between aggregate and individual dimensions of social reality in relation to crime in the city (see generally Farrington *et al.* 1993; also Bottoms 1993 for my own approach to this subject). Secondly, the social control dimension in Wikstöm's model is by implication restricted to surveillance or the lack of it ('direct social control'); but a more nuanced approach is needed here, for everyone knows of some parents, youth leaders, bar staff, etc. who are skilled at defusing trouble before it arises, or, conversely and unfortunately, of some occasions when the police have acted in such a way as to inflame a difficult situation and provoke offending. Thirdly and finally, it can be argued that, in conception at least, Wikström's model is too static; hence, for a more adequate explanatory tool, one would need to pay fuller attention to the *changes* (as well as the continuities) in the use by social actors of different districts within the city or (at the more micro-level as highlighted, for example, by the work of Sherman *et al.* 1989) to the constantly evolving character of particular streets, particular bars etc., in city centre locations.

With these modifications and developments, Wikström's outline model can be recommended as of very considerable value in the explanation of offence locations.

A Case Study: Offences in City Centre Public Houses

To try to illustrate concretely some of the issues touched upon in the preceding sub-section, it might be helpful to discuss a particular case study in environmental criminology, namely Hope's (1985: ch. 4) study of offences of disorder in city centre public houses in Newcastle-upon-Tyne. While this was a small study, and in places a little speculative because of lack of data, nevertheless it does illustrate very well some of the complex and interacting social factors that have to be taken into account in any full study of offence locations.

The focus of the study (which had a crime-preventative rationale) was on 'disorderly incidents' (N = 1,463) to which the police were called on Friday and Saturday nights,[28] over an eighteen-month period, in the central Newcastle police sub-division. The incidents were both temporally and spatially highly skewed. Temporally, 48 per cent of incidents occurred within a ninety-minute period just before, and for an hour after, the end of normal licensing hours (with a further smaller peak at the termination of 'special' (club) licensing). Spatially, disorders were concentrated in three particular areas: (i) a small area of four streets, with 15 per cent of the city centre's public houses, but 42 per cent of the disorderly incidents associated with public houses; (ii) a small area containing two large dance-halls, with contrasting musical and social styles; and (iii) the Metro underground rail system. (This kind of concentration in particular micro-locations within the city centre is, of course, once again highly congruent with the Minneapolis evidence of Sherman *et al.* 1989). In seeking to explain the disorders—both generally and in relation to the three specific 'trouble-spot' areas—Hope identified a number of relevant factors, including the following:

1. *Socio-cultural factors.* A striking characteristic of the whole Friday/Saturday city centre clientele was its *youth*, and Hope noted that this in itself constituted an important socio-cultural change from, say, the 1950s. In so far as there might now be less 'age-integrated' leisure than in previous generations, this might lessen informal social controls in group situations. At a more specific level, musical and social style was an important variable in customer choice of pub within the city centre (a fact well known to the pub owners), and this seemed to be a factor influencing the concentration of disorder in the first trouble-spot.
2. *Situational factors.* These included three factors associated with public houses: first, overcrowding in pubs; secondly, the spatial arrangements

[28] Friday and Saturday nights had been identified from previous research as the peak occasions for disorderly incidents.

within pubs; and thirdly, the nature of the social control exercised by bar staff (some much better than others at calming incipient trouble: see above). Additionally, Hope noted that the arrangement of *public space* in the city centre contributed to the level of disorder in all three trouble-spots—for example, the Metro system had large areas of space and few staff (factors deriving largely from its daytime use and the need to make a profit), so affording 'ample opportunities for trouble as people return home' (Hope 1985: 48); while in the second trouble-spot, large numbers of people simultaneously left both contrasting dance-halls at the end of 'special licensing' (2 a.m.), from exits only 50 yards apart.

3. *Urban management factors.* In this connection, Hope noted architectural/planning changes in the post-war period leading to, e.g. the creation of pedestrian precincts, multi-storey car parks, etc., in the city centre. 'All these arrangements are designed for the orderly, daytime population of the city, but it is apparent that the physical structure of the city centre . . . does not work nearly so well for the nighttime leisure population, which behaves differently . . . there is now a city centre which sometimes at night can seem like a "no man's land"' (Hope 1985: 51).
4. *The licensed trade.* Various specific features of the economics and regulation of the public house trade were raised by Hope under this heading, including the fact that 'not every pub can cater for the most "up-market" or best behaved sections of youth' (while all need to make a profit); and that 'staffing difficulties may force breweries to install inadequate, inexperienced or temporary managers and staff at some of their worst pubs' (Hope 1985: 52–3).

Within the terms of Wikström's model, the offences and incidents studied in Hope's research would of course be encompassed primarily under 'encounters and environments liable to provoke friction', and (to a lesser extent) 'relationships liable to provoke friction'; and both of these would be seen, within the model, as related to the types of activities occurring at specific premises, and the composition of the population in those places. While all these points are clearly valid and important, the Hope study also shows clearly why—as implicitly recommended in Herbert's model—the study of these specific patterns of Friday/Saturday night behaviour in micro-locations in Newcastle needs to be set within a broader understanding of allocative processes (e.g. as regards allocative decisions by city planners and, as regards management and style of pubs, the owning breweries) and also of broader macro-social developments (e.g. the development of an age-segregated weekend leisure culture).

EXPLAINING THE LOCATION OF OFFENDER RESIDENCE

We turn now to the problem of explaining the observed areal distribution of offender residence.

As seen in an earlier section, traditionally this subject was heavily dominated by the conceptualizations of the Chicago School; and the explanations of the Chicago School were themselves strongly influenced by the facts of *stability over time* in the distribution of areal offender rates, and in the nature of land use in different zones of the city. For this reason, as Robert Bursik (1986) has pointed out, Shaw and McKay, while aware of broader political forces, and of the non-market-orientated activities of business and industry, tended not to develop full analyses of those topics; hence 'it is easy to get the impression [from their work] that the distribution of delinquency is the natural outcome of economic competition for desirable space' (Bursik 1986: 61).

Evidence gathered since the Second World War, however, dealt a mortal blow to this general approach. As we saw earlier in this chapter (see Fig. 13.2), offender rates in post-war British cities have, given the different housing context, borne little resemblance to the Chicagoan concentric ring pattern. Even in Chicago, careful analysis by Bursik (1986) has now shown, first, that the old areal regularities have broken down (the 'assumption of ecological stability has not been warranted in Chicago since the 1940–50 period': p. 57); and secondly, that while the areas of the city that underwent the most rapid social change generally experienced considerable increases in delinquency (a finding that is 'consistent with the social disorganisation perspective': p.35), nevertheless, there were some atypical areas where this relationship did not hold (see further Taub *et al.* 1984, discussed in the next section). Analysis of such atypical areas then suggested that 'ecological theories would benefit from a consideration of dynamics external to local communities' (p. 35); in particular: 'An important theme of . . . recent work concerns the dynamics of political decision-making processes that can significantly alter the character (and ecological structure) of the city. A fuller consideration of these recent developments . . . is necessary if the ecological approach is to remain a viable approach in the future (Bursik 1986: 62).

We shall return to these broader issues later in the chapter. For the moment, we can simply note one important consequence of the above developments. This is that, while Shaw and McKay's social disorganization theory is still supported by some researchers as being useful in the explanation of offender rates in some urban sub-areas no serious scholar now supports—at least in any generalized fashion—the Chicago concentric ring theory and the formulation of urban process that went with it.

In order to see what might replace this approach in explaining offender rate variations, we shall look first at some statistical studies of the distribution of offender rates, and secondly at some more focused field research in local communities. Before turning to this evidence, however, it will be useful as a preliminary point to consider how, in principle, it could come about that area of residence and offender rates might be statistically related. This topic has been very usefully addressed by Wikström (1991: 130); developing his answer, the matter may be put in the following way.

First, area of residence and offender rates might be related because more or less crime-prone individuals or groups are distributed (by the dynamics of the local housing market) to certain areas. In this kind of correlation, however, the social life of the area itself does not affect the criminality levels of the residents. To take an extreme example in order to make the point, there are some small council estates (or parts of estates) in British cities which are reserved for elderly tenants; obviously, one would expect such areas to have low offender rates, for reasons unconnected with social processes within the area.

Secondly, however, in principle *the social life of the area might itself influence criminal motivation*; and this possible influence is itself of two types. The first type—described by Wikström (1991: 130) as 'short-term situational influences on criminal motivation',[29] might include such matters as friendship patterns among local youth, leading to one being influenced by others to commit an offence; or, perhaps, an older resident being talked into buying stolen goods at the local pub. In these instances, it can be assumed (for the sake of argument) that the relevant social interactions would not have occurred had the offender lived elsewhere; but also that the transaction is basically a 'one-off' affair, not necessarily affecting the person's general way of living. However, one may also postulate that, in principle, the social life of an area might have longer-term effects on a person's daily routines, thought processes, social activities, and even personality, such that his/her overall propensity to commit crime in certain situations is intrinsically affected. This kind of longer-term effect is obviously most likely to be manifested among young residents of an area, but the possibility of its occurring among older residents should not be ruled out.

In describing the first of the above possibilities, I referred to the operations of the local housing market as obviously relevant to the distribution of more or less crime-prone individuals to different areas. As we shall shortly see, one of my own central contentions is that the housing market is also the key to understanding the kinds of processes outlined in the

[29] 'Situational' is here used in a broad sense, and not in the restricted (opportunity-reducing) sense adopted in situational crime prevention theory.

second paragraph; but in order to see why, we must examine some research studies.

Statistical Studies of Offender Rate Distribution

When the study of criminology at the University of Sheffield began in the late 1960s, it was decided that it would be sensible to attempt, as a first major research project, a statistical study of recorded crime and offending in the city. Shortly before this project was begun, Rex and Moore (1967) had published an influential sociological analysis of Commonwealth migration to Britain, centred on empirical work in Birmingham. These authors were struck by the importance of the housing market in influencing the potential access of Commonwealth migrants to different districts within Birmingham, for example because building societies treated mortgage applications by immigrants with some suspicion, and also because the City Council operated a five-year waiting period before one could qualify for a council tenancy, even if housing need was otherwise established. In other words, Rex and Moore saw the detailed rules and social practices concerning access to particular kinds of housing (by ownership or tenancy) as of *general* sociological importance in shaping—in a major way—the population composition of different geographical areas, and this in turn was seen as having possibly significant subsequent effects on the kind of social community and social life developed in various districts.[30] These observations seemed to the Sheffield researchers to be of some importance. Hence, in the statistical study of offender data and Census data that was then undertaken, it was decided to try to operationalize Rex and Moore's insights—necessarily rather crudely, given the nature of the available data—by classifying each Census enumeration district on the basis of its predominant housing tenure type, and then seeing whether the resulting 'predominant tenure' variables were of importance in 'explaining' (statistically) the offender rates of urban sub-areas, when population data were also considered. The answer proved to be emphatically in the affirmative, and indeed a different regression equation had to be fitted for, on the one hand, areas which were predominantly 'private' (i.e. owner-occupied or privately rented) in their housing tenure, and, on the other hand, predominantly 'public' or 'council' housing areas (Baldwin and Bottoms 1976: ch. 4). It was also found, however, that there were major variations in offender rates *within* the range of areas that shared a predominant housing tenure type—for example, some council housing areas had very high offender rates, and some very low rates—

[30] They actually developed this insight through a specific concept of 'housing classes'. However, in subsequent debate and critique the concept of a 'class', tied to housing, has not seemed very helpful or appropriate to most urban sociologists.

and some preliminary more detailed exploration of the council sector revealed, *inter alia*, that there was no statistically significant relationship between the rate of tenant turnover on council estates and the offender rate (Baldwin and Bottoms 1976: 149–51, 169–71). These findings in general clearly suggested a potential importance for the housing market in explaining offender rates, but also (in the finding about residential mobility) indicated that one would have to look beyond the conceptualizations of the Chicago school—which, as we have seen, placed a special emphasis on residential mobility—if adequate sense were to be made of the data. This eventually led to more on-the-ground studies of particular areas in Sheffield, to be described in the next sub-section.

Following on from the Sheffield statistical analysis of offender rates, Wikström (1991) conducted a similar analysis for Stockholm; and, as the researchers had done in the Sheffield study, he followed the procedure of categorizing residential areas according to the predominant housing tenure of the dwellings in the area. He eventually adopted a path model approach, hypothesizing that housing tenure variables would feed through to population composition variables, with the whole providing some statistical explanation of the varying offender rates for different districts. The final path model for the total offender rate of areas is shown in Fig. 13.11. On the left-hand side of the diagram are shown the three main housing tenure variables (using Swedish housing categories). The three boxes in the centre of the diagram are labelled according to three aspects of population composition previously found to be important (in a factor analysis) in distinguishing different areas of the city according to social type;[31] and the whole was then found to explain about half the area variation in the total offender rates of different districts.

Wikström himself is at pains to point out that a statistical model of this kind cannot of itself disentangle the possible contributions of the two different aspects of variations in area offender rates that he had previously identified (i.e., in crude terms, 'population sifting' and 'area contextual effects on motivation': see above). The statistical model itself is of some interest, however, first in seeming to confirm, from an overall analysis of offender rates in Stockholm, some of the messages about housing tenure of the Sheffield study; and secondly in showing—again like the

[31] The three factors derived from the factor analysis were given names as shown in Fig. 13.11. The factor loadings for the 'social problems' factor have been given in note 14 above; factor loadings for the other two factors are shown in Wikström (1991: table 6.5, p. 123). In conducting the path analysis, Wikström did not, however, use the actual factor scores of these three factors; rather, he chose to use the major loading variable of each factor in order to facilitate the interpretation of findings (while still minimizing problems of multicollinearity). Hence, the actual single variables used in the path analysis were: (i) to represent 'familism': mean household size; (ii) to represent 'social problem areas': percentage of households receiving public welfare assistance; (iii) to represent 'socio-economic status': percentage of blue-collar workers. (See generally Wikström 1991: 156–7.)

Sheffield study—that the area offender rate is not by any means simply a reflection of the social class composition of the area, a point that is brought out clearly in Fig. 13.11. This last matter is of some general importance, since sceptics have not infrequently suggested that the study of high offender rate areas is simply the study of social class by another name; or, as Barbara Wootton vigorously expressed the matter in an earlier generation:

Even the most unprejudiced sociological eyebrows will hardly be raised at the discovery that delinquency tends to be concentrated in particular areas, and that in general these are the slummy ones . . . Ecological studies have thus shown a social and geographical distribution of offenders which conforms to expectations: hardly any new facts have emerged. (1959: 65, 73).

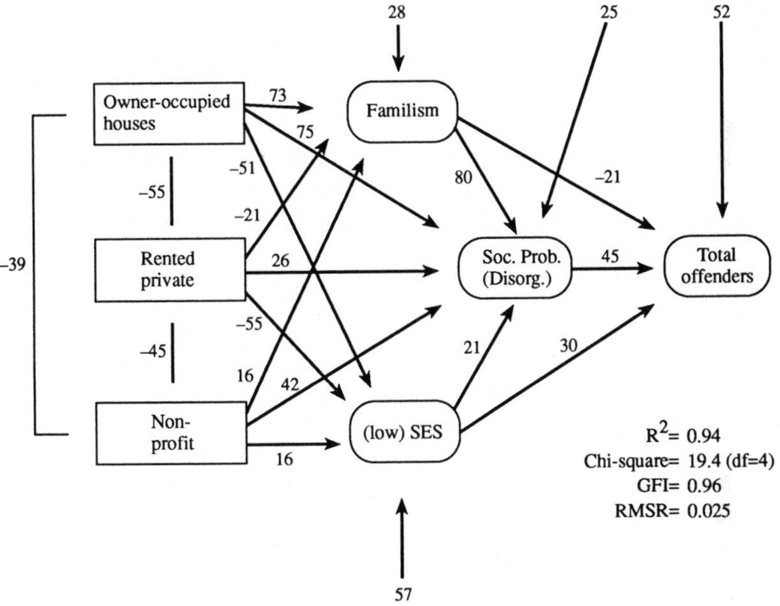

Fig. 13.11 Wilkström's path model of housing, population composition, and total offender rates in different districts of Stockholm
(Numbers on arrows linking boxes show path coefficients multiplied by 100. Floating numbers show proportion of unexplained rate variation for the relevant variable.)
Source: Wilkström (1991: 182).

Detailed Studies of Particular Areas

While the statistical studies of offender rates on a whole-city basis (in Sheffield and Stockholm) seem to suggest that one must go beyond social class in explaining differential offender rates, and seem further to suggest that the housing market is likely to be important in this respect, they are necessarily limited in their approach because they cannot address the qualitative aspects of social processes leading to the development of criminality in particular areas.

Work in Sheffield subsequent to Baldwin and Bottoms's (1976) statistical analysis did however attempt this.[32] In particular, three pairs of small areas with contrasting offender rates were selected on the basis of the prior statistical analysis, with each pair being (in the mid-1970s) of a different housing type, as follows:

Pair 1: Low-rise council housing
Two adjacent areas, one with a high offender rate, one with a lower rate.

Pair 2: High-rise council dwellings
Two adjacent areas, one with a high offender rate, one with a lower rate.

Pair 3: Privately rented areas
Two non-adjacent areas, one with a high offender rate, one with a lower rate. The high-rate area was also, in the mid-1970s, Sheffield's principal prostitution area.

These are the three pairs of areas referred to in Table 13.5 (on multiple victimization). I shall concentrate attention initially on the first of these pairs, as it was in the mid-1970s (the following account draws principally upon Bottoms *et al.* 1989; for a follow-up study of the same areas in the 1980s see Bottoms *et al.* 1992). Briefly, the original problem for explanation confronting the researchers was that these two small areas (population 2,500–3,000 each, and separated only by a main road), had (i) a 300 per cent difference in recorded offender rates, and a 350 per cent difference in recorded offence rates against individual residents and households, but (ii) no statistically significant differences at all on a set of key demographic variables (namely—sex; age; social class; ethnic origin; mean household size; percentage single; percentage male unemployment; age of termination of full-time education; and length of stay in current dwelling). Preliminary research (including adult victim and juvenile self-report studies) established that the crime and offender rate differences could not, for the most part, be regarded as artefactual. A further point of interest was that both areas had been built at approximately the same time (in the first quarter of the twentieth century), and both had, it

[32] For other detailed local British studies see for example Damer (1974); Gill (1977); Herbert (1982: ch. 5, summarizing several of the author's studies in Cardiff); Reynolds (1986).

seemed clear, begun as 'good', crime-free council areas. One of the estates (Stonewall) had retained this characteristic, but its neighbour (Gardenia) had 'tipped' sometime in the 1940s. Neither, however, was in any serious sense an 'area in transition'; rather, they were extremely settled, with 60 per cent of the adult residents in both areas having lived in their current dwelling for ten years or more.

The research team was unable to discover retrospectively exactly why Gardenia had tipped in the 1940s (though some speculative suggestions were made). But through detailed analysis of records in the local authority's housing department, plus ethnographic work in the areas, we were able to show that, once Gardenia had tipped, the local authority's rules of housing allocation had the unintended effects of maintaining the difference between the two areas,[33] and of ensuring that Gardenia attracted, as new tenants, predominantly (i) those in severe housing need, and (ii) those who had prior affective links with the area (relatives living on the estate, etc.). To some extent, therefore, housing allocative processes were drawing to the two estates new residents with a differential propensity to offend (i.e. the first of Wikström's two suggestions as to how offender rates and area of residence can be related was to an extent in operation). On the other hand, ethnographic work also showed that what Wikström has called 'area contextual characteristics' were certainly very much in evidence, and helped to influence the differential offender rate. These 'contextual characteristics' were very complex, and interactive, but included (in addition to the housing market context) certain physical geographical features; a mild criminal subculture in one part of the more criminal estate (Gardenia); the effects of the negative reputation of Gardenia on its residents and on potential residents; possibly a difference relating to the main schools serving the two areas; and some important differences in parental and peer socialization processes (see Bottoms *et al.* 1989: 67–75, esp. p. 74).

Three points are of special importance about this case study. First, it must be re-emphasized that, in terms of demographic variables related to social class (such as the Registrar-General's classification of social class, percentage unemployed, and age of completion of full-time education), these two areas were almost identical; hence, the study presents a major obstacle to those who wish to argue that differential area offender rates are always simply the product of macro-level aspects of social stratification, worked through to a local level. Secondly, very little in Shaw and McKay's conceptualization helps one in explaining the difference between Gardenia and Stonewall, not least since neither area had high population turnover. And thirdly, the researchers identified the

[33] Subsequently, however, there was some convergence between the two areas—but again this could be explained by housing market changes: see Bottoms *et al.* (1992).

operation of the local housing market as a key to understanding the areas (because this crucially affected the population composition of the areas, and the ease with which disatisfied tenants could move elsewhere); hence, this analysis reinforces David Herbert's (1982) emphasis, in his framework for a geography of crime (Fig. 13.10), on meso-level allocative mechanisms in society as being important in relation to area differences in crime and offender rates.[34] The operation of the local housing market, however, does not work in a stand-alone fashion, or only in relation to area population composition. Rather, the Sheffield researchers wished to stress that the workings of the housing market could have crucial secondary social effects—in terms of, for example, the nature of the relationships which subsequently developed in an area, or responses by outsiders (including social control agents, potential residents, etc.). Subsequently, some of these effects might themselves then have the potential to influence the housing market context of the area, e.g. by altering the area's perceived desirability, or perhaps escalating the number of residents wishing to leave. This complex interactive model is set out schematically in Fig. 13.12 (taken from Bottoms *et al.* 1992). It should be noted that the model has recently received significant implicit support from Hope and Foster's (1992) analysis of changes in criminality over time in another British council estate, but space precludes any detailed description of that study.

Despite its potential complexity when applied to a concrete empirical situation in a given area, the basic concept underpinning Fig. 13.12 is a simple one, and it links directly to the original insights of Rex and Moore (1967: see above). Leaving aside, for the moment, the important but minority problem of homelessness, everyone has to live somewhere; but most people do not have the resources to live exactly where they want. The housing market, in its various guises in different countries, powerfully shapes the choices made by individuals and families to live in particular areas (through mortgage availability, the bureaucratic rules of public housing and of housing societies, and so on). But once a household has settled in a given area, secondary effects on social life can occur, as postulated in Fig. 13.12; and these can include 'area contextual effects' on offending, as Wikström (1991) put it. Although other social processes are clearly identified in Fig. 13.12, the housing market can be regarded as central to the model, because it is the housing market that especially helps to determine households' decisions to move into and out of particular areas, from which all else follows. Once the dynamics of this model are grasped, it can be applied to any housing area, public or private. Indeed, a little reflection will show that the original formulations of Shaw

[34] It should be remembered (see earlier section) that offence and offender rates tend to be positively correlated in *residential* districts.

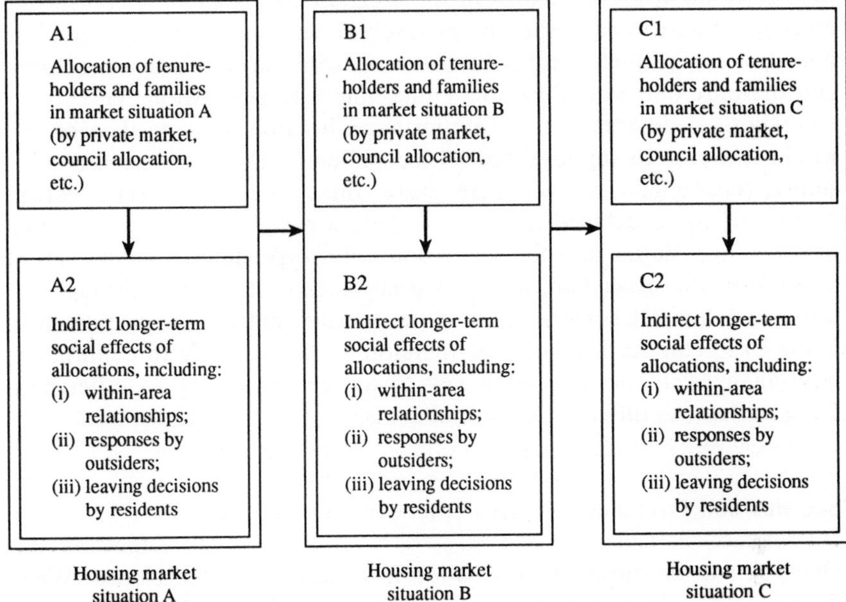
A1
Allocation of tenure-holders and families in market situation A (by private market, council allocation, etc.)
A2
Indirect longer-term social effects of allocations, including:
(i) within-area relationships;
(ii) responses by outsiders;
(iii) leaving decisions by residents
Housing market situation A
B1
Allocation of tenure-holders and families in market situation B (by private market, council allocation, etc.)
B2
Indirect longer-term social effects of allocations, including:
(i) within-area relationships;
(ii) responses by outsiders;
(iii) leaving decisions by residents
Housing market situation B
C1
Allocation of tenure-holders and families in market situation C (by private market, council allocation, etc.)
C2
Indirect longer-term social effects of allocations, including:
(i) within-area relationships;
(ii) responses by outsiders;
(iii) leaving decisions by residents
Housing market situation C

Fig. 13.12 Diagrammatic representation of the relationship between the potential effects of the housing market and residential community crime careers
Source: Bottoms et al. (1992: 120).

and McKay about area contextual effects on offending (in the 'zone in transition' and elsewhere) can readily be brought within this framework—but, conversely, the framework does not have the weaknesses of the Chicago School's zonal model of urban process.

I indicated earlier that, in the later stages of the Sheffield project, three pairs of areas (of contrasting housing types) were studied, with each pair having a high and a low offender rate area: (Gardenia and Stonewall were one of the pairs. Without discussing the other pairs in detail here, it is worth noting that the three high offender rate areas in the study were (in the 1970s) very different in social terms. Both the other two high rate areas had higher proportions of recent move-ins than Gardenia (indicative of greater overall residential mobility). Alone of the three areas, fewer than half of those living in the high-rise high-crime area (Skyhigh) said they felt they belonged to the area,[35] and a higher proportion than in any other area said they would like to move elsewhere: all this, together with other relevant evidence, suggested that residents in Skyhigh

[35] However, women respondents in the high-rate rented (prostitution) area also expressed alienation, to a degree similar to respondents of both sexes in Skyhigh.

were substantially alienated from the area, to a degree not shared in the other two areas. Meanwhile, the privately rented high-crime area was the only one of the three with substantial prostitution and drugs problems, and the only one with a sizeable ethnic minority population. These various points of difference are of importance, because Chicago theorization would lead one to suppose that all high offender rate areas should share similar characteristics, yet here were three that were very varied. Moreover, more detailed analysis of these areas showed that their high offender rate status, and the social and crime-type differences of each of them from the other two, could in every case be explained through the direct and indirect consequences of the housing market, as postulated in Fig. 13.12. This further analysis, therefore, tends strongly to confirm the housing market approach as a key to an understanding of differential offender rates in different residential areas.[36]

Socialization Processes and Area Offender Rate Differences

One point in the preceding discussion now needs to be developed. When discussing Gardenia and Stonewall, it was noted that there were some important differences in peer and parental socialisation processes as between the two estates. Since it is well known in the criminological literature that socialization processes can affect delinquency rates (the concentration here being upon parental socialization), it is not difficult to imagine some critics wishing to argue that much of the observed Gardenia–Stonewall area difference in criminality might be attributable to differential child socialization; the critics might then wish to pursue the case further by suggesting that the socialization difference was an *individual* effect, and hence that the extent to which there really were additional 'area contextual effects' in operation might be very doubtful (cf. Rutter and Giller 1983: 204–6).

This line of argument is, however, in my view ultimately flawed, because it fails to take account of the possibility that parental socialization processes might themselves be affected by area contextual characteristics. Yet exactly that possibility has been elaborated—in contradistinction to more traditional socialization theories—in Bronfenbrenner's (1979) so-called 'ecology of human development' frame of reference; and the Swedish criminologist Peter Martens (1990, 1993) has in recent years argued the case for the relevance of Bronfenbrenner's approach in criminological studies.

[36] There is no published full comparative analysis of all three high-rate areas in the Sheffield study, but see Bottoms and Wiles (1986) for the nearest equivalent; see also Bottoms and Xanthos (1981) for a fuller account of Skyhigh (there called CFH).

Bronfenbrenner particularly emphasizes that the child's development has to be seen in its *everyday context*; hence, he focuses less strongly than would some psychologists on purely psychological processes during the child's development, and more strongly on, as Martens (1993) puts it:

with *whom* the child *interacts* in day-to-day situations, the character of these interactions and in what ways persons outside the family can enhance or inhibit the quality of parent–child interaction. Hence, the focus is on . . . in Bronfenbrenner's own words, 'the actual environments in which human beings live and grow' (Bronfenbrenner 1979, p. xiv).

This 'actual environment' is then conceptualized in terms of a series of concentric circles (see Fig. 13.13), in which the innermost represents the micro-level contexts in which the child is involved at any one time; the middle circle represents all those circumstances potentially having an

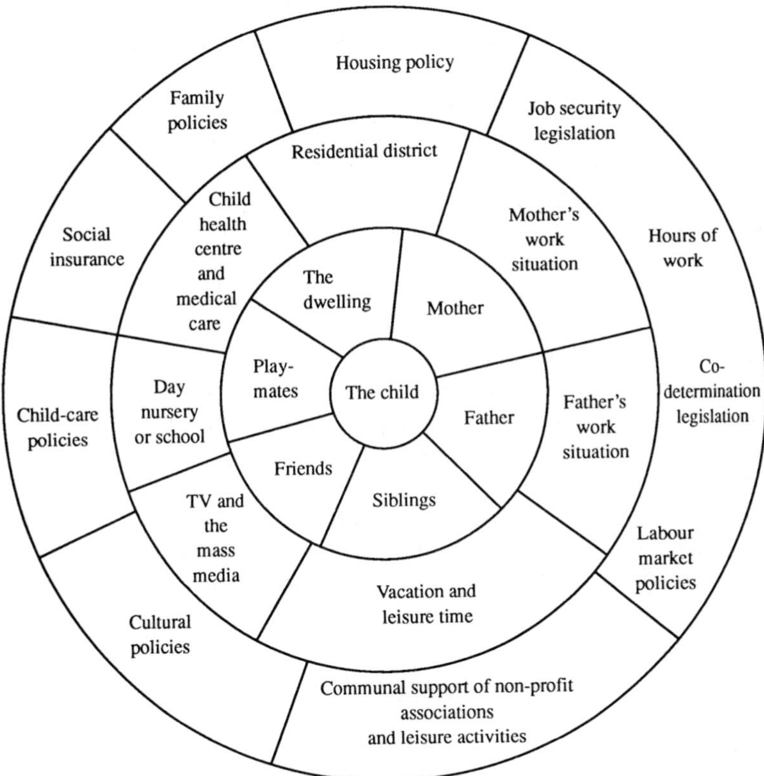

Fig. 13.13 Schematic representation of relevant structures in an 'ecology of human development' socialization model

Source: Martens (1993), drawing on a Swedish article by K. Sandquist.

indirect effect on these micro-level contexts (including parents' working status and conditions, local residential conditions, etc.); and the outer circle represents the macro-level context within which all this is set, and which obviously potentially affects the processes occurring in the middle circle. Among the consequences of all this, as Martens (1993) puts it, is that:

> the success of parenting can depend on the support parents receive in their community in the form of social networks (relatives, neighbours, friends, etc) or social services such as day nurseries and leisure centres. Parents living in a socially stable community have better outward conditions for their role than [other] parents.

At this point in the argument, one can begin to see some very interesting convergences between the way in which criminological understandings of *differential area offence rates* and of *differential area offender rates* have been developing. We saw in an earlier section that explanations of the location of offences now rely substantially, in various ways, on the concept of routine activities; but it was argued (via Herbert's framework: see Fig. 13.10) that such explanations needed to be set within a context of macro-social developments, and of meso-level allocative decisions by urban planners and others. As regards offender rates, it has been argued that the housing market (a crucial meso-level allocative mechanism) is of central importance, but that it has to be understood as operating in interaction with other social processes in the production of offender rates. Among those potential social processes is child socialization; and we have argued, via Bronfenbrenner and Martens, that child socialization should be seen not in purely psychological terms, but as potentially influenced by the area context. In understanding that area context, however, not only are the everyday and routine activities of parents and others crucial to the child's socialization; but those processes themselves have to be set within meso-level and macro-level aspects of the organization of the wider society (Fig. 13.13). It is, additionally, not hard to see that this kind of perspective offers a potentially very powerful explanatory framework, within which work on individual criminal careers can be brought together creatively with the offender-based aspects of environmental criminology (see generally Farrington *et al.* 1993).

Bringing Together Explanations of Offence Locations and Offender Locations

It cannot be claimed that environmental criminology has been particularly successful in integrating explanations of the location of offences and explanations of offender residence. At the time of the Chicago School, offender rates were emphasized to the virtual exclusion of offence rates, while more recently most environmental criminologists have focused their attention primarily on offence rates. Some researchers have, of course, considered both topics, especially when reviewing the field in general, but very few have paid serious attention to how one might best integrate explanations in the two sub-fields of study.

A recent general theory in criminology, by Gottfredson and Hirschi (1990) has, unusually, prioritized the integration of *offence explanations* and *offender explanations* as one of its major concerns. That feature of Gottfredson and Hirschi's work is one of its major strengths; but—unfortunately, from an environmental criminologist's point of view—very little attention is paid, within the theory, to issues of crime and place. A main thrust of Gottfredson and Hirschi's approach to offence–offender explanatory integration is to treat classicism as the master-framework for the understanding of offence commission, and positivism as the master-framework for the understanding of the social production of offenders; and they further argue that these two frameworks are compatible. In a recent essay (Bottoms 1993), I have concurred wholeheartedly with the view that offence studies and offender studies need to be brought more closely together (cf., for example, situational crime prevention's almost total neglect of the offender, and the absence of discussions about specific offences in the analyses of most criminal career researchers). However, I have also suggested that a more fruitful overarching theoretical approach than the classicist-positivist synthesis suggested by Gottfredson and Hirschi may be found in Anthony Giddens's (1984) structuration theory. This framework would have, I have suggested, the following advantages, among others:

1. It provides an integrated ontological framework for social theory which, despite criticisms that may be made of it, nevertheless offers 'the most systematic, interesting and sustained attempt so far found to develop an approach to social theory that transcends the dichotomies of determinism and voluntarianism, society and the individual, and object and subject' (Urry 1986).
2. A central feature of structuration theory is to argue that 'the basic domain of study of the social sciences . . . is neither the experience of the individual actor, nor the existence of any form of societal totality, but *social practices ordered across space and time*' (Giddens 1984: 2). Given this emphasis, both issues of *space*, and the concept of *routines*, are central to structuration theory in a way that is true of no other major recent approach to social theory; *prima facie*, therefore, the framework appears to offer much to environmental criminology, including the integration of offender and offence studies within an environmental context.

Space does not permit any further elaboration of these issues within the framework of this essay, though it should be noted that some features of structuration theory have been introduced at appropriate earlier points in this chapter, e.g. in discussing the work of Cohen and Felson (1979) and of Carter and Hill (1979). The most important message of this sub-section, however, is not specific to structuration theory: that message is simply to emphasize the general need for environmental criminology to provide a more adequately theorized integration of offence location studies and offender residence studies than it has usually achieved in the past.

COMMUNITY CHANGE AND CRIME

So far in this chapter, area influences have been described in a somewhat static fashion, although the interactive model shown in Fig. 13.12 contains within it the possibility of analysing dynamic changes in the housing market situations of particular areas, and the consequences of such changes.

In an important essay, Albert Reiss (1986) drew attention to the importance for criminology of changes in local communities, and he suggested that, analogously to the concept of the individual criminal career, one might speak in terms of local areas having 'community crime careers'. This is a concept with which Paul Wiles and I have worked in the context of the Sheffield study (see Bottoms and Wiles 1986, 1992; Bottoms *et al.* 1992); but, rather than use further Sheffield evidence here, I shall in this section consider the 'community crime career' idea using recent research studies from the United States. Because these studies cover only residential areas, and because offence and offender rates in residential areas tend to be positively correlated, I shall for convenience discuss here results relating to both *offender rate changes* and *offence rate changes*; however, as always, it is necessary in every instance to take careful note of which rate is being considered.

Schuerman and Kobrin (1986) carried out a statistical study of juvenile offender rates in different areas of Los Angeles for the period 1950–1970. They found evidence for a three-stage process which appeared to underpin the emergence of particular districts as high offender-rate areas over this period, and they were satisfied from the temporal patterning of the data that the causal influences were cumulative, and in the order specified. First, they argued, there were shifts in land use (for example, an increase in renting and decline in owner-occupation; and an increase in apartment dwellings). Secondly, there were changes in population-related features in areas (for example, a decline in total population size in the area; an increase, within the overall population, in the proportion of unrelated individuals; and an increase in residential mobility). Thirdly, there were changes in socio-economic status (more unskilled people; a higher proportion unemployed), and also in what Schuerman and Kobrin label, perhaps doubtfully,[37] 'subculture variables' (including an increase in the size of ethnic minority populations, increased proportions of ethnic minority females working, and ethnic minority members with advanced education). Hence, overall, these authors concluded that

> initial limited changes in land use induce a larger number of demographic changes, in turn fostering a still larger number of changes in the socio-economic features of the resident population . . . [and] ethnic, occupational and educational patterns representing shared adaptations to the set of background conditioning factors. (1986: 97).

This proposed causal model, derived purely statistically from census and offender data, of course fits extremely well with that postulated in the Sheffield study from more on-the-ground fieldwork experience (see Fig. 13.12). But perhaps of even more interest in the Los Angeles research was a further finding, namely, that it seemed to be

> the speed of structural change, rather than simply the fact of such change, that initiates the transition of city neighborhoods from a low to a high-crime status . . . [In particular] the high velocity of first-decade change primarily in socio-economic status and secondly in subculture that were highly related to the second-decade acceleration in the [offender] measure. (Schuerman and Kobrin 1986: 97–8)[38]

This emphasis on the speed of change raises particularly the issue of how areas 'tip' from low-crime to high-crime areas, sometimes quite quickly (as for example Gardenia seemed to do in Sheffield in the 1940s). This is an issue of some importance, not least since there is evidence from a variety of sources that tipping processes can often begin slowly and then rapidly accelerate.

One famous criminological hypothesis relevant to tipping processes is the so-called 'broken windows' hypothesis of James Q. Wilson and George Kelling (1982). According to these authors, there is at least a strong likelihood that signs of disorder in an area—such as broken windows, abandoned housing, litter, and graffiti—will undermine the subtle

[37] The authors admit that the census and administrative records to which they had access are not ideal for measuring this kind of variable, but nevertheless continue: 'the variables included such correlates of weakened social control as the ethnic composition of local populations, features of family organisation related to child neglect, and the kind of normative heterogeneity indicated by the presence of a population highly diverse in educational level. Variables indexing local subculture were drawn directly from these features' (Schuerman and Kobrin 1986: 71–2).

[38] I have substituted the word 'offender' for the authors' original of 'crime', since they were working with offender data.

and informal processes whereby communities normally maintain social control. For example, where signs of disorder are prevalent in an area, residents may shrink back into their own dwellings, and take no responsibility for what goes on in public spaces. Meanwhile, the increasing dilapidation of the public space means that it may become fair game for theft and/or vandalism, and may also act as an unintended invitation to those engaged in crime of a commercial or semi-commercial nature (drugs, prostitution, etc.) to come and 'trade' in the area.

The researcher who has been most active in seeking to investigate empirically the 'spiral of decay in American neighborhoods', as he calls it, is Wesley Skogan (1986, 1990: for some British evidence see also Hope and Hough 1988). Skogan believes that the study of disorder is a vital, but very neglected, topic in criminology. He distinguishes between physical and social disorders (physical = abandoned or ill-kept buildings, broken streetlights, litter, vermin, etc; social = public drinking, prostitution, sexual catcalling, etc.: Skogan 1990: 4), but goes on to find that the two sorts of disorder are strongly areally correlated (p. 51). Moreover, while 'disorder' might seem to be a concept much dependent on one's personal viewpoint, and therefore very differently perceived by different actors, in fact the area in which survey respondents lived turned out, in survey analyses, to be much more important as a predictor of the number of disorders they reported than did any personal characteristics of the respondents. (Younger respondents did, however, perceive more disorders in the same areas than did older respondents, probably because they used public space more often).

Skogan found, not surprisingly, that disorders tended to be most numerous in areas with low neighbourhood stability, poverty, and a high ethnic minority population. But the real interest of his research, for the purposes of this chapter, lies in his analysis of the consequences of disorder. Quite strong evidence of three impacts of disorder were found:

First, *'disorder undermines the mechanisms by which communities exercise control over local affairs'* (Skogan 1990: 65). On cross-sectional analyses, there was a negative relationship between the presence of disorder in an area and the extent to which residents were willing to help one another in a neighbourly way; and also in the extent to which residents engaged in simple crime-prevention activities such as property marking, or asking their neighbours to keep an eye on their home during an absence.

Secondly, *'disorder sparks concern about neighborhood safety, and perhaps even causes crime itself'* (Skogan 1990: 65). As we have seen, the evidence of Skogan's study was that disorder was statistically linked to areal poverty, ethnic minority residence, and social instability; not surprisingly, such areas tended also to have high crime rates. Disentangling the causal order of these variables is of course very difficult, especially in cross-sectional analyses, but a path model was presented (see Fig. 13.14), based on thirty areas for which robbery victimization data were available, and 'our data on urban neighborhoods are consistent with [this] causal diagram . . . there were no significant paths between those social and economic variables and neighborhood crime, except through disorder' Skogan does not wish to over-state the evidence for the conclusion that disorder might cause an escalation in local offence rates, but he certainly believes that the data oblige one to take this link seriously, at least as a significant hypothesis for future research.

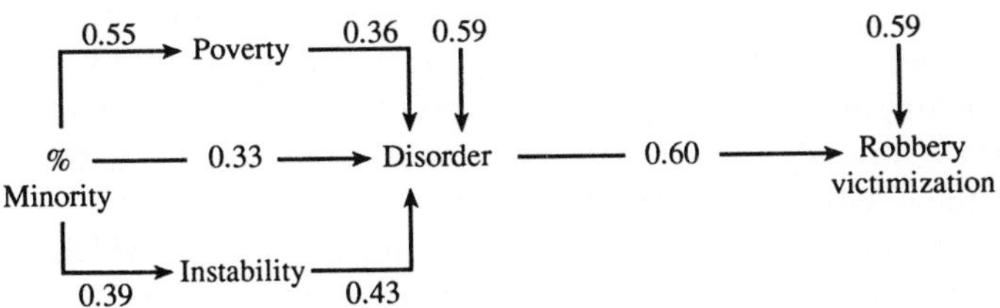

Fig. 13.14 Skogan's path model of area social characteristics, disorder, and robbery victimization in thirty American neighbourhoods
(Numbers on arrows linking boxes show path coefficients. Floating Numbers show proportion of unexplained rate variation for the relevant variable.)
Source: Skogan (1990: 75).

Thirdly, *'disorder undermines the stability of the housing market . . . [it] undercuts residential satisfaction, leads people to fear for the safety of their children, and encourages area residents to move away'* (Skogan 1990: 65). Drawing on work in the general field of urban sociology, Skogan suggests that selective out-migration from an area may be the most fundamental source of neighbourhood change. In the areas studied, there was a negative correlation between disorder and residents' degree of commitment to their area; moreover, this was related to moving intentions. Skogan goes on to note that these data probably underestimate the impact of disorder on local housing markets, since he had no data on perceptions of areas from anyone except area residents, and 'the stigma associated with high levels of visible disorder probably affects the perceptions and decisions of [potential in-migrants] as well' (1990: 84).

Overall, therefore, Skogan's research tends fairly clearly to support Wilson and Kelling's (1982) original 'broken windows' hypothesis. In the light of the Sheffield and Stockholm evidence, the fact that the housing market plays an important role within Skogan's theorization is also of great interest. Unfortunately, Skogan makes no direct attempt to link his housing market variables to the crime variables; on the basis of the

Sheffield and Stockholm experience, the likelihood is that they are in fact related, in an interactive way. Finally, Skogan's emphasis on out-migration from areas as an engine of neighbourhood change is undoubtedly of great importance, and it links strongly both to Sheffield evidence and to an earlier Chicago study, to which we must now turn.

Richard Taub and his colleagues (1984) begin their book with the observation that for many people, the relationship between crime (meaning here offence rates) and the deterioration of an area is obvious—crime causes deterioration. Their entire book is, however, in a sense an extended essay showing that this is an over-simplified conclusion. The authors are urban sociologists rather than criminologists, and their crime data and focus on crime are relatively restricted important parts of the volume being taken up with issues such as neighbourhood investment and the racial tipping of areas. Three key points, from a very complex argument, may however be selected as of special interest from the point of view of the environmental criminologist.

First, the authors discuss crime levels and the way in which they may affect people's perceptions of areas. The conclusion is that crime is certainly an issue in judging the quality of an area; however, these judgements are comparative rather than absolute (i.e. based on crime-related comparisons with other areas, not any ideal state). More importantly, the judgements made are essentially Gestalt assessments of the rewards and amenities (or disadvantages and lack of amenities) that the area offers, in which actual crime victimization levels are not necessarily the most important feature. Hence, in the empirical evidence of the study, an expressed intention to move out of the area was more strongly related, statistically, to measures of satisfaction with the general level of safety in the neighbourhood than it was to the actual level of criminal victimization. Moreover, two areas of Chicago were found where respondents from all ethnic groups (black, white, and hispanic) themselves rightly judged the actual risk of crime to be above average, *yet were satisfied with the level of safety in the neighbourhood* (Taub *et al.* 1984: 171–2).[39] One of these areas was the district where the University of Chicago is situated (Hyde Park–Kenwood). In this area Taub *et al.* 1984: 96–102) the university had itself spent enormous sums on urban renewal (and had been instrumental in obtaining federal funds and encouraging private investors towards the same end); the university and/or local citizens had also, *inter alia,* (i) pressurized the city authorities to enforce regulations against the multi-occupation of certain dwellings, (ii) provided low-cost second mortgages to encourage university staff to live in the area, (iii) assembled a large private security force with a radio link to the Chicago

[39] In the majority of areas studied, of course, these two variables (perceived risk of crime and satisfaction with level of safety) were negatively correlated.

Police Department, and (iv) created a fleet of buses, and installed emergency telephones at key points, to enhance feelings of personal safety. The net result of all this activity was an area which, despite being only 59 per cent white, was racially stable in population composition (no evidence of 'white flight'); and, a point of very great criminological interest, had rapidly appreciating property values despite a high crime rate. To repeat: residents and other users of an area make a Gestalt assessment of the rewards and amenities of an area, and the crime level is only one of the factors they take into account in deciding whether to live in or use the area. One should add that this finding probably does not disturb the conclusions from Skogan's study, since one might postulate that serious *disorder* (of the kind defined by Skogan) would almost certainly feature as a strong negative factor in most people's Gestalt assessment of an area.

Secondly, Taub and his colleagues devote some attention to the ways in which individuals make decisions relevant to neighbourhood decline. *Inter alia*, they propose, and find some empirical evidence for, a so-called 'threshold model' of neighbourhood change, which has consequences somewhat akin to a domino effect. Suppose, in a given area, that there are some signs that the area is beginning to deteriorate: do residents attempt to move?[40] Some (we can call them 'pioneers') will attempt to move anyway, even if no one else does, at the first hint of trouble—and maybe they would move on even if the area were not showing signs of difficulty. Some (such as the elderly who have lived in the area for very many years) will not move whatever anyone else does ('conservatives'). But perhaps some individuals and families in between these polar groups will in fact be influenced by the decisions of others. Some, maybe, are very anxious to protect their children, or their own finances, from an apparently bad future, and, while not natural 'first movers', they will try to leave as soon as they see a few other people doing so. Others, more cautiously, will wait a little to see if things improve; but when a lot of their neighbours begin to talk about moving, then they too will be influenced to join the exodus. A hypothetical 'threshold model' distribution of this type is shown in Fig. 13.15; in this imaginary situation, 30 per cent of the population are 'pioneers', and a further 30 per cent are 'conservatives' (shown respectively as 0.0 and 1.0 in the diagram). In between are shown those who will move if 20 per cent, 40 per cent, etc., of their fellow residents do. It is easy to calculate that, in this particular hypothetical distribution, 60 per cent of the relevant population will, by the end of the process, try to move from the area.

[40] The authors discuss threshold processes with reference to neighbourhood investment; however, it would appear that very similar arguments apply to moving decisions, and, in view of the importance of these decisions for neighbourhood change, I have therefore written with primary reference to them.

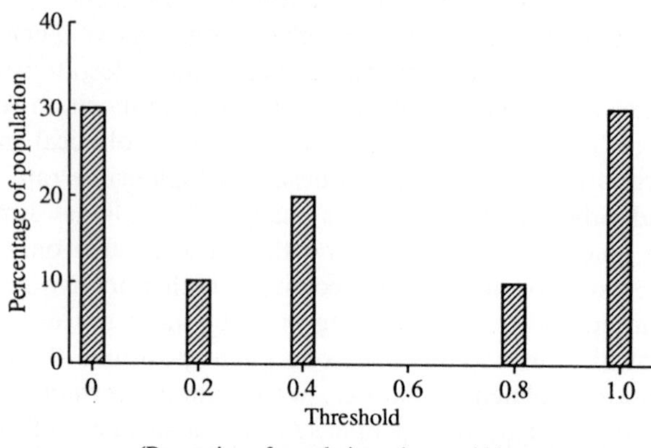

Fig 13.15 A Hypothetical 'threshold model' distribution
Source: Taub et al. (1984: 127).

The importance of this threshold model for present purposes is twofold. In the first place, it shows clearly how a 'tipping' process in an area can gather speed, and this re-emphasizes the importance of the 'velocity' dimension in Schuerman and Kobrin's results. Moreover, it shows, by implication, that once a tipping process is under way, there is very little that an individual can do to stop it, for an individual acting alone can have very little power to sway other individuals in an accelerating process of this kind. On the other hand, as Taub and his colleagues show, a corporate body can in fact influence the decisions of other individuals, and hence (in principle at least) halt a tipping process. The University of Chicago seems to have achieved this in Hyde Park–Kenwood (at least as regards a tipping process into urban decline, and a racial tipping process; though, in this case, the crime rate remained high). In another area studied in Taub *et al.*'s research (Beverly), not dissimilar success in halting a potential tipping spiral was achieved collectively by a community association, with substantial backing from local commercial interests. Interestingly, corporate decisions by local government agencies and other public bodies do not feature much in Taub *et al.*'s argument: but I shall hereafter assume, as is surely the case, that such agencies are also an important species of 'corporate body' within the framework of the valuable contrast made by these authors between individuals and corporate bodies.

These considerations lead directly on to the third and last main point to be emphasized from Taub *et al.*'s research. In their closing chapter, they offer a threefold approach to the understanding of neighbourhood change: such change is, it is suggested, always a product of the interaction between (i) ecological facts, (ii) individual decisions, and (iii) corporate decisions. 'Ecological facts' are defined as including (i) the potential employment base for neighbourhood residents, (ii) demographic pressures on the local housing market, (iii) the age and quality of the housing stock, and (iv) external amenities such as attractive physical locations (hills, lakes, etc).[41]. Taub *et al.* note that most previous theories of neighbourhood change have concentrated on ecological facts as the main explanatory variables, but they argue that this is an incomplete approach, as shown by some of their area case studies. For in reality:

> none of the factors influencing urban neighborhoods can be considered independently from the other two. Corporate decisions take into account the ecological facts; individual decisions take into account the ecological facts as well as corporate decisions; community organisations depend on individual and corporate contributions for survival; and so on (Taub *et al.* 1984: 187).

Finally, harking right back to the Chicago School, Taub *et al.* comment that, with hindsight, one can see only too clearly the central weakness of the urban model adopted:

> because early sociological theories [did] not make a place for the decision rules of individual and corporate actors, [they led] to the too-simple view that the neighborhoods in a city are somewhat interchangeable parts of a single, integrated urban system that operates according to univariate rules of evolution (Taub *et al.* 1984: 186)

Hence, ultimately, the study of community change and crime leads—just as did our following through of the implications of offence location studies and offender residence studies—to a linking together of micro-, meso-, and macro-social processes. Nothing else will provide an adequate framework for explanation. In the study of change, however, because one's focus is more long-term, it is perhaps easier to see the macro-level and the overtly political processes in operation; hence it is particularly important to remember, when studying other and perhaps more static issues in environmental criminology, that these macro-level and political forces are always present, even if not very visible in a particular piece of local research. As we saw at the beginning of the section on offender residence, very much the same message has emanated from Bursik's long-

[41] This definition of 'ecological facts' is not wholly unproblematic from a sociological point of view, since it contains some physical features (hills, the nature of the housing stock), and some social–structural features, such as the local employment base. However, it would not be difficult to create conceptual refinements which would deal with this difficulty, and the difficulty does not weaken the main thrust of Taub *et al.*'s argument.

term follow-up of the Shaw and McKay data on juvenile offender rates in Chicago.

ENVIRONMENTAL CRIMINOLOGY AND THE FUTURE

In bringing this chapter to a close, a few remarks on two rather diverse topics relevant to the future of environmental criminology might be helpful. These topics are the urban–rural contrast, and the changing nature of contemporary city life.

The Urban–Rural Contrast

In using the label 'environmental criminology', one is, by implication, drawing attention to the potential influence of differing environments upon various aspects of criminal behaviour. Apparently one of the most obvious of such influences is whether one lives in an urban or a rural environment, and criminological data of all kinds (police data, victimization surveys, self-report studies) consistently support the view that rates of crime and criminality in these differing kinds of community are very different indeed. Yet, in any serious sense, this must be one of the most under-studied topics in criminology, and, curiously, even environmental criminologists have shown very little sustained interest in it.[42]

Urban sociologists have, quite rightly, pointed out that, in a truly sociological sense, the urban–rural divide has now in many ways been eroded; by this they mean that even remote rural settlements are heavily influenced by the dominant urban culture of modern societies (via television, macro-economic developments, etc.). Despite this, the urban–rural differentiation in crime and offender rates has remained very clear. A re-examination of this issue, in the context of modern rural societies partly permeated by a metropolitan culture, could therefore have some general pay-off for criminological explanation.

The Changing Nature of Contemporary City Life

A traditional view as to why urban areas have more crime than rural areas suggests that two main factors are in operation: first, that urban areas generate more opportunities for crime; and secondly, that the weakened social bonds of urban societies increase aggregate criminality levels (control theory). In the late twentieth century, when the development of a consumer society has vastly increased the volume of easily transported yet

[42] For a brief but now somewhat dated discussion, see Baldwin and Bottoms (1976: introduction).

valued goods, but the social fabric of urban relationships often seems all too fragile both these factors seem very relevant to the problem of city crime. In consequence, many fear the 'nightmare scenario' of a society in which the average family is much more affluent than it was half a century ago, yet the feeling of order in public space, and even the sense of security within one's own dwelling, will have disappeared.

These fears may well be exaggerated, but the social processes related to them need to be taken seriously by modern environmental criminologists. For the truth is that the nature of contemporary city life is changing. Communications technology has made it possible for people to interact with one another easily across vast distances (by telephone, fax, air travel, etc.), and, concomitantly, it has become easier to move capital around the globe, so increasing the effective independence of large multinational corporations from direct control and regulation by single nation states, and increasing also the power of these corporations to outmanœuvre local labour resistances. These changes have had a number of important consequences for daily life in particular local areas, including (i) a decline in the importance of 'regional economies' in which economic, social, and political relations in a particular region are distinctively shaped by specifically local industries or trades; and (ii) an increased 'disembedding' of social relations from specifically neighbourhood contexts, as mobility renders it possible to build affective ties across distances—and, often enough, on the basis of individual choice rather than (as often in the past) upon membership of an identifiable and well-understood traditional local group such as an extended family or a church.[43] All these phenomena can be regarded as effects of the process referred to by Anthony Giddens (1984) as the radically increased *time–space distanciation* of the modern social world, i.e. 'the stretching of social systems across time–space'. There is, by now, a considerable literature on such matters (to take three very different examples, see e.g. Lash and Urry 1987, Harvey 1989; Giddens 1990), but it would stretch this chapter beyond its limits to discuss such issues in any detail here. Suffice it to say, therefore, that the issues very briefly touched upon here can have very profound consequences for social life—including crime and criminality—in specific local places, and that these consequences are researchable. To discuss the matter through the distinction between place and space (see note 4), *place* will continue to be of great importance in the environmental criminology of the future, and indeed very probably of enhanced

[43] See, in this connection, Giddens's (1990: 102) extremely interesting (if perhaps oversimplified) contrast between the main 'environments of trust' in pre-modern and in modern societies. In pre-modern societies, he suggests, these are: (i) kinship relations, (ii) the local community as a place, (iii) religious cosmologies, and (iv) tradition; in modern culture, they are (i) personal, intimate friendship relationships, (ii) abstract systems, and (iii) counterfactual thought.

importance, given the 'unevenness of development in a modernising economy' (to return to a quotation from Rosemary Mellor used at the beginning of this chapter).[44] At the same time, given the increased time–space distanciation of social systems, the social life of ordinary places and contexts may well have to be studied rather differently than in the days when local contexts were much more all-encompassing. To return again to another comment by Rosemary Mellor (1989: 253), increasingly it seems that 'localism *and* mobility define everyday life'; and the environmental criminology of the future—indeed, the criminology of the future––must ensure that it adequately tackles the implications of this dual trend. All this will, of course, need to be tackled *in addition to* the other prerequisites for an adequate environmental criminology, mentioned earlier in this chapter, such as improved integration of offence location and offender residence studies,and an adequate tying together of the interconnected macro-, meso-, and micro-level processes which underpin the commission of offences in particular places, and the social production of offenders.

Selected Further Reading

The following three books, taken together, perhaps offer the most accessible introduction to the main themes of modern environmental criminology:

P. J. Brantingham and P. L. Brantingham, eds., *Environmental Criminology*, Prospect Heights, III.: Waveland, 1991.

A. J. Reiss and M. Tonry, eds., *Communities and Crime.* Chicago: University of Chicago Press, 1986.

Wikstrom, P-O. H. *Urban Crime, Criminals and Victims: The Swedish Experience in an Anglo-American Comparative Perspective.* New York: Springer-Verlag, 1991.

The first two of these are edited books (the first originally appearing in 1981) containing a wide range of relevant essays. Wikstrom's book is a statistically-oriented analysis of the Swedish experience, in the light of a full examination of the American and British literature.

Recently, some scholars have shown interest in integrating research in environmental criminology with studies in the field of individual criminal careers. The following edited book, some chapters of which are not for beginners, is the best source for this nascent approach:

[44] These points are relevant to the debate about ghettoization, on which see Wiles (1992).

D. P. Farrington, R. J. Sampson and P-O. H., Wikstrom, eds., *Integrating Individual and Ecological Aspects of Crime*. Stockholm: National Council for Crime Prevention, 1993.

REFERENCES

ALIHAN, M. (1938), *Social Ecology*. New York: Columbia University Press.

ANDERSON, S., GROVE SMITH, C., KINSEY, R., and WOOD, J. (1990), *The Edinburgh Crime Survey: First Report*. Edinburgh: Scottish Office (Central Research Unit Papers).

BALDWIN, J. (1979), 'Ecological and Areal Studies in Great Britain and the United States', in N. Morris and M. Tonry, eds., *Crime and Justice: An Annual Review of Research*, vol. 1. Chicago: University of Chicago Press.

BALDWIN, J., and BOTTOMS, A. E. (1976), *The Urban Criminal*. London: Tavistock.

BENNETT, T., and WRIGHT, R. (1984), *Burglars on Burglary*. Aldershot: Gower.

BOTTOMS, A. E. (1993), 'Recent Criminological and Social Theory and the Problem of Integrating Knowledge about Individual Criminal Acts and Careers and Areal Dimensions of Crime', in D. P. Farrington, R. J. Sampson, and P-O. H. Wikstöm, eds., *Integrating Individual and Ecological Aspects of Crime*. Stockholm: National Council for Crime Prevention.

BOTTOMS, A. E., CLAYTOR, A., and WILES, P. (1992), 'Housing Markets and Residential Community Crime Careers: A Case Study from Sheffield', in D. J. Evans, N. R. Fyfe, and D. T. Herbert, eds., *Crime, Policing and Place: Essays in Environmental Criminology*. London: Routledge.

BOTTOMS, A. E., MAWBY, R. I., and WALKER, M. A. (1987), 'A Localised Crime Survey in Contrasting Areas of a City', *British Journal of Criminology*, 27: 125–54.

BOTTOMS, A. E., MAWBY, R. E., and ZANTHOS, P. (1989), 'A Tale of Two Estates', in D. Downes, ed., *Crime and the City*. London: Macmillan.

BOTTOMS, A. E., and WILES, P. (1986), 'Housing Tenure and Residential Community Crime Careers in Britian', in A. J. Reiss and M. Tonry, eds., *Communities and Crime*. Chicago: University of Chicago Press.

—— (1992), 'Explanations of Crime and Place', in D. J. Evans, N. R. Fyfe, and D. T. Herbert, eds., *Crime, Policing and Place: Essays in Environmental Criminology*, London: Routledge.

BOTTOMS, A. E., and XANTHOS, P. (1981), 'Housing Policy and Crime in the British Public Sector', in P. J. Brantingham and P. L. Branqingham, eds., *Environmental Criminology*. Beverly Hills: Sage.

BRANTINGHAM, P. J., and BRANTINGHAM, P. L. (1981*a*), *Environmental Criminology*. Beverly Hills: Sage.

—— (1981*b*), 'Notes on the Geometry of Crime', in P. J. Brantingham and P. L. Brantingham, eds., *Environmental Criminology*. Beverly Hills: Sage.

—— (1984) *Patterns in Crime*, New York: Macmillan.

—— (1991), *Environmental Criminology*, rev. edn. Prospect Heights, Ill.: Waveland.

BRANTINGHAM, P. J., and JEFFERY, C. R. (1981), 'Afterword: Crime, Space, and Criminological Theory', in P. J. Brantingham and P. L. Brantingham, eds., *Environmental Criminology*. Beverly Hills: Sage.

BRONFENBRENNER, U. (1979), *The Ecology of Human Development*. Cambridge, Mass.: Harvard University Press.

BULMER, M. (1984), *The Chicago School of Scociology*. Chicago: University of Chicago Press.

BURGESS, E. W. (1916), 'Juvenile Delinquency in a Small City', *Journal of the American Institute of Criminal Law and Criminology*, 6: 724–8.

BURQUEST, R., FARRELL, G., and PEASE, K. (1992), 'Lessons from Schools', *Policing*, 8: 148–55.

BURSIK, R. J. (1986), 'Ecological Stability and the Dynamics of Delinquency', in A. J. Reiss and M. Tonry, eds., *Communities and Crime*. Chicago: University of Chicago Press.

—— (1988), 'Social Disorganization and Theories of Crime and Delinquency: Problems and Prospects', *Criminology*, 26: 519–51.

CARTER, R. L., and HILL, K. Q. (1979), *The Criminal's Image of the City*. New York: Pergamon.

CLARKE, R. V. G. (1983), 'Situational Crime Prevention: Its Theoretical Basis and Practical Scope', in M. Tonry and N. Morris, eds., *Crime and Justice: An Annual Review of Research*, vol. 4. Chicago: Chicago University Press.

CLARKE, R. (1992), *Situational Crime Prevention: Successful Case Studies*. New York: Harvard and Heston.

COHEN, L. E., and FELSON, M. (1979), 'Social Change and Crime Rate Trends: A Routine Activities Approach', *American Sociological Review*, 44: 588–608.

COLEMAN, A. (1985), *Utopia on Trial: Vision and Reality in Planned Housing*. London: Hilary Shipman.

—— (1989), 'Disposition and Situation: Two Sides of the Same Crime', in D. J. Evans and D. T. Herbert, eds., *The Geography of Crime*. London: Routledge.

COOK, P. J. (1983), 'The Influence of Gun Availability on Violent Crime Patterns', in N. Morris and M. Tonry, eds., *Crime and Justice: An Annual Review of Research*, vol. 4. Chicago: Chicago University Press.

CRESSEY, D. (1964), *Delinquency, Crime and Differential Association*. The Hague: Nijhoff.

CROMWELL, P. F., OLSON, J. N., and AVARY, D'A. W. (1991), *Breaking and Entering: An Ethnographic Analysis of Burglary*. Newbury Park: Sage.

DAMER, S. (1974), 'Wine Alley: The Sociology of a Dreadful Enclosure', *Sociological Review*, 22: 221–48.

DAVIDSON, R. N. (1981), *Crime and Environment*. London: Croom Helm.

EVANS, D., and HERBERT, D. T., eds. (1989), *The Geography of Crime*. London: Routledge.

EVANS, D. J., FYFE, N. R., and HERBERT, D. T., eds. (1992), *Crime, Policing and Place: Essays in Environmental Criminology*. London: Routledge.

FARRELL, G. (1992), 'Multiple Victimization: Its Extent and Significance', *International Review of Victimology*, 2: 85–102.

FARRINGTON, D. P., and DOWDS, E. A. (1985), 'Disentangling Criminal Behaviour and Police Reaction', in D. P. Farrington and J. Gunn, eds., *Reactions to Crime*. Chichester: Wiley.

FARRINGTON, D. P., SAMPSON, R. J., and WIKSTRÖM, P-O. H., eds. (1993), *Integrating Individual and Ecological Aspects of Crime*. Stockholm: National Council for Crime Prevention.

FELSON, M. (1992), 'Routine Activities and Crime Prevention', *Studies on Crime and Crime Prevention: Annual Review*, 1: 30–4.

FIGLIO, R. M., HAKIM, S., and RENGERT, G. F., eds. (1986), *Metropolitan Crime Patterns*. Monsey, NY: Willow Tree Press.

FINESTONE, H. (1976), 'The Delinquent and Society: The Shaw and McKay Tradition', in J. F. Short, Jr, ed., *Delinquency, Crime and Society*. Chicago: University of Chicago Press.

GIDDENS, A. (1984), *The Constitution of Society*. Cambridge: Polity.

—— (1990), *The Consequences of Modernity*. Cambridge: Polity.

GILL, O. (1977), *LUKE STREET*. LONDON: MACMILLAN.

GOTTFREDSON, M. R. (1984), *Victims of Crime*: the Dimensions of Risk. Home Office Research Study no. 81, London: HMSO.

GOTTFREDSON, M. R., and HIRSCHI, T. (1990), *A General Theory of Crime*. Stanford: Stanford University Press.

HARRIES, K. D. (1981), 'Alternative Denominators in Conventional Crime Rates', in P. J. Brantingham and P. L. Brantingham, eds., *Environmental Criminology*. Beverly Hill: Sage.

HARVEY, D. (1989), *The Condition of Postmodernity*. Oxford: Blackweel.

HERBERT, D. (1982), *The Geography of Urban Crime*. London: Longman.

HOME OFFICE (1988), *The Five Towns Initiative: A Community Response to Crime Reduction*. London: Home Office.

HOPE, T. (1985), *Implementing Crime Prevention Measures*, Home Office Research Study no. 86. London: HMSO.

HOPE, T., and FOSTER, J. (1992), 'Conflicting Forces: Changing the Dynamics of Crime and Community on a "Problem" Estate', *British Journal of Criminology*, 32: 488–504.

HOPE, T., and HOUGH, M. (1988), 'Area, Crime and Incivity: A Profile from the British Crime Survey', in T. Hope and M. Shaw, eds., *Communities and Crime Reduction*. London: HMSO.

JANSON, C-G. (1993), 'Ecological and Individual Approaches in the Study of Crime and Delinquency', in D. P. Farrington, R. J. Sampson, and P-O. H. Wikström, eds., *Integrating Individual and Ecological Aspects of Crime*. Stockholm: National Council for Crime Prevention.

JEFFERY, C. R. (1971), *Crime Prevention through Environmental Design*. Beverly Hills: Sage.

KINSEY, R. (1985), *Merseyside Crime Survey: First Report*. Liverpool: Merseyside County Council.

KORNHAUSER, R. R. (1978), *Social Sources of Delinquency*. Chicago: University of Chicago Press.

LANDER, B. (1954), *Towards an Understanding of Juvenile Delinquency*. New York: Columbia University Press.

LASH, S., and URRY, J. (1987), *The End of Organized Capitalism*. Cambridge: Polity.

Liddle, M., and Bottoms, A. E. (1993), *The Five Towns Crime Prevention Initiative: Key Findings and Implications from a Retrospective Research Analysis*. London: Home Office.

Lowman, J. (1986), 'Prostitution in Vancouver: Some Notes on the Genesis of a Social Problem', *Canadian Journal of Criminology*, 28: 1–16.

Maguire, M., and Bennett, T. (1982), *Burglary in a Dwelling*. London: Heinemann.

Mannheim, H. (1965), *Comparative Criminology*. London: Routledge and Kegan Paul.

Martens, P. L. (1990), 'Family, Neighbourhood and Socialization', in P-O. H. Wikstrom, ed., *Crime and Measures against Crime in the City*. Stockholm: National Council for Crime Prevention.

—— (1993), 'An Ecological Model of Socialization in Explaining Offending', in D. P. Farrington, R. J. Sampson, and P-O. H. Wikström, eds., *Integrating Individual and Ecological Aspects of Crime*. Stockholm: National Council for Crime Prevention.

Matza, D. (1964), *Delinquency and Drift*. New York: Wiley.

Mawby, R. I. (1979), *Policing the City*. Farnborough: Saxon House.

—— (1989), 'Policing and the Criminal Area', in D. J. Evans and D. T. Herbert, eds., *The Geography of Crime*. London: Routledge.

Mayhew, H. (1862), *London Labour and the London Poor* , vol. 4: *Those That Will Not Work*. London: Griffin Bohn.

Mayhew, P., Clarke, R. V. G., Sturman, A., and Hough, J. M. (1976), *Crime as Opportunity*, Home Office Research Unit Study no. 34. London: HMSO.

Mellor, R. (1989), 'Urban Sociology: A Trend Report', *Sociology*, 23: 241–60.

Merrett, S. (1979), *State Housing in Britain*. London: Routledge and Kegan Paul.

Moriyama, T. (1993), 'Crime, Criminal Justice and Social Control: Why Do We Enjoy a Low Crime Rate?', paper presented to the British Criminology Conference, Cardiff.

Morris, T. P. (1957), *The Criminal Area: A Study in Social Ecology*. London: Routledge and Kegan Paul.

Newmann, O. (1973), *Dfensible Space*. London: Architectural Press.

Painter, K. (1992), 'Different Worlds: The Spatial, Temporal and Social Dimensions of Female Victimization', in D. J. Evans, N. R. Fyfe, and D. T. Herbert, eds., *Crime and Policing: Essays in Environmental Criminology*. London: Routledge.

Pease, K. (1993), 'Individual and Community Influences on Victimization and their Implications for Crime Prevention', in D. P. Farrington, R. J. Sampson and P-O. H. Wikström, eds., *Integrating Individual and Ecological Aspects of Crime*. Stockholm: National Council for Crime Prevention.

Polvi, N., Looman, T., Humphries, C., and Pease, K. (1990), 'Repeat Break and Enter Victimization: Time Course and Crime Prevention Opportunity', *Journal of Police Science and Administration*, 17: 8–11.

Poyner, B. (1983), *Design against Crime*. London: Butterworths.

Poyner, B., and Webb, B. (1992), *Crime Free Housing*. Oxford: Butterworths Architecture.

Radzinowicz, L. (1966), *Ideology and Crime*. London: Heinemann.

Ramsay, M. (1989), *Downtown Drinkers: The Perceptions and Fears of the Public in a City Centre*, Home Office Prevention Unit Paper no. 19. London: Home Office.

Reiss, A. J. (1986), 'Why Are Communities Important in Understanding Crime?', in A. J. Reiss and M. Tonry, eds., *Communities and Crime*. Chicago: University of Chicago Press.

Rengert, G., and Wasilchick, J. (1985), *Suburban Burglary*. Springfield, Ill.: Charles C. Thomas.

Rex, J., and Moore, R. (1967), *Race, Community and Conflict: A Study of Sparkbrook*. London: Oxford University Press.

Reynolds, F. (1986), *The Problem Housing Estate*. Aldershot: Gower.

Rhodes, W. M., and Conly, C. (1981), 'Crime and Mobility: An Empirical Study;, in P. J. Brantingham and P. L. Brantingham, eds., *Environmental Criminology*. Beverly Hills: Sage.

Robinson, W. S. (1950), 'Ecological Correlations and the Behavior of Individuals', *American Sociological Review*, 15: 351–7.

Rutter, M., and Giller, H. (1983), *Juvenile Delinquency: Trends and Prospects*. Harmondsworth: Penguin.

Sampson, A., and Phillips, C. (1992), *Multiple Victimization: Racial Attacks on an East London Estate*, Home Office Crime Prevention Unit Paper no. 36. London: Home Office.

Sampson, R. J., and Groves, W. B. (1989), 'Community Structure and Crime: Testing Social Disorganization Theory', *American Journal of Sociology*, 94: 774–802.

Schuerman, L., and Kobrin, S. (1986), 'Community Careers in Crime', in A. J. Reiss and M. Tonry, eds., *Communities and Crime*. Chicago: University of Chicago Press.

Sellin, T. (1938), *Culture, Conflict and Crime*. New York: Social Science Research Council.

Shaw, C. R., (1930), *The Jack Roller*. Chicago: University of Chicago Press.

Shaw, C. R., and McKay, H. D. (1931), *Social Factors in Juvenile Delinquency*. Washington, DC: US Government Printing Office.

—— (1942), *Juvenile Delinquency and Urban Areas*. Chicago: University of Chicago Press.

Sherman, L. W., Gartin, P. R., and Buerger, M. E. (1989), 'Hot Spots of Predatory Crime: Routine Activities and the Criminology of Place', *Criminology*, 27: 27–55.

Skogan, W. G. (1986), 'Fear of Crime and Neighborhood Change', in A. J. Reiss and M. Tonry, eds., *Communities and Crime*. Chicago: University of Chicago Press.

—— (1990), *Disorder and Decline: Crime and the Spiral of Decay in American Neighborhoods*. New York: Free Press.

Smith, L. (1989), *Domestic Violence: An Overview of the Literature*, Home Office Research Study no. 107. London: HMSO.

Smith, S. J. (1986), *Crime, Space and Society*. Cambridge: Cambridge University Press.

Snodgrass, J. (1976), 'Clifford R. Shaw and Henry D. McKay: Chicago Criminologists', *British Journal of Criminology*, 16: 1–19.

Sparks, R. F., Genn, H. G., and Dodd, D. H. (1977), *Surveying Victims*. Chichester: Wiley.

Taub, R., Taylor, D. G., and Dunham, J. D. (1984), *Paths of Neighbourhood Change*. Chicago: University of Chicago Press.

Taylor, R. B., and Gottfredson, S. (1986), 'Environmental Design, Crime, and Prevention: An Examination of Community Dynamics', in A. J. Reiss and M. Tonry, eds., *Communities and Crime*. Chicago: University of Chicago Press.

Tobias, J. J. (1972), *Crime and Industrial Society in the Nineteenth Century*. Harmondsworth: Penguin Books

Trickett, A., Osborn, D. R., Seymour, J., and Pease, K. (1992), 'What is Different about High Crime Areas?', *British Journal of Criminology*, 32: 81–9.

Urry, J. (1986), review of *The Constitution of Society* by Anthony Giddens, *Sociological Review*, 34: 434–7.

Walker, A., and Walker, C. (1987), *The Growing Divide: A Social Audit 1979–1987*. London: Child Poverty Action Group.

Wikström, P-O. H. (1990), 'Delinquency and the Urban Structure' in P-O. H. Wikström, ed., *Crime and Measures against Crime in the City*. Stockholm: National Council for Crime Prevention.

—— (1991), *Urban Crime, Criminals and Victims: The Swedish Experience in an Anglo-American Comparative Perspective*. New York: Springer-Verlag.

Wiles, P. (1992), 'Ghettoization in Europe?', *European Journal on Criminal Policy and Research*, 1: 52–69.

Wilson, J. Q., and Kelling, G. (1982), 'Broken Windows', *The Atlantic Monthly* March: 29–38.

Winchester, S., and Jackson, H. (1982), *Residential Burglary*, Home Office Research Study no. 74. London: Home Office.

Winkel, F. W. (1991), 'Police, Victims and Crime Prevention: Some Research-Based Recommendations on Victim-Orientated Interventions', *British Journal of Criminology*, 31: 250–65.

Wootton, B. (1959), *Social Science and Social Pathology*. London: Allen and Unwin.

PART 3

Crime Control and Criminal Justice

14

Crime Prevention

KEN PEASE

Each jurisdiction decides upon the scope of its criminal law. Crime comprises those actions which are deemed so damaging to the interests of the community that the state determines that it must take a direct role in identifying and acting against the criminal. Every crime is preventable by decriminalization of action, as for instance when sexual acts between consenting adult males in private became legal. It would in principle be possible to prevent all crime at a stroke, simply by repealing the relevant statutes. This means that, when we consider the prevention of crime, we are looking at a set of events joined only in their proscription by statute. With behaviour as diverse as murder and issuing false cheques, we should not look for universality in techniques of prevention.

Throughout the short history of their discipline, many criminologists trained in sociological traditions have been interested primarily in how the demands of the capitalist state have shaped the scope of the criminal law and the apparatus established to enforce it. Such a perspective places crime *control* at the margins of concern. In so far as scholars from such traditions have thought of it at all, crime prevention has been regarded as achievable only by changing large-scale economic and social arrangements. Self-evidently, such a position precludes empirical work on crime prevention, and discussion of it will not feature further in this chapter.

The view that society must be radically changed for crime control to occur may also be found among some practitioners within criminal justice, but there it has coexisted with the more popular rival view that the greatest prevention possibilities lie in changing the hearts and minds of established or potential offenders by control or reform. This view has been reflected in the rhetoric of offender change favoured by many sentencers and politicians. Long out of favour among academic criminologists, the revitalization of personal change as fashionable penology may be imminent (see Gendreau and Ross 1987 as a bell-wether of this revival). The tradition has the crucial advantage of being susceptible to empirical test.

I am grateful to my colleagues Graham Farrell and Coretta Phillips during the four weeks when I was preoccupied by writing this chapter, and to Sam Lloyd, Ian Hannant and Len Dyson of the Merseyside Police, whose work in establishing a programme to prevent some violent crime in the force's C Division meant that my mood while writing it was optimistic. Gloria Laycock's comments on an earlier draft were immensely helpful.

A third perspective on crime control, that it may be achieved by quite modest adjustments in the social and physical settings in which crime occurs, is of much more recent origin, but has generated a disproportionately large amount of good research and evaluation.

A useful categorization of approaches to crime prevention has been offered by Brantingham and Faust (1976) and later modified by Van Dijk and De Waard (1991). According to the Brantingham and Faust classification, *primary prevention* addresses the reduction of crime opportunities without reference to criminals or potential criminals. *Secondary prevention* addresses the change of people, typically those at high risk of embarking upon a criminal career, before they do so. It is concerned with the prevention of criminality rather than the prevention of crime. *Tertiary prevention* is focused upon the truncation of the criminal career, in length, seriousness, or frequency of offending; that is, it deals with the 'treatment' of known offenders.[1] Traditionally these ventures have taken place in parallel in Britain. In so far as anyone has led the way, the police have taken a leading role in primary prevention; local authority social work and youth services have assumed a leading role in secondary prevention; and the prison and probation services have led in tertiary prevention. The growth in multi-agency approaches to crime prevention has blurred these borders somewhat without redrawing them. In general, it is probably fair to say that the emphasis in crime prevention has moved from the tertiary towards the primary, and is moving back to become a combination at least of primary and secondary prevention strategies. Most space will be given over in this chapter to primary crime prevention. However, in recognition of cycles of fashion in crime prevention as elsewhere in criminal justice, secondary and tertiary prevention will also be discussed. This is particularly important in that the emerging study of criminal careers offers hitherto undreamed-of possibilities in the evaluation of secondary and tertiary prevention approaches.

THEORY, CRIME PREVENTION, AND THE THEORY OF CRIME PREVENTION

All theories of crime are also theories of crime prevention. They differ only in the scale of change necessary to achieve that end (for accounts of relevant theories see Kornhauser 1978; Lynch and Groves 1986; Lilly *et al.* 1989; Garland 1990). Theoretical positions originating in the work of

[1] Although the terms change with time, the construction of the field in this way does not. For instance, Henry Fielding's (1988 [1751]) classic *Enquiry into the Causes of the Late Increase of Robbers* is organized according to the distinction, with primary prevention followed by secondary followed by tertiary.

the French sociologist Durkheim regard crime prevention as undesirable, in that crime and reactions to it establish a kind of moral boundary-setting which is important for society to undertake. Others, the conflict theories, regard crime prevention as a flawed enterprise in that the important issues concern the scope and enforcement of criminal law as a manifestation of class interests, the only route to defensible prevention being via changes in social structure. These theories will not be discussed here, since within a limited compass it was deemed preferable to restrict attention to those theories within whose range of convenience primary crime prevention may be found. Notwithstanding that, one should never forget either the possible social benefits of shared outrage, or that one form of crime prevention is decriminalization, and that perhaps the first question for the would-be crime preventer is: 'Should the crime I intend to prevent be a crime in the first place?' There is also a valid place for conflict theories in the analysis of how crime prevention effort itself is deployed, that is, whether there are class or other sectional interests which shape the direction and extent of work designed to prevent crimes.

One of the ways in which theoretical traditions differ lies in the choice of what is to be explained. This is certainly the case in criminology. To oversimplify, one approach takes the motivated offender, and the other takes the crime event, as the thing to be explained. Theories which address the supply of motivated offenders differ from those which deal with crime opportunity. A person may become a motivated offender on the basis of genetic influences (Mednick *et al.* 1974), the experience of unfairness (Cloward and Ohlin 1960), strain (Cohen 1955; Merton 1957), social disorganization (Shaw and Mackay 1942), or choice of what will maximize personal benefits, and the social factors taken into account in constructing the relevant equation for oneself (exemplified by the control theory of Hirschi 1969). With the certain exception of genetic theory and the possible exception of control theory, the role of such theories in crime prevention has been declaratory, that is, to contend and seek to demonstrate that factors like unemployment and discrimination fuel crime rates. They may be used in justification of some secondary prevention projects (see Graham 1990 for a review) but often not in a way in which their originators would be likely to recognize. Indeed, 'community' crime prevention typically takes a more generic 'social problem approach . . . that seeks to reduce crime via the amelioration of the broad social conditions that breed criminal activity' (Lurigio and Rosenbaum 1986: 21). Theories like those mentioned above are concerned with the supply of motivated offenders; they posit the individual or social circumstances which fuel that supply. The default state of the properly socialized is non-criminal. Psychological theories which are concerned with the supply of motivated offenders, by contrast, regard the default state of at least some people as criminal. This is taken to be the expression of personality characteristics like extraversion (Eysenck 1970) or its close cousin impulsivity (Trasler 1972) in the anti-social personality (Farrington 1991: see also Farrington, Chapter 12, this volume).

Those sociological theories which regard crime as by and large a bad thing, and those psychological theories which contend that personality characteristics predispose to behaviour which is usually criminalized, have in common the attempted explanation of the supply of motivated offenders. Other theories take the supply of motivated offenders as given, and seek to explain variations in the level of crime by reference to other things. Hirschi (1986) explicitly argues for a division of responsibility in which theories of the kind touched upon above should (and clearly already do) focus on variations in criminality, and other theories focus upon the determinants of crime events. A similar distinction, with a similar conclusion, was offered by Bennett (1986). Although a division between the two types of theory is generally sensible, this should not obscure the significant points of contact between the two kinds of theory. For instance, the important topic of illegal drug use conflates elements of offender motivation with those of the immediate circumstances of offending. Bennett and Wright's (1986) research illustrates this. They showed that a smaller proportion of addicts reported non-drug crimes when receiving a prescription than in the period before receiving one. The 'artificial' generation of a motive to offend by the need to feed drug habits crosses the theoretical divide, since prescription practice (a feature of the immediate environment) determines the supply of motivated offenders. Some of the most interesting of the other areas of overlap concern the processes of recruitment into and desistance from crime. Both of these are underresearched, as is the fate of theoretical boundary zones generally. Finally in this category should be considered publicity campaigns, which may operate to demotivate a potential offender, or to recharacterize a situation as one offering less opportunity than was thought (see Winkel 1987 for a consideration of the effects of crime prevention campaigns).

Primary crime prevention has turned to theories of the crime event, rather than of the motivated offender, for its inspiration. The three theories of central interest for this kind of crime prevention are the lifestyle theory of Hindelang *et al.* (1978), the routine activities theory of Cohen and Felson (1979), and the rational choice theory of Cornish and Clarke (1986). These will be dealt with in a little more detail.

The origins of routine activities theory lie in the explanation of predatory crime, from which the range of application of the theory has been extended. The theory holds that three elements must converge in time and space for a crime to occur. These are a motivated offender, a suitable victim, and the absence of a capable guardian. As routine activity patterns disperse people away from their families and households, offenders will find targets with capable guardians absent. The decline of conventional communities also weakens the webs of informal social control which make for a multitude of capable guardians. Economic changes increase the number of suitable targets. Marcus Felson uses the number and portability of television sets as a surrogate for target availability. His advice to crime researchers and theorists (1986) makes clear why the theory appeals to the tacticians of primary crime prevention:

> Count television sets, monitor their portability, check their location. Examine travel patterns away from home; numbers of persons moving about with family, friends or strangers; adolescent activities with peers and parents; automobilization of youth; shopping patterns, parking patterns and so forth. Check household composition, housing types and patterns of occupancy of buildings and of ties among occupants. Look at hourly patterns of activity and where people are on the map. Check parental position vis-a-vis their own children and patterns of recognition among neighbours. Like physics and physiology, criminogenesis derives from a movement of physically bounded and identifiable entities about the physical world—movements that can be tracked according to map, clock, and calendar, and that from time to time assemble or disperse the four minimal elements in the web of informal crime control. (Felson 1986: 127–8)[2]

The lifestyle approach, as originally conceived by Hindelang *et al.* (1978), considered variations in rates of personal victimization. Lifestyle is deemed to be shaped by adaptations to role expectations and structural constraints. It incorporates routine daily activities, both locational and leisure. These determine likelihood of personal victimization because of the people with whom one associates and to whom one is exposed. Themes of research inspired by lifestyle theory have included differences in rates of victimization by age, sex, and ethnicity, and the usually high correspondence between the demographic characteristics of victims and offenders (e.g. Singer 1981). Lifestyle theory was modified by Garofalo (1987) to incorporate *direct* effects of societal structure upon victimization. This approach serves to recognize that people may be forced by the housing market to live in places which they would not choose, and whose hazards they experience independently of their lifestyle. Garofalo also inserts reactions to crime, target attractiveness, and individual differences as determinants of victimization risks. The first operates both directly and

[2] The three necessary conditions for crime referred to in the text were developed by Felson and expressed in the 1986 work cited as 'the web of informal crime control'. The elaboration of the original three into four elements occurred through considering controls on offender motivation in more detail, and introducing the concept of the 'intimate handler' of the offender, namely someone who may exercise informal control over a person motivated to offend.

as mediated through changes in lifestyle. The other two are described by Garofalo as variables that clearly merit inclusion but whose precise mode of operation has not yet been clarified.

Lifestyle theory differs from routine activities theory more in emphasis than in substance, for instance in that the concept of the capable guardian is more prominent in routine activities than in lifestyle theory. One way of deciding whether theories are really different is to see if, when both make predictions about the same thing, those predictions ever differ. The testing ground of lifestyle theory has tended to be cross-sectional data, and of routine activities longitudinal data, so the theories have not met 'head-on'. In the writer's tentative view, the theories are not clearly distinguishable in the predictions which they make. It may be that, in the future, clear differential predictions will be identified; or, alternatively, that the theories will be consolidated into a single 'lifestyle routines' theory.

The final theory to have shaped recent research in crime prevention has been that of Derek Cornish and Ron Clarke, and is known as rational choice theory. It begins with an assumption that

> offenders seek to benefit themselves by their criminal behaviour; that this involves the making of decisions and of choices, however rudimentary on occasion these processes might be; and that these processes exhibit a measure of rationality, albeit constrained by limits of time and ability and the availability of relevant information. (Clarke and Cornish 1985: 1)

Because offences differ very widely in their choice-structuring properties, the focus for Cornish and Clarke is upon the immediate situational context of a crime. The effect of the Clarke and Cornish approach is, *inter alia*, to focus upon the rich material to be yielded through interviews with offenders about what shaped their immediate behaviour. This enterprise, reviewed by Ekblom 1991*a*, has proven remarkably fruitful in generating crime prevention ideas (see e.g. Maguire 1982; Bennett and Wright 1984; Nee and Taylor 1988; Taylor and Nee 1988), and in understanding the way in which the structuring of offender choice will shape patterns of crime displacement (see Cornish and Clarke 1988*a*, *b*).

While the Clarke and Cornish formulation deals both with the initial decision to become involved in crime and with the decision to commit a particular crime in a particular context, its influence has tended to be greater in the second than in the first application. This second arm of the Clarke and Cornish approach complements lifestyle and routine activities theory by its injection of a consideration of how routine activities and lifestyle work at the point of offender choice. It has been criticized as being more applicable to instrumental than expressive crime (Trasler 1986, 1993).

SECONDARY AND TERTIARY PREVENTION: PROBLEMS AND OPPORTUNITIES

While primary prevention focuses on explaining the distribution of crime events, secondary and tertiary prevention concentrate upon changing the expressed criminality of those who already have, or have a high probability of acquiring, a criminal identity. It differs from community crime prevention approaches, described earlier, by being focused on the individual offender rather than on the community of which he or she is part—although the difference can become blurred. The whole balance of crime prevention effort directed at those who offend depends upon an understanding of how criminality is spread throughout the community. If the spread is somewhat even, secondary prevention measures directed at everyone would be indicated. If criminality is concentrated among a relatively small proportion of the population, rehabilitation or incapacitation become more attractive options. In fact, a case could be made for both these approaches. A high proportion of boys acquire at least one criminal conviction, indicating the high prevalence of criminality.[3] At the same time, a small proportion of frequent offenders commit a high proportion of crime. Focusing on the first of these facts serves to favour widely spread secondary prevention. Spotlighting the second serves to favour narrowly targeted tertiary prevention (Farrington 1992).[4]

The underpinning of secondary crime prevention comes from the predictability of the onset of a criminal career. This predictability lies both in the kind of child who will embark upon a criminal career, and the age at which he or she will do so. It is well established that those who are likely to be later classed as criminal can be roughly identified quite early in life. (For a full discussion of these issues see Farrington, Chapter 12, this volume.) Having parents who have a criminal record, being troublesome in school at age 8, having low intelligence, and being subject to poor housing and child-rearing are linked with being convicted at age 10–13 (Farrington 1986). This is not an artefact of the vicissitudes of official processing, since the same influences are predictive of self-reported delinquency. The factors which predict the onset of a criminal career are different in cases of late onset, when having an unstable job record, low family income, and an 'anti-establishment attitude' are the key predictors

[3] Although the gender difference in offending is less marked when self-reported offending is studied (Campbell 1981), it is enormous at both the conviction (Farrington 1981) and the imprisonment stage (Pease and Harvey 1987). It is regrettable that the primary British source of data on criminal careers dealt only with males.

[4] I am much indebted to David Farrington for letting me have a pre-publication copy of the work cited. The relevant part of the present chapter was entirely redrafted after reading it, and the debt will be obvious to any reader of both.

(Farrington 1986). Probably the age at which most males start offending is 14, and the age at which most stop is 23. As Farrington (1992) notes, these ages draw attention to times of life changes which may be linked to the probability of offending. Hastening or easing these life changes may yield a crime prevention harvest. Some of the options obviously are tractable only by social policy choices more generally, such as the provision of adequate and decent low-cost housing, and at this point secondary prevention merges imperceptibly into 'community' crime prevention (see Nelken 1985 for a critical discussion of 'community' crime prevention).

School-based programmes directed at the individual child and his or her parents are also available (see Kazdin 1987 for a review). However, whatever the intrinsic merits of such programmes, it is clear that many children identified as pre-delinquent do not embark upon criminal careers (see West 1982). The more widespread the provision made for secondary prevention, the more children are unnecessarily included. The more provision is restricted to children identified as being at high risk of delinquency, the more those who do embark on criminal careers will be excluded, and the greater the risk of labelling this highly selected group. There is a suggestion (Farrington 1977) that identification as an offender by formal processing may hasten and deepen involvement in crime, and it is arguable that this could also be true of official processing as pre-delinquent. To be set against this is the argument that early intervention, perhaps focused upon those predicted to become chronic offenders, may prove easier than intervention later. This is because the correlation between indices of anti-social personality measured increases with age (Farrington 1990), suggesting either decreasing measurement error or the consolidation of the anti-social personality in the absence of countervailing education.

Turning to tertiary prevention, uniformly harsh treatment of offenders would be inefficient in capturing those whose criminal careers are short in duration and infrequent and trivial in offences committed. Identification of those who will persist in crime is possible at the time of their first conviction since age at that point is a good predictor of length of criminal career (Farrington 1992). In the Cambridge longitudinal study, the average length of the criminal career of those followed up to age 32 proved to be six years, with an average age of desistance of 23 (Farrington 1992). Just as it is with career length, so it is with frequency. Indeed, the two go together. To oversimplify, much crime is committed by a small number of offenders who are generally versatile across crime types, and who offend frequently over a long period. Simply keeping high-rate offenders out of circulation could be expected to reduce the rate of crime generally, to say nothing of any deterrent or rehabilitative effects. This process, known as selective incapacitation, is less efficient than could be hoped. The first problem is that of recruitment into crime. There may be a parallel to the world of legitimate business, in which there are a limited number of opportunities taken up by the best businesspeople. If a plague suddenly wiped out all such entrepreneurs, the business opportunities they left behind would not thereafter be neglected. They would be taken up by other entrepreneurs being recruited into the market. This seems to be what happens in the illicit drug market, where the amount of money to be made is such that there is no shortage of willing recruits to become couriers or dealers. If this is true, locking up drug couriers and dealers, however frequently they offend, would have only a brief effect in disrupting the market, so lucrative is it for new recruits. As noted earlier, the issue of recruitment into crime as a career is a key area in which research is urgently needed.

A second problem with tertiary prevention by selective incapacitation is precisely the same as that advanced earlier in relation to secondary prevention. Offenders who commit a lot of crime do not come wearing T-shirts bearing the legend 'I commit a lot of crime'. For the purposes of selective incapacitation, offenders must be classified as high-rate offenders on the basis of imperfect evidence. Mistakes in that classification limit the effectiveness of the strategy. Every low-rate offender incorrectly classified as a high-rate offender suffers costly, unnecessary, and unfair custody. Every high-rate offender incorrectly classified as a low-rate offender means one extra highly active offender on the streets. High-rate offenders are rarer than low-rate offenders, and the prediction of rare phenomena in general is difficult, from earthquakes to athletes of Olympic potential. After arguably the most painstaking study of the potential of selective incapacitation, Haapanen concluded:

> Selective incapacitation policies hold only minimal potential for reducing levels of crime in society . . . While factors related to 'risk' of future high-rate criminal behaviour can be identified, the accurate identification of high-rate offenders using information available in official records does not appear possible at present. (1990: 142–3)

The position is contentious, and the literature generates inconsistent conclusions (see e.g. Chaiken and Chaiken 1984; Visher 1986).

Tertiary crime prevention is currently unfashionable. Incapacitation is not the lively issue it was a decade ago, and the spirit of British legislation on sentencing has moved with the 1991 Criminal Justice Act to primary emphasis on the seriousness of the offence and away from the more predictive criminal history of an offender. The perceived scope of tertiary crime prevention is probably at its nadir. It will rise again. An individual's criminal past remains the best predictor of his or her criminal future (see e.g. Nuttall *et al.* 1978; Ward 1987). In the past, special sentences such as preventive detention, corrective training, and the extended sentence have been reserved for those with long prior records (special sentences for habitual offenders are commonplace in North American jurisdictions). It is not realistic to expect courts long to forgo the incapacitation of those with lengthy criminal records. One of the central moral concerns, as Leslie Wilkins (1987) puts it, is the right not to be treated as a false positive. To clarify: we can succeed in identifying high-rate offenders (true positives) only be erroneously classifying some low-rate offenders as high-rate (false positives); if we are aware of this when we adopt a policy of selective incapacitation of high-rate offenders, we knowingly treat some low-rate offenders as high-rate offenders. We thus use them as means to an end, as necessary sacrifices to the wider good. This is morally questionable. On the other hand, there are those who argue that as a criminal record lengthens, the burden of responsibility shifts, with the offender no longer having the benefit of whatever doubts may persist (Walker 1980). Perhaps the fashion for tertiary prevention will be reinstated by consideration of 'recruiters'. These are offenders who repeatedly co-offend with those without criminal records, in other words, those who act as the recruiting officers for those on the threshold of a criminal career, but who may not otherwise have begun one. Sentencing enhancements may become officially accepted for this group of offenders, because they have a disproportionately large effect upon the prevalence of offenders and perhaps also upon the incidence of offending. More severe sentences for this group may be regarded as a kind of quarantine for the criminally contagious.

Tertiary prevention is the consequence of detection, conviction, and incarceration, either alone or in combination, according to how the process is presumed to work. Obviously detection is necessary for the later steps to take place. It is unfortunate that detection is thus only contingently linked with tertiary prevention, since it means that no 'pure' studies of the effects of detection upon crime rate can be considered. The tortuous process of taking an offender through the decision whether to caution, the Crown Prosecution Service, and the court, whatever its merits as social policy, confounds offender characteristics with effects of detection upon crime and criminality. Detection is the overlooked term in tertiary crime prevention, and consideration should be given into possible ways of estimating its actual and potential effectiveness in crime control.

PRIMARY CRIME PREVENTION

The Development of Research

The beginning of significant research attention to primary crime prevention in the UK can be dated fairly precisely at 1976. (For a succinct yet comprehensive review of British research and policy see Bottoms 1990.) That year saw the publication of Home Office Research Study no. 34, *Crime as Opportunity* (Mayhew *et al.* 1976). The research was inspired by data from quite a different area, that of suicide. The observation was that when natural gas was substituted for toxic town gas in British homes, the suicide method of preference, gas poisoning, ceased to be available. The *total* number of suicides decreased. This meant that people to whom a suicidal method of preference was denied did not necessarily choose an alternative. Some chose not to take their life at all. This pattern of incomplete substitution of suicide method reasserted itself when US regulations on catalytic conversion were introduced (see Clarke and Mayhew 1988 for an account of both effects). Ron Clarke, then of the Home Office Research and Planning Unit, opined that if this were true of a decision so fundamental as suicide, it might also be true of the decision to commit crime. If some reduction in suicide could be effected by removing some of the opportunities to kill oneself, could not some reduction in burglary or cheque fraud be effected by removing some of the opportunities to commit such crime? This led to a great deal of inquiry into opportunity reduction as the means of crime prevention. The first work in this tradition, published as the seminal *Crime as Opportunity*, referred to above, included research on the prevention of car theft by the introduction of steering-column locks (Mayhew *et al.* 1976, 1979).[5] It was shown that the compulsory fitting of steering-column locks to all cars in West Germany led to a reduction in the theft of cars, a reduction which was sustained over at least a decade. The compulsory fitting of steering-column locks to all *new* cars in the UK led to a reduction in the proportion of stolen cars which were new.

This research was quickly followed by other work stemming from the same group in the Home Office Research Unit and elsewhere. In a country where the levels of both recorded and unrecorded crime rise remorselessly, in part under the control of economic factors (Field 1991), it seems important to list the very substantial successes that have been achieved in crime control by primary prevention. Sometimes these can be serendipitous, such

[5] Much research in this area has been published more than once, in sources of varying degrees of convenient accessibility. The convention adopted has been to cite all known sources in the reference list.

as the effects on motorcycle crime of introducing the legal requirement for motorcycle riders to wear helmets (Van Straelen 1978; Mayhew 1991). More often they have been deliberate, and in the aggregate, the scale and variety of successful crime prevention enterprise are becoming impressive. At the risk of their enumeration becoming tedious, these achievements should be presented.

It was shown that some crime on underground stations could be prevented by the introduction of closed-circuit television cameras (Burrows 1979), as could bus vandalism (Poyner 1988, 1991), and shop thefts (Van Straelen 1978). It appears that some types of cheque fraud could be decimated by simply incorporating a photograph on cheque guarantee cards (Knutsson and Kuhlhorn 1981, 1992), and that fraud by inserting items other than coins into parking metres could be reduced by making the last item inserted in a meter visible to passers-by (Decker 1972, 1991). Simple precautions can substantially reduce some types of shop theft (Ekblom 1986). It has been shown that well-publicized domestic property marking can substantially reduce the incidence of burglary (Laycock 1985), that some obscene phone calls appear to have been deterred by allowing the display of calling numbers on victims' phones (Clarke 1991), that security screens may protect some vulnerable employees from robbery, whether in banks (Clarke *et al.* 1991), post offices (Ekblom 1987, 1991) buses (Poyner *et al.* 1988), or, more ambiguously, building societies (Austin 1988). Markus (1984) has demonstrated the effect of target-hardening upon thefts from public phone kiosks, a finding replicated and speculated upon by Challinger (1991). Laycock (1984) showed the effect of target-hardening on the reduction of burglaries in chemists' shops. Poyner (1991) showed the effect of formal and informal surveillance upon theft from cars in parking areas, and the pooling of street information to inform policing of a shipyard parking area was also effective in reducing thefts from cars (Eck and Spelman 1988, 1991). Programmes of diverse kinds have achieved reductions in levels of fare evasion (DesChamps *et al.* 1991; Van Andel 1989, 1991). Webb and Laycock (1992*a*) implicate publicity and management in crime reduction in one part of the London Underground. Smith and Burrows (1986) documented the effects of simple changes in management procedure on frauds in a hospital and on the prevention of abuses of car import regulations. The American Bar Association (1986) assessed the effects of a raft of measures upon drunk driving. Many other studies demonstrate the susceptibility of diverse types of crime to alleviation by relatively simple (albeit well-considered) opportunity reduction measures. There now exist handbooks of techniques which serve to offer a repertoire of prevention possibilities (see Davis 1986 on home burglary; Wesley and Wonat 1986 on management security procedures). These handbooks are useful but should be used to generate bespoke solutions in particular contexts, rather than general solutions which do not meet the detailed needs of a particular context.

A related product of the same emergent research tradition was a set of what could be termed risk analyses. Here the factors which determined risks of victimization were identified with clarity. Such studies belong in the tradition of primary prevention since they direct attention to those models of car or types of house which are most prone to victimization, and hence require extensive opportunity-reducing measures to be taken to protect them. The study of Manchester buses identified parts of buses which were most prone to criminal damage, a problem which was partially resolved by the introduction of vandal-proof materials in the vulnerable seats (Sturman 1976, 1980). Hauber (1978) identified those characteristics of public transport systems which were associated with high levels of fare evasion. Hope (1982, 1986) showed that features of school design were strongly linked to the probability of burglary victimization, with small, old, and compact schools being much less crime-prone than large, modern, and sprawling schools. Crime risks vary massively, for example by make of car (Burrows and Heal 1979, 1980; Houghton 1992), type of house (Winchester and Jackson 1982), and location and surveillability of phone kiosks (Mayhew *et al.* 1979, 1980). The pre-payment coin meter has been shown to be one of the most criminogenic features imaginable (Hill 1986). Hunter and Jeffery (1991) identify the characteristics of convenience stores which contribute to their robbery-proneness. Ekblom and Simon (1988) analysed patterns of crime and racial harassment in Asian-run shops, and Burrows (1988, 1991) rehearsed methods for the prevention of retail crime through analysis. Phillips and Cochrane (1988) described a crime-analytic approach to controlling crime and nuisance in a shopping centre, as did Smith (1987) in relation to crime in hospitals. Southall and Ekblom (1985) identified the characteristics of motor cars which made them vulnerable to crime, and Ekblom (1988) described the techniques of crime analysis which make for the identification of patterns, a process developed by Berry and Carter (1992). Figure 14.1 is reproduced from Ekblom (1988) as providing the most succinct statement of the processes involved in prevention through crime pattern analysis. In the particularly fascinating area of fraud prevention, Levi (1988) spells out a prevention strategy, and Levi *et al.* (1991) generate a very detailed set of technological and other solutions to cheque and credit card fraud. This last study well illustrates the dynamic of primary crime prevention, with changes in technology evoking changes in criminal method, which in turn evoke changes in technology. The introduction of smart cards in France, for example, led to offenders stamping on the card to disable the chip. A retailer, perceiving the card as faulty, then has recourse to manual methods with fewer safeguards,

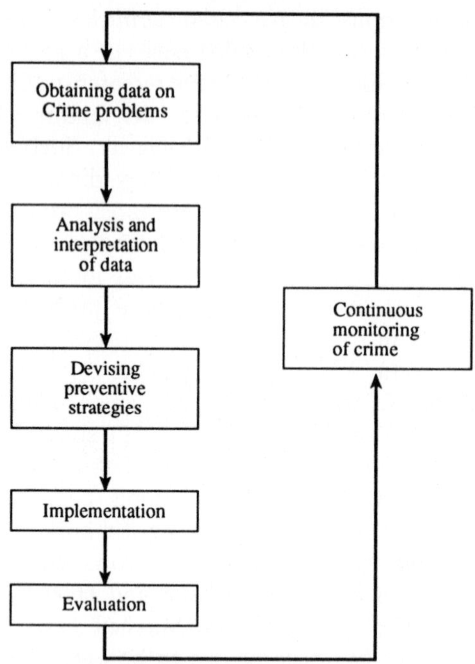

Fig. 14.1 The crime prevention process
Source: Ekblom (1988)

thus allowing frauds to occur. Responses to this tactic are also presented by Levi *et al.* Perhaps the only comparable depiction of the dynamics of primary crime prevention was by Walsh (1982), in his brief history of changes in safe design to respond to, and to anticipate, changes in criminal method.

These mainly British studies have occurred in parallel with similar North American research. For example, Lindsay and McGillis (1986) report an exceptionally well implemented and evaluated burglary reduction programme which succeeded in reducing rates of the offence. The distinctive North American contribution has lain in theory (two of the three theories detailed above are North American in origin, and all three were developed to maturity there), in meta-analyses of the effects of property marking, lighting, neighbourhood watch, security survey, and citizen patrols (which are more often depressing than otherwise; see Lurigio and Rosenbaum 1986), and in architectural effects on crime, reviewed superficially in the next section of this chapter. One other North American contribution worthy of mention is the recognition of crime 'hot spots', whose identification is the geographic sub-type of crime analysis generally (e.g. Sherman *et al.* 1989, Roncek and Maier 1991). These studies operate by pointing up time, place, and circumstance of concentrations of crime which might inform preventive efforts. Some British studies have used analyses which are in effect the identification of hot spots (or, perhaps more generally, temperature gradients) without using the term (Ramsey 1982, 1986; Ramsey and Heal 1982).

Architectural Determinism: An Important Detour

Special mention should be made of the tradition of architectural determinism pioneered by Jane Jacobs (1961) and C. Ray Jeffery (1971), whose most famous exponent was Oscar Newman (1972). Recent British interest in such work is spearheaded by Alice Coleman (1985). The tradition has recently been reviewed (Bannister 1991).

This tradition takes physical features of the built environment as intrinsically criminogenic, although its exponents vary in the proportion of any differences in rates of crime which are attributed to design and social factors. Newman's four features were

1. *territoriality*: the subdivision of places into 'zones of influence' to discourage outsiders and to encourage residents to defend their areas;
2. *surveillance*: the design of buildings to allow easy observation of territorial areas;
3. *image*: the design of buildings to avoid stigma in low-cost or public housing;
4. *environment*: the juxtaposition of public housing with safe zones.

Despite the criticisms of the Newman approach (reviewed by Mayhew 1979) on grounds of method and principle, it has been and remains an attractive approach, because it offers detailed advice on what to do about crime, which can be and has been put into practice. Rubenstein *et al.* (1980) identified the design approaches employed to make space more defensible, as follows:

(a) improving external lighting;
(b) reducing opportunities for offender concealment;
(c) reducing unassigned open spaces;
(d) locating outdoor activities in sight of windows;
(e) increasing designated walkways;
(f) increasing pedestrian activity.

Newman's earlier work has been heavily criticized on the basis of its unjustified generality (Mawby 1977) and its neglect of the role of social factors, both directly and in mediating the effects of architectural features (Merry 1981; Smith 1987; Taylor *et al.* 1980). In his later writings (e.g. Newman and Franck 1982) Newman acknowledges that resident characteristics are stronger predictors of crime levels than are design features, and defensible space notions have not fared especially well in the face of research evidence (Reppetto 1974; Waller and Okihiro 1978). Alice Coleman's (1985) forceful advocacy of the strong architectural determination of crime levels came at a time when the literature was suggesting a more complex picture. Furthermore, Coleman's eccentric use of statistical analysis leads her to conclusions which are not justified even on her own data (Smith 1986).

The tradition which emphasizes architectural features in the explication of crime levels has spawned a countervailing tradition of opposition to architectural determinism. It remains certain that some features of the environment are criminogenic and some criminocclusive (see, for example, Winchester and Jackson 1982; Poyner 1983; Bentvelsen and Van der Zon 1987). The danger of heat in advocacy of or opposition to architectural determinism is that the relevance of simple measures in design will be neglected.

One area of work which has been the focus of recent and fierce controversy is the alleged effects of street lighting upon crime and fear levels. A review of North American research shows conflicting findings (Fleming and Burrows 1986), and of British research very little effect of crime levels, but greater effects on fear of crime (Ramsey 1991). This is also the pattern suggested by the largest single British study (Atkins *et al.* 1991). Other research (Painter 1988, 1989*a*, *b*, 1991) suggests more substantial effects on crime rates in a more restricted area. The differences may be methodological in origin, or may indicate that lighting enhancement for crime prevention purposes should be restricted to extremely localized problem sites rather than uprated generally. What is needed is more very specific bespoke lighting solutions in small areas, probably in conjunction with other approaches, rather than uprating over a wide area.

Primary Crime Prevention: The Declining Years?

Studies of simple opportunity-reduction measures remain a valuable strand in the tradition. However, the picture has become less clear, and the practice of primary crime prevention has become less generally accepted in its simple form. There are three principal reasons for this.

1. The spectre of crime displacement, whereby crime is moved around rather than prevented, haunts the subject. If total, this could be held to render primary crime prevention useless.
2. Some commentators in the field judge that aspects of community or social structure are the basic causes of crime, and that techniques of crime prevention which do not address this point are hopelessly flawed.

3. Even when possibilities for opportunity reduction are obvious, there is attending much crime the lack of a motive to prevent it. Where circumstances indemnify victims against the consequences of falling victim to crime, opportunity reduction will not occur.

These three reasons for the recent modification of the opportunity-reduction tradition will be rehearsed in turn.

Crime displacement: conventional views

> There is little point in the policy-maker investing resources and effort into situational [crime] prevention if by doing so he merely shuffles crime from one area to the next but never reduces it. For this reason, the possibility of displacing crime by preventive intervention is a crucial issue for the policy-maker. (Heal and Laycock 1986: 123)

This 'crime shuffling' is what is *conventionally* meant by displacement. Consideration of displacement in these terms can induce a 'paralyzing extreme case pessimism' (Cornish and Clarke 1986: 3). This is because of the practical limitations upon the measurement of displacement. In essence, one can show complete displacement to have occurred, but one can never show complete displacement not to have occurred. The prudent researcher of domestic burglary prevention will examine rates of the same offence in areas contiguous with the project area. She may even look at the rate of the offence more generally in the police force area of interest. It is less likely that she will look at other property offences in contiguous areas, still less in the police force area as a whole. The probability that she will look still wider is effectively zero, since she is operating with a finite amount of money. Even if money were unlimited but displacement were to diverse offences and places, the effect would disappear into the normal variation in crime rates. Thus if some burglars turn to robberies close to home, some to robberies far from home, some to cheque fraud, some to drug-dealing, and so on, even total displacement would be undetectable. Thus total displacement is always something with which the extreme case pessimist can taunt the researcher, and never something that can be gainsaid.

In the above, the *conventionality* of the definition of displacement was stressed. The basic classification derives from Reppetto (1976) and will be presented here in the modified form used by Hakim and Rengert (1981). The classification is:

temporal: doing the intended crime at a different time;
spatial: doing the intended crime to the planned type of target in another place;
tactical: doing the intended crime using a different method; and
crime type/functional: doing a different type of crime from that intended.

Perpetrator displacement is a category added by Barr and Pease (1990). This occurs where a crime opportunity is so compelling that even if one person passes it up, others are available to take their place (as in stealing by finding, or drug supply).

There is an obvious overlap of these categories. For instance, spatial displacement must always be temporal displacement too. No one can be in two places at once! That apart, they strike the writer as an extraordinarily unimaginative categorization of the circumstances under which offenders change their minds, or have circumstances change their minds for them. This is not intended as a criticism of Reppetto, who laid the foundation, but of those of us who came after and failed to develop the classification.[6] Some space will be devoted to such a development, since it is of crucial importance for the assessment of crime prevention programmes.

Crime displacement or crime deflection?

Of the many flaws in the literature on crime displacement, perhaps the most fundamental is its failure to consider how crime patterns arise. Before crime gets displaced, it must get placed. Why is the pattern of crime as it is? In England and Wales, the 10 per cent of parliamentary constituencies with the highest crime incidence suffer thirty-five times the amount of crime as the 10 per cent with the lowest incidence, and the patterns can be more extreme depending on areal unit and crime type chosen (Trickett *et al.* 1992*a*, *b*). These patterns do not emerge by chance, but are a function of both attractive and repulsive forces. Traditionally, displacement has been seen as a repulsive process, whereby an initiative leads crime to go elsewhere. Stenzel (1977) noted that developments in an area can attract as well as repel crime, and this notion was more fully developed by Barron (1991*a*, *b*). The neglect of Stenzel's point for so long perfectly illustrates how circumscribed the perception of crime displacement has been. Indeed, the very assumption that a prevented crime will go elsewhere (displacement) rather than that other targets will also be protected by a kind of crime prevention halo (the free-rider effect) shows the partiality of the concept. The research clearly suggests that the free-rider effect can be substantial (see e.g. Miethe 1991; Clarke 1991).

Understanding crime placement in the first place offers more scope for crime prevention than starting with the existing pattern as given. Let us take the analogy of a piranha-infested river. The conventional literature is concerned with which pair of paddling legs the piranha will attack. The alternative perspective concerns itself with why there are more piranha in certain parts of the river.

[6] With some honourable exceptions, e.g. Brantingham (1986).

A second crucial flaw in the conventional consideration of displacement is to consider the movement of crime from one setting to another as necessarily a failure. To do so is clearly mistaken. This is why Barr and Pease (1990) preferred the word 'deflection' over 'displacement'. Deflection may be a success. Displacement is never referred to as a success. Crime deflection is benign when the deflected crime causes less harm or misery than the original crime. It may also be benign when there are surrounding social reasons for concentrating crime in particular locations. An obvious instance of this is prostitution. The existence of a distinct red-light area in cities away from residential areas offers the possibility of avoidance. Clearly located areas for drug-dealing offer similar, albeit more contentious, benefits. To persist with the piranha analogy, it has obvious benefits for the safety of river crossing generally to have all the piranha concentrated in one stretch of river. Schemes (piranha prevention programmes) which had the happy effect of such a concentration could not properly be deemed to have failed, even if the total population of piranha was undiminished. In short, the view that all displacement/deflection is bad and that all patterns of crime are equally desirable is naïve to the point of being bizarre. Displacement should be seen as a tool of social policy rather than as an unmitigated evil.

None of the above should be taken to suggest that displacement is typically close to total. Crimes are often closely distributed around an offender's home (Forrester *et al.* 1988), or around a particular purpose (like theft of a means of transport; see Mayhew *et al.* 1989), and this plausibly reduces the type and location of crime which should be scrutinized for displacement effects. Where that has been done, displacement has been shown to be very far from total. The argument advanced is rather that crime flux should be studied as a whole, and that states of affairs with numerically similar amounts of crime should not be regarded as equally desirable. If this were done, displacement would cease to be the *bête noire* of crime prevention attempts.

The re-emergence of community

Even within the strictest primary prevention perspective, social factors are always implicit. For example, target-hardening measures are relevant only if social conditions underpin them. The stoutest door will yield in time if no neighbour calls the police or intervenes. As noted earlier in this chapter, social disorganization has long been deemed a factor in determining levels of crime (see Shaw and McKay 1942), but the focus of the earlier tradition lay with the supply of motivated offenders rather than of criminal opportunities.

Alongside the classic crime-as-opportunity studies collected in *Designing Out Crime* (Clarke and Mayhew 1980) was a study by Sheena

Wilson whose significance lay, *inter alia*, in identifying child density as a determinant of levels of vandalism, thereby implicating the policy of housing departments in the allocation of families to dwellings. This role has also been emphasized in a series of studies performed in Sheffield by Tony Bottoms, Paul Wiles, and their colleagues (see Bottoms *et al.* 1989, Bottoms and Wiles 1991*a*). They contend:

> In order to understand and explain offending behaviour by residents of particular areas, it is vital to consider who lives in these areas; how they came to live there in the first place; what kind of social life the residents have created; how outsiders (including official agencies) react to them; and why they remain in the areas and have not moved (Bottoms and Wiles 1991*a*: 122).

The renewed emphasis on social factors in crime prevention has taken many forms. Hope and Shaw (1988) criticize some applications of primary crime prevention as suggesting that a community is under attack from without, rather than the more usual circumstance of being predated upon from within. King (1989) emphasizes the role of social crime prevention through local democratic channels, and contrasts the French approach, which incorporates such an emphasis, with the individualistic approach to crime prevention '*à la* Thatcher', and the latter's associated emphasis on opportunity reduction. Bottoms and Wiles (1991*b*) regard the neglect of people dynamics as a fault of Anglo-American criminology in general rather than of the UK in Thatcher's thrall.

Perhaps the most trenchant critique of a primary prevention tradition is offered by Currie (1988). He distinguishes two sometimes conflicting visions of what community crime prevention is, or should be. The two phases differ fundamentally in their conception of what a community is. Phase 2 emphasizes 'those more tangible structures and institutions that underlie and shape community attitudes' (1988: 281), and is less concerned with the offender as a focus of intervention. Perhaps most fundamentally, Phase 2 thinking differs in considering the place of crime in the scale of priorities for communities. Phase 1 thinkers,[7] says Currie,

> envision the community exerting its moral authority over bad people who seem to appear from nowhere, and who will surely take over if we don't wave the wand of traditional values at them—through tough policing, among other means. (ibid.: 282)

He contends that at its worst, Phase 1 thinking

> can slide into a kind of nostalgic voluntarism that exhorts shattered communities to pull themselves up by their own bootstraps, without help—and without money

[7] The exemplar of Phase 1 thinking which Currie uses is the work of James Q. Wilson and George Kelling rather than that of Ron Clarke's group, but it is clear that most of the work of the latter group and of others reviewed in the primary prevention section above would be characterized by Currie as exemplifying Phase 1 thinking.

. . . Phase 1 is no longer very impressive as a strategy against serious crime . . . The overselling of Phase 1 ideas has tangible and disturbing consequences: it diverts resources away from other things we might do, while offering facile but easily dashed hopes that quick solutions will stop crime. (ibid.: 284)

Phase 2, by contrast,

is more complicated in its understanding of crime and how communities might combat it. But . . . it is also far more promising, especially as a strategy for preventing *serious* crime, not merely reducing fear or taming neighbourhood incivilities. It is also, it is suggested, far more attuned to deeper and more fruitful criminological traditions. (ibid.: 282)

Extended consideration has been given here to the Currie critique for two reasons: first, I am unsure of what constitutes a Phase 2 approach, other than its complexity and its location of the crime problem alongside other social problems. Second, it seems to me that Currie caricatures (or is unaware of) the kinds of research done under Phase 1 traditions. Not all crime takes place in the kinds of shattered community whose image he evokes. There are many ways and places in which simple measures can be fruitful. Second, even in the shattered communities, it is far from clear that simple measures do not represent a kind of toehold on order through which a nucleus of community organization may be formed. It is a commonplace of change programmes that the first step should be the one most easily implemented, so that some experience of success may form the core of more ambitious efforts at change. None the less, the *Zeitgeist* of crime prevention has moved from the simple and situational to the complex and communal, and this has influenced and been reflected in the organizational arrangements for crime prevention activity.

Motives and implementations

Perhaps the greatest shortcoming in the literature on crime prevention is the assumption of the wish to prevent crime. This is particularly noticeable in relation to official reports and research. There is a chasm between possibility and achievement.

Some twelve years ago, I was driving home from a Young Offenders' Institution when two news items on the car radio illustrated the linkage. At the time, the favourite car for thieves was the Ford Cortina, because of its good performance and risible security. Many young car thieves were sent to detention centres. The two contiguous news items were the announcement of record profits for the Ford Motor Company, and the opening of two strict-regime detention centres, intended more effectively to reform or deter those detained. The link between the news items was that many of those who would be sent to those detention centres would be young car thieves. The cars they took would disproportionately be Ford

Cortinas. This was an instance in which tertiary prevention was intended as a substitute for primary prevention. What is more, the commercial choice which had visited the costs of police, court, and detention on the public purse had contributed, through small expenditure on car security, to record profits for the Ford Company. Levi *et al.*'s comment is central: 'We are acutely aware that if—as in pollution control—the "externalities" of costs to the public were taken into account, the costing of crime prevention in *every* sphere would take a different form' (1991: 1). Because public provision so effectively cushions corporate and insured crime victims from the costs of crime, even massively successful crime prevention measures cannot be guaranteed implementation. The spectacular reduction in cheque fraud after the incorporation of a photograph on cheque cards in Sweden (see above) has not led to such a measure being taken in the UK. Simple means exist for reducing credit card fraud (see Levi *et al.* 1991), which are not taken up. The range of simple car security measures which are technically possible mocks the range of what is offered. There is no doubt a threshold of cost above which simple crime prevention will come into play in commercial judgements, but that threshold is massively above the point at which the crime represents a significant social problem.

Sometimes, personal rivalries and ideological differences can subvert crime prevention efforts. They 'can increase social conflicts and provide a site for power struggles to be played out. Negotiating an agreement between conflicting groups is . . . often essential for the implementation of a crime prevention strategy' (Sampson 1991: 30). A local authority housing department's wish for quiet estates is in tension with its wish to have a ready location for problem families. A school may have its wish not to have its equipment stolen offset by the knowledge that the replacements would be more satisfactory. Individual victims, particularly if insured, may not feel compelled to prevent their own victimization. An interesting case study is offered by Mueller and Adler. They observe that as transatlantic passenger traffic by sea gave way to the aeroplane, an epidemic of losses of ocean liners occurred, most of them old and marginally maintained.

> It is clear to us that most of the losses were avoidable . . . Some vessels were overinsured at the time of loss. In several cases, the operators were or had been in the process of bankruptcy, or the vessel was declared to be unprofitable . . . Above all, there were the six liners en route to the ship breakers for scrap, some of whom sank close to their final destination. We have been unable to ascertain whether the insurance value of a ship destined for the breakers is greater than her scrap value. (1991: 105)

The same authors had identified a similar phenomenon when obsolete cargo ships sank in large numbers after the advent of ship containerization (Mueller and Adler 1985).

Put generally, the crime prevention motive interlocks with other motives, and usually occupies a subsidiary role. Carter writes:

> Ideally when deciding how much to spend on loss prevention the individual should allow for social costs and benefits but, as in other private economic decisions, he will normally be concerned only with items which affect his own pocket. At present after a theft the individual incurs only a little part of the cost of apprehending, convicting and punishing the thief (for example the cost of appearing in court); but neither does he receive a tax or rate rebate for taking precautions which are expected to reduce his demand on public services. (1974: 32)

This personal calculus is potentially modifiable by the operation of the insurance market, and the way in which the insurance market works merits some attention.[8] The unit of account for the police (and the victim) is the crime. The unit of account for the insurance industry is the pound sterling (Pease and Litton 1984). Insurers are concerned with making an overall profit on a class of business. They are thus not interested in risky small premium business because the anticipated cost of processing claims is too high. Thus, for whole areas, household insurance is effectively unavailable. These will by definition be the areas in greatest need of incentives towards crime prevention. Within areas in which insurance is available, the pressure to prevent crime will be exerted in proportion to the size of the possible loss.

Insurance incentives to prevent crime are thus exerted upon places where large losses are possible, that is, places which are numerically trivial when one counts crimes rather than pounds. There is a mismatch between where crime is and where insurance exerts its pressure to prevent crime. A side-effect of this is that insurance is given in those sectors of the market where there is most to gain by insurance fraud, as in the loss of passenger ships described earlier. No one knows the proportion of all property crime which is created by insurance (but see Litton 1990).

Insurers and influential citizens also to some extent shape police effort. The indirect effect of such shaping is to de-emphasize crimes with small losses and crimes with no losses. Crimes like domestic violence are those in which the human values of the police must prevail against the lack of direct pressures from sections of the public. An argument has been advanced that a closer matching of risk and insurance premiums would lead to the denial of insurance cover to those most at risk (Fenn 1986). Of course, the alternative view is that only when insurance operates as a motivator for risk reduction can it truly be called crime-preventive.

In short, insufficient attention has been given to the *pressure* on people to prevent crime. This is sometimes very meagre, sometimes absent. The

[8] For the best available account of insurance practice and crime prevention, see Litton (1990).

scope of simple situational measures of crime prevention must be measured against what is truly intended, not against the standard of that to which lip service is paid.

Even when there appears to be a real motive to prevent crime, failures of implementation intrude, and these have yielded some of the most tragicomic accounts in the literature. Implementation problems are reviewed by Hope (1985). Hope and Murphy (1983) describe many instances of implementation failure. A sensible and well-considered scheme of target-hardening directed at schools failed because:

the anti-climb paint used was applied too thinly—true to the traditions of painters but useless for the anti-climb purpose;

replacing tarmac underneath windows by greenery got as far as breaking up the tarmac;

replacing frequently broken windows by a proprietary material much more difficult to break was thwarted by the reluctance of local authority employees to store the new material;

finally, the overtime offered to caretakers at the most heavily victimized schools provoked resentment among their colleagues at other schools who did not have the same opportunity for making extra cash, so the patrols were discontinued.

In another project (Barker *et al.* 1992) a new sports area, upon completion, went overnight from being deemed so vulnerable that it required security patrols during the night to being regarded as capable of fending for itself without any oversight. Incidents like these do not make one sanguine about the status which the implementation of crime prevention would be afforded were it to come directly under local authority control.

Any crime prevention failure has to be ascribed to theory failure or implementation failure. If ascribed to theory failure, the implication is that no conceivable implementation could prove successful. If ascribed to implementation failure, the theoretical basis lives, to be reincarnated in more effective forms. The acute danger is that implementation failure is interpreted as theory failure, which closes off an avenue of possible application, or more often leads the technique's proponents into the myopic reproduction of the technique over time and place, unchanged by the lessons of research. This may be not because of what the research reveals, but because of how it is translated into media presentations and popular consciousness. This may be the fate of Neighbourhood Watch. The British evaluative research on the topic was scrupulous in choosing the best schemes for evaluation (Bennett 1987, 1990, 1991) and arguing that the appropriate next steps concerned the dynamics of how Neighbourhood Watch was supposed to work. In effect, Bennett concluded that implementation failure had occurred. None the less, reactions to the research were less thoughtful than the research itself. Its unthinking opponents persuade themselves that theory failure has been demonstrated. Its proponents continue to advocate it, despite the obvious implementation failures which descriptive research reveals (Husain 1988) and the variety of forms which it can take (Husain and Bright 1990).

CRIME PREVENTION: THE ORGANIZATIONAL BACKGROUND

In the quite recent past in England and Wales, crime prevention has come to be embodied in the employment by police forces of officers with special responsibility for preventing crime. The original specification of their work was hopelessly optimistic. Weatheritt (1986) quotes the ambitious and extensive brief which an Association of Chief Police Officers Working Party in 1979 gave to crime prevention officers (CPOs). Among the sixty-eight tasks which the working party thought should fall to the hapless CPOs were the following, each of which sounds like a full-time job on its own:

1. To cultivate a working two-way relationship between beat patrol officers and the crime prevention officer, and to encourage all officers to report matters of crime prevention interest.
2. To collect, coordinate, and disseminate crime prevention information and information on current trends in crime.
3. To inspect property where there are special or difficult security features, and to keep records of such visits to enable follow-up visits to be made at appropriate times.
4. To support and liaise with other departments of the force in the task of community relations and preventive policing and to cooperate with social agencies concerned with the welfare of children and young persons.
5. To give advice on security to builders and architects in the planning stages of buildings, and if necessary survey premises from plans; to maintain liaison with architects and local authority planning departments.

All this was to be done by a group of people who comprised on average 0.5 per cent of force strength (Weatheritt 1986).

The mismatch between the alleged primacy of crime prevention as a police purpose and its resourcing has been grotesque. The statement of the 1829 Act establishing the police states prevention to be its primary goal, and this is often quoted. Mocking those origins, the centre at which police crime prevention officers have been trained for the last twenty years is a Portakabin behind the headquarters of Staffordshire Police, until quite recently staffed by four officers, two at the rank of chief inspector and two of higher rank.[9] At the time of the last research to investigate the point (Harvey *et al.* 1988), there were police forces where crime prevention was handled by officers not given even the kind of basic training offered at Stafford. Perhaps the most telling statistic concerns the relationship between the amount of recorded crime in a force area and the proportion of the force's strength devoted to crime prevention. That relationship is *negative* and statistically significant. That is to say, those forces with the highest rates of recorded crime tend to be those with the lowest proportion of personnel effort devoted to crime prevention. It is almost as though crime prevention is a luxury to which forces may devote resources when there are no more pressing demands on their time. Writing in 1986, Weatheritt, in a section entitled 'What is wrong with crime prevention?', analyses the situation with some asperity in a passage worth quoting at length:

> Two histories of crime prevention can be written. There is the one of official reports and statements, the elevation of crime preventive objectives to be the primary purpose of policing, and the development of organisations and institutions for thinking about crime prevention and instigating action. Looked at from this perspective, the history is an encouraging one: not only does crime prevention receive strong rhetorical support, it also appears to rest on a sound base of institutional deliberation and activity.
>
> The other history of crime prevention goes behind the statements of intention to look at how far and in what ways preventive objectives have become part of day-to-day policing; . . . on what crime prevention officers do and how useful and effective this is . . . On these criteria, the achievements are less impressive . . . Whatever the expressed commitment of senior police officers and successive governments to the view that prevention is the primary object of policing, the crime prevention job remains an activity performed on the sidelines while the main action takes place elsewhere. (1986: 49)

Weatheritt's analysis criticizes the training of crime prevention officers for being unduly limited to the acquisition of knowledge about the armoury of security measures, applied unthinkingly, and not evaluated. She makes the pertinent point that in crime prevention there is nothing to show (literally) for success. This is anathema to the police culture, in which visible results are of paramount importance.[10]

The organizational position of crime prevention within the police service is also a matter of some dispute. Apart from the oddness of having a

[9] At the time of writing, this has increased to one assistant chief constable, one chief superintendent, four chief inspectors, and one sergeant. Extra civilian staff are to be recruited soon.

[10] The development of geographical information systems offers the best hope of changing this.

special title for crime prevention at all (Harvey *et al.* 1988 liken it to calling a goalkeeper in soccer a 'goals prevention officer', thus absolving the other ten players from defensive duties), there is strong feeling about whether crime prevention should be attached to the criminal investigation or community department of a force. Harvey *et al.* found that, whatever the organizational allegiance, 'activities described as crime preventive do not . . . permeate the force much beyond the designated officers' (1988: 88). They also cast doubt on the direct crime preventive impact of much of the work that was done. 'While social/community crime prevention can be dragged down into a candyfloss world of good public relations, physical crime prevention can likewise retreat into a ritualistic counting of surveys conducted, precautions advised and property marked' (ibid.: 91). They make the quite unrealistic, albeit interesting, recommendation that crime prevention enterprises be obliged to specify the causal route connecting the activities undertaken and the prevention of crime.

The leadership role of the police in crime prevention has been generally accepted, at least in European countries (see Pease 1979). Although the 1980s has witnessed a vogue for 'multi-agency' projects, the key role of the police persists. Given the centrality of police data sets, and the confidentiality surrounding their use, it is difficult to see how it could be otherwise. The police do remain the fundamental agency of primary crime prevention. To take but one example among many, the booklet issued to accompany the 1988 Home Office crime prevention campaign still assigned a qualified leadership role to the police (Home Office 1988). The Home Office Crime Prevention Unit, in the preface to its early reports, proclaimed its establishment 'with a view to promoting preventive action against crime. Included in its remit is a particular responsibility for the dissemination of information on crime prevention topics. The present series of occasional papers, while based largely upon research material, has been established primarily for practitioners whose work has a direct bearing on the reduction of crime.' In which department of the Home Office was this Unit set up? It was the Police Department, reinforcing yet again the primacy of the police in British crime prevention. In the last analysis, the police are guardians of the data on which any crime prevention initiative must rest, and their goodwill is a necessary component of any crime prevention activity. While virtually every public and private agency shapes the presenting problem of crime, their purposes are not centrally those of controlling crime, and their attitude to crime will be as a cost on their primary purpose. The 1980s witnessed a *perceived* diffusion of responsibility for crime prevention throughout the community. Heal (1991), the first Head of the Home Office's Crime Prevention Unit and a leading player in the development of crime prevention thinking over the last fifteen years, dates the change from:

> the beginning of Lord Whitelaw's period of office as Home Secretary. Allowing for some oversimplification, the most significant development of the time was the agreement secured across Whitehall that crime reduction was not solely the responsibility of the Home Office, but a concern of all central government departments (Home Office 1984). At local level, so the argument ran, all agencies had a part to play, not only the police. (Heal 1991: 257)

Heal identifies opportunity reduction as the engine of crime reduction at that stage in its evolution in England and Wales. Home Office Circulars 8/84 and 44/90 advocated the spread of crime prevention responsibility throughout the community, and this has been echoed in most official pronouncements of the 1980s and early 1990s. Heal notes the renewed emphasis on social factors evident in the mid-1980s.

> The crime prevention of the early 1980s prompted a series of questions and criticisms ranging from those driven by common sense to others inspired by political dogma. If nothing else, the criticisms demonstrated that situational prevention . . . was only a partial solution to the task of preventing crime. This recognition fuelled alternative thinking which focused not upon the physical situation within which crimes occur . . . , but upon the perpetrators of the crimes, and the social policies which bear on the lives of the perpetrators and the communities within which they live . . . What began to emerge was the hunt for a strategy which recognised the importance of both precipitating factors (e.g. the criminal opportunities for crime) and predisposing influences (the social and psychological needs and learned perceptions and attitudes of the individual which encourages him to exploit these opportunities). Within this broader strategy prevention might be set alongside the processes of detection, investigation and court disposal on the one hand, and care for the victim on the other, so forming a composite strategy for crime. (1991: 263–5)

Heal argues that the tasks facing crime prevention are to establish crime prevention in high-crime areas, to integrate social and physical measures against crime, and to move from a project approach to one in which crime prevention is routinely integrated into general policy issues. Major Home Office initiatives, like the 'Five Towns' and 'Safer Cities' initiatives, are called as evidence in the process. The agency 'Crime Concern' was established as a vehicle for collaborative thinking, and the voluntary organization NACRO's Safe Neighbourhoods Unit undertook projects of crime prevention. In 1991 the report of the Standing Conference on Crime Prevention of the Home Office (ordinarily known as the Morgan Report), entitled *Safer Communities*, made its key recommendation that 'in the longer term local authorities, working in conjunction with the police, should have clear statutory responsibility for the development and stimulation of community safety and crime prevention programmes, and for progressing at a local level a multi-agency approach to community safety' (Morgan Report 1991: 29).[11] The local authority should generate a Code of Practice, to include a portfolio of crime prevention activities. A sample portfolio is presented by the Morgan Committee and is reproduced here as Fig. 14.2.

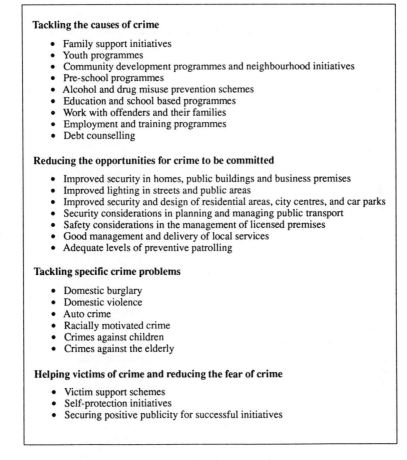

Tackling the causes of crime

- Family support initiatives
- Youth programmes
- Community development programmes and neighbourhood initiatives
- Pre-school programmes
- Alcohol and drug misuse prevention schemes
- Education and school based programmes
- Work with offenders and their families
- Employment and training programmes
- Debt counselling

Reducing the opportunities for crime to be committed

- Improved security in homes, public buildings and business premises
- Improved lighting in streets and public areas
- Improved security and design of residential areas, city centres, and car parks
- Security considerations in planning and managing public transport
- Safety considerations in the management of licensed premises
- Good management and delivery of local services
- Adequate levels of preventive patrolling

Tackling specific crime problems

- Domestic burglary
- Domestic violence
- Auto crime
- Racially motivated crime
- Crimes against children
- Crimes against the elderly

Helping victims of crime and reducing the fear of crime

- Victim support schemes
- Self-protection initiatives
- Securing positive publicity for successful initiatives

Fig. 14.2 A portfolio of community safety activities: some examples
Source: Morgan Report (1991)

[11] It is of interest that the Morgan Committee preferred the phrase 'community safety' over 'crime prevention' because the latter 'is often narrowly interpreted and this reinforces the view that it is solely the responsibility of the police' (Morgan Report 1991: 3). The extreme vagueness of the Morgan Committee's definition of community safety gives no confidence that the revised definition will provide a satisfactory focus for the work.

The development of crime prevention in its multi-agency persona in the 1980s is of a piece with the philosophy of the Conservative administration, praising and supporting the 'active citizen'. In his foreword to Hope and Shaw (1988), the Minister of State at the Home Office opined: 'At the very centre of our ideas on how to control crime should be the energy and initiative of the active citizen. His or her contribution must be mobilised and should be the core of the radical rethinking we need on prevention and control of crime' (Hope and Shaw 1988: v–vi). However, these approaches tend to marginalise crime itself. For instance, the three stated goals of the Safer Cities programme are

1. to reduce crime;
2. to lessen the fear of crime;
3. to create safer cities where economic enterprise and community life can flourish.

The second, and emphatically the third of these objectives have little to do with crime. The objectives are doubtless worthy, but the projects which form the substance of the programme reflect the frequent marginalization of crime. This is in part because it is simply easier to prevent fear of crime than crime itself, and easier yet to provide facilities justifiable in relation to the third objective.

FUTURES IN CRIME PREVENTION

Against a background of increasing numbers and rates of recorded and unrecorded crime, it seems absurd to be other than pessimistic about crime prevention. The sense of absurdity is heightened by reading the Home Office's regular news-sheet about crime prevention activities, *Crime Prevention News*, which contains a weird mixture of diverse activities, some of them connected by only the most tenuous of links with crime prevention. Yet there have been major successes in crime prevention work, which have simply not been generalized as they should. This appears to have been primarily a consequence of the absence of an adequate motivation to do so. The scale of successful property crime prevention effort now is probably as great as could realistically be expected in the absence of inducements to change that scale. Car tax differentials which penalize models which are most frequently stolen provide an instance of incentives which could be applied.

The exclusion of crimes against the person from the consideration of incentives derives from the strange fact that most research and evaluation from a crime prevention perspective has *relatively* neglected crimes of violence,[12] except in so far as this is attempted through the protection of place, as in lighting studies. Three reasons may be put forward for this:

1. People move, places don't. Victims of violence cannot be protected across places with any ease.
2. The expenditure of crime prevention energy has been moulded by the individual and corporate economic concerns of victims. Although violent crimes are acknowledged as more serious than crimes against property, economic interests and pressure on the police do shape crime prevention effort (Harvey *et al.* 1988).
3. Much violence occurs between intimates (Smith 1989; Stanko 1990). Crime prevention has typically been characterized as protecting victims against external dangers (Hope and Shaw 1988).

If primary crime prevention is to assume greater generality, it must research more fully into crimes of violence and crimes between intimates. This is beginning to occur, particular in relation to bullying and child sexual abuse. One way of moving in this direction involves the closer integration of victim support and conventional crime prevention.

Another relatively neglected area is that of victimless crime in general, and drug crime in particular. While some secondary and tertiary prevention programmes could be characterized as demand reduction, it will probably always be the case that less preventive effort will be directed towards crimes without victims.

An overlooked phenomenon in criminology has been the extent to which victimization concentrates not just upon particular geographic areas and particular social groups, but particular individuals.[13] This, Genn (1988) argues, is underestimated by victimization surveys. Farrell (1992) provides an excellent recent review of the data and it is from this work that much of what follows is adapted. For some kinds of crime, repeat victimization clearly occurs. These include domestic violence (almost by definition), embezzlement (where the employer–employee relationship is a necessary condition of the offence), and many kinds of fraud, including computer and cheque fraud. For these offences, it is self-evident that the prevention of repeat victimization would prevent most crime of the type. This is less obvious but equally true of commercial burglaries (Bloomer 1992), domestic burglaries (Polvi *et al.* 1990), racial attacks (Sampson and Phillips 1992), and serious property crimes against

[12] The obvious exception is the literature on gun control as a form of primary prevention of violent crime. The debate is similar to that on property crime in that issues of displacement appear to be central (see Zimring and Hawkins 1987). Some other exceptions are mentioned in Burrows (1991).

[13] There are exceptions to this neglect. As was so often true, Richard Sparks recognized its implications early (Sparks *et al.* (1977), as did Al Reiss (1980).

schools (Burquest *et al.* 1992). Furthermore, the same studies show there to be a very marked reduction in the rate of repeats over short periods of time after a first victimization. This is true for all the studies listed above, both where the phenomenon of repeat victimization is self-evident and where it is not. The point is illustrated in Fig. 14.3 by calls for police service after an incident of crime against schools. It will be seen that the rate of repeat calls for service diminishes to a very low level after a period of a few weeks from the first.[14] The practical significance of this is that, given that the period of elevated risk is quite closely circumscribed, special precautions can be taken over that time without an unrealistic, semi-permanent deployment of resources. The prevention of *repeat* victimization may thus prove to be a cost-efficient strategy of crime prevention generally, and some small developments in that spirit are already

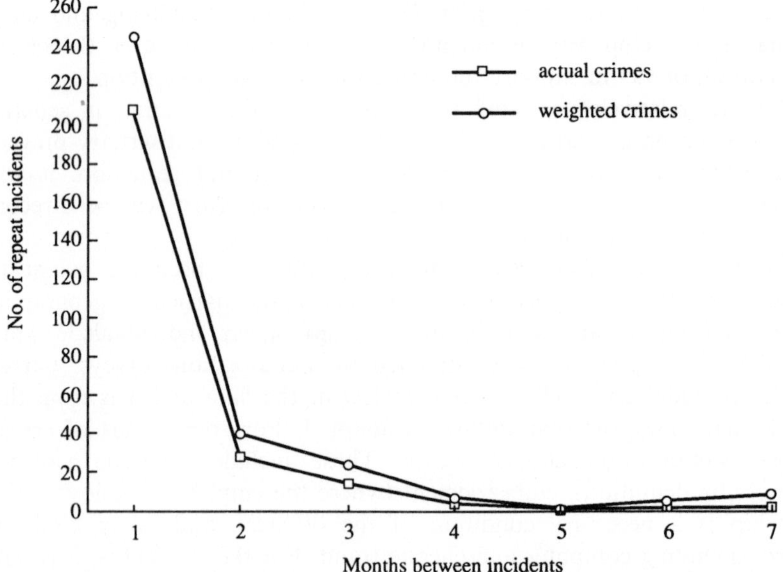

Fig. 14.3 Time-course of repeat school crimes: grouped thirty-day periods, Liverpool, 1990

[14] Fig. 14.3 contains two plotted lines. One is the actual number of crimes recorded. Looking at revictimization occurring within a month, some of the school crime in January 1990 might be repeats of crimes which occurred in December 1989. Similarly, the 'snapshot' of crimes in 1990 does not show that in 1991 some crimes will be committed which are revictimizations of 1990 crimes. What this means is that the number of repeat victimizations is underestimated. The second line in fig. 20.3 is weighted to account for this underestimation.

under way, involving the loan of silent alarms to people recently victimized in their homes, either by assault or burglary. The other advantages of the strategy, adapted from Pease (1990, 1991) are as follows:

1. Because it is based on a careful examination of the individual circumstances of a crime, it will tend to involve all the appropriate measures, social and physical, for the prevention of repeat victimization.
2. Preventing repeat victimization protects the most vulnerable social groups, without having to identify those groups as such, which can be socially divisive. Having been victimized already probably represents the least contentious basis for the claim to be given crime prevention attention.
3. Repeat victimization is highest, both absolutely and proportionately, in the most crime-ridden areas (Trickett *et al.* 1991), which are also the areas that suffer the most serious crime (Pease 1988). The prevention of repeat victimization thus *automatically* directs attention to the areas which need it most, rather than the converse, as is now the case (Harvey *et al.* 1988).
4. The rate of victimization offers a realistic scheduling for crime prevention activity. Preventing repeat victimization is a way of 'drip-feeding' crime prevention;
5. At least in England and Wales, the strategy addresses the way in which inequality of victimization rates has changed during the period covered by the British Crime Survey (Trickett *et al.* 1992). The increase in equality has been almost exclusively in the number of victimizations per victim, rather than in victim prevalence.
6. A high enough rate of victimization would tend to convert attention to repeat victimization into a community initiative, with the advantage over conventional community approaches of being rooted in real events suffered by citizens.

Whether or not the strategy advocated is adopted, it is clear that there have been enough primary crime prevention success stories to justify the belief that at many times and in many places, many crime problems are tractable. Often these achievements have been generated by special crime prevention projects. The project approach to crime prevention has many disadvantages. It is essentially artificial, with special arrangements, typically made by outsiders, being imposed upon an area. Yet there is reason to believe that successes in crime prevention are more often achieved than recognized. The present writer, Ralph Burquest, and Graham Farrell have begun to look at fast changes in recorded crime in one police force area. This phenomenon is referred to and discussed as 'crime flux' by Barr and Pease (1991), and is closely linked to the concept of a community's crime career (see Reiss 1986; Bottoms and Wiles 1991*a*). The argument is that at least a proportion of these changes represent real changes in crime. No doubt many more represent recording changes or other changes not part of deliberate crime prevention. There are many fast changes in the police force area studied, and analysis of these, it is hoped, will yield a swifter and fuller rate of return on successful crime prevention enterprise than has hitherto been enjoyed. The approach has the additional advantages of being restricted to activities which are realistic, because they were carried through, and reveal good crime prevention work (whether or not it was performed by personnel named as crime prevention officers) thereby allowing credit to be bestowed appropriately. The analysis of naturally occurring variation in circumstances where formal experimentation is difficult has a respectable tradition elsewhere in the social sciences, and it is surprising that it has not featured more in the literature of crime prevention.

ENDNOTE

If I could return to this topic in a decade, I would wish events to have progressed as follows. Specific primary prevention measures would continue to be applied as they became available, without being dismissed as simplistic. The issue of the motivation to prevent crime would have been addressed, and government and public opinion would have pressed for the implementation of simple crime prevention measures at the margins of what is regarded as economic to the victim (particularly the corporate victim). In this way the public costs, both financial and in hardship, consequent upon private decisions would be reduced. A more balanced crime prevention agenda by crime type and circumstance would have developed, giving appropriate weight to drug crime and to violence, in particular private violence. The prevention of repeat victimisation would have come to be recognised as a major strand in crime prevention strategy. By the analysis of fast changes in crime rates, numerous crime prevention successes would have been identified, common lessons learned, and the morale of crime preventers enhanced; and several chief constables would have taken office having spent the bulk of their service in force crime prevention departments. Perhaps it will take fifteen years.

Selected Further Reading

Clarke, R. V. ed., *Crime Prevention Studies*, vol 1. Monsey, New York: Criminal Justice Press, 1993.

Clarke, R. V., ed., *Situational Crime Prevention: Successful Case Studies.* New York: Harrow and Heston, 1991.

Felson Marcus, *Crime and Everyday Life.* London: Pine Forge Press, 1993.

REFERENCES

AMERICAN BAR ASSOCIATION (1986), *Drunk Driving Laws and Enforcement: an Assessment of Effectiveness.* Washington, DC: American Bar Association.

ATKINS, S., HUSAIN, S., and STOREY, A. (1991), *The Influence of Street Lighting on Crime and Fear of Crime*, Crime Prevention Unit Paper no. 28. London: Home Office.

AUSTIN, C. (1988), *The Prevention of Robbery at Building Society Branches*, Crime Prevention Unit Paper no. 14. London: Home Office.

BANNISTER, J. (1991), *The Impact of Environmental Design upon the Incidence and Type of Crime*, Central Research Unit Paper. Edinburgh: Scottish Office.

BARKER, M., PEASE, K., and WEBB, B. (1992), *Community Service and Crime Prevention: The Cheadle Heath Project*, Crime Prevention Unit Paper no. 39. London: Home Office.

BARR, R., and PEASE, K. (1990), 'Crime Placement, Displacement and Deflection', in N. Morris and M. Tonry, eds. *Crime and Justice: A Review of Research*, vol. 12. Chicago: University of Chicago Press.

—— (1991), 'A Place for Every Crime and Every Crime in its Place: An Alternative Perspective on Crime Displacement', in D. J. Evans, N. R. Fyfe, and D. T. Herbert, eds., *Crime, Policing and Place: Essays in Environmental Criminology*. London: Routledge.

BARRON, J. M. (1991*a*), 'Shuffling Crime Around: Offender Responses to Preventive Action', unpublished MA thesis, University of Manchester.

—— (1991*b*), 'Repulsive and Attractive Displacement', paper presented to the American Society of Criminology, San Francisco.

BENNETT, T. (1986), 'Situational Crime Prevention from the Offender's Perspective', in K. Heal and G. K. Laycock, eds., *Situational Crime Prevention: From Theory into Practice*. London: HMSO.

—— (1987), *An Evaluation of Two Neighbourhood Watch Schemes in London*, report to the Home Office. Cambridge: Cambridge University Institute of Criminology.

—— (1990), *Evaluating Neighbourhood Watch*. Aldershot: Gower.

—— (1991), 'Themes and Variations in Neighbourhood Watch', in D. J. Evans, N. R. Fyfe and D. T. Herbert, eds., *Crime, Policing and Place: Essays in Environmental Criminology*. London: Routledge.

BENNETT, T., and WRIGHT, R. (1984), *Burglars on Burglary: Prevention and the Offender*. Farnborough: Gower.

—— (1986), 'The Impact of Prescribing on the Crimes of Opioid Users', *British Journal of Addictions*, 81: 265–73.

Bentvelsen, T., and Van der Zon, F. (1987), *Petty Crime in High Rise Buildings Developed after the Second World War*. Delft: Delft University Press.

Berry, G., and Carter, M. (1992), *Assessing Crime Prevention Initiatives: The First Steps*, Crime Prevention Unit Paper no. 31. London: Home Office.

Bloomer, F. (forthcoming), 'Repeat Victimisations by Commercial Burglary in Lisburn', *Howard Journal.*

Bottoms, A. E. (1990), 'Crime Prevention Facing the 1990s', *Policing and Society*, 1/1; 3–22.

Bottoms, A. E., Mawby, R. I., and Xanthos, P. (1989), 'A Tale of Two Estates', in D. Downes, ed., *Crime and the City*. London: Macmillan.

Bottoms, A. E., and Wiles, P. (1991*a*), 'Housing Markets and Residential Community Crime Careers', in D. J. Evans, N. R. Fyfe, and D. T. Herbert, eds., *Crime, Policing and Place: Essays in Environmental Criminology*. London: Routledge.

—— (1991*b*), 'Explanations of Crime and Place', in D. J. Evans, N. R. Fyfe, and D. T. Herbert, eds., *Crime, Policing and Place: Essays in Environmental Criminology*. London: Routledge.

Brantingham, P. L. (1986), 'Trends in Canadian Crime Prevention', in K. Heal and G. Laycock, eds., *Situational Crime Prevention: From Theory into Practice*. London: HMSO.

Brantingham, P. J., and Faust, F. L. (1976), 'A Conceptual Model of Crime Prevention', *Crime and Delinquency*, 22: 130–46.

Burquest, R., Farrell, G., and Pease, K. (1992), 'Lessons from Schools', *Policing*, 8: 148–55.

Burrows, J. N. (1979), 'Closed Circuit Television and Crime on the London Underground', in P. Mayhew, R. V. Clarke, J. N. Burrows, J. M. Hough, and S. W. C. Winchester, eds., *Crime in Public View,* Home Office Research Study no. 49. London: HMSO. Repr. in R. V. Clarke and P. M. Mayhew, eds., *Designing Out Crime,* London: HMSO, 1980.

—— (1988), *Retail Crime: Prevention through Crime Analysis*, Crime Prevention Unit Paper no. 11. London: Home Office.

—— (1991), *Making Crime Prevention Pay: Initiatives from Business*, Crime Prevention Unit Paper no. 27. London: Home Office.

Burrows, J. N., and Heal, K. (1979), 'Police Car Security Campaigns', in J. Burrows, P. Ekblom, and K. Heal, eds., *Crime Prevention and the Police*. Home Office Research Study no. 55. London: HMSO. Repr. in R. V. Clarke and P. M. Mayhew, eds., *Designing Out Crime*. London: HMSO, 1980.

Campbell, A. (1981), *Girl Delinquents*. Oxford: Blackwell.

Carter, R. L. (1974), *Theft in the Market*, Hobart Paper no. 60. London: Institute of Economic Affairs.

Chaiken, M. R., and Chaiken, J. M. (1984), 'Offender Types and Public Policy', *Crime and Delinquency*, 30: 195–226.

Challinger, D. (1991), 'Less Telephone Vandalism: How Did It Happen?', *Security Journal*, 2: 111–19. Repr. in R. V. Clarke, ed., *Situational Crime Prevention: Successful Case Studies*. New York: Harrow and Heston, 1991.

Clarke, R. V. (1991), 'Deterring Obscene Phone Callers: The New Jersey

Experience', in R. V. Clarke, ed., *Situational Crime Prevention: Successful Case Studies*. New York: Harrow and Heston.

CLARKE, R. V., and CORNISH, D. (1985), 'Modelling Offenders' Decisions: A Framework for Policy and Research', in N. Morris and M. Tonry, eds., *Crime and Justice, An Annual Review of Research*, vol. 6. Chicago: University of Chicago Press.

CLARKE, R. V., FIELD, S. and MCGRATH, G. (1991), 'Target Hardening of Banks in Australia and Displacement of Robberies', *Security Journal*, 2: 84–90.

CLARKE, R. V., and MAYHEW, P. M., eds. (1980), *Designing Out Crime*. London: HMSO.

—— (1988), 'The British Gas Suicide Story and its Criminological Implications', in N. Morris and M. Tonry, eds., *Crime and Justice: An Annual Review of Research*, vol. 10. Chicago: University of Chicago Press.

CLOWARD, R. A., and OHLIN, L. (1960), *Delinquency and Opportunity*. New York: Free Press.

COHEN, A. K. (1955), *Delinquent Boys: The Culture of the Gang*. New York: Free Press.

COHEN, L. E., and FELSON, M. (1979), 'Social Change and Crime Rate Trends: A Routine Activity Approach', *American Sociological Review*, 44: 588–608.

COLEMAN, A. (1985), *Utopia on Trial*. London: Hilary Shipman.

CORNISH, D. B., and CLARKE, R. V., eds. (1986), *The Reasoning Criminal: Rational Choice Perspectives on Offending*. New York: Springer-Verlag.

—— (1988*a*), 'Understanding Crime Displacement: An Application of Rational Choice Theory', *Criminology*, 7: 933–47.

—— (1988*b*), 'Crime Specialization, Crime Displacement and Rational Choice Theory', in H. Wegener, F. Losel, and J. Haisch, eds., *Criminal Behaviour and the Justice System: Psychological Perspectives*. New York: Springer-Verlag.

CURRIE, E. (1988), 'Two Visions of Community Crime Prevention', in T. Hope and M. Shaw, eds., *Communities and Crime Reduction*. London: HMSO.

DAVIS, M. (1986), *Prevent Burglary: An Aggressive Approach to Total Home Security*. Englewood Cliffs, NJ: Prentice-Hall.

DECKER, J. F. (1972), 'Curbside Deterrence: An Analysis of the Effect of a Slug Rejectory Device, Coin View Window and Warning Labels on Slug Usage in New York City Parking Meters', *Criminology*, 9: 127–42.

—— (1991), 'Curbside deterrence?', in R. V. Clarke, ed., *Situational Crime Prevention: Successful Case Studies*. New York: Harrow and Heston.

DESCHAMPS, S., BRANTINGHAM, P. L. and BRANTINGHAM, P. J. (1991), 'The British Columbia Transit Fare Evasion Audit', *Security Journal*, 2: 211–18. Repr. in R. V. Clarke, ed., *Situational Crime Prevention: Successful Case Studies*. New York: Harrow and Heston.

ECK, J., and SPELMAN, W. (1988), *Problem Solving: Problem Oriented Policing in Newport*. Washington DC: Police Executive Research Forum/National Institute of Justice.

—— (1991), 'Thefts from Vehicles in Shipyard Parking Lots', in R. V. Clarke, ed., *Situational Crime Prevention: Successful Case Studies*. New York: Harrow and Heston.

Ekblom, P. (1986), *The Prevention of Shop Theft: An Approach Through Crime Analysis*, Home Office Crime Prevention Paper no. 5. London: Home Office.

—— (1987), *Preventing Robbery at Sub-Post Offices*, Home Office Crime Prevention Paper no. 9. London: Home Office.

—— (1988), *Getting the Best out of Crime Analysis*, Home Office Crime Prevention Unit Paper no. 10. London: Home Office.

—— (1991*a*), 'Preventing Post Office Robberies in London: Effects and Side Effects', in R. V. Clarke, ed., *Situational Crime Prevention: Successful Case Studies*. New York: Harrow and Heston.

—— (1991*b*), 'Talking to Offenders: Practical Lessons for Local Crime Prevention', in O. Nello, ed., *Urban Crime: Statistical Approaches and Analyses*. Barcelona: Institut d'Estudies Metropolitans de Barcelona.

Ekblom, P., and Simon, F. (1988), *Crime and Racial Harrassment in Asian-Run Small Shops: The Scope for Prevention*, Crime Prevention Unit Paper no. 15. London: Home Office.

Eysenck, H. J. (1970), *Crime and Personality*. London: Paladin.

Farrell, G. (1992), 'Multiple Victimisation: Its Extent and Significance', *International Review of Victimology*, 2: 85–102.

Farrington, D. P. (1977), 'The Effects of Public Labelling', *British Journal of Criminology*, 17: 112–25.

—— (1981), 'The Prevalence of Convictions', *British Journal of Criminology*, 21: 173–5.

—— (1986), 'Stepping Stones to Adult Criminal Careers', in D. Olweus, J. Block, and M. R. Yarrow, eds., *Development of Antisocial and Prosocial Behaviour*. New York: Academic Press.

—— (1991), 'Antisocial Personality from Childhood to Adulthood', *The Psychologist*, 4: 389–94.

—— (1992), 'Criminal Career Research: Lessons for Crime Prevention', in A. Solarz and V. Engwall, eds., *Studies on Crime and Crime Prevention*. Oslo: Scandinavian University Press.

Felson, M. (1986), 'Linking Criminal Choices, Routine Activities, Informal Control and Criminal Outcomes', in D. B. Cornish and R. V. Clarke, eds., *The Reasoning Criminal: Rational Choice Perspectives on Offending*. New York: Springer-Verlag.

Fenn, P. (1986), 'Insurance against Theft: A Market Contribution to Crime Prevention', in *Crime UK: An Economic and Policy Audit*. Oxford: Hermitage.

Field, S. (1991), *Trends in Crime and their Interpretation: A Study of Recorded Crime in Post-War England and Wales*, Home Office Research Study no. 119. London: HMSO.

Fielding, H. (1988 [1751]), *An Enquiry into the Causes of the Late Increase of Robbers and Related Writings*, ed. M. R. Zirker. Oxford: Clarendon Press.

Fleming, R., and Burrows, J. (1986), 'The Case for Lighting as a Means of Preventing Crime', *Home Office Research Bulletin*, 22: 14–17.

Forrester, D. P., Chatterton, M. R., and Pease, K. (1988), *The Kirkholt Burglary Prevention Demonstration Project*, Crime Prevention Unit Paper no. 13. London: Home Office.

Garland, D. (1990), *Punishment and Modern Society*. Oxford: Clarendon Press.

GAROFALO, J. (1987), 'Reassessing the Lifestyle Model of Personal Victimisation', in M. R. Gottfredson and T. Hirschi, eds., *Positive Criminology*. London: Sage.

GENDREAU, P., and ROSS, R. R. (1987), 'Revivification of Rehabilitation: Evidence from the 1980s', *Justice Quarterly*, 4: 349–407.

GENN, H. (1988), 'Multiple Victimisation', in M. Maguire and J. Pointing, eds., *Victims of Crime: A New Deal?* Milton Keynes: Open University Press.

GERAGHTY, J. (1991), *Probation Practice in Crime Prevention*, Crime Prevention Unit Paper no. 24. London: Home Office.

GRAHAM, J. (1990), *Crime Prevention Strategies in Europe and North America*. Helsinki: Helsinki United Nations Institute.

HAAPANEN, R. A. (1990), *Selective Incapacitation and the Serious Offender*. New York: Springer-Verlag.

HAKIM, S., and RENGERT, G. F. (1981), *Crime Spillover*. Beverly Hills: Sage.

HARVEY, L., GRIMSHAW, P., and PEASE, K. (1988), 'The Work of Crime Prevention Officers', in R. Morgan and D. J. Smith, eds., *Coming to Terms with Policing*. London: Routledge.

HAUBER, A. R. (1978), 'Fraud and Public Transport', *Research Bulletin*, no. 2. The Hague: Research and Documentation Centre, Netherlands Ministry of Justice.

HEAL, K. (1991), 'Changing Perspectives on Crime Prevention: The Role of Information and Structure', in D. J. Evans, N. R. Fyfe, and D. T. Herbert, eds., *Crime, Policing and Place: Essays in Environmental Crimonology*. London: Routledge.

HEAL, K., and LAYCOCK, G. K. (1986), *Situational Crime Prevention: From Theory into Practice*. London: HMSO.

HILL, N. (1986), *Pre-Payment Coin Meters: A Target for Burglary*, Crime Prevention Unit Paper no. 6. London: Home Office.

HINDELANG, M. J., GOTTFREDSON, M. R., and GAROFALO, J. (1978), *Victims of Personal Crime: An Empirical Foundation for a Theory of Personal Victimisation*. Cambridge, Mass.: Ballinger.

HIRSCHI, T. (1969), *Causes of Delinquency*. Berkeley: University of California Press.

—— (1986), 'On the Compatibility of Rational Choice and Social Control Theories of Crime', in D. B. Cornish and R. V. Clarke, eds., *The Reasoning Criminal: Rational Choice Perspectives on Offending*. New York: Springer-Verlag.

HOME OFFICE (1984), *Report of an Inter-Departmental Group on Crime*. London: HMSO.

—— (1988), *Practical Ways to Crack Crime*. London: Home Office.

HOPE, T. J. (1980), 'Four Approaches to the Prevention of Property Crime in Schools', *Oxford Review of Education*, 6: 231–40.

—— (1982), *Burglary in Schools: The Prospects for Prevention*, Home Office Research and Planning Paper no. 2. London: Home Office.

—— (1985), *Implementing Crime Prevention Measures*, Home Office Research Study no. 86. London: HMSO.

—— (1986), 'School Design and Burglary', in K. Heal and G. K. Laycock, eds., *Situational Crime Prevention: From Theory into Practice*. London: HMSO.

HOPE, T., and MURPHY, D. (1983), 'Problems of Implementing Crime Prevention: The Experience of a Demonstration Project', *Howard Journal,* 22: 38–50.

HOPE, T., and SHAW, M. (1988), 'Community Approaches to Reducing Crime', in T. Hope and M. Shaw, eds., *Communities and Crime Reduction*. London: HMSO.

HOPE, T., and SHAW, M., eds. (1988), *Communities and Crime Reduction*. London: HMSO.

HOUGHTON, G. (1992), *Car Theft in England and Wales: The Home Office Car Theft Index*, Crime Prevention Unit Paper no. 33. London: Home Office.

HUNTER, R. D., and JEFFERY, C. R. (1991), 'Environmental Crime Prevention: An Analysis of Convenience Store Robberies', *Security Journal*, 2: 78–83.

HUSAIN, S., and BRIGHT, J. (1990), *Neighbourhood Watch and the Police*. Swindon: Crime Concern.

JACOBS, J. (1961), *Death and Life of Great American Cities*. New York: Random House.

JEFFERY, C. R. (1971), *Crime Prevention through Environmental Design*. London: Sage.

KAZDIN, A. (1987), 'Treatment of Antisocial Behaviour in Children: Current Status and Future Directions', *Psychological Bulletin*, 102: 187–203.

KING, M. (1989), 'Social Crime Prevention à la Thatcher', *Howard Journal*, 28: 291–312.

KNUTSSON, J., and KUHLHORN, E. (1981), 'Macro-measures against Crime: The Example of Check Forgeries', *Information Bulletin, no. 1.* Stockholm: Swedish National Council for Crime Prevention. Repr. in R. V. Clarke, ed., *Situational Crime Prevention: Successful Case Studies*. New York: Harrow and Heston, 1992.

KORNHAUSER, R. (1978), *Social Sources of Delinquency*. Chicago: University of Chicago Press.

LAYCOCK, G. K. (1984), *Reducing Burglary: A Study of Chemists' Shops*, Crime Prevention Unit Paper no. 1. London: Home Office.

—— (1985), *Property Marking: A Deterrent to Domestic Burglary*?, Home Office Crime Prevention Unit Paper no. 3. London: Home Office. Repr. in K. Heal and G. K. Laycock, eds., *Situational Crime Prevention: From Theory into Practice*. London: HMSO, 1986.

LEVI, M. (1988), *The Prevention of Fraud*, Crime Prevention Unit Paper no. 17. London: Home Office.

LEVI, M., BISSELL, P., and RICHARDSON, T. (1991), *The Prevention of Cheque and Credit Card Fraud*, Crime Prevention Unit Paper no. 26. London: Home Office.

LILLY, J. R., CULLEN, F. T., and BALL, R. A. (1989), *Criminological Theory: Context and Consequences*. London: Sage.

LINDSAY, B., and MCGILLIS, D. (1986), 'Citywide Community Crime Prevention: An Assessment of the Seattle Programme', in D. P. Rosenbaum, ed., *Community Crime Prevention: Does It Work?* London: Sage.

LITTON, R. A. (1990), *Crime and Crime Prevention for Insurance Practice*. Aldershot: Avebury.

LURIGIO, A. J., and ROSENBAUM, D. P. (1986), 'Evaluation Research in Community Crime Prevention', in D. P. Rosenbaum, ed., *Community Crime Prevention: Does It Work*? London: Sage.

Maguire, M. (1982), *Burglary in a Dwelling*. London: Routledge.

Markus, C. L. (1984), 'British Telecom Experience in Payphone Management', in C. Levy-Leboyer, ed., *Vandalism Behaviour and Motivations*. Amsterdam: Elsevier-North-Holland.

Mawby, R. I. (1977), 'Defensible Space: A Theoretical and Empirical Appraisal', *Urban Studies*, 14: 169–79.

Mayhew, P. M. (1979), 'Defensible Space: The Current Status of a Crime Prevention Theory', *Howard Journal*, 18: 150–9.

—— (1991), 'Displacement and Vehicle Theft: An Attempt to Reconcile Some Recent Contradictory Evidence', *Security Journal*, 2: 233–9.

Mayhew, P. M., Clarke, R. V., and Elliott, D. (1989), 'Motorcycle Theft, Helmet Legislation and Displacement', *Howard Journal*, 28: 1–8.

Mayhew, P. M., Clarke, R. V., and Hough, J. M. (1976), 'Steering Column Locks and Car Theft', in P. M. Mayhew, R. V. Clarke, A. Sturman, and J. M. Hough, eds., *Crime as Opportunity*, Home Office Research Study no. 34. London: HMSO.

Mayhew, P., Clarke, R. V., Hough, J. M., and Winchester, S. W. C. (1979), 'Natural Surveillance and Vandalism to Telephone Kiosks', in P. M. Mayhew, R. V. Clarke, J. N. Burrows, J. M. Hough, and S. W. C. Winchester, eds., *Crime in Public View*, Home Office Research Study no. 49. London: HMSO.

Mayhew, P., Clarke, R. V., Hough, J. M., and Winchester, S. W. C. (1980), 'Natural Surveillance and Vandalism to Telephone Kiosks', in R. V. Clarke and P. M. Mayhew, eds., *Designing Out Crime*. London: HMSO.

Mayhew, P. M., Clarke, R. V., Sturman, A., and Hough, J. M. (1976), *Crime as Opportunity*, Home Office Research Study no. 34. London: HMSO.

Mednick, S. A., Schulsinger, F., Higgins, J., and Bell, B. (1974), *Genetics, Environment and Psychopathology*. New York: North Holland.

Merry, S. E. (1981), 'Defensible Space Undefended: Social Factors in Crime Control through Environmental Design', *Urban Affairs Quarterly*, 16: 397–422.

Merton, R. K. (1957), *Social Theory and Social Structure*. New York: Free Press.

Miethe, T. D. (1991), 'Citizen-Based Crime Control Activity and Victimisation Risks: An Examination of Displacement and Free Rider Effects', *Criminology*, 29: 419–40.

Morgan Report (1991), *Safer Communities: The Local Delivery of Crime Prevention through the Partnership Approach*. London: Home Office.

Mueller, G. O. W., and Adler, F. (1985), *Outlaws of the Ocean—The Complete Book of Contemporary Crime on the High Seas*. New York: Hearst Marine.

—— (1991), 'When Passenger Rates Go Down—So Do Passenger Liners: An Inquiry into the Opportunity of Sinking Wisely', *Security Journal*, 2: 102–7.

Nee, C., and Taylor, M. (1988), 'Residential Burglary in the Republic of Ireland: A Situational Perspective', *British Journal of Criminology*, 27: 103–18.

Nelken, D. (1985), 'Community Involvement in Crime Control', *Current Legal Problems*, 38: 239–61.

Newman, O. (1972), *Defensible Space: Crime Prevention through Urban Design*. London: Architectural Press.

—— (1976), *Design Guidelines for Achieving Defensible Space*, National Institute of Law Enforcement and Criminal Justice. Washington DC: US Government Printing Service.

NEWMAN, O., and FRANCK, K. A. (1982), 'The Effects of Building Size on Personal Crime and Fear of Crime', *Population and Environment*, 5: 203–20.

NUTTALL, C. P., *et al.* (1978) *Parole in England and Wales*, Home Office Research Study no. 38. London: HMSO.

PAINTER, K. (1988), *Lighting and Crime Prevention: The Edmonton Project*. London: Middlesex Polytechnic Centre for Criminology.

—— (1989*a*), *Lighting and Crime Prevention for Community Safety: The Tower Hamlets Study*. London: Middlesex Polytechnic Centre for Criminology.

—— (1989*b*), *Crime Prevention and Public Lighting with Special Focus on Women and Elderly People*. London: Middlesex Polytechnic Centre for Criminology.

—— (1991), *An Evaluation of Public Lighting as a Crime Prevention Strategy with Special Focus on Women and Elderly People*. Manchester: University of Manchester Faculty of Economics and Social Studies.

PEASE, K. (1979), *Reflection on the Development of Crime Prevention Strategies and Techniques in Western Europe*, Report to the United Nations CSDHA. (Available on request from the author, University of Manchester, M13 9PL.)

—— (1988), *Judgements of Offence Seriousness: Evidence for the 1984 British Crime Survey*, Research and Planning Unit Paper no. 44. London: Home Office.

—— (1990), 'Preventing Burglary on a British Public Housing Estate', *Security Journal*, 2: 73–7.

—— (1991), 'Preventing Burglary on a British Public Housing Estate', in R. V. Clarke, ed., *Situational Crime Prevention: Successful Case Studies*. New York: Harrow and Heston.

PEASE, K., and HARVEY, L. (1987), 'Prevalence of Imprisonment in England and Wales', *British Journal of Criminology*, 27: 65–9.

PEASE, K., and LITTON, R. (1984), 'Crime Prevention: Practice and Motivation', in D. J. Muller, D. E. Blackman, and A. J. Chapman, eds., *Psychology and Law*. Chichester: Wiley.

PHILLIPS, S., and COCHRANE, R. (1988), *Crime and Nuisance in the Shopping Centre: A Case Study in Crime Prevention*, Crime Prevention Unit Paper no. 16. London: Home Office.

POLVI, N., LOOMAN, N., HUMPHRIES, C., and PEASE, K. (1990), 'Repeat Break-and-Enter Victimisation: Time Course and Crime Prevention Opportunity', 17: 8–11.

POYNER, B. (1983), *Design against Crime: Beyond Defensible Space*. London: Butterworth.

—— (1988), 'Video Cameras and Bus Vandalism', *Security Administration*, 11: 44–51. Repr. in R. V. Clarke, ed., *Situational Crime Prevention: Successful Case Studies*. New York: Harrow and Heston, 1991.

—— (1991), 'Situational Crime Prevention in Two Parking Facilities', *Security Journal*, 2: 96–101. Repr. in R. V. Clarke, ed., *Situational Crime Prevention: Successful Case Studies*. New York: Harrow and Heston.

POYNER, B., WARNE, C., WEBB, B., WOODALL, R., and MEAKIN, R. (1988), *Preventing Violence to Staff*. London: HMSO.

Ramsey, M. N. (1982), *City-Centre Crime: The Scope for Situational Crime Prevention*, Home Office Research and Planning Unit Paper no. 10. London: Home Office.

—— (1986), *Preventing Disorder*, in K. Heal and G. K. Laycock, eds., *Situational Crime Prevention: From Theory into Practice*. London: HMSO.

—— (1991), *The Effect of Better Street Lighting on Crime and Fear: A Review*, Crime Prevention Unit Paper no. 29. London: Home Office.

Ramsey, M. N., and Heal, K. (1982), 'Crime Analysis: An Approach to Crime Prevention', *Police Research Bulletin*, 38: 23–37.

Reiss, A. J. (1980), 'Victim Proneness in Repeat Victimisation by Type of Crime', in S. E. Fienberg and A. J. Reiss, eds., *Indicators of Crime and Criminal Justice*. Washington: Bureau of Justice Statistics.

—— (1986), 'Why Are Communities Important in Understanding Crime', in A. J. Reiss and M. Tonry, eds., *Communities and Crime*. Chicago: University of Chicago Press.

Reppetto, T. A. (1974), *Residential Crime*. Cambridge, Mass.: Ballinger.

—— (1976), 'Crime Prevention and the Displacement Phenomenon', *Crime and Delinquency*, 22: 166–77.

Roncek, D., and Maier, P. A. (1991), 'Bars, Blocks and Crimes Revisited: Linking the Theory of Routine Activities to the Empiricism of Hot Spots', *Criminology*, 29: 725–54.

Rubenstein, H., Murray, C., Motoyama, T., Rouse, W. V., and Titus, R. M. (1980), *The Link between Crime and the Built Environment: The Current State of Knowledge*. Washington: National Institute of Justice.

Sampson, A. (1991), *Lessons from a Victim Support Crime Prevention Project*, Crime Prevention Unit Paper no. 25. London: Home Office.

Sampson, A., and Phillips, C. (1992), *Multiple Victimisation: Racial Attacks on an East London Estate*, Crime Prevention Unit Paper no. 36. London: Home Office.

Shaw, C. R., and Mackay, H. D. (1942), *Juvenile Delinquency and Urban Areas*. Chicago: University of Chicago Press.

Sherman, L. W., Gartin, P., and Buerger, M. E. (1989), 'Hot Spots of Predatory Crime: Routine Activities and the Criminology of Place', *Criminology*, 27: 27–55.

Singer, S. (1981), 'Homogeneous Victim–Offender Populations: A Review and some Research Implications', *Journal of Criminal Law and Criminology*, 72: 779–88.

Smith, L. J. F. (1987), *Crime in Hospitals: Diagnosis and Prevention*, Crime Prevention Unit Paper no. 7. London: Home Office.

—— (1989), *Domestic Violence*, Home Office Research Study no. 104. London: HMSO.

Smith, L. J. F., and Burrows, J. (1986) 'Nobbling the Fraudsters: Crime Prevention through Administrative Change', *Howard Journal*, 25: 13–24.

Smith, S. J. (1986), 'Utopia on Trial: Vision and Reality in Planned Housing', *Urban Studies*, 23: 244–6.

—— (1987), 'Design against Crime? Beyond the Rhetoric of Residential Crime Prevention', *Journal of Property Management*, 5: 146–50.

SOUTHALL, D., and EKBLOM, P. (1985), *Designing for Crime Security: Towards a Crime-Free Car*, Crime Prevention Unit Paper no. 4. London: Home Office.

SPARKS, R., GENN, H., and DODD, D. (1977), *Surveying Victims*. Chichester: Wiley.

STANDING COMMITTEE ON CRIME PREVENTION (1991), *Safer Communities: The Local Delivery of Crime Prevention through the Partnership Approach*. London: Home Office.

STANKO, E. A. (1990), 'When Precaution is Normal: A Feminist Critique of Crime Prevention', in L. Gelsthorpe and A. Morris, eds., *Feminist Perspectives in Criminology*. Milton Keynes: Open University Press.

STENZEL, W. W. (1977), *Saint Louis High Impact Crime Displacement Study*, paper given at the National Conference on Criminal Justice, February.

STURMAN, A. (1976), 'Damage on Buses: The Effects of Supervision', in Mayhew, P. M., Clarke, R. V., Sturman, A., and Hough, J. M., eds., *Crime as Opportunity*, Home Office Research Study no. 34. London: HMSO.

—— (1980), 'Damage on Buses: The Effects of Supervision', in R. V. Clarke and P. Mayhew, eds., *Designing Out Crime*. London: HMSO.

TAYLOR, R. B., GOTTFREDSON, S., and BROWER, S. (1980), 'The Defensibility of Defensible Space', in T. Hirschi and M. Gottredson, eds., *Understanding Crime*. London: Sage.

TAYLOR, M., and NEE, C. (1988), 'The Role of Cues in Simulated Residential Burglary', *British Journal of Criminology*, 28: 14–26.

TRASLER, G. (1972), 'Criminal Behaviour', in H. J. Eysenck, ed., *Handbook of Abnormal Psychology*. London: Putnam.

—— (1986), 'Situational Crime Control and Rational Choice: A Critique', in K. Heal and G. K. Laycock, eds., *Situational Crime Prevention: From Theory into Practice*. London: HMSO.

—— (1993), 'Conscience, Opportunity, Rational Choice, and Crime', in R. Clarke and M. Felson, eds., *Advances in Criminological Theory*. New Brunswick: Transaction.

TRICKETT, T. A., ELLINGWORTH, D., FARRELL, G., and PEASE, K. (1992*b*), 'Changes in the Inequality of Crime Distribution: England and Wales 1982–8', submitted to *British Journal of Criminology*.

TRICKETT, T. A., SEYMOUR, J., OSBORN, D., and PEASE, K. (1992*a*), 'What Is Different about High Crime Areas?', *British Journal of Criminology*.

VAN ANDEL, H. (1989), 'Crime Prevention that Works: The Case of Public Transport in the Netherlands', *British Journal of Criminology*, 29: 47–56.

—— (1991), 'The Care of Public Transport in the Netherlands', in R. V. Clarke, ed., *Situational Crime Prevention: Successful Case Studies*. New York: Harrow and Heston.

VAN DIJK, J. J. M., and DE WAARD, J. (1991), 'A Two-Dimensional Typology of Crime Prevention Projects: With a Bibliography', *Criminal Justice Abstracts*, 23: 483–503.

VAN STRAELEN, F. W. M. (1978), 'Prevention and Technology', in J. Brown, ed., *Cranfield Papers*. London: Peel Press.

VISHER, C. A. (1986), 'The Rand Inmate Survey: A Reanalysis', in A. Blumstein, J. Cohen, J. A. Roth, and C. A. Visher, eds., *Criminal Careers and Career Criminals*, vol. 1. Washington, DC: National Academy Press.

WALKER, N. (1980), *Punishment, Danger and Stigma*. Oxford: Blackwell.

WALLER, I., and OKIHIRO, N. (1978), *Burglary: The Victim and the Public*. Toronto: University of Toronto Press.

WALSH, D. P. (1982), 'An Appreciation of the Quest for Vulnerability in Victim Choice and its Consequences for Fortification', paper presented to the British Psychological Society, Welsh Branch, International Conference on Psychology and Law, Swansea.

WARD, D. (1987), *The Validity of the Reconviction Prediction Score*, Home Office Research Study no. 94. London: HMSO.

WEATHERITT, M. (1986), *Innovations in Policing*. London: Croom Helm.

WEBB, B., and LAYCOCK, G. K. (1992*a*), *Reducing Crime on the London Underground: An Evaluation of Three Pilot Projects*, Crime Prevention Unit Paper no. 30. London: Home Office.

—— (1992*b*), *Tackling Car Crime: The Nature and Extent of the Problem*, Crime Prevention Unit Paper no. 32. London: Home Office.

WESLEY, R. L., and WONAT, J. A. (1986), *Guide to International Loss Prevention*. Stoneham, Mass.: Butterworths.

WEST, D. J. (1982), *Delinquency: Its Roots, Careers and Prospects*. London: Heinemann.

WILKINS, L. T. (1987), 'Disparity of Dispositions: The Early Ideas and Applications of Guidelines', in M. Wasik and K. Pease, eds., *Sentencing Reform: Guidance or Guidelines?* Manchester: Manchester University Press.

WILSON, S. (1980), 'Vandalism and "Defensible Space" on London Housing Estates', in R. V. Clarke and P. Mayhew, eds., *Designing Out Crime*. London: HMSO.

WINCHESTER, S., and JACKSON, H. (1982), *Residential Burglary: The Limits of Prevention*, Home Office Research Study no. 74. London: HMSO.

WINKEL, F. W. (1987), 'Response Generalisation in Crime Prevention Campaigns', *British Journal of Criminology*, 27: 155–73.

ZIMRING, F., and HAWKINS, G. (1987), *The Citizen's Guide to Gun Control*. New York: Macmillan.

15

Policing and the Police

ROBERT REINER

INTRODUCTION: CRIMINOLOGY AND THE STUDY OF THE POLICE

In popular culture cops and robbers are a conceptual couple, the former perennially chasing the latter. In criminology until relatively recently this was not the case. For most of its history criminology has focused on robbers and other miscreants, but the activities of cops and the agencies of the criminal justice process generally were outside its conscious purview. The legal and criminal justice systems were taken for granted, even though they were responsible for making the laws the breaking of which was the research hunting ground of criminology, and corralled the captive populations of law-breakers who were the raw material for much criminological theory.

It was not ever thus. Prior to the rise of a positivist interpretation of criminology which coincided with the naming of the new discipline in the late nineteenth century (Garland 1985*a*, *b*, and chapter 1 in this volume), there flourished a variety of competing discourses about crime, criminals and control. In these 'proto-criminologies' the criminal justice system was at the centre of analytic and policy concern. Indeed, the so-called 'classical' school associated pre-eminently with Beccaria (Taylor *et al.* 1973: ch. 1; Vold and Bernard 1985: ch. 1; Roshier 1989) is often said not to be a 'criminology' in that it did not see the particularity of the criminal as its problematic (Garland 1985*b*). Instead it was concerned primarily with constructing a rational and efficient system of criminal law and justice.

At much the same time in the late eighteenth and early nineteenth centuries, there flourished a vigorous branch of political economy known as the 'science of police' (Pasquino 1978; Reiner 1988). This saw as its problematic the understanding of crime and disorder and the development of appropriate policies for its prevention and control. Its leading British exponent was Patrick Colquhoun, a Middlesex magistrate and architect of the first professional police force in Great Britain, created by the 1800 Thames River Police Act. Although Colquhoun is best known today as one of the precursors of Peel's Metropolitan Police, and lurks in the footnotes of police history alongside the Fieldings, Bentham, Chadwick, and others, 'police' in the modern sense of people in blue uniforms figured as only a relatively small part of his project.

The term 'police' was used then in a much broader way to connote the whole craft of regulating a social order by economic, social, and cultural policy. The criminal justice system *per se*—and *a fortiori* the police force—was only a residual aspect of this project. Policing in its contemporary interpretation was seen as merely a small part of the whole business of domestic government and regulation, all of which was relevant for the understanding and control of crime and disorder. This perspective was one widely shared by the leading political economists of the day, from Adam Smith (Smith 1978 [1763]) to Bentham, not to speak of Colquhoun himself, who wrote several works on political economy, such as *The Treatise on Indigence*, in addition to his better remembered and more directly influential *Treatise on the Police of the Metropolis*. (The most accessible and comprehensive discussion of Colquhoun's work is Radzinowicz, *History of English Criminal Law*, vol. 3, 1956.)

The birth of a positivist 'science of criminology' in the late nineteenth century largely eclipsed this earlier concern with the functioning of criminal law and justice. The problematic became the explanation of 'criminality', initially seen as a non-social defect of specific individuals (Garland 1985*a*, *b*). Even the subsequent development of sociological theories of crime in the early twentieth century did not remove the blinkers which excluded the functioning of policing and the criminal justice process from the intellectual province of criminology. There were, to be sure, lively debates about how criminology should interpret the concept of crime. Was it satisfactory merely to take over legalistic definitions, or was it necessary to develop more sociologically coherent and theoretically adequate concepts? The debate initiated by Sutherland about 'white-collar' crime (cf. Nelken, chapter 8 in this volume) came closest to a critical version of this issue. But while the conceptual ambit of the discipline was debated it was not suggested that the functioning of the police and other criminal justice institutions should be part of the research or theoretical concerns of criminologists.[1]

During the early 1960s an epistemological break occurred in the criminological enterprise, which sailed under the banners of 'labelling theory' and 'naturalism' and paved the way for new forms of radical and critical criminology (Taylor *et al.* 1973: chs. 5–9, 1975; Downes and Rock 1988 chs. 7, 8, 10; Garland, Young, and Rock, chapters 1, 2, 3 in this volume).

[1] The flourishing of penology as the empirical study of modes of punishing and/or treating offenders after sentence is not really an exception to this. It is the application of the premise of positivist criminology (that criminality has causes which can be understood) to the development of ameliorative techniques for curing or removing these causes.

The essential departure of the new approaches was to make problematic, intellectually as well as politically, the structure and functioning of criminal justice agencies, instead of or in addition to the people they labelled and processed as offenders. (The key references are Becker 1964; Lemert 1967.) Deviants were not special cases, rendered by their pathologies objects to the criminological gaze. They were human actors whose subjectivities were to be appreciated, not just corrected (Matza 1964, 1969). The other side of the picture was that the behaviour and practices of criminal justice agents were not to be taken for granted as an automatic professional response to pathological deviance. They had to be understood as interacting with deviants in ways that structured the phenomena of apparent criminality, and were themselves analytically and politically problematic and in need of 'correction' (Becker 1967 is most explicit in this). The police began to figure on the research agendas of criminologists and other social scientists as a particular aspect of this intellectual conjuncture.

In this chapter the development and findings of police research over the last thirty years will be reviewed. The next section will explore the origins and growth of research on the police. The main focus of this chapter will be research on the British police; however, because of the extensive cross-fertilization in the early years of police research in both countries, the next section will look at some classic American as well as British studies. The third section of the chapter will address the fundamental but all too frequently overlooked questions: What is policing and who are the police? What different forms can policing take? The fourth section will argue that the central concept underlying police research has been *discretion*, the recognition that the police do not automatically translate law into policing practice. The sources and significance of police discretion will be analysed. We will review the research on police work and organization in terms of three aspects of discretion: (1) What patterns are implicit in its exercise, and what are its social consequences? (2) How can these patterns be explained? (3) How can the operation of police discretion be shaped and controlled? Finally, in the concluding section of the chapter possible future trends in policing will be considered.

THE DEVELOPMENT OF POLICE RESEARCH

Police Research in the USA

Systematic analysis of and research about the police developed at roughly the same time, the early 1960s, on both sides of the Atlantic.[2] Its

[2] One influential sociological study of the police had been conducted earlier, by William Westley for his Ph.D. in the late 1940s. This was published as a book only in 1970,

emergence was prompted partly by political and cultural changes, and partly by theoretical developments in sociology and criminology.

In the USA the key motor driving the development of police research was the concern with civil rights, which was the dominant domestic political issue of the 1960s. This produced a multi-faceted recognition that police practice often departed from legal standards, and could result in abuse of rights and discrimination. The policy response, by both politicians and the judiciary, was to seek to close the gap by more tightly prescribing the requirements of due process of law (notably through the landmark Supreme Court decisions in *Miranda*, *Escobedo*, and other cases which collectively mounted a 'due process revolution'; cf. Graham 1970; Kaplan and Skolnick 1982: ch. 5).

The intellectual response by researchers in criminal law and criminology was to map the pattern of police practice, and analyse the sources of its deviation from the rule of law, so as to provide a more solid basis for the practical efforts to close the gap. Thus legal scholars demonstrated the sources and significance of police discretion to enforce or not to enforce the law (Goldstein 1960; Goldstein 1964; La Fave 1962, 1965; Davis 1969, 1975). At the same time sociological research probed the structuring of police deviation from due process values by the role, organization, culture, personality, and socialization of the police (Stinchcombe 1963; Skolnick 1966; Bittner 1967*a*, *b*; Bordua 1967; Niederhoffer 1967; Bayley and Mendelsohn 1968; Wilson 1968).

Within criminology, the 1960s were the heyday of 'labelling theory' and its shift of the spotlight on to the crime-producing consequences of criminal justice intervention. From this perspective studies emerged of the way in which the organizational and cultural biases of the police could produce or amplify deviance through their styles of intervention in particular situations. The police were seen as shaping the apparent social characteristics of crime and criminals by focusing on targets which reflected police stereotypes (Piliavin and Briar 1964; Werthman and Piliavin 1967).

The culmination of this early phase of US police research in the 1960s was the large-scale observational study mounted by Reiss and Black for

although two papers published in the 1950s were an important reference for the 1960s researchers in both Britain and the USA (Westley 1953, 1956, 1970). Apart from Westley's pioneering work, the only extensive body of writing on the police, apart from memoirs of celebrated detectives in the 'true crime' genre, was in history. Until the late 1960s, however, histories of the police were usually written by enthusiastic amateur police experts (notably Lee 1901; Reith 1938, 1940, 1943, 1948, 1952, 1956; Critchley 1967), not professional historians. A few academic authorities on criminal justice also contributed important work on the history of the police (Hart 1951, 1955, 1956; Radzinowicz 1948–68). Since the main inspiration for the enthusiastic amateurs' efforts was genuine admiration for the police, their works reflect a celebratory and uncritical perspective, and constitute an ideological, 'cop-sided' version of history (Robinson 1979; Reiner 1992*a*: ch. 1). This celebratory picture is reflected in most discussions on the British police until the late 1960s (Reiner 1989*b*).

the Presidential Commission on Law Enforcement, which was one of the products of the mid-1960s urban riots (Reiss 1968, 1971; Black 1970, 1972; Black and Reiss 1967, 1970). The Presidential Commission was also the precipitant of a profound alteration in the character and direction of police research in the USA after the late 1960s. This reflected a major change in the general politics of crime and criminal justice. In 1968 'law and order' displaced 'civil rights' as the major domestic political issue, championed by Richard Nixon's successful presidential campaign against Lyndon Johnson (Harris 1970). The debate about policing shifted away from concern about police deviation from legality towards more technical and managerial questions about police effectiveness in controlling crime and disorder (Rumbaut and Bittner 1979). The Presidential Commission on Law Enforcement set up the Law Enforcement Assistance Administration (LEAA), which poured money into police reform projects aimed at boosting police efficiency, and into research evaluating and developing these police efforts (Goulden 1970; Platt and Cooper 1974). This activity also received massive private financial backing from bodies like the Ford Foundation, which established the Police Foundation as a powerhouse of police research.

The result was a veritable police research industry, largely outside academia, although increasingly important as a source of financial support for research by academics as well. The more theoretical and the civil libertarian impulses which had produced the birth of police research were largely eclipsed by the huge growth of narrower policy-related and managerial work (Rumbaut and Bittner 1979). However, the earlier traditions of small-scale and detailed observational research did continue, as did some critical work, and efforts to develop a theoretical understanding of policing (Bittner 1970, 1974; Manning 1970, 1977; Van Maanen 1973, 1974; Manning and Van Maanen 1978; Bernstein *et al.* 1974—a rare example of a Marxist analysis of the American police).

In the 1980s the increasing influence of ideas of 'community policing' have resulted in something of a synthesis of these approaches. Instead of police efficiency and legal and community accountability being seen as contradictory concerns, in fundamental tension with each other, police leaders, policy-makers and researchers have increasingly argued that they are inextricably interdependent. In anything but the very short run, community support based on respect for civil rights and accountability is necessary for effective policing, not an impediment to it (Skolnick and Bayley 1986, 1988; Greene and Mastrofski 1988; Trojanowicz and Bucqueroux 1990; Moore 1992).

Police Research in the UK

Police research in Britain developed independently of the specifically American political concerns, but especially in its early years there was much mutual intellectual influence. The sources of British police research were a combination of changes in the politics of law and order since the 1950s, theoretical developments in criminology and sociology, and the shifting institutional context of social science research.

The growth of police research in Britain clearly reflects the trends in the politics of law and order which have occurred in the post-war period (Reiner 1989*b*). The 1950s were the heyday of cross-party consensus on law and order, as on other social issues (see Downes and Morgan chapter 5 in this volume). The police were generally regarded as national mascots, totems of patriotic pride, routinely referred to as role models for the world (Reiner 1992*a*; 57–60). The pedestal on which the police stood is illustrated by the popularity of the TV series *Dixon of Dock Green*, in which the central character was a kindly, avuncular PC who captured the cosy stereotype of the British bobby which then prevailed in the public imagination (Clarke 1983; Sparks 1992: 26–9; Reiner 1992*b*: 761).

The few books written about the police were within the same celebratory mode. They were the memoirs of senior detectives, like 'Fabian of the Yard', who had achieved celebrity status (Fabian 1950, 1954) or the efforts of enthusiastic amateur historians who came to applaud rather than analyse (see note 2 above). In the middle of the 1950s a journalist published a book on *Exploring English Character*, based on a survey he had conducted (Gorer 1955).[3] This found that the police officer represented the popular notion of the ideal male character, and was regarded as a model of decency (Gorer 1955: 311).

Towards the end of the 1950s a series of scandals aroused increasing public concern about the police. By 1959 this had reached a pitch where the Home Secretary was forced to announce during a parliamentary debate that he was establishing a Royal Commission to look at the role, organization, and accountability of the police (Critchley 1978: 270–4; Bottoms and Stevenson 1990; 1992: 25–7). This was the most sweeping official review of the structure and functioning of the police to take place since they were initially established in their modern form early in the nineteenth century, and the ensuing legislation, the Police Act 1964, continues to be the basis for the current pattern of accountability (Royal Commission on the Police 1962; Lustgarten 1986; Reiner 1991: ch. 2).

[3] As the 'sample' was a self-selected group of readers of a popular Sunday newspaper who responded to an appeal by the author, not too much can be claimed about its representativeness. For all its scientific limitations, however, the survey does arguably give some insight into respectable working-class opinion.

What is remarkable with the twenty/twenty vision of hindsight is the small-scale character of the incidents which were at that time seen as sufficiently momentous to warrant a major public inquiry.[4] This is itself testimony to the sacred aura which enveloped the police at that time (Banton 1964: 235–42). The Royal Commission mounted as part of its inquiry a large-scale national survey on police–public relations. This found 'an overwhelming vote of confidence in the police . . . No less than 83% of those interviewed professed great respect for the police' (Royal Commission on the Police 1962: 102–3).[5]

The earliest sociological research on the police in Britain developed in this context of increasing questioning of what had been widely seen as an exemplary national institution. The first empirical study of policing in Britain, Michael Banton's *The Policeman in the Community*, was published in 1964. It comprised an analysis of the role of the British police derived from data gathered by observation, interviews, and the keeping of time budgets by the police themselves in a Scottish force, as well as some comparative observations based on fieldwork in the USA (Banton 1964). Banton was well aware of the mood of increasing questioning of the police, and that his study would be seen as part of this climate. Indeed, his publishers were understandably eager to spice up the sales potential of the work by references in the blurb to police–public relations becoming 'a focus of national concern' and to 'popular reactions to certain well-publicised incidents'. However, Banton himself played down such

[4] Two cases involved allegations of assault by police officers. One concerned a dispute between the Chief Constable of Nottingham and the Watch Committee arising out of an investigation into alleged corruption among councillors. There were three cases of criminal or disciplinary proceedings against chief constables. These were not the serious matters they might appear at first sight. They occurred in small borough forces which today would constitute at most divisions, within the large forces with which we are familiar. The contemporary equivalents of the chief constables implicated would be chief superintendents or lower-ranked officers. The immediate trigger for the Royal Commission was a parliamentary debate arising out of an altercation at a traffic incident in Hyde Park in which the famous star of Whitehall farces, Brian Rix, became involved. By contrast, the 1980s were a decade of serious political conflict and debate about the police and policing issues, unprecedented in this century. None the less it was not until 1991 that the government had to break with its record of not having set up a Royal Commission since 1979. The Court of Appeal decision to uphold finally the appeal of the Birmingham Six, coming after mounting public controversy about the dramatic series of miscarriage of justice cases which began with the Guildford Four's successful appeal in 1979, has produced the Royal Commission on Criminal Justice announced in March 1991 (Rozenberg 1992).

[5] The Royal Commission was criticized at the time (e.g. Whitaker 1964: 15–17) as well as by subsequent critics (e.g. Brogden 1982: 204–5) for neglecting aspects of its own research which called into question its optimistic overall summary. It underplayed the findings of its survey of the police, which suggested that the rosy view of the state of police–public relations was not shared by the police themselves. The sample included only members of the adult population, at a time when the formation of self-conscious youth cultures was causing the police particular headaches with young people (Rock and Cohen 1970; Cohen 1972). None the less the survey is a rigorous study of the views of the broad mass of the population.

concerns in the preface which outlined his aims. He rebutted explicitly the assumption that he 'must be examining defects in police organisation and conduct'. Rather, he started from 'the idea that it can be instructive to analyse institutions that are working well in order to see if anything can be learned from their success' (Banton 1964: vii). Unlike much of the subsequent research on the police, Banton's study is inspired by scholarly questions of sociological theory rather than more immediate issues of policy or politics (Holdaway 1989 elaborates on this important point).

Banton's pathbreaking study was responsible for many ideas and approaches which have been returned to time and again in subsequent work.[6] It initiated what became the central research strategy of most subsequent British (and much American) work: detailed participant observation. Its account of the police role as primarily consisting of non-law enforcement 'peace-keeping' tasks has been echoed and developed in much subsequent work in Britain and around the world (from Cumming et al 1964 through Punch 1979*a* to Shapland and Vagg 1988). The peace-keeping role of the police arose as much from the tendency observed by Banton for the police to 'under-enforce' the law by exercising their discretion not to arrest as from the inherent character of the public's demand for police services.

The exercise of discretion by the police was informed primarily by their sense of the morality and the priority of different interventions which was embedded in the informal culture of the police themselves. The analysis of police culture pioneered by Banton—although the term itself is not used by him—identifies characteristics which have been replicated in many subsequent studies, notably the themes of police suspiciousness, internal solidarity, and social isolation (Skolnick 1966: ch. 3; Reiner 1992*a*: ch. 3). Banton's key analytic theme, the interpenetration of informal and formal social control, and the greater relative importance of the former, has only recently been re-emphasized (Shapland and Vagg 1988), shorn of the encumbrance of functionalist social theory within which Banton embedded it. Despite his eschewal of any concerns with scandal or muck-raking, Banton was acutely aware that there were severe threats developing to the comparatively benign and consensual mode of policing within the moral parameters of a community which he describes. He anticipated that the British police were in danger of losing the aura of the

[6] Banton's work influenced the development of American as well as British studies of the police. This was partly because, unlike most later research, it was comparative in approach. Banton's influence on such classic American police studies as Skolnick 1966, Wilson 1968, Bayley and Mendelsohn 1968, Reiss 1971, and Manning 1977 is apparent. The last of these is also one of the few pieces of research to incorporate study of more than one country, albeit reversing Banton's transatlantic trajectory in being an American scholar's analysis of British as well as American policing.

sacred with which they were invested and had to establish a new basis for the legitimation of their authority.[7]

These themes of Banton's initial study were developed by a number of young British researchers in the late 1960s and early 1970s who constituted the first generation of police research in this country (a useful volume giving samples of the work of most of them is Holdaway, ed. 1979).[8] Inspired by a variety of theoretical and political perspectives, several young sociologists followed Banton's lead and attempted to immerse themselves in police culture in order to describe and analyse the rules and meanings which constitute it. These studies resulted in a body of work which has provided an anchorage for understanding the crucial aspects of police occupational culture.[9]

It is impossible to sum up this rich tradition of detailed, largely observational, research without some distortion of the work of a diverse array of individual perspectives. The key theme was the charting of what industrial sociologists might call the *informal organization* of police work, echoing the importance in early American research of the discovery of discretion. It was demonstrated that the backstage life of the police, who are apparently the acme of a bureaucratic, rule-bound organization, disciplined to discipline others, was in fact a much more fluid world, seething with tensions, spontaneity, and deviance (although rule infractions discovered by prying sociologists were more likely to be the 'grass-eating' minor rule-bending type than the 'meat-eating' stuff of scandal). The police occupational world was constituted and informed by a complex set of informal meanings, norms, and understandings. The central fascination of these studies was the documentation of a variety of forms of illicit 'easing behaviour', and how the ingeniously varied interpretations of the 'Ways and Means Act' structured diverse patterns of deviation of the 'law in action' from the 'law in the books'. In short, police organization was

[7] In the optimistic scientific mood of the mid-1960s Banton sees more sociology in police training as a possible tool for this relegitimation. (This echoes the hope of the more optimistic founding fathers of the discipline in the nineteenth century that sociology could provide a new religion to integrate modern secular societies.) If only PC Dixon had read some Durkheim he might never have turned into Dirty Harry!

[8] The first generation of researchers were influenced by Banton's organizational activities as much as by his intellectual example. During the early 1970s Banton organized three conferences on 'The Sociology of the Police' at the University of Bristol (reported in Banton 1971, 1973, 1975). These were attended by most of the researchers on policing who were active in Britain at that time, as well as a few North American and European scholars. They were also attended by a number of senior police officers, facilitating the development of links which were invaluable for researchers seeking access to police organizations.

[9] The main examples are Cain 1973; Chatterton 1976, 1979, 1983; Holdaway 1977, 1979, 1983; Manning 1977, 1979—a leading American sociologist's analysis of Anglo-American policing; Reiner 1978*a*; Punch 1979*b*, 1985—observational studies of the Dutch police by a British sociologist. Although not directed at the analysis of police culture *per se*, Martin and Wilson 1969 and Lambert 1970 are two important works of the period looking at the police role which are congruent with the themes of Banton and the others.

shown to be a 'mock bureaucracy' (Gouldner 1954), with the quasi-militaristic drill and discipline of the station masking the discretion and deviance of the streets.

Although most of this research was inspired by scholarly rather than practical concerns, its political and policy implications were fairly evident (Cain 1979: 144–6). As summed up by Holdaway in his introduction to his volume assembling a representative sample of first-generation studies: 'One of the basic themes running through this book . . . is that the lower ranks of the police service control their own work situation and such control may well shield highly questionable practices' (Holdaway, ed. 1979: 12).

As the 1970s drew to a close the political aspects and implications of policing and police research in Britain were coming increasingly to the surface, reflecting a growing politicization of all aspects of national life and public policy. 'Law and order' became a central political issue, and an important ingredient of the Conservative victory in the 1979 general election (see chapter 5 in this volume). Researchers on police subculture began themselves to underline the political issues raised by their identification of the comparative autonomy of the police rank and file. 'If, in a British society itself pervaded by social inequality, we desire a more accountable police, then we will check police power and we cannot expect the police to do this themselves' (Holdaway, ed. 1979: 13). The police themselves were becoming a more overt pressure group on the political stage (Reiner 1978*a*: 268–9; 1980).

The greater salience of policing as a political and policy issue was reflected in the emergence in the late 1970s of two new strands of research on the police, which had not existed prominently until then. The most important development in the academic world was the proliferation of work from an explicitly critical or Marxist standpoint. Many of the first examples were influential historical studies of the role of the police in relation to class conflict (e.g. Storch 1975, 1976; Cohen 1979). Another key theme was the enhancement of police accountability (Brogden 1977, 1982; Hain 1979, 1980; Cowell *et al.* 1982; Jefferson and Grimshaw 1984). Others were more general critical analyses of the operation of policing as a means of state control (Bunyan 1976; Hall *et al.* 1978; Scraton 1985). Some of the first-generation sociological researchers began to publish more critical theoretical and political analyses (Cain 1977, 1979; Reiner 1978*b*, *c*).

The other new strand of police research which began to proliferate in the late 1970s as policing developed into a central political issue was policy-orientated research commissioned by government bodies or even the police themselves. A variety of official bodies began to stimulate an ever-widening stream of research directed towards answering problems of policing policy (Reiner 1989*b*, 1992*c*).

Although managerialist in origin, such studies are far from uniformly managerialist in style or conclusions. For example, one of the first pieces of independent research commissioned by a police force was the celebrated study of policing in London conducted for the Met by the Policy Studies Institute (Smith *et al.* 1983). This produced a 'warts and all' portrait which was significant in building up a head of steam for police reform initiatives. Much of the work produced by the Home Office Research and Planning Unit (HORPU) or the Police Foundation (an independent charity established in 1980 to promote police research) has questioned central assumptions of police policy and practice. The research commissioned by the Royal Commission on Criminal Procedure informed the attempts to buttress safeguards over the use of police powers which it recommended in its 1981 Report (which led to the Police and Criminal Evidence Act 1984). Much research in the early and mid-1980s was sponsored by radical Labour local authorities, notably the Merseyside and Islington Crime Surveys (Kinsey *et al.* 1986; Jones *et al.* 1986).

Official policy-orientated research is thus not necessarily uncritical or managerialist in inspiration. None the less there was a significant trend during the 1980s in which policy-orientated research eclipsed theoretically or critically inspired work, at any rate in the speed with which it multiplied. As police effectiveness and value-for-money considerations, rather than democratic or legal accountability, have come to dominate the political agenda with the increasing dominance of Thatcherite priorities in public policy debate, so the character of policy-orientated policing research has come to reflect this emphasis. Some theoretically inspired work still continues, and much policy-orientated work continues to be informed by liberal or even radical values, but the fastest growth areas are in managerialist studies of immediate policy issues. This work is increasingly often conducted by the police themselves, or by government agencies with responsibilities for policing, rather than by academic or independent research institutions (Reiner 1989*b*, 1992*c*).

In the rest of this chapter I will review the main findings of police research, in all its phases. To begin with, however, the next section will consider the conceptual issues: Who are the police, and what is policing?

'POLICE' AND 'POLICING'

Most research on the police has been concerned primarily with immediate policy matters and consequently has operated with a taken-for-granted notion of the police and their proper functions (Cain 1979). A particular mid-twentieth-century conception has tacitly been presumed as inevitable.

The police are mainly a body of people patrolling public places in blue uniforms, with a broad mandate of crime control, order maintenance, and some negotiable social service functions. They are supplemented by non-uniformed adjuncts concerned primarily with the investigation and processing of criminal offences and sundry administrative tasks.

While anyone living in a modern society has this intuitive notion of what *the police* are, understanding the nature and role of *policing*, especially over a broader span of space and time, requires some conceptual exploration of the taken-for-granted idea of police. Modern societies are characterized by what can be termed 'police fetishism', the ideological assumption that the police are a functional prerequisite of social order and that without a police force chaos or 'anarchy' would ensue.[10] In fact many societies have existed without a formal police force of any kind, and certainly without the present model. The contribution of the police to the control of crime and maintenance of order today is debatable, as studies of police effectiveness have suggested (Reiner 1992*a*: 146–56). The problematic nature of the present notion of the police is increasingly evident, because contemporary societies are characterized by a process of fragmentation and diffusion—sometimes dubbed 'greying'—of the police function (Shearing and Stenning 1983, 1984, 1987; Shearing 1992; South 1988; Spitzer and Scull 1977; Johnston 1991, 1992; Hoogenboom 1991; Reiner 1992*b*: 779–81).

It is important to distinguish between the ideas of 'police' and 'policing'. 'Police' refers to a particular kind of social institution, while 'policing' implies a set of processes with specific social functions. 'Police' are not found in every society, and police organizations and personnel can have a variety of shifting forms. 'Policing', however, is arguably a universal requirement of any social order, and may be carried out by a number of different processes and institutional arrangements.

The idea of policing is an aspect of the more general concept of social control. Social control is itself a complex and much debated notion. (See Cohen and Scull 1983 for a comprehensive discussion and a sample of essays on aspects of social control. Zedner 1993 is a succinct analysis of the varying usages of the concept.) In some sociological theories social control is seen broadly as everything that contributes to the reproduction

[10] An amusing exemplification of this is Morrison's analysis of the picture of the police in children's stories. Enid Blyton's *Mr Plod and Little Noddy*, for instance, describes the consternation in Toytown when PC Plod is put out of action for a while by an injury. 'Who is going to protect us against robbers?' wail the anxious inhabitants. It is inconceivable that order can be protected (until Noddy agrees to deputize for Mr Plod: see Morrison 1984). Similar conceptions of the necessity of the police underpin the widespread fears about police strikes, which are seen as inevitably producing disorder, a perception fuelled by horror stories about Boston in 1918, Liverpool in 1919, and Montreal in 1969. In fact numerous police strikes have occurred with little apparent effect on lawlessness (Ayres and Wheelen 1977; Reiner 1978*a*: 5–6).

of social order. This makes the concept all-encompassing, virtually coterminous with society. It would include all aspects of the formation of a culture and the socialization of the individuals who are its bearers. An example of this broad usage is Park and Burgess's classic sociology textbook, which declared that 'all social problems turn out finally to be problems of social control' (Park and Burgess 1929: 785). Therefore social control should be 'the central fact and the central problem of sociology' (ibid.: 42).

The problem with this broad concept of social control is its amorphousness. It fails to distinguish the specificity of what are ordinarily understood to be control processes as a sub-category of all social processes. This is that they are essentially negative, intended to prevent or react to threats to social order. As Cohen acerbically expressed it, the broader usage is 'a Mickey Mouse concept', and the term should be restricted to refer to 'the organised ways in which society responds to behaviour and people it regards as deviant, problematic, worrying, threatening, troublesome or undesirable' (Cohen 1985: 1–2).

In either its broad or its more specific interpretations the idea of social control may be regarded positively or negatively, according to whether a consensus or conflict model of society is espoused. In conservative versions of functionalist sociology (especially during the heyday of Parsonian functionalism in the 1950s), social control was seen as the necessary bulwark of the consensus which was seen to underpin the social order. Ensuring adequate control mechanisms in the face of threatening deviance or disintegration was a functional prerequisite of any viable society, although especially problematic in rapidly changing modern societies. Accomplishing adequate social control was seen as 'the major problem of our time' (Landis 1956).

The development of labelling theory and subsequent radical positions within criminology and the sociology of deviance changed the moral evaluation of social control institutions. Far from being seen as a necessary protection against deviance, social control came to be regarded as producing deviance through the effects of labelling and stigmatization (Becker 1964; Lemert 1967). Social control agents were seen as oppressors to be questioned and opposed (Becker 1967). More structuralist or Marxist versions of critical criminology saw these simple reversals of moral blame as merely making social control agents 'fall guys' for the inexorable working of a wider structure of power and privilege (Gouldner 1968; McBarnet 1979). All radical analyses, however, see social control at least in part as the oppressive maintenance of the privileged position of dominant groups—although more sophisticated critiques may see social control as inextricably intertwining the maintenance of universally beneficial order *and* social dominance and oppression (Marenin 1983).

The concept of policing is clearly closely related to that of social control, and is subject to the same variations in usage and interpretation. Indeed, a recent dictionary definition identifies policing as 'the function of maintaining social control in society' (Wilson 1993). However, as with the broad usage of social control, this wide definition of policing carries the danger of amorphousness. It misses the specificity of the idea of policing as it is ordinarily used to refer to a particular aspect of social control processes. Thus *punishment* is clearly an aspect of social control, but is usually regarded as something which should be kept separate from policing, even though any police intervention may be experienced as punitive by those who are policed. The police may in fact often exercise forms of kerbside punishment—the Rodney King case in Los Angeles, relating to an incident in 1991, being a notorious recent example (see Skolnick and Fyfe 1993)—but this is seen as scandalous in terms of a liberal democracy's values of legality (Skolnick 1966: ch. 1). Thus policing cannot usefully be analysed as coterminous with social control but must be seen as a specific phase or aspect of it.

The essential concept of policing relates to the idea of security through surveillance and the threat of sanctioning (Spitzer 1987; Shearing 1992). Policing implies the set of activities *directed* at preserving the security of a particular social order. That order may be regarded as one based on a consensus of interests, or a manifest and/or latent conflict of interests between social groups differentially placed in a hierarchy of advantage, or perhaps a complex intertwining of the two (Marenin 1983).

The above formulation emphasizes that policing activity is *intended* to secure social order. How effective any form of policing is, and its relationship to other elements in the preservation of social order, are moot points. Policing does not encompass all activities directed at guaranteeing social order. Thus it refers to a specific aspect of control processes, which excludes punishment as well as activities aimed at creating the conditions of social order in the first place (for example socialization, measures to secure family stability, encouragement of religion, or other forms of internalized ethical controls).

What is specific to the policing sub-set of control processes is that they involve the creation of systems of surveillance coupled with the threat of sanctions for discovered deviance—either immediately, or in terms of the initiation of penal processes, or both. The most familiar such system is of course the one denoted by the modern sense of police as discussed above: regular uniform patrol of public space coupled with *post hoc* investigation of reported or discovered crime or disorder.

Policing thus defined may be carried out by a diverse array of people and techniques, of which the modern idea of police is only one. Policing may be done by professionals employed by the state in an organization with an omnibus policing mandate—the archetypal modern idea of *the* police—or by state agencies with other primary purposes (like the Atomic Energy Authority Police, the Parks Constabularies, the British Transport Police, and other 'hybrid' policing bodies; cf. Johnston 1992: ch. 6). Police may be professionals employed by specialist private policing firms (contract security) or security personnel hired by an organization whose main business is something else (in-house security. See: Shearing and Stenning 1983; South 1988; Johnston 1992). Policing functions may be performed by citizens in a voluntary capacity within state police organizations, like the Special Constabulary (cf. Leon 1989; Gill and Mawby 1990); in association with the state police, like Neighbourhood Watch schemes (Bennett 1990; McConville and Shepherd 1992); or in completely volunteer bodies, like the Guardian Angels, and the many vigilante bodies which have flourished in many times and places. Policing functions may be carried out by state bodies with other primary functions, like the army in Northern Ireland, or by employees (state or private) as an adjunct of their main job (like *concierges* or shop assistants who also guard against theft). Policing may be carried out by technology, like security cameras or listening devices (although these can of course only be used in association with human operators at some point). These various policing strategies are proliferating today, even though it is only the state agency with the omnibus mandate which is still popularly understood by the label '*the* police'.

Until modern times policing functions were primarily carried out as a by-product of other social relationships and by citizen 'volunteers' or private employees. It has been shown by anthropological studies that many pre-literate societies have existed without any formalized system of social control or policing. A well-known cross-cultural study of the relationship between legal evolution and societal complexity in a sample of fifty-one pre-industrial societies found that 'elements of legal organisation emerge in a sequence, such that each constitutes a necessary condition for the next' (Schwartz and Miller 1964: 160). *Police* in the sense of a 'specialised armed force used partially or wholly for norm enforcement' were found in only twenty of the societies in the sample of fifty-one (ibid.: 161). These were almost all societies sufficiently economically developed to have monetary systems, and with a high degree of specialization including full-time priests, teachers, and official functionaries of various kinds. Police, the study found, appear 'only in association with a substantial degree of division of labour' (ibid.: 166), and are usually preceded by other elements of a developed legal system like mediation and damages.

It seems uncontentious that specialized policing institutions emerge only in relatively complex societies. They are not, however, a straightforward reflex of a burgeoning division of labour, as the Durkheimian undertones of Schwartz and Miller's analysis imply. While policing may originate in collective and communal processes of social control, specialized police forces develop hand in hand with social inequality and hierarchy. They are means for the emergence and protection of more centralized and dominant state systems (Spitzer 1975).

A valuable recent review of the anthropological literature concludes that the development of specialized police 'is linked to economic specialisation and differential access to resources that occur in the transition from a kinship- to a class-dominated society' (Robinson and Scaglion 1987: 109). During this transition communal policing forms are converted in incremental stages to state-dominated ones, which begin to function as agents of class control in addition to more general social control. The complex and contradictory function of contemporary police, as simultaneously embodying the quest for general and stratified order—'parking tickets' as well as 'class repression' (Marenin 1983)—is thus inscribed in their birth process.

British police ideology has rested upon the idea of a fundamental distinction between the British model of community-based policing and an alien, 'continental', state-controlled system (Mawby 1991, 1992). Conventional histories of the British police attempt to trace a direct lineage between ancient tribal forms of collective self-policing and the contemporary Bobby. 'Our English police system . . . rests on foundations designed with the full approval of the people, we know not how many hundreds of years before the Norman conquest' (Lee 1901: xxvii). The consequence of this populist pedigree is supposed to be a uniquely popular police force. 'Our national police has always been of the people and for the people' (ibid.: 61); 'The police are the public and the public are the police' (Reith 1956: 287).

Such claims have been characterized aptly as 'ideology as history' (Robinson 1979). It is true that many European systems of police did develop more overtly as instruments of state control (Chapman 1970). Revisionist histories, however, have emphasized the relationship between modern police development and the shifting structures of class and state in Britain as well as in the USA and other common-law systems (Silver 1967; Storch 1975, 1976; Miller 1977; Brogden 1982; Emsley 1983, 1991, chapter 4 in this volume; Scraton 1985; Reiner 1992*a*: chs. 1, 2). The supposedly benign 'British' model was in any case for home consumption only. A more militaristic and coercive model was from the outset exported to colonial situations, including John Bull's other island (Brogden 1987; Palmer 1988).

Although contemporary patterns of police vary considerably in detail, they have tended to converge increasingly around fundamentally similar organizational and cultural lines, without the qualitative distinctions of kind implied in traditional British police ideology (Mawby 1991, 1992; Bayley 1985). This is facilitated by the emergence of a new international group of technocratic police experts who are responsible for the diffusion of fashions in police thinking around the globe, as witnessed by the recent spread of enthusiasm for 'community policing' strategies (Skolnick and Bayley 1988).

It is problematic to define contemporary police mainly in terms of their supposed function (Klockars 1985). As Bittner has emphasized, the police are called upon routinely to perform a bewildering miscellany of tasks, from traffic control to combating terrorism (Bittner 1970; 1974). This has been a commonplace finding of empirical police research from the outset (Banton 1964; Cumming *et al.* 1964; Punch and Naylor 1973; Punch 1979*a*; Shearing 1984). The uniting feature of the tasks that come to be seen as police work is not that they are aspects of a particular social function, whether it be crime control, social service, order maintenance, or political repression; rather, it is that they all involve 'something that ought not to be happening and about which someone had better do something *now*!' (Bittner 1974: 30). In other words, policing tasks arise in emergency situations, usually with an element of at least potential social conflict. The police may invoke their legal powers to handle the situation, but more commonly they resort to a variety of ways and means to keep the peace without initiating legal proceedings (Bittner 1967).[11] None the less, underlying all their tactics for peace-keeping is their bottom-line power to wield legal sanctions, ultimately the use of legitimate force. 'A benign bobby . . . still brings to the situation a uniform, a truncheon, and a battery of resource charges . . . which can be employed when appeasement fails and fists start flying' (Punch 1979*a*: 116).

The distinctiveness of the police lies not in their performance of a specific social function but in being the specialist repositories for the state's monopolization of legitimate force in its territory. 'The policeman, and the policeman alone, is equipped, entitled and required to deal with every exigency in which force may have to be used' (Bittner 1974: 35). This should not be construed to imply that all policing is about the use of force. On the contrary, 'good' policing has often been seen as the craft of handling trouble without resort to coercion, usually by skilful verbal tactics (Muir 1977; Chatterton 1983; Bayley and Bittner 1984).

[11] The police are also not usually regarded as responsible for all elements of keeping the peace. Their task is the emergency response to threats of disorder, not the creation of its preconditions (although this has been implied in some very broad conceptions of community policing; see e.g. Alderson 1979). Waddington expresses the point well. 'The police are the social equivalent of the AA or RAC patrolmen, who intervene when things go unpredictably wrong and secure a provisional solution' (Waddington 1983: 34). In terms of this analogy, they are neither service station mechanics nor car markers nor road builders. However, like the AA they may legitimately advise on policies for which their work experience may be relevant as well as co-operating with other agencies to prevent future problems.

Nor are the police the only people who can use legitimate force. This remains the right (and in some circumstances the moral duty) of every citizen. There are many occupations where the potential for the legitimate use of force may arise with a fair degree of frequency, for example workers in the health or social services handling disturbed patients, or public transport staff who may have to deal with disorder. However, they are not 'equipped, entitled and required to deal with *every* exigency in which force may have to be used', in Bittner's previously cited definition (emphasis added). Indeed, other workers are likely to 'call the cops' at the earliest opportunity in troublesome situations, and use legitimate force themselves only as an immediate emergency measure in the interim.

To sum up, 'policing' is an aspect of social control processes which occurs universally in all social situations in which there is at least the potential for conflict, deviance, or disorder. It involves surveillance to discover actual or anticipated breaches, and the threat or mobilization of sanctions to ensure the security of the social order. The order in question may be based on consensus, or conflict and oppression, or an ambiguous amalgam of the two, which is usually the case in modern societies.

While policing may be universal, the 'police' as a specialized body of people given the primary formal responsibility for the use of legitimate force to safeguard security is a feature of only relatively complex societies. The police have developed in particular as a key institution in modern societies as an aspect of the rise of modern state forms. They have been 'domestic missionaries' in the historical endeavours of centralized states to propagate and protect a dominant conception of peace and propriety throughout their territories (Storch 1976).

This is not to say, however, that they have been mere tools of the state, faithfully carrying out tasks determined from above. Whether this is regarded as legitimate or not, all police forces have been characterized by the discretion exercised in particular by the lowest ranks in the organization, a discretion facilitated above all by the basic nature of police work as dispersed surveillance. The determination of police work in practice is achieved by the interplay of a variety of processes and pressures, among which formal policies determined at the top have historically been of relatively little significance. Many of these features of modern police organizations are currently under great challenge, and policing is undergoing profound changes in what many commentators have interpreted as a new 'postmodern' stage of social development (Reiner 1992*b*). These issues will be returned to in the conclusions of this chapter. Before that, the next section will analyse the concept of discretion and its functioning, which has been at the heart of police research since it began.

POLICE DISCRETION: ITS NATURE, OPERATION, AND CONTROL

A key intellectual underpinning of police research from the outset has been the 'discovery' of police discretion. Many jurisdictions have in the past denied the legitimacy of police discretion and refused to recognize its existence. Some continue to do so, especially outside the common-law tradition. In the USA many states adopted full enforcement statutes, requiring the police to initiate criminal proceedings whenever they had evidence of an offence (Allen 1984; Williams 1984*a*, *b*). From this perspective, the commonly observed tendency of the police to under-enforce the law by dealing with many incidents in a peace-keeping rather than law-enforcement style (Banton 1964) is illegal and scandalous.

The starting-point for empirical research on the police in the USA in the late 1950s and early 1960s was the recognition not only that the police regularly deviated from full enforcement of the law, but that this was both inevitable and arguably desirable (Goldstein 1960; La Fave 1962, 1965; Goldstein 1964; Davis 1969, 1975). Discretion was inevitable factually because the volume of incidents that could be regarded as breaches of the law would always outstrip police capacity to process them, so choices about priorities were inescapable. It was also inevitable as a matter of logic: translating general rules of law into enforcement decisions in particular situations could not be mechanistic and automatic, but required a process of interpretation of the meaning of the rules, implying an inherently subjective element. The exercise of discretion was also desirable in principle, to avoid the oppressiveness of invoking the full panoply of criminal law to deal with incidents which were commonly regarded as not warranting this.

The difficulty was that discretion opened the way for disparity and discrimination in legal decision-making. If police organizations did not operate in a mechanistic way to execute the rules laid down by legislatures and courts—if the 'law in action' deviated from the 'law in the books' (in the terminology of American legal realism)—it became important to understand the operation of the law in practice. This could be done only by empirical research on the reality of police work, aimed at understanding its dynamics and establishing a basis for more effective regulation of undesirable practices. Thus the recognition by American legal scholars of the existence of police discretion sparked a flurry of empirical studies of policing from a socio-legal perspective (most notably Skolnick 1966; Black and Reiss 1967; Bordua 1967; Wilson 1968; Black 1970, 1971; Reiss 1971).

In Britain the reality and desirability of police discretion had never been denied completely. In 1893, for example, a judge wrote in a criminal law training manual for constables:

Much power is vested in a police constable . . . Pray avoid harshness and oppression; be firm but not brutal, make only discreet use of your powers . . . You are not absolutely *bound* to arrest. You ought to exercise your discretion, having regard to the nature of the crime, the surrounding circumstances, and the condition and character of the accuser and the accused. (Sir Henry Hawkins, 'one of Her Majesty's Judges', in preface to Vincent 1893).

Nevertheless, although the wisdom (not to speak of the inevitability) of police discretion had long been accepted, there was a certain air of scandalous revelation when the early British sociological studies of the police emphasized its extent and the manner in which it could be exercised (for example Banton 1964: ch. 5; Lambert 1970: ch. 5; Young 1971; Cain 1971). The theme of these studies is encapsulated in the title of an article summing up the early British and American work: 'The Police Can Choose' (Lambert 1969).

Police discretion came to be seen as potentially problematic. Once the police were recognized as not mechanistically adhering to the rule of law the prospect of discrimination and other malpractices opened up. The answer to this, however, could not be the standard traditional response to revelations of police wrongdoing: slap on new rules and regulations, and/or enforce existing ones more rigorously. The implication of the sociological studies was that a strong measure of police discretion was inevitable because of the nature of police work, regardless of whether attempts were made to eliminate it or regulate it tightly. This was because the necessarily dispersed character of routine uniformed or plain-clothes police work gave it 'low visibility' from the point of view of police management or any outside regulatory bodies (Goldstein 1960). This was particularly true of decisions *not* to invoke the law, which might never be reviewed by anyone at all apart from the street-level police officer. In short, the patrol officer and detective were recognized to be 'street-level politicians' (Muir 1977) wielding enormous power, and effectively determining the policies in practice of the whole organization. Because of the low visibility of everyday police work, 'the police department has the special property . . . that within it discretion increases as one moves down the hierarchy' (Wilson 1968: 7).

The consequence of this seminal finding of the pioneering police research was that for many years studies were addressed only to understanding the dynamics of rank-and-file policing, and supervisory and senior management levels were almost completely neglected. The gap between 'street' and 'management' cops was emphasized (Ianni and Ianni 1983), and the real as opposed to formal action was supposed to emanate from the cultural imperatives of the former.

In the late 1970s a structuralist critique of this position began to develop, inspired mainly by the work of Doreen McBarnet (McBarnet

1978, 1979, 1981). This argued that the almost complete rule-scepticism implied by the then dominant sociology of the police mistakenly implied the virtual irrelevance of formal law and policy. It made the lowest-level police 'the "fall-guys" of the legal system taking the blame for any injustices' (McBarnet 1981: 156). This was misplaced, because although some degree of police discretion was inevitable, British law took an unnecessarily permissive stance towards police powers. These powers could and should be regulated more tightly in order to embody the principles of the rule of law in a set of specific legal rules specifying the legitimate limits of police practice in a clear, unambiguous, and strictly enforced way. By framing the powers of the police in elastic and vague rules, 'the judicial and political elites' effectively condoned those departures from due process legality which sociological studies of police work documented (and for which they blamed the rank-and-file police).

The implications of McBarnet's argument paved the way for more detailed studies of the interaction between variations in legal rules and police practice—for example, the now considerable body of research assessing the impact of PACE (the Police and Criminal Evidence Act 1984; cf. Reiner 1992*a*: ch. 6)—as well as studies of the supervisory and management ranks of the police (Currie 1986; Chatterton 1987; Grimshaw and Jefferson 1987: part IV; Reiner 1991). The rest of this section will review the results of research on the pattern of exercise of police discretion, its consequences, causation, and control.

The Operation of Police Discretion

The police routinely exercise discretion in the way they use their legal powers, and the law is usually under-enforced (Banton 1964), in the sense that clear evidence of violations will not result in criminal proceedings but in an informal (if any) intervention by the police aimed at peace-keeping rather than full law enforcement. This is indeed often lauded as a wise and desirable approach. The central premise of the policing philosophy advocated by Lord Scarman in his Report on the 1981 Brixton disorders (Scarman 1981)—which has become the conventional wisdom of the police elite since then (Reiner 1991: ch. 6)—was that public tranquillity should have a greater priority than law enforcement if the two conflicted. Discretion, 'the art of suiting action to particular circumstances', was the better part of police valour.

The problem with this is that research on police practice has shown consistently that police discretion is not an equal opportunity phenomenon. Some groups are much more likely than others to be at the receiving end of the exercise of police powers. A general pattern of benign under-enforcement of the law disguises the often oppressive use of police powers against unpopular or uninfluential and hence powerless minorities. Such groups have been described graphically as 'police property' (Cray 1972; Lee 1981): 'A category becomes police property when the dominant powers of society . . . leave the problems of the social control of that category to the police' (Lee 1981: 53–4). Not only are the 'police property' groups vulnerable to police harassment, the social powerlessness which makes them prey to the police also allows the police to neglect their victimization by crime. They tend to be over-policed and under-protected.

Studies of policing in all industrial societies and throughout modern police history show that the main grist to the mill of routine policing is the social residuum at the base of the social hierarchy (Brogden *et al.* 1988: ch. 6). Those who are stopped and searched or questioned in the street, arrested, detained in the police station, charged, and prosecuted are disproportionately young men who are unemployed or casually employed, and from generally discriminated against ethnic minorities. The police themselves recognize that their main business involves such groups, and their mental social maps delineate them by a variety of derogatory epithets: 'assholes' (Van Maanen 1978), 'pukes' (Ericson 1982), 'scum', 'slag' (Smith *et al.* 1983: iv. 164–5), 'prigs' (Young 1991). In turn, public attitude surveys show that such groups have the most negative views of the police (Smith *et al.* 1983: i. 314–15, iv. 162–8; Jones and Levi 1983; Hough and Mayhew 1983, 1985; Kinsey 1984; Jones *et al.* 1986; Crawford *et al.* 1990; Skogan 1990).

The basic organization and mandate of the police in an industrial society tends to generate this practical concentration on policing what has currently come to be signified as the underclass (Dahrendorf 1985: 98–107). Most police resources are devoted to uniformed patrol of public space (over 65 per cent, according to Tarling 1988: 5). It has long been recognized that the institution of privacy has a class dimension (Stinchcombe 1963). The lower the social class of a person, the more their social lives take place in public space, and the more likely they are to come to the attention of the police for infractions. People are not usually arrested for being drunk and disorderly in their living rooms, but they may be if their living room is the street. Detective work—the next most important concentration of police resources (about 15 per cent, according to Tarling 1988)—largely involves processing those handed over by uniform patrol. Even when it does not, detectives' clientele is still largely the same police property group of 'rubbish' or 'toe-rags' (Maguire and Norris 1992: 9–11), whose comparative lack of the rights conferred by the institutions of privacy exposes them more easily to detection.

The end result is that most of those handled by the police are from the 'police property' groups. This was demonstrated strikingly by a recent empirical study of custody in police stations (Morgan *et al.* 1990). This was based on observations of over 550 prisoners received into nine police stations (covering the full range of policing situations, from inner-city areas to remote rural locations), and the analysis of a random sample of over 1,800 custody records in these stations. It was found that the overwhelming majority of people detained at the police stations were drawn from the 'police property' group of the economically and socially marginal. Over half (55 per cent) had no paid employment (a few of these were retired people or housewives, but nearly all were unemployed). Most of the rest (a third overall) were in manual working-class jobs, predominantly unskilled ones. Only 6 per cent of the sample had non-manual occupations, and of these only one-third (i.e. 2 per cent overall) were in professional or managerial occupations. Most detainees were young (59 per cent under 25), 87 per cent were men, and 12 per cent were black. These data confirm that the weight of adversarial policing falls disproportionately on young men in the lower socio-economic and least powerful social groups.

The aspect of the differential use of police powers which has attracted the most analysis and controversy is the issue of racial discrimination. Numerous studies have shown that the police exercise their powers disproportionately against black people (Jefferson 1988; Reiner 1989*a*, 1993; Smith, chapter 22 in this volume). This has been well documented with respect to stop-and-search in the street (Willis 1983; Smith *et al.* 1983; Jones *et al.* 1986; Crawford *et al.* 1990; Skogan 1990); arrest (Stevens and Willis 1989; Smith *et al.* 1983; Jefferson and Walker 1992); and the decision to prosecute (Landau 1981; Cain and Sadigh 1982; Landau and Nathan 1983). While the evidence that black people are disproportionately at the receiving end of police powers is overwhelming, what remains contested is the extent to which this is due to differential offending or to discrimination by the police resulting from individual or institutionalized racism. The politically charged nature of this debate has often been reflected in the adoption of polarized either/or positions, though the evidence suggests that a complex interaction between police discrimination and social pressures generating disproportionate offending by young black people is the most plausible interpretation of the current pattern (Reiner 1989*a*, 1993; Smith chapter 22 in this volume).

It is also widely documented that ethnic minorities are disproportionately victimized by crime of all kinds, often due to racist motives, and that they perceive the police response as frequently inadequately sympathetic or effective. These problems are related to the issue of racial discrimination within the police force in the treatment of ethnic minority officers (Holdaway 1991). The evidence on race and policing will not be reviewed here in further detail, as it is discussed thoroughly by Smith in chapter 22 in this volume.

The issue of sex discrimination in policing has also been a vexed one in recent years. A fundamental difference between the debates about race and sex discrimination in policing is that whereas black people are disproportionately at the receiving end of police powers, the opposite is true of women. The very small proportion of female suspects or offenders at every stage of the criminal justice process is probably the most consistent pattern in the functioning of criminal justice systems, and feminist criminologists have rightly underlined the maleness of the overwhelming majority of processed offenders as perhaps the most important though usually overlooked feature of crime (see Heidensohn's discussion in chapter 21 of this volume). It does not follow that the police do not deal with women suspects or potential suspects in discriminatory ways. It has plausibly been suggested that police officers tend to regard women with a conventional imagery bifurcating them into either 'whores' or 'wives' (Heidensohn 1985: 58; Brogden *et al.* 1988: 119–20). A consequence could be that the low rate of formal processing of women as suspects could mask a complex web of discrimination. Some women may escape suspicion because of 'chivalry' placing them outside the frame of likely offenders in the stereotypes of investigating officers (Visher 1983; Morris 1987: 80–1), while others, such as teenage girls behaving in sexually precocious or deviant ways, or prostitutes, may be dealt with by the police at a lower threshold of entry into the system because they violate the officers' codes of acceptable behaviour, or may be seen paternalistically as in need of 'protection' from themselves (Brogden *et al.* 1988; Dunhill 1989). As Heidensohn concludes in chapter 21 in this volume, 'evidence on this topic is patchy, and conclusions necessarily tentative'.

There is much clearer evidence of discrimination at the expense of women in their treatment by the police as victims. Calls to domestic disturbances have always been a significant part of the police workload, but notoriously have tended to be treated by officers without recourse to criminal proceedings, even where evidence of assault is present (Dobash and Dobash 1979; Stanko 1985). 'Domestics' are seen as messy, unproductive, and not 'real' police work in traditional cop culture (Reiner 1978*a*: 177, 214–15, 244–5; Young 1991: 315–16). This issue has become highly charged in the last two decades, and around the world police forces have attempted to improve their response to domestic assaults, with debatable results (Edwards 1989; Hanmer *et al.* 1989; Sheptycki 1991, 1993; Dobash and Dobash 1992; Sherman 1992*a*). There has also been much concern about insensitive or even hostile treatment of rape victims, an issue dramatically highlighted a decade ago by a celebrated episode of Roger Graef's TV documentary on the Thames Valley Police which filmed a very disturbing interrogation of a rape victim (BBC 1, 18 January 1982). Despite considerable improvements since then (Blair 1985;

Temkin 1987: 158–62), the treatment of rape victims by police remains problematic (Hanmer *et al.* 1989).

It is also clear from a growing volume of evidence that women are discriminated against as police officers, in terms of career prospects as well as harassment in the job. Until less than twenty years ago discrimination within police forces was open and institutionalized in the existence of separate departments carrying out radically different functions. This itself followed from widespread resistance within (and outside) the force to the initial recruitment of policewomen in the early decades of this century (Carrier 1988). Since the Sex Discrimination Act 1975 women have been formally integrated into the same units as male officers. None the less the continuation of discrimination has been documented by numerous studies (Bryant *et al.* 1985; Jones 1986, 1987; Graef 1989: ch. 6; Young 1991: ch. 4; Heidensohn 1992; Walklate 1992). The issue of harassment and discrimination against women in the force has been vividly highlighted recently by the much publicized action brought by the former Assistant Chief Constable of Merseyside, Alison Halford, alleging discrimination against her in her attempts to gain promotion (Halford 1993). Many commentators have argued that the unequal employment and promotion of policewomen is important not only as an issue of justice, but also to dilute the machismo element in police culture which has been seen as an important source of abuse. As Heidensohn in chapter 21 of this volume makes clear, however, this argument is not firmly founded on research evidence that women officers police differently from their male colleagues, though it remains plausible (see also Heidensohn 1992).

Police discretion and the rule of law

An important ingredient of the rule of law is the principle of equality before the law. The above review of the evidence about the relationship between the operation of police discretion and social (especially racial) inequality supports the view that policing practice routinely departs from the principles of the rule of law. This conclusion is corroborated more generally by research evidence about the determinants of police decision-making in relation to their legal powers. From the outset this has demonstrated that the police in a liberal democracy are subject to a tension between the values of crime control and due process (in terms of the distinction introduced in Packer 1968; see also Sanders chapter 16 in this volume).[12] When subject to pressure to produce results in terms of effective law enforcement, the police will frequently cut corners in the procedures demanded by the principles of legality (Skolnick 1966 is the classic

[12] This tension is the obvious precipitating factor leading to miscarriages of justice, as demonstrated by recent *causes célèbres* such as the Guildford Four, the Birmingham Six, the Tottenham Three, and other cases (Woffinden 1989; Rozenberg 1992).

account of this, analysing the practices of Californian vice squad detectives in achieving convictions, often on the basis of legally improper tactics).

The space for this deviation between police practice and the rule of law is created of course by the low visibility of routine police work. This allows police officers considerable scope for the construction of *post hoc* accounts of their actions which are glossed in legally acceptable terms, even though these bear scant relationship to the real grounds for their decisions (Manning 1977, 1979; Chatterton 1979, 1983; Ericson 1981, 1982; Holdaway 1983). Observational studies have documented time and again that the decision-making process of police officers on the streets is not governed by the terms of legal discourse, even though these appear in the subsequent presentation of decisions in reports and paperwork (Smith *et al.* 1983: iv).

As argued above, the effective critique mounted by McBarnet and others against the extreme rule-scepticism implied in some early sociological studies of the police has shifted the analytic focus to the question of the interplay between legal rules and police practice, rather than seeing these as hermetically sealed distinct entities. The celebrated Policy Studies Institute research on policing London expressed the issue well in terms of distinctions among three sets of rules: 'working', 'inhibitory', and 'presentational' (Smith *et al.* 1983: iv. 169–72). 'Working' rules are those which underpin police practice. These derive largely from the informal culture of the police and bear a problematic relationship to official police policy and legal rules. 'Inhibitory' rules are those official rules which are perceived as likely to be effectively sanctioned and therefore influence practice even if they are not accepted as legitimate by the rank and file. 'Presentational' rules are those official rules which have no bearing on police practice, but which none the less provide the terms in which accounts after the event must be couched.

The implication of the early sociological research was that the low visibility of everyday police work opened up a discretionary space so that the working rules of police culture bore almost no relationship to official rules. Police policies and legal procedures amounted only to presentational rules specifying how reports should be written. They were not seriously inhibitory because of the *de facto* power provided by the low visibility and protective informal culture which shrouded deviation in a blue curtain of secrecy (Stoddard 1968). This conception of a deep gap between the law in action and the law in the books was questioned by McBarnet and the more structuralist analyses of police work which developed in the 1980s (McBarnet 1978, 1979, 1981; Ericson 1981, 1982; Shearing 1981*a*, *b*; Brogden 1982, 1983; Grimshaw and Jefferson 1987).

The 1980s in Britain also witnessed a thoroughgoing attempt to revamp police powers and legal procedures. In part this activity has purported to construct a regime of safeguards which aim to inhibit more effectively any deviation from the rule of law. The main landmark has been the Police and Criminal Evidence Act 1984, and the ongoing process of continuous assessment it generated (Zander 1991; Reiner 1992*a*: ch. 6; Sanders chapter 16 in this volume). In addition, senior police officers and HM Inspectorate of Constabulary have in recent years attempted to respond to a perceived decline in public confidence due to serious miscarriage of justice scandals by attempting to implement a cultural change in police forces, making them accept an ethical commitment to professional procedures (see for example the essays by senior officers in *Policing* 1991). The extent to which these strategies have succeeded has been subject to vigorous debate, and is largely still an open issue. The arguments will be reviewed in the section on control of discretion below. What the reform attempts themselves testify to, however, is the widespread deviation from the rule of law which has characterized policing.[13] Policing has largely reflected social power and reproduced social divisions rather than implementing impartial justice (Shearing 1981*a*; Lee 1981; Brogden *et al.* 1988: ch. 6). In the following section we will look at explanations of the pattern of operation of police discretion.

The Explanation of Police Discretion

Three broad approaches to explaining why police discretion operates as it does can be distinguished.

These are *individualistic*, *cultural*, and *structural* accounts.

Individualistic explanations

The most common concerns about police work have been about its action-orientation and impatience with legal procedural restraints, as well as the race and sex discrimination which studies have documented. These features have frequently been attributed to the idea that a peculiar kind of person is drawn to police work. In particular it has often been suggested that the police have personality patterns which predispose them to act in authoritarian ways. As the distinguished radical barrister (and now judge) Sir Stephen Sedley put it, 'the uniformed mind . . . tends frequently to be a mind for which authority has its special attraction, to

[13] Indeed, three of the leaders of current police attempts at self-reform testified to the past prevalence of 'noble cause' corruption—violation of legal procedures to achieve what was felt to be substantive justice—in a *Panorama* programme broadcast on 5 April 1993. This aroused much controversy and the chiefs were condemned for their disclosures by many rank-and-file officers (*Police Review*, 9 April 1993: 4–5, 15; 16 April: 13). However critical the response may have been of the wisdom of the chiefs' frankness, virtually no one challenged its accuracy.

which the helmet and the truncheon have a particular appeal' (Sedley 1985: 9).

A formidable body of research has been conducted to ascertain whether police work does attract people with distinctive personality characteristics, in particular authoritarianism. It is clear from many studies carried out in many different parts of the world at different times that police officers tend to have a particular constellation of attitudes which has been described as a 'police personality' (Balch 1972). The characteristics of this are in many respects similar to the psychological model of authoritarianism. What is debatable is whether this 'personality' reflects the pre-existing peculiarities of police officers as individuals, or whether it is the product of collective adjustment to the shared predicament of doing police work, a 'working personality' (Skolnick 1966: ch. 6).

This issue can only be resolved by comparing the characteristics of police recruits with control groups with similar general social characteristics. Much research attempting this has been conducted in the USA and Britain. One highly influential British study did conclude that police recruits were more authoritarian than civilian control groups (Colman and Gorman 1982). The findings of this research were sent to Lord Scarman during his inquiry into the 1981 Brixton disorders and informed his analysis which attributed such problems as racial discrimination to the failings of particular police officers rather than of the institution. However, Colman and Gorman's study has since been subject to extensive criticism on methodological grounds, especially because of the unrepresentative control groups used (Waddington 1982). Some other studies have also found disproportionate authoritarianism among police recruits (Brogden *et al.* 1988 14–15 cites examples).

The weight of research does not support the view that police recruits are more authoritarian than comparable civilian samples (McNamara 1967: 163–252; Niederhoffer 1967: 103–52; Bayley and Mendelsohn 1968: 14–30; Skolnick 1969: 252; Cochrane and Butler 1980; Brown and Willis 1985). Studies of the socialization of police recruits suggest the typical pattern is that, after a temporary liberalizing effect of initial training (Brown and Willis 1985; Fielding 1988), exposure to practical policing develops in officers a distinctive constellation of values and perspectives, akin to authoritarianism. This is better understood as a cultural adaptation to the exigencies of police work, however, than as the unfolding of a set of basic personality traits (Brogden *et al.* 1988: ch. 2; Reiner 1992*a*: ch. 3).

Cultural explanations

The impact of the informal culture of the rank and file is the most common explanation of police working practices found in the research literature. The first systematic formulation of this perspective was in Jerome Skolnick's seminal study of the work of detectives in California (Skolnick 1966: ch. 3). Synthesizing the findings of his own research and those of earlier studies, Skolnick argued that certain common tensions and problems inherently associated with the nature of the police task in liberal democracies generated a shared subculture among the police rank and file which facilitated the resolution of these difficulties.[14] The police in a liberal democracy are faced with a basic dilemma: they are under pressure to achieve results in the form of law enforcement, but are constrained by the requirements of the rule of law in the methods they use to reach their objectives. They are also visible embodiments of social authority, which exposes to them to perennial danger from those recalcitrant towards authority, as well as to ambiguities and tensions in all their social relationships. The combination of these inescapable elements of the police lot—authority, danger, pressure to achieve results without violating due process of law—gives rise to a common cultural reaction, a set of informal rules, rites, and recipes for coping.

Skolnick identified three main aspects of the cop culture, and subsequent studies have amplified these and suggested other features. (A detailed synthesis of these findings can be found in Reiner 1992*a*: ch. 3. British studies are wont to use the term 'canteen culture' to refer to the same phenomenon.) The three core characteristics of the police culture which Skolnick singled out for emphasis were suspiciousness, internal solidarity coupled with social isolation, and conservatism.

Suspiciousness is a common police attitude because it arises from the pressure to achieve results in the form of detection of offenders. It also results from the police concern with danger; people and places are constantly scrutinized to ascertain whether they present risks to the officer. Suspiciousness may also be deliberately cultivated as an aspect of police training, but fundamentally it is a way of coping with the pressures of the job. Although it is an inevitable aspect of policing, suspiciousness can raise many problems; above all, the tendency rapidly to assess the likelihood that people encountered may be offenders or dangerous makes the police particularly prone to operate with prejudiced stereotypes of potential 'villains' and 'troublemakers'. This is an important source of the discriminatory exercise of discretion which was discussed above.

Internal solidarity and *social isolation* are mutually reinforcing. Solidarity coalesces from the intense experience of confronting shared dangers and pressures, the need to be able to rely on colleagues in a tight spot, and the bonding resulting from having done so. Isolation is the

[14] Skolnick refers to this as a 'working personality', not a culture. But he is referring to a socially generated common set of values and perspectives, not a feature of individual psychodynamics. It thus seems more appropriate to use the term culture for this concept.

product of organizational aspects of the work, such as the shift system, the need to maintain social distance so as not to compromise a position of authority, and the wariness with which members of the public interact with authority figures. Even though police solidarity and isolation are inevitable to a degree, they have problematic consequences. Solidarity may act as a device for shielding wrongdoing from investigation by outsiders, even other police officers from different parts of the service. Social isolation can exacerbate the problem of the development of unrealistic or prejudiced stereotypes, determining the operation of discretion in discriminatory ways.

Conservatism in a moral and social rather than political sense is inherently related to the core police function of symbolizing and safeguarding authority. Charged with upholding the law and preserving public peace, the police are likely to have an elective affinity for a generally conservative outlook. Embracing change and empathizing with deviance are wont to generate a degree of cognitive dissonance in police officers. This is not to say that police officers can never be liberal in their sympathies and perspective, but it is unlikely to be the norm.

Political conservatism is less universal a feature of police culture, although it is certainly much more common than radicalism. Police officers have generally inclined to the right in their politics (Reiner 1992*a*: 191–4), but this leaning is subject to a countervailing structural tendency which has been manifest in some historical circumstances. The police are generally recruited from working-class origins, and some even have backgrounds in the labour movement (Reiner 1978*a*: 140, 149–50; Reiner 1991: ch. 4, 183–5). It has indeed been cogently argued that the formation of modern police organizations involved a complex process of *deradicalization* in which police officers were culturally torn away from their labour roots and sympathies (Robinson 1978).

Their own position as employees has generated conflicts and pressures which have resulted in most countries in the formation of police unions or similar representative associations (Reiner 1978*a*). While these have often been distant from, even hostile to, the general trade union and labour movements, at certain conjunctures their interests have coalesced, as happened for example in the period immediately following the First World War in both Britain and the USA. The Police Federation in England and Wales during the 1970s and 1980s became increasingly identified with the Conservative Party, playing a significant part in the Tories' successful capture of the law and order mantle in the 1979 general election. However, in recent years a variety of tensions have developed between the Conservative government and the police, primarily due to the increasing rigour with which policies to restrict public expenditure have begun to bite on the police (Rawlings 1989). The result has been an ever more evident *rapprochement* between the Police Federation and the Labour Party and concurrent alienation between the Tories and the police (see for example the account of the 1993 Police Federation Annual Conference in *Police Review*, 28 May 1993: 12–15). Despite the contradictory character of police politics, their culture undoubtedly remains predominantly conservative in a broad sense, and this is underpinned by the nature of the police role.

The sketch of police culture offered by Skolnick has been amplified and developed in several ways by subsequent analysts. Numerous studies have emphasized the important traits of *racism* and *machismo* as frequently encountered aspects of the police outlook, already adverted to by Skolnick in his account of police conservatism. (In the British context see for example Holdaway 1983; Smith *et al.* 1983; Graef 1989; Young 1991.) Others have emphasized the degree to which police officers often have a strong sense of commitment to the values of what they see as 'real' policing—fighting crime and catching criminals. Thus the pressure to produce results does not arise only from outside moral panics about law and order. Police officers often seem to have a sense of *mission* concerning their work, regarding it almost as a sacred duty, although this may be hidden behind a surface veneer of cynicism and resentment at obstacles inhibiting 'real' police work (Manning 1977; Reiner 1992*a*: 111–14). They are eager for action to achieve the ends of crime-fighting (Holdaway 1977, 1983). This connects back to the machismo element in police culture and is an important ingredient in discrimination against women within the force and the lack of seriousness with which crimes against women in the domestic context have often been regarded (Young 1991; Heidensohn 1992 and in this volume).

Researchers since Skolnick have not only amplified his account of the central characteristics of the core police culture. There has also been significant analysis of the structured variations in culture both within and among police forces.

Cultural variations within forces The rank structure and division of labour give rise to various permutations of the basic themes of police culture within police organizations. Added to these are variations due to age, gender, ethnic group, educational and social background, as well as individual personality. Although a distinctive police occupational culture along the lines indicated above has been depicted in numerous studies, it is certainly not monolithic and police officers exhibit its characteristics to varying degrees.

The most obvious cultural gulf is between the street-level officers and the management ranks. The latter have supervisory and disciplinary powers over the former. As the arbiters of the career prospects of the rank and file, the management strata in police forces clearly have potentially conflicting interests and perspectives on a number of issues. This is accentuated when (as was the case in British county forces until the Second World War) there is lateral entry of senior ranks and they come from more privileged social and educational backgrounds (Reiner 1991: ch. 2).

The divergent interests of different ranks are reflected in their organization into different representative associations (in Britain the Police Federation for ranks up to chief inspector, with more senior officers belonging to the Superintendents' Association or the Association of Chief Police Officers as appropriate). The roles of senior and street-level ranks are clearly very different. The former are mainly concerned with administration and with presenting a public face of acceptable standards of conduct to external audiences, rather than with the direct delivery of a service.

Senior officers will often be in an adversarial role *vis à vis* the rank and file, especially if scandals break out and complaints need investigation and adjudication. The rank and file often hold derogatory views of the administrative and managerial levels, who may be castigated as parasitic or hostile pen-pushers rather than 'real' police. Many studies both in Britain and abroad have emphasized this gulf between the cultures of 'street cops' and 'management cops' (Ianni and Ianni 1983; Punch 1983), which clearly introduces an important qualification into the picture of a solidary police culture.

None the less it is important not to lose sight of the common interests which unite all ranks in the police force. Officers at all levels share a stake in the status, reputation, and basic flourishing of the organization. When these are under threat there is a coalescence of interest and action. Thus since 1989 there has been a series of unprecedented common initiatives between the British police staff associations, concerned to counter a perceived decline in the public standing of the police and hostile government proposals for reorganization (notably those announced by the then Home Secretary Kenneth Clarke on 23 March 1993, aimed at restructuring the management and accountability of the police on a more 'business-like' basis). Even the normal cultural gulf between street and management cops may be analysed as something of a cynical, Faustian bargain. It allows management cops to do their business of presenting acceptable glosses of police practice to influential public audiences while being shielded from the more sordid aspects of street policing. Only when 'the wheel comes off' in a scandal does a token show of conflict between ranks occur.

In addition to the structured source of culture conflict based on the hierarchy of rank, the organizational division of labour produces systematic differences in the subculture associated with specialisms. The most hallowed is the perennial rivalry between uniform and detective branches. Each has a characteristic ideology which emphasizes the greater importance of its own role and an associated negative image of the other. Thus uniform branches will often stress the bedrock nature of their role in the organization, and that contrary to public impressions they actually apprehend the majority of offenders (Maguire and Norris 1992). The CID will be resented for taking over cases for court processing after the hard work of capture has already been accomplished, grabbing the glamour and the glory. For their part, detectives pride themselves on being at the heart of 'real' policing, dealing with crime and criminals, in particular the more serious cases (Hobbs 1988: chs. 4, 8). They will look down on the more humdrum peace-keeping, service, and low-level crime work of the patrol branches, and castigate those stuck there as plodding and dull 'woodentops'. In turn, both operational patrol and CID officers will have negative images of administrative personnel or specialists in branches like training or community relations, who are perceived as removed altogether from 'real' police work.

Although the main variations within police culture are rooted in the rank structure and specialist division of labour, differences in outlook and style are clearly discernible among groups of patrol officers at constable level, who constitute the majority of police officers. Several studies in different parts of the world and at different times have documented these. What is striking is the similarity of the types of subculture which have been depicted, even though these are referred to by different names in different studies (Reiner 1992*a*: 129–33). Four types of variation of the basic police culture have been pinpointed: a peace-keeper, a law-enforcer, an alienated cynic, and a managerially inclined professional. Essentially these correspond to different career aspirations and trajectories, based on variations in educational and social background as well as individual personality.

Peace-keepers are those who are committed to and fulfilled in the diverse jobs performed by patrol officers. They do not respond to trouble inevitably in terms of law enforcement. In Lord Scarman's terms they attach greater priority to maintaining public tranquillity than enforcing the law at all costs. They are as keen on the service role of the police as their control functions, although they neglect neither. *Law-enforcers* see 'real' policing as the control of crime and criminals. Service work and tasks like domestic disputes which are not easily assimilated into the perspective of cops vs. villains are disdained as tiresome distractions, 'rubbish'. The street cops should be left free to pursue villainy as they know best, but are hampered by outside do-gooders and their own bosses, the management cops, who are over-sensitive to legal niceties at the expense of substantive justice. *Alienated cynics* are officers who have become frustrated with failure in the job and are disenchanted with it altogether. They are merely serving out time until retirement pension requirements have been fulfilled, and they attempt to avoid work wherever possible. In police argot this type is often referred to as a 'uniform-carrier' or 'coat-hanger', wearing the uniform but not pursuing its purposes. Uniform-carriers seldom start that way. Usually they have become disillusioned by failure: either personal failure to be promoted or transferred to a desired specialism, or failure in a job, for example the acquittal of suspects the officer has invested effort in apprehending and 'knows' to be guilty. *Managerial professionals* are rank-and-file officers ambitious for promotion. In a form of anticipatory socialization they already exhibit attitudes associated with management rather than street cops. They see the virtue of all arrangements and policies ordained from on high and refrain from the general canteen chatter at the expense of the 'bosses'. If frustrated in his or her ambitions this type of constable is prime material for the uniform-carrying coterie. But for the moment they ape what are seen as the requisite attitudes of high rank and responsibility.[15]

Cultural variations among forces The emphasis of studies of police culture has been on those recurring characteristics of it which are found universally (at any rate to some degree) because they are a response to inevitable problems of the police work situation in contemporary societies. However the strength of, and balance among, features of police culture such as suspiciousness, solidarity, social isolation, and conservatism, can vary over time and from place to place. This variation among different organizations is a product of the particular social and political contexts in which forces operate, and may also be affected by deliberate management policies.

The first study to concentrate on the analysis of differences in the styles of whole police organizations was James Q. Wilson's *Varieties of Police Behaviour* (Wilson 1968). This distinguished among three departmental cultures found in Wilson's comparative research on eight forces in the USA, which he called the watchman, legalistic, and service styles. The styles were a product of departmental policy choices in part, but particular styles were only possible in conducive social and political contexts.

The *watchman* style emphasized order maintenance rather than law enforcement, and reflected the typical patrol officer's perspective writ large. Patrol officers had wide discretion in how they handled their beats. Professionalization and bureaucratization were hardly developed. The

[15] Senior officers are not themselves a monolithic group, although they may be perceived that way—as a faceless bunch of bureaucrats—by those they command. A variety of perspectives and styles can be found among them too, generated by variations in their working situations, career patterns, and individual personalities (Reiner 1991: ch. 12).

legalistic style emphasized universalistic and impartial law enforcement, with officers allowed no legitimate discretion over how rules and standards should be applied in different situations. The organization was highly bureaucratic and professional. The *service* style emphasized the provision of helpful services to citizens. The favoured reaction to deviance was the formal caution, not the (often benign) neglect of the watchman approach nor the automatic prosecution associated with the legalistic style. Public relations and community involvement were emphasized.

Each style was rooted in particular social and political preconditions. Legalistic departments had usually displaced watchman ones after a corruption scandal which brought in a reforming city administration concerned above all with formal law enforcement. Alternatively, they arose as a reflection of shifts in the balance of city power, favouring stable business groups with an interest in rational, universalistic authority as a framework for long-run planning. Paradoxically, argued Wilson, legalistic departments were most often accused of racial discrimination, despite the emphasis on impartial law enforcement. Their concern with law enforcement as a priority led to the adoption of more aggressive patrol tactics in inner-city areas which black residents perceived as harassment. The service style was possible only in middle-class suburban communities with a strong consensus on values and lifestyles.

Subsequent comparative studies of different forces have also demonstrated a range of variations in culture. Some have attributed these primarily to different policy choices by the police elite, others to the varying social and political contexts, or a mixture of both. A study of seventeen US cities in the late 1960s found that there was considerable variation in the extent to which their police practices were orientated to 'law and order' or 'civil rights' values. These were not explicable by differences in the individual demographic characteristics of the police officers: they were features of the departmental culture as a whole. To some extent the researchers found that the 'civil rights' approach was more common in areas where there was less conflict and the police had more opportunity for non-enforcement related interaction with citizens. However, the main factor appears to have been the ideologies of the police chief and the mayor (who usually was responsible for the chief's appointment). The more sympathetic these figures were to black people and their perspectives, the more policing practice was orientated towards 'civil rights' rather than 'law and order'. This suggests that policing styles can be significantly affected by political elites.

A number of British studies have also pinpointed cultural variations between forces. Cain's pioneering research in the 1960s demonstrated that there were significant differences in the cultures of a rural and a city force. The rural police were strongly integrated into their communities, but the city officers were more alienated from their publics and identified with each other. This difference between rural and urban police cultures has been a recurring theme of subsequent research, and clearly is a function of differing policing problems (Shapland and Vagg 1988; Shapland and Hobbs 1989; Young 1993).

A study comparing Devon and Cornwall with Greater Manchester when the two forces were led by chief constables whose perspectives characterized the opposite poles of policing philosophy, John Alderson and James Anderton, suggests that the rural/urban cultural difference may be accentuated by force policy (Jones and Levi 1983). Public ratings of the police in Devon and Cornwall were generally more favourable than in Greater Manchester, and police in the former also had a more accurate perception of public views than in the latter, suggesting a closer relationship. However, this was not solely the product of a general rural/urban difference. Plymouth had the lowest public satisfaction with the police in the Devon and Cornwall force area, suggesting that it is indeed harder to cultivate positive police–public relations in urban contexts. However, relations with the public appeared better than those found in relatively small country towns within the Greater Manchester force area, indicating that the overall culture of the force is also a significant factor.

A recent ethnographic study comparing two inner-city London police stations suggests that management *can* achieve discernible cultural change even in unpropitious circumstances (Foster 1989). In one station substantial changes in style and practice were introduced successfully, altering the culture in the direction intended by the Scarman Report with its philosophy of 'community policing', emphasizing the cultivation of community consent and placing greater priority on tranquillity than on law enforcement. The reason for the successful change was solid commitment and the support of the entire management hierarchy. In the other station the managerial and supervisory ranks were divided, and the attempt to introduce similar changes was frustrated by the resilience of the traditional police culture. A similar conclusion, suggesting the possibilities of reform even in tough city areas, is offered by a study of six innovative police chiefs in the USA in the 1980s who reorientated their departments towards a community policing culture (Skolnick and Bayley 1986).

The overall conclusion implied by the studies of variations in police culture is that although there are certain common tendencies which are generated by the basic features of police work in any contemporary industrial society, the strength and style of their manifestation can vary enormously. This is partly because of differences in social and political context, partly because of different management philosophies. Police culture is not a monolithic and invariant entity, but responsive to the social structure and official policy which may seek to mould it or to prevent certain cultural traits (like racial prejudice) affecting policing practice even if they cannot be eliminated entirely. This suggests that even though accounts of police culture may be descriptively true, and policing heavily influenced by the values and beliefs of that culture, explanations of police practice have to be rooted in a more fundamental structural level, which determines the culture itself.

Structural explanations

Structural explanations supplement rather than supplant cultural accounts. As we have seen, the major analyses of police culture, such as Skolnick's, do not represent this as a freestanding phenomenon into which successive generations of police are socialized as so many passive cultural dopes. The culture is generated and sustained by the problems and tensions of the police role, as it helps officers feel they can cope.

Although the culturally supported values and beliefs of police officers are an important element in explaining their practices, they are not the whole story. These values and beliefs are translated into action in concrete situations where other pressures have also to be taken into account. These include those rules of law and police policy which are effectively enforced and become inhibitory rules on police practice whatever the officers think of them in their hearts (Smith *et al.* 1983: iv 169–72). For example, officers who are racially prejudiced may none the less be restrained from acting in overtly discriminatory ways by clear and effectively sanctioned rules barring this (ibid.: ch. iv). The police may be resentful of some of the safeguards for suspects introduced by the 1984 Police and Criminal Evidence Act, but none the less will implement them to the extent that they are formulated in ways which can be and are effectively sanctioned by supervisors and/or the courts (Morgan *et al.* 1990; Reiner 1992*a*: 225–32). It is also clear that the content of police culture is not unchanging or impenetrable, and that a struggle for the hearts and minds of the rank and file, such as the Met's recent 'Plus' programme, may be capable of at least a limited degree of success.

Thus cultural analyses give an often accurate account of important immediate influences on police practice. But they must be supplemented by structural analyses of the police role (which underpins the culture), and of the context in which police work is carried out in order to ascertain what countervailing pressures are present inhibiting the straightforward translation of police values into operational practice.

Police work is structured by the core mandate and organization of the police within the social order. As argued above, the modern idea of police is of a body organized for the regular uniform patrol of public space coupled with *post hoc* investigation of reported or discovered crime or disorder. Police practice is fundamentally structured by the legal and social institution of privacy (Stinchcombe 1963). Privacy is socially patterned by class and gender. Certain groups—notably young men from socially and economically marginal groups who have restricted access to private areas for either work or leisure—are much more likely to lead their lives in public space than others. In our racially discriminatory social structures these groups are also disproportionately black. It is these groups who become 'police property' (Lee 1981), and disproportionately subject to coercive police powers (Brogden and Brogden 1984; Brogden *et al.* 1988: ch. 6; Jefferson 1988).

There is an isomorphism between the structure of power in a society and the mapping of the population as potential 'trouble' and hence suspicious in police culture (Norris 1989; Reiner 1992*a*: 117–21). This is because the content of police culture is a 'subterranean process in the maintenance of power' in a social order (Shearing 1981). Police culture is structured in a complex fashion by the place the police occupy in the social order, not an independent variable determining police practice (Ericson 1982; Brogden *et al.* 1988: ch. 3; Holdaway 1989; Fielding 1989; Reiner 1992*a*: ch. 3). The racism, sexism, impatience with legal formality, and other characteristics of police culture which have alarmed liberal critics are not simply manifestations of pathological authoritarian personalities, imported societal prejudices, excessive exposure to the *Sun*, or a self-sustaining canteen cowboy ethos. Such factors may overdetermine the character of police culture; but the basic determinant is the role the police are assigned, which is moral street-sweeping. Their control powers are primarily directed against the young, male, disproportionately black, economically marginal street population who threaten the tranquillity of public space as defined by dominant groups. Police prejudices are more a product than a cause of the differential use of police powers, which is itself a result of the socially structured nature of the police mandate (Manning 1971, 1977). The next section will consider how (if at all) this might be controlled.

The Control of Police Discretion

The English common law has developed a (controversial) doctrine which is generally referred to as constabulary independence. As stated in its strongest form by Lord Denning, this holds that a chief police officer,

> like every constable in the land . . . is not the servant of anyone, save of the law itself. No Minister of the Crown can tell him that he must, or must not, keep observation on this place or that; or that he must, or must not, prosecute this man or that one. Nor can any police authority tell him so. The responsibility for

law enforcement lies on him. He is answerable to the law alone. (*R.* v. *Metropolitan Police Commissioner, ex p. Blackburn* 1968 2 QB 136)[16]

The doctrine was summed up more pithily by a distinguished former chief constable and HM Chief Inspector of Constabulary: 'In operational matters a Chief Constable is answerable to God, his Queen, his conscience, and to no one else' (St Johnston 1978: 153; since this is said to derive from the fact that a chief officer still occupies the office of constable it is intended evidently to apply to all constables as well).

The doctrine of constabulary independence appears to give police officers in Britain a strong measure of legitimate discretion by contrast with jurisdictions where there is an ideal of full enforcement (Williams 1984*a*, *b*; Linnan 1984). The contrast is doubtless greater in jurisprudential theory than in social practice. As discussed above, the police inevitably exercise a degree of *de facto* discretion even when full enforcement statutes purport to operate. On the other hand, there are a variety of constraints upon the decision-making of the police in Britain. Indeed, it has long been an article of faith in the traditional view of the British police that they are exceptionally accountable despite—of indeed, because of—their independence of governmental institutions. As put by one of the most distinguished Metropolitan Commissioners of recent decades, Sir Robert Mark: 'The fact that the British police are answerable to the law, that we act on behalf of the community and not under the mantle of government, makes us the least powerful, the most accountable and therefore the most acceptable police in the world.' (Mark 1977: 56).

There are a variety of mechanisms by which police decision-making and discretion may be influenced. Two levels of decision-making can be distinguished in this regard: decisions taken by *individual officers* in the course of routine police work on a case-by-case basis; and *general policy* decisions about organizational matters and about how whole classes of cases should be dealt with.[17] These two levels are not hermetically sealed and distinct categories. The actual (as opposed to formal) policy of a

[16] It should be noted that these oft-cited words of Lord Denning are strictly speaking *obiter dicta* in the case under question. There has also been general agreement in the critical literature with Laurence Lustgarten's corrosive analysis that 'seldom have so many errors of law and logic been compressed into one paragraph' (Lustgarten 1986: 64). None the less, as Lustgarten himself states, however shaky a basis it may have had the doctrine of constabulary independence is now so firmly embedded in the tradition of the judiciary that they are unlikely to abandon it easily.

[17] This is superficially similar to the distinction between 'operational' and 'policy' matters which has come to be part of the common currency of interpretation of the Police Act 1964, even though the Act itself does not use these terms. The attempt to demarcate these two classes of decision sharply is doomed to failure. Purportedly policy decisions have implications for particular operations, while operational decisions are the individual atoms which constitute what *de facto* policy is. They may realize or sabotage formal policy. The attempted distinction is ideological rather than logical (Lustgarten 1986: 20–2; Reiner 1993).

police force is the product of myriad specific decisions by officers in individual incidents. As argued above in the discussion on discretion, these are problematically related to formal policy. On the other hand, all formal policy decisions have some effect on the structuring of individual decisions, even if it is only the need for street cops to find ways of covering up practices diverging from the principles espoused by management cops. None the less there are quite different mechanisms established for holding officers accountable for particular individual decisions, and for holding senior officers accountable for force policy.

Individual accountability

There are two principal channels for holding individual officers to account for alleged wrongdoing: the courts and the complaints process.

Legal accountability In traditional police ideology this is the main mechanism of police accountability in Britain (as the passage from Sir Robert Mark quoted above illustrated). Individual officers are accountable to the courts for the way that they have exercised their powers. Statute and common law on the one hand specify the powers available to the police for the accomplishment of their duties, but also, on the other, set limits on their legitimate use. The statutory powers of the police in the investigation of offences are largely consolidated in the Police and Criminal Evidence Act 1984, and in the arena of public disorder in the Public Order Act 1986. (For details of these Acts see respectively Zander 1991; and Smith 1987.)

One avenue of redress for individuals who believe they have been subject to a wrongful exercise of police powers has always been a civil action in tort against the particular constable. Until relatively recently this was usually not a practical possibility. The costs of the action have been prohibitive. In addition, police authorities were not vicariously liable at common law for the torts of constables. Since most police officers have limited personal means there was no financial incentive to sue. This has been altered by the extension of legal aid, coupled with the Police Act 1964 which did expose police authorities to vicarious liability for the wrongful actions of constables. This has made it much more worthwhile for people to take civil actions against the police for wrongful use of their powers. There has in recent years been a substantial growth of civil actions against the police, spurred also by lack of confidence in the complaints system, and substantial damages have sometimes beeen awarded to successful litigants (Clayton and Tomlinson 1987). However, the main channel of legal control over policing is by the routine safeguards over the exercise of police powers which have been developed by statute and case law.

PACE attempts for the first time to develop a comprehensive set of safeguards for suspects,[18] in the context of extended and rationalized powers for the investigation of offences. This is intended to achieve the 'fundamental balance' between adequate police powers and safeguards over their exercise which was the axiom that underlay the 1981 Royal Commission on Criminal Procedure (RCCP) Report, as well as PACE which was the Report's legislative culmination (albeit only after an exceptionally tortuous parliamentary passage: see Leigh 1986).

The exercise of any of the powers which PACE accords the police is governed by requirements which are set out partly in the Act itself, partly in the Codes of Practice which accompany it. These Codes specify detailed procedures for the police to follow concerning stop-and-search; search and seizure; detention and questioning of suspects; identification parades; and tape recording of interviews. Revised Codes, incorporating the fruits of experience, are supposed to be issued from time to time, the first of which came into effect on 1 April 1991 (Zander 1991: 60).

The RCCP sought to overcome the perennial problem of the low visibility of routine police work primarily by requiring that each exercise of a police power had to be recorded with reasons, as nearly contemporaneously as possible. PACE and the accompanying Codes of Practice rely heavily on this. For example, s. 1 of the Act extends powers to stop and search for stolen goods and a number of other prohibited articles, but requires that their exercise be justified by 'reasonable suspicion' and that the fact of and reasons for the search be recorded as soon as possible and made available to a suspect if its legality is challenged. The safeguards are underpinned by s. 67, which makes failure to comply with them a disciplinary offence. PACE also makes breaches of the Codes admissible as evidence in any criminal or civil proceedings, and gives judges a broad discretion to exclude evidence gathered in ways which would render the proceedings as a whole unfair (s. 78). In addition, PACE includes sections purporting to enhance police accountability more generally, for example through the complaints process and by community consultation.

During its protracted parliamentary passage, critics of PACE were particularly vexed about its reliance on internal police recording and discipline, and the largely discretionary role given the courts in overseeing the

[18] Prior to PACE limited protection for suspects was afforded by the Judges' Rules, a set of non-statutory administrative directions laying down procedures for questioning and taking statements originally formulated in 1912. These were much less detailed and rigorous than the Codes of Practice issued under PACE, and lacked the status derived from having a statutory underpinning. It was found by the 1977 Fisher Report into the Confait case that the Rules had little effect on the normal practices of the police. This was the immediate trigger for the establishment of the Royal Commission on Criminal Procedure which reported in 1981. The recommendations of the Royal Commission ultimately culminated in PACE, albeit with some considerable amendment (Leigh 1986).

procedures. Since the Act came into operation, however, criticism has come primarily from the police, who have complained regularly that the record-keeping and other procedural requirements hamper effective investigation. There has been an extensive programme of research evaluating the impact of PACE on police practice.[19]

Some studies emphasize the extent to which it remains the case that suspects fail to be accorded what are supposed to be their rights, and argue that the Act does not fundamentally erode the structural advantage which the police have in the investigation process, especially after a suspect is in police custody (McConville *et al.* 1991; chapter 16 in this volume). Others have suggested that the new procedures have made substantial changes in the treatment of suspects, even if there remains much scope for improvement. For example, the majority of suspects do not receive legal advice before being interviewed, despite the police being required to inform them of their rights. However, all studies concur in the finding that there has been a considerable increase in the proportion who do see a solicitor—at least a doubling (Maguire 1988; Brown 1989; Sanders *et al.* 1989; Morgan *et al.* 1990; Dixon *et al.* 1990). When the revised Codes of Practice added the requirement that suspects must also be informed that legal advice is available free of charge, the proportion taking it up increased further (Brown *et al.* 1992). The Royal Commission on Criminal Procedure which reported in June 1993, having been established as a result of the miscarriage of justice scandals in recent years recommended some further improvements in the safeguards for suspects.[20] It also appears to be the case that the courts in general have been more vigorous in excluding evidence gathered in violation of PACE procedures than they were under the old Judges' Rules (Feldman 1990).

On balance it appears that the regime of safeguards established in recent years has had some impact on police practice, inhibiting gross violations of suspects' rights. However, much of the change is doubtless presentational rather than substantive. The pressures on the police to achieve results have if anything intensified, and as Sanders rightly emphasizes in chapter 16 in this volume, it must be recognized that the police have an inevitably adversarial role in relation to suspects. The low visibility of police work will always place them in a position of power over suspects.

[19] The main studies are Maguire 1988; Brown 1989; Brown *et al.* 1992; and Mackenzie 1989; Sanders *et al.* 1989; Morgan *et al.* 1990; Bottomley *et al.* 1991; McConville *et al.* 1991. The overall debate and findings are summarized in Reiner 1992*a*: ch. 6.

[20] The Report of the Royal Commission on Criminal Justice (Runciman 1993) in the event disappointed many lawyers and civil libertarians by such controversial recommendations as limiting the right to choose trial by jury (*New Law Journal*, 9 July 1993: 981–3; *The Economist*, 10 July 1993: 13, 21–2). However, it did recommend some extended safeguards over police investigation and treatment of suspects, notably the video-taping of custody areas.

The extent of malpractice may be reduced by strict safeguards coupled with measures to expose backstage areas of policing to more scrutiny; but some discretion will always remain, as will the possibility of abuse. Legal accountability is inevitably limited by the low visibility and high discretion of police work.

The complaints process A statutory procedure for handling complaints against the police was first established by the Police Act 1964 (although many forces had already adopted similar systems long before this). The process specified by the 1964 Act relied entirely on internal police investigation and adjudication, although in serious cases these would be handled by officers from another force. The only independent element occurred in cases raising the possibility of criminal proceedings against an officer, when the papers were sent to the Director of Public Prosecutions (DPP) for a decision. For many years there was growing criticism of the absence of any independent element in the investigation and adjudication of complaints against the police.

The first step in this direction was taken by the Police Act 1976, establishing an independent Police Complaints Board (PCB) which reviewed the papers assembled by the police investigation and had the power to overrule a decision not to bring disciplinary charges. Although opposed by most police opinion—Sir Robert Mark resigned over the setting-up of the PCB—the system totally failed to command public confidence. Critics pointed to the impeccably Establishment character of PCB members, and to its complete lack of independent *investigative* powers. Reliant as it was on the case-file already constructed by the police, it is hardly surprising that the PCB almost never overturned the internal police decision not to bring charges in most cases.

In the late 1970s and early 1980s, as policing became embroiled in ever greater controversy, support for the idea of a completely independent complaints system grew, even in Establishment circles. The 1981 conversion of the Police Federation to the view that this was the only way to regain public confidence showed that this had become a widespread orthodoxy. An element of independence in the investigation, as well as adjudication of complaints, was finally achieved by PACE in 1984.[21] This replaced the PCB with the Police Complaints Authority (PCA). The PCA took over the adjudicatory powers of the PCB, but also acquired powers to supervise the police investigation in some cases. It is required to do so in complaints alleging death or serious injury caused by police abuse, and

[21] PACE introduced another important innovation in the complaints process which must also be mentioned. It established a system for the informal resolution of minor complaints, subject to the consent of complainant and police officer. This relieves the formal system of the pressure of having to investigate these cases, and also appears to achieve a higher level of complainant satisfaction (Corbett 1991).

empowered to do so in any other case where it considers it to be in the public interest. Other cases or categories of complaint may also be brought to the PCA's attention by the Home Office.

A major study evaluating the PCA suggests that it can operate effectively in its supervisory role, although resource constraints prevent more than token supervision in a few cases (Maguire and Corbett 1991). However, the same research—as well as other studies—shows that the system fails to command confidence among complainants, the police or the public at large (Maguire and Corbett 1991; Brown 1987). It seems clear that only a fully independent system could command widespread confidence, although chief constables remain convinced it would be less effective in reality (Reiner 1991: 286–300). Experience in other countries with independent systems shows that these can operate reasonably satisfactorily, although without necessarily sustaining more complaints than internal procedures, and consequently not satisfying critical opinion any better (McMahon and Ericson 1984; Loveday 1988; Goldsmith 1991).

The complaints process offers a possible avenue of redress for people wronged by the police, but it is doubtful whether it could ever function so effectively as to be a significant control over police discretion in the first place. No matter who does the investigating, complaints against the police are hard to sustain because of the low visibility of most encounters, which turns most cases into a head-on collision of testimony in which the complained-against police officer has the advantage at least of the benefit of the doubt.

Policy accountability

The discretion of the rank-and-file police officer is structured (although not determined) by the management style and policies developed by the chief officer in a force. What avenues are there for the public accountability of these policy decisions?

The present formal structure of police governance in England and Wales is set out primarily in the Police Act 1964 (which largely implemented the recommendations of the 1962 Report of the Royal Commission on the Police). The Act consolidated the so-called 'tripartite' system of accountability for the (currently forty-one) provincial forces in England and Wales. It left untouched the arrangements for the two London forces, the Metropolitan and the City of London Police, which remain much as they were when they were first founded in the 1820s and 1830s.

All these issues are currently under review. In March 1993 the then Home Secretary, Kenneth Clarke, announced proposals for sweeping changes, to be implemented together with the recommendations of the Sheehy Inquiry into Police Responsibilities and Rewards, and any relevant proposals emanating from the Royal Commission on Criminal Justice, both of which were expected to report in the spring. It was anticipated that a new Police Bill would set out fundamental changes in the organization of policing in the autumn of 1993. Mr Clarke's proposals may be modified by his replacement as Home Secretary by Michael Howard in May 1993, as well as by parliamentary and other debate. The discussion here is based on the present law, together with the Clarke proposals and leaks which emanated from the Sheehy Inquiry before its report.[22]

The present tripartite structure for provincial forces divides accountability among: chief constables, responsible for 'direction and control' of their forces; local police authorities, with the duty of 'maintenance of an adequate and efficient police force for the area' (s. 4); and the Home Secretary, who is expected to use a variety of powers to further the efficiency of policing throughout the country. In the provincial forces police authorities consist two-thirds of elected local councillors, and one-third of JPs (who are selected by the Lord Chancellor). In the Met there is no local police authority at all. Since the 1829 Metropolitan Police Act which established it, its Commissioners have been accountable directly to the Home Secretary as their police authority. The City of London force is accountable locally to the Common Council of the City of London (the Aldermen and Mayor).

Since the passage of the 1964 Act there has been vigorous debate about what its provisions really do and should imply (Marshall 1965, 1978; Lustgarten 1986; Reiner 1991: ch. 2). Until the late 1970s this dispute was conducted among academic and other commentators rather than the parties in the system itself. It seemed to be accepted by all participants that the role of police authorities was to be a sounding-board for the professional expert, the chief constable (Brogden 1977). Police authorities might exercise some influence over such broad policy matters as how the budget should be spent, but even on this and certainly on 'operational' issues they were generally content to accept the guidance of the chief. The Home Secretary's formidable powers remained largely dormant.

What broke up this cosy consensus was the increasing politicization of many policing issues in the late 1970s (Reiner 1992*a*: ch. 2). In 1991

[22] In the event both the White Paper *Police Reform* (Home Office 1993) and the Report of the Sheehy Inquiry (Sheehy Report 1993) were published at the end of June 1993. The recommendations of the Inquiry were very much as anticipated, and provoked a storm of protest from police staff associations and local government bodies (*Police Review*, 2 July 1993: 4–5, 12–13; 9 July: 4–5, 12–14; 16 July: 4–6, 12–15; *Police*, July 1993: 8–16, 26). The Police Federation organized a mass protest rally at Wembley on 20 July, and the AMA/ACC a joint conference in Westminster on 21 July. At the end of July press reports were suggesting that the new Home Secretary Michael Howard was considering dropping some of the more controversial proposals. Legislation was still planned for the autumn of 1993.

radical Labour councils were elected in most large cities, and the metropolitan police authorities which they controlled began to try to influence policing policy in a number of controversial areas, notably public order tactics in the urban disorders of that year (and later in the 1984–5 miners' strike and the 1985 disorders). Highly publicized conflicts occurred in several large cities between the chief constable and the police authority, most notably in Greater Manchester (McLaughlin 1990) and Merseyside (Loveday 1985). In London the Greater London Council (GLC) led a vigorous campaign to establish a local police authority for the capital, and its Police Committee was an important monitoring body covering Met policy carefully and critically, despite its lack of any statutory powers.

These clashes underlined the impotence of local police authorities within the tripartite system. Under the provisions of the Police Act 1964, in cases of dispute the Home Secretary acts as arbiter. Invariably, Home Secretaries supported the chief constables against the attempts of the police authorities to influence what chiefs described as 'operational' matters. To maintain the myth of local accountability, the Home Office has encouraged the proliferation of police–community consultative committees. These lack any power and have been widely characterized as 'talking-shops' which legitimate rather than challenge local police dominance over police authorities (Morgan 1989, 1992).

In the late 1980s the almost complete powerlessness of the local authority leg of the tripartite structure has been made manifestly clear by developments in statute and case law. The Local Government Act 1985 abolished the metropolitan authorities, replacing them with Joint Boards which have proved much more pliant to police leadership (Loveday 1991). In an important case in 1988 the Northumbria Police Authority sought a judicial review of the decision by the Home Secretary to make available plastic bullets for riot-control training to local forces where the police authority refused to sanction their purchase by the chief constable. The Court of Appeal rejected the Authority's case, holding that both under the 1964 Police Act and under the Royal Prerogative the Home Secretary had a duty to do what he felt necessary for preserving the Queen's peace, on advice from the chief constable and HM Inspectorate of Constabulary. This entitled the Home Secretary to override the police authority's views (*R.* v. *Secretary of State for the Home Department ex p. Northumbria Police Authority* 1988, *Weekly Law Reports* 590).

The tripartite structure is now one in which the local police authority enjoys only such influence as the other two parties, the chief constable and the Home Secretary, deem it wise to accord it. Most chief constables, however, tend to accept policies emanating from the Home Office as binding, even though they are formally merely advisory (Reiner 1991: ch.

11). This is not only because the Home Secretary controls most of the purse strings (since 1985 51 per cent of local police expenditure comes directly from Home Office funding, and much of the rest comes indirectly from central government in the shape of local taxation support grants). The Home Secretary also controls the various career aspirations chief constables may still entertain, such as appointment as an HM Inspector of Constabulary or even a knighthood or peerage. Few chief constables would be sanguine about crossing a Home Secretary, who is ultimately the dominant element in the tripartite structure.

The net effect of the proposals announced by Kenneth Clarke as Home Secretary in March 1993 would be to accentuate strongly this centralizing thrust which has become ever more apparent (Reiner and Spencer 1993). The elected councillor element on police authorities would go down from two-thirds to a half. The other half would be made up of JPs plus people appointed by the Home Secretary, who would also select the chairperson. The declared intention is to make police authorities more 'business-like', but the business they will be doing is that of central government rather than that of the local electorate. Mr Clarke also announced the intention to end the long anomaly whereby the Met does not have a local police authority. The new London authority was to have followed the lines of the reconstituted provincial ones, but it has been reported since that the capital's Conservative MPs are opposing this and that the likely outcome is an authority with members chosen entirely by the Secretary of State (the Northern Ireland model; cf. *Police Review*, 28 May 1993: 4). Although Mr Clarke did not announce amalgamations of forces into a smaller number of regional mega-forces (which had been widely predicted), he did indicate that he expected such mergers would take place in the future. This would further distance forces from local electorates and facilitate central influence.

The plans also included freeing chief constables from central government controls over how their budgets could be spent. However, this new independence is likely to be somewhat illusory. The Sheehy Inquiry recommended that all police officers be appointed on short-term contracts and subject to performance related pay (PRP). The criteria for successful performance, and the assessment of whether these have been satisfied, will be governed by the Home Secretary and the police authorities controlled by central government appointees. In effect this amounts to a formidably centralized system of control over policing. Without abandoning the constabulary independence doctrine in any formal way, the Home Secretary will colour the use of discretion by constables by setting and assessing the criteria for performance which will determine pay and job security. The two measures of performance indicated by Mr Clarke in his speech were crime clear-up rates and response times to public calls. Such targets are likely to become the ones to which all police efforts will be geared, at the expense of wider conceptions of quality of service or legitimacy. The possibilities for citizens influencing decision-making through their elected representatives will be even dimmer than they are at present.

CONCLUSION: THE FUTURE OF POLICING

British policing is facing momentous changes, as the previous section has already indicated. The architect of these changes, former Home Secretary Kenneth Clarke, claimed that they amounted to the most profound reorganization since Sir Robert Peel's original establishment of the Metropolitan Police in 1829. Granted some political licence for this hyperbole, there can be no doubt that the police have experienced themselves as in deep crisis in recent years. They are facing great upheavals, only partly as a result of the government's reorganization. This conclusion will attempt to analyse their predicament, and hazard a glance at the future. Although the concentration will be on the British police, the underlying pressures to which they are subject are found in other jurisdictions too.

One interpretation of the particularity of the crisis in British policing is indeed that the police are undergoing a normalization process. Having been in certain respects very different from other police forces, either in Europe or in the rest of the common-law world (Bayley 1985; Mawby 1991), they are now undergoing something of a convergence in organization and style. Facing similar domestic crime problems, and indeed confronting a common problem of growing international crime, police forces are adapting in similar ways, and this is facilitated by a direct diffusion of ideas and innovations through conferences, exchanges and increasing collaboration (Anderson 1989; Dorn *et al.* 1991; McLaughlin 1992; Anderson and den Boer 1992; Walker 1993).

The modern British police were established during the first half of the nineteenth century against widespread opposition across the social and political spectrum (Emsley 1991; chapter 4 in this volume; Reiner 1992*a*: ch. 1). As a way of overcoming this resistance, the architects of the British police tradition (Peel and the first two Metropolitan Commissioners, Rowan and Mayne), strove to construct a distinctive organizational style and image for the police (Miller 1977; Emsley 1991; Reiner 1992*a*; ch. 2). This emphasized the idea of the police as an essentially civilian body, minimally armed, relying primarily on the same legal powers to deal with crime as all citizens shared, strictly subject to the rule of law, insulated from governmental control, and drawn from a representative range of working-class backgrounds to facilitate popular identification. A recent official inquiry by the police staff associations succinctly summarized this conception: 'traditional British policing is relatively low in numbers, low on power, and high on accountability; . . . it is undertaken with public consent' (*Operational Policing Review*, 1990: 4).

This image of British policing did not develop because of some peculiar affinity of British culture with civic values, as some more conservative historians have suggested (Robinson 1979 offers a crisp critique of this interpretation). In colonial situations (including Ireland) British policing developed on an overtly militaristic model (Brogden 1987; Palmer 1988). The pacific image of the British bobby was a myth deliberately constructed in order to defuse the virulent opposition to the very idea of police which existed in early nineteenth-century Britain. That it succeeded owed at least as much to the more general long-term social process of greater social integration and consensus over the century between the 1850s and the 1950s as to any actions of the police themselves.

By the mid-1950s, however, the police had negotiated a huge degree of public support. This is attested to by the evidence of surveys and much contemporary documentation, indicating a high degree of popular trust, even affection, for the police (Reiner 1992*a*: 56–60). The police stood as symbols of the nation. Behind this facade there is much evidence from oral histories and memoirs that in the 'Golden Age' of consent to policing, the treatment of the 'police property' groups at the base of the social hierarchy was rough, ready, and uninhibited by notions of legality or justice (Mark 1978: chs. 2–4; Cohen 1979; White 1990; Brogden 1991; Young 1991). None the less, the high regard the population in general accorded the police in Britain was unparalleled in the experience of any other country.

In the last twenty-five years the process of growing acceptance of the police in Britain has been reversed. A number of changes have plunged them into acute controversy and conflict: corruption and miscarriage of justice scandals; accusations of race and sex discrimination; increasing public disorder and the militarization of police tactics (Jefferson 1990; Waddington 1991; Waddington 1992); rising crime and an apparently declining police ability to deal with it; decreasing public accountability as forces have grown larger, more centralized, and more reliant on technology (Reiner 1992*a*: ch. 2). In recent years the leaders of police forces have recognized this problem and tried to introduce reforms to deal with it. They have sought to professionalize management standards, improve training, streamline working procedures, and become more open to the public through consultation of various kinds. They have tried to reorientate the culture of policing around an explicit mission of service and ethos of consumerism (Reiner 1992*a*: 7; *Policing* 1991).

None of this self-engineered change has been sufficient to satisfy the government. As discussed above, the former Home Secretary Kenneth Clarke has launched a restructuring of police organization and accountability intended to make policing more 'business-like', according to standards set by central government and its local appointees. The police feel under attack as never before, and all the staff associations have strongly condemned the government's plans. At the annual conference of the Police Federation in May 1993 the ritual roasting of the Home Secretary contrasted strikingly with the enthusiastic reception for Labour's Tony Blair (*Police Review*, 28 May 1993: 12–13). The political alignments over policing appear to have turned full circle from the days when law and order was seen as a clear Tory issue, and the police were the pets of the Thatcher government (see Downes and Morgan chapter 5 in this volume).

The political space for this government confrontation with the police comes from the erosion of public support which was discussed above. The police are widely perceived as guilty of systematic malpractice as well as falling down on the job, despite generous treatment in terms of pay and conditions compared to other public services throughout the 1980s. This perception is largely exaggerated: malpractice was certainly prevalent in the past as well, though more readily covered up. Although police resources have increased they have been outstripped by the growing demands placed upon the police. Between 1981 and 1991 the total number of police officers in England and Wales rose by 6.3 per cent, from about 120,000 to 127,100, and the number of civilian staff rose by 24 per cent to nearly 47,000 (Barclay *et al.* 1993: 69). However, recorded crime increased by 96 per cent (Home Office 1992: 15), emergency (999) calls to the police by 72 per cent, and the number of vehicles on the road by 38 per cent (Association of Chief Police Officers 1993: 3). Clearly the growth in police personnel has nowhere near kept pace with the increased demand for police services. Whether justified or not, however, there has clearly been a decline in public confidence in the police, even though this remains robust compared to many other public institutions (Reiner 1992*b*: 762–4).

The prospects for reversing this decline by the government's new 'business-like' approach are dim. The government strategy rests upon a fundamental misconception of policing, which while common has for many years been called into question by research conducted by the Home Office itself. The premise underlying current initiatives is that, if properly organized, policing can have a significant impact on crime levels, deterring crime in the first place by uniform patrol, and detecting criminals efficiently after the event if crimes do occur. This can be referred to as the rational deterrent model of policing.

By this standard it certainly seems at first sight that the police in Britain are far less efficient and effective than they used to be, despite large increases in resources. In the period since the Second World War recorded crime levels have increased inexorably. In 1950 the police recorded about 500,000 offences; by 1992 this had increased to 5.4 million. While this increase may be due in part to increases in reporting by the public and recording by the police, the evidence of victim surveys (notably the Home Office British Crime Surveys) suggests that there has also been a substantial increase in victimization (Bottomley and Pease 1986; Mayhew and Maung 1992; chapter 6 in this volume). The proportion of these crimes which are cleared up by the police has fallen dramatically over the same period, from nearly 50 per cent to 29 per cent in 1991 (Home Office 1992: 25). While the clear-up rate is a notoriously inadequate measure of police performance (Audit Commission 1990), the decline in it has been politically damaging for the police, and has prompted the government's current policing initiatives.

There is, however, a substantial body of research evidence, much of it emanating from the Home Office Research and Planning Unit, suggesting that policing resources and tactics have at best a tenuous relationship to levels of crime or the clear-up rate (Clarke and Hough 1980, 1984; Reiner 1992*a*: 146–56). Innovative strategies may have some impact in particular situations but not on the overall levels of crime (Reiner 1992*a*: 153–6; Sherman 1992*b*). The police should be seen primarily as managers of crime and keepers of the peace; they are not realistically a vehicle for reducing crime substantially. Crime is the product of deeper social forces, largely beyond the ambit of any policing tactics, and the clear-up rate is a function of crime levels and other aspects of workload rather than of police efficiency.

Underlying the many specific causes of controversy over policing, such as malpractice, militarization, or apparently declining effectiveness, there is a deeper and more fundamental change in contemporary society, often labelled as 'postmodernity' (Reiner 1992*b*). We noted above that the rise of a specific organization specializing in policing functions coincides with the development of modern nation-states, and is an aspect of the process by which they sought to gain centralized control over a particular territory. This was particularly true of the British case, where bureaucratic police organizations came into being comparatively late by European standards and coincided with the historical trajectory towards greater social integration after the initial impact of the industrial revolution. The British police have always been unique on a comparative scale for concentrating in the same organization a variety of policing functions—crime prevention, detection, peace-keeping, public order maintenance, and the preservation of state security—which in other countries are divided among separate bodies. In all societies the symbolic functions of the police are at least as important as their direct instrumental effectiveness in dealing with crime and disorder (Manning 1977). This is particularly true in Britain, where the police came to stand—together with the monarchy, whose peace they are sworn to protect—as symbols of consensual and legitimate order.

The position of the police as an organization symbolizing national unity and order is threatened fundamentally by the advent of those social changes labelled as 'postmodernity'. The term has been used by social theorists from a variety of perspectives to refer to a complex set of cultural, social, and economic developments which are seen as fundamentally transforming the modern world into a new kind of social order. The most common theme of these analyses is the sense of fragmentation and pluralism. Whereas accounts of modernization reflect a Whig notion of unilinear progress, the postmodernist perspective calls into question any 'grand narrative' of historical development (Lyotard 1984).

Postmodern culture lacks any central reference-point or conception of the good life (Harvey 1989; Jameson 1992). The role of intellectuals is no longer that of 'legislators' mapping brave new worlds of progress but that of 'interpreters' of a pluralistic mosaic of lifestyles, none of which can trump the others in legitimacy. Consumerism becomes the driving force of action, the 'pleasure principle' displacing the Puritan asceticism and discipline which formed the cultural foundation of modern industrialism (Bauman 1987).

The social structure of postmodernity follows the same dynamic of fragmentation, dis-organization, pluralism, and decentring (Giddens 1990). As one of its leading theorists puts it: 'The postmodern order is split into a multitude of contexts of action and forms of authority . . . The nation state declines in importance and the cohesive totality is replaced by a multiplicity of sites of social reproduction' (Giddens 1992). Economic changes have transformed the economic and social framework, dispersing the centralized 'Fordist' production systems of modern times (Hall and Jacques 1989) and polarizing the class structure into what is often referred to as the 'two thirds, one-third society' (Therborn 1989). While the majority participate, albeit very unevenly and insecurely, in unprecedented levels of consumption, a substantial and growing 'underclass' is permanently and hopelessly excluded (Dahrendorf 1985: ch. 3; Galbraith 1992). Certainly with the political dominance of free-market economic policies there is no prospect at all of their incorporation into the general social order. In other words, the 'police property' group is far larger than ever before, and more fundamentally alienated. This economic fragmentation interacts with a long and complex process of cultural diversification, declining deference, erosion of moral absolutes, 'desubordination' (Miliband 1978) and growing 'anomia' (Dahrendorf 1985: ch. 2) to create a more turbulent, disorderly social world.

In this context, the British conception of the police as a body with an omnibus mandate, symbolizing order and harmony, becomes increasingly anachronistic. The British police are likely to move more towards the international pattern of specialist national units for serious crime, terrorism, public order, large-scale fraud, and other national or international problems. Local police providing services to particular communities will remain, but with sharp differences between 'service'-style organizations in stable suburban areas, and 'watchman' bodies with the rump duties of the present police, keeping the lid on underclass symbolic locations.

For those in society who can afford it, provision of security will be increasingly privatized, either in residential areas or in the 'mass private property' where more and more middle-class leisure and work takes place (Shearing and Stenning 1983, 1987; South 1988, Rawlings 1991; Johnston 1991, 1992; Shearing 1992). Specialized human policing in any form, however, will become a smaller part of an array of impersonal control processes built into the environment, technological control and surveillance devices, and the guarding and self-policing activities of ordinary citizens. *The* police will be replaced by a more varied assortment of bodies with policing functions, and a more diffuse array of policing processes. Police officers can no longer be totems symbolizing a cohesive social order which no longer exists. They will have to perform specific pragmatic functions of crime management and emergency peace-keeping in an effective and just way, or forfeit popular and political support.

Selected Further Reading

There are now a number of texts which synthesize and review the research and debates about policing in Britain. These include the following: R. Reiner, *The Politics of the Police*, 2nd edn (Hemel Hempstead: Harvester Wheatsheaf, 1992); M. Brogden, T. Jefferson, and S. Walklate, *Introducing Policework* (London: Unwin Hyman, 1988); S. Uglow, *Policing Liberal Society* (Oxford: Oxford University Press, 1988); M. Stephens, *Policing: The Critical Issues* (Hemel Hempstead: Harvester Wheatsheaf, 1988); N. Fielding, *The Police and Social Conflict* (London: Athlone, 1991).

Useful collections of readings giving representative samples of the research literature are: S. Holdaway, ed., *The British Police* (London: Edward Arnold, 1989); R. Reiner and J. Shapland, eds., *Why Police? Policing in Britain*, special issue of the *British Journal of Criminology*, 1987, 27/1; R. Morgan and D. Smith, eds., *Coming to Terms with Policing* (London: Routledge, 1989); M. Weatheritt, ed., *Police Research: Some Future Prospects* (Aldershot: Avebury, 1989); R. Reiner and M. Cross, eds., *Beyond Law and Order* (London: Macmillan, 1991); M. Tonry and N. Morris, eds., *Modern Policing* (Chicago: Chicago University Press, 1992).

For a general history see C. Emsley, *The English Police: A Political and Social History* (Hemel Hempstead: Harvester Wheatsheaf, 1991).

For accounts of police culture see P. Manning, *Police Work* (Cambridge, Mass.: MIT Press, 1977); S. Holdaway, *Inside the British Police* (Oxford: Blackwell, 1983); R. Graef, *Talking Blues* (London: Collins, 1989); M. Young, *An Inside Job* (Oxford: Oxford University Press, 1991).

The world of detectives is looked at in D. Hobbs, *Doing the Business: Entrepreneurship, the Working Class and Detectives in the East End of London* ((Oxford: Oxford University Press, 1988).

Accountability is examined in L. Lustgarten, *The Governance of the Police* (London: Sweet and Maxwell, 1986); R. Reiner, *Chief Constables* (Oxford: Oxford University Press, 1991); R. Reiner and S. Spencer, eds., *Accountable Policing: Effectiveness, Empowerment and Equity* (London: Institute for Public Policy Research 1993).

Developments in criminal procedure since the Police and Criminal Evidence Act 1984 are analysed in M. McConville, A. Sanders, and R. Leng, *The Case for the Prosecution* (London: Routledge, 1991).

The complaints system is considered in A. Goldsmith, ed., *Complaints against the Police: The Trend to External Review* (Oxford: Oxford University Press, 1991).

On issues of gender see J. Hanmer, E. A. Stanko, and J. Radford, eds., *Women, Policing and Male Violence* (London: Routledge, 1989); F. Heidensohn, *Women in Control? The Role of Women in Law Enforcement* (Oxford: Oxford University Press, 1992).

Race issues are considered in E. Cashmore and E. McLaughlin, eds., *Out of Order? Policing Black People* (London: Routledge, 1991).

Privatization is analysed in N. South, *Policing for Profit* (London: Sage, 1988); L. Johnston, *The Rebirth of Private Policing* (London: Routledge, 1992).

Public order tactics are debated by T. Jefferson, *The Case against Paramilitary Policing* (Milton Keynes: Open University Press, 1990); P. A. J. Waddington, *The Strong Arm of the Law* (Oxford: Oxford University press, 1991); D. Waddington, *Contemporary Issues in Public Disorder* (London: Routledge, 1992).

An academic journal published in Britain devoted to policing issues is *Policing and Society*, edited by Robert Reiner and Rod Morgan. Two quarterly British journals pitched primarily at a professional readership are *Policing* and *The Police Journal*. Regular police-related news is carried in the weekly *Police Review* and monthly *Police* (the magazine of the Police Federation).

REFERENCES

ALDERSON, J. (1979), *Policing Freedom*. Plymouth: Macdonald and Evans.

ALLEN, R. ed. (1984), *Discretion in Law Enforcement*, special issue of *Law and Contemporary Problems*, 47/4.

ANDERSON, M. (1989). *Policing the World.* Oxford: Oxford University Press.

ANDERSON, M., and DEN BOER, M., eds. (1992), *European Police Co-operation*. Edinburgh: University of Edinburgh Department of Politics.

ASSOCIATION OF CHIEF POLICE OFFICERS (1993), *Your Police: The Facts*. London: ACPO.

AUDIT COMMISSION (1990), *Effective Policing: Performance Review in Police Forces*. London: HMSO.

AYRES, R., and WHEELEN, T. (1977), *Collective Bargaining in the Public Sector*. Gaithersburg, Md: International Association of Chiefs of Police.

BALCH, R. W. (1972), 'The Police Personality: Fact or Fiction?', *Journal of Criminal Law, Criminology and Police Science*, 63/1: 106–19.

Banton, M. (1964), *The Policeman in the Community*. London: Tavistock.

—— (1971), 'The Sociology of the Police', *Police Journal*, 44/3: 227–43.

—— (1973), 'The Sociology of the Police II', *Police Journal*, 46/4: 341–62.

—— (1975), 'The Sociology of the Police III', *Police Journal*, 48/4: 299–315.

BARCLAY, G. C., DREW, C., HATTON, R., and ABBOT, C. (1993), *Digest 2: Information on the Criminal Justice System in England and Wales*. London: Home Office Research and Statistics Department.

BAUMAN, Z. (1987), *Legislators and Interpreters: Modernity, Postmodernity and Intellectuals*. Cambridge: Polity.

BAYLEY, D. (1985), *Patterns of Policing*. New Brunswick: Rutgers University Press.

BAYLEY, D., and BITTNER, E. (1984), 'Learning the Skills of Policing', *Law and Contemporary Problems*, 47/4: 35–60.

BAYLEY, D., and MENDELSOHN, H. (1968), *Minorities and the Police*. New York: Free Press.

BECKER, H. (1964), *Outsiders*. New York: Free Press.

—— (1967), 'Whose Side Are We On?', *Social Problems*, 14/3: 239–47.

BENNETT, T. (1990), *Evaluating Neighbourhood Watch*. Aldershot: Gower.

BERNSTEIN, S., PLATT, T., FRAPPIER, G., RAY, G., SCHAUFFLER, R., TRUJILLO, L., COOPER, L., CURRIE, E., and HARRING, S. (1974), *The Iron Fist and the Velvet Glove: An Analysis of the US Police*. Berkeley: Center for Research on Criminal Justice. (Third edn. 1982.)

BITTNER, E. (1967*a*), 'The Police on Skid Row: A Study in Peacekeeping', *American Sociological Review*, 32/5: 699–715.

—— (1967*b*), 'Police Discretion in the Emergency Apprehension of Mentally Ill Persons', *Social Problems*, 14/3: 278–92.

—— (1970), *The Functions of the Police in Modern Society*. Chevy Chase: National Institute of Mental Health.

—— (1974), 'Florence Nightingale in Pursuit of Willie Sutton: A Theory of the Police', in H. Jacob, ed., *The Potential for Reform of Criminal Justice*, 17–44. Beverly Hills: Sage.

Black, D. (1970), 'Production of Crime Rates', *American Sociological Review*, 35: 733–48.

—— (1971), 'The Social Organisation of Arrest', *Stanford Law Review*, 23: 1087–1111.

Black, D., and Reiss, A. (1967), 'Patterns of Behaviour in Police and Citizen Transactions', in US President's Commission on Law Enforcement and the Administration of Justice, *Studies in Crime and Law Enforcement in Major Metropolitan Areas*, Field Surveys III: 2. Washington, DC: US Government Printing Office.

—— (1970), 'Police Control of Juveniles', *American Sociological Review*, 35: 63–77.

Blair, I. (1985), *Investigating Rape: A New Approach for Police*. London: Croom Helm.

Bordua, D., ed. (1967), *The Police: Six Sociological Essays*. New York: Wiley.

Bottomley, A. K., Coleman, C., Dixon, D., Gill, M., and Wall, D. (1991), *The Impact of PACE: Policing in a Northern Force*. Kingston upon Hull: University of Hull Centre for Criminology and Criminal Justice.

Bottomley, K., and Pease, K. (1986), *Crime and Punishment: Interpreting the Data*. Milton Keynes: Open University Press.

Bottoms, A. E., and Stevenson, S. (1990), 'The Politics of the Police 1958–1970', in R. Morgan, ed., *Policing, Organised Crime and Crime Prevention* (British Criminology Conference Papers 4), 1–18. Bristol: Bristol University Centre for Criminal Justice.

—— (1992), 'What Went Wrong? Criminal Justice Policy in England and Wales 1945–70', in D. Downes, ed., *Unravelling Criminal Justice*, 1–45. London: Macmillan.

Brogden, A., and Brogden, M. (1984), 'From Henry VIII to Liverpool 8: The Unity of Police Street Powers', *International Journal of the Sociology of Law*, 12/1: 37–58.

Brogden, M. (1977), 'A Police Authority: The Denial of Conflict', *Sociological Review*, 25/2: 325–49.

—— (1982), *The Police: Autonomy and Consent*. London: Academic Press.

—— (1983), 'The Myth of Policing By Consent', *Police Review*, 22 April.

—— (1987), 'The Emergence of the Police: The Colonial Dimension', *British Journal of Criminology*, 27/1: 4–14.

—— (1991), *On the Mersey Beat: An Oral History of Policing Liverpool Between the Wars*. Oxford: Oxford University Press.

Brogden, M., Jefferson, T., and Walklate, S. (1988), *Introducing Policework*. London: Unwin.

Brown, D. (1987), *The Police Complaints Procedure: A Survey of Complainants' Views*. London: HMSO.

—— (1989), *Detention at the Police Station Under the Police and Criminal Evidence Act 1984*. London: HMSO.

Brown, D., Ellis, T., and Larcombe, K. (1992), *Changing the Code: Police Detention Under the Revised PACE Codes of Practice*. London: HMSO.

Brown, L., and Willis, A. (1985), 'Authoritarianism in British Police Recruits: Importation, Socialisation or Myth?', *Journal of Occupational Psychology*, 58/1: 97–108.

Bryant, L., Dunkerley, D., and Kelland, G. (1985), 'One of the Boys', *Policing*, 1/4: 236–44.

Bunyan, T. (1976), *The Political Police in Britain*. London: Quartet.

Cain, M. (1971), 'On the Beat: Interactions and Relations in Rural and Urban Police Forces', in S. Cohen, ed., *Images of Deviance*, 62–97. Harmondsworth: Penguin.

—— (1973), *Society and the Policeman's Role*. London: Routledge.

—— (1977), 'An Ironical Departure: The Dilemma of Contemporary Policing', in K. Jones, ed., *Yearbook of Social Policy in Britain*. London: Routledge.

—— (1979), 'Trends in the Sociology of Police Work', *International Journal of Sociology of Law*, 7/2: 143–67.

Cain, M., and Sadigh, S. (1982), 'Racism, the Police and Community Policing', *Journal of Law and Society*, 9/1: 87–102.

Carrier, J. (1988), *The Campaign for the Employment of Women as Police Officers*. Aldershot: Avebury.

Chapman, D. (1970), *Police State*. London: Macmillan.

Chatterton, M. (1976), 'Police in Social Control', in J. King, ed., *Control without Custody*, 104–22. Cambridge: Cambridge University Institute of Criminology.

—— (1979), 'The Supervision of Patrol Work under the Fixed Points System', in S. Holdaway, ed., *The British Police*, 83–101. London: Edward Arnold.

—— (1983), 'Police Work and Assault Charges', in M. Punch, ed., *Control in the Police Organisation*, 194–221. Cambridge, Mass.: MIT Press.

—— (1987), 'Assessing Police Effectiveness', *British Journal of Criminology*, 27/1: 80–6.

Clarke, A. (1983), 'Holding the Blue Lamp: Television and the Police in Britain', *Crime and Social Justice*, 19: 44–51.

Clarke, R., and Hough, M. (1984), *Crime and Police Effectiveness*. London: Home Office Research Unit.

—— eds. (1980), *The Effectiveness of Policing*. Farnborough: Gower.

Clayton, R., and Tomlinson, H. (1987), *Civil Actions against the Police*. London: Sweet and Maxwell.

Cochrane, R., and Butler, A. J. (1980), 'The Values of Police Officers, Recruits and Civilians in England', *Journal of Police Science and Administration*, 8/8: 205–11.

Cohen, P. (1979), 'Policing the Working Class City', in B. Fine, R. Kinsey, J. Lea, S. Picciotto, and J. Young, eds., *Capitalism and the Rule of Law*, 118–36. London: Hutchinson.

Cohen, S. (1972), *Folk Devils and Moral Panics*. London: Paladin; 2nd edn. 1980, Oxford: Martin Robertson.

—— (1985), *Visions of Social Control*. Cambridge: Polity.

Cohen, S., and Scull, A., eds. (1983), *Social Control and the State*. Oxford: Martin Robertson.

Colman, A., and Gorman, L. (1982), 'Conservatism, Dogmatism and Authoritarianism amongst British Police Officers', *Sociology*, 16/1: 1–11.

Corbett, C. (1991), 'Complaints against the Police: The New Procedure of Informal Resolution', *Policing and Society*, 2/1: 47–60.

COWELL, D., JONES, T., and YOUNG, J. eds. (1982), *Policing the Riots*. London: Junction Books.

CRAWFORD, A., JONES, T., WOODHOUSE, T., and YOUNG, J. (1990), *The Second Islington Crime Survey*. London: Middlesex Polytechnic Centre for Criminology.

CRAY, E. (1972), *The Enemy in the Streets*. New York: Anchor.

CRITCHLEY, T. A. (1978), *A History of Police in England and Wales*, 2nd edn. London: Constable. (First edn. 1967.)

CUMMING, E., CUMMING, I., and EDELL, L. (1964), 'The Policeman as Philosopher, Guide and Friend', *Social Problems*, 12/3: 276–86.

CURRIE, C. (1986), 'Divisional Command', *Policing*, 2/4: 318–24.

DAHRENDORF, R. (1985), *Law and Order*. London: Sweet and Maxwell.

DAVIS, K. C. (1969), *Discretionary Justice*. Urbana: University of Illinois Press.

—— (1975), *Police Discretion*. St. Paul: West Publishing.

DIXON, D., BOTTOMLEY, A. K., COLEMAN, C. A., GILL, M., and WALL, D. (1990), 'Safeguarding the Rights of Suspects in Police Custody', *Policing and Society*, 1/2: 115–40.

DOBASH, R., and DOBASH, R. (1979), *Violence against Wives*. London: Open Books.

—— (1992), *Women, Violence and Social Change*. London: Routledge.

DORN, N., SOUTH, N., and MURJI, K. (1991), 'Mirroring the Market? Police Reorganisation and Effectiveness against Drug Trafficking', in R. Reiner and M. Cross, eds., *Beyond Law and Order*, 91–106. London: Macmillan.

DOWNES, D., and ROCK, P. (1988), *Understanding Deviance*. Oxford: Oxford University Press.

DUNHILL, C., ed. (1989), *The Boys in Blue: Women's Challenge to Policing*. London: Virago.

EDWARDS, S. (1989), *Policing 'Domestic' Violence*. London: Sage.

EMSLEY, C. (1983), *Policing and its Context 1750–1870*. London: Macmillan.

—— (1991), *The English Police: A Political and Social History*. Hemel Hempstead: Wheatsheaf.

ERICSON, R. (1981), *Making Crime: A Study of Detective Work*. Toronto: Butterworths.

—— (1982), *Reproducing Order: A Study of Police Patrol Work*. Toronto: University of Toronto Press.

FABIAN, R. (1950), *Fabian of the Yard*. London: Naldrett.

—— (1954), *London after Dark*. London: Naldrett.

FELDMAN, D. (1990), 'Regulating Treatment of Suspects in Police Stations: Judicial Interpretation of Detention Provisions in the Police and Criminal Evidence Act 1984' *Criminal Law Review*: 452–571.

FIELDING, N. (1988), *Joining Forces*. London: Routledge.

—— (1989), 'Police Culture and Police Practice', in M. Weatheritt, ed., *Police Research: Some Future Prospects*, 77–88. Aldershot: Avebury.

FOSTER, J. (1989), 'Two Stations: An Ethnographic Analysis of Policing in the Inner City', in D. Downes, ed., *Crime and the City*, 128–53. London: Macmillan.

GALBRAITH, J. K. (1992), *The Culture of Contentment*. London: Sinclair-Stevenson.

GARLAND, D. (1985*a*), 'The Criminal and His Science: A Critical Account of the Formation of Criminology at the End of the Nineteenth Century', *British Journal of Criminology*, 25/1: 109–37.

—— (1985*b*), *Punishment and Welfare: A History of Penal Strategies*. Aldershot: Gower.

GIDDENS, A. (1990), *The Consequences of Modernity*. Cambridge: Polity.

—— (1992), 'Uprooted Signposts at Century's End', *The Higher*, 17 January: 21–2.

GILL, M., and MAWBY, R. (1990), *A Special Constable*. Aldershot: Avebury.

GOLDSMITH, A., ed. (1991), *Complaints against the Police: The Trend To External Review*. Oxford: Oxford University Press.

GOLDSTEIN, H. (1964), 'Police Discretion: The Ideal vs. the Real', *Public Administration Review*, 23: 140–8.

GOLDSTEIN, J. (1960), 'Police Discretion not to Invoke the Criminal Process: Low Visibility Decisions in the Administration of Justice', *Yale Law Journal*, 69: 543–94.

GORER, G. (1955), *Exploring English Character*. London: Cresset.

GOULDEN, J. (1970), 'The Cops Hit the Jackpot', *The Nation*, 23 November: 520–33.

GOULDNER, A. (1954), *Patterns of Industrial Bureaucracy*. London: Routledge.

—— (1968), 'The Sociologist as Partisan', *The American Sociologist*, May: 103–16.

GRAEF, R. (1989), *Talking Blues*. London: Collins.

GRAHAM, F. (1970), *The Due Process Revolution: The Warren Court's Impact on Criminal Law*. Rochelle Park, NJ: Hayden Book Co.

GREENE, J., and MASTROFSKI, S., eds., (1988), *Community Policing: Rhetoric or Reality?* New York: Praeger.

GRIMSHAW, R., and JEFFERSON, T. (1987), *Interpreting Policework*. London: Unwin.

HAIN, P., ed. (1979), *Policing the Police*. London: Calder.

—— (1980), *Policing the Police 2*. London: Calder.

HALFORD, A. (1993), *No Way Up the Greasy Pole*. London: Constable.

HALL, S., CRITCHER, C., JEFFERSON, T., CLARKE, J., and ROBERTS, B. (1978), *Policing the Crisis*. London: Macmillan.

HALL, S., and JACQUES, M., eds. (1989), *New Times: The Changing Face of Politics in the 1990s*. London: Lawrence and Wishart.

HANMER, J., RADFORD, J., and STANKO, E. A., eds. (1989), *Women, Policing and Male Violence*. London: Routledge.

HARRIS, R. (1970), *Justice: The Crisis of Law, Order and Freedom in America*. London: Bodley Head.

HART, J. (1951), *The British Police*. London: Allen and Unwin.

—— (1955), 'Reform of the Borough Police 1835–1856', *English Historical Review*, 70/3: 411–27.

—— (1956), 'The County and Borough Police Act 1856', *Public Administration*, 34/3: 405–17.

HARVEY, D. (1989), *The Condition of Postmodernity: An Inquiry into the Origins of Cultural Change*. Oxford: Blackwell.

HEIDENSOHN, F. (1985), *Women and Crime*. London: Macmillan.

HEIDENSOHN, F. (1992), *Women in Control? The Role of Women in Law Enforcement*. Oxford: Oxford University Press.

HOBBS, D. (1988), *Doing the Business: Entrepreneurship, The Working Class and Detectives in the East End of London*. Oxford: Oxford University Press.

HOLDAWAY, S. (1977), 'Changes in Urban Policing', *British Journal of Sociology*, 28/2: 119–37.

—— (1989), 'Discovering Structure: Studies of the British Police Occupational Culture', in M. Weatheritt, ed., *Police Research: Some Future Prospects*, 55–76. Aldershot: Avebury.

—— (1983), *Inside the British Police*. Oxford: Blackwell.

—— (1991), *Recruiting A Multi-Ethnic Police Force*. London: HMSO.

—— ed. (1979), *The British Police*. London: Edward Arnold.

HOOGENBOOM, B. (1991), 'Grey Policing: A Theoretical Framework', *Policing and Society*, 2/1: 17–30.

HOME OFFICE (1992), *Criminal Statistics: England and Wales 1991*, Cm 2134. London: HMSO.

—— (1993), *Police Reform*, Cm 2281. London: HMSO.

—— (1985), *Taking Account of Crime: Key Findings from the Second British Crime Survey*. London: HMSO.

HOUGH, M., and MAYHEW, P. (1983), *The British Crime Survey*. London: HMSO.

IANNI, E. R., and IANNI, F. (1983), 'Street Cops and Management Cops: The Two Cultures of Policing', in M. Punch, ed., *Control in the Police Organisation*, 251–74. Cambridge, Mass.: MIT Press.

IRVING, B., and MCKENZIE, I. (1989), *Police Interrogation*. London: Police Foundation.

JAMESON, F. (1992), *Postmodernism: Or the Cultural Logic of Late Capitalism?* London: Verso.

JEFFERSON, T. (1988), 'Race, Crime and Policing: Empirical, Theoretical and Methodological Issues', *International Journal of the Sociology of Law*, 16/4: 521–39.

—— (1990), *The Case against Paramilitary Policing*. Milton Keynes: Open University Press.

JEFFERSON, T., and GRIMSHAW, R. (1984), *Controlling the Constable*. London: Muller.

JEFFERSON, T., and WALKER, M. (1992), 'Ethnic Minorities in the Criminal Justice System', *Criminal Law Review*: 83–96.

JEFFERSON, T., WALKER, M., and SENEVIRATNE, M. (1992), 'Ethnic Minorities, Crime and Criminal Justice: A Study in a Provincial City', in D. Downes, ed., *Unravelling Criminal Justice*, 138–64. London: Macmillan.

JOHNSTON, L. (1991), 'Privatisation and the Police Function: From "New Police" to "New Policing"', in R. Reiner and M. Cross, eds., *Beyond Law and Order*, 18–40. London: Macmillan.

—— (1992), *The Rebirth of Private Policing*. London: Routledge.

JONES, S. (1986), 'Caught in the Act', *Policing*, 2/2: 129–40.

—— (1987), *Policewomen and Equality*. London: Macmillan.

JONES, S., and LEVI, M. (1983), 'The Police and the Majority: The Neglect of the Obvious', *Police Journal*, 56/4: 351–64.

JONES, T., MCLEAN, B., and YOUNG, J. (1986), *The Islington Crime Survey*. Aldershot: Gower.

KAPLAN, J., and SKOLNICK, J. (1982), *Criminal Justice: Introductory Cases and Materials*, 3rd edn. New York: Foundation Press.

KINSEY, R. (1984), *The Merseyside Crime Survey*. Liverpool: Merseyside County Council.

KINSEY, R., LEA, J. and YOUNG, J. (1986), *Losing the Fight against Crime*. Oxford: Blackwell.

KLOCKARS, C. (1985), *The Idea of Police*. Beverly Hills: Sage.

LA FAVE, W. (1962), 'The Police and Non-Enforcement of the Criminal Law', *Wisconsin Law Review*: 104–37, 179–239.

—— (1965), *Arrest: The Decision to Take a Suspect into Custody*. Boston: Little, Brown.

LAMBERT, J. (1969), 'The Police Can Choose', *New Society* 14/364: 430–2.

—— (1970), *Crime, Police and Race Relations*. Oxford: Oxford University Press.

LANDAU, S. (1981), 'Juveniles and the Police', *British Journal of Criminology*, 21/1: 27–46.

LANDAU, S., and NATHAN, G. (1983), 'Selecting Delinquents for Cautioning in the London Metropolitan Area', *British Journal of Criminology*, 23/2: 128–49.

LANDIS, P. A. (1956), *Social Control: Social Organisation and Disorganisation in Process*. Chicago: Chicago University Press.

LEE, J. A. (1981), 'Some Structural aspects of Police Deviance in Relations with Minority Groups', in C. Shearing, ed., *Organisational Police Deviance*, 49–82. Toronto: Butterworths.

LEE, M. (1901), *A History of Police in England*. London: Methuen.

LEIGH, L. (1986), 'Some Observations on the Parliamentary History of the Police and Criminal Evidence Act 1984', in C. Harlow, ed., *Public Law and Politics*. London: Sweet and Maxwell.

LEMERT, E. (1967), *Human Deviance, Social Problems and Social Control*. Englewood Cliffs, NJ: Prentice-Hall.

LEON, C. (1989), 'The Special Constabulary', *Policing*, 5/4: 265–86.

LINNAN, D. K. (1984), 'Police Discretion in a Continental European Administrative State: The Police of Baden–Württemberg in the Federal Republic of Germany', *Law and Contemporary Problems*, 47/4: 185–224.

LOVEDAY, B. (1985), *The Role and Effectiveness of the Merseyside Police Committee*. Liverpool: Merseyside County Council.

—— (1988), 'Police Complaints in the USA', *Policing*, 4/3: 172–93.

—— (1991), 'The New Police Authorities', *Policing and Society*, 1/3: 193–212.

LUSTGARTEN, L. (1986), *The Governance of the Police*. London: Sweet and Maxwell.

LYOTARD, J-F. (1984), *The Postmodern Condition*. Manchester: Manchester University Press.

MCBARNET, D. (1978), 'The Police and the State' in G. Littlejohn, B. Smart, J. Wakeford and N. Yuval-Davis, eds., *Power and the State*, 23–34. London: Croom Helm.

—— (1979), 'Arrest: The Legal Context of Policing', in S. Holdaway, ed., *The British Police*, 24–40. London: Edward Arnold.

McBarnet, D. (1981), *Conviction*. London: Macmillan.

McConville, M., Sanders, A., and Leng, R. (1991), *The Case for the Prosecution: Police Suspects and the Construction of Criminality*. London: Routledge.

McConville, M., and Shepherd, D. (1992), *Watching Police, Watching Communities*. London: Routledge.

McLaughlin, E. (1990), 'Community, Policing and Accountability: A Case Study of Manchester 1981–1988', Ph.D. thesis, University of Sheffield.

—— (1992), 'The Democratic Deficit: European Unity and the Accountability of the British Police', *British Journal of Criminology*, 32/4: 473–87.

McMahon, M., and Ericson, R. (1984), *Policing Reform*. Toronto: University of Toronto Centre of Criminology.

McNamara, J. (1967), 'Uncertainties in Police Work: The Relevance of Police Recruits' Backgrounds and Training', in D. Bordua, ed., *The Police*, 163–252. New York: Wiley.

Maguire, M. (1988), 'Effects of the "PACE" Provisions on Detention and Questioning', *British Journal of Criminology*, 28/1: 19–43.

Maguire, M., and Corbett, C. (1991), *A Study of the Police Complaints System*. London: HMSO.

Maguire, M., and Norris, C. (1992), *The Conduct and Supervision of Criminal Investigations*. London: HMSO.

Manning, P. (1971), 'The Police: Mandate, Strategies and Appearances', in J. D. Douglas, ed., *Crime and Justice in American Society*, 149–94. Indianapolis: Bobbs-Merrill.

—— (1977), *Police Work: The Social Organisation of Policing*. Cambridge, Mass.: MIT Press.

—— (1979), 'The Social Control of Police Work', in S. Holdaway, ed., *The British Police*, 41–65. London: Edward Arnold.

Manning, P., and Van Maanen, J., eds. (1978), *Policing: A View from the Streets*. Santa Monica: Goodyear.

Marenin, O. (1983), 'Parking Tickets and Class Repression: The Concept of Policing in Critical Theories of Criminal Justice', *Contemporary Crises*, 6/2: 241–66.

Mark, R. (1977), *Policing a Perplexed Society*. London: Allen and Unwin.

—— (1978), *In the Office of Constable*. London: Collins.

Marshall, G. (1965), *Police and Government*. London: Methuen.

—— (1978), 'Police Accountability Revisited', in D. Butler and A. H. Halsey, eds., *Policy and Politics*, 51–65. London: Macmillan.

Martin, J. P., and Wilson, G. (1969), *The Police: A Study in Manpower*. London: Heinemann.

Matza, D. (1964), *Delinquency and Drift*. New York: Wiley.

—— (1969), *Becoming Deviant*. Englewood Cliffs, NJ: Prentice-Hall.

Mawby, R. (1991), *Comparative Policing Issues*. London: Unwin.

—— (1992), 'Comparative Police Systems: Searching for a Continental Model . . .', in K. Bottomley, T. Fowles, and R. Reiner, eds., *Criminal Justice: Theory and Practice*, 108–32. London: Institute for the Study and Treatment of Delinquency/British Society of Criminology.

MAYHEW, P., and MAUNG, N. A. (1992), *Surveying Crime: Findings from the 1992 British Crime Survey*, Home Office Research and Statistics Department Findings 2. London: Home Office.

MILIBAND, R. (1978), 'A State of Desubordination', *British Journal of Sociology*, 29/4: 399–409.

MILLER, W. (1977), *Cops and Bobbies*. Chicago: Chicago University Press.

MOORE, M. (1992), 'Problem-Solving and Community Policing', in M. Tonry and N. Morris, eds., *Modern Policing*, 99–158. Chicago: Chicago University Press.

MORGAN, R. (1989), 'Policing By Consent: Legitimating the Doctrine', in R. Morgan and D. Smith, eds., *Coming to Terms with Policing*, 217–34. London: Routledge.

—— (1992), 'Talking about Policing', in D. Downes, ed., *Unravelling Criminal Justice*, 165–83. London: Macmillan.

MORGAN, R., MCKENZIE, I., and REINER, R. (1990), *Police Powers and Policy: A Study of Custody Officers*, Final Report to the Economic and Social Research Council. London: ESRC.

MORRIS, A. (1987), *Women, Crime and Criminal Justice*. Oxford: Blackwell.

MORRISON, C. (1984), 'Why PC Plod Should Come Off the Beat', *The Guardian*, 30 July: 8.

MUIR, W. K. (1977), *The Police: Streetcorner Politicians*. Chicago: Chicago University Press.

NIEDERHOFFER, A. (1967), *Behind the Shield*. New York: Doubleday.

NORRIS, C. (1989), 'Avoiding Trouble: The Police Officer's Perception of Encounters With the Public', in M. Weatheritt, ed., *Police Research: Some Future Prospects*, 89–106. Aldershot: Avebury.

PACKER, H. (1968), *The Limits of the Criminal Sanction*. Stanford: Stanford University Press.

PALMER, S. H. (1988), *Police and Protest in England and Ireland 1780–1850*. Cambridge: Cambridge University Press.

PARK, R., and BURGESS, E. (1929), *Introduction to the Science of Sociology*. Chicago: Chicago University Press.

PASQUINO, P. (1978), 'Theatrum Politicum: The Genealogy of Capital – Police and the State of Prosperity', *Ideology and Consciousness*, 4: 41–54.

PILIAVIN, I., and BRIAR, S. (1964), 'Police Encounters with Juveniles', *American Journal of Sociology*, 70/2: 206–14.

PLATT, A., and COOPER, L., eds. (1974), *Policing America*. Englewood Cliffs, NJ: Prentice-Hall.

POLICING (1991), *The Way Ahead*, special issue of *Policing*, 7/3.

PUNCH, M. (1979*a*), 'The Secret Social Service', in S. Holdaway, ed., *The British Police*, 102–17. London: Edward Arnold.

—— (1979*b*), *Policing the Inner City*. London: Macmillan.

—— (1983), 'Officers and Men', in M. Punch, ed., *Control in the Police Organisation*, 227–50. Cambridge, Mass.: MIT Press.

—— (1985), *Conduct Unbecoming: The Social Construction of Police Deviance and Control*. London: Tavistock.

PUNCH, M., and NAYLOR, T. (1973), 'The Police: A Social Service', *New Society*, 24/554: 358–61.

RADZINOWICZ, L. (1948–68), *A History of English Criminal Law* vols. 1–4. London: Stevens.

RAWLINGS, P. (1989), 'Creeping Privatisation? The Police, the Conservative Government and Policing in the Late 1980s', in R. Reiner and M. Cross, eds., *Beyond Law and Order*. London: Macmillan.

—— (1991), 'Creeping Privatisation? The Police, the Conservative Government and Policing in the Late 1980s', in R. Reiner and M. Cross, eds., *Beyond Law and Order*, 41–58. London: Macmillan.

REINER, R. (1978*a*), *The Blue-Coated Worker*. Cambridge: Cambridge University Press.

—— (1978*b*), 'The Police, Class and Politics', *Marxism Today*, 22: 69–80.

—— (1978*c*), 'The Police in the Class Structure', *British Journal of Law and Society*, 5/2: 166–84.

—— (1988), 'British Criminology and the State', *British Journal of Criminology*, 29/1: 138–58.

—— (1989*a*), 'Race and Criminal Justice', *New Community*, 16/1: 5–22.

—— (1989*b*), 'The Politics of Police Research', in M. Weatheritt, ed., *Police Research: Some Future Prospects*, 3–20. Aldershot: Avebury.

—— (1991), *Chief Constables*. Oxford: Oxford University Press.

—— (1992*a*), *The Politics of the Police*, 2nd edn. Hemel Hempstead: Wheatsheaf.

—— (1992*b*), 'Policing a Postmodern Society', *Modern Law Review*, 55/6: 761–81.

—— (1992*c*), 'Police Research in the United Kingdom: A Critical Review', in N. Morris and M. Tonry, eds., *Modern Policing*, 435–508. Chicago: Chicago University Press.

—— (1993), 'Race, Crime and Justice: Models of Interpretation', in L. Gelsthorpe and B. McWilliam, eds., *Minority Ethnic Groups and the Criminal Justice System*. Cambridge: Cambridge University Institute of Criminology.

REINER, R., and SPENCER, S., eds. (1993), *Accountable Policing: Effectiveness, Empowerment and Equity*. London: Institute for Public Policy Research.

REISS, A. J. (1971), *The Police and the Public*. New Haven: Yale University Press.

REITH, C. (1938), *The Police Idea*. Oxford: Oxford University Press.

—— (1940), *Police Principles and the Problem of War*. Oxford: Oxford University Press.

—— (1943), *British Police and the Democratic Ideal*. Oxford: Oxford University Press.

—— (1948), *A Short History of the Police*. Oxford: Oxford University Press.

—— (1952), *The Blind Eye of History*. London: Faber.

—— (1956), *A New Study of Police History*. London: Oliver and Boyd.

ROBINSON, C. D. (1978), 'The Deradicalisation of the Policeman', *Crime and Delinquency*, 24/2: 129–51.

—— (1979), 'Ideology as History', *Police Studies*, 2/2: 35–49.

ROBINSON, C. D., and SCAGLION, R. (1987), 'The Origin and Evolution of the Police Function in Society', *Law and Society Review*, 21/1: 109–53.

ROCK, P., and COHEN, S. (1970), 'The Teddy Boy', in V. Bogdanor and R. Skidelsky, eds., *The Age of Affluence 1951–1964*, 288–320. London: Macmillan.

ROSHIER, R. (1989), *Controlling Crime*. Milton Keynes: Open University Press.

ROYAL COMMISSION ON THE POLICE (1962), *Final Report*, Cmnd. 1728. London: HMSO.

ROZENBERG, J. (1992), 'Miscarriages of Justice', in E. Stockdale and S. Casale, eds., *Criminal Justice Under Stress*, 91–117. London: Blackstone.

RUMBAUT, R. G., and BITTNER, E. (1979), 'Changing Conceptions of the Police Role: A Sociological Review', in N. Morris and M. Tonry, eds., *Crime and Justice*, vol. 1, 239–88. Chicago: Chicago University Press.

RUNCIMAN, VISCOUNT (1993), *Report of the Royal Commission on Criminal Justice*, Cmnd. 2263. London: HMSO.

ST JOHNSTON, E. (1978), *One Policeman's Story*. Chichester: Barry Rose.

SANDERS, A., BRIDGES, L., MULVANEY, A., and CROZIER, B. (1989), *Advice and Assistance at Police Stations and the 24-Hour Duty Solicitor Scheme*. London: Lord Chancellor's Department.

SCARMAN, LORD (1981), *The Brixton Disorders*, Cmnd 8427. London: HMSO.

SCHWARTZ, R. D., and MILLER, J. C. (1964), 'Legal Evolution and Societal Complexity', *American Journal of Sociology*, 70/1: 159–69.

SCRATON, P. (1985), *The State of the Police*. London: Pluto.

SEDLEY, S. (1985), 'The Uniformed Mind', in J. Baxter and L. Koffman, eds., *The Police: The Constitution and the Community*, 5–10. London: Professional Books.

SHAPLAND, J., and HOBBS, R. (1989), 'Policing on the Ground', in R. Morgan and D. Smith, eds., *Coming To Terms with Policing*, 11–30. London: Routledge.

SHAPLAND, J., and VAGG, J. (1988), *Policing by the Public*. London: Routledge.

SHEARING, C. (1981*a*), 'Subterranean Processes in the Maintenance of Power', *Canadian Review of Sociology and Anthropology*, 18/3: 283–98.

—— ed. (1981*b*), *Organisational Police Deviance*. Toronto: Butterworths.

—— (1984), *Dial-A-Cop: A Study of Police Mobilisation*. Toronto: University of Toronto Centre of Criminology.

—— (1992), 'The Relation between Public and Private Policing', in M. Tonry and N. Morris, eds., *Modern Policing*, 399–434. Chicago: Chicago University Press.

SHEARING, C., and STENNING, P. (1983), 'Private Security: Implications for Social Control', *Social Problems*, 30/5: 493–506.

—— (1984), 'From the Panopticon to Disney World', in A. N. Doob and E. L. Greenspan, eds., *Perspectives in Criminal Law: Essays in Honour of John Ll. J. Edwards*, 335–49. Toronto: Canada Law Book Co.

—— eds. (1987), *Private Policing*. Beverly Hills: Sage.

SHEEHY REPORT (1993), *Report of the Inquiry into Police Responsibilities and Rewards*, Cm. 2280 I, II. London: HMSO.

SHEPTYCKI, J. (1991), 'Innovations in the Policing of Domestic Violence in London, England', *Policing and Society*, 2/2: 117–37.

—— (1993), *Innovations in Policing Domestic Violence*. Aldershot: Avebury.

SHERMAN, L. (1992*a*), *Policing Domestic Violence: Experiments and Policy Dilemmas*. New York: Free Press.

—— (1992*b*), 'Police and Crime Control', in M. Tonry and N. Morris, eds., *Modern Policing*, 159–230. Chicago: Chicago University Press.

SILVER, A. (1967), 'The Demand for Order in Civil Society', in D. Bordua, ed., *The Police*, 1–24. New York: Wiley.

Skogan, W. (1990), *The Police and Public in England and Wales: A British Crime Survey Report*. London: HMSO.

Skolnick, J. (1966), *Justice without Trial*. New York: Wiley.

—— (1969), *The Politics of Protest*. New York: Bantam.

Skolnick, J., and Bayley, D. (1986), *The New Blue Line*. New York: Free Press.

—— (1988), *Community Policing: Issues and Practices around the World*. Washington, DC: National Institute of Justice.

Skolnick, J., and Fyfe, J. (1993), *Above the Law: Police and The Excessive Use of Force*. New York: Free Press.

Smith, A. (1978 [1763]), *Lectures on Jurisprudence*. Oxford: Oxford University Press.

Smith, A. T. H. (1987), *Offences against Public Order*. London: Sweet and Maxwell.

Smith, D., Gray, J., and Small, S. (1983), *Police and People in London*, 4 vols. London: Policy Studies Institute.

South, N. (1988), *Policing for Profit*. London: Sage.

Sparks, R. (1992), *Television and the Drama of Crime*. Milton Keynes: Open University Press.

Spitzer, S. (1975), 'Punishment and Social Organisation: A Study of Durkheim's Theory of Evolution', *Law and Society Review*, 9/4: 613–37.

—— (1987), 'Security and Control in Capitalist Societies: The Fetishism of Security and the Secret Thereof', in J. Lowman, R. J. Menzies, and T. S. Palys, eds., *Transcarceration: Essays in the Theory of Social Control*, Aldershot: Gower.

Spitzer, S., and Scull, A. (1977), 'Privatisation and Capitalist Development: The Case of the Private Police', *Social Problems*, 25/1: 18–29.

Stanko, E. A. (1985), *Intimate Intrusions: Women's Experience of Male Violence*. London: Routledge.

Stevens, P., and Willis, C. (1989), *Race, Crime and Arrests*. London: HMSO.

Stinchcombe, A. (1963), 'Institutions of Privacy in the Determination of Police Administrative Practice', *American Journal of Sociology*, 69/2: 150–60.

Stoddard, E. (1968), 'The Informal Code of Police Deviancy: A Group Approach to Blue-Coat Crime', *Journal of Criminal Law, Criminology and Police Science*, 59/2: 201–13.

Storch, R. (1975), 'The Plague of Blue Locusts: Police Reform and Popular Resistance in Northern England 1840–1857', *International Review of Social History*, 20/1: 61–90.

—— (1976), 'The Policeman as Domestic Missionary', *Journal of Social History*, 9/4: 481–509.

Tarling, R. (1988), *Police Work and Manpower Allocation*, Home Office Research and Planning Unit Paper no. 47. London: Home Office.

Taylor, I., Walton, P., and Young, J. (1973), *The New Criminology*. London: Routledge.

—— eds. (1975), *Critical Criminology*. London: Routledge.

Temkin, J. (1987), *Rape and the Legal Process*. London: Sweet and Maxwell.

Therborn, G. (1989), 'The Two-Thirds, One-Third Society', in S. Hall and M. Jacques, eds., *New Times*, 103–15. London: Lawrence and Wishart.

Trojanowicz, R., and Bucqueroux, B. (1990), *Community Policing*. Cincinnati: Anderson Publishing.

Van Maanen, J. (1973), 'Observations on the Making of Policemen', *Human Organisation*, 32/4: 407–18.

—— (1974), 'Working the Street', in H. Jacob, ed., *The Potential for Reform of Criminal Justice*, 83–130. Beverly Hills: Sage.

—— (1978), 'The Asshole', in P. Manning and J. Van Maanen, eds., *Policing: A View from the Street*. Santa Monica: Goodyear.

Vincent, C. E. Howard (1893), *The Police Code and General Manual of the Criminal Law for the British Empire*. London: Francis Edwards and Simkin.

Visher, C. (1983), 'Gender, Police Arrest Decisions and Notions of Chivalry', *Criminology*, 21/1: 5–28.

Vold, G., and Bernard, T. (1985), *Theoretical Criminology*, 3rd edn. New York: Oxford University Press.

Waddington, D. (1992), *Contemporary Issues in Public Disorder* London: Routledge.

Waddington, P. A. J. (1982), 'Conservatism, Dogmatism and Authoritarianism in the Police: A Comment', *Sociology*, 16/4: 592–4.

—— (1983), 'Beware the Community Trap', *Police*, March: 34.

—— (1991), *The Strong Arm of the Law*. Oxford: Oxford University Press.

Walker, N. (1993), 'The International Dimension', in R. Reiner and S. Spencer, eds., *Accountable Policing: Effectiveness, Empowerment and Equity*, 113–71. London: Institute for Public Policy Research.

Walklate, S. (1992), 'Jack and Jill Join Up at Sun Hill: Public Images of Police Officers', *Policing and Society*, 2/3: 219–32.

Werthman, C., and Piliavin, I. (1967), 'Gang Members and the Police', in D. Bordua, ed., *The Police*, 56–98. New York: Wiley.

Westley, W. (1953), 'Violence and the Police', *American Journal of Sociology*, 59/1: 34–41.

—— (1956), 'Secrecy and the Police', *Social Forces*, 34/2: 254–7.

—— (1970), *Violence and the Police*. Cambridge: MIT Press.

Whitaker, B. (1964), *The Police*. London: Penguin.

White, J. (1990), *The Worst Street in London*. London: Routledge.

Williams, G. (1984*a*), *The Law and Politics of Police Discretion*. Westport: Greenwood Press.

—— (1984*b*), 'Police Rulemaking Revisited: Some New Thoughts on an Old Problem', *Law and Contemporary Problems*, 47/4: 123–84.

Willis, C. (1983), *The Use, Effectiveness and Impact of Police Stop and Search Powers*, Home Office Research and Planning Unit Paper no. 15 London: Home Office.

Wilson, C. (1993), 'Police', in W. Outhwaite, T. Bottomore, E. Gellner, R. Nisbet, and A. Touraine, eds., *The Blackwell Dictionary of Twentieth-Century Social Thought*, 475. Oxford: Blackwell.

Wilson, J. Q. (1968), *Varieties of Police Behaviour*. Cambridge: Harvard University Press.

Woffinden, B. (1989), *Miscarriages of Justice*. London: Coronet.

Young, J. (1971), 'The Role of the Police as Amplifiers of Deviancy', in S. Cohen, ed., *Images of Deviance*, 27–61. London: Penguin.

Young, M. (1991), *An Inside Job*. Oxford: Oxford University Press.

—— (1993), *In the Sticks: An Anthropologist in a Shire Force*. Oxford: Oxford University Press.

Zander, M. (1991), *The Police and Criminal Evidence Act 1984*, 2nd edn. London: Sweet and Maxwell.

Zedner, L. (1993), 'Social Control', in W. Outhwaite, T. Bottomore, E. Gellner, R. Nisbet and A. Touraine, eds., *The Blackwell Dictionary of Twentieth-Century Social Thought*, 585–7. Oxford: Blackwell.

16

From Suspect to Trial

ANDREW SANDERS

CRIME CONTROL AND DUE PROCESS

The principles underlying different criminal justice systems vary according to history, culture, and ideology. The adversary principle is an important characteristic of the English system and of other common law systems such as those of Australia, Canada, and the USA. This principle is often characterized as embodying the search for 'proof' rather than 'truth' (Damaska 1973). The search for 'truth' is usually said to be embodied in 'civil law' systems (such as the French), which are 'inquisitorial'.

To understand why 'proof' and 'truth' are not synonymous we may examine the 'due process' and 'crime control' models developed by Packer (1968) and Maguire and Norris (1992: ch. 4). We shall also see that the apparent opposition between 'proof' and 'truth' is not sustainable. No system corresponds exactly with either model (as no system is entirely adversarial or entirely inquisitorial), but in most systems the values of one or the other model appear to predominate. 'Due process' values prioritize civil liberties in order to secure the maximal acquittal of the innocent, risking acquittal of some guilty. 'Crime control' values prioritize the conviction of the guilty, risking the conviction of some (fewer) innocents and infringement of the liberties of some citizens to achieve the system's goals. Due process models tightly control the actions and effects of crime control agencies, while crime control models, with their concern for convictions and victims, do not.

A pure crime control system would prioritize the search for truth by adversarial law enforcement agencies at literally all costs. Police officers who 'know' that someone is guilty would either have this knowledge accepted as proof by a court or would be allowed to seek proof of it by any means. Put in this way, of course, the need for controls on crime control means becomes clear. Objective proof is needed, and law enforcement methods must be limited by humanitarian or libertarian standards even at the cost of knowledge. However, a pure due process system would prioritize proof and controls at literally all costs. Guilty verdicts would be allowed only on proof beyond literally all doubt, and law enforcement officials would need objective evidence before interfering with any civil liberties, however slight. And so we see the criminal justice system dilemma. Absolute proof, and completely innocuous methods of securing it, cannot be insisted upon. But simply to insist on uncontrolled discretion in the way the truth is sought is equally unacceptable. It is therefore impossible to view 'proof' and 'truth' as equally important, except in the simplistic sense of balancing the two.

This chapter aims, in part, to assess the extent to which criminal justice in England and Wales is characterized by adversarial due process. As soon as the police have any reason to suspect an individual an adversarial relationship is formed and due process protections, such as the caution against self-incrimination, are prescribed by law. This 'right of silence', along with the requirement of 'reasonable' suspicion for the exercise of coercive powers, is a key element in the due process model. On arrest the suspect is generally taken to a police station and detained. This requires further due process justification as civil liberties are further eroded by lengthy detention, interrogation, search of the suspect's home, fingerprinting, and so forth. The right of silence continues, bolstered by a right of access to lawyers and others. In order to charge, further evidence is required and further protections are provided—the Crown Prosecution Service (CPS) to vet the case and legal aid to prepare a defence. In order to convict there must be yet more evidence.

And so at each stage due process requirements become more stringent. Suspects may be believed to be guilty by the police, and may indeed be guilty 'in truth'. But in the absence of sufficient evidence (i.e. sufficient proof) due process requires that they be exonerated. At the final stage proof need not be absolute, but only 'beyond reasonable doubt'. Legal guilt and actual guilt are therefore not synonymous. Even in a due process system there will occasionally be legally guilty persons who are not 'actually' guilty, and many actually guilty persons who are not legally guilty. This puts the infamous 'miscarriage' cases of 1990–2—the Birmingham Six, Guildford Four, West Midlands Police Serious Crime Squad cases, and so forth—into perspective. All systems produce some cases like this. But how often do they occur, why do they occur, and are there adequate systems of review and appeal?

In crime control systems it might be thought that there would be more legally guilty persons who are not actually guilty, but fewer actually guilty persons who are not legally guilty. Crime control advocates argue, though, that crime control systems rely on professional experts (usually the police) to identify and secure evidence from suspects. Crime control is therefore more efficient not merely at identifying the guilty, but also at identifying the innocent (Walkley 1987: 5). More guilty verdicts could mean more actually guilty people being found guilty and fewer actually innocent people so found. However, this assumes that professional expertise really is that good; that the police can be trusted to find, rather than to manufacture, the evidence (and indeed that such a distinction between discovery and manufacture can be sustained); and that the overriding goal of the police will always be the discovery of the truth—as distinct from, for instance, gathering criminal intelligence, clearing the streets, defending themselves, or simply putting away known troublemakers.

This chapter will question these assumptions and, in so doing, will show that *both* due process *and* crime control ideologies are concerned to discover the 'truth'. The difference between them lies in the method of discovery. Doubts about police efficiency and propriety on the part of advocates of due process lead them to argue that the best method is the process of legal proof; while advocates of crime control argue that court processes and legal protections obstruct truth discovery.

POLICE DECISIONS 'ON THE STREET'

The due process origins of our system can be seen in the fact that, in the first decades after the establishment of the police, sufficient evidence to prosecute was needed before street powers could be exercised. Stop-and-search powers did not exist, and arrest was restricted to 'the apprehending or restraining of one's person in order to be forthcoming to answer an alleged or suspected crime' (Blackstone 1830: 289): arrested persons were to be taken directly before the magistrates, who decided whether to prosecute. In theory, then, police investigation had to take place *before* arrest rather than, as often happens now, after it. An arrest is now often made to *facilitate* investigation.

In reality many people used to be held by the police without formal arrest, and detention short of arrest ('helping the police with their enquiries') still continues (McKenzie *et al.* 1990). So, although most of the formal rules have become more strongly orientated towards crime control, this may simply represent rules being brought into line with an unchanging crime control reality. Thus rule changes do not necessarily change police practices, for better or worse. Whether or not, and the way in which, practices and rules correspond, is always an empirical matter.

The current legal position is now somewhere between the crime control and due process polarities. Both stop-and-search and arrest without judicial warrant are allowed for most 'normal' crimes (theft, burglary, serious assaults, sexual offences, drugs offences, public order offences, possession of offensive weapons, etc.). The power to stop-and-search is actually a bundle of powers: to stop a person or vehicle, to detain a person on the street, to question that person, and to make a superficial search of him or her. No time period is specified by legislation or case law, but no more than a few minutes would be usual. Arrest can be regarded as compulsory detention for rather longer in a police station.[1] The police must have 'reasonable suspicion' in order to exercise either power. The Code of Practice on stop-and-search issued by the Home Office under the authority of the Police and Criminal Evidence Act 1984 (PACE) states that 'there must be some objective basis' for the suspicion (para. 1.6), which 'can never be supported on the basis of personal factors alone' (para. 1.7). The 'objective' factors envisaged (which apply equally to arrest) include 'information received', someone 'acting covertly or warily', and someone 'carrying a certain type of article at an unusual time or in a place' where there have been relevant crimes recently (para. 1.6).

Discretion

Discretion is at the root of criminal justice practice. Police officers necessarily exercise discretion in deciding whether to stop and search and arrest. Some people look less 'suspicious' than others, and multitudes of actual or likely offences have to be prioritized. Minor offenders (prostitutes, unlicensed street traders, and so forth) are often simply ignored (Smith and Gray 1983). Research by Shapland and Vagg (1988) on public order, by Stanko (1985) on domestic violence, and by Clarkeson *et al.* (forthcoming) on violence in general shows that even in relatively serious situations arrest is less usual than no formal action. Similarly, when officers are able to be proactive (as compared to their usual reactive mode) they have to use discretion about the offences or offenders in which to invest scarce time. Discretion is also created as a consequence of the way offences are defined. Most offences require *mens rea* (a 'guilty mind') which, broadly, amounts to intent. Thus breaking someone's leg by tripping them up would be a crime if done deliberately but not if done accidentally. A police officer could make an arrest if she reasonably suspected the former, but not if she suspected the latter. However, since intent is so difficult to assess, officers have ample scope to arrest or not according to their preference. Discretion is also built into the definitions of other offences, such as public order offences and 'loitering' offences (Lustgarten 1987; McBarnet 1981).

Stop-and-search and arrest decisions are constrained only loosely by law because there are so many areas of judgement for the police. The powers themselves, based on reasonable suspicion, are ill-defined and subjective, the offences for which the powers are exercised are similarly ill-defined, and the police prioritize these offences for themselves. If discretion is not structured primarily by law, then, is it exercised arbitrar-

[1] There is no legal definition of either stop-and-search or arrest (see Bevan and Lidstone 1985: ch. 5; Sanders 1988*c*).

ily or is it structured by something else? Research on policing suggests four levels at which discretion is structured.

First, there are general policing goals. To say that a prime function of the police is to maintain order, control crime, and catch criminals may be trite, but it identifies a fundamental conflict between policing goals and the due process model. In so far as that model is an obstacle course it can only get in the way of policing goals. To expect the police to abide by due process standards voluntarily—without coercion through 'inhibitory' rules—is therefore unrealistic (Sanders 1992).

The second level is force policy. Different forces prioritize offences differently (Manchester, for example, at one time being 'hot' on vice) and place themselves on different parts of the community policing—fire-brigade policing continuum (Devon and Cornwall, for instance, being famous for the former). Walmsley (1978) analysed arrest and prosecution figures for homosexuality offences before and after the 1967 Sexual Offences Act (which partially legalized adult male homosexuality). Arrests were considerably higher after the Act than before. This was despite the fact that, assuming no change in the level of homosexual activity, the level of homosexual offences must have gone down as a result of the legal changes. It is likely that police forces were reluctant to arrest and prosecute while the law was the subject of debate, but no longer felt constrained under the new law.

Then there is 'cop culture' (discussed by Reiner 1985). Its elements of sexism and racism, and its stereotyping of people and groups of certain types (on 'rough' estates, with certain lifestyles, etc.) affect the way officers view society. Take the Code of Practice's reference to 'wary' actions and what is normal for certain 'times and places'. How one views these matters depends on one's culture and individual officers' own ways of mediating that culture. The final level, then, is that of the individual. As Reiner has pointed out, police officers are not representative of the population. They tend to be from social strata 'C1' and 'C2', to be more conservative than the average, and to be white and male. The homogeneity of this group, coupled with police training and socialization processes, enables 'cop culture' to be easily reproduced.

Patterns of Bias

The scope for bias in policing is provided by the weak constraints imposed on discretion by law. In the 1970s and 1980s concern at possible race bias, in particular, gave rise to several research studies. Smith and Gray, for example, found not only that there was no 'reasonable suspicion' in one-third of all stops which they observed, but that officers 'strongly tend to choose young males, especially young black males.

Other groups that they tend to single out are people who look scruffy or poor ('slag'), people who have long hair or unconventional dress (who, they think, may use drugs) and homosexuals' (1983: 436). This is classic cop culture stereotyping. Many patterns of bias could be discussed here (such as class, discussed by Reiner 1985: 127–9), but we will focus on race. Lord Scarman (1981) identified the mass use of stop-and-search on predominantly black youth as the 'trigger' for many of the inner-city riots of the early 1980s. Black people continue to receive disproportionate attention from the police. They constituted 16 per cent of all Metropolitan Police arrests in 1987, but comprised only 5 per cent of the capital's population (Home Office 1988). In Leeds in 1987, 6 per cent of arrests were of black people, who comprised just 3 per cent of the population (Jefferson and Walker 1992).

Willis's (1983) research produced similar results to that of Smith and Gray. The reasons which her officers recorded for stopping and searching were often based on the suspects' 'movements'. 'This category', Willis remarked, 'covered stops on grounds which police officers find it hard to specify.' This would be consistent with the crime control model if officers relied on intangible but reliable 'instinct' or 'experience', but the arrest rate (which was generally low at perhaps 10 per cent of all stops) was particularly low in the 'movements' cases. However, as stop-and-search is useful for intelligence-gathering (Brogden 1985; McConville *et al.* 1991), a low arrest rate is not inconsistent with crime control goals. It certainly appears that due process standards—even the minimal requirements of 'reasonable suspicion'—were rarely adhered to. These findings are, of course, consistent with research in the USA (see, for instance, Piliavin and Briar 1964; and, generally, Reiner 1985; ch. 4), which has similar rules on stop-and-search and arrest.

Willis found that black people were being stopped (although not arrested and prosecuted) disproportionately, also suggesting significant race bias. Indeed, following a review of several studies, mostly by Home Office researchers (e.g. Stevens and Willis 1979; Tuck and Southgate 1981; Field and Southgate 1982), Reiner (1985: 129) concludes that 'the weight of police activity' (including arrest) falls on black people and the 'lower working class' in general.[2] Reiner further concludes, as do other commentators such as Lea and Young (1984), that only part—an unquantifiable part—of this greater 'weight' of activity can be attributed to a greater involvement by black people in crime. If one adopts a 'labelling' perspective, 'objective' criminality and societal reaction to it

[2] The same could be said in general of the USA (see e.g. Bogolmony 1976). Further, although indirect, support for this view comes from a major study of race and sentencing in five Crown Courts (Hood 1992).

cannot easily be disentangled.[3] The important point, for our purposes, is that stop-and-search and arrest patterns are, at least in part, a product of police race and class stereotyping. However, Jefferson and Walker (1992) found that black arrest rates were higher than white arrest rates only in areas with relatively few black and Asian people. In areas with relatively high proportions of black and Asian people (where ethnic minorities comprise over 10 per cent of the population) white arrest rates were, if anything, higher. So, in so far as race bias does structure police decisions, that bias is mediated by (or a product of) other factors. These will be discussed further below.

Most of the research discussed so far was undertaken prior to the introduction of PACE in 1985. PACE gave more scope to the police 'on the street' by providing nationwide stop-and-search powers, extending powers of summary arrest, and so forth. But it also created new controls aimed at bringing police practices into line with the law. This could not, of course, prevent black people (or, indeed, homosexuals or 'slags') being disproportionately stopped where there is 'reasonable suspicion'. But it should, in principle, eradicate purely racist stops.

Police Working Rules

One of the major post-PACE studies of policing was carried out by McConville *et al.* (1991), who identify six police 'working rules' which structure police decision-making. The first is 'previous' (i.e. being known to the police). Sometimes this 'bureaucratic' mode of suspicion (Matza 1969) is sufficient on its own, as we saw Smith and Gray observe earlier: 'When you get to know an area, and see a villain about at 2.00 a.m. in the morning, you will always stop him to see what he is about.' (arresting officer, quoted in McConville *et al.* 1991: 24). The second concerns disorder and police authority. Dealing with disorder is a prime police task. Although Shapland and Vagg (1988) found that the police do not usually arrest when they intervene in disorderly incidents (as with domestic violence incidents), arrests are usual if the disorder does not cease. This is in part because of the challenge thereby presented to police authority, even if no specific charge fits the facts. Other working rules include consideration of the type of victim and his wishes (discussed further later), 'information received', and workload. But perhaps the most important working rule is 'suspiciousness'. This entails the suspect 'being in the right place at the right time', or being 'out of the ordinary' or 'uncooperative', or keeping the wrong company, or its being 'just a matter of instinct' on the

[3] The 'labelling' or 'societal reaction' perspective arose in the 1960s out of the symbolic interactionist tradition and became extremely influential in criminological theory as the first major reaction against criminological positivism. See Downes and Rock (1988).

officer's part, 'something undefinable' (all these phrases are from officers quoted in McConville *et al.* 1991: 26–8). This is Matza's (1969) other main mode of investigation.

The inability of police officers to tell McConville *et al.* precisely what made them suspicious confirms the continuing validity of the pre-PACE findings of Willis, Smith and Gray, Matza, and others. The other major study of post-PACE policing (by Bottomley, Coleman, and Dixon) came to similar conclusions, encapsulating them in the 'incongruity' principle (Dixon *et al.* 1989). These are precisely the kinds of consideration against which the Code of Practice (referred to above) cautions the police in its attempt to identify 'objective' factors which would satisfy a third party. But, as one officer put it to McConville *et al.* (1991), he would stop a suspect 'instinctively and then think about how he would satisfy a disinterested third party' (field notes). This suggests that the Code has altered the way officers account for their exercise of discretion, but not the way they actually *exercise* it. One form of incongruity is the presence of individuals of one ethnic group in an area predominantly made up of other ethnic groups. Jefferson and Walker's (1992) findings suggest that black people may be stopped and arrested primarily when they are incongruous—i.e. not in 'their own' areas. This accords with the more radical literature on social control and police (e.g. Brogden 1985; Scraton 1987) and is consistent with 'crime control' models in their broadest formulations.

Dixon *et al.* (1989) argue that non-adherence to due process standards is not so much wilful failure by police officers as the failure of due process standards to meet the reality of policing. Policing is about the creative use of experience in crime control. The development, and diminution, of suspicion is a dynamic process. It cannot, they argue, be reduced to compartmentalized legalistic steps dependent on precisely measured levels of evidence. The police police as best they can, reducing legal restraints to merely presentational significance. The effect of PACE on the operation of discretion is clearly limited. Police working rules gel with cop culture—stressing the importance of 'facing down' challenges to authority, investigating the incongruous, picking on 'known criminals', and so forth—far more than with PACE. This is not surprising, for police street work is intrinsically inquisitorial and orientated towards crime control (Sanders 1992).

Records and other Controls

It should not be surprising that PACE appears to have little impact on street policing, since it gives more, not less, power to the police. However, PACE incorporates more controls than operated hitherto, including requirements to tell suspects why they are being arrested or stopped, and to make records of the stop or arrest.

Since stop-and-search and arrest are of intrinsically low visibility (Goldstein 1960), no one apart from suspect and officer would usually know anything about a particular encounter. Most beat officers, for instance, see a supervisory officer just once per day on average, and this is usually at the beat officer's request (Shapland and Vagg 1988). Thus, in the same way that officers justify stops in terms of 'disinterested third parties' after the event, so written records can be constructed after the event (McConville *et al.* 1991: ch. 5). No longer are stops recorded as 'movements', but the reason for stops could be unchanged. Again, the account of the incident will correspond as much with legal expectations as with the reality of the incident (Scott and Lyman 1968; Ericson 1981).

Moreover, Willis (1983) found that around half of all stops were not recorded at all, and even fewer were recorded in the research of Bottomley *et al.* The less that is recorded the less accountable the officer is. But this is only a breach of PACE if PACE powers are actually exercised, that is, if the stop is not consensual. As with entry and search of premises, and even police station detention 'helping with enquiries', the police often characterize their exercise of powers ambiguously (Dixon *et al.* 1990; McConville *et al.* 1991: ch. 5). This gives them leeway and, if the encounter can be regarded as consensual, no record need be made. Not surprisingly, none of the research has found the new control and accountability mechanisms to be effective constraints on the exercise of these powers.

Arrest: Police- or Citizen-Initiated?

Unlike stop-and-search, arrest is rarely proactive; and only a small proportion of 'official' (i.e. non-consensual) stop-and-searches—17 per cent in 1986 and 1987—lead to arrest. Most police arrests usually follow information from, and complaints by, victims or witnesses (Shapland and Vagg 1988; Reiss 1971; Zander 1979; Steer 1980; McConville and Baldwin 1981). This is true even of CID work (Reiner 1985: 122). If few arrests are proactive, does discretion, and the patterns of bias which are reflected by it, play only a minor part in determining the shape of the official suspect population? Do claims that stereotyping and the 'mode of suspicion' structure the suspect population really 'not stand the test of empirical examination' (Steer 1980: 126)?

McConville *et al.* (1991) argue against Steer on several grounds. First, most of the studies cited above are based on indictable offences, missing out the summary offences (such as public order, prostitution, drunkenness, etc.) in which police initiative is more pronounced. Second, the issue is less who is influenced by stereotyping as whether the initiator—whoever he or she is—is so influenced. Store detectives stereotype (Cameron 1964, Murphy 1986), and doubtless 'ordinary' members of the public do too.

Most important of all, citizen initiation rarely takes the form of citizen arrest. More usually it is simply the transmission of information to the police. That information has to be sifted, evaluated, and acted upon (or not) by the police. In one American study only two-thirds of citizen complaints were taken seriously by the police (Black 1970). McConville *et al.* (1991: ch. 2) provide several examples where, even when the police did act upon complaints (for instance, by an ex-lodger and by a restaurateur), the way in which they acted—whether or not to arrest—was decided according to the working rules discussed earlier. In other words, police discretion and the exercise of judgement are still operative even when arrests are citizen-initiated. The same is true of information from informants, on which drug squads and regional crime squads depend (Maguire and Norris 1992). Information from the public is one resource among many which the police use in exercising discretion on the street.

DETENTION IN THE POLICE STATION

We have already noted that only in relatively recent years has the law moved in a crime control direction by allowing interference in the liberty of the citizen in the absence of sufficient evidence to prosecute. This movement was unplanned, *ad hoc*, and imprecise, giving rise to legal 'fudges' like 'helping police with their enquiries'. The Royal Commission on Criminal Procedure (1981) was therefore urged, on the one hand, to prohibit pre-charge detention (the due process position) and on the other to extend it (the crime control position). Meanwhile, research done for the Royal Commission showed that there was considerable regional disparity in the relative use of arrest/charge and summons (Gemmill and Morgan-Giles 1980). This suggested that arrest/charge—and the accompanying detention—was being over-used by many police forces. The Royal Commission wanted to reduce pre-charge detention, but to allow it when it was 'necessary': 'We do seek to alter the practice whereby the inevitable sequence on the creation of reasonable suspicion is arrest, followed by being taken to the station . . .' (para. 3.75). In this and other ways the Royal Commission attempted to satisfy both due process and crime control lobbies.[4]

[4] The Royal Commission on Criminal Justice (RCCJ) 1993 also attempted to balance due process and crime control. Extraordinarily, however, in ch. 1 it states that the acquittal of the guilty is as bad as the conviction of the innocent, which is a crime control

Detention without Charge

In line with the Royal Commission's recommendations, PACE provides that anyone at a police station should either be free to leave at will or be under arrest (s. 29). If the latter, there are clear time limits on how long a suspect can be held—normally twenty-four hours, but in exceptional cases up to thirty-six hours, or even ninety-six hours with the leave of the magistrates (ss. 41–4).

On arrest, all suspects, except in exceptional cases, should be taken directly to a police station (s. 30). It is then for the 'custody officer' (the old station sergeant, with an enhanced role and training) to decide whether or not the suspect should be detained. There are only two grounds for detention: in order to charge the suspect; or, where there is insufficient evidence to charge, in order to secure that extra evidence, but only where detention is *necessary* for that purpose (s. 37). In the words of the then Home Secretary, Douglas Hurd, the question is whether 'this detention was necessary—not desirable, convenient or a good idea but necessary.' (Hurd 1984: col. 1229).

The aims of these provisions should be clear. Being either arrested or free to go was designed to eliminate the travesty of voluntary co-operation encapsulated in the phrase 'helping the police with their enquiries'. Clear time limits were designed to ensure that both suspects and police knew what their respective rights and powers were, and to ensure that suspects were not intimidated by the prospect of indefinite detention. Detention only when 'necessary' was designed to reduce the numbers arrested and detained when summons procedures would be equally appropriate. And immediate transit to a police station where a custody officer then becomes responsible for the suspect, when detention is necessary, was designed to ensure that suspects did not remain in the hands of officers who might mistreat them.

Giving the police the powers which they ordinarily need (or are deemed to need), with greater powers in exceptional cases, is a crime control position. But there were due process elements, too: in setting absolute limits to detention; refusing to allow investigating officers to determine what is necessary in the interests of crime control; creating 'independent' custody officers; and having 'custody sheets' on all suspects recording the particulars of their detention, and so forth. Yet, like records of stop-and-search, this written 'evidence' of the encounter (providing objective evidence of what happened, to protect suspects against police fabrications) is written

position. Unfortunately the Report and most of its Research Studies were published too late to be fully taken into account in this chapter, although some references have been added at a late stage (see notes 7, 10, 14, 15, 18 below). References in the text to the 'Royal Commission' are to the Royal Commission on Criminal Procedure (1981) unless otherwise stated.

by the police against whom this is supposed to be a protection! Custody records and stop-and-search records suffer the same inevitable problems (McConville *et al.* 1991: ch. 5; Sanders and Bridges 1990).

Turning to the effect of these provisions, we will focus here on 'voluntary' attendance, the authorization of detention, and time actually spent in custody. McKenzie *et al.* (1990), as part of a wider study of custody officers in 1988–9, discovered that, as expected, two of the three police forces studied dealt with very few suspects as 'volunteers'. In the third force, though, about one third 'help police with their enquiries' as volunteers. A continuation of the pre-existing practice, common in rural areas, this was not just a matter of tradition: 'It's convenient because you set the time and . . . it avoids the time clock consideration. If arrest is necessary later, it doesn't count' (detective sergeant, quoted in McKenzie *et al.* 1990: 31). McKenzie *et al.* also observed the reception into detention of over 560 arrestees. In only one case—that of a suspect who was taken seriously ill—was detention not authorized. McConville *et al.* produced similar results from three different forces. When interviewed, custody officers often expressed surprise that the detention decision could be anything other than automatic (1991: ch. 3). Dixon, Bottomley, *et al.*, having found not one refusal of detention in their research, comment that 'reception into custody has become an essentially routinized process.' (1990: 130): most custody sergeants justify detention by simply writing out the words of PACE s. 37 verbatim. Some have even asked for a 'rubber stamp'! As with stop-and-search records, the effect of the new legal requirements is to produce appropriate accounts of events, rather than to alter the events themselves.

The incoherence of the law is a contributory factor. Arrest, contrary to the recommendation of the Royal Commission, may occur when there is 'reasonable suspicion', whether or not it is necessary. Yet the only reason for arrest is to secure detention (except in those few cases where the suspect could be charged immediately). Thus arrests can be lawfully made in circumstances where custody officers should decline detention and negate the arrest. Following the logic of McConville *et al.*'s argument, denial of detention would undermine officers' authority, and thus run counter to the working rules discussed above. In this situation, as with 'voluntary' attendance, working rules take precedence over legal rules. McKenzie *et al.* prefer to follow a bureaucratic argument, that it is easier and less likely to produce trouble for officers for detention to be authorized than not. These arguments are not incompatible, but McConville *et al.*'s argument is supported by the fact that nowhere are arrests being replaced by report for summons. Indeed, in urban areas at any rate, arrest is now the norm even for juveniles (Evans and Ferguson 1991).

Maguire (1988) found, in an early assessment of the effect of PACE, that most suspects were in custody for two to six hours, although this figure conceals great variation. This drop in detention length was confirmed by Brown's (1989) study of thirty police stations in 1987, and by Irving and McKenzie (1989). Brown found that 76 per cent of arrestees were held for less than six hours and 85 per cent for less than nine hours. Bottomley *et al.* (1991) found a slight increase in detention length between 1986 and 1987, but otherwise the results were similar. It seems that PACE has had no major effect on overall detention length, although both Brown and Maguire suggest that minor offenders now tend to be released sooner, and that some serious offenders are held for longer. Detention up to the normal limit of twenty four hours is rare, for confessions are usually forthcoming (or not) within six hours or so. Rarely, then, do time limits actually act as a constraint on the police. When suspects are detained for more than six hours the custody officer and other officers are supposed periodically to review detention. According to Dixon, Bottomley, *et al.* (1990) this is as routinized as the initial detention decision, though McKenzie *et al.* state that when custody officers are unhappy with an arrest they try to 'expedite' the processing. No information is provided, however, on how often this 'expedition' occurs, of what it consists, and on whether evidence gathering or the charge decision is affected.

Access to Legal Advice

The most striking due process provision of PACE is the provision, in ss. 58–9, of free legal advice to all suspects who request it. Information about this unambiguous right has to be provided by the custody officer to the suspect. Advice may be delayed in exceptional cases but not denied outright. Custody records state whether or not suspects were informed of their rights, whether or not suspects did request advice, and what (if anything) happened then. Both Brown (1989) and Sanders *et al.* (1989) found request rates of around 25 per cent and actual advice rates of around 20 per cent, although there were wide variations among police stations. This represents a massive increase over the pre-PACE situation—request and advice rates at around 7 per cent and 5 per cent respectively, according to Softley (1980)—but is still lower than one might have expected. Why should three out of four people reject an entirely free service? Why do one out of five requests fail?

First, Sanders *et al.* (1989) found that in a substantial minority of cases suspects were not informed (wholly or partly) of their rights. In these cases request rates were considerably lower than in the other cases. In some other cases suspects' requests were denied, ignored, or simply not acted upon. Sanders and Bridges (1990) estimated that in some 10.5 per cent of cases *which the police knew the researchers were observing* the police actually broke the law (the Code of Practice made under the authority of PACE). Custody records recorded some of these malpractices but failed to record the majority, underlining the point made in relation to the recording of reasons for stop-and-search and detention: records made by the police are an inevitably feeble safeguard for suspects against the police.

The same applies to the role of the custody officer as 'gatekeeper' for requests for legal advice. Sanders *et al.* (1989) found that in some 41.4 per cent of cases 'ploys' were used to attempt to dissuade suspects from seeking advice. These ploys ranged from the incomprehensible reading of rights to scare stories ('You'll have to wait in the cells until the solicitor gets here'). Other research, by Morgan *et al.* (n.d.), Dixon, Bottomley, Coleman, *et al.* (1990), and Maguire (1988), also found discouragement by the police, although these studies either did not quantify this or concluded that it occurred less often than Sanders *et al.* found. This is very much a matter of interpretation. Morgan *et al.* found 'active discouragement, leading questions, or incomplete statement of rights' in about 14 per cent of cases. In the rest, they say, rights were stated 'reasonably', but 'few suspects are in a "reasonable" frame of mind at the time. There is usually no attempt to make sure the statement has been understood.' Explanations again range from bureaucratic (Morgan *et al.*) to structural (giving effect to crime control goals through working rules: McConville *et al.*).

Sanders *et al.* found little statistical correlation between ploys and the take-up of advice, but Maguire (1988) rightly comments that for many suspects there is considerable 'elasticity of demand'. Legal advice is only one consideration among many others such as getting out of the station quickly (Sanders *et al.*, 1989). Thus ploys will have variable success. Also they are likely to be used most where it matters most to the police that a suspect does not see a solicitor, and where the suspect is most likely to ask for one. Ploys, along with solicitor unavailability, account for the request/advice gap. Dixon, Bottomley, *et al.* comment that solicitors complain frequently that, on arrival at the station, they are often 'informed by officers that the suspect has changed his/her mind, agreed to talk to them and confessed' (1990: 128).

There are many reasons why the request rate is relatively low, of which police ploys is only one. Suspects' negative attitudes towards solicitors was found to be another by Sanders *et al.*—which was not surprising, given the level of service documented by, in particular, McConville and Hodgson (1992). Advice is frequently provided by phone rather than in person, in many cases solicitors do not attend interrogations, and when they do they are usually passive. It would be a mistake to assume that police officers are generally hostile to legal advice, or that such advice is generally obstructive. These propositions are true only in some cases with some suspects and some solicitors. Dixon (1991*a*) shows that in most situations lawyers act 'for' suspects only in the most generalized terms. As McConville *et al.* (1991, ch. 8) and McConville and Hodgson (1992) also show, legal aid lawyers have a generally non-adversarial stance and take their lead from the police. Sometimes defence lawyers are actually sought by the police to put their case to recalcitrant suspects! Again, the extent to which due process ideology is actually operative is problematic even when, as here, the provision in question is unambiguously due process in character.

Police Interrogation

Interrogation has assumed ever greater importance in police investigation over the years. Nearly half of all detained suspects are now interrogated (Leng 1992: ch. 2). In part this is because, as we have seen, investigation now usually takes place after, rather than before, arrest. It is also a product of the requirements of substantive criminal law. Proof of *mens rea*—a guilty mind—requires knowledge of what was in the offender's mind, best secured through confession, so many interrogations centre on intention and recklessness (Sanders 1987; McConville *et al.* 1991: ch. 4; Evans 1992). Even when other ways of securing evidence are available, interrogation often serves as a 'short cut' and produces information about other offences and other offenders (Softley 1980).

The due process insistence on the prosecution proving its own case originally prohibited non-consensual interrogation, but this changed in 1912 when the Judges' Rules first allowed interrogation before charge. Confessions were invalid if secured 'involuntarily' or 'oppressively', but the 1981 Royal Commission, based on Irving's (1980) research, questioned how meaningful it was to talk of confessions given under conditions of involuntary detention being 'voluntary'. Following the Commission, the PACE Code of Practice on Detention and Questioning therefore set out specific basic standards for interrogation: the provision of proper heating, ventilation, breaks, access to solicitors and others, the taking of contemporaneous notes or tape recording, and so forth (Dixon, Bottomley, *et al.* 1990). Suspects may still refuse to answer questions,[5] though, as we have seen, PACE allows pre-charge detention to obtain 'evidence by questioning' (s. 37(2)). Thus the Code of Practice states that a police officer is 'entitled to question any person from whom he thinks

[5] The right to silence was, however, modified in Northern Ireland in 1988 (see Jackson 1991). The government established a working party for England and Wales with the same aim (Zuckerman 1989), but its report was overtaken by the events which led to the establishment of the Royal Commission on Criminal Justice.

useful information can be obtained . . . A person's declaration that he is unwilling to reply does not alter this requirement' (Note 1B). So, although suspects need not speak to officers (due process), officers may none the less attempt to persuade them to change their minds and to hold them, subject to the time limits, for as long as that takes (crime control). Given the importance attached by most suspects to the shortest detention possible (Sanders *et al.*, 1989: ch. 4) the pressures on suspects to speak are considerable.

How is evidence of guilt secured? First there are those many suspects who simply and speedily acquiesce, against whom there would often be plenty of evidence anyway (Irving and McKenzie 1989: s. 8; Moston *et al.* 1992). Secondly, many suspects are susceptible to 'deals' (confessions in exchange for favours or reduced charges): 'They always want to deal. When they're arrested they're immediately in the game of damage limitation' (CID officer, quoted by Maguire and Norris 1992: ch. 5). Then there are those who are intimidated by their situation—by being held against their will in 'police territory' where the environment is deliberately denuded of psychological supports (Driver 1968; Holdaway 1983; Walkley 1987), by being in fear of spending the night in the cells (Sanders *et al.* 1989), or by the employment of any number of 'tactics' against them (Irving 1980; Irving and McKenzie 1989; Softley 1980; Evans 1992; McConville and Hodgson 1992, ch. 7). Such tactics include offering inducements such as bail, claiming that there is overwhelming evidence against the suspect, using custodial conditions such as return to the cells, and so forth. Irving (1980) found that at least one tactic was used more often than not, two or more being frequently employed. Many officers try different tactics until they secure a result or give up, although others are not as flexible as one might expect (Moston *et al.* 1992). If they do not succeed in the initial interrogation, twenty-four hours (or more) allows time for further interrogation—there were two or more interrogations in 12 per cent of all interrogation cases in Leng's (1992) study, and 19 per cent in Brown's (1989) study.

Irving and McKenzie (1989) found that, following PACE, such tactics were, at first, used less frequently. But this was probably, in part, a temporary response to the requirement to take contemporaneous notes, now superseded in most cases by the tape recording of interrogations, for they found a 'partial reversion' to former practice even before tape recording became universal. Thus, in Evans's (1992) study of tape recorded interrogations, tactics were routinely used when admissions were not immediately forthcoming (although in only 20 per cent of all cases). As this was a study of juveniles, hence relatively unimportant offences and offenders, this finding is particularly significant, for tactics are used more in more serious cases (Irving and McKenzie 1989).

Extreme tactics are now unacceptable in formal interrogations since they are tape recorded. This gives rise to a fourth way of securing confession: through informal interrogation. The extent of this is controversial but its existence is not. Informal interrogation occurs on the way to the police station (the 'scenic route': McConville and Morrell 1983; Evans and Ferguson 1991; Hassan Khan's case, discussed by Kaye 1991: ch. 4; Maguire and Norris 1992: ch. 5); before and after formal interrogations (Sanders and Bridges 1990; McConville *et al.* 1991: chs. 4, 7; McConville 1992); and in the cells under the guise of 'welfare visits' (Dixon, Bottomley, *et al.* 1990). A classic instance is discussed by Leng (1992): a suspect having been silent throughout two interviews, the third opened with the officer stating, 'You have intimated that you wish to tell me about the matters which I have spoken to you about earlier.' Thus Irving and MacKenzie's claim (1988, p. 102) that custody officers 'were not prepared to allow any contact between suspect and investigating officer, save in the formal interrogation situation,' has not been confirmed by other researchers. Even were such control to be the norm (as Maguire 1988, Bottomley *et al.*, and Morgan *et al.* would argue), custody officers cannot control what happens before arrival at the station and what happens immediately before and after formal interrogations. Custody records are supposed to record the precise times at which interviews begin and end, but this does not prevent officers having 'a little chat to get things straight before I switch on the tape' (Evans and Ferguson 1991; see also Evans, 1992: 36; McConville 1992). It is precisely on confessions allegedly made 'informally' (but not repeated 'formally') that so many appeals have turned, especially in the West Midlands Police Serious Crime Squad investigation (Kaye 1991). To the extent that 'tactics' are now used less frequently in formal interrogations than they were before PACE, it is likely that they are now simply being used more under 'low visibility' conditions (Maguire and Norris 1992).

Coercion may occur too, in both informal and formal interrogations. This is inevitable under English law, for the job of the police interrogator is to elicit answers even from suspects who have declared a refusal to provide answers—in other words, to change their minds. Tactics are designed to do this, and not all tactics are of the 'carrot' variety: 'Sometimes it's necessary to shout at people . . . you have to keep up the pressure' (detective, quoted by McConville *et al.* 1991: ch. 4). Even interrogation practices which would be innocuous to most people are coercive to vulnerable people (Gudjonsson and MacKeith 1982). And even 'normal' people often make 'coerced-passive' confessions (McConville *et al.* 1991: ch. 4) as a result of leading questions (defended by Walkley 1987) and legal-closure questions (Irving 1985). Thus suspects get trapped into accepting they have 'stolen' when they in fact would put it in a different, exculpatory, way (see also Sanders *et al.* 1989: ch. 7; Evans 1992).

The sixth way of securing evidence of guilt is by 'gilding the lily' (Holdaway 1983; Maguire and Norris 1992). Controlling the manufacture of confession evidence has been a major aim of legal reform. The government tried, through PACE, to eliminate 'verballing' by requiring the contemporaneous recording of interrogations. When it was found, through ESDA tests (Kaye 1991), that hand recording was sometimes inaccurate, the requirement to tape record was introduced. And so, Sanders and Bridges (1990) argue, the police now informally interrogate more to avoid tape recording. While evidence of informal confessions, and uncorroborated confessions generally, is allowed to form the basis of convictions, these problems will remain. As one officer told Maguire and Norris (1992: 46–7), there was nothing to prevent him from distorting the contents of informal conversations 'if I was dishonest'.

Finally, false confessions. Just as not all 'informal' confessions are manufactured, not all manufactured confessions are false. On the other hand, false confessions can arise in the most controlled circumstances, although the less regulated the interrogation, the more likely they are to occur. Gudjonsson and MacKeith (1988) discuss various types of false confession arising from coercion, but coercion is not always necessary. Questioning taking the form of a supported direct accusation (i.e. an accusation with details of the crime itself) can lead to internalization by suggestible suspects whose subsequent 'confessions' will contain only the details provided by the police themselves (Moston 1992). Howsoever they arise, false confessions have been a feature of our system for many years (Williams 1979) and have led to perhaps thousands of innocent people being jailed even since PACE was introduced.[6]

It seems that PACE, like any other new law, has changed practices, but largely by shifting the unwanted behaviour instead of eradicating or even reducing it. Thus there is little violence now, but more use of other tactics and pressures. Formal interrogations are well controlled (good conditions, tape recording, custody records, access to lawyers and others, and so forth), but confessions purportedly given in 'informal' interrogations are still admissible; overt coercion has given way to the use of sophisticated legal-closure questions. Despite changes in police interrogation behaviour, Irving and McKenzie (1989) and Moston *et al.* (1992) report a small or non-existent drop in the confession rate since PACE was introduced.

Moston (1992) argues that police failure to verify confessions and avoid leading questions is a matter of technical competence and a failure of training. He distinguishes between inquisitorial and adversarial styles,

[6] See the evidence of bodies such as NACRO, Justice, and others to the Royal Commission on Criminal Justice. Some of the 'miscarriage cases' involved false and other manufactured confessions.

the latter being less reliable. McConville *et al.* (1991), on the other hand, start with the adversarial position of the police, arguing that making a case through interrogation is precisely their role. They aim not to identify verifiable facts, but to build a case. Like the rest of police investigation, McConville *et al.* argue, interrogation is a matter of construction. Facts are made, not discovered. An example is given by Maguire and Norris (1992: ch. 4), who report a CID sergeant saying that he had been taught, whenever he found someone carrying a knife, to induce them to say that it was for their own protection. This—unknown to the suspect—constitutes admission of the crime of carrying an 'offensive weapon'.

While the police do not seek false (or even coerced) confessions, McConville *et al.* argue that their adversarial role inevitably leads to the crime control value that this is a price worth paying. Technical solutions, such as video recording (Baldwin 1991) imply a bureaucratic explanation for false confessions and coercion and presuppose that due process is achievable. Even when solicitors or 'appropriate adults' attend interrogation, they rarely intervene, allowing the tactics and forms of coercion described earlier to continue (Dixon 1991*a*; Evans 1992: 48; McConville and Hodgson 1992). McConville *et al.*'s answer to miscarriages of justice based on false confessions is not to achieve 'better' or more 'objective' interrogation (as Moston argues), but—as in France (Leigh and Zedner 1992)—to prevent confession evidence forming the sole basis of convictions and to provide the defence with the same resources as are provided to the prosecution.[7]

The Right of Silence

Over half of all suspects who are interrogated either confess or make incriminating statements to the police (60, 54, and 75 per cent respectively in Softley 1980, Sanders *et al.* 1989, and Evans 1992 respectively). We have seen that the police have various methods of securing confessions, but these do not always work, and they work with varying success according to a wide range of factors—in particular, offence severity, prior legal advice, and strength of evidence (Moston *et al.* 1992*b*). Evans (1992) also found age and criminal record to be significant. Many suspects deny allegations. Both Moston *et al.* (1992b) and Leng (1992) found that the police are rarely successful in breaking down suspects' defences, despite the pressures and techniques discussed earlier, although Evans (1992: 49) found a strong statistical association between the use of persuasive tactics and confessions.

[7] The RCCJ was divided on the corroboration of confessions, but all members were sufficiently worried to agree that, if the law is not changed, juries should be warned by the judge of the danger of relying on uncorroborated confessions (1993: ch. 4).

From the due process point of view high confession rates are surprising. From the crime control viewpoint the question is why, in so many cases (especially serious cases), the police should be impeded by suspects' silence. Whether silence does impede the police turns principally on what, precisely, 'silence' is in this context; what the association is between silence and outcome; and in what ways the police are obstructed by silence.[8] Few suspects in the post-PACE studies exercise absolute silence (Willis *et al.* 1988: 2–4 per cent; Sanders *et al.* 1989: 2.8 per cent; Moston *et al.* 1993: 8 per cent; McConville and Hodgson 1992: 2.5 per cent). However, some suspects (a further 5.3 per cent in Sanders *et al.*) simply make flat denials, while others answer some questions and not others (11–15 per cent in Irving and McKenzie 1989, and a further 8 per cent in Moston *et al.* 1993). Silence often relates to questions about the involvement of others, and some suspects are silent at the start but then answer questions later (or vice versa). So studies which simply count the number of interviews in which questions were not answered at some point can be misleading: 12.3–23 per cent of interviews in the Home Office Working Group studies (Home Office 1989) were so identified.[9] Leng (1992), reanalysing McConville *et al.*'s (1991) data and taking these points into account, found a 'true' silence rate of 4.5 per cent.

Irving and McKenzie (1989: 239) report a drop in confessions for serious offences (but not for offences in general) and endorse (without supporting evidence) the police belief in a rise in the use of silence by offenders with serious records and/or who are suspected of serious offences. This was also endorsed by Moston and Williamson (1990), who, however, found little association between silence and charge, plea, or verdict (see also Moston 1992). Indeed, Leng (1992) found that in only a small percentage of 'no further actions' or acquittals was silence exercised, and that these negative outcomes rarely seemed to be a product of silence.

Silence could obstruct the police by denying them evidence on which to charge. But this is rare, for usually there is enough evidence to charge anyway, or the evidence is merely circumstantial and capable of being flatly denied (Leng 1992: ch. 3). Silence may also obstruct the police through 'ambush' defences. Here the issue is not really whether a suspect refuses to answer a question, but whether she is silent about alleged facts on which the particular defence relied upon was based. Again Leng (1992: ch. 5) alone has sought to quantify (and clarify) this. In only 20

[8] There are, of course, arguments of principle, both for and against the right, which do not turn on empirical matters. See Greer (1990); Easton (1991).

[9] See Leng (1992) for a penetrating analysis of these 'counting' problems in which he suggests that Moston *et al.* (1992*b*) and the Home Office Working Group overestimate the 'true' rate of silence by about 28 per cent.

per cent of acquittals following trial in his study (about 6 per cent of all acquittals, including dropped cases) were defences raised in court which were not raised in interview. But none of them were true ambushes and in only two of them was silence exercised. The successful defences amounted to interpretations of agreed facts (whether a knife or bat was an offensive weapon, whether an associate of a thief was an accomplice) or exculpatory statements to which the police would not listen. When genuine ambush defences were mounted (in between 1.7 and 5.1 per cent of all contested trials) they were unsuccessful. Thus most acquittals were the result of unanticipated, but not *unanticipatable*, defences. In preventing suspects from using interrogations as platforms for defences in court the police end up wrong-footing their own prosecutors.[10]

Detention: Some Conclusions

Rather than leading to less pre-charge detention following the 'creation of reasonable suspicion', the Royal Commission's scheme (enacted in PACE) has led to more detention. The formalization of pre-charge procedures was intended to protect suspects, and it may do so to some extent. But its unintended consequence has been to lead to more arrests (fewer suspects being held in limbo), more police station interrogation (instead of interviews at home), and the rushing (in some cases) of the charging process to beat the time limits.

On the broader impact of PACE on policing, researchers have reached different conclusions. Dixon *et al.* (1989) and McKenzie *et al.* (1990) argue that PACE is more significant than do McConville *et al.* (1991) and Sanders *et al.* (1989). Dixon *et al.* correctly argue that rules may impact differently, depending on their nature and the specific processes involved. But Holdaway (1983) argues that the police station is police territory *par excellence*, where one would *least* expect legal rules to change police working practices in the absence of new external constraints. The new constraints which are implicitly relied upon by Dixon *et al.* are access to lawyers—despite Dixon's (1991*a*) own scepticism about police station advice—tape recording of interrogation, custody records, and the general supervisory role of the custody officer. The strength or otherwise of these constraints is the key to this particular argument.

The miscarriages which led to the establishment of the Royal

[10] The RCCJ did not believe that the exercise of the right of silence in the police station was a major problem. Fearing that the disadvantages to the innocent would outweigh the advantages in relation to the guilty if the right of silence were altered, it recommended no change to the present rules. Although it did recommend changes in relation to defences in court which had not been raised earlier with the CPS (under proposed new pre-trial procedures), the Commission thought that it would be wrong to require suspects to forewarn the police of their defence(s) (1993: ch. 4).

Commission on Criminal Justice occurred before PACE. Would PACE have prevented them? Many of the people wrongly convicted were in custody for a long time before being charged, but lengthy detention is allowed by PACE. Access was usually delayed, but that is also allowed in such exceptional cases and often occurs when it is not allowed. The interrogations were often oppressive and uncontrolled but, again, we have seen that that is also common now. It is true that violence is never (or very rarely) used now, whereas it was a feature of the Guildford Four and Birmingham Six cases. Whether police tactics and intimidation effectively substitute for violence is arguable, but the release of the Cardiff Three came about because one suspect, in particular, 'confessed' to murder in 1988 after highly intimidatory questioning (*Guardian*, 11 December 1992). If miscarriages can be explained, crudely, by failure to adhere to due process (and it was this belief that led the Royal Commission in 1981 to condemn the most blatant crime control practices and to introduce more due process protection) we have to ask whether PACE will make such events less likely to occur in future than they have in the past.

PROSECUTION AND DIVERSION

When the police were first established they gradually took over responsibility for prosecution in the absence of any specific or exclusive prosecution powers or controls over their discretion. As arrest turned into a tool for (rather than the culmination of) investigation, pre-charge detention arose and the police developed various non-prosecution dispositions. There are now well over a million prosecutions per year, but many suspects are released from pre-charge detention with no further action (NFA). There are no official figures for NFAs, but McConville *et al.* (1991: table 10) found that 26 per cent of detained adults and 24 per cent of detained juveniles in their sample fell into the NFA category; 14 per cent of adults and 38 per cent of juveniles were cautioned, with most of the rest (58 per cent and 35 per cent respectively) prosecuted.

Many other agencies also prosecute. These include the Inland Revenue (IR), Department of Social Security (DSS), Health and Safety Inspectorate, Customs and Excise, Wages Inspectorate, and so forth. Although these agencies follow a diversity of policies and procedures (Lidstone *et al.* 1980) they all share a propensity not to prosecute. The DSS is the most prosecution-minded of the non-police agencies. The DSS mounted 8,090 prosecutions in 1986/7, compared to the IR's 459 in the same year (Cook 1989: ch. 7), despite the far greater number of tax offences. These agencies caution far more often than they prosecute, and NFA even more often than that (Sanders 1985a), although they do attempt to secure compliance with the law and/or secure financial compensation through informal negotiation (Hutter 1988; Richardson *et al.* 1983). Thus arrest does not necessarily lead to prosecution, and prosecution need not be the normal response to suspected crime.

No Further Action

NFA emerged when pre-charge detention became available to the police at a time when increasing emphasis was being placed on investigating crime after, rather than before, arrest. Even then, the law was unclear. Thus Wilcox, a former chief constable, wrote: 'If an arrest has been made on *prima facie* evidence of guilt the police feel that the safest course is to justify the action in court . . . [i.e. prosecute]' (1972: 107). Of course, not all arrests are, or were, made on the basis of such strong evidence; accordingly Steer (1980: table 4) found in his sample of cases an NFA rate in 1974 of 8.3 per cent (with a further 5.1 per cent 'NFA detected'). Changes in prosecution criteria (discussed below) have raised the threshold for prosecution which, assuming an unchanged level of arrests, would be expected to lead to more NFAs. Thus McConville *et al.* (1991) found the NFA rate to be around 25 per cent, suggesting a change in the pattern of police dispositions over the last preceding twenty years consistent with the crime control model. Police officers decide both whether to arrest and whether to charge, and they make release decisions themselves on the basis of their own criteria and on evidence collected and evaluated by themselves. Sifting is in the hands of the professionals. Procedural due process may be satisfied by different evidential thresholds for arrest and charge, but that for arrest falls short of substantive due process.

McConville *et al.* (1991: ch. 6) found that many arrests were a result of pressure from the public. If the police arrested reluctantly the outcome was often NFA, usually after consultation with the victim, regardless of the strength of evidence. The classic situation is domestic violence, made a low priority by stereotypical attitudes to victim and offender (Wasoff 1982; Stanko 1985). But there are many others. The police are not interested in non-homicidal violence in general, domestic or non-domestic, unless threats to order or their authority are involved (Sanders 1988*a*); other examples include non-violent disputes between neighbours (McConville *et al.* 1991: 107). Other reasons for NFA in cases where the police did find (or could have found) evidence include the doing of 'deals' with suspects, especially informants. And just as prosecution is sometimes used to protect the police against allegations of malpractice (Wilcox 1972) so in some circumstances NFA prevents the airing in public of events about which the police prefer to keep quiet (McConville *et al.* 1991: 111).

Some NFAs, of course, are simply cases in which the police would have liked to prosecute had they had more evidence. The obstacle here is rarely physical or legal, but simply one of resources. The police rarely seek evidence other than from eye witnesses, the victim, and the suspect himself. They could often investigate further but choose not to (Leng 1992). As we shall see, cases are a product of police work, and so the absence of a case is also a police product.

On the other hand, many NFAs are a product of purely speculative arrests. (McConville *et al.* 1991: ch. 2). Often the police accept that the suspect did not commit the offence or that there is no evidence—for instance, where the police 'trawled' local people with relevant previous convictions simply to eliminate them from a major rape enquiry; where suspects were arrested so that they could be held pending their questioning as witnesses; and also where *all* inhabitants of, and visitors to, a building where there had been a drugs raid were arrested, even though the building consisted of several self-contained flats (Leng 1992). In these types of case no due process standards, substantive or procedural, were adhered to. The working rules discussed earlier are the motor driving police dispositions.

Police Diversion

Large numbers of suspects are cautioned by the police: around 13 per cent of all adults found guilty or cautioned in 1990, a rise from around 4 per cent in 1978.[11] The Royal Commission on Criminal Procedure (1981: table 23.4) noted considerable variations in cautioning rates among police forces that could not be explained solely by offence variations (Sanders 1985*b*). As with arrest policies, police forces had their own cautioning policies. The Royal Commission was concerned both that cautionable offences were being prosecuted in some areas and that there was unjustifiable disparity among forces' use of cautioning and prosecution. The Home Office responded in 1985 with new guidelines which established clearer criteria for prosecution and caution: offence seriousness, previous convictions, dramatic mitigating circumstances, wishes of the victim, and so forth. However, both inter-force and intra-force disparity continued (Wilkinson and Evans 1990), because of the procedural arrangements for prosecution and caution (discussed below) and the guidelines themselves. The latter are vague (How serious an offence or record? What kinds of personal circumstance should be taken into account?), manipulable (the police themselves influence the wishes of victims: Edwards 1989, Ericson 1981), and non-prioritized (Are victims' wishes, suspect's circumstances, or offence seriousness to predominate?).

[11] The proportion of juveniles cautioned is far higher. For discussion see chapter 19 in this volume.

New guidelines were produced in 1990, but their impact is not likely to be any more significant, for the same reasons (Evans, 1991).

Diversion is none the less encouraged despite these problems, because it is cheaper than prosecution and because it avoids stigmatizing offenders. Drawing on labelling theory (e.g. Becker 1963), it is now generally accepted that prosecution and punishment can exaggerate criminal self-identity. The new caution guidelines exhort cautioning as 'reducing the risk that [offenders] will re-offend' (Home Office 1990: para. 5). Thus 'courts should only be used as a last resort, particularly for juveniles and young adults' (para. 7).

The cost-reduction and stigma-avoidance objectives would be undermined if cautions were used in cases which would not otherwise be prosecuted. The guidelines therefore warn, first, against 'net-widening' (para. 3). This occurs when cautions are used as alternatives to NFA rather than to prosecution (Ditchfield 1976; Morris *et al.* 1980; Cohen 1985; Pratt 1986). It is difficult to assess how widespread this is. Since NFA is a low-visibility option, and statistics on its use are not kept, we cannot compare the rising trend of cautions with the trend, whether up or down, of NFAs (Wilkinson and Evans 1990). Second, preconditions for caution (annex B, para. 2) are set out: that there is sufficient evidence to prosecute and that the suspect admits the offence and accepts the caution. Both Steer (1970) and Sanders (1988*b*) found that the preconditions (which predated the 1985 guidelines) were often ignored. Indeed, some suspects were cautioned precisely *because* there was insufficient evidence to prosecute! McConville *et al.* (1991: ch. 7), and Evans and Ferguson (1991) found that little had changed in more recent years. Over 20 per cent of the juveniles cautioned in the latter study, for instance, made no clear admission. The low-visibility nature of caution decisions also enables the police to use cautions as bargaining tools with suspects who would normally be prosecuted (McConville *et al.* 1991: ch. 6).

Both on the street and in the station, rules have little effect on police behaviour unless they are both enforceable and enforced (neither applying to cautioning) or coincide with police working rules. These controls often do not, for cautioning can serve crime control objectives. Cohen's original (1985) 'net widening' thesis was that less obviously coercive measures (the whole spectrum of 'community' policing and 'community' dispositions) were developing precisely in order to exercise more control over the suspect population. The police want to have on record suspects who are not prosecuted, and for these purposes legalistic questions of evidence and admission are trivial distractions. On this argument due process is subordinated to crime control in the practice of cautioning. Similarly, ostensibly cautionable cases are often prosecuted where this serves policing objectives; and the interests of the victim—often opposed to those of the suspect, as the guidelines acknowledge—are also subordinated to those of the police.[12]

The patterns of bias identified in street policing (race, class, and so forth) may also be evident in prosecution and diversion decisions. This certainly appeared to be so with juvenile decisions in the 1970s and 1980s (see chapter 19 in this volume), and may even have been true with adults in the 1980s (Sanders 1985*a*). The greater class bias is between police-enforced and other crime. Despite variations in the use of police cautioning the overwhelming pattern is, in adult cases, the use of prosecution instead of caution despite official guidelines urging otherwise. Both the police and other types of agency have near-absolute discretion. The police (dealing with mainly working-class crime use it one way, while most other agencies (dealing with mainly middle-class crime) use it in another. It is difficult to see how this can be justified in terms of offence seriousness, previous criminality, and so forth (Sanders 1985*a*; Cook, 1989), except, perhaps, in terms of a narrowly defined 'efficiency' (Hutter 1988). Efficiency, of course, is the crux of the crime control ideology. Thus the dispositions of both police and non-police agencies serve to further the different working rules of those different agencies.

Police Charging

In most cases the police now decide, following arrest, whether or not to charge. The usual threshold used to be a *prima facie* case. This, the Royal Commission on Criminal Procedure believed, led to many acquittals, and it recommended the more stringent criterion of 'a reasonable prospect of conviction'. Sanders (1985b, 1986) certainly found that weak evidence often led to acquittal, but also found that by no means all cases even passed the *prima facie* threshold. More recently, McConville *et al.* (1991: ch. 6) found the same in relation to the new threshold, and research by Zander for the Royal Commission on Criminal Justice confirms the continued prosecution of large numbers of weak cases (*Times*, 9 December 1992).

McConville *et al.* (1991) argue that the police continue to follow their working rules when making charge decisions, and follow American and English writers (such as Bittner 1967 and Chatterton 1976) in arguing that the charge—like stop-and-search, arrest, interrogation, and caution—is a resource for the police rather than an end in itself. Decisions to charge cases which are weak and to fail to charge cases which are strong are inconsistent and incomprehensible only in terms of the official guide-

[12] See e.g. Sanders (1988*a*) and Edwards (1989) on domestic violence, and Chambers and Millar (1983 1986) on sexual assault. This is discussed further by Zedner in chapter 25 in this volume.

lines. They are perfectly rational in terms of police working rules. This increases the acquittal rate, but convictions are only one dimension on the crime control scale. Acquisition of information (through interrogation which has then to be justified by charge); assertion of authority, protection of an officer against whom a complaint is expected: these are all reasons which McConville *et al.* (1991) found officers gave for charging with no regard for the rules.

Unlike cautions, which are usually decided by inspectors or more senior officers, charges are a matter for the arresting officer and custody officer. We have already seen that custody officers interpret their 'independence' to mean dispassion. This enables them to justify non-involvement in cases, thus actually *preventing* them from making meaningful detention or prosecution decisions. Thus McConville *et al.* (the only researchers to have looked at custody officers' charge decisions since Chatterton's (1976) early work, which reached similar conclusions about charge sergeants) found that 'I would go along with what the arresting officers have to say' was a typical view. As an arresting officer said: 'Perhaps by the book . . . "The custody officer will decide" sort of thing, but in practice it's different. He trusts your judgement' (McConville *et al.* 1991: 119–20). Very rarely do custody officers caution or NFA when the arresting officer wants a prosecution, or vice versa. And very rarely were senior officers involved until after prosecution by charge was initiated.

Custody officers are inevitably in a weak position in inquiring into evidential strength. If they try to evaluate arresting officers' evidence they have only one source of information from which to draw (apart from the suspect): that same arresting officer. Cop culture prevents the suspect from rising high on the hierarchy of credibility: 'I accept that [the officer's] got no cause to be telling lies and the other chap has' (McConville *et al.* 1991: 119). Arresting officers can, in other words, 'construct' their cases to achieve the results they want, and may even 'gild the lily' in the process (Ericson 1981; Holdaway, 1983). Case construction involves selection, interpretation, and creation of facts. Cases are constructed deliberately to appear strong, in accordance with adversarial principles (McBarnet 1981). Since the system is concerned more with legal truth than with actual truth, the police are also more concerned with the former, 'creating' facts which bear little relation to any reality which the suspect might recognize (Kaye 1991; Maguire and Norris 1992). Again, this is simply a continuation of the police role and processes revealed in study of interrogation and other policing practices.

It follows that, just as officers can secure cautions when NFA would be more in keeping with the rules, so they can secure charges when cautions would be more appropriate (and vice versa). Even when custody officers can secure extra relevant information (such as previous criminality) they usually do not do so (McConville *et al.* 1991: 121). Demeanour and the other factors influential at street level all play their part in the charge/caution decision and the inconsistency revealed by research is, again, explicable in part by the operation of working rules. The same factors apply with juveniles, despite relatively sophisticated juvenile liaison arrangements: many juveniles are still charged immediately, and even multi-agency juvenile bureaux still rely on police constructions.[13]

The Crown Prosecution Service

The Royal Commission realized that, left to their own devices, the police would not consistently apply the guidelines on evidential sufficiency and cautioning. To secure consistency, and to counterbalance extra police powers, it recommended establishing the Crown Prosecution Service (CPS). Apart from organizational and accountability matters with which we shall not be concerned here (on which see *Criminal Law Review* 1986), the government followed the Royal Commission's recommendations in the Prosecution of Offences Act 1985.

The CPS is built around the pre-existing system. The police continue to charge, summons, caution, and NFA as before. Once charged or summonsed, though, the accused becomes the responsibility of the CPS, which decides whether to continue the prosecution. The CPS is headed by the Director of Public Prosecutions (DPP), whose office had previously been responsible for national prosecutions of particular importance and for the prosecution of police officers. Many Crown Prosecutors had been police prosecutors, the only difference now being their new power to drop cases. The Code for Crown Prosecutors provides guidance on prosecution decisions in almost identical terms to those discussed before on evidential sufficiency and cautionability, so that poor police decisions can be corrected by the CPS.

Now that a 'realistic prospect of conviction' is the test for evidential sufficiency, conviction rates are key—if crude—performance indicators (National Audit Office 1989). Between 1985 and 1988 the percentage of cases ending in acquittal in the Crown Court went up slightly (from 16.7 to 17.6 per cent of cases). The percentage of cases ending in acquittal in the magistrates' courts in the same years, though, went up far more dramatically, from 12.5 to 23.8 per cent. Some of this increase can be attributed to the CPS dropping cases, but straight dismissals have also risen (McConville and Sanders 1992*a*), supporting McConville *et al.*'s (1991) findings in three police force areas. It was found that the CPS rarely dropped cases which were evidentially weak, and that when they did so

[13] See Evans and Ferguson (1991) and chapter 19 in this volume for further discussion of juvenile diversion.

this was usually on the initiative of the police and/or only after several court appearances.[14] McConville and Sanders (1992*a*) suggest three reasons for this: policy (the continuation of police working rules, shared by both prosecutors and police officers); the chance of a freak conviction (because verdicts are so hard to predict); and guilty pleas (just because a case is evidentially weak it does not follow that the defendant will contest the case; weak cases are continued in the—often correct—expectation of a guilty plea).

If the CPS is passive in relation to weak cases where case failure is a measure of institutional efficiency, it is not surprising to discover that it is even more passive in relation to cautionable cases. McConville *et al.* (1991) found no cautionable cases at all being dropped on grounds of cautionability alone, despite many similar cases being cautioned by the police. Again, where police working rules point to prosecution, the CPS is reluctant to stop the case (Gelsthorpe and Giller 1990). Doing so would also erode the conviction rate. That there is scope for diversion by the CPS was confirmed by the VERA Institute of Justice (Stone 1989), which found that the percentage of cases dropped on public interest grounds in the research area rose simply when this was being assessed; i.e. when CPS awareness of this possibility was heightened more cases of this type were identified. But, McConville and Sanders (1992*b*) argue, the CPS neither attempts nor wishes to raise consciousness of the issue among its personnel.

Regardless of the wishes or specific policies of the CPS nationally, the CPS is in a structurally weak position to carry out its ostensible aims primarily because of police case construction. The CPS reviews the quality of police cases on the basis of evidence provided solely by the police. This is like the problem of written records, where those who are being evaluated write their own reports. Cases being prosecuted are usually presented as prosecutable; the facts to support this are selected, and those which do not are ignored, hidden, or undermined. Thus weaknesses or cautionable factors, whether known by the police or not, often emerge only in or after trial (Leng 1992). This situation is exacerbated when the CPS relies on police summaries, which are very selective indeed (Baldwin and Bedward 1991). Moodie and Tombs (1982) in Scotland and Gelsthorpe and Giller (1990) in England cite prosecutors who agree that the police present them only with what seems relevant to them as prosecutors (as distinct from neutral intermediaries). Thus the VERA project found that

[14] Some additional evidence is provided by a study for the Commission by Block *et al.* (1993). They found that a high proportion of directed and ordered acquittals were predictably weak and should have been dropped at an early stage. In further but as yet unpublished research by Moxon and Crisp (cited in the Report, ch. 5), there is further evidence of cases being dropped only at a late stage.

when prosecutors were presented with information from non-police sources the discontinuance rate (on public interest grounds) rose from 1 per cent to 7 per cent (Stone 1989). The absence of national diversion schemes at the time of writing, despite the clear message of VERA, is striking.[15]

Attempts to resolve problems of due process and disparity in cautioning by using the CPS suffer another structural problem. Although cautionable cases which are prosecuted are in theory reviewable by the CPS, prosecutable (and NFA-able) cases which are cautioned are not. If the police decide to caution the case ends with them. However able or willing the CPS may be to deal with cases which should be cautioned, they cannot deal with cases which should *not* have been cautioned. This means that disparity will continue, and the violations of due process inherent in police cautioning procedures remain untouched by the CPS. As far as the cases in which the CPS is involved are concerned, the CPS appears to act as a police prosecution agency far more than as a 'ministry of justice'. This is hardly surprising in an adversarial system, but it does suggest that if suspects are in need of protection they will not find it in the CPS as presently constituted. Prosecutors could become adequate reviewers of either evidence or public interest only if placed in an entirely different structural relationship with the police. This would require fundamental changes in the adversarial system, and might even then be unsuccessful, if such impressionistic evidence as we have of continental systems (Leigh and Zedner 1992) is anything to go by.

PRE-TRIAL PROCESSES AND REMEDIES FOR MISCONDUCT

The criminal justice system is an integrated whole, so what happens at one stage of the process impacts upon—and often anticipates—other stages. Brief discussion of selected pre-trial processes and remedies is therefore appropriate to provide a rounded picture of the journey from suspect to trial.

Police Bail

After charge, the custody officer decides whether to release on bail or to hold the suspect in custody pending the next magistrates' court hearing (usually the next morning). Section 38 of PACE allows detention only if the suspect's real name and address cannot be ascertained, if he is

[15] However, the unpublished research by Moxon and Crisp referred to earlier (see note 14) does suggest that discontinuance on public interest grounds is now increasing, perhaps as a response to critical comment.

unlikely to appear in court to answer the charge, if he is likely to interfere with witnesses or further police investigations, or if he is likely to commit further significant crimes. Most of these provisions require the custody officer to predict what might happen if the suspect were released. However, the custody officer has to rely on what the investigating officers tell him and what little may be known about the suspect's previous record of appearing in court, offending on bail, and so forth. Also, suspects cannot prove that they would not have done something wrong had they been given the opportunity to do it. Thus decisions have to be taken quickly on the basis of inadequate information; although decisions are taken by independent officers to protect suspects from partisanship most of the information used will come from the very officers against whom protection is provided; and assessment of the quality of decision-making is almost impossible. So the initial bail/custody decision is entirely for the police, without real accountability.

This gives the police a powerful bargaining tool in interrogation. Although they should not offer 'inducements' (of which bail is one), this is a recognized interrogation 'tactic' (Irving 1980; McConville and Hodgson 1992: ch. 7), and the opportunity for informal 'chats' discussed above ensures that such negotiations need never take place in front of tape recorders or solicitors. McConville and Hodgson, for instance, report a suspect telling his solicitor: 'They [the police] said if I cough I'll get bail; if not then I'll be in court tomorrow' (1992: 79). Often 'bail bargaining' need not even be this explicit, since most suspects know—or think they know—that they can make deals on these lines, and ask 'will you get me bail?' (officer, quoted in McConville *et al.* 1991: 61).

Prior to PACE, bail was the principal currency of negotiation (see e.g. Dell 1971; Bottoms and McClean 1976; Softley 1980). Some recent research reports police officers claiming that PACE—the custody officer element in particular—has changed things (e.g. Dixon, Bottomley, *et al.* 1990; Irving and McKenzie 1989), but this is probably marginal. For bail bargaining, like so much police–suspect interaction, is 'all part of the relationship' (detective, quoted in McConville *et al.* 1991: 63). The building of relationships is a vital working rule, and, like other working rules, cannot simply be legislated away (Maguire and Norris 1992). Implicit bargaining over bail—leading to 'voluntary' confessions—is part of the differential power relationship between officer and suspect which leads suspects 'voluntarily' to agree to many similar things like stop-and-search, attendance at the station, search of premises, and so forth (Dixon, Coleman, and Bottomley 1990). The value of bail as currency is enhanced by the fear of being held overnight (Sanders *et al.* 1989: ch. 4). The power (and apparent power) of the police to deny bail is enhanced by the failure of many solicitors to attend the station and, when they do, to stay long.

Court Bail

Defendants who are granted police bail are not thereafter remanded in custody unless circumstances change. Defendants who are not granted police bail come before the magistrates as soon as possible, where bail may or may not be opposed by the police (through the CPS), and may or may not be requested by the defendant (usually through a solicitor). Although magistrates are independent their decisions are inevitably based on the information presented to them, and where the police have information justifying their own decision to hold suspects in custody they obviously present that information to magistrates with the aim of continued custody. Not surprisingly, magistrates tend to reach the same conclusions as the police (Simon and Weatheritt 1984), for they consider similar criteria and similar information. A magistrate, like a custody officer, has 'to come to a decision on the basis of probabilities and not certainties' (Hailsham, quoted in Zander 1988: 241). Overall, about 11–13 per cent of magistrates' cases are denied bail each year, in contrast to 19–22 per cent of those committed to the Crown Court (Morgan and Jones 1992).

One study found that, even when bail was refused, 38 per cent of magistrates' hearings took less than two minutes, and 87 per cent less than ten minutes (Doherty and East 1985). Either the information presented is considered hastily, or little information is provided. The more information from diverse sources which is presented, the more likely bail is to be granted. Bail information schemes, organized by local probation services, lead to the release of higher proportions of defendants than normal, demonstrating the partial (i.e. adversarial) approach of the police and the over-cautious approach of many courts. It seems that these schemes are more than paid for by the numbers of remanded prisoners thereby released, and the failure rate of the 'VERA offenders' was no greater than that of other offenders (Stone 1988). By 1991 bail information schemes covered over 100 magistrates' courts and fourteen prison establishments. As with diversion from prosecution, these schemes (also organized originally by VERA) shows the potential in the CPS for more independence if independent information is provided to it, for the CPS requests fewer custodial remands when these schemes are operating (Morgan and Jones 1992).

A suspect's being remanded in custody could obstruct defence work (including preparation of bail applications). Thus defendants remanded in custody are more likely to be convicted—and, if convicted, to be given custodial sentences—than those given bail (Bottomley 1973). But since not all defendants remanded in custody are convicted and given custodial sentences, some defendants who are legally innocent are held in custody, and some whose offence or circumstances do not warrant custodial sentences are also held in custody before sentence. Thus in 1986 54 per cent of defendants in custody in the magistrates' courts received non-custodial penalties, and a further 14 per cent were acquitted (Home Office 1986). On the other hand, 10–17 per cent of all persons released on bail commit further offences while at liberty (Morgan and Jones 1992). The initial police decision to grant bail or not has a major impact on the surrounding pre-trial processes, the prison population, and the use of police cells and police resources to house the consequent overflow from prison.

Guilty Pleas

The overwhelming majority of defendants plead guilty: 72 per cent of Crown Court defendants in 1989 (a substantial rise over previous years, according to Zander 1991), and 78.9 per cent of magistrates' courts defendants in 1987/8 (National Audit Office 1989). As McBarnet (1981) says, this is surprising in a system where one is presumed innocent until proved to be guilty. Why do so many defendants give up their right to put the prosecution to proof? The extensive American literature provides explanations ranging from bureaucratic to conflict models, with others centring on the historic role of defence agencies (see, for instance, McConville and Mirsky 1988, 1992). This wide range of perspectives was explored earlier in this chapter in relation to police and prosecution and will not be evaluated here. Rather than attempting to explain why (in common with the USA) England and Wales have a guilty plea system, we shall simply examine how it is secured.

Guilty pleas save police and CPS preparation and court time—and, of course, provide certain convictions in poorly constructed cases. Police and prosecutor pre-trial practices are therefore geared in large part to securing those guilty pleas. In general terms this means securing strong evidence (as would be needed were most pleas contested), in particular confessions. It is difficult for suspects to contest the guilt which they admitted to the police earlier, for it is assumed that no one would wrongly confess under normal conditions. Confessions, then, guarantee guilty pleas in all cases except those in which the suspect can convince a court (note the shift in the onus of proof) that the confession was obtained unlawfully or is otherwise unreliable. For as long as the law permits conviction on the basis of uncorroborated confession alone (which is not allowed in France and which has been questioned by the Royal Commission on Criminal Justice) the police will inevitably seek confessions without corroboration. The potential for police law-breaking (to secure confessions) and for false confessions (unverified by corroborative evidence but produced under pressure) is clear.

Defendants are encouraged to plead guilty through bargaining. Explicit plea bargaining over sentence with the judge is not permitted (Curran

1991) although the 'sentence discount' for pleading guilty is judicially acknowledged to be around 25–30 per cent (Thomas 1978: 51–2). Plea sometimes determines not just the length, but also the type of sentence (see the case of *Bird*, discussed by Curran 1991). Since no offences other than murder have fixed sentences in Britain, the difference between reducing sentence for a guilty plea and raising it for a not guilty plea is largely presentational, and the RCCJ has proposed that plea bargaining be made more explicit than it is currently.

We have seen that defence lawyers often fail to attend the interrogation, sending to suspects the due process message that it is the court, not police questioning, which is important (Sanders *et al.* 1989). However, this facilitates crime control practices at the police station and hence confessions, leaving little for the defence lawyer to do in court other than to mitigate on a guilty plea and to bargain. By failing to be adversarial in the police station, defence lawyers often deny their clients the opportunity to be adversarial in court. Some charges are often dropped or reduced—'adjusted', as some officers put it—in exchange for a plea. Both CPS and police make strenuous efforts 'to get a plea to something' (CPS, quoted in McConville *et al.* 1991: 166).

Defence lawyers frequently make commitments on behalf of their clients. Baldwin, in a study of pre-trial reviews, claimed that none of the bargaining he observed 'could fairly be described as improper' (1985: 97), which is surprising in view of his earlier findings (with McConville) to the contrary (Baldwin and McConville 1977). In fact Baldwin shows that defence lawyers frequently provide information to the prosecution which they need not, agree not to press their case when it might succeed, and agree to 'lean on' or 'pressure' their clients or 'beat them over the head'. This is the message of other recent English research too (e.g. Hansen 1986; McConville *et al.* 1991: ch. 8). The result is a remarkably high guilty plea rate, achieved with the co-operation of the legal defence community. What is regarded by Baldwin (1985: 85) as 'not standing on their rights' is in fact the defence failure to insist on due process. The crime control structure of arrest, interrogation, and prosecution practices, McConville *et al.* therefore argue, is concealed and legitimated by the defence community.

Does the abrogation of due process under the guilty plea system matter? The issues are similar to those encountered in relation to the right of silence. Some people plead guilty when they are innocent, often following a false confession (Davies 1970; Dell 1971; Baldwin and McConville 1977); Zander's Royal Commission research, conducted in 1992, suggests PACE has had little or no effect here. Some people feel aggrieved that legal rights appear to be only theoretical, thus undermining the legitimacy of the system. Sometimes the production of confessions and guilty pleas hides the absence of legal grounds for arrest, detention, prosecution, and so forth; this encourages 'fishing expeditions' by the police which impact not only on the legally guilty (whether factually so or not) but also on those held without charge (or prosecuted and acquitted) who should never have been deprived of their liberty without reasonable suspicion in the first place (McBarnet 1981; McConville *et al.* 1991; McConville and Mirsky 1992). Finally, the system is racially discriminatory: since black defendants contest their cases more often than do white defendants they get heavier sentences (Hood 1992).

And what if there were not pressures and incentives to plead guilty? Obviously the courts and prosecutorial agencies would require more resources. Cases would have to be more thoroughly prepared. Most important of all, as Dixon (1991b) argues in relation to the right of silence, the integration of street policing, police station procedures, and court processes would be dissolved.

Police Complaints Procedures

Discussion of street policing and police station procedures has revealed the disjunction between police working rules and legal rules, producing routine law breaking in relation to, for instance, reasonable suspicion in stops and arrests, access to solicitors, interrogation, and so forth. Then there are the more uncommon, but more serious, breaches of the law such as perjury, outright fabrication of confessions, 'gilding the lily', or the use or threat of violence.[16] Police and prosecution agencies simply attempt to achieve their institutional goals as efficiently as possible (Sanders 1992). It is because these rules aim to enforce due process values that they do not accord with working rules. To be inhibitory they would have to be supported by either moral force or threat. Police rhetoric tends to undermine the moral force of the law, so one is left only with sanctions (McConville *et al.* 1991: ch. 9). To understand fully why and how police practices operate on crime control lines we need to place them in the context of the sanctions available to victims of police law-breaking.

The only sanction available, for breaches of all laws, is the complaints and discipline procedure (see chapter 14 in this volume). Despite the introduction of the Police Complaints Authority (PCA) in 1985, very few complaints are substantiated. There are three possible explanations for this: that most complaints are unjustified; that most police investigations (and PCA scrutiny) are biased; and that evidence of malpractice cannot

[16] Kaye's (1991) discussion of the notorious West Midlands Police Serious Crime Squad includes many examples, some proven. Many also occurred in the notorious miscarriages revealed in 1990–2—the cases of the Guildford Four, Birmingham Six, Tottenham Three, Cardiff Three, Steven Kizco, Judith Ward, and so forth.

be obtained in most cases. The first two explanations are doubtless partially true. Regarding bias, the discrediting process discussed by Box and Russell (1975) in relation to the pre-PCA system is unaffected by changes in the structure of supervision. Even the Police Complaints Board (PCB) was aware of this, commenting that some officers say of some complainants (particularly in assault cases) that 'his previous record makes his evidence unreliable . . . it would be helpful if such conclusions were not preconceived but the result of the investigation.' (1980: paras 59–62). The PCA (and the PCB, DPP, and DCC) are in the same position as is the CPS *vis-à-vis* investigating police officers. Rather than reinvestigate, the PCA simply peruses a carefully constructed document. The discomfort felt by the PCB (and now the PCA) rarely allowed it to reverse negative findings, for, like the CPS, it receives information from the police alone.

Securing evidence of malpractice is the greatest problem. Since most alleged malpractice occurs on police territory, the very conditions which allow officers to break the law allow them to hide that fact from civilian witnesses, and 60 per cent of officers interviewed by Maguire and Corbett 'admitted the existence of something like a "code of silence" among junior officers . . .' (1991: 71). Thus the PCB and PCA view unsubstantiated complaints as complaints without sufficient evidence to support them rather than necessarily as unjustified complaints (Stevens and Willis 1981: ch. 1). Evidence can be hidden through PACE's self-validating procedures. Thus it is more difficult than hitherto to prove that unrecorded intimidatory interrogations occurred now that custody officers complete custody records which do not record such events, and which may not record the names of the officer involved.[17] Even the evidence required to bring disciplinary proceedings (let alone successfully to bring charges) must be 'beyond reasonable doubt'. Complaints have been unsuccessful in some of the most notorious miscarriage cases, such as *Confait* (discussed by the Royal Commission 1981), in which malpractices were revealed only some years after the event.

Many complainants are persuaded by police investigators to withdraw their complaints in the course of their investigation (Maguire and Corbett 1991: ch. 7), and many more are dissatisfied with the outcome. Most complainants interviewed by Maguire and Corbett thought 'that the PCA was on the side of the police' (1991: 176). Even the Metropolitan Police Commissioner acknowledges how little faith the public has in the PCA (*Guardian*, 25 April 1988). Hence many people are deterred from complaining in the first place.

The complaints system fails all due process tests (openness, not allow-

[17] This happened in a case secretly recorded for an ITV programme broadcast on 7 July 1992. See McConville (1992).

ing officials to be judges in their own cause, giving all parties a fair hearing, and so forth) and fails to deter the police from crime control practices in general and law-breaking in particular.[18] Like the rest of the system, black and working-class people seem to bear the brunt of its failings. This should only be surprising if we see complaints as the products of pathological 'bad apples'. If they are on the contrary regarded as normal reflections of policing practice (Goldsmith 1991), both the behaviour complained of and the closing of ranks preventing a high proportion of substantiation are to be expected in a crime control system. Moreover, as in other contexts, officers do not see the 'black letter' of the law as the dividing line between acceptable and unacceptable behaviour. As Maguire (1992) notes, police investigators probably do not consciously try to exonerate officers who 'overstep the mark', but 'the mark' is not a clear or unchanging line. It depends on the circumstances at the time, the police working rules being pursued, and the characteristics of the complainant.

Court-Based Remedies

Court-based remedies for police misconduct are of three kinds. First, there are criminal prosecutions. Some are initiated by the DPP following invocation of the complaints procedure, but there are other routes, including private prosecution. Such prosecutions are rare, not least because few types of police malpractice are actually criminal; however, prosecutions were brought against some of the officers in the Birmingham Six case.

Second, there are civil actions. Like private criminal actions these are expensive, lengthy, and difficult to win. However, proof on the balance of probabilities is all that is required, and civil actions have increased in number throughout the 1980s (this is perhaps more of a comment on the inadequacy of the other remedies than anything else; see Clayton and Tomlinson 1987). Wrongful arrest and false imprisonment are common civil actions in tort, but neither PACE nor any other legislation has created new torts (or crimes). Thus the 'right' to a lawyer is not a 'real right', for there is no court action available to enforce it or to seek compensation for its denial. The same is true of most unlawful interrogation (Sanders 1988*c*), the caution guidelines, and the Code for Crown Prosecutors.[19]

[18] The RCCJ expressed similar views, albeit in milder language, and recommended tougher discipline procedures for the police with a lower burden of proof (1993: ch. 3).

[19] Following early cases confirming the unfettered discretion of the police, two juveniles failed in 1991 to get their prosecutions judicially reviewed, despite their cases being clearly cautionable.

Thirdly, there is the exclusion in court of unlawfully obtained evidence. Only unreliable or oppressively obtained confession evidence is automatically excluded. Trial courts may hear other evidence at their discretion. Thus evidence arising from common forms of malpractice—unlawful stops, police-car interrogations, denial of access—may be used. The working rules used by courts to decide what to allow are difficult to determine. Although the courts exclude more evidence now than was the case before PACE, and do so more often than critics expected, in many cases where the right to legal advice is obstructed the decision to allow the evidence is upheld (Birch 1989; Feldman 1990; Sanders 1990). Neither courts nor Parliament adopt the American 'fruit of the forbidden tree' doctrine which is the hallmark of due process. Instead the emphasis is on the probative value of evidence, however it was obtained (up to a point): the crime control doctrine. In any case, most defendants plead guilty, few being encouraged to 'stand on their rights'. Excluding evidence can only help defendants who contest their cases. Hence defendants who are not prosecuted also fail to benefit from exclusionary rules. Yet they may still have suffered as a result of the abrogation of their rights, and police officers who are on 'fishing expeditions' or seeking information not related to the prosecution of the individual concerned will not be deterred by this possible problem.

Unlike complaints, court-based remedies are open and complainant-driven, as distinct from being police-driven. Their disadvantages, however, render them equally ineffective in preventing miscarriages of justice.

CONCLUSION

Criminal justice continually evolves in response to new ideas, new pressures, and new scandals. No system corresponds exactly with any one model and there are always gaps between rhetoric, rules, and reality. Criminal justice rhetoric is a response to public pressures; rules are designed for, rather than by, the agencies operating them; and reality represents those agencies' attempts to steer a course between those rules and their own priorities. Thus we have seen a largely due-process-based rhetoric, rules which (often incoherently) combine both crime control and due process, and a largely crime control reality. Inquisitorial faith in the crime-control-based fact-finding ability of the police and the CPS can be found alongside adversarial justification of their construction of cases to be as legally strong as possible without pursuing exculpatory lines of investigation. Even in court the presumption of innocence is compromised by the guilty plea system and bail systems whereby most decisions are made on the basis of police information. Due process requires legal representation, but crime control processes (in the station and through guilty pleas) thrive because legal representatives do not challenge them.

It is clear that if the police were forced to adhere faithfully to legal rules their crime control methods would be greatly modified; whether crime would be less well controlled is not so clear. It depends on how successful the police (and associated agencies) are in establishing actual guilt and innocence. The infamous miscarriages of justice of 1990–2 raise serious doubts about this, as do the less dramatic findings of research on unsuccessful stops, NFAs in the police station, and the failure of cases in court. Just because due process is a suspect-orientated way of establishing 'truth' it does not follow that it is a less effective one. As it is, law-breaking by the police and lesser failures of due process are tolerated by a system which fails to deter the police or to compensate the victims of those practices. Legal changes change some police practices at the margin, but often simply displace the unlawful activity of officials to another part of the system.

Whether the crime control reality of criminal justice is primarily a product of bureaucratic pressures or societal structures remains an open question, but the results are clear. Patterns of bias on the street—particularly concerning class and race—are reproduced throughout the system, so that in the prisons black people in particular are grossly overrepresented (Hood 1992). Cynicism about criminal justice abounds. The complaints system lacks credibility. Police rule-breaking is normal and not deviant. As labelling theory insists, criminals are best regarded merely as the legally guilty. Suspects are not a subset of the wider criminal population; rather, criminals are a subset of the wider (official) suspect population. How closely this relates to the 'actually guilty' population must remain a matter of speculation.

Prospects for change depend in part on one's view of the reasons for the predominance of crime control processes. Bureaucratic explanations, which focus on the values of particular institutions, produce more optimistic scenarios than do societal ones. The former influenced the 1981 Royal Commission and led to the PACE Act. On the other hand, law enforcement agencies do not all operate similarly. We saw how 'white-collar' law enforcement agencies generally avoid prosecution. They also avoid other trappings of crime control such as arrest, detention, oppressive interrogation, and so forth. Is this a sign of institutional 'best practice' to which other agencies could reasonably be expected to aspire? Would police forces still be recognizable as police forces if 'ethical interviewing' truly replaced current interrogation practices? Or does present practice simply reflect a society in which some of the most damaging criminals are treated in the most humane ways while those who are society's victims are treated as society's enemies so that, in time, they live up to their labels?

Selected Further Reading

D. Cook, *Rich Law, Poor Law*. Milton Keynes: Open University Press, 1989.

D. Dixon, C. Coleman and A. Bottomley, 'Consent and the Legal Regulation of Policing', *Journal of Law and Society*, 1990, 17: 345–62.

M. King, *Framework of Criminal Justice*. London: Croom Helm, 1981.

D. McBarnet, *Conviction*. London: Macmillan, 1981.

M. McConville, A. Sanders and R. Leng, *The Case for the Prosecution*. London: Routledge, 1991.

M. McConville and J. Hodgson, *Custodial Legal Advice and the Right of Silence*, Royal Commission on Criminal Justice Research Study no. 16. London: HMSO, 1992.

R. Reiner, *The Politics of the Police*, 2nd edn. Hemel Hempstead: Harvester Wheatsheaf, 1992.

A. Sanders, 'Rights, Remedies and the PACE Act', *Criminal Law Review*, 1988, pp. 802–12.

Royal Commission on Criminal Justice, *Report*. London: HMSO, 1993.

C. Walker and K. Starmer, eds., *Justice in Error*. London: Blackstone, 1993.

REFERENCES

Baldwin, J. (1985), *Pre-Trial Criminal Justice*. Oxford: Blackwell.

—— (1991), 'Videotaping in Police Stations', *New Law Journal*, 141: 1512–16.

Baldwin, J., and Bedward, J. (1991), 'Summarizing Tape Recordings of Police Interviewing', *Criminal Law Review*: 671–9.

Baldwin, J., and McConville, M. (1977), *Negotiated Justice*. Oxford: Martin Robertson.

Becker, H. (1963), *Outsiders: Studies in the Sociology of Deviance*. New York: Free Press.

Bevan, V., and Lidstone, K. (1985), *Police and Criminal Evidence Act, 1984*. London: Butterworths.

Birch, D. (1989), 'The Pace Hots Up: Confessions and Confusions under the 1984 Act', *Criminal Law Review*: 95–116.

Bittner, E. (1967), 'The Police on Skid-Row: A Study of Peace-keeping', *American Sociological Review*, 32: 699–715.

BLACK, D. (1970), 'Production of Crime Rates', *American Sociological Review*, 35: 733–48.

BLACKSTONE, W. (1830), *Commentaries*. London.

BLOCK, B., CORBETT, C., and PEAY, J. (1993), *Ordered and Directed Acquittals in the Crown Court*. London: HMSO.

BOGOLMONY, R. (1976), 'Street Patrol: The Decision to Stop a Citizen', *Criminal Law Bulletin*, 12: 544–82.

BOTTOMLEY, K., (1973), *Decisions in the Penal Process*. London: Martin Robertson.

BOTTOMLEY, K., COLEMAN, C., DIXON, D., GILL, M., and WALL, D. (1991), 'The Detention of Suspects in Police Custody: The Impact of PACE', *British Journal of Criminology*, 31: 347–64.

BOTTOMS, A., and MCCLEAN, J. (1976), *Defendants in the Criminal Process*. London: Routledge.

BOX, S., and RUSSELL, K., (1975), 'The Politics of Discreditability: Disarming Complaints Against the Police', *Sociological Review*, 23: 315–46.

BROGDEN, M., (1985), 'Stopping the People: Crime Control versus Social Control', in J. Baxter and L. Koffman, eds., *Police: The Constitution and the Community*, Abingdon: Professional Books.

BROWN, D. (1987), *Police Complaints Procedure: A Survey of Complainants' Views*. London: HMSO (HORS 93).

—— (1989), *Detention at the Police Station under the PACE Act*. London: HMSO (HORS 104).

CAMERON, M. (1964), *The Booster and the Snitch*. New York: Free Press.

CHAMBERS, G., and MILLAR, A. (1983), *Investigating Sexual Assault*. Edinburgh: HMSO.

—— (1986), *Prosecuting Sexual Assault*. Edinburgh: HMSO.

CHATTERTON, N. (1976), 'Police in Social Control', in J. King, ed., *Control without Custody*, Cambridge: Institute of Criminology.

CLARKESON, C., CRETNEY, A., DAVIES, G., and SHEPHERD, J. (forthcoming), *British Journal of Criminology*.

CLAYTON, J., and TOMLINSON, B. (1987), *Civil Actions Against the Police*. London: Butterworths.

COHEN, S. (1985), *Visions of Social Control*. Cambridge: Cambridge University Press.

COOK, D. (1989), *Rich Law, Poor Law*. Milton Keynes: Open University Press.

Criminal Law Review (1986), special issue on 'The New Prosecution Arrangements', 1–44.

CURRAN, P. (1991), 'Discussions in the Judge's Private Room', *Criminal Law Review*: 79–86.

DAMASKA, E. (1973), 'Evidentiary Barriers to Conviction and Two Models of Criminal Procedure: A Comparative Study', *University of Pennsylvania Law Review*, 121: 506–89.

DAVIES, C. (1970), 'The Innocent who Plead Guilty', *Law Guardian*, no. 57: 9–15.

DELL, S. (1971), *Silent in Court*. London: Bell.

DITCHFIELD, J. (1976), *Police Cautioning*. London: HMSO (HORS 37).

DIXON, D. (1991*a*), 'Common Sense, Legal Advice, and the Right of Silence', *Public Law*: 233–54.

DIXON, D. (1991*b*), 'Politics, Research, and Symbolism in Criminal Justice: The Right of Silence and the PACE Act', *Anglo-American Law Review*, 20: 27–50.

DIXON, D., BOTTOMLEY, A., COLEMAN, C., GILL, M., and WALL, D. (1989), 'Reality and Rules in the Construction and Regulation of Police Suspicion', *International Journal of the Sociology of Law*, 17: 185–206.

—— (1990), 'Safeguarding the Rights of Suspects in Police Custody', *Policing and Society*, 1: 115–40.

DIXON, D., COLEMAN, C., and BOTTOMLEY, A., (1990), 'Consent and the Legal Regulation of Policing', *Journal of Law and Society*, 17: 345–62.

DOHERTY, M., and EAST, R. (1985), 'Bail Decisions in Magistrates' Courts', *British Journal of Criminology*, 25: 251–66.

DOWNES, D., and ROCK, P. (1988), *Understanding Deviance*. Oxford: Oxford University Press.

DRIVER, P. (1968), 'Confessions and the Social Psychology of Coercion', *Harvard Law Review*, 82: 42–61.

EASTON, S. (1991), *The Right to Silence*. Aldershot: Avebury.

EDWARDS, S. (1989), *Policing Domestic Violence*. London: Sage.

ERICSON, R. (1981), *Making Crime*. London: Butterworths.

EVANS, R. (1991), 'Police Cautioning and the Young Adult Offender', *Criminal Law Review*: 598–609.

—— (1992), 'The Conduct of Police Interviews with Juveniles', Royal Commission on Criminal Justice, Research Study no. 8.

EVANS, R., and FERGUSON, T. (1991), *Comparing Different Juvenile Cautioning Systems in One Police Force*. London: Home Office, unpublished report.

FELDMAN, D. (1990), 'Regulating Treatment of Suspects in Police Stations', *Criminal Law Review*: 452–71.

FIELD, S., and SOUTHGATE, P. (1982), *Public Disorder*. London: HMSO (HORS 72).

GELSTHORPE, L., and GILLER, H. (1990), 'More Justice for Juveniles: Does More Mean Better?', *Criminal Law Review*: 153–64.

GEMMILL, R., and MORGAN-GILES, R. (1980), *Arrest, Charge, and Summons*. London.

GOLDSMITH, A., ed. (1991), *Complaints against the Police: A Comparative Study*. Oxford.

GOLDSTEIN, J. (1960), 'Police Discretion not to Invoke the Criminal Process: Low Visibility Decisions in the Administration of Justice', *Yale Law Journal*, 69: 543.

GREER, S. (1990), 'The Right to Silence: A Review of the Current Debate', *Modern Law Review*, 53: 709–30.

GREER, S., and MORGAN, R., eds. (1990), *The Right to Silence*. Centre for Criminal Justice, Bristol: University of Bristol.

GUDJONSSON, G., and MACKEITH, J. (1982), 'False Confessions', in A. Trankell, ed., *Reconstructing the Past*, Deventer, Netherlands.

—— (1988), 'Retracted Confessions: Legal, Psychological and Psychiatric Aspects', *Medicine, Science, and the Law*, 28: 187–94.

HANSEN, O. (1986), 'Newsbrief'. *New Law Journal*, 136: 601.

HOBBS, D. (1988), *Doing the Business*. Oxford: Oxford University Press.

HOLDAWAY, S. (1983), *Inside the British Police*. Oxford: Blackwell.

HOME OFFICE (1986), *Criminal Statistics*. London: HMSO.

—— (1988), *Criminal Statistics*. London: HMSO.

—— (1989), *Report of the Working Group on the Right of Silence*. London: Home Office, unpublished report.

—— (1990), *The Cautioning of Offenders*, Circular no. 59/1990. London: Home Office.

HOOD, R. (1992), *Race and Sentencing*. Oxford: Oxford University Press.

HURD, D. (1984), *Hansard*, House of Commons, Standing Committee E, 16 February.

HUTTER, B. (1988), *The Reasonable Arm of the Law? The Law Enforcement Procedures of Environmental Health Officers*. Oxford: Oxford University Press.

IRVING, B. (1980), *Police Interrogation: A Study of Current Practice*. London: HMSO.

—— (1985), 'Research Into Policy Won't Go', in E. Alves and J. Shapland, eds., *Legislation for Policing Today: The PACE Act*. Leicester: Leicester University Press.

IRVING, B., and MCKENZIE, I. (1988), *Regulating Custodial Interviews*. London: Police Foundation.

—— (1989) *Police Interrogation: The Effects of the PACE Act*. London: Police Foundation.

JACKSON, J. (1991), 'Curtailing the Right of Silence: Lessons from Northern Ireland', *Criminal Law Review*: 404–15.

JEFFERSON, T., and WALKER, M. (1992), 'Ethnic Minorities in the Criminal Justice System', *Criminal Law Review*: 83–95.

KAYE, T. (1991), *Unsafe and Unsatisfactory*. London: Civil Liberties Trust.

LEA, J., and YOUNG, J. (1984), *What is to be Done about Law and Order*? Harmondsworth: Penguin.

LEIGH, L., and ZEDNER, L. (1992), *A Report on the Administration of Criminal Justice in the Pre-Trial Phase in France and Germany*, RCCJ Research Study no. 1. London: HMSO.

LENG, R. (1992), 'The Right to Silence in Police Interrogation', RCCJ Research Study no. 10. London: HMSO.

LIDSTONE, K., HOGG, R., and SUTCLIFFE, F. (1980), *Prosecution by Private Individuals and Non-Police Agencies*. London: HMSO.

LUSTGARTEN, L. (1987), 'The Police and the Substantive Criminal Law', *British Journal of Criminology*, 27: 23.

MCBARNET, D. (1981), *Conviction*. London: Macmillan.

MCCONVILLE, M. (1992), 'Videotaping Interrogations: Police Behaviour on and off Camera', *Criminal Law Review*: 522–48.

MCCONVILLE, M., and BALDWIN, J. (1981), *Courts, Prosecution, and Conviction*. Oxford: Oxford University Press.

MCCONVILLE, M., and HODGSON, J. (1992), 'Custodial Legal Advice and the Right to Silence', RCCJ Research Study no. 16. London: HMSO.

MCCONVILLE, M., and MIRSKY, C. (1988), 'The State, the Legal Profession, and the Defence of the Poor', *Journal of Law and Society*, 15: 342–60.

McConville, M., and Mirsky, C. (1992), 'What's in the Closet: The Plea Bargaining Skeletons', *New Law Journal*, 142: 1373–81.

McConville, M., and Morrell, P. (1983), 'Recording and Interrogation: Have the Police got it Taped?', *Criminal Law Review*: 158–62.

McConville, M., and Sanders, A. (1992*a*), 'Weak Cases and the CPS', *Law Society Gazette*, 12 February: 24–5.

—— (1992*b*), 'Fairness and the CPS', *New Law Journal*, 142: 120–2.

McConville, M., Sanders, A., and Leng, R. (1991), *The Case for the Prosecution*. London: Routledge.

McKenzie, I., Morgan, R., and Reiner, R. (1990), 'Helping the Police with their Enquiries', *Criminal Law Review*: 22–33.

Maguire, M. (1988), 'Effects of the PACE Provisions on Detection and Questioning', *British Journal of Criminology*, 28: 19–43.

—— (1992) 'Complaints against the Police: where now?', unpublished paper.

Maguire, M., and Corbett, C. (1991), *A Study of the Police Complaints System*. London: HMSO.

Maguire, M., and Norris, C. (1992), *The Conduct and Supervision of Criminal Investigations*, RCCJ Research Study no. 5. London: HMSO.

Matza, D. (1969), *Becoming Deviant*. New Jersey:Prentice-Hall.

Moodie, S., and Tombs, J. (1982), *Prosecution in the Public Interest*. Edinburgh: Edinburgh University Press.

Morgan, R., and Jones, P. (1992), 'Bail or Jail?', in S. Casale and E. Stockdale, eds., *Criminal Justice under Stress*. London: Blackstone.

Morgan, R., Reiner, R., and McKenzie, I. (n.d.), *Police Powers and Policy: A Study of the Risk of Custody Officers*, report to ESRC. London.

Morris, A., Giller, H., Szwed, E., and Geack, H., (1980), *Justice for Children*. London: Edward Arnold.

Moston, S. (1992), 'Police Questioning Techniques in Tape Recorded Interviews with Criminal Suspects', *Policing and Society*, 3.

Moston, S., Stephenson, G., and Williamson, T. (1992), 'The Effects of Case Characteristics on Suspect Behaviour during Police Questioning', *British Journal of Criminology*, 32: 23–40.

—— (1993), 'The Incidence, Antecedents and Consequences of the Use of the Right to Silence during Police Questioning', *Criminal Behaviour and Mental Health*, 3: 30–47.

Moston, S., and Williamson, T. (1990), 'The Extent of Silence in Police Interviews', in S. Greer and R. Morgan, eds., *The Right to Silence*, Center for Criminal Justice, Bristol: University of Bristol.

Murphy, D. (1986), *Customers and Thieves*. Farnborough: Gower.

National Audit Office (1989), *Review of the Crown Prosecution Service*. London: HMSO.

Packer, H. (1968), *The Limits of the Criminal Sanction*. Stanford: Stanford University Press.

Piliavin, I., and Briar, S. (1964), 'Police Encounters with Juveniles', *American Journal of Sociology*, 70: 206–14.

Police Complaints Board (1980), *Triennial Report*. London: HMSO.

PRATT, J. (1986), 'Diversion from the Juvenile Court', *British Journal of Criminology*, 26: 212–33.

REINER, R. (1985), *The Politics of the Police*. Brighton: Wheatsheaf.

REISS, A. (1971), *The Police and the Public*. New Haven, Conn: Yale University Press.

RICHARDSON, G., OGUS, A., and BURROWS, J. (1983), *Policing Pollution*. Oxford: Oxford University Press.

ROYAL COMMISSION ON CRIMINAL JUSTICE (1993), *Report*. London: HMSO.

ROYAL COMMISSION ON CRIMINAL PROCEDURE (1981), *Report*. London: HMSO.

SANDERS, A. (1985*a*), 'Class Bias in Prosecutions', *Howard Journal of Criminal Justice*, 24: 176–99.

—— (1985*b*), 'Prosecution Decisions and the Attorney-General's Guidelines', *Criminal Law Review*: 4–19.

—— (1986), 'An Independent Crown Prosecution Service?', *Criminal Law Review*: 16–27.

—— (1987), 'Constructing the Case for the Prosecution', *Journal of Law and Society*, 14: 229–53.

—— (1988*a*), 'Personal Violence and Public Order: The Prosecution of Domestic Violence in England and Wales'. *International Journal of Sociology of Law*, 16: 359–82.

—— (1988*b*), 'The Limits to Diversion from Prosecution', *British Journal of Criminology*, 28: 513–32.

—— (1988*c*), 'Rights, Remedies and the PACE Act', *Criminal Law Review*: 802–12.

—— (1990), 'Access to Legal Advice and s. 78 PACE', *Law Society Gazette*, 31 October: 17–23.

—— (1992), 'Reforming the Prosecution System', *Political Quarterly*, 63: 25–36.

SANDERS, A., and BRIDGES, L. (1990), 'Access to Legal Advice and Police Malpractice', *Criminal Law Review*: 494–509.

SANDERS, A., BRIDGES, L., MULVANEY, A., and CROZIER, G. (1989), *Advice and Assistance at Police Stations and the 24 Hour Duty Solicitor Scheme*. London: Lord Chancellor's Department.

SCARMAN, Lord (1981), *The Scarman Report: The Brixton Disorders*. London: HMSO.

SCOTT, M., and LYMAN, S. (1968), 'Accounts', *American Sociological Review*, 33: 46–62.

SCRATON, P. ed. (1987), *Law, Order, and the Authoritarian State*. Milton Keynes: Open University Press.

SHAPLAND, J., and VAGG, J. (1988), *Policing by the Public*. London: Routledge.

SIMON, F., and WEATHERITT, M. (1984), *The Use of Bail and Custody by London Magistrates' Courts*. London: HMSO.

SMITH, D., and GRAY, J. (1983), *Police and People in London*. Aldershot: Gower.

SOFTLEY, P. (1980), *Police Interrogation: An Observational Study in Four Police Stations*. London: HMSO.

STANKO, E. (1985), *Intimate Intrusions*. London: Routledge.

STEER, D. (1970), *Police Cautions*. Oxford: Blackwell.

Steer, D. (1980), *Uncovering Crime: The Police Role*. London: HMSO.

Stevens, P., and Willis, C. (1979), *Race, Crime, and Arrests.* London: HMSO (HORS 58).

—— (1981), *Ethnic Minorities and Complaints against the Police*. London: Home Office.

Stone, C. (1988), *Bail Information for the Crown Prosecution Service*. New York: VERA.

—— (1989), *Public Interest Case Assessment*. New York: VERA

Thomas, D. (1978), *Principles of Sentencing*. London: Butterworths.

Tuck, M., and Southgate, P. (1981), *Ethnic Minorities, Crime and Policing*. London.

Walkley, J. (1987), *Police Interrogation*. London: HMSO (HORS 70).

Walmsley, R. (1978), 'Indecency between Males and the Sexual Offences Act 1967', *Criminal Law Review*: 400–7.

Wasoff, F. (1982), 'Legal Protection from Wifebeating', *International Journal of Sociology of Law*, 10: 187–204.

Wilcox, A. (1972), *The Decision to Prosecute*. London.

Wilkinson, C., and Evans, R. (1990), 'Police Cautioning of Juveniles: The Impact of Home Office Circular 14/1985', *Criminal Law Review*: 165–76.

Williams, G. (1979), 'The Authentication of Statements to the Police', *Criminal Law Review*: 6–23.

Willis, C. (1983), *The Use, Effectiveness, and Impact of Police Stop and Search Powers*. London: Home Office (RPUP 15).

—— (1988), *The Tape Recording of Police Interviews with Suspects*. London: HMSO (HORS 97).

Zander, M. (1979), 'The Investigation of Crime: A Study of Cases Tried in the Old Bailey', *Criminal Law Review*: 203–19.

—— (1988), *Cases and Materials on the English Legal System*. London: Weidenfeld.

—— (1991), 'What the Annual Statistics Tell Us about Pleas and Acquittals, *Criminal Law Review*: 252–8.

Zuckerman, A. (1989), 'Trial by Unfair Means: The Report of the Working Group on the Right of Silence', *Criminal Law Review*: 855–65.

17

Sentencing

ANDREW ASHWORTH

RATIONALES FOR SENTENCING

Sentencing amounts to the use of state coercion against a person for committing an offence. The sanction may take the form of some deprivation, restriction, or positive obligation. Deprivations and obligations are fairly widespread in social contexts—e.g. duties to pay taxes, to complete various forms, etc. But when imposed as a sentence, there is the added element of condemnation, labelling, or censure of the offender. In view of the direct personal and indirect social effects this can have, it calls for justification.

Much writing about the rationales of sentencing has focused on one or more particular justifications. In order to unravel punishment as a social institution, however, and to understand the tensions inherent in any given 'system', there is benefit in identifying the main thrusts of the several approaches. Among the issues to be considered are the behavioural and the political premises of each approach, its empirical claims, and its practical influence.

Desert or Retributive Theories

Retributive theories of punishment have a long history, including the writings of Kant and Hegel. In their modern guise as the desert approach, they came to prominence in the 1970s, to some extent propelled by the alleged excesses and failures of rehabilitative ideals (Bottoms and Preston 1980). Punishment is justified as the natural or appropriate response to crime, a fundamental intuitive claim, and its quantum should be proportionate to the degree of wrongdoing. The justification for the institution of punishment also incorporates the consequentialist element of needing to deter crime: without the institution, anarchy might well ensue (for a variety of modern writings, see von Hirsch 1976, 1986, 1990*a*; Duff 1986). The behavioural premise of desert is that individuals are responsible and predominantly rational decision-makers. The political premise is that all individuals are entitled to equal respect and dignity: an offender does not forfeit all rights on conviction, and has a right not to be punished disproportionately to the crime committed.

Proportionality is the key concept in desert theory. Cardinal proportionality requires that the overall level of the penalty scale should not be out of proportion to the gravity of the conduct: five years' imprisonment for shoplifting would clearly breach that principle, but beyond such extreme cases there is much room for debate. Social conventions and cultural traditions tend to determine what levels of sanction are thought appropriate in a particular national or historical context (cf. Downes 1988 on the Netherlands and England; Graham 1990 on Germany). Ordinal proportionality concerns the ranking of the relative seriousness of different offences. In practice, much depends here on the evaluation of conduct, especially by sentencers, and on social assumptions about traditional or 'real' crime (e.g. street crime) compared with new types of offence (e.g. city fraud, pollution). In theory, ordinal proportionality requires the creation of a scale of values which can be used to assess the gravity of each type of offence: other relevant factors, such as culpability, aggravation, and mitigation, must then be assimilated into the scale. This task, which is vital to any theory in which proportionality plays a part, is continuing (e.g. von Hirsch and Jareborg 1991; Ashworth 1992: ch. 4).

Deterrence Theories

Deterrence theories regard the prevention of further offences through a deterrent strategy as the rationale for punishing. As an exercise of state power, sentencing can be justified only by its consequences. The quantum of the sentence depends on the type of deterrent theory. There is little modern literature on individual deterrence, which sees the deterrence of further offences by the particular offender as the measure of punishment. A first offender may require little or no punishment. A recidivist might be thought to require an escalation of penalties. The seriousness of the offence becomes less important than the prevention of repetition. Traces of this approach can certainly be detected in modern sentencing practice, and some critics of desert theory claim that in taking (limited) account of prior record it incorporates a covert deterrent element (for discussion see Ashworth 1992*a*: ch. 6.2).

More attention has been devoted to general deterrence, which involves calculating the penalty on the basis of what might be expected to deter others from committing a similar offence. Major utilitarian writers such as Bentham (1789; and cf. Walker 1991) and economic theorists such as Posner (1985) develop the notion of setting penalties at levels sufficient to outweigh the likely benefits of offending. The behavioural premise is that of responsible and predominantly rational, calculating individuals. The political premise is that the greatest good of the greatest number represents the supreme value, and that the individual counts only for one: it may therefore be justifiable to punish one person severely in order to deter others effectively. Satisfactory empirical evidence of the effect of deterrent sentencing on individual behaviour is difficult to obtain. The conditions must be such that non-offending can safely be ascribed to the deterrent effect of the legal penalty rather than to any of the other myriad influences on people's conduct, such as the perceived risk of detection, the opinions of significant others, etc. (Beyleveld 1980; cf. Walker 1991). Few research findings meet that criterion, and those that do provide support for general deterrent sentencing in only a few types of situation (see Zimring and Hawkins 1973; Beyleveld 1979; Riley 1985; Harding 1990).

Rehabilitative Sentencing

Sentencing aimed at the reformation of the offender's character has a lengthy history, being evident in the early days of probation and of Borstal institutions. The rationale here is to prevent further offending by the individual through the strategy of rehabilitation, which may involve individual case-work, therapy, counselling, intervention in the family, etc. Still a leading rationale in many European countries, it reached its zenith in the United States in the 1960s and then declined spectacularly in the 1970s. Research by Martinson was widely represented as demonstrating that treatment programmes usually failed, swamping the more qualified judgement in an English survey by Brody and a subsequent clarification or retraction by Martinson himself (Martinson *et al.* 1974; Brody 1975; Martinson 1979). In terms of effectiveness, the true position is probably (as with deterrence) that certain rehabilitative programmes are likely to work for some types of offender in some circumstances. A humanitarian desire to provide help for those with obvious behavioural problems has ensured that various treatment programmes continue to be developed, and some authors have called for the rehabilitation of rehabilitative theory (see Cullen and Gilbert 1982; Hudson 1987; and discussion by von Hirsch and Ashworth 1992*a*: ch. 1).

Its behavioural premise is that some or many criminal offences are to a significant extent determined by social pressures, psychological difficulties, or other problems which impinge on individuals. The links with positivist criminology are strong. The political premise is that offenders are seen as unable to cope and in need of help from experts, and therefore (perhaps) as less than fully responsible individuals. The rehabilitative approach indicates that sentences should be tailored to the needs of the particular offenders, and places no limits on the extent of the intervention. It lays emphasis on the processes of diagnosis and treatment by trained professionals. In practical terms the pre-sentence report, formerly the social inquiry report, is an essential element in the pursuit of this approach.

Incapacitative Sentencing

The incapacitative approach is to identify offenders or groups of offenders who are likely to do such serious harm in the future that special protective measures should be taken against them. Programmes of selective incapacitation have focused on groups of recidivists (cf. Greenwood 1982; Blumstein *et al.* 1986), but in England the emphasis has been upon identifying individuals who are predicted to be likely to commit serious harm in the future. The discretionary sentence of life imprisonment has been used increasingly for this purpose, and the Criminal Justice Act 1991 authorizes 'public protection' sentences for violent and sexual offenders who are considered likely to do serious harm.

There is no behavioural premise for the incapacitative approach: it looks chiefly to the protection of potential victims, and can apply whether the offender is a rational calculator or is driven by pressures. The political premise is often presented as utilitarian, justifying incapacitation by reference to the greater aggregate benefit, but even a sentencing rationale which emphasizes the continuing rights of a person who has offended must deal with the possibility that those may conflict with the rights of a (potential) future victim. Some of these issues were examined in the Floud report, which also found that predictions of 'dangerousness' tended to be wrong more often than not (Floud and Young 1981; for different analyses cf. Bottoms and Brownsword 1982; Wood 1988). This repeatedly confirmed fallibility of predictive judgements (see also Brody and Tarling 1981; Monahan 1981) calls into question the justification for any lengthening of sentences on grounds of public protection, and yet the political pressure to have some form(s) of incapacitative sentence available to the courts has been felt in most countries. If this is the reality of penal politics, then there is surely a strong case for procedural safeguards to ensure that the predictive judgements are open to thorough challenge. The provisions of the Criminal Justice Act 1991 are inadequate in this respect (see further Ashworth 1992*a*: 163–7).

Restorative and Reparative Theories

These are not theories of punishment. Rather, their argument is that sentences should move away from punishment of the offender towards restitution and reparation, aimed at restoring the harm done and calculated accordingly. Restorative theories are therefore victim-centred (see e.g. Wright 1991), although in some versions they encompass the notion of reparation to the community for the effects of crime. They envisage less resort to custody, with onerous community-based sanctions requiring offenders to work in order to compensate victims, and also contemplating support and counselling for offenders to reintegrate them into the community. Such theories therefore tend to act on a behavioural premise similar to rehabilitation, but their political premise is that compensation for victims should be recognized as more important than notions of just punishment on behalf of the state.

Legal systems based on a restorative rationale are rare, but the increasing tendency to insert victim-orientated measures such as compensation orders into sentencing systems structured to impose punishment provides a fine example of Garland's observation that 'institutions are the scenes of particular conflicts as well as being means to a variety of ends, so it is no surprise to find that each particular institution combines a number of often incompatible objectives, and organizes the relations of often antagonistic interest groups' (1990: 282).

Social Theories

There has been a resurgence of writings which emphasize the social and political context of sentencing (for selected readings see von Hirsch and Ashworth 1992*a*, esp. ch. 7). Important in this respect are Garland's analysis of the theoretical underpinnings of historical trends in punishment (Garland 1990) and Hudson's argument in favour of a shift towards a more supportive social policy as the principal response to the problem of crime (Hudson 1987). Those who have been influenced by H. L. A. Hart's distinction between the general justifying aim of punishment (in his view, utilitarian or deterrent) and the principles for distribution of punishment (in his view, retribution or desert) (Hart 1968, esp. ch. 1) should consider the challenge to this dichotomy in Lacey's work. She argues that both these issues raise questions of individual autonomy and of collective welfare and that, rather than denying it, we should address this conflict and strive to ensure that neither value is sacrificed entirely at either stage (Lacey 1988). In developing this view she explores the political values involved in state punishment and argues for a clearer view of the social function of punishing.

The political philosophy underlying the work of Braithwaite and Pettit is what they term republicanism, at the heart of which lies the concept of dominion (Braithwaite and Pettit 1990; for a critique see von Hirsch and Ashworth 1992*b*). Its essence is liberty, not in the sense of simple freedom from constraint by others, but more in the form of a status of guaranteed protection from certain kinds of interference. This leads them to propose that punishments should increase the dominion of victims with the least loss of dominion to the offenders punished. Since dominion lays emphasis on reassuring citizens about the prospect of liberty, it might require preventative sentences based on deterrence or incapacitation. They refer to unspecified limits on severity, but not lower limits, and their view is that the censuring function of the criminal justice system can and should so far as possible be fulfilled by means other than punishment. There is thus no recognition of an individual's right not to be punished more than is proportionate to the seriousness of the crime: all depends on what will advance overall dominion, which might happen to be more or less in any individual case than the 'deserved' punishment.

Appraising the Rationales

In formal terms, the English sentencing system now contains an approximate hierarchy of rationales. According to the Criminal Justice Act 1991, desert is the primary rationale, except in the relatively rare cases where the conditions for imposing an incapacitative sentence are met. Deterrence may not be used to justify a disproportionately severe sentence. Rehabilitative considerations become important when choosing among community orders of a similar severity, and also serve as a justification for probation orders and supervision after early release from custody. Compensation orders appear to have priority over fines and not over custody. This legal framework is hardly conflict-free, but it establishes a greater degree of certainty than existed in the previous 'cafeteria-style' system in which sentencers usually had wide choices of approach.

In practical and in theoretical terms, however, the position is less clear-cut. Since punishment is a social institution, this means that discussions ought to take account of its relation to other social institutions, and the relationship of sentencing to other aspects of the criminal justice system. It also means that, in practice, the form and content of punishment in a given society are likely to reflect a historical mixture of political and social events and influences. The above summary of several rationales, necessarily brief and omitting much of their richness, has referred to the behavioural and the political bases of each one. Criminologists have also tended to evaluate the approaches in terms of their effectiveness, and doubts were expressed earlier about the efficacy of strategies of individual deterrence, general deterrence, rehabilitation, and incapacitation. In respect of the last two it may be possible to refine techniques for identifying suitable targets, but it is also important to note that the object of discussion is *marginal* preventative effects. Thus a sentencing system based on desert is likely to deter and incapacitate to a certain degree, and so the proponents of deterrent or incapacitative theories must seek to justify the search for extra increments of prevention, by reference to evidence of likely success and the types of measure which must be adopted in order to achieve that success. It is here that concrete evidence is wanting. (For a relatively optimistic view, see Walker 1985: chs. 7, 22.)

Even if there were satisfactory evidence of efficacy, however, there remain issues about the rights involved in punishment—notably, those of victims and of offenders. The victim's right to receive compensation from the offender is surely undoubted, but in what circumstances should it give way to the offender's interest in not being utterly impoverished for months or years to come? There is controversy about whether or not victims should be able to express an opinion on sentence to the court, but this surely overlooks the point that sentencing is a state function which should be determined by public policy rather than private preference. What rights should be accorded to offenders? Deterrence theory seems to regard individual offenders as mere units in the overall calculation; incapacitative theory may recognize a general right not to be punished more than is proportionate to the offence, but overrides this in situations which may be more or less well defined; and rehabilitative theory has often failed to recognize any such general right, since it has been invoked in support of indeterminate sentences. It may therefore be seen as a strength of desert theory that it limits punishment to what is proportionate, and proposes criteria for determining proportionality (e.g. von Hirsch and Jareborg 1991). Similar limits on state power out of respect for the rights of the offender are proposed in the republicanism of Braithwaite and Pettit (1991) and the communitarianism of Lacey (1988), although neither book works out the detailed implications.

The choice of one or more rationales for punishment may not dictate the level of punitiveness in a given country, especially in view of the sparse evidence on deterrent and rehabilitative efficacy. It has sometimes been argued that desert theory leads to harsh penalties, but there is no such connection (cf. Hudson 1987; von Hirsch 1990*b*). California has harsh penalties, whereas Finland and Sweden have relatively low levels of punitiveness, and yet all regard desert as the primary rationale. Much depends on the political climate and on the attitudes of key actors, but reductions in punitiveness may be better achieved through specific principles of restraint in the use of custody or even prison capacity constraints than through the promotion of a general rationale.

THE MECHANICS OF SENTENCING

In this part of the chapter some basic elements of the law and practice of sentencing are set out. The various stages of a criminal case are discussed, together with the procedures which surround the sentencing stage itself.

The Selection of Cases for Sentence

It is a commonplace that the courts pass sentence for only a small proportion of the crimes committed in any one year. According to the British Crime Survey, only some 40 per cent of offences committed are reported.[1] Police recording practices reduce that figure, so that only 26 per cent of all offences are recorded as such. Since over two-thirds of the offences are not 'cleared up' (i.e. traced to an offender) by the police, the figure is further reduced to a mere 7 per cent of offences committed. By no means all those offences which are cleared up result in the taking of official action, perhaps because the suspected offender is too young, perhaps because the evidence is not sufficiently strong. This reduces to 4 per cent of all crimes the numbers proceeded with (see Home Office 1991: 31). Overall about one-quarter of offenders are cautioned rather than prosecuted: that leaves 3 per cent of all offences in any one year which result in convictions and court sentences. This is not to suggest that sentencing is unimportant, for it may be thought to have a social or symbolic importance considerably in excess of the small proportion of crimes dealt with. But it does suggest the need for caution in assessing the effects of sentencing in preventing crime. Those theoretical rationales which look to the social consequences of sentencing may overestimate its potential for altering general patterns of behaviour.

The selection of cases for sentence is not merely a quantitative filtering process. There are also various filters of a qualitative kind, some formal, some informal. The role of the regulatory agencies is significant: the Health and Safety Executive, the Alkali Inspectorate, and the various pollution inspectorates do not record all breaches of the law as crimes (see e.g. Hawkins and Thomas 1984; Hutter 1988). These and other agencies, such as the Inland Revenue and the Customs and Excise, also have various means of enforcing compliance without resort to prosecution, such as warning notices or the 'compounding' of evaded tax and duty (see Sanders 1985). As for offences reported to the police, their decisions are formally regulated by a Home Office Circular on *The Cautioning of Offenders*.[2] Police cautioning increased considerably in the 1980s, but implementation of the official policy remains variable. The low visibility of crucial decisions (whether to warn an offender informally, or to take no further action, or to administer a formal caution, or to prosecute) leaves the police with ample leeway to advance their own working priorities above the concerns of the formal guidelines (see Sanders chapter

[1] Mayhew *et al.* (1989); note that their figures relate only to certain categories of offence, although most of the common offences are included.

[2] The latest is Home Office Circular no. 59/1990. For research which preceded and to some extent shaped the guidance, see Evans and Wilkinson (1990).

16 in this volume and, for recent research, McConville *et al.* 1991: chs. 5–6).

Where the police decide to prosecute, the Crown Prosecution Service has the power to drop the case if it is not in the public interest to proceed. As required by the Prosecution of Offences Act 1985, the Director of Public Prosecutions has published a Code for Crown Prosecutors which is intended to guide and to structure this discretion (for analysis see Ashworth 1987; Sanders 1988). The choice of charge may determine the level of court, and thereby affect sentencing, yet the police exercise considerable discretion at this point too. At the stage of plea the true extent of negotiated justice is not known, but there is no shortage of empirical evidence that negotiation is a familiar part of justice in magistrates' courts (Baldwin 1985) and in the Crown Court (Riley and Vennard 1988). Indeed, the Court of Appeal has frequently been called upon to rebuke judges for participating (see Curran 1991).

In summary, therefore, the offences for which the courts have to pass sentence are both quantitatively and qualitatively different from what might be described as the social reality of crime. The courts see only a small percentage of cases. Even if it may be assumed that these are generally the more serious offences, how they are presented in court may be shaped as much by the working practices and priorities of the police, prosecutors and defence lawyers as by any objective conception of 'the facts of the case' (see also Sanders chapter 16 in this volume).

Crown Court and Magistrates' Courts

Of the two levels of criminal court in England and Wales, the Crown Court deals with the more serious cases and the magistrates' courts with the less serious. The Crown Court sits as a trial court with judge and jury. However, most Crown Court cases involve a guilty plea (72 per cent in 1989), and these are dealt with by judge alone, since juries have no part in sentencing. The most serious Crown Court cases are taken by a High Court judge on circuit, but the majority of cases are taken by a circuit judge (full-time) or by a recorder or assistant recorder (part-time). The magistrates' courts are organized on a local basis: there are some 29,000 lay magistrates in England and Wales, and they usually sit in benches of three, advised by a justices' clerk. Typically a lay magistrate will sit in court one day a fortnight. There are also some fifty or more full-time stipendiary magistrates, together with some who sit part-time. Stipendiaries are professionally qualified full-time appointees, and most are assigned to metropolitan areas, where they tend to take the longer or more difficult cases.

What determines whether a case is heard in a magistrates' court or in the Crown Court? English law has three categories of offence. Indictable-only offences are the most serious group, and may only be dealt with in the Crown Court. Summary-only offences are the least serious group, and may only be dealt with in the magistrates' courts. Between them lies the category of offences triable-either-way. These are offences of intermediate gravity, which will generally be tried in a magistrates' court unless either the defendant elects to be committed for Crown Court trial (an absolute right, which accounts for some two-fifths of committals to the Crown Court), or the magistrates decide that the case should be committed to the Crown Court (three-fifths of cases). During the 1980s the magistrates' courts tended to commit an ever-increasing proportion of defendants to the Crown Court for trial, but the provisions of the Criminal Justice Act 1988 were designed to transfer some business away from the Crown Court and appear to have achieved that effect. Although it is widely believed that magistrates' courts are more prosecution-minded (Riley and Vennard 1988; Hedderman and Moxon 1992), magistrates' courts are limited in their sentencing to six months' custody, or twelve months on two or more convictions, and their sentences are comparatively much lower than those in the Crown Court.[3] Hand in hand with the transfer of business from Crown Court to magistrates' courts has gone a movement to relieve magistrates' courts of many traffic cases by enabling the police to issue fixed penalty notices. Thus in 1989 around 100,000 defendants were tried in the Crown Court, some 1.8 million people were prosecuted in the magistrates' courts, and a further 6.3 million fixed penalty notices were issued.

Maximum Sentences

Apart from a few common law offences which have no fixed maximum (e.g. manslaughter, conspiracy to outrage public decency), Parliament has generally provided the maximum sentence for each offence. Much statutory consolidation of criminal offences was completed in the mid-nineteenth century, and there have been several reforms of the criminal law since the late 1960s. Apart from that, maxima have been set at different times, in different social circumstances, and without any overall plan. Indeed, the statutory maxima set in the nineteenth century were much influenced by the traditional periods of transportation (see Thomas 1978; Radzinowicz and Hood 1985: ch. 15). Many had hoped that the Advisory Council on the Penal System would be able to improve the coherence of the system, but in its 1978 report on *Sentences of Imprisonment: a Review*

[3] Comparing two matched samples, Hedderman and Moxon (1992: 37) found that the Crown Court used custody three times as often as magistrates' courts and that the sentences were, on average, two and a half times as long as those given by magistrates' courts.

of Maximum Penalties it declined to revise the various statutory maxima, regarding the task as too controversial.[4]

Parliament continues to alter maximum sentences in a piecemeal way: for example, the Criminal Justice Act 1991 reduced the maxima for theft (from ten to seven years) and for non-residential burglary (from fourteen to ten years), and also increased the maxima for badger baiting (from three to six months) and for bomb hoaxes (from five to seven years). In practice, maximum penalties rarely have an impact on sentencing, but courts do sometimes 'steer by the maximum' by ensuring that sentences close to the maximum are reserved for the worst conceivable manifestations of that crime. It is likely that the changes in the 1991 Act are intended and will be received as symbolic, encouraging the courts to modify their customary sentencing levels for those crimes.

The Range of Available Sentences

Beneath the maximum penalty for the offence, the court usually has a wide discretion to choose among alternatives (see the following section). In England and Wales the range of alternatives is wider than in most other jurisdictions, but before they are considered two general points should be noted. First, the tradition is to create maximum penalties in terms of either a period of custody or an amount or level of fine: no offences have been assigned probation or community service as the maximum penalty. Second, since the mid-1960s there has been a tendency to enact broadly defined offences with relatively high maximum penalties: for example, in England and Wales there is a single offence of theft with a maximum of seven years' imprisonment, whereas in many other European countries there are grades of theft with separate maxima. The English approach leaves sentencers with much greater discretion (see Thomas 1974).

At the lowest level, the range of available sentences begins with absolute and conditional discharges, and binding over. Fines come next, and a compensation order should be considered in every case involving death, injury, loss, or damage. What are termed 'community sentences' by the Criminal Justice Act 1991 include probation orders, community service orders, combination orders (part probation, part community service), and curfew orders. Then come suspended sentences of imprisonment, and then imprisonment itself. For offenders aged 18–20 inclusive, the custodial sentence takes the form of detention in a young offender institution; suspended sentences are unavailable; and attendance centre

[4] It did, however, recommend the adoption of lower 'normal maxima', based on past practice, with a power to exceed them in exceptional cases. For discussion see Radzinowicz and Hood (1978).

orders can be made. All these forms of sentence are discussed further below. There are separate orders for juveniles and for mentally disordered offenders.

Discretion in Sentencing

Alleged inconsistencies in sentencing have been a frequent cause for concern. This might seem an obvious consequence of the expanse of discretion left by fairly high maximum penalties and the wide range of available sentences. But there is a paradox here. Many sentencers seem to place more emphasis on the restrictions on 'their' discretion than on the choices that remain. Judges have been critical of the various limits which Parliament places on their powers, e.g. previously the prohibitions on combining certain forms of sentence (such as probation with a fine or suspended sentence) and now the many 'technical' and often poorly expressed conditions imposed by the Criminal Justice Act 1991 (for similar criticism see also Thomas 1988). Courts are now under an obligation to consider making a compensation order in every case of death, injury, loss, or damage; and in drug trafficking cases a court is required to follow the prescribed statutory procedure for confiscation of the offender's assets. Even before some of these restrictions were imposed in the late 1980s, judges expressed themselves as having little choice in the sentences they passed: 'the least possible sentence I can pass . . .', 'I have no alternative but to . . .' (Ashworth *et al.* 1984: 53–4). To some extent this terminology may reflect the constraints imposed by Court of Appeal decisions, but it is more likely that it reflects self-generated constraints which stem from the attitudes and beliefs of the sentencer.

The paradox is that, despite these feelings of constraint, the sentencer's discretion is considerable in legal terms. The Criminal Justice Act 1991 seeks to impose a new structure and new restrictions, but there will still be room for choice in the length of custodial sentences and among the various community orders. Moxon's study of 2,000 cases yielded a model which is claimed to predict 80 per cent of Crown Court sentences, giving rise to the suggestion that 'differences between individual judges' did not have 'a particularly big impact on the *overall* pattern of sentences' (Moxon 1988: 64, emphasis in original). More quantitative and qualitative research into Crown Court sentencing will, it may be hoped, follow the implementation of the 1991 Act. Magistrates' courts have upper limits on their powers, but otherwise the choice among alternatives is little affected by Court of Appeal decisions (of which few are relevant). Just as Hood (1962) showed that some benches are 'probation-minded' and others are not, so Tarling (1979) demonstrated that among the thirty courts he surveyed the use of probation varied between 1 and 12 per cent, suspended sentences between 4 and 16 per cent, fines between 46 and 76 per cent, and so on. Significant elements of these variations remained after account had been taken of the different 'mix' of offences coming before the courts (Tarling *et al.* 1985). As Hood found in his study of motoring cases (1972), membership of a particular bench tends to be a major determinant of a magistrate's approach to sentencing. The influence of magistrates' clerks, who generally undertake the initial training of new magistrates, may be considerable (Darbyshire 1984). It is in these lower reaches of the sentencing system—the magistrates' courts and the lesser Crown Court cases—that the legal restrictions on sentencing (from Parliament or the Court of Appeal) impinge least and discretion is considerable.

While discretion is important to enable sentencers to take account of the wide and varying range of factors that might be relevant, it does leave decision-making open to irrelevant influences. For example, Hood's 1992 study has shown that at some courts black offenders are significantly more likely to receive custody than similarly situated white offenders. Farrington and Morris (1983) have shown, as have other studies, that the apparent leniency of sentences on women may conceal a trend of severity against a minority of female offenders.

Information about the Offence

Courts depend for their information on what they hear or what they are told. Since defendants in almost all cases in magistrates' courts and over 70 per cent of cases in the Crown Court plead guilty, the information is usually constructed for the court by the prosecutor or others. The main source of information about the offence is likely to be the statement of facts which the prosecutor reads out. It will usually have been compiled by the police, and the way in which it describes or omits certain factors may reflect a particular view of the offence, or perhaps a 'charge-bargain' struck with the police (see Sanders chapter 16 in this volume; also McConville *et al.* 1991: ch. 7). Sometimes the statement of facts may have been reconstructed, wholly or in part, by the prosecuting lawyer as a result of a change of plea or other negotiations (see chapter 16 in this volume). In addition to the prosecution statement of facts, the court may gather further information about the offence from the defence plea in mitigation, and perhaps from a pre-sentence report (formerly a social inquiry report). Any account of 'the facts' is likely to be selective, determined to some extent by the compiler's preconceptions. It is likely that judges and magistrates will be influenced by the selections made by those who inform them, as well as by their own preconceptions.

The prosecution's account of the facts may be disputed by the defence.

In a trial there is usually an opportunity to resolve these matters, but this is not always so: some facts relevant to sentencing are irrelevant to criminal guilt. The greatest difficulty arises where the defendant pleads guilty but only on the basis of a more favourable version of the facts than the prosecution presents. The courts have developed a procedure for resolving most such issues by means of a pre-sentence hearing, known as a 'Newton hearing' (after the leading case of *Newton* (1982) 4 Cr App R(S) 388), at which evidence is presented and witnesses may be heard. There is now a wealth of case law on the situations in which a 'Newton hearing' is necessary and on the procedures to be followed, but there remains a need for an authoritative commitment to the same evidentiary protections for the defendant as apply at the trial itself (see Wasik 1985*b*; Ashworth 1992*a*: ch. 11). The outcome can have a considerable effect on the length of a custodial sentence, and proper safeguards should therefore be introduced.

Information about the Offender

The court may obtain information about the offender from at least five sources: the police antecedents statement; the defence plea in mitigation, a pre-sentence report; a medical report; and the offender's own appearance in court.

The contents of the *police antecedents statement* are regulated by a Practice Direction from the Lord Chief Justice. The principal element is information about previous convictions, but there may also be reference to the defendant's age, education, employment, and domestic circumstances (for research on this see Shapland 1981: 123–30). The purpose of a *defence plea in mitigation* is to show the offender and offence in the best light. In practice, it appears that a realistic recognition of any aggravating factors may improve the credibility of what is said (Shapland 1981: ch. 5). Judges have tended to trust the factual basis of pleas in mitigation more than pre-sentence (social inquiry) reports, particularly because the latter may be prepared some weeks before the trial (Ashworth *et al.* 1984: 43–5).

The purpose of a *pre-sentence report* under the Criminal Justice Act 1991 is to assist the sentencer by summarizing the offence, by drawing on professional expertise to analyse the offender's behaviour and attitude to the offence, and (where applicable) by describing the community sentence under which, if the court were to choose such a course, the offender could most appropriately be supervised and the risk of future offending reduced (Home Office 1992). The form of the reports has been adapted in order to meet the expectations of sentencers. However, the demands on the probation service are considerable, not least in the task of assessing the seriousness of the offence, which is the key to so many decisions under the new Act (see Stone 1992).

A *medical report* is relatively rare, but a court may decide to call for one and section 4 of the Criminal Justice Act 1991 requires a court to obtain one before passing a custodial sentence if the defendant is or appears to be mentally disordered. The impact of *the offender's own appearance* and demeanour in court is difficult to gauge, but judges recognize that they take account of it and tend to feel that sentencing would be even more difficult if they did not see the offender in person (Cooke 1987: 58; Ashworth *et al.* 1984: ch. 3). This fifth source of influence serves to demonstrate that the impact of the reports, etc., received by a court may be mediated by the attitudes of the sentencer (see further Shapland 1987).

Representations on Sentence

Some of what is said by an advocate making a defence plea in mitigation will bear directly on the sentence. The tendency is not to mention particular sentences, but to refer more obliquely to 'a lenient course' (Ashworth *et al.* 1984: 44). The tendency at the sentencing stage has also been to avoid referring to Court of Appeal decisions, even though this is the practice in legal submissions during the trial itself. However, with the increase in numbers of 'guideline' judgments the practice may be changing: the Court of Appeal has said that it is the duty of advocates to refer the court to relevant guideline judgments and to ensure that an unlawful sentence is not passed (e.g. Panayioutou [1990] Crim LR 349; Komsta and Murphy [1990] Crim LR 434).

The English tradition is that the prosecutor plays no part in sentencing, in the sense that no sentence is 'asked for' or recommended. It is sometimes assumed that such a practice would lead to higher sentences, although this has not been the outcome in the Netherlands, where prosecutors recommend sentences and judges rarely exceed the recommendation (see van Duyne 1987: 144–5). There is no place in English procedure for the victim to make any representations on sentence: even as to the appropriate amount of a compensation order, the power to make representations is given to the prosecutor. In its 'Victim's Charter' the government recognized the issue of whether victims should be able to submit a 'victim impact statement' (VIS) or to make representations on sentence (see chapter 25 in this volume). During the 1980s the use of the VIS spread in various American and Australian states (see Hall 1991). However, there is a much stronger case for allowing a victim to submit a statement of the effect of the crime on him or her (subject to evidential safeguards for the offender), than for allowing the victim to express an opinion as to sentence (Ashworth 1992*b*). That is and should remain a matter of public policy rather than private preference.

Appeals against Sentence

A person who is sentenced in a magistrates' court may appeal to the Crown Court. The appeal is usually heard by a judge sitting with two magistrates, and it takes the form of a re-hearing. The Crown Court is then empowered to pass any sentence which the magistrates' court could have imposed, whether more severe or more lenient than the original sentence. The possibility of a more severe sentence tends to discourage appeals. Fewer than 1 per cent of offenders appeal, mostly those who have been sentenced to custody (Home Office 1990*b*: table 6.7). Where there is a disputed point of law, the defendant may appeal to the Divisional Court by means of case stated or for judicial review (see Wasik 1984).

A person sentenced in the Crown Court may appeal to the Court of Appeal (Criminal Division) on a point of law. Otherwise an offender may apply for leave to appeal against sentence to the Court of Appeal. Applications for leave to appeal are parcelled out to individual High Court judges: little is known about how these decisions are made. If an offender is granted leave to appeal, the Court will hear submissions, usually from defence counsel only, and increasingly including reference to other decided cases. The Court may substitute any sentence which is not more severe than the original sentence. The Court hears appeals from about 7 per cent of defendants sentenced in the Crown Court, about one-quarter of which succeed (Home Office 1990*b*: table 6.7).

There is no prosecution appeal against sentence in England and Wales. Such appeals exist in several other European and Commonwealth countries, but the closest approximation in English law is the power of the Attorney-General to refer to the Court of Appeal cases in which the sentence is thought to be unduly lenient. The power, introduced by the Criminal Justice Act 1988, has been invoked in some twenty-five cases per year. The Court of Appeal may increase the sentence if it is found to have been outside the normal range for the offence, and in a majority of referred cases it has increased the sentence.

English Sentencing Procedures

From this brief review, three main themes emerge. First, it is evident that other actors, apart from judges and magistrates, exert considerable influence on the sentencing process. Not only do the police and prosecutors select and shape the cases which come to court, but they (together with probation officers and defence lawyers) provide the courts with information which they have selected and constructed. There may also be suggestions, usually implicit, as to sentence. Second, what courts may receive in terms of information about the offence and the offender, and representations on sentence, is governed mostly by court practice and judicial decisions. Apart from pre-sentence reports, there is little legislative intervention in the field. The judges themselves have developed 'Newton hearings'. They could equally develop or modify other practices. And thirdly, there are several points at which the approach or attitude of the sentencer may be influential. Thus, despite the legislative restrictions recently introduced, there remains considerable room for different approaches to be taken by particular judges or particular benches of magistrates. More research on and analysis of the decision-making of sentencers is needed.

CUSTODIAL SENTENCING

The Evolution of a 'Tariff'

Maximum sentences are generally high, and English law has only one mandatory minimum sentence,[5] so that most day-to-day sentencing levels are little affected by legislative constraints. For Crown Court sentencing some normal ranges or starting-points have developed, often termed 'the going rate' by judges and 'the tariff' by others. Historically the idea of 'normal' sentences can be traced back at least as far as the 'Memorandum of Normal Punishments' drawn up by Lord Alverstone, the Lord Chief Justice, in 1901 (Thomas 1978; Radzinowicz and Hood 1986: 755–8). Since 1907 the Court of Criminal Appeal, and since 1966 its successor the Court of Appeal (Criminal Division), has adjusted and altered aspects of the tariff, as will be seen in the following two sections. However, the Court of Appeal's concentration on relatively severe and long sentences has led to suggestions that it exerts relatively little influence on day-to-day sentencing in the Crown Court for the majority of offences, which tend to be thefts, burglaries, deceptions, and handling stolen goods. Here, the 'going rate' stems from court practice. There appears to be less sense of a 'going rate' for offences which attract non-custodial sentences.

The same point is particularly true of the magistrates' courts, where Court of Appeal judgments have little relevance and little effect. In 1966 the Magistrates' Association introduced a list of suggested penalties for road traffic offences, in an attempt to foster consistency. In 1989 the

[5] Twelve months' disqualification from driving on conviction for drunk driving.

Association issued provisional guidelines for the sentencing of twenty frequent non-motoring crimes. In 1992 the motoring and non-motoring offence guidelines were brought together in a single document which proposes guidance within the terms of the 1991 Act. However, these guidelines have no legal force, and no research has been carried out into their effectiveness. So much depends, in the first instance, on the attitudes of key actors such as the local liaison judge, the justices' clerk, and the chairperson of the bench.

The Role of the Court of Appeal

Many appeals result in only a brief judgment on the facts of the case. Others raise a point of principle, and they are the judgments which tend to be reported. The reporting of Court of Appeal judgments on sentencing has increased since the 1960s, largely owing to the efforts of Dr David Thomas, who has also commented on many decisions. The publication of the first edition of his Principles of Sentencing in 1970 was a landmark in the development of a common law of sentencing. Since then judges have tended to refer to their previous decisions more often, and so a system of 'precedent' has begun to be established.

However, the Court of Appeal works under tremendous pressure, and almost all sentencing judgments are delivered *ex tempore*, without being reserved for consideration. Until 1988 the Court could only hear appeals by offenders who alleged that their sentence was too severe, and this led to a concentration of decisions on serious crimes and long prison sentences, with very few precedents on run-of-the-mill crimes and non-custodial sentences. In recent years the balance has slowly begun to alter, largely because the restrictions on custodial sentences for young offenders (introduced in 1982) required the Court of Appeal to examine the justifications for deciding that an offence is too serious for a non-custodial sentence.

It remains open to question, however, whether the Court of Appeal can fulfil both the role of deciding appeals in individual cases and the task of providing guidance for the lower courts. The latter task surely requires a body with the time and experience to consider the whole range of crimes in relation to the available sentences, criminal justice practices, and criminological knowledge. It is a policy function, for which a small number of senior judges working through long lists of cases might not be the most appropriate agency: see the final section of this chapter on 'Further Reform in England and Wales'.

Statutory Restrictions on Custodial Sentences

Section 1(4) of the Criminal Justice Act 1982 introduced restrictions on custodial sentences for offenders under 21 which were amended in 1988 and remained in force until 1992. For the first time, they required courts to justify their custodial sentences on grounds of the seriousness of the offence, the protection of the public, or a history of failure to respond to non-custodial sentences. The 1980s saw a spectacular decline in the use of custody for juveniles (from 7,900 in 1981 to 1,500 in 1991) and some decline for young adults, and the statutory restrictions on custody were regarded as one contributory factor. In the Criminal Justice Act 1991 legislative restrictions on custody have been introduced for offenders of all ages.

The scheme is as follows. A court may not impose a custodial sentence unless the case satisfies the custody threshold in section 1(2). The court must satisfy itself that the offence was so serious that only a custodial sentence can be justified. This may be seen as an application of the 'desert' or proportionality principle. The Court of Appeal dealt with myriad appeals on the equivalent provision for young offenders in the 1982 Act, but without much clear guidance being established.[6] The Court's first statement after the implementation of the 1991 Act was that an offence satisfies the custody threshold in section 1(2) if it 'would make right-thinking members of the public, knowing all the facts, feel that justice had not been done by the passing of any sentence other than a custodial one' (*Cox* (1993) 96 Cr App R 452 at 455). There is clearly a long way to go before practical guidance usable by sentencers is laid down.

Moxon's research into Crown Court sentencing shows that custody was significantly more likely where the victim was elderly, the offender was the ringleader, the offence was planned, or a weapon was used (Moxon 1988: 9). All these factors will be relevant as aggravating circumstances under the 1991 Act that make the offence more serious. Courts are free to take account of any mitigating factor, whether or not it has any bearing on the seriousness of the offence. In one of the first appeals after the 1991 Act, the Court held that the offence (reckless driving) was so serious that only custody could be justified, but then found that there were mitigating factors (the offender was 18, and had only one previous conviction) sufficient to take the case below the custody threshold (*Cox* (1993)). Perhaps the most contentious mitigating factor is the discount for pleading guilty, which amounts to one-quarter or even one-third off the length of a custodial sentence: it may even tip the scales towards a suspended sentence or community sentence—a potentially powerful factor in any

[6] Two of the leading decisions are *Hearne and Petty* (1989) 11 Cr App R (S) 316 and *Mussell* (1990) 12 Cr App R (S) 607.

plea negotiations (see further Ashworth 1992: 130–1 and the section above on 'The Selection of Cases for Sentence').

Two of the most controversial provisions in the 1991 Act have already been changed. The courts were very critical of the 'two offence rule' introduced by the 1991 Act: this applied whenever a court was sentencing an offender for several offences, and permitted the court to consider only the combined seriousness of any two of those offences when deciding on the type of penalty (e.g. prison, community sentence) that was deserved. The Criminal Justice Act 1993 has swept away this restriction. Judges, magistrates, and others were also critical of section 29 of the 1991 Act. Its effect was frequently mis-stated as 'courts are not allowed to take account of previous convictions', whereas the section was intended, more or less, to reflect the previous principle that a good record may mitigate while a bad record should not lead to a disproportionate sentence. The Criminal Justice Act 1993 replaces section 29 with a provision allowing courts to take account of any previous convictions of the offender or any failure of his to respond to previous sentences, when 'considering the seriousness of the offence'. The policy behind both these repealed sections of the 1991 Act was to prevent courts from imposing substantial sentences on people who commit a number of minor offences. Too little was heard of this policy (as distinct from the tortuous provisions of the Act) in 1991, and even less has been heard of it since. Moreover, the reappearance of the principle that courts may take account of the 'failure to respond to previous sentences' creates the risk that courts will once again impose custody largely because the person has already undergone various non-custodial sentences, rather than because the offence is really serious enough to merit it.

A second possible justification for custody under the 1991 Act is that it is necessary to protect the public from serious harm by the offender. This provision is only available where a court is dealing with someone for an offence involving sex, violence, or arson. The Act does define 'serious harm' and other key terms, but its definition of 'sexual offence' is defective. In effect, this is a 'dangerousness' provision, and decisions are bound to turn on fallible predictions of future misconduct (see further Floud and Young 1981; Monahan 1981; Brody and Tarling 1981).

If a case fails to satisfy the custody threshold, a non-custodial sentence must be given. If, however, it satisfies section 1(2), the duration of the custodial sentence is governed by section 2(2). Chiefly, this means that the length of sentence should be 'commensurate with the seriousness of the offence'. It was always likely that the courts would interpret this as confirming the 'tariff' or 'going rate' (see below), but it was startling to find Lord Taylor, the Lord Chief Justice, declaring that the new law does allow courts to take account of deterrence. He stated that the phrase 'commensurate with the seriousness of the offence' must mean 'commensurate with the punishment and deterrence that the offence requires' (*Cunningham* (1993) 96 Cr App R 422 at 425). He did accept, however, that an 'exemplary sentence' on a particular offender would be unlawful. Section 2(2)(b) of the Act expressly provides for the imposition of a longer-than-proportionate sentence where this is considered necessary to protect the public from serious harm and the offence is one of sex, violence, or arson. As with the initial decision to impose custody on this ground, the crucial factor is the prediction of dangerousness.

Proportionality and the Court of Appeal

The courts may be said to operate a kind of 'tariff' when calculating the length of prison sentences. A conventional 'going rate' for many offences has developed over the years, shaped and assisted by judgments of the Court of Appeal. The logic of the upper echelons of the tariff was considered by Lord Justice Lawton in his judgment in *Turner* (1975) 61 Cr App R 67. He started from the assumption that it would be absurd if an offender could receive longer sentences for armed robbery than for murder. So he estimated the number of years that a murderer without mitigating circumstances could expect to spend in prison, and then ranged the sentences for other serious offences just beneath that. He took the period for the murderer as fifteen years in prison, equivalent to a determinate sentence of twenty-two years (less the one-third remission which obtained in 1975). Just beneath this notional twenty-two years he placed a number of 'wholly abnormal' offences, such as political kidnapping and bomb attacks. He then held that armed robbery should be placed at the next level down, yielding around eighteen years for the two offences in that case. This scheme continues to apply more or less to the upper end of the 'tariff', but the lower reaches are less well settled.

The Court of Appeal's greatest achievement in exercising its policy function has been the formulation of about a dozen 'guideline judgments'. When Lord Lane was Lord Chief Justice he would occasionally take a particular case and, rather than giving a judgment on the facts alone, construct a judgment dealing with sentencing for all the main varieties of that particular crime. The first of these was in the case of *Aramah* (1982) 4 Cr App R (S) 407, where guidance was given on sentencing levels for the whole gamut of drugs offences, from large-scale trafficking down to possession of small amounts for individual use. A particularly well-constructed guideline judgment is that on rape in *Billam* (1986) 8 Cr App R (S) 48. The Lord Chief Justice established two starting points, of five years and eight years' imprisonment, according to the presence or absence of certain factors. He went on to enumerate eight aggravating factors, three mitigating factors, and certain factors which courts should not take into account. Although nothing was said about the weight to be given to the various aggravating factors (see Harvey and Pease 1987), the judgment is a significant advance on the amount of guidance available for most other crimes.

Guideline judgments are intended by the Lord Chief Justice to be binding on judges and magistrates, and it seems that they are so regarded. This method of guidance seems to have caused less judicial opposition than the systems in certain American states (see section below on 'International Patterns in Sentencing Reform'), probably because it has been developed *by* judges *for* judges, and because the guidance is in the familiar narrative form of a judgment. The Lord Chief Justice has used it both to supply guidance for relatively unusual crimes (e.g. drug trafficking in the early 1980s), and to alter sentencing levels where he believes that they have become too low or too high.[7] Lord Taylor has already shown that he intends to continue this approach, by delivering a guideline judgment on aggravated vehicle-taking (*Bird* (1993) 14 Cr App R (S) 343).

One advantage of guideline judgments is that they cover most manifestations of a particular crime at once, and produce more coherence than a series of separate judgments in different cases. The disadvantage is that relatively few such judgments have been delivered, covering only a small number of crimes, and that they do not consider proportionality of sentencing from one crime to another. There is no evidence of a judicial willingness to formulate guideline judgments for the offences which occupy most of the time of sentencers, e.g. theft, burglary, deception, and handling stolen goods. When the opportunity to give detailed guidance on burglary of dwellings was presented to Lord Lane in 1990 (*Mussell* (1990) 12 Cr App R (S) 607) he largely avoided the issue. Yet it is the custody borderline which is crucial to the success of the 1991 Act: what features make these common crimes so serious that only a custodial sentence would be adequate, and no community sentence sufficient? Moreover, there has been little recognition in recent Court of Appeal judgments of the special nature of deprivation of liberty as a punishment or of the conditions in English prisons. The various strictures of the Chief Inspector of Prisons and of the Woolf Inquiry have not been reflected, at any rate expressly, in the approach of the courts.

[7] e.g. sentencing levels were thought too low for rape (*Billam*, above) and for causing death by reckless driving (guideline judgment in *Boswell* (1984) 6 Cr App R (S) 257), and too high for social security fraud (guideline judgment in *Stewart* (1987) 9 Cr App R (S) 135).

International Comparisons and Proportionality

According to the Criminal Justice Act 1991 the primary rationale of sentencing should be proportionality, in the sense that sentences should be 'commensurate with the seriousness of the offence'. The guideline judgments, just considered, deal with proportionality within a particular offence, determining which forms of it are more serious and which forms less serious. They rarely consider whether the sentencing level for one crime is proportionate to the level for others: we have seen that only the *Turner* judgment in modern times has really attempted to take this general view, and that was confined to very serious types of crime.[8] Beyond these issues lies a more fundamental question of proportionality: is the overall sentencing level in this country too high or too low?

A possible answer can only be found by combining historical-cultural research with criminological research. A fine example of historical-cultural research may be found in Downes's comparative study of the Netherlands and England, identifying the various forces which have led since 1950 to a considerable lowering of sentence levels in the Netherlands and a raising of levels in England and Wales (Downes 1988). Acceptable sentence levels may depend on traditional conceptions, social change, and tolerance: they may also depend on political forces and media reporting. International comparisons of sentencing statistics are fraught with difficulty. The Council of Europe's figures show that England and Wales had during the 1980s a custodial rate of around 100 per 100,000, among the highest in Europe. The corresponding figure for France and Germany is around 80; for the Netherlands, about 40; and yet for the USA it is around 400 per 100,000. If the figures are adjusted to take account of crime rates, England moves closer to the European average, along with Germany and France (cf. Home Office 1991; Pease 1992). However, both of those other countries are making efforts to reduce their use of custody, and the figures are sufficient to raise questions about the current level of punitiveness. Could it be lowered without social catastrophe? Would recorded crime rates be expected to rise, or would the reaction of the mass media be more influential?

Custodial Sentences and Executive Release

In so far as 'public' reaction through the mass media restricts sentencing policy, it is instructive to consider the impact of remission and executive release. For many years until 1992, remission of one-third was deducted

[8] See the judgment of Lawton LJ in *Turner* (1975) 61 Cr App R 67, at 89–91, where he considered the relationship between sentences for murder and those for armed robbery and other heinous offences.

from every determinate custodial sentence. A person sentenced to three years' imprisonment would find that the date of release was calculated as two years, as soon as prison was entered. Parole was introduced in England and Wales in 1968, and by the early 1980s over 60 per cent of eligible prisoners were released on parole for some part of their sentence. In 1983 the government lowered the parole threshold to six months, so that anyone serving a custodial sentence of roughly twelve months or more was eligible for release on parole after six months or one-third, whichever was the longer. A streamlined procedure was introduced for those serving two years or less, with the result that some 78 per cent of them were released on parole before the two-thirds point of their sentence.

This may be seen as an example of the government taking action to reduce the effective length of custodial sentences for crimes which could not be described as really serious. The mass media seem to have made little of it, preferring to applaud measures taken at the same time to restrict the grant of parole to serious sexual and violent offenders and to restrict the release of certain murderers. The judiciary became concerned, however, at the erosion of their sentences which was resulting from the fact that some offenders spent little more than one-third of the announced sentence in prison. Judicial disquiet led to the appointment of the Carlisle Committee, which reported in 1988. Its recommendations are largely incorporated in the 1991 Act.

Under the Criminal Justice Act 1991, remission is abolished and parole is largely replaced by a system of early release. All those serving terms of under four years are conditionally released after one-half, subject to serving the unexpired balance if they are convicted of another offence which was committed during the second half of the full sentence. Additionally, those serving between one and four years will be subject to supervision on licence until the three-quarters point in their sentence. A system of discretionary parole will be retained for those serving four years and over, who may be so released after one-half of their sentence. Those not considered suitable for parole will be conditionally released after two-thirds of their sentence, and will be subject to supervision until the three-quarters point.

One result of the new arrangements is that every part of a custodial sentence counts for something. Conditional release means that the possibility of return to custody remains until the last day of the sentence pronounced in court. Moreover, all those serving longer than one year will receive some supervision on release. Another result, however, is that many of those serving sentences in the one- to three-year range might spend longer in prison, since under the pre-1992 arrangements most would have been released on or soon after the expiry of one-third of their sentence. The Carlisle Committee was insistent that there was no reason for a 'real' increase in the length of sentences, and urged that introduction of the reforms be accompanied by a strategy to reduce the level of sentences. The 1991 Act is silent on the point, but the Lord Chief Justice has issued a Practice Direction which states that judges should take account of the change in early release arrangements, without specifying details of how the calculations might be done.

Custodial Sentences in Magistrates' Courts

The 1991 Act's restrictions on sentencing apply equally to magistrates' courts, as did the former restrictions on custody for young offenders. Research shows that the magistrates' courts were slow to come to grips with the 1982 law (Burney 1985), but in the later 1980s lawyers began to use the statutory restrictions effectively in arguing appeals, and this seems to have filtered down to the magistrates' courts (Stanley 1988). However, the 1982 law and its interpretation in Court of Appeal decisions left considerable leeway to local courts, as does the 1991 Act. The finding of Parker *et al.* that different courts maintained different approaches to the use of custody (Parker *et al.* 1989; see also Hood 1962; Tarling 1979) is likely to remain relevant under the 1991 Act unless some specific and binding guidance is provided.

Many magistrates say that they rarely impose a custodial sentence. Since there are 29,000 magistrates this may well be true, but the custodial sentences imposed by magistrates' courts in 1989 amounted to some 55 per cent of receptions into prisons (although accounting for only 18 per cent of the prison population at any one time). One aim of the concept of 'community sentence' in the 1991 Act is to deal with many of those who would have received short custodial sentences by means of punishment in the community. For this policy the magistrates' courts will be a crucial testing ground. A more drastic approach would be to deprive magistrates' courts of the power to impose custodial sentences. However, this would inevitably result in a large increase in numbers of cases committed to the Crown Court, which would be not only administratively and financially unattractive to the government but also likely to result in a greater use of custody, since the Crown Court uses about seven times more custody in comparable cases than the magistrates' courts (Hedderman and Moxon 1992: 37).

Review of Policy and Practice

Government policy has been to advocate a twin-track policy of sentencing: sentences for serious offences involving sex, violence, or drugs should remain high, but the scale of penal response to non-serious offenders should be lowered (Home Office 1990*a*: para. 2.2). It is too early to assess whether the Criminal Justice Act 1991 will bring this about, but there is evidence that in the late 1980s the 'higher' track had already been put in place by the judiciary. Between 1984 and 1989 the number of prisoners serving over four years' imprisonment increased from 5,721 to 10,953. In the same years the number of juveniles sentenced to custody was declining steeply (from 6,700 to 2,000) and for young adults the numbers were beginning to fall (from 23,800 to 14,200). Indeed, the proportionate use of custody for adults began to decline after a steady rise throughout the 1980s. (all figures are from Home Office 1990*b*: tables 7.8, 7.20, 7.12.) It must be said that, save in respect of offenders aged under 21, there has been no evidence of a significant and sustained turn away from custodial sentencing. Moreover, the average length of sentences has been increasing, and the effect of the new provisions on early release is that many offenders will serve longer (particularly for sentences in the one- to two-year range) than hitherto. The new threshold test for custody introduced by the 1991 Act seems to be too blunt an instrument to achieve this effect: it leaves considerable discretion to the courts when taking the crucial decisions and, although discretion is necessary so that account can be taken of the varying facts of cases, the principles and policies which guide the courts in the exercise of that discretion are crucial. Just as the working philosophies of the police influence their exercise of discretion (see Reiner chapter 15 in this volume), so the working philosophies of magistrates and judges are likely to determine the impact of the 1991 Act. Much less is known about the working philosophies of the judges, because researchers have been kept at bay (Ashworth *et al.* 1984), and the training programmes for judges and for magistrates may have failed to overcome criticisms of the drafting of the Act and to imbue sentencers with a changed approach.

NON-CUSTODIAL SENTENCING

The Proliferation of 'Alternatives'

Since the mid-1960s successive governments have declared a policy of reducing the use of imprisonment. The general approach has been to create new forms of non-custodial sentence, such as the suspended sentence (1967), the community service order (1972), day training centres (1972), probation orders with Schedule 11 conditions (1982), and others for young offenders. The effect on custodial sentencing has not been significant. Apart from the day training centres, all these innovations may be regarded as successful in the sense that the courts have used them, but unsuccessful in the sense that they appear not to have used them in a way which reduces overall custody rates. One reason for this is that little guidance has been given to the courts about how the measures should be used. The Advisory Council on the Penal System remarked in 1970, when proposing the introduction of community service orders, that it could not 'predict' how the courts would use them (para. 37): clearly it did not see it as its function to formulate guidance. Bottoms (1981) has shown how the ambivalence in the use of the suspended sentence arose from the divergence between the government's hope that it would only be used in order to avoid custody, and the belief of many sentencers that it was simply a non-custodial measure reinforced with a specific deterrent.

Linked to these difficulties is that of the whole conception of an 'alternative to custody': many sentencers were sceptical of this notion, partly because these measures simply cannot be viewed as equivalent to incarceration, and partly because the law strictly required courts to decide on custody before considering an alternative, which seemed artificial. In the face of these perceived problems, the tendency has been to move away from the idea of 'alternatives to custody'. The 1990 White Paper refers instead to 'punishment in the community [as] an effective way of dealing with many offenders, particularly those convicted of property crimes and the less serious offences of violence, when financial penalties are insufficient. The punishment should be in the restrictions on liberty and in the enforcement of the orders' (Home Office 1990*a*: para. 4.3). The strategy seems to be to regard custodial sentences as requiring a special justification, over and above the case for a stringent community sanction. The origin of this lies in the 1988 Green Paper, which virtually invited the courts to say why they were not using the existing non-custodial measures and to indicate what kinds of community sanction they would use (Home Office 1988). The provisions of the 1991 Act, with their emphasis on more demanding orders which are more rigorously enforced, flow from this consultation.

Discharges

The least order a court can make on conviction is an absolute discharge.[9] Such orders are usually reserved for cases of very low culpability, or where the offender is ill, or where the court thinks the prosecution should not have been brought (Wasik 1985*a*). A conviction followed by a discharge does not rank as a conviction for any other purposes. The same applies to a conditional discharge: however, the condition is that the

[9] Powers of Criminal Courts Act 1973, ss. 7, 13, substituted by Criminal Justice Act 1991, Schedule 1.

offender is not convicted of another offence within a specified period (up to three years); if there is such a conviction, the offender is liable also to be resentenced for the original crime. Conditional discharges are quite widely used, amounting to some 15 per cent of adult male indictable offences in 1991 and some 34 per cent of adult female indictable offences. Their use has increased considerably in the 1980s, probably because of the decline in fining. Courts also have various powers to 'bind over' offenders, an order much used in some courts and little used in others (see Law Commission 1987).

Fines

Although the fine remains the most used sentence, even for indictable offences, its proportionate use has declined significantly in recent years—from 54 per cent in 1979 to 39 per cent in 1991 for adult males, and from 55 per cent to 28 per cent for adult females. The decline appears to be associated with the growth of unemployment in the 1980s, with courts being reluctant to fine unemployed offenders or feeling it inappropriate to fine them small amounts. The use of imprisonment for fine defaulters has, however, also declined during the 1980s: some 24,000 people were committed to prison for fine default in 1982, and 17,000 in 1988.

In an attempt to revive the use of the fine and to increase its fairness, the White Paper of 1990 announced and the 1991 Act introduced 'unit fines' into magistrates' courts. The essence of the scheme was that the court had to calculate the fine by assessing the seriousness of the offence on a scale of 1 to 50 units and then, in a separate inquiry, determine the offender's 'weekly disposable income' so as to decide how much the offender should pay per unit. Prior to the introduction of the Act there had been experiments in four magistrates' courts, suggesting that magistrates welcomed the new approach, that fines were perceived as fairer, and that fewer offenders were sent to prison in default of payment (Gibson 1989; Moxon *et al.* 1991). However, the statutory scheme introduced far higher maximum amounts per unit than the experiments. The higher fines that resulted attracted the attention of the mass media, which related the fines to the offence rather than to the offender's means. The approach of many newspapers implicitly rejected the notion that fines should be adjusted to the differing means of offenders. The government responded to the ensuing clamour by abolishing the entire system of unit fines in the Criminal Justice Act 1993, and for a returning to the broad principle that courts should take account of the financial circumstances of the offender. Despite the smooth operation of unit fines in other European countries, it was apparently decided not to amend the statutory scheme so as to bring it closer to the successful experiments. The change is likely either to put a strain on the framework of the 1991 Act, in that poor offenders may be thought unsuitable for fining and considered for the more demanding community sentences, or to result in a greater use of imprisonment for default as poor offenders prove incapable of paying their fines (see Shaw 1989; Morris and Gelsthorpe 1990).

Compensation Orders

Although there were miscellaneous powers previously, the present compensation order was introduced in 1972. In 1982 courts were allowed to use it as the sole order in a case, and courts were required to give priority to a compensation order over a fine if the offender had limited means. The 1988 Criminal Justice Act requires a court to consider making a compensation order in every case involving death, injury, loss, or damage, or to give reasons if it decides not to make an order. The total number of orders increased by 17 per cent between 1988 and 1989, with strong increases following convictions for violence (from 34 per cent up to 55 per cent in magistrates' courts and from 19 per cent up to 28 per cent in the Crown Court). (For detailed research see Moxon *et al.* 1992.) Reasons for not making an order might be that the offender has no assets, or that the offender has been given a custodial sentence and cannot therefore earn the money.

The contribution of compensation orders to greater justice for victims is important, but possibly more at a symbolic level than in terms of actual recompense for large numbers of victims: see further Zedner chapter 25. To some extent this is because compensatory principles inevitably come into conflict with other sentencing principles: for example, although compensation orders have priority over fines, the amount of a compensation order must still be reduced so as to be within the means of the offender.

Community Sentences

As described above, the language of alternatives to custody has now been replaced officially by references to punishment in the community. According to the scheme of the 1991 Act, there are four forms of community order for adult offenders: probation, community service, combination orders, and curfew orders. A court should not impose any such order unless satisfied that the offence is serious enough to warrant it. If it does decide to do so, it should ensure that the order or orders are (a) the most suitable for the offender, and (b) impose restrictions on liberty which are commensurate with the seriousness of the offence (Criminal Justice Act 1991, s. 6). This scheme is designed to bring the proportionality principle into non-custodial sentencing, while allowing some room for choices (e.g. between probation and community service) which reflect the perceived needs of the offender.[10] In most such cases a 'pre-sentence report' (the successor to the social inquiry report) will have been prepared by the probation service to 'assist' the court.

A probation order may be for between six months and three years. The basic order requires supervision by a probation officer. Five additional requirements are available to courts: residence, specified activities, attendance at a probation centre, mental treatment, or treatment for drug or alcohol dependency. Between 1981 and 1991 the use of probation orders increased from 6 per cent to 8 per cent for adult males, and remained at around 17 per cent for adult females. Some three-quarters of orders are completed satisfactorily (see further Vass 1990; Harris 1991).

A community service order may be for between 40 and 240 hours, requiring the performance of unpaid work during leisure hours. Between 1981 and 1991 the use of community service orders increased from 5 per cent to 8 per cent for adult males, and from 11 per cent to 14 per cent for males aged 17–20. Some three-quarters of orders are completed satisfactorily (see further Pease 1985; Vass 1990).

Combination orders were introduced by the 1991 Act. They may consist of 40–100 hours community service combined with one to three years of probation, with or without additional requirements. The 1990 White Paper envisaged that they might be used for persistent non-serious property offenders (Home Office 1990*b*: para. 4.16).

A curfew order is intended to restrict an offender's movements for between two and twelve hours per day for up to six months. Such orders have been available to juvenile courts since 1982 but have been little used. The 1991 Act provides for a curfew order to be combined with electronic monitoring in areas where the mechanism is available. The experiment with electronic monitoring was not a conspicuous success (Mair and Nee 1990), and there are formidable objections of principle to 'tagging' (see von Hirsch 1990*c*). Neither curfew orders nor electronic monitoring were introduced in October 1992, and it is unclear whether they will ever be introduced.

Pre-sentence reports should enable the courts to decide which measure is the most suitable in each case. But to decide what kind and length of order is 'commensurate with the seriousness of the offence' will be difficult. There is no stated hierarchy of community orders, and no notion that so many hours of community service is equivalent to probation with a requirement of attendance at a probation centre, etc. Since a workable system of proportionality requires both criteria for assessing the

[10] The proposals by Wasik and von Hirsch (1988) were influential; for a different approach see Morris and Tonry 1990.

seriousness of offences and a scale of the relative severity of the sanctions, there is an obvious deficiency in the machinery of the 1991 Act. Moreover, the Act sweeps away some earlier restrictions, enables courts to make two or more community orders in one case (if and when the curfew order is introduced) and allows them to add a fine. This creates a danger of 'cocktail' sentences, and research suggests that the more onerous a sentence is, the more likely it is to lead to breach (Home Office, *Probation Statistics*, various years).

Suspended Sentences

A sentence of imprisonment of two years or less may be suspended for a period of up to two years. If the offender is convicted of another offence committed during the operational period, the court must activate the suspended sentence in addition to the sentence for the new crime, unless it is 'unjust to do so'. Suspended sentences did not succeed in lowering the prison population following their introduction in 1967. Research showed that courts sometimes defied the law by imposing suspended sentences when immediate imprisonment would not be justifiable, and by imposing longer sentences when suspending (Bottoms 1981; Moxon 1988: 34–8). Although the suspended sentence is meant to be the most severe of non-custodial measures, it seems that many courts and offenders regard it as a 'let-off'. Suspended sentences were abolished for offenders under 21 in 1982, and abolition for adults has clearly been contemplated. The 1991 Act retains them in restricted form: a court may impose a suspended sentence only if immediate custody is justified and if there are 'exceptional circumstances' in favour of suspension. The Court of Appeal has confirmed the narrowness of the term 'exceptional', and it seems likely that suspended sentences will be passed infrequently. If a court does suspend, it must consider adding a fine or compensation order, to give the sentence an immediate sting (Home Office 1990*a*: paras. 3.19–3.22; s. 5 of Criminal Justice Act 1991).

Review of Policy and Practice

Whether the new approach of 'punishment in the community' will succeed in reducing the percentage of offenders sent into custody, where the previous approach of proliferating so-called 'alternatives to custody' failed, will depend on the practices of the courts. To what extent will Crown Court judges accept that persistent property offenders can be dealt with adequately by non-custodial means (see Ashworth *et al.* 1984)? Will they take the new 'community orders' seriously? Or will they remain sceptical, believing that the 1991 Act involves mere cost-cutting without regard to the human consequences? To what extent can the great variation in magistrates' courts' practices, well documented by research (e.g. Tarling *et al.* 1985; Parker *et al.* 1989), be reduced by the 1991 Act's criteria? Have the courts been given sufficient guidance to produce consistent decision-making and, if not, will the Court of Appeal supply further guidance? On what basis can senior appellate judges be expected to formulate guidance for non-custodial measures or for magistrates' courts?

Much will also depend on the reorientation of the probation service. The 1988 Green Paper fell little short of a threat to the probation service that if it failed to adapt to the new system of keenly enforced, well-regulated, and demanding penalties, some other agency would be found to do the work (Home Office 1988, esp. Part IV). Under the 1991 Act the probation service is subject to new 'national standards' for the content and enforcement of probation orders, community service orders, combination orders, and pre-sentence reports. These spell out details of expected practice on many issues, and can be expected to bind the probation service more tightly than ever before. This may be seen as a necessary step in persuading courts to make greater use of community sentences, but it leaves the probation service with the onerous tasks of producing more and better pre-sentence reports (see section above on 'Information about the Offender') and of containing more difficult offenders in the community (see Harris 1991).

It seems as though Cohen's earlier warnings have become more rather than less pertinent. His 1979 warnings of increased social control through net-widening, blurring, and the thinning of the mesh were questioned by Bottoms (1983), who showed that it was the fine rather than surveillance-based measures which increased in the 1970s. But the 1980s saw the decline of the fine and the rise of custody, community service, and probation. Cohen's thesis was thus rekindled (Cohen 1985; cf. Morgan 1983; Harris and Webb 1987) and the 1991 Act's reliance on punishment in the community—even to the extent of legislating for electronic surveillance—establishes its continued relevance. On one view this is the inevitable price for any element of progress in a society whose political system is much affected by punitive lobbies: the greater use of non-custodial sanctions can only be bought by making them tougher, and also perhaps by continuing to imprison certain groups of offenders for extremely long periods.

SENTENCING REFORM

Judicial Independence

For many years it has been argued that the fundamental constitutional principle of judicial independence makes it wrong for Parliament to 'interfere' with the sentencing discretion of the judiciary. However, the deceptive ambiguity of this argument was rightly denounced in the 1990 White Paper (Home Office 1990*a*: para. 2.1; see further Munro 1992; Ashworth 1992*a*: ch. 2): there is a difference between an impartial judiciary, which is fundamental, and the prohibition of legislation on sentencing, which is unfounded. There are several long-established legislative restrictions on sentence, and the Criminal Justice Act 1991 introduces a whole host of further restrictions. Parliament could, in theory, follow the legislatures of other countries and introduce mandatory minimum sentences for many offences which would leave hardly any judicial discretion. However, the American evidence suggests that such developments are far less effective, either in confining judges or in deterring potential criminals, than politicians suppose (Tonry 1992).

The Training of Sentencers

The Judicial Studies Board organizes seminars for newly appointed judges and refresher courses for other judges. The seminars tend to involve lectures on recent developments in legislation and in Court of Appeal decisions, and group discussions of particular issues (Judicial Studies Board 1991). The Board itself includes judges, civil servants, magistrates, and academics. The Board exercises a general superintendence over the training of magistrates through its Magisterial Committee, but it remains the case that most training of magistrates is undertaken locally. This practice may tend to confirm local bench traditions and the preferences of the local liaison judge and of the justices' clerk, who will usually lead the training.

Seminars and training days often succeed in bringing to light the current concerns of sentencers. Whether they conduce to consistency in sentencing depends partly on the amount of legislative and judicial guidance that is available—which, for many everyday sentencing decisions, is not great—and partly on the attitudes to sentencing which they foster (cf. Bond and Lemon 1979).

Structuring Discretion

While there are strong objections to mandatory sentences which remove all sentencing discretion, since they produce unfairness by requiring courts to treat different cases as if they were alike, there is a strong case for structuring the discretion of the courts in order to achieve certain goals. The 1991 Act attempts to do this by means of a framework of legislative restrictions. The government expressed the hope that the Court of Appeal would give further guidance to structure practical sentencing

(Home Office 1990*a*: para. 2.17). The Magistrates' Association has issued guidelines for the magistrates' courts, but these have no legal force (Magistrates' Association 1992). To what extent local courts will adopt these guidelines depends largely on the key actors mentioned above, local liaison judges and justices' clerks. Training cannot be expected to produce a consistency of approach unless there is sufficient guidance on practical sentencing issues which has been authoritatively agreed. The prospects of providing that in the present system, with so much local autonomy, seem slender.

How much of everyday Crown Court sentencing will be covered by Court of Appeal guidance remains problematic. Unstructured discretion leaves leeway to the personal preferences of the judge, and if the concept of the 'rule of law' has any stable meaning, it must exclude such preferences. While the English system does now have a leading principle—proportionality or 'desert'—the key concept of seriousness will remain open to diverse interpretations unless the Court of Appeal addresses itself to the formulation of guidance which covers the bulk of sentencing decisions, i.e. crimes such as theft, deception, burglary, and handling stolen goods.

International Patterns in Sentencing Reform

Recent years have seen major sentencing reforms in several countries, and reform proposals in many others (for discussion see Ashworth 1992*b*). Most attention has been focused on the various 'guideline systems' in the USA. Minnesota, Washington, and other states have introduced guidelines which indicate sentence ranges according to the type of offence and the criminal history of the offender. Usually there is a permanent sentencing commission to monitor practice, and often there is appellate review to determine the propriety of judicial departures from the guidelines (see Parent 1988; Frase 1990; and more generally Tonry 1987). Since 1987 there have been guidelines for federal sentencing, issued by the United States Sentencing Commission. These guidelines are more complex in their operation, and incorporate several mandatory minimum sentences introduced by Congress. Proponents regard them as sophisticated (e.g. Nagel 1990; Wilkins and Steer 1991), whereas opponents point to the absence of clear rationales, their subservience to previous practice, and their lack of concern for rising prison populations (e.g. von Hirsch 1988; Tonry 1991).

Closer to the approach taken in the English reforms are the systems introduced in Finland in 1976 and in Sweden in 1989. The Swedish statute states the aims and principles of sentencing, and leaves the courts to interpret and apply them to particular cases—the primary task being to assess the 'penal value' of the offence committed (see von Hirsch 1987; von Hirsch and Jareborg 1989). There is appellate review in Sweden, but there is no permanent sentencing commission. In Australia the report of the Law Reform Commission (1988) has not been implemented, but there have been some sentencing reforms in New South Wales, including the introduction of a computerized sentencing information system for use by judges, and there has been a major sentencing statute in Victoria following the Starke Report (Victorian Sentencing Committee 1988).

Further Reform in England and Wales

The Criminal Justice Act 1991 can be said to represent an advance in certain ways. (See also on this topic Ashworth 1992*a*: ch. 12; Cavadino and Dignan 1992: chs. 4, 10). It introduced a primary rationale for English sentencing (desert), and clarified the extent to which other 'aims', such as public protection, rehabilitation, and deterrence, should play a part. This may be expected to remove one source of inconsistency. The 1991 Act also introduced a framework of legislative restrictions on the use of custodial and community sentences which may succeed both in improving consistency and in reducing the use of custody for the less serious types of offence. The Act furthered 'truth in sentencing' by reforming parole and remission so as to ensure that all parts of a custodial sentence count for something. It is not difficult to conceive of other policies which Parliament might have pursued—notably, a significant reduction in the use of imprisonment—but at least the 1991 Act shows that legislative restrictions are possible. Will they work?

Much depends on the 'transmission mechanism' between general legislative policy and practical sentencing. The framework of the 1991 Act was created in the 'hope' that the court of Appeal would supply sufficient detailed guidance to lower courts. Is a court composed of a few senior judges the most suitable body for this task? They may have considerable experience of the most serious offences, but do they know enough about the 'ordinary' crimes which constitute the bulk of Crown Court and magistrates' court sentencing? Even if they have the knowledge, do they have a sufficiently wide perspective to exercise the policy-making function which this undoubtedly is—determining the relative severity of community orders, deciding whether particular orders are 'commensurate' with the seriousness of the offence? In the unlikely event that this breadth of experience can be claimed, do they have the time and resources to fashion sufficient guidance for all lower courts, while also operating as an appellate court? Questions of this kind prompted the call for the creation of a sentencing council to formulate detailed and practical guidance (e.g. Ashworth 1983, 1989; Justice 1990). Opponents criticized this as an attempt to import American-style guideline systems into this country, failing to take the point that a sentencing council for England ought to build on the best of English traditions in forms of guidance (e.g. narrative guideline judgments). The 1990 White Paper reaffirmed faith in the Court of Appeal and Judicial Studies Board to 'contribute to the development of coherent sentencing practice' (Home Office 1990*a*: para. 2.20). Since then, the creation of the Criminal Justice Consultative Committees (following the Woolf Report) has introduced a new forum for discussion among a wide range of criminal justice professionals.

What other policies might be pursued? The 1991 Act includes an oblique provision on non-discrimination in the criminal justice system, but it would have been preferable to have a clear and direct statement of principle.[11] The Act includes a few general principles of sentencing on previous convictions and multiple offenders without setting out all the relevant rules. The Act fails to declare a clear and general commitment to a policy of restraint in the use of custody, and says nothing on the relative severity of different forms of non-custodial measure. In these and many other respects, there is a growing need to develop authoritative guidance within the sentencing system. Moreover, as argued above, sentencing should not be regarded as an isolated and all-important function: it is substantially conditioned by decisions taken earlier in the criminal process, where clear and well-considered policies should also be devised and enforced. Equally, there is a need for research into the impact of rules and principles upon practical sentencing, for too often in criminological research it has been found that practices do not conform to the declared policies. A simple comparison of the amount and findings of research into the police (see Reiner chapter 15 in this volume) with those of research into sentencers shows the poverty of information on how the system actually works.

Selected Further Reading

A. Ashworth, *Sentencing and Criminal Justice*. London: Weidenfeld and Nicolson, 1992.

A. Ashworth, E. Genders, G. Mansfield, J. Peay, and E. Player, *Sentencing in the Crown Court*. Oxford: Oxford University Centre for Criminological Research, 1984.

[11] s. 95 (1) merely requires the Home Secretary to publish information which facilitates the performance by criminal justice personnel of their duty not to discriminate on improper grounds.

M. Cavadino and J. Dignan, *The Penal System: An Introduction*, chs. 2–4. London: Sage, 1992.

J. Floud and W. Young, *Dangerousness and Criminal Justice*. London: Heinemann, 1981.

D. Garland, *Punishment and Modern Society*. Oxford: Oxford University Press, 1990.

R. Hood, *Race and Sentencing*. Oxford: Oxford University Press, 1992.

N. Lacey, *State Punishment*. London: Routledge, 1988.

D. Moxon, *Sentencing Practice in the Crown Court*. Oxford: Oxford University Centre for Criminological Research, 1988.

C. Munro and M. Wasik, eds., *Sentencing, Judicial Discretion and Judicial Training*. London: Sweet and Maxwell, 1992.

K. Pease and M. Wasik, eds., *Sentencing Reform: Guidance or Guidelines?* Manchester: Manchester University Press, 1987.

D. Pennington and S. Lloyd-Bostock, *The Psychology of Sentencing*. Oxford: Centre for Socio-Legal Studies, 1987.

A. von Hirsch, *Censure and Sanctions*. Oxford: Oxford University Press, 1993.

A. von Hirsch and A. Ashworth, eds., *Principled Sentencing*. Edinburgh: Edinburgh University Press, 1993.

M. Wasik, *Emmins on Sentencing*. London: Blackstone, 1993.

REFERENCES

Advisory Council on the Penal System (1970), *Non-Custodial and Semi-Custodial Penalties*. London: HMSO.

—— (1978), *Sentences of Imprisonment: A Review of Maximum Penalties*. London: HMSO.

Ashworth, A. (1983), *Sentencing and Penal Policy*. London: Weidenfeld and Nicolson.

—— (1987), 'The Public Interest Element in Prosecutions', *Criminal Law Review*: 595–607.

—— (1989), *Custody Reconsidered*, Policy Study no. 104. London: Centre for Policy Studies.

—— (1992*a*), *Sentencing and Criminal Justice*. London: Weidenfeld and Nicolson.

—— (1992*b*), 'Sentencing Reform Structures', in M. Tonry, ed., *Crime and Justice*, vol. 16, 181–242. Chicago: University of Chicago Press.

Ashworth, A., Genders, E., Mansfield, G., Peay, J., and Player, E. (1984), *Sentencing in the Crown Court* (Oxford Pilot Study). Oxford: University of Oxford Centre for Criminological Research.

Australian Law Reform Commission (1988), *Sentencing*, Report no. 44. Canberra: Government Printer.

Baldwin, J. (1985), *Pre-Trial Justice in Magistrates' Courts*. Oxford: Oxford University Press.

Bentham, J. (1789), *Principles of Morals and Legislation*. London.

Beyleveld, D. (1979), 'Deterrence Research as a Basis for Deterrence Policies', *Howard Journal*, 18: 135–49.

—— (1980), *A Bibliography of General Deterrence*. New York: Saxon House.

Blumstein, A., Cohen, J., Roth, J., and Visher, C. (1986), *Criminal Careers and Career Criminals*. Washington, DC: National Academy Press.

Bond, R. A., and Lemon, N. (1979), 'Changes in Magistrates' Attitudes during the First Year on the Bench', in D. Farrington, K. Hawkins, and S. Lloyd-Bostock, eds., *Psychology, Law and Legal Processes*. London: Macmillan.

Bottoms, A. E. (1981), 'The Suspended Sentence in England, 1967–78', *British Journal of Criminology*, 21: 1–26.

—— (1983), 'Neglected Features of Contemporary Penal Systems', in D. Garland and P. Young, eds., *The Power to Punish*, 166–202. London: Heinemann.

Bottoms, A. E., and Brownsword, R. (1982), The Dangerousness Debate after the Floud Report', *British Journal of Criminology*, 22: 229.

Bottoms, A. E., and Preston, R. H. (1980), *The Coming Penal Crisis*. Edinburgh: Scottish Academic Press.

Braithwaite, J., and Pettit, P. (1990), *Not Just Deserts*. Oxford: Oxford University Press.

Brody, S. R. (1975), *The Effectiveness of Sentencing*, Home Office Research Study no. 35. London: HMSO.

Brody, S., and Tarling, R. (1981), *Taking Offenders out of Circulation*, Home Office Research Study no. 64. London: HMSO.

Burney, E. (1985), *Sentencing Young People*. Aldershot: Gower.

Carlisle, Lord (1988), *The Parole System in England and Wales*, Report of the Review Committee. London: HMSO.

Cavadino, M., and Dignan, J. (1992), *The Penal System: An Introduction*. Beverly Hills and London: Sage.

Cohen, S. (1985), *Visions of Social Control*. New York: Plenum.

—— (1979), 'The Punitive City', *Contemporary Crises*, 3: 339–63.

Cooke, R. K. (1987), 'The Practical Problems of the Sentencer', in D. Pennington and S. Lloyd-Bostock, eds., *The Psychology of Sentencing*, 57–60. Oxford: University of Oxford Centre for Socio-Legal Studies.

Cullen, F., and Gilbert, K. (1982), *Reaffirming Rehabilitation*. Cincinnati: Anderson.

Curran, P. (1991), 'Discussions in the Judge's Private Room', *Criminal Law Review*, 79–86.

Darbyshire, P. (1984), *The Justices' Clerk*. Chichester: Barry Rose.

Downes, D. (1988), *Contrasts in Tolerance*. Oxford: Oxford University Press.

Duff, A. (1986), *Trials and Punishments*. Cambridge: Cambridge University Press.

Evans, R., and Wilkinson, C. (1990), 'Variations in Police Cautioning Policy and Practice in England and Wales', *Howard Journal*, 29: 155–76.

Farrington, D., and Morris, A. (1983), 'Sex, Sentencing and Reconvictions', *British Journal of Criminology*, 23: 229–48.

Floud, J., and Young, W. (1981), *Dangerousness and Criminal Justice*. London: Heinemann.

Frase, R. (1990), 'Sentencing Reform in Minnesota, Ten Years After', *Minnesota Law Review*, 75: 1401–28.

Garland, D. (1990), *Punishment and Modern Society*. Oxford: Oxford University Press.

Gibson, B. (1989), *Unit Fines*. Winchester: Waterside Press.

Graham, D. (1990), 'Decarceration in the Federal Republic of Germany', *British Journal of Criminology*, 30: 150–70.

Greenwood, P. (1982), *Selective Incapacitation*. Santa Monica, Ca.: RAND Corporation.

Hall, D. (1991), 'Victims' Voices in Criminal Courts: The Need for Restraint', *American Criminal Law Review*, 28: 233–66.

Harding, R. (1990), 'Rational Choice Gun Use in Armed Robbery', *Criminal Law Forum*, 1: 427.

Harris, R. (1991), *Crime, Criminal Justice and the Probation Service*. London: Routledge.

Harris, R., and Webb, D. (1987), *Welfare, Power and Juvenile Justice*. London: Tavistock.

Hart, H. L. A. (1968), *Punishment and Responsibility*. Oxford: Oxford University Press.

Harvey, L., and Pease, K. (1987), 'Guideline Judgments and Proportionality in Sentencing', *Criminal Law Review*, 96–104.

Hawkins, K., and Thomas, J., eds. (1984), *Enforcing Regulation*. Boston: Kluwer-Nijhoff.

Hedderman, C., and Moxon, D. (1992), *Magistrates' Court or Crown Court? Mode of Trial Decisions and Sentencing*, Home Office Research Study no. 125. London: HMSO.

Home Office (1988), *Punishment, Custody and the Community*. London: HMSO.

—— (1990*a*), *Crime, Justice and Protecting the Public*. London: HMSO.

—— (1990*b*), *Criminal Statistics for England and Wales 1989*. London: HMSO.

—— (1991), *A Digest of Information on the Criminal Justice System*. London: Home Office.

—— (1992), *Probation Service National Standards for Pre-Sentence Reports*. London: HMSO.

Hood, R. (1962), *Sentencing in Magistrates' Courts*. London: Tavistock.

—— (1972), *Sentencing the Motoring Offender*. London: Heinemann.

—— (1992), *Race and Sentencing*. Oxford: Oxford University Press.

Hudson, B. (1987), *Justice through Punishment: A Critique of the Justice Model of Corrections*. London: Macmillan.

Hutter, B. (1988), *The Reasonable Arm of the Law*. Oxford: Oxford University Press.

Judicial Studies Board (1991), *Report 1987–1991*. London: HMSO.

Justice (1990), *Sentencing: The Way Forward.* London: Justice.

Lacey, N. (1988), *State Punishment*. London: Routledge.

Law Commission (1987), *Binding Over: The Issues*. London: HMSO.

McConville, M., Sanders, A., and Leng, R. (1991), *The Case for the Prosecution*. London: Routledge.

Magistrates' Association (1992), *Sentencing Guidelines*. London: Magistrates' Association.

Mair, G., and Nee, C. (1990), *Electronic Monitoring: The Trials and their Results*, Home Office Research Study no. 120. London: HMSO.

Martinson, R. (1979), 'New Findings, New Views: A Note of Caution on Sentencing Reform', *Hofstra Law Review*, 7: 243–60.

Martinson, R., *et al.* (1974), 'What Works? Questions and Answers about Prison Reform', *Public Interest*, 35: 22–54.

Mayhew, P., Elliott, D., and Dowds, L. (1989), *The 1988 British Crime Survey*. London: HMSO.

Monahan, J. (1981), *Predicting Violent Behaviour*. Beverly Hills and London: Sage.

Morgan, N. (1983), 'Non-Custodial Penal Sanctions in England and Wales: A New Utopia', *Howard Journal*, 22: 148–67.

Morris, A., and Gelsthorpe, L. (1990), 'Not Paying for Crime: Issues in Fine Enforcement', *Criminal Law Review*, 839–51.

Morris, N., and Tonry, M. (1990), *Between Prison and Probation*. Oxford: Oxford University Press.

Moxon, D. (1988), *Sentencing Practice in the Crown Court*, Home Office Research Study no. 103. London: HMSO.

Moxon, D., Corkery, J. M., and Hedderman, C. (1992), *Developments in the Use of Compensation Orders in Magistrates' Courts since October 1988*, Home Office Research Study no. 126. London: HMSO.

Moxon, D., Sutton, M., and Hedderman, C. (1991), *Unit Fines: Experiments at Four Courts*. London: Home Office.

Munro, C. (1992), 'Judicial Independence and Judicial Functions', in M. Wasik and C. Munro, eds., *Sentencing, Judicial Discretion and Judicial Training*, 13–32: London: Sweet & Maxwell.

Nagel, I. (1990), 'Structuring Sentencing Discretion: The New Federal Sentencing Guidelines', *Journal of Criminal Law and Criminology*, 80: 883–943.

Parent, D. (1988), *Structuring Criminal Sentences: The Evolution of Minnesota's Sentencing Guidelines*. London: Butterworths.

Parker, H., Sumner, M., and Jarvis, G. (1989), *Unmasking the Magistrates*. Milton Keynes: Open University Press.

Pease, K. (1985), 'Community Service Orders', in N. Morris and M. Tonry, eds., *Crime and Justice: An Annual Review*, vol. 6, 51–94. Chicago: University of Chicago Press.

—— (1992), 'Punitiveness and Prison Populations: University of Chicago Press. An International Comparison', *Justice of the Peace*, 156: 405–8.

Pennington, D., and Lloyd-Bostock, S., eds. (1987), *The Psychology of Sentencing*. Oxford: University of Oxford Centre for Socio-Legal Studies.

Posner, R. (1985), 'An Economic Theory of the Criminal Law', *Columbia Law Review*, 85: 1193–1231.

RADZINOWICZ, L., and HOOD, R. (1978), 'A Dangerous Direction for Sentencing Reform', *Criminal Law Review*, 713–24.

—— (1986), *The Emergence of Penal Policy in Victorian and Edwardian England.* London: Stevens.

RILEY, D. (1985), 'Drinking Drivers: The Limits to Deterrence', *Howard Journal*, 24: 241–56.

RILEY, D., and VENNARD, J. (1988), *Triable-Either-Way Cases: Crown Court or Magistrates' Court*, Home Office Research Study no. 98. London: HMSO.

SANDERS, A. (1985), 'Class Bias in Prosecutions', *Howard Journal*, 24: 176–99.

—— (1988), 'The Limits to Diversion from Prosecution', *British Journal of Criminology*, 28: 513–32.

SHAPLAND, J. (1981), *Between Conviction and Sentence*. London: Routledge.

—— (1987), 'Who Controls Sentencing? Influences on the Sentencer', in D. Pennington and S. Lloyd-Bostock, eds., *The Psychology of Sentencing*, 77–87. Oxford: University of Oxford Centre for Socio-Legal Studies.

SHAW, S. (1989), 'Monetary Penalties and Imprisonment: The Realistic Alternatives', in P. Carlen and D. Cook, eds., *Paying for Crime*, 29–45. Milton Keynes: Open University Press.

STANLEY, C. (1988), 'Making Statutory Guidelines Work', *Justice of the Peace*, 152: 648–50.

STONE, N. (1992), 'Pre-Sentence Reports, Culpability and the 1991 Act', *Criminal Law Review*, 558–67.

TARLING, R. (1979), *Sentencing Practice in Magistrates' Courts*, Home Office Research Study no. 98. London: HMSO.

TARLING, R., MOXON, D., and JONES, P. (1985), 'Sentencing of Adults and Juveniles in Magistrates' Courts', in D. Moxon, ed., *Managing Criminal Justice*, 159–74. London: HMSO.

THOMAS, D. A. (1970), *Principles of Sentencing*. London: Heinemann.

—— (1974), 'The Control of Discretion in the Administration of Criminal Justice', in R. Hood, ed., *Crime, Criminology and Public Policy*, 139–56. London: Heinemann.

—— (1978), *The Penal Equation*. Cambridge: University of Cambridge Institute of Criminology.

—— (1988), 'Sentencing: Some Current Questions', *Current Legal Problems*, 41: 115–34.

TONRY, M. (1987), *Sentencing Reform Impacts*. Washington, DC: National Institute of Justice.

—— (1991), 'The Politics and Processes of Sentencing Commissions', *Crime and Delinquency*, 37: 307–29.

—— (1992), 'Mandatory Penalties', in M. Tonry, ed., *Crime and Justice: A Review of Research*, vol. 16, 243–74. Chicago: University of Chicago Press.

VAN DUYNE, P. (1987), 'Simple Decision-Making', in D. Pennington and S. Lloyd-Bostock, eds., *The Psychology of Sentencing*, 143–58. Oxford: University of Oxford Centre for Socio-Legal Studies.

VASS, A. A. (1990), *Alternatives to Prison*. Beverly Hills and London: Sage.

VICTORIAN SENTENCING COMMITTEE (1988), *Report*, 3 vols. Melbourne: Government Printer.

von Hirsch, A. (1976), *Doing Justice*. New York: Hill and Wang.

—— (1986), *Past or Future Crimes*. Manchester: Manchester University Press.

—— (1987), 'Guiding Principles for Sentencing: The Proposed Swedish Law', *Criminal Law Review*: 746–55.

—— (1988), *Federal Sentencing Guidelines: The United States and Canadian Schemes Compared*, Occasional Papers from the Center for Research in Crime and Justice, no. 4. New York: New York University School of Law.

—— (1990*a*), 'Proportionality in the Philosophy of Punishment', *Criminal Law Forum*, 1: 259–90.

—— (1990*b*), 'The Politics of Just Deserts', *Canadian Journal of Criminology*, 32: 397–413.

—— (1990*c*), 'The Ethics of Community Sanctions', *Crime and Delinquency*, 36: 162–73.

von Hirsch, A., and Ashworth, A., eds. (1992*a*), *Principled Sentencing*. Boston: Northeastern University Press; Edinburgh: Edinburgh University Press.

—— (1992*b*), 'Not Not Just Deserts', *Oxford Journal of Legal Studies*, 12: 83–98.

von Hirsch, A., and Jareborg, N. (1989), 'Sweden's Sentencing Statute Enacted', *Criminal Law Review*, 275–81.

—— (1991), 'Gauging Criminal Harm: A Living Standard Analysis', *Oxford Journal of Legal Studies*, 11: 1–38.

Walker, N. D. (1985), *Sentencing: Theory, Law and Practice*. London: Butterworths.

—— (1991), *Why Punish?* Oxford: Oxford University Press.

Wasik, M. (1985*a*), 'The Grant of an Absolute Discharge', *Oxford Journal of Legal Studies*, 5: 211.

—— (1985*b*), 'Rules of Evidence at the Sentencing Stage', *Current Legal Problems*, 38: 187–210.

Wasik, M., and von Hirsch, A. (1988), 'Non-Custodial Penalties and the Principles of Desert', *Criminal Law Review*, 555–72.

Wilkins, W., and Steer, J. (1991), 'Relevant Conduct: The Cornerstone of the Federal Sentencing Guidelines', *South Carolina Law Review*, 41: 495–531.

Wood, D. (1988), 'Dangerous Offenders and the Morality of Protective Sentencing', *Criminal Law Review*, 424–33.

Wright, M. (1991), *Justice for Victims and Offenders*. Milton Keynes: Open University Press.

Zimring, F., and Hawkins, G. (1973), *Deterrence: The Legal Threat in Crime Control*. Chicago: University of Chicago Press.

18

Probation and Community Sanctions

TIM MAY

Changes in the criminal justice system in recent times have been not only rapid, but chaotic. Since the late 1960s, one of the dominant features of penal policy has been the need to reduce the pressure of overcrowding in prisons, primarily through reductions in the use of custody in sentencing decisions. The result has been a proliferation of 'alternatives to custody'—or, as the Criminal Justice Act 1991 refers to them, 'community sentences'. Driven, as they have been, as much by pragmatic and economic as by philosophical and principled arguments, initiatives in this area appear to be never-ending and confused in their aims, implementation, and day-to-day management. Attempts, therefore, to impose an evolutionary theoretical schema on the spread of community-based sentences must be treated with caution.

Two trends can be discerned in more recent developments, however: the movement from a 'welfare' to a 'punishment' model of community corrections; and the political call for community sentences to be 'tough' on offenders. As part of this change in emphasis, a new vocabulary has arisen, within which the idea of 'credibility' plays an important part. A rarely examined concept, it is applied frequently to the process of making community sentencing schemes acceptable in the eyes of the courts, who are further assumed to reflect society's opinion that offenders need not only to be punished, but to be punished in a manner which is visible in its exercise and consequences. One senior politician, reflecting this attitude, has noted in commenting upon community sentences that the vandal should be doing 'demanding work. Clearing up his neighbourhood. Scrubbing those graffiti off the walls, putting right the damage he has caused. That's what we want to see' (the Home Secretary addressing the Conservative Party Conference on 12 October 1988).

The main aim of this chapter is to build up a deeper understanding of how and why community sentences have arrived at their present stage, with particular emphasis upon changes in the probation service—the agency with statutory responsibility for their operation. This will be tackled in a number of different ways. First, I will examine the historical changes in government policy in relation to adult non-custodial penalties, which hold lessons for understanding the current tensions and contradictions within policy and practice (on juveniles, see Chapter 20 by

Gelstorpe and Morris in this volume). Second, I will consider the contemporary underlying rationale of punishment in the community. Third, following this theoretical discussion, I will consider the policies through which community sentences have been implemented and enforced, noting in particular the reactions of and implications for the work of the probation service. Fourth, the questions surrounding the cost and effectiveness of community-based schemes are considered. A final section will then draw these issues together.

A HISTORY OF COMMUNITY SENTENCING

The Growth of Probation

Histories of the beginning of the probation service and its role in the rise of community-based court disposals have already been written (Bochel 1976; Haxby 1978; Jarvis 1972; King 1969). However, these have tended to be descriptive and often have failed to discuss the outcomes of policy in relation to changes in political, social, and economic circumstances and the rising professionalism of groups within the criminal justice system. In order to counterbalance this approach, an historical account is needed to enable a greater understanding of the contemporary tensions in community sentencing policy to be reached (also see Garland 1985; McWilliams 1983, 1985, 1986, 1987; May 1991*a*, *b*; Young 1976).

It was in the latter part of the nineteenth century that the use of imprisonment as the 'normal' response to criminal activity began to be challenged. The English Temperance Society believed many criminal acts to be petty in nature, essentially temporary lapses into deviant activity caused by a combination of drink and personal moral weakness. Imprisonment, it argued, with its emphasis upon punishment and exclusion from the community, was not an appropriate response to such behaviour. It was in the search for an alternative approach that the idea of probation in the community began its development.

The key to the proposed solution lay in moral education to 'save' those offenders who were thought to lapse occasionally into criminal behaviour. Such offenders were not thought to suffer from an innate immorality, nor to be reacting to material deprivation. They had slipped from a righteous path and needed spiritual education to guide them back on to the 'straight and narrow'. With this concentration on the individual, suitable offenders were selected to be placed under the jurisdiction of volunteers known as 'police-court missionaries'.

The move to full-time officials dealing with offenders in the community was introduced in the 1907 Probation of Offenders Act. This Act made it possible for courts of summary jurisdiction to appoint probation officers who, in turn, were charged with duties to 'advise, assist, and befriend' those individuals whom the court regarded as suitable for a 'probation order'. It led to a significant increase in both probation orders and probation officers, a process accelerated by the 1925 Criminal Justice Act, which made it mandatory for every criminal court to have a probation officer attached to it. The numbers placed on probation rose from 15,094 in 1925 to 18,934 in 1933. In turn, increased emphasis on 'training' probation officers led to the development of therapeutic techniques for 'reforming' the offender in the community.

This change in method, away from religion and moral education to therapy, was sustained and rationalized by psychological studies detailing the 'abnormality' of offenders' personalities. Its aim was to 'normalize' offenders, outside the confines of the prison environment. No longer inspired by religious zeal, probation officers, social workers, psychiatrists, educationalists, and psychologists (to name a few) were the professionals whose jobs were created in the expansion of community-based sanctions. These changes had a direct bearing upon the ideological construction of the 'criminal': the technique of therapy aimed at reform of an individual who was in some sense 'sick', not at punishment of the 'wicked'.

The Emergence of 'Alternatives to Custody'

If 1907 and 1925 were significant dates in the rise of probation, the post-1945 period was important in a shift of focus to community-based sanctions as *alternatives to*, rather than *different in aim from*, custody. During this period, right up to the 1991 Criminal Justice Act, several changes took place in the purpose and function of community sanctions. This 'drift' was primarily the result of concern about three interrelated problems: the increasing levels of recorded crime, the custody rate, and the cost of imprisonment.

During the 1950s and 1960s, and to a lesser extent the 1970s, the elements of therapy within non-custodial penalties were consistently endorsed by professional groups involved in the criminal justice system, criminological studies, and various government-sponsored reports—one of the most significant of which was the Morison Committee Report (Home Office 1962). This Committee, which undertook a large-scale inquiry into probation, was set up by a reluctant Home Office in response to public anxiety over increasing crime rates and a frequently articulated belief that the probation order was a 'soft option'. In fact, as the Morison Committee noted with some concern, the relative use of probation by sentencers had fallen since the war. While endorsing the use of rehabilitative casework with offenders, its report also bowed to the critics by charging the probation officer with a clear duty to protect society and to ensure the good conduct of the probationer (Home Office 1962: para. 54).

The introduction, in the Criminal Justice Act 1967, of both parole and suspended sentences also marked significant developments in the history of non-custodial measures. Parole was intended not only to reduce the prison population, but to assist in the process of resettlement of the offenders in the community at a time in their sentence when a further period of incarceration would prove detrimental to their rehabilitation. However, it also incorporated elements of 'public protection' in the community, through the monitoring of parolees' progress by a probation officer to whom they were required to report on a regular basis.

Suspended sentences introduced a sentence of imprisonment held in 'suspension' in the community as long as no further offences are committed by the offender. If they commit a further offence, offenders are then liable to that sentence of imprisonment and a penalty for the new offence. (In 1989, 80 per cent of those breached for failing to comply with the conditions of a suspended sentence were sentenced to immediate custody: Home Office 1990*c*.) The suspended sentence, then, is designed as an 'alternative to custody'. The success of its main function, reducing the prison population, depends upon the courts using it in place of immediate custody for those who would otherwise receive a custodial sentence, though research suggests that, at least in its early years, it was used as often merely as an 'alternative to an alternative'.

The objective of replacing custodial with non-custodial penalties in order to reduce the prison population almost inevitably promoted a drift towards a more punitive epoch in community sentencing. Coupled with the cost of imprisonment, popular images of criminality, the desire for punishment, and criminological studies which were now questioning the 'rehabilitative ideal' upon which the techniques of therapy were based, it provided the impetus for more policy changes. It was in response to these conditions that the Wootton Committee reported in 1970 (Advisory Council on the Penal System 1970) with the recommendation for a new sentence of 'community work'. This proposal was certainly innovative. It offered not only a reformative element, but also punishment and restitution—albeit to the community, rather than directly to the victim(s). As an alternative to custody community service, like a suspended sentence, carries with it the threat of imprisonment in the event of a breach of conditions, while also satisfying the perceived public thirst for punishment as offenders pay back their debt to society by engaging in a variety of community work placements. The popularity with sentencers of this new penal measure has been considerable. In 1974, 928 community service orders were made; by 1981 this figure had reached 28,000 and by 1990 37,500.

Innovations in community-based sanctions continued throughout the 1970s and 1980s. Local probation committees were empowered to set up and run probation hostels and bail hostels (Powers of Criminal Courts Act 1973; Bail Act 1976). While probation hostels may house those on bail, their primary purpose is to enable magistrates to sentence individuals, as part of a probation order, to reside in a hostel for a specified period. Offenders then continue to be part of the community in an environment intended to assist in their rehabilitation. Further, in terms of the 'credibility stakes', magistrates are confident of their whereabouts and supervision. Within such an order, ideas of therapy are thus grafted on to the community surveillance of the offender.

'Day training centres' appeared in 1973 (Powers of Criminal Courts Act 1973: see Wright 1984) and were renamed day centres in 1982 (Criminal Justice Act 1982, s. 4A(1)(b)). Once again, the intention was to alter the perception, purpose, and aim of community-based sanctions. They are used most intensively in '4B orders', which are set up by local probation committees as part of the provision of a probation order and require full-time attendance at programmes in day centres, up to a maximum of sixty days. These may be specifically related to the offending behaviour and/or include drug and alcohol education schemes. Offenders may also be sentenced to refrain from certain activities as a condition of probation. These 'negative' requirements are controversial, due to the explicit controls involved: that is, the role of the probation officer in preventing offenders from undertaking certain actions, which the court specifies, while they are at 'liberty' in the community.

The introduction of day centres was again assumed to satisfy a need for more demanding community sentences by adding conditions to conventional probation orders. Meeting the stated aims of day centres means targeting those offenders processed through the courts who are 'at risk' of receiving a custodial sentence. The prison population is, in theory, reduced by persuading the courts to use more 'credible' community sentences.[1] Indeed, from 1979 to 1989 the number of probation orders grew by 54 per cent to 42,000. However, while the Crown-Court increased its use of community-based sentences, their use in magistrates' courts, which deal with nearly two-thirds of all indictable offences, remained unchanged (Home Office 1990*c*).

The effectiveness of such innovations clearly depends not just upon the probation services's targeting methods, but upon the willingness of the courts to use them as genuine alternatives to imprisonment. This depends, in turn, upon the 'culture' of the court. Running alongside these policy

[1] Because of the need to target those whose offences risk imprisonment by the court, day centre probation orders, along with community service orders and those schemes designed to target such offenders, are known as 'high-tariff' alternatives.

initiatives, therefore, have been a series of government attempts to encourage courts to use community sentences. Successive Criminal Justice Acts (1982, 1988, 1991) have contained increasingly specific guidance to sentencers on the factors that should be present before they consider passing a custodial sentence. For example, magistrates should ask themselves if there is a need to 'protect the public from harm' (Criminal Justice Act 1982, reiterated in Criminal Justice Act 1988, s. 123), and the current offence must be serious enough to justify a custodial sentence, it not being acceptable to imprison on the strength of a bad previous record (Criminal Justice Act 1991). Similarly, in *A Handbook for Courts on the Treatment of Offenders*, published by the Home Office, it is stressed that a custodial sentence 'should only be imposed when it is truly necessary . . . if it is necessary, the sentence should be as short as is consistent with the need of punishment.'

While the aim of reducing the rate of custody and the corresponding prison population might appear simple, its actual complexity cannot be overstated. Anomalies are produced not only by variations between the Crown Court and magistrates' courts, but by geographical variations in custodial sentencing practices: for example, the proportion of sentences that use a custodial option varies between 8 per cent and 39 per cent for adult males; 4 per cent and 16 per cent for adult females; and 4 per cent and 22 per cent for males between 17 and 21 years of age (May 1991*a*: 31). The judiciary and magistracy guard their autonomy with vigour. As a result, the suggestion that there should be a sentencing council issuing strong guidelines in order to reduce such variation is considered controversial.[2] Thus, it is largely the probation service that is held responsible for the success of these innovations through its ability to alter the sentencing patterns of courts. This requires convincing the courts to use alternatives to custody in place of imprisonment for suitable offenders. In order to ensure that the probation service achieves this task, a series of rules, statutory changes, and statements from the Home Office have added to a 'politics of penalty' as applied to alternatives to custody. To aid an understanding of this situation, attention is now turned to the rationale of these changes, before examining the politics of the enforcement and implementation of these schemes in recent years.

[2] Although the Conservative government has no plans to introduce such a council, the Labour Party in a White Paper on criminal justice (1990) drew up preliminary plans for a sentencing council. For a discussion of the issues involved see Ashworth (1989) and Thomas (1989).

THE RATIONALE OF PUNISHMENT IN THE COMMUNITY

As we have seen, the 'rehabilitative ideal', with its emphasis on the welfare and therapy of the individual offender, provided the justification for many non-custodial penalties. However, this justification was increasingly challenged as a result of two, sometimes contradictory, pressures. First, it was attacked on empirical grounds. It appeared that the rehabilitation of offenders was failing, and within both the Home Office Research Unit and the disciplines of the sociology of deviance and criminology, studies appeared which challenged the idea and operation of 'rehabilitation' (e.g. see Brody 1976; Croft 1978). Second, a change in political climate brought 'law and order' to the forefront of political debate, challenging not only the effectiveness of alternatives to custody, but also the legitimacy of the associated working methods: therapy had 'failed', now punishment was 'demanded'.

Although their theoretical explanations differ, there appears to be a broad consensus among scholars that over the past 100 years our society has been moving from an 'exclusionist' towards an 'inclusionist' form of social control (see Cohen 1985; Foucault 1977; Garland 1985, 1990; Ignatieff 1978). This has involved a broad shift in penal thinking from the emphasis on punishing the body in pre-eighteenth-century times, to the predominance of imprisonment (which segregated the offender from her or his community) in the nineteenth century, and then towards the form characteristic of contemporary society: punishment and control in the community.

Despite its location within the community, this form of social control and its rationale refuses to acknowledge the social basis of crime. Its tactic is to concentrate upon individual offenders, in isolation from their social environment and from questions about social, political, and economic justice. While this in itself is hardly a new feature of the criminal justice system, the extent to which the social dimension is disguised has been increased by the virtual abandonment by many contemporary criminologists of research into the social aspects and causes of crime, in favour of an 'administrative' approach to crime control. Young (1986) has called this a 'paradigm shift' or 'silent revolution', in which the agenda has shifted from the search for causes to the effectiveness of deterrence and control. The effects of this change on alternatives to custody have been more subtle and effective than even this analysis would predict.

The rationale of 'punishment in the community' perpetuates the abstraction of the individual from her or his environment by its silence on social issues and its concentration on the practices and techniques of the administration of community schemes. To take one example, is the apprehended offender 'jettisoned' into crime by social circumstances, or did she or he willingly 'jump'? This is an important question in sentencing decisions. In writing a social inquiry report on an offender for the court, the probation officer investigates her or his background in order to shed light on this question. However, if punishment is to be the core of community disposals and the prevailing ethos is 'responsibility' for one's actions, the social inquiry report which is used for this purpose seems like an anachronism. If people are to blame for their actions, do we need such reports, which are based in a welfare philosophy? If criminals are now constructed as 'responsible subjects', then they also have a 'right to be punished, not treated' (Cohen 1988: 122).

Attempts have been made to resolve this tension between social explanation and individual responsibility through administrative systems of community sentencing. Historically, we have moved from the determinism of psychological explanations (offenders as victims of forces beyond their control and in need of therapy) to a concept of individual freedom (full responsibility for individual actions, regardless of social circumstances, and therefore deserving of punishment). A concentration on the former in the era of rehabilitation was latterly criticized for removing from individuals both autonomy and responsibility for their actions, while placing power in the hands of welfare professionals. The new model, it is argued, replaces this with an emphasis on equal treatment and 'justice'. Yet who are the people whom these community schemes target? Are they a cross-section of society, impartially processed and targeted, as a 'neutral' criminal justice system would hold?

The criminal justice system is a nodal point of power relations within society which both reflects and perpetuates society's dominant assumptions. To assume that it is an impartial device built on consensus neglects the evidence that it is a mechanism of social control which is selective on class, race, and gender lines. Thus, when one examines the characteristics of persons who are sentenced to community schemes, not surprisingly, factors relating to class, race, and gender are prominent. For instance, the probation service has a current criminal caseload which stands at 129,000. Of those individuals, according to a recent report, 90,000 (70 per cent) do not have any employment and a further 15 per cent are either in training or not available for work (*NAPO News*, January 1992). While evidence on the causal link between unemployment and crime remains difficult to 'prove', Steven Box's (1987) authoritative study demonstrates that the link between income inequality and crime cannot be ignored by decision-makers in the criminal justice system.

The justice model of corrections, upon which the punishment in the community movement is built, does little to achieve any reduction in the crime rate by its refusal to acknowledge these social dimensions. Thus, in discussing the likely 'impact' that community sentencing can have in preventing reoffending, Whitehead, Turver, and Wheatley note that this is not 'a realistic objective for the probation service to pursue' (1991: 62). (Of course, this criticism can also be levelled against those who still adhere to the rehabilitative ideal with its concentration on offender abnormalities to the exclusion of the environmental factors which are associated with crime.)

The criminal justice system is also biased along the dimensions of race and gender, and this is reflected in the practices surrounding community sentencing (see e.g. Crow 1987; Carlen and Worrall 1987; Dominelli 1991; Eaton 1986; Mair and Brockington 1988; Scraton and Chadwick 1991; Waters 1990). The probation service, although committed to the eradication of these biases, is part of the system and the society which reproduce them. For this reason, the discretion which rests with probation officers and those responsible for administering the criminal justice system must be open to critical examination. As Eaton (1986: 61) concluded in her study of the courts' treatment of women: 'The practices of probation officers serve to disadvantage women by an endorsement of a model of family life which involves the oppression and exploitation of women.' Rather than confronting these issues of poverty, race, and gender, our system of criminal justice, as exemplified by the rationale of punishment in the community, has responded to such challenges by resorting to a particular mentality: 'the obsession with effectiveness, evaluation, classification, "what works"' (Cohen 1988: 26). By default, this approach 'brackets' the very issues which surround the complicated relationship between crime and society.

Aside from the predominant administrative mentality, criminologists' responses to the contemporary shift to non-custodial penalties have taken a variety of forms, none of them highly influential in the policy arena. Many have noted that government support for alternatives to incarceration is motivated by the desire to reduce public expenditure (Scull 1977, 1983). Others, reflecting upon the lack of impact of prison on the crime rate, have called for the abolition of the prison system either in general (Mathieson 1990) or for women in particular (Carlen 1990). There are also those who have simply ignored questions about the deterrent effect of imprisonment and focused upon its 'success' in symbolic terms as a mechanism of social control (Foucault 1977; Cohen 1985).

To sum up, the new era of punishment in the community is therefore concerned with the administration of community schemes, the production of information concerning their operation, and the punishment of the offender, all within a 'justice model of corrections' (see Hudson 1987). This emphasis has undermined the 'professional/therapeutic' movement in community sentencing and begun the 'punishment/administrative' phase

(May 1991*a*, *b*), where the community itself, rather than just the prison, has now become a place for punishment. How this change in thinking has been implemented in policy terms is the subject of the next section.

THE IMPLEMENTATION OF COMMUNITY SENTENCES

Changing the Discourse

It is dubious, although historically convenient, to place the beginning of 'punishment in the community' in the UK at a particular point in time—a popular date being 1979, with the election of a 'law and order' government. In fact, one can point to numerous forerunners of the philosophy. For example, the 1974 Younger Report suggested strengthening probation orders. Probation 'clients', it proposed, should no longer be required to give their consent to an order, and probation officers should have the power to detain clients for seventy-two hours if they 'thought it likely' that they would commit a further offence (Advisory Council on the Penal System 1974). Again, the ideas of 'intensive probation' and targeting 'high-risk' offenders had already been tested under the IMPACT study (Intensive Matched Probation and After-Care Treatment—see Folkard *et al.* 1976). Incidentally, in the contemporary enthusiasm for demanding alternatives to custody it should be noted that the results of this work were not exactly encouraging: 'All the findings of the IMPACT research were not completely negative, but IMPACT did nothing to suggest that treatment delivered to offenders within the context of a probation order was particularly effective at reducing recidivism' (Whitehead 1990: 14).

The suggestions of the 1974 Advisory Council Report were not implemented. Nevertheless, as the ideological climate changed, such ideas rapidly became more acceptable. The penal pessimism of the 'nothing works' variety, sustained by empiricist studies, permeated penal discourse in an environment of 'authoritarian populism' (Hall 1979). A change in the policy and mode of implementation of community sentences thus occurred, spurred on by reports of the injustices created by leaving so much discretion in the hands of welfare professionals (see Bean 1976; Wilding 1982). The movement away from the humanitarian underpinnings of the 'rehabilitative ideal' led to a concentration on the administrative technicalities of community sentencing: for example, targeting 'at risk' offenders by the use of 'risk of custody scales' and 'reconviction indicators' to see if these tools are effective in preventing future criminal acts.

All of the above is to be achieved under central government pressure to cash-limit the budgets of local probation services. This follows the government's Financial Management Initiative (see Humphrey 1987) and the work of the Audit Commission (1989). Cash-limiting probation service budgets is an idea which has now found its way into legislation (Criminal Justice Act 1991, part V).

In pursuing the implementation of punishment in the community, policy measures have become more prescriptive. As noted above, this has followed not only from changes in penal thinking, but also from criticisms of the degree of discretion which was thought to rest with those who ran such schemes during the rehabilitative period in community sentencing. The adherence of probation officers to the rehabilitative ideal has come to be considered an impediment to the effectiveness of punishment in the community: they are more concerned with helping, rather than punishing offenders (Willis 1986).

The practices of probation officers therefore produce effects perceived to be at odds with the intention of the new penal discourse. Attempts by the Home Office to define a range of penalties in a manner consistent with diverting offenders from custody consider such practices a problem. The difficulty is assumed to derive from the intransigence of a service whose historical legacy is that of an organization designed to cater for those for whom imprisonment was not an appropriate response, as opposed to functioning as an agency to reduce the prison population. Yet in the drive to measure the outcomes of innovations in community sentences, which has largely ignored the context in which they are implemented, no attempt has been made to examine the reasons, aside from professional intransigence, for the high degree of discretion which has always been so prominent. The need for discretion stems from experience in the day-to-day management of difficult and demanding environments. An authoritarian response by probation officers towards offenders becomes counterproductive in terms of reducing offending behaviour (see May 1991*a*: ch. 5). At the same time, it may increase the risk of violence against staff working alone in approved bail and probation hostels—an issue which has already generated industrial action in support of extra staffing in these settings (see *NAPO Newsletter*, April 1992).

If we subscribe to a top-down policy analysis of 'intention is equal to outcome' then there can be little doubt as to the effects of changes in recent years: the government is committed to new forms of punishment in the community and that is what has happened. However, problems of definition arise: What exactly constitutes an 'alternative', 'substitute', or 'community' sentence? Further, the implementation and practical operation of community-based sentences are variable. In the words of Vass (1990), there is a difference between the 'public' and 'private' worlds of alternatives to custody which is also substantiated by recent research on probation work (May 1991*a*: 109–39). Again, rather than examining the reasons for this state of affairs, a lack of uniformity in the implementation and operation of community sentences by the probation service is perceived by the government and the Home Office as a central impediment to their effective operation. The pursuit of uniformity in practice thus dominates the recent history of policies on alternatives to custody.

Messages from the Home Office attempt to limit variations in the implementation of community penalties by issuing guidelines and rules, using probation inspectors, introducing resource management information systems (RMIS), and cash-limiting probation budgets in an attempt to pursue efficiency, economy, and effectiveness in the probation service (see Audit Commission 1989; Home Office 1987). It is probation practice which, by default, is held officially responsible for these variations, and attempts to alter the working methods of the probation service are often believed to replicate the assumed efficient practices of the private sector (see Humphrey 1987, 1991).

Nowhere was the attempt to control local variations more clear than in the 1984 Home Office 'Statement of National Objectives and Priorities' for the probation services of England and Wales (SNOP). While noting the historical autonomy of magistrates, the employers of probation officers, in the running of probation areas, the statement nevertheless stipulated that programmes should 'reflect consistent principles which cannot just be determined locally' (Home Office 1984: 2). Nevertheless, this attempt to control local probation areas from the centre clearly begged questions concerning the autonomy of the judiciary from the executive. How, therefore, did the government effect local change in the face of this obstacle?

The answer was to circumvent probation committees, via devices such as SNOP, and to target policy changes on full-time probation personnel. Towards this end, it was stipulated that the appointment of chief probation officers must be approved by the Home Office (Probation Rules 1984, r. 28), which now charges them with the 'direction of the probation service in the area, for its effective operation and efficient use of resources' (Probation Rules 1984, r. 30). As for other full-time probation personnel, there has been provision to alter the practice of front-line staff who are in daily contact with offenders on supervision: the probation officer's practice of writing the format of, and ground covered in, pre-sentence reports (formerly called social inquiry reports) which are assumed to be influential in the process of sentencing (see Bottoms and Stelman 1988; Rawson 1982).

Paralleling these changes have been attempts to alter the practice of courts in respect of such reports: for instance, courts have been instructed that they should, except when the offence is triable only on indictment or they think it unnecessary, obtain a pre-sentence report (Criminal Justice Act 1991, s. 3)—despite it being questionable whether a report is of any influence at all in the decision-making process (see Bottoms and McWilliams 1986). As Raynor notes when drawing conclusions from a study of sentencing outcomes in relation to cases with and without social inquiry reports: 'In the long run the solution must probably involve changes in sentencing practice resulting from influences *other than* social enquiry reports: for instance, an extension to older adults of the kind of restrictions on custodial sentencing which have applied to young adults since 1982' (1991: 299, emphasis added).

Whatever the merits of these arguments, it is clear that central government considers the practice of pre-sentence report writing to be a central medium through which the effectiveness of the alternatives to custody industry might be enhanced (Home Office 1986). Despite evidence to the contrary, the inclusion in such reports of a recommendation of an alternative to custody for offenders 'at risk' of imprisonment is deemed influential in the court setting. To achieve this, it is argued, requires a change in the emphasis of report writing. All too often, it is believed, reports are more the application of social work theory to individuals (the welfare-based legacy of probation work) than of use to the courts in their decision-making.

Although this begs the question of who the client of the probation service is (the courts who seek to punish the offender, or the offenders whom the probation service has traditionally sought to help), a number of mechanisms have been used to alter the content of such reports, so that they unequivocally furnish the 'needs' of the court. As Harris (1992: 146) writes: 'In essence the new themes were that reports should be costed more carefully and concentrate on cases where there was a risk of custody or where a probation order was a possible outcome.' Among these mechanisms, SNOP (Home Office 1984) stands out alongside the Home Office circular on social inquiry reports (1986).

SNOP was a document which attempted to set the agenda for the implementation of alternatives to custody. Along with statutory changes in the Criminal Justice Act 1982, it was intended as a means for achieving the government's aims. SNOP prioritized the work of the probation service in both the provision of alternatives to custody and the preparation of social inquiry reports, the theme being to target offenders who were 'at risk' of imprisonment. This clearly represented a change of focus away from the traditional probation client, who was 'in need' of a social work service, towards those thought to represent such a 'threat' to society that a period of incarceration would be a justified response on the part of the courts. As such, SNOP stipulated that the probation service prioritize these ends in areas of its activity, even if this meant diverting resources from other areas of probation work such as prisoner through-care and divorce court welfare work.

The precise specification of how each local scheme was to be implemented and managed could not simply be set by central government or the Home Office, bearing in mind the role of magistrates as employers of probation officers. As a result, there were variations in probation areas' responses to SNOP (see Lloyd 1986). Nevertheless, the climate that these moves fostered certainly had an effect on the discussions which surrounded alternatives to custody. With government policy-making becoming more punitive and centralist in orientation, this was the framework within which discussions on community sentencing took place. In addition to SNOP, there were National Standards for Community Service, Green, White, and Blue Papers, plus 'Action Plans', all of which proposed or had implications for changes in community-based sentencing (Home Office 1988*b*, *c*; 1990*a*, *b;* 1991*a*, *c*; 1992). The change in climate led interested parties to produce a number of documents in response. The ensuing 'politics of penality' is characterized by a repeated anticipation of governmental thinking.

One attempt at unity in the face of these rapid and constant transformations in the government's statements on the probation service's purpose was *Probation: The Next Five Years* (ACOP *et al.* 1987). This was a collective endeavour by groups representing the probation service to formulate their own national policy on probation provisions. However, while it reaffirmed a commitment to aspects of probation service work which SNOP sought to marginalize, some commentators felt it did not go far enough in addressing basic differences of opinion within the service (Rumgay 1988). These differences stemmed from those who, on the one hand, believed in the provision of a social work service for 'clients' and those who, along with the government, believed the probation service was there to offer alternatives to custody for any 'offenders' whom the court sentenced to such schemes.

The question of whether the probation service provides a service to offenders for the purposes of their rehabilitation (stemming from the rehabilitative ideal) and/or welfare (recognizing the social dimensions of crime), or a service to the courts, is fundamental. The current punitive climate, fostered by the government, challenges a long history of theory and practice and therefore has led us into a politically charged situation in community sentencing. It is for this reason that the National Association of Probation Officers (NAPO) has moved further away from being an association concerned simply with the professional interests of its members towards taking on a more overt political campaigning role aimed at resisting or ameliorating the implications of the 'punishment in the community' era.

Although this debate reaches the philosophical foundations of the way our society deals with its law-breakers, the conflict, as argued above, has often been masked by administrative attempts to 'prove' that community sentencing is not only more cost-effective, but is as demanding and punitive as prison. To structure the debate in this way requires that alternatives to custody punish and are seen to punish offenders in the manner in which the current law and order climate demands, while also claiming to achieve this at less cost to the Exchequer.

It is not surprising, therefore, that soon after the publication of *Probation: The Next Five Years*, one of the three groups that co-authored the document broke ranks. The Association of Chief Officers of Probation (ACOP) published *More Demanding than Prison* (1988). The title was significant, given the increasingly punitive nomenclature surrounding the alternatives to custody debate. The document was intended to move the debate away from prison as the central focus of punitive thinking. With this end in mind, it suggested a new sentence known as the 'Community Restitution Order'. Its purpose was to target those offenders who were at risk of a custodial sentence. The 'demanding' nature of the sentence for offenders was emphasized (ACOP 1988: para. 15), as was the cost in relation to imprisonment—even though the document stressed that it was 'not primarily about costs' (para. 2).

In these proposals we see a fusion of two of the primary reference-points in the community sentencing debate: cost and effectiveness. While the proposals were not implemented, they represented part of the process of anticipating government proposals which, in this instance, were incorporated in the Green Paper significantly entitled *Punishment, Custody and the Community* (Home Office 1988*b*).

The debate thus became more firmly fixed within the parameters set by the government's justice model of corrections. As noted, the language that results stresses the efficiency, effectiveness, and economy of community sentences and the techniques utilized concentrate upon their administrative–technical dimension, thus bracketing the political features of criminal justice. Further, punishment no longer has to exclude the offender from the community as with a custodial sentence, but can take place within it.

The Criminal Justice Act 1991

The flagship legislation of the era of punishment and 'neo-rehabilitative' thinking is the Criminal Justice Act 1991. Continuing the transformation of the aims and rationale of community sentences, the Act emphasizes throughout the principle of matching the penalty to the severity of the offence. It takes the important further step of beginning to draw sharper distinctions between the types of offender who should be punished under the two sets of sanctions, imprisonment and community sentences.

Broadly speaking, the intention is that 'less serious' offenders—by which is largely meant perpetrators of non-violent crimes—will be punished within the community, while 'serious' offenders—primarily those who commit violent or sexual offences—will be incarcerated.

Much of the Act is concerned with restructuring and 'toughening up' the community sanctions to make them more suited to their new role. For example, probation orders, having been refashioned over the years with 'add-on' conditions for the punishment or training of the offender, are now routinely reinforced with conditions (Criminal Justice Act 1991, s. 9). In addition, the community service order with its mixture of penalty, reparation, and rehabilitation is now part of a new 'combination order' with probation.

The purpose of the combination order is to blend elements of probation, with its emphasis on the rehabilitation of offenders, with community service, with its emphasis on punishment. According to the traditional model of probation work, these two aims were considered to be in conflict; hence offenders were recommended for one or the other according to their suitability for these different regimes. However, as noted, pre-sentence reports now shift the focus of probation officers' report writing away from the diagnosis of offender needs, towards the sentencing requirements of the court. Of course, despite the court's need to take account of the seriousness of the offence before passing such an order (it should be an offence punishable by imprisonment), the questions as to whether breach rates will increase as a result, or whether combination orders will undermine the probation order, remain to be answered. Research on the consequences of this legislation will, no doubt, shed some light on these questions.

Curfew orders, which stipulate that an offender remain at a place specified by the courts for certain periods, may now be monitored by the fitting of electronic 'tags' to offenders (s. 13). This provision also permits an outlet for private enterprise within community sentencing: 'Electronic monitoring arrangements made by the Secretary of State under this section may include entering into contracts with *other persons* for electronic monitoring by them of offenders' whereabouts' (s. 13, emphasis added).

The fine, too, is looked at in a new way. An attempt is made to quantify the level of punishment it delivers, by relating it systematically to the means of the offender. The 1991 Act has now introduced the 'unit fine scheme' whereby the units of a fine correspond to the court's assessment of the seriousness of the offence, while the value attached to each unit takes account of the offender's weekly disposable income (s. 18).

In relation to these changes, the legislation can be regarded as Janus-faced. For some, it is said to compound current sentencing problems and undermine the spirit of probation (McWilliams 1992). For others, it offers an opportunity for a potential new lease of life for a beleagured probation service (McLaren and Spencer 1992). Whatever the merits of these arguments, a probation order is no longer passed by a court instead of punishment. It is now a sentence of the court and is intended to be demanding (read 'punishing').

The above noted, even as I write both the unit fine scheme and the attempts to restrict the courts' use of custody in the Act have come under criticism following its implementation. It remains to be seen exactly what the government does in reaction to the outcry by judges and magistrates that their powers to impose custodial sentences have been unduly limited. However, it is clear that the government is committed to changing these aspects of the legislation.

Set alongside alterations in bail and probation hostel provision and concern over their potential for privatization, the changes in community sentences may now be characterized in several ways. First, they have become more punitive. Second, they are subject to greater central government control. Third, the aspects of both welfare and professionalism that were applied to their management have been undermined. Fourth, they have recently allowed the concept of 'profit' to enter their management (Ryan and Ward 1990) and increasingly rely upon the use of volunteers in their administration (see Gill and Mawby 1990): for example, in the provision of community service schemes and offender housing projects. Indeed, under the Criminal Justice Act 1991, probation committees are now empowered to grant-aid voluntary organizations to assist in furthering community links in the resettlement and punishment of offenders.

THE EFFECTIVENESS OF COMMUNITY SENTENCING

The most obvious test of the 'effectiveness' of community sentences is to look at whether they achieve their now clearly defined goal of providing a genuine alternative to imprisonment and hence lead to a decrease in the use of custody (which, in turn, is assumed to lead to the more fundamental goal, in the present fiscal climate, of cutting back public expenditure on the criminal justice system).[3] Although the provisions of the 1991 Criminal Justice Act have not yet, at the time of writing, been in force long enough for their impact to be assessed, some general points can be made about ways in which community sentences have already resulted in

[3] In his study of the Afan project (a project using probation orders with special conditions), Raynor (1988: 168) estimated the cost at £60 per week per client. This compares with the average cost of sentences and orders, at 1989 prices, of prison at £288 per week, community service at £15 per week, and probation orders at £19 per week (Home Office 1991*b*).

'unintended consequences' (Mathieson 1983: 143) which are likely to be repeated in various forms in the future.

Particular clients are sought for these schemes in order that they be considered 'credible'. The targeted group consists of people who, in the absence of alternatives to custody, would have received a custodial sentence. However, if offenders other than these are given the community sentence, then the phenomenon of 'up-tariffing' has occurred. Community sentencing schemes would then not have reduced the prison population, but instead have extended the arm of formal social control. The outcome would then be an increase in the total number of people in these schemes, and eventually—because a certain proportion of those on community sentences will reoffend and be given a custodial sentence—even an increase in the prison population. A greater degree of formal intervention by the state and its agencies in people's everyday lives will then have taken place—a phenomenon described as 'net-widening' (Cohen 1979).

There is some evidence to suggest that this process has already occurred. In examining twenty years of sentencing trends in England and Wales, Bottoms (1987) finds an increasing trend in the courts' use of custody which, while influenced by higher rates of recorded crime, is not fully explained by this factor. Further, in a study of community service in Scotland, McIvor (1990) found that a community service order would have replaced a custodial sentence in only 42.4 per cent of cases. It appears, therefore, that alternatives are often not alternatives to custody, but simply alternatives to other alternatives.[4]

Despite the lack of effectiveness of community sentences in reducing the prison population at a national level, there has been evidence of diversionary potential and little evidence of net-widening or up-tariffing at a local level. For example, in an examination of intensive probation projects in Wales, Raynor (1988) found a degree of success in reducing reconviction rates among older offenders who had substantial criminal records. However, with younger offenders, who had less serious records but more reported personal problems, there was less success. The project was therefore 'more successful in achieving diversion . . . than in helping' (1988: 131). The implications are that simply targeting 'at risk' offenders appears to achieve little in terms of preventing crime. What is important is the type of work that is performed with offenders and the success of schemes in terms of assisting them in relation to the specific problems which may have led to offending in the first place. The latter point is

[4] The contradictions contained within the legislation on alternatives are exemplified in a dismissal by the Court of Appeal. A 19-year-old—with no previous convictions—was sentenced to a sixty-hour community service order for stealing a car radio. The Court of Appeal ruled that a CSO could be made under circumstances where a custodial sentence was not appropriate but that the hours should be short and the community service system should not be overloaded (*R.* v. *Zaman*. Reported in *Probation Journal* (1991), 38/3: 151).

important in terms of what realistically can be expected from community sentencing schemes. As argued previously, crime is linked with social, economic, and political circumstances and the probation service deals only with those offenders who are caught and processed. It follows that the ability of the probation service to have an effect on the overall crime rate, as well as the rate of imprisonment, will necessarily be limited.

If the ultimate aims of community sentencing include these broader goals of crime reduction, one has to ask whether it is productive for schemes to pursue all 'at risk' offenders at any price. Simply diverting people from custody is not, in itself, a sufficient condition for reducing criminal behaviour; it is the constructive work which can be undertaken as a result which is important. However, when the numbers of offenders on schemes is set as a condition of their perceived success and funding, this clearly has an effect on the running of schemes and what can realistically be achieved as a result. Cost and effectiveness are implicated, not mutually exclusive, each determining the outcome of the other.

In a 'measurement-obsessed' climate it therefore needs to be emphasized that there exist 'intangible outcomes'—the effects of schemes which are not amenable to a quantitative examination. These include the assistance offered to offenders in alleviating personal and financial problems and the importance not simply of reconviction, but the nature of that offence compared to the previous one and the circumstances surrounding it. Crude aggregate measures of outcome do not take account of the qualitative effects of such schemes; nor, even with increased sophistication, could they. Nevertheless, it is not simply a question of the numbers of offenders targeted for schemes (quantity) set alongside what is done for them when on those schemes (quality). The two interact. As a result of the government's increasing use of quantitative effectiveness as a condition of success, with occupancy of hostels and take-up of community schemes determining funding levels in the service, the qualitative dimension of work with offenders is directly affected (see May 1991*a*: ch. 5).

Concentrating on the qualitative dimension of community work with offenders brings us back to the operational discretion of probation officers which the government has sought to limit. The National Standards for Community Service (Home Office 1988*a*) provide an example of policy moves in this direction. While the aim of community service is not the same as that of a 4B probation order (community service is meant for those who do not have the degree of personal problems with which counselling or groupwork might assist), these standards have affected the qualitative dimension of community service schemes and resulted in an increase in breach rates.

The National Standards for Community Service were, along with the policies described so far, designed to reduce variation between probation areas in the management of schemes by centrally determining the type of work that an offender undertook when sentenced to community service. To this end, the Standards are replete with edicts for the probation officers who manage schemes and who, in turn, are supported by full-time non-probation-officer personnel and volunteers, who often oversee the community working parties themselves. In addition, the Standards stipulate that offenders should begin their placements in groups. By so doing, they have simply reinforced the group placements which the probation service was already using as a result of resource constraints (Vass 1984).

The above changes have rendered individual placements and the possibility of working with non-offenders less likely. They therefore undermine the spirit of the original Wootton Committee recommendations by making the idea of community service just an 'image' in the mind of offenders, because the recipients of the services which they provide are mostly unseen or simply absent when they undertake placements with other offenders. Thus McIvor's research on community service (1991), while noting the favourable disposition offenders often have towards community service, substantiates earlier comments that it is not targeting offenders and simply gaining 'numbers' for schemes that is significant for their success (however measured), but the experiences of people when undertaking them. Rather than concentrating on these issues, the Standards represent an authoritarian response which has resulted in an increase in the breach rates for community service orders (Lloyd 1991). This increase, in turn, has tested the credibility of schemes with magistrates, 'which will reduce the likelihood that higher tariff offenders would receive and/or be recommended probation for fear of "anticipated" failure' (Broad 1991: 99).

Little is achieved by increasing contacts between offenders and members of the community by simply cleaning graffiti from walls. Because of the emphasis on punishment in the community, transmitted through the national guidelines, and on 'tough' schemes, rather than 'challenging' ones, the effect is to distance offenders from the community, leading to such schemes being 'in', but not 'of', communities. In this way, the aims of reparation and resettlement in the community are undermined.

The issues with regard to community service are the same as with other diversionary schemes: at what price, in terms of the nature of the schemes, are offenders to be attracted from the courts, and what is done once the person is placed with that scheme? In considering these questions, it is a mistake to assume, as many have done, that these are mutually exclusive. If the court sentences someone to what it regards as a tough and demanding scheme, expectations alter accordingly. 'Demanding' is increasingly defined as punishing, which has no necessary connection with 'constructive'. If offenders regard community work placements as having no purpose except to take up their time, their compliance is unlikely to be forthcoming. As for the likely impact of the 1991 Criminal Justice Act, John Patten (the Minister of State at the Home Office) has said of community service orders: 'The punishment is in the degree to which the order restricts the offender's liberty and his freedom of choice' (Home Office 1992: 29). In the face of such a philosophy, offenders 'may well prefer the mindless anaesthetic of incarceration to the social useful efforts of community service' (Eadie and Willis 1989: 417).

Aside from the net-widening impact of the National Standards and their consequence for the qualitative dimension of community service work, the aims of reparation and rehabilitation are affected more generally by the contemporary social and political climate. It is difficult to imagine many communities being tolerant towards such schemes and thereby being more open to offenders, when they too have often been subjected to deprivation and marginalization as the result of radical changes in social policy provision in over a decade of social and political transformation.

SUMMARY

Other examples of community schemes could have been used in this chapter to illustrate the issues involved in appraising the effectiveness of community sentencing, as well as the discussion of its current underlying rationale. The purpose has been to introduce the history and issues surrounding community sentencing, and space precludes a more exhaustive review of substantive developments.

In drawing together the discussion, the changes which have taken place in the area of non-custodial penalties are clearly complicated, but may be summarized as follows. First, the traditional element of therapy, implemented by personnel within the probation service, has been seriously challenged by schemes whose emphasis is now upon the monitoring, punishment, and training of offenders within an 'administrative–technical' framework. Second, the degree of discretion accorded to those responsible for the implementation of non-custodial disposals has come to be viewed as a problem and is therefore increasingly circumscribed by central government policies, assisted by a movement towards a 'punishment–administrative', rather than 'professional–therapeutic', rationale of community sentencing. Third, in order to achieve both the first and second shifts in direction, central government is increasingly becoming involved in local schemes by the issuing of guidelines, rules, changes in statutory responsibilities, and cash-limiting of local probation service budgets. Fourth, the targeting of particular offenders who are 'at risk' of custody has led to a change in the characteristics of offenders sentenced to such schemes, with the consequence of 'up-tariffing'. Fifth, as a result of these changes, the community is now a sphere in which punishment is regarded as legitimately enacted and the visibility of these schemes is heightened by the justification that punishments are needed which fit the crime (the concept of proportionality). However, this also leads to offenders being 'in' but not 'of' communities, and undermines any constructive outcome in terms of reparation or rehabilitation—as discussed in relation to community service. Finally, although not implemented as yet, there still remains the possibility (now approved in statute following the provision in the 1991 Criminal Justice Act permitting the 'contracting out' of electronic tagging of offenders subject to curfew orders) that punishment in the community is to be increasingly privately, rather than publicly, administered.

It would be ironic that in the era of punishment in the community, voluntary groups may expand to fill a gap in provision as the probation service transforms to control, rather than care for, offenders and their families. The voluntary police-court missionaries, who were the first probation officers, could then return for the same reasons they first appeared. This time, however, it will be in a different guise.

Selected Further Reading

D. Bochel, *Probation and After-Care: Its Development in England and Wales*. Edinburgh: Scottish Academic Press, 1976.

R. Broad, *Punishment under Pressure: The Probation Service in the Inner City*. London: Jessica Kingsley, 1991.

N. Fielding, *Probation Practice: Client Support under Social Control*. Aldershot: Gower, 1984.

J. Harding, ed., *Probation and the Community: A Practice and Policy Reader*. London: Tavistock, 1987.

R. Harris, *Crime, Criminal Justice and the Probation Service*. London: Routledge, 1992.

D. Haxby, *Probation: A Changing Service*. London: Constable, 1978.

F. V. Jarvis, *Advise, Assist and Befriend: A History of the Probation and After-Care Service*. London: NAPO, 1972.

W. McWilliams and K. Pease, 'Probation Practice and an End to Punishment', *Howard Journal of Criminal Justice*, 29/1: 14–24.

T. May, *Probation: Politics, Policy and Practice.* Milton Keynes: Open University Press, 1991.

T. May, 'Under Siege: The Probation Service in a Changing Environment', in R. Reiner and M. Cross, *Beyond Law and Order: Criminal Justice Policy and Politics into the 1990s.* London: Macmillan, 1991.

P. Raynor, *Probation as an Alternative to Custody: A Case Study.* Aldershot: Gower, 1988.

P. Raynor, D. Smith and M. Vanstone, *Effective Probation Practice.* London: Macmillan, 1993.

R. Shaw and K. Haines, eds. *The Criminal Justice System: A Central Role for the Probation Service.* Cambridge: Institute of Criminology, 1989.

REFERENCES

ACOP (1988), *More Demanding than Prison.* Wakefield: The Association of Chief Officers of Probation.

ACOP, CCPC and NAPO (1987), *Probation: The Next Five Years: A Joint Statement by The Association of Chief Officers of Probation, Central Council of Probation Committees and National Association of Probation Officers.* London: ACOP, CCPC, NAPO.

Advisory Council on the Penal System (1970), *Non-Custodial and Semi-Custodial Penalties* (the Wootton Report). London: HMSO.

—— (1974). *Young Adult Offenders* (the Younger Report). London: HMSO.

Ashworth, A. (1989), 'Policy, Accountability and the Courts', in R. Shaw and K. Haines, eds, *The Criminal Justice System: A Central Role for the Probation Service.* Cambridge: University of Cambridge Institute of Criminology.

Audit Commission (1989), *The Probation Service: Promoting Value for Money.* London: HMSO.

Bean, P. (1976), *Rehabilitation and Deviance.* London: Routledge and Kegan Paul.

Bean, P., and Whynes, D., eds. (1986), *Barbara Wootton: Social Science and Public Policy. Essays in her Honour.* London: Tavistock.

Bochel, D. (1976), *Probation and After-Care: Its Development in England and Wales.* Edinburgh: Scottish Academic Press.

Bottoms, A. E. (1981), 'The Suspended Sentence in England 1967–1978', *British Journal of Criminology*, 21: 1–26.

—— (1987), 'Limiting Prison Use: Experience in England and Wales', *Howard Journal*, 26/3: 177–202.

Bottoms, A. E., and McWilliams, W. (1986), 'Social Enquiry Reports Twenty-Five Years after the Streatfeild Report', in P. Bean and D. Whynes, eds.,

Barbara Wootton: Social Science and Public Policy. Essays in her Honour, London: Tavistock.

BOTTOMS, A. E., and STELMAN, A. (1988), *Social Inquiry Reports: A Framework for Practice Development*. Aldershot: Wildwood House, Gower.

BOX, S. (1987), *Recession, Crime and Punishment*. London: Macmillan.

BROAD, R. (1991), *Punishment under Pressure: The Probation Service in the Inner City*. London: Jessica Kingsley.

BRODY, S. (1976), *The Effectiveness of Sentencing: A Review of the Literature*, Home Office Research Study no. 35. London: HMSO.

CARLEN, P. (1990), *Alternatives to Women's Imprisonment*. Milton Keynes: Open University Press.

CARLEN, P., and WORRALL, A., eds. (1987), *Gender, Crime and Justice*. Milton Keynes: Open University Press.

CHRISTIE, N. (1982), *Limits to Pain*. Oxford: Martin Robertson.

COHEN, S. (1979), 'The Punitive City: Notes on the Dispersal of Social Control', *Contemporary Crises*, 3: 339–63.

—— (1985), *Visions of Social Control*. Oxford: Polity.

—— (1988), *Against Criminology*. Oxford: Transaction.

CROFT, J. (1978), *Research in Criminal Justice*, Home Office Research Study no. 44. London: HMSO.

CROW, I. (1987), 'Black People and Criminal Justice in the UK', *Howard Journal*, 26/4: 303–14.

DOMINELLI, L. (1991), *Gender, Sex Offenders and Probation Practice*. Norwich: Novata Press.

EADIE, T., and WILLIS, A. (1989), 'National Standards for Discipline and Breach Proceedings in Community Service: An Exercise in Penal Rhetoric?', *Criminal Law Review*: 412–19.

EATON, M. (1986), *Justice for Women: Family, Court and Social Control*. Milton Keynes: Open University Press.

FOLKARD, M. S., SMITH, D. E., and SMITH, D. D. (1976), *Intensive Matched Probation and After-Care Treatment*, vol. 2: *The Results of the Experiment*, Home Office Research Study no. 36. London: HMSO.

FOUCAULT, M. (1977), *Discipline and Punish: The Birth of the Prison*. London: Allen Lane.

GARLAND, D. (1985), *Punishment and Welfare: A History of Penal Strategies*. Aldershot: Gower.

—— (1990), *Punishment and Modern Society: A Study in Social Theory*. Oxford: Oxford University Press.

GARLAND, D., and YOUNG, P., eds. (1983), *The Power to Punish*. London: Heinemann.

GILL, M., and MAWBY, R. (1990), *Volunteers in the Criminal Justice System: A Comparative Study of Probation, Police and Victim Support*. Milton Keynes: Open University Press.

HALL, S. (1979), 'Drifting into a Law and Order Society'. Cobden Trust Memorial Lecture.

HARRIS, R. (1992), *Crime, Criminal Justice and the Probation Service*. London: Routledge.

HAXBY, D. (1978), *Probation: A Changing Service*. London: Constable.

HOME OFFICE (1962), *Report of the Departmental Committee on the Probation Service* (the Morison Report), Cmnd 1650. London: Home Office.

—— (1984), *Probation Service in England and Wales: Statement of National Objectives and Priorities*. London: Home Office.

—— (1986), *Social Inquiry Reports*, Circular no. 92. London: Home Office.

—— (1987), *Efficiency Scrutiny of Her Majesty's Probation Inspectorate* (the Grimsey Report). London: Home Office.

—— (1988*a*), *National Standards for Community Service*. London: Home Office.

—— (1988*b*), *Punishment, Custody and the Community*, Cmnd 424. London: Home Office.

—— (1988*c*), *Tackling Offending: An Action Plan*. London: Home Office.

—— (1988*d*), *The Parole System in England and Wales* (the Carlisle Report). London: HMSO.

—— (1990*a*), *Crime, Justice and Protecting the Public*, Cmnd 965. London: HMSO.

—— (1990*b*), *Supervision and Punishment in the Community: A Framework for Action*, Cmnd 966. London: HMSO.

—— (1990*c*), *Criminal Statistics 1989: England and Wales*. London: HMSO.

—— (1991*a*), *Organising Supervision and Punishment in the Community: A Decision Document*. London: Home Office.

—— (1991*b*), *Digest of Information on the Criminal Justice System*. London: Home Office.

—— (1991*c*), *Action Plan for the Probation Service*. (Press Office). London: Home Office.

—— (1992), *The Probation Service: Statement of Purpose*. London: Home Office.

HUDSON, B. (1987), *Justice through Punishment: A Critique of the 'Justice' Model of Corrections*. London: Macmillan.

HUMPHREY, C. (1987), *The Implications of the Financial Management Initiative for the Probation Service*. Manchester: Manchester University Department of Accounting and Finance.

—— (1991), 'Calling on the Experts: The Financial Management Initiative (FMI), Private Sector Management Consultants and the Probation Service', *Howard Journal*, 30/1: 1–18.

IGNATIEFF, M. (1978), *A Just Measure of Pain: The Penitentiary in the Industrial Revolution, 1750–1850*. New York: Pantheon.

JARVIS, F. V. (1972), *Advise, Assist and Befriend: A History of the Probation and After-Care Service*. London: National Association of Probation Officers.

KING, J. (1969), *The Probation and After-Care Service*, 3rd edn. London: Butterworths.

KNAPP, M., ROBERTSON, E., and MCIVOR, G. (1992), 'The Comparative Costs of Community Service and Custody in Scotland', *Howard Journal*, 31/1: 8–30.

LABOUR PARTY (1990), *A Safer Britain: Labour's White Paper on Criminal Justice*. London: Labour Party.

LLOYD, C. (1986), *Response to SNOP: An Analysis of the Home Office Document, 'Probation Service in England and Wales: Statement of National Objectives and Priorities' and the Subsequent Local Responses*. Cambridge: Cambridge University Institute of Criminology.

LLOYD, C. (1991), 'National Standards for Community Service: The First Two Years of Operation', *Home Office Research Bulletin*, 31: 16–21.

McIVOR, G. (1990), 'Community Service and Custody in Scotland', *Howard Journal*, 29/2: 101–13.

—— (1991), 'Community Service Work Placements', *Howard Journal*, 30/1: 19–29.

McLAREN, V., and SPENCER, J. (1992), 'Rehabilitation and CJA 1991: A World Still to Win', *Probation Journal*, 39/2: 70–3.

McWILLIAMS, W. (1983), 'The Mission to the English Police Courts 1876–1936', *Howard Journal*, 22: 129–47.

—— (1985), 'The Mission Transformed: Professionalisation of Probation between the Wars', *Howard Journal*, 24/4: 257–74.

—— (1986), 'The English Probation System and the Diagnostic Ideal', *Howard Journal*, 25/4: 241–60.

—— (1987), 'Probation, Pragmatism and Policy', *Howard Journal*, 26/2: 97–121.

—— (1992), 'Death for Probation?', *Criminal Justice Matters* (Institute for the Study & Treatment of Delinquency), 9: 16.

MAIR, G. (1991), 'What Works—Nothing or Everything?', *Home Office Research Bulletin*, 30: 3–8.

MAIR, G., and BROCKINGTON, N. (1988), 'Female Offenders and the Probation Service', *Howard Journal*, 27/2: 117–26.

MARSHALL, T., and WALPOLE, M. (1985), *Bringing People Together: Mediation and Reparation Projects in Great Britain*. Research and Planning Unit Paper no. 33. London: Home Office.

MARTINSON, R. (1974), 'What Works? Questions and Answers about Prison Reform', *Public Interest*, 35: 22–54.

MATHIESEN, T. (1983), 'The Future of Control Systems', in D. Garland and P. Young, eds., *The Power to Punish*. London: Heinemann.

—— (1990), *Prison on Trial: A Critical Assessment*. London: Sage.

MATTHEWS, R., and YOUNG, J., eds. (1986), *Confronting Crime*. London: Sage.

MAWBY, R., and GILL, M. (1987), *Crime Victims: Needs, Services, and the Voluntary Sector*. London: Tavistock.

MAY, T. (1991*a*), *Probation: Politics, Policy and Practice*. Buckingham: Open University Press.

—— (1991*b*), 'Under Siege: The Probation Service in a Changing Environment', in R. Reiner and M. Cross, eds., *Beyond Law and Order: Criminal Justice Policy and Politics into the 1990s*. London: Macmillan.

MORRIS, N., and TONRY, M. (1990), *Between Prison and Probation: Intermediate Punishments in a Rational Sentencing System*. Oxford: Oxford University Press.

POINTING, J. ed. (1986), *Alternatives to Custody*. Oxford: Blackwell.

RAWSON, S. (1982), *Sentencing Theory, Social Enquiry and Probation Practice*. Norwich: University of East Anglia Social Work Monographs.

RAYNOR, P. (1988), *Probation as an Alternative to Custody: A Case Study*. Aldershot: Gower.

—— (1991), 'Sentencing with and without Reports: A Local Study', *Howard Journal*, 30/4: 293–300.

REINER, R., and CROSS, M., eds. (1991), *Beyond Law and Order: Criminal Justice Policy and Politics into the 1990s*. London: Macmillan.

RUMGAY, J. (1988), '"Probation—The Next Five Years": A Comment', *Howard Journal*, 27/3: 198–201.

RYAN, M., and WARD, T. (1990), 'Restructuring, Resistance and Privatisation in the Non-Custodial Sector', *Critical Social Policy*, 10/3: 54–67.

SCRATON, P., and CHADWICK, K. (1991), 'The Theoretical and Political Priorities of Critical Criminology', in K. Stenson and D. Cowell, eds., *The Politics of Crime Control*. London: Sage.

SCULL, A. (1977), *Decarceration—Community Treatment and the Deviant: A Radical View*. Englewood Cliffs, NJ: Prentice-Hall.

—— (1983), 'Community Corrections: Panacea, Progress or Pretence', in D. Garland and P. Young, eds., *The Power to Punish*, London: Heinemann.

SHAW, R., and HAINES, K., eds. (1989), *The Criminal Justice System: A Central Role for the Probation Service*. Cambridge: University of Cambridge Institute of Criminology.

SINGER, L. (1989), *Adult Probation and Juvenile Supervision*. Aldershot: Gower.

STENSON, K., and COWELL, D., eds. (1991), *The Politics of Crime Control*. London: Sage.

THOMAS, D. A. (1989), 'Constraints on Sentencers?' in R. Shaw and K. Haines, eds., *The Criminal Justice System: A Central Role for the Probation Service*, Cambridge: University of Cambridge Institute of Criminology.

VASS, A. (1984), *Sentenced to Labour: Close Encounters with a Prison Substitute*. St Ives: Venus Academica.

—— (1990), *Alternatives To Prison: Punishment, Custody and the Community*. London: Sage.

WATERS, R. (1990), *Ethnic Minorities and the Criminal Justice System*. Aldershot: Gower.

WHITEHEAD, P. (1990), *Community Supervision for Offenders: A New Model of Probation*. Aldershot: Avebury.

WHITEHEAD, P., TURVER, N., and WHEATLEY, J. (1991), *Probation, Temporary Release Schemes and Reconviction*. Aldershot: Avebury.

WILDING, P. (1982), *Professional Power and Social Welfare*. London: Routledge and Kegan Paul.

WILLIS, A. (1986), 'Help and Control in Probation', in J. Pointing, ed., *Alternatives to Custody*, Oxford: Blackwell.

WRIGHT, A. (1984), *The Day Centre in Probation Practice*. Norwich: University of East Anglia Social Work Monographs.

YOUNG, A. (1976), 'A Sociological Analysis of the Early History of Probation', *British Journal of Law and Society*, 3: 44–58.

YOUNG, J. (1986), 'The Failure of Criminology: The Need for a Radical Realism', in R. Matthews and J. Young, eds., *Confronting Crime*, London: Sage.

19

Imprisonment

ROD MORGAN

INTRODUCTION

Every year some 100,000 people are committed to the more than 130 prisons and young offender institutions in England and Wales (Scotland and Northern Ireland have separate prison systems).[1] There are currently between 45,000 and 50,000 people in prison and over 34,000 people are employed to make sure they stay there. It all costs a great deal of money: a little over £1.4 billion in 1991/2, nearly 16 per cent of total public spending on the so-called law and order services. In 1991 it cost on average £438 per week to keep someone in prison (Home Office 1992*d*).

The system has grown substantially since 1945. In 1946 there were about forty prisons, approximately 15,000 prisoners, and approximate 2,000 staff (Home Office 1947). Most observers would agree that many aspects of daily prison life have changed greatly for the better. No longer are there rows of convicts hand-sewing mailbags in silence, the flogging triangle and the bread and water dietary punishments have long since gone, many restrictions on prisoners' contacts with their families have been phased out, and there is a reasonable prospect that what used, until relatively recently, to be the universal practice of 'slopping out' will soon be a thing of the past. Much has not changed, however. Practically all the old Victorian prisons in use in 1946—e.g. Wandsworth, Pentonville, Brixton, Dartmoor, Manchester, Leeds, Liverpool, Parkhurst, Wakefield—are still in use today and would be almost as familiar now to their regular occupants of half a century ago as they were then. The legal framework within which prisons operate—the Prison Act 1952 and the Prison Rules 1964—has changed little, despite the frequent amendment of the latter. Male prisoners still wear shabby ill-fitting prison garb of blue, grey, or brown and prison officers retain their military uniforms of dark blue with flat peaked hats, though there is now talk of allowing all

[1] Most of the quantitative data drawn on in this introductory section are taken from the annual reports of the Prison Service. These are invaluable sources, currently issued in three volumes, covering a prose account of the work of the Service; prison statistics; and statistics of offences against discipline and punishments. At the time of writing the most recent volumes are: Home Office 1991*a*, 1992*a*, and 1992*b*, all relating to 1990.

prisoners to wear their own clothes (females have long since been permitted to) and of 'demilitarizing' staff uniforms. Moreover, some things have undoubtedly got worse. There was no overcrowding in the late 1940s. In the following four decades, in spite of the conversion to prison use of war-time camps and country houses in the immediate post-war period, and the steady commissioning of purpose-built prisons from the 1950s onwards, the growth in the prison population outstripped the additional places coming on stream. The system was on average 0.5 per cent overcrowded in the 1950s, and 5.4, 8.5, and between 10 and 15 per cent overcrowded in the 1960s, 1970s, and 1980s respectively. In the 1980s there began the largest prison building programme since the mid-nineteenth century. By 1994, 19,500 places will have been added to the system since 1979, twenty-one new prisons providing 11,300 places and further accommodation on existing sites providing an additional 8,200 places (*Hansard*, 1 April 1993, written answer no. 61). Yet the hopes of the government that this expansion would see an end to overcrowding have not yet been fulfilled and still look precarious.

Nor are prisons now as orderly as they were in the past. Concerted acts of prisoner indiscipline were rare half a century ago (Fox 1952: 160) and staff industrial action unheard-of. Today prison disturbances are commonplace and controlling prison officers has in recent years become almost as difficult a task for prison managers as controlling prisoners. The 1970s and 1980s saw a litany of serious industrial disputes and prisoner disorders leading to the two major official inquiries—the May Committee in 1978–9 and the judicial inquiry conducted by Lord Justice Woolf in 1990–1—the reports of which became landmarks for analysts of prisons policy (May Committee 1979; Woolf Report 1991).

One of the reasons for this transformation in the prisons climate is the dramatic change in the character of the prison population. In the 1940s custodial sentences were used proportionately more often by the courts than is the case today (Bottoms 1987), but the sentences were typically short compared to now. In 1945 approximately 80 per cent of the offenders sentenced to custody were serving six months or less, life sentences were rare, and prisoners serving determinate sentences of over ten years almost unknown. Moreover, the vast majority of prisoners—almost 90 per cent—were convicted of property, not violent, offences. Of the daily average prison population fewer than 20 per cent of sentenced prisoners were serving eighteen months or more.

The picture today is very different. Fewer than 40 per cent of offenders sentenced to custody serve sentences of six months or less, and the number of offenders given life or determinate sentences of more than ten years is such that at any one time there are now more than 4,000 of them in prison. The majority of custodial sentences are still for property rather than violent offences (a little over three-quarters if robbery is excluded) but more than two-fifths of the average daily sentenced population is in prison for an offence involving violence. The prison population has become more intractable as the proportionate use of imprisonment has fallen and prisons are undoubtedly more difficult to manage today than they were in the past.

The result is that prisons are seldom out of the news. Prisons tend, as successive Home Secretaries have testified, to dominate ministerial in-trays. The fact that prisons remain overcrowded in spite of the enormous cost of the recent prison building programme; are a constant management headache; are a conspicuous failure in terms of the subsequent behaviour of those committed to them (approximately two-thirds of all young offenders and almost a half of all adults are reconvicted at least once within two years of release (Home Office 1990*a*: ch. 9)); and are of questionable value in terms of public protection (because so small a proportion of those responsible for offences are caught, convicted, and imprisoned—see Mayhew *et al.* 1989). This has meant that there is perennial debate about the purpose of imprisonment. And once the purpose of imprisonment is called into question there is inevitably debate about what constitutes a sensible rate of imprisonment. Though international comparisons are fraught with difficulties (Pease 1991), all three British jurisdictions rely on the use of imprisonment more than almost any other Council of Europe member state. In 1988 ninety-seven persons were incarcerated per 100,000 population in England, compared to eighty-five in Germany, eighty-one in France, sixty-five in Belgium, and forty in the Netherlands (Council of Europe 1990). There are other countries with higher incarceration rates—the USA, China, South Africa, and some of the former Warsaw Pact nations, for example—but these countries have markedly different crime rates, histories, or political cultures. They do not make comfortable penal bedfellows. The countries with which we generally like to compare ourselves in Europe and elsewhere generally make less use of imprisonment.

Should we, as some politicians and judges argue, be relatively unconcerned about the size of our prison population and focus rather on the rising tide of serious crime against which the courts have a duty to protect the public by locking up more offenders for longer? And if locking up more offenders means that conditions in prisons are less than ideal, should we conclude that this is no more than prisoners deserve? Or does the prison, as others argue, reflect a punitively British obsession, an expensive anachronism, and a largely chimerical crime control device, the use of which we could significantly reduce without risk to anyone? Should we regard poor prison conditions as a bar to our claims to be civilized and a misuse of state power against vulnerable and disadvantaged minorities? What after all should prisons be like: dark deterrent statements of the consequences of committing crime; training camps in citizenship; or protective therapeutic communities for damaged and sometimes dangerous offenders?

We cannot examine these complex questions exhaustively in this chapter (some are touched on elsewhere in this volume—see, especially, the chapter by Andrew Ashworth). Rather, the aim here is to provide brief introductions to five key questions. What objectives should prison administrators set themselves? What is the character of the prison population and how is it changing? How are prisons organized and made accountable? How do the dynamics of prison life affect objectives? And how might prisons change in the near future? The discussion will focus largely on the situation in Britain. However, prisons, like other social institutions, operate in an increasingly international stream of policy development. Some references will therefore be made to initiatives and analyses from elsewhere.

Finally, to conclude this introduction, it is necessary to say something about two vital questions that this chapter will not address. The first concerns the rate at which imprisonment is used. Practically all commentators, be they politicians, sentencers, or academic analysts, claim to support the use of imprisonment only as a last resort when no other measure will suffice and, to the extent that they decide the issue, maintain that this is the basis of their decision-making. But the degree to which imprisonment is resorted to varies greatly over time and between jurisdictions (Rutherford 1984; Council of Europe 1990). The evidence suggests that these variations cannot straightforwardly be explained by reference to changing fashions in the philosophy of punishment subscribed to by sentencers, or crime rates, or demographic factors, or levels of economic activity, or public policy considerations. Though factors subsumed by these headings—unemployment or the supply of prison places, for example—have undoubtedly influenced the rate of imprisonment in some countries in some periods (for a thorough review of the literature and the American data, see Zimring and Hawkins 1991), the use of imprisonment is a complex issue almost certainly explained by variable contextual factors (for example, see Downes 1988 for a detailed examination of recent penal policy in the Netherlands and in England and Wales). I favour less resort to custody in England; but how best to achieve that object is beyond the scope of this chapter.

What is clear is that critics of the relatively high incarceration rate in Britain need to be acutely aware of a second issue, the complex appeal and function of imprisonment. Prisons are central to contemporary 'penality', that is, our ideas about and practices of punishment (Garland and Young 1983). It follows that imprisonment, like punishment, needs to be approached from a variety of angles—as a technical means to an end, as a coercive relationship, as an instrument of class domination, as a form of power, and as an expression of collective moral feeling ritually expressed (see Garland 1990 for a review of the sociological literature). And to the extent that imprisonment serves several social functions (see Cavadino and Dignan 1992 for a brief review of different sociological hypotheses) this suggests that attempts radically to shift the rate at which we imprison offenders are unlikely to succeed simply by proclaiming the utilitarian shortcomings of the enterprise. This debate is also beyond the scope of this chapter. What is certain is that even those commentators who proclaim themselves 'abolitionists' neither advocate nor foresee an end to the use of imprisonment for some offenders (Mathieson 1974; Mathieson 1990). Prisons will continue to exist. It follows that their operation requires detailed analysis.

THE MISSION

What are prisons for? The question can be answered in different ways. The most fundamental approach to the issue is to distinguish the legal uses to which imprisonment is put. We can distinguish three uses: the *custodial*, the *coercive*, and the *punitive*. Prisoners refused bail and held before trial (unconvicted 'trials' and 'remands'), or convicted but not yet sentenced (generally awaiting medical or pre-sentence reports, the 'unsentenced'), are held in custody for no other reason than to ensure that the course of justice proceeds to its conclusion and that the public, victims, witnesses, and sometimes suspects themselves are protected against the likelihood of harm in the interim. Moreover, a small number of non-criminal prisoners—those held under the Immigration Act, for example—are held in prisons pending completion of inquiries or execution of an administrative decision. There is no justification for holding such *custodial* prisoners in conditions more oppressive than is warranted by the fact of custody itself: either they are not eligible for punishment (the unconvicted are subject to the presumption of innocence) or, if convicted, the court has not yet determined that loss of liberty is the appropriate sentence.

Prisoners held *coercively*—nowadays almost entirely fine defaulters—are kept in prison for as long as they fail to comply with a court order that they pay a financial penalty or some other payment enforced by the court. As soon as they meet their obligations in the community, or once the custodial period in lieu of payment is served, they are released. In this case the prison, in the form of both the loss of liberty itself and possibly also conditions in custody, is being used in an attempt to pressurize the offender into conforming.

Finally, there are prisoners held *punitively*—nowadays the great majority—as a sanction for offences of which they stand convicted. Since the abolition of the death penalty in 1965 imprisonment has been the most serious penalty the courts can impose, though in fact it has been the principal penalty for serious crime ever since the decline of various corporal punishments in the eighteenth century and the phasing out of transportation in the nineteenth century (McConville 1981; Radzinowicz and Hood 1990). The development of the modern prison arose out of its transition from a *custodial* and *coercive* to a *punitive* institution (Ignatieff 1978). The punishment of imprisonment for sentenced prisoners *might* comprise both loss of liberty *and* harsh living conditions. In the nineteenth century prison conditions were deliberately punitive, designed to reflect the 'less eligibility' of prisoners (see McConville 1981: 417–19). Today prison administrators disavow such purposes, reiterating Paterson's famous dictum that offenders are sent to prison 'as a punishment, not *for* punishment' (Ruck 1951: 23). However, it is difficult to square conditions and practices in many prisons with this disavowal and 'less eligibility' remains a potent political if not administrative imperative (Garland 1990). Further, it is clear that custodial prisoners, in spite of the presumption of innocence, tend both in Britain and elsewhere to be viewed by prison staff as sentenced prisoners in waiting (Fox 1952: 286): their living conditions are generally among the worst to be found in the system (King and Morgan 1976; Morgan 1993).

A distinction needs to be drawn between the reasoning which leads sentencers to send offenders to prison and the objectives pursued by those who manage prisons. Ideally the two should be consistent and spring from the same principles. But they are not the same and hitherto sentencers have generally not been required to spell out the rationale for their decisions. Whatever the varied motives of sentencers, prison administrators have practically to manage prisons in an efficient and positive manner with regard to the welfare of staff as well as prisoners. Their main point of reference is the Prison Rules (SI 1964, no. 388), the first two of which enjoin the encouragement of 'good and useful lives', the promotion of 'self-respect', and the development of 'personal responsibility'. This formula came in for a good deal of criticism in the 1970s. The criticism was prompted partly by loss of confidence in rehabilitative thinking, stemming from empirical evidence that rehabilitative programmes were largely ineffective (Lipton *et al.* 1975; Brody 1976), combined with the observation that the rehabilitative perspective had led to considerable discretionary powers being granted to executive agencies, the exercise of which contravened the rules of procedural justice (American Friends Service Committee 1971; Morris 1974).

In Britain it was argued that the treatment and training paradigm adopted by the Prison Department in fulfilment of Prison Rule 1 was dangerous not least because it was obviously appealing; it suggested that prisons, despite all the indications to the contrary, were positive establishments fulfilling a noble purpose (King and Morgan 1980: ch. 1). If imprisonment could be justified on the grounds that it could make prisoners less likely to offend in the future, then sentencers were more likely to be deluded into using imprisonment for this purpose. On this basis longer and indeterminate sentences had been argued for in preference to short and determinate sentences, so that the authorities would have time to do their remedial work and offenders could be released when treatment or training had successfully been undertaken (this was part of the rationale for introducing parole—see Maguire 1992). Thus, argued King and Morgan, treatment and training militated against a more parsimonious use of custody within a 'justice' rights-based framework. According to this view the aims of sentencers and prison managers, though analytically separable, cross-fertilize.

In their critique of Rule 1, which they gave in their evidence to the May Committee, King and Morgan claimed that 'treatment and training' was a rhetorical doctrine that had never squared with the primitive reality of prison life. Rule 1 was so vague that it had never been operationalized. Indeed, it was inspired by aspirations incapable of fulfilment, something that prison staff had always known. Moreover, it quite arbitrarily excluded remand and trial prisoners from view. Far better, they argued, to try to turn the concept of 'humane containment'—the term grotesquely coined by the Prison Department to describe what they offered in local prisons—into a reality. For King and Morgan the term 'humane containment' was preferable to 'treatment and training' precisely because it was practical and prosaic: 'because [it] may fail to fire the imagination', so it might 'prevent the excesses of the past' (1980: 38). They argued that, properly—rather than cynically—considered, 'humane containment' was completely consistent with a 'justice model', and could embrace three major principles. These were:

1. *Minimum use of custody*: 'Imprisonment should be used only as a last resort, when other forms of sentence have been exhausted, or are clearly inappropriate having regard to the nature of the offence . . . [and] that custody should be used for the minimum length of time consistent with public safety' (ibid.: 34). This principle, as Bottoms (1990) has argued, concerns sentencing policy rather than prison management.
2. *Minimum use of security*: 'Prisoners should be subject to only that degree of security necessary to safeguard the public against any realistic threat' (King and Morgan 1980: 37).
3. *Normalization*: 'As far as resources allow, and consistent with the

constraints of secure custody, the same standards which govern the life of offenders in the community should be held to apply to offenders in prison' (ibid.: 37).

King and Morgan further argued that there was need for a new set of Prison Rules and a comprehensive review of the Standing Orders and Circular Instructions which are issued to governors by the Prison Service Headquarters on the interpretation of the Prison Rules. This was because policy objectives needed to be spelt out: there was 'need to specify the standards against which they are to be measured, and the strategies to be used for achieving them' (ibid.: 30).

King and Morgan's propositions did not convince the May Committee. The Committee, in two much-quoted passages, judged King and Morgan's argument to have 'much force' but concluded that

> there is a danger that it may throw out the good with the unattainable . . . Further, as one group of witnesses pointed out to us, 'humane containment' suffers from the fatal defect that it is a means without an end. Our opinion is that it can only result in making prisons into human warehouses—for inmates and staff. It is not, therefore, a fit rule for hopeful life or responsible management. (May Committee 1979: para. 4.24)

> In our view mere 'secure and humane containment' is not enough. Prison staff cannot be asked to operate in a moral vacuum and the absence of real objectives can in the end lead only to the routine brutalisation of all the participants. (ibid.: para. 4.28).

Nevertheless, the Committee agreed 'that the rhetoric of "treatment and training" has had its day' (ibid.: para. 4.27). They proposed that Rule 1 be replaced by a statement of 'positive custody' in which the purpose of detention of convicted prisoners 'shall be to keep them in custody which is both secure and yet positive', the duty of the authorities being to 'create an environment which can assist [prisoners] to respond and contribute to society as positively as possible', to 'preserve and promote . . . self respect', minimize security and the harmful effects of custody, and prepare prisoners for release (ibid.: para. 4.26).

In response, King and Morgan trenchantly dismissed the May Committee formulation. 'Positive custody', they maintained, had 'no real meaning': it was more concerned with the 'generation of hope than . . . the generation of objectives' and was therefore as rhetorical as 'treatment and training' (King and Morgan 1980: 29). It did not cover unconvicted prisoners. It imposed no 'obligations on the prison authorities' and conferred 'no rights on prisoners. Indeed it would always be open to the authorities to justify any activity by intentions rather than results' (ibid.). 'What the May Committee appeared not to recognise is that prisons have sometimes been inhuman warehouses' (ibid.: 25).

This retort has undoubtedly carried the weight of critical opinion since 1980: the May Committee formula has not been officially adopted and the penal pressure groups and most academic commentators have weighed in on the side of positive rights for prisoners (Richardson 1985) and timetables for the introduction of legally enforceable minimum standards for prison conditions (Casale 1984; Maguire *et al.* 1985, part two; Casale and Plotnikoff 1989). Nevertheless, King and Morgan were unable to rescue the slogan 'humane containment' from its original, cynical application to the local prisons which were increasingly deprived of resources and programmes and in which *nothing* positive was happening. This led Ian Dunbar, then a Prison Department Regional Director, to conclude:

> Although [humane containment focuses on prison life] more directly and exclusively than does the treatment model . . . in practice it has led to even greater disillusionment. At least the treatment model gave the service something to believe in and some hope. Humane containment has led to the cynicism of human warehousing. (Dunbar 1985: 7)

Likewise Vivien Stern, Director of the National Association for the Care and Resettlement of Offenders (NACRO) and in most respects an advocate of the reformist agenda set out by King and Morgan, was nevertheless worried by the 'moral vacuum' argument. 'Treatment and training' *had* had its day, but neither 'positive custody' nor prisoners' rights and enforceable standards had been adopted; and the management-orientated Statement of Tasks adopted by the Prisons Board in 1984 (reprinted in Train 1985) seemed insufficient. The list of 'tasks' were all 'about the means, but not about the ends. Such a moral vacuum soon fills up with cynicism and defeatism' (Stern 1987: 229). The problem, Bottoms argued, was that 'humane containment' was too barren a concept; it was present rather than future-orientated, it would fail to motivate staff, it invested no hope in the enterprise, it was 'ontologically insufficient' (Bottoms 1990).

In fact, as the appearance of a 'Statement of Tasks' made clear, the Prisons Board, in the absence of any political prompting to amend the statutory framework, adopted a formula which owed more to the requirements of the government's Financial Management Initiative (FMI) than to the penal debate. The FMI required of all public sector services a statement of objectives, means for measuring performance, and devolution to managers of control over those resources which determine their capacity to set and attain objectives (Prime Minister 1982). In the Prison Department, as in other departments, the emphasis was on the three Es—Economy, Efficiency, and Effectiveness—performance indicators, and the rest of the FMI baggage-train. Thus the preamble to the Statement of

Tasks was narrowly technical—'to use with maximum efficiency the resources of staff, money, building and plant made available . . . in order to fulfil . . . the relevant provisions of the law' (Train 1985). There then followed a bald statement of what was legally required: delivering the untried and unsentenced to court; keeping everyone in secure custody; providing prisoners with 'as full a life as is consistent with the facts of custody, in particular . . . the physical necessities of life'—health care, work, education, exercise, opportunity to practice religion, etc; and enabling prisoners 'to retain links with the community and where possible assist them to prepare for their return to it' (ibid). This statement was what the FMI required; but, like 'humane containment', it was not inspirational. Further, it provided no rights and laid down no standards. Yet ironically it set in train the management initiatives and information systems for which King and Morgan had argued. It did not answer the question: What are prisons for? But it did begin to focus attention on the question: What services are being delivered to prisoners? The inevitable result was that as more sophisticated data began to emerge about how little was being delivered, and at what cost, so the debate eventually returned to broader purposes and how staff could be persuaded to change what was being delivered. The catalyst that got the debate going again was trouble, this time in the shape of the disorders at Strangeways Prison, Manchester and other prisons in April 1990. Though given the potentially limited remit of inquiring into the events leading up to the disturbances, and the measures taken to bring them to a conclusion, Lord Justice Woolf embarked on a wide-ranging inquiry which made 'identifying the task of the Prison Service' a central question (Woolf Report 1991; Morgan 1991).

Many commentators will find Woolf's discussion of the purposes of imprisonment disappointing. There is no review of the debate as it has developed. Further, contrary to most current opinion, Woolf finds merit in the May Committee's statement of 'positive custody' and, with two caveats, endorses the Prison Service's current Statement of Purpose which is displayed outside all establishments: 'Her Majesty's Prison Service serves the public by keeping in custody those convicted by the courts. Our duty is to look after them with humanity and to help them lead law abiding and useful lives in custody and after release.' Woolf's two caveats are vital, however. First, he is critical of the absence of any reference to justice (Woolf Report 1991: paras. 10.16–10.44). Second, he does not agree that the Statement adequately covers the unconvicted and unsentenced (ibid.: paras 10.45–10.64).

Woolf's use of the term justice is arguably too broad (see Morgan 1992*a*), but, significantly, it ties together sentencing and prisons policy. Woolf maintains that when the Prison Service says it 'serves the public' it does so by more than simply keeping in custody those committed by the courts. It does so best by furthering the objectives of the criminal justice system (with the rest of which the Service tends to be ill co-ordinated—Woolf Report 1991: para. 10.16), namely, by preventing crime. That means at the very least by looking after prisoners with humanity. It also means safeguarding prisoners' 'civil rights which are not taken away expressly or by necessary implication' (*Raymond* v. *Honey* 1982, 759, quoted in Woolf Report 1991: para. 10.22). It also means minimizing 'the negative effects of imprisonment which make reoffending more likely'; requiring 'the offender to confront and take responsibility for the wrong doing which resulted in his . . . imprisonment'; providing the 'prisoner with an opportunity to obtain skills which will make it easier to obtain and keep employment and enable him to maintain his family and community contacts'; ensuring 'that life in prisons . . . [is] as close to life outside as the demands of imprisonment permit'; and seeing 'that the prisoner is properly prepared for his return to society' (para. 10.29). Woolf states categorically that this does not mean 'a return to what came to be known as the treatment model' (para. 10.34). Imprisonment is not justified for reformative purposes, nor is 'being a criminal . . . a creative condition'. However, 'we regard it as part of the Prison Service's role to ensure . . . that a prisoner . . . should have an opportunity of training', for if prisoners are released 'in an embittered and disaffected state' then the criminal justice objective of preventing reoffending is undone (paras. 14.8–14.9). Thus:

> If the Prison Service contains [the] prisoner in conditions which are inhumane or degrading . . . then a punishment of imprisonment which was justly imposed will result in injustice . . . it is the Prison Service's duty to look after prisoners with humanity. If it fulfils this duty, the Prison Service is partly achieving what the Court must be taken to have intended when it passed a sentence of imprisonment.' (para. 10.19)

It may be useful to retrace our steps at this point and summarize an argument implicit in these passages and elsewhere in the Woolf Report. Woolf takes for granted why sentencers send offenders to prison and addresses the logical consequences for prison administrators. He assumes that Paterson's dictum is no longer penological rhetoric but has come into its own as a statement of what sentencers use prisons for. In this he is endorsing an influential Prison Department Working Party on the Management of Long-Term Prisoners which reported in 1984: 'Imprisonment itself . . . is the punishment inflicted by law and no further available hardship should be imposed on a prisoner except by way of formal disciplinary action' (Home Office 1984: para. 108).

How valid is Woolf's assumption that sentencers, not prison

administrators, intend the punishment of imprisonment to comprise loss of liberty alone? Woolf provides a partial explanation, but there are at least two ways in which the question can be fully answered on his behalf. First (the rationale most fully spelt out in the Woolf Report), there is the proposition that sentencers are familiar with the Prison Rules and the various statements of purpose which in recent years the Prison Service has produced. It follows that when passing a sentence of imprisonment sentencers must intend it to comprise an experience congruent with what Parliament and the Prison Service have outlined: if it does not then, as Woolf puts it, a sentence 'justly imposed will result in injustice' (para. 10.19). Though empirically dubious, this argument is in theory impeccable. The courts no longer have available to them a range of differentiated custodial sentences—detention centres, Borstal training, imprisonment, corrective training, and preventative detention—each with its own regimen. There is now a single custodial sentence for adults and another for young offenders, and impoverished prison conditions are repeatedly deprecated by the ministers and department responsible for them. We are therefore entitled to assume that sentencers are cognisant with official intentions regarding the single class of sentenced prisoners that remains.

The second justification for Woolf's assumption is more complicated. There is arguably what I shall term a 'new realism' in sentencing theory. In England this new realism can be discerned in the various government statements that preceded the introduction of the Criminal Justice Act 1991 and the provisions within the Act. It has three ingredients. First, that sentencers are not justified in sentencing offenders to custody on the grounds that custody will in some sense enable them to be made better. If treatment, training, or rehabilitation is the object, it is accepted that these outcomes are more likely to be accomplished by the offender remaining in the community (Home Office 1990*b*: para. 2.7; see Home Office 1991*b*: para. 1.28). Second, though deterrence in the general educative sense of the term continues to command support, the idea of deterrence in its more individualistic calculative sense (as regards both potential offenders and offenders undergoing punishment, particularly imprisonment) has lost credibility (see Home Office 1990*b*: para. 2.8). It is no longer believed that making prison conditions more unpleasant will better deter ex-prisoners from reoffending or dissuade potential offenders from committing crime. Further, what the Home Office refers to as the 'attrition rate'—the statistically low likelihood that particular categories of offenders will have their offences reported and will be apprehended, prosecuted, convicted, and sentenced to a penalty of a given type (see Home Office 1993: 29)—makes much deterrence theory implausible. It also suggests that the public is made only very marginally more safe from crime by more offenders being put in prison (see Brody and Tarling 1980). Thus, third, the current sentencing orthodoxy (set out in sections 1 and 2 of the Criminal Justice Act 1991) is that the primary objective for sentencing is denunciation of and retribution for crime, supplemented in certain circumstances by the need for public protection. The penalty of imprisonment is simply loss of liberty. The government claims, therefore, to be committed to Paterson's dictum and maintains that though imprisonment cannot be justified by the prospect of improving offenders, nevertheless the Prison Service must 'do everything it can, consistent with maintaining a person's loss of liberty, to help make imprisonment a positive and constructive experience' (Home Office 1990*b*: para. 2.9). Woolf's accusation of injustice, then, most appropriately applies to the manifest failure of the Prison Service universally to provide prison regimes consistent with the new realism in sentencing.

In conclusion, 'humane containment' has been judged too stark a prospect and 'positive custody' too woolly. An alliance has been forged between 'new realism' in sentencing theory and a 'neo-rehabilitative' approach to prisons administration. Justice is the underlying leitmotif. Terms hitherto considered incompatible have been brought together. The state has a duty to *facilitate* rather than *coerce* treatment or training (Morris 1974), and prisoners can legitimately expect (may possibly establish a right to) facilities whereby they can begin to address whatever personal shortcomings and social disadvantages are associated with their offending behaviour. This is what Rotman describes as a rights model of rehabilitation, 'humanistic and liberty-centred' as opposed to 'authoritarian and paternalistic' (Rotman 1986). The model emphasizes the view that the legal rights that prisoners retain as citizens generate feelings of dignity and self-worth, that prisoners are legally responsible individuals and must be treated accordingly, that the state has a duty to ensure that prisons are not destructive environments, and that potentially self-improving facilities and programmes are not provided at the discretion of the administration to be downgraded whenever it is administratively convenient or judged ineffective.

This rights approach to treatment and training has implications for the morale of prison staff. It is generally agreed that the quality of life for prisoners depends crucially on their relationships with prison officers. Prison officers, it is argued, will best be motivated to treat prisoners well if two conditions are satisfied: first, if they are given practical tasks that they understand, value, and can perform (King and Morgan 1980; Dunbar 1985); second, if those tasks instil hope and the belief that what custodial staff do comprises more than simply locking people up in civilized conditions or otherwise: to put it another way, if those tasks emphasize the intrinsic worth of prisoners as persons capable of transforming themselves for a more worthwhile future (Bottoms 1990). In so far as the rights approach to rehabilitation emphasizes standards to be attained and programmes to be delivered by a more active and skilled staff, then arguably it provides the vision which the Service has so conspicuously lacked since the demise of the paternalistic rehabilitative approach. Moreover, if the Prison Service creates for prisoners a safe, humane, and positive environment, and if prisoners are presented with meaningful choices, then there is at least a prospect that they will choose to make positive use of their time behind bars—in which case prisons will be better places in which to work as well as live.

However much agreement there is about what the Prison Service mission should comprise, there continues to be a good deal of argument about how it should be implemented. Is the present Service statement of objectives adequate or should it be more detailed? Should prisoners' entitlements be enforceable by judicial review or should they be able to claim damages in the event of breaches of the rules? Should programmes for prisoners be prison-specific, delivered by the Prison Service, or should community-based agencies service prisons as part of their remit? These questions will continue to generate controversy and are returned to below.

WHO ARE THE PRISONERS?

British prisoners are overwhelmingly young, male, socially and economically disadvantaged repetitive property offenders. In all respects the British prison populations reflect the character of prisoner populations in other advanced industrialized democratic jurisdictions. If the primary function of the police is to sweep the streets of the most readily identifiable (and thus vulnerable) offenders, then the function of the prison system is repeatedly to contain the most intractable part of the residue. Prisons have accurately been described as 'penal dustbins'. Prisoners from socially privileged backgrounds attract disproportionate media attention largely because of their rarity. Prisons—their staff, culture, occupants, and, prior to the modern use of green field sites, physical location—have largely been a feature and hazard of working-class life. Only governors have traditionally been 'gentlemen', and invariably their reminiscences betray their identification with that strange animal, the 'toff' prisoner thrust into an alien underclass world (see Priestley 1989: 40; Blake 1927: ch. 6; Clayton 1958: ch. 8).

When discussing the character of the prison population a clear distinction must be drawn between 'receptions' and 'average daily population' (ADP). Most custodial experiences are surprisingly transitory. If all categories of prisoner are included then the overwhelming majority are in prison for a matter of days, weeks, or months rather than years. If sentenced prisoners—those prisoners in prison the longest are considered alone, then, if remission for good behaviour and parole are taken into account, approximately 85 per cent are released within twelve months of their receipt (the average time served by prisoners with determinate sentences of between eighteen months and three years in 1990 was 11.7 months—see Home Office 1992*a*: table 4.16). However, the ADP is very different. Longer-term prisoners dominate prisons both numerically and, more importantly, culturally. Of the sentenced ADP, approximately 46 per cent are serving sentences of more than three years, meaning that they will be in prison for more than a year, many very much longer, a few for most of their lives.

The contrast between prison receptions and the ADP is becoming more marked. In a prescient article Bottoms described a policy process whereby attempts are made to distinguish 'ordinary', 'mundane', or 'non-threatening' offenders from 'serious', 'exceptional', and 'dangerous' offenders (Bottoms 1977). He termed this process bifurcation, one function of which is to reassure the public by locking up the latter for longer while increasingly catering for the former by means of what are now termed 'community penalties'. The Criminal Justice Act 1991, s. 2(6) explicitly provides for bifurcation: violent or sexual offenders are singled out as candidates eligible for custodial sentences longer than their 'just deserts' if there is need to protect the public from serious harm. In fact bifurcation has been pursued for some time and its impact is clearly illustrated in the changing character of the prison population. In spite of the increase in recorded crime and crime cleared up, the number of sentenced prisoners received annually has risen little in recent years. Yet, as Fig. 19.1 illustrates, there has been a significant increase in the proportion of prisoners received with long sentences. Particularly striking has been the increase in the number of prisoners serving *very* long sentences. In 1980 fifty-five adult prisoners were received with determinate sentences of more than ten years. In 1990 the corresponding number was 186 (Home Office 1992*a*: tables 4.11, 5.11). Life-sentence prisoners have also become more numerous. In 1965, when the death penalty was abolished, seventy-six new life-sentence prisoners were received. By 1970 the figure had reached 135, by 1980 217, and by 1990 229 (ibid.: table 8.4). By contrast, both the number and proportion of prisoners received with sentences of less than twelve months had markedly declined.

The increase in the number of long-term prison receptions, and the increased length of those long-term sentences (a long-term sentence is statutorily defined as one of four years or more: Criminal Justice Act 1991, s. 33), has been matched by an increase in the proportion of sentences actually served in prison. In 1980, for example, the average time

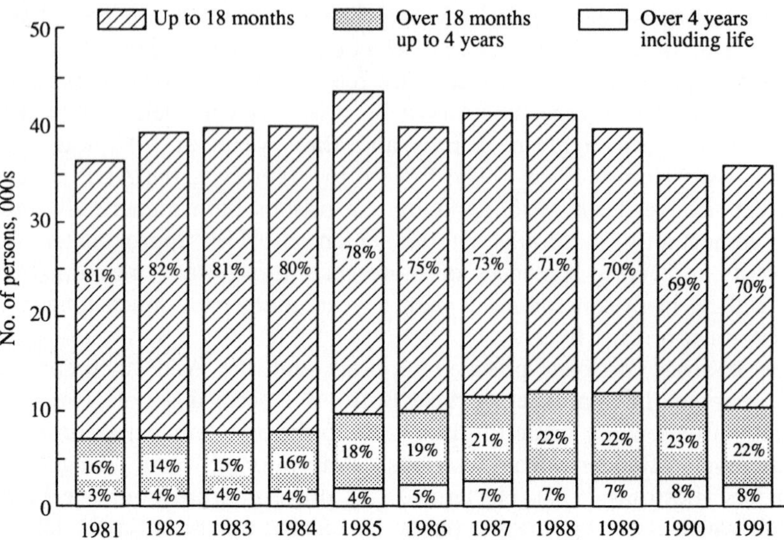

Fig 19.1 Receptions of adult males under sentence of immediate imprisonment, by length of sentence, 1981–1991

Source: Home Office 1992*a*: figure 4(b).

served by life sentence prisoners released on licence was 10.3 years. In 1990 the average duration was thirteen years, the highest ever recorded (ibid.: table 8.5). The evidence indicates that both murderers (for whom the life sentence is mandatory) and discretionary life-sentence prisoners are now generally required to remain longer in custody before being conditionally released.

The clearest evidence of the operation of bifurcation in executive release policy is provided in Table 19.1. It is apparent that the dividing-point is around the four years mark. Prisoners serving sentences of three years or less have gradually been required to serve proportionally less of their sentences, while those with sentences of more than five years have served proportionally more of their sentences. Prisoners with sentences of around four years are being released at roughly the same point in their sentences as a decade ago.

It follows that bifurcation in sentencing and executive release policy has impacted the prison population at three levels, generating an increase in the proportion of receptions serving long-term sentences; an increase in the length of those long-term sentences; and an increase in the proportion of those longer long-term sentences being served. The consequence has been a dramatic change in the composition of the ADP (see Fig. 19.2). In

Table 19.1 Average time served by adult male prisoners discharged from determinate sentences on completion of sentence or on licence, by length of sentence, 1981–1991 (England and Wales)

Length of sentence[a]	Average time served, and percentage of sentence served in custody, under sentence											
	1981		1982		1983		1984		1985		1986	
	Mths	(%)	Mths	(%)	Mths	(%)	Mths	(%)	Mths	(%)	Mths	(%)
Up to 3 months	1.2	(60)	1.2	(60)	1.2	(61)	1.2	(60)	1.2	(60)	1.2	(58)
Over 3 months up to 6 months	3.2	(59)	3.2	(60)	3.2	(60)	3.2	(60)	3.2	(60)	3.1	(59)
Over 6 months up to 12 months	6.0	(60)	5.9	(60)	5.8	(58)	5.6	(56)	5.4	(54)	5.3	(53)
Over 12 months up to 18 months	8.6	(60)	8.6	(59)	8.5	(58)	7.6	(52)	6.6	(45)	6.8	(42)
Over 18 months up to 3 years	13.3	(53)	12.9	(52)	12.8	(52)	11.3	(46)	10.1	(41)	11.8	(43)
Over 3 years up to 4 years	22.1	(48)	21.4	(47)	20.8	(46)	20.2	(44)	21.1	(47)	21.7	(48)
Over 4 years up to 5 years	28.7	(49)	27.2	(47)	27.3	(47)	28.0	(48)	29.2	(50)	29.6	(51)
Over 5 years up to 10 years	40.5	(49)	41.3	(49)	40.6	(49)	42.5	(53)	45.0	(55)	45.8	(55)
Over 10 years less than life	74.7	(46)	73.5	(47)	70.4	(44)	80.4	(49)	101.5	(59)	86.3	(56)

Length of sentence[a]	Average time served, and percentage of sentence served in custody, under sentence									
	1987		1988		1989		1990		1991	
	Mths	(%)	Mths	(%)	Mths	(%)	Mths	(%)	Mths	(%)
Up to 3 months	1.1	(52)	0.8	(41)	0.8	(42)	0.8	(42)	0.9	(42)
Over 3 months up to 6 months	2.7	(51)	2.2	(42)	2.3	(42)	2.2	(43)	2.3	(43)
Over 6 months up to 12 months	4.8	(48)	4.0	(40)	4.2	(41)	4.1	(41)	4.2	(41)
Over 12 months up to 18 months	6.8	(41)	6.8	(41)	6.5	(39)	6.8	(41)	6.9	(42)
Over 18 months up to 3 years	11.8	(43)	11.8	(43)	12.0	(43)	11.7	(42)	11.8	(42)
Over 3 years up to 4 years	21.7	(48)	21.5	(47)	22.3	(49)	21.5	(48)	22.3	(49)
Over 4 years up to 5 years	28.7	(49)	29.2	(50)	29.3	(50)	28.9	(50)	28.4	(49)
Over 5 years up to 10 years	46.7	(55)	44.9	(54)	45.3	(54)	43.9	(53)	44.9	(53)
Over 10 years less than life	89.3	(54)	96.4	(59)	87.3	(53)	87.8	(58)	87.2	(49)

[a] On discharge; the sentence may change after reception if there are further charges or an appeal.

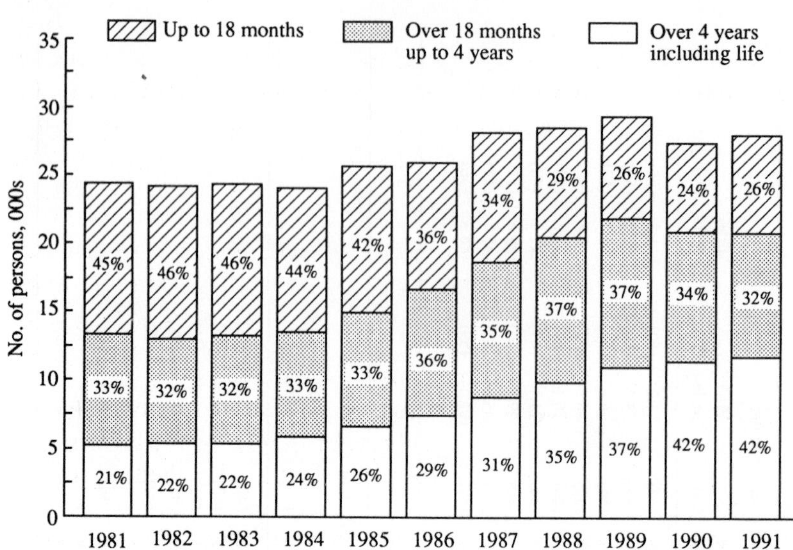

Fig 19.2 Population of adult males under sentence on 30 June, by length of sentence, 1981–1991

Source: Home Office 1992*a*: figure 4(a).

the mid-1960s when, as we shall see, security considerations first came to the fore in prisons administration, some 11 per cent of the sentenced ADP (young and adult, male and female) was serving sentences of four years or more, including life (Home Office 1966: table E.2). By 1980 the proportion had risen to 22 per cent and by 1990 to 46 per cent (Home Office 1992*a*: table 1.9). The actual numbers tell the story even more dramatically. In 1964 there were only 1,256 prisoners serving sentences, including life, of more than five years (Home Office 1966: table E.2). By 1990 there were more than twice as many prisoners (2,704) serving life sentences alone, and almost eight times as many (9,603) serving more than five years, including life (Home Office 1992*a*: table 1.9).

One explanation for the population trends described above lies in the introduction in 1967 of parole (superimposed on an existing policy which had been in existence since 1940 of one-third automatic remission for good conduct on all determinate sentences) and its development since. After a cautious beginning, when parole was seen very much as a privilege to be earnt by prisoners who had reached a 'recognisable peak in their training' (Home Office 1965), executive release was gradually liberalized (for detailed accounts see Carlisle Report 1988; Maguire 1992). Following initiatives by two Home Secretaries, Roy Jenkins in 1974 and Leon Brittan in 1983, an increasing proportion of short- and medium-sentence prisoners received parole almost routinely. Indeed, after 1987 all prisoners serving sentences of twelve months or less were automatically released without assessment at the half-way point in their sentences. In the case of Leon Brittan's initiative, however, this liberalization at the lower end of the sentence range was balanced by a much tougher policy for certain categories of longer-term prisoner, a policy which was highly controversial because it effectively involved ministers making sentencing decisions. It was announced that parole would not normally be granted at all to prisoners serving over five years for violent offences or drug-trafficking, that ministers would set a minimum tariff period to be served by life-sentence prisoners, dependent on the circumstances of their offence, and that special categories of lifer—those convicted for the murder of police or prison officers, the sexual or sadistic murder of children, murder by firearms in the course of robbery, or murder in the furtherance of terrorism—would not normally be released until they had served at least twenty years.

The policy of ministers setting a minimum tariff period to 'meet the interests of deterrence and retribution' was modified in 1987 in the case of discretionary life sentences (following *R.* v. *Secretary of State for the Home Department, ex p. Handscombe* (1991), *The Times*, 4 March) such that the recommendations of the judiciary were strictly adhered to. In the case of mandatory life sentences for murder, however, ministers, typically junior ministers, continued to determine the tariff to be served and, as evidence given to a House of Lords Select Committee showed, ministers typically altered upwards the tariffs recommended by trial judges and the Lord Chief Justice (House of Lords 1989; see also Maguire *et al.* 1984).

Not surprisingly, the Brittan rules proved highly controversial. They removed discretion from the Parole Board, involved ministers rather than judges deciding what certain sentences should be, and exacerbated the less than consistent gulf between sentences passed and sentences served. The policy also had consequences for control in prisons: it did terrible damage to the morale of both staff and prisoners, as prisoners brought back from open prisons and long-termers now felt they had little to lose. In 1987–8 the parole system was thoroughly reviewed by the Carlisle Committee, whose recommendations were, with certain important exceptions, adopted and incorporated within the Criminal Justice Act 1991. The most important ingredients in the new system, which came into force in October 1992, are abolition of remission combined with automatic conditional release at the half-way point of sentences under four years; Parole Board responsibility for release decisions for prisoners serving determinate sentences of between four and seven years, the threshold for release being the half-way point in sentences with conditional release up to the three-quarter point; and continued involvement of the Home Secretary in release decisions of sentences of seven years or more, though the Brittan rules have been abolished. All the indications are, therefore, that the build up of the long-term prison population will continue. The Prison Service has to cater to the needs of the majority of committals, for whom the experience of custody is transitory, within a prison system which, on a day-to-day basis, has to accommodate prisoners of whom an ever-increasing number must regard the prison as their home. There is a tension between the needs of the two groups.

Imprisonment has hitherto been experienced largely by the young. In 1990 34 per cent of untried receptions, 40 per cent of convicted but unsentenced receptions, and 26 per cent of sentenced receptions were under 21 years of age. Of adult prisoners received under sentence, 60 per cent were under 30 years of age. Young men in their twenties dominate life in most prisons. This is not surprising. Though crime (at least the sort of crime that leads to conviction) is very largely the activity of adolescents and young adults, the fact that sentences of imprisonment have generally been imposed on repeat offenders (the Criminal Justice Act 1991, s. 29, called that policy into question) means we should expect the modal age of prisoners to be higher than that of convicted criminals generally. Almost 80 per cent of the ADP for whom the information was recorded in 1990 had three or more convictions and over a third had eleven or more convictions (Home Office 1992*a*: table 4.2). The modal age of sentenced male and female prisoners was 25 or 26.

Nevertheless, the age profile of the prison population is changing, both that of receptions and the ADP. The number of very young prisoners has been sharply reduced in recent years and the proportion of middle-aged and even elderly prisoners has risen. This is partly a consequence of the successful policy determination to reduce the custody in Prison Service establishments of juveniles and to carry the impetus of that effort over to young adults (the minimum age for a sentence of detention in a young offender establishment is 15 for both boys and girls, but the government is committed to ending remands in prison of male juveniles aged 15 or 16, the remanding of girls under 17 having already been ended. The number of juveniles aged 16 or less received for an immediate custodial sentence in 1990 was 1,520, the lowest number for many years and approximately a fifth of the number in 1980. The number of males aged 16 or less received on remand in 1990 was also the lowest for ten years and, given the furore caused by the tragic suicide in prison of two 15-year-olds in 1990 and 1991, it can confidently be predicted that the number will be further reduced until the local authority social service departments are made wholly responsible for the pre-trial custody of juveniles.

Though the population of adults in their early twenties received under sentence has increased, younger prisoners tend to have shorter sentences. The consequence of the changing pattern of receptions, therefore, is that the ADP is ageing: in 1980 almost half the ADP was aged under 25 years and approximately 13 per cent was aged 40 years or more; in 1990 the proportions were 39 and 16 per cent. There are now almost 400 prisoners at any one time over 60 years of age.

Prisoners are overwhelmingly male—94.7 per cent of all receptions and 96.5 per cent of the ADP. Moreover, since it has long been the policy for women to be housed in institutions exclusively for women (though some remand prisons accommodate males and females in separate wings), and because, until relatively recently, women prison officers have been employed exclusively to work with female prisoners, culturally most prisons remain overwhelmingly masculine bastions. The character of the female prison population is in some respects different from that of the male population. This is not the place to examine whether, *ceteris paribus*, women are more or less likely to be imprisoned than men, but it is clear that the male and female prison populations differ in some important respects relevant to criminal justice (see Carlen 1990). First, the ratio of remand to sentenced prisoners differs. Twenty-four per cent of the female ADP comprises remands, compared to 21.2 per cent for men, in spite of the fact that the average remand period for women is significantly shorter than for men (forty-one compared to fifty-four days in 1990). The principal explanation for the disparity is that a higher proportion of female than male custodial remands precede, where the defendant is convicted, a non-custodial sentence (Home Office 1992*a*: ch. 2; how great is the difference is unclear, because a high proportion of outcomes are not recorded). Sentenced women prisoners also differ from men. They are typically older (a much lower proportion of both receptions and ADP are under 21); serving shorter sentences (24.7 compared to 15.7 per cent of the ADP serving sentences of one year or less); less likely to be serious recidivists (53 per cent of the ADP for which the information is available have none or only one or two previous convictions, compared to 21 per cent of males); and markedly less likely to have committed offences of violence (19 compared to 45 per cent of the adult ADP having committed violent offences including robbery and sexual offences). Some writers, notably Carlen (1990), suggest that these differences in the character of the male and female prison populations indicate that despite the small number of women in prison there is a powerful case for there being even fewer.

It is difficult to evaluate the extent to which prisoners are now much more intractable than they once were, the contention generally advanced by prison staff. Certainly a slightly higher proportion of those received under sentence have been convicted of crimes of violence (including sexual offences and robbery) than was the case ten years ago, and because sentences—particularly those for violent offences—are now longer and parole is less readily given for longer sentences, a substantially higher proportion of the sentenced ADP has been convicted of offences of violence. However, the limited data available (there are no data recorded on the previous convictions of almost half of all sentenced receptions) suggest that the prison population is not more recidivist today than it was a decade ago (Home Office 1992*a*: table 4.9, compared to Home Office 1981*a*: table 4.3). Nevertheless it is clear, as we have seen, that major prison disturbances are now more common. Further, to the extent that prisoner disciplinary proceedings reflect the incidence of prisoner offences (which they may not) or are an index of stability (which arguably they are), then certainly the number of offences against the Prison Rules punished per head of population has risen in recent years, and the increase has been in every type of establishment except those for women, where the number has fallen but still remains far higher than that for men (Home Office 1992*b*: table 2).

What is clear is that the prison population is socially and economically disadvantaged relative to the population generally. There has recently been conducted by the Office of Population Censuses and Surveys on behalf of the Home Office the most comprehensive survey ever of the prison population (Walmsley *et al.* 1992).[2] Prisoners are disproportionately black (15 per cent of male and 23 per cent of female prisoners, compared to less than 5 per cent of the general population) and working-class (83 per cent of male prisoners are from manual, partly skilled, or unskilled groups, compared to 55 per cent of the population generally). These broad structural characteristics are compounded by more telling signs of social stress. An astonishingly high proportion of prisoners, 26 per cent, say they have been in local authority care below the age of 16. For prisoners under 21 the figure is 38 per cent. This compares with approximately 2 per cent for the population generally. There is also evidence of the fragility of prisoners' family relationships. A much higher proportion of prisoners than one would expect from their age profile and social background were cohabiting and many fewer were married at the time of their incarceration compared to the population at large. At the time of interview the differences were greater still, suggesting the breakdown of relationships as a result of imprisonment. Further, though a high proportion of prisoners had dependent children living with them prior to imprisonment (32 per cent of males and 47 per cent of females), a significant proportion at the time of interview said their children were being looked after by their ex-spouse or ex-partner (27 per cent of men

[2] For earlier partial surveys of the prison population see Banks and Fairhead 1976; Fairhead 1981; Mott 1985.

and 19 per cent of women with children) and, in the case of women prisoners, the majority (52 per cent) said their children were being looked after by relatives or were in care or with foster parents (12 per cent). The survey did not investigate why so many prisoners were taken into care when children, but the evidence suggests that many children of prisoners are destined to suffer the same disadvantageous start in life (see Shaw 1992 for a general review).

Many prisoners have generally precarious toeholds on life outside prison. Some 13 per cent had no permanent residence prior to their incarceration (they were roofless, or living in a hostel or some other temporary accommodation), and of those who had a permanent residence and were not living with their parents, two-thirds were living in rented accommodation, nowadays very much a minority form of tenure. Unsurprisingly, prisoners are no better placed in the employment market. Forty-three per cent said that they left school before the age of 16 (compared to 11 per cent of the population generally), and of the remainder very few continued education beyond 16. Forty-three per cent had no educational qualifications whatsoever (many of these prisoners are functionally illiterate) and only 8 per cent had qualifications beyond 'O' level. A third were unemployed before their imprisonment, two-fifths of those under 25: almost three times as many as one would expect to find in the population generally.

The mental health of prisoners has been a perennial cause for concern. In 1991 the most comprehensive survey of the mental health of the sentenced population ever undertaken (Gunn *et al.* 1991) estimated that of adult males and females 2.4 and 1.1 per cent respectively were suffering from psychoses; 5.8 and 15.4 per cent from neuroses; 8.8 and 16.1 per cent from personality disorders; and 1.0 and 2.6 per cent from organic disorders. Moreover, almost a quarter of all males and approaching one-third of all females were regular substance abusers or were substance-dependent. Thus, though the incidence of serious psychiatric illness or disorder is small—the data suggest that there are approximately 700 sentenced prisoners suffering psychotic illness in the system at any one time—it appears that approximately two-fifths of all males and two-thirds of all females have pronounced psychiatric or behavioural problems. The remand population almost certainly exhibits more acute problems. Though the methodology adopted by the most recent survey of remand prisoners does not permit overall estimates to be generated, referrals to prison doctors in three prisons over six months produced over 200 prisoners suffering from some form of psychosis or mental handicap (Dell *et al.* 1991). Most of these prisoners had been remanded in custody not because of the seriousness of their alleged offences, but because of their need for social or psychiatric help: as the authors of the survey pointed out, 'remands in custody are an inefficient, ineffective and inhumane way of securing psychiatric assessment and treatment' (ibid.: 423).

In conclusion, prisoners are drawn disproportionately from groups that are socially and economically marginal to the life of the community, though it is not clear to what extent their marginality preceded or followed their typically repeated convictions. What is certain is that imprisonment is not likely to enhance their life chances. Further, the personal inadequacy of many prisoners compounds the vulnerability which is a general characteristic of prison life and which makes it essential to turn to an age-old question: *Quis custodies custodiet*? Who guards the guards?

ORGANIZATION AND ACCOUNTABILITY

Prisoners and prisons bring together characteristics always likely to provoke controversy. Prisoners stand condemned legally, are judged deficient morally, and are of little account politically. They are drawn, as we have seen, disproportionately from the ranks of the underprivileged. Prisons are relatively closed and 'total institutions' (Goffman 1968). Since the essence of imprisonment is loss of liberty, it is all too easy for a prison service to adopt secretive and restrictive policies, ostensibly in fulfilment of its mandate. When prisoners protest, their pleas are often not heard or, when heard, not listened to. Winston Churchill can have little claim to stand in the first rank of protectors of domestic civil liberties, but he was surely correct when he maintained, in a much-quoted passage, that 'the mood and temper of the public in regard to the treatment of crime and criminals is one of the most unfailing tests of the civilisation of any country' (*HC Debates*, col. 1354, 20 July 1910). If that be true then the accountability of any prison system is an acid test of its acceptability: to ensure that prisoners are being treated well, we have first to establish how they are treated.

Expenditure on prisons since 1979 has risen by more in real terms than that on almost any other central government service. Yet, in spite of the massive building programme of the 1980s, and the greatly improved staff/prisoner ratio, all the evidence suggests that the delivery of measured services to prisoners either had not improved or had deteriorated (Morgan 1983; King and McDermott 1989, 1991, 1992). Further, the litany of serious prison disturbances was immensely costly. It was partly because the prison budget appeared to be a bottomless pit, and partly because the government was in any case committed to greater competition in the provision of public services, that the unthinkable became the thinkable: it was proposed that the management of prisons be privatized (Ryan and Ward 1989; see also chapter 5 in this volume). In April 1992 a new purpose-built prison for remand prisoners, the Wolds, opened under the management of Group 4 Security, and a second 'privatized' new prison, Blakenhurst, opened in early 1993 under the management of UK Detention Services. The Criminal Justice Act 1991, s. 84, provides for the management of any prison to be contracted out to any agency the Secretary of State thinks appropriate. In 1993 the Home Secretary invited tenders for the running of existing as well as new prisons, including Strangeways Prison, Manchester, which had been rendered uninhabitable in April 1990 by the longest siege and most serious riot in English penal history, and subsequently substantially rebuilt. Further, in April 1993, the Prison Service became an agency outside the Home Office. These radical administrative developments will have profound implications for the running of prisons and their general accountability.

From 1877, when they were brought wholly under central government control, until the opening of the Wolds in 1992, prisons in England had been the sole undivided financial and administrative responsibility of the Home Secretary: until 1962 via the Prison Commission, and subsequently by the Prison Department, a department within the Home Office (renamed the Prison Service in the mid-1980s). The Prison Service was reorganized in 1990. The 130-odd institutions are grouped in a more or less geographically proximate fashion into fifteen areas, each headed by an area manager. The supreme executive body is the Prisons Board, chaired by the Director General who is accountable to the Secretary of State, who is in turn answerable to Parliament. It remains to be seen whether agency status, and the recruitment from the commercial world of a Director General, Mr Derek Lewis, with no previous experience of prisons, will lead to a change in these administrative arrangements, but it will be surprising if the number of staff employed in headquarters and central services—currently 2,550 or 8 per cent of all Prison Service staff (Home Office 1991*a*: para. 228)—is not drastically reduced.

The administration of prisons is governed by statute, the Prison Act 1952. This lays down the general duties of the prison authorities; provides for personnel; defines what a prison is; and, most importantly, empowers the Minister to make rules for the management of prisons. Such rules are exercisable by statutory instrument. The current rules date from 1964 (SI no. 388, as amended) and elaborate on issues covered in the Act. They state the purpose of prisons; describe aspects of prison regimes (e.g. exercise, cells, privileges) and decision-making (e.g. parole, early release); cover staff and prisoner disciplinary procedures; and define the duties of prison boards of visitors (for a detailed discussion of the Rules see Prison Reform Trust 1993).

The Prison Service is required to produce an annual report for the Minister to lay before Parliament and, as we have seen (note 1), this now comes in three parts. Current annual reports contain far more information than they are statutorily required to, but it is nevertheless difficult to judge from them whether conditions in prisons have got better or worse. For example, there are data on crowding and the number of prisoners sharing with one or two others cells designed for single occupancy, and on the average hours per prisoner spent at work or on education or training. These data are uninformative, however, about conditions in any particular establishment or about such important aspects of regimes as time spent out of cell, clothing changes, or the generosity of visiting arrangements. The Prison Service is committed to the systematic collection of regime monitoring data, but these have so far not been published (except for Home Office 1991*b*: table 1) and have hitherto been methodologically suspect (see Morgan 1992*b*).

The absence of detailed data on the quality of prison regimes would arguably not matter were the Prison Rules to lay down specific conditions and facilities to which prisoners were entitled. But they seldom do. The Rules are ungenerous in their provisions, are generally not specific and, even where specific, usually grant prison managers extensive discretion as to whether facilities will be given (Zellick 1981; Richardson 1993*a*). Moreover, the courts have held that breaches of the Prison Rules do not provide the basis for an action for breach of statutory duty and that the Rules do not vest prisoners with any special rights (*Hague* v. *Deputy Governor of Parkhurst Prison* [1991] 3 All ER 733, confirming *Arbon* v. *Anderson* [1943] KB 252). Moreover, after a period of speculation, the House of Lords has ruled that an action for false imprisonment is not available to prisoners challenging the conditions of their otherwise lawful custody (*Hague* [1991], confirming *Williams* v. *The Home Office* (no. 2) [1981] 1 All ER 1211). Though there is a well-established principle that the prison authorities owe a duty of care to prisoners (*Ellis* v. *Home Office* [1953] 2 QB 135), and though prisoners have been paid compensation, it is agreed that actions based on generally bad custodial conditions are unlikely to succeed (Feldman 1993). When challenged, governors or the Home Office will claim that they are doing their best in difficult circumstances and liability for negligence is unlikely to be found in the face of such submissions. There is another route, namely judicial review, by which legal intervention may be sought and which, as we shall see, has enjoyed some success in relation to the making of certain decisions by the prison authorities. But before that avenue is explored, what have been the living conditions of which the Prison Rules provide the merest sketch and about which the British courts have very largely maintained a hands-off posture?

It should be said at the outset that many British prisons provide imaginative prisoner programmes delivered by committed staff in physical settings and relaxed atmospheres which are arguably in the first rank of any prison system in Europe and a good deal better than many (for an overview of European and some other prison systems see Van Zyl Smit and Dunkel 1991). Most prisons in England, Scotland, and Northern Ireland are modern, are not overcrowded, have good facilities, and are not prone to major disorder. There is a dark side, however. Some prisons are old, ill-resourced, and insanitary, and many of them have until recently been grossly overcrowded. In 1980 the then Director General of the Prison Department described the prison conditions in some of the institutions for which he was responsible as an 'affront to civilised society' (Home Office 1981*a*: 2). Where are the 'bricks of shame' about which Stern, quoting Oscar Wilde's 'Ballad of Reading Gaol', has written (1987) and how have they been laid down and allowed to remain?

Now that the courts have only a single custodial sentence available to them, albeit distinguished by whether the offender is under or over 21 years of age, the Prison Service is able to adopt a simple administrative classification for its estate. There are two main types of institutions. First, there are the local prisons and remand centres whose primary task is to receive prisoners from and deliver prisoners to the courts and to assess and allocate those prisoners serving sentences sufficiently long for it to have been held sensible that they be allocated. Second, there are the prisons to which sentenced prisoners are allocated, the young offender institutions (YOIs) and, for adults, the training prisons. YOIs and training prisons are further subdivided into closed and open institutions. In fact this subdivision reflects a prisoner security classification and, by implication, the level of security which institutions are considered able to provide. All sentenced prisoners are security classified A, B, C, or D according to a scheme adopted in 1966 on the recommendation of Lord Mountbatten, following his investigation of some notorious breaches of security (Mountbatten Report 1966). Category A prisoners, whom Mountbatten envisaged would comprise no more than 120, but whose number had drifted up to between 400 and 500 by the early 1990s, are those 'whose escape would constitute a danger to the public, the police or the security of the state'. Category D prisoners are those suitable for open conditions, that is, those who may be trusted to stay there and whose escape would not excite public anxiety. Category B and C prisoners are those required to be held in closed conditions providing more or less security. Trial and remand prisoners are, with the exception of a few provisionally categorized as A, all assumed to be Category B. It follows that local prisons and remand centres which, broadly speaking, must cater for anyone committed by the courts, are essentially Category B establishments, though in most local prisons some specially strengthened cells and areas are set aside for a few Category A prisoners.

The allocation of sentenced Category A prisoners has been the subject of a long-running controversy (King and Elliott 1977; King and Morgan 1980). Mountbatten recommended that they be confined to a single purpose-built fortress, but on the recommendation of a committee chaired by Professor Radzinowicz (Advisory Council on the Penal System 1968) it was decided that they should be dispersed among a few high-security prisons, the majority of whose occupants would be Category B or even C. In fact, as we shall see, Category A prisoners have never been wholly accommodated in the so-called 'dispersal prisons'—pre-existing high-security units were retained and others developed—and the dispersal policy has been subtly modified so that there is now less dispersal than Radzinowicz envisaged (Home Office 1984; Prison Service 1991).

It is increasingly common for institutions to have multiple functions (e.g. male prisons to have a small unit for females, adult prisons to have a wing for young prisoners, training prisons to include a small section for trial and remand prisoners). This is an important development which, in the light of Lord Justice Woolf's recommendation that there be developed 'community prisons' (Woolf Report 1991: paras. 11.49–11.68), is likely to become more common. It follows that it becomes more and more difficult precisely to delineate the numbers and characteristics of different types of institutions. It is a feature of penal institutions that their titles and functions change rather more frequently than their facilities and culture.

At the time of writing there are approximately thirty predominantly local prisons for males (though two contain small units for women) and one or two training prisons that have small units for remand prisoners. There are about a dozen remand centres for trials and remands under 21 years of age, two-thirds of which are part of a local prison or YOI complex. Two male remand centres cater also for females. There are approximately sixty male training prisons, six of which are high-security dispersal prisons and ten of which are open prisons. There are between twenty-five and thirty YOIs—the number is gradually being reduced in response to the decreasing number of committals—of which eight are open. Finally, there are sixteen prisons that wholly, partly, or occasionally accommodate women, though the hub of the women's system is a single multi-functional local prison, Holloway Prison in London, which accommodates almost a third of the female prison population (for a recent account of Holloway see Casale 1989). Prisons for women are also open or closed.

About these approximately 130 institutions it is possible to generalize as follows. More than a quarter of the estate—about thirty-five institutions—comprises Victorian, generally radial, institutions. Most of these Victorian prisons fulfil functions today similar to those they met almost one and a half centuries ago. Most are local prisons in major cities or administrative centres, originally built as city or county gaols. One or two—like Dartmoor and Parkhurst—are on isolated sites, a reflection of their former function to house convicts awaiting transportation, for which central government was responsible. They are now training prisons, with a regional or national role. The open training prisons and YOIs are invariably former military camps, residential institutions or country houses converted to penal use in the late 1940s and 1950s when the increase in the prison population was responded to as cheaply as possible. Most of the remaining institutions, over half of the total, are purpose-built prisons constructed in or since the 1950s. Virtually no prisons were built in the first half of the twentieth century.

The local prisons, then, with the exception of those opened since Belmarsh in East London in 1991, are all Victorian and urban, and include among their number the largest prisons in the system. Pentonville, the original 'model prison' opened in 1844, now has certified normal accommodation (CNA) for 750 prisoners but regularly houses up to 1,000. Strangeways Prison, Manchester, which at the time of the riot in April 1990 had a CNA of 970 but in fact accommodated 1,600 prisoners, was the largest prison in England. By contrast, the closed training prisons are mostly modern purpose-built institutions of medium size (280–500) on green-field sites. The exceptions are the former local prisons such as Maidstone, Preston, and Wakefield which, as the Chief Inspector of Prisons often points out, are training prisons in little more than name. Open prisons and YOIs, for men and women alike, are a motley collection of camps and converted buildings, invariably rural, many of them small (fewer than 200 places), and, according to the Prison Service, often not cost-effective. Were the prison population to fall significantly, many of them would no doubt be closed.

This pattern of investment in building reflects the Prison Service's historical commitment to treatment and training. The training prisons and YOIs have represented the Service's noble (albeit misguided) mission and historically have been given the lion's share of the resources. Further, when the Service has been under population pressure, the training sector has largely been spared overcrowding. Overcrowding has always, as a matter of policy, been concentrated in the local prisons where, in treatment and training terms, it was expected that nothing much could happen. In the local prisons have been held those prisoners excluded from the noble mission: the untried and unsentenced, because they are legally ineligible for treatment and training; those sentenced prisoners serving short sentences, for whom there has been held to be insufficient time to achieve anything; and the seriously recalcitrant, judged to be beyond the training pale. Over time the local prisons became the dumping grounds for many of those prisoners with whom the training prisons could not cope, those administratively segregated or 'inappropriately allocated' (see Woolf Report 1991: paras. 12.221–12.263).

The Prison Service's explanation for the overcrowding of the local prisons is that Victorian prisons with large cells designed for single occupancy under the 'separate' system (see Ignatieff 1978, ch. 4; McConville 1981; Radzinowicz and Hood 1990) can be overcrowded in a way that modern prisons with smaller cells designed largely for sleeping in cannot. There is an element of truth in this, and one or two of the older training prisons were allowed to become overcrowded when system overcrowding was at its worst. But this explanation is belied by the fact that the modern purpose-built remand centres with their small cells were crowded in the same manner. Concentrating crowding in remand establishments was managerially convenient and prejudiced the noble mission of the Service least. The attention of untried prisoners is focused largely on their cases and prospects: they are orientated to life beyond the walls and are therefore least likely to protest against their living conditions—or so it seemed before the disturbances in 1986 and since (Morgan 1993). By contrast, the prison is for long-term prisoners their home and any depreciation in their quality of life is jealously guarded against, if necessary by collective violent protest. The consequence is that those prisoners who on any criterion should have been given the least oppressive conditions, the untried subject to the presumption of innocence, have typically had the most impoverished regimes (King and Morgan 1976; Casale and Plotnikoff 1990; Morgan 1993) and vice versa. References to conditions that constitute 'an affront to civilised society' are invariably references to the Victorian local prisons.

What does this mean in terms of day-to-day practice? The best array of up-to-date descriptions of the quality of prisoners' lives in particular institutions is provided in the inspection reports of Her Majesty's Chief Inspector of Prisons.[3] In report after report, successive Chief Inspectors have chronicled the 'degrading' and 'insanitary' accommodation and slopping-out procedures; the 'enforced idleness'; the prolonged daily cellular confinement; the miserable conditions in which visits are held; and the general absence of facilities or prisoners' access to facilities (see Her Majesty's Chief Inspector of prisons [HMCIP] 1988, 1990*a*, 1990*b*, 1992, 1993 for particularly graphic recent examples). About the position of the untried there is general agreement. They generally get the least facilities

[3] Among earlier detailed descriptions of prison life are several research studies (Morris and Morris 1963; Emery 1970; Sparks 1971; Bottoms and McClintock 1973; King and Morgan 1976; King and Elliott 1977; Jones and Cornes 1977; Carlen 1983), some excellent prisoner, though regrettably no good staff, autobiographical accounts (Benney 1948; Norman 1958; Curtis 1973; Caird 1974; Boyle 1977, 1984; Peckham 1985), and a few structured anthologies of prisoner and prison staff descriptions and viewpoints (Parker 1970, 1973; Priestley 1989; Padel and Stevenson 1988; Casale 1989).

and are most oppressively confined. They are the 'forgotten people' (HMCIP 1989: para. 4.30), held in conditions that are 'completely insupportable' (House of Commons Home Affairs Committee 1981: para. 54), 'the worst . . . the prison system has to offer' (Stern 1987: 33). Most damningly, the Council of Europe Committee for the Prevention of Torture (the CPT) which, by virtue of the UK's ratification of a convention of the same name, undertook a visit of inspection of places of detention in August 1990 (for a full account of the operational practice of the CPT see Evans and Morgan 1992), concluded that conditions in Brixton, Leeds, and Wandsworth Prisons—all three Victorian local prisons—amounted to 'inhuman and degrading' treatment (Council of Europe 1991*a*). The Committee adopted a cumulative view of the adverse conditions they found. Thus conditions that might in themselves not be inhuman and degrading become so when combined with others. The building blocks in their judgement were three: overcrowding (of which the worst case found was three prisoners occupying a cell designed for one); lack of integral sanitation (prisoners having to defecate and urinate in plastic pots without privacy in front of cellmates); and lack of out-of-cell activities (some prisoners were confined to their cells for twenty-two and a half hours per day).

The phrase 'inhuman and degrading', employed for the first time in a published CPT report, cannot have been used lightly: it suggests that the conditions might be held to breach Article 3 of the European Convention for the Protection of Fundamental Human Rights. In fact it cannot be said that, if petitioned, the European Court of Human Rights (ECHR) would find such a breach: the CPT is not a judicial body and is guided by authorities other than the developing jurisprudence of the ECHR. None the less the CPT judgement is highly significant, first because it comes from an impartial international body and second because the British government's repudiation of the appellation (Council of Europe 1991*b*) contradicts what numerous British authorities have found the conditions described by the Committee to be. Certainly the conditions described by the CPT are not consistent with Prison Rules 1 and 2, with their references to encouraging useful lives, self-respect, and a sense of personal responsibility.

It might be argued that during the 1980s critical opinion of prisons policy became monomaniacally obsessed with the chronically bad physical conditions in the local prisons. This is not surprising. The building programme further improved conditions in the training prison sector, with the consequence that the state of the local prisons was thrown into ever starker relief. Moreover, as the increased system capacity was soaked up by the rise in the prison population, so the prospect of an end to overcrowding in the local prisons came to look like a mirage. The majority of persons experiencing imprisonment never saw anything but their local prison (Sparks 1971), and the courts maintained their hands-off policy regarding prisoners' general quality of life. Thus, raising basic standards in local prisons and remand centres became the litmus test for radical change. The penal pressure groups and prison staff associations unanimously pressed for the adoption of a code of minimum living standards which, set alongside a clearly delineated timetable for implementation, would in the end be incorporated in a new set of Prison Rules and made legally enforceable (Casale 1984; Gostin and Staunton 1985; Casale and Plotnikoff 1989, 1990). Part of the case for such a code of standards was that the effectiveness of all the grievance-ventilation and accountability mechanisms depended on there being a rudder by which various scrutineers could be induced to steer. This applied as much to the Inspectorate of Prisons as to prison boards of visitors and senior managers handling complaints within the Prison Service.

The present prisons inspectorate has existed since 1981 and is probably the single lasting achievement of the May Committee on whose recommendation it was set up (1979: 92–6). Before 1981 the prisons inspectorate was part of the management of the Prison Department and its reports were confidential. Today HMCIP, though part of the Home Office, is outwith the Prison Service and is directly responsible to the Home Secretary (see Morgan 1985 for an account of the creation and early operation of the Inspectorate). To that extent the inspectors can be said to be independent. The Chief Inspector is charged with reporting to the Minister 'on the treatment of prisoners and conditions in prison' (Prison Act 1952, s. 5a(3)), and does so by conducting regular inspections of prisons; undertaking occasional thematic reviews of aspects of policy; and investigating major incidents. All his reports are published and, as we have seen, many are severely critical and attract a good deal of media attention. However, it can be argued that the Chief Inspector's critiques sometimes lack policy bite because it is not clear by what standards he concludes that provisions are 'impoverished', 'degrading', or 'unacceptable'. On the occasions when his criteria and solutions are made precise, as in HMCIP's unequivocal denunciation of 'slopping out' (HMCIP 1989, and as co-author of Part II of the Woolf Report 1991: para. 11.105), the impact has been considerable. The Home Secretary has undertaken to advance the date jointly recommended by Lord Justice Woolf and HMCIP by which 'slopping out' should end (Home Office 1991*b*: para. 6.7).

Every prison in England and Wales is served by a board of visitors: a body of lay volunteers, currently appointed by the Secretary of State, and the last vestigial link with the days when most prisons were administered by local government. Until recently (April 1992) the boards had three functions: inspecting the state of the prison; hearing prisoner grievances; and undertaking disciplinary hearings of more serious charges. The third function was long held by critics to be incompatible with the first and second and the principal reason why the boards' 'watchdog' role was so poorly developed (Martin 1975; Justice 1983; Maguire and Vagg 1984; Prior Report 1985). This criticism, plus evidence that in spite of procedural improvements following the decision in 1979 that board hearings were subject to judicial review[4] there nevertheless remained major shortcomings in the quality of justice dispensed by boards (Light and Mattfield 1988; Morgan and Jones 1991), led to the recommendation that boards no longer be involved in disciplinary proceedings (Woolf Report 1991: paras. 14.363–14.435).[5] It remains to be seen whether boards, relieved of their disciplinary function and the close identification with local management to which the disciplinary role was said to lead, will be more willing publicly to criticize conditions or staff (boards, with some commendable exceptions, have repeatedly been accused of failing to act decisively during prison disturbances to protect prisoners from staff reprisals—see Home Office 1977; Thomas and Pooley 1980; Martin 1980; Woolf Report 1991: paras. 8.124–8.126). Nor is it clear that they will develop a less parochial and more collective voice in order to address the structural problems which give rise to poor conditions (Maguire and Vagg 1984; Vagg 1985).

[4] In 1975, in the first case (*Fraser* v. *Mudge* (1975) 3 All ER 1036) in which the courts looked at prison disciplinary hearings, the Court of Appeal held that prisoners were not entitled to legal representation. Hearings were said to be like summary disciplinary hearings in the armed forces. Likewise in 1978 the Divisional Court (*R.* v. *Board of Visitors of Hull Prison ex p. St Germain* (1978) 2 WLR 598) held that prison disciplinary hearings were not subject to judicial review. This decision was overturned by the Court of Appeal (*R.* v. *Board of Visitors of Hull Prison ex p. St Germain* (1979) 1 All ER 701), thereby opening up the prospect that this and other cases be decided by the courts on their merits. Five years later it was held (*R.* v. *Secretary of State ex p. Tarrant and another* (1984) 1 All ER 799) that though prisoners were not entitled to legal representation, Boards had a discretion to grant it, that they should exercise that discretion properly and in certain circumstances should grant it. (For reviews of legal intervention in disciplinary proceedings see Fitzgerald 1985; Prior Report 1985; Richardson 1993*a*.)

[5] Prior to April 1992 there were in effect three levels at which offences committed in prison could be dealt with. If they were relatively minor they were dealt with by governors whose powers of punishment were limited to twenty-eight days' loss of remission: 95 per cent of cases were dealt with by governors. If they were more serious they could be committed to the Board of Visitors, whose powers were limited to 120 days' loss of remission (prior to 1986 there was no limit to the amount of remission that boards could remove in the case of grave offences). In the case of serious offences against the prison disciplinary code (Prison Rule 47) that were also *prima facie* criminal offences, the prison authorities could refer the matter to the police who might in turn refer it to the Crown Prosecution Service with a view to prosecution. In April 1992 the middle tier was removed, meaning that the maximum punishment which could be imposed in internal proceedings was reduced from 120 to twenty-eight days' loss of remission, which, with the abolition of remission with the implementation in October 1992 of the Criminal Justice Act 1991, became twenty-eight days' deferred release.

It has been argued that boards of visitors, like HMCIP, will best develop their inspectoral role if they have clear standards by which to judge what they find and a national president to broaden their recruitment, organize their training, and inculcate good inspection practices with respect to those standards (Woolf 1991: para. 12.180; following opposition from board members the Home Secretary has announced that he will not now appoint a president for boards of visitors). This may be true also of boards' credibility with prisoners in respect of complaints. Prisoners have always been able to complain about any aspect of their custody to their board of visitors, to their governor, or to the Secretary of State by way of petition (in fact petitions were dealt with by a unit within the Prison Service headquarters). In 1990, following a series of reports (Ditchfield and Austin 1986; HMCIP 1987*a*; Home Office 1989), a new grievance system was introduced. The new integrated hierarchical system is designed, *inter alia*, to reduce the delays which characterized previous arrangements. Prisoners are now expected to complain first to unit managers or the duty governor or to the board of visitors, with the option, if they are dissatisfied with the outcome, of taking the matter further to the area manager. At all levels time limits for replies have been introduced and replies must be reasoned and in writing. Prisoners may still take up their complaints externally (to a member of parliament or to the 'ombudsman', or by seeking judicial review in the domestic or European courts), but these relatively time-consuming avenues are likely to be considered appropriate only for more serious complaints of particular types.

No systematic evaluation of the new complaints system has yet been conducted, though early reports on particular institutions from HMCIP suggest that the time limits are often breached. Critics, who suggest that the new arrangements mean only that prisoners get negative replies more quickly, agree with Lord Justice Woolf's observation that the system lacks a truly independent element. Woolf endorses the proposal (HMCIP 1987*a*; Home Office 1989*b*) that there be an independent 'complaints adjudicator' at the apex of the system (Woolf 1991: paras. 14.326–14.362). This proposal goes beyond the suggestion that there be a specialist prisons ombudsman whose remit would be restricted to cases involving maladministration (Birkinshaw 1985): Woolf's complaints adjudicator would be able to deal with any grievance and would also act as a final tribunal of appeal in relation to the internal disciplinary proceedings now handled entirely by governors. The government initially gave no undertaking to accede to Lord Justice Woolf's proposal (Home Office 1991*b*), but following the issue of a consultation paper (Prison Service 1992*b*), the decision has been made to appoint an independent adjudicator who will be known as the Prison Ombudsman. At the time of writing the incumbent is being appointed and his or her office will begin operation at the end of 1993.

Woolf's response to the prison standards debate was very different from the sentiments underlying Lord Godard's famous statement that 'it would be fatal to all discipline in prisons if governors and warders had to perform their duty with the fear of an action before their eyes if they in any way deviated from the rules' (*Arbon* v. *Anderson* [1943] KB 252), or Lord Denning's observation thirty years later that 'if the courts were to entertain actions by disgruntled prisoners, the governor's life would be made intolerable' (*Becker* v. *Home Office* [1972] 2QB 407). Much of the Woolf Report comprises an account of the intolerable conditions with which *prisoners* have to live and the absence of justice in prisons. Nevertheless, it is clear that Woolf did not favour excessive judicial intervention in prison life, certainly nothing approaching the extraordinary litigiousness of the US system (Jacobs 1980; Morgan and Bronstein 1985) which is nowhere replicated in Europe (Van Zyl Smit and Dunkel 1991). However, Woolf was clearly keen to extend the modest degree of judicial intervention which the domestic and European courts have undertaken in recent years (particularly in relation to disciplinary proceedings and prisoners' access to courts and lawyers).[6] In order to take up the general question of prisoners' living conditions, an issue about which the courts have hitherto shown singular reticence, Woolf favoured an interlocking hierarchy of 'contracts' or 'compacts'—between the Chief Executive of the Service and the Minister, between area managers and governors, between governors and officers, and between governors and prisoners—setting out the resources and facilities to be provided for a stated prison population. This would permit, in the case of prisoners, 'legitimate expectations' to be generated (Woolf Report 1991: para. 12.129), which 'could provide a platform for an application for judicial review' were those expectations unreasonably not met (ibid.: para. 12.123). However, prisoner contracts should not be drawn up in such a way that they would give prisoners private rights leading to awards of damages if breached. Further, were contracts to lead, as Woolf hoped, to the promulgation of aspirational standards, to a system of accrediting prisons for having achieved those standards (as happens in the USA) and, eventually, to the incorporation of those standards in a new set of Prison Rules, Woolf

[6] Regarding disciplinary hearings see note 4 above. Apart from disciplinary hearings, judicial intervention has been greatest and has had most practical effect with regard to prisoners' correspondence and access to the courts, both areas of direct interest to the legal profession. Initial headway was made in Strasbourg by the European Court of Human Rights (ECHR). For example, the case of *Silver* v. *UK* (1983: 5 EHRR 347) led to significant changes in the system of censorship. Domestic concessions to European decisions have been made neither willingly nor swiftly but the government has had to bow to pressure in the end. Moreover, the British courts have been gradually influenced by the positions adopted by the ECHR: subsequent decisions about prisoners' correspondence, for example, have paid heed to the *Silver* decision. See Feldman 1993, Richardson 1993*a* for detailed discussion of reported cases and their policy impact.

does not favour those new Rules vesting private rights in prisoners. They would be enforceable only by judicial review (ibid.: para. 12.117).

Nevertheless, Woolf considered that prisoners should be given reasons, in writing if they reasonably request it, 'for any decision which materially and adversely affects them' (ibid.: paras. 14.300, 14.307). Were this done it would be a considerable change from the present position in which prisoners can be and are transferred in large numbers, without explanation, to prisons relatively distant from their homes as part of normal 'training' allocation, better to distribute prisoner numbers within the prison estate, or as an administrative control measure. Prisoners may also be administratively segregated for control reasons under Rule 43; hitherto prisoners have had no entitlement to be given reasons for either their initial security classification or the reviews of their security classification which take place from time to time. All these decisions critically affect the quality of prisoners' lives. The manner in which such decisions are made would be significantly altered if Woolf's recommendations were pursued in respect of the development of 'community prisons', (ibid.: paras. 11.49–11.68) and of sentence planning in a manner which fully encouraged prisoner responsibility (ibid.: paras. 14.57–14.83; King 1993), and if the proportion of prisoners in high-security categories were significantly reduced as successive reviewers of the system have recommended (King and Morgan 1980: ch. 3; Prison Department 1981; Morgan 1983; Home Office 1984; HMCIP 1984; Scottish Prison Service 1990; Hadfield and Lakes 1991).

Woolf argued that the degree to which there can be a stable relationship between the expectations of prisoners and the services delivered by prison officers on prison landings is ultimately dependent on there being a compact between the Minister and the Chief Executive of the Prison Service, comprising a prospective statement covering the year ahead setting out objectives, tasks, and resources (Woolf Report 1991: paras. 12.47–12.48). The purpose is to address the perennial complaint of prison administrators that they are unable to control the demands made on them: the corollary of the observation that the sentencers who directly determine the size of the prison population have no responsibility for the consequences of their decisions. Of course, politicians indirectly determine the size of the prison population and directly determine the resources allocated to prison administrators (Rutherford 1984). Woolf's compact is designed to make that political fact clear for all to see, and yet insulate the Service from day-to-day political interference. For much the same reason, Woolf recommended that there be introduced a prison rule that no prison hold more prisoners than 3 per cent above its CNA, except temporarily, or following the laying by the Minister of an authorizing certificate before both Houses of Parliament (ibid.: paras. 11.141–11.142).

The purpose is to ensure that decisions to overcrowd are seen to be high-profile political decisions rather than stealthy administrative decisions about which commentators learn only after the event. The government, not surprisingly, has said that it will consider introducing such a rule when there is equilibrium between prison system capacity and the size of the prison population—i.e. when there is no further any pressing need for it (Home Office 1991*b*.: para. 6.13).

Woolf was agnostic about whether the Prison Service should become an agency, but agency status was entirely consistent with his other recommendations and, not surprisingly, the government, after taking further managerial advice (Lygo 1991), decided on this course in both England and Scotland. The decision was uncontroversial and marked a return to the *status quo ante* 1963, when the Prison Commission outwith the Home Office ran prisons (Thomas 1972, 1980). More controversial, however, was the decision by the government to privatize the management of whole prisons. Privatization now enjoys a good deal of pragmatic support from those who see it as a backdoor means of quickly establishing higher standards and thus enhancing accountability (Taylor and Pease 1989; see Logan 1990 for a general review of the arguments for and against the privatization of prisons). Moreover, the contracting out of particular services within prisons—for example, education and training (for which tenders are being received at the time of writing), escorts (for which specific provision is made in the Criminal Justice Act 1991), employment workshops, food, clothing, and maintenance—can be seen as the normalization of prison regimes for which critics have long pressed (King and Morgan 1980). Contractors could take various forms, profit-making or otherwise. However, critics of privatization, particularly those critical of the commercial management of whole institutions, maintain that it is wrong in principle to derive profits from imprisonment. Further, they fear that the vested commercial interests that will be built up will serve to extend resort to custody. Moreover, they doubt that financial savings will accrue: the costs to contractors will never be comparable to those incurred by the state. The latter will always have to provide a back-up service in the event of the contractor losing control (this contingency is specifically provided for by the Criminal Justice Act 1991, s. 88) and the state service will almost certainly be left with responsibility for the high-security and more intractable, and thus more costly, sectors of the system.

The latter point is crucial, because the Prison Service has become preoccupied (as have other systems in Europe—see Van Zyl Smit and Dunkel 1991; Muncie and Sparks 1991) with the containment and control of a relatively small but growing number of long-term and allegedly 'dangerous' or 'disruptive' prisoners (see Bottoms and Light 1987). Thirty years ago there was no talk of dangerous prisoners and no maximum-security accommodation in the system. Now there exist almost 3,000 places in the dispersal prisons, plus the network of special security and special (control) units (SSUs and SUs), of which there are currently three each. The terminology represents an important distinction. Prisoners who are a *security* risk are not necessarily a *control* problem. Indeed, though the two occasionally overlap, quite the contrary. Many prisoners who have the personal capacity and external organizational backing to escape from relatively secure prisons—international drugs racketeers, for example—are often model prisoners (though according to Laycock (1983: 33) over 70 per cent of terrorists were considered by staff to be involved in subversive activity). Conversely, some prisoners who are judged to present a profound danger to the public were they to escape are themselves at risk within the prison community. For example, there are now more than 3,000 sex offenders in prison, many of them segregated for their own protection (almost 2,000 prisoners were subject to protective segregation under Prison Rule 43 or Young Offender Rule 46 in 1991—see Home Office 1991*a*, para. 16) or held in the vulnerable prisoner units (VPUs) of which there are currently thirteen.

The proliferation of special prisoner statuses and units poses problems for procedural and substantive justice. It also complicates the question of standards and upsets the balance of incentives and disincentives for good behaviour (Home Office 1984). Model prisoners may, in King and Elliot's phrase (1977), be held in an 'electronic coffin' if considered a security threat (see Walmsley 1989 for a review of the history and operation of the SSUs) or suffer an indefensibly impoverished regime in segregation if they are repeatedly attacked by fellow prisoners (Priestley 1981; Prison Reform Trust 1990). Conversely, some special units may absorb such disproportionate resources, afford so many privileges, and gain such a prestigious reputation that the envy and opposition of the service is excited because it is said that the occupants are being rewarded for their bad behaviour.[7] How to create conditions within which security and order can be achieved with respect to long-term and difficult prisoners, yet create a ladder of opportunity whereby those prisoners who at no stage present problems can be rewarded, and high-security prisoners will wish to be recategorized and transferred to less secure conditions, is the single most difficult management issue confronting the Prison Service (Home Office 1984; Dunbar 1985; Scottish Prison Service 1990). Before considering

[7] The most famous example of the marginalization of a special unit concerned the Barlinnie prison Special Unit, Glasgow (see Boyle 1977; Carrell and Laing 1982; Boyle 1984; Coyle 1987, 1991; Cooke 1989). In England Grendon Underwood prison, a prison which provides a psychiatrically orientated therapeutic regime which has not been replicated elsewhere, has to some extent suffered the same process (see Genders and Player 1989*b*).

how the English Prison Service is addressing that issue, and what the future shape of the system is likely to be, we need first to consider the social dynamics of prison life.

THE SOCIOLOGY OF PRISONS

Prisons represent the power of the state ultimately to coerce, and order within prisons may in the last resort rest on the use of force by staff. Yet disorder is not the norm of prison life. Order in prisons, as in any other social setting, is negotiated (McDermott and King 1988). The negotiation is not between equals; yet order within prisons is for the most part achieved with the consent, albeit the grudging consent, of prisoners who invariably far outnumber the prison officers who guard them. Disturbances may have become a perennial feature of the British penal landscape, but most prisons are orderly most of the time. By the same token, the 80,000 offences against the prison disciplinary code that are punished each year belie the fact that staff and prisoners generally coexist relatively harmoniously: frictions are for the most part resolved through more subtle accommodations or, occasionally, through the use of what the Prison Officers' Association once described honestly as the 'alternative disciplinary system' (1984: 2). These assertions prompt the question as to what counts as order within prisons and whose standpoint prevails.

The sociological literature on prisons points to the existence of a prison culture—a set of attitudes and a way of doing things—in which both prisoners and prison officers have roles. This literature is for the most part American and is largely based on studies of long-term prisoners in relatively high-security prisons. It is questionable, therefore, to what extent that literature applies to Britain and to all prisons within Britain. Few social scientists have been permitted to set up their anthropological huts on British prison landings,[8] and though a good deal can be learnt about life in prison from the autobiographical accounts of prisoners, few prisoners have written analytically about the minutiae of daily life.[9] Prison staff, retired or serving, have contributed even less to the literature and to our understanding.[10]

[8] The most prominent exceptions have been the Morrises (Morris and Morris 1963), King and colleagues (King and Morgan 1976; King and Elliott 1977; King and McDermott 1989, 1992); Carlen (1983); and Bottoms and colleagues (Bottoms and McClintock 1973; Hay *et al.* 1990). Though not allowed to set up their hut on a landing, Cohen and Taylor (1972) gathered rich material on long-term prisoners' experience of custody by running an educational class within a prison.

[9] Notable recent British exceptions have been Caird (1974), Boyle (1977, 1984), and Peckham (1985). There is of course a rich international literature of prison writings, of which the most important recent analytical example is Serge (1970).

[10] As far as I am aware no British prison governor or officer, retired or serving, has

To the extent that prisons exhibit a specific culture there has been a long-standing debate as to whether it is of primarily indigenous or imported origin. The indigenous approach is represented by Sykes's classic account of the *Society of Captives* (1958) and Goffman's seminal discussion of *Asylums* (1968). Both writers stress the distinctiveness of prison life (Sykes specifically and Goffman generally in relation to what he calls 'total' institutions—prisons, closed psychiatric hospitals, detention camps, etc.) because of its encompassing character, relatively shut off as prisoners are from the world at large. Within this tradition the prison has been seen as a more or less closed social system in which it is the task of one group of persons, the prison officers, to manage or process another group, the prisoners. Sykes's focus is on the 'pains of imprisonment'—the various deprivations that living in prisons involves—while Goffman's stress is on the dynamics of mortification—the transformation of the self—that allegedly results from entering a 'people-processing' institution. In both accounts the prisoner is described as being under psychological assault, with the usual supports for and expressions of personal identity—possessions, control over personal appearance, autonomy of movement, personal privacy and security, etc.—being severely diminished. Prisoners may develop individualistic responses to these stresses, responses ranging from escape attempts or playing the role of the barrack-room lawyer to psychological withdrawal or intensive autodidacticism. However, for Sykes the distinctive aspect of the prison culture—largely, though not entirely, its emphasis on prisoner solidarity against staff—represents a functional response to these social and psychological assaults: a means by which the rejected can reject their rejectors (McCorkle and Korn 1954) and thus maintain a degree of self-esteem. According to this view, the more that prisoners adopt a cohesive stance, the more the pains of imprisonment can be mitigated for everyone. This process represents a paradox. Some of the relative deprivations of prison life are the result of staff attempts to maintain external security and internal order. Yet to some extent the pains of imprisonment stimulate a solidaristic counter-culture subversive of official objectives. Thus the apparently total power of staff is compromised by their need to reach an accommodation with their charges in order that routine tasks be accomplished. In this way, whatever purposes prisons officially pursue—treatment and training,

written about his experience since Miller (1976) and Cronin (1967): neither of these accounts, or indeed those of predecessors (see Priestley 1989 for an anthology), is particularly analytical or repays attention, except in ways the authors probably did not intend. By contrast, several of the best-known American contributions to the sociology of prisons literature have come from persons with direct involvement in prisons administration: Clemmer (1940) was a senior prisons administrator; Morris (1974) was appointed a 'special master' by a court to oversee the implementation of an order relating to a prison; and, most recently, Dilulio (1987), a former warden, has reflected generally on the business of *Governing Prisons*.

rehabilitation, deterrence, and so on—are in practice undermined by the daily reality of the negotiated settlements which take place between prison officers and prisoners. This suggests that in reality prisons are unlikely to be about the pursuit of noble missions: they are ultimately about practical survival in settings which, because inherently coercive, have extreme potential for instability and disorder.

The problem with indigenous accounts of prison culture is that they fail to provide any ready explanation of change other than the sort of minor shifts from crisis to equilibrium which might occur within a closed system. For example, indigenous accounts do not explain the more fundamental changes in operational policy and prisoner response which, as we have seen, have taken place in British prisons since 1945 or, more dramatically, which occurred in American prison systems in the wake of the black civil rights movement in the 1960s. By contrast, importationist theorists stress the connection between relationships within prisons and those outside—for example, changes in political expectations, the legitimacy of authority and legal culture (see Jacobs' classic study of *Stateville* Prison, Illinois: Jacobs 1977). Importationists also highlight the degree to which the cultural norms to which prisoners subscribe, and the individual roles within prison they adopt, are extensions of subcultures of which they were a part, or roles that they occupied, before being incarcerated (Irwin and Cressey 1962; Irwin 1970). According to this approach the prison culture is not peculiar to the prison at all: it is both a microcosm of the wider society and a sort of career continuation of the criminal culture of the streets from which a high proportion of prisoners are drawn. Thus Irwin and Cressey identify a 'thief subculture' outside prison which stresses group loyalty and toughness: to the extent that there is group solidarity between *some* prisoners within prison, then this 'convict' or 'prisoner' subculture is both an extension of that street culture *and* an adaptation in response to the contingencies of life inside.

Today the indigenous and importationist perspectives are seen not as contradictory but as complementary (Carroll 1974; Jacobs 1979). Moreover, whatever is to be learnt from the American literature, British prisons are unlikely to exhibit the same cultural patterns as have been found in the USA. There has not, for example, been sophisticated organized crime in Britain on the scale found in the USA; nor, with one or two notable exceptions in particular cities, have criminal street gangs regularly employing life-threatening violence been a normal feature of British crime, and thus their influence has not been felt within prisons. Further, as we have seen, maximum-security prisons, of the kind which are widely employed for the mainstream prison population in some US states (Texas, for example: see Martin and Ekland-Olson 1987), have only recently become part of the English system, and even today only a small proportion of the prison population is housed in such conditions. Finally, though British society is riven by deeply engrained class differences and, since the mass immigration from the Caribbean and the Indian subcontinent in the period since 1945, racial divides, Britain is nevertheless a relatively homogeneous society culturally. There are not the fundamental cleavages which in the USA have historically separated the African-American from the white population and in more recent times, the Hispanic from the English-speaking community. These cleavages have fatally dominated the American prison scene to an extent hitherto undreamt-of in Britain and, indeed, Western Europe. It may not be surprising, therefore, that Mathieson's (1965) study of a Norwegian prison (Norway almost certainly has less of a criminal subculture and less organized crime than Britain, and is not noted for its tough prisons) failed to reveal much in the way of prisoner solidarity. On the contrary, prisoners were relatively weak and isolated: they were vulnerable to the discretionary favours which the staff were in a position to distribute.

The British 'sociology of prisons' literature has drawn on both the indigenous and importationist accounts and has emphasized the complexity and varied quality of prison communities: researchers, critical of stereotypical portrayals of staff and prisoners, have argued that both groups adapt to the particular circumstances in which they find themselves. Total institutions may be characterized by social relations and 'ways of doing things' that are different from those prevailing in the world outside, but prisons nevertheless differ a good deal along all the regime dimensions that Goffman (1968) provisionally identified (see Jones and Cornes 1977: ch. 4; King and McDermott 1989). Further, it is clear that the regimes which different groups of prisoners experience differ considerably within prisons (King and Morgan 1976; ch. 3): this is evident also from many of the institutional reports of HMCIP. Thus, while prisoners' responses to custody may owe much to their previous institutional and criminal careers, they are also shaped by the length of their sentences (see e.g. Sapsford 1983, on life-sentence prisoners), the physical restrictions to which they are subject (see Cohen and Taylor 1972, on a high-security unit), and whatever opportunities and facilities (or lack of them) the prisons provide (King and Elliott 1977; Hay *et al.* 1990).

By the same token, it is clear from the dismally limited literature on prison staff that the background characteristics of prison officers have changed a good deal in recent years, as have their working conditions. Officers now, as in the past, generally join the Service in their late twenties or thirties, after spells in other occupations. But whereas the overwhelming majority used to be recruited from the armed forces, usually as regulars rather than from national service, this is seldom the case today (Morris and Morris 1963: ch. 4; Jones and Cornes 1977: ch. 7; Marsh *et al.* 1985). Twenty years ago, virtually no prison officers had any educational qualifications. Today the indelibly working-class culture of the majority, shaped now by previous experience of manual or clerical work rather than military discipline, is blended with a sizeable minority of recruits with 'A' levels or degrees (26 per cent in 1985; see Marsh *et al.* 1985: table 3.6) seeking advancement within an integrated career structure. Moreover, the simple world of the 'gentleman' governors and prison 'screws' of the 1940s and 1950s has been complicated by the employment of women in all institutions and at all levels, and the importation of specialists who, in the 1960s and 1970s at least, took on the majority of the plum 'treatment and training' tasks—education, social work, and the various therapies with which the Service flirted (Thomas 1972: ch. 9). It needs always to be remembered that prison officers typically spend a far higher proportion of their lives in prison than do their charges. They also have a culture, shaped by their previous experience and the increasingly complicated managerial context within which they operate. The living conditions of prisoners are the working conditions of prison officers.

In criminal career terms, indigenous and importationist factors may reinforce each other. Clemmer (1940), a pioneer American analyst of the prison community, wrote of the process of 'prisonization', the gradual destructive socialization of prisoners into the norms of prison life which make it difficult for them successfully to adapt to law-abiding life outside, thereby possibly deepening criminality. The idea of prisonization, which most researchers have rejected on the grounds that it posits too mechanical and linear a process, bears a close resemblance to the idea of institutionalization, a syndrome which analysts of closed mental hospitals have employed to describe the adjustment, with pathological consequences, of patients to stultifying regimes (see Barton 1959). Most of the prison studies identify a minority of prisoners whose reaction to custody is one of extreme social withdrawal or retreatism, but such prisoners appear to be in a minority (see Morris and Morris 1963: 173–4). However, there are abundant references to prisoners learning or knowing how to 'do time' passively 'behind their doors', and the prisoners adopting this approach are said typically to be 'old lags' who have been imprisoned on many previous occasions and who are resistant to more open regimes, enhanced association, and the like (see Morris and Morris 1963: 172–3; King and Elliott 1977: 241–4). These recidivist prisoners may well be said to be 'institutionalized' or 'prisonized' within a penal tradition which was still the norm when the Morrises undertook their study of Pentonville in the early 1960s, and which still lives on in many of the local prisons where most short-sentence prisoners continue to do their time today.

To the extent that there is a prisoner culture it is plausible to see it as the product of utilitarian responses which different groups of prisoners, depending on their background, reputation, offence, and length of sentence, make to the pressures and opportunities arising out of captivity. There may be an informal code of not 'grassing' to staff, but there is also as much rivalry and hatred in prisons as there is comradeship (Morris and Morris 1963: 168). Moreover, there are plenty of ways in which prisoners can and do inform staff about those prisoners whose behaviour they may wish to control, either for reasons of power play or simply to prevent a breakdown in the orderliness which most prisoners and staff have a vested interest in preserving. All the British studies emphasize with Sykes that one of the worst aspects of prison life is having to live with other prisoners. This may be because fellow prisoners are 'dirty in their personal habits, socially unpleasant or guilty of crimes which other prisoners regard as revolting' (Morris and Morris 1963: 168–9), or because of a lack of privacy within a highly restricted physical space (Cohen and Taylor 1972: 80–1), or because of the discomforting strategies which colleagues adopt to cope with whatever time they have to serve (King and Elliott 1977: ch. 8), or for reasons of racial prejudice (Genders and Player 1989*a*).

Clearly there are moral and power hierarchies within prison communities. One of the reasons why most prisoners are keen that order, however tenuous, should be maintained (and, as a corollary, do not wish to get involved in any incident if it erupts), is that major disturbances provide perfect opportunities to settle scores and confirm moral hierarchies (see e.g. Woolf 1991, section 3, for a graphic account of the riot in April 1990 at Strangeways Prison, Manchester). It is doubtful that British prisoner communities can be simply characterized in class analogy terms in which the gangsters constitute a ruling class and the sex offenders (or 'nonces') a lumpenproletariat (Genders and Player 1989*b*): the categories 'gangster' and 'sex offender' are themselves problematic and subject to subtle qualifications relating to the nature of a prisoner's original offence and the reputation he or she establishes and maintains within prison (Cohen and Taylor 1972: ch. 3). Nevertheless, it is clear that certain categories of sex offenders, particularly those who have committed offences against children, are generally preyed on and anathematized (to the extent that they have to request segregation or are segregated), and that established professional criminals who have experienced prison before, who are generally older and are doing longer than average sentences, tend within training prisons to be the 'top men' (King and Elliott 1977: 254–6). But social prominence within the prison community is a complex matter. Whereas Irwin's professional Californian thieves were allegedly orientated to the outside world, King and Elliott's 'top men' had as few outside contacts as their 'retreatists'. Nor were they heavily involved in the prisoner culture of barter in contraband goods and power cliques. On the contrary, their reputation enabled them to secure good positions (attractive cell locations and valued jobs) and non-interference from prisoners and staff alike, so that they were able to 'do their own bird' in relative peace and security. The prisoners prominent in 'jailing' activities—regarded by the 'top men' as 'hotheads', 'tearaways', and 'Borstal boys'—were on the whole younger, shorter-sentence prisoners whose criminal careers were disorganized (ibid.: 250–2).

It follows that power structures within prisons vary a good deal according to the nature of the prison (there has, for example, been virtually no research attention given to the predatory behaviour which, according to HMCIP, dominates some young offender and low-security adult institutions—see HMCIP 1992*b*, *c* for two recent examples) and depend less on a rigid class structure and rather more on a fluid pattern of competing groups based on ethnic and regional affinities as well as prior friendships and 'business' interests (Hay *et. al.* 1990: para. 5.63). This conclusion makes comprehensible the fact that attempts at predicting where trouble will occur and who will spark it off, or participate in incidents once they have started, have borne little fruit. Ditchfield's wide-ranging review (1990) of the literature on disturbances and control in prisons found there was little evidence that the likelihood of incidents could straightforwardly be related to such factors as overcrowding, architectural design, or prisoner facilities, though changes, both positive and negative, likely to destabilize power structures and relationships seemed to increase the likelihood of disorder (see also Adams 1992: chs. 5–7). Moreover, attempts by prison psychologists to identify prisoners likely to be control problems, or to find common features among those prisoners identified by governors as control problems and transferred to special units, have not been conspicuously successful (see Williams and Longley 1987; and a critical review by King and McDermott 1990). Nor, despite references by senior prison administrators to disorder-prone 'toxic mixes' in their reviews of some recent prison disorders (see HMCIP 1987*b* on disturbances at Wymott and Northeye in 1986; also Ditchfield 1990: ch. 4), was the Woolf Inquiry able to identify a pattern among the prisoners prominent in the 1990 disturbances. There was, as Lord Justice Woolf concluded, 'no single cause of the riots and no simple solution or action which will prevent rioting' (Woolf Report 1991: para. 9.23), nor was there any basis on which prisoners could be categorized for 'control' as opposed to 'security' purposes (ibid.: paras. 9.43–9.50). The fact 'that a prisoner who creates control problems in one prison, may behave with complete propriety in another' (ibid.: para. 9.48) suggested to Woolf that more attention needed to be paid to the quality of relationships between prisoners and staff, to the nature of regimes, to procedural justice, and to day-to-day fairness (ibid.: section 9).

This is in line with what analysts of the prison community have long maintained: namely, that 'order' and 'control' are not synonymous (Young 1987). Given his broader insight it is unfortunate, therefore, that Woolf employed 'control' rather than 'order' in his troika of objectives—'security', 'control', and 'justice'—to be kept in balance (ibid.: paras. 9.19–9.23; see Morgan 1992*a* for commentary). For whereas control measures may be designed to achieve order, they tend often to produce the reverse outcome. This is the essence of King and McDermott's (1990) critical analysis of the use of transfers to control 'troublesome' prisoners and of Hay *et al.*'s (1990) comparison of the staff–prisoner dynamics in two dispersal prisons.

There are three lessons to be derived from such research. First, though there are undoubtedly a few prisoners whose response to most penal situations is so disruptive or aggressive—the extreme case being prisoners who have killed within prison—that they must for a time be placed in special units, attention needs most to be paid to trouble-generating *situations* and *procedures* rather than to the relatively illusive 'disruptive' population. Removal of 'troublesome' prisoners is seldom a solution. Such prisoners are labelled and often go on to confirm their labels (Boyle's autobiographical accounts, 1977 and 1984, are object lessons in this process) and the situation within which their troublesome behaviour was first identified typically generates further trouble (Hay and Sparks 1991). Second, and following logically from the first, it is the regime experienced by the 'mainstream' population which has crucially to be got right. It is within mainstream situations that trouble sporadically occurs and, as we have seen, the proliferation of special units disrupts the ladder of incentives and disincentives on which the stability and fairness of the whole system ultimately rests. Third, positive relationships between prisoners and basic grade prison officers are critical to the quality of prisoners' lives. This suggests, to take the crime-preventative analogy adopted by Hay *et al.* (1990), that benefits are likely to flow from adopting a 'social' rather than 'situational' control strategy, in effect what Dunbar (1985) has termed 'dynamic security'. This involves devising 'active' regimes for prisoners in which prison officers are positively involved *with* prisoners in the delivery of programmes, services, and facilities between which prisoners may exercise a degree of responsible choice. It is not without significance that the same lessons are implicit in the developing literature on suicide prevention in prison (Lloyd 1990). There are a few prisoners who recognizably feel so suicidal that they can be identified and focused measures taken to prevent them taking their own lives (Prison Service 1992*a*; Liebling 1992). The latter should not involve segregation in an environment within which suicide is made physically impossible: by definition, 'strip cells' of the sort that used regularly to be employed can only deepen the slough of despond. More importantly, a high proportion of prison suicides are not predictable: they occur more or less randomly within the mainstream population. The solution is to enhance the quality of life for all prisoners in an attempt to mitigate the pressures which give rise to suicidal tendencies (HMCIP 1990*b*). This focus on general prison standards was central to the Woolf Report.

THE FUTURE

In his oral evidence to the Woolf Inquiry, the then Director General of the Prison Service maintained:

> The life and work of the Prison Service have, for the last twenty years, been distorted by the problem of overcrowding. That single factor has dominated pressure on staff, and as a consequence has soured industrial relations. It has skewed managerial effort . . . away from positive developments. The removal of overcrowding is . . . an indispensable pre-condition of sustained and universal improvement in prison conditions . . . the canker of overcrowding must be rooted out.[11]

This explanation of the ills that have beset the English system is over-simplified, not least because overcrowding and resources could arguably have been managed in a different manner. Nevertheless, there is no doubt that system overcrowding makes the reallocation of priorities and resources more difficult: there is literally less room for manœuvre. It follows that the future likely shape of the prison system depends heavily on whether there is a political will to bring the size of the prison population into better balance with the prison estate. At the time of writing (early 1993) the prison system is for the first time in almost half a century not overcrowded: there are approximately 2,000 more places than prisoners. This does not mean that institutional overcrowding has been eliminated: on the contrary, because there is need for a margin of approximately 5 per cent of places to cope with contingencies such as damage and refurbishment, and because the estate is currently not well matched to the geographical and legal pattern of court committals, there remains a good deal of under- and overoccupation of establishments. In the longer term, the prospects for an end to prison overcrowding hang in the balance. It is unclear what the impact of the Criminal Justice Act 1991 will be for sentencing policy (the parole changes alone will increase the population, but may be offset by reductions in the sentencing tariff—see chapter 17 in this volume); the government has been less than robust in rebutting a sustained police campaign about 'offences while on bail' with possibly

[11] Evidence of Mr Chris Train: transcript of Seminar D, Day 6, Lord Justice Woolf's Inquiry into Prison Disturbances, City University, 22 October 1990: 5.

adverse consequences for the size of the remand population (see Morgan and Jones 1992); the extensive prison building programme of the 1980s is coming to an end; and the latest Home Office projections suggest that the prison population will rise to 57,500 by the year 2000 (Home Office 1992c). By far the largest percentage increase is predicted for the remand population. Were this population increase allowed to occur then, without a further building programme, there will be system overcrowding into the twenty-first century. If that were to happen it seems improbable that the structural reforms recommended by Lord Justice Woolf would be implemented.

The government has claimed to have accepted practically all that Woolf proposed (Home Office 1991*b*: para. 13). However, no timetable has been set down for the implementation of Woolf's core propositions, neither has the government undertaken to increase spending, or refrain from clawing back the Prison Service budget in the event of the prison population being reduced. It is said only that the 'necessary changes must be taken forward gradually over the coming years' and that 'not everything can be afforded immediately' (ibid.: para. 3). Further, even where temporal targets have been specified, it is far from clear, in the absence of precise standards, what they mean. For example, the government has made much of the fact that it has advanced from February 1996 to December 1994 the date by which Woolf recommended that slopping out should end (ibid.: para. 6.7). But what does having 'full access to sanitation' mean, and are all the possible arrangements acceptable which, once introduced, would enable the government to say that they have honoured their undertaking? For example, sharing a small cell containing a relatively unscreened lavatory, of the sort which HMCIP describes being introduced in some establishments (see HMCIP 1992*a*), is arguably not much less demeaning than sharing a cell without sanitation: it involves, as some commentators have put it, living in a lavatory.

It is precisely this sort of critique which makes it essential that explicit physical and regime standards be promulgated and their attainment monitored. There is policy movement on this front. For example, at the time of writing consultation documents on a method for formulating standards are being circulated and the government has undertaken to 'prepare a model regime for local prisons and remand centres, taking particular account of the needs for unconvicted prisoners' (Home Office 1991*b*: para. 7.17). A draft of that model regime has been written (Prison Service 1991) and its contents very largely reproduce the unprecedentedly high regime standards stipulated in the tender documents circulated to potential contractors for the management of the first privatized prisons (Home Office 1991*d*, 1992*e*). However, whereas the Wolds is already delivering these superior standards, senior Prison Service officials have talked of the passage of twenty to twenty-five years before state-run local prisons will be able to achieve the same standards: this estimate, which was lent credibility by the Home Secretary,[12] has done nothing to inspire confidence that lessons have been learnt from the disturbances of 1990 and that change is being sought with urgency. Meanwhile, deplorable physical conditions and impoverished regimes continue to be reported by HMCIP—the latest to be published concern Lewes Prison (HMCIP 1992*d*) and Cardiff Prison (HMCIP 1993)—and disturbances continue (a major riot took place at Reading Remand Centre in December 1992). If the government and Prison Service pursue a three-track standards policy, as currently appears to be the case—the contracted-out sector, the local prisons and remand centres, and the rest—that would seem to be a recipe bound to promote substantive and perceived inequity likely to lead to further trouble with both prisoners and staff.

Some of the structural reforms recommended by Woolf will undoubtedly take time and are not without their operational problems. For example, Woolf's proposition that the vast majority of prisoners be held throughout their time in custody in redesignated 'community prisons' (prisons physically proximate to their occupants' community ties and in which links with families and local services will be positively encouraged—Woolf Report 1991, para 11.63) could be operationalized in one of two ways. In those parts of the country where there are relatively few committals it could mean single establishments serving comprehensive multi-functional purposes: such prisons would have to be sub-divided to cater for men and women, young and old, untried, convicted, and sentenced. In urban areas generating many committals and already well supplied with institutions, the maintenance of institutional specialization would be compatible with the concept of the community prison. Even so, there are several policy dilemmas to resolve. For example, because the integration of convicted and unconvicted prisoners has historically been to the detriment of the latter, many commentators maintain that the convicted and unconvicted must be rigidly segregated, ideally in different institutions (see Home Office 1991*b*: para. 5.19; Morgan 1993). For much the same reason, some feminist commentators are opposed to the accommodation of women within the same establishments as men (Tchaikovsky 1991; Carlen 1992). Further, some parts of the country (London in particular) generate many more committals than there are institutions and

[12] The address by the then Home Secretary, Mr Kenneth Baker, to the Annual General Meeting of the Prison Reform Trust, July 1991; comments made by a senior Prison Service official to a seminar on the 'Model Regime' paper at Newbold Revel Training College, December 1991 (these comments are not recorded in the official account of the seminar—Directorate of Inmate Programmes, *Report on the Seminar on the Model Regime for Local Prisons and Remand Centres, 16–18 December 1991*, Regime Management Report no. 5, Prison Service, 1992).

bed-places: unless some prisoners are removed to more distant locations then plausible 'community prisons' will be intolerably overcrowded.

The government has quite reasonably argued, therefore, that Woolf's proposals involve 'competing aims' which, in the short term at least, 'may be irreconcilable' (Home Office 1991*b*, para 5.5). For example, the more that prisons are specialized, or different categories of prisoners are separated from each other, the less likely it is that the estate will be used efficiently, that overcrowding will be prevented, and that prisoners will be kept as close to their community ties as possible. There has to be some flexibility. If prisoners are to be treated as responsible individuals, and given reasons for decisions as Woolf recommended that they should, then it would seem desirable that some of the dilemmas to which the government has drawn attention should be resolved by asking prisoners to make choices. For example, women may have to choose between being held in a multi-functional establishment close to home (thereby permitting family visits with ease) but with relatively poor facilities, and transfer to a distant specialist establishment for women providing a superior regime. The system of 'sentence planning', which the Service claims now to be introducing (Home Office 1991*b*: paras. 7.15–7.19), should involve a shift towards decision-making *by* rather than *for* prisoners. Their choices must not, however, be between equally unacceptable alternatives.

This raises, in conclusion, the whole question of prisoners' contracts, pilot schemes for which are already reported to be in operation (ibid.: para. 7.20). The problem, from the prisoner's standpoint, with the concept of contracts is that the public law doctrine of 'legitimate expectations' to which Lord Justice Woolf referred, is a desperately fragile one. It is, as Richardson (1993*b*) puts it, a 'notoriously flexible' doctrine on which to hang hopes of redress with regard to general prison conditions. To have a legitimate expectation to some programme or facility is not to have a right to it. It seems unlikely, therefore, that were the Prison Service to plead operational difficulties—a surge in the prison population, an industrial dispute, the loss of accommodation as a result of a disturbance, for example—the courts would decide that the expectations must be satisfied. Moreover, contrary to Woolf's high hopes, contracts may turn out to be more of a means to control individual prisoners *by* the authorities than they will prove a mechanism for effective remedy and structural change for prisoners *against* the authorities. The 'compacts' (a term the Service appears to favour over 'contracts') with which the Service is experimenting are described in terms reminiscent of contracts with clients in a social work context. They set out what facilities are to be provided and what is expected in return. The compact may provide the basis for a complaint against the authorities on the one hand or for withdrawal of facilities or disciplinary measures on the other. Such contracts may turn out to be accompanied by generally improved conditions. But there is nothing inherent in the way the device is being adopted which either implies or assures that outcome. It is not at all clear that the legacy of Woolf will be what he intended.

Selected Further Reading

Discussions of imprisonment ideally take place within the broader context of the debate on the philosophy and sociology of punishment: Nigel Walker's *Why Punish* (Oxford: Oxford University Press, 1991) is an excellent introduction to the former question and David Garland's *Punishment and Modern Society* (Oxford: Oxford University Press, 1990) provides a masterly overview of the major theorists who have explored the latter issue.

The current organization of imprisonment is heavily influenced by past practice. Michael Ignatieff's *A Just Measure of Pain* (London: Macmillan, 1978) provides an inspirational account of the emergence of imprisonment as the principal penalty for serious crime at the end of the eighteenth and beginning of the nineteenth centuries, and Sir Leon Radzinowicz and Roger Hood's *The Emergence of Penal Policy in Victorian and Edwardian England* (Oxford: Clarendon Press, 1990) and Sean McConville's *A History of English Prison Administration* (London: Routledge, 1981) provide detailed scholarly accounts of the development of imprisonment.

As far as the contemporary use and organization of imprisonment is concerned, there is no substitute for becoming familiar with the annual report of the Prison Service on the *Work* of the Service and the Home Office Research and Statistics Department's annual volume of *Prison Statistics*. There is no independent up-to-date academic text on the organization of prisons in the UK, though Michael Cavadino and James Dignan's *The Penal System: An Introduction* (London: Sage, 1992) and Vivien Stern's *Bricks of Shame: Britain's Prisons* (Harmondsworth: Penguin, 1987) provide accessible and critical accounts of aspects of the system. Equally surprising is the absence of a British text reviewing the sociology of the prison, though the topic is introduced in several of the research monographs cited in this chapter. The *Report* of the Woolf Inquiry into the riots at Strangeways and elsewhere in 1990 is essential reading for those interested in the current agenda for change, though it is not an easy text with which to get to grips because of the inexcusable absence of an index.

Imprisonment is ultimately an experience which only those who have been incarcerated can adequately relate. Victor Serge's *Men in Prison*

(London: Gollancz, 1970), Rod Caird's *A Good and Useful Life* (London: Hart-Davies, 1977), Jimmy Boyle's *A Sense of Freedom* (London: Canongate, 1977) and Audrey Peckham's *A Woman in Custody* (London: Fontana, 1985) are among the best recent analytical accounts.

REFERENCES

ADAMS, R. (1992), *Prison Riots in Britain and the USA*. New York: St Martins Press.

ADVISORY COUNCIL ON THE PENAL SYSTEM (1968), *The Regime for Long-Term Prisoners in Conditions of Maximum Security* (Radzinowicz Report). London: HMSO.

AMERICAN FRIENDS SERVICE COMMITTEE (1971), *Struggle for Justice: A Report on Crime and Punishment in America*. New York: Hill and Wang.

BANKS, C., and FAIRHEAD, S. (1976), *The Petty Short-Term Prisoner*. Chicester: Howard League and Barry Rose.

BARTON, R. (1959), *Institutional Neurosis*. Bristol: John Wright.

BENNEY, M. (1948), *Gaol Delivery*. London: Longmans Green.

BIRKINSHAW, P. (1985), 'An Ombudsman for Prisoners', in M. Maguire, J. Vagg, and R. Morgan, eds., *Accountability and Prisons: Opening Up a Closed World*, 165–76. London: Tavistock.

BLAKE, W. (1927), *QUOD*. London: Hodder and Stoughton.

BOTTOMS, A. E. (1977), 'Reflections on the Renaissance of Dangerousness', *Howard Journal*, 16/2: 70–96.

—— (1987), 'Limiting Prison Use: Experience in England and Wales', *Howard Journal*, 26/3: 177–202.

—— (1990), 'The Aims of Imprisonment', in *Justice, Guilt and Forgiveness in the Penal System*, Edinburgh University Centre for Theology and Public Issues, Paper no. 18. Edinburgh.

BOTTOMS, A. E., and LIGHT, R. (1987), *Problems of Long-Term Imprisonment*. Aldershot: Gower.

BOTTOMS, A. E., and MCCLINTOCK, F. H. (1973), *Criminals Coming of Age*. London: Heinemann.

BOYLE, J. (1977), *A Sense of Freedom*. Edinburgh: Canongate.

—— (1984), *The Pain of Confinement: Prison Diaries*. Edinburgh: Canongate.

BRODY, S. (1976), *The Effectiveness of Sentencing*, Home Office Research Study no. 35. London: HMSO.

BRODY, S., and TARLING, R. (1980), *Taking Offenders out of Circulation*, Home Office Research Study no. 64. London: HMSO.

CAIRD, R. (1974), *A Good and Useful Life*. London: Hart-Davis.

CARLEN, P. (1983), *Women's Imprisonment*. London: Routledge.

—— (1990), *Alternatives to Women's Imprisonment*. Milton Keynes: Open University Press.

—— (1992), *Prisons for Women*, Open University Course Material, D 803 A5. Milton Keynes: Open University.

Carlisle Report (1988), *The Parole System in England and Wales: Report of the Review Committee* (Carlisle Report), Cm. 532. London: HMSO.

Carrell, C., and Laing, J., eds. (1982), *The Special Unit, Barlinnie: It's Evolution through its Art*. Glasgow: Third Eye Centre.

Carroll, L. (1974), *Hacks, Blacks and Cons*. Lexington: Lexington Books.

Casale, S. (1984), *Minimum Standards for Prison Establishments*. London: National Association for the Care and Resettlement of Offenders.

—— (1989), *Women Inside: The Experience of Women Remand Prisoners in Holloway*. London: Civil Liberties Trust.

Casale, S., and Plotnikoff, J. (1989), *Minimum Standards for Prisons: A Programme for Change*. London: National Association for the Care and Resettlement of Offenders.

—— (1990), *Regimes for Remand Prisoners*. London: Prison Reform Trust.

Cavadino, M., and Dignan, J. (1992), *The Penal System: An Introduction*. London: Sage.

Clayton, G. F. (1958), *The Wall is Strong: The Life of a Prison Governor*. London: John Long.

Clemmer, D. (1940), *The Prison Community*. New York: Holt, Rinehart and Winston.

Cohen, S., and Taylor, L. (1972), *Psychological Survival*. Harmondsworth: Penguin.

Conservative Party (1979), *Manifesto*. London: Conservative Party.

Cooke, D. J. (1989), 'Containing Violent Prisoners: An Analysis of the Barlinnie Special Unit', *British Journal of Criminology*, 29/1: 129–43.

Council of Europe (1990), *Prison Information Bulletin*, no. 15. Strasbourg: Council of Europe.

—— (1991*a*), *Report to the United Kingdom Government on the Visit to the United Kingdom Carried Out by the European Committee for the Prevention of Torture and Inhuman or Degrading Treatment or Punishment from 29 June 1990 to 10 August 1990*. Strasbourg: Council of Europe.

—— (1991*b*), *Response of the United Kingdom Government to the Report of the European Committee for the Prevention of Torture and Inhuman or Degrading Treatment or Punishment on its Visit to the United Kingdom from 29 July 1990 to 10 August 1990*. Strasbourg: Council of Europe.

Coyle, A. (1987), 'The Scottish Experience with Small Units', in A. E. Bottoms and R. Light, eds., *Problems of Long-Term Imprisonment*, 228–48. Aldershot: Gower.

—— (1991), *Inside: Rethinking Scotland's Prisons*. Edinburgh: Scottish Child.

Cronin, H. (1967), *The Screw Turns*. London: Longman.

Curtis, D. (1973), *Dartmoor to Cambridge*. London: Hodder and Stoughton.

Dell, S., Grounds, A., James, K., and Robertson, G. (1991), *Mentally Disordered Remanded Prisoners: Report to the Home Office*. Cambridge: University of Cambridge.

DiIulio, J. (1987), *Governing Prisons: A Comparative Study of Correctional Management*. New York: Free Press.

Ditchfield, J. (1990), *Control in Prisons: A Review of the Literature*, Home Office Research Study no. 118. London: HMSO.

Ditchfield, J., and Austin, C. (1986), *Grievance Procedures in Prison*, Home Office Research Study no. 91. London: HMSO.

Downes, D. (1988), *Contrasts in Tolerance: Post-War Penal Policy in the Netherlands and England and Wales*, Oxford: Oxford University Press.

Dunbar, I. (1985), *A Sense of Direction*. London: Prison Service.

Emery, F. E. (1970), *Freedom and Justice within Walls: The Bristol Prison Experiment*. London: Tavistock.

Evans, M., and Morgan, R. (1992), 'The European Convention for the Prevention of Torture: Operational Practice', *The International and Comparative Law Quarterly*, 41: 590–614.

Fairhead, S. (1981), *Persistent Petty Offenders*, Home Office Research Study no. 66. London: HMSO.

Feldman, D. (1993), *Civil Liberties and Human Rights in England and Wales*. Oxford: Oxford University Press.

Fitzgerald, E. (1985), 'Prison Discipline and the Courts', in M. Maguire, J. Vagg and R. Morgan, eds., *Accountability and Prisons: Opening Up a Closed World*, 29–45. London: Tavistock.

Fox, L. (1952), *The English Prison and Borstal System*. London: Routledge.

Garland, D. (1990), *Punishment and Modern Society: A Study in Social Theory*. Oxford: Oxford University Press.

Garland, D. and Young, P. (1983), 'Towards a Social Analysis of Penality', in D. Garland and P. Young, eds. *The Power to Punish*, 1–36. London: Heinemann.

Genders, E., and Player, E. (1989*a*), *Race Relations in Prison*. Oxford: Clarendon Press.

—— (1989*b*), *Grendon: The Study of a Therapeutic Community within the Prison System*, a report to the Home Office. Oxford: Oxford Centre for Criminological Research.

Goffman, E. (1968), 'The Characteristics of Total Institutions', in *Asylums*. Harmondsworth: Penguin.

Gostin, L., and Staunton, M. (1985), 'The Case for Prison Standards: Conditions of Confinement, Segregation and Medical Treatment', in M. Maguire, J. Vagg, and R. Morgan, eds., *Accountability and Prisons: Opening Up a Closed World*, 81–96. London: Tavistock.

Gunn, J., Maden, A., and Swinton, M. (1991), *Mentally Disordered Prisoners*. London: Institute of Psychiatry.

Hadfield, R., and Lakes, G. H. (1991), *Summary Report of an Audit of Custody Arrangements for Category A Prisoners and of an Inquiry into DOC I Division*. London: Home Office/Prison Service.

Hay, W., and Sparks, R. (1991), 'Maintaining Order in the English Dispersal System', in K. Bottomley and W. Hay, eds., *Special Units for Difficult Prisoners*. Hull: University of Hull Centre for Criminology and Criminal Justice.

Hay, W., Sparks, R., and Bottoms, A. E. (1990), *Control Problems and the Long-Term Prisoner: A Report for the Home Office*. Cambridge: University of Cambridge Institute of Criminology.

Her Majesty's Chief Inspector of Prisons (1984), *Prisoner Categorisation Procedures*. London: Home Office.

—— (1987*a*), *A Review of Prisoners' Complaints*. London: Home Office.
—— (1987*b*), *Report of an Inquiry into the Disturbances in Prison Service Establishments in England between 29 April and 2 May 1986*, HC 42. London HMSO.
—— (1988), *HM Remand Centre Risley*. London: Home Office.
—— (1989), *Prison Sanitation*. London: Home Office.
—— (1990*a*), *HM Prison Brixton*. London: Home Office.
—— (1990*b*), *Suicide and Self-Harm in Prison Service Establishments in England and Wales*, Cm. 1383. London: HMSO.
—— (1990*c*), *HM Prison Leeds*. London: Home Office.
—— (1992*a*), *HM Prison Canterbury*. London: Home Office.
—— (1992*b*), *YOI Feltham*. London: Home Office.
—— (1992*c*), *HM Prison Acklington*. London: Home Office.
—— (1992*d*), *HM Prison Lewes*. London: Home Office.
—— (1993), *HM Prison Cardiff*. London: Home Office.
Home Office (1947), *Report of the Commissioners of Prisons and Directors of Convict Prisons for the Year 1946*, Cmd. 7271. London: HMSO.
—— (1965), *The Adult Offender*, Cmnd. 2852. London: HMSO.
—— (1966), *Report on the Work of the Prison Department: Statistical Tables*, Cmnd. 2957. London: HMSO.
—— (1977), *Report on Inquiry into the Cause and Circumstances of the Events at HM Prison Hull 31 August to 3 September 1976* (the Fowler Report). London: HMSO.
—— (1981*a*), *Annual Report of the Work of the Prison Department 1980*, Cmnd 8228. London: HMSO.
—— (1981*b*), *Prison Statistics England and Wales 1980*, Cmnd 8372. London: HMSO.
—— (1984), *Managing the Long-Term Prison System: The Report of the Control Review Committee*. London: HMSO.
—— (1989*a*), *Report of the Work of the Prison Service, April 1988–March 1989*, Cmnd. 835. London: HMSO.
—— (1989*b*), *An Improved System of Grievance Procedures for Prisoners' Complaints and Requests: Report of a Working Group*. London: Home Office.
—— (1990*a*), *Prison Statistics England and Wales 1989*, Cmnd. 1221. London: HMSO.
—— (1990*b*), *Crime, Justice and Protecting the Public*, Cmnd. 965. London: HMSO.
—— (1991*a*), *Report on the Work of the Prison Service April 1990–March 1991*, Cmnd. 1724. London: HMSO.
—— (1991*b*), *Custody, Care and Justice: The Way Ahead for the Prison Service in England and Wales*, Cmnd. 1647. London: HMSO.
—— (1991*d*), *Tender Documents for the Operating Contract of Wolds Remand Prison*, Schedule 2 and 3. London: Home Office.
—— (1992*a*), *Prison Statistics England and Wales 1990*, Cmnd. 1800. London: HMSO.
—— (1992*b*), *Statistics of Offences against Prison Discipline and Punishments England and Wales 1990*, Cmnd. 1651. London: HMSO.

Home Office (1992*c*), *Projections of Long-Term Trends in the Prison Population to 2000, Home Office Statistics Bulletin* 10/92. London: Government Statistical Service, Home Office.

—— (1992*d*), *Costs of the Criminal Justice System*, vol. 1: *The Crown Court*. London: Home Office.

—— (1992*e*), *Tender Documents for the Operating Contract of HM Prison Blakenhurst*, Schedule 3a. London: Home Office.

—— (1993), *Digest 2: Information on the Criminal Justice System in England and Wales*. London: Home Office.

House of Commons Home Affairs Committee (1981), *The Prison Service*, vol. 1, HC 412, 1980/1. London: HMSO.

House of Lords (1989), *Report of the Select Committee on Murder and Life Imprisonment*, HL 78, 1988/9. London: HMSO.

Ignatieff, M. (1978), *A Just Measure of Pain*. London: Macmillan.

Irwin, J. (1970), *The Felon*. Englewood Cliffs, NJ: Prentice-Hall.

Irwin, J., and Cressey, D. (1962), 'Thieves, Convicts and the Inmate Culture', *Social Problems*, 10/2: 145–55.

Jacobs, J. (1977), *Stateville: The Penitentiary in Mass Society*. Chicago: University of Chicago Press.

—— (1979), 'Race Relations and the Prisoner Sub-Culture', in N. Morris and M. Tonry, eds., *Crime and Justice: An Annual Review of Research*, vol. 1, 1–28. Chicago: University of Chicago Press.

—— (1980), 'The Prisoners' Rights Movement and its Impacts, 1960–1980', in N. Morris and M. Tonry, eds., *Crime and Justice: An Annual Review of Research*, vol. 2, 429–70. Chicago: University of Chicago Press.

Jones, H., and Cornes, P. (1977), *Open Prisons*. London: Routledge.

Justice (1983), *Justice in Prisons*. London: Justice.

King, R. D. (1993), 'Order, Disorder and Regimes in the Prison Services of Scotland and England and Wales', in E. Player and M. Jenkins, eds., *Prisons After Woolf*. London: Routledge.

King, R. D., and Elliott, K. (1977), *Albany: Birth of a Prison—End of an Era*. London: Routledge.

King, R. D., and McDermott, K. (1989), 'British Prisons 1970–1987: The Ever-Deepening Crisis', *British Journal of Criminology*, 29: 107–28.

—— (1990), 'My Geranium is Subversive: Some Notes on the Management of Trouble in Prisons', *British Journal of Sociology*, 41: 445–71.

—— (1991), 'A Fresh Start: Managing the Prison Service', in R. Reiner and M. Cross, eds., *Beyond Law and Order*, 134–57. London: Macmillan.

—— (1992), 'Security, Control and Humane Containment in the Prison System in England and Wales', in D. Downes, ed. *Unravelling Criminal Justice*, 96–118. London: Macmillan.

King, R., and Morgan, R. (1976), *A Taste of Prison: Custodial Conditions for Trial and Remand Prisoners*. London: Routledge.

—— (1980), *The Future of the Prison System*. Aldershot: Gower.

Laycock, G. (1983), 'Highly Dangerous Offenders', *Home Office Research Bulletin*, no. 15: 32–5.

Liebling, A. (1992), *Suicides in Prison*. London: Routledge.

Light, R., and Mattfield, K. (1988), 'Prison Disciplinary Hearings: the Failure of Reform', *Howard Journal*, 27: 266–82.

Lipton, D., Martinson, R., and Wilks, J. (1975), *The Effectiveness of Correctional Treatment*. New York: Praeger.

Lloyd, C. (1990), *Suicide and Self-Injury in Prison: A Literature Review*, Home Office Research Study no. 115. London: HMSO.

Logan, C. H. (1990), *Private Prisons: Pros and Cons*. New York: Oxford University Press.

Lygo, R. (1991), *Management of the Prison Service: A Report for the Home Secretary*. London: Home Office.

McConville, S. (1981), *A History of English Prison Administration*, vol. 1: *1750–1877*. London: Routledge.

McCorkle, L., and Korn, R. (1954), 'Resocialisation within the Walls', *Annals of the American Academy of Political and Social Science*, 293: 88–98.

McDermott, K., and King, R. D. (1988), 'Mind Games: Where the Action is in Prisons', *British Journal of Criminology*, 28: 357–77.

—— (1989), 'A Fresh Start: The Enhancement of Prison Regimes', *Howard Journal*, 28: 161–76.

Maguire, M. (1992), 'Parole', in E. Stockdale and C. Casale, eds., *Criminal Justice under Stress*, 179–209. London: Blackstone.

Maguire, M., Pinter, F. and Collis, C. (1984) 'Dangerousness and the Tariff: the Decision-making Process in Release from Life Sentences', *British Journal of Criminology*, 24: 250–68.

Maguire, M., and Vagg, J. (1984), *The 'Watchdog' Role of Boards of Visitors*. London: Home Office.

Maguire, M., Vagg, J., and Morgan, R., eds. (1985), *Accountability and Prisons: Opening Up a Closed World*, London: Tavistock.

Marsh, A., Dobbs, J., Mont, J., and White, A. (1985), *Staff Attitudes in the Prison Service*. London: HMSO.

Martin, J. (1975), *Boards of Visitors of Penal Institutions* (the Jellico Report). Chichester: Barry Rose.

—— (1980), 'Maintaining Standards: Who Guards the Guards?' in R. King and R. Morgan, eds., *The Future of the Prison System*, 159–99. Aldershot: Gower.

Martin, S. J., and Ekland-Olson, S. (1987), *Texas Prisons: The Walls Came Tumbling Down*. Austin, Texas: Texas Monthly Press.

Mathieson, T. (1965), *The Defences of the Weak*. London: Tavistock.

—— (1974), *The Politics of Abolition: Essays in Political Action Theory*. Oxford: Martin Robertson.

—— (1990), *Prison on Trial*. London: Sage.

May Committee (1979), *Report of the Committee of Inquiry into the United Kingdom Prison Services*, Cmnd 7673. London: HMSO.

Mayhew, P., Elliott, D., and Dowds, L. (1989), *The 1988 British Crime Survey*, Home Office Research Study no. 111. London: HMSO.

Miller, A. (1976), *Inside, Outside*. London: Queensgate.

Morgan, R. (1983), 'How Resources are Used in the Prison System', in *A Prison System for the '80s and Beyond: The Noel Buxton Lectures 1982–3*, 21–42. London: National Association for the Care and Resettlement of Offenders.

Morgan, R. (1985), 'Her Majesty's Inspectorate of Prisons', in M. Maguire, J. Vagg, and R. Morgan, eds., *Accountability and Prisons: Opening Up a Closed World*, 106–23. London: Tavistock.

—— (1991), 'Woolf: In Retrospect and Prospect', *Modern Law Review*, 54: 713–25.

—— (1992*a*), 'Following Woolf: The Prospects for Prisons Policy', *Journal of Law and Society*, 19: 231–50.

—— (1992*b*), 'Regime Monitoring for Prisoners', *Prison Report*, Spring.

—— (1993), 'An Awkward Anomaly: Remand Prisoners', in E. Player and M. Jenkins, eds., *Prisons After Woolf*. London: Routledge.

Morgan, R., and Bronstein, A. (1985), 'Prisoners and the Courts: The US Experience', in M. Maguire, J. Vagg, and R. Morgan, eds., *Accountability and Prisons: Opening Up a Closed World*, 264–80. London: Tavistock.

Morgan, R., and Jones, H. (1991), 'Prison Discipline: The Case for Implementing Woolf', *British Journal of Criminology*, 31: 280–91.

Morgan, R., and Jones, S. (1992), 'Bail or Jail?', in E. Stockdale and S. Casale eds., *Criminal Justice Under Stress*, London: Blackstone.

Morris, N. (1974), *The Future of Imprisonment*. Chicago: University of Chicago Press.

Morris, T., and Morris, P. (1963), *Pentonville: A Sociological Study of an English Prison*. London: Routledge.

Mott, J. (1985), *Adult Prisons and Prisoners in England and Wales 1970–1982: A Review of the Findings of Social Research*, Home Office Research Study no. 84. London: HMSO.

Mountbatten Report (1966), *Report of the Inquiry into Prison Escapes and Security*, Cmnd 3175. London: HMSO.

Muncie, J., and Sparks, R. (1991), 'Expansion and Contraction in European Penal Systems', in J. Muncie and R. Sparks, eds., *Imprisonment: European Perspectives*. London: Harvester Wheatsheaf.

Norman, F. (1958), *Bang to Rights*. London: Secker and Warburg.

Padel, U., and Stevenson, P. (1988), *Insiders: Women's Experience of Prison*. London: Virago.

Parker, T. (1970), *The Frying Pan*. London: Hutchinson.

—— (1973), *The Man Inside*. London: Michael Joseph.

Pease, K. (1991), 'Does England and Wales Use Prison More than Other European Countries?', paper presented to British Society of Criminology Annual Meeting, York.

Peckham, A. (1985), *A Woman in Custody*. London: Fontana.

Priestley, P. (1981), *Community of Scapegoats*. Oxford: Pergamon Press.

—— (1989), *Jail Journeys: The English Prison Experience 1918–1900*. London: Routledge.

Prime Minister (1982), *Efficiency and Effectiveness in the Civil Service*. London: HMSO.

Prior Report (1985), *Report of the Departmental Committee on the Prison Disciplinary System*. London: HMSO.

Prison Department (1981), *Report of Working Party on Categorisation*, P5 Division. London: Prison Department.

PRISON OFFICERS' ASSOCIATION (1984), *The Prison Disciplinary System: Submissions to the Home Office Departmental Committee on the Prison Disciplinary System*. London: Prison Officers' Association.

PRISON REFORM TRUST (1990), *Sex Offenders in Prison*. London: Prison Reform Trust.

—— (1993), *Prison Rules: A Working Guide*. London: Prison Reform Trust.

PRISON SERVICE (1991), *The Control Review Committee 1984: Implementation of the Committee's Recommendations*, Directorate of Custody. London: Home Office/Prison Service.

—— (1992*a*), *Caring for Prisoners at Risk of Suicide and Self-Injury: The Way Forward*. London: Prison Service.

—— (1992*b*), *Consultation Paper: Independent Complaints Adjudicator for Prisons*. London: Prison Service.

—— (1992*c*), *Model Regime for Local Prisons and Remand Centres*. London: Prison Service.

RADZINOWICZ, L., and HOOD, R. (1990), *The Emergence of Penal Policy in Victorian and Edwardian England*. Oxford: Clarendon Press.

RICHARDSON, G. (1985), 'The Case for Prisoners' Rights', in M. Maguire, J. Vagg, and R. Morgan, eds., *Accountability and Prisons: Opening Up a Closed World*, 46–60. London: Tavistock.

—— (1993*a*), *Law, Custody and Process: Prisoners and Patients*. London: Hodder and Stoughton.

—— (1993*b*), 'From Rights to Expectations', in E. Player and M. Jenkins, eds., *Prisons After Woolf*. London: Routledge.

ROTMAN, E. (1986), 'Do Criminal Offenders Have a Constitutional Right to Rehabilitation?', *Journal of Criminal Law and Criminology*: 1023–68.

RUCK, S. K., ed. (1951), *Paterson on Prisons: Being the Collected Papers of Sir Alexander Paterson*. London: Arthur Murray.

RUTHERFORD, A. (1984), *Prisons and the Process of Justice*. Oxford: Oxford University Press.

RYAN, M., and WARD, T. (1989), *Privatization and the Penal System: The American Experience and the Debate in Britain*. Milton Keynes: Open University Press.

SAPSFORD, R. (1983), *Life Sentence Prisoners*. Milton Keynes: Open University Press.

SCOTTISH PRISON SERVICE (1990), *Opportunity and Responsibility*. Edinburgh: Scottish Prison Service.

SERGE, V. (1970), *Men in Prison*. London: Gollancz.

SHAW, R., ed. (1992), *Prisoners' Children: What are the Issues*? London: Routledge.

SPARKS, R. F. (1971), *Local Prisons: The Crisis in the English Penal System*. London: Heinemann.

STERN, V. (1987), *Bricks of Shame: Britain's Prisons*. Harmondsworth: Penguin.

SYKES, G. (1958), *The Society of Captives*. Princeton: Princeton University Press.

TAYLOR, M., and PEASE, K. (1989), 'Private Prisons and Penal Purpose', in R. Mathews, ed., *Privatising Criminal Justice*. London: Sage.

TCHAIKOVSKY, C. (1991), 'Mixed Prisons: Misogynistic and Misguided', *Prison Report*, 16.

THOMAS, J. E. (1972), *The English Prison Officer since 1850*. London: Routledge.

—— (1980), 'Managing the Prison Service', in R. D. King and R. Morgan, eds., *The Future of the Prison Service*, 134–58. Aldershot: Gower.

THOMAS, J. E., and POOLEY, R. (1980), *The Exploding Prison*. London: Junction Books.

TRAIN, C. (1985), 'Management Accountability in the Prison Service', in M. Maguire, J. Vagg, and R. Morgan, eds., *Accountability and Prisons: Opening Up a Closed World*, 177–86. London: Tavistock.

VAGG, J. (1985), 'Independent Inspection: The Role of Boards of Visitors', in M. Maguire, J. Vagg, and R. Morgan, eds., *Accountability and Prisons: Opening Up a Closed World*, 124–40. London: Tavistock.

VAN ZYL SMIT, D., and DUNKEL, F., eds., (1991), *Imprisonment Today and Tomorrow: International Perspectives on Prisoners' Rights and Prison Conditions*. Deventer: Kluwer.

WALMSLEY, R. (1989), *Special Security Units*, Home Office Research Study no. 109. London: HMSO.

WALMSLEY, R., HOWARD, L., and WHITE, S. (1992), *The National Prison Survey 1991: Main Findings*, Home Office Research Study no. 128. London: HMSO.

WILLIAMS, M., and LONGLEY, D. (1987), 'Identifying Control—Problem Prisoners in Dispersal Prisons', in A. E. Bottoms and R. Light, eds., *Problems of Long-Term Imprisonment*. Aldershot: Gower.

WOOLF REPORT (1991), *Prison Disturbances April 1990: Report of an Inquiry by the Rt Hon. Lord Justice Woolf (parts I and II) and His Honour Judge Stephen Tumin (Part II)*, Cm. 1456. London: HMSO.

YOUNG, P. (1987), 'The Concept of Social Control and its Relevance to the Prisons Debate', in A. E. Bottoms and R. Light, eds., *Problems of Long-Term Imprisonment*, 97–114. Aldershot: Gower.

ZELLICK, G. (1981), 'The Prison Rules and the Courts', *Criminal Law Review*: 602.

ZIMRING, F. E., and HAWKINS, G. (1991), *The Scale of Imprisonment*. Chicago: Chicago University Press.

20

Juvenile Justice 1945–1992

LORAINE GELSTHORPE AND ALLISON MORRIS

In the early nineteenth century in England and Wales, the dominant response to delinquent and deprived youth was to deal with them in quite distinct ways. Policies during much of the twentieth century, on the other hand, sought to erode this distinction. Now, at the time of writing, these two groups of young people have been distinguished again and are dealt with in quite different legislation. Our task in this chapter is to review and explain these developments.[1]

The conventional way of looking at changes in juvenile justice policy and practice is to see them as a reflection of changing perceptions of crime and juvenile offenders. Such an approach provides only a superficial understanding. Changes in legislation reflect social and political debates and struggles and, in a sense, debates around juvenile justice issues are also sites of political struggle. They are inextricably bound up with changes occurring in the social and economic order and with political debates within which that social order (re)produces itself. Clarke (1975), for example, has argued that 'youth' is a social category which has the power to carry a deeper message about 'the state of society', about social and political changes, without actually employing or engaging in an overtly political discourse. Thus debates about 'youth crime' or 'juvenile justice' are rooted in civil society (Gramsci 1971) rather than in the political realm, but the underlying message remains undoubtedly political.

SETTING THE SCENE

A brief historical sketch serves as a necessary introduction to the complex issues which underlie half a century of juvenile justice policies and practices. At common law, the age of criminal responsibility was 7 years until

The authors are grateful to Andrea Tisi and Maggie Lee for their efficient and good-humoured assistance with the preparation of the references.

[1] Developments in Scotland have been very different and for this reason are not discussed here, though some information is included in the Note at the end of the chapter. Developments in Northern Ireland have broadly followed those in England though, on occasion, they have taken a different turn. These are also not discussed in this chapter, but again some information is included in the Note at the end of the chapter.

1933. In England and Wales, juveniles between 7 and 14 were presumed incapable of crime and it was for the prosecution to prove that they knew that their conduct was wrong.[2] Sparing the penalties of law merely on account of age would have weakened the deterrent force of law. Accordingly, juveniles accused of crimes were treated as adults at both trial and disposition stages—they could be executed, transported, and imprisoned.

The need for special jurisdiction over juvenile offenders was first mooted in the early nineteenth century when liberal-minded magistrates began to question the efficacy of sending juveniles under 14 to prison while awaiting trial for minor offences. As a consequence of this concern, a parliamentary Bill was introduced in 1840 to allow magistrates to try and to sentence juveniles under 12 immediately. The Bill never became law because it was considered unconstitutional: it denied juveniles the right to a jury trial. Thus an attempt to achieve separate justice for juveniles was rejected because it did not accord with the methods deemed suitable for adults. It was not until the 1879 Summary Jurisdiction Act that the number of juveniles in prison was markedly reduced—through various measures designed to try most juveniles at magistrates' courts (Morris and McIsaac 1978).

Reformatory and Industrial schools established by voluntary effort (Carlebach 1970) contributed to an overall reduction in the use of prison for juveniles. As a general rule, however, juveniles were still subject to the rigours of the penal system because of the 'prior imprisonment' rule (juveniles had to serve fourteen days in prison in expiation of their crimes before moving on to these institutions). This continued to undermine beliefs in differences in cause and kind between adult and juvenile crime.

It was not until the 1908 Children Act that the principle of dealing with juvenile offenders separately from adult offenders finally took root. But the establishment of the juvenile court (initially special sittings of the magistrates' court from which the public were excluded)[3] reflected a primarily *symbolic* change in attitude towards the juvenile offender. In spite of changes achieved through the activities of the philanthropic societies, the juvenile courts remained criminal courts and the procedures were essentially the same as for adults.

Herbert Samuel, introducing the Children Bill, stated that it was founded upon three principles which are often taken to mark the beginnings of a welfare perspective: juvenile offenders should be kept separate

[2] The age of criminal responsibility was raised to 8 in 1933 and subsequently to 10 in 1963. Though English law distinguishes between children, that is, those aged 10–13, and young persons, that is those aged 14–16, for ease of reading the term 'juvenile' is used to apply to both unless the context demands a distinction to be made.

[3] Some areas around the country had already adopted this practice prior to the Act.

from adult criminals and should receive treatment differentiated to suit their special needs; parents should be made more responsible for the wrongdoing of their children; and the imprisonment of juveniles should be abolished. These principles to some extent reflect the wider context of the Act which was concerned with, for example, inspection of premises which cared for infants and protecting children from the hazards of drinking, smoking, and moral contamination. (There are six Parts to the Act, only one of which deals explicitly with juvenile offenders.) But closer scrutiny of Samuel's words confirms that, far from being a simple reflection of humanitarian ideas and welfare principles, the Act also reflected ideas and principles derived from concerns about criminal justice and crime control: conflict and ambivalence were embedded in the concept of the juvenile court. Samuel argued that the 'courts should be agencies for the rescue *as well as* the punishment of juveniles' (emphasis added); and parental responsibility was encouraged because parents could not be allowed to 'neglect the upbringing of their juveniles, throw on society a child criminal and escape scot free' (Fansara HC, vol. 183, cols. 1435–6). Even the abolition of the imprisonment of juveniles cannot be seen to be an unalloyed reflection of humanitarian ideals. It was said that 'imprisonment would destroy the deterrent value if used too soon'.

Another legislative development confirmed the shift in thinking about what to do with juvenile offenders. The Probation of Offenders Act 1907 endorsed the principle of supervising (principally juvenile) offenders within the community, thus consolidating the extensive arrangements which had already developed informally. But while imprisonment for juveniles under 14 was ended in 1908, the Crime Prevention Act of the same year set up specialized institutions in which rigid discipline and training in work were to be provided in a secure environment. The first of these was at Borstal in Kent; it subsequently gave its name to numerous similar establishments. It is important to understand the social significance of these pieces of legislation. All were shaped by concerns about the declining birth rate, the physical state of the nation following the Boer War (Davin 1978), and the need to limit the effects of underemployment among the young (Thomson 1950; Webb and Webb 1909).

The juvenile courts retained their original character and structure until the Children and Young Persons Act 1933. This implemented the recommendations of the 1927 Molony Committee,[4] namely that there be a specially selected panel of magistrates to deal with juveniles and that the age

[4] The Molony Committee (The Departmental Committee on the Treatment of Young Offenders) was set up in 1925 to examine the 'treatment' and 'protection' of young offenders up to the age of 21 and carried out a critical review of the juvenile courts (Home Office 1927). For a more detailed discussion see Morris and McIsaac (1978) and Rutherford (1986).

of criminal responsibility be raised from 7 to 8. The Act also dictated that magistrates were to have regard to 'the welfare of the child'. The juvenile court was to act in *loco parentis*, establishing itself as the forum capable of adjudicating on matters of family socialization and parental behaviour, even if no 'crime' as such had been committed (Morris and McIsaac 1978: Rutherford 1986). This marked a departure from ideas of 'criminal justice', 'crime control', and full criminal responsibility for behaviour towards a focus on welfare and treatment to suit the needs of each individual child. But the legislation also confirmed that the *court* was the appropriate place in which to deal with juveniles.

These contradictory considerations were reflected in other developments leading up to the Second World War. Borstals, for example, under attack because of allegations of brutality, gradually became detached from their penal roots and were increasingly modelled on public schools. They took a new welfare/treatment direction (Hood 1965) and this philosophy was promoted throughout the 1930s. At the same time, other types of institutions were increasingly used. The number of juveniles in approved schools (established in 1933) rose, as did the number in remand homes.[5] However, by the end of the 1930s, there was evidence of a revitalized emphasis on punishment. In particular, the Magistrates' Association seemed determined to keep alive their idea for a new sentence of 'young offender's detention' which was intended to provide a sentence 'midway' on the tariff between Borstal and probation.[6] Further support for this came from the departmental committee on corporal punishment (the Cadogan Committee) which could conceive of abolishing corporal punishment only if it were to be replaced with other measures to strengthen the authority of the courts (Home Office 1938).

Supporters of this more punitive perspective were generally frustrated in their attempt to turn back the tide. The appointment in 1937 of Sir Samuel Hoare as Home Secretary by the Conservative government led not to an increased emphasis on punishment but to the promotion of proposals in the 1938 Criminal Justice Bill to transform further the treatment of juveniles in the criminal justice system. Hoare, no doubt encouraged by his ancestral connections to both Elizabeth Fry and Sir Fowell Buxton, who in 1816 had founded the Society for the Reformation of

[5] The 1933 Children and Young Persons Act had removed the distinction between reformatory and industrial schools to establish a single class of 'approved schools'. Remand homes were introduced in the same Act to provide a place of custody for juveniles charged with offences and not released on bail, juveniles who were required to be lodged in a 'place of safety' (that is, juveniles alleged to be in need of care, protection, or control), juveniles whose cases were adjourned for reports, and juveniles admitted to a remand home for a short period of detention. The use of remand homes changed with successive pieces of legislation.

[6] This was first introduced around the time of the 1908 Act. See Bailey (1987: ch. 1) for a detailed discussion.

Prison Discipline, proposed an end to imprisonment for all those under 16, restrictions on imprisonment for those between the ages of 16 and 20, attendance centres for those between the ages of 12 and 21, and 'Howard Houses' (offering accommodation and supervision for young offenders between the ages of 16 and 21 and the opportunity to work in the community). Judicial corporal punishment was to be abolished. These proposals all marked a clear departure from notions of punishment. Hoare's Bill was abandoned in 1939, however, because of events leading to the onset of war.

JUVENILE JUSTICE 1945–1970

Between 1945 and 1970, Britain experienced both Labour (1945–51 and 1964–70) and Conservative (1951–64) administrations for approximately equal amounts of time. This might have been expected to lead to radical shifts from one set of policies to another. But the closing years of the Second World War saw the development of a broad cross-party consensus with regard to the creation of a post-war 'welfare state' which endured for some time. This involved state intervention in the economy in order to maintain full employment, with supporting policies on housing, unemployment and sickness benefit, health, and child care (Marshall 1975). These were shared between the parties (though with some differences in emphasis). The word 'Butskellism' was coined to reflect these similarities (Taylor 1981; Bottoms and Stevenson 1992; see also chapter 5 in this volume).[7]

This was a period of major social change, with increases in the gross domestic product and personal incomes (after a period of austerity in the immediate post-war period); low unemployment rates; changes in housing away from largely privately rented accommodation to both local authority housing and owner-occupied housing; increases in the number of married women working and young people entering higher education. At the same time, the rate of births to teenage mothers rose; divorce became easier to obtain; church attendance declined; and cars and televisions increasingly became regular features of family life (Halsey 1988; Marwick 1982).

This, then, was the context for a new phase in juvenile justice: there was a broad political consensus which provided a backcloth for consensus also with regard to criminal and juvenile justice policy. For a time, the

[7] The word refers to successive Chancellors of the Exchequer from different political parties: Hugh Gaitskell, Labour (Chancellor, 1950–1; subsequently Leader of the Labour Party, 1955–63) and R. A. Butler, Conservative (Chancellor, 1951–5; subsequently Home Secretary, 1957–62, and Foreign Secretary, 1963–4).

particular party in power made little difference—so such so that, in 1964, George Brown, then Chairman of the Labour Home Policy Committee, felt able to say that crime was 'not a subject on which there is great Party political conflict' (in the foreword of the Longford Report, which turned out to be a most contentious document). Nevertheless, despite the emerging welfarist perspective, the war years saw a new clamour for an unequivocally punitive perspective towards young offenders. In 1942, for example, John Watson, widely regarded as a progressive juvenile court chairman, called for a new type of punishment to bring offenders to their senses and to act as a deterrent. The Magistrates' Association renewed its demands for a new short custodial sentence and the advisory committee set up to consider the treatment of offenders in 1944 under the chairmanship of Mr Justice Birkett endorsed the idea which found its way into the Bill preceding the 1948 Criminal Justice Act.

The contrast, then, between the 1930s—when official opinion had largely resisted the use of institutions for young people specifically as a punishment and had seen them much more as places of treatment—and the 1940s is remarkable. In the 1930s, the discussions had been about removing young people from prison and offering more appropriate non-institutional alternatives. A Conservative Home Secretary had rejected the proposition that there be introduced what later became known as the detention centre. In the 1940s, however, despite an awareness of the effects of wartime circumstances (bombing, sleeping in tube stations, evacuation problems, poor home circumstances because of the bombings, and so on—see Rose 1989), the Government affirmed punishment and in 1948 a Labour Home Secretary accepted the idea of detention centres, that is custodial institutions which emphasized discipline, hard work, and military-style regimes.

Quite different trends are apparent during this period. During the war, some 20,000 juveniles had been described as 'unbilletable' because of behavioural or temperamental difficulties (Ministry of Health 1944). For some researchers and writers, this war-time experience only confirmed what they already knew in terms of the effects of parental separation and poor family circumstances (Bowlby 1946, 1952). What is ironic is that, newly alerted to these difficulties, the mental health authorities prepared radical changes to their services to deal with troubled and troublesome young people which reflected care and help, in the form of child guidance clinics, child psychiatric clinics, and hostels. Further, the post-war Labour government enacted the Children Act 1948. While the Act did not directly concern juvenile offenders, it created a child-care service and this service was instrumental in the gradual merging, as far as social policy and action were concerned, of the neglected and the juvenile offender into one category: juveniles in need of care (see the Curtis Committee Report:

Home Office 1946). Meanwhile, those specifically charged with the task of dealing with crime and offenders pressed on with strategies that emphasized punishment. In 1950, a special 'punishment Borstal' was established and two years later harsher regimes were recommended throughout the Borstal system.

From this point onwards, developments become exceptionally complex. As Bottoms and Stevenson (1992) point out, the story began with a letter to *The Times* on 16 March 1955 signed by, among others, Mrs Rosamund Fisher (the wife of the Archbishop of Canterbury), Dr John Bowlby (eminent child psychiatrist), Margery Fry (a celebrated penal reformer), and Eileen Younghusband (a leading social work thinker). Their theme was 'the urgent need for reorientating the social services towards the maintenance of the family', not least because they believed juvenile crime often resulted from family breakdown. They called for the setting up of a committee of inquiry whose terms would be broad enough 'to include all causes of family breakdown, with positive recommendations for their prevention and alleviation'. Their letter was followed up by a delegation to the Home Office.

At the same time the Magistrates' Association, possibly influenced by the actions of the so-called 'Fisher group', pressed the Home Office for a review of 'the procedure in juvenile courts and the treatment of juveniles coming before them'. The Home Office, under a Conservative government, responded by setting up in 1956 a departmental committee (the Ingleby Committee) to consider the issues posed by both groups.

In one sense, the resulting Ingleby Report (Home Office 1960) merely endorsed the existing structure of the juvenile court, though there were recommendations to strengthen the powers of the court by allowing magistrates to sentence young persons directly to Borstal. However, the committee also proposed that the age of criminal responsibility be raised from 8 to 12, thereby replacing criminal with care proceedings for the younger age group. In 1963, as a legislative compromise, the age of criminal responsibility was raised to 10 in the Children and Young Persons Act.

But there is a broader point to be taken from the deliberations at this time. Critics of the Ingleby Report focused primarily on the missed opportunity for creating a unified family service. These critics were, politically speaking, from the left, and their reflections on the need for a single service eventually paved the way—after Labour regained power in 1964—for a whole series of developments which led to a radical rethink of the juvenile court and of ways of dealing with juvenile offenders. First, there was the publication of *Crime: A Challenge to US All*, the report of a Labour Party Study Group produced some months before the Labour Party came to power in 1964 and known after its chairman as the Longford Report.

A fundamental principle underlying the group's thinking was that 'delinquents are to some extent a product of the society they live in and of the deficiencies in its provision for them' (Labour Party 1964: 28). It also believed that the machinery of the law was reserved for working-class youth and that those from other social classes were dealt with by other means. The group's proposals, therefore, were that 'no child in early adolescence should have to face criminal proceedings', that criminal proceedings were 'indefensible' where the offence was trivial, and that serious offences were themselves indicative of 'the child's need for skilled help and guidance' (ibid.: 24). One further issue was clear: juveniles had no personal responsibility for their offences. The group's aim, therefore, was to take juveniles out of the criminal courts and the penal system and to treat their problems in a family setting through the establishment of family advice centres, a family service, and, for a minority, a family court.

This thinking formed the basis of the Labour party's subsequent White Paper *The Child, the Family and the Young Offender* (Home Office 1965), which would have entailed the abolition of the juvenile court and its replacement by a non-judicial 'family council', linked to a unified 'family service'. But there was concerted opposition to these proposals from magistrates, lawyers, and probation officers who, commentators believe, did not want to lose the chance of working with young offenders in their fast-developing professional service (Rutherford 1986; Harris and Webb 1987; Pitts, 1988).

In response to this opposition, the Labour Government produced a second White Paper, *Children in Trouble* (Home Office 1968). In this second attempt to promote reforms, the government leaned heavily on the expertise of the Home Office Child Care Inspectorate (Pitts 1988) and, as a result, the language used (though not all of the underlying sentiments) changed. The appropriate response was one which depended on 'observation and assessment', 'a variety of facilities for continuing treatment', 'increased flexibility', and 'further diagnosis'. And this White Paper, while holding on to some of the more radical features of the earlier attempt at reform, managed to produce proposals which were largely acceptable to political, administrative, and professional constituencies. The cost of this was the retention of the juvenile court.

The 1969 Children and Young Persons Act which ensued thus dictated that juveniles under 14 were not to be referred to the juvenile court solely on the grounds that they had committed offences (thus bringing Britain into line with many other European countries). Rather, where it could be established that such juveniles were not receiving the care, protection, and guidance a good parent might reasonably be expected to give, it was proposed that 'care and protection' proceedings should be brought. Criminal proceedings were to be possible against juveniles aged 14–16 who had committed offences, but only after mandatory consultation had taken place between the police and social service departments. The expectation was that these juveniles would also, in the main, be dealt with under care and protection proceedings.

Integral to these proposals was an increase in the role of the local authority social worker. There was to be mandatory consultation between the police and local authority social services prior to proceedings in the juvenile court and increased social work with families and juveniles on both a compulsory and a voluntary basis. Moreover, considerable power was to be placed in the hands of social workers to vary and implement the dispositions made by the magistrates. Magistrates were no longer to make detailed decisions about the kind of treatment appropriate for juveniles; instead, this task was to be given to social workers.

A second main thrust of the Act was an attempt to curtail magistrates' power to make use of custodial sentences. Prior to the Act, magistrates had been able to remit juveniles of 15 and over to the Crown Court with a recommendation that the judge impose a sentence of Borstal training. Magistrates had no direct power to sentence juveniles to substantial periods in custody. The Act sought to prevent all those under 18 from being remitted to the Crown Court in this way. Further, detention centres and attendance centres were to be replaced by a new form of treatment—Intermediate Treatment—and the form which this would take was also to be determined by social services (Bottoms *et al.* 1990).

Overall, the general aim of the Act was to make the commission of an offence no longer a sufficient ground for intervention—that is, to 'decriminalize' the court's jurisdiction to reduce the number of juveniles appearing before the juvenile court—that is, to divert juveniles wherever possible—to abolish detention centres and Borstals and replace them with community measures—that is, to encourage de-institutionalization. In this way, the government sought to blur the distinction between the 'deprived' and the 'depraved'. Put very simply, the juvenile court was to become a welfare-providing agency, but also an agency of last resort: referral to the juvenile court was to take place only where voluntary and informal agreement could not be reached between social workers, juveniles, and their parents (Morris and McIsaac 1978).

THE CONSTRUCTION OF WELFARE

Why did the 1969 Children and Young Persons Act take the form that it did? Why did a welfare perspective assume prominence at this particular time—a question all the more intriguing, given the explicit moves away from such a perspective in other jurisdictions[8]—with an emphasis on decriminalization, diversion, and de-institutionalization.

We referred earlier to Clarke's (1975) depiction of nineteenth-century debates on juvenile justice policy as political metaphors. The same point can be made with respect to debates surrounding the Children and Young Persons Act 1969. Bottoms (1974: 322) identifies as important in understanding the precise content of the Act the 'conjunction of interests and ideology between the Labour party and those in key positions in social work'.

We have already described the main themes running through the Longford Report and the two Labour government White Papers in the 1960s. In brief, the language changed from the promotion of egalitarianism and the avoidance of discrimination and stigma to the language of treatment.[9] There was a shift from (but, importantly, not an abandonment of) 'an expression of general social democratic ideology' to an acceptance of a particular social work ideology (Bottoms 1974: 328).

Labour Party writings about crime were more than recommendations about how to deal with crime. They were both shaped by and promoted broad-based socialist ideologies.[10] To this extent, the Children and Young Persons Act 1969 can legitimately be described as part and parcel of a legislative programme geared to the development of what was believed to be a more just society. We need to make these links more explicit.

Crossman (1952: 27) has described the main tasks of socialism as distributing responsibility and enlarging freedom of choice. This has traditionally involved, through fellowship and cooperation, working towards a more egalitarian distribution of incomes and wealth, the abolition of the class system, the pursuit of social justice and the elimination of poverty, primarily through fiscal, social, and educational policy—often summed up in the catchphrase 'equality, liberty, and fraternity'. In practical terms, this meant public ownership of essential services, equal opportunity in education, economic equality in work, full employment, and industrial democracy, Capitalism was to be not so much rejected as made bearable.

[8] See, for example, debates at the time of the USA (President's Commission on Law Enforcement and the Administration of Justice 1967).

[9] Such language was not new. For example, a report published in 1945 in the Fabian Research Series (Donington 1945) advocated the abolition of the juvenile court and its replacement with a welfare council modelled on Scandinavian lines and the establishment of observation centres in order to find out 'everything about the child' (1945: 14). See aslo Donnison and Jay (1962).

[10] Many examples of this are found in publications in the Fabian Research Series. For this period, see e.g. Jones (1959) on prison reform and Morris (1960) on prison after-care. For later periods, see May (1980) and Downes (1983). The Longford Report was not strictly a report *of* the Labour Party but rather a report *to* it. The group had been asked to 'assemble all the relevant facts, consider them objectively, and draw on the expert advice of many others who are directly concerned with these problems'. However, it is undoubtedly a political document.

However, during the 1960s, there was an increasing awareness that these objectives—in particular, the abolition of poverty and a reduction in the differences between the living standards of the rich and the poor—were not being fully realized. First, poverty was 'rediscovered'. Abel-Smith and Townsend (1965), for example, found that a substantial proportion of the population was living below national assistance level and that nearly a third of the poor were juveniles. Consequently, socialist intellectuals (e.g. Titmuss 1968; Crossman 1972) argued that the answer to poverty and social inequalities lay in the universal provision of essential services, for otherwise there would exist a two-tier system in which many—the poor—would be treated as second-class citizens. The reorganization of social services was part of that universal provision.[11] Thus social services were to deal with the family as a whole and were to be available for all who wished to make use of them. To borrow Donnison and Stewart's distinction, the provision was not a 'problem families service' but a 'family casework service' (1958: 7).

Second, it was realized that there were individuals who somehow or other had fallen through this net of provision—'secondary poverty' in Crosland's terms (1963: 81–101). Delinquency was one of the many expressions of 'secondary poverty' and its underlying social and psychological causes had also to be addressed. In doing so, Crosland referred to the need to get advice from psychiatrists, sociologists, and social psychologists and he predicted that the aid required would be individual therapy, casework, and preventative measures.

The conceptions of delinquency and the appropriate responses to it found explicitly in the Longford Report and implicitly in the first White Paper are situated within a similar framework: an acceptance of the accomplishments of the post-war reconstruction, but an acceptance too of the failure of the state to meet the needs of certain juveniles. Socialist ideals and the rejection of the consequences of capitalism are quite apparent in the language of the Longford Report. The study group set out its objectives in the first chapter:

> All of us have some responsibility to our neighbours, individually and collectively: all of us share rights which, in a perfect society would be equal . . . As socialists . . . [we] are concerned with justice both for the community and for those who offend against it. But we have also been concerned with two refinements of this simple antithesis—with the forestalling and prevention of crime . . . so that the forces of justice need to be invoked and used as economically as possible; and—a dimension beyond 'pure' justice—with care for the offender as a human being . . .

[11] See the report of the Seebohm Committee in 1968 (Home Office *et al.* 1968). It recommended a new local authority department which would provide a family-orientated service and which would 'enable the greatest possible number of individuals to act reciprocally, giving and receiving services for the well-being of the whole community' (ibid.: 11). Its recommendations were subsequently enacted in the Local Authority Social Services Act 1970.

A society which fails in its obligations to many of its citizens must not be surprised if some of them do not keep its rules. (Labour Party 1964: 4)

Explicitly, the group acknowledged 'serious gaps' in the supposedly universal services of the welfare state and that 'poverty, squalor and social inadequacy' still existed on a considerable scale. Importantly, however, this was through no fault of those who suffered from them. But although the group accepted that deprivation was a factor in crime (because individuals living in such circumstances were more likely both to yield to temptation and to be caught), it entered a caveat: 'on the whole, criminals do not come from stable and closely knit working class families, however poor their circumstances' (ibid.: 5). Thus it was *deficiencies* in the working-class family that the group identified as a major cause of crime: 'chronic or serious delinquency in a child is . . . evidence of lack of the care, the guidance and the opportunities to which every child is entitled' (ibid.: 21). This was the logic which led to the proposals for family advice centres and a family service. It was their role to provide 'special help and support' for those families who needed more from the welfare state (again, through no fault of their own) but who had not requested it. This emphasis on bolstering the family is well captured in the group's claim that 'a happy and secure family life is the foundation of a healthy society and the best safeguard against delinquency and anti-social behaviour' (ibid.: 16).

A theme repeated over and over again was that the provision of these services was no more than what was already available to 'parents with ample means'. But it was not only the provision of services which was believed to be discriminatory; the 'machinery of the law' was too. Thus the group expressed the view: 'The parent who can get such help for his child on his own initiative can almost invariably keep the child from court. It is only children of those who are not so fortunate who appear in the criminal statistics' (ibid.: 24). The group wanted to avoid 'the branding of a child . . . as a criminal, whatever offence he might have committed' (ibid.). It was in society's interests that such children should receive the treatment they needed 'without any stigma or any association with the penal system' (ibid.). For the great majority of juveniles who offended, therefore, the group envisaged that their needs would be met by agreement between the family service and their parents. Only a minority (where agreement could not be reached) would have to appear in a court, and this would be a much changed court: a family court. The emphasis and atmosphere of this court was to be 'essentially human': the welfare of the family as a whole was to be a primary consideration.

However, there was another strand to the group's theorizing about crime. Reference was also made to the importance of 'the values that prevail among those that dominate society'. Where these were 'personal advancement' and 'ruthless self interest', individuals were not trained in 'social responsibility'. The logic of this led the group to identify 'the get-rich quick ethos of the affluent society' as a major reason for crime. To address this problem it was necessary to 'substitute the ideal of mutual service and work towards a society in which everyone has a chance to play a full and responsible part' (ibid.: 5). Thus, in the chapter entitled 'Forestalling Delinquency', there is a wide range of proposals referring to the need for improvements in health, housing, education, social security, and so on.[12] The group's political agenda emerges most clearly here as it makes explicit that the social value of these proposals was *intended* to go beyond the prevention of delinquency to 'promote the health, happiness and well-being of the whole family' (ibid.: 20). Implicitly, therefore, the group's remedies for juvenile crime were no different from remedies in other areas of policy: social unity (inequality led to crime), social justice (inequality was inequitable), social efficiency (otherwise abilities were wasted), and individual self-realization (inequality prevented the realization of potential).

The first White Paper endorsed wholeheartedly the importance of the family in the causes of delinquency (and many other social problems): it was 'the right place to begin' (Home Office 1965: 3). And although there is no explicit political content to this document, it generally accepted the main principles underlying the recommendations of the Longford Report: sparing children the stigma of criminality and providing appropriate treatment without the need for a court appearance. Its main purpose was 'to take . . . [those] under the age of 16 as far as possible outside the ambit of the criminal law and of the courts, and to make, if possible with the agreement of their parents or guardians, such arrangements for their welfare as . . . appropriate' (ibid.: 12). In the mechanism chosen, however, it differed significantly from the Longford Report. Instead of simply families and social workers working together to identify what was required, this would be the task of family councils. These would be made up of social workers and 'other persons selected for their understanding and experience of children and, in particular, for their awareness of the problems facing the children and adults likely to come before them'

[12] Hastings and Jay (1965) echoed these themes in their subsequent tract *The Family and the Social Services*, published by the Fabian Society. They also argued that, despite advances in health, education, housing, and welfare, 'a tragic tale of failure' was revealed in terms of protecting the family and that here lay 'the seedbed of anti-social attitudes, and sometimes of delinquency' (1965: 4). They believed that the behaviour of children (offenders and non-offenders alike) was almost always 'a direct reflection' of family problems. Consequently they also advocated Family Advice Centres which would allow families to take 'responsibility for their own well-being by seeking help and advice at an early stage rather than waiting at home for problems and social workers to overwhelm them' (1965: 9).

(ibid.: 6). Cases in which agreement could not be reached would be referred to a family court—an approach not dissimilar to that advocated by the Kilbrandon Committee in Scotland (Scottish Home and Health Department and Scottish Education Department, 1964). The reason for this shift is unclear, though Morris (1989), a member of the Labour Party study group chaired by Long Longford, expresses the view that this White Paper might have been closer to their proposals but for the publication of the Kilbrandon Committee's report. Nor was it clear whether these 'other persons' would be drawn from the general public (as in Kilbrandon's proposals) or from the 'experts'—psychologists, pychiatrists, and the like. And this White Paper seems also more acutely aware than the Longford Report of the need to make gestures towards anticipated (political and popular) opposition. It states quite explicitly that 'there is no intention to deal lightly with young offenders—quite the contrary' (Home Office 1965: 12). What was needed was firm discipline as well as constructive treatment.

Children in Trouble is altogether a more sophisticated document than *The Child, The Family and The Young Offender*. First, it accepted that most juveniles got involved in delinquency: 'it is no more than an incident in the pattern of a child's normal development' (Home office 1968: 4). For some, however, it was 'a response to unsatisfactory family or social circumstances, a result of boredom in and out of school, an indication of a maladjustment or immaturity, or a symptom of a deviant, damaged or abnormal personality' (ibid.: 4). The conception of delinquency was not only a broader one, therefore, but one in which full assessment and diagnosis was required. We had to know *which type of offender* we were dealing with. Consequently the appropriate course of action would have to be variable, flexible, and continuing. The influence of the current rhetoric of social work is undeniable here. However, this second White Paper did not abandon the significance attached to the role of the family. We also had to know *which type of family* we were dealing with and so, equally, the proposals were designed to encourage and help parents to fulfil their responsibilities.

Secondly, even more explicit gestures were made in this White Paper to right-wing opinion: references are made to 'the interests of society', the need for 'firm and consistent discipline', and the fact that children required 'control as well as help' (ibid.: 16). And, crucially, the juvenile court was preserved. These proposals—and their enactment in 1969—to some extent, therefore, reflect a political compromise, though the language of politics is absent. We see here, then, the coming together of political (implicit) and social work (explicit) influences.[13]

[13] Criminological influences are also apparent. Trevor Gibbens, a psychiatrist at the Maudsley psychiatric hospital in London, and Terence Morris, a sociologist at the London

THE OPPOSITION TO WELFARE

Changes in the post-war economy also had consequences perceived negatively by some. The burgeoning of the economy had led to an influx of labour from Commonwealth countries, particularly the West Indies and the Indian sub-continent. This ultimately led to race relations tensions in some urban areas. Also, a series of youth cultures ('teddy boys', 'bikers', 'mods and rockers', and so on) emerged, demonstrating both the increased economic emancipation of the young and the commercialization of that market, and on occasion their members got into trouble. Though their perceived profiles were far worse than their actual behaviour, there were confrontations with the police and consequent 'moral panics' about young people (Cohen 1973). From the late 1950s onwards there were other tensions, too, which ultimately combined to contribute to the fracturing of the political consensus. This period saw the development of the Campaign for Nuclear Disarmament, the emergence of the women's movement, and more explicit protests by the young (about students' rights and the Vietnam War, for example). Moreover, from 1955 onwards there was a wholly unexpected and unprecedented rise in the crime rate (McClintock and Avison 1968). Thus the stage was set for political dissensus: consensus gave way as racial and social tensions and recorded crime increased and pressed in on previously shared social policy developments (see also chapter 5 in this volume).

The stage was also set for a very different conception of social order and of the appropriate response to juvenile offenders. The writings of the Conservative Party (see e.g. Cooper and Nicholas 1963, 1964) depict the law-breaker as choosing to commit offences and as doing so out of personal iniquity and promoted by 'demands' or 'desires' exacerbated by the welfare state rather than from social inequality.[14] Neither psychological nor social conditions were viewed as relevant to understanding criminal behaviour.[15] Consequently, juvenile offenders were viewed as personally

School of Economics, were both members of the Labour Party study group chaired by Lord Longford. In other Fabian Society documents (e.g. Hastings and Jay 1965), explicit reference was made to the research of John Bowlby (1946, 1952). A number of other criminologists were actively involved with the Labour party and/or the Fabian Society—for example, Herbert Mannheim, Barbara Wooton, Pauline Morris, and Howard Jones.

[14] Conservative Central Office published two influential reports in the 1960s which give clear statements of Conservative Party policy on crime: *Crime and Punishment* (1961) and *Putting Britain Right Ahead* (1965). In addition, the Conservative Political Centre also published in the 1960s a number of reports and papers on crime which, though not official Conservative Party policy, can be broadly taken as indicative of Party thinking.

[15] The report *Crime in the Sixties* (Cooper and Nicholas 1963) distinguished between 'probable causes' and 'possible causes'. Among the former were included a decline in moral standards and of family influence, increased opportunities for crime, the shortage of police,

responsible for their actions—although, depending on their age, parents might share in this responsibility in that they had failed both to discipline their young and to inculcate in them 'basic' values. Thus a key role in preventing and controlling crime was assigned to the family which, it was believed, had been systematically undermined by socialism because it had taken away the responsibility from families to provide for their members. Thus 'family responsibility' was given a different force and meaning from that found in comparable Labour Party writings. Deficiencies in the family were to be remedied through discipline and external controls, not through support and services. Parents were to be held responsible for the offences of their children by making them pay, quite literally. The appropriate response to the delinquent was correction through discipline and punishment. The role of the courts—and the actual and symbolic powers of the magistracy—were also viewed as important in preserving respect for the law, ensuring parental responsibility and making juvenile offenders accountable for their actions. Academic criminologists contributed very little to this 'law and order' ideology (for a discussion of this point see Brake and Hale 1992).

As a result, the Conservative Party was always opposed to the philosophy underlying the Longford Report, the 1960s White Papers, and the subsequent legislation. In making sense of Conservative ideology about crime, we find its roots, as with our exploration of Labour Party ideology, in the core values of Conservatism. According to Durham (1989: 50), Conservatism rests on a belief in 'human fallibility'—humans, as a result of their 'proneness to evil', need government—and on a reliance on tradition—established customs and traditions are preferred to radical social change. (This concern is easily translated into a concern with national identity and was effectively so used by Enoch Powell in the late 1960s.) Conservatism is also said to uphold both authority and liberty. Hogg explains this apparent paradox by arguing that it is only under the rule of law and a settled government that liberty can be enjoyed (quoted in Durham, 1989: 51). In essence, Conservatives prefer to limit state controls (defence, law and order, and a minimum standard of welfare are viewed as the main tasks appropriate for government action), to cut government spending, to expand free enterprise, and to privatize (eventually) even essential services. Through these strategies, society is believed to be better off, both materially and morally, as they encourage competition and competition means progress. Substantial government intervention is viewed as socially disruptive (because 'wants' get translated into 'rights'), as wasteful of resources (because it stimulates false 'demands'), as promoting economic inefficiency (through weakening competition), and as

the leniency of the courts, and the increase in immigration; among the latter, the lack of discipline in schools, boredom, and the breakdown of local communities.

removing individual freedom. There is an acceptance of the government's role in the provision of certain services but this is as a last resort, a safety net, and only for those in 'real' need. Individuals are responsible for themselves and this includes providing for themselves. The government's responsibility is only to provide a framework which enables each person to achieve his or her best. In Macleod's words, 'on our banners we will put "opportunity", an equal opportunity for men to make themselves unequal' (1958: 14). It is not surprising, therefore, that the Conservative Party was united in its opposition to the Children and Young Persons Act.

THE PRACTICE OF JUVENILE JUSTICE IN THE 1970S: THE ECLIPSE OF WELFARE?

We have argued that policy debates in the 1960s were ideological battlegrounds in which power struggles took place among the political parties for the eventual satisfaction that their values would dominate in current policy. But this struggle impinged on the practice and practitioners of juvenile justice too. On the 'right', for example, alliances were drawn between the Conservative Party and the Magistrates' Association (and possibly the Police Federation, though this is less clear-cut); and on the 'left', alliances were drawn between the Labour Party, social workers, and liberal reform groups. Ideological differences provided the ammunition: policies for equality of opportunity were posed against those for achieving equality of results; the responsibility of juvenile offenders was set against their need for help; measures of punishment were contrasted with measures for treatment. Under the banner of 'the best interests of the child', these ideological and professional differences were provided with a public forum.

Thus the Children and Young Persons Act 1969 was a compromise in two fundamental ways. First, in design, it promoted both diversion *from* courts and the provision of welfare *in* courts. And second, by design, it perpetuated these competing conceptions of juvenile offenders and of how best to deal with them (this is apparent in the changes which occurred in the second White paper and which, at the time, silenced the opposition). The full machinery of courtroom adjudication was retained for those who saw juvenile offenders as responsible and who believed in the symbolic and deterrent value of such appearances. At the same time, an emphasis on social welfare (through an enlarged role for social workers and the introduction of certain dispositions) was retained for those who saw juvenile offenders as the product of social circumstances. The sphere of influence of these competing conceptions was not, however, mutually exclusive; nor were the people charged with operating the new Act—social workers, magistrates, and the police—isolated actors with a single conception of offenders or of how best to deal with them. Thus these conceptions collided at key points in the process: prosecution, adjudication, determination of the disposition, and implementation of the disposition. As Morris and Giller write, 'the history of the 1969 Act is the history of the operation of these different conceptions in practice' (1979: 19).

The Act was never fully implemented. Like many Acts of Parliament, certain sections in the Children and Young Persons Act 1969 were to be implemented at some future date. However, a Conservative government replaced the Labour one in 1970 and the Conservatives made it clear that they would not fully implement the Act. So, from its beginnings, the Act in practice reflected compromise. And when the Labour Party were re-elected in 1974, it was no longer politically or popularly viable to implement the Act in full. Thus new welfare measures were added on to, but did not replace, the old punitive ones. Thorpe *et al.* (1980: 22) describe this as 'vertical integration'. The consequence was that, on occasions, the two systems collided.[16]

More broadly speaking, two opposing trends—first an increase in punitive dispositions generally and in custodial dispositions in particular, and second an increase in the use of diversion—occurred in the 1970s. Neither is overtly linked with welfare; quite the contrary, in fact. But both were undoubtedly created by the consequences of perceptions of welfare—or, more accurately perhaps, by perceptions of those promoting welfare practices. A third and paradoxical trend also occurred: a decline in the use of welfare-orientated dispositions despite the intentions underlying the Act.

Towards Custody

Fines, attendance centre orders, and custodial sentences were increasingly relied on by magistrates, particularly for 14–16-year-old boys, at the expense of welfare and community-based alternatives, the precise operation of which was in the hands of social workers (see Table 20.1 for changes in the number of juveniles given various dispositions between 1970 and 1979 and Fig. 20.1 for trends in the use of custody over this period).

The increase in the use of custody could have been explained by an

[16] See the research findings on the operation of care orders of: Zander 1975; Thorpe *et al.* 1980; Cawson 1981; Giller and Morris 1981. A direct consequence of social workers' and magistrates' different 'views' of the care order was the increased use of penal sanctions. Social workers also contributed to this by the provision and content of social inquiry reports. See Thomas 1982; Millichamp *et al.* 1985; Duncan 1985.

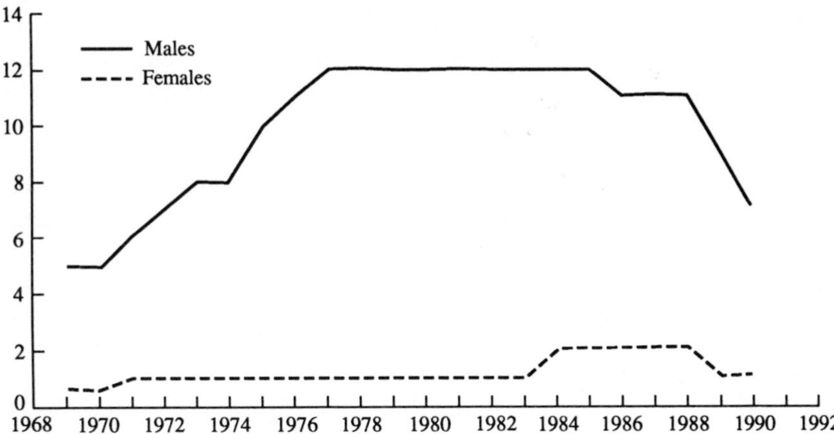

Fig. 20.1 Percentages of offenders aged 14–16 given custodial penalties for indictable offences, by sex, 1989–1990

For the period up to 1975 this includes remits to the Crown Court for consideration for Borstal training and detention centre orders; from 1975 to April 1983, detention centre orders and Borstal training; from May 1983 to October 1988, sentences to youth custody and detention centres; and from October 1988, sentences of detention in young offender institutions.

increase or changes in the nature of juvenile crime,[17] but an analysis by the DHSS (1981) showed that only one-sixth of this increase in custody could be so explained. The report also showed that, throughout the 1970s, those given custodial penalties had not necessarily previously experienced the full range of non-custodial penalties available to the courts. This was particularly so for boys given detention centre orders. Changes in the use of custody reflected changes in sentencing practice, not in juvenile crime.[18]

Towards Diversion

Parallel with the growth in custody went a quite contradictory trend towards diversion. Diversion in the form of warnings by the police has been a significant factor since the early 1970s and remains a dominant

[17] Indeed, this 'moral panic' about juvenile crime took place against a backdrop of declining juvenile crime rates. Though the annual criminal statistics showed that recorded juvenile crime increased to a peak in the mid-1970s, they then showed a decrease in the late 1970s.

[18] This rapid growth in the use of custodial measures was paralleled by a growth in the number of secure places within the child-care system. For a critique see Millham *et al.* 1978; Cawson and Martell 1979.

trend in current juvenile (and criminal) justice policies. In 1970, 35 per cent of known juvenile offenders were being cautioned; by 1979, this figure had increased to 50 per cent. These figures were considerably higher for both girls and children.[19] See Table 20.1 for changes in the number of juveniles cautioned and found guilty between 1970 and 1979 and Fig. 20.2 for the trends in cautioning over this period.

Table 20.1 Percentage increases and decreases in the number of juvenile offenders cautioned and given various sentences for indictable offences, by age and sex, 1970–1979

	Boys		Girls	
	Under 14	14–17	Under 14	14–17
Cautioned	+36	+91	+143	+190
Found guilty	–31	+15	–17	+30
Discharged	–28	+13	–14	+32
Fined	–24	+12	–4	+51
Given attendance centre orders	–5	+109	–	–
Given supervision orders	–44	–14	–28	+7
Given care orders	–34	–42	–11	+12
Remitted to Crown Court (for Borstal training)	–	+56	–	+121
Given detention centre orders	–	+155	–	–

This expansion in police cautioning prompted two concerns: the tendency of diversion practices to 'net-widen' and hence to expand rather than limit social control (Ditchfield 1976; Farrington and Bennett 1981); and the discriminatory nature of decision-making (Farrington and Bennett 1981; Fisher and Mawby 1982). There was some evidence, for example, that black youths were less likely to be cautioned than white youths (Landau 1981; see also chapter 22 this volume).

Another form of diversion was also introduced in the late 1960s: Intermediate Treatment (IT). This term was first mentioned in the 1968 White Paper (Home Office 1968) and subsequently came to mean any intervention through community-based programmes of supervised activity, guidance, and counselling. The primary objective was to reduce the level of juvenile offending by addressing the needs of juvenile offenders or potential juvenile offenders (it was also intended to reduce the need for residential/institutional care or custody, but had little impact in this respect until considerably later). In design and in practice, IT was also 'expansionist' (for a description of practice at that time see Thorpe *et al.*

[19] For 10–13-year-old girls the comparable figure was 85 per cent; for 14–16-year-old girls it was 59 per cent; and for 10–13-year-old boys it was 66 per cent.

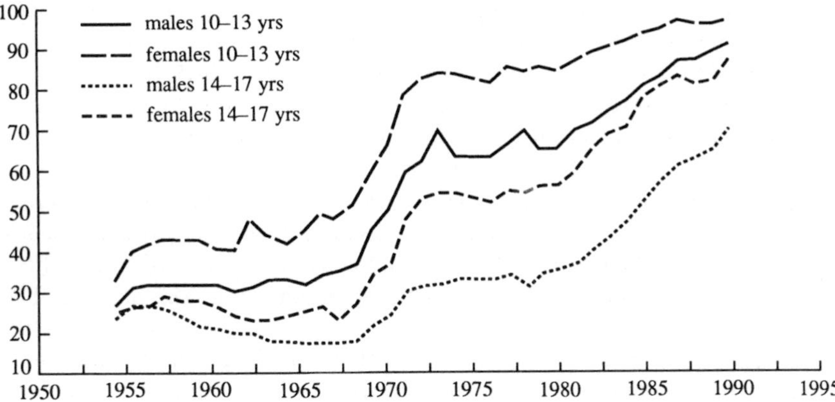

Fig. 20.2 Percentages of juvenile offenders cautioned, by sex and age, 1954–1990

1980). This was particularly so with respect to girls, who were more likely than boys to be involved in IT schemes on a voluntary basis and for reasons other than the commission of offences. This is a general feature of girls' involvement in the juvenile justice system (for a review, see Morris 1987: 94–100).

The Decline of Welfare

We have shown that even at its 'birth' in the 1960s there was considerable opposition to a welfare response to juvenile offending, especially by the Conservative Party and allied interest groups. And it is clear that juvenile practice under the 1969 Act could hardly be characterized as welfare-orientated (see Table 20.1).

The relevance of a welfare perspective for *certain* juvenile offenders (identified on the basis of their offences) was also questioned in the mid-1970s (House of Commons Expenditure Committee 1975; Home Office *et al.* 1976). In effect, the perspective underlying the 1969 Act was deemed to have failed; in reality, it had never been tried. But its 'moment' had gone. Indeed, Smith (1984: 36) argues thoughtfully that, in some senses and in retrospect, the 1969 Act represented an end, not a beginning.[20]

How, then, can we explain these developments and the refusal to put

[20] As noted earlier, the Labour Party regained power in 1974 and survived, after a further general election in 1975, until 1979, but there was no attempt to implement the 1969 Act fully. This was due in part to the narrowness of the victory, in part to the existence of more pressing issues (it was a period of industrial unrest, high unemployment, and reduced public expenditure), and in part to the fact that, given the 'moral panics' about juvenile crime, such changes were no longer popularly or politically feasible.

into practice the socialist ideals intended fundamentally to change juvenile justice in the 1970s? We have already mentioned increasing social tensions and crime rates as contributing factors. More explicitly, state authority believed it faced unprecedented challenges which led to the erosion of those ideals. Hall *et al.* (1978) refer not only to moral panics about crime rates, but also to the fact that the inter-class truce, grounded in full employment and free collective bargaining, was decidedly shaky at the end of the 1960s and early 1970s with the 'three-day week' and 'flying pickets'. A fresh wave of immigration (Asians from Kenya) also fuelled the growing political, social, and economic crisis and, indeed, highlighted the ideological struggles. The moment of harsh truth had arrived. The state was perceived to be under threat.

It is no accident that many of those subject to these moral panics were women, blacks, and young people. Morris and Gelsthorpe (1981), for example, have speculated that at least some of the increase in women's recorded offences during the 1970s was artificial, due to changed perceptions of women and of women's crime among the police and the public. It was believed, because of the debates around the women's movement, that women's roles had changed in ways that were threatening and challenging to the social order and this resulted in more women being brought within the control of the criminal justice system. In much the same way, Hall *et al.* (1978) refer to the 'creation' of the offence of mugging and link supposed increases in mugging to more generalized fears about young blacks. Whatever the truth, many on the right believed that it was not appropriate to shift authority into a more coercive gear. Stuart Hall summed up this mood in a lecture to the Cobden Trust in 1979: 'We are now in the middle of a deep and decisive movement towards a more disciplinary, authoritarian kind of society. This shift . . . has gathered pace through the 1970s and is heading towards some sort of interim climax' (1979: 3). The combination of social changes and challenges had led to a crisis in legitimate authority which had to be both explained away and dealt with (Hall *et al.* 1978).

The 'explanation' was that the police and other 'policing' agencies had been prevented from 'doing their job' by industrial dissidents, political and social deviants (hippies, homosexuals, 'scroungers', and the like), and criminals (Box 1987; Hall *et al.* 1978). 'Dealing with' it involved refusing fully to implement the 1969 Children and Young Persons Act. The subsequent developments in juvenile justice policy in the 1970s symbolized the increasing separation of political ideologies. The focus on crime rates masked other social tensions and became the stage on which political tensions were played out. In practice, this meant that responses to juvenile offenders became 'bifurcated' (Bottoms 1974), so that 'tough' (persistent) offenders were dealt with in 'tough' ways and 'young inexperienced' offenders were dealt with in a minimal fashion to maximize the chances of their growing out of crime without further state intervention. High custody rates and high cautioning rates existed side by side.

There was ideological continuity between the 'liberal progressives' of the 1940s and those arguing for reforms in the 1960s, but the social and political context had changed. While the 'liberal' ideas had posed no threat in the 1940s, they increasingly came to be seen as challenges to traditional legal tenets and institutions (Bailey 1987). And, given this context of social changes and social challenges, the right preferred firm responses within existing frameworks rather than new and untested frameworks based on social work principles (Bottoms and Stevenson 1992).

JUVENILE JUSTICE IN THE 1980S: THE 'MOMENT' OF CRIME CONTROL'?

Since the mid-1970s, it is argued, a new 'underclass' in British society, often homeless and without employment, has appeared (Morris 1989). The welfare state has not fulfilled the expectations held out for it; and the social and economic policies at the centre of the post-war reconstruction were in crisis by the mid-1970s as world recession and unemployment took root. The Thatcherite solution was to move to create a new populist consensus around the themes of freedom, choice, self-reliance and enterprise, morality, responsibility, and nationhood (Brown and Sparks 1989: introduction). This new right thinking consequentially reflected a revival of interest in liberal political economy and a reconsideration of immigration, industrial disputes, social security abuse, high taxation, state bureaucracy, and, crucially in this context, crime and punishment. Levitas shows how these themes were pulled together: 'The real innovation of Thatcherism is the way it has linked traditional conservative concerns with the basis of authority in social institutions' (1986: 6). We can see this in the field of juvenile justice.

In the 1980s in England and Wales, as elsewhere, there was an explicit revival of traditional criminal justice values. It is no accident that this coincided with and was fuelled by the electoral campaigns and eventual election of a Conservative government with a large majority. The 'need to stand firm against crime' was especially apparent in the electoral campaigns of the Conservative Party in 1979, where it presented itself as the party which would and could take a strong stand against crime, in contrast to the Labour Party, which was presented as excusing crime and as sympathetic to offenders (for more detail, see chapter 5 in this volume).

The key points of the message used in this 1979 campaign were: the need to protect victims from offenders irrespective of their age (it is no accident that the growth of the 'victims' movement' also dates from around this period); the need to reduce the high level of recorded crime and the allegedly increased seriousness of crime, particularly among juveniles; and the need to alleviate growing concerns about both individual and neighbourhood safety (especially in light of the emergence of areas in which values and culture were diverse). Hence, in its electoral pamphlet *Now is the Time to Choose* (Conservative Political Centre 1979), the Conservative Party listed six steps which were essential for Britain's recovery; greater respect for 'law and order' was one of these. The day after its publication, Sir Keith Joseph made it clear that he and his party rejected claims that deprivation led to crime and that the responsibility for crime lay with society. Rather, the major blame lay with 'attitudes that have grown out of fashionable Socialist opinion' and with parents. In this speech, he explicitly referred to the need to amend the Children and Young Persons Act 1969. At different times and by different individuals throughout the campaign, the Labour government was presented as anti-police, as condoning law-breaking, and as having ineffective policies for crime control. The Conservatives, on the other hand, would 'place a barrier of steel' (Margaret Thatcher, quoted in Clarke and Taylor 1980: 101) against 'the ruthless' (by this she meant pickets, muggers, and some Labour politicians). Specifically, the political rhetoric referred to 'young thugs' who were to be sent to detention centres for a 'short, sharp shock'; secure places for juveniles were to be increased and the number of attendance centres expanded. And later that year, after the Conservatives had won the election, the new Home Secretary made good some of the electoral promises: two detention centres were, on an experimental basis, to adopt tougher regimes.[21] A few years later, a White Paper—*Young Offenders* (Home Office 1980)—was introduced which set the scene for further changes.

Both this White Paper and the resulting legislation—the Criminal Justice Act 1982—attacked the root of the social welfare perspective underlying the 1969 Act, although the White Paper did endorse the expansion of diversion and shortened the minimum period of custody for which a boy could be held in a detention centre, demonstrating yet again how opposing tendencies coexist. Both documents represented a move away from treatment and lack of personal responsibility to notions of punishment and individual and parental responsibility. They also represented a move away from executive (social workers) to judicial decision-making, and from the belief in the 'child in need' to the juvenile criminal—what Tutt (1981) called 'the rediscovery of the delinquent'.

[21] This experiment subsequently failed to the extent that reconviction rates were no lower than in other detention centres and the young men involved were reported actually to have enjoyed the regime (National Association for the Care and Resettlement of Offenders 1985; Muncie 1990).

Overall, the government attempted to toughen and tighten up the provisions of the 1969 Act. In brief, the 1982 Act made available to magistrates three new powers of disposal: youth custody; care orders with certain residential requirements; and community service. Further, there were three major changes to existing powers: periods in detention centres were shorter, restrictions on activities could be included as part of supervision orders, and it was to become normal practice to fine parents rather than the juvenile.

There was at the same time an increasing disillusionment among academics with positivist approaches to crime, beginning in the USA in the 1960s but not taking root in England and Wales until the late 1970s (see e.g. Morris and McIsaac 1978; Morris *et al.* 1980; Taylor *et al.* 1980). Instead, academics and pressure groups like Justice for Children promoted an alternative perspective, often referred to as a 'justice' or 'just deserts' approach (see e.g. Morris *et al.* 1980; Taylor *et al.* 1980), and this had some influence on policy proposals—as for example, in the report of the Parliamentary All-Party Penal Affairs Group (1981) and the report of the Black Committee (Department of Health and Social Services *et al.* 1979) on juvenile justice in Northern Ireland.

To some extent the principles underlying a justice perspective are the obverse of those underlying a welfare perspective: an emphasis on the gravity of the offence and not on the juvenile's underlying needs; on responsibility, accountability, and free will and not on determinism; on equality of sanction and not on individualized treatment; on determinacy of sanctions and not on indeterminacy of treatment; on formality and not on informality; on due process and procedural safeguards and not on executive decision-making; and so on.

They are also closely allied in many respects to a 'crime control'/'law and order' ideology, and traces of both can be seen in the eventual shape of the Criminal Justice Act 1982. Thus legal representation became mandatory in certain situations (where a custodial penalty was being considered); the provision of social inquiry reports was also mandatory in these situations, reflecting the fact that social welfare considerations were not abandoned entirely; and the imposition of care orders or custodial sentences had to be justified. Thus the Act was not simply a reflection of the Conservative government's successful 'law and order' campaign; it was more complex. There was also general agreement by the early 1980s that some kind of change was necessary to reverse the unanticipated consequences of the 1969 Act and to take account of demands to provide 'justice for juveniles.'[22]

[22] The Labour Party was uncomfortably quiet throughout this period. There were, however, a number of attempts from the left to attempt to address the balance. A tract written by John May and published by the Fabian Society in 1980, for example, attempted to revive

THE PRACTICE OF JUVENILE JUSTICE IN THE 1980s

Probably the most notable feature of the early 1980s in this field was bifurcation, and much of the effort expended since then has been devoted to counteracting the negative consequences of this trend.

Limiting Custody and Residential Care

Contrary to the predictions of academic commentators (see e.g. Morris and Giller 1981), the number of 14–16-year-old boys found guilty of indictable offences and sentenced to custody declined dramatically during the 1980s, from 6,900 in 1979 and 7,700 in 1981 to 1,900 in 1989 and 1,400 in 1990 (see Table 20.2 and Fig. 20.1). However, much of this decline was gradual. It was not until 1986 that it was marked,[23] and the most dramatic fall was that between 1988 and 1989. Also, the proportionate use of custody hardly changed until 1989—custodial penalties made up 12 per cent of juvenile court dispositions in 1979 and remained at that figure until dropping to 11 per cent in 1986. It stayed at that level until 1988 and only fell to 9 per cent in 1989 and to 7 per cent in 1990. It is also less clear that the custody rates of young blacks fell so markedly. Blacks are known to have been overrepresented in the custodial population since the Prison Department began to publish statistics on the ethnic origins of those in custody, and, according to NACRO (1989*a*), young blacks were under-represented in 'alternatives to custody' schemes (see also chapter 22 in this volume).

Over this same period, the decline in the use of custody for 14–16 year old girls is less clear cut: the number remained relatively stable at around 100 (see Table 20.2 and Fig. 20.1). However, it dropped to under 50 in 1981, 1982, and 1988. It returned to 100 in 1989 but fell back below 50 again in 1990. This means that, over this period, the proportionate use of custody for girls increased from 1 per cent in 1979 to 2 per cent in 1984.

interest in juvenile crime by emphasizing 'the fraternity of the socialist . . . the least mentioned member of the socialist trinity of liberty, equality and fraternity, yet . . . the most important in any discussion of a socialist penal policy' (May 1980: 14). May continued to advocate current ideas in juvenile justice policy—decarceration, diversion, decriminalization, and the reduction of opportunities to commit crime—but proposed also a new order for courts: the sponsorship order—'a kind of cross between intermediate treatment . . . supervision . . . and fostering'. However, just how much ground had been passed to the right is apparent in the recommendation that sponsorship orders would supplement and not replace punitive sanctions (though Borstals and detention centres would be abolished, May suggests instead 'junior prisons' for serious offenders) and that the justification for the sponsorship order would be premised on the gravity of the offence (not the needs of the juvenile).

[23] The actual numbers were as follows; 7,100 in 1982; 6,700 in 1983; 6,500 in 1984; 5,900 in 1985; 4,300 in 1986; 3,900 in 1987; 3,200 in 1988; 1,900 in 1989; and 1,400 in 1990.

Table 20.2 Percentage increases and decreases in the number of juvenile offenders cautioned and given various sentences for indictable offences, by age and sex, 1980–1989

	Boys		Girls	
	Under 14	14–17	Under 14	14–17
Cautioned	–36	+18	–60	–1
Found guilty	–83	–67	–90	–71
Discharged	–53	–44	–75	–43
Fined	–92	–81	–100	–86
Given attendance centre orders	–83	–64	–	–66
Given supervision orders	–89	–62	–100	–79
Given care orders	–93	–96	–100	–100
Given custody	–	–74	–	0

It remained at this level until 1989 when it again dropped to 1 per cent, where it remained in 1990. (See Fig. 20.1 for trends in the use of custody over this period.)

Decreases in the number of care orders and in their proportionate use occurred more rapidly (see Table 20.2). Thus 1,200 10–13-year-old boys and 2,100 14–16-year-old boys found guilty of indictable offences were given care orders in 1981—that is, 8 per cent and 3 per cent respectively of those sentenced in the juvenile court for indictable offences. The comparable figures for girls were 100 and 400—that is, 8 per cent and 6 per cent respectively of those sentenced in the juvenile court for indictable offences.[24] By 1990, for boys, the numbers had dropped to fewer than 50 for 10–13-year-olds and to 100 for 14–16-year-olds (that is, 2 per cent and 1 per cent respectively of those sentenced); for girls it had dropped to fewer than 50 for both age groups (that is, 3 per cent and 1 per cent respectively of those sentenced).

How is this decline in the use of custody and care orders and the rate of decline to be explained? Early research on the impact of the criteria introduced in the 1982 Criminal Justice Act intended to restrict the use of custody showed that they were not very significant: magistrates failed to follow statutory procedures (Burney 1985; Parker *et al.* 1989). The research also questioned the belief that legal representation increased the provision of justice for juveniles. Gradually, however, case law on what amounted to an offence sufficiently 'serious' to warrant custody emerged. Lawyers in certain areas took a more active stance and the criteria used in justifying custody were further tightened up in the Criminal Justice Act 1988 (for a description see Stanley 1988; Dodds 1986, 1987; Allen 1991).

Changes in the 1982 Criminal Justice Act also required changes in social work practice. They forced social workers and probation officers to reconsider the provision and content of social inquiry reports and to reform the provision and content of Intermediate Treatment. Though the original form of IT continued to be available (as part of a supervision order) a new format was also introduced in the 1982 Act—the 'supervised activity requirement'. The significance of this was that the control and content of the order shifted to magistrates. This was an explicit attempt to increase magistrates' confidence in such orders as realistic alternatives to custody.

According to Bottoms *et al.* (1990), IT practitioners were evolving at the same time a 'new style of working' which meant a move away from a concentration on meeting the social and emotional needs of juveniles to a perspective which focused more on the offence. They also began to focus more on the provision of IT as a 'high tariff' option specifically aimed at those at risk of residential care or custody.[25] Thus IT gradually (in the 1980s) developed into a mechanism geared to solve some of the consequences of the ideology which had produced it—for example, to reduce the number of care orders imposed. Particularly influential in this respect was a group of academics from Lancaster University (Thorpe *et al.* 1980).

But despite all these efforts, and although the number of custody declined (at least for boys), the proportionate use of custody remained remarkably stable until 1989, at least at a national level,[26] though, in some areas, 'alternative to custody' packages were effective (NACRO 1989*a*). It is only when we look at the proportionate use of custody for the whole of the known juvenile offender population that we see a very marked reduction: from 8 per cent in 1981 to 1 per cent in 1990.[27] This indicates that it was the impact of diversion (cautioning) practices rather than deinstitutionalization (IT) practices,[28] the increased use of

[24] The biggest drop for boys in both age groups occurred between 1982 and 1983; for 10–13-year-old girls it was post-1983, and for older girls the decline was gradual.

[25] This shift is usually characterized as a move from an emphasis on prevention in the 1970s to 'the new orthodoxy' (Jones 1984) in the mid-1980s.

[26] Again, this took place against a backdrop of a declining juvenile crime rate. Recorded juvenile crime increased in the early part of the 1980s, reaching a peak in 1985, but then decreased again. Thus the rate per 1,000 decreased between 1985 and 1989 by one-third for boys and by nearly a half for girls (Farrington 1992).

[27] The numbers for girls are too small to be calculated accurately.

[28] The use of supervision orders has declined markedly for 10–13-year-old boys and girls: from 21 per cent and 26 per cent respectively of those dealt with by the courts in 1980 to 16 per cent and 13 per cent respectively of those dealt with by the courts in 1990. The picture is the same for 14–16-year-old girls; the comparable figures are 15 per cent and 19 per cent. For 14–16-year-old boys, on the other hand, there has been a steady increase in the use of supervision orders: from 16 per cent of those dealt with by the courts in 1980 to 20 per cent of those dealt with by the courts in 1990. Also, there is at least some evidence that those involved in 'alternatives to custody' programmes would not have been at risk of custody at all (Bottoms 1987; Parker *et al.* 1989).

fines,[29] compensation,[30] or community service,[31] the introduction of criteria to restrict the use of custody or legal representation,[32] which reduced custody.

The Continued Expansion of Diversion

Throughout the 1980s, diversion was repeatedly affirmed in Government documents (e.g. Home Office 1980), consultative documents (Home Office 1984), circulars to the police (e.g. Home Office 1985), and in the Code of Practice for prosecutors (Crown Prosecution Service 1986). In these various documents, it was made clear that prosecution should not occur unless it was 'absolutely necessary' or as 'a last resort' and that the prosecution of first-time offenders where the offence was not serious was unlikely to be 'justifiable' unless there were 'exceptional circumstances'. Prosecution was to be regarded as 'a severe step'. This principle was echoed in local police force procedures. Thus the proportion of 14–16-year-old boys cautioned for indicatable offences increased from 34 per cent in 1980 to 69 per cent in 1990.[33] The comparable figures for 10–13-year-olds boys were 65 per cent and 90 per cent.[34] (See Fig. 20.2 for trends in the use of cautioning over this period. It is clear from Table 20.2, however, that the number of juveniles cautioned has declined since 1980, except for boys aged 14–17.)

Home Office Circular 14/1985 explicitly referred to the dangers of 'net-widening' and encouraged the use of 'no further action' or 'informal warnings' instead of formal cautions; and, since then, the number of juveniles brought into the juvenile justice system *has* declined. There has been a reduction both in the number of juveniles prosecuted—it is very rare

[29] The proportion of juvenile offenders fined has decreased gradually since the early 1980s years for both age groups and both sexes. This is so despite the introduction of provisions that the payment of a fine could be ordered against a parent. In 1990, such an order was made in 22 per cent of cases where children were fined and in 12 per cent of cases where young persons were fined. These figures represent a decline over recent years. In 1986, for example, the comparable figure for all juveniles was 21 per cent; in 1990, it was 12 per cent.

[30] The proportion of cases where compensation orders have been made against parents has similarly declined, from 29 per cent in 1986 to 17 per cent in 1990.

[31] Community service orders have increased gradually for 14–16-year-old boys from 3 per cent in 1984 to 4 per cent for 1985 and 1986 and to 5 per cent for each year since then. For 14–16-year-old girls, it has fluctuated between 1 per cent and 2 per cent.

[32] The proportion of juveniles represented by legal aid has, however, increased markedly: from 35 per cent in 1981 to 55 per cent in 1986 and 74 per cent in 1989. There is little recent research on the impact of this representation.

[33] The comparable figures for 14–16-year-old girls were 58 per cent and 86 per cent respectively.

[34] The comparable figures for 10–13-year-old girls were 85 per cent and 96 per cent respectively.

for juveniles under 14 to appear in court[35]—and in the rate of known juvenile offending (see Fig. 20.3). This was particularly marked in some areas (for Northampton, see Bowden and Stevens 1986; for Kent, see Stanley 1988).

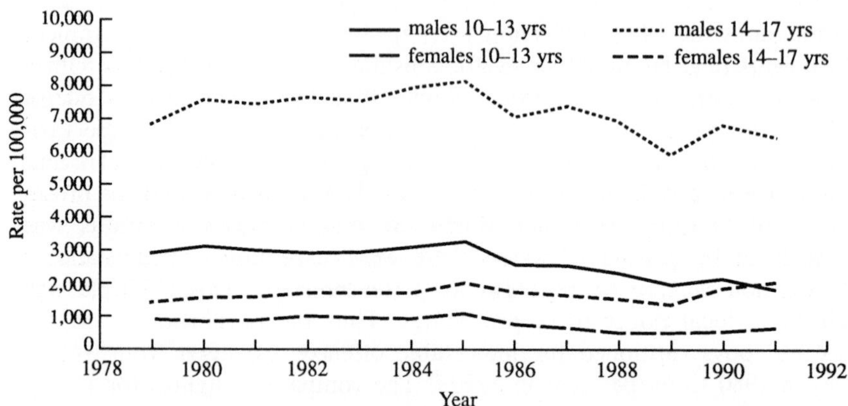

Fig. 20.3 Known juvenile offender rates per 100,000 population, 1979–1991

There are a number of reasons why net-widening is not now occurring. First, there is a declining youth population.[36] Second, there is evidence of changes in police practices. For example, in many police areas 'instant cautions' have been introduced. These are given to minor and/or first offenders usually within seventy-two hours of the offence. Many areas have also now introduced inter-agency consultation as a forum for deciding what action it is appropriate to take for particular juvenile offenders in their area.[37] Most police areas also now say that they will give 'multiple cautions' if each new offence meets the criteria in the guidelines,

[35] Three thousand children were dealt with in the juvenile court in 1989, and 2,800 in 1990, compared with 18,200 in 1979.

[36] The number of persons in the population aged 10–16 gradually declined during the 1960s and reached a trough in 1967; it then increased again to a peak in 1978 but then decreased to a further trough in 1990. It is, however, predicted to increase again in the 1990s.

[37] The police, probation, social services, education, and youth services can all be represented at these meetings. Although consultation was promoted in the 1969 Children and Young Persons Act as mandatory before the prosecution of a juvenile could take place, the relevant section was never implemented and so, originally, consultation developed spasmodically and on an *ad hoc* basis. But now consultation and such meetings are relatively common, though they appear in a variety of guises. The panels make joint recommendations but the actual decision whether or not to prosecute remains with the police. Many of these panels provide various schemes in addition to a simple warning (for example, befriending, compensation, counselling, activities, reparation, and the like). For a critique, see Davis *et al.* 1989).

though in practice multiple cautions are very rarely given (Evans and Wilkinson 1990).[38] Prosecution is the norm after one or two cautions, except in exceptional circumstances. But the major reason for the reduction in the number of juveniles subject to official processing is the expansion of informal (that is, unrecorded) cautions in some police force areas. In Northampton, for example, in 1985, 86 per cent of juveniles who came to the notice of the police were either prosecuted or formally cautioned. The comparable figure for 1989 was only 30 per cent. It is for this reason that Farrington (1992) argues that the reduction in recorded juvenile crime over this period is illusory and due to changes in police practices rather than changes in juvenile crime, though it is not clear how common this practice is. Wilkinson and Evans (1990) examined practice in fifteen police areas and found that in eleven areas informal warnings were given.[39] The extension of their use is clearly envisaged in the National Standards for Cautioning produced by the Home Office in 1990 (Annex B, Circular 59/1990).[40]

We can sum up the 1980s in this way. In 1979, the Conservative Party made crime a major election issue. The emphasis was on re-establishing 'Victorian values' in opposition to the legacy of the supposed permissiveness of the 1960s and its 'soft' approach to crime. Indeed, as McLennon (1987) has argued, it was not merely that left-wing and liberal writers failed to see the problems inherent in 'soft' approaches to crime, discipline, education, and so on, but that those 'soft' approaches were seen as contributing to permissiveness and all its unwelcome, politically unpalatable effects (see also Taylor 1981). In such a supposedly demoralizing culture, crime and violence were seen as 'out of control': hence the need for 'law and order' policies to reassert the virtue and necessity of authority, order, and discipline and attempts to realign relationships between the state and civil society as a whole.

[38] In a national survey carried out by Evans and Wilkinson (1990), the majority of those cautioned were first offenders—the range lay between 63 per cent and 84 per cent; some were second offenders—the range was from 13 per cent to 20 per cent. Only between 2 per cent and 6 per cent had been cautioned three times and between 1 per cent and 3 per cent had been cautioned four times.

[39] Social services also continued to deal informally with 'at risk' juveniles, especially girls, through IT. For a critique see Tutt 1987.

[40] The Crown Prosecution Service (CPS), introduced in 1986, was also intended to have a role in diverting juveniles (and adults) from prosecution, but its impact has been minimal. The proportion of cases discontinued has remained low (see the annual reports of the Crown Prosecution Service; also Gelsthorpe and Giller 1990). The high level of absolute or conditional discharges in the juvenile court also may indicate that prosecution is not yet being used as a last or exceptional resort. In 1990, half of 10–13-year-old boys and two-thirds of 10–13-year-old girls appearing before the court were dealt with in this way. For the older age group, too, discharges were common: in 1990, almost a third of 14–16-year-old boys and more than a half of 14–16-year-old girls were dealt with in this way. The comparable figures for 1980 were 18 per cent and 28 per cent respectively.

But also in the 1980s the relevance of the role of the police and prisons in accomplishing this task was recognized as more limited than had been at first envisaged, and debate continues about both the causes of and solutions to crime. There were a number of different sources for this new-found modesty (see in particular Reiner and Cross 1991). For example Rutherford (1989) points to the obvious failure of the system in its task and the heavy expenditure involved. A more sinister view is that the utilization of unofficial networks of control is a more effective way of spreading discipline throughout the social order (Foucault 1977; Cohen 1979; Pratt 1989). We cannot here explore these complex issues, but what is clear is that the 1990s began with a renewed call for a coordinated and shared response to juvenile offenders amid concerns about youth unemployment, lawlessness, joy-riding, homelessness, and riots on the streets.

JUVENILE JUSTICE IN THE 1990S: THE RETURN TO CONSENSUS?

Differences in the titles of the relevant White Papers and legislation in the 1960s and the 1980s reflect changes in ideological approach over this period. Provisions with respect to juveniles have appeared since the 1980s in Criminal Justice Acts (in 1982, 1988, and 1991), and in the 1990s discussions of juvenile justice policy have been within White Papers dealing broadly with criminal justice policy (see, for example, *Crime, Justice and Protecting the Public* Home Office, 1990*b*). And, since October 1992, the juvenile court has become the *youth* court.

Juveniles are also affected by the 1989 Children Act which came into force in October 1991. This represents a major structural alteration to the law concerning the welfare of juveniles and covers an enormous range of matters previously dealt with in different legislation. The law affecting juveniles who offend is only touched upon, but the resulting changes, together with the Act's underlying sentiments about the nature of the relationship between the state, children, and their parents, have significant implications for juvenile offenders.

The most important of these is the cessation of the use of the care order as a disposal available to the court in criminal proceedings and the removal of the offence condition in proceedings justifying state intervention in the life of a family. This change at once recognizes the enormous decline in the use made of the care order, the inappropriateness of a care order in criminal proceedings, the principle of determinacy in sentencing, and the importance that the government gives to parental responsibility (Harris 1991).[41] New rules also provide for the transfer of care proceed-

[41] While the government has abandoned provision to remove juveniles from their homes, it has drawn up new requirements to enable juveniles to live in local authority accommoda-

ings from the juvenile court. These are now heard in a renamed 'family proceedings' court; the newly named youth court deals only with criminal proceedings. This change in name forcefully symbolizes the separation of the 'deprived' and the 'delinquent'.

The Government has also argued that the change in name to the youth court reflects the changing age balance of the offenders who appeared in the juvenile court: most of those under 14 are now dealt with without bringing them before a court. However, the government has also decided to include 17-year-olds in the youth court. The reasons underlying this decision were an awareness that 16- and 17-year-olds were dealt with differently in terms of the use of custody and that these differences could not readily be explained by differences in their crime patterns. This change in the youth court's jurisdiction, however, is not due simply to benevolent intentions, since 16- and 17-year-olds are to be dealt with as 'near adults' (Home Office 1990*b*), and we have no information yet on the extent to which custody for 17-year-olds has declined. The reasons for the change are basically pragmatic: the vast increase in diversion has meant a marked decline in the juvenile court population and economic expediency demanded some change 'to keep courts busy'. A less cynical interpretation is that the change is designed to implement the principles embodied in the United Nations Standard Minimum Rules for the Administration of Juvenile Justice and the United Nations Convention on the Rights of the Child. These provide that a child—defined as a person of below 18 years—shall be entitled to be dealt with under a jurisdiction separate from that for adults and should be subject to a range of penalties and dispositions that take into account his or her welfare and are different from those available for older offenders (United Nations 1985, 1989).

However, this explanation does not stand up in the light of changes with regard to the sentencing framework and sentencing options introduced in the Criminal Justice Act 1991. The framework established to limit the use of custody is the same as that for adult offenders: sentencers must consider first on the basis of the gravity of the offence committed (and one other offence) whether or not custody is justified—what is generally referred to as the 'threshold test' and, if it is, they then consider all the offences for which the offender is currently before the court in order to make the amount of custody commensurate with these offences—what is generally referred to as fixing the appropriate point on the tariff. And the sentencing options hardly reflect a welfare perspective, but rather one

tion for a specified period up to a maximum of six months which can be added to supervision orders in criminal proceedings. Critics suggest that the criteria governing the new requirement are so tightly drawn that they may render the disposal inapplicable as an alternative to a custodial sentence for the small numbers of juveniles who, towards the end of the 1980s, received a care order (NACRO 1989*b*).

of punishment and parental responsibility. For example, the so-called 'community penalties' have been decidedly 'toughened up'. The number of hours within a community service order have been extended and fines have been increased (with provision to take into account parents' means where parents are made liable). The Act also confers a power to order the payment of a fine by a parent or guardian in the case of a young person aged 16 and above, and gives courts the power to bind over parents or guardians if it is thought that it would be desirable in the interest of preventing further offences; if the court does not use this power, it must state its reasons in open court. There are also two new orders, a combination order and a curfew order, the latter of which might be enforced by electronic monitoring (Ashworth *et al.* 1992*a*).

Recent changes in juvenile justice policy are inextricably linked with wider criminal justice policy and social changes. Some of those affecting juveniles reflect the government's weddedness to the notion of 'just deserts' (Ashworth *et al.* 1992*b*), concerns about the cost of custody, and a desire to cut public expenditure. Some also reflect recognition of the demands of the victims of crime (Rock 1990). There is general (though not necessarily financial) sponsorship of mediation schemes to reinforce this (Marshall and Merry 1990); and at the same time there is continued emphasis on parental responsibility for their children's offending (Allen 1990) and an emphasis on shared responsibility. The Morgan Committee (Home Office 1991), for example, promoted the continued growth in inter-agency working and collaboration between state and voluntary or private agencies to deal with offenders.

The emphasis on parental responsibility obviously reflects key Conservative principles of responsibility and authority. It also reflects fears of a growing population of under-educated, unemployed, or unemployable young people. For example, one study shows the United Kingdom to have the lowest rate of full-time participation in education or training for 16–18-year-olds out of thirteen countries examined (Central Statistical Office 1990). Official statistics also show that there is an increasing disparity between income groups and that one in four children is currently living in poverty (*Guardian*, 16 July 1992). This emphasis on parental and individual responsibility thus masks wider structural causes of crime. Street battles between young people and the police are explained away as a symbol of moral decay and reprehensible anti-authority attitudes rather than a sign of alienation, hopelessness, the decline in physical surroundings, unemployment, recession, and depression. Indeed, the 'underclass' identified in the 1980s is increasingly a *youthful* underclass—potentially a new 'dangerous class' (Chapman and Cook 1988).

Inter-agency approaches can also be interpreted in different ways, reflecting the hydra-like qualities of state control (Pratt 1989) or social and economic expediency. There are some negative side-effects to multi-agency approaches to dealing with young offenders (such as the tendency to develop new or multiple routes *into* systems; the term 'transinstitutionalism' has been coined to reflect this phenomenon—see Children's Society 1991). But there is cause for optimism too. Towards the end of the 1980s, practitioners appeared to be in the ascendancy in controlling, from the ground, what happened to juvenile offenders and there was what Nellis has described as a 'successful revolution' (Nellis 1991) in terms of ameliorating an apparently harsh governmental response to juvenile offenders by 'managing' to keep many of them out of the system. The figures on the use of custody and residential care reflect this success. The central challenge for juvenile justice practitioners in the 1990s, of course, goes beyond consolidating the successes of previous years, but the Acts brought into play at the beginning of this decade do leave considerable discretion with practitioners. There is scope for the anti-custody drive to be continued.[42]

The arguments are clearly no longer about 'welfare', 'crime control', or 'justice'; and the new philosophies, where discernible among practitoners, cannot be allied to the political right or left as they once could. Indeed, there is every indication that the 1990s begin with a return to the consensus on crime that marked the post-war era. The manifestos for the 1992 election revealed little difference in the political parties' respective responses to crime and conceptions of justice (Conservative Political Centre 1992; Labour Party 1992).[43] Indeed, it appears that 'Majorism' has had the effect of moving Conservatives to the left and that the rhetoric of control and punishment is mellowing; the Labour Party, on the other hand, appears to have moved to the right and there seems to be a new, shared realism among party members of different persuasions that punishment and responsibility (including parental responsibility) are at the core of concerns about juvenile justice.

In both rhetoric and practice, the formal arrangements for juvenile—

[42] Rutherford (1989) has identified five major points which contributed to changes in this sphere in the 1980s: (1) the local nature of some initiatives; (2) practice-led initiatives; (3) the focus on process rather than programmes (that is, targeting offenders at the 'deep end'); (4) inter-agency collaboration; and (5) the development of an anti-custody ethos among practitioners.

[43] The 1992 electoral campaign was remarkable for the similarity in the ways in which the major parties talked about crime. Both now focus on prevention and understanding the roots of criminality; and even Labour Party politicians now refer to individual responsibility and the need for punishment. There remain, however, some differences in emphasis. Kenneth Baker, the Home Secretary at the time of the 1992 election, rejected unemployment and deprivation as explanations of criminal behaviour, whereas Roy Hattersley, Deputy Leader of the Labour Party and shadow Home Secretary, continued to stress social factors, including poverty (*Public Eye*, BBC2, 27 March 1992).

or, more accurately, youth—justice are increasingly becoming linked with other social institutions and processes (schools, the family, neighbourhood, work) and there is ostensible concern among political parties and politicians to make strong connections between these processes where preventative and healing resources are perceived ultimately to reside. It remains to be seen whether or not this commitment remains at a rhetorical level and whether or not the right or the left will offer effective support to those social institutions in which both parties are placing their faith.

FURTHER READING

For an account of early developments in juvenile justice, readers may like to consult Morris and McIsaac, *Juvenile Justice?* (1978). *Understanding Juvenile Justice* by Morris and Giller (1987) provides a useful account of developments, debates, and empirical research. Similarly, *Justice through Punishment* (Hudson 1987) reflects a critical understanding of 'welfare' and 'justice' debates which have been the hallmark of juvenile justice developments in England and Wales. The second edition of *Growing Out of Crime* (Rutherford 1992) offers a critical account of policy and practice developments with regard to juvenile justice and contains some useful comments on the new era—heralded by the Criminal Justice Act 1991 and the introduction of the youth court. For a detailed description of the workings of the youth court, see Ashworth *et al.*, *The Youth Court* (1992*b*).

NOTE: SCOTLAND

Juvenile justice in Scotland has taken a completely different direction from England and Wales since the 1960s. While moves to abolish the juvenile court in England and Wales were fiercely resisted, similar ideas in Scotland were accepted—a remarkable achievement given the country's strong Calvinist traditions, traditions which stress individual responsibility and the punishment of wickedness. Indeed, Scotland has managed to implement, at least in theory, a social welfare approach.

In 1961, the Secretary of State for Scotland set up a committee, chaired by a High Court Judge (Lord Kilbrandon) to 'consider the provisions of the law of Scotland relating to the treatment of juvenile delinquents and juveniles in need of care or protection or beyond parental control and, in particular, the constitution, powers and procedures of courts dealing with such juveniles'. The committee, which reported in 1964 (Scottish Home and Health Department and Scottish Education Department 1964), began with the assumption that juveniles appearing before the juvenile court—whatever the reason for their appearance—were all exhibiting the varied symptoms of the same difficulties. It stated that in terms of actual needs, the legal distinction between juvenile offenders and children in need of care or protection was—looking to the underlying realities—very often of little practical significance. The Kilbrandon Committee's recommendations, and subsequently the White Paper *Social Work and the Community* (Scottish Education Department *et al.* 1966), led to the Social Work (Scotland) Act 1968, which heralded welfare tribunals staffed by lay people. This is not to suggest that the adoption of a welfarist perspective occurred without debate; but whereas interested parties in England and Wales lost the battle, in Scotland they won (for a detailed discussion of developments, see Morris and McIsaac 1978).

Children's hearings, as these are called, are concerned only with disposition. There is a complete separation between the judicial and disposition functions. If the juvenile or parents deny the commission of the offence, the case is referred by a Reporter (whose initial function it is to decide on the basis of reports, whether or not the juvenile referred to them by the police, social work, or education department is 'in need of compulsory measures of care') to the Sheriff Court for the offence to be proved. If the juvenile or parent objects to the decision made by the children's hearing regarding disposition, they can also appeal to the Sheriff Court. In both these instances, the parents and the juvenile are entitled to legal aid (This is not available before a children's hearing.)

This system applies to juveniles under the age of 16, although, if they enter the system before 16, they remain within it until the age of 18 unless the children's hearing terminates its jurisdiction. (The age of criminal responsibility in Scotland is 8, as opposed to 10 in England and Wales and Northern Ireland). The children's hearing can either discharge the referral by the Reporter or impose a supervision order, which may include residential conditions. The hearing has continuing jurisdiction; cases are reviewed annually. In contrast to the system in England and Wales, the lay panel has no power to fine the juvenile or his/her parents, to impose a custodial penalty, or to remit the juvenile to the Sheriff Court for sentence.

There is a considerable amount of research on the operation of the children's hearing system (Morris and McIsaac 1978; Martin *et al.* 1981; Asquith 1983; Adler 1985), though much of it is now quite old and may not accurately reflect current practice. That research raised questions about the observance of procedural safeguards, civil liberties, and patterns of communication and participation in the hearings.

Needless to say, developments in Scotland deserve a chapter of their own. We have been able here merely to indicate the salient point of departure from developments in England and Wales. In the absence of more recent material, readers will be well served by the references noted above. Kearney's *Children's Hearings and the Sheriff Court* (1987) provides a good descriptive account of the legal procedures involved in dealing with juvenile offenders in Scotland. Murray and Hill (1991) discuss the divergence of the Scottish and English systems, especially with regard to the development of the children's hearings system.

NOTE: NORTHERN IRELAND

Developments in Northern Ireland are similarly deserving of a separate chapter. The Children and Young Persons Act (Northern Ireland) 1968 provides the current legislative framework for dealing with juvenile offenders and children deemed to be in need of care, protection, and control. This legislation reflects a situation similar to that which pertained in England and Wales prior to the Children and Young Persons Act 1969.

The juvenile court remains the judicial forum in which any statutory intervention into the lives of children and young persons takes place. The court is presided over by a magistrate who has at least six years' experience as a practising lawyer, assisted by two members of a lay panel. Disposals available to the juvenile court are: fines, absolute and conditional discharges, committal to a training school, committal to the care of a fit person order, supervision or probation orders, attendance centre orders, committal to a remand home, a period in a young offenders' centre, and community service (for those juveniles who have reached the age of 16).

In 1976, a committee under the chairmanship of Sir Harold Black was established to review legislation and services relating to the care and treatment of children and young people. Its report was published at the end of 1979 (Department of Health and Social Services *et al.* 1979). The committee, influenced in the main by the 'Justice for Children' lobby, made some radical suggestions including the separation of the juvenile justice and welfare systems. Within the juvenile justice system, it was suggested that disposals should be determined by the offence alone and not be affected by any 'welfare' considerations. Also, custodial disposals were to be reserved for the serious and persistent offender, determinate, and served in a single secure unit replacing the existing training school system. Successive administrations accepted the Black Committee's recommendations 'in principle', but the proposed changes have been repeatedly postponed. Moreover, it may be argued that the original proposals have been considerably diluted. Black's recommendations for determinate sentencing and for a fixed number of custodial places, for example, appear to have bitten the dust. However, a Children and Young Persons Order dealing with some aspects of child care may give effect to at least some of the Black Committee's proposals.

Material on the Northern Ireland juvenile justice system appears to be thin on the ground, but interested readers should consult: Caul *et al.*, (1983) *The Juvenile Justice System in Northern Ireland.* McQuoid and Bloomer (1991) provide some detail on the operation of juvenile justice in Northern Ireland by describing sentencing in Craigavon juvenile court 1985–9. Their essay also offers some comment on the 'diversion from court' scheme in operation.

REFERENCES

ABEL-SMITH, B., and TOWNSEND, P. (1965), *The Poor and the Poorest*. London: G. Bell & Sons.

ADLER, R. (1985), *Taking Juvenile Justice Seriously*. Edinburgh: Scottish Academic Press.

ALLEN, R. (1990), 'Punishing the Parents', *Youth and Policy*, 31: 17–20.

—— (1991), 'Out of Jail: The Reduction in the Use of Penal Custody for Male Juveniles', *Howard Journal*, 30/1: 30–53.

ASHWORTH, A., CAVADINO, P., GIBSON, B., HARDING, J., RUTHERFORD, A., SEAGO, P., and WHYTE, L. (1992*a*), *Criminal Justice Act 1991:* Legal Points. Winchester: Waterside Press.

—— (1992*b*), *The Youth Court*. Winchester: Waterside Press.

ASQUITH, S. (1983), *Children and Justice: Decision-Making in Children's Hearings and Juvenile Courts*. Edinburgh: Edinburgh University Press.

BAILEY, V. (1987), *Delinquency and Citizenship*. Oxford: Oxford University Press.

BOTTOMS, A. E. (1974), 'On the Decriminalisation of English Juvenile Courts', in R. Hood, ed., *Crime, Criminoloy and Public Policy*. London: Heinemann.

—— (1987), 'Limiting Prison Use: Experience in England and Wales', *Howard Journal*, 26: 177–202.

BOTTOMS, A. E., BROWN, P., MCWILLIAMS, B., MCWILLIAMS, W., and NELLIS, M. (1990), *Intermediate Treatment and Juvenile Justice: Key Findings and Implications from a National Survey of Intermediate Treatment Policy and Practice*. London: HMSO.

BOTTOMS, A. E., and STEVENSON, S. (1992), 'What Went Wrong? Criminal Justice Policy in England and Wales, 1945–1970', in D. Downes, ed., *Unravelling Criminal Justice*. London: Macmillan.

BOWDEN, J., and STEVENS, M. (1986), 'Justice for Juveniles: A Corporate Strategy in Northampton', *Justice of the Peace*, 24 May: 326–9; 31 May: 345–7.

BOWLBY, J. (1946), *Forty-four Juvenile Thieves: Their Characters and Home Lives*. London: Bailliere, Tindall & Cox.

—— (1952), *Maternal Care and Mental Health: A Report Prepared on Behalf of the World Health Organization*. Geneva: World Health Organization.

BOX, S. (1987), *Recession, Crime and Punishment*. Basingstoke: Macmillan Educational

BRAKE, M., and HALE, C. (1992), *Public Order and Private Lives: The Politics of Law and Order*. London: Routledge.

BROWN, P., and SPARKS, R., eds. (1989), *Beyond Thatcherism: Social Policy, Politics and Society*. Milton Keynes: Open University Press.

BURNEY, E. (1985), *Sentencing Young People*. Aldershot: Gower.

CARLEBACH, J. (1970), *Caring for Children in Trouble*. London: Routledge and Kegan Paul.

CAUL, B., PINKERTON, J., and POWELL, J. (1983), *The Juvenile Justice System in Northern Ireland*. Ulster Polytechnic: The Polytechnic Series.

CAWSON, P. (1981), *Young Offenders in Care*. London: Department of Health and Social Security.

CAWSON, P., and MARTELL, M. (1979), *Children Referred to Closed Units*, DHSS Research Report no. 5. London: HMSO.

CENTRAL STATISTICAL OFFICE (1990), *Social Trends 20*. London: HMSO.

CHAPMAN, T., and COOK, J. (1988), 'Marginality, Youth and Government Policy in the 1980s', *Critical Social Policy*, 8/1: 41–64.

CHILDREN'S SOCIETY (1991), *Psychiatric Admissions: A Report on Young People Entering Residential Psychiatric Care*. London: The Children's Society.

CLARKE, A., and TAYLOR, I. (1980), 'Vandals, Pickets and Muggers: Television Coverage of Law and Order in the 1979 General Election', *Screen Education*, 31: 99–111.

CLARKE, J. (1975), *The Three Rs—Repression, Rescue and Rehabilitation: Ideologies of Control for Working Class Youth*. Birmingham: Birmingham University Centre for Contemporary Cultural Studies.

COHEN, S. (1973), *Folk Devils and Moral Panics: The Creation of Mods and Rockers*. St Albans: Paladin.

—— (1979), 'Notes on the Dispersal of Social Control', *Contemporary Crises*, 3: 339–63.

CONSERVATIVE POLITICAL CENTRE (1961), *Crime and Punishment*. London: CPC.

—— (1965), *Putting Britain Right Ahead*. London: CPC.

—— (1979), *Now is the Time to Choose*, Electoral Pamphlet. London: CPC.

—— (1992), *The Best Future for Britain*, Conservative Party manifesto. London: CPC.

COOPER, B., and NICHOLAS, G. (1963), *Crime in the Sixties*. London: Conservative Political Centre.

—— (1964), *Crime and the Labour Party*. London: The Bow Group.

CROSLAND, R. (1963), *The Future of Socialism*. London: Cape.

CROSSMAN, R. (1952), *The New Fabian Essays*. London: Turnstile Press.

—— (1972), *Inside View: Three Lectures on Prime Ministerial Government*. London: Jonathan Cape.

CROWN PROSECUTION SERVICE (1986), *Code of Practice for Prosecutors*. London: CPS.

DAVIN, A. (1978), 'Imperialism and Motherhood', *History Workshop*, 5: 9–65.

DAVIS, G., BOUCHERAT, J., and WATSON, D. (1989), 'Pre-Court Decision-Making in Juvenile Justice', *British Journal of Criminology*, 29: 219–34.

DEPARTMENT OF HEALTH AND SOCIAL SECURITY (1981), *Offending by Young People: A Survey of Recent Trends*. London: DHSS.

DEPARTMENT OF HEALTH AND SOCIAL SERVICES, NORTHERN IRELAND OFFICE AND DEPARTMENT OF EDUCATION (1979), *Report of the Children and Young Persons Review Group* (The Black Report). Belfast: HMSO.

DITCHFIELD, J. (1976), *Police Cautioning in England and Wales*, Home Office Research Study no. 37. London: HMSO.

DODDS, M. (1986), 'The Restrictions on Imposing Youth Custody and Detention Centre Sentences', *Justice of the Peace*, 7 June: 359–62.

—— (1987), 'The Restrictions on Imposing Youth Custody and Detention Centre Sentences—Some Recent Cases', *Justice of the Peace*, 19 September: 597–600.

DONINGTON, H. (1945), *The Care of Homeless Children*, Fabian Research Series Pamphlet. London: Fabian Society.

DONNISON, D., and JAY, P. (1962), *The Ingleby Report*, Fabian Research Series 231. London: Fabian Society.

DONNISON, D., and STEWART, M. (1958), *The Child and the Social Services*, Fabian Research Series 231. London: Fabian Society.

DOWNES, D. (1983), *Law and Order: Theft of an Issue*, Fabian Tract 490. London: Fabian Society.

DUNCAN, I. D. (1985), 'Social Work and Probation Court Reports: A Junior Detention Centre Perspective', unpublished paper.

DURHAM, M. (1989), 'The Right: The Conservative Party and Conservation', in L. Tivey and A. Wright, eds., *Party Ideology in Britain*. London: Routledge.

EVANS, R., and WILKINSON, C. (1990), 'Variations in Police Cautioning Policy and Practice in England and Wales', *Howard Journal*, 29/3: 155–76.

FARRINGTON, D. (1992), 'Trends in English Juvenile Delinquency and Their Explanation', special issue of *International Journal of Comparative and Applied Criminal Justice*, 16/2: 151–68.

—— and Bennett, T. (1981), 'Police Cautioning of Juveniles in London', *British Journal of Criminology*, 21/2: 123–35.

FISHER, C., and MAWBY, R. (1982), 'Juvenile Delinquency and Police Discretion in an Inner City Area', *British Journal of Criminology*, 22: 63–75.

FOUCAULT, M. (1977), *Discipline and Punish: The Birth of the Prison*. London: Allen Lane.

GELSTHORPE, L., and GILLER, H. (1990), 'More Justice for Juveniles: Does More Mean Better?', *Criminal Law Review*, March: 153–64.

GILLER, H., and MORRIS, A. (1981), *Care and Discretion: Social Workers' Decisions with Delinquents*. London: Burnett Books/Andre Deutsch.

GRAMSCI, A. (1971), *Selections from Prison Notebooks*. London: Lawrence and Wishart.

HALL, S. (1979), *Drifting Into a Law and Order Society*, The Cobden Trust Human Rights Day Lecture 1979. London: The Cobden Trust.

HALL, S., CRITCHER, C., JEFFERSON, T., CLARKE, J., and ROBERTS, B. (1978), *Policing the Crisis: Mugging, the State and Law and Order*. London: Macmillan.

HALSEY, A. (1988), *British Social Trends since 1900*, 2nd edn. London: Macmillan.

HARRIS, R. (1991), 'The Life and Death of the Care Order (Criminal)', *British Journal of Social Work*, 21: 1–17.

HARRIS, R., and WEBB, D. (1987), *Welfare, Power, and Juvenile Justice*. London: Tavistock.

HASTINGS, S., and JAY, P. (1965), *The Family and the Social Services*, Fabian Tract no. 359. London: Fabian Soceity.

HOME OFFICE (1927), *Report of the Departmental Committee on the Treatment of Young Offenders*, chaired by T. Molony, Cmd 283. London: HMSO.

—— (1938), *Report of the Departmental Committee on Corporal Punishment*, chaired by E. Cadogan, Cmd 5684. London: HMSO.

—— (1946), *The Care of Children Committee Report*, chaired by Miss M. Curtis, Cmd 6922. London: HMSO.

—— (1960), *Report of the Committee on Children and Young Persons*, chaired by R. Ingleby, Cmnd 1191. London: HMSO.

HOME OFFICE (1965), *The Child, the Family and the Young Offender*, Cmnd 2742. London: HMSO.

—— (1968), *Children in Trouble*, Cmnd 3601. London: HMSO.

—— (1980), *Young Offenders*, Cmnd 8045. London: HMSO.

—— (1984), *Cautioning by the Police: A Consultative Document*. London: Home Office.

—— (1985), *Home Office Circular 14/1985: The Cautioning of Offenders*. London: Home Office.

——1990*a*), *Home Office Circular 59/1990: The Cautioning of Offenders*. London: Home Office.

——(1990*b*), *Crime, Justice and Protecting the Public: The Government's Proposals for Legislation*, Cm 965. London: Home Office.

——(1991), *Safer Communities: The Local Delivery of Crime Prevention through the Partnership Approach*, Report of the Standing Conference on Crime Prevention chaired by J. Morgan. London: Home Office.

HOME OFFICE, DEPARTMENT OF EDUCATION AND SCIENCE, DEPARTMENT OF HOUSING AND LOCAL GOVERNMENT, AND DEPARTMENT OF HEALTH (1968), *Report of the Committee on Local Authority and Allied Personal Social Services* (The Seebohm Committee), Cmnd 3703. London: HMSO.

HOME OFFICE, WELSH OFFICE, DHSS, AND DES DEPARTMENT OF HEALTH AND SOCIAL SECURITY, AND DEPARTMENT OF EDUCATION AND SCIENCE (1976), *Children and Young Persons Act 1969: Observations on the Eleventh Report from the Expenditure Committee*. London: HMSO.

HOOD, R. (1965), *Borstal Reassessed*. London: Heinemann.

HOUSE OF COMMONS EXPENDITURE COMMITTEE (1975), *Eleventh Report: The Children and Young Persons Act 1969*. London: HMSO.

HUDSON, B. (1987), *Justice through Punishment*. Basingstoke: Macmillan Educational.

JONES, H. (1959), *Prison Reform Now*, Fabian Research Series no. 203. London: Fabian Society.

JONES, R. (1984), 'Questioning the New Orthodoxy', *Community Care*, (October): 15–17.

KEARNEY, B. (1987), *Children's Hearings and the Sheriff Court*. London: Butterworths.

LABOUR PARTY (1964), *Crime: A Challenge to Us All*, Report of a Labour Party Study Group, chaired by F. Longford. London: Labour Party.

—— (1992), *It's Time to Get Britain Working Again*, Labour Party election manifesto. London: Labour Party.

LANDAU, S. (1981), 'Juveniles and the Police', *British Journal of Criminology*, 21/1: 27–46.

LEVITAS, R., Ed. (1986), *The Ideology of the New Right*. Cambridge: Polity.

MCCLINTOCK, F., and AVISON, N. (1968), *Crime in England and Wales*. London: Heinemann Educational.

MACLEOD, I. (1958), 'The Political Divide', in P. Goldman, ed., *The Future of the Welfare State*. London: Conservative Political Centre.

MCLENNON, G. (1987), 'Sociological Theories of Crime: From Disorganisation to Class and Beyond', in *Thinking About Crime: Theories of Crime and Justice*, Open University D3104 Course Booklet. Milton Keynes: Open University.

McQuoid, J., and Bloomer, S. (1991), 'A Portrait of Juvenile Crime: Craigavon Juvenile Court Statistics 1985–1989', in T. Booth, ed., *Juvenile Justice in the New Europe*. Sheffield: University of Sheffield Joint Unit for Social Services Research and Community Care Magazine.

Marshall, T. (1975), *Social Policy*. London: Hutchinson.

Marshall, T., and Merry, S. (1990), *Crime and Accountability: Victim/Offender Mediation in Practice*. London: HMSO.

Martin, F., Fox, S., and Murray, K. (1981), *Children Out of Court*. Edinburgh: Scottish Academic Press.

Marwick, A. (1982), *British Society since 1945*. Harmondsworth: Penguin.

May, J. (1980), *Justice, Welfare and Juvenile Delinquents*, Fabian Tract no. 472. London: Fabian Society.

Millham, S., Bullock, R., and Hosie, K. (1978), *Locking up Children: Secure Provision within the Childcare System*. Farnborough: Saxon House.

Millichamp, D., Payne, D., and Thomas, H. (1985), 'A Matter of Natural Justice', *Community Care*, 13 June: 25–7.

Ministry of Health (1944), *Hostels for 'Difficult' Children*. London: HMSO.

Morris, A. (1987), *Women, Crime and Criminal Justice*. Oxford: Blackwell.

—— (1981), 'Young Offenders: Law and order and the Child-Care System', *Howard Journal*, 20/2: 81–9.

—— (1987), *Understanding Juvenile Justice*. London: Croom Helm.

Morris, A., and Gelsthorpe, L. (1981), 'False Clues and Female Crime', in A. Morris and L. Gelsthorpe, eds., *Women and Crime*, Cropwood Series no. 13. Cambridge: University of Cambridge Institute of Criminology.

Morris, A., and Giller, H. (1979), *What Justice for Children?*. London: Justice for Children.

Morris, A., Giller, H., Szwed, E., and Geach, H. (1980), *Justice for Children*. London: Macmillan.

Morris, A., and McIsaac, M. (1978), *Juvenile Justice?* London: Heinemann.

Morris, P. (1960), *Prison After Care: Clarity or Public Responsibility?*, Fabian Research Series no. 218. London: Fabian Society.

Morris, T. (1989), *Crime and Criminal Justice since 1945*. Oxford: Blackwell.

Muncie, J. (1990), 'Failure Never Matters: Detention Centres and the Politics of Deterrence', *Critical Social Policy*, 10: 53–66.

Murray, K., and Hill, M. (1991), 'The Recent History of Scottish Child Welfare', *Children and Society*, 5/3: 266–81.

National Association for the Care and Resettlement of Offenders (1985), *Tougher Regimes in Detention Centres: The Evaluation Report*. London: NACRO.

—— (1989*a*), *Replacing Custody*. London: NACRO.

—— (1989*b*), *The Children Act: Implications for Juvenile Justice*, Briefing Paper. London: NACRO.

Nellis, M. (1991), 'The Last Days of "juvenile" justice?', in P. Carter, T. Jeffs, and M. Smith, eds., *Social Work and Social Welfare*, Yearbook 3. Milton Keynes: Open University Press.

Parker, H., Sumner, M., and Jarvis, G. (1989), *Unmasking the Magistrates: The 'Custody or Not' Decision in Sentencing Young Offenders*. Milton Keynes: Open University Press.

Parliamentary All-Party Penal Affairs Group (1981), *Young Offenders: A Strategy for the Future*. Chichester: Barry Rose.

Pitts, J. (1988), *The Politics of Juvenile Crime*. London: Sage.

Pratt, J. (1989), 'The Punishment of Juveniles and the Commodification of Time', in S. Jones, ed., *British Criminology Conference Proceedings*. Bristol: Bristol and Bath Centre for Criminal Justice.

President's Commission On Law Enforcement and the Administration of Justice (1967), *Task Force Report: Juvenile Delinquency and Youth Crime*. Washington, DC: US Government Printing Office.

Reiner, R., and Cross, M., eds. (1991), *Beyond Law and Order: Criminal Justice Policy in the 1990s*. Basingstoke: Macmillan.

Rock, P. (1990), *Helping Victims of Crime: The Home Office and the Rise of Victim Support in England and Wales*. Oxford: Clarendon Press.

Rose, N. (1989), *Governing the Soul: The Shaping of the Private Self*. London: Routledge.

Rutherford, A. (1986), *Growing Out of Crime*. Harmondsworth: Penguin.

—— (1989), 'The Mood and Temper of Penal Policy: Curious Happenings in England during the 1980s', *Youth and Policy*, 27: 27–31.

—— (1992), *Growing Out of Crime: The New Era*, 2nd edn. Winchester: Waterside Press.

Scottish Education Department, Scottish Home and Health Department (1966), *Social Work and the Community: Proposals for Re-organising Local Authority Services in Scotland*. Edinburgh: HMSO.

Scottish Home and Health Department and Scottish Education Department (1964), *Report of Committee on Children and Young Persons*, chaired by Lord Kilbrandon, Cmnd 2306. Edinburgh: HMSO.

Smith, D. (1984), 'Law and Order: Arguments for What?' *Critical Social Policy*, issue 11 (Winter), pp. 33–45.

Stanley, C. (1988), 'Making Statutory Guidelines Work', *Justice of the Peace*, 8 October: 648–50.

Taylor, I. (1981), 'Crime Waves in Post-War Britain', *Contemporary Crises*, 5: 43–62.

Taylor, L., Lacey, R., and Bracken, D. (1980), *In Whose Best Interests?* London: Cobden Trust/MIND.

Thomas, H. (1982), 'The Road to Custody is Paved with Good Intentions', *Probation Journal*, 29: 92–7.

Thomson, D. (1950), *England in the Twentieth Century*. Harmondsworth: Penguin.

Thorpe, D., Smith, D., Green, C., and Paley, J. (1980), *Out of Care*. London: Allen and Unwin.

Titmuss, R. (1968), *Commitment to Welfare*. London: Allen and Unwin.

Tutt, N. (1981), 'A Decade of Policy', *British Journal of Criminology*, 21/4: 246–56.

—— (1987), 'Response to the Review of Intermediate Treatment in Scotland', *Viewpoints*, 43. Glasgow: Intermediate Treatment Resource Centre.

United Nations (1985), *Standard Minimum Rules for the Administration of Juvenile Justice* (The Beijing Rules), General Assembly Resolution 40/33 of 29 November 1985. Geneva: UN.

—— (1989), *The Convention of the Rights of the Child* (Geneva: Defence for Children International and the United Nations Children's Fund).

WEBB, S., and WEBB, B., eds. (1909), *The Public Organisation of the Labour Market* (Being Part III of the Minority Report of the Poor Law Commission). London: Longmans.

WILKINSON, C., and EVANS, R. (1990), 'Police Cautioning of Juveniles: The Impact of Home Office Circular 14/1985', *Criminal Law Review*, March: 165–76.

ZANDER, M. (1975), 'What Happens to Young Offenders in Care', *New Society*, 24 July: 185–7.

PART 4

Social Dimensions of Crime and Justice

21

Gender and Crime

FRANCES HEIDENSOHN

Any account of the connections between gender and crime must begin by confronting a paradox. This is that while these links have long been known to take distinctive forms wherever crime has been systematically recorded, their significance was ignored and marginalized throughout much of the history of criminology. In the latter part of the twentieth century, however, the situation was transformed; from being a criminological Cinderella, this topic became the focus of a great deal of attention and the source of some of the major developments in the field. In order to cover the subject of gender and crime, then, it is important to explain its prehistory and standing as well as addressing the extensive material which appeared in the modern period of high fertility.

First it is necessary to clarify the terms being used and to outline the main aspects of the subject which will be covered in this chapter. Longman's English Dictionary (1984) defines gender simply as 'sex', but for social scientists 'sex' and 'gender' are usually differentiated. 'Sex' is commonly used to describe the innate biological characteristics of humans, constituting their femaleness or maleness. 'Gender', on the other hand, covers the social characteristics and usages associated with one sex or the other. Since such roles and customs can vary and be modified, it follows that 'masculine' and 'feminine', the terms applied to the respective genders, are much more flexible than 'female' and 'male'. It is possible, for example, to describe a woman's clothing as 'masculine' or a man as having a 'feminine sensibility'. (Biological sex can, of course, be altered too, but this usually requires drastic surgical and pharmaceutical intervention as well as presenting the individual concerned with vast social and legal obstacles to surmount.)

Of course, the definition of what is a woman (or a man) is by no means always straightforward (Edwards 1984). Once one begins to consider the meaning of gender roles to individuals and groups, the situation becomes very complex. It has been increasingly recognized, for instance, that differences between the experiences of ethnic groups may be as great as those between men and women (Arnold 1990; Chigwada 1991). In this chapter I try as far as possible to acknowledge such differences where they matter, as well as noting and analysing the important similarities between categories and persons.

In practice, most social enquiry is concerned with issues of both sex and of gender, although the second term is used more often because it covers both aspects of innate and acquired characteristics and the interaction between them and society. In the case of crime there is an elision made between the two forms of categorization which has considerable salience for the study of this field. For as long as systematic records of crime have been kept the sex of offenders has been noted. Indeed, sex has sometimes had significance as a legal category in relation to criminal acts. While criminal law broadly applies equally to women and to men, there have been, and still are, some exceptions. Male homosexual acts have generally been defined as criminal in most western countries, while lesbian acts have not. Criminal codes often treat prostitution activities of males and females differently. Under English common law women charged with felony (except murder and treason) committed in the presence of their husbands could rely on the presumption that they acted under compulsion (Mannheim 1965: 691–3) until this provision was abolished in 1925.

Noting the sex of offenders was necessary primarily for routine purposes in the criminal justice system, especially once segregation was practised in prisons (Smith 1962; Zedner 1991). Obviously, sex can be registered only for known offenders, and thus data on this topic are subject to even more limitations than those considered in general elsewhere in this volume (see Maguire chapter 6 and Zedner chapter 25 in this volume). Despite these reservations, certain trends and patterns in female criminality as compared with male have long been observed. In summary, these are:

1. Women commit a small share of all crimes.
2. Women's crimes are fewer, less serious, and more rarely professional than men's.
3. In consequence, women are represented in very small numbers in penal establishments.

The attentive reader will see at once that I have moved from discussing the question of sex and gender to a focus on *women*, or women compared with men. This shift reflects what has happened historically in the history of criminology, although, as I shall argue later in this chapter, masculine gender and its relation to crime became an area of increasing interest in the late twentieth century. There is a marked contrast between this situation and that which obtained during what can be described as the prehistory of this subject. As I have already suggested, a grasp of this history is important in understanding more recent developments.

THE PREHISTORY OF GENDER AND CRIME

It has often been asserted that the subject of women and crime suffered from criminological neglect until the late twentieth century. While this statement is broadly true, it does need some qualification. Female criminality was *relatively* neglected and was treated in certain very specific ways. Much more notable is the almost total absence of what two modern writers describe as 'questions (which) now occupy a central role in research on gender and crime . . . the *generalizability problem* . . . and the *gender ratio problem*' (Daly and Chesney Lind 1988: 508, emphasis in original). By the generalizability problem they mean 'whether theories generated to describe men's . . . offending can apply to women', while the gender ratio question is 'why females commit less crime than males' (ibid.).

Accounts of female criminality published during the nineteenth century and the earlier twentieth century can be usefully divided into two groups: practical criminologies, and essays at theory which were frequently characterized by their psychological or biological reductionism. By practical criminologies I mean that range of mainly Victorian studies which dwelt on women's social and moral position and especially their vulnerability to 'falling' into crime and deviance. They were written by prison chaplains (Horsley 1887), doctors (Acton 1857), journalists (Mayhew 1861), lawyers (Pike 1876), and amateur social scientists concerned with 'denouncing casinos and dancing saloons as sources of female corruption' (cited in Zedner 1991: 61). As Zedner points out, many of these descriptions locate the origins of female crime in the same sources as those of male crime: variously, poor urban conditions and moral weakness. Most, however, she notes, regarded women as more vulnerable than men because their 'purity' and hence their whole moral being could be at risk.

Later in the nineteenth century, women criminals became, as did their male counterparts, the subjects of enquiry of positivist criminology. Lombroso and Ferrero's *The Female Offender* (*La Donne Deliquente*, 1895) is the best-known example of this trend and the only one generally cited. Their study does deal, albeit crudely, with both the gender ratio and the generalizability problem. In the case of the latter, they failed to find the numbers of 'born female criminals' marked by physical, atavistic traits which they had anticipated. They argued that *all* women were less evolved than men, and thus closer to primitive types, but also that natural selection had bred out the criminal tendencies among women, since more 'masculine' women did not find sexual partners.

Most of the flaws in positivism, and the inadequacies of Lombroso's methods, are represented in this work. It is however, notable for several features. First, it was frequently used to represent psychological and biodeterminist theories of female crime. Secondly, it survived and was cited as a convincing commentary on female criminality (Mannheim 1965) long after comparable work on males had been rejected (Heidensohn 1985) and has, it has been argued, cast a long shadow over women's penal treatment (Dobash *et al.* 1986). Both of the key problems of gender and crime are tackled in *The Female Offender*, but it is characteristic of so much of this literature, and other related types of work, that such issues are not discussed in studies of male offenders. Another feature of Lombroso's work was that, as modern scholarship has demonstrated, it was a contribution to a range of complex debates about criminality and social control in late nineteenth-century and early twentieth-century Europe (Beirne 1988; Garland 1985), in which Lombroso was subject to serious challenge. What is fascinating is that, while the force of some of these criticisms was overestimated (see, for instance, Beirne's (1988) appraisal of *The English Convict* as unsuccessful), evaluations of Lombroso and Ferrero have been much more neglected. Frances Kellor, an American sociologist, conducted comparative studies which did not substantiate Lombroso's findings and indeed showed social and environmental factors to be much more important (see also Pollock-Byrne 1990 for a review of a range of such US studies).

The consequence of this was a scenario reminiscent of *Sleeping Beauty*. Whereas the rest of the criminological world moved on from positivism, embracing in particular a series of sociological theories of crime and deviance, female crime was cut off from most of this development as though by thickets of thorn (Smart 1977; Leonard 1982). Those few studies which did appear in the first half of the twentieth century seem very isolated and lack a base. Pollak's work (1950) I have characterized (Heidensohn 1985) as curiously outside and unrelated to all the fervour of work of that time on 'strain' theory and subcultures. It exists in an ahistoric limbo in which women, as domestic servants and full-time housewives, commit *more* crime than men, but keep this hidden through devious means and by exploiting men's innate chivalry. This relative neglect and isolation in research on female crime was a major target of criticism for the many, and many varieties of, feminist criminologists who were to transform work on this subject in the late twentieth century. Their primary focus was on women and crime, and their central theme was that in ignoring women's experiences of crime, both as perpetrators and as victims the subject was impoverished (Smart 1977; Heidensohn 1968, 1985). Implicitly, however, this criticism also extends to the limitations of all studies of crime which do not address questions of gender. In order to demonstrate how central these questions are we shall now look in detail at evidence and analysis of the configurations of gender in three areas: crime, criminal justice, and punishment. Given the emphases in past and recent studies in these areas, the main focus will be on women, but comparisons will also be made between women and men and the importance of gender to each topic will also be addressed.

WOMEN, MEN, AND CRIME

'Women commit much less crime than men do' is a statement that has achieved the status of a truth universally acknowledged. Closer examination leads, however, to some qualification. On most comparisons, the differences are remarkable and robust, and, as we shall see, appear to be valid. Throughout the 1980s in England and Wales the rates of offending (measured as persons found guilty or cautioned for indictable offences) per 100,000 of population were always over 1,000 for males, but well under 500 for females (see Fig. 21.1, Table 21.1). Expressed in another way, women's share of serious offending during the same decade varied between 14 per cent and 18 per cent (Home Office 1990, 1992). Yet another approach is to assess the relative likelihood of being convicted

Table 21.1. Women's involvement in crime by category

Crime	Percent of Total Arrests
Murder and nonnegligent manslaughter	12.5%
Forcible rape	1.2%
Robbery	8.1%
Aggravated assault	13.3%
Burglary	7.9%
Larceny/theft	31.1%
Motor vehicle theft	9.7%
Arson	13.7%
IOther assaults	15.1%
Forgery and counterfeiting	34.4%
Fraud	49.5%
Embezzlement	38.1%
Stolen property	11.6%
Prostitution	84.8%
Drug abuse violations	14.9%
Offenses against family and children	17.4%
(Other crime categories excluded)	

Source: Uniform Crime Report U.S. Department of Justice

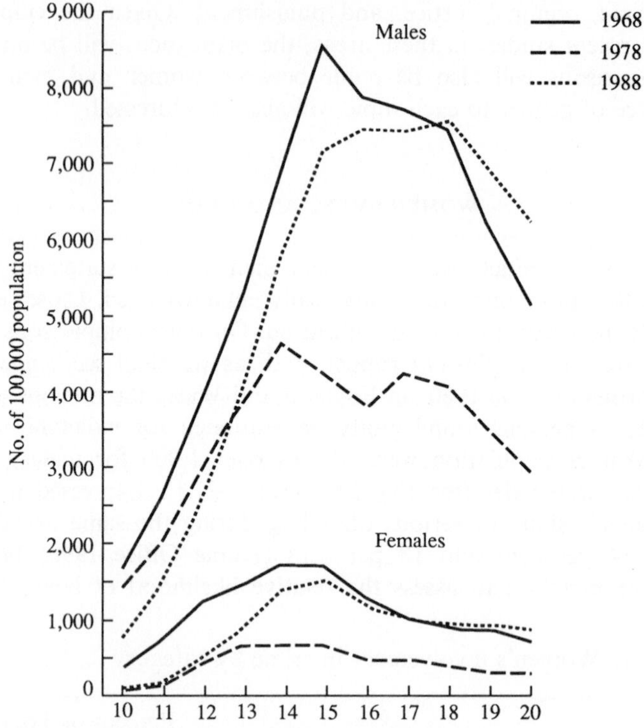

Fig. 21.1 Persons under 21 found guilty of, or cautioned for, indictable offences, per 100,000 population, by age group (England and Wales)
Source: Criminal Statistics 1991 HMSO London

over a lifetime: Farrington (1981) suggested that 43 per cent of men, but fewer than 15 per cent of women, were likely to be convicted of a serious offence during their careers.

Such differences seem to be common across a variety of nations and cultures. In surveying material on Europe, I found that 'crime is still an activity overwhelmingly dominated by men in all European countries. In France in 1986 . . . of persons . . . dealt with in criminal proceedings 81.27% were male and 18.73% female . . . in Germany . . . 79.5% were male and 20.5% female' (Heidensohn 1991: 57). Similar, or lower shares, can be found in the Netherlands and Scandinavia. Figures given in the US *Uniform Crime Reports* (US Department of Justice 1984–) also show that women made up less than 20 per cent of those arrested. This apparently consistent pattern has led some commentators to suggest that women offenders are 'only 10 per cent of the trouble'. However, when one considers different types of offence and changes over time, a more complex and qualified picture emerges. Some very diverse writers have suggested that women mainly confine themselves to sexually delinquent acts (Lombroso and Ferrero 1895; Thomas 1923; Cohen 1955). On the contrary, women contribute to all types of offending, but their share varies considerably. Taking figures of violent offenders for England and Wales during the 1980s, women's share rose slightly from 9 per cent in 1979 to 11.2 per cent in 1989 (Home Office 1990). In other types of crime, there is considerable variation. Similar 'shares' can be found under other jurisdictions, although they are by no means always the same. Thus, in the nearest equivalent figures for England and Wales, those of offenders found guilty or cautioned for indictable offences, in none of the categories does the female share reach half the total (Home Office 1990).

The question whether female crime was rising at a faster rate than male, and whether the female share was thus going up, has been a highly contended criminological issue since the 1970s. Indeed, this is one of the few topics to do with women and crime to excite widespread attention (Heidensohn 1989*a*: ch. 5). The issue was first raised by Freda Adler (1975)—and, in a more modified form by Rita Simon (1975)—who argued

(a) that female crime rates had been rising more rapidly in the late 1960s and early 1970s;
(b) that women offenders were changing their patterns of offending to more 'masculine' styles, becoming more aggressive and violent; and
(c) that this was due to the growth of the modern women's movement: in short, that 'liberation causes crime'.

These contentions have been much discussed and analysed. Two aspects of the thesis need to be distinguished: that of rising female crime rates, and that of the influence of feminism. As to the first, no very clear picture emerges; and, given what we know of the limitations of such data (see Maguire chapter 6 in this volume), great caution is necessary. Smart (1979), for instance, taking long time series for England and Wales, finds that female crime rates were already rising at a faster rate than male long before the advent of the modern women's movement, although Austin (1981) is critical of some of her interpretation. Smart also pointed out the dangers to which interpretations of figures on female criminality are additionally subject: because numbers are so small they are highly susceptible to shifts in policing, recording, and other policies. Further, measuring percentage changes may give an exaggerated view—an increase from five to ten cases is a 100 per cent rise.

Steffensmeier (1978) in the USA and Box (1983) and Box and Hale (1983) in Britain reviewed figures and found a stable female share of violent offending but some increase in property crimes of a conventional, petty kind. This led Steffensmeier to conclude that 'the new female criminal is more a social invention than an empirical reality'. Authors who tried to define and measure female emancipation and to test its relationship with crime experienced difficulty and are scarcely convincing (Box and Hale, 1983). They found little plausible linkage. Critics of this view have argued that a theory of marginalization or impoverishment would be more plausible (Chapman 1980; Carlen 1990).

Modern historical work on crime has experienced a renaissance and studies of women offenders have been one element of this. They enrich, and also complicate, the patterns of crime we are trying to unravel. Writing of Britain in the eighteenth century, McLynn says that 'only 12 per cent of the accused in the home counties in 1782–7 were female' (1989: 128). Others have pointed out, none the less, that women participated in food riots in the pre-modern period (Beattie 1975). Figures for these, and earlier, periods need to be treated with even more circumspection than those from the contemporary period. In particular, they record such phenomena as 'the criminal classes'; Zedner notes that 'Overall there was a considerable decline in those designated as the "criminal classes". Over the period 1860–90 they fell by more than half. The number of women fell at roughly the same rate as men, remaining at around a fifth of the total in this category over the period' (1991: 20). She concludes that this relatively low rate was due to the exclusion of prostitutes, vagrants, and tramps. In terms of convictions, Zedner notes that 'overall, women's crimes made up a steady 17% of all summary convictions' (1991: 34), with drunkenness, assault, and larceny the commonest types of offence. In contrast to the steady state in summary jurisdiction, 'over the second half of the nineteenth century, women formed a declining proportion of those proceeded against by indictment . . . (from 27% of the total in 1867 to only 19% by 1890)' (1991: 36). Zedner's detailed work on nineteenth-century data confirms on the whole the 'modest share' view of female as compared with male crime. She also notes some reporting of a decline in convictions of women for serious offences by the end of the century (1991: 23).

Other writers have asserted that women's share of criminality declined relatively in certain modern periods (Mannheim 1965; Feest 1985). Boritch and Hagan (1990), using one of the longest time series, from 1850 to 1950 in Toronto, document such a trend and claim that this was due to the success of moral entrepreneurs of the first wave of feminism, who provided diversion from criminality and stigma through non-punitive interventions in women's lives. Jones also records a fall in female crime: 'The mid Victorian years witnessed a concerted campaign against the crime and violence associated with "women of the streets" and a sustained fall in reported female attacks on property and persons, especially by the very young' (1982: 7). Most historians are more cautious and/or rely on changed practices of recording, controlling, and classifying crime and misdemeanours (Walkowitz 1980), 'chivalry' arguments (McLynn 1989), views about the changed nature of femininity in Victorian Britain (Zedner 1991), or combinations of all three.

Too Few to Count?

Women's low share of recorded crime can be substantiated, with certain reservations. While for decades, as I pointed out above, this finding proved to be of little interest to criminologists, the situation changed in the 1970s and considerable efforts were expended in searching for the hidden iceberg of female crime. Pollak had, of course, already (1950) insisted that hidden female crime far exceeded revealed and concealed male crime, but he did not evince any new sources of material, relying instead on assertions about thefts by domestic servants. Several modern writers have sought to demonstrate a similar point, albeit less dramatically, by using self-report studies, 'bystander' or observer accounts, or victim surveys (Smith and Visher 1980; Gold 1970; Mawby 1980; Pratt 1980; Burney 1990; Hindelang 1979; and see Box 1983 for a review). While many of these researchers did find 'hidden' female crime, they also found hidden male crime too, and do not suggest that the ratios derived from official data should be reversed.

Domestic 'Secrets'

Our understanding of other features of the gender ratio has not, in any case, remained static. The subject of victimization, and the contributions of feminists, among others, to its 'discovery', are covered elsewhere in this volume (see Zedner chapter 25). It is important to note how the focus on the 'private' harms perpetrated within the home in domestic violence and the physical and sexual abuse of children alters the gender ratio adversely for men, since they are largely, though not exclusively, the offenders in such crimes. While measures of incidence are shadowy, victim surveys do suggest that there are low reporting rates for such offences and yet a high rate of distress (Jones *et al.* 1986; Hanmer and Saunders 1984; Stanko 1990). Serious sexual crimes such as rape also have low reporting rates because of women's fear of shame and of police and court procedures (see Zedner chapter 25 in this volume). Some attempts have been made to redress the gender 'imbalance' in such private and personal crimes. Dobash and Dobash (1992: 258 ff.) review family violence research in the USA which seeks to show that there is an equivalence in violence between spouses, with husbands more likely to be victims than wives. The Dobashes also review what they call 'violence-against-women research' and conclude that empirical studies conclusively support an asymmetric view which further imbalances the gender ratio.

Other related topics have also been considered in this way. Child sexual abuse by women, including mothers, has been the subject of some concern, even though the proportion of women carrying out such acts is still acknowledged to be very small. Research on abuse of children in the home by the British National Society for the Prevention of Cruelty to Children (Creighton and Noyes 1989) is significant in that their data enable comparisons to be made of the relative risks to which children are exposed with parents, step-parents, etc. This study, based on some 8,274 children on NSPCC registers, indicates the *suspected* abusers. In the period covered (1983–7), natural mothers were implicated in 33 per cent and natural fathers in 29 per cent of the physical injury cases. When the figures were adjusted to take account of which parent the child lived with, then the natural fathers were implicated in 61 per cent and mothers in 36 per cent of cases. Moreover, these figures, as the authors point out, make no allowance for the proportional time spent with children and especially not of time alone with them. Such findings, based as they are on observations and not on police evidence or court verdicts, may be even less robust than official crime records. Nevertheless, even if they do record assumptions rather than acts, there is perhaps some significance in their consistency with all the other material noted in this section.

WOMEN IN THE CRIMINAL JUSTICE PROCESS

Women and Policing

The nature and tasks of modern policing have been much discussed, in both academic and public debate (Reiner 1985; Reiner and Shapland 1987; and see Reiner chapter 15 in this volume). In particular, the culture of police agencies and the impact this has on their activities have been anatomized as based on macho values, stressing aggression, sexism, and racism, and giving status to serious crime work (Smith and Gray 1983; Young 1991). There are differing views on how far attitudes derived from such values affect police in their work with citizens (Smith and Gray 1983). What is not in doubt is that many researchers, as well as representatives of minority groups and, increasingly, the general public, have become critical of police behaviour towards citizens and suspects. The police themselves have recognized this and have tried to alter their policies and procedures in response.

Police operate within a very considerable range of discretion, processing only a proportion of incidents and citizens through to a full criminal charge (and being limited at that stage by the Crown Prosecution Service). How women fare in such encounters is another considerably contested area and one on which it is much harder to reach conclusions than on criminal behaviour. No record exists of *all* police–public encounters. However, there are significant differences between the sexes in reported contacts. Thus, in the Policy Studies Institute survey of policing in London (Smith and Gray 1983), more men than women (63 per cent to 51 per cent) had had recent contacts with the police. Class and race complicated the issue: 87 per cent of unemployed men, but only 16 per cent of Asian women, reported direct encounters. Surveys do show that frequent contact with the police lowers the esteem in which they are held and this may help to explain the slightly greater support for police among women. It is police treatment of *men* from ethnic minorities (including the Irish) that has been most strongly linked to the 'cop culture' discussed above.

Women, it has been argued by many writers, benefit from the values to which the cop culture gives rise (Morris 1987: 80–1). They are seen as in need of protection, not punishment, and accorded the respect of chivalry. Indeed, this view was long adduced in explanation of lower rates of recorded female crime (Mannheim 1965). More recent work suggests a more complex picture in which 'demeanour' (Piliavin and Briar 1964) is a key factor in determining police reactions, as well as seriousness of offence and recidivism (Harris 1992).

Gender appears to be only one factor in determining police decisions: 'To be older, apologetic and "respectable" is as advantageous for men as for women and gender is only one of many variables to consider in the complex process of police arresting behaviour' (Harris 1992: 95). However, there does not appear to be a neatly constructed demonology from least to most deviant, cross-tabulated by sex, demeanour, and aggression. If there were, as Visher noted (1983: 19), then violent women offenders would be at one extreme, yet they do not seem so to feature (and see Allen 1987).

The opposite view to that of the police as 'knights in shining armour' has been advocated by a growing number of observers in the 1980s and 1990s. These fall broadly into two groupings: those who have examined police treatment of women and girls as *victims*, especially of domestic violence and sexual crimes; and those who have encountered the police as members of 'deviant' groups, such as political protestors, and members of sexual and other minorities. Female victimization is discussed in detail elsewhere in this book (see Zedner chapter 25), as are the reported attitudes and practices to female victims of the police and other agencies, and the changes, or attempted changes, in procedures made in response to widespread criticism. Several writers suggest that police officers transfer their low evaluation of women as victims to women as offenders and respond to them as women and thus as inferior (Jones 1987; see Dunhill 1989 for a selection). The louder 'voices' which many women have sought to express as a result of modern feminism have given graphic details of some experiences (e.g. Reynolds 1991).

It is difficult to establish how far such accounts represent examples of women being treated differentially *as women*, or rather in the same way as men are also treated by official control agencies because they are all offenders. Certainly, women as victims of certain kinds of crime report distinctive fears, distress, and trauma. They also describe the additional problems of being interrogated by male officers whose gender may seem a threat, and this being compounded by unsympathetic and disparaging treatment. However, from this recognition the confident assertion that women offenders are also policed in harsh and stereotypical ways is a large leap—and one, moreover, that involves the fallacy of overprediction. If the police were particularly ill-disposed and punitive towards women then, logically, there should be *more*, not fewer, women criminalized and processed as deviant. In short, evidence on this topic is patchy, and conclusions necessarily tentative. It is clear that cautioning is used more heavily for female than for male offenders. Yet this seems to arise mainly from the less serious and less frequent nature of female offending.

Several groups of deviant women have reported particularly repressive treatment by the police and accused them of especially harsh treatment. Prostitutes have long complained, and more recently campaigned, as have others on their behalf, about such treatment. The nineteenth-century Contagious Disease Acts, and the opposition organized against them (Petrie 1971), have been followed by a series of such groupings in the twentieth century (see below). Høigård and Finstad, in their study (1992) of street prostitution in Norway, describe the women's fear of police brutality, sexual advances, and failure to offer protection against dangerous clients. McLeod outlines a somewhat different pattern in Britain. Harassment and entrapment were reported, but also a degree of accommodation (1982: 106). Evidence given by police representatives themselves to a parliamentary committee showed disparaging views of women who prostitute themselves (cited in Heidensohn 1985: 55–6).

While street prostitutes are one, untypical, group of women who have frequent contact with the police, the converse is true of the other deviant women who make complaints about how the police have treated them. The militant suffragettes were among the first political protesters to object to police manhandling of them, a tradition carried on by the Greenham Common women and other demonstrators (Strachey 1978;

Young 1990). What distinguishes these accounts from those of men is that they often allege sexual abuse and humiliation. These are still more marked in the episodes recounted by lesbian, Irish, and black women (e.g. Natzler, O'Shea, Heaven, Mars 1989). Organizations which monitor such policing grew in the 1970s and 1980s, but were then affected by cuts in aid to voluntary organizations (Greater London Council 1985). While such stories are harrowing it is, without systematic monitoring, impossible to tell how typical they are, or how gender-specific. Many accounts have parallels in the histories of male offenders, although sexual abuse and humiliation are usually reserved for homosexual men.

Most discussions of these issues are based on the sexist notion that all police officers are male and the stereotyped one that 'the police' are a unified body with common aims and procedures. In fact, in both Britain and the USA some 10 per cent of officers overall are women, as are a much higher proportion of basic grade officers, whom the public and petty offenders meet first (Heidensohn 1992*b*). Women's entry into policing in both countries was promoted in the late nineteenth and early twentieth century precisely to provide protection to female and juvenile offenders and victims which, it was felt, they did not receive from an all-male force (Carrier 1988; Feinman 1986). For more than fifty years, until integration in the 1970s, small numbers of female officers worked in this fashion in both systems.

Both the pioneer policewomen of the early days and present-day women officers report extensive harassment and abuse by their male colleagues (Heidensohn 1992*b*). Young (1991) has given an extensive account of such attitudes and behaviour in a British force. Other writers have, however, questioned how typical such accounts of conventional machismo now are (e.g. Walker 1985), while elsewhere researchers have found some signs of changes (Steel and Lovrich 1987; Martin 1990).

Very little work has been done to establish whether female officers treat female offenders in distinctive ways (for reviews see Heidensohn 1985, 1992). Carey (1977) found no differences. Studies of these issues are bedevilled by complications characteristic of this area in general. First, numbers of both women offenders and women officers are very small. Second, their range is neither broad nor typical of the full scope of either offending or policing. Third, women officers are still, despite integration, deployed in stereotypical tasks, e.g. in child protection teams. Further, a whole series of questions has to be raised about gender-specific and gender-neutral perceptions and experiences. Some studies, for instance, report women as being more punitive towards their own sex (Worrall 1990). But women in law enforcement agencies handle all their cases within a male-dominated system. They may either be more censorious or feel the need to appear so (see Heidensohn 1992, for one such episode).

There are further questions, raised increasingly in more thoughtful analyses, to do with both variations within groups and systems, and standards and perceptions of fairness and appropriateness. As I have suggested elsewhere (1985, 1987), women are policed by the same agencies, and using the same laws, as men are. Some, however, perceive and protest about their treatment in distinctive ways. In part this seems to be due to their experience of much greater levels of informal social control outside the formal agencies. Husbands, partners, families, social workers, the church, can all be seen as giving particular attention to assuring the conformity of women (Heidensohn 1985).

Gender is, in short, a variable of some significance in debates about policing. Primarily this is because official policing has been seen as an extremely masculine occupation, reserved for men. As a result, women's experience of it may be more or less harsh, appropriate or inappropriate, largely, though not entirely, depending on how far this situation has been remedied. Because it was long assumed, in Britain especially, that gender-based policing was normal, its failures in this and other respects have been tackled only late in the twentieth century.

Women and Sentencing

We have already observed that gender differences in crime are most sharply apparent in recorded patterns of offending. With some important exceptions, it is these differences which are reflected in sentencing patterns. Most notably, the numbers of women in prison are small at any one time (about 1,200–1,500 during the 1980s). Moreover, they form a very small percentage of the total prison population, which is overwhelmingly male (the ratio is around 30:1). However, the numbers of women sentenced to immediate imprisonment grew faster than comparable figures for males for much of the 1980s, although there was a fall for both from 1987 to 1990. Many women in prison are there as untried or unsentenced prisoners and it has been argued, since many of the former are not subsequently imprisoned, that women are subject to 'punitive remands' (Heidensohn 1985). Whereas nearly 20 per cent of males convicted of indictable offences go to prison, only 5 per cent of females do so. (All figures are taken from the government's *Criminal Statistics*: see Home Office 1990, 1992).

Courts appear to use the full range of the tariff less for women than for men, despite their apparent suitability for alternative dispositions (Moxon 1988). About one-fifth of adult female offenders are the subject of probation orders, very few receive community service orders, and the use of fines declined during the 1980s, while discharges were used more widely. Alternatives to women's imprisonment have been developed at the local level (Carlen 1990), but have not yet led to its abolition.

At first sight, then, gender might not seem to be a key variable in sentencing. Rather, women's low levels of offending, consisting mainly of property related and non-violent crimes, could be seen as the basis for their treatment. However, as I shall discuss below, arguments both about chivalry being afforded to women and about their being, under some circumstances, more punitively dealt with, have been pursued in modern academic and popular debate (Kennedy 1992). It is certainly true that females fit awkwardly, if at all, into most parts of the criminal justice system, and present puzzles and problems to it. Typically perhaps, the Home Office *Criminal Statistics* volumes (1992, etc.) give far less detail (and no graphics) on the sentencing of women than on that of men.

FEMINIST APPROACHES TO CRIMINOLOGY

Gender Ratios and Gender Questions

The gender ratio problem, according to Daly and Chesney Lind, leads to the following queries: 'Why are women less likely than men to be involved in crime? Conversely, why are men more crime-prone than women? What explains gender differences in rates of arrest and in variable types of criminal activity?' (1988: 515). They express some scepticism about finding answers to such questions, given the limitations of existing data, and juxtapose what they call gender ratio scholarship to work on generalizability, that is on questions of theory: 'Do theories of men's crime apply to women? Can the logic of such theories be modified to include women?' (ibid.: 514). They insist that the two sets of questions need to be 'bracketed' together (ibid.: 519). How have explanations of male and female criminality developed, and how far in practice have answers to these questions been found?

Criminology and Feminist Perspectives

I have already suggested that there was a prehistory to the study of this field. Its modern cultivation can be said to have started in the late 1960s as one of the by-products of modern second-wave feminism. Definitions of feminism abound (Michell and Oakley 1986; Stanley and Wise 1983) and will not be rehearsed here. Being 'woman-centred' and stressing the importance of gender in social structures and relations are at least two key components. As far as criminology is concerned, there are, if anything, greater problems. Gelsthorpe and Morris (1988) seek to define a canon of work which has certain core features, although in a later account they suggest a diversity of perspectives (Gelsthorpe and Morris, 1990), while Smart (1990) doubts both the possibility and the validity of such an enterprise. I am sceptical about an 'add and stir' approach, simply mixing feminism into criminology, I do recognize that considerable contributions have been made to the field by scholars who would accept a feminist label, and that this may be one way of defining it (Heidensohn 1985, 1989*a*).

Precise demarcations may elude us. Of the changes in assumptions, above all in this part of the subject, and of the massive contribution to the literature, there can be no question. Scholars from other perspectives began to write much more extensively about gender at the very end of the twentieth century. In particular, major mainstream texts notably started to include gender as a key theme (Braithwaite 1989; Hagan 1989). What is striking, however, is that they were doing so *in response to* the criticisms raised by feminists and also to the sheer volume and range of work which they had produced. I therefore make no apology for starting with these perspectives and will include other contributions within that framework.

Developments in Research on Women: Pioneering and Consolidation

It is useful, if arbitrary, to divide feminist criminological studies into two phases: of pioneering and of consolidation. The pioneers defined the agenda for the study of gender, which remains broadly unaltered. Consolidation has seen a range of studies produced in response to that agenda. It is now possible also to suggest what the future might possibly hold.

In articles published in the late 1960s, Marie Andrée Bertrand (1969) and I (Heidensohn 1968) drew attention to the neglect of women in the study of crime and to the stereotyped distortions which were imposed on their female subjects by those few authors who did address this topic. There was a widespread tendency, for example, to sexualize all female deviance and to ignore any rational or purposive part of it. It was the gender ratio problem which provided the stimulus for these critiques: 'the patterns . . . of male and of female deviance were long ago observed, . . . nevertheless, the focus of research has been very much away from this particular area' (Heidensohn 1968: 160–1). It was this lack which was emphasized in all the early pioneer work. More precisely perhaps, two aspects were stressed: 'Orthodox, control-oriented criminology . . . has virtually ignored the existence of female offenders . . . An important consequence of this lack of development has been the total neglect of any critical analysis of the common-sense perceptions of female criminality informing classical . . . and contemporary studies' (Smart 1977: 3). In short, women's *absence* from the literature and/or *distortion* of their experiences when present were the accusations levelled at criminologists.

Successive studies from this phase filled out this picture. Leonard (1982) examined major theorists in detail, showing how their ideas failed to deal with the gender gap and urging that women might be fitted back in again. Millman (1982) analysed in depth the appreciative stance of labelling theorists such as Howard Becker (1963). Central to Becker's approach was to take the perspective of the deviant as social critic; yet in discussing jazz musicians' wives it was the men's viewpoint alone which he quoted.

Unexplored assumptions about, and stereotyping of, female offending received heavy criticism. The determinist psychobiology of Lombroso and Ferrero, Thomas and Pollak, was attacked by Heidensohn (1968), Klein (1976), and Smart (1977). What was seen as more significant by all these writers was the survival, and even the continued flourishing, of such ideas well into the end of the twentieth century. Not only was this approach alive and well in academic studies, but it still affected the treatment of women offenders in Britain (Carlen 1983; Dobash *et al.* 1986) who were treated as sick or mad in ways not applied to men.

Although such pioneering projects first began in the late 1960s, and Smart's key work was published in 1977, similar studies continued to appear after the initial phase, consolidating and expressing the key ideas more confidently (Heidensohn 1985; Morris 1987; Naffine 1987). They also proposed ways in which feminist contributions to criminology might advance and alter the arid and unsatisfactory positions which they had criticized. Such proposals included much more research on women and crime (Heidensohn 1968, 1970) and the more vigorous application of criminological theories (Morris 1987). In fact the development of feminist perspectives in criminology (and in related approaches which have responded to them) have followed several paths. There is no coherent body of work, nor is it comprehensive, but its impact has been considerable. It can be usefully grouped under three broad headings:

1. *Acts*: The ways in which gender affects criminal activity.
2. *Treatment and gender:* How women (as compared with men) experience the criminal justice and penal systems.
3. *Concepts*: The concepts and approaches which have been developed to provide theories of the relationships of gender to crime and criminology.

Acts

In the 1970s Smart (1977) suggested that women's crimes had been ignored because they did not constitute a major social problem. She was concerned about the consequences of possible exposure, fearful of what I later called the 'Falklands factor', the dire consequences of moving from the periphery to the centre of world attention. Many aspects of female offending have been studied since then. Female criminals have found their own voices (Carlen 1985; Reynolds 1991); observers have presented the perspectives of women who murder their husbands (Browne 1987), who are prostitutes (McLeod 1982; Miller 1986), who are members of violent gangs (Campbell 1981, 1984), who take crack cocaine (Maher 1990), or who are involved in other serious forms of offending (Daly 1993). Many of these studies are characterized by giving offending women a voice, and are small-scale and ethnographic in approach. They need to be related to some of the larger-scale surveys noted above. Three characteristics are attributed to female offending in these studies. They suggest that women do act with a sense of agency, if sometimes a distinctive one; that their offences constitute purposive action; and finally, they contribute to the (re)discovery of female iniquity.

Agency

Much of the 'prehistoric' work on women cited above stressed the irrational nature of their actions. Their behaviour was determined by their physiology or their instincts. Such ideas have not been absent from more modern debate, for example in relation to the effects of menstruation (Dalton 1980), although caution is expressed now (Vanezis 1991). In contrast, the majority of modern studies have emphasized how rational and purposive were the women offenders whom they studied.

Carlen, for example, in a series of ethnographic studies of convicted women in the UK, has shown how they are caught in two constricting structures, the gender bind and the class bind, and yet how their choices to offend and of the type of offence were often made on the basis of carefully weighted consideration: 'Property crime was chosen because certain types (e.g. shoplifting and cheque fraud) were seen to be so "easy" and because women, most women expressed inhibitions about engaging in prostitution' (1988: 34). She does stress also the variety of the offending patterns and the short-term nature of their rewards (1988: 45). Such emphasis is found in other kinds of deviant activities too. Many social researchers have sought to challenge the view of drug users as 'dope fiends'—helpless addicts, hooked after one shot or smoke and at the mercy of evil pushers (Pearson 1987; MacGregor 1989). While women drug users have been studied far less often, the same notion of at least initial choice occurs: 'In analysing the career of the woman addict, I found her career is inverted and that is the essence of its social attraction' (Rosenbaum 1981: 11). Maher, using her field research among young crack-cocaine users in New York, is highly critical of the official response which defines pregnant women who use crack as irresponsible and criminal (1990). She argues that many of them manage their lives well and that in most cases they deliver healthy infants.

In a somewhat similar way, McLeod (1982) and Miller (1986) suggest that prostitution is one kind of reasonable, if restricted and ultimately destructive, choice made by some women whose other options are very circumscribed. Even grave violence, such as homicide, has been depicted as the 'last option' when no others exist in battering relations, when, it is argued, 'women . . . are extremely knowledgeable about the patterns of violence in their relationships' (Browne 1987: 184). Such views are supported by several appraisals of historical material on violence perpetuated by women which shows that they were, even in the eighteenth and nineteenth centuries, able to make skilful use of conventions about femininity to obtain leniency (McLynn 1989; Hartmann 1977; Jones 1991; Heidensohn 1991).

Contributions from all these sources suggested the development of what Daly has termed the 'leading scenario' for a typical entry for women into a career of petty crime: one, that is, based on constrained choices due to poverty, poor education, etc. Daly herself, however, has argued that it is possible to find a variety of 'pathways' to criminality for women. As well as what she terms the 'street woman' scenario, she also records two other major routes to crime which are distinctive for women. One is via a relationship with a violent man, the second through connections with friends or partners who use or sell drugs (1993). Such work and its insights are still unfolding and large areas remain unexplored.

The (re)discovery of iniquity

The study of female offenders has undergone various phases since the 1960s. During one of these, far more attention was devoted to women as victims than as perpetrators of crime. This was true at both an academic level (Stanko 1984, 1990; Hanmer and Saunders 1984; Dobash and Dobash 1979, 1992) and also at a practical, policy level, where refuges for victims of domestic violence were set up (Pizzey 1973), rape crisis centres founded (Anna T 1988), and helplines for victims of sexual abuse instituted (Parton 1992). For many, this remains the most important contribution which modern feminism has made to criminology and criminal justice. It is credited by Young with being a key factor in the shaping of left realism (1986).

Crucial although this development was (it is explored more fully by Zedner in chapter 25 in this volume), it did mean in effect that offending by women was much less a focus of enquiry. In the late 1980s and early 1990s, however, this changed, and the range and variety of female crime were explored rather more fully; particular attention was given to violence committed by women. Again, this was stimulated in part by a confrontation with older debates which were re-emerging in new forms. The notion of the especially evil woman, the 'witch' of mythology, had stalked the texts of earlier writers such as Lombroso and Ferrero and Pollak. Adler and Simon had put forward the notion of a new, ruthless female criminal. The new factors lay in the approach taken, for example, by the American 'family violence' school, who argued (Dobash and Dobash 1992), contrary to the arguments of many researchers in the field of domestic violence, that as many women abused their husbands or partners as did the latter their wives and partners. Several notable court cases also focused on aspects of female offending, including those dealing with a female serial killer, and a notorious child death in New York which raised questions about women's acceptance of, or collusion in, the abuse of children (Johnson 1991). The prominence of child abuse and child sexual abuse cases also led, as Parton (1992) points out, to a focus on family interaction and the roles played by mothers in such cases. Several thorough journalistic studies covered women's involvement in international terrorism (MacDonald 1991) and homicide (Jones 1991; Reynolds 1991), while a spate of books appeared covering aspects of female violence (Lloyd 1993; Krista 1993). For the most part, these did not attempt to theorize women's participation in violence, although one approach did suggest that gender roles in the use of legitimate violence were important in understanding women's low share of such actions (Heidensohn 1992*a*).

Treatment

Much modern research on women and crime is marked by its engagement with debates from the past. This is nowhere more true than in relation to women's experiences of the criminal justice and penal systems. One old and commonly held view of why women's crime rates were so low was that the police, the courts, and other agencies extended 'chivalry' towards them. As a result they were protected from the full rigour of the law (Mannheim 1965). Of course, we have already seen that the sex: crime ratio differential is related more to a smaller 'pool' on which agencies may draw. Nevertheless, discussions have focused on this topic and a series of concepts which modify the notion of chivalry have been advanced and discussed. These include the notions of double deviance and double jeopardy, of stigma, and of the importance of formal and informal controls in the lives of women.

Chivalry

Several authors have reviewed and/or researched the respective treatment of women and men by the courts. Smith (1988), reviewing the British literature, was unable to come to a clear-cut conclusion about whether men and women were treated in different ways by the courts, although the proposal of systematic chivalric bias is supported only by Allen's study (1987), which showed violent women offenders receiving more sympathetic and individualized treatment for serious crimes for which men got no comparable understanding. Other British researchers have found a more complex pattern in which courts appear to have somewhat conventional and stereotyped views of gender roles which they then reinforce with conviction and sentencing. Farrington and Morris (1983) found that apparent court leniency towards women was due to their lesser criminal records, while Eaton (1986) noted that men *and* women conforming to conventional roles were better treated than the unconventional, such as homosexuals or single mothers. She stressed that gender expectations differed and that women were supposed to take much more responsibility than men for home-making and for domestic morality. Carlen (1983) also found Scottish sheriffs distinguishing between 'good' and 'bad' mothers and being prepared to sentence them accordingly. Worrall (1990) discerned a still more complex situation in which various agents and agencies contrived to play down and almost to 'lose' female offenders in the system.

In the USA, Daly (1989*a*) found that it was children and the family, rather than women themselves, who were the focus of chivalry, or 'judicial paternalism', as the courts sought to support and conserve the fabric of society. In marked contrast Player (1989), in studying crime in an inner-city area, found that black women were more likely to be stopped and questioned than white women were, and that the police had different perceptions of them.

Double deviance and double jeopardy and stigma

Women's low share of criminality is so well known that it has significant consequences for those women who do offend. They are seen to have transgressed not only social norms but gender norms as well. As a result they may well, especially when informal sanctions are taken into account, feel that they are doubly punished. Carlen (1983, 1985) notes the prevalence of informal punishment of women by their partners. Several observers have stressed that concern over the anomalous position of deviant women leads to excessive zeal in their treatment, in remands in custody for reports, and in more medicalized interventions (Heidensohn 1981; Edwards 1984). Such approaches are particularly marked towards young girls whose minor sexual misdemeanours seem to be consistently more harshly handled than those of boys (Chesney Lind 1986; Parker *et al.* 1981; Webb 1984; Cain 1989; and see Gelsthorpe and Morris chapter 20 on juveniles in this volume). Such bias is not, as Gelsthorpe emphasizes (1989: 147) the sole determining factor in the way young people are handled by agencies. Other variables, such as organizational features, are important as well.

Much evidence has accumulated to suggest that women suffer especially from the stigma associated with deviance. I have discussed the negative and positive forces that affect this (Heidensohn 1985). There are relatively few positive role models of the good old villain-type for women to emulate. At the same time, the damage done to women who lose their characters is widely stressed in fictions of all kinds. At a practical level, women who offend risk losing their homes and children more readily than do men, who may have wives to stand by them (Shaw, ed. 1991). The plight of women drug couriers from abroad sentenced to long terms in European gaols illustrates this most effectively. They are often selected because they are of good character, but this does not mitigate their sentences nor prevent them losing homes and children and facing additional punishment on release (Green 1991).

Much of the sense of injustice felt by women who come before the courts stems from their perceptions of such agencies as male-dominated and unsympathetic to them (Heidensohn 1986; Scutt 1981). Such feelings have been much increased by the greater publicity now given to crimes, especially violent crimes, against women and what are often perceived as inappropriate reactions to them (Edwards 1989). Such reactions are by no means consistent; they vary by age, ethnic background, and social class, and whether a woman has herself been a victim (Schlesinger *et al.* 1992). What research does make clear is the considerable effect victimization can have on women's world views (Stanko 1990; Walklate 1989).

Prison for women

Prison studies of institutions for men were started much earlier than similar work on women (Sykes 1956; Cressey 1961). However, once the first studies had been completed in the USA in the 1960s (Ward and Kassebaum 1966; Giallombardo 1966), this is one area in which there has been something of a catching-up exercise. Those pioneer studies insisted that the penal life of women was distinctive: largely because of their small numbers and restricted provision, female felons in the USA felt the pains of imprisonment, the loss of family and home, more acutely and therefore set up alternative sexual relationships with one another (Ward and Kassebaum 1966) or formed 'pseudo-families' to replace their missing kin. Subsequent research has focused on a series of critical issues:

1. Are women 'too few to count' in the prison system, making their part an uneconomic and worthless activity?
2. Do regimes for women have special characteristics?
3. Do women respond differently to imprisonment.

Women, as the discussion above makes clear, are almost too few to count in the prison system. In England and Wales they constitute under 2,000 of prisoners at any one time out of some 50,000. Ratios in other countries are similar (Pollock-Byrne 1990). There tend to be two models of provision in the west. In federal systems such as Canada (Shaw 1991) and Germany (Heidensohn 1991), women tend to be incarcerated in small, scattered units. They lack basic facilities for education and work. In central systems, such as France and the UK, they are concentrated in larger units and are often remote from family and friends (Cario 1985; Heidensohn 1991). The USA manages to combine both sets of disadvantages, with federal penitentiaries too far away for women to sustain relationships with their children and local correctional facilities which suffer from being overcrowded and inadequate.

Historically, women have usually been subject to broadly the same prison system as men, but with distinctive variations introduced from time to time. Welfare objectives have sometimes been to the fore, especially in the nineteenth century and in relation to women in moral danger. Rafter (1983) has catalogued the history of one such institution in the USA and noted how the lofty intentions of its founders led to its becoming additionally repressive of its female inmates, who were infantilized by middle class maternalism.

Zedner describes the parallel history of two schemes in Britain primarily designed for women. Like the Massachusetts example studied by Rafter, these had aims which were thought especially appropriate for women: diversion from the penal system, care and welfare of offenders, and provision of moral protection. In the first programme, from 1898 to 1914, a number of inebriate reformatories for habitual female drunkards were founded. The official assumption was 'that the female inebriate was the greatest problem and must therefore, be the main focus of their work' (Zedner 1991: 233), and the purpose of the project 'quite simply, to create of the enfeebled and degraded drunk a model of healthy, domesticated femininity' (ibid.: 237). In consequence a special system was set up with much emphasis on fresh air, clean living, and close supervision. The experiment failed.

> Having defined the female inebriate primarily as a moral offender, reformatories operated on the premise that, by providing a sufficiently propitious environment and benign moral influences her cure could be achieved. Finding, instead, women resiliently resistant to the intentions of the regime, or so feeble-minded as to be irredeemable, the very momentum of the endeavour collapsed. (ibid.: 263)

This initiative was followed by another in which assumptions about female deviance had changed, and now centred on 'feeblemindedness' as a prime cause of female crime and deviance—and, indeed, wider social evils (Simmons 1978). Again, women, because of their reproductive role, were the especial focus of such policies, in which containment was emphasized (Zedner 1991: 296). It was the undermining of its key assumptions which damaged this approach irreparably, although not before many women had been institutionalized to protect society and themselves.

As Zedner points out, such case histories are highly instructive. They show, first, that when women are made the subjects of special penal treatment it frequently results in the development of benevolently repressive regimes for them which emphasize dependency and traditional femininity and fail to provide the skills which could aid rehabilitation. Secondly, such programmes tend to be determined by the assumed characteristics and needs of women, rather than by well-explored evidence. Such cases are not merely found in the past. The rebuilding of Holloway Prison for women in Britain during the 1970s was based on views about women offenders being physically or mentally sick, or both, and thus needing a therapeutic environment. The case was not proven and the design of the prison proved unsatisfactory and controversial (RAP 1972; Heidensohn 1975). Ironically, it was its lack of adequate psychiatric facilities for treating disturbed women which was the focus of most concern (Carlen 1985; Padel and Stevenson 1988).

Research in women's prisons in Britain in the 1980s and 1990s stressed both the distresses and discomforts common to men and women and certain features largely suffered by the latter. Women in prison are still less likely than men to receive good education, training, and job opportunities and more likely to have to carry out domestic tasks. This is, however, part of a wider policy which tends to define criminal women as doubly deviant, needing additional pressures to conform and be rehabilitated (Carlen 1983; Dobash *et al.*, 1986). Petty modifications—no uniforms, better decor—soften the contours of the women's system but do not alter its basic shape.

There have, nevertheless, been changes, sometimes as the result of growing awareness of women's changing position in society. Some innovative schemes have been developed in the USA, such as the Bedford Hills programme in New York State, which enables children to stay with their mothers for a vacation. Pollock-Byrne (1990) also notes a range of other family visits and community programmes in the USA which have altered the prison experience for women. Even in Britain's centralized system, where it is harder to experiment, there have nevertheless been clear signs of innovation (Women's National Commission 1991), especially at Holloway Prison.

Carlen (1990) has argued that imprisonment for women should be abolished or, at any rate, reduced to use for just a small number, for an experimental period of five years. This would have value not only for women but for men and for the whole of the system, since women would be a suitable experimental group as they are seen as less threatening and less deserving of punishment than men.

The literature on responses to imprisonment is vast and, unsurprisingly, dominated by studies of men. There are, to oversimplify, two major areas of interest: prisonization; and inmate subcultures. By the first is meant how far prisoners become adapted to their prisons and thus unable to cope with the outside world (Sykes 1956). The earliest sociological studies (Sykes 1956; Irwin and Cressey 1962) observed that (male) prisons in the USA were notable for the prevalence of inmate subcultures. These were characterized by distinctive slang or argot and by a range of role types, such as Schrag's 'square johns, right guys, cons and outlaws' (1961). Two kinds of explanation are offered for this phenomenon. Sykes' 'pains of imprisonment' argument (1956) was that prisoners responded to the losses they felt in prison—of liberty, security, privacy, sex, etc.—by setting up compensating structures and roles. Irwin and Cressey (1962), on the other hand, favour external influences as causative, insisting that prisoners being their pre-prison criminal values with them.

Much research on prisons for women in the USA has used the now rather aged features of such studies to explore women's reactions. Some important sex differences are found in responses to imprisonment, especially in subcultures. As noted above, studies in the 1960s noted the salience of sexual and emotional relations in female correctional establishments. Several studies found women's commitment to inmate codes to be less than men's (Tittle 1969; Kruttschitt 1981). In Scotland, Carlen (1983) found little evidence of inmate solidarity, or indeed of the presence of subcultures. One of the paradoxical conclusions of a review of research on female subcultures is that they are weaker and more diffuse than the male (Pollock-Byrne, 1990); yet, certainly in Britain, women perceive the pains of imprisonment as sharper and react with much greater vehemence against them than men (Heidensohn 1975, 1981; Casale 1989; Mandaraka-Sheppard 1986; Carlen 1985). A higher proportion of women are charged with disciplinary offences, doses of tranquillizers prescribed are higher, and there is a significant incidence of self-mutilation.

However, as Pollock-Byrne points out, the US subculture studies should be read with two caveats. They all use comparisons with males as a baseline, assuming, for instance, that men and women experience the same deprivations when in prison. Secondly, there is more evidence that in establishments for both sexes there have been considerable changes which have altered subcultural patterns. Race is one very important one (Arnold 1991); another is the closer ties developed with communities, which have lessened inmate isolation. Clark and Boudin (1990), for instance, report as two inmate participants on a programme for AIDS/HIV education at a New York State prison which broke down many conventional barriers.

It is often derisorily observed that the pursuit of research by social scientists has only one certain conclusion: that more such projects should be undertaken. Reviewing the considerable body of work on women's experience in prison, and indeed on the whole of the criminal justice system, such a reaction does come to mind. One of the main reasons is that, as in so many topics concerning women, close observation has revealed diversity, complexity, and sometimes contradiction. While there *are* common features of women's contribution to crime they have, it seems less in common in how they experience society's reaction to it. Black women in the US, native women in Canada and Australia all experience distinctive forms of penality from white women. Within such categories, too, class 'normality' and family situation may all also play a part. One of the pioneer projects of feminist criminology was to seek theoretical explanations which would help in understanding female criminality. Decades on from that era it is important to recast the original questions but no less vital to consider the answers, as we shall do in the next section.

Concepts and Continuing the Critique: Theorizing Women and Crime

The title of my first contribution to this field was 'The deviance of women: a *critique* and an *enquiry*' (Heidensohn 1968, emphasis added). My enquiry concerned the lack of interest in sex differences in recorded criminality and in female deviance in itself; my critique was of the limitations of existing explanations of these two matters. These two points still serve as useful guides for considering the considerable range of conceptual studies which have appeared since then. There is now, when one enquires of bibliographies and data bases, much to consider of an explanatory kind. However, it is still vital to engage in a dialogue with mainstream criminology, especially about the assimilation of ideas about gender.

This area has been, as I trust all I have already written about it has indicated, one of the most fruitful and dynamic in the whole of criminology. It is not, then, surprising that its theoretical development has proceeded through considerable challenge and debate. In the section that follows I shall outline, in summary, some of the key contributions and also indicate how they are part of a continuing debate. As in all such debates, there has never been full, clear discussion of every issue; there is no great master script covering all roles and perspectives.

One summary of work in feminist criminology divided its conceptual concerns into the *gender gap* and the *generalizability problem*. Some theorists have attempted to deal with these issues; however, the most significant work of feminist theorists is to be found in *explanations of female criminality*. Partly, however, because of problems in developing such approaches and also because of wider difficulties and developments, there is another (growing) category of criminological *feminist sceptics* who proffer no answers but ask further and profounder questions.

The gender gap and generalizability

We have already noted the main contributors to theories about the gender gap, the so called 'liberation causes crime' theorists (Adler 1975; Simon 1975), and the consequent debates about their views. This approach is one of the few perspectives on female crime to have been subjected to thorough empirical testing, indeed, to have been disproved (Box 1983; Box and Hale 1983; Austin 1981; Smart 1979; Steffensmeier 1980). Strictly speaking, the 'liberation hypothesis' was not a single coherent theory; indeed, Adler and Simon differ in key aspects of their approaches, although both see increased equality for women as a key variable in causing their patterns of criminal behaviour.

However, Adler contended that the battle to emancipate women had been won by the mid-1970s and thus male and female behaviour was converging, with females resembling males more and more by becoming aggressive and violent. Simon, on the other hand, suggested an opposite situation and outcome. Women's opportunities had not yet expanded very much; when they did so, their violence would diminish and their property crimes increase with their growing opportunities. Both approaches fail when tested because they do not fit statistical trends, because criminal women are among those least likely to be affected by feminism (and those most affected by it, middle-class white women, are the least likely to be criminal), and because criminal women tend to score highly on 'femininity' scores whereas 'masculine'-scoring women are less delinquent (Naffine 1987). These ideas are not supported, then, by the evidence. 'Yet ironically it is around this theme that a considerable debate has focussed, putting female criminality into mainstream discussion' (Heidensohn 1989: 95).

Much of the initial critique of criminology's failure to address the issues of gender and of women was directed at the limits of conventional theories. They could not for the most part account for the gender gap and broke down when applied to women as well as men, usually because they overpredicted female crime. Some critics went on to suggest that some criminological theories could be applied to women with success if only they were developed or modified (Leonard 1982; Morris 1987). Indeed, this was a criticism Greenwood (1981) made of feminist criminologists: that they merely wished to add women back in. In practice it is hard to find examples of this, although Smith and Paternoster (1987) have suggested that 'gender-neutral' theories of delinquency should be developed and try to do this in a study of marijuana use. They take factors from classic theories of male delinquency and conclude that 'factors that influence participation decisions and the frequency of marijuana use are similar for males and females' (1987: 156).

This does not, however, explain the differences in recorded and in self-reported narcotic offences. Nor does it explain why many other researchers find gender-specific theories important in just such areas (Auld *et al.* 1986; Rosenbaum 1981).

Gender theories

In the early days of work on women Carol Smart issued a warning: 'In the movement towards developing a feminist perspective a critique of sexism is vital, but in itself a critique alone cannot constitute a new theoretical approach . . . In particular more research is needed in the area of women and crime' (1977: 183). This has in fact turned out to be the agenda for most of those who have contributed to this field. Once more it will be helpful to adopt a taxonomy within which we can group the work we are reviewing. This would include studies of patriarchy, of social and economic marginalization, and of control; and finally there is a group of feminosceptics who have focused particularly on epistemological issues.

Patriarchy

Patriarchy is simply 'the rule of fathers'; but defining it and using it as a concept has not proved at all simple for feminists—who have none the less used it frequently. Many writers have tried to define and refine it (Mitchell and Oakley 1986; Walby 1989). Quite often it appears to signify the rule of men or the power of men, and especially the use of this rule or power against women. On the whole patriarchy, or male power, is not used very much as a direct explanation of female crime. The concept is employed nevertheless in at least two important ways: to explain women's experience of the criminal justice system, and to explain the gendered nature of much criminal victimization, especially from violence and abuse within the home.

Indeed, it is from concern about women's treatment as victims in the processes of the criminal justice system and their experience of 'family law' that much of the evidence comes which has led, as Dobash and Dobash put it, to 'some feminist activists and scholars [arguing] that it is impossible to use the law and legal apparatus to confront patriarchal domination and oppression when the language and procedures of these social processes and institutions are saturated with patriarchal beliefs and structures' (1992: 147). Victims and victimization are topics covered fully elsewhere in this volume (see Zedner chapter 25). It is only the elision of the issues which I wish to discuss here. Susan Edwards, whose earlier work (1984) did emphasize sexist aspects of criminal justice, puts this view forcefully:

> A consideration of patriarchy has been central to an understanding of sex/gender division within the law . . . the criminal justice process . . . and policing . . . it is the precise juncture of bourgeois and male interest which constitutes the cornerstone of women's experience and corresponding oppression. In everyday experience women's need for protection, women's voice as victims of crime, as criminal offenders and as victims of the law has been totally eclipsed (Edwards 1989: 13).

Carol Smart (1989) has gone furthest in arguing that 'it is important to think of non-legal strategies and to discourage a resort to law as if it holds the key to unlock women's oppression' (1989: 5). Boldly she concludes: 'A main purpose of this book has been to construct a warning to feminism to avoid the siren call of law. But of equal importance has been the attempt to acknowledge the power of feminism to construct an alternative reality to the version which is manifested in legal discourse' (1989: 160). In fact, the Norwegian lawyer, Tove Stang Dahl, has argued for just such a parallel system to be set up beside the traditional system (1987) and indeed herself set up and ran a department of women's law at the University of Oslo.

In the 1980s there was widespread discussion of the work of Carol Gilligan (1982, 1987), who argued that men and women differ in approaches to moral questions, with men stressing 'justice' as an independent concept while women focus more on a relational notion of caring. I used Gilligan's dichotomy as the basis of an ideal-type model of two types of justice system: the *Portia* (rational, judicial, and masculine) and the *Persephone* (relational, informal, and feminine), and explored what the effects of using such an alternative system might be. The conclusion was that such approaches had been adopted at certain times and had not always been beneficial (Heidensohn 1986). Daly, in a review of this and other applications of Gilligan's difference discourse, disagrees with this approach and concludes:

> In canvassing feminist scholarship for ways to rethink the problem of justice for men and women accused of crime, I find little guidance . . . I would like to see a feminist conception of criminal justice which maintains a focus on women's lives and on redressing harms to women, but which does not ignore those men who have been crippled by patriarchal, class and race relations. (1989a).

These comments could serve as the basis for the whole of this series of perspectives. What these studies amount to is a sophisticated critique of the administration of justice and the structures in which it operates. Clearly, there are certain gender-specific forms of discrimination rife within it. However, as Gelsthorpe (1989: 137–45) goes to great lengths to point out, it is impossible to try to demonstrate the existence of a conspiracy behind such practices. It is even more difficult to relate them etiologically to women's crime, since although women can be shown to be more socially and economically oppressed than men, their experience of the system as perpetrators, rather than as victims, is far less. Where links can be made is through social construction theories which actually deconstruct the meanings of concepts such as rape (Rafter 1990) or, as in Zedner's work quoted above, those of 'inebriation' and 'feeblemindedness' as applied to women. As Zedner's work (1991) shows, redefinitions of female deviance can diminish their apparent deviance or increase it. This is not, of course, solely due to the operation of the criminal justice system. On the contrary, many other features of the *Zeitgeist* contribute: culture, values, changes in medical science. Politics and the media have also played crucial roles in such developments, as Young (1990), for example, shows in her analysis of the media reactions to the women protesters at the Greenham Common air base in Britain in the 1980s. She argues that the criminal justice system and the media rely on each other's definitions of deviance.

This set of approaches informs much writing on women and crime. It leads us to question some of the most basic assumptions about law, justice, and punishment in our society and to raise queries about unstated 'patriarchal' values. However, it is also then essential to question all the other implicit parts of the system and we are likely, as Daly points out, to need to raise at least as many points about what happens to men, especially if they are young, poor, and come from minorities, as we do about women.

Marginalization

Economic explanations of criminal behaviour go back at least as far as Bonger and, albeit implicitly, to Marx as well (Taylor *et al.* 1975). More recently, critical criminologists insisted on the criminogenic capacities of capitalist societies (ibid.). *Critical Criminology* omits all consideration of gender, yet this is surely a crucial test for such theories since women are generally poorer than men in most societies, especially capitalist ones, and have suffered more in modern recessions (Millar and Glendinning 1989). Some writers researching female crime have put forward a variation of such approaches in arguing that deviant women are an especially marginalized group.

Part of the reason for proposing this perspective is to counteract the liberation hypothesis discussed earlier. Chapman (1980) stressed that the rise in female property crime was due to women's poverty, and especially to the problem of single mothers, a growing proportion of the poor. In an empirical study Jurik (1983) found support for such findings. A series of studies undertaken by Carlen in Britain (1983, 1985, 1988) elaborate on this theme. She concludes:

> The analyses presented here claim only to indicate that, under certain, relatively rare *combinations* of otherwise general economic and ideological conditions, some women are more likely than not to choose to break the law and/or be imprisoned. Such analyses do *not* assume or imply that the women involved have no choice. (1988: 162; emphasis in original)

Scandinavian authors have also suggested that female crime is linked to what they have called 'expulsion', that is, exclusion from ordinary economic and social life. They see women as more helpless in this respect than men because of their childcare role and their dependency on men or the state for welfare. Like Carlen, they stress what she calls the 'gender bind' as well as the 'class bind', that is, the twin structures which support conventional social roles, although, unlike Carlen, they do not emphasize that many younger female delinquents find fun and excitement in their activities (Heidensohn 1991).

Such approaches, while they usefully balance and counteract the notion of the 'new' female criminal, are beset with several problems. Most offences, especially property offences, are committed by girls of 15, not mothers in their twenties with several children. Secondly, as Pollock-Byrne puts it, they must face 'the same criticisms with which all economic theories must contend—namely, how to account for the large numbers of poor people who do not steal' (1990: 25). Obviously, as Carlen suggests, poverty can be an important factor in the choice of women's criminal careers. It then often reinforces such choices by limiting others. Yet, as Daly showed in her study cited above, other factors, such as abuse in childhood and marriage, or relationships with men with associations with drugs, are also important. None of these offender-based, somewhat positivist approaches can answer certain important queries, namely, are the situations of those not convicted of crimes necessarily different? In short, do these explanations fulfil necessary and sufficient conditions of theorizing; or have they, perhaps, not addressed the right questions?

Control and Conformity

A quite different approach has been adopted by a number of other writers who have sought to understand female criminality. So called 'control theory' was developed originally by Hirschi (1969) and his colleagues, who sought to explain delinquency by the failure of social bonding processes. The emphasis shifted from deviance and what caused it to conformity and what impaired it. Hirschi's work has been much criticized, notably for its weak theoretical base, although it appears to have empirical support from large survey studies (for a review see Downes and Rock 1988).

In various modified forms, control theories have been applied to women because 'an examination of female criminality and unofficial deviance suggests that we need to move away from studying infractions and look at conformity instead, because the most striking thing about female behaviour . . . is how notably conformist to social mores women are' (Heidensohn 1985: 11). In the same book I suggested that women were subject to a series of pressures and rewards to conform to which men were not. Informal sanctions discourage women and girls from straying far from proper behaviour: parents will disapprove or impose sanctions, as will gossip, ill repute, and male companions. Fear of crime, harassment, and stigma all aid this process. A range of other commitments—to children, family, community, etc.—occupy women much more fully than they do men. Finally, public images and culture encourage daring deviance in men, but suggest that deviant women are punished (ibid.: chs. 5, 9). Hagan and colleagues (1979) have also offered gender-specific versions of their general control theory, arguing that girls are much more subject to controls within the family than boys are. Extensive empirical testing of various related hypotheses produced somewhat inconclusive results. Hagan in his Canadian study found more informal control of girls and more formal control of boys, and some predictive value for his hypothesis. Others found, however, that while greater social bonds among girls (and women) explained some of the sex: crime ratio differences, they did not do so fully (Smith 1979; Mawby 1980). Further, some of the differences were not in the expected direction. Thus girls who were 'masculine' in their identification in the last of these studies were *less* delinquent than indeterminate or 'feminine' girls (Norland *et al.* 1981).

These approaches do at least try to account for the gender gap and to present a generalizable theory of a kind, even though it seems to have only limited explanatory power, since the operation of the bonds is not fully theorized. Naffine is especially critical of such approaches because they depict females as essentially passive (1987: 68–70), whereas male delinquency is glorified as active and defiant. She misses, I think, the rising tide of comment on women's own contribution to social control, especially of their own sex. In *Women and Crime* (Heidensohn 1985) I discussed it at some length, noting women's higher investment in conformity and stability. More recently, a spate of studies have focused on women's role as social control agents, both historically (Carrier 1988; Boritch and Hagan 1990; Daly 1988) and in modern times (Zimmer 1986; Martin 1980, 1989; Jones 1986; Heidensohn 1989*a*, 1992*b*). In a complex analysis, Worrall has suggested that women offenders do act within the criminal justice system to alter their own fates, although they are able to do so only because, as women, they confront *two* systems of social control. 'They are effectively offered a contract which promises to minimize the consequences of their criminality by rehabilitating them within the dominant discourses of femininity (that is, domesticity, sexuality and pathology). Despite these programmes of feminization, such women it is argued, attempt to resist such construction by exploiting the contradictions of official discourses' (1990: 163).

Almost all the empirical testing of control theories has been conducted with juvenile subjects. Measures of delinquency often include relatively minor infractions, such as truancy and under-age drinking. This does limit the value of such studies where adults and more serious crimes are concerned. Gender-specific social control is, nevertheless, a widely cited component of most efforts to discuss women and crime. There is also clearly scope within such an approach to ask about many further issues: the control of males, for instance, or the role of women in control.

In reviewing theories of female criminality advanced in recent times, Pollock-Byrne makes a succinct if gloomy point: 'Unfortunately feminist criminology has not offered any comprehensive theory to supplement those it has criticized' (1990: 25). It is hard to disagree with this. Despite a considerable body of work in the field, theoretical crocks of gold have still failed to appear. What has developed is a much more sustained and sophisticated critique and several important conceptual contributions which still have some scope in application. For the most part, the debate is still with older and existing theories and with the development of second-order constructs. This does not merely reflect poverty of imagination; indeed, it is truer to say that something of an epistemological crisis has affected social science and feminism, and studies of crime are implicated.

Feminosceptics

Much modern feminist debate in social science has focused on methodological issues. How should women be studied? What is feminist analysis? Numbers of articles and books have sought to respond to these questions and several scholars have applied the answers specifically to the study of gender and crime. These debates are complex, subtle, and sometimes arcane and are beyond the scope of this chapter. What I do wish to do is to draw attention to the proposals made by several scholars who have tackled the epistemological crisis. What characterizes them all, to some degree, is their scepticism about either the past of this field or its future. Smart mounts the most devastating attack on criminology: 'It is very hard to see what criminology has to offer feminism' (1990: 84). This contrasts with what she sees as the value and influence of feminist post-modernism on analyses of women's experiences (1990: 83). It is also in contrast to other possible approaches, such as feminist empiricism and what is termed 'standpointism' (Harding 1986). The latter is based in experience and on the argument that only a shared perspective with the subject gives a researcher adequate insight and knowledge. Smart favours the deconstruction of everything, insisting that no meanings should be taken for granted.

Cain in the same volume tries also to describe what she calls the 'successor science' and lays down criteria for its operation (1990: 125–40). Somewhat confusingly, she calls her approach 'realism'.

Rafter (1990) also advocates a ruthless deconstruction of all laws, concepts, etc., as does Bertrand (1991). Once again, the source of this continuing critique is outside criminology, although in these examples it is debates within feminism itself which have fuelled these developments. *La lutte continue*, no doubt, without resolution of the issues, although these developments suggest yet further room for growth and dynamism.

CONCLUSIONS: *ALICE IN WONDERLAND* AND *ALICE THROUGH THE LOOKING GLASS*

An intelligent enquirer who has followed the growth of this topic during the late twentieth century may feel that she has, *inter alia*, moved from the world of *Alice in Wonderland* to that of *Alice Through the Looking Glass*. It is possible to construe all the modern work on women and crime as a great heap of glistening treasure. There is diversity, great range, rich material. It is possible to find the answers to many questions. There are still many puzzles and absurdities, but it is even possible to use key concepts to explain the studied world. Yet one of the main lessons which recurs throughout all the texts, articles, and reports is simple yet stunning in its implications. That is, that Alice should be in the other strange place, through the glass where everything is reversed or upside down.

Then it becomes clear that we have to ask different questions. Not what makes women's crime rates so low, but why are men's so high? Such questions are being asked in a few places (Kersten 1991; Stanko 1993), but they are the crucial ones, intellectually and politically. There is already a new *policy* agenda for law and order which highlights the gendered nature of much personal crime: domestic violence, rape, child abuse, etc. It is in the impact of such studies that its effect should be found.

There has been a significant shift in the study of crime because of feminist perspectives on it. New ideas have been developed. The most important contribution of all, however, was to see the centrality of gender to crime and to press for that. We know a vast amount about women and crime viewed through the prism of gender. Far less is known about men and crime and therefore I have concentrated on the first in this chapter. In the spirit of simple equality, I hope to affect a redistribution of interests next time such a chapter is required.

Selected Further Reading

K. Daly & M. Chesney Lind, 'Feminism and Criminology' *Justice Quarterly*, 1988.

M. Eaton, *Justice for Women?*, Milton Keynes: Open University Press, 1986.

L. Gelsthorpe & A. Morris (eds.), Feminist Perspectives in Criminology: Buckingham, Open University Press, 1990.

L. Gelsthorpe & A. Morris 'Feminism and Criminology in Britain', *British Journal of Criminology*, 1988.

F. Heidensohn, *Women & Crime*, London: Macmillan, 1985.

C. Smart, Women, Crime and Criminology, London: Routledge and Kegan Paul, 1977.

E. Stanko, Everyday Violence, London: Pandora (1990).

REFERENCES

ACTON, W. (1857), *Prostitution: Considered in its Moral, Social and Sanitary Aspects in London and Other Large Cities and Garrison Towns*. London: Frank Cass.

ADLER, I. (1975), *Sisters in Crime*. New York: McGraw-Hill.

ALLEN, H. (1987), *Justice Unbalanced.* Milton Keynes: Open University Press.

ANNA, T. (1988), 'Feminist Responses to Sexual Abuse: The Work of the Birmingham Rape Crisis Centre', in M. Maguire and J. Pointing, eds., *Victims of Crime*. Milton Keynes: Open University Press.

ARNOLD, R. (1991), 'Processes of Victimization and Criminalization of Black Women', *Social Justice*, 17/3: 153–66.

AULD, J., DORN, N., and SOUTH, N. (1986), 'Irregular Work, Irregular Pleasures: Heroin in the 1980s', in R. Matthews and J. Young, eds., *Confronting Crime*. London: Sage.

AUSTIN, R. L. (1981), 'Liberation and Female Criminality in England and Wales', *British Journal of Criminology*, 21/4.

BEATTIE, J. M. (1975), 'The Criminality of Women in Eighteenth Century England', *Journal of Social History*.

BECKER, H. S. (1963), *Outsiders: Studies in the Sociology of Deviance*. London: Macmillan.

BEIRNE, P. (1988), 'Heredity versus Environment', *British Journal of Criminology*, 28/3: 315–39.

BERTRAND, M. A. (1969), 'Self-Image and Delinquency: A Contribution to the Study of Female Criminality and Women's Image', *Acta Criminologica*, January.

BERTRAND, M. A. (1991), 'Advances in Feminist Epistemology in the Field of Social Control', paper delivered to the meeting of the American Society of Criminology, San Francisco.

BORITCH, H., and HAGAN, J. (1990), 'A Century of Crime in Toronto: Gender, Class, and Patterns of Social Control, 1859 to 1955', *Criminology*, 20/4: 567–99.

BOX, S. (1981), *Deviance, Reality and Society*. London: Holt, Rinehart and Winston.

—— (1983), *Power, Crime and Mystification*. London: Tavistock.

BOX, S., and HALE, C. (1983), 'Liberation and Female Criminality in England and Wales', *British Journal of Criminology*, 23/1.

BRAITHWAITE, J. (1989), *Crime, Shame and Reintegration*. Cambridge: Cambridge University Press.

BROWNE, A. (1987), *When Battered Women Kill*. London: Collier Macmillan.

BUCKLE, A., and FARRINGTON, D. (1984), 'An Observational Study of Shoplifting', *British Journal of Criminology*, 24/1.

BURNEY, E. (1990), *Putting Street Crime in its Place*. London: Centre for Inner City Studies, Goldsmiths' College.

—— ed. (1989), *Growing up Good*. London: Sage.

CAIN, M. (1990), 'Realist Philosophy and Standpoint Epistemologies, or Feminist Criminology as a Successor Science' in L. Gelsthorpe and A. Morris, eds., *Feminist Perspectives in Criminology*. Buckingham: Open University Press.

CAMPBELL, A. (1981), *Girl Delinquents*. Oxford: Blackwell.

—— (1984), *The Girls in the Gang*. Oxford: Blackwell.

CAREY, K. (1977), 'Police Attitudes to Women Offenders', paper presented to British Sociological Association Conference.

CARIO, R. (1985), 'La Criminalité des Femmes: Approche Differentielle', doctoral thesis, Université de Pau et des Pays de l'Adur.

CARLEN, P. (1983), *Women's Imprisonment*. London: Routledge and Kegan Paul.

—— ed. (1985), *Criminal Women*. Oxford: Polity

—— (1988), *Women, Crime and Poverty*. Milton Keynes: Open University Press.

—— (1990), *Alternatives to Women's Imprisonment*. Milton Keynes: Open University Press.

CARLEN, P., and WORRALL, A., eds. (1987), *Gender, Crime and Justice*. Milton Keynes: Open University Press.

CARRIER, J. (1988), *The Campaign for the Employment of Women as Police Officers*. Aldershot: Avebury/Gower.

CASALE, S. (1989), *Women Inside: The Experience of Women Remand Prisoners in Holloway*. London: Civil Liberties Trust.

CHAPMAN, J. (1980), *Economic Realities and the Female Offender*. Lexington, Mass.: Lexington Books.

CHESNEY-LIND, M. (1986), 'Women and Crime: The Female Offender', *Signs*, 12/1: 78–96.

CHIGWADA, R. (1991), 'The Policing of Black Women', in E. Cashmore and E. McLaughlin, eds., *Out of Order*. London: Routledge.

CLARKE, J., and BOUDIN, K. (1990), 'Community of Women Organize Themselves to Cope with the AIDS Crisis: A Case Study from Bedford Hills Correctional Facility', *Social Justice*, 17/2: 90–109.

COHEN, A. K. (1955), *Delinquent Boys*. London: Free Press.

COHEN, S., and SCULL, A., eds. (1983), *Social Control and the State*. Oxford: Blackwell.

CREIGHTON, S. J., and NOYES, P. (1989), *Child Abuse Trends in England and Wales 1983–1987*. London: NSPCC.

CRESSEY, D. R., ed. (1961), *The Prison*. New York: Holt, Rinehart and Winston.

DALTON, K. (1980), 'Cyclical Criminal Acts in the Premenstrual Syndrome', *Lancet*, 2: 1070–1.

DALY, K. (1988), 'The Social Control of Sexuality: A Case Study of the Criminalization of Prostitution in the Progressive Era', *Research in Law, Deviance and Social Control*, 9: 171–206.

—— (1989*a*), 'Rethinking Judicial Paternalism: Gender, Work–Family Relations and Sentencing', *Gender and Society*, 3/1: 9–36.

—— (1989*b*), 'Criminal Justice Ideologies and Practices in Different Voices: Some Feminist Questions about Justice', *International Journal of the Sociology of Law*, 17: 1–18.

—— (1990), 'Reflections on Feminist Legal Thought. *Social Justice*, 17/3: 7–24.

—— (1992), 'Women's Pathways to Felony Court: Interrogating and Leading Feminist Scenario of Women's Law Breaking', in *Proceedings of the International Conference on Women, Law and Social Control*, held at Mt. Gabriel, Quebec, 1991. British Columbia: International Centre for Comparative Law Reform, University of British Columbia.

—— (1993), *Gender, Crime and Punishment*. New Haven: Yale University Press.

DALY, K., and CHESNEY-LIND, M. (1988), 'Feminism and Criminology', *Justice Quarterly*, 5/4: 498–538.

DOBASH, E. R., and DOBASH, R. (1979), *Violence against Wives*. London: Open Books.

—— (1992), *Women, Violence and Social Change*. London: Routledge.

Dobash, R. P., Dobash, R. E., and Gutteridge, S. (1986), *The Imprisonment of Women*. Oxford: Blackwell.

DOWNES, D. M., and ROCK, P. E. (1988), *Understanding Deviance*, 2nd edn. Oxford: Oxford University Press.

DUNHILL, C., ed. (1989), *The Boys in Blue: Women's Challenge to the Police*. London: Virago.

EATON, M. (1986), *Justice for Women?* Milton Keynes: Open University Press.

EDWARDS, S. M. (1984), *Women on Trial*. Manchester: Manchester University Press.

—— (1989), *Policing 'Domestic' Violence*. London: Sage.

ENISELE, H. (1981), *Female Criminality in the Federal Republic of Germany*. Strasbourg: Council of Europe.

FARRINGTON, D. (1981), 'The Prevalence of Convictions', *British Journal of Criminology*, 21/2: 173–5.

FARRINGTON, D. P., and MORRIS, A. M. (1983), 'Sex, Sentencing, and Reconviction', *British Journal of Criminology*, 23/3.

FEEST, J. (1985), 'Frauenkninmalität', in G. Kaiser, *et al.*, eds., *Kleines Kriminologisches Wörterbuch*. Heidelberg: Müller.

FEINMAN, C. (1986), *Women in the Criminal Justice System*. New York: Praeger.

FIGUERIA-MCDONOUGH, J. (1984), 'Feminism and Delinquency', *British Journal of Criminology*, 24/4.

GARLAND, D. (1985), *Punishment and Welfare*. Aldershot: Gower.

GELSTHORPE, L. (1989), *Sexism and the Female Offender*. Aldershot: Gower.

GELSTHORPE, L., and MORRIS, A. (1988), 'Feminism and Criminology in Britain', *British Journal of Criminology*, 28/2.

—— eds. (1990), *Feminist Perspectives in Criminology*. Buckingham: Open University Press.

GENDERS, E., and PLAYER, E. (1986), 'Women's Imprisonment: The Effects of Youth Custody', *British Journal of Criminology*, 26/4.

GIALLOMBARDO, R. (1966), *Society of Women: A Study of a Woman's Prison*. New York/London: Wiley.

—— (1974), *The Social World of Imprisoned Girls*. New York: Wiley.

GILLIGAN, C. (1982), *In a Different Voice*. Cambridge, Mass.: Harvard University Press.

—— (1987), 'Moral Orientation and Moral Development', in E. Kittay and D. Meyers, eds., *Women and Moral Theory*. Totowa, NJ: Rowman and Littlefield.

GOLD, M. (1970), *Delinquent Behaviour in an American City*. Belmont, Ca.: Brooks Cole.

GREATER LONDON COUNCIL (1985), *Breaking the Silence*. London: GLC Women's Equality Group.

GREEN, P. (1991), *Drug Couriers*. London: Howard League for Penal Reform.

GREENWOOD, V. (1981), 'The Myth of Female Crime', in A. Morris and L. Gelsthorpe, eds., *Women and Crime*. Cambridge: Cambridge University Institute of Criminology.

HAGAN, J. (1989), *Modern Criminology: Crime, Criminal Behaviour and its Control*. New York: McGraw-Hill.

HAGAN, J., SIMPSON, J. H., and GILLIS, A. R. (1979), 'The Sexual Stratification of Social Control: A Gender-Based Perspective on Crime and Delinquency', *British Journal of Sociology*, 30.

HANMER, J., and SAUNDERS, S. (1984), *Well-Founded Fear*. London: Hutchinson.

HARDING, S. (1986), *The Science Question in Feminism*. Ithaca, NY: Cornell University Press.

HARRIS, R. (1992), *Crime, Criminal Justice and the Probation Service*. London: Routledge.

HARTMAN, M. (1977), *Victorian Murderesses*. London: Robson Books.

HARVEY, L., and PEASE, K. (1987), 'The Lifetime Prevalence of Custodial Sentences', *British Journal of Criminology*, 27/3: 311–15.

HEIDENSOHN, F. M. (1968), 'The Deviance of Women: A Critique and an Enquiry', *British Journal of Sociology*, 19/2.

—— (1970), 'Sex, Crime and Society', in G. A. Harrison, ed., *Biosocial Aspects of Sex*. Oxford: Blackwell.

—— (1975), 'The Imprisonment of Females', in S. McConville, ed., *The Use of Imprisonment*. London: Routledge and Kegan Paul.

—— (1981), 'Women and the Penal System', in A. Morris and L. Gelsthorpe, eds., *Women and Crime*. Cambridge: Cambridge University Institute of Criminology.

—— (1985), *Women and Crime*. London: Macmillan; New York: New York University Press.

—— (1986), 'Models of Justice: Portia or Persephone? Some Thoughts on Equality, Fairness and Gender in the Field of Criminal Justice'. *International Journal of the Sociology of Law*, 14.

—— (1989*a*) *Crime and Society*. Basingstoke: Macmillan.

—— (1989*b*) *Women in Policing in the USA*. London: Police Foundation.

—— (1991), 'Women and Crime in Europe', in F. Heidensohn and M. Farrell, eds., *Crime in Europe*. London: Routledge.

—— (1992*a*), 'Danger, Diversion or a New Dimension?', paper delivered at seminar on Women and Violence, University of Montreal, Quebec, February.

—— (1992*b*), *Women in Control? The Role of Women in Law Enforcement*. Oxford: Oxford University Press.

HINDELANG, M. (1979), 'Sex Differences in Criminal Activity', *Social Problems*, 27.

HIRSCHI, T. (1969), *Causes of Delinquency*. Berkeley: University of California Press.

HØIGÅRD, C., and FINSTAD, L. (1992), *Backstreets Prostitution: Money and Love*. Oxford: Polity.

HØIGÅRD, C., and SNARE, A. (1983), *Kvinners Skyld*. Oslo: Bakgater.

HOME OFFICE (1990), *Criminal Statistics 1989*. London: HMSO.

—— (1992), *Criminal Statistics 1990*. London: HMSO.

HORSLEY, J. W. (1887), *Jottings from Jail: Notes and Papers on Prison Matters*. London: T. Fisher Unwin.

IRWIN, J., and CRESSEY, D. (1962), 'Thieves, Convicts and the Inmate Culture', *Social Problems*, 10/3: 145–7.

JOHNSON, J. (1991), *What Lisa Knew*. London: Bloomsbury.

JONES, A. (1991), *Women Who Kill*. London: Gollancz.

JONES, D. (1982), *Crime, Protest, Community and Police in Nineteenth Century Britain*. London: Routledge.

JONES, S. (1986), *Policewomen and Equality*. London: Macmillan.

—— (1987), 'Women's Experience of Crime and Policing', discussion paper (mimeo), Centre for the Study of Community and Race Relations, Brunel University.

JONES, T., MACLEAN, B., and YOUNG, J. (1986), *The Islington Crime Survey*. Aldershot: Gower.

JURIK, N. (1983), 'The Economics of Female Recidivism', Criminology, 21/4: 3–12.

KELLOR, F. (1900*a*), 'Psychological and Environmental Study of Women Criminals', *American Journal of Sociology*, 5: 527–43.

—— (1900*b*), 'Criminal Sociology: Criminality Among Women', *Arena*, 23: 516–24.

KENNEDY, H. (1992), *Eve was Framed*. London: Chatto and Windus.

KERSTEN, J. (1989), 'The Institutional Control of Girls and Boys', in M. Cain, ed., *Growing Up Good*. London: Sage.

KERSTEN, J. (1991), 'A Cross-Cultural Debate of Crime and its Causes in Australia, Germany and Japan', paper presented to Australian and New Zealand Criminology Conference, Melbourne, Australia.

KLEIN, D. (1976), 'The Aetiology of Female Crime: A Review of the Literature', *Issues in Criminology*, 3: 3–30.

KRUTTSCHITT, C. (1981), 'Prison Codes, Inmate Solidarity and Women: A Re-examination', in M. Warren, ed., *Comparing Female and Male Offenders*. Newbury Park, Ca.: Sage.

LEONARD, E. B. (1982), *A Critique of Criminology Theory: Women, Crime and Society*. New York/London: Longman.

LLOYD, A. (1993), *Women and Violence*. Harmondsworth: Penguin.

LOMBROSO, C., and FERRERO, W. (1895), *The Female Offender*, with an introduction by W. D. Morrison. London: T. Fisher Unwin.

LONGMAN'S ENGLISH DICTIONARY (1984), London: Longman.

MACDONALD, E. (1991), *Shoot the Women First*. London: Fourth Estate.

MACGREGOR, S., ed. (1989), *Drugs and British Society*. London: Routledge.

MCLEOD, E. (1982), *Women Working: Prostitution Now*. London: Croom Helm.

MCLYNN, F. (1989), *Crime and Punishment in the Eighteenth Century*. Oxford: Oxford University Press.

MAHER, L. (1990), 'Criminalizing Pregnancy—The Downside of a Kinder, Gentler Nation?', *Social Justice*, 17/3: 111–35.

MANDARAKA-SHEPPARD, A. (1986), *The Dynamics of Aggression in Women's Prisons in England*. Aldershot: Gower.

MANNHEIM, H. (1965), *Comparative Criminology*. London: Routledge and Kegan Paul.

MARTIN, S. E. (1989), *Women on the Move—A Report on the Status of Women in Policing*, Police Foundation Report. Washington, DC: Police Foundation.

—— (1990), *On the Move—The Status of Women in Policing*. Police Foundation. (Washington, 1990).

MARTIN, S. E. (1980), *Breaking and Entering*. Berkeley, Ca.: University of California Press.

MATTHEWS, R., and YOUNG, J., eds. (1986), *Confronting Crime*. London: Sage.

MAWBY, R. (1980), 'Sex and Crime: The Results of a Self-Report Study', *British Journal of Sociology*, 31/4: 525.

MAYHEW, H. (1861), *London Labour and the London Poor*, 4 vols. London.

MILLAR, J., and GLENDINNING, C. (1989), 'Gender and Poverty', *Journal of Social Policy*, 18/3: 363–83.

MILLER, E. (1986), *Street Woman*. Philadelphia: Temple University Press.

MILLMAN, M. (1982), 'Images of Deviant Men and Women', in M. Evans, ed., *The Woman Question*. London: Fontana.

MITCHELL, J., and OAKLEY, A., eds. (1986), *What is Feminism?* Oxford:Blackwell.

MORRIS, A. (1987), *Women, Crime and Criminal Justice*. Oxford: Blackwell.

MORRIS, A., and GELSTHORPE, L., eds. (1981), *Women and Crime*, Cropwood Conference Series, no. 13. Cambridge: University of Cambridge Institute of Criminology.

MOXON, D. (1988), *Sentencing Practice in the Crown Court*, Home Office Research Study no. 103. London: HMSO.

MUKHERJEE, S. K., and SCUTT, J. A. (1981), *Women and Crime*. London: Australian Institute of Criminology/George Allen and Unwin.

NAFFINE, N. (1987), *Female Crime*. Sydney: Allen and Unwin.

NATZLER, C., O'SHEA, M., HEAVEN, O., and MARS, M. (1989), all in C. Dunhill, ed., *The Boys in Blue: Women's Challenge to the Police*. London: Virago.

NORLAND, S., WESSEL, R. C., and SHOVER, N. (1981), 'Masculinity and Delinquency', *Criminology*, 19/3: 421.

PADEL, V., and STEVENSON, P., eds. (1988), *Insiders: Women's Experience of Prison*. London: Virago.

PAHL, J. (1978), *A Refuge for Battered Women: A Study of the Role of a Women's Centre*. London: HMSO.

PARKER, H., CASBUM, M., and TURNBULL, D. (1981), *Receiving Juvenile Justice*. Oxford: Blackwell.

PARTON, N. (1992), *Governing the Family*. Basingstoke: Macmillan.

PEARSON, G. (1987), *The New Heroin Users*. Oxford: Blackwell.

PETRIE, G. (1971), *A Singular Iniquity—The Campaigns of Josephine Butler*. London: Macmillan.

PIKE, L. (1876), *A History of Crime in England*. London: Smith Elder.

PILIAVIN, I., and BRIAR, S. (1964), 'Police Encounters with Juveniles', *American Journal of Sociology*, 70: 206.

PIZZEY, E. (1973), *Scream Quietly or the Neighbours Will Hear*. Harmondsworth: Penguin.

PLAYER, E. (1989), 'Women and Crime in the City', in D. Downes, ed., *Crime in the City*. London: Macmillan.

POLLAK, O. (1950), *The Criminality of Women*. New York: A. S. Barnes/Perpetua.

POLLOCK-BYRNE, J. (1990), *Women, Prison and Crime*. Belmont, Ca.: Wadsworth.

PRATT, M. (1980), *Mugging as a Social Problem*. London: Routledge Kegan Paul.

RADICAL ALTERNATIVES TO PRISON (1972), *Alternatives to Holloway*. London: Christian Action Publications.

RAFTER, H. N. (1983), 'Chastizing the Unchaste: Social Control Functions of a Women's Reformatory 1894–31', in S. Cohen and A. Scull, eds., *Social Control and the State*. Oxford: Blackwell.

—— (1990), 'The Social Construction of Crime and Crime Control', *Journal of Research in Crime and Delinquency*, 27/4: 376–89.

REINER, R. (1985), *The Politics of the Police*. Brighton: Harvester Wheatsheaf.

REINER, R., and SHAPLAND, J. (1987), 'Introduction: Why Police?', *British Journal of Criminology*, Special Issue on Policing in Britain, 27/1: 1–4.

REYNOLDS, A. (1991), *Tight Rope*. London: Sidgwick and Jackson.

ROSENBAUM, M. (1981), *Women on Heroin*. New Jersey: Rutgers University Press.

SCHLESINGER, P., DOBASH, R. E., and DOBASH, R. P. (1992), *Women Viewing Violence*. London: British Film Institute.

SCHRAG, C. (1961), 'A Preliminary Criminal Typology', *Pacific Sociological Review*, 4/2: 11.

SCUTT, J. A. (1981), 'Sexism in Criminal Law', in S. K. Mukherjee and J. A. Scutt, eds., *Women and Crime*. London: AIC/Allen and Unwin.

SHAW, M. (1991), *The Federal Female Offender*. Solicitor General of Canada, no. 1991–3. Ottawa: Office of the Solicitor General.

SHAW, R., ed. (1991), *Prisoners' Children: What are the Issues?* London: Routledge.

SIMMONS, H. G. (1978), 'Explaining Social Policy: The English Mental Deficiency Act of 1913', *Journal of Social History*, 11/3.

SIMON, R. J. (1975), *Women and Crime*. Toronto/London: Lexington Books.

SMART, C. (1977), *Women, Crime and Criminology*. London: Routledge and Kegan Paul.

—— (1979), 'The New Female Criminal: Reality or Myth?', *British Journal of Criminology*, 19/1.

—— (1989), *Feminism and the Power of Law*. London: Routledge.

—— (1990), 'Feminist Approaches to Criminology; or Post-Modern Woman Meets Atavistic Man', in L. Gelsthorpe and A. Morris, eds., *Feminist Perspectives in Criminology*. Buckingham: Open University Press.

SMITH, A. D. (1962), *Women in Prison*. London: Stevens and Sons (Library of Criminology).

—— (1979), 'Sex and Deviance: An Assessment of Major Sociological Variables', *Sociological Quarterly*, 20: 183.

SMITH, D., and GRAY, J. (1983), *Police and People in London*, 4 vols. London: Policy Studies Institute.

SMITH, D., and PATERNOSTER, R. (1987), 'The Gender Gap in Theories of Deviance: Issues and Evidence, *Journal of Research on Crime and Delinquency*, 24: 140–72.

SMITH, D. A., and VISHER, A. C. (1980), 'Sex and Involvement in Deviance/Crime: A Quantitative Review of the Empirical Literature', *American Sociological Review*, 45: 691–701.

SMITH, L. J. F. (1988), 'Images of Women—Decision-Making in Courts', in A. Morris and C. Wilkinson, eds., *Women and the Penal System*, Cropwood Conference Series, no. x. Cambridge: Cambridge University Institute of Criminology.

STANG DAHL, T. (1987), *Women's Law: An Introduction to Feminist Jurisprudence*. Oxford: Oxford University Press.

STANKO, E. (1984), *Intimate Intrusions*. London: Routledge and Kegan Paul.

—— (1990), *Everyday Violence*. London: Pandora.

—— (1993), *Men and Crime*. Milton Keynes: Open University Press.

STANLEY, L., and WISE, S. (1983), *Breaking Out*. London: Routledge and Kegan Paul.

STEEL, B. S., and LOVRICH, N. P. (1987), 'Equality and Efficiency Trade-offs in Affirmative Action: Real or Imagined? The Case of the Feminine in Policing', *Social Science Journal*, 24/1.

STEFFENSMEIER, D. J. (1978), 'Crime and the Contemporary Woman: An Analysis of Changing Levels of Female Property Crime, 1960–75', *Social Forces*, 57.

—— (1980), 'Assessing the Impact of the Women's Movement on Sex-Based Differences in the Handling of Adult Criminal Defendants', *Crime and Delinquency*, 26: 344–57.

STRACHEY, R. (1978), *The Cause*. London: Virago.

SYKES, G. (1956), *Society of Captives*. Princeton, NJ: Princeton University Press.

TAYLOR, I., WALTON, P., and YOUNG, J. (1973), *The New Criminology*. London: Routledge and Kegan Paul.

—— (1975), *Critical Criminology*. London: Routledge and Kegan Paul.

Thomas, W. I. (1923), *The Unadjusted Girl*. Boston: Little, Brown.

Tittle, C. (1969), 'Inmate Organization: Sex Differentiation and the Influence of Criminal Sub-Cultures', *American Sociological Review*, 34: 492–505.

US Department of Justice (1984), *Uniform Crime Reports*. Washington, DC: US Department of Justice.

Vanezis, P. (1991), 'Women, Violent Crime and the Menstrual Cycle: A Review', *Medicine, Science and the Law*, 31/1: 11–14.

Visher, C. A. (1983), 'Gender, Police Arrest Decisions and Notions of Chivalry', *Criminology*, 21: 5–28.

Walby, S. (1989), 'Theorising Patriarchy', *Sociology*, 23/2: 213–34.

Walker, R. (1985), 'Racial Minority and Female Employment in Policing', *Crime and Delinquency*, 31/4: 555–72.

Walklate, S. (1989), *Victimology*. London: Unwin Hyman.

Walkowitz, J. (1980), *Prostitution and Victorian Society*. Cambridge: Cambridge University Press.

Ward, D. A., and Kassebaum, G. G. (1966), *Women's Prison*. London: Weidenfeld.

Webb, D. (1984), 'More on Gender and Justice: Girl Offenders on Supervision', *Sociology*, 18.

Women's National Commission (1991), *Women and Prison*. London: Cabinet Office.

Worrall, A. (1990), *Offending Women*. London: Routledge.

Young, A. (1990), *Femininity in Dissent*. London: Routledge.

Young, J. (1986), 'The Failure of Criminology: The Need for a Radical Realism', in R. Matthews and J. Young, eds., *Confronting Crime*. London: Sage.

Young, M. (1991), *An Inside Job*. Oxford: Oxford University Press.

Zedner, L. (1991), *Women, Crime and Custody in Victorian England*. Oxford: Oxford University Press.

Zimmer, L. (1986), *Women Guarding Men*. Chicago: University of Chicago Press.

22

Race, Crime, and Criminal Justice

DAVID J. SMITH

Most accounts explain law as a formalized and abstracted version of custom. All social groups somehow impose constraints on their members, and all social life involves a network of reciprocal obligations, which must somehow be enforceable. Constraints and obligations imply rules (whether implicit or explicit); and while most enforcement will be informal, effective constraints must ultimately depend on public rituals which act out what Rousseau called the 'general will' of the people. Among relatively small, especially pre-literate, groups, these controls can be exercised by custom, and the customs can be transmitted by oral tradition. As groups become larger, and social organization more complex, custom becomes formalized and abstracted into written law.

It follows that law and law enforcement are most coherent and easily understood within a homogeneous society having a single religious, cultural, and moral tradition. The more culturally homogeneous a society is, the closer the correspondence will be between custom (together with its infinitely complex apparatus of informal controls) and the concepts and ritualized processes of the criminal justice system. To the extent that a society is culturally heterogeneous, the perceptions, expectations, and scale of values built into the criminal justice system must be removed from the diverse traditions of all of the different ethnic groups, or must chiefly reflect the culture of the dominant group, or else must be confused and contradictory.

The ethnic dimension in crime and criminal justice therefore highlights the fundamental relationship between morals, social expectations, and informal controls, on the one hand, and the law and the criminal justice process on the other. The law seeks to impose a universal framework on more or less diverse groups which may differ in their perceptions and definitions of deviance, in the methods they use to control it, and in their readiness to appeal to the formal legal process.

Especially in the case of post-colonial nations, power is distributed very unequally between ethnic groups. Furthermore, the majority group has a unique connection with the moral, religious, and cultural tradition which shaped the legal system. The universal framework of law is closely connected with the concept of a nation. As Gilroy puts it:

Law is primarily a national institution, and adherence to its rule symbolizes the imagined community of the nation and expresses the fundamental unity and equality of its citizens. Beyond this general level, the importance of law and constitution in Britain is understood to be a unique and important cultural achievement. As Britain, stressed by crisis, has moved in the direction of a 'law and order' society, popular politics have infused legality with the capacity to articulate the very core of national identity. (1987: 74)

Yet if the law is thought to express national identity, neither the law nor the corresponding sense of identity grew out of a tradition that included the present-day ethnic minorities. Their treatment under the law is therefore the sharpest test of the capacity of the tradition to evolve and adapt. Unlike, for example, France, Britain does not have an official ideology of assimilation. The tradition can therefore afford to become more catholic, to incorporate certain elements of ethnic minority traditions, to respond to the specific needs of ethnic minorities, while seeking to find a new balance and coherence.

METHODOLOGY AND EPISTEMOLOGY

The Concept of Equal Treatment

The ideal of justice is abstract and universal. The principle that everyone is equal under the law is fundamental to our system. Of course, individuals acquire specific rights and obligations (such as the rights of the freeholder and the obligations of the employer), and the decision in any individual case takes account of a complex and unique set of circumstances. But the legal system tries to deal with unique cases by applying universal rules and by making judgements anchored in general principles. In modern times, any rule or principle implying that members of one social group should be treated less favourably than members of another has been considered wrong and in conflict with the fundamental values of the system.

Among the most important questions to be asked about criminal justice is how close it comes to the ideal of treating everyone equally. To the extent that the system falls short of this ideal, it is either inconsistent and incoherent, or systematically discriminatory; either way it is unjust, and loses legitimacy. A central objective of research must therefore be to establish how far different ethnic groups are treated equally.

There is room for considerable discussion about what is meant by equal treatment in this context. At one end of the scale there is the view that equal treatment means the impartial application of existing rules and principles regardless of the outcome. At the other end of the scale, there is the view put forward, for example, by Hudson (1993) that any policies, rules, or procedures that have the effect of punishing a higher proportion of one social group than of another are unjust, and that law and policy should be adjusted so as to achieve equal outcomes (say, in terms of the proportion imprisoned) for different ethnic groups or social classes.

It is difficult to defend either of these extreme views. Ensuring that equal proportions of different social groups are punished has never been seen as an objective of the criminal justice system, and does not seem a valid interpretation of the ideal of equality before the law. It is deeply ingrained in our tradition that the verdict in individual cases depends on the evidence, while the sentence depends on the seriousness of the offence and the previous record of the offender. What is meant to determine the pattern of law enforcement by the police and other official agencies is much more open to doubt; but few would accept the idea that either enforcement or the decisions of the courts should have the primary aim of achieving equality of outcome for different social groups. That would imply unequal treatment of individuals, and it would mean that an increase in the rate of offending among any social group would be accompanied by a decline in the proportion of offenders within that group who were penalized.

On the other hand, the view that equal treatment means impartial application of existing rules and principles seems equally questionable. Some of these rules or principles may work to the disadvantage of a particular ethnic group, yet could be changed without the sacrifice of any fundamental objective. For example, Afro-Caribbeans may tend to be remanded in custody rather than bailed because their family circumstances tend not to meet criteria commonly used in making decisions about awarding bail; and people remanded in custody are more likely to be convicted than those awarded bail, probably because people in prison find it more difficult to prepare a defence. The justification for using family circumstances as a criterion for awarding bail is not clear, and these criteria could probably be changed so as to reduce the disadvantage to Afro-Caribbeans without the sacrifice of any fundamental principle.

These two polar views about what constitutes equal treatment are similar to the two opposing models of justice implied in discussion of anti-discrimination law. McCrudden *et al.* (1991) describe them as the *individual justice model* and the *group justice model* of legislation against race and sex discrimination. On the *individual justice model*,

> it is argued that the aim of the legislation is to secure the reduction of discrimination by eliminating from decisional processes illegitimate considerations based on race which have harmful consequences for individuals. The model concentrates on cleansing the process of decision making, and is not concerned with the result except as an indicator of a flawed process. It is also heavily individualistic in its

orientation: it concentrates on securing fairness for the individual. It does not appear to depend on a recognition of social classes or groups. It is also generally expressed in universal and symmetrical terms: blacks and whites are equally protected.

On the *group justice model*, by contrast,

> the basic aim is the improvement of the relative economic position of blacks, whether to redress past subordination and discrimination, or out of concern for distributive justice at the present time . . . The model depends on the recognition of social classes or groups. It is often expressed in asymmetrical terms as focusing on the betterment of blacks in particular and is less concerned with protection for whites. (McCrudden *et al.* 1991: 5, 6)

The aims of these polar models of anti-discrimination legislation conflict in important ways, and the actual legislation represents a compromise between them. The main element of the group justice model incorporated within the Race Relations Act 1976 and the Sex Discrimination Act 1975 is the concept of *indirect discrimination*: the use of a condition or requirement which is such that a considerably smaller proportion of one than of another group can comply with it, which is to the other's detriment, and where the person using the condition or requirement cannot show it to be justified. The concept of indirect discrimination belongs within the group justice model to the extent that it is concerned with the outcomes for groups resulting from the application of some rule or principle. However, conflict with the individual justice model is minimized by the qualification that criteria working to the disadvantage of a particular ethnic group may always be used as long as they can be justified. The Commission for Racial Equality (1985, 1991) has recommended that the balance should be shifted a little further towards the group justice model by changing the word 'justified' to 'necessary'.

At present the decisions at certain key stages of the criminal justice process do not fall within the provisions of the anti-discrimination legislation, although there have been calls for this to be changed (Commission for Racial Equality 1991). Sentencing is excluded 'because a judge enjoys a general immunity from suit when acting in his judicial capacity' (Hood 1992). Decisions by other officials (for example, a police officer's decision to make an arrest) may also be excluded, because the Acts are concerned with the provision of goods, facilities, and services, and it may be held that these officials are not providing such services. Also, persons acting on behalf of the Crown may be excluded from the provisions of the anti-discrimination legislation: the key case (*Amin* v. *Entry Clearance Officer, Bombay* (1983), 2 AC 818) was concerned with immigration officials, but the principle could presumably be extended to others acting on behalf of the Crown, such as police officers. The state of the law on these points is far from clear, but in practice enforcement of the Race Relations Act has not extended to most aspects of the criminal justice process.

However, in approaching the central question how far different ethnic groups are treated equally by the criminal justice system it seems right to apply a concept of equal treatment that finds the same balance as the Race Relations Act between individual justice and group justice. That means analysing the criminal justice process as if it were subject to the provisions of the Race Relations Act. On this interpretation, equal treatment goes well beyond the individual justice model. Hence, practices, rules, and criteria which are apparently neutral, but in practice work to the disadvantage of a particular ethnic group, and cannot be justified, amount to unequal treatment under the proposed definition. On the other hand, this concept of equal treatment does not imply equality of outcomes (for example, that an equal proportion of each ethnic group should be imprisoned), nor does it place greater emphasis on the protection of ethnic minorities than on the protection of whites. Within this framework of analysis, equal treatment does not mean the same treatment. Hence there is room for different treatment of groups according to their specific needs: for example, for the police and other agencies to take special action to meet the needs of ethnic minorities as victims of racial attacks.

Establishing whether Ethnic Minorities are Treated Equally

As will be set out in more detail later, in Britain a much higher proportion of people of Afro-Caribbean and black African origin than of other ethnic groups are in prison. There is a similar contrast between rates of imprisonment of black and white people in the USA and in Australia and Canada (Tonry forthcoming). In several other European countries there are large differences in the rate of imprisonment between ethnic groups. (For example, see Tournier and Robert 1991 for an analysis of the French statistics.) In the broadest terms, two kinds of explanation can be put forward for these striking differences. On the one hand it may be suggested that the different ethnic groups are unequally treated at various stages of the criminal justice process. On the other hand it may be suggested that rates of crime are much higher among certain ethnic minority groups than among the white majority.

In broad terms, the balance of evidence from the large amount of research carried out in the USA is that while black people are treated somewhat unequally by the criminal justice process, in large part the difference in rates of imprisonment arises because crime rates are substantially higher among black than among white people. (Wilbanks 1987, while setting out to make this case, provides the fairest and most complete evaluation of the evidence that is available.) A strategy that has been used to resist this conclusion is to maintain that no evidence will ever be sufficient to decide the issue. For example, Reiner (1993) argues that no method 'can conclusively pin down the chimera of "pure" discrimination which is sought for'. In his view:

> The main problem with either statistical or qualitative analysis of criminal justice practice is the inability to control all other relevant variables apart from 'race'. Statistical analyses in particular invariably attempt to establish discrimination by seeking to show that there is a residual element of differentiation in the treatment of black people which is not explicable by 'legally relevant' factors . . .
>
> It is inconceivable that this approach could ever conclusively establish racial discrimination. The most obvious problem is the practical impossibility of holding constant more than a few 'legally relevant' variables. This means that it is always open to analysts of different persuasions to characterise any remaining differences in treatment as (so far) unexplained variation rather than discrimination.

One interpretation of this argument is that the statements that the crime rate is higher among black than among white people, or that the criminal justice system discriminates against black people, are the expression of 'essentially contested propositions', meaning propositions that will always be contentious and that some will resist at all costs. On that interpretation, Reiner is simply saying that some of the participants in discussion on this subject will never be convinced by reasoned argument on the basis of evidence. This echoes Lewis Carroll's demonstration in his essay 'What the Tortoise Said to Achilles' that a person cannot be *forced* to accept a logical inference. It is, of course, true that no argument can ever be conclusive, in the sense that people can go on resisting it as long as they wish to; also, as Reiner emphasizes, people have particularly strong motives for resisting argument and evidence on the subject of race and crime. If everyone responded in that way, there would not be enough consensus for social science to tackle the issues. However, this chapter is written for those (surely the majority of scholars) who do not wish to resist *at any cost* the proposition that crime rates vary between ethnic groups, or that the criminal justice system is biased against black people.

On a more straightforward interpretation, the argument that 'none of these methods (or indeed any other methods) can conclusively pin down the chimera of "pure" discrimination' is an argument against the possibility of social science. Moreover, since it does not turn on special attributes of social as opposed to physical or biological science, it is an argument against the possibility of science in general.

An argument of that kind would be based on a misconception of the scientific enterprise. Science does not aspire to godlike certainty: that would be more characteristic of religious fanaticism. All it provides is the best explanations in the light of available evidence (this is a crude summary of the views of Karl Popper: 1959, 1963). Before putting forward a theory (for example, that the criminal justice process discriminates against Afro-Caribbeans), the social scientist need not have considered every other possible explanation. It is up to the scientific community to put forward alternative explanations, and to devise ways of choosing between competing ones. The best theories will be those that explain the most, and which best survive intensive criticism and marshalling of evidence.

To draw a brief comparison, it seemed inconceivable before the late nineteenth century that the age of the earth could be established, yet Kelvin insisted that the problem could be tackled by applying the accepted principles of physics and making use of available measurements. The estimate depends on a calculation of the speed of cooling since the earth was formed. Critics of Kelvin's model pointed out that he had failed to take account of a number of variables, in particular convection within the earth's core. Kelvin's estimates turned out to be wrong by orders of magnitude when allowance was made for these additional factors. However, it was Kelvin's pioneering work, and in particular his insistence that the problem could be tackled, that paved the way for subsequent advances. Further criticisms may yet lead to further refinements, but in the meantime, the theory that the earth is four and a half billion years old is a good one, and certainly the best we have got. Of course the figure can never be established beyond doubt. Yet if Kelvin had not insisted that the problem could be tackled, we would still be stuck with the biblical creation myth.

In each of his reviews, Reiner (1989, 1993) has concluded that unequal treatment accounts for a substantial part of the overrepresentation of Afro-Caribbeans and Africans among the prison population, even though he maintains that the evidence can never be conclusive. At first sight, this seems contradictory, although on one interpretation he is only saying 'this is a reasonable view, but some people will never be convinced'. In any case, it seems that he is willing to draw conclusions, even though he believes these conclusions must remain in some sense infinitely contestable. In that context, the theory that the conclusions are infinitely contestable does not seem to matter very much, yet this is a strategy that loosens the chains of logic: it legitimates the expression of views that need not, in the end, be justified, on the argument that no evidence could ever be sufficient.

The propagation of the myth that nothing can ever finally be said is damaging to the development of any subject. It does not cause the practitioners of the discipline to become silent, but rather encourages them to believe that anything goes, because no absolutely guaranteed standards apply. In particular, the insistence that no evidence can ever be totally conclusive discourages people from thinking of new ways of testing theories which might make a major contribution to the development of the subject. For example, victim survey data have recently been used to test the theory that offences committed by ethnic minorities are more likely to be reported to the police than those committed by white people (Shah and Pease 1992). Writers who argue that 'crime' is an infinitely problematic concept, and that there is no completely reliable way of interpreting the statistics of recorded crime, would have discouraged this recent advance. People could equally well have said 200 years ago that from looking at the sky there is no completely reliable way of telling how far away the stars are—and in fact they did.

Interaction Effects

The high rate of criminal convictions among certain ethnic minority groups may be in part the result of a sequence of interactions between members of the minority group and the authorities, particularly the police (this idea is developed in more detail in Smith 1991). The point can be illustrated through the case of Rodney King, a black man who was severely beaten by a group of white police officers in the course of arresting him in Los Angeles in 1991. Clear evidence of the beating was provided by an amateur video tape played at the first trial of the four police officers in 1992, but in spite of this an all-white jury acquitted them. The acquittal was followed by widespread riots in Los Angeles, in which black people committed hundreds of violent offences against police officers and ordinary citizens, destroyed and damaged large amounts of property, and looted many shops. When the four police officers were retried in 1993, two of them were found guilty, and this time the city stayed calm. The sequence of interactions was: (1) Rodney King commits traffic offences; (2) white police officers seek to arrest him; (3) probably assuming that they are racially prejudiced against him, King does not immediately obey the order to 'prone out'; (4) white police officers respond with excessive and unlawful force; (5) because video-tape evidence is (exceptionally) available, the police officers are prosecuted; (6) an all-white jury is selected; (7) it arrives at a manifestly biased verdict of not guilty; (8) a huge number of offences are committed by black people in protest at the verdict. Of course, the sequence could continue indefinitely with (9) many of these black people are arrested; (10) some resist arrest and the police respond with excessive and unlawful force . . .

In this sequence, racial prejudice and discriminatory actions at several points in the criminal justice process are the immediate cause of an escalating criminal response among black people; also, hostility to the police and courts among black people at each stage is an immediate cause of an increasingly prejudiced and unfair response by the criminal justice system.

It is reasonable to say that unequal treatment of black people by the criminal justice system was a cause of the Los Angeles riots, hence a cause of the high crime rate among black people; and that the high black crime rate was a cause of unequal treatment of black people (but no excuse).

It is these interaction effects, rather than the problem of 'controlling for all of the variables', that pose the greatest challenge to researchers in the field. The problem is that crime emerges from a series of interactions, yet one of the forces shaping those interactions is unequal treatment by the criminal justice system itself. This is enough to tempt some commentators to say that black crime is constructed by white racism. The contention of this chapter is that sweeping generalizations of that kind do not lead towards greater understanding. Instead of giving an ideological summary, the task for research is to describe and analyse the interactions in detail. In order to do this, it is necessary to accept that crime is crime, even when it is caused, in part, by injustice. The Los Angeles police officers did assault Rodney King, and they were wrongly acquitted, and these injustices were part of a pattern of racial discrimination. Equally, the rioters did commit arson, theft, assault, and murder.

ETHNIC MINORITIES IN BRITAIN: THE BACKGROUND TO CRIMINAL JUSTICE

According to the 1991 census, which for the first time included a question on ethnic origin, 5.5 per cent of the population of Britain belonged to an ethnic minority group at that time. Among these, three broad groups can be identified: black people, who made up 1.6 per cent of the population, among whom 0.9 per cent originated from the Caribbean; south Asians, who made up 2.7 per cent, among whom 1.5 per cent originated from India, 0.9 per cent from Pakistan, and 0.3 per cent from Bangladesh; and other minorities, which accounted for 1.2 per cent, among whom 0.3 per cent were of Chinese origin, while 0.4 per cent were other Asians.

Ethnic minorities have a distinctly younger age structure than the majority white population. For example, all ethnic minorities accounted at the census date for 6.93 per cent of the population aged 16–24, compared with 5.5 per cent of all age groups, and 2.7 per cent of those aged 45 and over. Because most crime is committed by males up to the age of 30, it is important to take account of the unusual age structure of the ethnic minority groups when evaluating their recorded crime rates.

The ethnic minorities counted in these statistics are those which are perceived by the majority to be physically distinct, and which are visually identifiable. The vast majority of these people are either themselves migrants, or descendants of people who migrated to Britain since the Second World War. Although the migration from the Caribbean got under way in the early 1950s, most of the inflow happened more recently. Thus, a national survey carried out in 1974 showed that among adults of south Asian and Caribbean origin, only 1 per cent at that time had been born in Britain; only 22 per cent had come to Britain before 1960 (Smith 1977: 27, table A1). The present-day minority population is much larger than in 1974, and includes many people whose families came after that date.

It was the Race Relations Act 1968 which first made it unlawful to discriminate on grounds of race, colour, or ethnic or national origins, in the provision of goods, facilities, and services. A pioneering research project carried out in 1966–7, before the Act was passed, showed that racial discrimination 'ranged from the massive to the substantial' (Daniel 1968). The research particularly concentrated on recruitment to employment and private rental of accommodation, but some other fields were also covered less intensively. Three methods of research were used. First, a survey was carried out of immigrants in six towns, and respondents were asked about their experiences of racial discrimination. Second, field experiments were conducted in which teams of actors, each one belonging to a different ethnic group, applied for the same job, or to rent the same accommodation. Third, interviews were conducted with managers or officials in organizations which had been proven to discriminate (from the results of a field experiment) and with others who were in a position to discriminate if they so wished. It was the combined results of these three lines of inquiry which led irresistibly to the conclusion that racial discrimination was widespread.

A further finding of this study is crucial to any analysis of crime among ethnic minorities. Both the field experiments and the interviews with actual and potential discriminators showed no difference in the extent or nature of discrimination against different specific groups, as long as these were considered to be racially distinct from the majority population. The study demonstrated that perceived 'colour' was the important factor, by including a Turkish Cypriot actor in the experiments. Discrimination against the Turkish Cypriot was radically lower than against the Afro-Caribbean, Indian, or Pakistani, but there was no difference in the level of discrimination against these last three groups. The Indian and Pakistani respondents in the survey were much less likely than the Afro-Caribbeans to say they had encountered discrimination, but Daniel showed that this was because of the radically different survival strategies adopted by south Asians compared with Afro-Caribbeans in Britain. Afro-Caribbeans came from islands whose institutions had been modelled on the British pattern. Their only language was English, and they did not realize how different their English was from British dialects. In coming to Britain, many thought they were going to 'the mother country'. They thought they belonged to the same culture, did not expect to encounter hostility and rejection, and were therefore open and outgoing in their attitude in the initial period. South Asians, by contrast, came from countries where Britain had in a brief period of colonial rule changed the superstructure of government without influencing the culture or institutions in a fundamental way. People in the Indian subcontinent continued to speak their own languages (although some added English), to practise their religions, and to conduct their family and economic life in ways that were little influenced by the colonists. When the migrants came to Britain, they therefore expected to rely on the resources of their own family or community.

The effect of these contrasting attitudes was marked. Afro-Caribbeans, expecting much more of British people, adopted a far more outgoing style of life: they were likely to apply for a job at a firm they had never heard of before, and where no other black people were working; or to apply cold to rent accommodation. South Asians looked for job opportunities through their established social networks, and from the beginning made extraordinary efforts to buy rather than rent accommodation. Daniel's experiments showed that the level of discrimination against members of the two groups was the same, where they put themselves in the same situation. But in reality, the Afro-Caribbeans placed themselves in situations in which they might face discrimination more often than south Asians did. They were therefore more likely to encounter face to face the hostility and rejection that south Asians avoided.

Levels of discrimination against south Asians and Afro-Caribbeans in comparable situations were the same, but personal experience of discrimination, and awareness of it, was substantially greater among Afro-Caribbeans. Subsequent research in the 1970s (Smith 1977) and 1980s (Brown 1984; Brown and Gay 1986) confirmed that the initial pattern continued. None of the field experiments carried out in Britain has yet shown any difference in the level of discrimination against south Asians on the one hand compared with Afro-Caribbeans on the other. Of course, none of this experimental research has been concerned with decision-making by the criminal justice process. However, it is an important part of the background to discussion of criminal justice issues that British people generally (presumably including victims of crime, police officers, and magistrates) show an undifferentiated tendency to discriminate against anyone perceived to be racially distinct.

In the 1960s, the migrants were largely concentrated in unskilled and semi-skilled manual jobs in the main conurbations and the textile towns of Lancashire and Yorkshire. Initially, a large proportion of south Asians had little English, and even today a substantial minority (around 20 per cent) do not speak English well. The south Asian population was always diverse, with a substantial minority of high educated people together with a larger proportion having little or no education. From 1969 onwards the migration of Asians from east Africa swelled the number who were well educated and who had experience of managing businesses. More recently, migration from Bangladesh has introduced a group of generally poor Asians with little education. By contrast, Afro-Caribbeans were always a more homogeneous population in social, economic, and cultural terms. Very few were uneducated, but few had higher education qualifications obtained in the West Indies. From the beginning, a high proportion of the men were skilled manual workers, and that remains the case today.

The process of development for ethnic minorities from the 1960s to the present time has been one of increasing differentiation (Jones 1993). There are increasing differences between specific minority groups, and also between members of each particular group. People of African-Asian and Indian origin now have a profile similar to that of white people in terms of educational qualifications and job levels. On the other hand, the Muslim groups (principally those of Pakistani and Bangladeshi origin) are at a substantial disadvantage in terms of job levels, rate of unemployment, educational and job qualifications, income, and standard of living (Jones 1993). Afro-Caribbeans occupy an intermediate position. In cultural terms, the specific ethnic minorities have always been more different from each other than each group is from the white majority. What they had in common was the racial discrimination and hostility displayed by white people and institutions. The different groups adopted entirely different strategies in response to this treatment. The outcome is that the original cultural differences, and the differences in human and financial capital between the groups, have proved far more influential than the hostility and discrimination directed impartially at all groups perceived to be racially distinct. As a result, the socio-economic positions of the specific minority groups are drawing further apart.

The sequence of field experiments suggests that there was a substantial decline in racial discrimination following the Race Relations Act 1968, but that discrimination nevertheless continued at a fairly high level. No further declines in the level have been recorded since 1974, although the latest experiments were carried out in 1986. These showed that about 40 per cent of south Asian and Afro-Caribbean job applicants were refused an interview where a similarly qualified white applicant was offered one (Brown and Gay 1986).

It is not, of course, possible to construct a time series of information about treatment of ethnic minorities by the criminal justice system, or about crime rates among ethnic minorities. However, it is clear that *con-*

cern about high crime rates among Afro-Caribbeans is relatively recent. In a report published in 1972, the Home Affairs Committee of the House of Commons on Race Relations and Immigration expressed some disquiet about difficult relations between the police and young Afro-Caribbeans, but on the whole tended towards the view that Afro-Caribbeans were less criminal than whites; certainly, two chief constables put forward that view in their evidence to the Committee (House of Commons Home Affairs Committee 1972). The years between 1972 and 1976 'saw the definition of blacks as a low crime group turned round 180 degrees' (Gilroy 1987: 92). Giving evidence to the Home Affairs Select Committee in the 1975/6 session, the Metropolitan Police made it clear that they considered that crime rates were high among Afro-Caribbeans, and also complained about anti-police campaigning by black activist groups (House of Commons Select Committee on Race Relations and Immigration 1976: 182). As Gilroy (1987) points out, this swing in official opinion was probably the result of a series of high-profile confrontations between the police and Afro-Caribbeans. Gilroy lists the 1970 conflict around the Mangrove restaurant, Notting Hill (London); the 1971 conflict at the Metro Club (Notting Hill); the Bonfire Night riots in Chapeltown, Leeds, in 1973, 1974, and 1975; the conflicts between police and black youth at Brockwell park (south London) at various times in the 1970s; and the riots at the Notting Hill Carnival in 1976, 1977, and 1978.

In the context of disturbances such as these, the Metropolitan Police provided statistical evidence in its 1976 submission to the Home Affairs Committee to support the proposition that there was a specific crime problem among ethnic minorities. These statistics showed the number of people arrested for certain types of offence who belonged to all 'non-white' groups lumped together, and the race of offenders according to victims' reports. Non-violent thefts and violent robberies were lumped into a single category, which rapidly became known as 'mugging', with the false implication that violence was involved in all cases. The proportion of offenders for this category of thefts and robberies who were non-white was apparently high. From this point onwards, public discussion of the threat of rising crime was linked with discussion of racial conflict and with the perceived problem of crime among Afro-Caribbeans. It has been argued that the growing public and police perception of black people as criminal was closely connected with the conception of 'mugging' and its promotion in the media as a typically black crime (Hall *et al.* 1978).

In the 1980s, relations between black (Afro-Caribbean) people and the police were at the forefront of public consciousness. There were a considerable number of disturbances expressing hostility by black people towards the police: St Paul's, Bristol, in 1980; protests against police handling of the investigation into the Deptford fire, culminating in the Black People's Day of Action on 2 March 1981; the Brixton disorders in April of that year; the further, serious public disorder in July 1981 in Southall, Liverpool (Toxteth), the Moss Side area of Manchester, and the West Midlands; the disorders in the Lozells and Handsworth areas of Birmingham in September 1985; and that at Broadwater Farm in October 1985. These disturbances led to various official and unofficial reports: the Scarman Report on the Brixton disorders (Scarman 1981); the report by Bennet Hytner on the Moss Side disturbances; the report by Julius Silverman on the Handsworth disturbances, commissioned by Birmingham City Council (Silverman 1986); the Broadwater Farm Inquiry, commissioned by the London Borough of Haringey. This period also saw the publication of the Policy Studies Institute (PSI) report on *Police and People in London* (Smith 1983*a*, *b*; Small 1983; Smith and Gray 1983), which attracted headline coverage of its account of relations between the police and ethnic minorities. In the space of ten years, therefore, there was a swing from muted official concern about relations between Afro-Caribbeans and the police, together with an official view that crime rates among ethnic minorities were the same as among whites, or lower, to anti-police riots in which black people played the major part, and an official view (backed up by some limited statistical evidence) that rates for certain types of crime were high among Afro-Caribbeans.

Throughout the period, it was Afro-Caribbeans, and not south Asians, who were highlighted in public discussion of crime and disorder. The famous conflicts in the 1970s revolved around Afro-Caribbean clubs and cultural events such as the Notting Hill Carnival. The anti-police riots of the 1980s took place in areas of Afro-Caribbean concentration (such as St Paul's in Bristol, Brixton in south London, and Moss Side in Manchester); while white people as well as Afro-Caribbeans took part, there is little evidence that south Asians were involved. Many south Asian shopkeepers were victims in the 1985 riots in the Lozells and Handsworth areas of Birmingham.

As will be shown in more detail later, south Asians have been at least as subject to racial attacks as Afro-Caribbeans throughout the 1970s and 1980s. This is further evidence, in addition to the results of experiments on racial discrimination, to show that prejudice and hostility among the public at large is just as great against south Asians as against Afro-Caribbeans. Nevertheless, it is only Afro-Caribbeans, and not south Asians, who have become associated in public debate and in the public mind with predatory crime.

In the 1990s, the Muslim groups (originating from India as well as from Pakistan and Bangladesh) have become more active, assertive, and politically organized as a consequence of the Salman Rushdie affair. This development has been associated with the growth of specifically anti-Muslim prejudice. There are some early indications that public debate may come to focus on Muslim involvement in crime: for example, this was one theme of a BBC *Panorama* programme transmitted in April 1993 on 'Britain's new Muslim Underclass'.

ETHNIC MINORITIES AS SUSPECTS AND OFFENDERS

The criminal justice process can be regarded as a sequence of decisions starting with behaviour that someone considers to be deviant or offensive, and ending with the punishment of an offender. A number of choices are available at every stage on the route between the two points. Most of these result in the matter being dropped or resolved or in action being taken by methods other than criminal justice process. Hence the number of remaining cases successively diminishes from one stage to the next. One reason why the process takes this form is that people and organizations have a number of resources and sanctions to deploy against deviant and offensive behaviour, of which criminal justice is only one. Many matters which could potentially be treated as crime are never referred to the criminal justice system at all. Many others are initially referred, but are later dealt with in some other way instead. If criminal justice is regarded as a resource for dealing with deviant or offensive behaviour, then other resources are often more easily available, cheaper, quicker, and more efficient. Indeed, the system is so inefficient that most reported crimes that do remain to be processed cannot result in a conviction even with the current large expenditure on the police, other investigatory and regulatory agencies, and the courts.

The decisions made at each stage determine which incidents and individuals remain within the system to be processed at the next stage. In that sense, the various stages are linked. For example, the acquittal rate partly depends on the selection of cases that get to court; and the acquittal rate could vary between ethnic groups because weak cases are more likely to reach trial where the defendant belongs to one ethnic group rather than another.

Because the system takes this form, the ideal piece of research to test whether ethnic minorities are equally treated would be longitudinal. It would start by identifying deviant or offensive behaviours (which might be found to vary in pattern and incidence between ethnic groups) and would then follow their treatment through the criminal justice system and by other methods. In practice, no longitudinal research design of this kind could ever be comprehensive. One reason is that identifying the behaviours in question before they are referred to the criminal justice process would be impossible in many cases. For example, obstructing a police officer in the course of his duties is a behaviour that exists from the time that the police officer decides to make an arrest. It is not feasible to inquire how many potential offences of this kind occurred, but were not proceeded with. In practice, although longitudinal research could probably cover some fairly large stretches of the whole process, no research of that kind has yet been attempted. However, by studying each stage separately, much progress can be made towards showing whether there is equal treatment at that stage and how much contribution any unequal treatment makes to overrepresentation of ethnic minorities at the end of the whole process.

In summarizing the research results, it would be neat to start at the beginning of the sequence and move towards the end. However, the ethnic composition of the prison population must be examined first, because it provides striking evidence of something that needs to be explained.

The Prison Population

Statistics of the prison population by ethnic group were first published for 1985 and have been published annually since. These are a count of the population on a reference date: no statistics on the flow of people into prisons ('receptions') by ethnic group have yet been published. The prison population on a reference date of course reflects both the number admitted into prison, and the length of their sentences.

Table 22.1 The male and female prison population by ethnic group, % (England and Wales, 1985 and 1991)

	Males Prison		GP[a]	Females Prison		GP[a]
	1985	1991	1991	1985	1991	1991
White	83.1	83.5	92.9	77.8	67.9	92.5
West Indian, Guyanese, African	8.0	10.3	1.8	12.1	22.8	2.0
Indian, Pakistani, Bangladeshi	2.3	3.0	3.4	1.8	1.7	3.4
Chinese, Arab, mixed origin	2.2	2.0		3.2	4.3	
Other, not known	4.5	1.1		3.2	3.2	
N	45,926	43,210		1,577	1,544	

[a] General population aged 16–39.
Sources: Home Office *Statistical Bulletin*, 17/86; *Prison Statistics England and Wales, 1991*; *Census of Population, 1991.*

Table 22.1 shows the proportion belonging to each ethnic group among all prisoners, including young offenders as well as adults, and prisoners on remand as well as sentenced offenders. Afro-Caribbeans and black Africans (grouped together in the available statistics) are heavily overrepresented among the prison population compared with their numbers in the general population, whereas this is *not* true for south Asians. The National Prison Survey shows that 84 per cent of the prison population in 1991 consisted of people aged 17–39 (Walmsley *et al.* 1992: 9, table 1). It is therefore appropriate to compare the prison population with the general population within this age band. In 1991, the black groups (those of West Indian, Guyanese, and African origin) were 10.3 per cent of the male prison population, compared with 1.8 per cent of the general population aged 16–39 according to the 1991 census. Females are only a small proportion of the prison population: they accounted for a mere 3.4 per cent in 1991. However, the black groups formed an astonishing 22.8 per cent of this small female prison population. A substantial proportion of these black female prisoners are foreign 'mules' caught bringing drugs into Britain (Green 1991). Among sentenced female black prisoners, nearly half were sentenced for drugs offences, compared with 15 per cent of white female prisoners.

The statistics lump together people of Indian, Pakistani and Bangladeshi origin. This group forms a slightly smaller proportion of the prison than of the general population in the case of males, and a distinctly smaller proportion in the case of females. The other groups (people of Chinese, Arab, and mixed origin) seem to be overrepresented among the prison population, but this is hard to interpret since the category is so heterogeneous, and it is not possible to make an exact comparison with census data.

Between 1985 (when these statistics first became available) and 1991, there was some increase in the proportion of prisoners belonging to the black groups. This increase was particularly marked in the case of females, probably reflecting an increase in the number of drugs 'mules' arrested.

The black groups account for about the same proportion of prisoners on remand as of those under sentence (see Table 22.2). However, by 1991 they accounted for a considerably smaller proportion of sentenced young offenders than of sentenced adults, although they had accounted for about the same proportion of these two groups in 1985.

These comparisons between the prison population and the general population show that the black groups are heavily overrepresented in prison; this can be demonstrated more clearly by calculating the rate of imprisonment per head of population in the relevant age groups (see Table 22.3). Among adult males, the rate of imprisonment is about the same for south

Table 22.2 The male prison population by ethnic group, % (England and Wales, 1985 and 1991)

	On remand		Sentenced			
			Young offenders		Adults	
	1985	1991	1985	1991	1985	1991
White	75.8	83.3	86.4	87.9	84.6	83.4
West Indian, Guyanese, African	10.0	10.9	8.4	6.8	7.0	10.6
Indian, Pakistani, Bangladeshi	2.4	2.5	1.4	2.5	2.6	3.0
Chinese, Arab, mixed origin	2.4	2.3	2.3	2.4	2.1	1.8
Other, not known	9.5	1.0	1.5	0.5	3.7	1.2
N	9,531	8,876	10,104	5,683	26,083	28,283

Sources: Home office *Statistical Bulletin*, 17/86; *Prison Statistics England and Wales, 1991.*

Asians and whites, but nearly seven times as high among blacks. This contrast is slightly stronger among adult remand prisoners than among sentenced prisoners. Among young males, the rate of imprisonment is markedly lower for south Asians than for whites, but 5.4 times as high for blacks as for whites.

The great majority of prisoners (78 per cent in 1991) are under sentence, while the remainder are on remand or have been convicted but not yet sentenced. For those under sentence, the published statistics show the type of offence they committed according to ethnic group. For each group of offences, these have been used to calculate rates of imprisonment per head of population in the relevant age band (see Table 22.3). The rate of imprisonment for black males is much higher than for white males for every group of offences, but there are wide variations between offence groups. About twenty-seven times as many black as white adult males per head of population are in prison for drugs offences, and eight to nine times as many for rape and for robbery. On the other hand, this ratio is comparatively low for burglary (about 3) and for sexual offences other than rape (1.5). Among south Asian adult males, the rate of imprisonment for drugs offences is also very high—about four times as high as among white men; but the rate of imprisonment of south Asian men for burglary is particularly low, at around one-fifth the rate for white men.

In broad terms, the pattern for young offenders is similar. Young black males have exceptionally high rates of imprisonment for rape, robbery, and drugs offences—eleven to twelve times the rate for young white males in each case. Again, the contrast is least marked in the case of burglary.

Table 22.3 Rate of imprisonment of males by ethnic group (England and Wales, 1991): adults, rates per 10,000 population aged 20–39; young offenders, rates per 10,000 population aged 17–19

	Ethnic origin			
	A	B		
	White	Black[d]	S. Asian[e]	B/A
Adult Males				
All prisoners[a]	43.7	294.0	47.3	6.7
On remand[b]	8.5	61.3	7.7	7.2
Sentenced	35.0	223.3	36.4	6.4
Offence[c]				
Violence against the person	7.5	39.0	9.0	5.2
Rape	1.6	13.9	2.4	8.7
Other sexual offences	2.2	3.3	0.9	1.5
Burglary	5.1	14.7	1.0	2.9
Robbery	3.8	31.1	2.4	8.2
Theft and handling	3.0	13.5	2.1	4.5
Fraud and forgery	0.9	5.7	2.3	6.3
Drugs offences	2.0	53.0	8.5	26.5
Other offences	3.4	14.4	2.9	4.2
Young Males				
All prisoners	54.0	292.8	34.1	5.4
On remand	13.6	79.5	8.3	5.8
Sentenced	40.4	213.4	25.8	5.3
Offence[c]				
Violence against the person	5.8	35.6	5.4	6.1
Rape	0.8	9.4	1.8	11.8
Other sexual offences	0.4	1.1	0.7	2.8
Burglary	10.2	18.3	1.8	1.8
Robbery	4.9	63.3	4.5	12.9
Theft and handling	4.7	20.0	1.4	4.3
Fraud and Forgery	0.2	1.1	0.7	5.5
Drugs offences	0.7	7.8	1.3	11.1
Other offences	4.7	10.0	2.0	2.1

[a] Includes young convicted unsentenced prisoners and young non-criminal prisoners.
[b] Includes young convicted unsentenced prisoners.
[c] Covers offences with immediate custodial sentence only (this is the great majority).
[d] West Indian, Guyanese, black African (prison statistics); black Caribbean, black African (population statistics).
[e] Indian, Pakistani, Bangladeshi.
Sources: Prison Statistics England and Wales, 1991; Census, 1991

While the prison statistics lump together people of Indian, Pakistani, and Bangladeshi origin, the National Prison Survey provides more detailed information for 1991. This shows that the proportions of Indians and Bangladeshis in the prison population were about the same as in the general population, but that Pakistanis were overrepresented in the prison population to some extent (Walmsley *et al.* 1992: 11). Sampling error prevents an exact estimate of this overrepresentation, but it cannot be very marked, particularly if the age structure of the Pakistani population is taken into account. It is important to note that this slight tendency to overrepresentation among the prison population does not apply to all Muslim groups: Bangladeshis are a clear exception.

The prison statistics show that by the end of the criminal justice process, black people (Afro-Caribbeans and black Africans) are far more likely to be undergoing the most severe penalty available—a prison sentence—than white people. Equally striking, they show that south Asians are no more likely to be in prison than white people. Finally, they show that the contrast in rates of imprisonment between black and white people varies dramatically according to the type of offence. The evidence about the outcome of the criminal justice process at the final stage therefore strongly raises the question whether black people are equally treated. Answering that question is much more difficult, but the pattern of results within the prison statistics themselves already gives some purchase.

First, it is highly significant—but has generally been ignored by most commentators—that rates of imprisonment are no higher among south Asians than among white people. As set out earlier, racial discrimination against south Asians, for example in employment and housing, is just as prevalent as it is against Afro-Caribbeans. Other manifestations of hostility, such as racial attacks, are also at least as common against south Asians as against Afro-Caribbeans. It follows that any generalized notion of 'racism' is incapable of explaining the high rate of imprisonment of Afro-Caribbeans. Some commentators, such as Reiner (1989, 1993) and Hudson (1993), have simply ignored this fundamental point. Others, such as Jefferson (1993), recognize its importance but seek to preserve the theory that 'racism' explains the criminality of ethnic minority groups by postulating that the forms of racism directed against south Asians and Afro-Caribbeans are different. The problem with this approach is that if 'racism' takes such extremely different forms it loses its coherence as a concept. Also, there is as yet little evidence of differentiated forms of racial hostility directed at specific groups.

Second, it is also potentially important that the contrast in rates of imprisonment between black and white people varies so starkly according to the type of offence. If the overrepresentation of black people among prisoners is the result of bias at various stages of the criminal justice process, then the contrast in rates of imprisonment between black and white people should be greatest for offences whose detection depends on proactive investigation and the use of discretion; the contrast should be least for offences where victims generally do not know the ethnic group of the offender, and where police or other investigatory agencies have to decide whether to investigate before they know the ethnic group of the offender. This analytic point is similar to one made by Wilbanks (1987: 65) about the pattern of arrests according to offence. In fact, some of the main features of the observed pattern do fit the theory that black people end up in prison because of selective reporting of offences and discretionary law enforcement. The high rate of imprisonment of black people for drugs offences is particularly telling. Arrests for drugs offences notoriously arise from the exercise of police discretion, and it is easy for police and customs officers to target law enforcement in this field at a particular ethnic group. The relatively low rate of imprisonment of black people for burglary also fits the theory. Householders do not know the ethnic group of the burglar when they decide to report a burglary to the police; and there is little the police can do to target efforts to improve the clear-up rate for burglaries on offences committed by black people.

Even the prison statistics on their own can therefore point towards two conclusions. First, the high rate of imprisonment of Afro-Caribbeans is unlikely to be purely the result of bias at various stages of the criminal justice process, because south Asians, like Afro-Caribbeans, suffer substantial racial hostility and discrimination, but do not show abnormally high rates of imprisonment. Second, the pattern of offences for which black people are imprisoned fits the theory that their high rates of imprisonment arise in part because of selective reporting of offences by members of the public and selective law enforcement by the police and other agencies. Nevertheless, such an explanation can only be partial, since even for burglary there remains a 3:1 difference between black and white men in rate of imprisonment, although reporting and law enforcement in this case can be targeted against black people to only a limited extent.

Victims' Reports

So far the analysis has established that the final outcome of the criminal justice process is a very high rate of imprisonment of black people (but *not* of south Asians). The next step is to return to the beginning of the process, and to consider the limited evidence on how the disparity arises at each successive stage.

Some offences, such as obstructing a police officer in the execution of his duty, are generated by the decisions of officials; others, such as possession of drugs, only come to notice as a result of action by officials.

However, apart from drugs and traffic offences, the great bulk of offences processed by the police and the courts first come to notice as a result of victims' reports. The great majority of crime victims (well over 90 per cent) are, of course, white; and although black offenders tend to choose black or south Asian victims, it is likely that about 85 per cent of offences committed by black people are on white victims (calculated from Mayhew *et al.* 1989: 47, table 1.3). A possible theory, therefore, is that because of racial hostility or fear, white victims are more strongly motivated to report an incident to the police if they think the offender was black. A grave problem for such a theory, of course, is that racial hostility among the general public is directed just as much against south Asians as against black people. Nevertheless, it is important to consider whether there is specific evidence to support it.

Victim survey data show that in only about one-third of cases can the victim say something about the offender. (See e.g. Smith 1983*a*: 71. In this survey of Londoners carried out in 1981, 36 per cent of victims could say something about the offender.) The remaining two-thirds of cases are not relevant to the hypothesis that victims are more likely to report offences committed by black people, since the victim's reporting behaviour could not have been influenced by the ethnic group of the offender in these cases. This substantially reduces the scope for victim's reporting behaviour to have an influence.

Among offenders who *are* described by victims, there is a substantial overrepresentation of black people. The PSI survey of Londoners carried out in 1981 found that the offender was described as 'black' in 24 per cent of cases, and as 'Asian' in 3 per cent of cases. This implied that black people (taken to include black Africans as well as Afro-Caribbeans) were 'represented among offenders about four times as strongly was would be expected from their representation in the general population' (Smith, 1983*a*: 73). It also implied a substantial underrepresentation of Asians among offenders described by victims at that time. The findings of the British Crime Survey (BCS) are broadly in agreement. For example, the 1988 BCS showed that 8 per cent of offenders described by white victims were 'black', while 2 per cent were Asian (Mayhew *et al.* 1989: 47, table 1.3). At that time, all the 'black' groups accounted for around 1.6 per cent of the population of Britain, so offenders described by white people as 'black' were overrepresented by a factor of 5:1. Asians were, again, somewhat underrepresented among the offenders described by victims.

A combined analysis of the 1982, 1984, and 1988 BCS data shows little difference in the proportion of incidents reported to the police according to whether the offender was described as white or non-white (Shah and Pease 1992). This analysis was confined to offences of personal violence (including sexual assaults and robbery). In detail, the probability of an incident being reported to the police was related to its seriousness in combination with the described race of the offender, but none of these differences was large, and they tended to cancel out. For example, where the offence caused no injury, it was rather more likely to be reported to the police if the offender was non-white than white (36 per cent compared with 25 per cent). However, where the offence caused injury requiring medical attention, the opposite was the case (non-white offender 54 per cent, white offender 61 per cent). The matter becomes still more complicated when other characteristics of the incidents are considered, such as whether a weapon was used, and whether the offence was committed by a single person. In any case, the overall effect of the perceived race of the offender on reporting to the police was small.

It may be suggested that the victim survey findings are somehow influenced by differential recall: a tendency for respondents to recall or fail to recall incidents according to whether the offender was black. If the perceived race of the offender does influence recall, then this would be likely to have some effect on the distribution of the incidents recalled over time: for example, respondents might take longer to forget about incidents involving a black than a white offender. However, Shah and Pease have shown that the distribution over the recall period of the incidents described by BCS respondents does not vary according to the perceived race of the offender: for example, it is not the case that recalled incidents involving a black offender tend to be less recent (Shah and Pease 1992: 198–9, table 6).

Three points emerge from this analysis of evidence about the first stage of the criminal justice process. First, if victims are more likely to report incidents to the police where the offender is perceived to be black, this can have an influence in only about one-third of cases involving individual victims, for in the remaining two-thirds of cases the victim cannot describe the offender. Second, black people are heavily overrepresented among offenders described by victims before the criminal justice process begins: that is, among the descriptions in victim surveys which include incidents that were and were not reported to the police. In fact, in incidents described in the 1988 BCS, 9 per cent of offenders were perceived to be 'black', and in 1987 (the recall period of the survey), 9 per cent of the prison population of England and Wales were black. Third, there is little or no difference in the proportion of incidents reported to the police according to whether the offender is perceived to be black. These findings suggest that differential reporting to the police is not a significant factor leading to the criminalization of black people, and that much of the difference in rate of criminalization between black and white people arises at the earliest possible stage: when the offence is observed, and before it is reported.

Against this, there is one piece of indirect evidence on reporting rates (Stevens and Willis 1979; Shah and Pease 1992). From analysis of statistics on recorded crimes of violence in 1975 produced by the London police, Stevens and Willis showed that a much smaller proportion of black on white crimes than of other types caused injury. Where the attacker was described by the white victim as non-white, there was no injury in 50 per cent of cases, which was twice as high as for other encounters. One possible explanation of this pattern is that victims report to the police assaults by non-whites which would be too trivial to report when committed by whites. However, this conflicts with the BCS evidence summarized above, and as Shah and Pease (1992) point out, because these statistics relate to recorded crime, the observed pattern could be a reflection of police recording behaviour. The likely explanation is that 'some offences are recorded by the police as having been committed by non-whites or as involving assaultive behaviour when the event was not reported to them in these terms' (Shah and Pease 1992: 193).

Police Stops

Among those offenders who are processed by the criminal justice system, a considerable proportion are drawn into the net through the exercise of discretionary powers by the police, particularly stop-and-search. Thus, a survey of London police officers carried out in 1982 showed that 23 per cent of arrests arose from a stop (Smith 1983*b*: 81, table V.3). The proportion of arrests arising from a stop was particularly high for driving offences (64 per cent), taking and driving away a vehicle or vehicle theft (47 per cent), and drugs offences (39 per cent) (Smith 1983*b*: 87, table V.6). At that time, most of the stop-and-search powers were not consolidated within national legislation, although a variety of local powers existed. Consequently, police practice on stops may have varied widely between different parts of the country, and the use of stop-and-search was probably greater in London than in most other places. Since the Police and Criminal Evidence Act 1984 (PACE) came into force, police throughout England and Wales have had authority to stop persons or vehicles on the reasonable suspicion that they would find stolen goods or prohibited articles, and to carry out searches of vehicles and persons stopped. Other legislation also gives police authority to stop and search for other reasons, for example to look for controlled drugs. Although up-to-date statistics are not available, it seems likely that a substantial proportion of arrests now result from stops throughout the country. Clearly the overrepresentation of black people at later stages in the process could in principle arise partly because the police use their discretion to stop a larger proportion of black people than of other ethnic groups.

Pattern

A survey carried out in three parts of Manchester in 1980 found no significant difference between Afro-Caribbeans and whites in terms of the proportion who had been 'stopped, searched or arrested' within the last year, or in the number of times this had happened (Tuck and Southgate 1981). These data do not distinguish between stops and arrests, and because of the rather small sample sizes, the 1.43:1 ratio between the 10 per cent of Afro-Caribbeans and the 7 per cent of white people who were 'stopped, searched, or arrested' does not reach statistical significance. This survey covered a single police division which extended over parts of five wards and had a population of 33,000. Other studies, which have all covered larger and more heterogeneous areas than this, have found differences in stop rates between black and white people. Willis (1983) analysed stops recorded at four police stations (she estimated that about half of the stops actually carried out were recorded). The recorded stop rates were two to three times as high for black people as for the general population. There were also huge differences in overall stop rates between the four police stations, although the contrast in stop rates between black and white people remained much the same. The PSI survey of Londoners carried out in 1981 found that the proportion stopped in the previous twelve months was 24 per cent for Afro-Caribbeans, 17 per cent for whites, and 7 per cent for south Asians. Also, among those who had been stopped at all, Afro-Caribbeans had on average been stopped twice as often as white people. The stop rate among young males aged 15–24 was found to be very high. Within this group, 66 per cent of the Afro-Caribbeans had been stopped an average number of 4.1 times in twelve months, while 44 per cent of the whites had been stopped an average number of 2.6 times (Smith 1983*a*: 96–100). National data are available from the 1988 BCS, which was carried out well after national stop powers were consolidated in PACE. Within the fourteen-month reference period, 15 per cent of white people, 20 per cent of Afro-Caribbeans, and 14 per cent of south Asians said they had been stopped by the police. The difference in stop rate between Afro-Caribbeans and white people or south Asians remains significant within a multivariate model including the following variables: age, income, sex, vehicle access, occupation, tenure, urban versus rural area (five types), length of education, marital status, and whether unemployed (Skogan 1990: 28).

In general, the PSI survey of Londoners carried out in 1981 and the 1988 BCS show a highly consistent pattern of relationships between a range of characteristics and the likelihood of being stopped by the police. The most important factors are age and sex. Among males aged 16–24, the BCS found that 48 per cent had been stopped (this compares with 44 per cent of young white males in the PSI survey); and this rose to 56 per cent among young Afro-Caribbean males (compared with 66 per cent in the PSI survey). Both surveys found that the unemployed are considerably more likely to be stopped than others.

Jefferson (1988) and Walker (1987) have suggested that the study of parts of Manchester (Tuck and Southgate 1981) failed to find a difference in stop rates between Afro-Caribbean and white people because it was carried out in a relatively small and homogeneous area. They believe that what is being observed in the BCS and the PSI London survey is differences in policing practice between types of area: for example, higher stop rates in disadvantaged urban settings where concentrations of Afro-Caribbeans tend to be high. Jefferson (1993) suggests in particular that the style of policing is more a response to the social and housing composition of the area than to the ethnic group of potential suspects. Whatever the merits of this argument in general terms, it is not needed to explain the Tuck and Southgate findings. These do not relate to stops alone, and as Skogan points out (1990: 53) they do not necessarily indicate a different ratio between the rate of police–initiated encounters among Afro-Caribbean and white people from that shown by the BCS: the sample size in the Tuck and Southgate study was simply too small to demonstrate a contrast of the order shown by the BCS.

In a later article, Jefferson *et al.* (1992) used police records of stop-and-searches to compare parts of Leeds where ethnic minorities accounted for more versus less than 10 per cent of the population. (PACE requires the police to make a record where a member of the public is stopped *and* searched, and these are the records used by Jefferson *et al.* The earlier survey findings referred to stops as a whole, a far more inclusive category.) They find that in areas of *low* ethnic concentration, the stop rate is *higher* for black than for white or south Asian people, whereas in areas of *high* ethnic concentration, the stop rate is *lower* for black than for white or south Asian people. However, the 1981 PSI survey of Londoners showed no difference in stop rates (all stops, regardless of whether there was a search) among either Afro-Caribbeans or south Asians according to the concentration of ethnic minorities in the local area, defined as a census enumeration district (ED), which contains on average 150 households. Also, the survey showed no difference in stop rates among white people according to the concentration of ethnic minorities in the ward where they lived (unpublished data available from the author on request).

As part of the same study, a survey was carried out within EDs in Leeds in which 10 per cent or more of households were estimated to be non-white. Roughly equal numbers of black, south Asian, and white people were interviewed in each ED. As EDs are very small areas, this design produces a sample of black and south Asian people, together with a sample of white people who live nearby. The sample of white people is therefore (deliberately) highly unrepresentative of white people generally. The survey findings show that the stop rate (in 1987) was *lower* among black and south Asian people than among white people living nearby. Jefferson and Walker (1992, 1993) interpret these findings as showing that stop decisions are influenced by the social characteristics of very small areas, and that the stop rate among Afro-Caribbeans tends to be higher than among white people in other studies only because of the characteristics of the small areas where Afro-Caribbeans live. The problem with this interpretation, however, is that the individual characteristics of those rather few white people who live in areas of high ethnic concentration tend to be unusual, and the pattern of results may reflect their unusual individual characteristics rather than the social composition of the area. Thus, for example, Jefferson and Walker's results show that a much higher proportion of their white than of their ethnic minority sample are in privately rented households and have been living in the area for less than three years. What their results may chiefly show is that a comparison between black and white people living in the same enumeration districts is not very helpful.

On balance, there is a consistent body of evidence to show that Afro-Caribbeans are more likely to be stopped than white people or south Asians. These differences are not very marked, and are much smaller than the differences in rates of imprisonment. They probably do make some contribution to explaining the high rate of imprisonment of Afro-Caribbeans, but they can explain only a small part of it. That is not only because the ethnic differences in stop rates are relatively small, but also because this kind of policing generates less than one-quarter of arrests.

Decision

Given that black people (but *not* south Asians) are more likely to be stopped by police than white people, the question that arises is how police officers take these decisions, and whether they amount to unequal treatment of black people. As Skogan (1990: 32) points out, the most important factor here is that the vast majority of stops do not produce an arrest or prosecution (although, because such a vast number of stops are carried out, a considerable proportion of arrests arise from stops, as set out earlier). The implication of the low 'strike rate' is that the exercise of this kind of police power is highly discretionary. The law requires in principle that the police officer should have 'reasonable suspicion' to justify stopping or searching someone, but in practice this criterion is extremely weak, and largely unenforceable. The 1988 BCS shows that of those stopped on foot, only 4 per cent were arrested, and 3 per cent were prosecuted. The comparable figures for those involved in traffic stops were 1 per cent arrested and 10 per cent prosecuted—the prosecutions being mainly fixed penalty and vehicle defect notices (Skogan 1990: 32). The low 'strike rate' is confirmed by local surveys in Merseyside (Kinsey 1985) and London (Smith 1983*a*), and by earlier national estimates from police records (Willis 1983).

Because the criteria that determine whether a stop is justified are weak, vague, and unenforceable, the question whether the relatively high stop rate for black people amounts to unequal treatment is very hard to answer. The PSI survey of Londoners found that the proportion of stops leading to an arrest or to an offence being reported was the same for Afro-Caribbeans and white people (Smith 1983*a*: 116). Assuming that arrests and reported offences are backed up by evidence, this shows that the higher stop rate for Afro-Caribbeans is 'justified by results', and does not, therefore, amount to unequal treatment. Of course, that assumption may be contested, but to the extent that it is false, the problem is fabrication of evidence against Afro-Caribbeans rather than an unjustifiably high stop rate.

No observational studies have been carried out on a sufficient scale in Britain to provide the basis for a quantitative analysis of police decisions to stop. In the course of extensive observational research on policing in London, Smith and Gray (1983) observed a total of 129 stops. In 18 per cent of cases the person was seen to commit a traffic offence and in half of the cases the researchers judged there was some other specific reason for 'reasonable suspicion', while they judged that there was no reason at all to make the stop in one-third of cases. On a number of occasions, stops made for no reason did produce a 'result'. Smith and Gray concluded that 'it is clear from the way that police officers talk about stops that the question of what their legal powers may be does not enter into their decision-making except in the case of rare individuals' (1981: 233). Specific reasons for making a stop, apart from traffic offences, were that a person was running, hurrying, or loitering, was rowdy or drunk, or was driving in an erratic manner. Where there was no specific reason, the criteria that police officers used were ones they associated with the chance of getting a 'result'. They tended to choose young males, especially young black males; people who look scruffy or poor; people who have long hair or unconventional dress; and homosexuals. They also tended to choose cars with several young males in them, old cars, and certain specific car models (believed to be often stolen). The researchers gained the impression that whether the person was Afro-Caribbean was a criterion, but that other criteria were more important.

The 1981 survey of Londoners found that people who had been stopped thought the police had good reasons for stopping them in 59 per cent of cases (Smith 1983*a*: 112). A lower proportion of Afro-Caribbeans (38 per cent) than of white people (59 per cent) or south Asians (62 per cent) thought there was a good reason for the stop.

The 1988 BCS found that once stopped, Afro-Caribbeans were substantially more likely to be searched than white people or south Asians (Skogan 1990: 34). In the case of traffic stops, this difference remained significant after controlling for the effects of a number of factors, including past arrests, within a multivariate model.

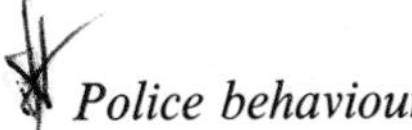

Police behaviour

The 1988 BCS found that about one-quarter of those stopped by the police while on foot, and about one in five of those involved in a traffic stop, thought the behaviour of the police had been impolite. Afro-Caribbeans were much more likely than white people or south Asians to think the police had been impolite, and this difference remained after controlling for a range of other factors (Skogan 1990: 36). In particular, people were more critical of police behaviour if the stop led to some sanction (such as arrest or a reported offence); but this did not explain the difference between Afro-Caribbeans and white people. Respondents were more likely to think the police had been polite where a reason was given for the stop, a finding which replicates the 1981 London survey (Smith 1983*a*). Again, this did not explain the difference between Afro-Caribbean and white people.

The 1981 London survey found little or no difference between ethnic groups in the proportion who said the police explained the reason for the stop (Smith 1983*a*: 107–9). A smaller proportion of Afro-Caribbeans than of white people or south Asians thought the police were polite, and that they behaved in a fair and reasonable manner, but these differences were not striking (ibid.: 12). From their observational work as part of the same study, Smith and Gray (1983) concluded that where people were stopped, the encounter was fairly relaxed and friendly in the great majority of cases. While the survey showed that for 19 per cent of stops people thought the police had not behaved in a fair and reasonable manner, the researchers judged from their observations that the police behaved aggressively in a smaller proportion of cases than that, but a failure to give an explanation might underlie people's responses in some cases.

Smith (1983*a*) conducted an intensive analysis of the relationship between critical views of the police (the belief that they fabricate evidence, use unnecessary violence, etc.) and patterns of contact with them. This showed a strong correlation between the amount of contact (of any kind) and critical views, although a later analysis (unpublished) showed that service contacts, primarily as a victim of crime, were only associated with negative views if those specific contacts were negatively evaluated. Within this general framework, stops tended to dominate the picture as (mildly) adversarial contacts that are very large in quantity and associated with critical views of the police. In a survey of parts of Leeds, Jefferson and Walker (1993) also found a relationship between the number of times stopped and critical views. From these findings it is likely that the large-scale practice of stop-and-search, and the disproportionate stopping of Afro-Caribbeans, have been among the causes of hostility between Afro-Caribbeans and the police. However, both the Leeds and London studies show that the relatively high level of criticism of the police among Afro-Caribbeans compared with white people cannot be wholly explained by their personal encounters with the police (see Smith 1991 for further discussion of this point on the basis of the London findings).

Arrests

No national statistics are available on the ethnic group of persons arrested, but data are available for London (the Metropolitan Police District) starting in 1975. These cover arrests for notifiable offences (that excludes minor including most traffic offences) that were followed by further action (caution, referral to juvenile bureau, or charge). In 1975, these statistics showed that 12 per cent of persons arrested were black, compared with 4 per cent of the London population, and 3 per cent were south Asian, which was the same as the proportion of south Asians in the London population. By 1987, the proportion of those arrested who were black had risen to 18 per cent, compared with just over 5 per cent (aged 10 or over) in the London population, while the proportion who were south Asian had risen to 5 per cent, which was again the same as the proportion of south Asians in the London population (Home Office 1989*a*). The proportion of those arrested who are black varies little according to the offence, except that it is extraordinarily high for robbery and other violent theft (54 per cent in 1987) and for non-violent thefts from the person (51 per cent).

For certain offences between 1975 and 1985, the Metropolitan Police also recorded the ethnic origin of the offender from the victim's description. For these offences, there is a fairly close correspondence between the proportion of offenders described as non-white by victims and the proportion of people arrested who were non-white (see Table 22.4). It is notable that both for persons arrested and for offenders as described by victims, the proportion who are non-white is much lower in the case of assaults than in the case of robberies and snatches. The statistics cover only a few specific offences, and they may well be influenced by police recording practices. None the less, they suggest that there was little or no tendency for the arrest rate *per offender* to be higher for black than for white suspects.

Table 22.4 Ethnic group of offender from victims' descriptions compared with ethnic group of persons arrested, % (London, 1985)

	Offender	Persons arrested	
	Non-white	Black	Asian
Assaults	17	22	5
Street robbery of personal property	65	60	3
Other robbery	45	37	2
Theft from the person, snatches only	54	64	4

Source: Home Office *Statistical Bulletin*, 5/89.

Disregarding the victim's descriptions of offenders, the London statistics show such a large difference in arrest rates *per head of population* between black and white people that an explanation substantially in terms of biased policing is implausible. Walker (1987) hints at this conclusion, but adds that 'this must be a subjective judgement'. That considerably understates the strength of the evidence. Using the 1983 statistics, Walker calculates that if the actual rate of burglary by black and white offenders were the same, then the arrest statistics would imply that black burglars had four and a half times the chance of being arrested compared with white burglars. That is a wholly implausible hypothesis, because police action against burglars is so ineffective. The police are incapable of increasing the arrest rate for burglary by more than a small amount. Even if they could substantially increase the burglary arrest rate, they would not be able to target such an increase on black people with any degree of accuracy. The relatively high rate of stops of black people (see the previous section) would produce a few extra arrests of burglars, but the effect would be trivial in the context of a 4.5:1 ratio in arrest rates. The only other conceivable strategy would be to arrest black people more or less at random and charge them falsely. Unless the courts are completely corrupt, this would result in a radical difference in acquittal rates between black and white defendants in burglary cases, but there is no such difference. In the case of robbery, Walker calculates that if actual rates of offending were the same for black and white people, the statistics imply that the rate of arrest was fourteen times higher for black than for white robbers in 1983. There is more that the police could do in the case of robbery to target an increase in detections of black people, but the scope for this is nevertheless limited, and the hypothesis of a fourteen-fold increase is obviously absurd.

On any reasonable assessment, therefore, the London statistics reflect a much higher rate of offending among black than white people. Unfortunately, they do not resolve the issue as to whether there is bias in policing practice. The comparison between victims' reports and arrest statistics (Table 22.4) tends to suggest that the overall effect of any such bias is fairly small, but this evidence is fragmentary.

A study by Stevens and Willis (1979) used multivariate techniques to compare the black, Asian, and white arrest rates in seventeen districts within the Metropolitan Police District as a whole. Although the objective of the analysis is not entirely clear, it may have been to establish whether areas containing high proportions of black people tend to have high crime rates (as measured by arrests) after allowing for the influence of other socio-demographic characteristics of the areas. However, the actual analyses reported do not provide a convincing answer to this question.

Walker (1992) analysed the arrest rates of males aged 11–35 in six police sub-divisions within Leeds during a six-month period in 1987, when police recorded whether people arrested were white, black, or Asian. Like other elements within this research programme, this analysis compares white and black people living in the same very small areas (census enumeration districts, containing 150 households on average). As already argued in the section on stops, the purpose of making such comparisons is unclear. In the high ethnic concentration EDs (those with more than 10 per cent 'non-white households'), the arrest rate for black people was lower than for white people, while in the lower-concentration EDs the arrest rate was higher for black than for white people. This mirrors the pattern shown for stops (see earlier section). As before, the likely explanation is that white people in areas of high ethnic concentration are an unusual and high-crime group. In the city as a whole, the arrest rate was more than twice as high for black as for white people.

In the PSI London survey, respondents were asked whether they had ever been arrested, and whether they had been arrested in the past five years. Because respondents have strong motives for concealment, and for other reasons, these questions were not expected to produce good estimates of arrest rates, but where respondents said they had been arrested in the past five years, they were asked detailed questions about each of the last three occasions.[1] The sample size is rather small (137 people gave

[1] It is stated in the report that 'there are strong motives for concealment' and that 'it is fair to assume that there are people in the survey who have been arrested but deny it' (Smith 1983*a*: 118). Walker (1987) argues that the survey data show much lower arrest rates than the official statistics. In fact, estimated arrest rates cannot be derived from the data

accounts of a total of 169 arrests), but large enough to form a reasonable basis for generalization.

> A statistical analysis of the pre-coded questions shows that in 47 per cent of cases people thought the police were behaving unreasonably in arresting them; in 59 per cent of cases, people had criticisms to make of the way the police behaved towards them; in 26 per cent of cases they thought a police officer said something rude or insulting to them; in 22 per cent of cases they said that police officers used force or hit them, in 18 per cent of cases unjustifiably in the person's opinion; in 20 per cent of cases people thought the police threatened them or put unfair pressure on them in some other way; and in 47 per cent of cases people thought they were treated unfairly overall in connection with the arrest. (Smith 1983*a*: 312)

Thus, a substantial proportion of people who said they had been arrested had serious criticisms to make of the way they were treated. From the accounts that respondents also gave in their own words, a substantial proportion made very specific allegations against the police, ones involving gross misconduct in many cases. However, Afro-Caribbeans were no more likely than white people to think they had been badly treated or to make serious allegations of this kind: in fact, if anything, the answers given by Afro-Caribbeans were more favourable to the police. The number of south Asians who said they had been arrested was too small for any conclusion to be drawn in their case.

Decision to Prosecute

A majority of arrests overall lead to the arrested person answering in court to a criminal charge or charges, but a substantial minority of

shown in the report (Smith 1983*a*: 118 ff.) so it is unclear where Walker's 'PSI-based' arrest rates come from. Estimates were not attempted because it was assumed that a small proportion of people are arrested a large number of times, and that these people will (a) tend not to be included in surveys, (b) tend not to tell the truth, and (c) find it hard to remember about all their arrests over a five-year period. A further, serious, problem is that at any given time a substantial proportion of this often-arrested group will be in prison, and therefore ineligible for inclusion in a survey of people in private households. In spite of these problems, it was judged that the survey could provide reasonably accurate estimates of the proportion of stops leading to an arrest, because these questions used a twelve-month recall period (instead of the five years for arrests generally) and because the population of people stopped is large and unlikely to have highly unusual characteristics. Because not all respondents admitted to arrests that had actually occurred, there is clearly the possibility of bias when comparing experience of arrest between ethnic groups. All that can be said about this is that the comparisons will have some validity unless the tendency to deny experience of arrest is stronger among members of one ethnic group than another. Also, the problem will not be serious unless a substantial proportion of those who have been arrested deny all experience of arrest, rather than simply failing to report some of the arrests that have occurred.

arrested persons do not end up in court.[2] In the case of juveniles (aged up to 17) official policy since the 1970s has increasingly encouraged alternatives to prosecution, chiefly formal cautions. Currently, only about one-third of arrests of juveniles lead to a prosecution. Under the Home Office *Guidelines on Cautioning* it is an absolute requirement that the accused person should admit the offence if a caution is to be granted. The guidelines also say that both the offence and the offender's past record should be taken into account. Within these rather wide constraints, different police forces have adopted different criteria for deciding whether to caution or charge juveniles; and there is wide scope for the exercise of discretion by individual officers in applying force-wide criteria, since the decision to charge rather than caution cannot be challenged by the accused or by any independent person or authority.

In a proportion of cases (probably around 5 per cent) the police decide to take no further action following an arrest: that is, they release the person without issuing a charge or caution.

Not everyone charged with an offence ultimately stands trial. The most important factor here is that following the establishment through the Prosecution of Offences Act 1985 of a Crown Prosecution Service independent of the police, the prosecuting authority may decide that the evidence is insufficient to justify a prosecution.

Unfortunately, evidence on the flow of cases from arrest to prosecution is fragmentary. It is here that longitudinal studies are particularly needed, but they have not yet been carried out. In principle it is entirely possible that following an arrest ethnic minorities are more likely than white people to be prosecuted. This is a large potential source of inequality in the case of juveniles, since most juvenile offences do not result in a charge. Because a relatively high proportion of arrested adults are prosecuted, the scope for bias in their case is not as great, but it must still be substantial.[3]

The very limited data available about the treatment of ethnic minorities at this important stage of the process relate mainly to juveniles. The Commission for Racial Equality (1992) summarized the early results of ethnic monitoring in seven police forces of the processing of juvenile suspects, although so far useful data were available for only five of these forces. In four of the five areas, a considerably higher proportion of Afro-Caribbean than of white juvenile suspects were prosecuted. In Bristol during a twelve-month period starting in September 1989, '51–57

[2] A large number of prosecutions—nearly all for minor, especially traffic, offences—originate from the police reporting an offence, followed by a summons, without the suspect ever being arrested. However, in the vast majority of cases involving more serious (notifiable) offences, the criminal process is started by an arrest, so the analysis here concentrates on the path from arrest to prosecution.

[3] I have not been able to find good data on the proportion of arrested adults who are prosecuted, but this is likely to be well over half.

per cent of ethnic minority young people were prosecuted compared with 34 per cent of White Europeans' (CRE 1992: 9). In Kensington and Chelsea and in Hounslow (London) in the first six months of 1990, '64 per cent of Afro-Caribbeans, 50 per cent of Others, and 36 per cent of White young people were prosecuted' (ibid.: 10–11). In the West Midlands in 1991, '48 per cent of Afro-Caribbeans, 75 per cent of Asians, 48 per cent of Others, and 55 per cent of Whites [all juveniles] were diverted from the courts' (ibid.: 13). In Leeds and Huddersfield, during the nine months starting with October 1989, '27 per cent of Asians, 58 per cent of Blacks, 55 per cent of Others, and 41 per cent of Whites were prosecuted' (ibid.: 15). Only in Northamptonshire was there no difference between ethnic groups in the proportion of juvenile suspects prosecuted.

The data from these monitoring exercises were not consolidated or subjected to intensive analysis. However, from certain limited analyses reported, it seems likely that the difference in treatment between ethnic groups may be explained by the proportion denying the offence (there is evidence that this is higher for Afro-Caribbeans than for whites), the proportion having previous convictions (higher among Afro-Caribbeans than whites in some areas), and the proportion already on bail or warrant or still subject to conditional discharge (apparently higher among Afro-Caribbeans than whites in the West Midlands).

A few more detailed studies have been reported of the police processing of juvenile suspects, but even the most recent of these (Landau and Nathan 1983) uses data that are now fifteen years old. The processing of juvenile offenders has changed substantially over those fifteen years, so there is no knowledge, based on systematic research, of the operation of current policies and practices. Landau (1981) and Landau and Nathan (1983) examined police decisions on juvenile suspects made during the last quarter of 1978 in five police divisions in London. At that time there was a two-stage procedure. At Stage A, the police either charged immediately (19.6 per cent of cases) or referred the case to the juvenile bureau (80.4 per cent). At Stage B, the bureau either decided to charge after all (37.9 per cent), to caution (36.3 per cent), or to take 'no further action' (6.2 per cent). The first paper considered Stage A, while the second considered Stage B. The analyses compared black (Afro-Caribbean and black African) juveniles with whites; south Asians, and other ethnic groups, were excluded. At the first stage, a substantially higher proportion of black than of white juveniles was immediately charged, and this applied to every type of offence except auto crime. In the context of a multivariate model including age, sex, offence, area (two boroughs included in each of three areas), and previous offences, there remained a substantial difference in the probability of immediate charge between black and white juveniles. As Walker (1987) points out, the analysis did not take account of social class. At the second stage, the minority (6.2 per cent) for whom no further action was taken were unaccountably excluded. Among the remainder, 53.7 per cent of the whites, compared with 39.7 per cent of the blacks, were cautioned. A substantial difference remained between black and white juveniles in the probability of being cautioned in the context of a logistic regression model including the following independent variables: previous criminal record: offence; ethnic group; whether a 'latch-key child' (that is, according to the official record, left on their own without parental control on a regular basis); age; area (three groups of two boroughs). Sex and tenure of accommodation (a proxy for social class) were also investigated, but were only weakly related to whether the juvenile was cautioned or charged, and were not included in the final model. The probability of a caution was higher for white than for black juveniles for all six types of offence except 'traffic and other'. Although white were more likely than black juveniles to be charged immediately with car crimes at Stage A, this was compensated for by Stage B, where they were much more likely to be cautioned.

In the second of the two articles, Landau and Nathan (1983) included an interesting discussion of the principles underlying juvenile justice, and considered the implications of their findings in the light of those principles. If police decisions on the processing of juvenile suspects are to be made on the basis of formal rationality, as interpreted by Weber (1954), then only 'legal variables' should be taken into account (previous criminal record, the nature and seriousness of the offence, whether the offence is admitted). However, it can be argued that the principle guiding the juvenile justice system is substantive justice (on the model of Weber's substantive rationality) rather than formal justice. In that case, it is important to distinguish between variables that reflect legitimate criteria of substantive justice, such as the character and social circumstances of the suspect, and other non-legal variables that cannot be legitimate criteria, such as sex, ethnic group, and social class.

Against that background, the variables included in Landau and Nathan's analysis can be sorted into three groups: criteria of formal justice (the offence, previous criminal record); criteria of substantive justice (age, whether a latch-key child); and illegitimate criteria (sex, ethnic group, tenure, area). The analysis shows that variables of all three types have an important influence on the outcome, but previous criminal record (a criterion of formal justice) has the strongest effect.

Landau and Nathan described the illegitimate criteria as discriminatory, by which they meant directly discriminatory. They recognized that the use of substantive criteria could work to the disadvantage of black juveniles: for example, a higher proportion of the black juveniles were charged partly because a higher proportion were classified as 'latch-key children'. Following the Race Relations Act 1976 (enacted seven years before the article was published) the use of such a criterion might be described as indirect discrimination, if it is thought that the criterion cannot be justified. Landau and Nathan concluded that the system should revert to emphasizing criteria of formal justice, so that 'a more balanced representation of blacks among juveniles sent to court may be achieved' (1983: 147).

Landau and Nathan made an interesting contribution, but the discussion needs to be taken further. From their results it looks as though direct discrimination is considerably more important than indirect discrimination as a cause of the difference in cautioning rate between black and white juveniles. For example, their model suggests that among latchkey children aged 10–14 in area 2 who were accused of crimes of violence, the probability of being cautioned was 0.663 for white children compared with 0.271 for black children (Landau and Nathan 1983: table 4). It follows that a reversion to formal criteria (for example, abandoning the criterion of parental control) would not make much difference. In any case, what is most distinctive about police decisions on juveniles is that they lie outside the system of formal justice, since they cannot be challenged or reviewed by a court. In those circumstances, the distinction between formal and substantive criteria may not have much importance, since even the application of the formal criteria cannot be formally challenged. The problem for policy is to find a way of changing the way the police use their wide discretion in this matter; Landau and Nathan's analysis does not demonstrate that the best way to do this is to revert to legalistic principles of decision-making.

A study of juveniles from one London police division referred to the juvenile bureau in 1973 showed no significant difference in the proportion cautioned between whites and non-whites (Farrington and Bennett 1981). This result is not enlightening, since the non-white group included south Asians (who probably had a high rate of cautioning) and Afro-Caribbeans (who probably had a low rate). A study of juveniles in Bradford (Mawby *et al.* 1979) showed a higher rate of cautioning for Pakistanis than for Indians or non-Asians, but this result is hard to interpret, as there was no analysis by offence type.

In broad terms, there is clear evidence that a higher proportion of Afro-Caribbean than of white juvenile suspects is prosecuted. This seems to occur mainly because of direct discrimination, but also because of the application of intelligible criteria which may or may not be justifiable but which work to the disadvantage of Afro-Caribbeans. In the case of adults, there is less scope for discrimination at this stage, because a much higher proportion of adult suspects are prosecuted. For adults, there is no detailed evidence about the extent of discrimination at this stage.

While the available statistics are not detailed, there is clear evidence that in London the overall proportion of persons arrested who are subsequently prosecuted is only slightly higher for ethnic minorities than for white people. This can be shown by comparing persons arrested in London in 1985 with persons proceeded against for indictable offences at magistrates' courts in 1984 and 1985. Eighteen per cent of persons arrested were black, compared with 19 per cent of persons prosecuted; 3 per cent of persons arrested were south Asian, compared with 4 per cent of persons prosecuted; and 4 per cent of persons arrested belonged to some other ethnic minority group, compared with 5 per cent of persons prosecuted (Home Office 1989*b*: table 1). The discussion above has concentrated on cautioning rates for juveniles, but juveniles account for only about 10 per cent of the cases that come to court. The general picture is dominated by adults, and the overall London statistics indicate that bias in decisions about prosecution has little significance as an explanation of the overrepresentation of Afro-Caribbeans in the prison population. However, the results for juveniles may have wider significance, if interactions with the police and courts in youth are an important influence on the development of an adult criminal career.

The Courts

The process prior to sentencing

All persons prosecuted should initially appear in the magistrates' courts. Summary offences (the least serious) can only be dealt with in the magistrates' courts. Indictable-only offences (the most serious) have to be tried in the Crown Court, and the task of the magistrates is to decide whether the case should be committed for trial there, or dropped. Triable-either-way offences can be dealt with either in the magistrates courts or in the Crown Court. At the hearing in the magistrates' court, the defendant may elect for trial in the Crown Court. Also, the magistrates may commit the case for trial in the Crown Court if they feel that their own court is not able to deal with it adequately.

Which court the defendant is tried in his important implications for the outcome of the case. A high proportion of defendants in the magistrates' courts plead guilty, and a high proportion are found guilty, whereas a higher proportion in the Crown Court plead not guilty, and a higher proportion are acquitted. However, the penalties imposed by the Crown Court tend to be more severe. Hence, any tendency for ethnic minorities to be tried in the Crown Court rather than in magistrates' courts could lead to a relatively high rate of imprisonment for those groups.

A small proportion of cases never get started in the magistrates' courts, either because the defendant fails to appear, or because the case is withdrawn for lack of evidence. Walker (1988), using data for London in 1983, found that a slightly higher proportion of cases against young black than against young white men (aged 14–16) were withdrawn for lack of evidence (9 per cent compared with 6 per cent). She found no difference of this kind for men aged 17–25 (Walker 1989).

It is fairly well established that a higher proportion of cases against black people (Afro-Caribbeans and black Africans) than against whites are dealt with by the Crown Court. Statistics have been published for London in 1984 and 1985 covering prosecutions for indictable offences: that includes indictable-only offences (which must be tried in the Crown Court) and triable-either-way offences, but excludes summary offences. Among males, the proportions committed for trial at the Crown Court were 27 per cent for whites, 36 per cent for blacks, 35 per cent for south Asians, and 27 per cent for other ethnic groups (Home Office 1989*b*: table 2). Also, a higher proportion of black females than of white females were committed for trial at the Crown Court, although the proportion of south Asian females and of females belonging to other ethnic groups committed for trial was lower than for whites (ibid.: table 3). This general pattern is confirmed by an analysis of prosecutions of boys aged 14–16, and another of men aged 17–25, in London in 1983 (Walker 1988, 1989); and by a survey of defendants in Leeds magistrates' courts in 1988 (Brown and Hullin 1992).

The tendency for black defendants to be tried at the Crown Court may arise partly because of the distribution of offences: for example, a relatively high proportion of black defendants are charged with robbery, and a high proportion of robbery cases (over 80 per cent) are tried at the Crown Court. However, this is not the main explanation, since the difference remains within broad offence types, with the exception of robbery, where it is reversed. The proportion of black defendants committed for trial at the Crown Court is particularly high in the case of sexual offences (57 per cent of black compared with 32 per cent of white males in London, 1984 and 1985: Home Office 1989*b*: table 3). That may be because a relatively high proportion of the alleged sexual offences in the case of black defendants are rapes.

The anomalous finding for robbery is significant, since it has been argued (Blom-Cooper and Drabble 1982) that black people tend to be charged with robbery in circumstances where a white person would be charged with theft. That would mean that robbery offences tend to be less serious in the case of black than white defendants, which would explain why a smaller proportion of these cases against black people go to the Crown Court.

It is well established that among cases going to the Crown Court, the proportion that *must* be tried there (because the offence is indictable only) is higher for black male than for white male defendants (Hood 1992: 51, table 5; Walker 1989: 359, table 8). Hood's study of cases heard in the Crown Court at five locations in the West Midlands in 1989 also shows that the proportion involving triable-either-way offences where the defendant *elected* for trial at the Crown Court is not significantly higher for black males (8 per cent) than for whites (11 per cent). Citing some other as yet unpublished findings, Hood suggests that there may be considerable regional variation in committal of triable-either-way offences (1992: 52 n.). However, a study of cases heard by magistrates' courts in Leeds in 1989 confirms the West Midlands pattern; it shows that a higher proportion of Afro-Caribbean than of white defendants were committed for trial at the Crown Court, but this reflected the pattern of committals by magistrates, and not the choices of defendants. The same study also showed that in deciding to commit to trial at the Crown Court, magistrates were in the vast majority of cases following the recommendation of the Crown Prosecution Service (Brown and Hullin 1992: 51).

Hood found that a considerably higher proportion of the black (23 per cent) than of the white male defendants (11 per cent) pleaded not guilty at trial. This confirms earlier indications from Walker's (1989) data for London.

Persons to be prosecuted can be summoned to the magistrates' court and tried immediately, and this is what happens with many summary offences. However, for more serious offences (triable-either-way or indictable-only) the usual sequence is arrest, remand by the police either on bail or in custody, hearing at the magistrates' court, remand by magistrates either on bail or in custody pending a full hearing in the magistrates' court, or committal for trial at the Crown Court either on bail or in custody. If there is more than one hearing at the Crown Court, that court may also remand on bail or in custody. Whether ethnic minority defendants are more likely than white defendants to be remanded in custody at any stage is important for two reasons. First, imprisonment before trial is serious in itself, and a higher likelihood of imprisonment before trial, if not shown to be justifiable, would be unequal treatment of a particularly serious kind. Second, defendants in prison find it more difficult to prepare a defence than those at liberty, and there is evidence (Hood 1992) that they receive stiffer sentences.

The London statistics for 1984 and 1985 (Home Office 1989*b*: table 3) show that a higher proportion of black (9 per cent) and south Asian (8 per cent) than of white men (5 per cent) accused of indictable offences were committed in custody by magistrates for trial at the Crown Court. The difference remains for each group of offences considered separately, except for robbery.

Walker (1989) has conducted a detailed analysis of remands at every stage for her database of London cases in 1983 involving males aged 17–25. In the case of both police remands and remands by magistrates at some stage, a higher proportion of black than of white defendants were remanded in custody. For example, of those remanded by magistrates before trial for indictable-only offences, 53 per cent of the black men aged 17–20 were remanded in custody at some point, compared with 41 per cent of the whites; in the case of those aged 21–25 the comparable figures were 61 per cent for black men and 48 per cent for white men (Walker 1989: 363, table 14). In the case of police remands, these differences were smaller. There were indications, however, from Walker's results, that these different rates of remand in custody could be justified by the later decisions in the cases. The police were much more likely to remand in custody than magistrates, so it could be argued that many of the police remands in custody were unjustified. However, allowing for that difference of policy, there was a high degree of consistency between police and magistrates: for example, very few defendants bailed by police were later remanded in custody or given a custodial sentence by magistrates. The police decisions about black and white defendants could be justified in the sense that they tended to predict later decisions by magistrates. Similarly, magistrates' decisions about remands tended to predict the final outcome of cases in the magistrates' courts.

> The conclusion is that more blacks than whites were kept in custody by the police and by the magistrate before conviction or sentence, but there was no difference between blacks and whites with regard to whether this was justified in terms of the later outcome. The final custodial decision (sentence or remand for Crown Court trial or sentence) had the same relationship to earlier custody for the two race groups. However, the combination of remand and final decision leads to a higher proportion of blacks in custody. (Walker 1989: 364)

Walker's data showed no difference between black and white men aged 17–20 in the proportion remanded in custody by the Crown Court, although there was a difference (12 per cent compared with 8 per cent) for those aged 21–25.

The London statistics show little or no difference for all age groups combined in the rate of acquittal between ethnic groups either at the magistrates' courts or at the Crown Court (Home Office 1989*b*: tables 5, 6). There were, however, some differences in acquittal rates for certain indictable offences. The most striking of these was that among males tried at the Crown Court for criminal damage 44 per cent of blacks, 38 per cent of south Asians, but only 27 per cent of whites were acquitted. Similarly, Walker's findings for males aged 17–25 prosecuted in London in 1983 show little or no difference overall in acquittal rates between ethnic groups (Walker 1989). However, her findings for boys aged 14–16 show a higher rate of acquittal for blacks than for whites, both at the magistrates' courts and at the Crown Court (Walker 1988: 448, table 6). For both courts combined, 15.3 per cent of young black defendants were acquitted completely, compared with 9.5 per cent of whites and 10.9 per cent of south Asians.

Hood's study of cases at the Crown Courts in five West Midlands locations in 1989 concentrates on sentencing, but some information is provided about acquittal rates. Among male defendants at the five courts combined, the acquittal rates were 9.1 per cent for whites, 11.1 per cent for blacks, and 16.7 per cent for south Asians and others (Hood 1992: calculated from table 1, p. 32). However, there was considerable variation among the five courts. At one of them (Dudley) the acquittal rate was higher among whites (9.2 per cent) than among blacks (6.2 per cent), whereas at three courts (Coventry, Warwick, and Stafford), acquittal rates were considerably higher among blacks than among whites: for male defendants at these three courts combined, the acquittal rates were 9.1 per cent for whites, 21.3 per cent for blacks, and 26.9 per cent for south Asians and others.

While these data about acquittal rates are not national, they do cover the two largest areas of ethnic minority settlement (London and the West Midlands). They indicate that there is, if anything, a tendency for acquittal rates to be higher among ethnic minorities than whites, with considerable variation between individual courts. No study has tried to evaluate verdicts by ethnic group according to the state of the evidence, or other characteristics of the case or the defendant: hence the pattern of acquittals is hard to interpret. The fact that acquittal rates do not vary widely overall among ethnic groups suggests a considerable degree of consistency between earlier stages of the criminal justice process and the decisions of the courts. For example, if black people are more often accused than white people because of bias on the part of the public or the police, then the evidence against black defendants should be weaker than against white defendants; and assuming that the courts apply tougher evidential standards than the public or the police (a fair assumption, since a considerable proportion of defendants are acquitted) the weaker evidence against black defendants should be reflected in higher acquittal rates. This suggests that the high rate of prosecution of black people is unlikely to result from massive bias at stages before a case reaches court. The small overall difference in acquittal rates between ethnic groups is consistent with the theory of massive bias at earlier stages *only* on the assumption that the decisions of the courts are also massively biased against black people (or that they are more or less random).

Sentencing

London statistics on prosecutions for indictable offences in 1984 and 1985 (Home Office 1989*b*) show that there was no significant difference between sentences imposed in magistrates' courts on white and black offenders, but that south Asians and members of other ethnic minority groups were much more likely than whites or blacks to be fined and less likely to be given a custodial sentence. At the Crown Court, however, 57 per cent of black offenders were given immediate custody, compared with 51 per cent of whites, 50 per cent of south Asians, and 49 per cent of other ethnic groups. The high figure for blacks was due to the higher proportion given youth custody (19 per cent of blacks compared with 11 per cent of whites). Analysis by age of the offender and offence group (the only other information available in these official statistics) explains a part of these differences, but considerable variation between ethnic groups in the use of custody remains within offence groups for each age group considered separately.

Among males aged 14–16, the largest differences in the proportion receiving immediate custodial sentences were for sexual offences (21 per cent for blacks compared with 4 per cent for whites), robbery (43 per cent compared with 34 per cent) criminal damage (29 per cent compared with 11 per cent), and drug offences (13 per cent compared with 5 per cent). The difference for robbery is striking in view of the evidence that robberies committed by blacks tended to be of a different and less serious nature. For example, 22 per cent of the white robbers were sentenced at the same time for additional firearms offences, compared with 8 per cent of the black robbers.

Among males aged 17–20, the proportions receiving immediate custodial sentences were 27 per cent of blacks, 20 per cent of whites, 17 per cent of Asians, and 14 per cent of other ethnic groups. Considerable differences remained when offence groups were considered separately. The largest difference was for sexual offences, where 58 per cent of blacks compared with 17 per cent of whites received immediate custodial sentences.

Among males aged 21 and over, the proportion receiving immediate custodial sentences was again higher for blacks (27 per cent) than for whites (23 per cent) or south Asians (21 per cent) and other ethnic minorities (14 per cent). Again the differences remained when offence groups were considered separately, and once more the largest difference was for sexual offences.

A recurring feature of these results is that black men are far more likely than white men to be given custodial sentences for sexual offences. This is partly because a higher proportion of these sexual offences were rapes where the offender was black (24 per cent) than where he was white (3 per cent). However, as already observed, the converse pattern exists in the case of robbery (robberies committed by white men are more serious); yet black men were still more likely than white men to receive immediate custody for robbery. For the most part, the difference in sentences imposed on black and white men cannot be explained by the offence, as far as that is known from the official statistics.

Among those receiving sentences of immediate custody at the magistrates' courts, there was no difference in average sentence length between ethnic groups. At the Crown Court, south Asians received considerably longer custodial sentences, on average, than whites. Also, young black males (aged 17–20) received longer custodial sentences than young white males, although there was no similar difference among those aged 21 or more. The Home Office suggests that 'the longer sentence length for Asians reflect[s] the high proportion of drug trafficking offenders' (1989*b*: para. 24). A separate table shows that among those convicted of drugs offences, the specific offence was drug trafficking for 64 per cent of Asians compared with 17 per cent of whites and 27 per cent of blacks (ibid.: table 18). However, it has not been demonstrated that this accounts for the longer custodial sentences imposed on Asians.

From the limited information available in these statistics, it is not possible to tell whether the sentences imposed reflect equal or unequal treatment of different ethnic groups. A number of studies have pursued this question (McConville and Baldwin 1982; Crow and Cove 1984; Mair 1986; Moxon 1988; Voakes and Fowler 1989; Hudson 1989; Brown and Hullin 1992; Hood 1992). However, as Hood (1992) has convincingly argued, the earlier studies had serious limitations which for the most part prevent any definite conclusions being drawn from them on the central question under consideration. Hood's study of sentencing in the Crown Court in five West Midlands locations collected far more extensive information than the others about the cases and offenders, and used far more powerful analytic methods, so it is at present the best available source. Its main limitation (but also a strength in analytic terms) is that it does not cover sentencing by the magistrates' courts. Some up-to-date information about that is, however, available from Brown and Hullin's study in Leeds.

There were 2,884 sentenced male offenders in Hood's sample, of whom 48.9 per cent were sentenced to custody. Over the five courts covered by the study, 56.6 per cent of the blacks were sentenced to custody, compared with 48.4 per cent of the whites and 39.6 per cent of the Asians. However, there were substantial variations between the individual courts. Most of the cases were heard at two of the courts, Birmingham and Dudley, which between them accounted for 89 per cent of sentenced male offenders. At Birmingham, 52 per cent of the blacks compared with 45 per cent of the whites were sentenced to custody, whereas at Dudley 65 per cent of the blacks compared with 48 per cent of the whites were sentenced to custody. There were also substantial differences between individual judges in the relative sentences they imposed on blacks and whites. However, there were considerable differences between the three ethnic groups in terms of the three types of variables that could justifiably have influenced the sentencing decision: how the case had been processed to date, the type of offence, and the prior history of offending. Also, there were some differences between ethnic groups in their personal and social characteristics, some of which might be considered relevant, especially if sentencing is meant to be influenced by considerations of substantive (as well as formal) justice.

A tabular analysis suggested

> that differences in the use of custody were not evident when the case characteristics were generally regarded as the most serious and where there was consequently little room to exercise discretion in choosing between custody and an alternative sentence. They do suggest, however, that where there was room to exercise greater discretion, the racial factor was associated with a pattern in the use of custody which was disadvantageous to blacks and that the degree of this disadvantage was much more evident at the Dudley courts than at Birmingham. (Hood 1992: 65)

More detailed and precise results were obtained by carrying out several types of multivariate analysis. One method, for example, was a logistic regression analysis in which the dependent variable was whether or not the offender had been sentenced to custody. The independent (or predictor) variables described the legal process, the characteristics of the offence, and the prior history of offending. In more detail, they included the most serious offence of which convicted, the mode of trial (main offence triable only on indictment or either way), whether remanded in custody when appeared for sentence, plea, number of charges of which convicted, outstanding court orders, violence in the offence, degree of injury, motive for violence, effect of violence, amount of financial loss involved, vulnerability of victim, number of previous convictions, previous custodial history for similar type of offence, and previous breach of community service order. Each of these items was found to be significantly related to the probability of custody, and the logistic regression model reflected the best possible method of predicting whether there would be a custodial sentence from this combination of variables. In the context of this model, it was found that the probability of custody remained 5 per cent higher for black than for white men, while it remained 5 per cent lower for south Asian men than for white men. The raw difference in use of custody between ethnic groups was reduced after taking account of the process, offence, and prior record variables, but it did not disappear. The difference between black and white men was significant at the 93 per cent level of confidence.

Differences in the use of custody between ethnic groups were found to be greatest where the judges' discretion was greatest: that is, for offences at a middling level of seriousness. In fact, for each type of offence examined, there was no such difference for the most serious offences or for the least serious ones.

All of the difference between ethnic groups occurred among those aged 21 or over: there was no difference for young offenders. Also, there was no difference in custody rate between black and white offenders in employment: the differences were confined to those who were unemployed. This happened because 'being unemployed was a factor significantly correlated with receiving a custodial sentence if the defendant was black but not if he was white or Asian' (Hood 1992: 86). A higher proportion of the black male defendants pleaded not guilty than of the whites (23 compared with 11 per cent), and a not guilty plea was associated overall with an increased probability of custody. However, because of the detailed pattern of the relationships, the difference in pleas between ethnic groups did not help to explain the difference in the use of custody.

In the context of the multivariate model, there was a large difference between sentencing practice at Dudley and Birmingham. At Dudley, black defendants were considerably more likely than white defendants to receive custody, and this applied fairly consistently to all of the individual judges. At Birmingham, overall black and white defendants were equally likely to receive custody, but there was variation between individual judges, such that some tended to favour whites, while others tended to favour blacks, and these biases cancelled each other out.

Among adult males given custodial sentences, these sentences tended to be considerably longer for south Asians and blacks than for whites. This was partly because south Asians and blacks were more likely to plead not guilty than whites, and because of the detailed characteristics of their case and prior record, summed up as the seriousness of the offence. Those pleading not guilty were given considerably longer sentences on average. Among those who pleaded guilty, there was little difference in length of sentence between ethnic groups after controlling for the seriousness of the offence. Among those who pleaded not guilty, however, sentences were considerably longer for blacks and Asians than for whites after allowing for the seriousness of the offence.

Hood estimated that in the West Midlands, 24.4 per cent of the male prison population was black, compared with 3.8 per cent of the population at large: a ratio of 6.4:1. He estimated that 70 per cent of this difference was accounted for by the number appearing for sentence, taking account of all stages prior to sentence, but not the profile of offences; 10 per cent 'by the more serious nature of the offences and other legally relevant characteristics of the charges on which black defendants were convicted'; 7 per cent by greater use of custody than expected (after taking account of legally relevant variables); and 13 per cent 'by lengthier sentences, which appears to be entirely due to a greater propensity to plead not guilty, and to the lengthier sentences for those who did so' (1992: 130). This means that 7 per cent of the overrepresentation of blacks in the prison population was explained by direct discrimination in sentencing. A further proportion may be explained by indirect discrimination, if it is considered that some of the criteria currently used are not justifiable, but that argument would have to be made by far more detailed consideration of individual criteria.

Hood's data show that a higher proportion of offences committed by black and south Asian men than by white men came to light as a result of proactive policing, for example stop-and-search, or discovery at the scene of the crime. Although this cannot be quantified, the findings suggest that some of the overrepresentation of blacks does occur because policing is targeted on them. More of the south Asians and blacks than of the whites had legal advice at the police station, which may help to explain why more pleaded not guilty, and consequently tended to receive lengthier sentences. An important factor associated with the greater use of custody for blacks was that they were more likely to be remanded in custody when they were sentenced. This higher probability of being remanded in custody could not be wholly explained by variables known to be legally relevant to the bail/custody decision. The proportion who had no social inquiry report prepared on them varied significantly between south Asian men (43 per cent) and blacks (42 per cent) on the one hand, and whites (28 per cent) on the other. Most of this variation occurred because a higher proportion of the ethnic minorities had signalled their intention to plead guilty. Most of the difference in use of custody between black and white men arose among those for whom no social inquiry report was prepared, but it is not clear that a failure to prepare a report is the causal factor.

No study comparable to Hood's (which covers only the Crown Court) has been carried out of race and sentencing in magistrates' courts. As mentioned above, London statistics for 1984 and 1985 (Home Office 1989*b*) show no difference in sentences imposed on black and white offenders, although those imposed on south Asians were less severe. A recent study by Brown and Hullin (1992) of sentencing in magistrates' courts in Leeds found no significant difference overall in sentences imposed according to ethnic group. Although differences between ethnic groups did appear within certain sub-groups (for example, Afro-

Caribbean females were more likely to receive custodial sentences than white females) these could probably be explained by the use of justifiable criteria (offences committed by Afro-Caribbean females tended to be more serious than those committed by white females). The information collected by this study was relatively limited, and the analysis was not sufficient to address the question whether discrimination had occurred. However, together with the London statistics, these findings do suggest that the extent of any racial discrimination in sentencing is considerably less in the magistrates' than in the Crown Court.

Conclusions

At the end of the criminal justice process, black people (Afro-Caribbean and black Africans) are about seven times as likely to be in prison as white people or south Asians. In principle, this could reflect a difference in the rate and pattern of offending between the ethnic groups, or bias against black people at various stages of the criminal justice process. Both may be true, but in that case it is important to establish the relative importance of each type of explanation.

Although the evidence is unsatisfactory and incomplete, a number of broad conclusions can be drawn from the foregoing analytical review.

1. There is evidence of bias against black people at various stages: in the targeting of proactive law enforcement; in the decision to prosecute juveniles; and in sentencing by the Crown Court. Also, the pattern of offences for which black people are arrested and imprisoned is consistent with the theory that they tend to be the targets of proactive law enforcement.

2. Most of these decisions are not covered by the Race Relations Act, but the concept of racial discrimination can in principle be applied to them. In large part, the biases identified amount to direct discrimination. Indirect discrimination—the application of criteria which work to the disadvantage of black people, and are not justified—is probably much less important. Many of the criteria used at various stages of the process do work against black people, but in most cases it would be hard to argue that they are unjustified.

3. Although bias against black people has been demonstrated at several stages, the magnitude of these biases is small compared with the stark contrast in rates of arrest and imprisonment between black and white people. The theory that this stark contrast is mainly or entirely caused by cumulative bias at each different stage of the criminal justice process can on existing evidence be shown to be implausible.

(a) This theory would predict a steady increase in the proportion of black people among suspects and offenders from the earliest to the latest stage of the process. In fact, the proportion of black people is about the same among suspects as described by victims, persons arrested, and the prison population.

(b) Arising directly from the first point, it is impossible to account for the high representation of black people at early stages (for example, according to victims' reports) in terms of bias.

(c) Even at stages where bias has been demonstrated, its potential impact is fairly limited. For example, proactive law enforcement does target black people to some extent: but most clear-ups do not result from proactive law enforcement, and most proactive law enforcement cannot be targeted on black people. Hence the total effect of this bias must be modest, especially in relation to the stark differences in rates of arrest and imprisonment between black and white people. To take another example, black juveniles are considerably more likely than comparable white juveniles to be prosecuted rather than cautioned, but there is no evidence of a similar difference in the case of adult offenders, who account for 90 per cent of the cases coming before the courts. Hence, the bias in cautioning of juveniles, though important, has only a small significance as an explanation of the difference in rates of imprisonment between black and white people.

(d) While proactive law enforcement targeted on black people can help to explain the arrest rates for certain offences (notably, robbery) it cannot for others (such as burglary) where proactive law enforcement cannot for the most part be targeted on black people and is in any case singularly ineffective.

(e) Contrary to what has been stated by some commentators (for example, Reiner 1989, 1993) it is not the case that bias has been demonstrated at every stage of the process. Most notably, black people are, if anything, more likely to be acquitted than white people. There is not a steady accumulation of bias from one stage to the next.

(f) If there is massive bias at earlier stages of the process (such as the decisions to report to the police, to arrest, and to prosecute) then the evidence will tend to be much weaker where the defendant is black than where he or she is white. Unless there is also massive bias against black defendants in court, the acquittal rate should therefore be radically higher for black than for white defendants, but in fact it is about the same or slightly higher. Given the facts on acquittal rates, massive bias at earlier stages can only exist if there is also massive bias in the courts. Most observers would consider that to be implausible.

A fair assessment of the limited evidence is that while substantial bias against black people has been demonstrated at several stages of the process, in large part the difference in rate of arrest and imprisonment between black and white people arises from a difference in the rate of offending.

4. However, this high rate of offending among black people may be partly the consequence of mutually hostile interactions with the police and other authorities. Racial prejudice among the authorities may be one factor leading to escalating hostility in these encounters. Thus, high crime rates among black people may possibly be explained partly in terms of labelling and deviance amplification, and racial prejudice among the authorities may be important in initiating and maintaining such a system of interaction. Racial prejudice and discrimination may be important in explaining why the crime rate *is* high among black people, although it is not important in explaining why it is *not*.

5. South Asians—collectively the largest part of the ethnic minority population—are not overrepresented among offenders described by victims, persons arrested, or the prison population. No bias has been demonstrated against them at any stage, and at various points they tend to be favoured compared to white or black people. In other contexts, south Asians are just as much subject to racial hostility and discrimination as black people. The bias against black people that has been demonstrated within the criminal justice system is therefore different from that existing in other contexts such as employment. It is not adequately described as part of a generalized 'racism'. More plausibly it springs from a perception of black people specifically, as distinct from other ethnic minorities, as a threat to law and order. Those perceptions are both justified by reality, since crime rates are in fact relatively high among black people, and help to shape that reality, since racial hostility and discrimination will through a sequence of interactions cause black crime rates to rise still further.

CRIMINAL JUSTICE INSTITUTIONS

This section considers the policies, practices, and organizational dynamics of criminal justice institutions as they impinge on ethnic minorities. There is far more relevant research on the police than on the other institutions, but some brief comments will be made on the probation service, the courts, and the prisons.

The Police

Attitudes and behaviour of working groups

It is a well-established research finding that there are high levels of racial prejudice among working groups of police officers (Lambert 1970; Cain

1973; Reiner 1978; Smith and Gray 1983; Holdaway 1983; Graef 1989). From extensive observational research, the PSI study of London policing found that:

> Although there were variations in the extent of racial prejudice and racialist talk between different groups of officers and individuals and at different times (there was an increase at the time of the 1981 riots), these things are pervasive: they are, on the whole, expected, accepted and even fashionable. Senior officers seldom try to set a different tone (though they do on occasion) and there were some cases where they initiated racialist talk and kept it going. (Smith and Gray 1983: 335)

There is also extensive research to show that hostility towards ethnic minorities is a pervasive feature of police culture in the USA (Skolnick 1966; Bayley and Mendelsohn 1968; Westley 1970). However, the large-scale observational study carried out by Black and Reiss in the late 1960s (Black and Reiss 1967; Reiss 1971) suggested that rude, hostile, or violent behaviour by police officers was unrelated to the race of suspects after other factors were taken into account. Among these other factors, the race of the victim was important, since black victims tended to be insistent in demanding tough action against the person they accused, who tended also to be black.

Similarly, the PSI researchers in London concluded that:

> Racial prejudice is presumably one of a number of factors conducive towards bad behaviour by police officers, but it is probably not a fundamental one. Police behaviour is best explained by the structure of rewards and constraints within which police officers operate; only at exceptional times (such as the riots of 1981) does retribution against a particular ethnic group become an end in itself for police officers. (Smith and Gray 1983: 111)

The observational work, although extensive, could not be analysed by quantitative methods, so the effects of the many variables involved in any police–public encounter could not be separately identified. However, the researchers concluded that 'although the thing cannot be definitely proved, we are fairly confident that there is no widespread tendency for black or Asian people to be given greatly inferior treatment by the police' (1983: 128). This conclusion from observational research was supported by the results of the survey of Londoners, which showed that assessments by people belonging to ethnic minority groups of *specific encounters* with the police were no more unfavourable than those of white people, although Afro-Caribbeans were far more critical than white people or Asians in response to questions about the extent of police misconduct *in general terms* (Smith 1983*a*).

The PSI researchers qualified their main conclusion on police behaviour towards ethnic minorities in various ways. The research established that Afro-Caribbeans were more likely to be stopped by police than white people or south Asians. The researchers concluded that 'police officers tend to make a crude equation between crime and black people, to assume that suspects are black and to justify stopping people in these terms' (Smith and Gray 1983: 128). Yet the distribution of persons stopped according to ethnic group was in line with the distribution of offenders according to victims' descriptions; and the proportion of persons stopped who were subsequently arrested and charged, or reported for an offence, was the same for all ethnic groups. Hence, while racial hostility was part of the rhetoric of justification used by working groups of police officers to account for their stop-and-search behaviour, it would also be possible to construct a more rational explanation.

At the same time, the survey of Londoners showed a strong relationship between adversarial encounters with the police, particularly repeated stops, and hostile views. Smith and Gray argued that the massive use of stop-and-search in London was a mistaken policy because it produced relatively poor rewards for a large expenditure of resources, while increasing the hostility of young people, especially young black people, towards the police. This view was reinforced when a stop-and-search campaign in Brixton codenamed 'Swamp 81' was identified as an important factor precipitating the first round of riots in 1981 (Scarman 1981). Of course, the decision to mount such a campaign in an area of high Afro-Caribbean concentration—especially in the area that had come to symbolize the Afro-Caribbean community in the popular mind—sprang from a specific concern about black crime which had been encouraged by the police from the mid-1970s onwards. However, most stops, even in 1981, were not part of special campaigns on the pattern of 'Swamp 81', and most were very little influenced by policy from outside small working groups of police officers.

The other major qualification that the PSI researchers made to their general conclusion arose from their observations from within the Metropolitan Police during the 1981 riots and in their aftermath. During that period, Afro-Caribbeans became the focus of intense hostility among working groups of police officers in London. Nationwide, almost 4,000 people were arrested in the disorders of July 1981, and of the 3,704 for whom data were available, 21 per cent were black (Afro-Caribbean or African), 5 per cent were south Asian, and 67 per cent were white (Home Office 1981). However, the PSI researchers were observing in areas of high ethnic concentration in London, where around two-thirds of people arrested belonged to ethnic minority groups. The perception of police officers in these areas that they were under attack from black people specifically was not unreasonable. Racial hostility (on both sides) was an essential element of the confrontation, but the PSI researchers suggested that the actions of the police would have been much the same if they had been under attack from some other group such as 'skinheads armed with petrol bombs'.

In recent years there have been a number of allegations in individual cases of police misconduct in which racial hostility was clearly a motive, and some have been proven. However, this is consistent with the view based on research evidence that racial antagonism does not substantially influence the *pattern* of behaviour among working groups of police officers.

Policing policy and the climate of relations with black people

The attitudes and behaviour of working groups of police officers unfold within a much wider framework. It has been argued that there are a number of predisposing conditions of the mutual hostility between the police and ethnic minorities: a history of immigration control justifiably regarded as racist, continuing racial attacks and harassment, high black unemployment, and conflict over cannabis (Smith 1991). It is widely agreed that before the mid-1970s, there was no public perception of a link between ethnic minorities and crime, and little public awareness of hostile relationships between the police and ethnic minorities (see e.g. Lea and Young 1982; Benyon 1986; Solomos 1989; Reiner 1989). A number of factors came together from the mid-1970s to change public perceptions, and to bring about what Benyon calls a 'spiral of decline' in relations between black people and the police. One factor, according to the police view, was an actual increase in crime committed by Afro-Caribbeans. The evidence for this is fragmentary, but it would be implausible to suggest that no such increase occurred. However, many commentators have maintained that policing policy, and the way that senior police officers conducted the public debate about race and crime, played a crucial role in stigmatizing black people and starting the downward spiral in police/black relations (Lea and Young 1982; Benyon 1986; Gilroy 1987). Aspects of policing policy that commentators cite are heavy-handed policing of major black cultural events, especially the Notting Hill Carnival from 1976 onwards; highly visible policing of black neighbourhoods that have acquired symbolic significance, such as All Saints' Road in west London; raids on black clubs and subsequent outcries over alleged miscarriages of justice; deployment of the notorious 'sus' (suspicious person) law against black people, before its abolition in 1981; subsequently, special stop-and-search operations targeting areas of high ethnic concentration (for a comment on 'sus' and stop-and-search, see Brogden 1981). In addition to these actions, the police intervened in public debate, most decisively by publishing statistics on black involvement in street crime in evidence to a House of Commons Select Committee in 1976. This was crucial in creating the conditions for what many commentators describe as a 'moral panic' about black crime, especially 'mugging' (Hall *et al.* 1978). By 1979 the senior ranks within the Metropolitan Police were certainly aware of serious problems developing in relations with black people, and some senior officers recognized that the actions of the police had contributed to the growing crisis: it was that awareness which led the Metropolitan Police Commissioner to initiate the study of *Police and People in London* by the Policy Studies Institute in late 1979.

It has often been observed that racial prejudice among working groups of police officers was entrenched well before black crime was highlighted by the senior ranks (Lambert 1970 provides evidence of this). From the mid-1970s, however, the prejudices of working groups were legitimated to some degree by statements and actions at the top. The PSI researchers found that middle management seldom acted to counter racist talk, and sometimes initiated it (Smith and Gray 1983: 125). Reiner's more recent research among chief constables found that they tended to see black people as a source of crime and disorder (Reiner 1991: 206).

Policing actions as a cause of black hostility

Black hostility to the police is located in experience, in the sense that people explain or elaborate their hostility in terms of concrete examples of police misconduct, or a pattern of policing that is thought to be unjust. Black people have on average substantially more adversarial encounters with the police than white people, and a considerably higher proportion of their contacts are adversarial (where they are being treated as suspects or offenders rather than offered a service). At the same time, black people are considerably more critical of the police (in general terms) than white people or south Asians. Finally, there is a strong relationship between the level of contact with the police, especially adversarial contact, and holding critical views. Hence black hostility to the police is associated with a pattern of adversarial contact (Smith 1983; Skogan 1990; Jefferson and Walker 1992). At the same time, the nature of particular encounters, according to the reports of the individual people concerned, is much the same for all ethnic groups, and the nature of the service provided is much the same for all ethnic groups, if rather better than average for West Indians (Smith 1991).

However, more detailed analysis shows that the actions of the police as they are reflected in encounters with black people cannot wholly explain black people's hostility. A reanalysis of the 1981 London survey has shown that the association between critical views and adversarial encounters with the police was much less strong among people of West Indian origin than among others. Further, the biggest contrast in views of the police between white people and Afro-Caribbeans was among those who have no experience of adversarial contact. Both of these findings suggest that personal experience was not the critical factor explaining the high level of criticism of the police among Afro-Caribbeans. The analysis can be refined by distinguishing those adversarial encounters in which the person thought the police behaved badly, discourteously, or unreasonably. The results show that it was indeed these negatively evaluated encounters that were associated with critical views. However, again the views of West Indians varied much less than those of whites according to the number of negatively evaluated encounters, and when the number of negatively evaluated encounters was held constant, the West Indians remained substantially more hostile to the police than white people (Smith 1991). Jefferson and Walker's (1992) analysis of their data for Leeds produced findings consistent with those from the earlier London survey.

In seeking to explain this pattern, Smith (1991) suggests that the police tend to be seen as the symbol of an oppressive white authority, and that black people do not rely mostly on personal experience to confirm this perspective: they are receptive and sensitive to information from other sources. On this view, black hostility to the police is akin to a political force, and part of the assertion of identity by a social and cultural group. Gaskell and Smith (1985) have shown that among young black people criticism of the police is fairly distinct from criticism of other central institutions, and they conclude that black hostility to the police is not an aspect of hostility to most of the dominant institutions of a predominantly white society (see also Gaskell 1986). This suggests that the police have come to occupy a special place in the myths of origin of black people in Britain. It is the police rather than any other institution that have come to symbolize those features of white authority to which black people see themselves as opposed.

In recent years police leaders have tried to change these perceptions by making public demonstrations of support for policies intended to benefit ethnic minorities or race relations. For example, various initiatives have been taken (mainly in London) to improve the quality of the police response to racial harassment; increasing emphasis has been placed on recruiting ethnic minorities into the police force; and in March 1993 the new Metropolitan Police Commissioner, Mr Paul Condon, made opposing racism within the police force the subject of his first major speech.

Ethnic minorities in the police force

The number of people from ethnic minority groups in British police forces remains low. In March 1992 they represented just over 1 per cent of the police strength of England and Wales, compared with 5 per cent of the general population (Home office 1992). This is in spite of a number of recruitment campaigns targeting ethnic minorities over a period of fifteen years or more. The first national advertising campaign in 1976 produced thirty-two applications but none led to an appointment. In his report on the 1981 riots, Lord Scarman argued that 'the composition of our police forces must reflect the make-up of the society they serve' (Scarman 1981: 76) and recommended that increased representation of minority groups should be achieved through special initiatives but without lowering entry standards. The Home Office responded by setting up a working party, whose report (Home office 1982) recommended a number of active measures to recruit members of ethnic minority groups. A number of forces introduced special initiatives over the next few years, but progress remained slow. Following the urban riots in 1985, the Home Office launched a further set of proposals (Home Office 1986*a*, *b*). Circulars on equal opportunities and on ethnic minority recruitment were issued a few years later (Home Office 1989*c*, 1990), but 'the general trend of recruitment nevertheless remains slow, reflecting a continuing reluctance of qualified people from minority ethnic groups to join the police service' (Holdaway, 1991*a*: 367).

Several research projects have given consistent accounts of the reasons for this reluctance (Smith and Gray 1983; Wilson *et al.* 1984; Holdaway 1991*a*, *b*). Because of antagonism between the police and Afro-Caribbeans, many black people see joining the police as going over to the enemy. Many south Asians regard policing as a low-status job. Ethnic minority officers face at best continual racist banter and at worst abuse and harassment from their white colleagues; they also have to cope with racist responses from white members of the public, and with disapproval from members of their own group. According to Holdaway (1991*a*, *b*), a major reason for the small success of recruitment campaigns is a failure by police management to tackle racism within the force. In addition, positive action to recruit ethnic minorities had been limited in most forces, and had failed to use available resources: for example, only four out of the forty-three forces had used their community or race relations staff to plan or carry out positive action on recruitment.

Lord Scarman's argument was that the police force should represent the ethnic diversity of the country. That seems an important symbolic gesture which would mean that the police are not in opposition to the minority communities but are of them and partly belong to them. Whether the recruitment of ethnic minorities beings short-term practical benefits has not been investigated in Britain. The one aspect of this question that has been intensively investigated in the USA is the use of deadly force. Although the total number of killings by police officers in American cities declined in the 1970s, when there were large increases in the number of black police officers, black people remained much more at risk of being killed by a police officer than white people. In fact, the 'kill rate' is much higher for black than for white police officers, although the research findings suggest that this is because black officers are assigned to black precincts, and because, living in high-crime areas, they are more likely to kill people off duty (Fyfe 1981; Sherman 1983).

The Probation Service

The three key functions of the probation service are providing information and advice to decision-makers in the criminal justice system, usually in the form of social inquiry reports (amounting to 300,000 a year) provided for the courts; working constructively in the community with offenders on supervisory orders under a wide range of statutes; and working with people in custody to prepare for their eventual release (Mavunga 1993). The limited information available about the way the probation service impinges on ethnic minorities is largely confined to social inquiry reports and their influence on the decisions of the courts. In principle, there is a serious risk that social inquiry reports will lead to discrimination against ethnic minorities. Referring back to the discussion in Landau and Nathan (1983), this is because these reports are part of a system of substantive rather than formal justice; they are intended to guide the courts in making discretionary decisions on the disposal of offenders found guilty. The reports and the conclusions drawn from them do not depend on formal criteria. They are the accounts prepared by a particular professional group of the history and background of offenders, and their judgements about how those offenders would respond to various sanctions or treatments. They may be expected, therefore, to reflect the cultural and value perspective of those professionals, who are overwhelmingly white.

There is evidence from small-scale studies carried out in the 1980s that social inquiry reports did at that time tend to reflect racial stereotypes (Whitehouse 1983; Pinder 1984; Waters 1988). It seems likely that this must influence the sentencing of offenders belonging to ethnic minority groups, but there is no convincing evidence to support this theory as yet. A potentially more important factor is that before the Criminal Justice Act 1991 social inquiry reports were generally not prepared on defendants who were expected to plead not guilty. Several studies have shown that the proportion of cases in which no social inquiry report was prepared was substantially higher for ethnic minorities than for white people (Voakes and Fowler 1989; Walker 1989; Hood 1992). This arose (prior to the Criminal Justice Act 1991) mainly because black and south Asian defendants were more likely to plead not guilty. Hood's study (which covered the Crown Court only) showed that the contrast in use of custody between black and white defendants arose entirely among those for whom there was no social inquiry report. Hood was not able to demonstrate that if there had been social inquiry reports on more of the black defendants the contrast in custodial sentences would have been reduced. What his findings do demonstrate, however, is that where there was a social inquiry report there was no difference in sentences between black and white defendants.

The limited evidence suggests that while social inquiry reports tend to reflect racial stereotypes held by those compiling them, this has little or no effect on the final outcome; but that prior to 1991 ethnic minority defendants may have tended to be at a disadvantage because *no* social inquiry report was compiled on them.

A survey of probation staff in post at the end of 1987 recorded 2.6 per cent as coming from ethnic minorities (Home Office 1992). A system of regular ethnic monitoring of staff has recently been established. The probation service first began to give attention to ethnic minority issues in 1983, when the Central Council of Probation Committees produced a report, *Probation: A Multi-Racial Approach*. In 1987, the Association of Chief Officers of Probation established an anti-racism committee, and in 1988 the Home Office issued a circular, *Probation Service Policies on Race*, which gave advice on policy, recruitment, training, employment, and service delivery.

The Courts and the Legal Professions

The results of research on the decisions of the courts were summarized in an earlier section. Hood's (1992) study of the cases in the Crown Court in five West Midlands towns and cities showed that there were differences between individual courts (as also between individual judges) in the degree of bias in sentencing against black defendants. This suggests that there are properties of a court as an organization which bring about or prevent discrimination against ethnic minorities, although there is no information about what these properties might be.

In general, representation of ethnic minorities among legal practitioners is rather low. According to the Home Office (1992), 2 per cent of solicitors are from ethnic minorities. However, statistics published by the Law Society suggest that the proportion is much higher among recent entrants. For example, 13 per cent of those admitted to the roll in 1991 were from ethnic minorities; 5 per cent of these were Hong Kong Chinese lawyers qualifying to practise in England, but the remainder amount to 8 per cent of those admitted, whereas ethnic minorities account for about 5 per cent of the general population (Law Society 1992). A current survey of law students suggests that 12 per cent are from ethnic minority groups

(Halpern 1993).[4] Hence, the representation of ethnic minorities among solicitors can be expected to rise in future. King and Israel (1989) found, however, that law graduates from ethnic minorities (except for the Chinese) were much less likely than white graduates to be articled with a commercial firm of solicitors, and this is a strong indication that their career progress will tend to be slower.

A relatively high proportion of barristers (6 per cent) are from ethnic minorities, but only 0.9 per cent of QCs (Home Office 1992). A recent report has shown that ethnic minority students on the Bar Vocational Course achieve substantially poorer results than white students, although the reasons for this poorer performance are not clear (Dewberry 1993). The Council for Legal Education has set up a Committee of Inquiry into Equal Opportunities on the Bar Vocational Course to investigate the pattern of results, the teaching and assessment methods used, and the complaints of individual students. It is alleged by the Society of Black Lawyers that people from ethnic minorities who qualify at the end of the course have difficulty in finding a pupillage in chambers offering good training and experience.

According to the Home Office (1992: 23), 'there were no clerks to the justices from the ethnic minorities, while a survey has shown that 2 per cent of magistrates are from the ethnic minorities. There are believed to be 3 judges from the ethnic minorities, 7 recorders and 7 assistant recorders.' King and May (1985) identified a number of reasons for the failure to recruit more black magistrates, including lack of contact with minority group organizations, a preference for middle-class people from mainstream organizations, an assumption that minority group magistrates should 'represent' their community, a fear that this would be against the interests of justice, vaguely specified requirements that left wide room for prejudiced judgements, and a failure to use people from ethnic minorities as selectors. Since King and May's study, the Lord Chancellor has publicly committed his department to a policy of making the magistracy more representative of local populations (Lord Chancellor's Department 1988). Some moves have also been made towards including ethnic minority issues among subjects covered in magistrates' training.

Prisons

There is wide scope for racial discrimination within prison establishments and within the prison system more broadly. Conditions vary radically

[4] This estimate is based on a large sample of students on graduate law courses and on the postgraduate common professional examination course through which graduates in non-law subjects become eligible to train to become solicitors or barristers. Only students paying home as opposed to overseas fees are included.

from one prison establishment to another, and there is a system for allocating prisoners to particular establishments that takes account of a range of criteria including the nature of the offence, the length of the sentence, and the offender's prior record. In principle, this allocation system could discriminate against ethnic minorities. The ethnic composition of the prison population varies widely between establishments, but no study has yet analysed ethnic composition in relation to the conditions and regimes obtaining at different establishments. The one detailed study so far published (Genders and Player 1989) is based on case studies of three establishments, with some more limited information about a further two.

As Genders and Player point out, it was established in 1987 by the case of *Alexander* v. *The Home Office* that the provisions of the Race Relations Act 1976 do apply to prison establishments (see *Equal Opportunities Review* 1987). The court upheld Alexander's claim that the repeated refusal of a job while he was in Parkhurst Prison on the grounds that he was black amounted to unlawful discrimination. Although the case could not be brought under the employment provisions of the statute because prison work did not count as employment, the court held that prison work was covered under the heading of providing goods, facilities, and services. The same logic could presumably be applied to other aspects of prison conditions and régimes.

Starting in 1981, a series of Home Office circulars on race relations in prisons has demonstrated an increasing level of concern. The first (Home Office 1981*a*) was mild in tone and presented race relations as more a potential than an actual problem. It recommended that a race relations liaison officer should be appointed in each prison; an addendum published in 1982 spelt out the liaison officer's role in more detail. A second circular published in 1983 presented race relations as an issue of immediate rather than potential importance, and signalled a commitment to actively pursuing the objective of fair treatment. It targeted derogatory language and allocation of work and training for special attention, and emphasized the need to attract more ethnic minority staff. A further circular published in 1986 emphasized the need for prisons to issue a race relations policy statement and make it widely known. Finally in 1988 the Home Office issued an addendum to the 1983 circular on the need to avoid racially offensive remarks and derogatory language in written reports on inmates. This was a response to the *Alexander* case which had revealed the following passage from an assessment report prepared at Wandsworth: 'He displays the usual traits associated with his ethnic background, being arrogant, suspicious of staff, anti-authority, devious and possessing a very large chip on his shoulder which he will find very difficult to remove if he carries on the way he is doing.'

Genders and Player found that in two of the establishments they studied in detail, the race relations liaison officer had been active in putting the race relations policy into practice. At Duxton, for example, 'he had taken a high-profile "proactive" approach. He regularly monitored the ethnic composition of the inmate population and their representation in different wings, their allocation to different jobs, and the proportion subject to disciplinary proceedings . . . He was vigilant in his opposition to the use of racist language and he challenged the under-employment of Black inmates in some work tasks' (1989: 38). At the third establishment, however, the approach had been much less active and energetic.

The study showed that prison staff tended to have highly unfavourable stereotypes of black (but not south Asian) prisoners, and that many features of these stereotypes were contradicted by evidence gained from interviewing both black and white prisoners. For example, whereas prison officers generally thought that black prisoners were alienated from education and vocational training, black prisoners were in fact more likely to have taken courses in further education outside prison, to have attended classes in prison, and to have completed vocational courses in prison.

Genders and Player provide evidence of various kinds of racial discrimination within the establishments they studied. From a self-report study they found no significant difference between ethnic groups in the proportion who had been involved in serious confrontations with staff or violent conflict with other inmates. However, among those who had been involved in such incidents, a higher proportion of the ethnic minority than of the white inmates had been subject to formal disciplinary action of some kind. An analysis of written assessments contained in standard classification forms also suggested racial discrimination. 'For example, of those prisoners who had disciplinary offences recorded against them during previous spells in custody, none of the Asians, but 27 per cent of the Whites, and as many as 44 per cent of the Whites, and as many as 44 per cent of the Blacks were assessed as being resistant to authority.' There was also evidence of discrimination in the allocation of inmates to jobs. For example, at one of the establishments, jobs were divided into 'best' and 'worst' categories on the basis of inmates' ratings. Only 14 per cent of ethnic minority inmates were engaged on work parties that fell within the 'best' job category, compared with 45 per cent of whites. Also, interviews conducted with work supervisors showed that those with responsibility for popular jobs had few inmates from ethnic minorities in their parties, while those responsible for unpopular jobs had many. Genders and Player conclude that 'racial discrimination is intrinsic to the social organization of prisons. In addition to being the product of a few racially prejudiced individuals, it is also the consequence of a complex interaction between racial stereotyping and the attempts by prison staff to achieve the multifarious and sometimes conflicting goals of the institution' (1989: 131).

The national prison survey 1991 is potentially an important source of information about the treatment of ethnic minorities in prisons (Walmsley *et al.* 1992). However, further analysis will be required to show whether the findings support the theory that ethnic minorities are unfairly treated. The survey shows that a smaller proportion of black Caribbean prisoners than of those from other ethnic groups thought that prison officers treated them well (29 per cent of black Caribbeans, compared with 43 per cent of whites). Also, black Caribbean prisoners were less likely than others to say that the prison governor treated them well.

ETHNIC MINORITIES AS VICTIMS OF CRIME

Rates of Victimization

The British Crime Survey 1988 shows that rates of victimization are distinctly higher among both Afro-Caribbeans and south Asians than among white people, both for household crimes and for personal crimes (Mayhew *et al.* 1989: 42, table 11). Among Afro-Caribbeans, the differences are particularly marked for burglary (10.3 per cent of Afro-Caribbeans compared with 5.6 per cent of whites victimized during the reference period), for bicycle theft (8.4 per cent compared with 4.2 per cent of owners), for assault (7.3 per cent compared with 3.4 per cent), and for robbery or theft from the person (3.3 per cent compared with 1.1 per cent). In the case of Asians, the differences are most marked for household vandalism (7.5 per cent compared with 4.7 per cent), vehicle vandalism (13.7 per cent compared with 9.4 per cent), threats (5.3 per cent compared with 2.5 per cent), and robbery or theft from the person (3.0 per cent compared with 1.1 per cent).[5]

The risk of victimization tends to be strongly associated with characteristics of the area of work or residence, and after these area characteristics have been taken into account, the differences in risks between ethnic minorities and white people are considerably reduced. To some extent, therefore, the relatively high risks of victimization suffered by ethnic minorities are associated with the areas where they live. This was demonstrated by Mayhew *et al.* (1989), using logit models with the risk of victimization as the dependent variable. Three of these models included south Asians and whites only. In the two cases of threats and vandalism, the area characteristics associated with victimization were captured by a scale composed of the following highly correlated variables: neighbourhood cohesion, time the respondent has lived in the area, likelihood of

[5] All of these differences are significant at the 95 per cent level of confidence, taking account of sample design effects in calculating standard errors.

moving from the area, housing conditions, and (in the case of vandalism only) level of incivilities. It can be seen that this is not a true ecological variable: it partly reflects the individual's circumstances, aspirations, and perceptions of the area. Hence it would not be accurate to say that characteristics of the area which are common to all residents partly explain the difference in victimization between whites and Asians. It would be more accurate to say that the relatively high level of victimization among Asians is bound up with the way they and white people perceive the area where they live. In the case of contact theft, the significant area characteristic is simply inner-city versus the rest. Separate models were computed for Afro-Caribbean and white respondents only. In the case of burglary and assault, the significant geographical characteristics were again captured by complex scales which partly reflect individual circumstances and perceptions. In the case of contact theft, the relevant area characteristic was again inner-city versus the rest. (Mayhew *et al.* 1989: 83–6, tables B1–B6).

These same models also included a number of other, rather heterogeneous, variables, such as sex, age, job level (manual versus non-manual), marital status, tenure, whether unemployed, and number of evenings spent outside the home. It was found that the ethnic differences were considerably reduced in the context of a model including a number of these variables (in detail the variables included varied between one model and the next). These findings seem difficult to interpret because the models were not designed to test any clearly specified hypothesis about the difference in rate of victimization between ethnic groups. Among the variables included, some would have an entirely different status from others in any *explanatory* model: for example, the association of victimization with youth seems quite different from its association with perceived incivilities in the area. To the extent that the difference in victimization between ethnic groups is a function of differences in age profiles, this does suggest that it is not due to ethnicity. However, the parallel argument does not apply in the case of perceived incivilities. In that case, the statistics might mean that Asians tend to be confined to areas that are actually disordered and unsafe, or that those subject to high risks of victimization tend to perceive the area to be unsafe, or both. These explanations would be consistent with the theory that being Asian is a factor leading to a high rate of victimization. In other words, the association with perceived incivilities, or with the other features included in the residential scale, does not 'explain away' the ethnic differences.

In the case of Afro-Caribbeans, the relatively high level of victimization is connected with the relatively high crime rate. Most crime is committed near to where the offender lives, and either on people the offender knows or on others in similar circumstances (for example, belonging to the same social class or ethnic group). It is interesting, for example, that victimization is particularly high among offenders (Smith 1983*a*). Hence, it is not surprising that black-on-black crime accounts for a substantial proportion of the victimization of black people. Confining the analysis to the minority of cases where the victim could describe the offender, he or she was described as black by 8 per cent of white victims, 38 per cent of Afro-Caribbean victims, and 19 per cent of Asian victims. The offender was described as Asian by 2 per cent of white victims, no Afro-Caribbean victims, and 12 per cent of Asian victims (Mayhew *et al.* 1989: 47, table 13).

The pattern of victimization by ethnic group shown by the PSI survey of Londoners carried out in 1981 was different from that shown by the 1988 BCS for England and Wales. In London the rate of victimization was about the same among Afro-Caribbeans and white people, but considerably *lower* among Asians. However, the PSI survey, like the BCS, showed that Afro-Caribbeans were *more* likely to be victims of contact theft than white people. The low level of victimization of Asians found in London as a whole in 1981 may reflect the numerical strength in London of middle-class Asians living away from the inner-city areas. Working-class Asians are relatively more numerous outside London. The Islington Crime Survey carried out in 1985 showed about the same rate of victimization among Asian and white people within that relatively small, inner, and deprived part of London, but it showed a considerably higher rate of victimization among black people (Jones *et al.* 1986).

Victims and the Police

The 1988 BCS found little difference between ethnic groups in the proportion of victims who reported the incident to the police. A higher proportion of Asian and Afro-Caribbean than of white people reported burglaries and vandalism in the home, but this 'seems largely explained by higher levels of loss and damage' (Mayhew *et al.* 1989: 28). The PSI London survey in 1981 similarly found no significant differences between ethnic groups in the proportion of victims who reported incidents to the police (Smith 1983*a*: 76).

The 1988 BCS found that satisfaction after reporting to the police was lower among ethnic minorities than among white people:

> 61 % of white victims said they were 'fairly' or very' satisfied with the way the police had dealt with the matter, as against 49% of Afro-Caribbeans and 44% of Asian victims. Both Afro-Caribbean and Asian victims were more likely than whites to feel that the police did not do enough. Afro-Caribbean victims more often perceived impoliteness or unpleasantness on the part of the police, and they were more likely to feel that the police should have apprehended the offender.

Asian victims were relatively more dissatisfied because the police did not appear to be interested. (Mayhew *et al.* 1989: 28–9)

Levels of satisfaction shown by the 1981 London survey were generally higher, though again ethnic minorities, in this case especially the Asians, were less likely to be satisfied than white people. The proportion who were 'very satisfied' was 45 per cent among white people, 36 per cent among Afro-Caribbeans, and 18 per cent among south Asians. In marked contrast to the 1988 BCS, however, the 1981 London survey showed that the police appeared to have been more active and successful where the victim was Afro-Caribbean than white. 'Where the victim was a West Indian, the police were more likely to take some action, to make a full investigation, to move quickly and to catch the offender than where the victim was white or Asian' (Smith 1983*a*: 84). Possibly this contrast arises because the PSI survey asked more concrete and factual questions than the BCS, so that the BCS findings reflect general anti-police attitudes among ethnic minorities (especially Afro-Caribbeans) rather than police actions in the particular case.

In the 1988 BCS respondents were asked whether they had taken action about incidents they had observed in the past five years. Over 10 per cent in each case had observed instances of shoplifting, vandalism, and 'serious fights', while a few (3 per cent) had observed theft from parked cars. The proportion who had reported such incidents to the police ranged from around one-quarter (for stealing from cars and vandalism) to around one-tenth (for shoplifting and serious fights). The proportion who had reported such incidents to the police did not vary between ethnic groups (Skogan 1990: 48). Both smith (1983*a*) and Tuck and Southgate (1981) found on the basis of hypothetical questions ('*would* you call the police') that Afro-Caribbeans were less inclined to do so than others, although the differences were not large. Again, the answers to the hypothetical questions may reflect attitudes that are not expressed in behaviour. Smith also asked hypothetically about willingness to serve as a witness and appear in court, and here found a more marked difference between the responses of Afro-Caribbean and white respondents. The Islington Crime Survey, using closely similar hypothetical questions, found a lower level of willingness to help the police than the PSI survey for London as a whole, and a sharper contrast between white people on the one hand and both Afro-Caribbeans and south Asians on the other (Jones *et al.* 1986: 139–45).

Racially Motivated Crime and Harassment

The best evidence—that from the 1988 BCS—suggests that south Asians and Afro-Caribbeans are at considerably higher risk than white people of being victims of a number of kinds of crime. To some extent, this is because they fall into demographic groups (for example, the young) which are at higher than average risk. It is also associated with the actual and perceived characteristics of the areas where ethnic minorities live, although, as argued above, this does not 'explain the difference away'. In addition, Afro-Caribbeans have an elevated risk of crime *victimization* because *offending* rates among Afro-Caribbeans are several times higher than among white people, and a considerable proportion of the crimes committed by Afro-Caribbeans are on Afro-Caribbean victims.

However, another reason why rates of victimization are high among ethnic minorities is that they are the objects of some racially motivated crimes. They may also be the victims of a pattern of repeated incidents motivated by racial hostility, where many of these events on their own do not constitute crimes, although some crimes may occur in the sequence, so that the cumulative effect is alarming and imposes severe constraints on a person's freedom and ability to live a full life. Racial harassment is the term that is used to describe a pattern of repeated incidents of this kind.

Genn (1988) and Bowling (1993) have pointed out that victim surveys have not been designed to describe patterns which develop over time. Instead, they have up to now aimed to categorize and count discrete incidents using definitions parallel to those applied by the courts. This is most appropriate for crimes such as car theft or burglary, where most incidents *are* discrete from the viewpoint of the victim. It is least appropriate for crimes which take place within a continuing relationship (family violence, incest) or within a restricted social setting (the school, the workplace, the street).

A further difficulty in studying racially motivated crime or racial harassment is establishing racial motivation. One approach is to accept the victim's view; another is for an observer to make a judgement based on a description of the facts. Definitions used vary in the emphasis given to these two types of criterion, and in other detailed ways, so that it is often difficult to compare the results from different studies.

Although racial attacks and harassment, on any reasonable definition, are ancient phenomena, they have 'arrived relatively late on the political policy agenda and thence onto the agenda of various statutory agencies' (FitzGerald 1989). The first major report on the subject, *Blood on the Streets*, was published by Bethnal Green and Stepney Trades Council in 1978. Since then there has been an official report by the Home Office (1981*b*) based on statistics of incidents recorded by the police; a report by the House of Commons Home Affairs Committee (1986), which has also recently initiated a further inquiry; and two reports by an Inter-Departmental Group set up to consider racial attacks (Home Office

1989*c*, 1991). National statistics on racial incidents recorded by the police have been regularly reported in *Hansard.* Very few national survey-based statistics have become available, the main sources being the third PSI survey of racial minorities carried out in 1982 (Brown 1984) and the British Crime Survey (Mayhew *et al.* 1989). There has been a much larger number of local studies and initiatives, but most will not be cited here because they tend to have severe limitations as sources of hard information. The same can be said of the reports compiled by the Commission for Racial Equality and the Greater London Council on this subject.

As FitzGerald points out, the Home Office study of 1981 is generally used as a benchmark for the national scale of the problem. However, these statistics are virtually useless as a measure of racially motivated crime and racial harassment, because they are derived from police records. Later research has shown that most of these incidents are not reported to the police (especially the low-level harassment that forms part of a cumulative pattern); also, there is likely to be a large amount of 'noise' in the way the police record and classify these incidents. Despite their severe limitations, statistics based on police records may perhaps be of use as an indication of trends over time. The number recorded in London has risen from 1,945 in 1985 to 3,373 in 1991; in the rest of England and Wales, it rose from 3,955 to 4,509 over the same period (*Hansard*, HC, 17 December 1992, vol. 216, no. 79, col. 443).

The PSI's 1982 survey of racial minorities did not attempt to capture racial harassment, but asked about two types of crime victimization: physical attack or molestation, and burglary or damage to property. From detailed descriptions of the incidents (including the ethnic origin of the persons concerned) the researcher identified those where there was a probable racial motive. The classification did not, therefore, primarily depend on the victim's view as to whether there was a racial motivation. In most cases of burglary and damage to property, there were few clues as to whether there might have been a racial motivation: for example, the ethnic group of the offender was usually unknown. The analysis therefore concentrated on assaults. Over a 16–18-month period, there were ten cases among the 4,833 people asked these questions of interracial assaults where a racial motive or racial background was specifically mentioned; there were a further twenty-eight unprovoked interracial assaults with no stated motive, many of which were probably motivated by racial hostility, and eighteen other incidents involving interracial assault (Brown 1984: 260, table 134). Even on the most restrictive definition (counting only the ten assaults where the motive was plainly racist), the survey showed an incidence of racial attacks around ten times that revealed by the statistics derived from police records and published in the 1981 Home Office report.

The PSI survey also tapped views of the ethnic minorities on racial attacks. Among both Afro-Caribbeans and south Asians, the balance of opinion was clearly that racist attacks and insults had got worse over the previous five years. A majority of Afro-Caribbeans, and a substantial minority of south Asians, believed they could not rely on the police to protect them (Brown 1984: 261–2, tables 135–6).

In the 1988 BCS, 24 per cent of offences reported by south Asians, and 15 per cent of those reported by Afro-Caribbeans, were racially motivated in the respondent's view. Types of incident most often seen as racially motivated were vandalism, physical and sexual assaults, and threats (Mayhew *et al.* 1989: 47–8).

Local surveys have adopted various definitions, but have generally been more inclusive, and have tried to cover low-level harassment as well as criminal offences. They tend to suggest that racial harassment, on a broad definition, is a problem affecting a high proportion of south Asians and Afro-Caribbeans. For example, a survey in the London borough of Newham in 1986 suggested that one in four of Newham's black residents had experienced some form of racial harassment in the previous twelve months (London Borough of Newham 1987). A survey carried out in Plaistow, east London, in 1989 found that between one in five and one in six Afro-Caribbean and Asian men and women suffered a racial incident in an eighteenth-month period; about one in twelve of white people said they had experienced a racial incident (Saulsbury and Bowling 1991). These incidents covered a wide range of seriousness; some were one-off events, while others were part of a pattern. 'Some of those interviewed mentioned the effect that persistent door-knocking, egg-throwing, damage to property, verbal abuse, threats and intimidation had on victims, even though the events may not look serious as individual "incidents"' (Saulsbury and Bowling 1991: 118). A much higher level of racial victimization was found in a study of an east London local authority housing estate where there is a history or racial abuse (Sampson and Phillips 1992). Over a period of six months, there was an average of four and a half attacks against each of thirty Bengali families, although seven families were not attacked, while six families were attacked twelve or more times. A sequence of incidents recorded for one family was: stones thrown, chased; threatened and prevented from entering flat; punched and verbal abuse; attempted robbery; chased by gang of youths; stones thrown, chased; common assault.

The problems of definition and of evidence in this field are severe, and no ready solutions are in sight. However, from available evidence it is likely that racially motivated crimes form an important although fairly small proportion of offences committed against members of ethnic minority groups. In addition, racial harassment (a pattern of criminal and non-criminal attacks, threats, and insults) probably affects a substantial proportion (but well under half) of the ethnic minority population, but a much higher proportion in certain areas.

CONCLUSION

Returning to the broad perspective established at the beginning of this chapter, the process of gaining acceptance for a single, universal standard of law applicable equally to all ethnic groups seems in some ways to be well advanced. Ethnic group is by no means the most important characteristic influencing rates of offending or victimization, or the way people interact with the police, the probation service, or the courts. Sex and age are far more important predictors, and social class is also probably more important. Although Afro-Caribbeans are considerably more hostile to the police than white people or Asians, the contrast between age groups is much starker. The ethnic minorities do not reject the criminal justice system or deny its legitimacy. As victims of crime, or as bystanders, they are just as likely as white people to report matters to the police.

On the other hand, it cannot be claimed that ethnic minorities are treated equally with white people at each stage of the criminal process. In the past, claims of unequal treatment have tended to be exaggerated, and hence to lose credibility. The rate of imprisonment of black (Afro-Caribbean and African) people is many times higher than for white people, but the evidence suggests that in part this reflects a large difference in rates of offending. In smaller part, it reflects discrimination at various stages of criminal process. That discrimination has most clearly been demonstrated in sentencing by the courts.

In the economic sphere, there is at least as much discrimination against south Asian as against black people. By contrast, the criminal justice process discriminates against black people, but not against south Asians. In all probability, actual rates of offending are no higher among south Asians than among white people, but considerably higher among black people.

So far there is little evidence from the tradition of empirical social science that helps to explain why discrimination in the field of criminal justice should be directed against black and not south Asian people, or why the rate of offending should be considerably higher among black people than among the white majority and other minority groups. That is because the facts have not generally been acknowledged, and the theoretical problems that they raise have not been considered legitimate. At present the best that can be done is to suggest possible explanations that might be explored by future research.

It seems likely that the two main findings are linked: that is, discrimination against black minorities interacts with high rates of offending by those same groups. It was suggested towards the beginning of this chapter that crime arises from a sequence of interactions, and that in certain sequences racial hostility on one side and antagonism to authority on the other become mutually reinforcing. Within this sequence of interactions, actual rates of offending among black people begin to rise, which in turn causes an increase in racial hostility and discrimination. It can well be imagined that the interaction between racial stereotypes, discrimination, antagonism to authority, and actual rates of offending among black people produces a cycle of deviance amplification. These effects would be magnified by the large-scale conflicts between black people and the police that have become so salient since the late 1970s and have acquired intense significance for young black people (Small 1983).

Despite the claims that some have made, researchers have not demonstrated that there is a steady cumulation of discrimination through each stage of the criminal justice process. However, a more relevant perspective would be the life cycle of the individual. For the young black male, there may be a cumulation of interactions which greatly increase the likelihood of entanglement with the criminal justice process and subsequent criminality.

It will also be important to consider broader causes of crime. Black people tend to live in areas of social stress, where crime rates among all ethnic groups are high; they have a much higher rate of unemployment overall than white people, and a lower standard of living, and a higher proportion of them are in poverty (Jones 1993). However, certain other racial minority groups—south Asian Muslims, in particular—are more disadvantaged in these respects than black people, yet have much lower crime rates. It would be fruitful to focus in future research on this striking difference.

It would be wrong to assume that these contrasts are a permanent feature of the social scene. Concern about crime among black people did not appear until the mid-1970s, although it is difficult to say whether there was an actual increase in the black crime rate around that time. Recent research (Jones 1993) has shown some improvement in the conditions of life of black people in Britain over the ten years up to 1990. There is currently a striking increase in the number of black people going into higher education. Along with such changes, it is entirely possible that the proportion of young black people who are criminalized will decrease. It is also, unfortunately, possible that the crime rate will rise among south Asian Muslims who arrived in Britain more recently than migrants from the West Indies, and who currently suffer greater social and economic disadvantages.

Nevertheless, the difference in rate of imprisonment between black and south Asian people is so striking that it can hardly be explained by differences in economic hardship or in the timing of the migration. What the difference may possibly indicate is that the outgoing and integrative strategy initially adopted by migrants from the Caribbean was met by rejection leading to conflict, which the more separatist and inward-looking strategy of south Asians tended to avoid. Of course, these broad generalizations greatly oversimplify the great range of adaptations made by different groups over more than one generation, but they may contain a kernel of truth.

As well as reviewing the treatment of ethnic minorities as offenders and suspects, this chapter has also considered their experience as victims of crime. They are found to be at higher risk of crime victimization than white people. In some areas especially, they are likely to be subject to repeated racist attack and harassment. The most important improvement in the service provided by criminal justice agencies to ethnic minorities would be better protection from attacks and harassment that are racially motivated and which therefore threaten the ethnic minorities' right to exist and their identity as British citizens.

A review of the policies and practices of criminal justice institutions shows that there is much more that they could do to ensure that racial minorities are treated fairly and given a service corresponding to their needs. Racial prejudice is widespread among the police, and probably also among other practitioners within the criminal justice system. It is clear that prejudice is not translated directly into behaviour, but it would be implausible to suggest that it has no influence. Racial stereotyping has been shown to be common in social inquiry reports prepared by probation officers, although the main cause of disadvantage to black people is the failure to prepare a report at all. The Home Office has become increasingly conscious of the substantial race relations problems in prisons, and a major study funded by the Home Office demonstrated that in the late 1980s some policies and practices in prisons were discriminatory (Genders and Player 1989).

With the exception of barristers, ethnic minorities are severely under-represented among practitioners within every part of the criminal justice system. Increasing the number of people from ethnic minorities working within the system is desirable in itself, but is not the key to securing equal treatment for ethnic minorities. If it is to be achieved at all, equal treatment has to be delivered by the majority of police officers, probation officers, magistrates, and judges who will be white even when the ethnic minorities are proportionately represented.

Selected Further Reading

E. Genders and E. Player, *Race Relations in Prisons*. Oxford: Clarendon Press, 1989.

R. Hood, *Race and Sentencing*. Oxford: Clarendon Press, 1992.

S. F. Landau and G. Nathan, 'Selecting Delinquents for Cautioning in the London Metropolitan Area', *British Journal of Criminology*, 1983, 23/2: 128–49.

R. Reiner, 'Race Crime and Justice: Models of Interpretation', in L. Gelsthorpe and W. McWilliam, eds., *Minority Ethnic Groups and the Criminal Justice System*. Cambridge: Cambridge University Press, 1993.

W. Skogan, *The Police and Public in England and Wales: A British Crime Survey Report*, Home Office Research Study no. 117. London: HMSO, 1990.

D. J. Smith and J. Gray, *Police and People in London: The PSI Report*. Aldershot: Gower, 1985.

M. A. Walker, 'Interpreting Race and Crime Statistics', *Journal of the Royal Statistical Society*, 1987, A150, Part 1: 39–56.

W. Wilbanks, *The Myth of a Racist Criminal Justice System*. California: Brooks/Cole, 1987.

REFERENCES

Bayley, D., and Mendelsohn, H. (1968), *Minorities and the Police*. New York: Free Press.

Benyon, J. (1986), 'Spiral of Decline: Race and Policing', in Z. Layton-Henry and P. B. Rich, eds., *Race, Government and Politics in Britain*. London: Macmillan.

Bethnal Green and Stepney Trades Council (1978), *Blood on the Streets*. London: Bethnal Green and Stepney Trades Council.

Black, D., and Reiss, A. (1967), *Studies of Crime and Law Enforcement in Major Metropolitan Areas*. Washington, DC: US Government Printing Office.

Blom-Cooper, L., and Drabble, R. (1982), 'Police Perception of Crime: Brixton and the Operational Response', *British Journal of Criminology*, 22: 184–7.

Bowling, B. (1993), 'Racist Harassment and the Process of Victimization: Conceptual and Methodological Implications for the Local Crime Survey', in J. Lowman and B. D. MacLean, eds., *Realist Criminology: Crime and Policing in the 1990s*, Vancouver: Collective Press.

Brogden, A. (1981), '"Sus" is Dead: But What About "Sas"?', *New Community*, 9/1: 44–52.

BROWN, C. (1984), *Black and White Britain: The Third PSI Survey*. London: Heinemann.

BROWN, C., and GAY, P. (1986), *Racial Discrimination: 17 Years After the Act*. London: Policy Studies Institute.

BROWN, I., and HULLIN, R. (1992), 'A Study of Sentencing in the Leeds Magistrates' Courts: The Treatment of Ethnic Minority and White Offenders', *British Journal of Criminology*, 32/1: 41–53.

CAIN, M. (1973), *Society and the Policeman's Role*. London: Routledge.

CENTRAL COUNCIL OF PROBATION COMMITTEES (1983), *Probation: A Multi-Racial Approach*, London: CCPS.

COMMISSION FOR RACIAL EQUALITY (1985), *Review of the Race Relations Act 1976: Proposals for Change*. London: CRE.

—— (1991), *Review of the Race Relations Act*. London: CRE.

—— (1992), *Cautions* v. *Prosecutions: Ethnic Monitoring of Juveniles by Seven Police Forces*. London: CRE.

CROW, I., and COVE, J. (1984), 'Ethnic Minorities and the Courts', *Criminal Law Review*: 413–17.

DANIEL, W. W. (1968), *Racial Discrimination in England*. Harmondsworth: Penguin.

DEWBERRY, C. (1993), *A Further Analysis of the Relative Pass Rates of White and Ethnic Minority Students Examined for the 1991–92 Vocational Course for Intending Practitioners*. London: Birkbeck College.

EQUAL OPPORTUNITIES REVIEW (1987), *Law Reports 15* (September–October): 36–7.

FARRINGTON, D. P., and BENNETT, T. (1981), 'Police Cautioning of Juveniles in London', *British Journal of Criminology*, 21: 123–35.

FITZGERALD, M. (1989), 'Legal Approaches to Racial harassment in Council Housing: The Case for Reassessment;, *New Community*, 16/1: 93–105.

FYFE, J. (1981), 'Who Shoots? A Look at Officer Race and Police Shooting', *Journal of Police Science and Administration*, 9/41: 367–82.

GASKELL, G. (1986), 'Black Youth and the Police', *Policing*, 2/1: 26–34.

GASKELL, G., and SMITH, P. (1985), 'Young Blacks' Hostility to the Police: An Investigation into its Causes', *New Community*, 12/1: 66–74.

GENDERS, E., and PLAYER, E. (1989), *Race Relations in Prisons*. Oxford: Clarendon Press.

GENN, H. (1988), 'Multiple Victimization', in M. Maguire and J. Pointing, eds., *Victims of Crime: A New Deal?*, 90–100. Milton Keynes: Open University Press.

GILROY, P. (1987), *There Ain't No Black in the Union Jack: The Cultural Politics of Race and Nation*. London: Hutchinson.

GRAEF, R. (1989), *Talking Blues*. London: Collins Harvill.

HALL, S., CRITCHER, C., CLARKE, J., JEFFERSON, T., and ROBERTS, B. (1978), *Policing the Crisis*. London: Macmillan.

HALPERN, D. (1993), *Law Students' Survey: Second Year*. London: Policy Studies Institute.

HOLDAWAY, S. (1983), *Inside the British Police*. Oxford: Blackwell.

—— (1991*a*), *Recruiting a Multiracial Police Force*. London: HMSO.

—— (1991*b*), 'Race Relations and Police Recritment', *British Journal of Criminology*, 31/4: 365–82.

HOME OFFICE (1981*a*), *Prison Department Circular Instruction 28/1981*. London: Home Office.

—— (1981*b*), *Racial Attacks: Report of a Home Office Study*. London: Home Office.

—— (1982), *Statistical Bulletin*, 20/82. London: Home Office.

—— (1983), *Prison Department Circular Instruction 56/1983*. London: Home Office.

—— (1986*a*), *Prison Department Circular Instruction 32/1986*.

—— (1986*b*), *The National Conference of Police Recruiting Officers, 14–15 October, Record of Proceedings*. London: Home Office.

—— (1986*c*), *National Conference of Recruiting Officers, Letter from Mr Douglas Hogg, MP, Parliamentary Secretary of State at the Home Office, to All Chief Constables*. London: Home Office.

—— (1988), *Probation Service Policies on Race*, Home Office Circular No. 75/88.

—— (1989*a*), *Crime Statistics for the Metropolitan Police District by Ethnic Group, 1987: Victims, Suspects and Those Arrested, Home Office Statistical Bulletin*5/89. London: Home Office.

—— (1989*b*), *The Ethnic Group of Those Proceeded Against or Sentenced by the Courts in the Metropolitan Police District in 1984 and 1985, Home Office Statistical Bulletin* 6/89. London: Home Office.

—— (1989*c*), *The Response to Racial Attacks and Harassment: Guidance for the Statutory Agencies. Report of the Inter-Departmental Racial Attacks Group*. London: Home Office.

—(1989*d*), *Equal Opportunities Policies in the Police Service*, Home Office Circular no. 87/1989. London: Home Office.

—— (1990), *Ethnic Minority Recruitment into the Police Service*, Home Office Circular no. 33/1990. London: Home Office.

—— (1991), *The Response to Racial Attacks: Sustaining the Momentum. The Second Report of the Inter-Departmental Racial Attacks Group*. London: Home Office.

—— (1992), *Race and the Criminal Justice System: A Home Office Publication under Section 95 of the Criminal Justice Act 1991*. London: Home Office.

HOOD, R. (1992), *Race and Sentencing*. Oxford: Clarendon Press.

HOUSE OF COMMONS HOME AFFAIRS COMMITTEE (1986), *Racial Attacks and Harassment*, Session 1985–86, HC 409. London: HMSO.

HOUSE OF COMMONS SELECT COMMITTEE ON RACE RELATIONS AND IMMIGRATION (1972), *Police/Immigrant Relations*, HC 71. London: HMSO.

—— (1976), *The West Indian Community*, HC 180. London: HMSO.

Hudson, B. (1989), 'Discrimination and Disparity: The Influence of Race on Sentencing', *New Community*, 16/1: 23–34.

—— (1993), 'Penal Policy and Racial Justice', in L. Gelsthorpe and W. McWilliam, eds., *Minority Ethnic Groups and the Criminal Justice System*. Cambridge: Cambridge University Institute of Criminology.

JEFFERSON, T. (1988), 'Race, Crime and Policing: Empirical, Theoretical and Methodological Issues', *International Journal of the Sociology of Law*, 16: 521–39.

—— (1993), 'The Racism of Criminalization: Policing and the Reproduction of the Criminal Other', in L. Gelsthorpe, and W. McWilliam, eds., *Minority Ethnic Groups and the Criminal Justice System*. Cambridge: Cambridge University Institute of Criminology.

JEFFERSON, T., and WALKER, M. A. (1992), 'Ethnic Minorities in the Criminal Justice System', *Criminal Law Review*: 83–95.

—— (1993), 'Attitudes to the Police of the Ethnic Minorities in a Provincial City', *British Journal of Criminology*, 33/2: 251–66.

JEFFERSON, T., WALKER, M., and SENEVIRANTNE, M. (1992), 'Ethnic Minorities, Crime and Criminal Justice: A Study in a Provincial City', in D. Downes, ed., *Unravelling Criminal Justice*. London: Macmillan.

JONES, T. (1993), *Britain's Ethnic Minorities*. London: Policy Studies Institute.

JONES, T., MACLEAN, B., and YOUNG, J. (1986), *The Islington Crime Survey: Crime, Victimization and Policing in Inner-City London*. Aldershot: Gower.

KING, M., and ISRAEL, M. (1989), 'The Pursuit of Excellence, or How Solicitors Maintain Racial Inequality', *New Community*, 16/1: 107–20.

KING, M., and MAY, C. (1985), *Black Magistrates*. London: Cobden Trust.

KINSEY, R. (1985), *Final Report of the Merseyside Crime and Police Surveys*. Liverpool: Merseyside County Council.

LAMBERT, J. (1970), *Crime, Police, and Race Relations*. Oxford: Oxford University Press.

LANDAU, S. (1981), 'Juveniles and the Police', *British Journal of Criminology*, 21/1: 27–46.

LANDAU, S. F., and NATHAN, G. (1983), 'Selecting Delinquents for Cautioning in the London Metropolitan Area', *British Journal of Criminology*, 23/2: 128–49.

LAW SOCIETY (1992), *Annual Statistical Report*. London: Law Society.

LEA, J., and YOUNG, J. (1982), 'The Riots in Britain 1981: Urban Violence and Political Marginalisation', in D. Cowell, T. Jones, and J. Young, eds., *Policing the Riots*, 5–20. London: Junction Books.

LONDON BOROUGH OF NEWHAM (1987), *Report of a Survey of Crime and Racial Harassment in Newham*. London: L. B. Newham.

LORD CHANCELLOR'S DEPARTMENT (1988), *Report of a Survey of the Ethnic Composition of the Magistracy*. London: Lord Chancellor's Department.

MCCONVILLE, M., and BALDWIN, J. (1982), 'The Influence of Race on Sentencing in England', *Criminal Law Review*: 652–8.

MCCRUDDEN, C., SMITH, D. J., and BROWN, C. (1991), *Racial Justice at Work: The Enforcement of the 1976 Race Relations Act in Employment*. London: Policy Studies Institute.

MAIR, G. (1986), 'Ethnic Minorities, Probation, and the Magistrates' Courts', *British Journal of Criminology*, 26/2: 147–55.

MAVUNGA, P. K. (1993), 'Probation: A Basically Racist Service', in L. Gelsthorpe and W. McWilliam, eds., *Minority Ethnic Groups and the Criminal Justice System*. Cambridge: Cambridge University Institute of Criminology.

MAWBY, R. I., MCCULLOCH, J. W., and BATTA, I. D. (1979), 'Crime among Asian Juveniles in Bradford', *International Journal of the Sociology of Law*, 7: 297–306.

MAYHEW, P., ELLIOTT, D., and DOWDS, L. (1989), *The 1988 British Crime Survey*, Home Office Research Study no. 111. London: HMSO.

MOXON, D. (1988), *Sentencing Practice in the Crown Court*, Home Office Research Study no. 103. London: HMSO.

PINDER, R. (1984), *Probation Work in a Multi-Racial Society: A Research Report*. Leeds: University of Leeds Applied Anthropology Group.

POPPER, K. R. (1959), *The Logic of Scientific Discovery*. London: Hutchinson.

—— 1963), *Conjectures and Refutations: The Growth of Scientific Knowledge*. London: Routledge and Kegan Paul.

REINER, R. (1978), *The Blue-Coated Worker*. Cambridge: Cambridge University Press.

—— (1991), *Chief Constables*. Oxford: Oxford University Press.

—— (1993), 'Race, Crime and Justice: Models of Interpretation', in L. Gelsthorpe and W. McWilliam, eds., *Minority Ethnic Groups and the Criminal Justice System*. Cambridge: Cambridge University Institute of Criminology.

REISS, A. (1971), *The Police and the Public*. New Haven: Yale University Press.

SAMPSON, A., and PHILLIPS, C. (1992), *Multiple Victimisation: Racial Attacks on an East London Estate*, Police Research Group, Crime Prevention Unit Series, Paper no. 36. London: Home Office.

SAULSBURY, W., and BOWLING, B. (1991), *The Multi-Agency Approach in Practice: The North Plaistow Racial Harassment Project*, Research and Planning Unit Paper no. 64. London: Home Office.

SCARMAN, LORD (1981), *The Brixton Disorders 10–12 April 1981: Report of an Inquiry by the Rt Hon. the Lord Scarman, OBE*, Cmnd 8427. London: HMSO.

SHAH, R., and PEASE, K. (1992), 'Crime, Race and Reporting to the Police', *Howard Journal*, 31/3: 192–9.

SHERMAN, L. W. (1983), 'After the Riots: Police and Minorities in the United States, 1970–1980', in N. Glazer and K. Young, eds., *Ethnic Pluralism and Public Policy*. Lexington: Heath; London: Heinemann.

SILVERMAN, J. (1986), *The Handsworth/Lozells Riots, 9, 10, 11 September 1985: Report of an Inquiry by Mr Julius Silverman*. Birmingham: Birmingham City Council.

SKOGAN, W. (1990), *The Police and Public in England and Wales: A British Crime Survey Report*, Home Office Research Study no. 117. London: HMSO.

SKOLNICK, J. (1966), *Justice Without Trial*. New York: Wiley.

SMALL, S. (1983), *Police and People in London, II: A Group of Young Black People*. London: Policy Studies Institute.

SMITH, D. J. (1977), *Racial Disadvantage in Britain*. Harmondsworth: Penguin.

—— (1983*a*), *Police and People in London, I: A Survey of Londoners*. London: Policy Studies Institute.

—— (1983*b*), *Police and People in London, III: A Survey of Police Officers*. London: Policy Studies Institute.

—— (1991), 'The Origins of Black Hostility to the Police', *Policing and Society*, 2: 1–15.

SMITH, D. J., and GRAY, J. (1983), *Police and People in London, IV: The Police in Action*. London: Policy Studies Institute.

SOLOMOS, J. (1989), *Race and Racism in Contemporary Britain*. London: Macmillan.

STEVENS, P., and WILLIS, C. (1979), *Race, Crime and Arrests*, Home Office Research Study no. 58. London: HMSO.

Tonry, M. (forthcoming), 'Racial Disproportion in US Prisons', *British Journal of Criminology*,

Tournier, P., and Robert, P. (1991) *Étrangers et Délinquances: Les Chiffres du Débat*, Paris: Harmattan.

Tuck, M., and Southgate, P. (1981), *Ethnic Minorities, Crime and Policing: A Survey of the Experiences of West Indians and Whites*, Home Office Research Study no. 70. London: HMSO.

Voakes, R., and Fowler, Q. (1989), *Sentencing, Race and Social Inquiry Reports.* Bradford: West Yorkshire Probation Service.

Walker, M. A. (1987), 'Interpreting Race and Crime Statistics', *Journal of the Royal Statistical Society*, A 150, Part 1: 39–56.

—— (1988), 'The Court Disposal of Young Males, by Race, in London in 1983', *British Journal of Criminology*, 28/4: 441–59.

—— (1989), 'The Court Disposal and Remands of White, Afro-Caribbean, and Asian Men (London, 1983)', *British Journal of Criminology*, 29/4: 353–67.

—— (1992), 'Arrest Rates and Ethnic Minorities: A Study in a Provincial City', *Journal of the Royal Statistical Society*, A 155, Part 2: 259–72.

Walmsley, R., Howard, L., and White, S. (1992), *The National Prison Survey 1991: Main Findings*, Home Office Research Study no. 128. London: HMSO.

Waters, R. (1988), 'Race and the Criminal Justice Process: Two Empirical Studies on Social Inquiry Reports and Ethnic Minority Defendants', *British Journal of Criminology*, 28/1: 82–94.

Weber, M. (1954), *Max Weber on Law in Economy and Society*, ed. M. Rheinstein. Cambridge, Mass.: Harvard University Press.

West Midlands County Council (1986), *A Different Reality: An Account of Black People's Experiences and their Grievances before and after the Handsworth Rebellion of September 1985*. Birmingham: West Midlands County Council.

Westley, W. (1970), *Violence and the Police*. Cambridge, Mass.: MIT Press.

Whitehouse, P. (1983), 'Race, Bias and Social Enquiry Reports', *Probation Journal*, 30/2: 43–9.

Wilbanks, W. (1987), *The Myth of a Racist Criminal Justice System*. Monterey, Ca: Brooks/Cole.

Willis, C. F. (1983), *The Use, Effectiveness and Impact of Police Stop and Search Powers*, Home Office Research and Planning Unit Paper no. 15. London: Home Office.

Wilson, D., Holdaway, S., and Spencer, C. (1984), 'Black Police in the United Kingdom', *Policing*, 1/1: 20–30.

23

Mentally Disordered Offenders

JILL PEAY

Current policy is disarmingly straightforward: 'Mentally disordered offenders should, wherever appropriate, receive care and treatment from health and personal social services rather than in custodial care' (Reed Report 1991: Community Group para. 2.1). It mirrors a humanitarian view widely held since the introduction of the Mental Health Act 1959 and underlined by the Butler Report; namely that 'In making a hospital order the court is placing the patient in the hands of the doctors, forego-ing [*sic*] any question of punishment and relinquishing from then onwards its own controls over them' (Butler Report 1975: para. 14.8). Where mentally disordered people offend, punishment and protection are not overriding criteria, nor even necessarily relevant ones. Diversion and treatment are paramount. Or are they? A contrary view, reflecting the darker side of public conceptions of the mentally disordered offender, was captured by Rubin (1972: 398): 'certain mental disorders [are] characterized by some kind of confused, bizarre, agitated, threatening, frightened, panicked, paranoid or impulsive behaviour. That and the view that impulse (i.e. ideation) and action are interchangeable support the belief that all mental disorder must of necessity lead to inappropriate, anti-social or dangerous actions.' This view finds expression in the arrangements for discretionary life sentences for offenders of an 'unstable' character (*R.* v. *Hodgson* (1967) 52 Cr App R 113) who are in a 'mental state which makes them dangerous to the life or limb of members of the public' (*R.* v. *Wilkinson* (1983) 5 Cr App R (S) 105 at 109). It emerges also in the *Report on Mentally Disturbed Offenders in the Prison System*, where it was noted, in the context of transferring prisoners to hospital for treatment, that 'the response to the needs of individual mentally disturbed offenders has to take account of the legitimate expectation of the public that government agencies will take appropriate measures for its protection' (Home Office/DHSS 1987: para. 3.6). It is also evident in the new arrangements under the Criminal Justice Act 1991; although proportionality in sentencing is the leading principle, with sentences being 'calculated on the basis of what the person deserves for the offence committed, and not lengthened for any supposed deterrent or rehabilitative reasons' (Ashworth 1992: 229), there is a limited—but important—exception for violent and sexual offences where it is 'necessary to protect the public from serious harm' (s. 2(2)(b)). Indeed, a further 'polluting' late amendment in the House of Lords arguably has the potential to exclude mentally disordered offenders from being tied into the proportionality principle central to Part I of the Act (see s. 28(4)(a)).

It is paradoxical that, on the one hand, calls for diverting the mentally disordered offender from the damaging effects of the criminal justice system grow louder, demanding earlier and ever earlier diversion; yet, on the other hand, concerns remain about some discharged mental patients and the likelihood of their reoffending. What is more curious is that such concerns persist despite repeated demonstrations that for mentally disordered offenders 're-offending rates are in fact no higher than for any other class of offender' (Murray 1989: iii).

Much of the confusion arises because of the tensions inherent across both the continuum of ordered–disordered behaviour and that of law-abiding–law-breaking behaviour. Notions of care/treatment are seen as peculiarly appropriate for the seriously disordered, provided such condition does not also arise in conjunction with offending of a worrying nature. Similarly, notions of protection/punishment are traditionally confined to serious offenders, again assuming an absence of obvious disorder. Yet these tensions are confounded where it is argued (or denied) that disorder and offending exist side-by-side in one individual, or, more confusingly still, interact. The questions posed by the handling of those mentally disordered offenders isolated as meriting 'special' provision, whichever limb of the bifurcated policy (special care or special control) is adopted, cannot be answered readily. Moreover, 'special' provision arguably manifests itself in special discrimination (Campbell and Heginbotham 1991).

The conflict is essentially one between welfarism and legalism, with legalism prevailing at the serious offending end and welfarism at the seriously disordered end. Gostin (1986: v) distinguishes the two approaches thus: legalism occurs 'where the law is used to wrap the patient in a network of substantive and procedural protections against unjustified loss of liberty and compulsory treatment', whereas welfarism occurs where 'legal safeguards are replaced with professional discretion which is seen as allowing speedy access to treatment and care, unencumbered by a panoply of bureaucracy and procedures'. Gostin argues that the Mental Health Act 1983, which encompasses both the mentally disordered non-offender and the mentally disordered offender, achieves a balance between the two principles, retaining welfarism as established by the 1959 Act, but enhancing safeguards for patients' rights in such areas as treatment without consent (the Act established the Mental Health Act Commission) and continued detention of offender patients (Mental Health Review Tribunals—MHRTs—acquired the power to discharge restricted patients). This balance is arguably least satisfactory when resolving the dilemmas posed by mentally disordered offenders. Both pre-trial diversion and post-treatment discharge highlight the difficulties. Most notably, the High Court ruling in *R.* v. *Merseyside Mental Health Review Tribunal ex p. K* [1990] 1 All ER 694, as upheld by the Court of Appeal, stated that K, a restricted patient, was not entitled to an absolute discharge, even though there was no evidence of current mental disorder, since there was a liability to relapse. This philosophy of 'once ill, always ill' is strikingly at odds with a criminal justice approach that strives to deal with offenders on the basis of what they have done, rather than who they are. This, in turn, impels the criminal justice system to focus on the philosophy of a just measure of punishment, in the recognition that offending behaviour may be no more than an adapted response to an environment which may or may not change, independent of any individual measure of pain. In stark contrast, mental health professionals are arguably more interested in the enduring features of individuals, placing the individual at the centre of the problem and thereby providing the justification for treatment.

It is evident that a chapter devoted to 'mentally disordered offenders' cannot focus discussion on the needs of some single, easily identifiable group. This chapter will do little more than chart a path through muddied waters, muddying them further as it passes. Although textbook authors and editors may wish to confine the mentally disordered to a single chapter and the law may, in isolated places, achieve a coherent strategy, neither confinement nor coherence is evident where an overview is attempted. The mentally disordered are not a class and the law, practitioners, policy-makers, and the caring professions will mix and match philosophies in response to the problems created by *individual* offender-patients. Accordingly, notions of justice, treatment, and, indeed, the very existence of a group of 'disordered offenders' will harry this chapter.

The chapter is divided into nine sections. The first examines the concept of mentally disordered offenders: do such offenders constitute an isolated category meriting special provision, or do the issues this 'group' raise have wider implications for the study of criminology? The second addresses problems of definition: what do the various stages of the criminal justice process include or exclude from the gamut of definitions applying to the 'mentally disordered offender'? Third, are mentally disordered offenders a minority group? What is their incidence and to what extent are such offenders intertwined with conventional custodial populations? Fourth, why are such offenders to be found in custodial care, given the long-standing policy of diversion? The fifth section examines attempts to place the offender-patient in non-penal settings, addressing issues of diversion and transfer. Section six considers mental disorder as a defence, with discussion of recent limited statutory changes stemming from issues of due process and dissatisfaction with mandatory disposals. The seventh section covers the fundamental justification for separate provision—treatment—with an examination of a key problematic group, namely psychopathic offenders, who straddle the ordered–disordered offending continuum. The eighth section tackles hidden agendas—bifurcation; detention for protective purposes in the name of treatment; due process at discharge/release—and the ninth formulates some conclusions.

MENTAL DISORDER AND OFFENDERS: A CASE FOR SPECIAL PROVISION?

Confronting the topic of 'mentally disordered offenders' demands painful examination of a number of key areas. First, and perhaps not surprisingly, the list of contributors to this tome includes five women (and twenty-one men). The numerical imbalance is striking, but the distribution of topics is perhaps more telling. Juvenile justice, gender, victims, and the mentally disordered are the women's lot. Soft topics? Marginal topics? Or topics which are superficially self-contained? Topics which perhaps have a common thread of being 'inconvenient' for theories of criminology? Or topics where discriminatory treatment of offenders can be justified? Or just Cinderella areas?

It might, of course, be argued that such an allocation stems from the very nature of 'criminology'. Imbued with values of the male, adult, mentally healthy, and non-victimized, criminology perceives the other as marginal. Such views have been advanced elsewhere (Young 1991). It is my contention in this chapter that the lessons to be learnt from how we deal conceptually, practically and in principle with those deemed 'mentally disordered offenders' have as much to say about topics regarded as central to, or ranging across, the scope of criminology as they have to say about 'marginal' groups.

To argue for the existence of a discrete group of mentally disordered offenders presupposes a category of mentally ordered offenders. This does not deny the mental element in all crimes, but merely assumes some to be rational and some unacceptable. As Lord Devlin noted with reference to the insanity defence,

> It is reason which makes a man responsible to the law, reason and reason alone. It is reason which gives him sovereignty over animate and inanimate things. It is what distinguishes him from the animals, which emotional disorder does not; it is what makes him man; it is what makes him subject to the law. So it is fitting that nothing other than a defect of reason should give complete absolution (Smith and Hogan 1988: 200)

But such a clear-cut division is problematic. In the area of so-called 'normal offending', defences are frequently advanced or mitigations constructed which draw on elements of 'diminished responsibility', 'unthinking' behaviour, or merely a response to extreme social stress. Yet few of these offenders would wish for the special treatment which may follow a finding of 'defect of reason'. Why not? Is it a recognition of the punishing aspects of such treatment? Or a desire not to be stigmatized along with the helplessly mad? Or merely that some level of disordered thinking should alleviate punishment, if not excuse it altogether?

'Complete absolution' is clearly a legal nicety. Mentally disordered offenders find themselves confined in hospitals, prisons, therapeutic regimes within prisons, and, most notably, within the remand population. The disorders offenders present at court create opportunities at defence and mitigation, but problems thereafter for those into whose care or custody they are sent. Mentally disordered offenders exist in one shape or form across the entire criminal justice system, and 'disorder' may be found to a greater or lesser extent—partly dependent on the incentives for its construction—throughout offending populations.

Accordingly, one theme which runs through this chapter arises out of a plea that the mentally disordered offender be treated as a person first, as an offender second, and as mentally disordered third. Prioritization of one aspect (the mentally disordered element) of an individual's make-up readily leads to neglect of other, perhaps more pertinent, aspects. As the Reed Committee in its interim report (hereafter 'Reed Report') recognized (1991: overview para. 7.ii), mentally disordered people may have other special needs—addressed in a subsequent report (Reed Report 1992)—which are arguably as important in respect of their special status within the criminal justice system. As the 1991 Report details, such categories may include: people from black and ethnic minority groups; women; the elderly; children and adolescents; sex offenders; substance misusers; people with personality (or psychopathic) disorders; people with sensory disabilities; people with brain damage; people with learning disabilities (the new term for mental handicap); and arguably also the homeless. There is no pure form of mentally disordered offender. To assume that there is would be both to mislead and to negate the transparent and frequently reiterated need for flexibility within the mental health and criminal justice agencies. Hence, flexibility is required not only in respect of the movement of people between available resources, but also in the conceptualization of 'mentally disordered offending', for without it, the gap between expectations and provision cannot be bridged.

THE PROBLEM OF DEFINITION

Hoggett (1990: 145), who admirably details the interactions between the mentally disordered offender and the criminal justice system at all of its stages, notes that 'the fact that a person who is alleged to have committed a criminal offence may be mentally disordered can affect the normal process of the law at several points'. These crisis points are sketched below. No attempt is made to replicate the detail of Hoggett's (1990) analysis, but some key themes emerge which reflect how an individual's mental state may affect his or her prosecution, conviction, disposal, treatment, and release.

What is meant by mental disorder is, however, problematic. Definitions of mental disorder act like a concertina, expanding and contracting in order to accommodate different client groups with little or no coherent theme. Their mismatch frequently results in anomalies; for example, the presence of a disorder of a particular form may be sufficient for compulsory admission to hospital, but its absence in the same form may be insufficient to bring that period of detention to an end.

In order to illustrate the effects of this concertina, it is necessary to go into the statutory provisions in some detail. Those familiar with, and those who do not wish to become confused by, this legal exposition could skip several paragraphs.

The Mental Health Act 1983 s. 1(2) defines mental disorder as 'mental illness, arrested or incomplete development of mind, psychopathic disorder *and any other disorder or disability of mind*' (emphasis added), and then goes on to provide definitions of severe mental impairment, mental impairment, and psychopathic disorder. The definition of psychopathic disorder in s. 1(2) as 'a persistent disorder or disability of mind (whether or not including significant impairment of intelligence) which results in abnormally aggressive or seriously irresponsible conduct on the part of the person concerned' is peculiarly problematic, neither corresponding with psychiatric definitions of personality disorder nor absolving itself of a tautological association with behaviour likely to be criminalized. Although mental illness constitutes one of the four narrow, but key, classifications, the Act provides no definition of it. However, s. 1(3) does make clear that a person may not be dealt with under the Act as suffering from mental disorder 'by reason only of promiscuity or other immoral conduct, sexual deviancy or dependence on alcohol or drugs'. This last sub-section serves to exclude from treatment under the Mental Health Act many of those deemed mentally disordered by psychiatrists yet who are currently located within prison populations (see Gunn *et al.* 1991*a*).

Broadly, the 1983 Act may be conceived of as establishing two tiers of mental disorder: first, mental illness and severe mental impairment; second, psychopathic disorder and mental impairment. To invoke many of the sections of the 1983 Act in respect of this second tier (e.g. a hospital order under s. 37; transfer from prison to hospital under s. 47) it is necessary to satisfy an additional criterion that medical treatment in hospital be 'likely to alleviate or prevent a deterioration' of the individual's condition. Notably, this treatability requirement does not always have to be satisfied (e.g. MHRTs determining whether or not to discharge a patient under s. 72 only have to 'have regard' to it). In addition to these two tiers, there is the catch-nearly-all phrase 'mental disorder'.

Some alleged offenders may be diverted into hospital, with a civil admission constituting a real alternative to involvement with the criminal justice system. For admission under either s. 2 (for assessment—twenty-eight days' duration) or s. 4 (cases of emergency—seventy-two hours' duration) the presence of *mental disorder* 'of a nature or degree which warrants detention of the patient in hospital' is sufficient. Similarly, s. 136 (mentally disordered persons in a public place—removal to a place of safety) requires the person to appear to a police constable to be suffering from mental disorder and to be in immediate need of care or control. All of these sections are accordingly broadly inclusive. Under s. 3 (admission for treatment—six months' duration) the criteria are somewhat narrower: the patient must be suffering from one of the four categories above *and*, in the case of psychopathic disorder or mental impairment, the treatability criterion must be satisfied.

For a hospital order, a therapeutic post-conviction order, the criteria in respect of the definition of mental disorder are the same as those in s. 3 noted above, but the court must also be of the opinion under s. 37(2)(b), 'having regard to all the circumstances including the nature of the offence and the character and antecedents of the offender, and to other available methods of dealing with him, that the most suitable method of disposing of the case is by means of an order under this section'. This makes medical evidence favouring a therapeutic disposal a necessary prerequisite, but not necessarily a determining factor. The courts may choose to punish or protect in the face of medical evidence, even given the additional option of attaching a restriction order under s. 41 where 'necessary for the protection of the public from serious harm'. Indeed, *R.* v. *Birch* (1989) 90 Cr App R 78 CA makes clear that a restriction order can be made by the courts even where the medical evidence is that the offender is not regarded as dangerous. A hospital order with restrictions attaches limits to psychiatrists' control over the subsequent release of the patient and, with the exception of the MHRT's power to discharge, places all control over the movements of the patient subject to the restriction order with the Home Secretary. Notably, in 1988/9 there were in total only 501 hospital orders under s. 37(1) and 301 restriction orders; the vast bulk of 'disordered' offenders do not receive a therapeutic disposal, even though their sentence may be mitigated, if not absolved, by their mental state (for detailed review see Ashworth and Gostin 1984; Verdun-Jones 1989).

Remand to hospital for treatment under s. 36 requires mental illness or severe mental impairment, while s. 35 remand to hospital for reports and s. 38 interim hospital orders may be satisfied by the broader classifications of mental illness, severe mental impairment, mental impairment, or psychopathic disorder—with no treatability criterion.

For transfer from prison to hospital under s. 47, for persons serving sentences of imprisonment, there must be mental illness, severe mental impairment, mental impairment, or psychopathic disorder (with the latter two satisfying the treatability criterion). But for other prisoners, e.g. remand prisoners, their transfer under s. 48 demands both the first tier classifications of mental illness or severe mental impairment *and* that the prisoner be in 'urgent need' of medical treatment in hospital. Interestingly, the Reed Report (1991: Prison Advisory Group para. 6.6(c)) recommends that s. 48 be amended to widen its scope so as to offer provisions for transfer of remand prisoners similar to those set out in s. 47 for sentenced prisoners. In any event, transfer provisions account for only a tiny number of mentally disordered offenders each year (in 1988, ninety-four restriction directions and twenty-seven without restrictions under s. 47).

Other possible routes into psychiatric care are a finding of 'unfit to plead' (a legal test; see below); or cases where mental disorder provides a defence, for example not guilty by reason of insanity, or a partial defence, for example manslaughter by reason of diminished responsibility. Although not greatly used, both insanity verdicts and findings of 'unfit to plead' heavily feature offenders with diagnoses of schizophrenia, perhaps conforming best with classic lay notions of mental illness. Hence, mentally disordered offenders within the hospital system are a mixed bag.

Within the prison system, the situation may be even more problematic. The Reed Report (1991: Prison Advisory Group para. 2.1) recognizes three groups of disordered offenders: first, those meeting the four narrow classifications under the 1983 Act and needing in-patient treatment; second, those falling within ICD9 criteria (World Health Organization 1978: International Classification of Diseases) but not meeting Mental Health Act criteria or requiring in-patient treatment; and third, those 'who ask for the help of the caring agencies within the prison system'. Quite where alcohol and drug abuse falls is not clear.

Regrettably, therefore, the term 'mentally disordered offender' means many things to many people. The Reed Report glossary (1991: Overview) specifies the mentally disordered offender as 'a mentally disordered person who has broken the law. In identifying broad service needs this term is sometimes loosely used to include mentally disordered people who are alleged to have broken the law.' But even this definition is less helpful than it seems; it would exclude those deemed not guilty by reason of insanity and is unclear as to whether it applies only to the most recently caught and convicted or whether the label constitutes a lifelong attribution.

Finally, the Reed Report (1991: Community Advisory Group para 1.6) recognizes three categories: (1) alleged offenders to be diverted into the health and social services and away from the criminal justice system; (2) mentally disordered offenders discharged or diverted from hospital or prison; and (3) non-offenders in the community who are vulnerable and may need assistance to prevent their offending. The third category would permit intervention for non-offenders predicted as likely to offend.

Clearly this is an area of acute terminological inexactitude. Yet mental disorder is not a once-and-for-all classification; some disorders can come and go, and frequently do so at inconvenient points in an offender's history. Criminal justice agencies must be sufficiently flexible to accommodate such individuals' needs, in much the same way as hospitals should be sufficiently secure to accommodate those whose intermittently violent behaviour makes them unattractive to a wholly open local hospital. To deal with individuals as *either* offenders *or* mentally disordered, or, perhaps worst of all, as mentally disordered offenders, may negate both the right to treatment and the nascent right to a proportional measure of punishment. Heralded by Bottoms and Brownsword (1983: 21), drawing on Dworkin's theory of rights, the right to a proportional measure of punishment would yield a '*prima facie* right to release for the prisoner at the end of his normal term', applying—in the absence of '*vivid* danger'—equally to the alleged 'dangerous offender'. Too often, paternalistic assumptions about the 'mental disorder' element, and protective/predictive ones about the offending element, leave prisoner-patients with more than their 'just' deserts.

In terms of an individual's treatment needs, the facilities available, the desire and reluctance of the caring professions to treat, their ability to enforce treatment and to continue to detain, no one set of rules applies. So there is unlikely to be any one easy solution.

MENTALLY DISORDERED OFFENDERS: A MINORITY GROUP?

An examination of the extent of mental disorder within the prison population (1) details the range of disorders recognized by psychiatrists among an offending population, (2) underlines the irrelevance to many of these offenders of their mental disorder (since it has not resulted in their being subject to special provisions—even though offenders may be assessed as being in need of treatment and thought likely to benefit from it) and (3) re-emphasizes the central point that offenders with mental disorder are not a minority group of only marginal concern to the criminal justice system.

Mental disorder is not confined to the hospital population. In the remand population, the process of referral to prison for psychiatric reports results in an even higher recorded incidence of mental disorder (Dell *et al.* 1991) than in the sentenced population.[1] Recent research (Gunn *et al.* 1991*a*) indicates that 37 per cent of sentenced prisoners were suffering from mental disorder. In absolute terms, this means 13,594 mentally disordered offenders at June 1988. Clearly, this is no marginal group. Equally, the available total of fewer than 2,500 secure beds for patients detained under the Mental Health Act means that the hospital system and the caring services—even taking account of the additional 900 'locked' beds at district level—are not, and cannot be, the starting point for an examination of 'mentally disordered offenders'.

The research by Gunn *et al.* (1991*a*) entailed a survey of *sentenced* prisoners in England using a 5 per cent sample of men serving six months or more: 1,365 adults and 404 young offenders agreed to take part (the survey of women is excluded from the 1991 publication). Of the sample, 37 per cent had psychiatric disorders diagnosed by the psychiatric survey team, with diagnoses reaching far wider than Mental Health Act classifications, to include, for example, drug and alcohol abusers. They found: 23 per cent substance misuse, 10 per cent personality disorder, 6 per cent neurosis, 2 per cent psychosis, 0.8 per cent organic disorders.[2] Treatment needs were also assessed, with 3 per cent judged as requiring transfer to hospital for psychiatric treatment; 5 per cent as requiring treatment in a therapeutic community setting (primarily those with personality disorder, deemed suitable for treatment at places such as Grendon Prison or the Henderson Hospital and/or drug or alcohol rehabilitation centres); and 10 per cent as being in need of further psychiatric assessment or treatment within prison. The authors argued:

[1] Of 242 prisoners formally classified as having committed suicide between 1980 and 1989, 54 per cent were on remand (Fennell 1991: 340). Fennell (1991: 333), citing Dooley (1990), further notes that one-third of all the prisoners who had committed suicide between 1972 and 1987 had a history of mental disturbance and one-quarter had a previous psychiatric in-patient admission.

[2] The figures do not add up since each individual could have up to three conditions diagnosed. Notably, for personality disorder the figure probably represented an underestimate, since it was based solely on an offender's previous history. The survey of women may be found in Gunn *et al.* (1991*b*).

By extrapolation the sentenced prison population includes over 700 men with psychosis and around 1100 who would warrant transfer to hospital for psychiatric treatment. Provision of secure treatment facilities, particularly long term medium secure units, needs to be improved. Services for people with personality, sexual and substance misuse disorders should be developed both in prisons and the health service. (Gunn *et al.* 1991*a*: 338)

Are these figures shocking in absolute terms? Arguably, yes. But perhaps more worryingly, the problem is in no sense new or surprising. The survey reported in 1991 was, in effect, a rerun of a survey of the south-east prison population conducted in 1972 (Gunn *et al.* 1978). This earlier study found 31 per cent with psychiatric disorders, of whom 2 per cent were psychotic. This high level of disorder (in its broadest sense) but 'low' level of psychosis (the latter comparable with that in the community) is a common finding of such surveys.[3]

WHY ARE MENTALLY DISORDERED OFFENDERS IN PRISON?

It is important to remember that the level of mental disorder in the general population, using the equivalent diagnostic criteria, has been estimated at between 15 and 17 per cent (Gunn 1992, citing studies by GPs in London area; Office of Population, Censuses and Surveys 1986)—making the level of identifiable disorder within the sentenced prison population (Gunn *et al.* 1991*a*) only just over twice the level that would be expected by chance. Although the majority of those with psychosis in prison are chronic cases, prison may exacerbate underlying psychiatric conditions or precipitate breakdown in vulnerable individuals. Or, as Gunn (1992) put it, 'People are sent to prison to damage them.' Certainly, twelve of the thirty-seven inmates recommended for hospital treatment for mental illness or organic disorder (Gunn *et al.* 1991) had developed their illness *after* imprisonment, underlining the need for some transfer mechanism even if all those with disorders classifiable under the Mental Health Act were correctly identified at the point of sentence. But equally, considering the number and variety of hurdles that mentally disordered offenders have to jump in order *not* to be diverted from the prison population, an incidence of 37 per cent suggests a number of

[3] Prins (1990: 249), quoting the NACRO 1987 figures, noted that during the year ending 31 March 1986 14,228 prisoners were referred to prison psychiatrists. It was estimated that on any one day there could be 1,500 male prisoners who were formally mentally disordered, with 250 of these being mentally ill. Equally, the Report of the Interdepartmental Working Group (Home Office/DHSS 1987) described a census carried out on 1 October 1986 which found that 1,497 prisoners serving six months or more imprisonment (i.e. 4.8 per cent of the sentenced male population) were judged to suffer from mental disorder within the terms of the Mental Health Act.

additional hypotheses. First, these filters may fail effectively to identify and divert. Although psychiatric evidence was not considered at trial in the cases of seven of twenty-five men who were ill at the time of their offence (twenty-four of whom were known to their local psychiatric service), this may have been attributable not so much to a failure of identification as to a recognition that treatment in hospital was not a probable outcome in any case. Certainly, eighteen of the twenty-five were judged unsuitable for treatment in hospital, usually because of their difficult or violent behaviour. As has been argued in respect of the remand population (Dell *et al.* 1991), the courts perceive a need for a psychiatric referral which ultimately is not matched by those providing the services, who define their role in a more limited way. Where the courts cannot force doctors to accept patients for treatment, prison sweeps up.

Secondly, the incidence of 37 per cent may be substantially accounted for by the tautological relationship between personality disorder/drug/alcohol/sexual problems and offending behaviour (495 men appeared in these groups, of whom 174 were thought to require further assessment or transfer to a therapeutic community or hospital). This would both make the absolute numbers of mentally disordered offenders higher than the incidence of mental disorder in the community and, as the authors assert, contribute to the prison population where disagreements among doctors about treatability and the lack of suitable facilities for those suffering from personality disorder and sexual deviation resulted in resort to prison by default. Of course, the mismatch between the narrow criteria for Mental Health Act disposal at the point of sentence and the subsequent broad clinical diagnosis of disorder will have further exacerbated these figures.

But, of the thirty-four prisoners diagnosed as psychotic, thirty were deemed likely to receive adequate care only in an NHS hospital, where drugs could be administered on a compulsory basis, victimization by other prisoners avoided, and unpredictable violence or incidents of self-harm better controlled. Notably, eight of the thirty-four had been referred for transfer by the prison doctor or were awaiting a bed and a further seventeen had been identified as psychotic but had not been placed on a transfer list. A cynical view might be that there is little point placing an offender on a transfer list when there is no realistic prospect of a bed becoming available.

Here is the heart of another problem. There simply are not enough secure beds. For, although 2 per cent psychosis diagnosed in the sentenced population is low in absolute terms, as the authors note, it represents some 730 men at any one time requiring transfer to hospital—primarily, to a medium-secure bed. Yet, by January 1991, there were only

635 permanent Regional Secure Unit (RSU) beds—far short of the 2,000 minimum recommended by Butler's Interim Report (1974) and the 1,000 accepted as an initial target by the DHSS (in 1974). Even the three special hospitals provide only 1,700 secure beds (Fennell 1991: 344), and of the 1,800 patients detained subject to restriction orders who would have gone straight to hospital from the courts, two-thirds of these are in special hospital beds, leaving little spare capacity for transferred prisoners.

It was evidently not before time when the government announced that there was to be a sixfold increase in the money available for building medium secure psychiatric units (i.e. from £3 million to £18 million in 1992/3) to meet the shortfall of 400 places in medium-secure units (*Guardian*, 28 January 1992). But even this may be insufficient. The Reed Report (1991: Overview para. 22) identified the required provision of medium-secure beds, designed for patients who are too ill for prison, but insufficiently ill for special hospitals, at a level of 1,500; so even with the new injection of money, the system will be 500 places short. And before the additional beds are provided by the regions, they will undoubtedly want assurance that money will be available not only for capital costs but also for revenue finance. It is unlikely that the shortfall identified in 1974 will evaporate in the foreseeable future.

However, the reality is perhaps more as Shapland (1991: 2) notes: 'We shall always have mentally disordered offenders in what we are currently calling the penal system not because of lack of facilities, but because of intrinsic contradictions in our ideas about mental disorder and its relation to offending.' Although the sentencing of mentally disordered offenders is predicated on notions of diversion and treatment, there has always been the possibility of recourse to a penal disposal where there are elements of culpability (or predicted dangerousness) which require punishment (or control), as most recently espoused in *R.* v. *Birch* (1989).

The prospects for reform of offenders following such disposals are recognized as bleak (Home Office 1990*a*: para. 2.7). 'For most offenders, imprisonment has to be justified in terms of public protection, denunciation and retribution. Otherwise it can be an expensive way of making bad people worse.' Accordingly, diversion in its various forms is regarded as the most appropriate route for the 'deserving' mentally disordered offender.

CORRECTLY LOCATING THE MENTALLY DISORDERED OFFENDER: DIVERSION AND TRANSFER

One of the more telling anomalies emerges from the disparity between the government's stated policy of treating and caring for the mentally disordered offender outwith custodial care and the numbers of mentally disordered offenders still to be found in custody who could benefit from care and treatment under alternative regimes. The intention of Home Office Circular no 66/90, *Provision for Mentally Disordered Offenders*, was twofold: first, to draw to the attention of criminal justice agencies those legal powers relevant to the mentally disordered; second, to reinforce the desirability of ensuring the best use of resources and to ensure that the mentally disordered were not prosecuted where this was not required by the public interest. Where prosecution was necessary, Circular 66/90 stressed the importance of finding non-penal disposals wherever appropriate. Clearly, however effective diversion schemes become, there will always be mentally disordered offenders in the penal system, either because of late onset of the disorder or because the nature of the offending/disorder makes a penal disposal inevitable. Such offenders are not denied access to treatment. Provision exists for treatment within prison (on a voluntary basis),[4] transfer within the prison system to a more appropriate environment, e.g. Grendon Underwood Prison, or temporary transfer into the hospital system. These options are discussed below.

Diversion

The Mental Health Act 1983 attempted to rectify the partial failure of the 1959 Act to realize a treatment-based approach by introducing measures to divert offenders into the hospital system at an earlier stage. Hence, s. 35 permitted remand to hospital for reports (but not compulsory treatment); s. 36 provided for remand to hospital for treatment; and s. 38 initiated interim hospital orders. All these provisions were designed to ensure early identification of those with mental disorders in need of treatment and appropriate disposal of them, with interim hospital orders designed to avoid the difficulty that could arise out of the 'once-and-for-all' disposal to hospital under s. 37. The interim hospital order lasts, with renewals, up to a maximum of six months, at which point the court may make a full hospital order or any other available disposal. In effect, it permits hedging of bets. Although a punitive order should not follow where 'instant cure' at hospital occurs, a punitive approach may be adopted where it becomes apparent that no cure is possible.

However, none of these orders has been frequently used by the courts. Fennell (1991: 337–9) notes that there were only thirty-four s. 36 orders in 1988/9, and although there were 328 s. 35 orders in the same period, this compares very unfavourably with the 5,569 psychiatric reports carried out by prison medical officers following remand in 1989. Indeed,

[4] Even those offenders certifiable as transferable under the provisions of the 1983 Act cannot be treated under its provisions on a compulsory basis while still in prison.

recent research on mentally disordered remanded prisoners by Dell *et al.* (1991) noted that courts remand in custody essentially for psychiatric and social reasons, rather than for reasons of public safety or the seriousness of offence—as the denial of bail implies. The Reed Report (1991: Prison Advisory Group para. 3.3) recommends that 'the appropriate powers in the Bail Act 1976 and Magistrates' Court Act 1980 should be reviewed with a view to amendment or repeal' to prevent magistrates sending the accused to prison solely for medical reports—a practice regarded as wrong in principle and an unjustifiable use of the prison system. Such limitations on magistrates' powers might result in an increase in their limited use of s. 35, although clearly not all offenders would fit the necessary Mental Health Act classifications, nor would sufficiently secure provisions necessarily be available. Equally, as Fennell notes (1991: 338) if all those offenders currently remanded to prison were remanded to hospital, it would result in a 30–35 per cent increase in the numbers of compulsory admissions to hospitals.

By the end of the 1980s, and partly in recognition of the under-use, non-use, and delay these provisions entailed, a movement developed towards even earlier assessment and diversion. Court-based psychiatric assessments (not dissimilar to the duty solicitor schemes) enabled the courts to receive speedy medical advice and to ensure that, where appropriate arrangements could be made, mentally disordered offenders would be admitted to hospital (1) as a condition of bail; (2) under s. 35(2)(b) of the Mental health Act 1983 by magistrates following conviction, or where the magistrates were satisfied before conviction that the accused did the act or made the omission charged and was suffering from one of the four narrow classifications; (3) under s. 35 if the accused consents; (4) using civil powers of admission under s. 2 or s. 3; (5) by a hospital order under s. 37; (6) by a psychiatric probation order; or (7) under s. 36 (remanding to hospital for treatment).[5]

Although these schemes (Blumenthal and Wessely 1992) all take different forms, they share the innovative and proactive approach of getting psychiatrist, Crown Prosecution Service (CPS), mentally disordered alleged offender, and sentencer together at court. They aim to prevent offenders having to be remanded in custody for reports merely because they do not enjoy stable community ties or because of the absence of bail hostels; ultimately, disposal into a custodial setting should be avoided where a therapeutic one would be more appropriate. The Reed Report (1991: Community Advisory Group para. 2.37(x)) recommends that 'there

[5] Curiously, s. 36 precludes those charged with murder. This is particularly odd since many of these accused will ultimately be convicted of manslaughter and some receive hospital orders. Equally, they have a high risk of suicide in prison whilst on remand (West 1965). Accordingly, s. 36 makes little sense in either principle or practice.

should be nationwide provision of court psychiatrist or similar schemes for assessment and diversion of mentally disordered offenders'. This recommendation notably comes on top of a series of recommendations to ensure earlier and earlier diversion, including diversion from police stations as a place of safety under s. 136, specialized bail hostels, and extension of the 'public interest' case assessment. As para. 2.25 notes: 'comprehensive and reliable information about the suspect's mental condition' should be available so that the CPS may consider the desirability of proceeding against a person who is mentally disordered.

Such an overall approach, which implies exemption from prosecution, is not without its problems. Some commentators believe that those with mental handicap should be prosecuted and held responsible where responsibility exists (Carson 1989). Although the Code for Crown Prosecutors already requires the CPS to consider a defendant's mental condition, disorder *per se* is not regarded as a sufficient basis for not proceeding. Indeed, the Home Office Circular no. 66/90, paralleling the Code, distinguishes in para. 6 those forms of mental disorder made worse by the institution of proceedings and those which come about by reason of instituting proceedings. It has also been suggested (Robertson 1988) that the presence of disorder may make prosecution more likely where a guilty plea is anticipated. Hence it is important to distinguish the additional safeguards all mentally disordered people should enjoy under the Codes of Practice and the Police and Criminal Evidence Act (PACE), while in police custody, from the decision to prosecute. In the latter instance, the presence of mental disorder may act as a mitigating factor and pre-empt prosecution, or it may act as an incentive to proceedings being taken.

Curiously, under PACE, the presence or suspicion of mental disorder, as defined in the Mental Health Act 1983 (i.e. including psychopathic disorder) should trigger all of the protections and additional rights to which the mentally vulnerable are entitled in police custody, including the right to have an appropriate adult present during questioning (Code C, paras. 1.4, 3.9, 3.12, 11.14). It would be interesting to know how frequently the police's definition of a 'psychopath' impels them to adhere to these special protections for the mentally disordered under PACE. The work of Gudjonsson *et al.* (1993) underlines the likelihood of false confessions being made by vulnerable individuals, but this may be another area where the mismatch between different agencies' expectations for, and definitions of, 'the mentally disordered' impedes the full protection to which that group is entitled in law.

Thus, the public interest in ensuring that the offence will not be repeated needs to be weighed against that of the welfare of the person in question. Equally, there are difficulties concerning potential net-widening;

such schemes work best for trivial offences which might, in the absence of an assured diversion scheme, have never even come before the courts.[6] And there are problems of due process (e.g. the question of being unfit to plead: see below) where the earlier involvement of psychiatrists will inevitably favour welfarism over legalism; are alleged offenders being made offers they cannot refuse? Finally, as Fennell notes (1991: 336–7); assuming that an offender is prepared to be diverted, 'hospital authorities and local authorities have considerable discretion as to whether to accept responsibility for that person. If he is a persistent petty offender, or is potentially disruptive, he is unlikely to be afforded priority status in the queue for scarce resources.' With the drop at district level in in-patient beds for the adult mentally ill from around 150,000 in the 1950s to approximately 63,000 in the early 1990s, and a reluctance by some to see offender-patients integrated with 'non-offenders', diversion and community care may have real limits to their ability to absorb all those whom the courts might wish so to allocate.

Ultimately the debate concerns the need to balance care and control in different measures at an individual level. But doing so in the community is arguably even more fraught with difficulty than doing so in an institutional setting. Psychiatric probation orders attempt such a balance and, with 980 orders in 1988, they represent numerically one of the most popular disposals for the mentally disordered offender. But, like guardianship orders, they lack the element of compulsory treatment, at present confined to those detained in hospital. As Fennell (1992) details, the campaign for a community treatment order has fluctuated in momentum; but since such a provision would be in keeping with current notions of punishment in the community, the possibility of the courts developing common law principles, so as to provide a basis for compulsory community treatment of patients who refuse voluntary treatment, remains.

Transfer to hospital

Transfer to hospital, with or without a restriction direction, has a history plagued with difficulties. Again the basic premise is difficult to contest, namely that detention in prison is inappropriate for those whose mental disorder is sufficiently serious to justify transfer to hospital. Yet the absolute number of transfers of s. 48 remand prisoners to hospital reached a maximum of eighty-five in 1988, but ranged downwards to nine in 1978; transfer of sentenced prisoners between 1968 and 1988 never rose above 130 annually and was consistently under 100 per year for the

[6] James and Hamilton (1992) found that such schemes can result in a fourfold increase in those referred pre-plea—largely accused of minor offences—with the charge being sorted out with the CPS rather than involving a psychiatric remand.

majority of that period (figures illustrated in Grounds 1991: 56). As a proportion of those requiring treatment and being transferable, these figures do not suggest that the premise is reflected in practice.

A number of factors may help to explain why transfer has been so problematic (Grounds 1991). Clearly, there are difficulties in moving patients on from the special hospitals into conditions of lesser security because of the shortage of RSU beds; this creates a logjam, making fewer beds available in the special hospitals for transferred prisoners. Offender-patients tend to remain in conditions of greater than necessary security for longer than is justifiable. Nothing can be done to make an RSU, a local hospital, or the local authority accept a patient who is agreed to be ready to proceed to a less secure environment.[7] Equally, there can be problems with remission to prison where the RMO says a patient is suffering from psychopathic disorder but is untreatable, or is mentally ill and, having responded to medication in hospital, is predicted as being likely to refuse to continue with treatment in a prison environment where no compulsion can be used. Clearly, a policy of flexible transfer will succeed only where the psychiatric system is geared up to meet increased demand: in the context of reduced psychiatric beds and under-provision of secure facilities, this looks unlikely.

Grounds (1990) argues that, ultimately, transfer may be motivated as much by a desire to protect the public as by a wish to ensure that the patient receives the care he or she needs. Yet, as he notes (1991: 67), the purpose of the legislation 'is not preventative detention beyond sentence, but the enabling of hospital treatment during sentence'; that particular groups, for example Afro-Caribbeans, are overrepresented among s. 47 transfer may rightly result in their feeling aggrieved about potential misuse of the legislation. Grounds (1990) noted the trend during the period 1960–83 towards later transfer; during the last decade of the operation of the 1959 Act, a third of transfers to Broadmoor were made in the last month before the prisoner's earliest date of release and one in eight in the final week. Moreover, progressively longer periods passed as prisoners waited for transfer: in the period 1974–83 one in four patients waited for a year before transfer following a positive recommendation. This picture hardly represents the speedy and flexible system now demanded, even given Broadmoor's peculiar difficulties.

Use of the hospital system as a basis for preventive detention, and disregard of the rights of would-be patient-offenders under both the 1959

[7] Notably, the Reed Report (1991: Prison Advisory Group para. 3.13) raises the power of the Home Secretary to direct admission of a prisoner *without* the agreement of hospital managers and recommends its greater use where this is in the interests of the prisoner-patient. If it is acceptable for a prisoner to be admitted without the approval of the clinicians expected to provide treatment under s. 47(1), the arguments for retaining such agreement under s. 37(4) look less compelling.

and 1983 Acts, has placed transferred patients in a disadvantageous position. As Grounds (1990) argues, prior to the 1959 Act their detention in Broadmoor continued only up to the expiry of their sentence; thereafter, they had to be discharged or sent to county asylums for further treatment. After 1959 they could be detained on a notional hospital order *after* their prison sentence expired. And such patients enjoyed fewer safeguards than those admitted under civil provisions.[8] Although there was recourse to review by an MHRT, such a safeguard is unsatisfactory where the test to be applied does not equate to that for a new admission. Hence, the late transfers which troubled the Butler Committee (1975: para. 3.42) as being only 'almost entirely theoretical' were, as noted scathingly by Grounds, clearly there in practice—both numerically and in respect of due process. When respected author-practitioners make such comments, the time has arrived for serious reappraisal. Fears which such activity reflect will not evaporate with another policy statement about 'treatment of mentally disordered offenders'.

Fennell (notably writing prior to the Reed Report) concludes his thorough review of diversion of mentally disordered offenders from custody with the comment that 'it is likely that, despite current policies of diversion, significant numbers of mentally disordered offenders will remain in prisons, and therefore there is an urgent need to consider how a humane and therapeutic psychiatric service might be provided within the prison system' (1991: 333). And here is the nub of the problem: if mentally disordered offenders cannot be neatly packaged and swept into the caring system, some means of offering effective 'treatment' (if not compulsory treatment, anathema to psychiatrists) within prison will have to be considered. But, if treatment is provided for the mentally disordered offender, why not to other offenders? Those others make up 63 per cent of the sentenced population; are they any less deserving of the opportunity for change?

Hence the possible resurgence of a treatment movement within criminology; although its genesis may derive equally well from disillusionment with just deserts and humane containment for what is evidently a 'damaged' population, the presence and proportion of mentally disordered offenders in the prison population constitutes a compelling force. Although the view was ominously expressed (Home Office 1991: para. 1.28) that 'offenders are not given sentences of imprisonment by the courts for the purposes of ensuring their rehabilitation', attempts to

[8] For example, the involvement of an independent person (approved social worker or nearest relative) and the requirement that admission occur within fourteen days of certificate. For transfer, the certificate would just be delayed; examination could have occurred many months earlier. Certainly, in the 1970s and 1980s patients were transferred on the basis of out-of-date reports.

reform specific groups remain on the agenda; their implications and rationale demand examination.

MENTAL DISORDER AT TRIAL

The presence of mental disorder may permit specific charges to be brought (e.g. infanticide) or qualified defences used (diminished responsibility) to obviate the mandatory life sentence which follows a murder conviction. Mental disorder either at the point of trial ('unfit to plead') or at the point at which the offence was committed (the 'M'Naghten Mad') had, until recently, irrevocably determined the disposal of such individuals: namely, indefinite detention in a psychiatric hospital. Arguably, all these four areas discussed below represent crisis points for legal theory in that the consequences of a full application of the law would or did constitute intolerable outcomes for 'needy' individuals, attributable directly to the court's lack of discretion. Importation of psychiatric reasoning and the construction of concepts of responsibility enabled offenders to be dealt with primarily on the basis of their medical condition rather than on the basis of their criminal behaviour, resulting in treatment on the basis of who they were, rather than what they had done. Of course, the danger is that once deference to psychiatric notions is permitted, welfarism need no longer be tempered by legalism (see below) and outcomes which challenge notions of justice can arise.

Long-standing dissatisfaction with the arrangements for the 'insane' and 'unfit', and, in particular, with counsel's advice to clients to avoid such outcomes by pleading guilty to offences they may not have committed or which the prosecution may not have been able to establish, led to considerable pressure to amend the law. Although the Mental Health Act 1983 improved the theoretical position of these patients—in that they could be discharged by MHRTs where the presence of continuing disorder could not be established—their numbers remained minimal (Mackay 1991).[9] Given that the purpose of both unfitness findings and the insanity verdict is to protect vulnerable individuals and excuse defendants not fully responsible for their crimes from punishment, their under-usage was an indictment of the law. Pressure for reform ultimately resulted in the Criminal Procedure (Insanity and Unfitness to Plead) Act 1991 (hereafter 'the 1991 Act').[10] Although the grounds for such determinations remain

[9] Although the tiny number per year—consistently six or fewer for insanity—makes statistical inferences problematic.

[10] The Act came into force on 1 January 1992. Its effect is confined to Crown Court decisions as it relates only to trials on indictment. White (1991: 503), writing prior to the 1991 Act, asserted that it is proper for the magistrates to entertain a defence of insanity and, if successful, the proper verdict is an unqualified acquittal (followed by committal under the

the same, the consequences that follow have changed radically, with the 1991 Act increasing the court's disposal options to include:

- an admission order (equivalent to a hospital order);
- an admission order with restrictions (which may be indefinite or of fixed length);
- guardianship;
- a supervision and treatment order;
- absolute discharge.

Infanticide

The Infanticide Act 1938 (passed prior to introduction of the defence of diminished responsibility) created a special category of offence under s. 1(1) where a woman causes the death of her child of under twelve months when her mind was 'disturbed by reason of not having fully recovered from the effect of giving birth to the child or by reason of the effect of lactation consequent upon the birth of the child'. It enables the court to avoid the mandatory life sentence for murder and to impose instead whatever penalty it thinks fit. Although a defence of diminished responsibility encompasses a wider group of victims, including those over twelve months and the children of others, a charge of infanticide provides a defence where a mother kills in circumstances of extreme stress arising out of, for example, poverty, social deprivation, failure of bonding, or otherwise being unable to cope with a new baby. Although such psychiatrically endorsed and facilitated usage comes dangerously close to making 'adverse social conditions a defence to child killing' (Smith and Hogan 1988: 363), the Criminal Law Revision Committee (1984: paras. 103–6) wished to ratify such use by extending the offence to cover stresses caused by 'circumstances consequent to the birth'. As Hoggett (1990: 172) questions, should such stresses amount to an excuse, and if so, why should they not apply to fathers as well, or to others provoked to kill by intolerable circumstances, currently falling outside the ambit of provocation?

Diminished Responsibility

The Homicide Act 1957 s. 2(1) enabled a defendant to be found not guilty of murder, but guilty of manslaughter, by reason of diminished responsibility where the defendant could establish that 'he was suffering from such abnormality of mind (whether arising from a condition of arrested or retarded development of mind or any inherent causes or

1983 Act where appropriate). The position in the magistrates' court remains, as White asserts, unclear.

induced by disease or injury) as substantially impaired his mental responsibility for his acts and omissions in doing or being a party to the killing'. The abnormality test—'a state of mind so different from that of ordinary human beings that the reasonable man would term it abnormal' (Lord Parker CJ in *R.* v. *Byrne* [1960] 2 QB 396 at 403)—is sufficiently wide to include a gamut of disordered states, even if transient. It includes the failure to resist an impulse where, although the ability to resist was present, it was substantially less than that of an ordinary man and the offender could not resist or could not have resisted without substantial difficulty. Arguably, it provides a psychiatrist's charter at trial; similarly, the substantial responsibility test implies that it is possible to have degrees of responsibility. And if there can be lesser degrees of responsibility, why should the defence be confined to murder? The explanation lies, of course, with the mandatory life sentence for murder—but this is not a justification for limiting such a defence if logical in itself.

Recent research (Maierkatkin 1991; Wilczynski 1991) suggests that 'gender blindness' (Koe 1992) in the law may manifest itself not only in statutory provision in respect of infanticide, but also in the way in which defences, equally open to both men and women, are employed in cases of spousal homicide or filicide. Broadly, the qualified defences of diminished responsibility and provocation are regarded in law as excuses—with the focus being on the actor—while self-defence is a justification and focuses on the act; where successful it provides a complete defence. Yet women make more use of 'psychiatric defences' such as diminished responsibility, while men (and increasingly, in the USA, women as well; see Raeder 1992) resort to self-defence or lack of intent to kill. The upshot is that women are more likely to receive psychiatric disposals and men penal sentences. Hence 'men are bad and normal, women are mad and abnormal' (Wilczynski 1991).[11] The pathologizing of women via infanticide, diminished responsibility, and, arguably, provocation, rather than utilizing self-defence—which leaves an offender with a normal response to abnormal circumstances rather than an abnormal response to common circumstances (giving birth/woman battering)—may help to explain why women surface in the prison statistics at the ratio of 28:1 with men, whereas in special hospitals the ratio is 5:1. Hence, gender rather than mental disorder may be the pre-eminent factor for ensuring that women be treated on the basis of who they are rather than what they have done. Departure from the normal principles of criminal law at present pathologizes women's behaviour, when a better solution might be to abolish the

[11] The recent decision of the English Court of Appeal in *R.* v. *Ahluwalia* [1992] 4 All ER 889 CA (*Guardian*, 5 August 1992) to remit a 'battered woman' case for retrial on the issue of diminished responsibility, rather than extending the interpretation of provocation so as to encompass 'battered woman syndrome', affirms this view.

mandatory life sentence for murder. Currently, practice requires the distortion of concepts to accommodate legal solutions.

Unfit to Plead

The Criminal Procedure (Insanity) Act 1964 did not provide a test to be applied when determining whether a person was 'unfit to plead'. Eastman (1990) argued that psychiatrists sought an interpretation via the legal criteria for fitness (*R.* v. *Pritchard* [1836] 7 C & P 303), namely, that the defendant 'can plead to the indictment, be of sufficient intellect to comprehend the proceedings so as to make a proper defence, know that he might challenge any one of the jurors to whom he may object and comprehend the details of the evidence'. Unfitness cannot merely be equated with certifiability; indeed, the legal criteria 'do not fit neatly with any diagnostic criteria' (Chiswick 1990: 174). Eastman (1990) also asserted that a significant psychiatric distortion occurred under the 1964 Act towards a finding of fitness, with the result that many were in practice tried when unfit, and many more when not maximally fit. Although such psychiatric manipulation would avoid indefinite detention in hospital without trial, it failed to achieve the objectives of the 1964 Act, namely, that an individual should be protected from the ordeal of trial if his or her mental state might cause that trial to be unfair.

Between 1979 and 1989 only 229 unfitness findings were recorded, with the numbers consistently declining, reaching a mere eleven in 1989 (Mackay 1991). A similar survey (Grubin 1991) between 1976 and 1988 found 295 cases; over 50 per cent had a primary diagnosis of schizophrenia, with a further 23 per cent being mentally handicapped (or brain-damaged). Over a third of the total alleged offences were of a mild or nuisance level. In Mackay's (1991) sample, over 70 per cent were sent to local hospitals or RSUs. Of the total sample, 30 per cent were remitted for trial during the research period, with 11 per cent ultimately being found not guilty. Of those 159 patients not remitted, over 40 per cent of those sent to special hospitals, and over 24 per cent of those in local hospital and RSUs, were still in hospital at the time of the survey. Forty patients had been discharged. Concerns about the decline in use of the plea, the inflexibility of the disposal, and the failure to resolve the accusation of offending (where a finding of unfitness arose there was no determination of the facts, despite the triviality of the cases) were powerful reasons for change.

The 1991 Act requires unfitness to be determined by a jury on the evidence of two or more doctors, one of whom is approved. If the defendant is found unfit, then a (new) jury will consider on the basis of such evidence adduced by both prosecution and defence whether the person did the act or made the omission charged. During this 'trial of the facts' there will be no examination of the intention of the accused, who will be assured legal representation, via a court appointment if necessary. If the jury are satisfied that the *actus reus* is not made out, then the accused shall be acquitted. If made out, and the accused remains unfit, then the court will have access to the increased range of disposals—except where the offence alleged is murder, in which case an indefinite restriction order is mandatory.

Not Guilty by Reason of Insanity

For a verdict of not guilty by reason of insanity to be brought, it must be established that the accused falls within the ambit of the M'Naghten Rules, their essence being that the accused 'at the time of the committing of the act . . . was labouring under such a defect of reason, from disease of the mind, as not to know the nature and quality of the act he was doing, or, if he did know it, that he did not know he was doing what was wrong' (1843) 10 Cl & F 200 at 210. The Rules provide a legal test of responsibility for the mentally disordered. Insanity in the medical sense is not sufficient for the defence, although mental disorder *per se* at the point of the act alleged to constitute a crime is clearly a prerequisite. Curiously, as Mackay (1990: 251) observes, the verdict could result under the 1964 Act even in the absence of medical evidence.

Although the insanity defence was rarely used (Dell 1983) and was regarded by some as 'obsolete' (Smith and Hogan 1988: 185), recent research challenged such widely held beliefs. Mackay (1990), looking at cases over a fourteen-year period up to 1988, revealed that the verdict occurred primarily not in murder cases, but in other non-fatal offences against the person of an unprovoked nature. Schizophrenia was overwhelmingly the commonest diagnosis (in 51 per cent of the sample). Curiously, in the light of legal scholars' preference for the first limb of the M'Naghten Rules ('did not know the nature or quality of the act'), in the bulk of the sample (over 57 per cent) the second limb of the test ('did not know that it was wrong') accounted for the verdicts. This may, of course, be partly attributable to the failure to distinguish between lack of knowledge of legal wrong (as required by law) and lack of knowledge of moral wrong (frequently a better fit with the facts of the sample). But, as Mackay notes (1990: 251), 'the general impression gained . . . was that the wrongness issue was being treated in a liberal fashion by all concerned, rather than in the strict manner regularly depicted by legal commentators' (see e.g. Dell 1983; Verdun-Jones 1989).

Equally contrary to widely held beliefs, of the forty-nine special verdicts, two accused were immediately released by the courts, one successfully appealed against the special verdict; and of the remaining forty-six, only 40 per cent went to special hospitals, with 53 per cent going to local hospitals or RSUs. For this last group, the disposal was clearly *not* the psychiatric equivalent of a life sentence, with ten (of twenty-six) patients being discharged within nine months. For the special hospital patients, periods of detention were longer, with 50 per cent not having been discharged by 1991 and 50 per cent being detained for periods up to nine years. Given that fear of disposal was thought to be the main reason for non-use of the insanity verdict, such fears may have been misplaced or exaggerated. But, where such fears resulted in defendants pleading guilty to avoid the disposal, the situation demanded a remedy. Undoubtedly, the figures of six or fewer insanity verdicts a year suggest that there are a number of offenders who might have benefited from the 'not guilty' verdict had they not been deterred by the consequences into pleading guilty.

Under the 1991 Act a jury verdict of not guilty by reason of insanity will require evidence from two or more medical practitioners (one approved in the field of mental disorder). For all acquittals—again with the exception of those arising out of murder charges, where the disposal will remain the equivalent of a hospital order with indefinite restrictions—the court's disposal options are to be increased in line with those following a finding of unfit to plead.

MENTAL DISORDER AND TREATMENT

Treatment is the fundamental justification for separate provision for mentally disordered people who have committed offences. But it is not readily clear what is meant by treatment, or what treatment is attempting to alter: the 'underlying disorder'; the offending behaviour; or the link, if any, between the two? And if the target of treatment is the likelihood of criminal behaviour *per se*, the justification for treatment will not be confined to a 'mentally disordered' sub-group of offenders. Accordingly, an examination of this relationship and any resultant failure to establish causality might undermine the whole basis for treatment. This leads into the discussion in the final section on protection.

Indeed, if efforts to describe, classify, and treat the mentally disordered offender are aimed at a change of offending behaviour rather than fundamentally at the disorder, this would help to explain the focus on questions concerning predictions of reoffending. In respect of one particularly problematic group discussed below, those with 'psychopathic disorder', the government's recent attempts to rationalize the law stemmed from concerns not about treatment, justice, or due process, but about reoffending by those psychopathic offenders released 'prematurely' from the hospital system. Ultimately, the attempt to extend control over these offenders by, if necessary, prolonging their detention, fell by the wayside, but only in the context of a recognition that the proposals might have led to less control and not more (Peay 1988).

What is the Relationship between Mental Disorder and Offending Behaviour?

As Prins (1990) has amply demonstrated, the relationship between mental abnormality and criminality is an uncertain one. Prins summarizes the principal psychiatric classifications of disorder and illustrates the forms of offending which may be associated with them—or, indeed, be less likely to arise where individuals are suffering from particular disorders—concluding (1990: 256): 'Most psychiatric disorders are only very occasionally associated with criminality.' Prins also illustrates well the difficulties of establishing cause and effect in this troubled area: 'We are trying to make connections between very different phenomena, and these phenomena are the subject of much debate concerning both substance and definition' (1990: 247).

Another emphasis in the literature concerns the relationship between mental disorder and violence (Monahan 1992; Wessely and Taylor 1991). Although many have resisted the idea that mental disorder may be a risk factor for the occurrence of violence (Monahan and Steadman 1983) and question the logic of why those with paranoid delusions should be any more or less likely to attack their tormentors than those who are in fact being tormented, the ground has recently shifted. Tentative demonstrations based on survey data that lack of control and associated violent behaviour may be a prerogative of the *currently actively psychotic* (Swanson *et al.* 1990; Link *et al.* 1993) should be treated with necessary circumspection and in the context of knowledge that the overwhelming correlates of violence are male gender, youth, lower socio-economic class, and the use/abuse of alcohol or drugs and not the diagnosis of major mental disorder. None the less, Wessely and Taylor's (1991: 222) assertion regarding violent offences among schizophrenics with delusional presentation of long duration that 'the single most effective prevention measure would be a better standard of after-care' bears reflection.

In contrast, merely weighing the contribution of Bluglass and Bowden in *Principles and Practice of Forensic Psychiatry* (1990)—another 'handbook', with chapters on everything from Amok to Sexual Asphyxia (regrettably, nothing on Zealotry)—might lead one to conclude that there is no form of criminal behaviour without a psychiatric element. It provides a comprehensive state-of-the-art review—and not one I plan to reproduce here. I merely wish to make a couple of observations pertinent to this path of medicalized explanations.

First, offence categories among 'disordered offenders' mirror those of 'normal' populations, the only differences being that the disordered populations are slightly less likely to be convicted of offences of violence and slightly more likely to have committed property offences.[12] Sexual offences and those involving drugs enjoy identical percentages for both groups in the study by Gunn *et al.* (1991*a*). Of course, given the level of disorder among the sentenced population, this is what any study of sentenced populations should demonstrate. Images of axe-wielding maniacs are based on highly visible and intuitively attractive evidence, but are not statistically replicable.[13]

Second, the Institute of Psychiatry has recently redefined 'forensic psychiatry' to mean 'the prevention and treatment of the effects of victimisation in relation to mental disorder', crudely summarized as 'all our patients are victims' (Gunn 1992). The implication that all or many of the offending population have themselves been offended against constitutes another form of medicalized explanation of their behaviour. Although Gunn (1992) believes that the study of personality development/disorder, including abuse, will help us to understand crime in some individuals, can correlation and causation be so readily disentangled (Player 1992)? How can it be determined what the relevance of the victimization was to the individual, if observations are based on psychiatric contact with those who have offended, or offended and volunteered themselves as 'damaged'—seeking some psychiatric explanation for their behaviour? Offenders are, after all, only too willing to have their behaviour treated as a manifestation of themselves—to be 'treated' for who they are. Hence Lisa Corless, 19, a known gas inhaler, convicted of murdering an 84-year-old widow by battering her to death, was reported as saying 'Now they know me for what I am and not for what I have done' (*Guardian*, 23 August 1991). As inconvenient as this interpretation may be for criminologists seeking to avoid discriminatory treatment for the 'mentally disordered', it provides a powerful illustration of the preparedness of offenders to be victims. The scene is set: offenders desire to accommodate and incorporate psychiatric explanations of their behaviour; victimization in one form or another—like the mother–child relationship—is a common,

[12] Although the latter includes robbery, which in law requires violence, the Oxford study of offences of violence (Genders 1991) illustrates the minimal level of violence frequently associated in practice with 'robbery' charges.

[13] A cautionary note is advisable. The sentenced population is a skewed sub-sample; the remand population might reveal a different picture (Taylor and Gunn 1984). Levels of suicide (from despair or disorder) and the incidence of disorder are significantly higher among remand populations (Dooley 1990). And statistical account should be taken of the offences committed by those found in hospital, but never prosecuted.

if not universal, experience; psychiatrists are heavily reliant on what their clients tell them (see below); offending is widespread. All of the ingredients are present to permit a restructuring of experiences as explanations or excuses.

Or is the victim–offending relationship merely coincidental? The danger is twofold. First, once criminologists start down this path it is hard to see where it ends. Are not all offences equally open to medicalization? Even seemingly comprehensible property offences may, especially where trivial items are involved, require some less readily accessible explanation than mere acquisitiveness. Second, a medicalized explanation precedes a medicalized solution. But if treatment is adopted and then fails, is the next step to throw away the key?

Psychopathic Disorder

There is likely to be some association between disorders of personality and criminality, since the legal definition of psychopathic disorder under the 1983 Act includes the element that the disorder has resulted in 'abnormally aggressive or seriously irresponsible conduct'. In essence, it is a legal category defined by persistently violent behaviour. The 'criminal' behaviour attracts attention to the offender, who may subsequently be diverted into care. This, in turn, creates therapeutic and conceptual difficulties for the psychiatric profession (Grounds 1987). But it is important to stress that people suffering from 'psychopathic disorder' rarely find themselves subject to civil commitment, which would be expected if the disorder were genuinely problematic for the individual. Perhaps the 'mythical' personality type—ruthless, cold, uncaring, and egocentric—actually benefits the entrepreneur.

The Reed Committee recognized the lack of medical agreement about the diagnosis and treatability of psychopathic disorder (1991: Overview para. 9). Coid (1989: 755) noted: 'The sheer range of psychopathology makes it more appropriate therefore to think of the psychopathic disorders rather than a single entity.' Undoubtedly, there is a need to separate clinical definitions (of personality disorders) from legal definitions (of psychopathic disorder).

Despite the confusion, 'some working concept of psychopathy is necessary for the use of those involved in this field' (Prins 1991: 124). That provided by Roth (1990: 449), for which he claims wide consensus, is noteworthy:

> It comprises forms of egotism, immaturity, aggressiveness, low frustration tolerance and inability to learn from experience that places the individual at high risk of clashing with any community that depends upon co-operation and individual responsibility of its members for its continued existence. It has a characteristic sex

distribution, age of onset, family history of similar symptoms and disorders and family constellations and influences that show a large measure of consistency in their course and outcome . . . One purpose of describing psychopathic personalities in longitudinal as well as cross-sectional perspective is to intervene in the early formative years . . . The treatments so far discovered achieve a relatively low rate of success. This does not justify abrogating responsibility for the care of psychopathic individuals.

But agreeing criteria for diagnosis does not necessarily ensure consistent application, classification, or identification of treatment needs. The legal definition of psychopathic disorder, given its mismatch with psychiatric definitions of personality disorder and its inherent vagueness, is likely to frustrate validity and reliability in diagnosis.[14]

This illustrates well the dilemma in which the psychiatric profession now finds itself. As Ghosh (BBC Radio 4, *File on Four*, 21 January 1992) has argued, the 1959 Act came about in an era of psychiatric optimism. Treatments for mental disorder were available and psychiatrists could concern themselves with treating aberrant behaviour. This led to an assumption that the pathology of aberrant behaviour was equally open to psychiatric expertise, and aberrant behaviour could be deemed to include psychopathic disorder. By the time of the 1983 Act, therapeutic pessimism had set in, and psychiatrists were increasingly wary of being asked to accept psychopathic offenders for treatment when they recognized that they were really offering detention and control: hospital as prison. None the less, psychopathic disorder remained one of the four key organizing categories within the Act. The 'treatability' test under the 1983 Act was one attempt to alleviate this difficulty. The psychiatric profession would only be expected to offer treatment to those they could realistically hope to help; the untreatable, even if clearly disordered, were to receive penal disposals—with the probability of a determinate sentence, the likelihood of release without 'treatment', and the possibility of subsequent reoffending. Paradoxically, the psychiatric profession now finds itself criticized for a failure to provide control and containment.[15]

Even under the 1983 Act, though, the legal definition of psychopathic disorder remained so vague as to permit considerable psychiatric discretion. Although the figures for decreased numbers of offenders suffering

[14] Equally, one eminent forensic psychiatrist (Gunn 1992) has recently departed from all accepted wisdom about the early onset of the disorder to argue that personality disorder can start in middle life following years of normal behaviour—with the illustration of 'Zeebrugge Man'—and may never get better; hence the late onset, incurable psychopath.

[15] The McReady case (*Guardian*, 7 December 1991) concerned a habitual sex offender who killed only a month after release from a prison sentence and was subsequently gaoled for life following a conviction for manslaughter by reason of diminished responsibility. McReady had sought medical treatment during his previous prison sentence, but had been refused treatment (even though diagnosed as psychopathic by special hospital doctors).

from psychopathic disorder in the special hospitals and those for decreased admissions for this group indicate the partial success of the treatability criterion in excluding offender-patients, confusion within the profession prevails. Some argue that the label 'psychopathic disorder' adds nothing to an understanding of the condition—and indeed, doubt the existence of an underlying medical condition at all. Some judge the label to be 'little more than a moral judgement masquerading as a clinical diagnosis' (Blackburn, cited in Prins 1991: 119). Others argue that the term has outlived its legal usefulness. Yet others recognize a disorder, but doubt whether any psychiatric intervention could be successful; while yet others (e.g. Coid 1989) argue that an attempt should be made to continue to treat selected psychopathic offenders.[16]

Here is the difficulty. What is it that treatment is designed to alter: underlying pathology or reoffending rates? Equally, the profession is unable to say with any confidence how long treatment will take, what the nature and extent of it must be, what outcome is likely, whether the treatment will work, or whether—on completion—it has worked. As Chiswick (*Everyman*, BBC1, 8 March 1992) has poignantly argued, psychiatrists are dependent on those with psychopathic disorder disclosing their feelings; if they choose not to do so, there are no objective measures by which to assess 'recovery'. But the point requires elaboration. Failure to disclose presupposes an offender-patient not only being sufficiently 'insightful' but also being able to predict his or her own behaviour. If the Kirkman affair has any lessons, it must be that after seventeen years of successful treatment, how could either psychiatrist *or* patient have been expected to predict the unique circumstances preceding the offence?[17] There are inherent limits to treatment. The whole area remains a quagmire, underlining how little is known about treating 'criminality' *per se*.

Treatment in Prison

Cynics might argue that facing up to the improbability of imprisonment having a reforming influence has gone hand in hand with an acceptance that inferior care is inevitable. Dr Brian Cooper, in evidence to a General

[16] MacCulloch notably claims success in respect of reducing reoffending, with 75 per cent of his study group not committing serious offences in a period of follow-up on discharge from special hospital over a period lasting in some cases up to ten years; reoffending for a similar group of untreated releases from prison was in the region of 60–70 per cent (BBC Radio 4, *File on Four*, 21 January 1992).

[17] In the Kirkman case (West Midlands Regional Health Authority 1991), following seventeen years of treatment in both a special hospital and the Reaside Clinic (RSU), a programme of carefully structured release, a stable relationship, and confidence among psychiatrists that he was ready for release, Kirkman killed a woman on his first day following discharge. He had touched her leg while assisting her with some repairs at her flat, panicked, and stabbed her. He subsequently committed suicide while on remand.

Medical Council hearing into the case of a prison doctor charged with the neglect or inappropriate treatment of four of her patients (*Guardian*, 7 March 1992), stated that Brixton's medical F-wing was 'a human warehouse where humans are stored, labelled and catalogued. There is not the care you would expect for a psychotic patient.' Similarly, in *Knight* v *Home Office* (1990) 3 All ER 237; 140, NLJ 210, it was noted that 'there may be circumstances in which the standard of care falls below that which would be expected in a psychiatric hospital without the prison authority being negligent'. Clearly, even without the inability to impose medication, prison is no place for psychotic patients. But what about the potential in prison for the treatment of other mentally disordered offenders?

There has recently been a resurgence of effort in respect of one category, namely sex offenders (see Reed Report 1992: Report of the Official Working Group on Services for People with Special Needs, discussion paper 4). This is not a movement confined to the UK, with papers being presented to the Eighteenth International Congress on Law and Mental Health in Vancouver on sex offender treatment programmes, but it is one that merits careful examination, not least because of the paucity of clinical evidence that treatment reduces reoffending (Player 1992). In 1985 the decision was made that Grendon Underwood (psychiatric) Prison should specialize in 'sociopaths', short-term acute management, lifer career plans, and sex offenders; a unit appropriate to the needs of this last group has recently opened, adopting Grendon's therapeutic community approach where offenders are forced to face up to their crimes. The treatment programme at the prison has been charted by Genders and Player (1989) and the therapeutic elements of the programme detailed. Notably, Grendon has few discipline problems with what is a highly problematic population and accordingly works well as a form of control. One poignant factor they identify as underpinning Grendon's success is the knowledge, by all concerned, that the rest of the prison system provides a very different form of containment.

Yet Genders and Player's most crucial observations concern reconviction. Why, they ask, should progress in therapy lead to a reduction in future criminality? There is no logical reason why it should. Any progress at Grendon represents only a small part of the prison experience; 'is it feasible to expect Grendon, or any form of psychotherapy alone, to induce changes in an individual's personal and social functioning which, in and of themselves, result in changes to his social situation or structural position in society?' (1989: 141). Hence the predictability of Gunn and Robertson's (1987) finding of *no* significant differences in reconviction rates, in respect of either frequency or severity of offending, between Grendon releases and a matched control group. Grendon's 'successes', as

Genders and Player point out, may alter their behaviour only in respect of how they deal with problems, which may or may not have led them into criminal difficulties in the past. That may, in itself, be a sufficient justification for the treatment endeavour, but it should not be confused with questions of reoffending. Nor, as Player (1992) cautions, where the emphasis is on the unobtainable 'quick fix', should the risk of a shift towards more draconian methods of control be ignored.

This minefield may be crudely summarized:

1. 'Treatment' may mean many different things, ranging from the administration of anti-psychotic medication to the acquisition of social survival skills.
2. If the relationship between the disorder and the offending behaviour is not primarily causal, there is less justification for excusing from punishment—the 'mad and bad' theory—and offenders should remain entitled to protection of their rights as offenders, while not being denied access to treatment.
3. Even if there is some causal element, there is no reason why punishment for the partially responsible (and hence partially guilty) should not be combined with treatment, where requested.
4. Successful treatment for a disorder may have no bearing on future criminality; mentally disordered offenders should accordingly be entitled to proportionality in the length of custody; release should not be determined on the basis of predictions of future offending (in the way it plays no part in release from a determinate sentence).
5. As Campbell and Heginbotham (1991: 135) argue, where an offender is treatable and there is some causal connection between the disorder and the offending behaviour, then there may be less (or no) justification for continued detention after treatment.

PROTECTION, RELEASE, AND REOFFENDING

The discussion so far has paid scant regard to Rubin's axe-wielding image of the first page, and arguably rightly so, since although mentally disordered offenders have the capacity to commit the most serious offences, the frequency and regularity with which they do is minimal in comparison with other forms of offending. Indeed, they are much more likely to kill themselves than others. But the publicity value of serious offending and its influence over those practitioners and policy-makers who make decisions about mentally disordered offenders is enormous.

Concepts of dangerousness and its alleged association with mental disorder abound in the academic literature and in the rhetoric of sentencing; repeatedly, attempts have been made to single out that group of 'worrying' offenders and permit special protective sentences for them. Here is not the place for a review of that literature (Floud and Young 1981; Radzinowicz and Hood 1981; Peay 1982; Bottoms and Brownsword 1983; Prins 1986; Wood 1988). Suffice it to say that academics and policy-makers have been fiercely divided on both predictive statistical grounds—the 'will it work?' approach—and on questions of rights—should it be allowed to work? For the moment that debate has been silenced (arguably stunned into silence) by the introduction of the Criminal Justice Act 1991. Although the approach broadly adopted is that custodial sentences shall be commensurate with the seriousness of the offence, three exceptions can be identified. First, s. 1(2)(b) permits custodial sentences on protective grounds for offences of a violent or sexual nature, even where those offences are not in themselves serious. Second, s. 2(2)(b) builds on this exception by permitting courts to sentence, 'where the offence is a violent or sexual offence, for such longer term (not exceeding that maximum) as in the opinion of the court is necessary to protect the public from serious harm from the offender'. Although courts will have to give reasons, there are few constraints beyond offence type for this 'know it when you see it' approach to dangerousness. Certainly, there is no place for any of the offender's offence history prerequisites so beloved in the academic literature; although previous serious offending is no reliable guide to reoffending, it arguably constitutes the 'best of a bad bunch' of predictors. The absence of a requirement for prior serious offending is alarming.[18] Third, there is the exception to proportionate sentencing for mentally disordered offenders (i.e. pathology-based) in s. 28(4)(a): '(4) Nothing in this Part shall be taken—(a) as requiring a court to pass a custodial sentence, or any particular custodial sentence, on a mentally disordered offender.' Like s. 2(2)(b) noted above, this section assumed its present form rather late in the parliamentary process, arguably polluting the principles of the Act as set out in the 1990 White Paper, *Crime, Justice and Protecting the Public* (Home Office 1990*a*). Discerning its purpose should normally be possible from the accompanying debates in the House of Lords. Regrettably, however, there is little to be gleaned there either, since discussion of the relevant clause of the specific amendment (no. 71: April 1991 at 1620) was linked with amendment no. 17 (now in the Act as s. 4, requiring the courts to obtain medical reports before passing a custodial sentence on an offender who is, or appears to be, mentally disordered). Yet, when explaining the purpose of

[18] Para. 3.13 of the preceding White Paper (Home Office 1990*a*) was even more strident: 'There are a small number of offenders who become progressively more dangerous and who are a real risk to public safety. Some will be mentally disordered and can be detained under mental health legislation.' Moreover, it had been proposed that restrictions on the use of custody would not apply to the most serious crimes tried only in the Crown Court—even where not justified by the actual offence seriousness.

amendment no. 17, Earl Ferrers stated that the courts 'should not pass a custodial sentence if that would adversely affect an offender's mental condition and his treatment'. The spirit accordingly was restrictive, but the letter of the amendment passed did not achieve a constraining effect; indeed, an opposition amendment (no. 25, 16 April at 1350) which explicitly sought that objective was successfully opposed by the government because of its resource implications. Equally, amendment no. 23 was opposed on the grounds that it would deny the courts the opportunity to impose custodial sentences to protect the public, and any more prescriptive approach, requiring hospitals to accept offenders for treatment, was perceived as undermining the therapeutic nature of the doctor–patient relationship (26 March at 1054).[19] Meanwhile, what found its way on to the statute book as s. 28(4)(a) seemingly slipped by without explicit discussion. In summary, on the face of it s. 28 excludes proportionate sentencing; this may not have been its principal purpose. But conspiracy theorists, who see the protective intent of s. 2 arising out of ignorance and political dogma, fear that s. 28 may permit, in a resource-constrained world, protective sentences for the mentally disordered. Has axe-wielding found its place in the Act?

Mentally disordered offenders, as with all offenders, are overwhelmingly not dangerous. But some individuals in all groups are dangerous; it is their identification which is the practical stumbling-block. The arguments for limited special measures have their attractions, if only to deal with that small but worrying group about whom unsubstantiable fears of future offending abound. Moreover, the arguments for bifurcation in the field of mentally disordered offenders are inherently appealing, because of the *quid pro quo* of diverting into humanitarian care all those offenders for whom a penal sentence would be inappropriate.

A number of difficulties arise out of acceptance of such notions. First, protective imperatives can infect the way in which decisions are made about the release of even non-offenders among the detained psychiatric population; fear of future offending can lead to inappropriate denial of release (Peay 1989: 184). It can also lead to inappropriate transfer of prisoners to hospital where continued detention, rather than immediate treatment needs, appears to be the prevailing motive (Grounds 1990). It can also result in offender-patients with diagnoses of psychopathic disorder being detained in hospital for periods commensurate with their offence rather than on the basis of assessed recovery from their disorders—the

[19] This is curiously at odds with the Home Secretary's existing power under the Mental Health Act 1983 s. 47 to direct the transfer of prisoners to hospitals for treatment, a power the Reed Report recommended should be used more frequently where hospitals proved recalcitrant.

supposed justification (Dell and Robertson 1988). Protective confinement appears to be self-justifying.

There have, however, been some chinks in this analysis. Paralleling the concern of lawyers about the position of restricted patients under the Mental Health Act 1959, resulting ultimately in the case of *X* v. *UK* (1981) 4 EHRR 181 and the substantial enhancement of patient safeguards under the 1983 Act, unease about the position of discretionary life prisoners—another group whose mental state has affected their sentence—has resulted in this group gaining enhanced review procedures. The discretionary life-sentenced population make up approximately one-fifth of the total lifer population—the rest being mandatory life sentences. For the one in five due process will rule.

Following reluctantly from the decisions of the European Court of Human Rights (ECHR) in *Weeks* v. *UK* (1988) 10 EHRR 293 and *Thynne, Wilson and Gunnell* v. *UK* 1989 190 of Series A European Court of Human Rights (Richardson 1991),[20] the government extended the powers of the parole board under the Criminal Justice Act 1991, so that in future it will take the final decision about release in life sentence cases. The board will be explicitly concerned with assessing future dangerousness; it will have to be satisfied under s. 34 'that it is no longer necessary for the protection of the public that the prisoner should be confined'. Spelling out the involvement of predictions of dangerousness is, of course, a first step in ensuring that such predictions are made with due regard to the rights of an offender not to be unjustifiably detained. A second necessary step is to ensure procedural fairness; arrangements are already in hand in respect of discretionary lifers, and there have been undertakings that reasons for other early release decisions will be given (Wasik 1992: 256).

Broadly, these provisions place the life-sentence prisoner on the same footing as restricted patients applying to MHRTs. In this respect, all the problems which bedevil tribunals are likely to be replicated (Peay 1989).[21] The burden of proof militates against release—how can an offender prove

[20] Weeks's life sentence was imposed for purposes of social protection because of his mental instability and potential dangerousness. Denial of regular access to a body which had the power to release him breached article 5(4) of the European Declaration on Human Rights: 'Everyone who is deprived of his liberty by arrest or detention shall be entitled to take proceedings by which the lawfulness of his detention shall be decided speedily by court and his release ordered if the detention is not lawful.' In *Thynne, Wilson and Gunnell* v. *UK* the ECHR made plain that *Weeks* was of general application to all discretionary life-sentence prisoners detained on the basis of mental disorder and dangerousness; at some point in a life sentence the punitive element would expire, leaving detention on the grounds of continued dangerousness the sole criterion. The Court argued that this must change over time; accordingly a mechanism for review must exist.

[21] For example, what will be the position of those who continue to protest their innocence? The parole board likes prisoners to be honest about their feelings, but the Home Office likes admissions of guilt as an index of assessing future risk to public.

that he is safe when in conditions of security?[22] Moreover, having improved the position of the discretionary lifer, disparities emerge with those serving the mandatory life sentence and long determinate sentences. There is evidence that the progress made in response to the position of the mentally disordered offender will influence these groups too, in favour of greater procedural fairness; already the Court of Appeal's decision in *Doody, Smart, Pierson and Pegg* (*Guardian*, 7 May 1992) that mandatory lifers should have the right to know the minimum time to be served as recommended by the trial judge has been affirmed by the House of Lords.

Welfarism and legalism may strain in different directions; protectionism and due process may do likewise; but it appears that back-door protectionism is to be repeatedly challenged by up-front due process, a movement deriving from the so-called mentally disordered offender, but ultimately to extend to all.

CONCLUSIONS

If the basic premise of this chapter is accepted, namely, that mentally disordered offenders are not, and should not be treated as an isolated category, the conclusions that follow are of broader significance.

First, effort should be devoted to developing a pluralistic model of the criminal justice system. This has been discussed in detail elsewhere (Peay 1993). Piecemeal tinkering may provide solutions for the problems posed by specific offenders; it is insufficient as a basis for addressing problems across the ordered–disordered offending continuum.

Second, if the mentally disordered cannot be effectively identified and marginalized, diversion and transfer can never be the solution. Resource allocation needs to be conducted across the board, not in respect of a limited number of beds for potentially difficult offender-patients.

Third, and stemming from this, it is unrealistic to confine treatment to hospital settings. Lord Justice Woolf (Woolf Report 1991) and the Chief Inspector of Prisons (Tumim 1990) have both stressed the need—despite *Knight* v. *Home Office* (1990)—to provide psychiatric services in prison equal to those in mental hospitals. The Reed Report (1991: Overview para. 20) recommends contracting in a full mental health care service from the NHS. Whether, as in the USA (Miller 1992), due process safe-

[22] Edward Fitzgerald, who took the cases of discretionary lifers to the ECHR, has argued that the onus should be on the Home Office to convince the board that an applicant should remain in prison. This mirrors Richardson's (1991) view that the burden of proof should be located clearly in such cases, as either on the detaining authority to prove the existence of a real risk after release or on the decision-making body to satisfy itself of the existence of such a risk.

guards for the mentally disordered will be closely followed by the right to treatment in prison, and its more problematic flip side, compulsory treatment in prison, are open questions. What is clear is the need to think more carefully about the circumstances under which treatment will be offered, to whom, and what the consequences will be where it is deemed unsuccessful or inappropriate. A pluralistic model would require the same limitations on intervention for all offenders and, arguably, the principle of proportionality could constitute a sound foundation for greater fairness between offenders.

Fourth, the justifications for singling out sub-sections of 'disordered offenders' for special treatment are many. But special treatment can readily become special control; to be seduced by the notion that risk can be managed through the containment of identifiable individuals is to allow discriminatory treatment for that group, while failing to tackle the roots of the problem. It is a false dawn.

Finally, the failure to agree on a definition of what constitutes a mentally disordered offender, or to apply it consistently even if criteria could be agreed, is likely to result in there being a mismatch of expectations among the various personnel and agencies dealing with such offenders. As Watson and Grounds (1993) have observed, greater liaison combined with overcoming the boundaries between different parts of the criminal justice and health agencies will be insufficient for as long as the discrepancy in expectations remains. Pursuing a pluralistic model may go some way towards addressing these fundamental problems.

Selected Further Reading

Helpful 'setting the scene' books and articles on mentally disordered offenders are: A. Ashworth and L. Gostin, 'Mentally Disordered Offenders and the Sentencing Process', *Criminal Law Review*, 1984: 195–212; P. Fennell, 'Diversion of Mentally Disordered Offenders from Custody', *Criminal Law Review*, 1991: 333–48; B. Hoggett, *Mental Health Law*, 3rd edn., ch. 5 (London: Sweet and Maxwell, 1990); Reed Report, *Review of Health and Social Services for Mentally Disordered Offenders and Others Requiring Similar Services* (Department of Health/Home Office, September 1991; for lighter reading see only the 'Overview'); S. Verdun-Jones, 'Sentencing the Partly Mad and Partly Bad: The Case of the Hospital Order in England and Wales', 12 *International Journal of Law and Psychiatry*, 1989, 12: 21.

Provocative papers on mental disorder, violence, and dangerousness are: J. Monahan, 'Mental Disorder and Violent Behaviour. Perceptions and Evidence', *American Psychologist*, 1992, 47: 511–21; J. Floud and

W. Young, *Dangerousness and Criminal Justice*. London: Heinemann, 1981.

Relevant works on issues of rights and justice are: G. Richardson, 'Discretionary Life Sentences and the European Convention on Human Rights', *Public Law*, 1991: 34–40; A. Bottoms and R. Brownsword, 'Dangerousness and Rights', in J. W. Hinton, ed., London: Allen and Unwin, 1983; T. Campbell and C. Heginbotham, *Mental Illness: Prejudice, Discrimination and the Law*. Aldershot: Dartmouth, 1991; S. Dell and G. Robertson, *Sentenced to Hospital: Offenders in Broadmoor*, Maudsley Monographs no. 32. London: Institute of Psychiatry, 1988; A. Grounds, 'Detection of "Psychopathic Disorder Patients" in Special Hospitals: Critical Issues', *British Journal of Psychiatry*, 1987, 151: 474–78.

A provocative paper on treatment of sex offenders is E. Player, 'Treatment for Sex Offenders: A Cautionary Note', *Prison Service Journal*, 1992, 85: 2–9.

For the facts on incidence, see D. H. Grubin, 'Unfit to Plead in England and Wales 1976–1988: A Survey', *British Journal of Psychiatry*, 1991, 540–8; J. Gunn, A. Maden and M. Swinton, 'Treatment Needs of Patients with Psychiatric Disorders', *British Medical Journal*, 1991, 303: 338–41.

On way forward, see J. Peay, 'A Criminological Perspective', in W. Watson and A. Grounds, eds., *Mentally Disordered Offenders in an Era of Community Care*. Cambridge: Cambridge University Press, forthcoming.

REFERENCES

ASHWORTH, A. (1992), 'Face the 1991 Act' (editorial), *Criminal Law Review*: 229–31.

ASHWORTH, A., and GOSTIN, L. (1984), 'Mentally Disordered Offenders and the Sentencing Process', *Criminal Law Review*: 195–212.

BLUGLASS, R., and BOWDEN, P., eds. (1990), *Principles and Practice of Forensic Psychiatry*. Edinburgh: Churchill Livingstone.

BLUMENTHAL, S., and WESSELY, S. (1992), 'The Extent of Local Arrangements for the Diversion of the Mentally Abnormal Offender from Custody', Report submitted to the Department of Health from the Institute of Psychiatry and King's College Hospital Medical School, London.

BOTTOMS, A., and BROWNSWORD, R. (1983), 'Dangerousness and Rights', in J. W. Hinton, ed., *Dangerousness: Problems of Assessment and Prediction*. London: Allen and Unwin.

BUTLER, Lord (1974), *Interim Report of the Committee on Mentally Abnormal Offenders*, Cmnd 5698. London: HMSO.

—— (1975), *Report of the Committee on Mentally Abnormal Offenders*, Cmnd 6244. London: HMSO.

CAMPBELL, T., and HEGINBOTHAM, C. (1991), *Mental Illness: Prejudice, Discrimination and the Law*. Aldershot: Dartmouth.

CARSON, D. (1989), 'Prosecuting People with Mental Handicaps', *Criminal Law Review*: 87.

CHISWICK, D. (1990), 'Fitness to Stand Trial and Plead, Mutism and Deafness', in R. Bluglass and P. Bowden, eds., *Principles and Practice of Forensic Psychiatry*. Edinburgh: Churchill Livingstone.

COID, J. (1989), 'Psychopathic Disorders', *Current Opinion in Psychiatry*, 2: 750–6.

CRIMINAL LAW REVISION COMMITTEE (1984), 15th Report: *Sexual Offences*, Cmnd 9213. London: HMSO.

DELL, S. (1983), 'Wanted: An Insanity Defence that Can be Used', *Criminal Law Review*: 431.

DELL, S., GROUNDS, A., JAMES, K., and ROBERTSON, G. (1991), 'Mentally Disordered Remanded prisoners: Report to the Home Office (unpublished).

DELL, S., and ROBERTSON, G. (1988), *Sentenced to Hospital: Offenders in Broadmoor*, Maudsley Monographs 32. London: Institute of Psychiatry.

DOOLEY, E. (1990), 'Prison Suicide in England and Wales, 1972–87', *British Journal of Psychiatry*, 156: 40–5.

EASTMAN, N. (1990), 'Unfit to Plead: The Test of being "Under Disability"', paper presented to Law Society's Mental Health Sub-Committee Conference, London, 8 June.

FENNELL, P. (1991), 'Diversion of Mentally Disordered Offenders from Custody', *Criminal Law Review*: 333–48.

—— (1992), 'Balancing Care and Control: Guardianship, Community Treatment Orders and Patient Safeguards', *International Journal of Law and Psychiatry*, 15: 205–35.

FLOUD, J., and YOUNG, W. (1981), *Dangerousness and Criminal Justice*. London: Heinemann.

GENDERS, E. (1991), 'Types of Violent Crime', Report to the Home Office. Oxford: Centre for Criminological Research, University of Oxford.

GENDERS, E., and PLAYER, E. (1989), 'Grendon: A Study of a Therapeutic Community within the Prison System', Report to the Home Office. Oxford: Centre for Criminological Research, University of Oxford.

GOSTIN, L. (1986), *Mental Health Services: Law and Practice*. London: Shaw and Sons.

GROUNDS, A. (1987), 'Detection of "Psychopathic Disorder Patients" in Special Hospitals: Critical Issues', *British Journal of Psychiatry*, 151: 474–8.

—— (1990), 'Transfers of Sentenced Prisoners to Hospital', *Criminal Law Review*: 544–51.

—— (1991), 'The Transfer of Sentenced Prisoners to Hospital 1960–1983', *British Journal of Criminology*, 31/1: 54–71.

GRUBIN, D. H. (1991), 'Unfit to Plead in England and Wales 1976–1988: A Survey', *British Journal of Psychiatry*, 158: 540–8.

GUDJONSSON, G., CLARE, I., RUTTER, S., and PEARSE, J. (1993), *Persons at Risk during Interview in Police Custody: The Identification of Vulnerabilities*,

Research Study no. 12, Royal Commission on Criminal Justice. London: HMSO.

Gunn, J. (1992), 'Psychiatry and Criminology: A Reconciliation', paper presented to the British Society of Criminology AGM, London, 29 January.

Gunn, J., Maden, A., and Swinton, M. (1991*a*), 'Treatment Needs of Patients with Psychiatric Disorders', *British Medical Journal*, 303: 338–41.

—— (1991*b*) *Mentally Disordered Prisoners*. London: Home Office.

Gunn, J., and Robertson, G. (1987), 'A Ten-Year Follow-Up of Men Discharged from Grendon Prison', *British Journal of Psychiatry*, 151: 674–8.

Gunn, J., Robertson, G., Dell, S., and Way, C. (1978), *Psychiatric Aspects of Imprisonment*. London: Academic Press.

Hoggett, B. (1990), *Mental Health Law*, 3rd edn. London: Sweet and Maxwell.

Home Office/Department of Health and Social Security (1987), *Report of the Interdepartmental Working Group of Home Office and DHSS Officials on Mentally Disturbed Offenders in the Prison System in England and Wales*. London: Home Office/DHSS.

Home Office (1990*a*), *Crime, Justice and Protecting the Public*, Cm. 965. London: HMSO.

—— (1990*b*), *Report of an Efficiency Scrutiny of the Prison Medical Service*, vol. 2, October. London: Home Office.

—— (1991), *Custody, Care and Justice*. London: HMSO.

James, D., and Hamilton, L. (1992), 'Setting up Psychiatric Liaison Schemes to Magistrates' Courts: Problems and Practicalities', *Medicine, Science and Law*, 32: 167–76.

Koe, H. (1992), 'Domestic Violence, Gender Blindness and Concepts of Criminal Responsibility', paper presented to the MA Criminal Justice Seminar Programme Brunel University, 2 March.

Link, B., Cullen, F., and Andrews, H. (1993), 'Violent and Illegal Behaviour of Current and Former Mental Patients Compared to Community Controls', *American Sociological Review*, 57/3: 275–92.

Mackay, R. D. (1990), 'Fact and Fiction about the Insanity Defence', *Criminal Law Review*: 247–55.

—— (1991), 'The Decline of Disability in Relation to the Trial', *Criminal Law Review*: 87–97.

Maierkatkin, D. (1991), 'Postpartum Psychosis, Infanticide and the Law', *Crime, Law and Social Change*, 15/2: 109–24.

Mental Health Act Commission (1989), *Third Biennial Report, 1987–1989*. London: HMSO.

Miller, R. D. (1992), 'Economic Factors Leading to Diversion of the Mentally Disordered from the Civil to the Criminal Commitment Systems', *International Journal of Law and Psychiatry*, 15: 1–12.

Monahan, J. (1992), 'Mental Disorder and Violent Behaviour: Perceptions and Evidence', *American Psychologist*, 47: 511–21.

Monahan, J., and Steadman, H. (1983), 'Crime and Mental Disorder: An Epidemiological Approach', in M. Tonry and N. Morris, eds., *Crime and Justice: An Annual Review of Research*, vol. 4, 145–89. Chicago: University of Chicago Press.

Murray, D. J. (1989), *Review of Research on Re-offending of Mentally Disordered Offenders*, Research and Planning Unit Paper no. 55. London: Home Office.

Office of Population, Censuses and Surveys (1986), *Morbidity Statistics from General Practice: Third National Study 1981–82*. London: HMSO.

Peay, J. (1982), 'Dangerousness: Ascription or Description?', in P. Feldman, ed., *Developments in the Study of Criminal Behaviour*, vol. 2: *Violence*. Chichester: Wiley.

—— (1988), 'Offenders Suffering from Psychopathic Disorder: The Rise and Demise of a Consultation Document', *British Journal of Criminology*, 28: 67–81.

—— (1989), *Tribunals on Trial: A Study of Decision-Making Under the Mental Health Act 1983*. Oxford: Clarendon Press.

—— (1993), 'A Criminological Perspective', in W. Watson and A. Grounds, eds., *Mentally Disordered Offenders in an Era of Community Care*. Cambridge: Cambridge University Press.

Player, E. (1992), 'Treatment for Sex Offenders: A Cautionary Note', *Prison Service Journal*, 85: 2–9.

Prins, H. (1986), *Dangerous Behaviour, the Law and Mental Disorder*. London: Tavistock.

—— (1990), 'Mental Abnormality and Criminality: An Uncertain Relationship', *Medicine, Science and Law*, 30/3: 247–58.

—— (1991), 'Is Psychopathic Disorder a Useful Clinical Concept? A Perspective from England and Wales', *International Journal of Offender Therapy and Comparative Criminology*, 35/2: 119–25.

Radzinowicz, L., and Hood, R. (1981), 'A Dangerous Direction for Sentencing Reform', *Criminal Law Review*: 756–61.

Raeder, M. (1992), 'Evidentiary Procedural and Substantive Ramifications of Premenstrual Syndrome and Battered Women Syndrome', paper presented to 'Reform of Evidence', a conference of the Society for the Reform of Criminal Law, Vancouver, August.

Reed Report (1991), *Review of Health and Social Services for Mentally Disordered Offenders and Others Requiring Similar Services*. London: Department of Health/Home Office.

—— (1992), *Review of Health and Social Services for Mentally Disordered Offenders and Others Requiring Similar Services*. London: Department of Health/Home Office.

Richardson, G. (1991), 'Discretionary Life Sentences and the European Convention on Human Rights', *Public Law*: 34–40.

Robertson, G. (1988), 'Arrest Patterns among Mentally Disordered Offenders', *British Journal of Psychiatry*, 153: 313–16.

Roth, M. (1990), 'Psychopathic (Sociopathic) Personality', in R. Bluglass and P. Bowden, eds., *Principles and Practice of Forensic Psychiatry*. Edinburgh: Churchill Livingstone.

Rubin, D. (1972), 'Predictions of Dangerousness in Mentally Ill Criminals', *Archives of General Psychiatry*, 27: 397–407.

Shapland, J. (1991), 'Where Do We Put Them? Coping with Mentally Disordered Offenders', paper presented to the British Criminology Conference, York, July.

SMITH, J. C., and HOGAN, B. (1988), *Criminal Law*, 6th edn. London: Butterworths.

SWANSON, J., HOLZER, C., GANJU, V., and JONO, R. (1990), 'Violence and Psychiatric Disorder in the Community: Evidence from the Epidemiological Catchment Area Surveys', *Hospital and Community Psychiatry*, 41: 761–70.

TAYLOR, P., and GUNN, J. (1984), 'Violence and Psychosis. I: Risk of Violence among Psychotic Men', *British Medical Journal*, 288: 1945–9.

TUMIM, S. (1990), *Suicide and Self Harm in Prison Service Establishments in England and Wales*, Report of a Review by Her Majesty's Chief Inspector of Prisons for England and Wales, Cm. 1383. London: HMSO.

VERDUN-JONES, S. (1989), 'Sentencing the Partly Mad and Partly Bad: The Case of the Hospital Order in England and Wales', *International Journal of Law and Psychiatry*, 12: 1–27.

WASIK, M. (1992), 'Arrangements for Early Release', *Criminal Law Review*: 252–61.

WATSON, W., and GROUNDS, A., eds. (1993), *Mentally Disordered Offenders in an Era of Community Care*. Cambridge: Cambridge University Press.

WESSELY, S., and TAYLOR, P. (1991), 'Madness and Crime: Criminology versus Psychiatry', *Criminal Behaviour and Mental Health*, 1: 193–228.

WEST, D. J. (1965), *Murder Followed By Suicide*. London: Heinemann.

WEST MIDLANDS REGIONAL HEALTH AUTHORITY (1991), *Report of the Panel of Inquiry Appointed to Investigate the Case of Kim Kirkman.*

WHITE, S. (1991), 'Insanity Defences and Magistrates' Courts', *Criminal Law Review*: 501–11.

WORLD HEALTH ORGANIZATION (1978), *Mental Disorders: Glossary and Guide to their Classification in Accordance with the Ninth Revision of the International Classification of Diseases, Injuries and Causes of Death.* Geneva: WHO.

WILCZYNSKI, A. (1991), 'Images of Parents who Kill their Children', paper presented to the British Criminology Conference, York, July.

WOOD, D. (1988), 'Dangerous Offenders, and the Morality of Protective Sentencing', *Criminal Law Review*: 424–33.

WOOLF, Lord Justice (1991), *Prison Disturbances April 1990, Report of an Inquiry by the Rt Hon. Lord Justice Woolf (Parts I and II) and His Honour Judge Stephen Tumin (Part II),* Cm. 1456. London: HMSO.

YOUNG, A. (1991), 'Feminism and the Body of Criminology', paper presented to the British Society of Criminology, York, July.

24

Youth, Crime, and Society

GEOFFREY PEARSON

I have three objectives in this chapter. The first is to situate the preoccupation with youthful crime within its social and historical contexts. The second is to explore in a little more depth in the main body of the text some of the key issues in the study of youth crime, particularly as these have been developed in the interplay between British and North American traditions of research and theory since the 1939–45 world war. Finally, I hope to focus attention on different ways of addressing the vexed question of why it is that adolescence appears to be the 'peak age' for criminality.

In pursuit of these aims, the plan of the chapter is as follows. In an introductory section I will offer a brief overview of the history of the concept of 'juvenile delinquency' and some of the methods of inquiry adopted in its study. This historical context casts considerable doubt over the easy contrasts which are so often struck between the lawlessness of youth today and the law-abiding conformity of earlier generations. The following section explores some of the central contributions of North American criminology to the study of juvenile crime, particularly those flowing from the urban sociology of the Chicago School and the different varieties of subcultural theory and research which have proved so influential. Next, there is a discussion of how this work was received within British criminology, where a distinctive subcultural tradition was fashioned in the post-war years which resulted in a number of illuminating ethnographic studies, together with theoretical and empirical innovations which embraced not only youth crime but also the study of youth cultures. Flowing from this, the penultimate section examines the applications of labelling theory to youthful misconduct, as a means of addressing the question to what extent young offenders are 'abnormal' and 'deviant' when compared with their peers; or whether, to pose an alternative viewpoint, youthful misconduct is more or less a common currency among the rising generation and that it is only some young people (but not others) who emerge as committed criminals because of the way in which they become ensnared within the criminal justice system and its stigmatizing processes. This dichotomy, it seems to me, describes an uneasy tension within both contemporary criminology and the wider supporting culture of British society, whereby there is a tendency to see juvenile crime both as the problem of a tiny hard core of persistent offenders and as a symptom of an entire generational process of moral decline. Finally, in my concluding remarks I will suggest that the field of inquiry and its root assumptions might be in need of a radical overhaul, and point to some possible directions in rethinking the commonly held association between 'youth' and 'crime'.

There will therefore be a certain unevenness in the approach adopted, which leans heavily towards a historically informed sociology of youth, youth cultures, and youth crime. I will, for example, not be concerned with traditions of research and theory which locate the origins of juvenile crime in family breakdown or supposedly abnormal systems of family functioning, intra-familial communication, and socialization.[1] Nor will I

[1] The often vigorous debate on the family and juvenile crime is one with a long history. For the early Victorians of the mid-nineteenth century, it was already commonplace to assert that juvenile delinquency was a direct consequence of the perceived decline of parental control, broken homes, and the absence of working women from the home. Directly similar accusations were brought against the working-class family in the late 1890s and the early years of the twentieth century, and have been repeated periodically at times of social anxiety about the youth question (cf. Pearson 1983). In the course of the twentieth century this moral discourse on the family was combined with a variety of social-scientific research and theorizing on family life and delinquency. One of the most important landmarks in this development was the 'maternal deprivation' thesis proposed by John Bowlby, who claimed that a history of broken family life was common in the lives of juvenile thieves, and then more generally that the absence of adequate maternal care in early childhood resulted in the production of an 'affectionless' character type who was more prone to criminality (Bowlby 1946, 1952, 1953).

Bowlby's work has been subjected to various forms of criticism, both scientific and ideological. Summarizing a complex body of evidence, Michael Rutter (1972) was to show that although emotional harm could result from disruptions in early childhood, the 'maternal deprivation' thesis had been much overstated. Family influences nevertheless remain important in more recent 'criminal career' research (West and Farrington 1973, 1977; chapter 12 in this volume). Even so, as Junger-Tas (1992) has observed, the 'broken home' is an unhelpful 'umbrella' concept which conflates too many different aspects of family life. For example, a review of fifty previous research studies by Wells and Rankin (1991) indicated that in most of these the family had been judged against a simple measuring-stick as either 'broken' or 'unbroken', whereas a more useful approach might be to distinguish between types of family structure as against family processes and relationships: thus turning the attention towards the quality of family life, the character of parental supervision, 'parenting skills', and so on (Riley and Shaw 1985; Utting *et al.* 1993). Associated concerns with behaviour disorders resulting from the physical and sexual abuse of children within intact families confirms the inadequacies of the 'broken home' concept (Cicchetti and Carlson 1989).

However, one central difficulty with this area of concern is that the debate remains rootedly ideological. Feminist critiques have identified the ways in which Bowlby's maternal deprivation thesis formed part of an ideological effort to reconstruct the 'normal' family in the immediate post-war period, and to encourage women to return to their 'traditional' roles after the excitements of the 1939–45 war years when working women had made a vital contribution to the war effort (Riley 1983; Mitchell 1975). The independence of women with children (whether as working mothers or single parents) is a frequent sub-text of the discourse on the 'broken' home. Amid the renewed moral panic on juvenile crime of the early 1990s, in one particularly embittered attack on single parenthood it is asserted that even in impoverished neighbourhoods it is 'families without fatherhood' which are the root cause of

address research and theory which relies upon genetic, biological, or neuropsychological research (cf. Moffitt 1990).

This emphasis (or bias) in my approach is explicitly informed by what I take to be the central directions of human self-understanding with regard to youthful crime: namely, that law-breaking among young people in 'western' societies is regarded as a normal feature of life-cycle development, rather than as an 'aberrant' or 'deviant' phenomenon. As Talcott Parsons (1942: 606) described it in one of the earliest formulations of the notion of an adolescent 'youth culture', when contrasted with the responsibility assumed in adult roles 'the orientation of the youth culture is more or less specifically irresponsible'. I do not, necessarily, accept this view as given fact. Indeed, the brief auto-critique of the field of inquiry which is found in the conclusion will suggest that there are good reasons to question such a view, and that the commonly held youth–crime connection is itself an ideological belief-system associated with the consequences of living with modernity.

FORGOTTEN HISTORY: JUVENILE CRIME AS PERPETUAL NOVELTY

Our understanding of the problem of youth crime and youthful misconduct is bedevilled by a lack of attention to its history. A profound historical amnesia has settled around the youth question, whereby it is imagined that in the past young people were orderly, disciplined, and well behaved. The problem of youth crime then appears as one that is entirely unprecedented. It is understood as a result of recent social changes, involving a pattern of complaint linking youthful crime to the 'permissive society'; the break-up of the family and community; the dwindling power of parents, teachers, magistrates, and policemen; the lack of respect among the young for authority in all its forms; and the incitements of demoralizing popular entertainments such as television violence and video nasties which lead to imitative 'copy-cat' crime.

The complaint is entirely familiar, invariably expressed in a generational time-scale which links the perceived erosion in moral standards to events of 'twenty or thirty years ago' or 'since the war'. For example:

> That's the way we're going nowadays. Everything slick and stream-lined, everything made out of something else. Celluloid, rubber, chromium-steel everywhere

crime among the young (Dennis and Erdos 1992). This is a position deeply reminiscent of North American debates on the role of the female-headed black household in generating ghetto crime which, whatever the intention, have invariably distracted attention from the structural poverty and discrimination which afflict black families and black communities (Wilson 1987; Murray 1984). In spite of these persistent ideological backdrops, however, what can be said with a fair degree of confidence is that the hollow notion of the 'broken home' has been unpacked and rendered both more complex and less rhetorical by social research.

. . . radios all playing the same tune, no vegetation left, everything cemented over . . . There's something that's gone out of us in these twenty years since the war.

Or again:

The passing of parental authority, defiance of pre-war conventions, the absence of restraint, the wildness of extremes, the confusion of unrelated liberties, the wholesale drift away from churches, are but a few characteristics of after-war conditions.

We know these different versions of the 'post-war blues' well enough. It is a structure of feeling which has commonly been linked to successive post-war 'crime waves' and spectacular youth cultures such as the Teddy Boys of the 1950s, the Mods of the early 1960s, the Skinheads of the late 1960s and early 1970s, and their successors. The immediate conceptual difficulty, however, is that both of these complaints against 'post-war' decline come from before the Second World War. The first is from George Orwell's pre-war novel *Coming Up For Air* (1939); the second is from a Christian youth worker, James Butterworth, describing in *Clubland* (1932) the difficulties heaped upon him in the 'post-war' years in his work among young people in the Elephant and Castle district of working-class south London. Nor should the historical irony be allowed to pass that, twenty years later, it was from this same area of south London that the 'Teddy Boy' phenomenon would emerge, amid widespread public concern that this was an entirely novel and un-English phenomenon resulting from 'Americanizing' influences of rock-and-roll music and post-war 'affluence' (cf. Fyvel 1963). As Richard Hoggart had described the 1950s 'juke box boys' in *The Uses of Literacy* (1958: 248), they were 'boys between fifteen and twenty, with drape-suits, picture ties, and an American slouch'.

North American culture, specifically in the form of the cinema, had already been identified as a criminogenic force among British youth in the 1920s and 1930s, as in a King George's Jubilee Trust report of 1939:

A Never-never land of material values expressed in terms of gorgeous living, a plethora of high-powered cars and revolvers, and unlimited control of power . . . of unbridled desire, of love crudely sentimental or fleshly, of ruthless acquisition, of reckless violence . . . It is an utterly selfish world . . . It is a school of false values and its scholars cannot go unscathed. (Morgan 1939: 242)

The baleful influence of North American modernity, signified most powerfully by the 'movies', was thus seen as leading to novel generational conflicts. F. R. Leavis was among those to express the deep concerns of the inter-war years as these focused on the family, community, and the rising generation. 'Change has been so catastrophic,' he wrote in 1930, that it 'has, in a few years, radically affected religion, broken up the family, and revolutionised social custom': 'the generations find it hard to adjust themselves to each other, and parents are helpless to deal with their children . . . It is a breach of continuity that threatens . . . It is a commonplace that we are being Americanised' (Leavis 1930: 6–7).

The inter-war years had also been a period of great change in the juvenile justice system. As indicated by Victor Bailey in *Delinquency and Citizenship* (1987), it was an era in which many of the reforming principles were established which nowadays tend to be regarded as aspects of 'post-war' permissiveness. Bailey (1987: 117) describes how in the mid-1930s 'a vigorous controversy burst forth' between 'reformers' and 'reactionaries' on the question of the 1933 Children and Young Persons Act, which was widely condemned by the 'reactionaries' as a system of 'sentimental justice' which had weakened the authority of the courts and led to an upsurge in juvenile crime. Generally speaking, in fact, we find an extraordinary symmetry between pre-war and post-war complaints about the rising generation:

> Relaxation of parental control, decay of religious influence, and the transplantation of masses of young people to new housing estates where there is little scope for recreation and plenty for mischief . . . a growing contempt by the young person for the procedures of juvenile courts . . . The problem is a serious challenge, the difficulty of which is intensified by the extension of freedom which, for better or worse, has been given to youth in the last generation. (Morgan 1939: 166, 191)

As I have described at some greater length in *Hooligan: A History of Respectable Fears* (1983), these uncanny resemblances between 'pre-war' and 'post-war' forms of expression echo across a much longer connected history of complaint against young people whereby successive generations have understood juvenile crime as an entirely unprecedented phenomenon which reflects the breakdown of tradition. One common way of stating these perceived discontinuities is in strictly generational terms—hence the popular slogans 'twenty or thirty years ago' or 'since the war'. However, nor can social scientific enquiry exempt itself entirely from these deeply ingrained social attitudes. The idea of the disruption of custom and tradition brought about by modernity, for example, is one of the organizing principles of sociology. Where the idea of youthful crime as a symptom of social breakdown is enshrined in certain kinds of social theory, however, the time-scale is more likely to invoke longer-term developments such as 'urbanization', 'industrialization', and 'modernity'.

Even so, these historical formulations are difficult to square with the historical record since there was already widespread concern with 'unruly apprentices' in pre-industrial England, together with a broader set of early modern European preoccupations with youthful misconduct (Pearson 1983: ch. 8; Gillis 1974; Davis 1971). Of the infamous London apprentices of the seventeenth and eighteenth centuries, Smith (1973: 149,

157) has suggested that they 'were thought of as a separate order or subculture' and that they 'displayed many of the characteristics which have been ascribed to twentieth century youth'. Various attempts were made to regularize the conduct of apprentices, banning them from participation in football games, playing music, or drinking in taverns (Pearson 1983: 193). The length of their hair was another focus for periodic conflict between the generations, and one typical order of 1603 had required that they should not 'weare their haire long nor locks at their eares like ruffians' (Dunlop 1912: 192). The outcomes of these struggles between masters and apprentices were not always settled in the favour of the masters; nor was the apprenticeship system always above blame, since there were instances of great cruelty against the young. As Dorothy George (1966: 269) observed: 'The theory that masters in general exercised a wholesome discipline over apprentices seems to have been theory only'.

As Pinchbeck and Hewitt (1969) make clear, more generalized complaints against the delinquency of children and young people had been commonplace in pre-industrial 'Merrie' England. In 1678, for example, Firmin was among those who expressed his shock at 'the rudeness of children' in the London streets where one found 'whole companies at play, where they shall wrangle or cheat one another, and upon the least provocation swear and fight for a farthing; or else they shall be found whipping of horses . . . throwing of dirt or stones into coaches, or at the glasses' (quoted in Pinchbeck and Hewitt 1969: 104). Nearly a century later, in 1758 Sir John Fielding could be found rehearsing a directly similar lament against 'the numberless, miserable, deserted, ragged and iniquitous pilfering Boys that at this Time shamefully infested the streets of London' (quoted ibid.: 111).

It was, however, to be amid the experiences of the urban and industrial revolutions of the early nineteenth century that more distinctively 'modern' forms of complaint about juvenile crime began to be heard—and heard often. 'The factory system,' wrote Samuel Smiles in 1843, 'however much it may have added to the wealth of the country, has had the most deleterious effect on the domestic condition of the people. It has invaded the sanctuary of the home and broken up the family and social ties' (quoted in Smiles 1879: 60). It is questionable whether the home ever had been a 'sanctuary' for the common people, but the accusation was almost routine in the nineteenth century. A decade earlier the Reverend Edward Irving, in a solemn treatise on *The Last Days*, had claimed proof for his assertion 'that disobedience to parents is a strong and striking characteristic of the present times' in 'the amazing increase of juvenile depredations and felonies' (1828: 81). 'Is not every juvenile delinquent the evidence of a family in which the family bond is weakened and loosened?' Irving had asked himself.

The destruction of what were held to have been previously intact traditions of family and community, resulting in widespread juvenile depravity in the manufacturing districts, was to become a common currency in the mid-nineteenth century as philanthropists such as Mary Carpenter and Matthew Davenport Hill busied themselves in their endeavours to rescue the children of the poor from crime and immorality (Pearson 1983: ch. 7; Radzinowicz and Hood 1990: ch. 6). Social opinion on the causes of juvenile crime would remain divided in the later decades of the nineteenth century, involving a complex interplay of traditional moral arguments which stressed the lack of discipline and religious instruction, the emphasis on social and environmental influences, and hereditary notions of juvenile crime which were strengthened by the popularity of Darwinism (Wiener 1990; Radzinowicz and Hood 1990; Garland 1985). It was in the mid-nineteenth century, however, that a recognizable pattern of complaint was established: that young criminals were getting younger; that they were symptomatic of the breakdown of the family; that young people were becoming precociously independent; and that juvenile crime often assumed a form which imitated the dramas which children had witnessed at the cheap theatres and music halls (Pearson 1983: ch. 7).

By the 1870s it was not uncommon for supporters of the reformatory school movement to claim that the problem of juvenile crime had been defeated (Radzinowicz and Hood 1990: ch. 7). This brief interlude of social optimism, which was not universally shared, was to be shattered in the late Victorian and Edwardian years, which were to be consumed by a massive wave of anxiety about the nation's youth. It was in the late 1890s that the term 'hooligan' entered into common English usage (Pearson 1983: chs. 4, 5). Interlocking fears about youthful crime, the failure to reproduce stable work habits among the young, and a perceived decline in both the physical and moral condition of the rising generation prompted a number of controversies and schemes of social reclamation, including Baden-Powell's Boy Scout movement which was launched in 1908 (Gillis 1974, 1975; Springhall 1977; Humphries 1981; Hendrick 1990; Bristow 1991; Pearson 1989). It was a constant accusation in these years that young people had 'tasted too much freedom' and that they had 'emancipated themselves from all home influence and restraints' (Braithwaite 1904: 189; Gorst 1901: 213). Reginald Bray, who was by no means an unsympathetic observer, went so far as to state that 'the city-bred youth is growing up in a state of unrestrained liberty', further alleging that 'the habits of school and home are rapidly sloughed off in the new life of irresponsible freedom' and that 'the large amount of money he has to spend on himself is by no means an unmixed benefit' (Bray 1911: 102–3, 205).

This was also an era, however, in which a new sensitivity was introduced into the understanding of youthful crime and misconduct in the form of a number of closely observed quasi-ethnographic studies of the lives of young people—such as those by Alexander Paterson (1911), Charles Russell (1905), E. J. Urwick (1904), Arnold Freeman (1914), and Reginald Bray (1904, 1907)—which were a considerable advance on the distant and sometimes clouded imaginings of the early Victorians. As one consequence of this closer and more detailed observation it became clear that working-class youth in some of Britain's cities had established what we would now call a 'youth culture' with its own distinctive clothing style and a penchant for territorial gang fights and assaults on police officers (Pearson 1989; 1983 ch. 5). The 'Hooligan' dress style in London consisted of bell-bottom trousers cut tight at the knee, heavily ornamented leather belts, neck-scarves, a peaked cap, and short-cropped hair with a donkey fringe. In other cities, similar gangs were known by different names. In Birmingham, they were called 'Peaky Blinders', while in Manchester and Salford they were known and feared as 'Scuttlers' and also as 'Ikes' or 'Ikey Lads'. Among the various descriptions of these gangs and their habits, a Police Court Missioner, Alex Devine, offered a detailed account from 1890 of the Salford Scuttler and his dress style of 'narrow-go-wide' trousers, 'puncher's cap', and narrow-toed brass-tipped clogs. Devine was particularly struck by the ornamental designs which adorned the Scuttlers' leather belts:

> Many of these belts are very curious, bearing remarkable designs upon them. These are made by the insertion of a large number of pins, which are used to form a design the whole length of the belt. The pins are inserted into the leather, then broken off, and filed down to a level with the leather. These designs include figures of serpents, a heart pierced with an arrow (this appears to be a favourite design), Prince of Wales' feathers, clogs, animals, stars, etc., and often either the name of the wearer of the belt or that of some woman. (Devine 1890: 2).

The similarities with the ways in which young people in the later years of the twentieth century would adorn leather jackets with metal stud designs seem unmistakable. What is equally unmistakable is that whereas we think of 'youth cultures' as a novel development deeply characteristic of the post-war years in Britain, they have been observable for a century or more—reflecting the dominant and unhelpful tendency whereby a historical amnesia is cast around the youth question, so that youth cultures and youth crime assume the appearance of ever-increasing outrage and perpetual novelty.

SOCIAL STRUCTURE, CITY, SUBCULTURE: YOUTH IN THE UNDERCLASS

Some of the earliest responses to the problem of juvenile crime in mid-nineteenth-century England had understood it to be a symptom of the explosive forces of the urban and industrial revolutions. These, it was often supposed, had uprooted the pre-industrial customs and traditions of community and family, and supplanted them with the unnatural arrangements of the factory system of labour and the teeming anonymity of the city. Fierce controversies were engaged in at the time and in later years of the century as to whether crime, which was seen as the result of these changes, was a moral or a material condition. Was poverty at the root of crime in the slums of the manufacturing districts? Or was it drink and depravity which spurred on the 'dangerous classes'?

The same vast alterations of the social landscape arrived some decades later in the northern cities and manufacturing centres of the USA, prompting distinctive sociological approaches to crime, the city, and social structure in the early years of the twentieth century. Both the work of Robert Merton in his essay on 'Social Structure and Anomie' (1938), which offered a general theory of deviant conduct, and that of the Chicago School of Sociology in the 1920s and 1930s, were to have a decisive influence on subsequent inquiries into juvenile delinquency. The purpose of this section is to trace the main contours of these developments.

Some aspects of the Chicago School's work were to reproduce preoccupations directly similar to those of the English Victorians, albeit in a social-scientific mode. Wirth's essay 'Urbanism as a Way of Life' (1938), for example, which offered a grand synthesis of the Chicago position, was deeply troubled by the psychological and social disorientations of city life, with its fleeting human contacts and overcrowding of the senses, leading to a disintegration of the moral order, social incohesion, and crime (cf. Smith 1980). This devastating image of the city could easily have been confused with the proclamations of the North American philanthropist and moral crusader Jane Addams, who frequently gave vent to the commonplace fears and bafflement of an earlier generation:

> The social relationships in a modern city are so hastily made and often so superficial, that the old human restraints of public opinion, long sustained in smaller communities, have also broken down. Thousands of young men and women in every great city have received none of the lessons in self-control which even savage tribes imparted to their children. (Addams 1912: 104)

In other respects, however, the Chicago School was to develop a body of work which edged away from this luridly undifferentiated pessimistic urban vision. Statistical methods were devised and deployed in order to map the social ecology of crime and deviance, and ethnographic studies portrayed in careful detail the varied lifestyles of the hobos and tramps, the Jewish ghetto, the cultural mosaic of the lower North Side of the city with its contrasts of middle-class prosperity and rooming-house poverty, the taxi-dance-hall racket where patrons bought tickets to dance with the girls, and the delinquent gangs which were found in profusion in the Chicago of the 1920s (Hannerz 1980).

In terms of the Chicago ethnographic legacy, two pioneering works on delinquency stand in sharp contrast. The first is Frederic Thrasher's *The Gang* (1927), which described and analysed no fewer than 1,313 gangs of different types in the city of Chicago. The second is Clifford Shaw's *The Jack-Roller* (1930), which employed autobiographical techniques to offer the life-history or 'own story' of a delinquent boy named Stanley. In his introduction to a later edition of *The Jack-Roller*, Howard Becker (1966: xv) suggests that personal documents such as this allow a means of 'putting ourselves in Stanley's skin' so that we 'become aware of the deep biases about such people that ordinarily permeate our thinking' and can 'begin to ask questions about delinquency from the point of view of the delinquent'. In a wide-ranging review of ethnographic and 'oral history' methods as applied to delinquency, Bennett (1981) has suggested that there is a line of continuity which stretches from the work of Henry Mayhew in Victorian London in terms of the rhetorical means by which oral histories offer this possibility of conversation and dialogue across the divides of social class, enabling the conventional world to glimpse the enduring humanity of those belonging to powerless and marginalized groups.

By contrast, Thrasher's *The Gang* is now generally recognized to be something of a curiosity in social-scientific terms. Given its ambitious scope to study as many as 1,313 Chicago gangs, it is as one might anticipate a sprawling and unruly book, full of detailed observations culled from a variety of sources, with little in the way of connecting argument and utterly devoid of any explicit account of the methods used to collect its data. Some sources suggest, for example, that Thrasher performed magic tricks to gain the confidence of his informants. Further confusion is added by the fact that many of the gangs studied were not delinquent gangs at all, but varied from a small network of 'dope-peddlers' serving North Side Chicago to formally organized social and athletic clubs with several hundred members. Thrasher nevertheless offered some fascinating observations on the internal structures of gangs, their systems of morality, and (where crime and violence are concerned) their modes of conduct. However, a major difficulty with *The Gang* is its stress on the 'disorganization' of the environment in which gangland flourished, as against clear indications of varying modes of social organization within these gangs, albeit ones different from those prevailing in the conventional social order.

The Chicago School employed a variety of methods in its programme of social research, including the spatial mapping of juvenile delinquency which had been pioneered by Clifford Shaw in 1929 and culminated, through a series of major studies in collaboration with Henry McKay, in their jointly authored *Juvenile Delinquency and Urban Areas* (1942). Their work is generally recognized as a criminological landmark, in spite of criticisms of some aspects of their method and further developments in 'criminal area' research (cf. Brantingham and Brantingham 1984). Essentially, what Shaw and McKay established was that juvenile crime was not evenly distributed throughout the city, but that it tended to be concentrated in what we might now call the 'inner city'. This 'delinquent area' was one which was also characterized by low family income, housing decay, high infant mortality rates, and high rates of both mental disorder and tuberculosis. A largely neglected Chicago School study by Bingham Dai (1937) also indicated a concentration of opium use in the same areas of the city, and later research confirmed high rates of heroin misuse among young men (Finestone 1957; Kobrin and Finestone 1968). One further social factor identified by Shaw and McKay (1942) was that the 'delinquent area' contained a high proportion of either foreign-born or black people, although they also pointed out that high rates of delinquency had been recorded in these areas of the city for some decades, across which several different ethnic groups had formed the predominant population in these neighbourhoods during successive periods of immigration and settlement.

Clearly, the incidence of juvenile crime was closely linked to a variety of measures of social deprivation. The theoretical interpretation of this relationship which Shaw and McKay adopted was that of 'social disorganization': communities weakened by economic forces and cultural heterogeneity, resulting in a low resistance to crime and deviance. As Downes (1966: 71) has pointed out, this involved a somewhat tautological position, 'the rate of delinquency in an area being the chief criterion for its "social disorganisation" which in turn was held to account for the delinquency rate'. Moreover, for all its strengths, the work of Shaw and McKay reproduced and continued a central contradiction of the Chicago legacy, which was that while the ethnographic studies portrayed complex forms of 'low-life' social organization, since these involved values and lifestyles which were unconventional they must be deemed 'dis-organized'. It was a conceptual difficulty neatly summed up William F. Whyte in his 1940s study *Street Corner Society*, which depicted the lives of 'corner boys' in an Italian slum neighbourhood of Boston: 'The middle-class person looks upon the slum district as a formidable mass of confusion, a social chaos. The insider finds in Cornerville a highly organised and integrated social system' (1981 [1943]: xvi).

The work of Shaw and McKay was nevertheless to be deeply influential in the subsequent development of theories of juvenile crime which developed the notion of the 'cultural transmission' of a delinquent subculture, hence perpetuating high levels of crime and deviance within poor neighbourhoods from generation to generation. Restatements and refashionings of the subcultural thesis such as Cohen's *Delinquent Boys* (1955), Cloward and Ohlin's *Delinquency and Opportunity* (1960), Short and Strodtbeck's *Group Processes and Gang Delinquency* (1965), Suttles' *The Social Order of the Slum* (1968), and Miller's 'Lower Class Culture as a Generating Milieu of Gang Delinquency' (1958) were part of this North American criminological tradition which involved criticisms and departures from the Chicago tradition, while maintaining its impetus (cf. Short 1968, 1976).

The other looming presence in this body of work is that of Robert Merton. In his 1938 essay 'Social Structure and Anomie', Merton had proposed that different forms of deviance arose out of the 'strain' between America's cultural system and its social structure. Thus, to abbreviate a complex argument, American culture described itself as an open society in which possibilities of upward social mobility ('from log cabin to White House') were universally available; whereas its social structure was one which limited the possibilities of wealth acquisition and upward mobility to certain social groups, others being excluded. The legitimate 'ends' prescribed by the society (wealth and prosperity) therefore did not correspond to the available 'means' (honest toil). Some forms of deviance such as theft and property crime were hence described by Merton as 'innovative' means by which to deliver the promised ends of the American Dream. Others, such as drug misuse or 'hobo' lifestyles, were grouped together as 'retreatist' adaptations by which people opted out of the conflict between ends and means, attempting neither to achieve the good life by honest toil nor to short-circuit wealth acquisition through illicit means.

There are various forms of criticism of Merton's 'anomie' theory and the resulting typology of deviance (cf. Downes and Rock 1982; Taylor *et al.* 1973). It nevertheless offers a succinct theoretical formulation which would predict, for example, the greater likelihood of juvenile crime among the poorest sections of society. A point which is often overlooked is that, although Merton made no attempt to consider gender relations, his theory would also predict why women commit much less crime than men (cf. Leonard 1982). This is because for women the dominant culture prescribes marriage and motherhood as the desired ends of life, and not monetary success. Hence, young women are on this account subject to less social 'strain' than young men, since access to these ends is not restricted by reasons of lower social class (cf. Goode 1959).

Merton's position was, however, to be challenged in a number of ways within the developments of North American subcultural theory. Albert Cohen in *Delinquent Boys* (1955) was the first to draw together a distinctive theory of the 'delinquent subculture', although he found Merton's stress on monetary gain to be inappropriate given the non-utilitarian character of the subculture. Cohen argued that the delinquent subculture was organized around vandalism, truancy, fighting, and 'having a lark', and that when delinquent boys indulged in theft it was often 'for the hell of it'. Much time was spent 'hanging around', 'chewing the fat', and 'waiting for something to turn up' (cf. Corrigan 1976). For Cohen, the central problem which the delinquent subculture attempted to resolve was that of a working-class boy growing up in a class-based society. The subculture was thereby a means to 'get even' within an uneven society, and crucially to establish and demonstrate status and achievement within an alternative set of values. Similar concerns were much in evidence in Miller's (1958) thesis that the adolescent street-corner gang's philosophy was organized around the 'focal concerns' of lower-class culture: trouble, toughness, smartness, and excitement which through participation in the gang allowed boys to achieve autonomy, belonging, and status.

By contrast, Cloward and Ohlin (1960) developed a position which relied much more directly upon Merton's contribution, and which distinguished between different kinds of delinquent gangs: 'criminal', 'conflict', and 'retreatist'. If Merton had stressed the way in which deviance arose through blocked opportunity structures at a societal level, for Cloward and Ohlin the subcultural differentiation of juvenile gangs was the result of varied opportunity structures at both societal and neighbourhood level. At the societal level, they endorsed the position of Merton and Cohen that lower-class youths were excluded from legitimate opportunities by reason of social class position and race. However, where illegitimate opportunities were concerned, these varied from one neighbourhood to the next. Thus, the central focus of the 'criminal' subculture was property crime, and this type of delinquent gang thrived in those neighbourhoods where there was an adult criminal subculture into which successful young thieves and robbers could be recruited through a form of apprenticeship. 'Conflict' gangs arose in neighbourhoods where neither legitimate opportunities nor access to stable criminal opportunity systems existed, and the focus of their activities was fighting and the assertion of territorial supremacy. 'Retreatist' subcultures were those which engaged in drug misuse and were seen by Cloward and Ohlin, following Merton, as 'double failures' who were unable to succeed by either legitimate or illegitimate means, as a consequence of either what Merton had termed 'socially structured barriers' or 'internalized prohibitions' against the illegitimate structures of opportunity.

One remaining challenge to the subcultural thesis was whether the delinquent subculture was as completely separate from the dominant culture, and oppositional to it, as was usually supposed. For Cohen, although the youthful offender understood the difference between right and wrong, and therefore did not completely lose touch with conventional norms and values, the delinquent subculture was nevertheless directly oppositional: 'The delinquent subculture takes its norms from the larger culture but turns them upside down. The delinquent's conduct is right, by the standards of his subculture, precisely *because* it is wrong by the norms of the larger culture' (Cohen 1955: 28). Cloward and Ohlin, for their part, described an evolutionary process whereby the delinquent's first hesitant steps in law-breaking would be tinged with guilt, but through the experiences of arrest and conflict with the law, and through contact with other juveniles sharing these experiences, he would become separated from convention and more steadily committed to delinquent values.

The strongest line of opposition to these ways of thinking was provided by Sykes and Matza (1957), who suggested a social mechanism by which the delinquent could engage in deviant acts without rejecting conventional morality, but also without suffering incapacitating guilt. This was by the use of a variety of 'techniques of neutralization'. These included the denial of responsibility (e.g. 'It was an accident'); the denial of injury ('They can claim on the insurance'); the denial of the victim ('He was asking for it'); and the condemnation of the condemners ('The system stinks'). An interesting variety of this kind of distancing tactic, by which a deviant identity is managed and conventional values are neutralized, is offered in a study by Reiss (1961) of delinquent boys who engaged in homosexual acts for money on a regular basis, but through a variety of tactics avoided defining themselves as either prostitutes or homosexuals.

In a later paper, Matza and Sykes (1961) developed a different line of critique of those subcultural theorists who had stressed the difference between delinquent and non-delinquent values. In the leisure values of the middle class, they suggested, there were a number of responses and pursuits which were closely akin to supposedly delinquent values, and which thus formed a 'subterranean' value system within the dominant culture. Delinquency and the dominant culture were therefore not oppositional. For example, the pursuit of 'kicks'—held by subculturalists to be a core delinquent value—also had its place in respectable society. 'The search for adventure, excitement and thrill is a subterranean value', Matza and Sykes argued (1961: 716), that 'often exists side by side with the value of security, routinisation and the rest. It is not a deviant value, in any full sense, but must be held in abeyance until the proper moment and circumstances for its expression arrive.' Rather than deviating from these values, the delinquent merely accentuates and 'caricatures' the subterranean value system of the wider culture. 'His vocabulary is different, to be sure, but kicks, big time spending and "rep" have immediate counterparts in the value system of the law-abiding' (ibid.: 717).

Matza was subsequently to develop these fragmentary critiques into a full-blown theory of delinquency which opposed not only the subculture thesis, but any form of sociological or psychological reasoning which implied that the delinquent was constrained and compelled by external or internal forces into a fully different and committed deviant life project. In *Delinquency and Drift* (1964), the delinquent was someone who, through the deployment of techniques of neutralization, and equally through a self-legitimating sense of injustice in the world, could be set adrift from conventional values and commitments—if only partially and temporarily. One crucial difficulty for positivistic, causal theories of all kinds was that most juvenile delinquents did not go on to become adult career criminals. 'Positive criminology accounts for too much delinquency,' Matza argued (1964: 21–2), and predicts 'far more delinquency than actually occurs', thus yielding 'an embarrassment of riches which seemingly goes unmatched in the real world.' Delinquents were not, as suggested by positivist criminology, 'radically differentiated from the rest of conventional youth'. If they had been, 'then involvement in delinquency would be more permanent and less transient, more pervasive and less intermittent than is apparently the case'.

By way of conclusion to this theory of delinquent 'drift', it was further allowed by Matza (1964: 29–30) that although most delinquents were probably 'delinquent drifters', a minority were 'neurotically compulsive and some in the course of their enterprise develop commitment' to adult criminal careers. Because these were more 'sensational and dramatic' than the ordinary delinquent, it was Matza's view that 'the extraordinary delinquent has received greater attention in both mass media and criminological theory'. Stating that his book was to be regarded as 'not a plea for the delinquent but a plea for a reassessment of his enterprise', Matza confirmed his position as joker in the pack by arguing with exquisite irony that the foregoing arguments did not make the 'delinquent drifter' any less of a problem, even though he was 'far less likely to become an adult criminal': 'Though his tenure is short, his replacements are legion.'

THE BRITISH SUBCULTURALIST TRADITION: YOUTH CRIME AND YOUTH CULTURES

By comparison with this vigorous North American sociological legacy within criminology, until the 1960s the position in Britain was relatively impoverished. In the 1940s and early post-war years there had been a number of studies of young people which touched either directly or indirectly on juvenile crime, although these are now of limited interest except in points of detail and in the overall tendency of this body of research to link youthful crime with poverty and social deprivation (e.g. Bagot 1941; Carr-Saunders *et al.* 1942; Cameron 1943; Mannheim 1948; Ferguson 1952; Ferguson and Cunnison 1951, 1956; Willcock 1949).

It was John Barron Mays in his account of juvenile delinquency in Liverpool, *Growing Up in the City* (1954), who first located a British delinquency study in the subculturalist tradition. In a work which bears clear traces of the influence of Shaw and McKay, Thrasher, and William Foote Whyte, he portrayed delinquency as 'almost a social tradition' and a normal aspect of growing up in the Liverpool slums'. He wrote that 'delinquency is not so much a symptom of maladjustment as of adjustment to a subculture in conflict with the culture of the city as a whole' (1954: 147). It was thus 'merely one aspect of the behaviour pattern of underprivileged neighbourhoods . . . characterised by a long history of poverty, casual employment and bad housing'. Though methodologically naïve in certain respects, Mays nevertheless offered a vivid account of the everyday contexts of youthful delinquency with a fine eye for detail. The appendix on the social organization of football games contested by numerous street teams, for example, was in itself a little gem of a study reminiscent of much earlier English observations on the passion for football among working-class youths, such as Charles Russell's *Manchester Boys* (1905), Alexander Paterson's *Across the Bridges* (911) from South London, and Arnold Freeman's *Boy Life and Labour* (1914) from Birmingham (cf. Pearson 1989).

Delinquent 'subcultural' values were much in evidence in any number of post-war British research studies, such as Willmott's (1966) account of adolescent boys in London's working-class East End, and in that of school life by Hargreaves (1967), which described a 'delinquescent' subculture which while not explicitly and actively delinquent offered the potential for delinquent conduct. It was not, however, until the appearance of David Downes's *The Delinquent Solution* (1966) that British sociological criminology came of age. Undertaking a thorough review and critique of the North American legacy, and interrogating it against the British experience, this work constituted both a path-breaking study of the social and economic contexts of juvenile delinquency in London and a rare example of comparative criminology. Primarily, Downes indicated that there were a number of ways in which the British experience of the 1950s and early 1960s differed significantly from that of the USA: for example, the virtual non-existence of the organized criminal 'gang' structure, the absence of a working-class 'retreatist' subculture of drug misuse; and the different racial composition of working-class neighbourhoods and friendship networks. It would be of considerable interest to take the detailed observations on English working-class youth networks offered by Downes, and to reassess them against the experiences of the subsequent thirty years, although it is an indication of the scope of his achievement that this would be an enterprise far too ambitious for the present undertaking. My aim will be more limited, namely to identify some of the ways in which the subculturalist thesis has been developed and ratified by social research in Britain; and also to indicate points of linkage between the British and American research which have shown the received versions of the subculture thesis to be flawed in certain respects.

The tendency for juvenile offenders to be most heavily concentrated in areas of social deprivation provided one focus for British social research, although the outcomes of these studies tended to depart from the spatial model of crime proposed by the Chicago School. Terence Morris's Croydon study *The Criminal Area* (1957) suggested that it was public housing estates rather than the 'interstitial zone' of the inner city which provided a home for juvenile crime; and public-sector housing developments were also identified as high juvenile crime areas by research in Leicester (Jones 1958), Bristol (Spencer 1964), and London (Wallis and Maliphant 1967). The spatial ordering of juvenile crime was given powerful confirmation in the Sheffield study by Baldwin and Bottoms (1976) which was later to unravel some of the mechanisms of the housing market and public-sector housing allocation policies which led to these crime-clustering effects (Bottoms and Wiles 1986; Bottoms *et al.* 1989). Gill (1977) also demonstrated how housing policies could contribute to the development of a 'delinquent area' in a Merseyside study which combined ethnographic methods with an account of the evolution of the notorious reputation of the 'Luke Street' neighbourhood. The intersections of youthful crime, subculture, and local definitions of territory have thus been understood as central issues in both British and North American criminology (Suttles 1968; Armstrong and Wilson 1973; Hope and Foster 1992; Forsyth *et al.* 1992).

In the decade or so following the publication of *The Delinquent Solution*, a number of British field studies were to explore different facets of youthful subcultures of crime and violence (cf. Brake 1980; Hall and Jefferson 1976; Mungham and Pearson 1976). Undoubtedly, one of the outstanding ethnographic studies from this period was Howard Parker's *View from the Boys* (1974), which offered a richly textured account of young men and boys in an inner-city Liverpool neighbourhood who had developed a specialized and financially rewarding pattern of crime in the form of the theft of car radios (or 'catseyes') which briefly enabled them to enjoy the 'good times' before either settling down to marriage and family life, or going to prison (Parker 1974, 1976). Paul Willis (1972, 1978) offered a different focus for ethnography in his various studies of popular music, the social meaning of the motorbike, and patterns of drug use among hippies. In his book *Learning to Labour* (1977), on the other hand, Willis explored through field research in a Midlands secondary school how working-class youths developed an oppositional subculture against formal educational values. Whereas in the work of Albert Cohen and others this type of 'anti-school' subculture had been described as 'delinquent', in Willis's treatment the concept of 'criminality' proved to be too narrow to describe what was seen as an expression of a more generalized conflict within a class-divided society. For Willis, the rejection of the middle-class values of the school by 'the lads' offered a form of preparation for the shop-floor culture of the manual working class, so that through a rehearsal of many of the core values and activities of the shop-floor culture, subverting the value system of the school was a type of 'anticipatory' occupational socialization. Similar preoccupations offered the focus for Paul Corrigan's *Schooling the Smash Street Kids* (1979), based on fieldwork in the city of Sunderland in the north-east of England, which examined why young people 'muck about' in the classroom, or simply refuse to attend school at all and become truants, and interpreted these phenomena as a form of inarticulate resistance to compulsory schooling (cf. Carlen *et al.* 1992). If studies such as those of Willis and Corrigan edged away from 'criminality' as the organizing conceptual principle for understanding youthful misconduct, James Patrick's *A Glasgow Gang Observed* (1973) described a subcultural style which fully embraced and celebrated the values of violent confrontation and machismo which were personified in the semi-heroic figure of the local 'hard man'. By contrast, the more gentle 'hippie' subculture which briefly visited Britain in the late 1960s and early 1970s was glimpsed in studies which, in common with that of Paul Willis, tended to take the use of 'soft' drugs such as cannabis and hallucinogens as their focus (Young 1971*a*, *b*, 1973; Plant 1975; Willis 1978).

The core themes of these studies—fighting, thieving, and drug misuse—might seem to offer some justification for the relevance of Cloward and Ohlin's (1960) gang typology—'conflict', 'criminal', and 'retreatist'—to the British experience. Downes (1966) had, of course, been highly suspicious of such a position, and although subsequent developments must modify one's stance it remains true that North American subculturalist theory has limited application to Britain. There are surprisingly few detailed accounts, for example, of career-criminal youth subcultures. In the one notable example, Parker (1974) describes both how the success of the car-radio theft operation developed by 'The Boys' depended upon the inner-city location of their neighbourhood, which offered an abundant supply of targets in the form of commuters' parked cars during the day, together with the existence of 'older fellers' in the neighbourhood who acted as middlemen in order to 'fence' stolen radios. If this seems to conform to a 'criminal' opportunity structure, however, Parker also makes it clear that the 'The Boys' grew up in a neighbourhood which had formerly been renowned for toughness and fighting, a 'conflict gang' tradition which the younger generation had renounced unless it was necessary to defend honour or to protect oneself.

If the 'criminal' orientation of delinquent subcultures such as these was more likely, as Downes suggested, to be opportunistic than 'traditional', where a 'conflict' orientation is concerned fighting has certainly been a focal concern of successive post-war British youth cultures—Teddy Boys, Mods, and Skinheads (Cohen 1972; Rock and Cohen 1970; Hall and Jefferson 1976; Mungham and Pearson 1976). Fights between neighbourhoods gangs, involving disputes over 'turf' and territory, were a particularly strong feature of the Skinhead subculture in the late 1960s and early 1970s (Clarke 1976). Fighting and rowdyism were also a recurring theme in the rivalries between youthful supporters of football clubs which manifested themselves in the form of 'football hooliganism' (Taylor 1971; Marsh *et al.* 1978). In the case of football, moreover, the conflict orientation is deeply traditional and can be traced back to the origins of the professional game in the late nineteenth century (Pearson 1983; Dunning *et al.* 1988). Racist violence also provided an intermittent thread within British youth subcultures, from the Teddy Boy involvement in the Notting Hill and Shepherds Bush race riots in late 1950s London to the Skinhead gangs of the late 1960s and beyond (Pearson 1976*b*; Fryer 1984: 378 ff; Daniel and Mcguire 1972; Robins and Cohen 1978).

In the case of 'retreatist' subcultures, where Downes had found little or no evidence of drug use among working-class youth, the British experience has been mixed. Britain had been a 'late developer' in terms of illicit drug use, and although there were some pockets of both cannabis use and heroin use in London jazz clubs in the 1950s (Spear 1969), the only evidence of extensive working-class involvement in illicit drug use was the 'Purple Hearts' craze among Mods in the mid-1960s. The 'Boys' in Parker's Liverpool study had access to cannabis which some of them used on a regular basis as part of having a 'good night out', but they seemed generally reluctant to try other drugs such as LSD or those in pill and capsule form. It was Martin Plant's *Drugtakers in an English town* (1975) which offered one of the earliest confirmations through social research of illicit drug use among young people in Britain, approximately divided at that time between 'weekend hippies', whose drug preferences were confined to cannabis and hallucinogens, and an emerging poly-drug culture which was devoted to a variety of drugs in pill and powder form. Prior to this there had been little in the way of social research on drug misuse in Britain, other than of the relatively small heroin scene which until the late 1970s was confined almost entirely to London (Stimson and Oppenheimer 1982; Pearson 1991*a*).

None of this added up, however, to a 'retreatist' youth subculture. Admittedly, some patterns of heroin use identified in London in the late 1960s and early 1970s conformed to an isolationist, retreatist pattern (Stimson 1973). However, the problems with the notion of the 'retreatist' subculture are conceptual rather than empirical, and are not confined to the British experience. The shortcomings of the Mertonian concept of 'retreatism' which had been adopted by Cloward and Ohlin have been clearly demonstrated in both Britain and the USA (Pearson 1987*b*). In particular, the notion of 'retreatism' as the organizing principle of drug subcultures was explicitly refuted by subsequent North American research which focused on the highly active and entrepreneurial lifestyles which street addicts must maintain in order to support a drug habit and 'take care of business' (Feldman 1968; Preble and Casey 1969; Rosenbaum 1981; Johnson *et al.* 1985; Williams 1989). In the context of Britain's heroin epidemic of the 1980s, research among young heroin users in working-class neighbourhoods provided ample confirmation for the view that an energetic delinquent lifestyle organized around various hustles and 'scams' was invariably a central feature of the heroin subculture (Burr 1987; Pearson 1987*a*; Parker *et al.* 1988; Gilman and Pearson 1991). Subsequently, with the emergence of the all-night dance-venue 'rave' culture of the late 1980s and early 1990s, which is strongly associated with the use of stimulant drugs such as Ecstasy (MDMA) and its chemical affiliates, we encounter another youthful British drug subculture which, while it might be self-enclosed and 'retreatist' in terms of its adopted value positions, also offers a form of short-run hedonism which is compatible with the pursuit of conventional roles and lifestyles in both working-class and middle-class cultures and occupations (Pearson *et al.* 1991; Redhead 1993). In a recent ethnographic study of how young intravenous drug users in Glasgow have responded to the risk of HIV infection, McKeganey and Barnard (1992) make it abundantly clear that high-risk practices such as sharing injecting equipment must be understood as a means of expressing loyalty and solidarity, and as a reflection of traditional communal values of 'sharing' scarce commodities and 'making do', rather than as the result of adherence to 'deviant' or 'pathological' value systems.

Quite apart from this vigorous ethnographic tradition, there were a number of theoretical innovations within the post-war British approach to youth subcultures. Given a more traditionally class-based system of political representation and trade unionism than in the USA, it was hardly surprising that some of the consensual assumptions of North American criminology would be called into question. One expression of this was the National Deviancy Conference which had been formed in 1968 in opposition to positivist criminology, and which fashioned a radicalized blend of labelling theory, interactionism, and phenomenological 'naturalism' in the early 1970s (Cohen 1971; Taylor and Taylor 1973). More specifically, the idea of generational subcultures as a classless phenomenon, which had become a dominant view in the 'affluent' society of the post-war years, was rejected and shown to be inadequate in attempting to explain the cultural preferences of young people (Murdock and McRon 1973, 1976*a*).

A body of work which was to be highly influential in the development of a distinctive British approach to the study of youth crime and youth cultures was that of the Centre for Contemporary Cultural Studies at the University of Birmingham, where a group of young researchers, brought together by Stuart Hall, were to make a number of decisive contributions to both field research and theoretical development (Hall and Jefferson 1976; Hall *et al.* 1978, 1980; Clarke *et al.* 1979). Some of the work of the Birmingham Centre was directly concerned with 'deviant' youth subcultures, as in those aspects of Paul Willis's writings which focused on motorbike gangs, drug use among hippies, and the development of an oppositional counter-culture among working-class schoolboys (Willis 1972, 1977, 1978). Willis's contribution also pointed, however, along with that of Hebdige, towards a quite different conceptual framework from that devised in North America; one which located the study of youth within the broader vision of cultural studies (Hebdige 1979; Willis 1990).

An early, formative essay on youth subcultures in east London by Philip Cohen (1972, 1980) was to prove to be a seminal contribution to the development of the Centre for Contemporary Cultural Studies and others who were influenced by the Centre's work (cf. Brake 1980). Cohen situated the emergence of the 'Mod' and 'Skinhead' styles of the 1960s in the context of the social and economic changes which had been visited upon the working-class neighbourhoods of the East Eng in the post-war years. These involved a number of linked alterations to working-class aspirations in terms of housing, the job market, educational opportunities, and leisure. Where housing was concerned, 'slum clearance' had resulted in large-scale migrations to new housing estates. Changes in the local economy and educational opportunities meant that new possibilities of upward social mobility were offered to some, while others languished in the de-skilled and evaporating job opportunities offered by the labour market of London's dwindling dockland. In terms of leisure, the 'communal' spaces offered by the traditional pastimes of the multi-generational kinship network, the corner pub, and the street were also transformed, as a newly 'privatized' form of nuclear family came to be juxtaposed with more remote and centralized leisure facilities.

The working-class community, as described by Cohen, was thus faced with a central contradiction between the promise of an upwardly mobile consumer society and the memories and impoverished remnants of an older working-class lifestyle. These contradictions faced by the 'parent culture', Cohen argued, formed the backcloth against which the younger generation was to fashion successive youth styles such as those of the Mods and the Skinheads. It was the 'latent function of subculture', Cohen suggested (1972: 23), 'to express and resolve, albeit "magically", the contradictions' which existed at an ideological level between 'traditional working class puritanism and the new hedonism of consumption' and at an economic level 'between a future as part of the socially mobile elite, or as part of the new lumpen'. Thus the Mods, with their neat appearance, scooter-bike mobility, and pretensions to an affluent night-clubbing lifestyle, explored the cultural possibilities of the upwardly mobile option; whereas the Skinheads, with cropped hair and a clothing style which caricatured that of the traditional working attire of the manual labourer, explored the downward option while also 'magically' retrieving communal space through the emphasis on territorial gang fights and the physical defence of the 'End' at the football stadium (cf. Clarke 1976).

Cohen's contribution, together with those of Paul Willis (1972) and Dick Hebdige (1979) thus offered a means of 'reading' the dress fashions, musical preferences, and lifestyles adopted by different youth cultures in the post-war years (Clarke and Jefferson 1976; Murdock and McCron 1973; Taylor and Wall 1976; McRobbie 1989). It was a position often expressed within a neo-Marxist, specifically Gramscian, conceptual framework; although it was also possible to discern in Phil Cohen's paper the echo of Robert Merton's emphasis on the 'strain' between culturally prescribed aspirations and structurally limited opportunities—except that, in the work of the Birmingham Centre, the 'innovation' which 'magically' resolved the tension was to be found in a cultural and stylistic mode of expression, rather than through property crime.

In addition to these achievements, the Birmingham Centre was also to offer a significant challenge to racist stereotypes of youthful crime in Britain in the late 1970s and early 1980s (Hall *et al.* 1978; Centre for Contemporary Cultural Studies 1982; Gilroy 1987), while opening up the much neglected question of the cultural and subcultural contexts of the lives of young women and girls (McRobbie and Garber 1976; Women's Studies Group 1978; McRobbie 1978, 1980, 1991; McRobbie and Nava 1984; Griffin 1985).

Quite apart from the contributions of the CCCS, there were a number of studies relevant to the question of black youth (Cashmore and Troyna 1982). Ken Pryce's *Endless Pressure* (1979) indicated, through fieldwork in the African-Caribbean community of Bristol, how the familiar themes of status-frustration and blocked opportunities were compounded by racism and 'resolved' by hustling and the celebration of cultural forms such as reggae. Ernest Cashmore in *Rastaman* (1979) focussed on the Rastafari faith in Britain, although paying more attention to its formal aspects of religious organization than to its looser subcultural affiliations ('reggae', 'locks' and 'weed') among black British youth in the 1970s. As part of the Policy Studies Institute study of policing in London, Stephen Small (1983) undertook a study of young black people's lifestyles, together with their attitudes towards the police and experiences of racist policing. In a novel approach using socio-linguistic techniques, Roger Hewitt (1986) illuminated the workings of inter-racial friendships and how racism might be combated on a day-to-day basis among adolescents in south London. A more conventional ethnographic approach informs the disturbing commentary offered by David Robins (1992) on 'Satellite City', a multi-racial housing estate in London where amid the fallen hopes and survival strategies of an embattled and impoverished community young men act out exaggerated and often self-destructive versions of masculinity. And Heidi Safia Mirza's *Young, Female and Black* (1992) followed young black women through their experiences in the classroom, into the world of work and the creation of effective identities of black womanhood. Nevertheless, questions of 'race' and ethnicity were to remain relatively unexplored within British studies of youth subcultures, in spite of the fact that black youth acted as an almost demonic focus for the law-and-order movement of the 1970s and 1980s (Solomos 1988; Pitts 1988; Cashmore and McLaughlin 1991).

Reflecting the dominant trend in criminology, subcultural approaches to youth studies have rested upon often unstated gender-specific theoretical assumptions of masculinity (McRobbie 1980; Dorn and South 1982). Research on the subcultural contexts of the lives of young women and girls has benefited both from more generalized studies of how the experiences of family, school, and work are negotiated by young women (Griffin 1985; Mirza 1992) and how they cope with issues of femininity and sexuality (McRobbie 1991; Lees 1986; Hudson and Ineichen 1991), and from feminist studies which are more tightly focused on the involvement of young women in crime (Carlen 1988; Campbell 1981; Cain 1989).

While it is generally accepted that young women are less visible in the public sphere than young men, a question which divides some of this work is whether young women form themselves into 'gangs', or whether their friendship networks are more likely to take the form of a one-to-one 'best friend' relationship (Campbell 1981; McRobbie and Garber 1976). What has been made clear by Angela McRobbie's work in particular is that the 'culture of femininity' operates in ways directly similar to the masculine 'delinquent subculture', as a means by which working-class girls devise an oppositional 'anti-school' culture of insubordination. A related set of questions within the 'cultural studies' approach involves the ways in which the culture of femininity is reproduced and enacted in the lives of young women and girls though dress styles, dance and music, and dominant forms of body image which are promoted by the 'youth media' and social movements directed towards the shaping of femininity—matters which have also been addressed in some historical research (McRobbie 1991; McRobbie and MacCabe 1981; MacRobbie and Nava 1984; Dyhouse 1981; Gorham 1982).

In many respects, however, it would be inappropriate to follow these lines of development in a text which is devoted to the study of crime and criminality, since there is nothing illegal in the adoption of subcultural styles and preferences, even though when these assume the forms of outrageous hairstyles, precocious expressions of sexuality, or ear-splitting musical forms, they might sometimes be seen by an older generation as 'deviant' and a shocking departure from 'tradition'.

There are two sides to this dilemma. It is one thing to demonstrate, as in some of what Short (1991: 506) describes as a 'new generation' of North American gang studies, that the motivations of members of a subculture are in many respects conventional (Williams 1989; Williams and Kornblum 1985; Jankowski 1991; Hagedorn 1988). This is portrayed most vividly in Williams and Kornblum's *Growing Up Poor* (1985), which offers a voice to the different adaptations of lifestyle and socio-economic choices (including crime and prostitution) which are made by young people in the poverty-stricken cities of the USA; and again in Terry Williams's *The Cocaine Kids* (1989), where in spite of their deep involvement in cocaine use and dealing in New York's West Harlem, the aspirations of gang members were essentially conventional—financial security, home comforts, status, prestige, respect. As Williams describes it (1989: 132), in spite of their involvement in drugs and crime these are no more than 'struggling young people trying to make a place for themselves in a world few care to understand and many wish would go away'.

It is another thing, however, to imply as do some British youth culture studies that adherence to subcultural values is 'normal' in the sense that all young people conform to these 'deviant' subcultures. Indeed, one of the weaknesses of these subcultural developments within post-war British sociology was that the focus on 'spectacular' youth cultures such as the Teddy Boys and Skinheads risked the implication that all young people of a particular generation and class fraction were active 'carriers' of the style or culture—which is not the case. As suggested by Murdock and McCron (1976*b*), it was to a large extent because of the fact that 'contemporary subcultural analysis has its roots in delinquency research' that it had tended to focus on 'the deviant rather than the conventional, on working class adolescents rather than those from the intermediate and middle classes, and . . . on boys rather than girls'.

The point is well made in Richard Jenkins's study *Lads, Citizens and Ordinary Kids* (1983), which concerned youth lifestyles on a large Belfast housing estate. Jenkins attempted to shift the focus of youth subcultural research away both from criminological concerns and from a narrow preoccupation with youth styles in the leisure sphere to include both participation in the labour market and also, through some attention to courtship, to the question of how young people make the transition towards home-building and parenthood. Moreover, even within the study of a single neighbourhood Jenkins illustrated the ways in which different groups of young people gravitated towards different subcultural styles: the 'Lads', who were recognizably the near-delinquent youths so often in the centre of the researcher's field of vision; the 'Citizens', who aspired towards upward social mobility; and those who when asked for their subcultural affiliations replied simply that they were 'Ordinary Kids'. The single-minded preoccupation in the mass media and elsewhere with spectacular youth cultures is one means by which youth as a generation can be defined as 'deviant'. Unwittingly, perhaps subcultural criminology sometimes risked doing the same.

'NORMALITY' AND 'DEVIANCE' THE LABELLING TRADITION

A final question flowing from considerations such as these is to what extent delinquent youth can be distinguished from their non-delinquent peers. Is it that delinquency is a collective expression of the experiences of class, community, culture, and subculture? Or are juvenile delinquents best approached in individual terms as radically different from other young people?

An emphatic expression of the latter view is offered by West and Farrington in one of the most authoritative 'criminal career' studies, where it is argued that 'convicted criminals are not typical representatives of their class':

> Without in any way contradicting the importance of social and cultural factors in determining the incidence of delinquency . . . the individual characteristics of the offender also play a large part . . . They [i.e. convicted offenders] differ from the norm in character, attitude and style of life. We had not expected to find that young men convicted once or twice for theft, or for driving off someone else's vehicle, would be much different from their unconvicted contemporaries, but we were proved wrong. The occurrence of a criminal conviction . . . points to a constellation of characteristics among which aggressiveness, irregular work habits, immoderation in the pursuit of immediate pleasure, and lack of conventional social restraints are the most prominent. Even youths with only one conviction were significantly different from their peers, and the minority with several convictions were conspicuously deviant in many respects. (West and Farrington 1977: 160)

A quite separate tradition, resting on different bodies of evidence, is in sharp disagreement with this view. Youthful infractions of the law are seen as entirely commonplace, and the difference between delinquents and non-delinquents is understood not as a difference in psychological character but as a consequence of whether or not the young person has become entangled in the criminal justice system (e.g. Werthman and Piliavin 1981). It is not my intention to arbitrate between these different positions, nor to attempt to resolve their differences. My more modest aim is simply to state their existence as one of the fractures within criminology's field of vision.

The view that involvement in crime is common among young people can be expressed in a number of ways. Adolescence is often seen as a turbulent phase in the life cycle where the predisposition to commit crime is most common. Is juvenile crime, then, merely a 'normal' aspect of social and psychological development in western societies? One of the most powerful justifications for the view that crime is commonplace in adolescence is the way in which the official criminal statistics, with all their imperfections, have for many years indicated that the peak age for offending hovers around the mid-teens, at the point of transition from school to work, with some more recent evidence showing a slight shift towards 17–18 years for the peak age (cf. Home Office 1988; 86; 1990: 93; Farrington 1986, 1992.) Self-report studies have also consistently indicated that the majority of boys (but fewer girls) admit to having committed some kind of offence during their adolescent years. In one typical self-report study Joanna Shapland (1978) found that approximately one-quarter of boys admitted to stealing school property at age 11–12 years, as against almost two-thirds of the same boys when re-interviewed at age 13–14 years. Acts of a fairly trivial nature were found to be even more common, with 96 per cent of boys at both 11 and 14 years admitting to some act of trespass, and 80 per cent having entered a bar for drinking while under age. By contrast, although a substantial proportion (somewhat less than half) of them had stolen from a large store, only 8 per cent had broken into a shop in order to steal.

These kinds of evidence are, at face value, impressive. Whether they indicate anything specifically 'criminogenic' about the adolescent phase of development, however, must remain questionable. There are considerable areas of bias in public perceptions of juvenile crime. Symptomatic is a recent Home Office study of what is described as 'the nature and extent of car crime' (Webb and Laycock 1992) which, while pointing to evidence that between one-half and two-thirds of 'car crime' offenders were below the age of 20 years, makes reference only to theft of and from motor vehicles, thus neglecting potentially dangerous practices which are widespread among adult drivers such as speeding or driving while under the influence of alcohol. This is not to deny the emergence in some localities of youthful subcultures which centre on the motor car and the risks and excitements of 'twocking' or 'joy-riding' (Spencer 1992; Light *et al.* 1993). However, the problem reflects a more general bias in the criminal statistics and the preoccupations of mainstream policing which pay scant attention to types of illegalities such as theft from the workplace and tax evasion which, by definition, are criminal opportunities that are unavailable to juveniles.

To place this kind of stress on the way in which dominant social definitions of what constitutes serious 'crime' can distort our perceptions is to invoke one version or another of labelling theory. The labelling tradition emphasizes the ways in which 'crime' and, more generally, 'deviance' are social constructions. That is to say, following Howard Becker's definition (1963: 8–9), deviance 'is created by society' through the ways in which 'social groups create deviance by making the rules whose infraction constitutes deviance, and by applying those rules to particular people and labelling them as outsiders'. In one sense, this is no more than obvious: what constitutes a crime is governed by laws, and laws can be (and are) changed, so that 'crime' is always a potentially changeable and negotiable category. Where young people are concerned, for example, the age of criminal responsibility governs whether acts of misconduct can be prosecuted as crimes. Also, the commission of certain kinds of acts by young people (riding a motorbike, purchasing cigarettes or alcohol, engaging in sexual activity) are defined as crimes although, since these are 'status offences', the same acts committed by adults would not be. Under extreme circumstances, social definitions of even the most serious forms of crime are suspended: when young men go to war, killing is no crime.

Labelling theory also directs attention to more specific and commonplace ways in which the enforcement of law and social regulation is itself socially constructed. Police encounters with juveniles, for example, are influenced by whether the suspect has a 'deviant' hairstyle, is wearing a leather jacket, is walking with an over-confident strut, or is black (cf. Piliavin and Briar 1964). As Werthman and Piliavin (1981: 162) point out, discretion in police work can err both ways: on the side of lenience if it is felt 'that contact with the unsavory clientele of a juvenile hall [i.e. court-house] would damage an otherwise positive attitude towards the law', whereas 'if the officer decides that the offender is a "punk", a "persistent troublemaker", or some other version of a thoroughly bad boy, he may well decide to make an arrest'. Discretion merges into discrimination: 'A "delinquent" is therefore not a juvenile who happens to have committed an illegal act. He is a young person whose moral character has been negatively assessed' (ibid.: 162). A variety of social stereotypes are thus reproduced and reinforced within the criminal justice system. Indeed, more generally the dominant social definition and social imagery of deviance are regarded by labelling theorists as a consequence of the interaction between officialdom and reality (Young 1971*a*)—although it becomes questionable in this way of thinking what 'reality' is, other than the symbolic interactive processes which define social reality (Cicourel 1968; Rock 1973). In a more politicized version of this tradition, 'crime' is no more than the social definitions and prescriptions of those with the power to define, although it could be argued that this implies an unwarranted passivity on the part of deviant actors (Walton 1973; Taylor *et al.* 1973).

One vital application of the labelling tradition was to draw attention to the role played by the mass media in the shaping of the dominant imagery of crime and deviance (Chibnall 1977; Cohen and Young 1973), including the way in which 'moral panics', to use Stanley Cohen's evocative phrase, create 'folk devils' out of flimsy events. Selective media reporting thus demonized youth cultures and youthful misconduct in the early 1960s and established authoritative versions of 'Mods' and 'Rockers', just as in the 1950s mass media typifications had been created of the outlandish and violent image of the 'Teddy Boy' (Cohen 1973*a*; Rock and Cohen 1970). In a cultural context where it sometimes appeared that to be young in itself constituted a reason for being regarded as one of the 'usual suspects', the youth–Crime connection is cemented in both social imagery and official statistics. To be both black and young is to have one's social identity criminalized to the point of social extinction (Hall *et al.* 1978; Gilroy 1982). Likewise, the experience of young women and girls within the criminal justice system is that of a double stigmatization, since patriarchal assumptions dictate that offending behaviour is both unlawful and 'un-ladylike' (Chesney-Lind 1973; Carlen 1987).

Labelling theory thus came to provide the basis of a powerful cultural and political critique of the bedrock of both criminological theory and the social organization of the criminal justice system (Pearson 1975*a*). Its application was particularly relevant to those social groups who were relatively powerless, such as the young, and it pointed to the potentially damaging and stigmatizing influences of the application of criminal law in the form of 'deviance amplification'. It thus offered justification for diversion schemes, a stance to be defined by Edwin Schur (1973) in one of the more extreme expressions of the sentiment as 'radical non-intervention', where the aim was to be to 'leave the kids alone wherever possible'. By pointing to the crucial role of the definitional process in fashioning deviant typifications, labelling theory also made available the idea of constructing competing social definitions of deviance which contested the dominant belief that youthful misconduct was a motiveless pathology and placed a contrasting emphasis on its social meaning and rationality (Cohen 1937*b*; Pearson, 1976*a*). Although this tendency was to some extent implicit in the theoretical imperatives of labelling theory and symbolic interactionism, it was undoubtedly reinforced by the cultural politics of the late 1960s and early 1970s, where stigmatized social groups devised positive image slogans such as 'Gay is good' and 'Black is beautiful' and thus adopted a defiant expression of self-identity (Pearson 1975*a*, *b*). Effectively, what this position stated was that if young people were drawn into various forms of crime and deviance to such an extent that this was almost 'normal', then this should be construed not as a failure on their part but as a form of social commentary on the constraints placed upon them and even as a crypto-political form of protest (Goodman 1960; Horowitz and Liebowitz 1968).

This 'radical' deviancy theory opened up a series of complex divisions on the youth question which can only be hinted at here. Its appeal to the rationality and 'free will' of the deviant actor rested partly on the path-breaking theoretical stance which had been developed by David Matza in *Delinquency and Drift* (1964) and *Becoming Deviant* (1969), Works which enjoyed a commanding reputation in the late 1960s and early 1970s. Its assumption that there might often be a thread of rationality in youthful misconduct also reflected, however, a 'romanticized' structure of feeling: if young people vandalized schools and high-rise flats, for example, this was a response to bad schooling and dehumanized architecture. The implicit rational-actor stance of radical deviancy theory was thus a highly politicized one which bore little if any relationship to the rational-actor stance of the emerging 'situational' crime prevention model (e.g. Clarke and Mayhew 1980), which proved to be thoroughly uninterested in criminal motivation. In outlining their 'rational choice perspective', Cornish and Clarke (1986: vii) merely had this to say about motivation:

'Situational crime prevention leaves open the question of criminal disposition.' As the influence of the cultural politics of the 1960s and 1970s waned, a similar shift was to take place in politically informed criminologies of the left. At first this was observable in the rejection of the romanticized 'Robin Hood' characterization of youthful vandals and hooligans which stressed the fact that working-class communities were most often victimized by working-class criminals (Young 1975; Platt 1978) and led to the 'left realist' approach which entered into a sympathetic alliance with victimology, resulting in a corresponding lack of interest in the offender's perspective and the motives and meanings of crime. In attempting to fashion a new populist inner-city politics towards law and order under the slogan of 'taking crime seriously', the 'left realist' position was also to jettison labelling theory's scepticism towards officially constructed crime rates, together with its critical stance towards the contribution of the mass media in the generation of moral panics (cf. Jones *et al.* 1986).

In their lack of interest in the motivation and meaning of criminal acts, however, these developments in British criminology of the late 1970s and 1980s did no more than reflect Howard Becker's own agnostic formulation of deviant motivation which had been so influential within the labelling tradition. Arguing that questions such as 'Why do they do it?' were unimportant, since people committed crimes or used drugs for all manner of different and often conflicting reasons, Becker suggested that it was only in the process of committing deviant acts and dealing with the stigmatizing social reaction to deviant acts that what had been 'vague impulses and desires' settled down into a stable pattern of action and motivation. 'To put a complex argument in a few words,' wrote Becker (1963: 42), 'instead of deviant motives leading to deviant behaviour, it is the other way around; the deviant behaviour in time produces the deviant motivation.' If crime and deviance were relatively common during adolescence, in other words, then they were also, as David Matza (1964: 22) had indicated, much more 'transient' and 'intermittent' than had been allowed by positivistic causal explanations of either a sociological or a psychological nature. Many young people might commit 'criminal' and 'deviant' acts, but they did not become criminals and deviants unless they were caught and branded and drawn into the criminal justice system, whereupon they learned the lessons of deviant motivation from the labelling process.

The lack of attention to the initial motivation for criminal and deviant acts, which in some versions of 'administrative' and 'realist' criminology has become a complacent orthodoxy, was one of the inherent theoretical limitations of labelling theory itself (Taylor *et al.* 1973). It nevertheless offered a significant challenge to criminology and the criminal justice system, pointing to the ways in which the stigmatizing influence of the law might transform juvenile pranks into committed criminality. As Ed Lemert (18=967: v) had put it in one of the touchstone formulations of 'social reaction' and 'labelling' theory:

> This is a large turn away from the older sociology which tended to rest heavily upon the idea that deviance leads to social control. I have come to believe that the reverse idea, that is, social control leads to deviance, is equally tenable and the potentially richer premise for studying deviance in modern society.

Labelling theory had been embraced in these terms as an entirely novel theoretical formulation of the deviant question. It was also, as David Matza (1969: 80) described it, an 'ironic' formulation in that social control systems and professional interventions were directly implicated in the manufacture of deviance and criminality: 'The very effort to prevent, intervene, arrest, and "cure" persons of their alleged pathologies may . . . precipitate or seriously aggravate the tendency society wishes to guard against.' Labelling theory was thus the inheritor of an ancient tradition of humanist critique of the corrupting power of state institutions and legal processes, which can be traced through successive waves of penal reform since the late eighteenth century (Pearson 1991*b*). Because here there was a distinct echo of a much older current of feeling; as John Howard had expressed the irony of the penal system in *The State of the Prisons* in 1777:

> In many of our gaols you can see (and who cannot see it without pain?) boys of 12 or 14 eagerly listening to the stories told by practised and experienced prisoners . . . How directly contrary this is to the intention of our laws with regard to these prisoners; which certainly is to correct and reform them. Instead of which, their confinement doth notoriously promote and increase the very vices it was designed to suppress. (Howard 1977 [1777]: 20–1)

THE YOUTH–CRIME CONNECTION: LIVING WITH MODERNITY

Although the relationship between youthfulness and crime is firmly cemented in both the public imagination and the received traditions of criminology, a concluding question must be whether or not the social preoccupation with the youth–crime connection can be entirely justified. In this final section I will therefore address some of the internal difficulties in what we mean by both 'youth' and 'crime', together with the ways in which these are commonly yoked to the troublesome concept of 'modernity'. My aim is to suggest ways in which the apparently firmly embedded youth–crime connection might be an aspect of our cultural self-understanding of living with modernity, which is itself in need of correction and redress.

The first requirement is to note that 'youth' and 'crime' are both highly elastic social categories. As we have seen, it is 'labelling theory' which offers the most explicit version of the essentially arbitrary nature of definitions of 'crime' and 'deviance'. Nevertheless, the recognition that variations in law and custom—whether between different societies and cultures, or across historical time—result in the improvisation of new categories of crime, or the deletion of older ones, has a much longer history. Mid-nineteenth-century critiques of the extent to which official criminal statistics could offer a reliable indication of actual trends in criminal activity in England, for example, sometimes based their case on an appeal to the shifting sands of legal definitions of 'crime'. Without succumbing to an unnecessarily extreme version of cultural relativism (cf. Pearson 1993), all this and more would have to be encompassed within an effective legal anthropology.

'Youth' is another flexible social category, most conveniently understood as the transitional period between 'childhood' and 'adulthood'. John Gillis in his book *Youth and History* (1974), which draws essentially on European and North American experiences, has mapped out in some detail the ways in which 'youth' as a social category passed through various shifts of meaning as pre-industrial society was transformed by the social, economic, and demographic changes of the urban and industrial revolutions. In pre-industrial Europe, 'what they commonly called "youth" was a very long transition period, lasting from the point at which the very young child first became somewhat independent of its family, usually about seven or eight, to the point of complete independence at marriage, ordinarily in the mid- or late twenties' (Gillis 1974: 2). In this pre-industrial era, Gillis argues, 'youth' nevertheless enjoyed considerable independence. Through the extension of compulsory education and other means in the latter half of the nineteenth century young people, especially young people of middle-class origin, became thus bequeathing to the twentieth century what has become its recognizable social definition of 'youth'. It is therefore essentially a residual category, subject to the changing historical definitions of both 'child' and 'adult' status. Close attention to the evidence of social anthropology would, of course, extend the available range of definitions of child, youth, and adult.

Given the flexibility enjoyed by these two social categories, it is all the more remarkable that 'youth' and 'crime' are twinned in so many discussions on the criminal question. It is indisputable that official criminal statistics identity youth as the peak age for committing criminal acts, but what does this statistical correlation of 'youth' and 'crime' mean and how should it be interpreted? The identification of 'crime' and 'youth' is often felt to be a distinctively modern phenomenon, belonging to the late twentieth century. It is nevertheless a social preoccupation possessed of a much longer history, and successive generations have discovered and rediscovered the 'youthfulness' of crime since the time when criminal statistics were first gathered together and analysed in the early to mid-nineteenth century. Although the correspondence between 'youth' and 'crime' has often been understood as a consequence of the turbulence of adolescence, some doubts must be placed against this 'psychological' explanation, since the idea that adolescence is a time of 'storm and stress' is itself one of the changing cultural definitions of 'youth'. It seems equally likely that criminal statistics (which are always frail indicators of actual patterns of crime) contain large numbers of young offenders for other reasons to do with how the process of gathering criminal statistics (involving implicit definitions of 'crime') is itself socially organized. For example, young people are under more rigorous systems of control and surveillance, principally through the institutions of the family and school, with the result that their actions are more publicly accessible and observable than those of adults. One might also speculate that young offenders are by definition less experienced and thus more easily caught—and hence more visible within the known age profile of recorded offences and apprehended offenders. Or one might attend to the ways in which the criminal statistics involve systematic biases of definition. Vast numbers of illegalities—principally involving theft from the workplace and the 'hidden economy' from which young people are largely excluded—are themselves excluded and ignored in the official criminal statistics, thus resulting in an unintended de-emphasis of 'crimes' committed by adults. The routine act of potentially endangering life by driving a motor care either recklessly or under the influence of alcohol—which, by reasons of patterns of car ownership, overwhelmingly involve respectable citizens of formal adult status—is also rendered somehow morally less objectionable than other more 'deviant' and 'youthful' styles of violent conduct such as fighting or rowdyism. Equally, young offenders will be only marginal within that other vast and unfathomed criminal category of 'domestic violence'—although young people will often be victims of violence in the home. However, it is symptomatic of the social equation underlying the youth–crime connection that it finds its dominant expression in youth as the perpetrators of crime, and that the subject of children and young people as the victims of crime is a largely neglected topic. Indeed, we must ask what this extraordinary blind spot says about our culture which pretends to such an interest in the welfare of the child. Research on the 'child as victim' rather than the 'child as offender' has belatedly revealed sometimes quite serious levels of criminal victimization by adults, in both the public and domestic spheres, which provides further justification for calling into question the usual ways of stating the preoccupation with youth and crime (Anderson *et al.* 1990; Morgan and Zedner 1992).

However, the already compelling youth–crime connection is rendered all the more potent when the question of 'modernity' is entered into the equation. Indeed, 'youth' itself is commonly understood as a metaphor of social change, and also as a symbol of the troubles associated with change and the process of modernity—not solely in the post-war years, as has been often assumed (cf. Smith 1975), but across a much wider sweep of the modern era.

Modernity is a disquieting phenomenon, as illustrated by Marshall Berman's vibrant thesis *All that is Solid Melts into Air* (1983). To be 'modern' means to live in a moving world which promises much, but which in order to deliver its promise must destroy and trample underfoot the familiar landmarks of the 'form of life' into which each successive generation is born. Accordingly, for an older generation the experience of modernity is one of loss and regret. The world is understood to be falling apart, as the previously existing taken-for-granted universe into which the older generation had been socialized is displaced by new sets of landmarks and assumptions.

'Youth' is both a signifier of these unwelcome changes, and their embodiment. The rising generation is not only 'new'; it has no option other than to embrace the present and its implied future in whatever terms it is presented, if it is to make its way in the world. What the older generation experiences in the novelty of modernity as deteriorated and unfamiliar is therefore sensed by the young as both familiar and whole; whereas what the rising generation senses as tired and worn in the past is regretted by the old as the loss of integrity. The 'folk memory' of the past which emerges from these complex social processes is thus a selective tradition which we know as 'nostalgia'. It is a felt relationship to the past which is cleansed of disorder and moral complexity. Within this selective tradition, 'crime' has become one of the controlling metaphors of social change and social breakdown in the modern era. The youth–crime–modernity equation is thereby sealed within the ways in which the biological life cycle is understood and enacted within the conditions of modernity. Uncertainty is in the future; certainty is in the past. 'I think morals are getting much worse,' says a 60-year-old woman, 'There were no such girls in my time as there are now. When I was four or five and twenty my mother would have knocked me down if I had spoken improperly to her.' A persuasive lament, no doubt, although it is one to which our response must necessarily become more complex when it is recognized that this was part of the evidence marshalled by Lord Ashley before the House of Commons to promote a system of moral education for the children of the poor as long ago as 1843 (*The Times*, 1 March 1843).

These concluding remarks are merely intended to suggest ways in which the common youth–crime connection might be deconstructed. We simply do not have the evidence—in the form of government-sponsored statistics, social surveys, reliable self-report studies, etc.—to state with any confidence the actually existing relationships between 'youth' and 'crime'. The youth–crime connection should therefore be approached as one which, although it is a firmly embedded aspect of cultural self-understanding in the modern era, remains subject to the self-reflexive reordering and alteration of all aspects of culture. Indeed, one might even envisage a culture in which the youth–crime connection was entirely dissolved: namely, a culture which defined young people as exempt from prosecution within the criminal law by virtue of their shortage of experience of moral affairs. Under such circumstances, young people might still (indeed, would) sometimes do wrong and conduct themselves improperly. They might also commit certain acts which would be defined as crimes if committed by adults. It would nevertheless be impossible for 'youth' to be 'criminals'.

Selected Further Reading

M. Brake, *The Sociology of Youth Cultures and Youth Subcultures*. London: Routledge, 1980.

R. A. Cloward and L. E. Ohlin, *Delinquency and Opportunity: A Theory of Delinquent Gangs*. New York: Free Press, 1960.

A. K. Cohen, *Delinquent Boys: The Culture of the Gang*. New York: Free Press, 1955.

S. Cohen, *Folk Devils and Moral Panics*. London: Paladin, 1973.

D. Downes, *The Delinquent Solution*. London: Routledge, 1966.

J. R. Gillis, *Youth and History*. New York: Academic Press, 1974.

S. Hall and T. Jefferson, eds., *Resistance through Rituals*. London: Hutchinson, 1976.

N. McKeganey and M. Barnard, *AIDS, Drugs and Sexual Risk*. Milton Keynes: Open University Press, 1992.

A. McRobbie, *Feminism and Youth Culture*. London: Macmillan, 1991.

D. Matza, *Delinquency and Drift*. New York: Wiley, 1964.

H. S. Mirza, *Young, Female and Black*. London: Routledge, 1992.

H. J. Parker, *View from the Boys*. London: David and Charles, 1974.

G. Pearson, *Hooligan: A History of Respectable Fears*. London: Macmillan, 1983.

G. Pearson, *The New Heroin Users*. Oxford: Blackwell, 1987.

C. R. Shaw, *The Jack-Roller: A Delinquent Boy's Own Story*. Chicago: University of Chicago Press, 1930.

C. R. Shaw and H. McKay, *Juvenile Delinquency and Urban Areas*. Chicago: University of Chicago Press, 1942.

J. F. Short, jun., ed., *Gang Delinquency and Delinquent Subcultures*. New York: Harper and Row, 1968.

J. Springhall, *Youth, Empire and Society: British Youth Movements 1883–1940*. London: Croom Helm, 1977.

W. F. Whyte, *Street Corner Society*. Chicago: University of Chicago Press, 1943.

T. Williams, *The Cocaine Kids*. New York: Addison-Wesley, 1989.

T. Williams and W. Kornblum, *Growing Up Poor*. Lexington: Lexington Books, 1985.

P. Willis, *Learning to Labour*. London: Saxon House, 1977.

P. Willis, *Profane Culture*. London: Routledge and Kegan Paul, 1978.

J. Young, 'The Role of the Police as Amplifiers of Deviance, Negotiators of Reality and Translators of Fantasy', in S. Cohen, ed., *Images of Deviance*. Harmondsworth: Penguin, 1971.

REFERENCES

Adams, J. (1912), *A New Conscience and an Ancient Evil*, New York: Macmillan.

Anderson, S., Kinsey, R., Loader, I., and Smith, C. (1990), *Cautionary Tales: A Study of Young People and Crime in Edinburgh*. Edinburgh: University of Edinburgh Centre for Criminology.

Armstrong, G., and Wilson, M. (1973), 'City Politics and Deviancy Amplification', in I. Taylor and L. Taylor, eds., *Politics and Deviance*. Harmondsworth: Penguin.

Bagot, J. H. (1941), *Juvenile Delinquency: A Comparative Study of the Position in Liverpool and England and Wales*. London: Cape.

Bailey, V. (1987), *Delinquency and Citizenship: Reclaiming the Young Offender 1914–1948*. Oxford: Clarendon Press.

Baldwin, J., and Bottoms, A. E. (1976), *The Urban Criminal: A Study in Sheffield*. London: Tavistock.

Becker, H. S. (1963), *Outsiders*. New York: Free Press.

—— (1966), 'Introduction', in C. R. Shaw, *The Jack-Roller: A Delinquent Boy's Own Story*. Chicago: University of Chicago Press.

BENNETT, J. (1981), *Oral History and Delinquency: The Rhetoric of Criminology*. Chicago: University of Chicago Press.

BERMAN, M. (1983), *All that is Solid Melts into Air: The Experience of Modernity*. London: Verso.

BOTTOMS, A., MAWBY, R. I., and XANTHOS, P. (1989), 'A Tale of Two Estates', in D. Downes, ed., *Crime and the City: Essays in Memory of John Barron Mays*. London: Macmillan.

BOTTOMS, A. E., and WILES, P. (1986), 'Housing Tenure and Residential Community Crime Careers in Britain', in A. J. Reiss and M. Tonry, eds., *Communities and Crime*. Chicago: University of Chicago Press.

BOWLBY, J. (1946), *Forty-Four Juvenile Thieves: Their Characters and Home Life*. London: Balli–re Tindall and Cox.

—— (1952), *Maternal Care and Mental Health*. Geneva: World Health Organization.

—— (1953), *Child Care and the Growth of Love*. Harmondsworth: Penguin.

BRAITHWAITE, W. J. (1904), 'Boys' Clubs', in E. J. Urwick, ed., *Studies of Boy Life in Our Cities*. London: Dent.

BRAKE, M. (1980), *The Sociology of Youth Cultures and Youth Subcultures*. London: Routledge and Kegan Paul.

BRANTINGHAM, P., and BRANTINGHAM, P. (1984), *Patterns in Crime*. New York: Macmillan.

BRAY, R. A. (1904), 'The Boy and the Family', in E. J. Urwick, ed., *Studies of Boy Life in Our Cities*. London: Dent.

—— (1907), *The Town Child*. London: Fisher Unwin.

—— (1911), *Boy Labour and Apprenticeship*. London: Constable.

BRISTOW, J. (1991), *Empire Boys: Adventures in a Man's World*. London: HarperCollins.

BURR, A. (1987), 'Chasing the Dragon: Heroin Misuse, Delinquency and Crime in the Context of South London Culture', *British Journal of Criminology*, 27/4.

BURT, C. (1925), *The Young Delinquent*. London: University of London Press.

BUTTERWORTH, J. (1932), *Clubland*. London: Epworth.

CAIN, M., ed. (1989), *Growing Up Good: Policing the Behaviour of Girls in Europe*. London: Sage.

CAMERON, C., ed. (1943), *Disinherited Youth: A Survey 1936–1939*. Edinburgh: Constable.

CAMPBELL, A. (1981), *Girl Delinquents*. Oxford: Blackwell.

CARLEN, P. (1987), 'Out of Care, into Custody: Dimensions and Deconstructions of the State's Regulation of Twenty-two Young Working Class Women', in P. Carlen and A. Worrall, eds., *Gender, Crime and Justice*. Milton Keynes: Open University Press.

—— (1988), *Women, Crime and Poverty*. Milton Keynes: Open University Press.

CARLEN, P., GLEESON, D., and WARDHAUGH, J. (1992), *Truancy: The Politics of Compulsory Schooling*. Milton Keynes: Open University Press.

CARR-SAUNDERS, A. M., MANNHEIM, H., and RHODES, E. C. (1942), *Young Offenders*. Cambridge: Cambridge University Press.

CASHMORE, E. (1979), *Rastaman*. London: Allen and Unwin.

Cashmore, E., and McLaughlin, E., eds. (1991), *Out of Order? Policing Black People*. London: Routledge.

Cashmore, E., and Troyna, B., eds. (1982), *Black Youth in Crisis*. London: Allen and Unwin.

Centre for Contemporary Cultural Studies, ed. (1982), *The Empire Strikes Back: Race and Racism in 70s Britain*. London: Hutchinson.

Chesney-Lind, M. (1973), 'Judicial Enforcement of the Female Sex Role: The Family Court and the Female Delinquent', *Issues in Criminology*, 8/2.

Chibnall, S. (1977), *Law-and-Order News: An Analysis of Crime Reporting in the British Press*. London: Tavistock.

Cicchetti, D., and Carlson, V., eds. (1989), *Child Maltreatment: Theory and Research on the Causes and Consequences of Child Abuse and Neglect*. Cambridge: Cambridge University Press.

Cicourel, A. V. (1968), *The Social Organisation of Juvenile Justice*. New York: Wiley.

Clarke, J. (1976), 'The Skinheads and the Magical Recovery of Community', in S. Hall and T. Jefferson, eds., *Resistance through Rituals*. London: Hutchinson.

Clarke, J., Critcher, C., and Johnson, R., eds. (1979), *Working Class Culture: Studies in History and Theory*. London: Hutchinson.

Clarke, J., and Jefferson, T. (1976), 'Working Class Youth Cultures', in G. Mungham and G. Pearson, eds., *Working Class Youth Culture*. London: Routledge and Kegan Paul.

Clarke, R. V. G., and Mayhew, P. (1980), *Designing Out Crime*. London: HMSO.

Cloward, R. A., and Ohlin, L. E. (1960), *Delinquency and Opportunity: A Theory of Delinquent Gangs*. New York: Free Press.

Cohen, A. K. (1955), *Delinquent Boys: The Culture of the Gang*. New York: Free Press.

Cohen, P. (1972), 'Subcultural Conflict and Working Class Community', *Working Papers in Cultural Studies*, no. 2. Centre for Contemporary Studies, University of Birmingham.

—— (1980), 'Subcultural Conflict and Working Class Community', in S. Hall, D. Hobson, A. Lowe, and P. Willis, eds., *Culture, Media, Language: Working Papers in Cultural Studies, 1972–79*. London: Hutchinson.

Cohen, S. (1973*a*), *Folk Devils and Moral Panics*. London: Paladin.

—— (1973*b*), 'Protest, Unrest and Delinquency: Convergences in Labels and Behaviour', *International Journal of Criminology and Penology*, 1.

—— ed. (1971), *Images of Deviance*. Harmondsworth: Penguin.

Cohen, S., and Young, J., eds. (1973), *The Manufacture of News: Social Problems, Deviance and the Mass Media*. London: Constable.

Cornish, D. B., and Clarke, R. V. (1986), *The Reasoning Criminal: Rational Choice Perspectives on Offending*. New York: Springer-Verlag.

Corrigan, P. (1976), 'Doing Nothing', in S. Hall and T. Jefferson, eds., *Resistance through Rituals*. London: Hutchinson.

—— (1979), *Schooling the Smash Street Kids*. London: Macmillan.

Dai, B. (1937), *Opium Addiction in Chicago*. Chicago: Chicago University Press.

DANIEL, S., and MCGUIRE, P., eds. (1972), *The Paint House: Words from an East End Gang*. Harmondsworth: Penguin.

DAVIS, N. Z. (1971), 'The Reasons of Misrule: Youth Groups and Charivaris in Sixteenth Century France', *Past and Present*, 50.

DENNIS, N., and ERDOS, G. (1992), *Families without Fatherhood.* London: IEA Health and Welfare Unit.

DEVINE, A. (1890), *Scuttlers and Scuttling*. Manchester: Guardian Printing Works.

DORN, N., and SOUTH, N. (1982), *Of Males and Markets: A Critical Review of 'Youth Culture' Theory*, Research Paper 1, Centre for Occupational and Community Research. London: Middlesex Polytechnic.

DOWNES, D. (1966), *The Delinquent Solution: A Study in Subcultural Theory*. London: Routledge and Kegan Paul.

DOWNES, D., and ROCK, P. (1982), *Understanding Deviance*. Oxford: Clarendon Press.

DUNLOP, O. J. (1912), *English Apprenticeship and Child Labour*. London: Unwin.

DUNNING, E., MURPHY, P., and WILLIAMS, J. (1988), *The Roots of Football Hooliganism: An Historical and Sociological Study*. London: Routledge and Kegan Paul.

DYHOUSE, C. (1981), *Girls Growing Up in Late Victorian and Edwardian England.* London: Routledge and Kegan Paul.

FARRINGTON, D. P. (1986), 'Age and Crime', in M. Tonry and N. Morris, eds., *Crime and Justice: A Review of Research*, vol. 7. Chicago: University of Chicago Press.

—— (1992), 'Criminal Career Research in the United Kingdom', *British Journal of Criminology*, 32: 521–36.

FELDMAN, H. W. (1968), 'Ideological Supports to Becoming and Remaining a Heroin Addict', *Journal of Health and Social Behaviour*, 9.

FERGUSON, T. (1952), *The Young Delinquent in his Social Setting: A Glasgow Study*. London: Oxford University Press.

FERGUSON, T., and CUNNISON, J. (1951), *The Young Wage-Earner: A Study of Glasgow Boys*. London: Oxford University Press.

—— (1956), *In their Early Twenties: A Study of Glasgow Youth*. London: Oxford University Press.

FINESTONE, H. (1957), 'Cats, Kicks, and Colour', *Social Problems*, 5.

FORSYTH, A. J. M., HAMMERSLEY, R. H., LAVELLE, T. L., and MURRAY, K. J. (1992), 'Geographical Aspects of Scoring Illegal Drugs', *British Journal of Criminology*, 32: 292–309.

FOSTER, J. (1990), *Villains: Crime and Community in the Inner City*. London: Routledge.

FREEMAN, A. (1914), *Boy Life and Labour: The Manufacture of Inefficiency*. London: King.

FRYER, P. (1984), *Staying Power: The History of Black People in Britain*. London: Pluto.

FYVEL, T. R. (1963), *The Insecure Offenders*. Harmondsworth: Penguin.

GARLAND, D. (1985), *Punishment and Welfare: A History of Penal STrategies*. Aldershot: Gower.

George, M. D. (1966), *London Life in the Eighteenth Century*. Harmondsworth: Penguin.

Gill, O. (1977), *Luke Street: Housing Policy, Conflict and the Creation of the Delinquent Area*. London: Macmillan.

Gillis, J. R. (1974), *Youth and History: Tradition and Change in European Age Relations 1770–Present*. New York: Academic Press.

—— (1975), 'The Evolution of Juvenile Delinquency in England, 1880–1914', *Past and Present*, 67.

Gilman, M., and Pearson, G. (1991), 'Lifestyles and Law Enforcement', in D. K. Whynes and P. T. Bean, eds., *Policing and Prescribing: The British System of Drug Control*. London: Macmillan.

Gilroy, P. (1982), 'Police and Thieves', in Centre for Contemporary Cultural Studies, ed., *The Empire Strikes Back: Race and Racism in 70s Britian*. London: Hutchinson.

—— (1987), *'There Ain't No Black in the Union Jack': The Cultural Politics of Race and Nation*. London: Hutchinson.

Goode, W. J. (1959), 'The Theoretical Importance of Love', *American Sociological Review*, 24.

Goodman, P. (1960), *Growing Up Absurd*. New York: Vintage Books.

Gorham, D. (1982), *The Victorian Girl and the Feminine Ideal*. London: Croom Helm.

Gorst, J. (1901), *The Children of the Nation*. London: Methuen.

Griffin, C. (1985), *Typical Girls? Young Women from School to the Job Market*. London: Routledge and Kegan Paul.

Hagedorn, J. M. (1988), *People and Folks: Gangs, Crime and the Underclass in a Rustbelt City*. Chicago: Lake View Press.

Hall, S., Critcher, S., Jefferson, T., Clarke, J., and Roberts, B. (1978), *Policing the Crisis: Mugging, the State, and Law and Order*. London: Macmillan.

Hall, S., Hobson, D., Lowe, A., and Willis, P., eds. (1980) *Culture, Media, Language: Working Papers in Cultural Studies, 1972–79*. London: Hutchinson.

Hall, S., and Jefferson, T., eds. (1976), *Resistance through Rituals*. London: Hutchinson.

Hannerz, V. (1980), *Exploring the City: Inquiries Towards an Urban Anthropology*. New York: Columbia University Press.

Hargreaves, D. (1967), *Social Relations in a Secondary School*. London: Routledge and Kegan Paul.

Hebdige, D. (1979), *Subculture: The Meaning of Style*. London: Methuen.

Hendrick, H. (1990), *Images of Youth: Age, Class, and the Male Youth Problem 1880–1920*. Oxford: Clarendon Press.

Hewitt, R. (1986), *White Talk Black Talk: Inter-Racial Friendship and Communication amongst Adolescents*. Cambridge: Cambridge University Press.

Hoggart, R. (1958), *The Uses of Literacy*. Harmondsworth: Penguin.

Home Office (1988), *Criminal Statistics England and Wales, 1987*, Cm 498. London: HMSO.

—— (1990), *Criminal Statistics England and Wales, 1989*, Cm 1322. London: HMSO.

HOPE, T., and FOSTER, J. (1982), 'Conflicting Forces: Changing the Dynamics of Crime and Community on a "Problem" Estate', *British Journal of Criminology*, 32: 488–504.

HOROWITZ, I. L., and LIEBOWITZ, M. (1968), 'Social Deviance and Political Marginality: Towards a Redefinition of the Relation between Sociology and Politics', *Social Problems*, 15/3.

HOWARD, J. (1977) [1777]), *The State of the Prisons*. London: Professional Books.

HUDSON, F., and INEICHEN, B. (1991), *Taking it Lying Down: Sexuality and Teenage Motherhood*. London: Macmillan.

HUMPHRIES, S. (1981), *Hooligans or Rebels? An Oral History of Working Class Childhood and Youth*. Oxford: Blackwell.

IRVING, E. (1828), *The Last Days: A Discourse on the Evil Character of These Our Times*. London: Seeley and Burnside.

JANKOWSKI, M. S. (1991), *Islands in the Street: Gangs and American Urban Society*. Berkeley: University of California Press.

JENKINS, R. (1983), *Lads, Citizens and Ordinary Kids: Working Class Youth Lifestyles in Belfast*. London: Routledge and Kegan Paul.

JOHNSON, B. D., GOLDSTEIN, P. J., PREEBLE, E., SCHMEIDLER, J., LIPTON, D. S., SPUNT, B., and MILLER, T. (1985), *Taking Care of Business: The Economics of Crime by Heroin Abusers*. Lexington: Lexington Books.

JONES, H. (1958), 'Approaches to an Ecological Study', *British Journal of Delinquency*, 8/4.

JONES, T., MACLEAN, B., and YOUNG, J. (1986), *The Islington Crime Survey*. Aldershot: Gower.

JUNGER-TAS, J. (1992), 'Changes in the Family and their Impact on Delinquency', *European Journal on Criminal Policy and Research*, 1/1.

KOBRIN, S., and FINESTONE, H. (1968), 'Drug Addiction among Young Persons in Chicago', in J. F. Short jun., ed., *Gang Delinquency and Delinquent Subcultures*. New York: Harper and Row.

LEAVIS, F. R. (1930), *MASS CIVILISATION AND MINORITY CULTURE*. CAMBRIDGE: MINORity Press.

LEES, S. (1986), *Losing Out: Secuality and Adolescent Girls*. London: Hutchinson.

LEMERT, E. M. (1967), *Human Deviance, Social Problems and Social Control*. New Jersey: Prentice-Hall.

LEONARD, E. B. (1982), *Women, Crime and Society: A Critique of Criminological Theory*. New York: Constable.

LIGHT, R., NEE, C., and INGHAM, H. (1993), *Car Theft: The Offender's Perspective*. Home Office Research Study no. 130. London: HMSO.

MCKEGANEY, N., and BARNARD, M. (1992), *AIDS, Drugs and Sexual Risk*. Milton Keynes: Open University Press.

MCROBBIE, A. (1978), 'Working Class Girls and the Culture of Femininity', in Women's Studies Group, Centre for Contemporary Cultural Studies, *Women Take Issue: Aspects of Women's Subordination*. London: Hutchinson.

—— (1980), 'Settling Accounts with Subcultures: A Feminist Critique', *Screen Education*, 39.

—— (1991), *Feminism and Youth Culture: From 'Jackie' to 'Just Seventeen'*. London: Macmillan.

McRobbie, A. ed. (1989), *Zoot Suits and Second-Hand Dresses: An Anthology of Fashion and Music*. London: Macmillan.

McRobbie, A., and Garber, J. (1976), 'Girls and Subcultures: An Exploration', in S. Hall and T. Jefferson, eds., *Resistance through Rituals*. London: Hutchinson.

McRobbie, A., and McCabe, T., eds. (1981), *Feminism for Girls*. London: Routledge and Kegan Paul.

McRobbie, A., and Nava, M., eds. (1984), *Gender and Generation*. London: Macmillan.

Mannheim, H. (1948), *Juvenile Delinquency in an English Middletown*. London: Kegan Paul.

Marsh, P., Rosser, E., and Harré, R. (1978), *The Rules of Disorder*. London: Routledge and Kegan Paul.

Matza, D. (1964), *Delinquency and Drift*. New York: Wiley.

—— (1969), *Becoming Deviant*. New Jersey: Prentice-Hall.

Matza, D., and Sykes, G. M. (1961), 'Juvenile Delinquency and Subterranean Values', *American Sociological Review*, 26/5.

Mays, J. B. (1954), *Growing Up in the City: A Study of Juvenile Delinquency in an Urban Neighbourhood*. Liverpool: Liverpool University Press.

Merton, R. K. (1938), 'Social Structure and Anomie', *American Sociological Review*, 3.

Miller, W. B. (1958), 'Lower Class Culture as a Generating Milieu of Gang Delinquency', *Journal of Social Issues*, 15/1.

Mirza, H. S. (1992), *Young, Female and Black*. London: Routledge.

Mitchell, J. (1975), *Psychoanalysis and Feminism*. Harmondsworth: Penguin.

Moffitt, T. E. (1990), 'The Neuropsychology of Juvenile Delinquency: A Review', in M. Tonry and N. Morris, eds., *Crime and Justice: A Review of Research*, vol. 12. Chicago: University of Chicago Press.

Morgan, A. E. (1939), *The Needs of Youth*. Oxford: Oxford University Press.

Morgan, J., and Zedner, L. (1992), *Child Victims: Crime, Impact, and Criminal Justice*. Oxford: Clarendon Press.

Morris, T. P. (1957), *The Criminal Area: A Study in Social Ecology*. London: Routledge and Kegan Paul.

Mungham, G., and Pearson, G., eds. (1976), *Working Class Youth Culture*. London: Routledge and Kegan Paul.

Murdock, G., and McCron, R. (1973), 'Scoobies, Skins and Contemporary Pop', *New Society*, 23 (29 March).

—— (1976*a*), 'Youth and Class: The Career of a Confusion', in G. Mungham and G. Pearson, eds., *Working Class Youth Culture*. London: Routledge and Kegan Paul.

—— (1976*b*), 'Consciousness of Class and Consciousness of Generation', in S. Hall and T. Jefferson, eds., *Resistance through Rituals*. London: Hutchinson.

Murray, C. (1984), *Losing Ground: American Social Policy, 1950–1980*. New York: Basic Books.

Orwell, G. (1962 [1939], *Coming Up For Air*. Armondsworth: Penguin.

Parker, H. J. (1974), *View from the Boys: A Sociology of Down-Town Adolescents*. London: David and Charles.

—— (1976), 'Boys Will Be Men: Brief Adolescence in a Down-Town

Neighbourhood', in G. Mungham and G. Pearson, eds., *Working Class Youth Culture*. London: Routledge and Kegan Paul.

PARKER, H., Bakx, K., and Newcombe, R. (1988), *Living With Heroin: The Impact of a Drugs 'Epidemic' on an English Community*. Milton Keynes: Open University Press.

PARKER, H., Casburn, M., and Turnbull, D. (1981), *Receiving Juvenile Justice: Adolescents and State Care and Control*. Oxford: Blackwell.

PARSONS, T. (1942), 'Age and Sex in the Social Structure of the United States', *American Sociological Review*, 7.

PATERSON, A. (1911), *Across the Bridges*. London: Edward Arnold.

PATRICK, J. (1973), *A Glasgow Gang Observed*. London: Eyre Methuen.

PEARSON, G. (1975*a*), *The Deviant Imagination*. London: Macmillan.

—— (1975*b*), 'Misfit Sociology and the Politics of Socialisation', in I. Taylor, P. Walton, and J. Young, eds., *Critical Criminology*. London: Routledge and Kegan Paul.

—— (1976*a*), 'In Defence of Hooliganism', in N. Tutt, ed., *Violence*. London: HMSO.

—— (1976*b*), '"Paki-Bashing" in a North East Lancashire Cotton Town: A Case Study and Its History', in G. Mungham and G. Pearson, eds., *Working Class Youth Culture*. London: Routledge and Kegan Paul.

—— (1983), *Hooligan: A History of Respectable Fears*. London: Macmillan.

—— (1986), 'Perpetual Novelty: A History of Generational Conflicts in Britain', in D. Dowe, ed., *Jugendprotest und Generationkonflikt in Europa im 20, Jahrhundert*. Bonn: Verlag Neue Gesellschaft.

—— (1987*a*), *The New Heroin Users*. Oxford: Blackwell.

—— (1987*b*), 'Social Deprivation, Unemployment and Patterns of Heroin Use', in N. Dorn and N. South, eds., *A Land Fit for Heroin? Drug Policies, Prevention and Practice*. London: Macmillan.

—— (1989), '"A Jekyll in the Classroom, a Hyde in the Street": Queen Victoria's Hooligans', in D. Downes, ed., *Crime and the City: Essays in Memory of John Barron Mays*. London: Macmillan.

—— (1991*a*), 'Drug Control Policies in Britain', in M. Tonry, ed., *Crime and Justice: A Review of Research*, vol. 14. Chicago: University of Chicago Press.

—— (1991*b*), 'Control Without Custody', *Bulletin of the Scottish Association for the Study of Delinquency*, June 1991.

—— (1993), 'Pharmacology and Fashion: The Uses and Misuses of Cultural Relativism in Drug Policy Analysis', *European Journal on Criminal Policy and Research*, 1/2.

PEARSON, G., Ditton, J., Newcombe, R., and Gilman, M. (1991), '"Everything Starts with an E": An Introduction to Ecstasy Use by Young People in Britain', *Druglink*, 6/6.

PILIAVIN, I., and BRIAR, S. (1964), 'Police Encounters with Juveniles', *American Journal of Sociology*, 70/2.

PINCHBECK, I., and Hewitt, M. (1969), *Children in English Society*, vol. 1: *From Tudor Times to the Eighteenth Century*. London: Routledge and Kegan Paul.

PITTS, J. (1988), *The Politics of Juvenile Crime*. London: Sage.

PLANT, M. (1975), *Drugtakers in an English Town*. London: Tavistock.

PLATT, A. (1978), 'Street Crime—A View from the Left', *Crime and Social Justice*, 9.

PREBLE, E., and Casey, J. J. (1969), 'Taking Care of Business: The Heroin User's Life on the Street', *International Journal of the Addictions*, 4/1.

PRYCE, K. (1979), *Endless Pressure: A Study of West Indian Lifestyles in Britain*. Harmondsworth: Penguin.

RADZINOWICZ, L., and HOOD, R. (1990), *The Emergence of Penal Policy in Victorian and Edwardian England*. Oxford: Clarendon Press.

REDHEAD, S., ed. (1993), *Rave Off: Politics and Deviance in Contemporary Youth Culture*. Aldershot: Avebury.

REISS, A. J., JUN. (1961), 'The Social Integration of Peers and Queers', *Social Problems*, 9/2.

RILEY, D. (1983), *War in the Nursery: Theories of the Child and Mother*. London: Virago.

RILEY, D., and SHAW, M. (1985), *Parental Supervision and Juvenile Delinquency*, Home Office Research Study no. 83. London: HMSO.

ROBINS, D. (1992), *Tarnished Vision: Crime and Conflicts in the Inner City*. Oxford: Oxford University Press.

ROBINS, D., and COHEN, P. (1978), *Knuckle Sandwich: Growing Up in the Working-Class City*. Harmondsworth: Penguin.

ROCK, P. (1973), *Deviant Behaviour*. London: Hutchinson.

ROCK, P., and COHEN, S. (1970), 'The Teddy Boy', in V. Bogdanor and R. Skidelsky, eds., *The Age of Affluence*. London: Macmillan.

ROSENBAUM, M. (1981), *Women on Heroin*. New Jersey: Rutgers University Press.

RUSSELL, C. E. B. (1905), *Manchester Boys*. Manchester: Manchester University Press.

RUTTER, M. (1972), *Maternal Deprivation Re-Assessed*. Harmondsworth: Penguin.

SCHUR, E. M. (1973), *Radical Non-Intervention: Re-Thinking the Delinquency Problem*. Englewood Cliffs: Prentice-Hall.

SHAPLAND, J. M. (1978), 'Self-Reported Delinquency in Boys Aged 11 to 14', *British Journal of Criminology*, 18/3.

SHAW, C. R. (1930), *The Jack-Roller: A Delinquent Boy's Own Story*. Chicago: University of Chicago Press.

SHAW, C. R., and MCKAY, H. (1942), *Juvenile Delinquency and Urban Areas*. Chicago: University of Chicago Press.

SHORT, J. F., jun. (1991), 'Poverty, Ethnicity, and Crime: Change and Continuity in US Cities', *Journal of Research in Crime and Delinquency*, 28/4.

—— ed. (1968), *Gang Delinquency and Delinquent Subcultures*. New York: Harper and Row.

—— (1976), *Delinquency, Crime, and Society*. Chicago: University of Chicago Press.

SHORT, J. F., jun., and STRODTBECK, F. L. (1965), *Group Processes and Gang Delinquency*. Chicago: University Press.

SMALL, S. (1983), *Police and People in London, II: A Group of Young Black People*. London: Policy Studies Institute.

SMILES, S. (1879), *Character*. London: Murray.

SMITH, A. C. H. (1975), *Paper Voices: The Popular Press and Social Change, 1935–1965*. London: Chatto and Windus.

SMITH, M. P. (1980), *The City and Social Theory*. Oxford: Blackwell.

SMITH, S. R. (1973), 'The London Apprentices as Seventeenth Century Adolescents', *Past and Present*, 61.

SOLOMOS, J. (1988), *Black Youth, Racism and the State: The Politics of Ideology and Policy*. Cambridge: Cambridge University Press.

SPEAR, H. B. (1969), 'The Growth of Heroin Addiction in the UK', *British Journal of Addiction*, 64.

SPENCER, E. (1992), *Car Crime and Young People on a Sunderland Housing Estate*, Crime Prevention Unit Paper no. 40. London: Home Office.

SPENCER, J. (1964), *Stress and Release on an Urban Estate*. London: Tavistock.

SPRINGHALL, J. (1977), *Youth, Empire and Society: British Youth Movements 1883–1940*. London: Croom Helm.

STIMSON, G. V. (1973), *Heroin and Behaviour*. Shannon: Irish University Press.

STIMSON, G. V., and Oppenheimer, E. (1982), *Heroin Addiction: Treatment and Control in Britain*. London: Tavistock.

SUTTLES, G. D. (1968), *The Social Order of the Slum: Ethnicity and Territory in the Inner City*. Chicago: University of Chicago Press.

SYKES, G. M., and Matza, D. (1957), 'Techniques of Neutralisation: A Theory of Delinquency', *American Sociological Review*, 22.

TAYLOR, I. (1971), 'Soccer Consciousness and Soccer Hooliganism', in S. Cohen, ed., *Images of Deviance*. Harmondsworth: Penguin.

TAYLOR, I., and TAYLOR, L., eds. (1973), *Politics and Deviance*. Harmondsworth: Penguin.

TAYLOR, I., and WALL, D. (1976), 'Beyond the Skinheads: Comments on the Emergence and Significance of the Glamrock Cult', in G. Mungham and G. Pearson, eds., *Working Class Youth Culture*. London: Routledge and Kegan Paul.

TAYLOR, I., WALTON, P., and YOUNG, J. (1973), *The New Criminology*. London: Routledge and Kegan Paul.

THRASHER, F. M. (1927), *The Gang: A Study of 1,313 Gangs in Chicago*. Chicago: University of Chicago Press.

URWICK, E. J., ed. (1904), *Studies of Boy Life in Our Cities*. London: Dent.

UTTING, D., BRIGHT, J., and HENRICSON, C. (1993), *Crime and the Family: Improving Child-Rearing and Preventing Delinquency*, Occasional paper no. 16. London: Family Policy Studies Centre.

WALLIS, C. P., and MALIPHANT, R. (1967), 'Delinquent Areas in the County of London: Ecological Factors', *British Journal of Criminology*, 7/3.

WALTON, P. (1973), 'The Case of the Weathermen: Social Reaction and rAdical Commitment;, in I. Taylor and L. Taylor, eds., *Politics and Deviance*. Harmondsworth: Penguin.

WEBB, B., and LAYCOCK, G. (1992), *Tackling Car Crime: The Nature and Extent of the Problem*, Crime Prevention Unit Paper no. 32. London: Home Office.

WELLS, L. E., and RANKIN, J. H. (1991), 'Families and Delinquency: A Meta-Analysis of the Impact of Broken Homes', *Social Problems*, 38/1.

WEST, D. J., and FARRINGTON, D. P. (1973), *Who Becomes Delinquent*? London: Heinemann.

—— (1977), *The Delinquent Way of Life*. London: Heinemann.

WERTHMAN, C., and PILIAVIN, I. (1981), 'The Police perspective on Delinquency', in E. Rubington and M. S. Weinberg, eds., *Deviance: The Interactionist Perspective*, 4th edn. New York: Macmillan.

WHYTE, W. F. (1981) [1943], *Street Corner Society: The Social Structure of an Italian Slum*, 3rd edn. Chicago: University of Chicago Press.

WIENER, M. J. (1990), *Reconstructing the Criminal: culture, Law, and Policy in England, 1830–1914*. Cambridge: Cambridge University Press.

WILLCOCK, H. D. (1949), *Mass Observation Report on Juvenile Delinquency*. London: Falcon Press.

WILLIAMS, T. (1989), *The Cocaine Kids*. New York: Addison-Wesley.

WILLIAMS, T., and KORNBLUM, W. (1985), *Growing Up Poor*. Lexington: Lexington Books.

WILLIS, P. (1972), 'The Motorbike within a Subcultural Group', *Working Papers in Cultural Studies*, no. 2. Centre for Contemporary Cultural Studies, University of Birmingham.

—— (1977), *Learning to Labour: How Working Class Kids Get Working Class Jobs*. London: Saxon House.

—— (1978), *Profane Culture*. London: Routledge and Kegan Paul.

—— (1990), *Common Culture: Symbolic Work at Play in the Everyday Cultures of the Young*. Milton Keynes: Open University Press.

WILLMOTT, P. (1966), *Adolescent Boys of East London*. London: Routledge and Kegan Paul.

WILSON, W. J. (1987), *The Truly Disadvantaged: The Inner City, the Underclass, and Public Policy*. Chicago: University of Chicago Press.

WIRTH, L. (1938), 'Urbanism as a Way of Life', *American Journal of Sociology*, 44.

WOMEN'S STUDIES GROUP, CENTRE FOR CONTEMPORARY CULTURAL STUDIES (1978), *Women Take Issue: Aspects of Women's Subordination*. London: Hutchinson.

YOUNG, J. (1971*a*), 'The Role of the Police as Amplifiers of Devianc, Negotiators of Reality and Translators of Fantasy', in S. Cohen, ed., *Images of Deviance*. Harmondsworth: Penguin.

—— (1971*b*), *The Drugtakers*. London: Paladin.

—— (1973), 'The Hippie Solution: An Essay in the Politics of Leisure', in I. Taylor and L. Taylor, eds., *Politics and Deviance*. Harmondsworth: Penguin.

—— (1975), 'Working Class Criminology', in I. Taylor, P. Walton, and J. Young, eds., *Critical Criminology*. London: Routledge and Kegan Paul.

25

Victims

LUCIA ZEDNER*

INTRODUCTION

Studying victims has become one of the growth industries of criminology. Since the 1980 there has been an extraordinarily rapid increase in national and local victim surveys and in studies of the impact of crime, of victim needs and services. Academic research has been mirrored and encouraged by the growth of dynamic and influential groups set up to help victims and to promote their interests. Feminist organizations such as Rape Crisis Centres and the Women's Refuge Movement, providing support for sexually assaulted and battered women, have been influential in raising awareness of these specific groups (Corbett and Hobdell 1988). Victims more generally have been taken up by the national organization Victim Support, which offers emotional support and practical services. While the victims' lobby in Britain is less highly politicized than the rights-orientated victims' movement in the USA led by NOVA—the National Organization for Victim Assistance (Elias 1986), it is apparent that victims have now established a high profile both in criminal justice policy and in criminology. As Maguire has noted, 'In their everyday decision making, police officers, prosecutors, judges, probation officers, and parole boards are frequently enjoined—and, increasingly, compelled—to pay heed to victims' interests as well as to those of the community and the offender' (Maguire 1991: 363). Innovations in policing policy, in provisions for victim-witnesses before and during trial, in compensation by the state and from the offender all attest to the combined influence of academic research and effective lobbying.

This chapter will examine the origins and genesis of studies in 'victimology' and the development of mass and local victimization surveys, upon which much of our knowledge and understanding of victims are based. It will go on to examine research findings on the 'costs of crime': not least the fear it generates; the constraints consequently placed on lifestyles and mobility; and its direct impact on those who are its victims.

* The author is very grateful to Andrew Ashworth, Leonard Leigh, Paul Rock, Martin Wright, and the editors for their comments and criticisms on drafts of this chapter.

The chapter will survey research aimed at identifying the psychological, physical, and financial harms suffered by victims and at assessing their need for emotional support, as well as for practical and financial assistance. The progress of the victim movement in responding to these needs and in providing services will also be analysed. Finally, this chapter suggests that the growth of interest in victims has had the effect of opening to scrutiny the very purpose of the criminal justice system and the place of victims within it. Mediation schemes to enable victims and offenders to seek resolution of their conflict, and the expansion of offender and state compensation, are some of the more important manifestations of this change. At a more theoretical level, reorientation of the criminal justice process towards the victim connotes a shift in penological thinking from classical retributivism towards ideas of reparative justice. The chapter will conclude by outlining some of the problems, both philosophical and practical, entailed by this conceptual shift.

CLASSICAL STUDIES IN VICTIMOLOGY

Interest in victims has a long history. The term 'victimology' appears to have been coined in 1949 by the American psychiatrist Frederick Wertham, who called for 'a science of victimology' which would address itself to the sociology of the victim (Wertham 1949). It is, however, the work of his contemporary Hans Von Hentig, *The Criminal and his Victim* (1948), which is now widely regarded as the seminal text in developing victim studies. Highly critical of the traditional offender-orientated nature of criminology, Von Hentig proposed a new, dynamic approach challenging the conception of the victim as passive actor by adopting an interactionist stance. This focused simultaneously both on those characteristics of victims which might be said to have precipitated their suffering and on the relationship between victim and offender. He argued 'The law . . . makes a clear-cut distinction between the one who does and the one who suffers. Looking into the genesis of the situation, in a considerable number of cases, we meet a victim who consents tacitly, co-operates, conspires or provokes' (Von Hentig 1948, quoted in Fattah 1989: 44). By classifying victims into typologies based on psychological and social variables he suggested that certain individuals were 'victim-prone'.

Others took up these notions of victim-precipitation and victim-proneness. Mendelsohn, for example, sought to identify those personal characteristics which made some people more susceptible to victimization than others (Mendelsohn 1956). Drawing on existing explanations of accident causation, he attempted to quantify the extent of the victim's 'guilty contribution to the crime'. This moralistic approach went beyond the merely descriptive exercise of developing victim typologies to assign degrees of culpability, developing a classification with categories ranging from the 'completely innocent' to the 'most guilty victim'. This form of 'victim blaming' was later to attract considerable criticism. But Mendelsohn's intent was less to exculpate the offender than to devise an explanatory model on the basis of which preventive programmes might be devised to reduce the extent and severity of victimization.

Not until Wolfgang's classic study *Patterns in Criminal Homicide* (1958) were Von Hentig's ideas subjected to systematic, empirical testing. Wolfgang defined victim-precipitated offences as those 'in which the victim is a direct, positive precipitator in the crime' (Wolfgang 1958). Examining police records of 588 homicides in Philadelphia in the years 1948–52, he calculated that 26 per cent of known homicides resulted from victim-initiated resort to violence. The conclusion of his work, that some crime was victim-precipitated, inspired many subsequent studies replicating his approach (for example, Amir 1971; Hindelang *et al.* 1978). Miers has identified the main characteristics of this early victimology as follows: 'firstly, the persistent search for factors inhering within individuals that increase their susceptibility to victimisation; secondly, the almost exclusive focus within victimological studies upon crimes against the person; and thirdly, the perennial concern with the question of victim participation in crime' (Miers 1989*a*: 8). While these studies were as much concerned with developing victim typologies as with identifying the extent and nature of victim precipitation, it is this latter aim, with its emotive connotations of victim-blaming, that continues to attract criminological attention.

Perhaps the most controversial application of Wolfgang's model of victim precipitation is Amir's *Patterns of Forcible Rape* (1971). Amir analysed 646 forcible rapes recorded by the police in Philadelphia and concluded that 19 per cent were victim-precipitated. Amir's study provoked considerable disquiet and has been criticized on both methodological and ideological grounds. His definition of precipitation is broad and vague, encompassing all those instances in which 'the victim actually—or so it was interpreted by the offender—agreed to sexual relations but retracted . . . or did not resist strongly enough when the suggestion was made by the offender. The term also applies to cases in which the victim enters vulnerable situations charged sexually' (Amir 1971: 262). This shift, from recognizing victim–offender interaction as a precipitating factor in crime to reascribing blame to the victim in rape cases, was heavily criticized by the newly emergent feminist movement. Methodological criticisms were also made. Since only a small proportion of rapes are reported (Temkin 1987: 9), Amir's reliance on police records necessarily presents a very partial picture. Moreover, reports contained within police files cannot be taken as unproblematic accounts. It could be argued that such reports tell us as much about police attitudes to rape victims as they do about the etiology of the crime. Finally, Amir's inference that those who accorded with his definition were in some sense 'asking for it' has been condemned for ignoring 'the profound and long-term effects which rape has on victims (nightmares, fear, shame, guilt, powerlessness, depression and the like)' (Morris 1987: 174).

The chief difficulty with Amir's study (and others which followed its model) is that it conflates the careful analysis carried out by Wolfgang of the dynamics of individual crimes with a more generalized reattribution of responsibility to the victim. It moves from recognizing that risk of victimization is correlated with factors such as social background, time, and place to victim-blaming. In short, as Anttila noted, its seems to suggest 'that victims of assault have no one except themselves to blame if they deliberately walk in dark alleys after dark' (Anttila 1974: 7). It is this apparent endorsement of the common view that 'nice girls' do not get raped which has been deemed most objectionable about this approach.

More recently, Fattah has defended the hypothesis of victim-precipitation, arguing that in a rigorously pursued, value-free social science there is no reason why it should entail victim-blaming. Although it has been used carelessly in the past, he argues, it is basically sound as an explanatory tool (Fattah 1979, 1991). Others have been less sanguine about its utility, arguing that its explanatory powers are simply inadequate. And a new generation of feminist criminologists (of which more below) have condemned the tendency for victim-precipitation studies to lead to value-laden victim-blaming (Morris 1987: 173–4, Walklate 1989: 4–5). The narrow concentration of early victim studies on reassigning responsibility for crime offered few new, coherent theoretical insights (Rock 1986: 72–3) and produced little by way of empirical findings other than that *some* victims bear *some* responsibility for *some* crimes (Miers 1989*a*: 15). It is therefore perhaps not surprising that, throughout the 1960s and much of the 1970s, mainstream criminology remained firmly wedded to offender-orientated studies.

MASS VICTIMIZATION SURVEYS

One of the most important factors in regenerating criminological interest in victims was the development of the victim survey. In America in the 1960s earlier micro studies of individual victims were overtaken by mass victimization surveys designed to uncover the unreported 'dark figure' of crime. Pilot studies carried out on behalf of the US President's Crime Commission 1967; (Ennis 1967; Reiss 1967) were followed up by annual National Crime Surveys (NCS) carried out by the Bureau of Justice

Statistics. The core findings of the annual NCS have been characterized as follows: 'that the bulk of events uncovered by the surveys are relatively trivial, that criminal victimization of the types measured is relatively rare, and that there is a large amount of repeat victimization' (Gottfredson 1986: 251). Only as a consequence of later studies on the impact of victimization were these rather sanguine conclusions to be revised.

In Britain, the first major survey was carried out in London by Sparks, Genn, and Dodd (Sparks *et al.* 1977). In addition to attempting to ascertain the extent and nature of unreported crime, it also asked questions about victims' perceptions of crime and attitudes to the criminal justice system. In so doing it may be said to have set the agenda for many subsequent surveys and smaller-scale, qualitative studies.

Nationally, crime surveys have been funded and administered by central government. The first British Crime Survey reported in 1983, drawing on a representative sample of over 10,000 people over the age of 15. Its main aim was to estimate the extent of crime independently of statistics recorded by the police. In addition it collected data on 'factors predisposing people to victimisation; the impact of crime on victims; fear of crime; victims' experiences of the police; other contacts with the police; and self-reported offending' (Mayhew and Hough 1983). It has been replicated three times, reporting in 1985, 1989, and 1992 (Hough and Mayhew 1985; Mayhew *et al.* 1989; Mayhew and Maung 1993). The first Scottish Crime Survey was carried out in 1983 (Chambers and Tombs 1984) and, more recently, an ambitious cross-national crime survey was carried out using comparable surveys in fourteen countries (Van Dijk *et al.* 1990). These new macro studies aim to quantify the true volume of victimization and to identify the social, economic, and demographic characteristics of the victim population. Their technique typically involves asking large samples of the population, nationally or in a given area, questions about crimes committed against them over a specified period—generally six months or a year. Non-household and non-personal offences (such as vandalism, shoplifting, and fraud) are excluded from BCS questionnaires. Information is collected about personal and property crimes committed (the time and place of the incident, its impact, whether or not it was reported to the police) and about the victims (their age, sex, race, social class, and their consequent attitudes and behaviour) (Crawford *et al.* 1990: 2–3).

Perhaps the most significant finding elicited is that, as anticipated, crimes reported to the police represent only a small fraction of those which occur. The first British Crime Survey found that around only one in four crimes of property loss and damage and around only one in five offences of violence were recorded in the official statistics. The 1988 BCS estimated that there were 13,292,000 household and property offences—

four times more than the number recorded by the police (Mayhew *et al.* 1989). This figure was 12 per cent more than the BCS estimate in 1985 and 21 per cent more than in 1983. Interestingly, the percentage of crimes reported to the police has increased steadily since the BCS began from 31 per cent in 1981 to 43 per cent in 1991 (Mayhew and Maung 1992: 1).

The 1992 BCS found that while the chance of being a victim of a minor offence was high, the risk of suffering a more serious offence was small (Mayhew and Maung 1992). Theft was the most common offence, and vehicle theft particularly so—over a third (36 per cent) of all incidents revealed by the BCS involved theft of, or from, or criminal damage to, a vehicle. Burglaries, on the other hand, made up only 9 per cent of crimes, violent offences (wounding and robbery) made up 5 per cent, and common assaults another 12 per cent (Mayhew and Maung 1992). To take one, much quoted, example from the 1989 BCS, the 'statistically average' adult can expect to have his home burgled once every thirty-seven years, or have the family car stolen once every fifty years. While comforting to the general public, such figures are less than informative since they gloss over major geographical, social, and economic differences. Risk of victimization generally is closely related to geographical area, and risk of personal victimization correlated with age, sex, and patterns of routine activity such as going out in the evenings and alcohol consumption. For example, although over a quarter of vehicle owners suffered some form of crime against their vehicle, risk was closely related with living in cities, especially inner cities, parking in the street at night, living in council property, and driving a good deal. More striking still are the correlates of burglary. The risk of being burgled was found to be five times higher in urban areas than elsewhere. Flats were at greater risk than houses, end-of-terrace than mid-terrace houses, and council than owner-occupied homes.

Crimes of violence also correlate closely with specific variables. Data from the 1988 BCS show that robbery is twice as likely to occur to those under 45 than those over 45 and to men than women. Living in inner cities and going out at night also increase the risk of victimization. Men make up the bulk of assault victims (80 per cent). Most at risk are those who are single, under 30 years old, drink heavily several evenings a week, and who assault others. Assaults were reported to occur most often in places of entertainment such as pubs and clubs, secondly in the workplace, and thirdly in the home. However, such estimates do not take into account the likelihood that domestic assaults are underreported even in crime surveys. The findings of the 1988 BCS that victims know their assailant in a third of cases and that a sixth of assailants are relatives, partners, or former partners are almost certainly an underestimate (for reasons discussed below).

For many types of crime, both Afro-Caribbeans and Asians tend to be more at risk than whites. This may be explained in part by the fact that they are overrepresented in social and age groups particularly prone to crime. Members of ethnic minority groups are disproportionately likely to be council tenants, or to live in younger households in socially disadvantaged areas. Asians were more likely to suffer victimization by groups of strangers. Twenty-seven per cent of crimes against Asians involved four or more offenders, compared with 19 per cent against white people and 11 per cent against Afro-Caribbeans. Members of ethnic minority groups were more likely to suffer serious offences than whites: levels of monetary loss or damage were higher and, for Asians at least, injuries in cases of assault or robbery tended to be slightly more severe (Mayhew *et al.* 1989: ch. 5). The BCS asked respondents whether they considered crimes against them to have a racial element. Asians were more likely to do so, considering 24 per cent of offences to be racially motivated, while Afro-Caribbeans saw only 15 per cent as being so. Assaults, threats, and vandalism were those offences most often thought to be committed for racial reasons.

This new generation of victim surveys proved to be a valuable resource widely welcomed by criminologists. It is arguable that they radically restructured the criminological agenda. None the less, many methodological problems have been identified both by independent commentators and by the surveyors themselves. An initial difficulty lies in identifying a sample which is in some measure representative of the population. Past samples for the British Crime Surveys have been drawn from the electoral register, a source known to underrepresent ethnic minorities, the young, and the less socially stable—all groups particularly prone to victimization. Even among those actually approached, non-respondents may include disproportionate numbers of victims. Mindful of these methodological problems, the 1992 BCS drew its sample from the Postcode Address File (a listing of all postal delivery points), a source likely to produce a more representative sample than the electoral register.

Victim surveys are also problematic as a measure of crime in that they enumerate only those incidents for which individuals are able and willing to identify themselves as victims. For this reason they tend to concentrate on physical and sexual assaults (though even these may not be readily revealed to an interviewer) and personal or household property crime. They necessarily ignore the entire gamut of corporate, environmental, and, more mundanely, motoring offences. Nor can they easily uncover crimes against organizations such as company fraud, shoplifting, or fare evasion (Hough and Mayhew 1983: 3–4). Crimes in which the 'victim' is complicit, such as drug offences, gambling, and prostitution are also unlikely to be revealed since this would entail confession to offences for which respondents may themselves face prosecution. Crimes where the victim and offender are known to each other are less likely to be reported to the interviewer, especially if the offender is a relative or a member of the household. In the case of domestic violence or sexual assault, the offender may even be present when the interview takes place. Even where this is not the case, the common assumption that 'real crime' is something that occurs only between strangers is likely to inhibit the revelation or recognition of much physical and sexual violence committed against women. As a consequence this 'hidden violence', as Stanko characterizes it (Stanko 1988), is likely to be significantly undercounted in all but the most sensitive crime surveys. The latest British Crime Survey revealed only fifteen cases of sexual assault among the 5,500 women surveyed (Mayhew *et al.* 1989), a figure recognized by its authors and critics alike to be a gross underestimate.

The popular reporting of national crime surveys tends also to create a distorted picture of the distribution of crime. By ignoring geographic and social differentials, press reports have generally implied that the risk of victimization is uniformly low. Further distortion may result from the fact that educated, middle-class respondents appear better able to understand the questions posed and more willing to report offences to the interviewer. Further down the social scale, respondents may be so regularly exposed to crime that they fail to recognize activities as criminal or have difficulties in recalling all the offences perpetrated against them. Where the period under survey is more than a few months, problems of recall are likely to become especially marked. Victims may forget less serious incidents or may have difficulties in remembering whether a more distant occurrence fell within the specified time period.

LOCAL CRIME SURVEYS

Seeking to overcome some of the perceived inadequacies of the national surveys, local crime surveys have been carried out in Merseyside (1985), Islington (1986, 1990), Hammersmith and Fulham (1989), and Edinburgh (1990). By focusing on particular localities these surveys attempted to pinpoint the higher levels of crime prevailing in socially deprived inner-city areas; to highlight the disproportionate victimization of women, of members of ethnic minority groups, and of those lower down the social scale; and to set crime in its broader social context by including questions about racial and sexual harassment, drug abuse, and other forms of anti-social behaviour (Crawford *et al.* 1990: 4). Questions about victims' encounters with the police and their assessment of police response have also been included to elicit public perceptions of police priorities and service delivery, and their opinions concerning the control and accountability of police forces. New questions also address the role of other agencies in responding to crime, for example local authority social services and housing departments and the work of Victim Support schemes.

The nature and scope of these questions partly reflects a desire to establish the social context of victimization. More problematically, they are intended to create a database to be used in auditing police performance, allocating resources to combat particular crime problems, and developing policy initiatives. These policy-orientated goals arose partly from the fact that the 'second generation' crime surveys were funded for the most part by radical local authorities committed to addressing problems faced by socially marginalized members of the communities they served. As Rock has commented, these local authorities were 'powerful patrons' whose pragmatic concern with problems of policy obliged those carrying out these local crime surveys to become 'the new administrative criminologists of the left' (Rock 1988: 197).

In describing the trends and patterns of victimization, local surveys have, above all, documented the uneven distribution of risk, showing that certain age or social groups and particular residential areas are far more frequently subjected to crime than others. The Merseyside Crime Survey, for example, found that the incidence of burglary on Merseyside was three times higher than in the rest of England and Wales (Kinsey 1984: 5); and the second Islington Crime Survey (ICS) found that 12 per cent of its respondents had been burgled, compared to only 7 per cent of respondents to the latest British Crime Survey (Crawford *et al.* 1990: 10). Curiously, while the BCS found a marked disparity between physical assaults against whites (5.5 per cent) and Afro-Caribbeans (9 per cent), the second ICS found no appreciable difference between these groups (7 per cent and 6 per cent respectively). How one interprets such findings is open to doubt. It may be that Afro-Caribbeans in Islington are so exposed to violence that they tend to underreport assaults against them. Alternatively, it may be that the high concentration of ethnic minority populations in this inner London borough levels out disparities in the victimization of whites and blacks. Such a possibility draws attention to the difficulties of comparing local studies of highly deprived, inner-city areas with the findings of national (rural and urban) surveys.

Local victimization surveys have shown themselves to be more sensitive than national surveys in revealing incidents of sexual assault. The first two British Crime Surveys revealed only one (unreported) case of attempted rape and seventeen and eighteen cases of sexual assault respectively in the 1983 and 1985 reports (Hough and Mayhew 1983, 1985). In stunning contrast, the first Islington Crime Survey estimated 1,200 cases of sexual assault in Islington during the period under review (Jones *et al.*

1986). Such disparities suggest major flaws in the wording of questions in the national survey and possibly also in the demeanour and approach of interviewers. Insensitivity in either sphere is unlikely to do much to uncover areas of 'hidden crime'. In displaying greater sensitivity both to local variation and to the feelings of victims themselves, this new generation of victim surveys has had greater success in revealing differential patterns of victimization.

The notion of 'differential victimization' has been studied with reference not only to geographic, social, and economic variables but also to race and sex. We have seen above that women's personal experiences of crime may be less readily documented by mass victimization surveys. To rectify this, feminist researchers have carried out a number of studies of personal crimes against women (Dobash and Dobash 1979; Hanmer and Saunders 1984; Hall 1985; Stanko 1988). Dobash and Dobash studied over 1,000 cases of domestic violence. Despite the gender-neutral character of this term, they found that over three-quarters of cases involved husbands assaulting their wives. Only ten cases involved attacks on husbands by wives (Dobash and Dobash 1979). They found that only 2 per cent of women reported the crime to the police, others preferring instead to seek help from friends or relatives.

Sexual offences against women have also received increasing attention, initially in American studies but more recently also in Britain. One landmark study, *Ask Any Woman* (Hall 1985), carried out in London suggested that a third of respondents had been raped or sexually assaulted, though it has since been subject to methodological criticism. A study carried out in Leeds (Hanmer and Saunders 1984) used a much broader definition of sexual violence and found that 59 per cent of women had been sexually assaulted at least once in the previous year, while Radford found that as many as 76 per cent of women had experienced some form of sexual violence over the previous year (Radford 1987).

These surveys suggest levels of sexual crime against women far higher than those revealed by national victim surveys and infinitely higher than those indicated by police records. Hall, for example, found that only 8 per cent of those respondents claiming to have been raped and 18 per cent of those alleging sexual assault had reported their victimization to the police (Hall 1985). Yet the considerable variation in the findings of these different surveys highlights a central difficulty in ascertaining the true extent and nature of sexual victimization. As Morris has pointed out, 'most of us believe we know what rape is, but our knowledge is derived from social not legal definitions' (Morris 1987: 165). The common perception is that 'true rape' involves a stranger using threats or weapons, at night in a dark or isolated place, against a sexually inexperienced woman who in the struggle suffers severe bruising or other physical signs of injury. The role of the media in creating and reinforcing these stereotypes may partly explain why victims whose experiences do not fit the prescribed pattern fail not only to report but even to recognize them as rape (see Soothill and Walby 1991). Even where they do, prevailing assumptions about rape foster feelings of guilt and self-blame which also inhibit victims from reporting. As a consequence, the sensitivity of survey questions and the approach and demeanour of the interviewer may dramatically alter response rates.

The example of rape victims may be seen to highlight wider problems inherent in victim surveys: not least the problem of how respondents come to perceive themselves as victims and why it is that some who have been subjects of crimes fail to recognize themselves as victims? Which offences remain in the memory of the respondent to be reported to the surveyor and which, and for what reasons, are simply forgotten? The conclusion by Reiss that 10 per cent of crimes reported to the police in the USA are not reported to those conducting victim surveys must make us wary of seeing the findings of victim surveys as in any way representing the 'true' figure of crime (Reiss 1986).

In switching attention from offenders to victims, it could be argued that victim surveys did no more than suggest a new subject area for positivist criminology. Revelations about offences least likely to be reported to the police, such as sexual assault and domestic violence, may have reconstituted our picture of crime. The findings that victims of violence tend to share many characteristics with offenders, or that property offences are committed more often against the less well-off than the wealthy, bring into question many prevailing assumptions about victimization. But the counting of crimes and detailed descriptions of the age, sex, socio-economic and geographical characteristics of victims could be said to do no more than provide a new measure of crime and a new set of portraits, in many ways parallel to those previously drawn of offenders.

Yet victim surveys have typically gone beyond the counting of unreported offences to ask questions about perceptions of and reactions to crime. In so doing they provide the basis for the development of a new theoretical framework organized around questions about the attributes of crime victims, societal attitudes to crime, and the effects of crime on the community. Two areas, in particular, have caught the criminological imagination and furnished the agenda for much subsequent research. These are fear of crime among the public generally and the impact of crime upon those who are its victims.

FEAR OF CRIME

Interest in fear of crime originated in the United States in the 1960s during a period of race riots and growing urban violence. But it was the victim survey which, by providing data about the extent and severity of such fear, pinpointed an entirely new area for criminological inquiry (Maxfield 1984; Garofalo 1979; Skogan 1986*a*, *b*). Although clearly a corollary to interest in victimization, fear of crime is now recognized as a distinct social problem extending well beyond those who have actually been victimized to affect the lives of all those who perceive themselves to be at risk. Moreover, although fear of crime is closely related to levels of crime, and tends to increase as crime rises, it exists independently and cannot be seen as a mere function of levels of criminal activity at any given time. This recognition of fear of crime as a distinct area of inquiry raises theoretical problems: What it is we mean by the term? To what exactly is it a reaction? What are its social correlates? Who is most vulnerable to fear, when, and why? Ironically, the very carrying out of crime surveys may serve to increase sensitivity to the risks of crime. Situating questions about fear within a crime survey may consequently elicit higher levels of apparent anxiety than would otherwise prevail.

Generally, the term 'fear of crime' has been used to refer to perceived threats to personal safety rather than threats to property or more generalized perceptions of risk (Maxfield 1984: 3). An immediate problem is how to control for variations in respondents' willingness to admit to such fears. Socialization alone is likely to make men less willing to admit to such feelings than women. Another major methodological difficulty is how to phrase questions so as to identify the nature and level of this fear without distorting the data by importing other anxieties. Questions in crime surveys typically ask 'How safe do you feel walking in your neighbourhood alone at night?' But, phrased in this way, such a question may also elicit answers relating to a given neighbourhood, fear of the dark, or other non-crime-related dangers. Or again, answers may reflect respondents' attitudes to their own physical strength or weakness. The construction of fear of crime may then be as closely related to feelings of power or vulnerability as it is to calculated perceptions of actual risk.

Crime surveys have produced problematic data that appear to show that levels of fear are far from closely correlated with risk. Young working-class men who spend a great deal of leisure time outside the home, particularly those who habitually visit pubs, may be most at risk but admit to very little fear, whereas women and the elderly commonly express profound anxiety despite lower levels of risk. The first British Crime Survey found, for example, that in inner-city areas 60 per cent of women, but only 27 per cent of men, over the age of 61 felt 'very unsafe' when alone after dark (Hough and Mayhew 1983: 23). Highlighting the weak correspondence between fear and risk, the BCS focused on the apparent irrationality of fears disproportionate to risk.

Suspicious that such findings were an administrative attempt to diminish the seriousness of crime as a social problem by discounting fear of crime as 'irrational', many criminologists have examined the relationship between risk and fear (Young 1988; Skogan 1986*b*; Crawford *et al.* 1990). The authors of the Islington Crime Survey asked respondents both about their fears and about the 'probability of crime in the next year'. They found that although some people worry a good deal about crime, they appear to be well informed as to the likelihood of becoming a victim (Jones *et al.* 1986: 9). The second Islington Crime Survey went even further in attempting to identify the social and structural causes of people's fear (Crawford *et al.* 1990: 40). It sought to differentiate between fear of crime on the street, on public transport, and in the home, to develop gender-specific understanding of fear, to focus on those groups expressing highest levels of fear, and to examine the ways in which personal behaviour determined and was itself affected by perceptions of risk.

If risk assessment is not the sole determinant of fear, then other causal factors must be sought. Fear of crime is primarily an urban phenomenon and may be seen as a reaction to 'local incivilities' such as poor street lighting, vandalism, boarded-up buildings, youths loitering on street corners, drunks, and other signals of a hostile environment (Crawford *et al.* 1990: 82). Other correlates include perceptions of 'moral decline', anxiety among whites about the influx of racial minorities, or other changes to their neighbourhood (Skogan 1986*b*: 138). This more diffuse sense of insecurity may be exacerbated by past personal experiences, by socialization, media portrayal of crime, or the perceived inadequacy of policing (Garofalo 1979: 82). Ironically, crime prevention efforts, whether by the police, Home Office literature, or media campaigns, may raise popular perceptions of risk and so stimulate increased fear.

Gender-specific analyses have been developed by feminist criminologists such as Stanko (Stanko 1985 and 1988) to explain women's greater fear of crime. First, since crimes against women, particularly sexual offences and assaults occurring within the home, are least susceptible to discovery or revelation, women, and particularly girls, may suffer far higher levels of victimization than revealed even by crime surveys. The assumed 'irrationality' of women's fears, when judged against only that level of risk known to the surveys, may be all too rational a reflection of 'hidden violence' (Stanko 1988: 40). Secondly, merely counting offences takes no account of the differential impact of actual or potential violation. Racial harassment suffered by members of ethnic minority communities may involve incidents individually too 'minor' to be reported or recorded but which, when repeated over time, profoundly blight the lives of their victims (Cooper and Pomeyie 1988). For those living in predominantly white communities, isolation may make them feel even more vulnerable. Women and the elderly may also be 'unequal victims' in that the physical, psychological, or economic costs of crime may be much greater for them than for other more robust or more affluent individuals (Crawford *et al.* 1990: 70). The lower risks faced, if indeed they are lower, are more than offset by this greater vulnerability to the impact of crime.

Lifestyles and Mobility

These findings have led criminologists to consider the ways in which individual's lifestyles are altered and life choices constrained by fear of crime. Several models of fear-related behaviour have been identified (see e.g. Skogan 1986*a*). To the degree that they consider risks to be unacceptable, some individuals may withdraw from social life. Other people assess the costs and benefits of modifying their behaviour to achieve some reasonable level of risk and delimit their lifestyle accordingly. Yet here again behavioural responses are not tied solely or exactly to risk. The wealthy may be no more at risk, and in many situations are arguably less so, but they have the resources to take precautionary measures such as installing burglar alarms to their homes or taking taxis in preference to public transport.

A prime example is the development of Neighbourhood Watch schemes in settled 'affluent suburban areas, high-status non-family areas and in areas of modern family housing with higher incomes' (Mayhew *et al.* 1989: 52)—areas known to be less vulnerable to crime. The geographical spread of these schemes illustrates the way in which alleviating fear may be correlated to income rather than risk. One of the underlying purposes of Neighbourhood Watch (NW) is to enable communities to develop some sense of control over crime and so enjoy increased security and lower levels of fear. Interpreting the success of NW in this respect is complicated by the fact that those joining, often as a result of having been burgled in the past, tend to be more anxious initially than non-scheme members. While it appears that members do enjoy feelings of being better protected as a result of their efforts (for example, installing home security devices) this does not seem to effect any marked diminution in levels of fear (Bennett 1987). The 1988 BCS found that 60 per cent of NW members were 'very or fairly worried about being the victim of burglary' compared to only 55 per cent of non-members (Mayhew *et al.* 1989: 59). Since this discrepancy does not appear to be explained solely by other fear-related factors (such as age, sex, perceptions of risk) it may be that anxiety is reinforced through the heightened sensitivity to danger brought about by belonging to NW schemes (Mayhew *et al.* 1989: 59–60).

The relationship between fear of crime and quality of life is also problematic. For example, fear may be an important factor in inhibiting mobility. Of respondents to the second Islington Crime Survey, nearly two-thirds gave fear of crime as a reason for not going out and 41 per cent gave it as a considerable part of the reason. However, other factors may also be at work, not least physical disabilities, financial restrictions, having nowhere to go, or preferring to stay at home in the evenings with friends or family (Crawford *et al.* 1990: 59). The extent to which behaviour is limited by fear of crime varies considerably from avoiding certain places to never going out at night unaccompanied. Even those willing to go out at night alone report developing elaborate strategies of safekeeping: parking in well-lit areas, monitoring walking routes home, developing strategies for avoiding or deflecting potential violations.

Both the BCS and the ICS found substantial differences in the impact of fear of crime on the lifestyles of men and women. The first Islington Crime Survey found that 36 per cent of women, compared to only 7 per cent of men, never went out after dark for fear of crime. This avoidance behaviour, in the view of the authors of the ICS, 'limits their participation in public, to the extent of a virtual curfew' (Crawford *et al.* 1990: 91). Less well documented is the effect of racial harassment against members of the ethnic minorities. Yet the experience of Victim Support in responding to victims of racial harassment has revealed that 'many victim families end up living like prisoners in their homes or being forced to move away from a familiar environment; children are unsettled and both their education and social life suffer; women are scared to go about the normal tasks . . . and also feel insecure in their own homes' (Cooper and Pomeyie 1988: 85).

IMPACT OF VICTIMIZATION

So far we have considered fear of crime and its consequences among the population generally. We now turn to consider the impact of personal victimization. The earlier, large-scale crime surveys tended to suggest that, in general, effects on victims were relatively mild and/or transitory. For example, Hindelang, Gottfredson, and Garofalo found that their respondents' lives were only altered in minor, mostly ephemeral ways by the experience of victimization (Hindelang *et al.* 1978). The mass of petty property offences would appear to engender little or no emotional trauma. Similarly, Sparks, Genn, and Dodd suggest that most victimization is no more than minimally disruptive since much crime consists of attempts, or results in little by way of loss or physical injury (Sparks *et al.* 1977). The British Crime Surveys have each included questions about the impact of victimization and have concluded that relatively little harm was suffered by most respondents. The first BCS found that at the time of the crime only 11 per cent were 'very much' affected and 17 per cent were 'quite a lot' affected by the time of the interview these proportions had fallen to only 2 per cent and 5 per cent respectively (Hough and Mayhew 1985).

More recently, smaller-scale, qualitative studies have suggested that victimization entails greater costs than the mass crime surveys had implied. Large-scale studies have been criticized as unreliable guides to crime's impact in that their respondents include very small numbers of serious crime victims and much larger populations of victims of petty infractions. As a consequence, aggregate results 'tend to wash or attenuate the overall effect of crime' (Lurigio 1987: 454). To rectify this tendency, qualitative research has focused on particular types of crime or specific victim groups. Studies have been carried out, for example, on burglary victims (Maguire 1980; Maguire and Corbett 1987), on victims of violence (Shapland *et al.* 1985; Stanko 1988), on rape victims (Burgess and Holstrom 1974; Chambers and Millar 1983), and on child victims (Finkelhor 1979, 1986; Morgan and Zedner 1992*a*). These studies, by concentrating on the more serious types of offence, have highlighted the acute stress and adverse physical, practical, or financial effects suffered by many victims.

Limitations arise from the fact that there has been little attempt to compare victimized with non-victimized groups in order to ascertain how far attitudes and experiences are attributable to victimization alone. Nor has there been any serious attempt to undertake longitudinal research which would allow pre- and post victimization comparisons. And as yet little comparative work has been done on the impact of different kinds of victimization or on the impact of victimization on different kinds of people (Skogan 1986*b*: 136).

Analysis of the impact of crime has been organized around types of impact and persistence of effects over time. Studies have shown that the vast majority of victims suffer in some way in the immediate aftermath of crime. Research by Lurigio in the United States found that most 'crime victims suffer from adverse, short-term psychological consequences as a result' (Lurigio 1987: 464). In Britain, Maguire found that 83 per cent of the burglary victims in his study experienced strong reactions on discovering that their homes had been invaded and that 65 per cent were still aware of some continuing impact on their lives four to ten weeks later (Maguire 1982: 126–31). Perhaps surprisingly, Maguire found that when asked about the worst aspect of burglary, only 32 per cent of victims spoke of loss or damage, while 41 per cent cited feelings of intrusion and 19 per cent feelings of emotional upset.

Personal crimes such as physical and sexual assault commonly entail still longer-term effects. Shapland *et al.* studied 300 victims of assault, robbery, or rape. They found that 75 per cent of victims of violence were still mentioning some effect at the 'outcome interview' two and a half years after the offence (Shapland *et al.* 1985: 98–9). Rape victims and victims of sexual abuse during childhood have been found to suffer persisting effects for many years afterwards (Burgess and Holstrom 1974; Morgan and Zedner 1992*a*: 44–5). Resick, in an American study, commented that rape victims experienced profound distress for several months after the crime and that 'many continue to experience problems with fear, anxiety, and interpersonal functioning for years after the event' (Resick 1987: 474). Unsurprisingly, sexual assault victims seem to recover more slowly than victims of other types of crime, suffering emotional disturbance, sleeping or eating disorders, feelings of insecurity or low self-esteem, or troubled relationships for months or even years after the event (Maguire and Corbett 1987: Smith 1989*a*; Kelly 1988).

The types of effect victims are likely to suffer obviously vary according to the crime. Assaults may entail physical injury, shock, loss or damage to property, time off work, and financial losses (Shapland *et al.* 1985: 97). The impact of burglary is more likely to be emotional (involving feelings of shock, insecurity, violation, etc.), financial, or practical (loss of property, disruption, mess, broken doors or windows) (Maguire 1980). Child sexual abuse may inflict few visible or tangible injuries but is liable to induce profound feelings of 'fear, revulsion, shame and guilt' (Morris 1987: 191). In the longer term child-abuse victims may suffer impaired self-esteem, school learning problems, withdrawal, and regressive behaviour (Finkelhor 1986: 152–63). While reactions are to a considerable extent crime-specific, most studies suggest that some degree of psychological distress is the dominant reaction among crime victims. At its most severe, this distress has been formally recognized by psychologists as 'post-traumatic stress disorder'—a clinical condition whose symptoms include anxiety, depression, loss of control, guilt, sleep disturbance, and obsessive dwelling on the crime itself (Burgess and Holstrom 1974; Jones *et al.* 1987).

Recent studies have sought to explain the differential impact of victimization, in order to understand why some victims are more severely affected than others by apparently similar crimes. Skogan has identified a number of key factors in determining the differential impact of crime: isolation, resources, vulnerability, and previous experience (Skogan 1986*b*: 140–3). Isolated people are not only more fearful of crime but are likely to suffer higher levels of stress when victimized. Thus those who live alone, with few friends or no close family, tend to feel the impact of crime more acutely than those who are well supported (Maguire 1980). Criminal damage, theft, and burglary are all likely to place heavier burdens on those with fewer financial resources, particularly because these are the very groups least likely to be insured against such loss. Generalized feelings of vulnerability among certain groups, such as women, ethnic minorities, and the elderly, also appear to magnify the impact of crime. Lack of ability to resist or to defend oneself against an attacker may amplify pre-existing feelings of vulnerability. For children, a burglary of the family home may be a shocking invasion of the one place they perceived to be secure from the terrors of the world and may entail trauma quite out of proportion to the physical damage or loss of property incurred (Morgan and Zedner 1992*a*: 63–4). Apart from feelings of vulnerability, actual physical weakness may result in victims suffering more serious injuries or taking longer to recover from assaults than those who are more robust (Garofalo 1977).

The significance of previous experience is perhaps most difficult to calculate. Multiple or series victimization appears to compound the impact suffered with each repeated occurrence and a minority of individuals are so repeatedly victimized that it becomes virtually impossible to distinguish the impact of discrete crimes from the generally impoverished quality of their life (Genn 1988). Racial harassment is a good example here. Although little academic research has yet been carried out on the extent of racial harassment in schools and colleges, the Commission for Racial Equality (1988) suggests that it is 'widespread and persistent'. For those who suffer continual 'name-calling and racial insults and abuse, graffiti . . . and racial violence varying from slapping, punching, jostling, and assault to maiming', the cumulative impact is far greater than any account of each individual incident would suggest (Commission for Racial Equality 1988: 7). Aside from previous crimes, other non-crime-related life experiences may also be influential in determining the impact of crime. The death of a relative; divorce, separation, or other family trauma; illness, or pre-existing psychological problems may amplify or be amplified by the impact of crime.

Just as factors external to the crime may be relevant in determining its impact, so the consequences of crime extend beyond the incident itself. Considerable expenses may be incurred as a direct result of the crime for the replacement of uninsured property, for medical care, counselling, or funeral costs. Other expenses arising less directly may none the less be considerable. Some victims are driven to move house as a consequence of a traumatic burglary or to escape continuing attacks or harassment. Some lose earnings or even risk their job after missing time from work for court attendances or due to crime-related illness or depression (Shapland *et al.* 1985: 104–5; Resick 1987). Many crimes may place considerable stress on family relations. Domestic violence may lead to the break-up of the family. The consequent dislocation not only affects those who are the direct victims but also impinges on those other members of the household who are its 'indirect victims'—most commonly the children (Morgan and Zedner 1992*a*: 28–31).

The wider impact of crime on secondary or 'indirect' victims is increasingly recognized in the literature. The most obvious example is that of the families of murder victims (Black and Kaplan 1988; Pynoos and Eth 1984). Although they are not primary victims they suffer perhaps the most profound trauma of any crime victim. The trauma of sudden bereavement is often compounded by the viciousness of the attack or the senselessness of the killing. For those who witness homicide or other non-fatal assaults, feelings of shock or guilt for failing to intervene may be profound, and onlookers, too, may be victims (Victim Support 1991; Pynoos and Eth 1984). The mass of other less serious offences may also create 'indirect victims'. For example, over a third of the 400,000 households burgled every year include children who, though rarely recognized as victims, may be distressed or even traumatized as a result (Morgan and Zedner 1992*a*). At its worst the impact of crime on those who are witnesses or obliged to live with its consequences may be such that they should properly be recognized as victims in their own right.

The impact of corporate or business crime upon its victims is perhaps least recognized of all. Most victims of fraud are, by its very nature, unaware that they have been victimized at all or unwilling to recognize that they have been duped (Box 1983: 17). Criminal negligence leading to workplace injuries and deaths is rarely recognized as crime. Large-scale incidents involving loss of life tend not to be popularly perceived not as crimes but as 'disasters'—witness *Piper Alpha*, Zeebrugge, and Bhopal. It is perhaps not surprising, then, that victims of 'white-collar' crime have only recently become the subject of criminological enquiry (Levi and Pithouse 1988; Levi 1992).

VICTIMS' NEEDS

The relationship between impact of crime and need is highly problematic. Those suffering the highest levels of harm or loss do not necessarily have correspondingly high needs. They may enjoy a supportive environment, be innately resilient, or otherwise be able to overcome the effects of victimization. On the other hand, victims suffering objectively less serious crimes may require greater support if they are vulnerable or isolated. Criminological understanding of victims' needs is largely reliant on views expressed by victims themselves—a source which is necessarily problematic (Mawby 1988: 132–3; Maguire 1991: 403–6). Vocal, determined, or well-connected victims may do much to colour perceptions of need, ironically at the expense of those whose needs are greatest but whose very vulnerability or inability to ask for help ensures their silence. Educated, informed, and resourceful individuals are better placed to seek out help, be it practical assistance, information, or advice on future crime prevention. For these reasons, Shapland and her colleagues argue that needs as expressed by victims cannot be seen as 'actual' or 'objective' assessments (Shapland *et al.* 1985: 112).

Victims' expressions of need are determined in part by their cultural background, their expectations, and their knowledge as to what services may be available to them. Those ignorant of the existence of available help may express only a diffuse, vague need for emotional support where others would specifically identify their desire for voluntary or professional counselling. The provision of services, too, plays a part in determining victims' needs. Expert-led innovations in the provision of support in turn drives victim expectations. While researchers have attempted to identify and even to calibrate the needs of specific groups of victims (Shapland *et al.* 1985; Maguire and Corbett 1987), the task must be a relativist one. How levels of need are to be assessed remains a matter of fiercely contested debate.

While most attention has focused on emotional impact and psychological needs, victims may also need practical help, information, and financial support. Practical needs tend to be short-term and relatively easily satisfied. The mending of windows or replacement of keys and broken locks following a burglary are obvious examples (Maguire 1982). Longer-term practical help may be required following the most serious offences: transportation to and from hospital for the treatment of injuries (Shapland *et al.* 1985), help with child-care following rape (Morgan and Zedner 1992*a*), or refuge from domestic violence (Smith 1989*b*). Provision of information for victims has also been identified as a major and, as yet, largely unmet need. In the immediate aftermath of crime this may entail no more than advice on crime prevention, insurance, or compensation claims. But for more serious crimes, the progress of police investigations, prosecution decisions, and the dates and outcome of any trial are all likely to be a source of considerable interest and concern. Studies by Maguire and Corbett (1987), Shapland *et al.* (1985), and Newburn and Merry (1990) reveal the importance attached by victims to being kept informed of the progress of 'their case'. Largely as a result of these research findings, the Home Office issued a Circular in 1988 (no. 20/1988) calling on police and prosecutors to make improvements in the way victims are kept informed. These innovations have been monitored by Newburn and Merry, who called for the introduction of a reliable system for providing victims with information, both as a matter of routine and in response to personal enquiries (Newburn and Merry 1990). *The Victim's Charter* (Home Office 1990) reiterated the importance of keeping victims informed. Given limits to resources, identifying types and quantifying levels of need in this way remains of central concern to those attempting to develop services for victims.

THE VICTIM MOVEMENT

In the USA, a strongly rights-based victim movement emerged in the 1960s and 1970s. Largely conservative in outlook, often seeking a more punitive response to offenders, it was in some states associated with demands for the retention or reintroduction of the death penalty. Dissatisfied with the existing responses to victims, the movement demanded a reorientation of the criminal justice system to take account of the needs and, increasingly, the 'rights' of victims.

In Britain, the central organ of the victim movement, Victim Support (formerly the National Association of Victim Support Schemes, NAVSS) has a very different history and orientation. Beginning life as a local initiative in Bristol in 1974, Victim Support grew dramatically in the following decades (Rock 1990). In 1991 it numbered 370 affiliated schemes nationwide, calling on the services of over 7,000 volunteers who, in the preceding year, made contact with almost 600,000 victims. Despite this impressive rate of growth, the political impact of Victim Support has been relatively low-key, for a number of reasons. Victim Support as an organization seems anxious to be considered politically neutral, partly, no doubt, to maximize its pool of volunteers and of potential donors, and cross-party political support and partly to maintain its charitable status. Unlike its American counterpart NOVA, Victim Support has concentrated more on securing practical advantages for victims than on formulating statements on victims' rights. Its code of practice expressly forbids commenting on the sentencing of offenders, except in relation to compensation. Where it has sought legislative change, it has avoided overt political lobbying, preferring to work more effectively behind the scenes to bring pressure to bear on issues such as services to victims by the police, compensation, and provision for the victim in court (Rock 1990, 1991). Good working relations with the Home Office and the police have perhaps proved more effective channels for change than attempts to win the interest of politicians.

The main thrust of Victim Support's endeavour is in providing services to individual victims at a local level. It works from the assumption that many crime victims are likely to be traumatized by their experience and that support from friends, family, or neighbours may be insufficient or simply unavailable. Given the considerable difficulty in identifying those most badly affected, the local schemes operate an 'outreach' service. This mainly takes the form of 'crisis intervention' by volunteers contacting victims directly to offer a 'shoulder to cry on', practical services, and information. The means of contacting victims varies between letters, doorstep visits, or (more rarely) telephone calls. Maguire and Corbett found that while 90 per cent of those receiving unsolicited visits invited the caller in to talk and half went on to discuss their feelings in depth or ask for practical help, only 7 per cent of those contacted by letter responded at all (Maguire and Corbett 1987). Outreach is more expensive in terms of volunteers' time and scheme resources but its obvious advantages in sparing the victim from having to ask for help has made it the dominant model of Victim Support work.

Each local scheme operates under the guidance of a management committee; a central co-ordinator liaises with the police daily to collect details of victims which are then distributed to a pool of volunteers who make contact and offers of help (Holtom and Raynor 1988). While this model forms the basis of Victim Support's organization, strong links with the community ensure considerable diversity of local policy and practice. Inner-city urban schemes are fashioned by different crime patterns, social and economic problems, and political imperatives from their rural counterparts. The availability of volunteers also plays a part in determining the level of service a scheme is able to offer. Inner-city areas with the highest crime rates lack an established middle-class community from which a pool of volunteers might readily be recruited. In rural areas, on the other hand, volunteers may be required to travel considerable distances to respond to victims in need. While the movement has become increasingly centralized, the national organization is far from imposing consistency or overcoming unevenness of provision in many areas. This said, levels of victim satisfaction with support when it is offered appears to be high (Shapland *et al.* 1985).

In its early days, Victim Support focused mainly on victims of 'conventional' crimes such as burglary, robbery, and theft: crimes generally committed by strangers. More recently, it has worked increasingly with the victims of seuxal and violent crime, often committed by those known to them. In its Annual Report for 1990/1 the director, Helen Reeves, estimated that Victim Support made contact with half of those reporting rape and half of the families of murder victims. Work with such victims inevitably tends to be of a very different nature from the general pattern of short-term 'crisis intervention', involving instead long-term support, often by a pair of specially trained volunteers, over months or even years.

One area into which Victim Support has until recently remained unwilling to venture is that of domestic violence, on the grounds that to use its traditional method of sending volunteers into the victim's home was inappropriate and placed the volunteer at risk. Support for victims of domestic violence has largely been the preserve of the women's movement. The first women's 'refuge' was established at Chiswick by Erin Pizzey in 1972 for battered women. It was quickly emulated across the country as small, underfunded refuges proliferated, clearly fulfilling an unmet need in providing emergency accommodation for women fleeing from abusive partners. In the course of one year alone (1977/8), 11,400 women and 20,850 children were taken in by 150 refuges (Binney *et al.* 1985). The refuge movement has maintained a precarious position, partly reliant on local authority funding yet often in conflict with conventional statutory services.

'Rape crisis' centres developed out of the same wave of re-emergent feminism in the 1970s, on a similar model to that of refuges. Rape crisis centres were first opened in London in 1976 and in Birmingham in 1979. By 1988 there were forty such centres in operation, offering emotional support and legal and medical advice to women who have been sexually assaulted or raped (Anna T. 1988). With few funded posts, reliant mainly on the work of volunteers, rape crisis centres offer a 24-hour telephone helpline and provide face-to-face counselling. Committed also to educating and informing the public about rape, these centres have been loath to accept the use of the term 'victim'. Their objection rests on the grounds that 'using the word "victim" to describe women takes away our power and contributes to the idea that it is right and natural for men to "prey" on us' (London Rape Crisis Centre 1984: ix). Replacing the term victim with 'survivor', rape crisis campaigners have deliberately differentiated their response from that of the rest of the victim movement (Kelly 1988). Although based upon diverse feminist beliefs, the general commitment of rape crisis centres to radical feminism and their deep suspicion of police attitudes to rape has limited the interplay between their work and that of other voluntary and criminal justice agencies (Anna T. 1988).

Victim Support, women's refuges, and rape crisis centres are far from enjoying coherence of outlook, organization, or method. The 'victim movement' is ideologically heterogeneous. Relations between the various agencies range from close co-operation to barely concealed hostility. As Van Dijk has observed from an international perspective, 'the movement's demands and achievements do not flow from a well-defined victimological theory, or in fact from any social theory at all' (Van Dijk 1988). Despite, or perhaps because of, this heterogeneity, the combined impact of these endeavours has been enormous.

VICTIMS IN THE CRIMINAL JUSTICE SYSTEM

The role of the victim within the criminal justice system attracts increasing attention among criminologists and policy-makers alike. Without the co-operation of the victim in reporting crime, in furnishing evidence, in identifying the offender, and in acting as a witness in court, most crime would remain unknown and unpunished. The reliance of the criminal justice system on the victim has proved to be a powerful bargaining tool for those seeking to further recognition of victims' needs and, to a lesser extent, rights. This political impetus is important in so far as much of the criminological research into victims has been funded, promoted and, in many cases, even instigated, by central or local government.

That victims became a focus for political concern may be related to the profound and growing sense of disillusionment across political parties with the ability of the criminal justice system to 'do anything' about crime. By contrast, concern for the victim promised relatively easy, high public relations benefits (Rock 1990). Across the political spectrum, those on the left saw support and compensation to victims as a natural extension to national insurance and liberal reformers saw policies for victims as an important corollary to welfarism, while conservative interest has been characterized as representing the softer face of the 'law and order lobby'. The financial backing given to Victim Support by the Conservative government during the 1980s has been seen as entirely consistent with their wider search for lost community, to encourage 'active citizenship' through the agency of good neighbours fulfilling their social obligations through voluntary work. In 1990, the Home Office announced a 'Victim's Charter' which lays down the rights of victims, specifying how they are to be treated and what standards they have a right to expect, for example, information about the progress of their case, about trial dates, bail, and sentencing decisions (Home Office 1990). Pressure for the recognition of victims' rights has also been influential at the international level. In 1985, the General Assembly of the United Nations adopted a 'Declaration of the Basic Principles of Justice for Victims of Crime and Abuse of Power'. The Declaration lays down basic standards for the treatment of victims, including the right to information and fair treatment, consideration of their views, restitution and compensation, and the provision of victim services. The Council of Europe has also been active in this area endorsing a 'Convention on State Compensation' for victims of violent crime in 1983 and making a series of recommendations on the role of the victim in criminal law and the criminal process, on assistance to victims, and on crime prevention (Joutsen 1987).

The political impetus to championing the rights of victims has played a major part in raising the profile of the victim from 'forgotten actor' to key player in the criminal justice process. Research on victims' experiences of the criminal process has suggested that, at best, prosecution, conviction, and sentence may have a powerful cathartic effect in relieving victims' feelings of complicity and guilt (Adler 1988: 140). Depending on the sanction meted out, victims may benefit from compensation for their losses and harms suffered, or may enjoy feelings of increased security when a threatening offender is incarcerated. On the other hand, insensitive questioning by police, inadequate provision of information, delays, or unexplained decisions by the prosecution service to drop a case or reduce a charge may each entail further suffering. At worst, the impact of the criminal process may be tantamount to 'secondary victimization' (Maguire and Pointing 1988: 11).

As the first point of contact with the criminal justice system, the police play an important role in shaping the victim's experience. The first British Crime Survey found that satisfaction with the police response was generally good but that the young, particularly young males, tended to be more critical (Mayhew and Hough 1983). Shapland and her colleagues modified this view by showing that while initial levels of satisfaction with the police were generally high, these tended to decline steadily as the case progressed (Shapland *et al.* 1985: 83–9; see also Newburn and Merry 1990). Dissatisfaction arose from police failure to keep victims informed, perceived inefficiency, unhelpfulness, or unfairness. Disillusionment was a product, therefore, of a growing feeling that 'the police did not care and were not doing anything' (Shapland *et al.* 1985: 85). In a bid to respond to such criticisms, the Home Office is now carrying out regular surveys of public satisfaction with police services.

Partly as a result of adverse publicity following a television documentary about the investigation of a rape by Thames Valley Police in 1982, the Home Office called on all police forces to review procedures for the treatment of victims. As a result, many forces developed a so-called 'specialist response' to women and child victims of sexual offences. They introduced special interview suites in police stations and trained teams of women police officers to respond to sexual assault victims with greater sensitivity. In responding to child abuse victims, a pioneer scheme by the Metropolitan Police in the London Borough of Bexley to establish joint interviewing by police and social workers has provided a model of 'inter-agency co-operation' which has been copied widely (Metropolitan Police and Bexley Social Services 1987). Beyond these specialist areas of innovation, however, little has changed in respect of police attitudes or response to victims. Specially trained 'victim liaison' or 'community involvement unit' police officers exist in some forces but their work still tends to be regarded as outside the remit of 'real' policing. Police officers' primary concern to solve crimes and elicit admissible evidence has led to criticisms of their consequent failure to show sympathy to victims (Maguire 1985; Shapland *et al.* 1985). Partly as a result of this research, training for all new police recruits on 'handling victims' has now been introduced.

Given these innovations in respect of victims of sexual assault, it is perhaps not surprising that they appear to be more satisfied with the police than victims of physical assault or robbery (Shapland *et al.* 1985: 87). For the mass of property crimes where a suspect is never located, it may be that there is little more the police can do than inform the victim as to the reasons for ceasing their inquiries (Newburn and Merry 1990). However, in the case of more serious offences, victims look for sensitivity in the conduct of interviews, in the collecting of forensic evidence, and in the handling of identification procedures, and for information about developments in the investigation. Since the introduction of the Crown Prosecution Service, the police simply may not have information about prosecution decisions or court dates. As a consequence, the victim's desire to be kept informed about the progress of 'their' case remains largely unmet.

Unlike jurisdictions such as France or Germany, where victims have considerable rights to participate in the prosecution or to present civil claims within the criminal process, in Britain victims have little role other than as a source of evidence. Nor do victim-witnesses enjoy representation by counsel as in many jursidictions in the USA, or the protection of US Victim/Witness Protection statutes. In Britain, the role of the victim in the prosecution is largely limited to that of witness in court. Most attention has been focused on the plight of rape victims and the extent to which they, quite as much as the defendant, are placed on trial (Temkin 1987: 6–8). While under the Sexual Offences (Amendment) Act 1976 s. 2 sexual history evidence is excluded except where admitted at judicial discretion, permission to admit such evidence appears to be readily given (Temkin 1987: 121). Where admitted it is used to blacken the victim's character and throw doubt upon her testimony that consent to sexual intercourse was not given. Yet the trauma experienced by victims under cross-examination is not confined to sexual offences. McBarnet has argued that the feelings of degradation experienced by many victims in court is not incidental, but rather structural to the proceedings (McBarnet 1983). In court, the victim is no more or less than a witness and as such is placed in a position of vulnerability—at the mercy of questioning by defence counsel and prosecution alike. The adversarial nature of advocacy and the legal rules surrounding the construction of 'truth' mean that victim-witnesses are liable to find themselves treated harshly by all sides. Whereas the defendant can choose to remain silent and not to disclose information as to his history and character, the victim enjoys no such protection.

Increasing attention to the plight of 'vulnerable' witnesses (particularly children in sexual abuse cases) has led to innovations in court procedure and changes in the rules of evidence. In many courts where children are involved, judges may remove wigs and robes or come down from the bench; barristers too may derobe; quietly spoken victim-witnesses may be provided with microphones; and most recently, provision has been made for the use of screens, live video-links, and pre-recorded video-taped interviews, all intended to reduce the stress to victims (Morgan and Zedner 1992*a*: 128–44, 1992*b*; Spencer 1990). But these innovations are far from universal.

Other victim-witnesses generally enjoy little special treatment though they too may find the experience of giving evidence traumatic. In recognition of their needs, Victim Support has instigated a number of Crown Court Witness Services, modelled in part on American victim-witness assistance programmes. Following the American model, volunteers provide advice, information, and emotional support to those victims waiting to be called as witnesses (National Association of Victim Support Schemes 1988). For witnesses obliged to wait in crowded, inhospitable areas, often for interminable periods, the presence of volunteers has been recognized as 'comforting and congenial, a symbolic end to their solitary and pariah status' (Rock 1991). The Victim's Charter (Home Office 1990) gave a commitment to improve facilities for victim-witnesses called to court, to reduce waiting times by improving listing systems, and to take the special needs of the victim into account in the construction of new court buildings; but progess in achieving these aims is likely to be slow.

In the USA the legal rights of victims have been greatly strengthened by the introduction of legislation passed by local and federal government since the early 1980s (Maguire 1991: 379). The right to make 'victim impact statements' now exists in at least forty-three states. These are primarily used in setting the level of compensation, but also inform sentencing decisions more generally. Even greater influence is accorded to 'victim statements of opinion', which allow the victim to indicate what sentence he or she would deem appropriate. Some states also require that victims be consulted prior to any plea-bargaining or decisions pertaining to parole.

In England demands for victims to have any influence over prosecutorial discretion, the acceptance of a plea, or the length of sentence have been far less forthcoming. Even when such demands have been heard they have generally been met with resistance. If the wrong committed is a matter of public rather than merely private interest, should the victim be entitled to any say about whether or to what extent sanctions are to be imposed? Arguments raised in favour of increased victim participation in the criminal justice process include: recognition of their status as a party to the dispute (Christie 1977); reduced risk of inflicting further psychological harm on the victim; greater victim co-operation and thereby the improved efficiency of the system; better information about harms suffered and thereby closer proportionality in sentencing (Von Hirsch and Jareborg 1991). However, equally forcible arguments have been raised against allowing victims a greater say. These include: limitations on prosecutorial discretion; the danger that the victim's 'subjective' view undermines the court's objectivity; disparity in sentencing of similar cases depending on the resilience or punitiveness of the victim (Ashworth 1993); and finally, that to increase their involvement may entail further burdens on victims while raising their expectations unrealistically (Reeves 1984). In practice, as we have seen, in England emphasis has been on the more sensitive treatment of victims within the criminal justice process, with little sustained demand being made for any extension of their role in areas of police, prosecutorial, or judicial discretion.

SHIFTING CONCEPTIONS OF CRIMINAL JUSTICE

The proliferation of research about victims has raised larger questions about the very purpose of criminal justice and the place of the victim within it. Victim surveys have revealed that the public are not so punitive as had been expected and that many victims would welcome the opportunity to seek some reparation or even reconciliation in place of traditional punishment (Hough and Moxon 1985). Such evidence, together with the growing disillusionment of academics, policy-makers, and criminal justice professionals with the existing paradigm of punishment, has prompted discussion of models of reparative justice reorientated towards the aims of mediation and restitution (Barnett 1977; Wright 1982, 1991).

In its purest form, mediation seeks to provide a way of resolving disputes without recourse to the courts, allowing both parties to retain control and to voice their grievances under the supervision of a mediator, whether a trained professional or lay volunteer (Davis 1992; Davis *et al.* 1987; Marshall 1991). The mediator makes no decisions and any resolution is reached by the mutual agreement of the two parties. In practice, the form and organization of mediation schemes varies considerably, from operating as a direct alternative to adjudication, through 'court-based' schemes taking referrals from the courts prior to sentencing as in South Yorkshire (see e.g. Smith *et al.* 1988), to meetings between groups of victims and offenders already in custody as at Rochester Youth Custody Centre (Launay 1985).

Mediation schemes were first introduced in Britain at the end of the 1970s. They have developed gradually, if slowly; by 1990 fourteen such schemes were in operation, bringing victims and offenders together on a one-to-one basis or in groups to hold regular discussions. Their aims are similarly various: from providing victims with some tangible reparation and offenders with the hope of a reduced sentence, through providing a conduit for communication, to allowing both parties to understand one another better and, possibly, to resolve their conflict. A study by the Home Office over two years (1985–7) found that in six schemes dealing with juveniles cautioned by the police, 57 per cent of all agreements involved some sort of explanation and apology with just over 25 per cent involving material reparation (Marshall 1991: 9). Although mediation has obvious attractions, sceptics have questioned whether it can really operate 'in the shadow of the court'. Victim Support has warned of the additional burdens it may place on the victim in terms of time, goodwill, and energy (Reeves 1984). While mediation may have achieved some success in respect of crimes of low seriousness, it is doubtful whether it could really substitute for formal adjudication in the case of serious crime.

The paradigm of restitution rests on the recognition that crime is not only a wrong against society but often represents also a private wrong done by the offender to a specific victim. Historically, it is argued, the state has 'stolen' the dispute from the hands of victims and offenders, and, in so doing, has usurped the right of the victim to seek recompense for harms suffered (Christie 1977; Ashworth 1986; Wright 1991: 1–9). Restorative theories of justice argue that compensating individual victims (but less often the wider community) should be the primary aim of the criminal justice system (Barnett 1977; Wright 1991; Davis 1992). To quote Barnett, a leading proponent of restitution: 'Justice consists of the culpable offender making good the loss he has caused . . . Where we once saw an offense against society, we now see an offense against an individual' (Barnett 1977: 287–8). This, it is claimed, would reduce reliance on negative, solely punitive disposals and institute in their place positive attempts to rectify the specific harm caused by crime. Pure restitutionists, like Barnett, deny altogether the value of punishment and demand only that the offended party receive just compensation. In practice, pure restitution has nowhere overthrown the paradigm of punishment; instead, restitutive principles are incorporated somewhat awkwardly into the existing punitive framework. The stigmatizing and deterrent qualities of punishment are retained but, alongside traditional punishments, provision is made for compensation to identifiable victims.

Compensation is made through both the state-funded Criminal Injuries Compensation Scheme (CICS) and via compensation orders payable by the offender (Miers 1991). It is arguable that the initial impetus to these developments was largely negative, spurred on by the feeling that if punishment was failing to deter or to rehabilitate then at least some limited good might be achieved by compensating victims for the wrongs they have suffered. State-funded compensation was set up as early as 1964 in the form of the CICS, which makes discretionary payments to victims of unlawful violence. It has been suggested that state-funded compensation is based on the premise that the state is under an obligation to maintain law and order, that the commission of crime may be said to result from a failure to fulfil that duty, and therefore that compensation is payable accordingly (Council of Europe convention on 'Compensation for Victims of Violent Crime', 1983). In Britain, payments seem to be made on behalf of the community more as an expression of public sympathy than out of any clear sense of duty (Newburn 1989). More cynically, it might be argued that compensation is paid partly in recognition of the state's reliance on the victim's co-operation in bringing offenders to justice. For the victim, engagement with the criminal justice process entails further costs: the time, energy, and stress of assisting the police with their investigation and, for a few at least, the trauma of giving evidence as a witness in court. State-funded compensation may be said to represent 'payment' to victims for their co-operation in the criminal justice process (Barnett 1977: 285) or as compensation for the further costs or 'secondary victimization' suffered as in consequence.

Provision was made for the CICS to be placed on a statutory footing by the Criminal Justice Act 1988, but this did not appear to signify any marked change in the administration of the scheme. Victims must still report to a responsible authority and co-operate with the police, they must 'come with clean hands', and the offender must not benefit from any payment (Miers 1989: 39). These provisions have been criticized on a number of grounds, not least because they may serve to exclude those who are unwilling to pursue prosecution, however justifiable their reasons. They also deny funds to those whose assailant shares their home and might therefore benefit. The CICS board retains considerable discretion, much of it beyond the bounds of public scrutiny, and its workings remain remarkably opaque to outside observers. Compensation remains, broadly speaking, available only to victims of violence, though why they should be singled out for help denied to other victims remains a matter of debate (Ashworth 1986; Duff 1987).

Similarly obscure are the grounds on which awards are made; the process by which the level of harm is calculated; and who is or is not deemed an appropriate or 'deserving' recipient of state aid. Under the scheme as originally set up, the board was able to withhold or reduce compensation if it considered that 'having regard to the conduct of the applicant before, during or after the events giving rise to the claim or to his character or way of life . . . it is inappropriate that a full award, or any award at all be granted' (Newburn 1989: 4). Criticisms of this provision led to its omission in s. 112(2) of the Criminal Justice Act 1988, though the Board retains discretion to take into account previous convictions (even those having no causal relation with the injury which is the subject of a claim) (Miers 1989*b*). Where an applicant can be seen to have attracted assault through his own provocative conduct or where he has convictions for serious offences, however unconnected with the offence in question, then compensation will generally be withheld.

The police may play a significant role as 'gatekeepers' in deterring would-be recipients from applying, in failing to inform those they consider inappropriate claimants about CICS, or in giving information to the Board which calls into question the legitimacy of claims (Shapland *et al.* 1985: ch. 7; Newburn and Merry 1990). Without some strategy for ensuring that all victims are routinely informed of the existence of CICS, the police may effectively deprive victims of access to compensation, though Victim Support has sought to ensure that all victims receive leaflets about CICS. In contrast to this unregulated exclusion of 'undeserving victims', those who fulfil the stereotypical picture of a worthy or deserving recipient may receive awards even though the injuries they have sustained are relatively slight. Newburn draws attention to the Board's willingness to compensate little old ladies even where the harm suffered falls below the minimum award, now £1,000 (Newburn 1989). Despite research evidence as to the relative rarity of elderly women being violently robbed or assaulted, the 'poor, innocent little old lady' would appear to continue to represent the 'ideal victim' in the mind of the state (Newburn 1989: 15).

Victim recourse to the CICS has increased dramatically in recent years: the number of applications rose from 22,000 in 1979/80 to 53,650 in 1989/90 (Barclay 1991: 22). The number of awards paid out by the Board for England and Wales over the same decade (excluding Scotland) rose more slowly from 17,500 to 27,800. Hence, while 80 per cent of applicants received awards in 1980, ten years later the proportion had fallen to 52 per cent. In addition, the increased burden on the administrative resources of the Board has led to massive delays in the handling of applications so that in 1989/90 barely a fifth of claims were settled within one year (Barclay 1991). This said, £109.3 million was paid out to victims in 1990/1, a 50 per cent increase on the previous year, and it is projected that spending will rise to £161 million by 1994–5.

Compensation payable by the offender was introduced in the Criminal Justice Act 1972 which gave the courts powers to make an ancillary order for compensation in addition to the main penalty in cases where 'injury, loss, or damage' had resulted. The Criminal Justice Act 1982 made it possible for the first time to make a compensation order as the sole penalty. It also required that in cases where fines and compensation orders were given together, the payment of compensation should take priority over the fine. These developments signified a major shift in penological thinking, reflecting the growing importance attached to restitution and reparation over the more narrowly retributive aims of conventional punishment. The Criminal Justice Act 1988 furthered this shift. It required courts to consider the making of a compensation order in every case of death, injury, loss, or damage and, where such an order was not given, imposed a duty on the court to give reasons for not doing so. It also extended the range of injuries eligible for compensation. These new requirements mean that if the court fails to make a compensation order it must furnish reasons. Where reasons are given, the victim may apply for these to be subject to judicial review.

Figures for the use of compensation orders suggest that the need for the criminal justice system to recognize and respond to the harms suffered by victims has firmly established itself in the minds of the courts. In 1989, 55 per cent of offenders sentenced in magistrates' courts for offences of violence, 39 per cent for burglary, 42 per cent for robbery, 53 per cent for fraud and forgery, and 66 per cent for criminal damage were ordered to pay compensation (Barclay 1991:20). Overall, 28 per cent of those sentenced for indictable offences in magistrates' courts were ordered to pay compensation. In the Crown Court the figure was much lower: only 14 per cent of those sentenced (partly due to the fact that compensation orders are not normally combined with custodial sentences). In 28 per cent of offences of violence, 10 per cent of burglary, 21 per cent of fraud and forgery, and 25 per cent of criminal damage a compensation order was made. This said, difficulties remain in determining what constitute reasonable grounds for failing to make an order. Where an order is made, problems arise in determining the degree of harm caused and, therefore, the level of compensation payable.

The 1991 Criminal Justice Act contains a number of provisions which directly or indirectly encourage an even greater role for compensation. The maximum sum to be ordered by magistrates' courts was increased from £2,000 to £5,000 per offence, so allowing for a much higher total sum to be awarded—and, incidentally, encouraging the retention of a larger number of cases by magistrates' courts (Wasik and Taylor 1991). Where offenders are social security claimants, payment of compensation can now be deducted at source from income support. The attachment of compensation orders to suspended sentences is encouraged. And perhaps more obliquely, the introduction of unit fines, which require disclosure of offenders' means and ability to pay, will probably encourage the courts to make more compensation orders, for larger sums, than before. Unhappily, the 1991 Act does not address the intended relationship between its primary commitment to just deserts (proportionality) and these significant moves towards reparative aims. The possibility of developing conceptions of crime seriousness based on the assessment of harm to identifiable victims may provide a partial solution, but as yet it is no more than a matter for academic debate (Von Hirsch and Jareborg 1991).

The problems entailed in reorientating the criminal justice system towards the victim in this way have not passed unobserved (Ashworth 1986, 1991; Duff 1988; Miers 1992). Objections to restitution focus primarily upon the argument that it has no penal character and that to secure reinstatement to the victim is no more than the enforcement of a civil liability. Restitution fails, in short, to acknowledge the distinction between civil and criminal law. It ignores the broader social dimension of crime: that it is not only the victim but also society that has been wronged. More pragmatically, it may lack the deterrent or punitive impact necessary to control crime. Moreover, to make restitution the sole aim of criminal justice would be effectively to decriminalize the mass of 'victimless' offences. Finally, and perhaps most importantly, Ashworth has concluded that a reparative approach 'ignores one cardinal element in serious crimes—the offender's mental attitude . . . Criminal liability and punishment should be determined primarily according to the wickedness or danger of the defendant's conduct . . . on what he was trying to do or thought he was doing, not upon what actually happened in the particular case' (Ashworth 1986: 97). To focus on the harm done to the victim risks undermining the relationship between moral wrong and penal sanction. It substitutes valuations of harm for the question of intent upon which criminal liability is traditionally based. Attempts, conspiracy, conduct crimes (such as careless driving), precursor offences (such as possessing firearms or explosives), fraud, and theft (which requires no more than 'the intention permanently to deprive') are all deemed to be criminal irrespective of any harm done. To make harm the central determinant of criminal liability and repayment to identifiable victims the primary goal of criminal justice would involve a major reorientation of both our criminal law and our system of punishment.

Fundamental questions remain unresolved: Should compensation be welcomed as a move towards a reparative system of criminal justice which seeks to place the victim on a equal footing with the offender? Or should reparation remain merely ancillary to the 'proper purpose' of punishment? How far are developments regarding compensation based on a coherent view of the rights and responsibilities of victim, offenders, and the state? Is it possible that victims' claims to justice have been overstated in recent years? And what are the implications of reparative models of justice for the mass of 'victimless' crimes?

CONCLUSION

Victims attract a level of interest, both as a subject of criminological inquiry and as a focus of criminal justice policy, unimaginable a decade ago. Far from being simply a compartmentalized topic for research, the recognition of victims has resulted in a major reorientation of criminological thinking. This conceptual shift has made it less and less easy for radical criminology to play down crime as a social problem—labelling theory, for one, will surely never assume quite the same status again. Victim surveys have profoundly altered our picture of crime by uncovering a vast array of hidden offences, many against the most vulnerable and least vocal members of society. And, increasingly, pressure from voluntary and professional agencies ensures the recognition of victim needs and the importance of victim services.

Reorientation of the criminal justice process towards the victim is as yet in its infancy but significant changes have already occurred, most importantly in respect of compensating harms. At a time when desert-based sentencing is gaining increasing sway, simultaneous demands for a more victim-orientated criminal justice system challenge conventional means of assessing the gravity of offences. The proper priority between victim-orientated and desert-based sentencing is far from being resolved. The implications of introducing the victim into that delicate balance between the state and offender, between offence and penalty, will surely be key issues for the future.

Selected Further Reading

R. E. Barnett, 'Restitution: A New Paradigm of Criminal Justice', *Ethics*, 1977, 87: 279–301.

N. Christie, 'Conflicts as Property', *British Journal of Criminology*, 1977, 17: 1–15.

Home Office, *Victim's Charter: A Statement of the Rights of Victims*. London: Home Office, 1990.

M. Joutsen, *The Role of the Victim of Crime in European Criminal Justice Systems: A Crossnational Study of the Role of the Victim*. Helsinki, 1987.

M. Maguire and C. Corbett, *The Effects of Crime and the Work of Victim Support Schemes*. Aldershot: Gower, 1987.

M. Maguire and J. Pointing, eds., *Victims of Crime: A New Deal?* Milton Keynes: Open University Press, 1988.

R. I. Mawby and M. L. Gill, *Crime Victims: Needs, Services, and the Voluntary Sector*. London.

P. Mayhew, D. Elliot, and L. Dowds, *The 1988 British Crime Survey*. London: HMSO, 1989.

J. Morgan and L. Zedner, *Child Victims: Crime, Impact, and Criminal Justice*. Oxford, 1992.

P. Rock, *Helping Victims of Crime: The Home Office and the Rise of Victim Support*. Oxford, 1990.

J. Shapland, J. Willmore, and P. Duff, *Victims and the Criminal Justice System*. Aldershot: Gower, 1985.

J. Van Dijk, P. Mayhew, and M. Killias, *Experiences of Crime across the World: Key Findings of the 1989 International Crime Survey*. The Netherlands, 1990.

S. Walklate, *Victimology*. London, 1989.

M. Wright, *Justice for Victims and Offenders*. Buckingham, 1991.

REFERENCES

ADLER, Z. (1988), 'Prosecuting Child Sexual Abuse: A Challenge to the Status Quo,' in M. Maguire and J. Pointing, eds., *Victims of Crime: A New Deal?* Milton Keynes.

AMIR, M. (1971), *Patterns of Forcible Rape*. Chicago.

ANDERSON, S., GROVE SMITH, C., KINSEY, R., and WOOD, J. (1990), *The Edinburgh Crime Survey: First Report*. Edinburgh.

ANNA, T. (1988), 'Feminist Responses to Sexual Abuse: The Work of the Birmingham Rape Crisis Centre', in M. Maguire and J. Pointing, eds., *Victims of Crime: A New Deal?* Milton Keynes.

ANTTILA, I. (1974), 'Victimology: A New Territory in Criminology', *Scandinavian Studies in Criminology*, 5: 3–7.

ASHWORTH, A. (1986), 'Punishment and Compensation: Victims, Offenders and the State', *Oxford Journal of Legal Studies*, 6: 86–122.

—— (1992), *Sentencing and Criminal Justice*. London.

—— (1993), 'Victim Impact Statements and Sentencing', *Criminal Law Review*: 498–509.

BARCLAY, G., ed. (1991), *A Digest of Information on the Criminal Justice System*. London.

BARNETT, R. E. (1977), 'Restitution: A New Paradigm of Criminal Justice', *Ethics*, 87: 279–301.

BENNETT, T. (1987), *An Evaluation of Two Neighbourhood Watch Schemes in London*. Cambridge.

Binney, V., Harkell, G., and Nixon, J. (1985), 'Refuges and Housing for Battered Women', in J. Pahl, ed., *Private Violence and Public Policy*. London.

Black, D., and Kaplan, T. (1988), 'Father Kills Mother: Issues and Problems Encountered by a Child Psychiatric Team', *British Journal of Psychiatry*, 153: 624–30.

Box, S. (1983), *Power, Crime and Mystification*. London.

Box, S., Hale, C., and Andrews, G. (1988), 'Explaining Fear of Crime', *British Journal of Criminology*, 28/3: 340–56.

Burgess, A. W., and Holstrom, L. L. (1974), *Rape: Victims of Crisis*. Bowie, Md.

Chambers, G., and Millar, A. (1983), *Investigating Sexual Assault*. Edinburgh.

Chambers, G., and Tombs, J. (1984), *The British Crime Survey Scotland*. Edinburgh.

Christie, N. (1977) 'Conflicts as Property', *British Journal of Criminology*, 17: 1–15.

Clarke, A. H., and Lewis, M. J. (1982), 'Fear of Crime among the Elderly', *British Journal of Criminology*, 22/1: 49–62.

Commisssion for Racial Equality (1988), *Learning in Terror: A Survey of Racial Harassment in Schools and Colleges*. London.

Cooper, J., and Pomeyie, J. (1988), 'Racial Attacks and Racial Harassment: Lessons from a Local Project', in M. Maguire and J. Pointing, eds., *Victims of Crime: A New Deal?* Milton Keynes.

Corbett, C., and Hobdell, K. (1988), 'Volunteer-Based Services to Rape Victims: Some Recent Developments', in M. Maguire and J. Pointing, eds., *Victims of Crime: A New Deal?* Milton Keynes.

Crawford, A., Jones, T., Woodhouse, T., and Young, J. (1990), *Second Islington Crime Survey*. Middlesex.

—— (1986), 'The Ideal Victim', in E. A. Fattah, ed., *From Crime Policy to Victim Policy*. London.

Davis, G. (1992), *Making Amends: Mediation and Reparation in Criminal Justice*. London.

Davis, G., Boucherat, J., and Watson, D. (1987), *A Preliminary Study of Victim–Offender Mediation and Reparation Schemes in England and Wales*, Home Office Research and Planning Unit Paper no. 42. London.

Dobash, R., and Dobash, R. (1979), *Violence against Wives: A Case Against Patriarchy*. New York.

—— (1984), 'The Nature and Antecedents of Violent Events', *British Journal of Criminology*, 24: 269–88.

—— (1992), *Women, Violence and Social Change*. London.

Duff, P. (1987), 'Criminal Injuries Compensation and "Violent" Crime', *Criminal Law Review*: 219–30.

—— (1988), 'The "Victim Movement" and Legal Reform', in M. Maguire and J. Pointing, eds., *Victims of Crime: A New Deal?* Milton Keynes.

Elias, R. (1986), *The Politics of Victimization: Victims, Victimology and Human Rights*. New York.

Ennis, P. H. (1967), *Criminal Victimization in the United States: A Report of a National Survey*. Washington, DC.

FATTAH, EZZAT A. (1979), 'Some Recent Theoretical Developments in Victimology', *Victimology*, 4/2: 198–213.

—— ed. (1986), *From Crime Policy to Victim Policy*. London.

—— (1989), 'Victims and Victimology: The Facts and the Rhetoric', *International Review of Victimology*, 1: 43–66.

—— (1991), *Understanding Criminal Victimization*. Scarborough, Ontario.

FINKELHOR, D. (1979), *Sexually Victimized Children*. New York.

—— (1986), *A Sourcebook on Child Sexual Abuse*. New York.

FRIEDRICHS, D. O. (1983), 'Victimology: A Consideration of the Radical Critique', *Crime and Delinquency*, 29/2: 283–94.

GAROFALO, J. (1979), 'Victimization and the Fear of Crime', *Journal of Research in Crime and Delinquency*, 16: 80–97.

GENN, H. (1988), 'Multiple Victimization', in M. Maguire and J. Pointing, eds., *Victims of Crime: A New Deal?* Milton Keynes.

GOTTFREDSON, M. R. (1984), *Victims of Crime: The Dimensions of Risk*, Home Office Research Study no. 81. London.

—— (1986), 'Substantive Contributions of Victimization Surveys', *Crime and Justice*, 7: 251–87.

HALL, R. (1985), *Ask Any Woman*. Bristol.

HANMER, J., and SAUNDERS, S. (1984), *Well Founded Fear*. London.

HINDELANG, M., GOTTFREDSON, M., and GAROFALO, J. (1978), *Victims of Personal Crime: An Empirical Foundation for a Theory of Personal Victimization*. Cambridge, Mass.

HOLTOM, C., and RAYNOR, P. (1988), 'Origins of Victim Support: Philosophy and Practice', in M. Maguire and J. Pointing, eds., *Victims of Crime: A New Deal?* Milton Keynes.

HOME OFFICE (1990), *Victim's Charter: A Statement of the Rights of Victims*. London.

HOUGH, M., and MAYHEW, P. (1983), *The British Crime Survey: First Report*. London.

—— (1985), *Taking Account of Crime: Key Findings from the Second British Crime Survey*. London.

HOUGH, M., and MOXON, D. (1985), 'Dealing with Offenders: Popular Opinion and the View of Victims', *Howard Journal*, 24: 160–75.

JONES, D., PICKETT, J., OATES, M. R., and BARBOR, P. (1987), *Understanding Child Abuse*. Basingstoke.

JONES, T., MACLEAN, B., and YOUNG, J. (1986), *The Islington Crime Survey*. Aldershot.

JOUTSEN, M. (1987), *The Role of the Victim of Crime in European Criminal Justice Systems: A Crossnational Study of the Role of the Victim*. Helsinki.

KAISER, G., KURY, H., and ALBRECHT, H-J., eds. (1991), *Victims and Criminal Justice: Victimological Research: Stocktaking and Prospects*. Freiburg-im-Breisgau.

KELLY, L. (1988), *Surviving Sexual Violence*. Oxford.

KINSEY, R. (1984), *Merseyside Crime Survey: First Report*. Liverpool.

—— (1985), *Merseyside Crime and Police Surveys: Final Report*. Liverpool.

LAUNAY, G. (1985), 'Bringing Victims and Offenders Together: A Comparison of Two Models', *Howard Journal*, 24/3: 200–12.

LEVI, M., and PITHOUSE, A. (1988), *The Victims of Fraud*, Report of the Economic and Social Research Council. London.

—— (1992), 'The Victims of Fraud', in D. Downes, ed., *Unravelling Criminal Justice*. London.

LONDON RAPE CRISIS CENTRE (1984), *Sexual Violence: The Reality for Women*. London: LRCC.

LURIGIO, A. J. (1987), 'Are All Victims Alike? The Adverse, Generalized, and Differential Impact of Crime', *Crime and Delinquency*, 33: 452–67.

MCBARNET, D. (1983), 'Victim in the Witness Box: Confronting Victimology's Stereotype', *Contemporary Crises*, 7: 293–303.

MACDONALD, J. (1971), *Rape: Offenders and their Victims*. Springfield, Ill.

MAGUIRE, M. (1980), 'The Impact of Burglary upon Victims', *British Journal of Criminology*, 20/3: 261–75.

—— (1982), *Burglary in a Dwelling*. London.

—— (1985), 'Victims' Needs and Victims' Services', *Victimology*, 10: 539–59.

—— (1991), 'The Needs and Rights of Victims of Crime', in M. Tonry, ed., *Crime and Justice: A Review of Research*, vol. 14: 363–433. Chicago.

MAGUIRE, M., and CORBETT, C. (1987), *The Effects of Crime and the Work of Victim Support Schemes*. Aldershot.

MAGUIRE, M., and POINTING, J., eds. (1988), *Victims of Crime: A New Deal?* Milton Keynes.

MARSHALL, T. (1984), *Reparation, Conciliation and Mediation*. London.

—— (1991), 'Victim–Offender Mediation', *Home Office Research Bulletin*, 30: 9–15.

MAWBY, R. I. (1988), 'Victim's Needs or Victim's Rights: Alternative Approaches to Policy-Making', in M. Maguire and J. Pointing, eds., *Victims of Crime: A New Deal?* Milton Keynes.

MAWBY, R. I., and GILL, M. L. (1987), *Crime Victims: Needs, Services, and the Voluntary Sector*. London.

MAXFIELD, M. G. (1984), *Fear of Crime in England and Wales*, Home Office Research Study no. 78. London.

MAYHEW, P., ELLIOT, D., and DOWDS, L. (1989), *The 1988 British Crime Survey*. London.

MAYHEW, P., and HOUGH, M. (1983), 'Note: The British Crime Survey', *British Journal of Criminology*, 23: 394–5.

MAYHEW, P., and MAUNG, N. A. (1992), 'Surveying Crime: Findings from the 1992 British Crime Survey', *Home Office Research Findings*, no. 2.

—— (1993), *The 1992 British Crime Survey*. London.

—— (1988), *Explaining Fear of Crime: Evidence from the 1984 British Crime Survey*, Home Office Research and Planning Unit Paper no. 43. London.

MENDELSOHN, B. (1956), 'Une nouvelle branche de la science bio-psycho-sociale: Victimologie', *Revue internationale de criminologie et de police technique*, 10–31.

METROPOLITAN POLICE AND BEXLEY SOCIAL SERVICES (1987), *Child Sexual Abuse: Joint Investigative Programme: Final Report*. London.

MIERS, D. (1989*a*), 'Positivist Victimology: A Critique,' *International Review of Victimology*, 1: 3–22.

—— (1989*b*), 'The Criminal Justice Act 1988: The Compensation Provisions', *Criminal Law Review*: 32–42.

—— (1991), *Compensation for Criminal Injuries*. London.
—— (1992), 'The Responsibilities and the Rights of Victims of Crime', *Modern Law Review*, 55/4: 482–505.
MORGAN, J., and ZEDNER, L. (1992*a*), *Child Victims: Crime, Impact, and Criminal Justice*. Oxford.
—— (1992*b*) 'The Victim's Charter: A New Deal for Child Victims?', *Howard Journal*, 31/4: 294–307.
MORRIS, A. (1987), *Women, Crime and Criminal Justice*. Oxford.
NATIONAL ASSOCIATION OF VICTIM SUPPORT SCHEMES (1988), *The Victim in Court*. London.
NEWBURN, T. (1989), *The Settlement of Claims at the Criminal Injuries Compensation Board*, Home Office Research Study no. 112. London.
NEWBURN, T., and MERRY, S. (1990), *Keeping in Touch: Police–Victim Communication in Areas*, Home Office Research Study no. 116. London.
PIZZEY, E. (1974), *Scream Quietly or the Neighbours Will Hear*. London.
PYNOOS, R. S., and ETH, S. (1984), 'The Child Witness to Homicide', *Journal of Social Issues*, 40/2: 87–108.
RADFORD, J. (1987), 'Policing Male Violence', in J. Hanmer and M. Maynard, eds., *Women, Violence and Social Control*. London.
REEVES, H. (1984), 'The Victim and Reparation', *Probation Journal*, 31: 136–9.
REISS, A. J. (1967), *Studies in Crime and Law Enforcement in Major Metropolitan Areas*. Washington, DC.
—— (1986), 'Official Statistics and Survey Statistics', in E. Fattah, ed., *From Crime Policy to Victim Policy*. London.
RESICK, P. A. (1987), 'Psychological Effects of Victimization: Implications for the Criminal Justice System', *Crime and Delinquency*, 33/4: 468–78.
RIZZO, M. J. (1979), 'The Cost of Crime to Victims: An Empirical Analysis', *Journal of Legal Studies*, 8/1: 79–205.
ROCK, P. (1986), *A View from the Shadows*. Oxford.
—— (1988), 'The Present State of Criminology in Britain', *British Journal of Criminology*, 28/2: 188–99.
—— (1990), *Helping Victims of Crime: The Home Office and the Rise of Victim Support in England and Wales*. Oxford.
—— (1991), 'The Victim in Court Project at the Crown Court at Wood Green', *Howard Journal*, 30/4: 301–10.
SHAPLAND, J. (1984), 'Victims, The Criminal Justice System and Compensation', *British Journal of Criminology*, 24/2: 131–49.
SHAPLAND, J., WILLMORE, J., and DUFF, P. (1985), *Victims and the Criminal Justice System*. Aldershot.
SKOGAN, W. G. (1986*a*), 'The Fear of Crime and its Behavioural Implications,' in E. Fattah, ed., *From Crime Policy to Victim Policy*. London.
—— (1986*b*), 'The Impact of Victimization on Fear', *Crime and Delinquency*, 33: 135–54.
SMITH, D., BLAGG, H., and DERRICOURT, N. (1988), 'Mediation in South Yorkshire', *British Journal of Criminology*, 28/3: 378–95.
SMITH, L. J. (1989*a*), *Concerns about Rape*, Home Office Research Study no. 106. London.

SMITH, L. J. (1989*b*), *Domestic Violence: An Overview of the Literature*, Home Office Research Study no. 107. London.

SOOTHILL, K., and WALBY, S. (1991), *Sex Crime in the News*. London.

SPARKS, R., GENN, H., and DODD, D. J. (1977), *Surveying Victims*. London.

SPENCER, J. (1990), *Children's Evidence in Legal Proceedings: An International Perspective*. Cambridge.

STANKO, E. A. (1985), *Intimate Intrusions*. London.

—— (1988), 'Hidden Violence against Women', in M. Maguire and J. Pointing, eds., *Victims of Crime: A New Deal?* Milton Keynes.

TEMKIN, J. (1987), *Rape and the Legal Process*. London.

VAN DIJK, J. (1988), 'Ideological Trends within the Victims Movement: An International Perspective', in M. Maguire and J. Pointing, eds., *Victims of Crime: A New Deal?* Milton Keynes.

VAN DIJK, J., MAYHEW, P., and KILLIAS, P., (1990), *Experiences of Crime across the World: Key Findings of the 1989 International Crime Survey*. Deventer.

VIANO, EMILIO C. (1985), 'Theoretical Issues and Practical Concerns for Future Research in Victimology', *Victimology: An International Journal*, 10: 736–50.

VICTIM SUPPORT (1991), *Supporting Families of Murder Victims*. London.

VON HENTIG, H. (1948), *The Criminal and his Victim*. New York.

VON HIRSCH, A., and JAREBORG, N. (1991); 'Gauging Criminal Harm: A Living-Standard Analysis', *Oxford Journal of Legal Studies*, 11/1: 1–38.

WALKLATE, S. (1989), *Victimology*. London.

—— (1990), 'Researching Victims of Crime: Critical Victimology', *Social Justice*, 17/2: 25–42.

WASIK, M., and TAYLOR, R. D. (1991), *Blackstone's Guide to the Criminal Justice Act 1991*. Oxford.

WERTHAM, F. (1949), *The Show of Violence*. New York.

WOLFGANG, M. (1958), *Patterns in Criminal Homicide*. New York.

WRIGHT, M. (1982), *Making Good*. London.

—— (1991), *Justice for Victims and Offenders*. Buckingham.

WRIGHT, M., and GALWAY, B., eds. (1989), *Mediation and Criminal Justice*. London.

YOUNG, J. (1988), 'Risk of Crime and Fear of Crime: A Realist Critique of Survey-Based Assumptions', in M. Maguire and J. Pointing, eds., *Victims of Crime: A New Deal?* Milton Keynes.

ZEDNER, L. (1992), 'Sexual Offences', in S. Casale and E. Stockdale, eds., *Criminal Justice under Stress*. London.

Index